P9-EMB-699

THE OLIVER WENDELL HOLMES DEVISE
HISTORY OF THE SUPREME COURT
OF THE UNITED STATES

General Editor: PAUL A. FREUND

THE
Oliver Wendell Holmes
DEVISE

HISTORY OF
THE SUPREME COURT
OF THE UNITED STATES

VOLUME I

THE OLIVER WENDELL HOLMES DEVISE

History of the

SUPREME COURT

of the United States

VOLUME I

Antecedents and Beginnings to 1801

By Julius Goebel, Jr.

NEW YORK

The Macmillan Company

Collier-Macmillan Ltd.

LONDON

Contents

Illustrations

James Wilson

John Blair

James Iredell

Thomas Johnson

William Paterson

Samuel Chase

Oliver Ellsworth

Bushrod Washington

Alfred Moore

FOLLOWING PAGE 674

Edmund Randolph

William Bradford

Charles Lee

William Lewis

William Rawle

Jared Ingersoll

Alexander J. Dallas

William Tilghman

Edward Tilghman

Peter S. Du Ponceau

Samuel Dexter

Jacob Read

Documents

DOCUMENTS

Foreword

WHEN OLIVER WENDELL HOLMES, JR., Associate Justice of the Supreme Court, died in March 1935 at the age of ninety-three, he left to the United States of America his residual estate, amounting to approximately $263,000. Since such a bequest was unusual, there was no ready formula for utilizing this money. The subsequent deliberations among government leaders about a suitable disposition of the gift were interrupted by the onset of the Second World War, with the result that for many years the money remained in the Treasury, untouched and uninvested. Finally, in 1955, an act of Congress (P.L. 84–246) established the Oliver Wendell Holmes Devise Fund, consisting of the original bequest augmented by a one-time appropriation in lieu of interest. The act also created the Permanent Committee for the Oliver Wendell Holmes Devise to administer the fund. The Committee consists of four public members appointed by the President of the United States for an eight-year term and the Librarian of Congress as Chairman *ex officio*.

The principal project supported by the Holmes bequest, as stipulated in the enabling act, has been the preparation and publication of a history of the Supreme Court of the United States. The present volume is part of that series. Intended to fill a gap in American legal literature, the multivolume history has been planned to give a comprehensive and definitive survey of the development of the Court from the beginning of the nation to the present. Paul A. Freund, Carl M. Loeb University Professor, Harvard University, has served as editor in chief. The authors, of whom Julius Goebel, Jr., George Welwood Murray Professor Emeritus of Legal History, Columbia University School of Law, is one, have devoted many years to the research and writing.

The operation of the Permanent Committee has been dependent upon the services of the distinguished men who have contributed their time, their wisdom, and their practical assistance as members of the Committee. Their names appear below.

In the early days of the Committee, Joseph P. Blickensderfer was Administrative Editor and Special Assistant to the Chairman. Dr. Blickensderfer contributed much imagination, enthusiasm, and hard work to plans for the publication of the history of the Supreme Court and later to preparations for the Holmes Devise lecture series also supported by the Committee. Following Dr. Blickensderfer's death in 1960, the late Lloyd Dunlap served as Administrative Editor for the years 1961–64. Since then the responsibility for the office of the Permanent Committee has been assigned to Mrs. Elizabeth E. Hamer, Assistant Librarian of Congress, who is assisted by Mrs. Jean Allaway as Administrative Officer for the Devise.

As Chairman *ex officio* of the Committee that has sponsored this work, I am happy to see the plans for the Oliver Wendell Holmes history of the Supreme Court come to fruition. This volume and its companions will form an appropriate tribute to the great Justice whose legacy has made possible their publication.

L. Quincy Mumford
LIBRARIAN OF CONGRESS

PERMANENT COMMITTEE FOR
THE OLIVER WENDELL HOLMES DEVISE
(TERMS OF EIGHT YEARS EXCEPT FOR INITIAL APPOINTMENTS)

Charles T. McCormick	1956–58 (two-year term)
Edward S. Corwin	1956–60 (four-year term)
George L. Haskins	1956–58 (six-year term but resigned 10/7/58)
Virgil M. Hancher	1956–64
Frederick D. G. Ribble	1958–66
Ethan A. H. Shepley	1959–67
Nicholas Kelley	7/8/60–7/22/60
Jefferson B. Fordham	1961–69
Harry H. Ransom	1964–72
Herbert Wechsler	1966–74
Robert G. McCloskey	1967–69
J. A. C. Grant	1970–78
Alfred H. Kelly	1970–78

Editor's Foreword

T HE SUPREME COURT of the United States is on any count an extraordinary creation, remarkable in each of its major functions. It stands, in the first place, as the head of a system of federal courts, Circuit and District, separate from the courts of the states yet possessing jurisdiction in many cases concurrent with that of the state tribunals. The Court, moreover, is the supreme judicial arbiter of the constitutional order, exercising appellate authority for this purpose over both state and federal courts. And finally, the Court is vested with power in its original (as contrasted with its appellate) jurisdiction to resolve controversies between two or more states themselves. It is an awesome mission, reflecting the concern of the Framers and the members of the first Congress for maintaining the rule of law and the supremacy of the Constitution and laws passed pursuant to it, and manifesting a faith that, as a multiplicity of interests would diffuse the conflicts bound to persist in the Union, structured institutions and procedures for adjudication would domesticate them.

But remarkable as was the conception of the Supreme Court in the federation, it was not devoid of ancestry. Continuity with the past, as Justice Holmes reminded us, is not a duty, it is only a necessity. The flash of genius that produces a patentable invention does not dissolve the linkages of tradition and experience. The theme of the present volume is the lineage of the Court and its business in the first decade of its existence.

Professor Goebel has brought to this formidable task his immense learning in the formative eighteenth-century period of American law. Building on his resources of scholarship and insight he has traced the influences that shaped the federal judiciary—the traditional practices of the local courts in England and the procedures in the colonial and early state courts in America. These sometimes labyrinthine explorations, conducted with hard-won command of the terrain, provide a foundation for understanding the practice and process of the federal Circuit Courts, whose decisions were not only reviewable by the Supreme Court but were actually participated in by individual members of that Court. For circuit riding was a major function of the Justices, as it was surely the most onerous branch of their duties, exposing them to "the dangers and miseries of overturned vehicles, runaway horses, rivers in full flood or icebound, and scruffy taverns." Such was the heavy price of bringing the Justices literally to the people.

The other principal function of the Court, the maintenance of the constitutional order and the settlement of disputes between the states, likewise had its antecedents. The Privy Council in England, the Court of Appeals in prize cases under the Articles of Confederation, the commission for boundary disputes among the states, the state judicial systems themselves, all pass in review as prologue to the Constitutional Convention and Article Three, the ratifying conventions in the states, and the legislation of the first Congress giving structure to the federal judicial establishment.

The early years of the Court have come to be overshadowed by the towering figure of John Marshall. And yet the Justices who served during the twelve years before the fourth Chief Justice came to the bench were faced with issues of great moment, even with disputes over governmental powers under the Constitution, which they adjudicated with sagacity and no little learning. The reader of Professor Goebel's masterful account is not likely to forget that there were indeed brave men before Agamemnon.

Paul A. Freund

Preface

W HEN THE SUPREME COURT of the United States held its first
term, February 1790, in the city of New York there was no
expectation that the establishment of federal judicial power would add
a certain splendor to the development of American law. Indeed, in the
very recent past the provisions for the judicial in the new Constitution
had been under assault, nowhere more bitterly than in the state of New
York. Some change of attitude had occurred only after Congress had
effected a species of historical transfusion in the first statutes organizing
the federal judiciary by drawing upon the laws and practices of the
several states to vitalize the functioning of the new system. The force
and effect of this can be appreciated only by taking into account the
relative antiquity of native experience with law administration and its
diversities. These were factors that were to make difficult the development of a federal jurisprudence; nevertheless their embracement promised
a better chance of survival than if a scheme unrelated to extant realities
had been contrived.

In Thomas Jefferson's first catalogue of his library (1783) the
laws of the American states other than his own were classified as
"Foreign Laws." This insular outlook was shared by lawyers in other
jurisdictions; it derived from the fact that as colonies each had had an
identity impressed upon it by the circumstances of its founding that
was to develop into a jealous particularism. In the most venerable of
the continental colonies basic ideas about the judicial structure and the
procedures, original and appellate, had become settled long before the
Crown instituted an effective watch and ward over colonial enactments
and saw to it that as respects the judicial there should be the least impairment of the *status quo*.

In any jurisdiction reached by royal mandates, acts of assemblies
were subjected to tests of law and policy, all conceived to be ingredients

of the imperial constitution. Disallowance awaited transgression. The colonials had no stomach for such control, but they became so far conditioned to the notion that legislation must consist with certain standards that this became part of the total experience that shaped the doctrine of constitutional supremacy. This was to be embodied in many of the first state constitutions.

Two incidents of royal policy contributed to the perpetuation of local diversities. One was the prohibition upon legislative erection of new courts except for small causes, a policy that served to perpetuate the existing structure of colonial courts. The second and less effective policy was the subjection of acts meddling with procedure to the test of conformity with the common law. For one reason or another a variety of legislative experiments escaped the axe, and consequently some new departures from the English canon were to survive. The novelties for which the bar and the judges alone were responsible never suffered systematic scrutiny, for the Crown never formally imposed upon the judiciary as it did upon the legislatures the standard of common law conformity. This was a dispensation favorable to the Americanization of what the colonials appropriated from the stores of the common law— a process highly selective, depending, as one might expect, upon local political traditions and the accidents of juristic controversy. There was never, as some myth-makers would have us believe, a wholesale reception.

Colonial judiciaries were, however, not utterly immune from surveillance, for their judgments or decrees were in principle subject to review on appeal to King in Council. This was in practice a more or less latent possibility, for the appellate jurisdiction was so regulated that in relation to the quantum of American judicial business, only the most resolute and affluent litigant was likely to pursue his remedy. Nevertheless, determinations of great constitutional import were made on appeal that affected some of the most politically vocal colonies. To the very end such appeals remained a contingency of which counsel on this side of the water were well advised to be aware.

When royal government came to an end, judicial power in its plenitude devolved upon the new states, and encompassed matter such as the chancery jurisdiction, hitherto a preserve of the Crown, and the admiralty jurisdiction, once a flower in what Francis Bacon called the "garland of prerogatives" that had become the subject of parliamentary regulation. The so-called reception provisions of state constitutions and statutes assured the continuing vigor of the common law as practiced or as a fundamental source of reference. It was from this aggregate, conserved by intense local pride, that surrenders were to be sought in the national interest.

At the outset, the national interest was the successful prosecution

of the war and then the recognition of independence. It was in connection
with the former that the Continental Congress, the *de facto* organ of the
rebel colonies, assumed appellate jurisdiction (1775) in cases of prize
adjudicated in state courts—a first exercise of "federal" judicial authority. There were to be instances of state resistance to this assertion
of jurisdiction and the fact that the instrument that was to convert the
de facto confederation into one *de jure* empowered the Congress to
establish a Court of Appeals in cases of captures did not subdue the
recalcitrants. It was all of four years before all the states ratified the
Articles of Confederation. Yet, even after this occurred, the appellate
jurisdiction was challenged and an attempt was made in Congress (1784)
to have vacated all sentences.

The belated attack on the appellate jurisdiction in cases of captures
at sea was one of the accumulating events that convinced the leading
advocates of union of what they called the "imbecility" of the Confederation. Indeed, the coming of peace made manifest that the American's hitherto perilous situation had been in Edmund Randolph's
words "the cement of our union." The details of disintegration and the
steps taken to bring this to a halt are familiar history. Ironically enough,
it was the states acting independently that furnished the impetus for
constitutional reform.

A federal judiciary was not, in eighteenth-century parlance, the
most "interesting" problem facing the delegates to the Constitutional
Convention of 1787. Although everyone was aware of the fact that the
nation's foreign affairs were suffering from the shortcomings of state
administration of justice, ideas regarding a federal establishment were
long amorphous. There was never any doubt about a Supreme Court,
but the inferior courts were a real bone of contention. Perhaps even
more than the scope and heads of federal jurisdiction, the problem of
making the judicial an independent branch of government fully coordinate with the other branches was to engage the Convention. This
was not quickly done, for the image of the English judge whose participation in government was not confined to judicial duties haunted the
delegates who sought to have Supreme Court Justices share in the veto
power. Even after agreement seemed to have been reached that their
role with respect to enactments should be confined to the review of
statutes for repugnancy to the supreme law, there was a last-ditch effort
to make a privy councillor of the Chief Justice.

The decision that the adoption of the new frame of government
should be the act not of the Continental Congress, but of the people
for whom the Convention purported to speak, was to precipitate prolonged and searching inquiry into the expedience and soundness of the
proposed instrument of union. As might be expected of a litigious
populace quick to appeal and one widely conversant with the operations

xvii

of courts, the inquest into the judicial was at once intelligent and prejudiced, critical and immensely informative. It has in the past been but little regarded for its impact, yet it led to the formulation of the Bill of Rights; it profoundly influenced the provisions of the first Judiciary Act. Both must be accounted to be the prime achievements of the first session of the first Congress. Both owed their strength to the fact that they were retrospective—the Bill of Rights because it put beyond controversy the quiet possession of rights of which the colonials believed that they then had been deprived and had fought a war to secure; the Judiciary Act because it was constructed in so many of its parts from long-seated law and usage.

One thing the ratification discussions had made clear was the need for some sort of *modus vivendi* between state and eventual federal judicial establishments. In exercise of the constitutional authority to ordain and establish courts inferior to the Supreme Court, the Judiciary Act provided for District and Circuit Courts; significantly, however, it also provided for the exercise of concurrent jurisdiction by state courts in certain species of actions. The safeguard against a possible centrifugal effect was the lodgment in the Supreme Court of a power of review of judgments in the highest state courts for alleged repugnancy to the laws, treaties or Constitution of the United States. There were also sops to Cerberus in the shape of monetary limitations: the direction that the laws of the states be the source of reference for decisions in trial at common law, and that jury service be governed so far as practical by state laws. A final yielding to state pride was the later rejection by the Senate of a proffered scheme of uniform federal procedure and the passage of a Process Act making mandatory state forms.

A problem to which only opponents of the Constitution had given tongue was the difficulty if not impossibility of administering justice over a territory, which miserable means of communication made vaster than in fact it was. In combination with the clamor over the probable expense of a federal system, it became evident that some form of judicial visitation such as prevailed in England and in some states was desirable. The scheme devised was to associate the District judge with two, later one, of the Justices of the Supreme Court to hold and keep the Circuit Court in each district within a designated circuit. This was an inimitable idea, but it imposed intolerable travel burden upon the visiting Justices. They were, furthermore, the least pampered of any government servants. No clerks were allotted them, no allowance for travel. The Judiciary and the Process Acts between them required that they acquire a command of state law, and as in every instance this was a memory jurisprudence, they had to put their trust in the attendant District judge. In centers like Boston, New York and Philadelphia, where the bar possessed a high level of competence, the ardors of advocacy invited conflicts of memory

xviii

difficult for a Justice reared in a different legal culture to resolve and consequently tended to induce judicial reliance on English book law. The business of the Circuit Courts was one of steady growth that exacted a heavy toll on a Justice's energies. It was here that the power of review of state and federal legislation was first exercised; here that the defects of the statutory regulation of admiralty appeal were first laid bare. It was from the Circuit Courts that the bulk of the causes to come before the Supreme Court on error came, and although the practice developed that a Justice who sat on a case at Circuit refrained from participating in the Supreme Court decision thereon, it is difficult not to believe that in conference he might supplement the record.

The criminal jurisdiction of the Circuit Courts was insulated by the fact that the Congress did not see fit to provide for error—not even in prosecutions for misdemeanor long permitted in English law. Criminal procedure was left by Congress so far at large that in this area the Circuit Courts were free within the limits of the Bill of Rights to effect a reception of common law practices. The list of crimes against the United States was an attenuated one, and but for the addition of the Sedition Act in 1798, the administration of the criminal law was a matter neither of public solicitude nor of great public interest. It was a partisan wrath over the enforcement of this new act that was to bring on a calculated wave of criticism against the Circuit Courts and eventually to raise the issue of a federal common law, to lead to an attempted disherison of judicial review and to become a ponderable factor in the later assault upon the federal judicial.

Because the Justices moved about the country, the press of the 1790's reflects a widespread interest in their doings on circuit, but the public was illy informed of their work in the Supreme Court. Indeed, it was not until 1798 that the first reports of decisions from a professional hand became available, to be followed in 1799 by a second volume. These publications were a boon to the bar at large, for at long last there were at hand rulings of the Court on appellate practice; certain fundamentals were settled during the first decade of the Court's existence and this portion of the business that came before it must be accounted one of its major achievements. Procedure, after all, is something savored only by the connoisseur and is devoid of the spice that a dash of politics can lend a litigated cause. With such the text of the Constitution proved redolent.

The Supreme Court's first encounter with what developed into a politically explosive cause arose in *Chisholm, Exr. of Farquhar v. the State of Georgia* where it undertook to exercise original jurisdiction in an action against a state by a citizen of another state. The majority of the Justices decided that the meaning of the clause in Article III was plain, which, indeed, it was, although this answer had been evaded throughout the ratification debates. Judgment was duly entered for the plaintiff. Because similar suits against states were already on the docket, the repercussions were profound, and there ensued in the states a resurgence of the pretensions to sovereignty that had bedevilled the formulation and ratification of the Constitution. The contested jurisdiction was expunged by the eventual ratification of the Eleventh Amendment; until this happened, the Court, nevertheless, abided by its precedent.

Among the woes from which the old Confederation government suffered had been the disposition of the new states not to discharge their debts—as if this were a perquisite of newly found sovereignty—and, of even greater embarrassment, to impede the performance of treaty obligations. The so-called diversity jurisdiction conferred upon the federal judicial had been contrived among other reasons to provide a forum where British creditors could pursue their claims without impediment as covenanted in the treaty of peace. Suits for collection, nevertheless, remained obstructed by earlier state statutes allowing discharge of debts paid into state treasuries. Once more the sovereignty argument was paraded in the debt case of *Ware v. Hylton* where it was determined that such acts had been voided by the treaty of peace—the first great affirmation of the supremacy of treaties over state law. The fact that at the same term the Court held constitutional the federal carriage duties—a form of taxation volubly opposed by states' rights advocates—did nothing to smother a growing belief that the federal judiciary was a "foreign" jurisdiction.

What the Supreme Court contributed toward defining the grant of maritime and admiralty jurisdiction was achieved likewise in an atmosphere of political tension, the result of emotions aroused by the wars growing out of the French Revolution. The basic problem of the Court was to establish judicially the obligations inherent in the national policy of neutrality in relation to competing claims of treaty rights, and to resolve conflicting views of the law of nations. This was an awesome task in the face of the sharp divisions of public opinion that swiftly developed into party programs, and the accusations of malfeasance emanating from one of the belligerent powers.

The Supreme Bench remained steadfast in its adherence to the conception that it was a court of justice independent of and coordinate with other branches of government, which it declined to advise and upon which it would not trespass. Neither was it disposed to enlarge its powers beyond what the Constitution seemed explicitly to authorize. In no particular was this more plainly manifested than in the reserve it displayed when urged to exercise supervisory powers over the federal judiciary. The outlook of the Justices was national—it could hardly be otherwise, for the experience of nearly all of them reached back to the

pre-Revolutionary troubles through the travails of the Confederation
and the founding of the Constitution. They gave the Court a tone that
was to persist into another era.

Except as research has dictated some deviations, this volume has
followed in the main the specifications of the plan submitted by the
Permanent Committee for the Oliver Wendell Holmes Devise. It reflects
necessarily the writer's long engagement with problems of the transplantation of law and his belief that even those matters professionally
least beguiling to lay people are part and parcel of intellectual history.
Consequently, the provenance of ideas and the use to which such were
put has seemed to us more worthy of investigation than what may be
called the "outward and visible" aspects of the judiciary such as how it
was housed or the apparel of judges. About these matters others have
written. It has been sought, further, to deal with our evidence at first
hand without regard to anachronous assumptions or sentiments. The
difficulty of estimating men and events in terms of their own times is
close to insuperable. Yet in anything concerning the administration
of the law, it is the virtue of the relevant sources within a given span of
years that these are susceptible of assessment in the context of the
period. A decade and more spent with the muniments of eighteenth-
century law practice has emboldened us to make the attempt.

JULIUS GOEBEL, JR.

Acknowledgments

U PON THE COMPLETION of a work of research a final and pleasurable duty is the tender of thanks to the many who have given aid and comfort. This writer is particularly indebted to the members of the Permanent Committee for the Oliver Wendell Holmes Devise and to its administrative officers—the late Dr. Joseph P. Blickensderfer, the late Mr. Lloyd A. Dunlap, Mrs. Elizabeth E. Hamer and Mrs. Jean D. Allaway —for many favors. Dean William C. Warren of Columbia University School of Law arranged that our undertaking be designated a University project, a benefit that has facilitated our work in many ways. The staffs of the Columbia University libraries and of all the federal repositories— The Manuscript Division of the Library of Congress, the National Archives and the various Federal Record Centers—have all gone out of their way to assist our researches. This has also been our happy experience at the various state and city repositories—the Connecticut State Library, the Massachusetts Archives, the New York State Library, the Boston Public Library, the New York Public Library, Astor, Lenox and Tilden Foundations and the Division of Old Records in the Office of the New York County Clerk.

At all the historical societies and other private collections mentioned in the list of manuscripts the writer and his assistants have received innumerable courtesies in particular from Mr. John D. Cushing, Librarian of the Massachusetts Historical Society. Requests to quote from manuscript sources have been uniformly granted and we are happy to express our gratitude for these permissions to the following:

The Beverly Historical Society, Beverly, Massachusetts, for an excerpt from a letter of Nathan Dane.

The William L. Clements Library, University of Michigan, Ann Arbor, Michigan, for the use of Robert R. Livingston's notes on the Constitution and the Anthony Wayne Papers.

The College of William and Mary in Virginia for matter from the Monroe Papers and the Tucker-Coleman Collection in the Earl Gregg Swem Library.

Columbia University for items in the Jay Papers.

The Maryland Historical Society for a quotation from Samuel Chase's Charge Book.

The Massachusetts Historical Society for quotations from the Cushing, Knox, Pickering, R. T. Paine and miscellaneous manuscripts.

The Newport Historical Society, Newport, Rhode Island, for quotations from letters in the Loan Office Letter Book and Custom House Letter Book.

The New York Historical Society for quotations from the Bancker Papers, the James Duane Papers, the Richard Harison Papers, the Rufus King Papers, the Lamb Papers, the Livingston Papers, the McKesson Papers and the Joseph Reed Papers.

The New York Public Library, Astor, Lenox and Tilden Foundations, for quotations from Gilbert Livingston's notes on the New York Convention.

The Historical Society of Pennsylvania for quotations from the Peter Du Ponceau Letterbooks and his Form Book, the Richard Peters Papers, the Shippen Papers and the William Rawle Papers.

Mr. Thomas Pinckney, Mrs. Langbourne M. Williams and Mrs. M. M. Pinckney for liberty to consult the Pinckney Family Papers.

The Library of the University of Virginia for quotations from letters of Chase and others in the Lee Family Papers.

Yale University Library for quotations from the notes of Sir William Lee in the Osborn Collection.

Acknowledgments for permission to reproduce portraits appear with the illustrations themselves. The writer is most grateful to Miss Helen Sanger of the Frick Art Reference Library for her assistance in the process of selection.

For the examination of the widely dispersed federal judicial records the writer has had the help of a succession of former students. He is especially indebted to Mr. Robert L. Crawford, to Mr. Gerald Mac D. Shea, to Mr. Hugh C. Humphreys, now of the New York bar, and to Mr. Donald J. McLachlan, now of the Illinois bar, for his analysis and reports on the Revolutionary War Prize Appeals and the Supreme Court Appellate Case Papers. Mr. McLachlan also prepared the statistical tables of Supreme Court appellate practice.

A great deal is owed to friends and former colleagues. The late Mr. David J. Mays of the Virginia bar drew our attention to various useful items, and Mr. Harold L. Russell, Jr., of the Georgia bar pursued inquiries into the survival of early rules of court in that state. On all difficult points of practice, United States District Judge Jack B. Weinstein has

ACKNOWLEDGMENTS

given constant expert counsel; Professor Joseph Henry Smith of Columbia Law School has helped to solve difficult questions of admiralty appeals. Professor Gerald Gunther, now of Stanford University Law School, read and made many affirmative suggestions for the betterment of Chapter V. For advice on divers historical problems the writer is indebted to two distinguished historians, Professor Harold C. Syrett, editor of *The Papers of Alexander Hamilton*, and Professor Emeritus Dorothy Burne Goebel. Miss Winnifred Bowers and Miss Betty J. Thomas, associate editors of *The Law Practice of Alexander Hamilton*, have given invaluable editorial aid in the preparation of the manuscript. Finally, the writer's thanks are due to our editor Ray A. Roberts of The Macmillan Company, to Professor Herbert Wechsler of the Columbia Law School and to our editor-in-chief Professor Paul A. Freund for their great interest and encouragement.

Antecedents and Beginnings
to 1801

CHAPTER I

The Path of the Law—
Old World to New

WHEN THE FIRST colonies were planted on the North American continent, the judicial had come to occupy a position of pre-eminence in the English constitution unmatched in any other European country. This position was owed not alone to the high degree of professional competence traditional in the superior courts and the respect in which their judgments were held. It derived also from the centuries-old distribution in depth of court-keeping functions, and from the fact that duties of attendance and of participation by freemen had insured popular engagement in the business of law administration. The diffusion of jurisdiction by feoffment, by royal grant, by force of ancient usage and by statute had brought into being a plethora of courts. As a result, whether in borough, manor, hundred or county, ordinary men took part in the dispensing of justice as an incident, so to speak, of daily life. Because ordinary men fared forth in such numbers to people the New World, there were to be planted here the same beliefs, indeed convictions, respecting the role of the judicial process that prevailed in England. Eighteenth century lawyers made much of the idea intimated by Chief Justice Holt that an Englishman carries his law with him to a new country.[1] This was a convenient if sometimes troublesome fiction.

---

[1] In Blankard v. Galdy, Holt K. B. 341 (1693), Holt is reported saying, "In the case of an uninhabited country newly found out by English subjects, all laws in force in England, are in force there. . . ." See also the reports in 2 Salkeld 411; 4 Modern 222; Comberbach 228. In Dutton v. Howell, Shower P. C. 24 (1693/4), this statement was elaborated by Sir Bartholomew Shower to the effect that when Englishmen go to an uninhabited country the common law must be presumed to be their rule for this is their birthright. The idea is made a matter of imperial constitutional law in the so-called Privy Council Memorandum, 2 Peere Williams 75 (1722), when the Master of the Rolls laid it down: "That if there be a new and uninhabited country found out by English subjects, as

Closer to truth, because demonstrable, is the proposition that what went with the adventurers was what Montesquieu called the spirit of the laws.

If in contemplating the dispositions first made in the pristine seaboard communities it seems not a little pretentious to speak of a spirit of the laws, nevertheless, as one observes the directions taken in colonial efforts to establish a rule of law, one finds exemplified the notion of Montesquieu that independently of the laws made by men, a complex of principles is unceasingly operative that determines their institutions and indeed their legislation.[2] There were many details of English seventeenth century law that appear to us to have been less than admirable, even as they did to the colonists. Yet there is no denying the suzerainty of the great fundamentals—the supremacy of the law, the prescription of certainty, the orderly determination of controversies and, above all, the dominating concept of due process. These people, high and humble, exhibited a preoccupation with operations of the law that irresistibly recalls their Norman ancestors. It was not only, as noticed, that they shared in its administration, but they were also uncommonly litigious, and in the recurrent adversarial situations vis-à-vis the Crown, in which particular and eventually all colonies became embroiled, it was to the books of the law that they turned for munitions.

These involvements with the law had implications beyond the execution of civil justice and the determination of *meum et tuum*. We are prone to forget in our times that in English jurisprudence litigated questions of constitutional right were questions of private law, raised by private law procedures and settled as matters of general law.[3] This, a legacy of the Middle Ages, was still the mode in the colonial period. All the great cases involving such issues that came from the plantations to the Privy Council for final adjudication are standing proof of this. The law at large thus assumes a position of focal importance in the life of the little polities of America, and we must therefore make some inquiry into how it was planted here and how were shaped the institutions by which it was administered. This is a phenomenon of growth

---

the law is the birthright of every subject, so, wherever they go, they carry their laws with them."

The underlying notion—viz., that law is personal—is very old; cf. John Edward Austin Jolliffe, *The Constitutional History of Medieval England, from the English Settlement to 1485* (London: A. and C. Black, 1937), 5, 97; Heinrich Mitteis, *Der Staat des Hohen Mittelalters; Grundlinien einer vergleichenden Verfassungsgeschichte*

des Lehnszeitalters, 4th ed. (Weimar: H. Böhlaus Nachfolger, 1953), 139.

[2] Montesquieu, *Spirit of the Laws* (Dublin: 1751), Bk. I, cc. 1 and 2.

[3] Albert Venn Dicey, *Introduction to the Study of the Law of the Constitution*, 8th ed. (London: Macmillan and Co., 1923), 191. Further references in J. Goebel, "Constitutional History and Constitutional Law," 559–60.

as much a matter of American intellectual as of political history, reaching its eighteenth century climax in the great appeal to the intelligence of the people when the new federal Constitution was offered to them in 1787. Except that a high degree of knowledgeability about the partition of jurisdiction and the appellate process could have been premised, the provisions in the Constitution for the judicial would never have been debated on the rare and often technical level that it was. All this will be later explored, but first of the genesis of the premise.

THE TRANSPLANTATION OF THE LAW

SAVE FOR A few leaders, what the first generations of settlers thought about the law and the institutions that served it was in particulars very different from the notions entertained by sovereign authority for which spoke the experts who drafted the first charters and later the governors' commissions, when the Crown itself took a hand in government overseas. The models for the charters were the forms used for the trading companies that themselves were variants of domestic corporate charters. One clause in these complex instruments conveyed the power to make laws, provided the same were not repugnant to the law of England.[4] This was the standard form by which certain types of corporations were vested with power to make by-laws.[5] In the chartered and proprietary colonies, all of which were to be thus limited, the clause was the warrant pursuant to which local legislatures functioned. In the royal provinces this authority was embodied in a clause of the

---

[4] This can probably be accounted for by the traditions established in the chartering of early overseas trading companies. John Wheeler, who was secretary of the great Merchant Adventurers Company, in his *Treatise of Commerce* (1601), 24–25, describes the authority of the governor and assistants of this company as encompassing the ending and determination of all civil cases, questions and controversies among the members as well as others who might "prorogate the Jurisdiction" of the company and its court—"without appeale, provocation or declination." This was in substance granted by the charter of Henry VII in 1505, an instrument presumably supplanted by Elizabeth's charter of 1564 which granted powers of judicature but had no such provision. The charter of Elizabeth also contained a

clause requiring that ordinances be not contrary to English laws and statutes. For the two charters see George Cawston and Augustus Henry Keane, *The Early Chartered Companies (A. D. 1296–1858),* (London and New York: E. Arnold, 1896), 249, 254. See also the charter to the Eastland Company, in M. Sellers, *Acts and Ordinances of the Eastland Company,* Camden Society *Publications,* 3d ser. (1906), XI, 142, 145; and that to the Levant Company, in R. Hakluyt, *Principall Navigations, Voyages and Discoveries of the English Nation . . . ,* V, 192. On the objective of the companies to secure judicial "facilities" overseas, see W. Cunningham, *Growth of English Industry and Commerce,* I, 416.

[5] *E.g.,* workhouses and hospitals, by St. 39 Eliz. I, c. 5 (1597).

3

governor's commission. No such reservation was written respecting the exercise of judicial power.[6] Presumably royal officials anticipated that this would be exercised in accordance with common law standards. It is, however, conceivable that observance of these standards was deemed to be assured by the existence of the King's prerogative to hear appeals from his demesnes. Yet of this there is no evidence. For in the early decades of colonization there was only the most tentative gesture toward extending appellate authority over any of the new enterprises.[7] It is only after the Restoration that conscious efforts began to exploit this royal prerogative. So far as the continental colonies are concerned, it is not until the reforms of William III that the full impact of appellate control was to be experienced.

The net result of the early English policy, as it was projected in the charters, was that as respects anything relating to the judiciary, insofar as this rested upon colonial enactment, a certain degree of conformity with English law was expected. As respects anything on which there was no specific legislation, the colonists were initially left to their own devices. As it turned out, a truly impressive mass of detail—forms, modes of procedure and rules of substance—was put into effect without any legislative direction whatever. This free dealing with the mechanics and, indeed, the principles of justice was to give a peculiar quality to the first stage of the introduction of English law in America. Many individual peculiarities have been attributed to the effects of the frontier, as if the prospect of forests yet to be felled and the circumambient savages together were to have as immediate an impact on the texture of the immigrants' ideas as they had upon their struggles to settle and survive.[8]

---

[6] An exception may be construed in the short-lived Virginia charter of 1609 which provided that ordinances and proceedings, in which the governor and officials in case of necessity had discretion, must be agreeable to English law. F. N. Thorpe, *Federal and State Constitutions, Colonial Charters, and Other Organic Laws . . .* (1909), VII, 3790, 3801 (hereafter cited as Thorpe, *Constitutions and Charters*). Similar is the limited exception, because of its temporary character, in the charter to William Penn (1681) where laws relating to property "as well for the descent and enjoyment of lands, as likewise for the enjoyment and succession of goods and Chattles and likewise as to Fel-

onies" were to follow the general course of the law of England until altered by Penn and the freemen of the province. *Ibid.,* 3035 at 3038–39.

[7] In 1638, by the terms of the projected restoration of a corporate government in Virginia. 1 *Acts of the Privy Council of England, Colonial Series, 1613–1783,* No. 403 (hereafter cited as *APC Col.*).

[8] See the citations to adherents of the frontier theory collected in J. Goebel and T. Naughton, *Law Enforcement in Colonial New York,* xix–xx; add C. Rossiter, *Seedtime of the Republic,* 27, and Daniel Joseph Boorstin, *The Americans: The Colonial Experience* (New York: Random House, 1958), 25–26.

4

I: *The Path of the Law*

This phantasy does not take into account the state of affairs in the England these men had left. For the dispersion of jurisdiction already mentioned had had the result that, viewed in the large, the law of England was a composite of divers ingredients some of which were rudimentary indeed if measured by the standards of the common law—the creation of the King's courts at Westminister. The common law, of course, was the most important component of this English law. It was important in the sense that within the domain carved out by statutes, by commissions, by writs, by process mesne, and finally, and above all, by the pronouncements of its oracles, the common law courts—King's Bench, Common Bench and Exchequer—asserted and in general maintained a paramountcy in the administration of justice. There were areas where this supremacy was invaded—in the criminal law by Star Chamber, on the civil side by the Privy Council, and by Chancery, which ruled its own bailiwick of equity, remaining a rival, but in a peculiar and limited sense. The common law was the law of the reports and of the great commentaries, and because of the accessibility of this learning, assumptions have been made about the degree to which in England it had permeated or controlled the lives of the subject. This view does not take into account the myriad inferior courts that administered local enactments and a variety of usages, some of great antiquity, some reflecting, ofttimes clumsily, central court law. These were the courts frequented by masses of people for reasons of convenience and economy or because, as in the case of tenant farmers, they would otherwise have been remediless. If the procedure in some burghal courts approached in sophistication the standards of Westminster Hall, that in rural jurisdictions still abode in a relative state of innocence. All of such jurisdictions were subject to supervision by the central courts, through devices for removal of causes or by way of review. But this was so much at the whim of litigants that however important in theory, in practice control was most adventitiously exercised.

It was with this heterogeneous body of local law from the backwaters of the mainstream of the common law that the bulk of the immigrants had had immediate experience. It was from recollections of this experience, from approval or distaste of incidents of mother institutions, that the laymen who manned the courts fashioned the jurisprudence of the infant colonies.[9] In some communities where the law books of the

---

[9] This view of the first stage of reception was set forth in J. Goebel, "King's Law and Local Custom in Seventeenth Century New England," 416–48. There is further matter relating to early developments in New York in Goebel and Naughton, *Law Enforcement in Colonial New York,* at 64, 332–34, 386–90. Joseph Henry Smith, ed., *Colonial Justice in Western Massachusetts, 1639–1702: The Pynchon Court Record . . .* (Cambridge,

Old Testament were held in higher esteem than Dalton's *Countrey Justice* or Kitchin's *Jurisdiction of Courts Leet*—two breviaries for English local court-keepers—some rules of substance of biblical origin were enacted. But barring a very few hardy survivals, this aspect of early law-making left no lasting impress.

If the first phase of American legal development exemplifies the age-old phenomenon of the homing hearts of colonists undertaking to install in the new environment something of what they had forsaken, the second phase is a manifestation of the power of finished art to displace the artless. When lawyers in England discovered in the latter decades of the seventeenth century that the profession need not starve in the New World, the process of remaking provincial law began. Many of these immigrant lawyers were not notably proficient. But they had some training in the common law itself, and were obviously better able to extract meaning from Coke's *Institutes*, to say nothing of the case law, than some parson or planter. It thus became inevitable that the forms and practices current in the royal courts at Westminster and so the body of the common law itself should crowd out the more rudimentary practices and rules first imported and put to use. Owing to the nature of colonial record keeping, this process of displacement is most easily traced in the field of pleading and practice, in conveyancing and the application of English land law. By the beginning of the eighteenth century it is clear that in the superior courts of jurisdictions like New York and Maryland, the hegemony of the common law was assured. In others, like Connecticut, it had not yet completely established itself.

The colonial reception of the common law itself appears to have been an achievement of the bar, although in attributing this feat to the lawyers it is only proper to indicate that we have much more and better evidence of their learning and capacity than of the judges'. The lawyers were forever compelled to produce briefs. But the reporting of any decision was unusual, and it was more or less a matter of chance that here and there some individual would trouble to do so. This almost casual attitude toward native judicial pronouncements may be laid in large measure to the well-nigh utter dependence upon English case law. The reason for this dependence was not alone the availability of published abridgments and reports, but also the deference colonial lawyers were ready to pay to the opinions of courts regarded as peerless.

The whole business of propagating the common law from these

Mass.: Harvard University Press, 1961), 157, and George Lee Haskins, *Law and Authority in Early Massachusetts: A Study in Tradition and* *Design* (New York: Macmillan, 1960), 167–77, agree with the statement in the text.

English sources was in its earlier stages reflexive. It is only later, when at particular junctures the ancient conception of the common law as the subjects' birthright is argued, that lawyers become self-conscious about what they had been doing. So far as Crown policy was concerned, there was every reason not to exercise compulsion that the common law as such be introduced and made effective in the colonies. Otherwise the King's prerogative over the laws in his demesnes would have come to an end, for it was a rule of law that once the common law as such was introduced, it lay with Parliament to make alterations.[10] The Crown, nevertheless, in its dealings with colonial enactments indicated clearly enough that it was intolerant of antic deviations from common law standards.[11] Beyond this, there was of course the control implicit in the exercise of appellate authority of which American lawyers became well aware. But as we shall shortly notice, this did not touch the criminal law, and because of various limitations did not directly affect the great bulk of litigation.

The making over of the law and practice in the colonies in the image of the common law was conditioned by many factors: geography, the availability of professional skill and, above all, the way in which jurisdiction was partitioned. This last deserves particular comment here, for the patterns followed in the arrangement and distribution of jurisdiction in the several colonies contributed to the establishment of distinctly American beliefs regarding the disposition of judicial power. What was done in colonial times determined arrangements in the states upon independence, and the sum of this experience was to affect profoundly the shape of the federal system.

It has been commented in a context irrelevant to our subject that "the English are past masters at holding together odd bits and pieces of incompatible systems and at drawing lines that seem quite arbitrary even to sympathetic friends."[12] No words could better describe the patchwork quilt of English law-enforcing agencies at the time when James Stuart became king. Whether or not the first builders of our commonwealths were aware of the illogic of the institutional scheme they were forsaking, they proceeded to set up their courts in a way at once rational in design and suitable to their needs.[13] Incompatibilities like

---

[10] Calvin's Case, 7 Coke Rep. 1 at 17b.

[11] E. B. Russell, *The Review of American Colonial Legislation by the King in Council*, 149 *et seq.* With reference to legislation regarding the judiciary, see J. H. Smith, "Administrative Control of the Courts of the American Plantations," 1210–53.

[12] B. Minchin, *Outward and Visible*

(London: Darton, Longman and Todd, 1961), 343.

[13] Design emerges in the penultimate stages of organization, for it is apparent that initially in the first colonies—Virginia, Maryland and Massachusetts—the steps taken to provide for more than a single central court were contingent upon the dispersion of settlements. The country courts

the vice-admiralty jurisdiction that were thrust upon them they suffered. But historical accidents, like the probate jurisdiction and Chancery, they managed in some provinces partially to adapt and incorporate in their systems. In other provinces, as in New York and New Jersey, these jurisdictions gained foothold because the inhabitants were powerless to effect change.[14]

---

were entrusted with jurisdiction sufficient to their needs and presumably with regard to the capacities of personnel. Inevitably the supervisory authority and the ultimate appellate power were reserved to an agency at the center of colonial affairs. There is a good account of the Virginia development in P. A. Bruce, *Institutional History of Virginia in the Seventeenth Century*, I, 478 *et seq.* For Maryland, see the account by J. H. Pleasants, ed., *Proceedings of the Provincial Court of Maryland, 1663–1666* (*Archives of Maryland*, 1932), XLIX, vii *et seq.* For Massachusetts, 1639–1702, see Smith, *Colonial Justice in Western Massachusetts*, at 65–88.

New York's judicial system after conquest was the first deliberately planned scheme (probably by Colonel Nicolls and the secretary of the province) and was in large degree an adaptation of the Bay Colony system. It was a scheme imposed by authority with the semblance of popular agreement. A second planned system where there was no attempt to get agreement was that instituted for the Dominion of New England into which New York and New Jersey were embodied. On both of these, see Goebel and Naughton, *Law Enforcement in Colonial New York*, at 16–23, 60–69.

[14] The fate of probate jurisdiction was various. For example, in Virginia it was placed in the county courts in 1645 where it remained. I W. W. Hening, comp., *The Statutes at Large, Being a Collection of all the Laws of Virginia from . . . 1619* [to 1792], (1809–23), 302 (hereafter cited as Hening, *Va. Stats.*). In Maryland the Provincial Court and the county courts exercised the jurisdiction until 1673 when the Prerogative Court was established. A court of delegates was specially commissioned to review

causes. See *Archives of Maryland* (1932), XLIX, xv; E. E. MacQueen, "The Commissary in Colonial Maryland," *Maryland Historical Magazine*, 25: 190, 1930. The act of 1681 (*Archives of Maryland* [1889], VII, 195) made the Prerogative Court competent to deal even with wills that "Concerne Title to Land," notwithstanding English law and custom.

In Massachusetts probate powers were given to the county courts in 1649 and 1652, two magistrates and the recorder being given authority to take proof of wills when the county courts were not sitting. W. H. Whitmore, ed., *Colonial Laws of Massachusetts* (Boston: 1889), 200–201 (hereafter cited as *Col. Laws Mass.*). After the second charter, county Probate Courts were established from which appeal lay to governor and council, to whom the powers of Ordinary were committed by charter. On the similar development in New Hampshire, see Elwin Lawrence Page, *Judicial Beginnings in New Hampshire, 1640–1700* (Concord: New Hampshire Historical Society, 1959), 152–63. Connecticut also set up an independent Probate Court, and the jurisdiction was so far integrated that appeals lay to the Superior Court and thence to the assembly. *Acts and Laws, of His Majesties Colony of Connecticut in New-England, 1702–1729* (1729), 24, 62, 128. In Rhode Island probate and administration were vested in town councils with appeal to governor and council. *Acts and Laws of His Majesty's Colony of Rhode-Island, and Providence-Plantations in America, 1663–1736* (1730–36), 5. Pennsylvania established its Orphans Court in 1683; and despite the vicissitudes of the judiciary laws, there the probate jurisdiction remained with appeal to the Supreme Court. S.

THE COLONIAL JUDICIARY

THE PRINCIPLE EMPLOYED in the establishment of courts was the distinction between inferior and superior jurisdiction—something that could not be carried out to logical fulfillment in England because of the dominance of property concepts of jurisdiction and of the tyranny of long history. The colonials' approach made possible an approximation of a hierarchical ordering of their courts. The inferior-superior

George *et al.*, eds., *Charter to William Penn, and Laws of the Province of Pennsylvania Passed between the years 1682 and 1700* (1879), 180 (hereafter cited as *Charter and Laws Prov. of Pa.*); 2 *The Statutes at Large of Pennsylvania from 1682 to 1801*, 17 vols. (Harrisburg, Pa.: W. S. Ray, State Printer, 1896-1915), Vol. 2-16 compiled by James T. Mitchell and Henry Flanders, Commissioners, 199; 3 *ibid.*, 14.

Equity courts as such did not exist in New England. In Massachusetts, New Hampshire and Rhode Island some equity powers were exercised in common law courts, although in 1741 a brief attempt was made in the latter colony to use a separate court. J. R. Bartlett, ed., *Records of the Colony of Rhode Island and Providence Plantations in New England*, V, 27, 76. Initially in Connecticut the General Assembly exercised equity powers, sometimes through committee. J. H. Trumbull and C. J. Hoadly, eds., *The Public Records of the Colony of Connecticut, 1636-1776*, V, 152, 444; *ibid.*, VIII, 107, 152, 213, 239, 312, 434. Pennsylvania, having originally committed equity powers to the common law courts, maintained a separate court briefly on the basis of a governor's proclamation but abandoned it; see Albert Smith Faught, ed., *The Registrar's Book of Governor Keith's Court of Chancery of the Province of Pennsylvania, 1720-1735* (Harrisburg, Pa.: Pennsylvania Bar Association, 1941). Virginia had also committed equity powers to the county courts and to the General Court which had probably exercised such before the former courts were empowered; see

1 Hening, *Va. Stats.*, 302 (1645), 345 (1647). Maryland made provision for a Chancery Court in 1638 (*Archives of Maryland* [1883], I, 49), but it would appear from the records that the Provincial Court long continued to exercise equity jurisdiction. In 1694 the royal governor set up a Chancery Court (*ibid.*, XX, 136-37, and see *ibid.*, XXVI, 283; thenceforward it remained a separate establishment.

The situation in these royal provinces was the result of the fact that the governor was commissioned as Ordinary, and since he was given custody of the Great Seal of the Province he assumed powers as Chancellor. In New York there had been early legislation giving Chancery powers to the governor (1683) and to governor and council (1691). 1 *Colonial Laws of New York from the Year 1664 to the Revolution* (1894), 125 at 128, 226 at 230 (hereafter cited as *Col. Laws N.Y.*). Lord Bellomont's Court Ordinance of 1699 did not continue this (2 *Laws of the State of New-York, Revised . . .* [1813], App. V). Governor's ordinances issued in 1701, in 1704 and in 1711 established Chancery as a separate court where the governor was Chancellor (*ibid.*, App. No. VII; Ms. Minutes Provincial Council of New York, VIII, 254, 268, and Ms. Minutes, XI, [NYSL]). On the early single court for equity and common law causes in New Jersey, see Preston W. Edsall, ed., *Journal of the Courts of Common Right and Chancery of East New Jersey, 1683-1702* (Philadelphia: American Legal History Society, 1937), introduction. As

9

dichotomy was in the main determined by monetary limitations of the amount in controversy in civil actions, the seriousness of the crime in criminal proceedings. The test of original or appellate jurisdiction was not chosen, chiefly, we believe, because the paradigm of King's Bench, a court of both original and appellate jurisdiction, was in the end not to be ignored. The colonists themselves fixed what may be called the structural principles of their judiciaries in the first decades after settlement and before effective controls were imposed on them by the Crown. There were marked resemblances in the several establishments, because there was some borrowing, but chiefly because the conditions precedent for action were everywhere roughly identical. When active intervention by the Crown began in the latter years of Charles II's reign, so much of the prerogative had been conveyed to so many grantees that it was only in the royal colonies that the King's mandates could operate immediately. On the mainland there was at first only one such province—Virginia. But the ambit of royal orders soon increased as one by one jurisdictions fell into the King's hands. By 1754 only the two corporate colonies, Connecticut and Rhode Island, proprietary Maryland and the Lower Counties (Delaware) were virtually immune from administrative interference by the Crown in their law-making.

---

in New York, when New Jersey became a royal province the Chancery rested on a governor's ordinance. R. S. Field, *Provincial Courts of New Jersey*, New Jersey Historical Society *Collections*, (1849), III, 113; William May Clevenger and Edward Quinton Keasbey, *The Courts of New Jersey: Their Origin, Composition and Jurisdiction* (Plainfield, N. J.: New Jersey Law Journal Publishing Company, 1903), 119–21.

In North Carolina the governor and council sat as a court of Chancery. For early examples, see W. L. Saunders, ed., *Colonial Records of North Carolina, 1662–1776*, I, 422, 435, 454; for later, *ibid.*, V, 654, 811. The early vicissitudes of Chancery in South Carolina are related in Anne King Gregorie, ed., *Records of the Court of Chancery of South Carolina, 1671–1779* (Washington, D.C.: American Historical Association, 1950), 5–7. The establishment by statute of the governor and a majority of the council to be a court of Chancery took place in 1721. T. Cooper and D. J. McCord, Comps., 7 *Statutes at Large of South Carolina, 1662–1838*, (1836–41), 163.

In both New York and New Jersey the governor's authority as Ordinary was exercised by surrogate. See E. B. O'Callaghan and B. Fernow, eds., *Documents Relative to the Colonial History of the State of New-York* (1853–87), VII, 830, 927 (hereafter cited as *Docs. Rel. Col. Hist. N.Y.*); Clevenger and Keasbey, *The Courts of New Jersey, Their Origin, Composition and Jurisdiction*, 128–30, 136. In the "remote" counties of New York, legislation approved by the Crown designated the Courts of Common Pleas as surrogates to take proof of wills. 1 *Col. Laws N.Y.*, 300 (1692); 3 *ibid.*, 780 (1750). For a similar diffusion of authority in New Jersey, see Clevenger and Keasbey, *The Courts of New Jersey, Their Origin, Composition and Jurisdiction*, 128–29.

In South Carolina the governor himself sat as Ordinary; see Ms. Record of the Proceedings of the Court of the Ordinary, 1764–1771, at 50 (S. Car. Hist. Soc.).

I: *The Path of the Law*

The royal administrative control over colonial government was exercised positively through directions in the commission and instructions to royal governors, and negatively through the process of review of colonial enactments. The basic policies with respect to the judiciary as set forth in commissions and instructions were formulated and fixed under the last Stuarts, and typically Stuart they were. The subsidiary policies developed in the review of local legislation dealing with the courts were chiefly the product of the eighteenth century. What was laid down in the commission was of prime importance, because this instrument came to be regarded as the constitution of the royal province.[15] Not only did it provide the frame of government, but for technical reasons of law indicated in the margin the privileges and jurisdictions granted were conceived to be irrevocable.[16] The order to call an assembly was among

---

[15] The idea appears as early as 1677 in an opinion on a Jamaica law by Attorney General Sir William Jones that "by the constitution of that Government as it is founded on His Majesty's Commission the said act is totally void." Ms. Journal of the Lords Committee of Trade and Plantations (rough minutes), II, 238, Nov. 6, 1677 (LC). It appears also in 1679, in a report of the Lords Committee of the Privy Council on Jamaica, in the restricted sense of a frame of government (1 *APC Col.*, No. 1274). The Crown law officers in the eighteenth century treat the effect of the commission as instituting a constitution. G. Chalmers, Comp., *Opinions of Eminent Lawyers on Various Points of English Jurisprudence*, I, 180, 204, 220–21 (hereafter cited as Chalmers, *Opinions*). And see further the 1722 report of the Board of Trade, in *Docs. Rel. Col. Hist. N.Y.*, V, 495, 606. The notion is well settled by 1764 when Thomas Pownall's *Administration of the Colonies* appeared (see 1765 edition, 54). Pownall, however, adds the gloss that the instructions also were a component. The seating of the idea that the commission was a constitution was furthered by the fact that after the early years of the eighteenth century the form and content of the instrument became close to immutable. Only the commissions to the Massachusetts governors did not conform to the pattern used in other royal colonies because of limitations contained in the charter of 1691. These commissions are printed in A. Matthews, ed., *Massachusetts Royal Commissions, 1681–1774*.

[16] The commission was in the form of letters patent issued under process of the Great Seal—the traditional method by which the Crown delegated any prerogative. The rule of irrevocability, which applied as well to charters as to commissions, rested upon the very old rule of the integrity of a royal grant *ex mero motu*, provided there had been no false surmise or deception of the Crown. As we shall see in the next chapter, however, abuse of privileges might lead to forfeiture of the charter. There was, though, a peculiar exception to the normal rule of reversion of privileges in such circumstances into the hands of the Crown. In the Case of the Abbot of Strata Mercella, 9 Coke Rep. 24a at 25b (1591), it had been held that when a privilege, liberty, franchise or jurisdiction "was at the beginning erected and created by the King, and was not any such flower before in the garland of the Crown," such privilege became appendant to the possession and there could be no reversion to the Crown. This doctrine was argued in a South Carolina case of 1759 where it was claimed that the surrender of the patent by the proprietors effected only a transfer of the soil and that the liberties granted in the patent remained. Wil-

the grants, and from this the inhabitants derived their right to legislate. The judiciary was, however, put beyond the assembly's reach, for the power to erect and constitute courts was vested in governor and council, creatures of the King.

When this provision first appeared in a commission,[17] the Crown was bent upon opening and assuring the way to appeals "to our Royall Person," and furthermore, difficulties had arisen over the local judicial enforcement of acts of trade. Either or both of these reasons may account for the reservation.[18] The intention to keep intact the royal prerogative is further evidenced by an instruction that no new courts should be erected without royal orders.[19] This had, of course, the effect of a qualified toleration of the *status quo*. Yet it was not a mandate upon which the inhabitants could base any claim of right. The instructions were "private rules" for the direction of the governor, were "not to be exposed to public view,"[20] and the manner of issuance was such that none

---

liams Adm'r. d.b.n. v. Watson's Ex'rs., Ms. Journal So. Car. Court of Common Pleas, 1754–1763, *sub* Nov. term 1759 (printed in part in Goebel, *Cases and Materials on the Development of Legal Institutions*, 285–86).

The rules about deception of the Crown were developed with respect to grantees. So far as the commission was concerned, the inhabitants of a province were not grantees but beneficiaries; hence these rules were obviously not applicable to them. They were, in any event, regarded as bound by the letters patent; see J. Vaughan, *Process out of the Courts at Westminster into Wales* (1677), 400, 401. The rule of irrevocability is reiterated by Mansfield in Campbell v. Hall, 20 T. Howell, *State Trials*, 239 at 320 (1774).

[17] The commission to Atkins of Barbados (1673), in L. W. Labaree, ed., *Royal Instructions to British Colonial Governors, 1670–1776*, II, 809 (hereafter cited as Labaree, *Royal Instructions*).

[18] For later commissions, see 1 Albert Stillman Batchellor and Henry Harrison Metcalf, eds., *Laws of New Hampshire, including Public and Private Acts and Resolves and the Royal Commissions and Instructions . . .* , 10 vols. (Manchester, N. H.: The John B. Clarke Co., 1904–22), 48, to Cranfield (1682); *ibid.*, 501,

Allen (1691/2); *ibid.*, 612, Bellomont (1699); *Docs. Rel. Col. Hist. N.Y.*, III, 623, Sloughter (1689); Field, *Provincial Courts of New Jersey*, App. B, Cornbury of New Jersey (1702); Labaree, *Royal Instructions*, II, 816, Glen of South Carolina (1739).

[19] Labaree, *Royal Instructions*, I, No. 421. First instituted by instructions to Dutton of Barbados, Ms. Journal of the Lords Committee of Trade and Plantations, III, 187, Aug. 6, 1680 (LC Trans.).

[20] So described by the Board of Trade in 1701. *Calendar of State Papers, Colonial Series, America and West Indies*, (1701), No. 627 (hereafter cited as *CSP Col.*). The policy was settled two decades earlier by the Lords Committee of Trade and Plantations on the point of exhibiting instructions to the Jamaica Assembly. Ms. Journal of the Lords Committee of Trade and Plantations, III, 151, Mar. 5, 1679/80 (LC Trans.).

The injunction of secrecy was impractical to be observed with any consistency because circumstances made necessary disclosure of such regulations as those on trade or appeals. In June 1752 the Board of Trade, in a circular, described the instructions as "calculated in general for the support of His Majesty's Prerogative and protection of his subjects in their just rights, for the

of the rules of law which gave the commission its constitutional quality applied.[21]

Except as he had divested himself by charter, the King never relinquished as a matter of record the prerogative asserted over the creation of courts, saving a grudging concession that assemblies might erect courts for small causes.[22] Nevertheless, in practice the policy generally pursued was to leave undisturbed existing judicial arrangements. The colonists themselves were, indeed, much more disposed to disturb things than was the Crown, provoking frequent disallowance of such legislative experiments. On only four occasions was resort had to the powers granted in the commission by governor and council in the mainland colonies later to become united. Only twice was there direct prerogative action by the Crown.

The first occasion on which the Crown intervened directly was after the Massachusetts patent had been vacated, and James II set up the Dominion of New England (1686–89) which eventually included both New York and New Jersey as well as the four New England colonies. In the first commission[23] sole but limited legislative power was vested in governor and council and the power to erect courts was specifically mentioned. The first ordinance was promulgated by President Joseph Dudley and a council of New Englanders in 1686.[24] It effected a simplification of the earlier Massachusetts system, and without disturbing the inferior-superior court pattern, set at the apex a Superior Court. The commission allowed appeals to governor and council in cases involving over £100. In the second commission, to Governor Sir Edmund Andros, enlarged legislative powers were conveyed.[25] Andros, an experienced colonial administrator, and his council issued a second ordinance (1686/7) dealing with the judiciary that was essentially a modification of the earlier one.[26] What was new was the separation of

---

establishing and preserving good government in his Colonies." *Docs. Rel. Col. Hist. N.Y.*, VI, 760. It is clear from the tenor of the circular that the instructions were binding only on the governor. For litigation of the constitutional question, *infra*, c. II, p. 82.

[21] The instructions issued under the sign manual and signet, the process by which the personal acts of the Crown were authenticated. The complex of rules of law governing public acts under the Great Seal was not applicable.

[22] By a circular letter to governors, Apr. 20, 1703, *CSP Col.* (1702–03), No. 590.

[23] The commission of October 1685

to Dudley is in 1 *Laws of New Hampshire*, 94.

[24] *Ibid.*, 102.

[25] The commission of June 1686, in *ibid.*, 146. A second commission to Andros issued Apr. 7, 1688, covering New York and New Jersey. *Ibid.*, 226; *Docs. Rel. Col. Hist. N.Y.*, III, 537.

[26] A Chancery Court was also erected; and a small causes act was separately promulgated. The ordinance and the act, in 1 *Laws of New Hampshire*, 190, 194; *Public Records of the Colony of Connecticut*, III, 411, 414. The proofs for the actual introduction of the machinery in New York are in Goebel and Naughton, *Law Enforcement in Colonial New*

criminal and civil jurisdiction at the inferior level, and the bestowal on the Superior Court of the powers of King's Bench, Common Pleas and Exchequer. This was an addition of great moment, for in discarding the English precedent of a dispersal of jurisdiction at the superior level, it affirmed the American practice of concentration. Furthermore, the explicit reference to the English central courts could not be without its effects upon the reception of the common law by making relevant the jurisprudence of these courts. That Andros intended this is clear from a report rendered in 1690.[27] The requirement that the Superior Court make the circuit of former jurisdictions was presumably to further uniformity in the law.

The significance of the Andros ordinance is not to be estimated by the brief interval of its vigor as law but by the aftereffects. Both in Massachusetts and New Hampshire it served as the model for the judicial system instituted by legislation in the last decade of the seventeenth century.[28] In New York, where Governor Sloughter apparently did not grasp the purport of his commission, the assembly set up a court structure virtually identical with that instituted by Andros (1691).[29] Subsequently, when the assembly sought to decentralize the system, the governor intervened by ordinance in 1699 to perpetuate the *status quo*.[30] Five years later, after the surrender of New Jersey to the Crown, Governor Cornbury by ordinance restored the scheme there introduced by Andros.[31] In both provinces the judiciary thereafter rested upon ordinance.

The final occasion when the home authorities took the initiative was upon the institution of royal government in Georgia. The plan of government was prepared in England[32] and the provision for the judiciary formally voted by governor and council in 1754.[33] Except as

---

York, at 22–23; and for New Jersey, see Edsall, *Journal of the Courts of Common Right and Chancery of East New Jersey, 1683–1702*, at 25, n. 54.

[27] *Docs. Rel. Col. Hist. N.Y.*, III, 722.

[28] I *Laws of New Hampshire*, 541 (1692), 660 (1699). I *Acts and Resolves, Public and Private, of the Province of the Massachusetts Bay* (1869–1922), 72 (1692), 369–75 (1699), 464 (1701) (hereafter cited as *Acts and Resolves Prov. of Mass. Bay*).

[29] I *Col. Laws N.Y.*, 226 (1691), 303 (1692), 359 (continued in 1695) and 380 (1697).

[30] The text of Governor Bellomont's ordinance is in 2 *Laws of the State*

of New-York, Revised . . . (1813), App. V.

[31] Field, *Provincial Courts of New Jersey*, App. C.

[32] By the law officers of the Crown; see Historical Manuscripts Commission, *Fifth Report* ("Shelburne Papers"), 230. It was considered at length by the Board of Trade attended by the agents for Georgia. *Journal of the Commissioners for Trade and Plantations*, Jan. 1749/50–Dec. 1753 (1932), 376–78.

[33] A bill was prepared by the provincial attorney general. The proceedings are in A. D. Candler, comp., *Colonial Records of the State of Georgia*, VII, 28–88. For an account, see P. S. Flippin, "The Royal Gov-

a provision was made for courts for small causes,[34] jurisdiction over both civil and criminal causes was concentrated in two central courts. This was only a qualified recognition of the inferior-superior court principle, but the colony was then Lilliputian and not ready for a more elaborate organization.

In none of the instances where the judiciary had been established by fiat (with the possible exception of Georgia) was there a basic departure from the pattern that had become distinctively American. The fact that the most radical reorganization, that of Andros, was subsequently accepted by the assemblies of Massachusetts, New Hampshire and New York is indication enough. The Crown had shown no disposition to rebuild the colonial judiciary in the image of the English establishment and, beyond holding separate civil and criminal business, had indulged the colonials' initial design for the judicial. As we have seen, it was not prepared to indulge second thoughts, and consequently the institutional pattern remained remarkably stable throughout the eighteenth century until the Revolution.

The resemblances in the judicial structure as among the several colonies has already been noticed. The differences related to the number of stages in the hierarchy of courts to the ultimate colonial appellate level, and to the lines drawn between inferior and superior jurisdiction as respects nature and extent. After 1753 the final locus of appeal within the colonies was the governor and council in all the royal provinces, except Massachusetts.[35] In the two proprietary provinces, the Supreme Court in Pennsylvania and the Court of Appeals in Maryland performed this function. In the two corporate colonies, Connecticut and Rhode Island, the Assembly was the final resort. It may be remarked that there appears to have been no prejudice against a final review by bodies in which laymen sat in a judicial capacity. There was, after all, the precedent of the House of Lords.[36]

Two factors were involved in settling what original jurisdiction was allocated to inferior courts. There were considerations of public convenience, inevitable because of geography and the difficult state of communications. There was, secondly, in various colonies an antipathy to the centralization of justice. This sentiment was one with which royal officials had no sympathy, and when provincial assemblies sought to

---

ernment in Georgia, 1752–1776: The Judicial System and Administration," *Georgia Historical Quarterly*, 10:251, 1926.

[34] In 1760 the assembly enacted a small causes law. *Colonial Records of the State of Georgia*, XVIII, 372; amended in 1762, *ibid.*, 501.

[35] Because of the peculiar wording of the Massachusetts charter, only in probate cases did governor and council act as an appeal court owing to the vesting of powers as Ordinary.

[36] See T. Beven, "Appellate Jurisdiction of the House of Lords," *L.Q. Rev.* 17:357, 365 *et seq.*, 1901.

give it practical effect, they experienced the full force of the royal policy against erecting "new courts."[37]

Although the colonial inferior courts served much the same purpose as did the English local courts, providing convenient forums for petty litigation, the resemblance goes no further. For over here there was no complex of indigenous custom rooted in remote centuries, and little local enactment of a nature to form the basis of a particular law and practice.[38] These inferior tribunals were intended to be part of a more integrated system than was the case in England, and they were susceptible of integration because despite early experiment in certain colonies, property concepts of jurisdiction never gained a foothold here.[39] The conditions for ultimate reception of common law from the ground

[37] For example, the controversy in New York that led to the court ordinance of 1699. In the act of 1695 the assembly, over protest by Governor Fletcher, committed trial of land titles to the county inferior Courts of Common Pleas. 1 *Col. Laws N.Y.*, 359; *Journal of the Legislative Council of New York* (1861), I, 86. Subsequently, the assembly in 1699 attempted to convert the central Supreme Court into a county court (*Journal of the Legislative Council*, I, 140), upon which Governor Bellomont issued the ordinance on which the New York establishment thereafter rested. The struggle over decentralization in Pennsylvania is related in J. H. Smith, "Administrative Control of the Courts of the American Plantations," 1210 at 1217.

[38] Not even in chartered cities where ordinance powers for local purposes were exercised; *e.g.*, New York, on which see A. E. Peterson and G. W. Edwards, *New York as an Eighteenth Century Municipality*, 230, 391. Some eighteenth century ordinances for Philadelphia are in Brown and Williams, comps., *Digest of Laws and Ordinances Concerning Philadelphia, 1701–1904*, (Philadelphia: J. L. H. Bayne, 1905). Of similar cast are the Boston town ordinances; see those scattered in *Reports of the Record Commissioners of the City of Boston: Boston Town Records, 1700–1728, 1729–1742, 1742–1757, 1758–1769, 1770–1777* (1883–87).

Ordinance-making by local bodies

in England, *e.g.*, the manorial leets, was very ancient and there is a sprinkling of Yearbook cases relating thereto. The ordinance-making of justices of the peace in England very obviously influenced developments in America. On this see S. and B. Webb, *English Local Government . . . The Parish and the County*, 535 *et seq.* The nexus with America is most clearly indicated in Virginia practice; see Bruce, *Institutional History of Virginia in the Seventeenth Century*, II, c. 32. Massachusetts town ordinance-making is discussed in A. B. MacLear, *Early New England Towns* (New York: Columbia University Press, 1908), 106–36; for New York, see Goebel and Naughton, *Law Enforcement in Colonial New York*, at 36–42.

[39] On the experiment with manorial courts in Maryland, see J. H. Johnson, *Old Maryland Manors*, Johns Hopkins University *Studies in History and Political Science* (1883), VII. On the short-lived experiment in New York, J. Goebel, *Some Legal and Political Aspects of the Manors in New York* (Baltimore: 1928). The preposterous "Fundamental Constitutions of Carolina" (1669), drafted by philosopher John Locke and Lord Chancellor Shaftesbury, contemplated transplanting the property concept of jurisdiction (Thorpe, *Constitutions and Charters*, V, 2772); and so did the Penn charter (1681) which licensed erection of manors with court-keeping privileges (*ibid.*, 3042–43).

up were thus highly favorable. The extent to which these local courts remained havens for practices introduced during the early decades of colonization when so much of local English usage was transplanted has never been studied. One may hazard that these were only slowly extirpated, although some of the crudities and ineptitudes of the early eighteenth century are easily mistaken for vestiges of the past. These were, in any event, matters for missionary work by the bar.

To what degree accomplished and experienced lawyers were likely to be engaged in inferior court litigation and exercise their amending hands depended, of course, upon whether or not business of consequence could be conducted at this level. Clearly in provinces like New Jersey and New York, where causes exceeding very limited amounts were removable from the local Courts of Common Pleas to the respective Supreme Courts,[40] proffered retainers for country trials would be less than tempting. Litigation here would be handled by country lawyers— of no great parts in early days as surviving pleadings indicate. Or, as was later the case with John Jay and Gouverneur Morris, newly fledged barristers might appear in these courts to try out their wings.[41] The possibility of review by writ of error or certiorari, of course, had a minatory effect upon inferior courts inducing compliance with common law forms and rules so far as lay within the capacities of practitioners.

Other provinces, like Massachusetts, Pennsylvania and Virginia, vested their county courts with broad original jurisdiction.[42] There was

---

[40] In New Jersey, by the Cornbury Ordinance (1702), causes over £10 involving land titles or anything relating thereto. The Hunter Ordinance (1714) permitted removal of any cause, and this was continued by the Burnet Ordinances of 1724, 1725 and 1728. In New York causes involving over £20 were removable under the terms of the Bellomont Ordinances. The device used was an ingenious adaptation of the *habeas corpus ad respondendum* which removed both adversary and record.

[41] See Ms. Minutes Court of Common Pleas, Westchester County, 1723–1773, particularly during the year 1770 (Westchester County Clerk's Office, N.Y.).

[42] For Massachusetts, 1 *Acts and Resolves Prov. of Mass. Bay*, 369 (1700), 459 (1701), where actions were excluded when the King was a party. In Pennsylvania the successive disallowances of judiciary acts in-

volved a paring down of Common Pleas powers, although when the Act of 1722 was finally allowed, the powers were still very large. The 1701 act conveyed criminal jurisdiction (except for treasons and what were classified as grand felonies) and all forms of action as well as equity jurisdiction. *Charter and Laws Prov. of Pa.*, 311. Governor Evans' interim ordinance (*ibid.*, 319) cut off the criminal jurisdiction, but left common law and equity jurisdiction as before. In the 1722 act (*ibid.*, 387) the equity jurisdiction was not mentioned, the short-lived Chancery Court being then in operation.

In Virginia the earliest legislation regarding county courts is obscurely worded—all suits to the value of one hundred pounds of tobacco; see 1 Hening, *Va. Stats.*, 125 (1624). In 1642/3 the minimum limit for actions was two hundred pounds of tobacco. Then in 1645 the county courts were

thus no reason why possible rewards might not be adequate to tempt members of the "urban" bar. Yet John Adams' remembrance of Massachusetts country practice as being in "the hands of Deputy Sheriffs, Pettyfoggers and even Constables" indicates the contrary.[43] Things may have been on a better footing in Pennsylvania. The fact that James Wilson was content to practice in the country for years[44] suggests this. And, for Virginia, so do the casebooks of Thomas Jefferson, who had a considerable practice in local county courts which possessed a substantial common law as well as an equity jurisdiction.[45]

The reworking of procedure in the inferior courts so that it bore some resemblance to practice in the superior courts tended to promote in each colony a certain degree of uniformity in what writers were then fond of calling the "unwritten law." A comparison of early eighteenth century local records with those immediately prior to the Revolution shows a measurable advance in technical proficiency. The fact, however, that the bench in these rural inferior courts was in all colonies predominantly lay could not but have a retarding effect. This situation had further, we believe, a direct bearing upon the frequency with which litigants sought review of the causes in superior courts. This is a matter on which statistics are wanting, but it is apparent from the amount of colonial legislation designed to limit the appellate process that the inhabitants at different times and places were minded to resort to it too freely for public convenience.[46] It is clear, furthermore, from the tenor and amount of writing on and discussion of the appellate jurisdiction, when the ratification of the federal Constitution was being debated, that the problem excited general interest to a degree explicable only on the basis of familiarity with, if not expert knowledge of, its scope.

---

given full jurisdiction over all causes in law and equity (*ibid.*, 303). This was cut down in 1661/2 to cases involving more than 20*s.* or two hundred pounds of tobacco (2 *ibid.*, 72). In the revision of 1710 this jurisdiction was reaffirmed. Minor civil actions were committed to single justices of the peace (3 *ibid.*, 504, 507). That Chancery cases in the county courts were handled with some professional skill in the late colonial period is indicated by certain petitions and bills in Chancery preserved among the Ms. Tucker-Coleman Collection (Earl Gregg Swem Library, The College of William and Mary in Virginia); see Randolph v. Royall (1753), Fairley v. Fairley (1762), in "Chester-

field County Court Papers, 1753–1786"; Scott v. Newell (1766), Walker v. Woodlief (1772), in "Prince George County Papers, 1703–1785."

[43] L. H. Butterfield, ed., *Diary and Autobiography of John Adams*, III, 274 (hereafter cited as *Adams Papers*).

[44] C. P. Smith, *James Wilson, Founding Father, 1742–1798*, 37, 46–49.

[45] Ms. Jefferson Register of Cases, and Ms. Fee Book, both in The Huntington Library, San Marino, Calif. Dr. Julian P. Boyd, editor of *The Papers of Thomas Jefferson*, kindly loaned us his transcripts of both manuscripts.

[46] *Infra*, n. 158.

APPELLATE DEVICES: THE ENGLISH PARADIGMS

IT WILL BE USEFUL here to consider the appellate devices current in the colonies, for what may be described as political thinking about the structure of the judicial was to some extent molded by the nature of these devices and the use to which they could be put. This thinking was largely the result of experience with the review of civil actions at common law. Consequently, it is with the mechanics of this that we will be concerned. The English common law furnished two major devices—the writ of error and the certiorari. In eight of the colonies a third device was to be developed—an adaptation to new uses of a procedure in the English Quarter Sessions Courts, the so-called appeal.

The writ of error had been perfected in the course of the thirteenth century as a means of reforming a judgment in a King's court, the record of which was otherwise unimpeachable.[47] Although something was owed to more ancient procedures for controlling judgments of local courts, the chief debt of the writ of error proceeding was to the canon law. But unlike the appeal of Roman and canon law, that was by definition the transit of a cause once determined from a lower to a superior court, the proceeding in error was conceived as original, and, indeed, the writ issued from Chancery as an original. The form of the writ[48] once settled, it remained virtually unaltered until modern times.[49] On its face the writ discloses something of its nature and limitations. It alleges that "in the record, and process, and also in the giving of judgment" in a certain cause, manifest error has intervened to the injury of the complainant, and states the Crown's willingness that the error, if any, be corrected and justice be done thereupon to the parties. It directs that if judgment has been given, the record and process "with all things touching them" be transmitted under seal of the judge to whom the writ is directed, for inspection of the matter transmitted and to do what of right ought to be done.

What would come before the reviewing authority by appellant's assignment of errors was restricted by the nature of the common law record—writ, mesne process, pleadings, issue, jury process, the verdict

---

[47] The origin has been traced in J. Goebel, "Matrix of Empire," introduction to J. H. Smith, *Appeals to the Privy Council from the American Plantations*, xxv–xxxviii.

[48] For the form of the writ, see *Registrum Brevium*, 4th ed. (1687), 17, 132; see also Fitzherbert, *Natura Brevium*, 9th ed. (1794), 24D.

[49] There were certain minor deviations of language when the use of Latin and Law French was abolished by statute in 1731 (4 Geo. II, c. 26). The Englished form is in Blackstone, *Commentaries on the Laws of England*, 1771 ed., III, App., xxi (hereafter cited as Blackstone, *Commentaries*).

and the judgment. Since the word "processus" in the pristine Latin form of the writ of error is ambiguously "proceedings" or "process," it is conceivable that something more than the instruments issued to secure attendance may have been intended. If this was the case, the writ was not so read, and a statute was needed to make the proceedings in error more effective. This was done by the Statute of Westminster II (1285)[50] which provided for the bill of exceptions, viz., the privilege of taking exceptions to judicial rulings that, if denied, were to be inscribed by the objector and judicially sealed. The statute anticipates that sealed objections be embodied in the roll of the case, but if not, makes provision for their exemplification by the plaintiff in error, in which event the judge is required to affirm or deny his seal.

Because of the nature of the record which was requisitioned by the writ of error, and upon which the judgment was founded, the proceedings in error were from the first concerned only with questions of law.[51] Where a cause was tried on issues of fact, there never was a question of going behind the verdict. The King's judges had always treated as conclusive the results of any method of proof, provided there were no procedural irregularities, whether the method was compurgation, ordeal or battle, and eventually trial by the country, viz., the true speaking of the men of the vicinage on controverted facts.[52] The fact that the witness quality of the jury had become virtually obliterated[53] when the verdict was reached on the basis of proofs adduced at trial, in particular through "witnesses indifferent," as an old statute has it,[54] did nothing to alter the status of the verdict in error proceedings except insofar as it may have rested upon judicial misdirection in the admission of evidence or comment on its effects. It was precisely here that the bill of exceptions proved its usefulness.

---

[50] 13 Edw. I, c. 31.

[51] This is manifest from the structure of the common law record where all the details related culminate in the formula judgment *ideo consideratum est* (therefore it is considered) by the court. On this see Coke, *Littleton*, 39a, 168a, 288b.

[52] On the petit jury as a "method of proof," see F. Pollock and F. W. Maitland, *History of English Law*, 2d ed. (Cambridge: Cambridge University Press, 1898, reprint 1923), II, 621 *et seq.*; W. Holdsworth *History of English Law* (1927), I, 316–17. It should be added that the century-long habit of royal judges of treating the fact-finding of any inquest as conclusive, barring misspeak-

ing or perjury, was not without influence in the posture taken toward verdicts on trial.

[53] A vestige, of course, was the challenge to the array for want of hundredors, the theory being that they were needed "for their better notice of the cause." Coke, *Littleton*, 157a. By St. 27 Eliz. I, c. 6 (1584) two hundredors in personal actions sufficed, and in 1705 it was enacted that if the jury came from the body of the county it was sufficient (4 Anne, c. 16, §6). Not until 6 Geo. IV, c. 50, §13 (1825) was the requirement of hundredors on criminal juries abolished.

[54] 27 Hen. VIII, c. 4 (1535).

I: *The Path of the Law*

The conventional bill of exceptions in the late seventeenth and eighteenth centuries was in narrative form and embodied an account of the tenor of the evidence adduced by one or both litigants and objections either to its admission or to rulings on its legal effect—usually in the course of a charge to the jury.[55] If the bill was not attached to the record, the pleadings were set out. Exceptions were taken at trial. The instrument specifying the errors in law which a plaintiff in error alleged were embodied in an assignment of errors after judgment. The importance of such assignments is indicated by the numerous precedents set out in the books of Entries, the practitioners' form books.[56]

Proceedings in error had originally been conceived as a remedy against unjust judgments, and although debased by men "prying with eagles' eyes," as Coke put it,[57] for errors in form, the underlying ethical concept that a judgment should be just was never obliterated. The remedy, apart from serving as a safeguard against adjudication of individual rights on the basis of mistakes in law, was manipulated as a means of arriving at the right rule, a consideration of crucial importance in a system of law that rested on precedent.[58] Error was not a device designed generally to supervise the administration of justice. The writ ran only to courts of record proceeding according to the course of the common law. This, as a practical matter, limited proceedings chiefly to cases in the two central courts at Westminster, or in the Assizes or those heard by virtue of royal commission.[59] Since the King's courts were, in the old phrase, theoretically *pari gradu* (of equal rank),[60] the

---

[55] Examples of forms, in J. Lilly, *Modern Entries,* 1723 ed., 250–51, 273; Fabrigas v. Mostyn, 20 Howell, *State Trials,* 82 at 189–93 (1774); F. Buller, *An Introduction to the Law Relative to Trials at Nisi Prius,* 7th ed. (1817), 317 (Trinity term, 3 Geo. III). A later example is in W. Tidd, *Forms of Practical Proceedings in the Courts of King's Bench, Common Pleas, and Exchequer of Pleas,* 6th ed. (1824), 374.

[56] Coke, *Booke of Entries* (1614), s.v. Error.

[57] Higgen's Case, 6 Coke Rep. 44b at 46a.

[58] To this end was admirably adapted the convention developed in the central courts that the judgment was arrived at by argument among the judges. This may be taken in its origin as a projection into the realm of the law of scholasticism's method of disputation. This is evident in many Yearbook cases and was carried into modern times by Plowden in his *Commentaries* (1550–80) and, of course, by Coke in his *Reports.* For some comment, see M. Hemmant, ed., *Select Cases in the Exchequer Chamber, 1461–1509,* Selden Society Publications (1945), LXIV, xvi–xvii.

[59] And in a few other courts, *e.g.,* in a County Palatine, Coke, *The Fourth Part of the Institutes of the Laws of England,* 1809 ed., 214, 218 (hereafter cited as Coke, *Fourth Institute*); in Wales, in pleas real and mixed, by 34 & 35 Hen. VIII, c. 26, §113 (1542).

[60] And see here the discussion in *Ex Parte* Fernandez, 10 C.B. (n.s.) 3 (1861), where the distinction made in M. Bacon, *A New Abridgment of the Law,* 3d ed. (1768), s.v. Courts D, between courts of record that are

writ of error had to be treated as a special commission[61] and the scrutiny of the record for errors of law as a new proceeding. There was no question of setting one court over another as a sort of schoolmaster.

To adapt English proceedings in error to a system based, as was the colonial, on the distinction of superior and inferior courts both as a matter of theory and, lamentably, of quality, involved a change in opinion about the writ's function.[62] For although the end of doing justice *inter partes* remained, the procedure assumed the aspect of a species of supervision by relative proficiency over unproficiency. Maryland seems to have been the first province to employ the writ (post-1660),[63] and at various dates thereafter in the ensuing fifty years there is practical reception or legislation in other colonies. But the "law of errors" as it stood in England around the beginning of the eighteenth century was not the simplest matter to adapt to colonial uses. For one thing, the procedure had become encrusted with a mass of highly technical learning. Much of this was dispensable here in the early stages of reception, but like anything embalmed in the books was susceptible to being exhumed to make difficulties for judges new to their tasks. In the second place, the procedure was, in particulars, too narrow to be fully effective as a supervisory device. This was the criticism of a leading Maryland lawyer in 1697. He believed that there should be greater latitude in assigning errors than in England "and the merits of the Cause [ought] to be more inquired into by the Judges" because judges and juries were disposed to be moved more by personal feelings toward litigants than by the merits, or by the law.[64]

If colonial judges and lawyers had been prepared to experiment

---

more principal and less principal was repudiated as to courts of Assize (hereafter cited as Bacon, *Abridgment*).

[61] Coke, *The Second Part of the Institutes of the Laws of England,* 1809 ed., 40 (hereafter cited as Coke, *Second Institute*).

[62] Although there was an obvious difference in grade between a court of record like the General Quarter Sessions of the Peace and King's Bench, there were only a few English cases which speak of error to "inferior" courts of record; *e.g.,* Ap-Richarde v. Jones, 2 Dyer 250 (1566); Roe v. Hartly, Cro. Eliz. 26 (1584). It is not until the eighteenth century that this notion gains real foothold. Thus the anonymous *Law of Errors* (1703), c. XVIII, "Errors of Judg-

ment in Inferior Courts"; and following this, Matthew Bacon's *Abridgment* (first published 1736-59), *s.v.* Error, where the writ is defined as a commission to judges of a superior court by which they are authorized to examine the judgment given in an inferior court. None of the cases cited supports this definition.

[63] *Proceedings of the Provincial Court of Maryland, 1663-1666 (Archives of Maryland, 1932),* XLIX, 358 (1664/5), contains the first recognizable writ. In two earlier cases it is possible the formal writ was employed; see *ibid.,* 122 (1663), 330 (1664).

[64] Charles Carroll, in *Proceedings of the Council, 1694-1697 (Archives of Maryland, 1900),* XX, 439.

with certiorari, the other long-established writ for review, they might have made of it something more suited to their needs than the writ of error. They seem, however, to have settled for using certiorari as it was commonly employed in England. Originally, certiorari had been the most flexible of mandates as the variety of precedents in the form books indicates.[65] The underlying principle was the old one that it was the King's prerogative to have certified to him the record of any of his courts.[66] Certiorari was, therefore, one of the family of prerogative writs and it did not entirely lose this quality even when in certain situations it lay virtually as of course.

In the hands of the King's Bench certiorari became one of the chief instrumentalities by which this court's power of superintendence over the administration of justice was exercised. The writ came to be used at an early date to remove causes,[67] in particular indictments, for trial in a form other than the one where proceedings had been begun. Since the writ was structurally susceptible of various applications, the removal form was adapted with minor changes for purposes of review.[68] It contained no allegation of error, stating only that "for certain causes" the King wished to be certified upon the record and process of the case. Like the writ of error it required that judgment should have been rendered, and commanded the transmission under seal of record, process and all things touching them.

The certiorari for review was peculiarly associated with the control of the conglomerate of powers exercised by the justice of the peace.[69] In the process of converting these functionaries into mainstays of county government in England there had been conferred upon them acting singly, by twos, or threes or fours, a heterogeneous complex of police and general administrative duties. These powers could be exercised summarily, and in two notable instances, forcible entries and riots, the justices were themselves authorized to make inquest on the basis of which conviction would be had.[70] The nature of the record of orders

---

[65] Fitzherbert, *Natura Brevium,* 81C, 147B, 242B–48E.

[66] For the reason precisely that they were *his* courts and the records were unimpeachable. Leges Henrici, 31, 4 and 49, 4; Glanvill, *De Legibus et Consuetudinibus regni Angliae,* G. Woodbine, ed. (New Haven: Yale University Press, 1932), VIII, 8, 9.

[67] For a form of removal, Fitzherbert, *Natura Brevium,* 245C–F.

[68] For a form of certiorari to review, *ibid.,* 242B.

[69] On the early use, see B. H. Putnam, *Proceedings before the Justices*

of the Peace in the Fourteenth and Fifteenth Centuries, Edward III to Richard III (London: Spottiswoode, Ballentyne and Co., 1938), lxiv *et seq.*

[70] In forcible entries the founding statutes were 5 Ric. II St. 1, c. 8 (1381), 15 Ric. II, c. 2 (1391), and 8 Hen. VI, c. 9 (1429); for later statutes, W. Hawkins, *Pleas of the Crown,* 2d ed. (1724), I, c. 64. A single justice, upon notice of forcible entry, holding or detainer, was empowered to arrest the offenders at the place and make a record upon view. This was a sufficient conviction, on

or convictions by justices of the peace was such that a writ of error would not have been appropriate. In consequence, the certiorari was employed, and since the bill of exceptions was entirely associated with common law proceedings in error, it was not available in certiorari proceedings. The eventual judicial explanation of the distinction between error and certiorari was that where a court of record or judge acted according to the course of the common law a writ of error would lie on their judgments. But where they acted in a summary way or in a new course different from the course of the common law, error did not lie but certiorari.[71]

Both the writ of error and certiorari came into general use in colonies that fashioned their procedure most closely on common law models. But one may suppose that the certiorari was the form of review with which the first generations of settlers, at least the more substantial of them, were most familiar. For in England the writ served as the only available means of securing relief at the hands of a superior court of an oppressive order such as fixing rates, binding apprentices, settling paupers, bastardy or summary convictions—all matters within the periphery of ordinary human experience. An order could be certified directly to King's Bench, but would also lie thereto after an intermediate review by the General Quarter Sessions of the Peace.

In its social significance such intermediate review greatly overshadowed employment of the older forms, because it was so universally resorted to that in eighteenth century England this business nearly crowded the original jurisdiction of General Sessions off the books.[72] To this procedure the name of "appeal" was popularly attached at an early date, and given currency by the manuals composed for the use of justices of the peace. The procedure was made available in a long succession of English statutes beginning in the second half of the sixteenth century, and as the variety and number of duties loaded upon the justices out of Sessions was increased, the amount of appeal business rose in due ratio.[73] Indeed, the appeal became, in the words of two

---

the basis of which offenders could be imprisoned and make fine. See further W. Lambard, *Eirenarcha* (1614), 136. The basic riot statute was 13 Hen. IV, c. 7 (1411). Two justices with the sheriff were empowered to make a record upon view which again was sufficient basis for summary conviction. Without the sheriff, a single justice could only attempt to disperse the rioters and cause inquest to be made by a jury.

[71] Groenvelt v. Burwell, 1 Salkeld

263 (1698).

[72] Webb, *English Local Government . . . The Parish and the County*, at 420, n. 1.

[73] The germ of the appellate procedure may have lain in the practice where a single justice issued an order and the person affected was often put under recognizance which was certified to Quarter Sessions. There, depending upon the form, the individual might make his objections. The first statute clearly indicating the appellate

profound students of English county government, "the almost universal right of the aggrieved party."[74] It was a writless procedure and was initiated at the prayer of defendant. It involved no more than that the full bench of justices of the peace in Sessions would examine the order, information and examination, if any, and determine whether to confirm, alter or reverse. Since the justice out of Sessions was competent both as to law and fact, review by the full bench was on a much broader basis than was possible in a strict common law procedure.

The institution of the justice of the peace was everywhere transplanted to this country, and along went the traditional statutory functions to which the colonial assemblies made constant additions. Surveillance by the superior courts, but even more, the distribution and use of the many English handbooks on the office of justice of the peace, assured adherence here to the details of English procedures. Against this species of justice almost every inhabitant was likely to brush, be he ever so law-abiding. The effect of this experience had, we believe, much more to do with establishing in men's minds ideas about law enforcement and in particular about the "right of appeal," in whatever species of litigation or prosecution they might be embroiled, than did the older forms of review. The records of local courts that we have examined indicate a frequent resort to the appeal, although this did not reach the almost pathological dimensions that it did in England.

APPELLATE DEVICES: AMERICAN INNOVATIONS

So MUCH FOR the seating of the English Sessions appeal as it related to administrative orders and convictions for petty offenses. By the same name and at a very early date there was instituted in three colonies, Virginia, Maryland and Massachusetts, a procedure for reviewing civil actions that appears to us to have been adapted from the Sessions appeal. There is no question that the American legislation and

---

authority of Quarter Sessions is 14 Eliz. I, c. 5 (1572), which authorizes review of rates fixed by justices, churchwardens and others. And see here, 39 Eliz. I, c. 3 (1597); 43 Eliz. I, c. 2, §§5 and 6 (1601). The statute 18 Eliz. I, c. 3, §2 (1576), dealing with bastardy, provides for two justices to make orders regarding punishment and support, and to require persons not performing to give surety for appearance before the full bench. The great extension of appellate authority is made in the 1601 revision of the poor law, where the binding out of apprentices, settlement of poor rates and "any other act" of justices of the peace are made reviewable. The term "appeal" in the statutes begins after the Restoration; see 13 & 14 Car. II, c. 12, §2 (1662), and 22 Car. II, c. 1, §6 (1670).

[74] Webb, *English Local Government . . . The Parish and the County*, at 420.

practice could have been in imitation of the English Chancery appeal, for this was still, so to speak, *in ventre sa mere* when the first American enactments were put on the books. At this time the process of copying the incidents of English local laws and procedures was in full spate. The Sessions appeal consequently seems the most likely source, unless one is prepared to concede a greater degree of inventiveness than is otherwise observable in procedural matters. But whatever the source, the "appeal" of civil actions was soon to become firmly established in ten American colonies and to enjoy a brief life in an eleventh. The Massachusetts version was to be the model for Connecticut, Rhode Island and New Hampshire. And because the first code in New York, the Duke's Laws (1665), was largely derived from the Massachusetts Bay Laws, these may be taken to have been the source of the appeal used in the newly conquered province.[75] With the reorganization of the judiciary there in 1683 and the introduction of the writ of error, the New York appeal came to an end.

In the South there does not appear to have been resort to a mother statute, although it is possible that Maryland and later North Carolina may have been influenced by Virginia practice. These colonies eventually all used the writ of error, and the appeal procedure was influenced by this fact. Where, as in Virginia and later Pennsylvania, equity powers were bestowed on inferior courts, the adaptability of the appeal is obvious. The developments have never been exhaustively investigated, but they deserve to be because of their effect upon American thinking about the review process. We can perforce give only an incomplete sketch, indicating chiefly how the various procedures differed from those traditional in England.

The New England appeal was the most complex of all the various adaptations. It is first mentioned in the Massachusetts legislation of 1636 setting up courts in the counties, and is embalmed in the Body of Liberties (1641).[76] There was further legislation in succeeding years. As matters stood in the Code of 1648, the magistrates of the appellate court were competent to hear matters of law, but matters of fact had to be considered by bench and jury.[77] At this time, as later, all evidences

---

[75] The provision of the Duke's Laws is in 1 *Col. Laws N.Y.*, 11. The first volume of the Proceedings of the Court of Assizes, 1665–1672, was burned. A Ms. Calendar in the New York Public Library shows a lively appeal business. *The Proceedings of the General Court of Assizes, 1680–1682*, New-York Historical Society *Collections* (1912), XLV, 3–38, indicates a review of proceedings including verdict. The numerous cases do not show use of a jury at the appellate step.

[76] N. B. Shurtleff, ed., *Records of the Governor and Company of the Massachusetts Bay in New England*, I, 169; *Col. Laws Mass.*, 41.

[77] *The Laws and Liberties of Massachusetts* (1648), introd. by M. Farrand (reprint 1929), 2.

were required to be in writing "for presidents" and for purposes of review.[78] In 1654 it was enacted that judgment had to be on former evidence.[79] The right of appeal lay from judgments of single magistrates to county courts and from county courts to the Court of Assistants.

After the second Massachusetts charter (1691) and the reorganization of the judiciary there was a recodification of the law in an act of 1701[80] that was substantially taken over by New Hampshire. Appeals were provided for from inferior Courts of Common Pleas to the Superior Court. An appellant was required to produce in the latter court attested copies of writ, judgment and all the evidence, and also to file a declaration of his reasons with the clerk of the former court who would attest it and turn it over to appellant for delivery to the court where the appeal was to be tried. In the appellate court each party was allowed the "benefit of any new and further plea and evidence." The feature of trial by jury on the appeal was preserved.

Although the courts in Massachusetts seem to have thought that their appeal was in the nature of writ of error proceedings,[81] it cannot be regarded as even a perversion of such. The manner of initiating an appeal resembles that used to bring a case to General Sessions and not a proceeding begun by mandate. Even the wonderfully ample record could not substitute for a bill of exceptions, for it contained nothing of proffered but rejected evidence. Furthermore, the appeal had a strange bedfellow indeed—the so-called bill of review. This procedure had been originally conceived of as a new trial on the basis of new evidence. When new evidence and pleas came to be permitted in appeals, the bill of

---

[78] *Ibid.*, 46; and see the Code of 1660, *Col. Laws Mass.*, 187–89.

[79] *Col. Laws Mass.*, 122. Appellant filed "reasons" for appeal which have a certain bucolic resemblance to assignments of error. For samples see 3 J. F. Cronin, ed., *Records of the Court of Assistants of the Colony of the Massachusetts Bay, 1630–1692* (1928), 42–43 (1656), 50 (1657), 75–76 (1659/60), 88 (1659/60), 112 (1660/61). Further examples are scattered in *Records of the Suffolk County Court, 1671–1680*, Colonial Society of Massachusetts Publications (1933), XXIX, XXX. See also Browne v. Dever (1683), in Ms. Mass. Archives (Judicial 1683–1724), XL, 1–2; Nourse v. Endicott (1682), *ibid.*, 37–39. The "reasons" for appeal were abolished in January 1741/2 (2 *Acts and Resolves Prov. of Mass. Bay*, 1086).

[80] 1 *Acts and Resolves Prov. of Mass. Bay*, 464. Earlier acts embodying similar provisions had been disallowed (*ibid.*, 285, 373).

[81] There was statutory provision for writ of error (*ibid.*, 73, 284, 372–73), but there is reason to suppose that it was rarely used. The judges of the Superior Court decided in 1703 that appeals were in the nature of writ of error proceedings; this, however, was based on a much earlier opinion formulated when there was no statutory writ of error. Ms. Mass. Archives (Judicial 1683–1724), XL, 744–45. In 1725 Boston lawyer John Read informed John Winthrop that in the opinion of Judge Dudley, "all thoughts of a Writ of Err are utterly vain here, seing [sic] there is no such practice at all among us." *Winthrop Papers*, VI, 419–20.

review, far from being interred, was given fresh statutory life.[82] By this device a second trial of the cause, whether at the first instance or at the appellate stage, was allowed at which the record of the first trial as well as new pleas and evidence were considered, and again there was trial by jury. With these two procedures it was possible to keep a litigation in train at least through three trials, as happened in the notorious case of *Vassall v. Fletcher*.[83]

It is unnecessary to elaborate on the practice of the other three New England colonies, all of which initiated the appellate procedures of Massachusetts Bay. All were peopled by Massachusetts men, and despite the fact that in two colonies these were religious dissidents, all copied the procedures faithfully. In this respect the Bible Commonwealth was more successful in exporting its law than its theology. There are indications that in Rhode Island there was an initial gesture toward common law practices, but if such were ever used, they quickly gave way to the appeal-review scheme.[84] No important variants appear in Connecticut legislation, and the seventeenth century muniments of proceedings before the Court of Assistants might have been enrolled in Boston. But in the eighteenth century the writ of error makes its appearance and becomes a competitor of the appeal.[85] New Hampshire

---

[82] Originally enacted in 1642, *Col. Laws Mass.*, 197; carried forward in the 1701 statute, 1 *Acts and Resolves Prov. of Mass. Bay*, 466.

[83] The proceedings are in a pamphlet, *The State of the Action Brought by William Fletcher against William Vassall for Defaming Him* (Boston: 1753). A copy is in the New-York Historical Society. This was a defamation action in the Inferior Court of Common Pleas where, on failure of plaintiff to produce evidence, judgment was for defendant. This was affirmed on appeal to the Superior Court. Then, upon a bill of review, Fletcher introduced a mass of evidence and recovered £2,000.

[84] In its first code of laws in 1647 attaint and error were specified in the schedule of fees (*Records of the Colony of Rhode Island*, I, 207–08). However, in 1650 an order was passed providing for appeal or "rehearing" of causes (*ibid.*, 222–23). And in the following year it was enacted that appeals would go to the General Court; reviews could be had in the same court which had heard the case (*ibid.*,

237). A law of 1680 required the filing of "reasons" for appeal; see *Laws and Acts of Her Majesties Colony of Rhode Island, and Providence-Plantations, 1636–1705* (Rider, facsimile), 60–61. By a 1690 enactment it was required that copies of "the whole case" be submitted; see *Acts and Laws of His Majesty's Colony of Rhode-Island, and Providence-Plantations, 1663–1736* (1730–36), 34. When the courts were reorganized, provision was made in 1729 for appeals from the inferior Courts of Common Pleas to the Superior Court. As in Massachusetts, "reasons" for appeal were filed (*ibid.*, 190). In an act passed at the June session 1732 (*ibid.*, 247–48), the "rehearing" became the review. The proceeding was by writ of review. The act of 1745 regulating use of such writ is in *Acts and Laws . . . of Rhode-Island, 1745–52* (1752), 7.

[85] Connecticut made provision in 1639 for appeal before judgment and execution, following by a few years Massachusetts introduction of the remedy. *Public Records of the Colony of Connecticut*, I, 37. In 1664 it was

was jurisdictionally dependent on the Bay Colony from 1641 until the Crown took over in 1679. The influence of Massachusetts procedural notions persisted, nevertheless, for when New Hampshire recast its regulation of civil actions in 1701, a recent Massachusetts act was used as a model.[86]

The New Englanders were obviously happy with their appellate scheme. The voice of criticism came from without. The visiting Englishman Bennett, who wrote a sketch of judicial administration in the Bay Colony around 1740, was frankly appalled by the system of appeals and reviews which he believed led to great inconveniences and prejudicial delays. He did not conceive that an appeal, in any recognizable sense, was involved, but rather a series of new trials.[87] This was, of course, inevitable with the consistent use of juries. Whatever encomium of jury trial it may have been that was responsible for making the twelve men the constant attendants of the bench, it is clear that opinion in New England regarded this to be indispensable. And it may be remarked that this complete commitment goes far to explain what may be called the jury trial syndrome in this region.

Old as was the New England appeal, the Virginia version antedates it, for the first enactment dates from 1624.[88] In the course of the next century and a quarter there was intermittent legislation induced partly by the policy of setting appealable minima expressed in pounds of tobacco, the price of which fluctuated, and partly by the need of check-

---

enacted that a jury was discretionary on appeal. The records of the Court of Assistants, 1671–1702, indicate a consistent use of jury. See the transcripts in the unpublished thesis by N. B. Lacy, "Records of the Court of Assistants of Connecticut, 1665–1701" (New Haven, Conn.: Yale University, 1937); *e.g.*, Armstrong v. Reinolds, *sub* Oct. 10, 1671; Blackman v. Walker, Hawley v. Judson, *sub* May 2, 1672; Hawley v. Brinsmade, *sub* May 25, 1675. At the court held May 30, 1682, six appeals were heard, all with jury. There was a steady accretion of appeal and review business. For a good example of triple jury trial, see the original action, the review in the same county court, and eventually an appeal in the Court of Assistants in the case of Allyn v. Pratt, *ibid.*, *sub* Oct. 6, 1687. In 1711, when the judicial system was reorganized, provision was made for writs of error as well as appeals to the

Superior Court which replaced the old Court of Assistants. In 1728 it was enacted that writs of error must be brought within three years. *Acts and Laws, of His Majesties Colony of Connecticut in New-England, 1702–1729* (1729), 167, 354.

[86] The early New Hampshire appeal is discussed in Page, *Judicial Beginnings in New Hampshire, 1640–1700*, at 96–101. The act of 1701, patterned on the Massachusetts law, in 1 *Laws of New Hampshire*, 704–05.

[87] J. J. Bennett, "History of New England," Mass. Hist. Soc. *Proc.*, 5: 108, 119–20, 1st ser., 1862.

[88] 1 Hening, *Va. Stats.*, 125. The appeal lay from monthly courts to governor and council. In March 1642/3 appeals were provided from monthly courts to Quarter Court (as the General Court was then called), and thence to the General Assembly. *Ibid.*, 272. Further details, *infra*, n. 89.

ing abuse of the remedy. Prior to 1705 appeals would lie even before judgment, but in that year a statute put an end to this.[89] There appears to have been fairly lively traffic in appeals, for a surviving volume of General Court records shows a total of ninety-nine cases in the period 1670–78. It would appear that the review resembled common law proceedings in error, for there are no signs of trials *de novo* as in New England.

In the course of the eighteenth century there appeared in Virginia two rival methods of review, the supersedeas and the writ of error, to which we shall come in a moment. The statutes are not particularly revealing as to the circumstances when one or the other was appropriate, and the destruction of General Court records has deprived us of evidence of practice.[90] As for appeals, it would appear from the statutes that in cases under £20 appeals would touch only matters of "right." In cases where the claim exceeded £20 but was under £50 errors of form and

---

[89] An act of 1660 provided that appeals lay only after judgment. 1 Hening, *Va. Stats.*, 541. This seems to have been repealed *sub silentio* by the revision of 1662. 2 *ibid.*, 65. The General Court minutes for 1674 have two cases which appear to be appeals before judgment, and two years later a case is definitely noted as an appeal before judgment. H. R. McIlwaine, ed., *Minutes of the Council and General Court of Colonial Virginia, 1622–1632, 1670–1676* (1924), 366, 369, 452.

In the act of 1705 and subsequent acts, only appeals after judgment, decree or sentence are provided for. 3 Hening, *Va. Stats.*, 287, 299; 5 *ibid.*, 467, 481 (1748); 6 *ibid.*, 325, 338 (1753).

[90] The act of 1705 specifically introduces the supersedeas (3 *ibid.*, 302) and provides that proceedings upon it shall be the same as for appeals. In England the chief use of the supersedeas was to stay execution. The writ of error was, of course, by implication a supersedeas. The only English uses of the supersedeas for review purposes that we have noticed were in connection with the forcible entry proceedings. Here, where justices of the peace had awarded restitution of the premises after indictment for a forcible entry, if the insufficiency of the indictment was established the

same justice could supersede the order; otherwise it lay with King's Bench. Dyer 187; Hawkins, *Pleas of the Crown* (1777 ed.), I, c. 28, §61. It was also used after judgment when the sheriff held plea for 40s. or more. Fitzherbert, *Natura Brevium*, 239H.

It may be conjectured that the Virginians hit upon supersedeas as a review device, not only because of the local court background, but also because it is nowhere indicated that on appeal execution was stayed.

The 1705 act does not authorize writs of error, although it mentions that in all causes above £50 or ten thousand pounds of tobacco, and in all real actions, errors might be assigned in form or substance "in like manner as is permitted by the law of England in the prosecution upon writs of error." 3 Hening, *Va. Stats.*, 301. It is likely that the writ of error was introduced in Virginia, as in New York, by the lawyers and without benefit of statute. This is suggested by a case report by Barradall where a doubt was raised regarding appeal or supersedeas in an action brought under the Small Causes Act (1 Geo. II). It was argued that a subject was entitled to a writ of error as a matter of common right. The writ was granted. 2 R. T. Barton, ed., *Virginia Colonial Decisions*, (1909), B34.

substance were appealable if pressed in the inferior courts. In actions over £50 and in all real actions a full review of all errors of form and substance was permitted. The notice of appeal had to be filed with the inferior court in term time. Appellant had to assign errors but what went up to General Court is not clear, for a 1753 statute merely states that a clerk must keep record of pleadings "and other matters relating thereto."[91] For what retrospective probative value evidence shortly after the Revolution may possess, it would appear that the reviewing court could look into matters *dehors* the record.[92] By the terms of the 1753 statute certain risks attached to the appeal remedy, for any appellant if cast was liable to 15 percent damages, or if he prevailed, a fixed sum of 50s. and costs was due respondent.

Both supersedeas and writ of error issued after judgment and in term time. They did not lie *ex debito justitiae* but upon petition. An attorney practicing in General Court had to certify sufficient matter of error was set forth in an assignment of errors, but it lay with the governor and two judges to order issuance of the writ.[93] Unlike the appeal, the error proceedings carried no penalties or extra charges. So far as we can determine, only matters of law were considered in proceedings on either of these writs.

There is the possibility that Maryland which also had an appeal procedure may have been in Virginia's debt, for the use of this remedy began after it had been instituted in Virginia. But unlike Virginia, here both writ of error and appeal seem to have come into use simultaneously. Initially, an appeal involved a new trial.[94] This was cut off by an act

---

[91] 6 Hening, *Va. Stats.*, 325.

[92] The evidence at our disposal is meagre. Most of it relates to the strictures with which exact compliance with technical details of filing, bond, etc., was enforced by the courts. *E.g.*, the letter of St. George Tucker, Aug. 20, 1787, regarding the loss of benefit of appeal if bond were not filed in time, Ms. Tucker-Coleman Collection, box and folder "Virginia High Court of Chancery" (Earl Gregg Swem Library, The College of William and Mary in Virginia). Wood v. Thrift, Nov. 17, 1789, where the General Court refused to entertain an appeal when only one of two appellants had signed the bond, *ibid.*, unbound volume containing 1788 docket and brief reports of General Court cases. On the point in the text, the General Court, Oct. 13, 1786, relying upon an earlier unnamed General Court case of 1779,

entertained an appeal where (1) the judgment was altered after the appeal was filed, (2) there was an omission in the verdict and (3) there was a mistake in the verdict; see Posey v. Curtis' Admin'rs., *ibid.*, bound volume of ms. reports of cases, p. 15.

[93] There are examples of such certifications post-1776 in the Ms. Tucker-Coleman Collection. *E.g.*, Braxton v. Beall, Mar. 26, 1786, folder (mislabeled) "High Court of Chancery, 1764–86"; Peachy and Ford v. Cryer, Aug. 18, 1787, box and folder "Virginia High Court of Chancery."

[94] For examples, *Proceedings of the Provincial Court of Maryland, 1663–1666 (Archives of Maryland, 1932)*, XLIX, 16 (where new trial is apparent from the bill of costs), 54–56, 81–84, 258–60, 272; *Proceedings of*

of 1678[95] which was viewed as unsatisfactory,[96] but there was no reversion to the old ways. Judge Bond, who has commented on early appellate jurisdiction, believes that eventually substantial differences between writ of error and appeal in common law cases came to an end.[97] But it appears to us that some advantage remained for litigants who used the appeal. No writ was required. A transcript of the record was filed with the clerk of the Court of Appeals together with "reasons"; the subsequent gambits followed standard error proceedings. It is conceivable that the "reasons" were not identical with the assignment of error in proceedings begun by writ of error, for these "reasons," as in Virginia, may have encompassed questions of "right." One case published by Judge Bond indicates clearly enough that matter not in the record was thus brought to the attention of the appellate court.[98]

The North Carolinians' earliest legislation dates from the year 1715 and provided for both appeal and writ of error.[99] On appeal, security was required of appellant; the justices were directed to cause the clerk to transcribe the proceedings and certify them to the reviewing court. According to a rule of the General Court, appellant "was required" to serve appellee with "errors" within a certain time.[100] Governor Burrington reported in 1731 that the great advantage of the procedure was that since the appeal was made at the inferior court, no writ was required and appellee had immediate notice.[101]

In 1746 the procedure was drastically revised.[102] The writ of error became a remedy limited to the defendant, and it lay with the county

---

the Provincial Court, 1666–1670 (Archives of Maryland, 1940), LVII, 72–73, 129, 250, 359; Proceedings of the Provincial Court, 1670–1675 (Archives of Maryland, 1952), LXV, 299; Proceedings of the Provincial Court, 1679–80/1 (Archives of Maryland, 1961), LXIX, 219 (where the record indicates permission to appeal was given by the county court).

[95] Proceedings and Acts of the General Assembly of Maryland, 1678–1683 (Archives of Maryland, 1889), VII, 71.

[96] In messages in 1681 from governor and council to the assembly, ibid., 222, 224; the reason being that the county lawyers were so unskilled that on error causes would undoubtedly be reversed, whereas on appeal the merits could be gone into at a new trial.

[97] C. T. Bond, ed., Proceedings of the Maryland Court of Appeals, 1695–1729, (1933), xxix–xxx.

[98] Tench v. Hopkins (1695), ibid., 61; the errors complained of, at 68. And compare the appeal, Blangey v. Harris (1680), in Proceedings of the Provincial Court, 1679–80/1 (Archives of Maryland, 1961), LXIX, 296–300.

[99] State Records of North Carolina, XXIII, 67.

[100] Ms. Minutes General Court of North Carolina, 1725–1751, sub Apr. 1, 1727. Apparently "errors" could be filed on the basis of something resembling a stipulation of the parties; see Pollock v. Worley, ibid., sub Nov. 3, 1727. (North Carolina Department of Archives and History, Raleigh, N.C.)

[101] Colonial Records of North Carolina, III, 183.

[102] State Records of North Carolina, XXIII, 265.

court to allow it. Appeals in the county court were available to both parties. The security required of appellant was to include "condemnation money," as in Virginia. The transcript of the record had to be filed with the General Court and a trial *de novo* was there to be held or at the Assize to which the record would be sent. Unlike the New England appeal, no new plea or evidence was authorized. This statute was disallowed by the Crown in 1754 for reasons that had nothing to do with appeals.[103] The system was continued by a second act of 1754 which again was disallowed.[104] But finally in 1762 a statute was enacted which passed muster.[105]

Of all the colonies, Pennsylvania had the spottiest experience with the appeal. The remedy was early introduced; one may hazard in imitation of the scheme of the Duke's Laws under which some settlements had lived before Penn's patent issued. Judicial records indicate that it lay in the discretion of the trial court to grant the remedy,[106] but in 1698 allowance was made mandatory by statute if the debt or damage amounted to £10 or more.[107] This act makes clear that hereafter what was involved in any appeal was a retrial of the cause at a higher instance. All of this early legislation was belatedly disallowed. Indeed, the provincial assembly's attempts to settle a judiciary suffered a series of dis-

---

[103] *Colonial Records of North Carolina*, V, 108.

[104] *Ibid.*, VI, 26.

[105] *State Records of North Carolina*, XXIII, 563. In an act of 1721 by which South Carolina established county and precinct courts provision was made for "appeals" to the General Court, viz., Court of Common Pleas, held at Charleston (7 *Stats. at Large South Carolina*, 166). The procedure stipulated was modeled on that used in Virginia. However, the author of the Ms. Observations on the Present State of the Courts of Judicature in His Majesty's Province of South Carolina (LC), a treatise composed *c.* 1740, states that attendance on these local courts was as burdensome and attended by as many disorders as too soon become disused. From this writer's comments on the Virginia system it is inferable that appeals as there used were unknown in South Carolina.

[106] *Records of the Court of Chester County, Pennsylvania, 1681–1697*, Colonial Society of Pennsylvania *Publications* (1910), 215 (1690), 243 (1691), 249 (1691), 273 (1692),

279 (1693), 326 (1694); *Records of the Courts of Quarter Sessions and Common Pleas, Bucks County, Pennsylvania, 1684–1700*, Colonial Society of Pennsylvania *Publications* (1943), 100 (1688), 199 (1688), 169 (1692), 174 (denied 1692), 246 (1690), 280 (1693). At Newcastle, permission or refusal of appeal is noted; see *Records of the Court of New Castle on Delaware, 1681–1699*, Colonial Society of Pennsylvania *Publications* (1935), II, 72 (1683), 115 (1685), 130 (1686), 157 (1687), 159 (1687), 209 (1694). In a 1687 case, Gramton v. Woollaston, the would-be appellant was ordered to give reasons for appeal; these were held insufficient and the appeal denied (*ibid.*, 151, 154–55). Woollaston then obtained an order from the President and Council of Pennsylvania ordering stay in further proceedings. The court refused to "Depart from their first Judgments of Court there being no Law to compell them so to doe . . ." (*ibid.*, 161).

[107] *Charter and Laws Prov. of Pa.*, 225.

allowances until 1722, and the establishment rested upon governors' ordinances in the interim between each disallowance and new legislation.[108]

The eighteenth century pattern of review was settled by an act of 1701 that was disallowed in 1705, but the pattern was maintained by the ordinances. The 1701 statute introduced proceedings in error.[109] The appeal was thereafter confined to equity causes in the inferior courts although alongside it flourished the Sessions appeal as it existed in England for review of administrative orders. This appears to have been the inspiration for a new form of appeal introduced in 1735.[110] A single justice of the peace was empowered to hear cases of small debts. From his judgment an appeal was allowed to the local courts of Common Pleas where issues of fact were to be decided by a jury. This provision was not, we believe, inspired by the New England practice, but was devised as a check on the bench. No more than in England were the worthies named in the colonial commission of the peace picked from the pillars of the county—there is too much evidence to the contrary. We know from the torrent of discussion about the virtues of jury trial in the decade before the Revolution, and subsequently when the Constitution was submitted, how much importance was attached to the jury as a check on the judge.

In certain particulars the Pennsylvania law influenced a New Jersey Small Causes Act (£5) of 1748 which gave parties the option of a six-man jury in the trial before a single justice if more than 40s. was involved.[111] Appeals were allowed to the inferior Court of Common Pleas where more than 20s. was at issue but not if there had been jury

---

108 Discussed in J. H. Smith, "Administrative Control of the Courts of the American Plantations," 1210, 1217–22.

109 Charter and Laws Prov. of Pa., 311.

110 4 Stats. at Large Pennsylvania, 291, enacted for three years; re-enacted in 1739, ibid., 339; in 1742/3, ibid., 370; in 1745/6 with amendment, 5 ibid., 22.

111 1 S. Nevill, Acts of the General Assembly of the Province of New-Jersey, 1702–1752 (1752), 388. The 1748 act was continued in 1756, and the procedure was written into a £6 small causes act of 1775. S. Allinson, Acts of the General Assembly of the Province of New-Jersey, 1702–1776 (1776), 210 and 468, respectively.

In East Jersey, before the province was taken over by the Crown, there is some indication as early as 1672 of appeals being used after the model of the Duke's Laws (A. Leaming and J. Spicer, eds., Grants, Concessions, and Original Constitutions of the Province of New Jersey, 2d ed. [1881], 56). Provision for appeals was made in the "Fundamental Constitutions" of 1683 (ibid., 164), but it appears from the Journal of the Court of Common Right that the writ of error was the proceeding actually used (Edsall, Journal of the Courts of Common Right and Chancery of East New Jersey, 1683–1702, at 167, 258, 259, 264, 272, 282, 304, 305). In West Jersey provision was made in 1685 for appeals from magistrates to county courts (Leaming and Spicer, Grants, Concessions, and Original Constitutions of the Province of New Jersey, 510). In 1693

trial. At the appellate stage, when more than 40*s*. was at stake, jury trial in Common Pleas was mandatory.

The final colonial introduction of the appeal was enacted by the Georgia assembly, again in a Small Causes Act, in 1760. This statute provided an "appeal" from the so-called Court of Conscience held by a justice, but it is clear that only a rehearing was involved. A clarifying amendment of 1762 stipulated an appeal to the General Court which was empowered to examine process and witnesses' depositions or to order a new trial before itself.[112]

Although the American appeals flew in the face of strict common law tradition, in the colonies where a superior court was constituted the appellate forum they were probably a more effective means of supervision than the classic common law forms. Whether or not they were susceptible of promoting the growth of the law—something English error proceedings certainly achieved—is open to doubt, but in the period which we have had under consideration, when the autochthonous development of the law was in the hands of the legislatures, the energies of superior courts were devoted to the appropriation and settling of the incidents of English law. The appeals to inferior courts from orders or judgments of justices of the peace were, if we are to believe the critics of the inferior bench, an indifferent supervisory device and one hardly calculated to advance the law.[113] There is no question but that they served to promote general awareness of the appellate process and, as in England, a consequent belief in a "right" of appeal.

THE SUPREME APPELLATE AUTHORITY—
THE PRIVY COUNCIL

THE COLONISTS, for all their pains in elaborating appellate structures, their inventiveness with appellate devices and their zeal in resort-

---

a Court of Appeals was created, but the act is not specific as to the nature of the appeal procedure. It would appear that appeals from magistrates' courts were in the nature of rehearings; see H. Reed and G. Miller, eds., *The Burlington Court Book* (1944), 341. The entries of Court of Appeals proceedings are uninformative.

[112] The original act, in *Colonial Records of the State of Georgia*, XVIII, 372; the amendment, *ibid.*, 501.

[113] See the complaints of Governor Moore of New York to Lord Shel-

burne, Oct. 1, 1767 (*Docs. Rel. Col. Hist. N.Y.*, VII, 978); and the 1758 memorial of the New York lawyers (*Journal of the Legislative Council of New York* [1861], II, 1323). See also the report in 1771 of Richard Jackson, counsel of the Board of Trade, concerning a New Jersey act (*APC Col.*, V, No. 191). In North Carolina the assembly prepared an address to the Crown on the miserable quality of local justice, May 23, 1760 (*Colonial Records of North Carolina*, VI, 414).

ing to these, were nevertheless not fated to exercise complete and exclusive control over their litigation. Since medieval times there had inhered in the King the prerogative of entertaining and disposing of applications for relief from judgments alleged to be unjust. Within the realm the writ of error had of course been the instrument by which this power had been exercised. But since originals issuing from Chancery were not conceived to run without the realm, this writ had not been available even in a demesne as close-lying as Wales.[114] Instead, the prerogative of review *extra regnum* had been variously handled, by commission or by King in Council.[115] At the time when settlement of America began, the loss of all the continental European possessions had whittled down the appellate jurisdiction to the causes emanating from the Channel Islands. It was on this archaic foundation that the extension of appellate authority over the plantations was to rest.[116]

Why lands peopled by English subjects under warrant of the Crown should not have been directly embraced in the orbit of the English judicial establishment at the appellate stage requires explanation. When the first colonial charters passed the seals, and long beyond, the medieval concept of lordship was still dominant as respects the relation of the King to lands where he was suzerain. The places in the New World were his demesnes, his possessions, which, through indulgence of a fiction, he was deemed to hold by right of conquest. The notion survived even the great upheaval of the Puritan Revolution and, as we shall see, the whole apparatus of imperial administration was set up and elaborated on this premise.[117]

Not until the first charter to the Duke of York (1664)[118] did the Crown reserve in explicit terms its right to hear appeals, although it is clear from the instructions shortly issued to the commissioners sent to Massachusetts Bay that the Crown conceived that it possessed the power even if not reserved.[119] There was to be argument that there inhered in the King the right to receive and determine appeals irrespective of reservations—more to the heart of a losing litigant than of his opponent or of the courts in colonies where the royal prerogative was resisted. There was, further, the imposing authority of Coke, "for as much as an appeale

---

[114] C. J. Vaughan, in Craw v. Ramsey (1670), Vaughan 274, and *Process into Wales, ibid.*, 395, state the contrary, but historical evidence supports the statement in the text. See the writer's review of R. Schuyler, *Parliament and the British Empire* (1929), in *Colum. L. Rev.*, 30:273, 1930.

[115] See Goebel, "Matrix of Empire,"

introduction to Smith, *Appeals to the Privy Council from the American Plantations*, xli–xlix.

[116] Smith, *Appeals to the Privy Council from the American Plantations*, c. I.

[117] *Infra*, c. II, pp. 60 *et seq.*

[118] 1 *Col. Laws N.Y.*, 1 at 2.

[119] The commission is in *Docs. Rel. Col. Hist. N.Y.*, III, 64.

is a naturall defence, it cannot be taken away by any prince or power"[120] —a dictum which qualified an appeal to be classed as one of the rights and liberties of Englishmen, guaranteed in many a charter. There were jurisdictions, however, which did not see it that way. Such objections were not to stay the hands of the Crown.

It was characteristic of English official thinking that, confronted with new problems, in preference to experiment, the lumber room of old institutional paraphernalia should be made to yield the means of proceeding. So it was to be with the exploitation of appellate authority in the New World. The Privy Council was settled upon as the agency because there it had been in the past that the King's prerogative in demesnes without the realm had been administered. There was to be questioning whether or not the Statute 16 Charles I, c. 10, which had extirpated the Privy Council's judicial authority within the realm, had not also ended its appellate jurisdiction without. But even during the great Civil War hearing of Channel Island appeals had kept animate this vestige of conciliar judicial authority. This took a fresh lease on life with a great bulk of such cases when Charles II at length ascended the throne. On the basis of this precedent the Privy Council was to become the supreme appellate court for the plantations.[121]

From the vantage point of three centuries later it seems curious indeed that the theory and methods of a scheme rooted in medieval times and developed in connection with lands that each cherished a jurisprudence of its own were to be applied to communities that would be moving toward a general reception of the common law. But clearly, if precedent had to be guiding, the King would not have been safeguarding his prerogatives if choice had fallen upon the House of Lords, or the King's Bench to which Irish causes came by writ of error.[122] Furthermore, as things developed, the law in the plantations was to be persistently viewed as a species of foreign law[123]—which, indeed, in New England and New York it surely must have seemed when in the last decade of Charles II's reign appeals began to come in from the New World.

The difficulties of setting the Privy Council as a final appellate

---

[120] Coke, *Fourth Institute*, 340.

[121] On this, Smith, *Appeals to the Privy Council from the American Plantations*, at 3–5, 37–40.

[122] From King's Bench in Ireland; see Fitzherbert, *Abridgment*, s.v. Error, 89 (5 Edw. II); 75 (19 Edw. III).

[123] See the statement of Mansfield C. J., in Mostyn v. Fabrigas, 1 Cowper 161 at 174 (KB 1774), that in Privy Council "they inform themselves, by having the law [of the colonies] stated to them." On the proof of foreign laws, Fremoult v. Dedire, 1 Peere Williams 429 (1718). That in certain respects the colonies were regarded as foreign countries, King v. Speke, 3 Salkeld 358 (1689); Colepepper's Case, 1 Ventris 349 (1680).

court over various jurisdictions where the judicial structure had been locally contrived without reference to such ultimate stage of review were soon apparent. Measures had to be taken to effect some sort of integration and to settle the conditions under which recourse could be had.[124] This involved, first of all, efforts through commissions and instructions to the governors of royal provinces, to settle the course of review within the provinces. Since governor and council appear to have been viewed as a Privy Council *in parvo*, this body was to be the ultimate local resort.[125] This was a necessary decision of policy since there was a disposition in some of these colonies to settle this power in their assemblies. A second policy decision was to place a monetary limitation upon the appellate jurisdiction of provincial governor and council. This amounted to a drastic break with common law tradition for never had the amount in controversy or of recovery been used as a measuring rod to determine the right to bring a writ of error or certiorari. But the Crown carried the principle of limitation further by setting even higher appealable minima to qualify a cause to be taken to the Privy Council. This is one point where the influence of the rules governing Channel Islands appeals is patent, for as early as Elizabeth's reign the monetary limitations had been placed on these, and what is more, certain classes of cases had been excluded from review.

Nothing could illustrate better the power of indurated administrative tradition than the extension to New World demesnes of the policy of limiting appeals developed for the Channel Islands. Two factors in particular should have dictated an examination *de novo* of the wisdom of such restriction. Not only were the physical conditions of access to the seat of appeals in no way comparable, but there existed the difference between an old and settled jurisdiction and one in process of being established. Nevertheless, the Privy Council, although aware of resistance

---

[124] On the measures taken, Smith, *Appeals to the Privy Council from the American Plantations*, at 77–88.

[125] This emerges from the discussion in June 1676 in the Lords Committee on the petition of Giles Bland who had been fined without jury trial by the Virginia governor and council. Bland's counsel argued that every Englishman was supposed to carry the benefit of the laws of England along with him. The Lords admitted that they themselves were bound by the restraints of St. 16 Car. I, c. 10, but there was uncertainty if that law extended to so bind the Virginia Council. Doubts were ex- pressed on whether the provincial council had full powers, although it was conceded that that body was clothed with many authorities which had been exercised and allowed. The Lord Privy Seal was particularly doubtful on attributing the Privy Council's powers to Virginia since it was not "an ancient colony." The consensus appears to have been that it would be difficult to support a government in such a remote location if there were not extraordinary powers in the provincial council for emergent occasions. Ms. Journal of the Lords Committee of Trade and Plantations, I, 14 (PRO: CO 391/1; LC Trans.).

to the assertion of royal appellate jurisdiction in America, and, indeed, while in the thick of a struggle to enlarge royal prerogative over colonial legislation, set a pattern for appellate authority that fell short of asserting the prerogative in its plenitude.[126]

From the governors' commissions and instructions drafted at this time it appears that a mere reservation of right by the Crown, as had been done in the Duke of York's charter, was not deemed appropriate or sufficient. In the commission to Cutt of New Hampshire (1679) the existence of a recalcitrant temper overseas is recognized by the provision that "it shall and may be lawfull" for persons aggrieved to appeal to King in Council judgments or decrees involving title to realty and personal actions above the value of £50. This language is again used in the commission to Cranfield (1682), Cutt's successor.[127] But in 1680, in an instruction sent to Barbados, the appeal is treated as a "liberty," namely, a privilege of the subject, not to be impeded, although in the same paragraph the monetary minimum of £100 is set.[128] This same treatment of the appeal as a liberty of the subject is used under James II in the commission to Dongan of New York (1686) and Andros of the Dominion of New England (1688).[129] Why the hand of authority should have seen fit to wear the glove of liberty is not clear, unless to overcome colonial resistance. It was to be discarded, but not before the "liberty of Appeale" was imbedded in the Massachusetts charter of 1691.

The experiments with imperial administration during the years 1660–96 are significant chiefly in this, that the foundations were laid upon which the structure of eighteenth century controls was to be set. The volume of plantation appeals prior to 1696 was relatively insignificant—short of sixty identifiable appeals emanating thence and affirmative action being taken only in twenty-six cases.[130] And for one reason or another, some problems of jurisdiction, in particular the vice-admiralty appeals, were left unsettled, certain questions of procedure remained unresolved. Apart from the short-sighted decision to cleave to the Channel Islands precedents, already commented upon, the sharpest criticism to be leveled at dispositions made in this period is the ineptness of choice of governor and council to be the *dernier ressort* in the

---

126 On this, *infra*, c. II, pp. 73–82.
127 N. Bouton, ed., *Documents and Records Relating to the Province of New Hampshire, 1623–1776*, (1867–73), I, 373, commission to Cutt; *ibid.*, 433, commission to Cranfield.
128 Labaree, *Royal Instructions*, I, No. 443.
129 *Docs. Rel. Col. Hist. N.Y.*, III,

377, commission to Dongan; *ibid.*, 538, commission to Andros. The earliest instruction to the West Indies is blunter; see Labaree, *Royal Instructions*, I, No. 443.
130 Smith, *Appeals to the Privy Council from the American Plantations*, at 129–30.

royal colonies. There must have been some who asked of what avail the pleader's art, the command of the subtleties of precedents, if in the end a cause was to be reviewed by a group of individuals chosen not for their mastery of law but because they were King's men.[131] Since the Privy Council itself was a body overwhelmingly lay, a judgment carried to the ultimate stage of review of necessity would twice pass through the hands of amateurs before being finally settled. The reasons of administrative control that dictated the designation of governor and council are obvious. But this was a decision that no less obviously was unlikely to forward the indigenous development of the law.

The system under which the seaboard colonies were to live until the American Revolution and which for a while thereafter was to affect opinion about appellate jurisdiction was the result of a reorganization in 1696. So far as the Privy Council itself was concerned, the hearing of appeals by a select committee was abandoned and the function vested in a committee of the whole. All the Lords or any three of them were competent to this end.[132] But a change of even greater significance for law administration was the creation of a new and ancillary body, the Lords Commissioners for Trade and Plantations, commonly known as the Board of Trade.[133] Composed of a few ministers of state whose attendance was desultory, and a group of working appointees, the Board of Trade became the central agency for supervising the details of running an empire. For our purposes the most significant item was the control over colonial enactments, of which we shall later have more to say.[134]

A number of important policy changes affecting colonial litigation were initiated following the reorganization. In the first place, efforts were made to establish Crown appeal jurisdiction as something to which all colonies were subject. Except as this prerogative to hear appeals had been reserved in a charter, it existed as of course only in the royal colonies. In the case of the two corporate colonies no such reservation had been made. Connecticut was to be a place of resistance, but Rhode Island was to furnish more appeals than any other continental colony. As for the proprietary colonies, there was a reservation in Penn's charter,[135] and a provision susceptible of being read as such had been written

---

131 Their appointment being controlled by the Crown. The policy was initiated after Virginia became a royal colony; see H. Osgood, *The American Colonies in the Seventeenth Century,* III, 78–79. A list of nominees and appointees in various royal colonies 1680–1720 is in 2 *APC Col.,* App. II.

132 The order of Dec. 11, 1696, is in 2 *APC Col.,* No. 657.

133 The commission establishing the Board, May 15, 1696, is in *Docs. Rel. Col. Hist. N.Y.,* IV, 145–48. The circumstances leading to the action are discussed in O. M. Dickerson, *American Colonial Government,* 20 et seq.

134 *Infra,* c. II, pp. 60 et seq.

135 Thorpe, *Constitutions and Charters,* V, 3038.

into the Carolina patent.[136] The Maryland charter had contained no reservation, but in 1690 it had been taken into the King's hands and it would appear that after the proprietor was restored in 1715 the royal instructions which had regulated appeals were treated as still applicable.[137]

The maneuvers to promote central appellate authority were but one phase of the attempts to bring some organization to an empire badly structured because of jurisdictional diversities. Not all of the measures taken were well considered and, as will be noticed, there was uncritical reliance upon the decisions taken under the Stuarts. One of the changes that was lacking in political sagacity was the transfer of directions on appeals from the governor's commission (the instrument used for the continental colonies) to his instructions.[138] This had constitutional implications, which, if not immediately appreciated, were soon to be as the opinion gained strength that the governor's commission served as a constitution in the royal provinces. But the instructions were a more flexible medium for expressing the royal will than was the commission and it was probably for this reason that they were settled upon for directions about appeals. Nevertheless, the decision to do so subtracted something of constitutional solidity from the appellate process.

There was apparently no re-examination at this time of the question of an appealable minimum. This had already become fixed for the continental colonies at £300 and there it remained until 1753 when the amount was raised to £500.[139] A later explanation of this revision by the Board of Trade does not account for this particular change and it does not appear that appeal business from the plantations in the preceding decade was heavy enough to have induced the restriction. The new instruction included some exceptions and, as a matter of practice, appeals were admitted below the minimum. But the equitable approach on occasion did not remedy the inherent defect of the rule of limitation. No systematic control of the doings of the judiciary overseas was possible under the rule of the appealable minimum and, obviously, the possibility of securing conformity with English law was foreclosed. If the Americans had felt that the "liberty to appeal to Our Royal Person" was truly one of those rights and liberties of Englishmen over which they were perennially aroused, there might have been some consistent complaint. But generally they seem to have been content, and when

---

[136] *Ibid.*, 2752.
[137] Smith, *Appeals to the Privy Council from the American Plantations*, at 255.

[138] See the instructions in Labaree, *Royal Instructions*, I, Nos. 445–50.
[139] *Ibid.*, No. 453.

they came to organize their own Supreme Court, they promptly resorted to the monetary limitation.[140]

Although American legislation both before and after the Revolution was influenced by the long-sustained policy regarding the conditions under which appeals could be brought to Privy Council, the procedure before that body left no demonstrable mark upon the growth of American practice. This is not surprising, for barring a very few exceptions colonial lawyers had only a hearsay knowledge of its particulars. For once a litigation had been guided through the hierarchy of provincial courts and put on shipboard, so to speak, for its final adventures at the last stage of appeal, local counsel rarely had direct professional dealings with the cause until the final Order in Council reached these shores. Furthermore, although Privy Council appellate procedure had a long history of its own, it lay outside the mainstreams of English practice, which most of the colonies were in process of imitating. To one familiar with the details of the then current review procedures at common law or equity, the Privy Council procedure could not but seem a strange pastiche.

Since the exercise of appellate jurisdiction by King in Council was based on the vestigial remains of its judicial authority—that relating to the Channel Islands—the procedures for the presentation and argument of a cause were those traditionally employed in cases there arising.[141] An eighteenth century lawyer would find resemblances to the newly developed equity appeals and at points there were perceptible ghostly traces of writ of error procedure. The preliminaries took place in the plantations with the admission or allowance of an appeal at the colonial court of last instance.[142] This was something foreign to the common law and was the result of the limitations on appealable minima, the directions about entering appeals within fourteen days, the posting of security effectively to prosecute and, eventually (1727), stay of execution. Whether or not the allowance was intended to be no more

---

[140] In the Judiciary Act of 1789, 1 U.S. Stats., 73.

[141] The brief account in the text following is based on Chapter V of Joseph H. Smith's *Appeals to the Privy Council from the American Plantations*, the definitive study of Privy Council procedure. B. Knollenberg, *Origin of the American Revolution, 1759–1766* (New York: Macmillan Co., 1960), 299, n. 13, refers to Smith's book as "largely superseding" other studies. It should be evident to anyone who may examine these that the supersession is utter and complete.

[142] Although instructions of Charles II's time speak of permitting appeals (Labaree, *Royal Instructions*, I, No. 444), the standing instructions for the continental colonies until 1727 (*ibid.*, Nos. 446, 449) are not explicit and the formal admission was to be inferred from the specification of conditions. The circular instruction of 1727 regarding suspension of execution speaks of admission of appeals, and the revised instruction of 1753 does likewise (*ibid.*, Nos. 450, 453).

than a formality, the tribunal appealed from could and sometimes did refuse to allow. In this situation the subject was at liberty to file with the Privy Council a petition for leave to appeal—the so-called *doleance*, another ancient indigene of Channel Islands appeal procedure. This was of particular importance in cases originating in jurisdictions not reached by royal instructions.[143] The Council itself would decide if leave should be granted. If it so ruled, the cause would be set down as a perfected appeal in course. The colonials resorted to *doleance* where there had been arbitrary denials of appeal, failure to meet appealable minima or conditions for appeal had been imposed below.

A petition to the fountain of justice, for such a *doleance* was, may seem ineffably medieval, yet this was still characteristic of ultimate appellate jurisdiction in English cases. For petition to the Crown was a condition precedent to review in Parliament of a King's Bench judgment,[144] and so too of a Chancery decree until the House of Lords secured the privilege of being directly petitioned.[145] Inevitably, and in the face of official emphasis upon the colonial subject's right to appeal, the normal course of bringing a cause before the Privy Council was by "petition and appeal," a requirement which served to underline the permissive character of the jurisdiction.[146]

With his "petition and appeal" the appellant was required to file a tenor of the record below under seal. This was a burden sometimes difficult properly to discharge, for the Council did not have available a mandate like the writ of error to order the record and proceedings from the colonial trial court of last instance. Appellant was thus cast upon the good offices of the court below and its staff, and what was supplied him for exemplification was sometimes a deliberately attenuated record.

Usage fixed at a year and a day the time to prosecute with effect, but this was a rule laxly enforced. The Council required proof that respondent had been summoned, but no entry of appearance was necessary. On the unusual occasions when this was deemed essential, notice might be ordered posted at the Royal Exchange or some plantation coffee house[147]—an expedient which anticipated by decades the notorious service by publication on the island of Tobago that so exercised Lord Ellenborough.[148] Neither in King's Bench nor in the House of

---

[143] As, *e.g.*, Connecticut, whence emanated Winthrop v. Lechmere, *infra*, c. II, pp. 73 *et seq.*

[144] Coke, *Fourth Institute*, 21; still observed in the eighteenth century, W. Tidd, *Practice of the Courts of King's Bench, and Common Pleas*, 9th ed. (1828), II, 1141.

[145] Hargrave's preface to his edition of Hale, *Jurisdiction of the Lords House, or Parliament, considered according to antient records* (1796), ccxxi.

[146] A specimen is printed in Smith, *Appeals to the Privy Council from the American Plantations*, at 272, n. 2.

[147] *Ibid.*, 275–77.

[148] Buchanan v. Rucker, 9 East 192 (1808).

Lords was the appearance of defendant in error essential to proceed to judgment.[149] The form of summons was essentially an invitation to appear to hear the errors on the record[150] and it was at defendant's option if he would plead or demur.

So far as actual hearing before the Lords Committee of the Council was concerned, the resemblance to proceedings in the House of Lords is very striking. The parties submitted printed "cases" which contained statements of the facts and issues, concluding with a brief summary of the reasons why reversal or affirmance was prayed. Precedents were rarely cited in these "cases" but it appears from notes of the hearings before the Lords Committee of the Council that counsel entered at large into expositions of law. Counsel were invariably English barristers and very frequently personages at the head of their profession. The Committee deliberated its decision *in camera*. Its function was to report to the Privy Council in such manner and form that the conclusions could be embodied in an Order in Council. We know from notes of the arguments kept by counsel and others attending hearings that in the course of such the judges made important rulings on points of law. It appears also that on occasion, if not invariably, a statement of the reasons of law on which the report was based would be made, very probably at the time when the Lords Committee concluded its report and announced it.[151] The evidence of this is by no means free from some doubt. Yet it is clear from reports sent in by colonial agents or parties' solicitors that some circulation of what was decided took place.

The reasoned decision delivered by members of the Lords Committee was in no sense part of the case since its duty was merely to advise the Crown and to cast the advice in terms appropriate to a final Order in Council. This was the concluding judicial act, and must be esteemed to be such despite the fact that administrative decisions

---

[149] Tidd, *Practice of the Courts of King's Bench, and Common Pleas*, II, at 1172-73.

[150] The *scire facias ad audiendum errores*. The form of King's Bench is in *Thesaurus Brevium*, 2d ed. (1687), 229. On the practice in the House of Lords see Hale, *Jurisdiction of the Lords House, or Parliament . . .*, at 148-51.

[151] The most persuasive piece of evidence is the report of the case of Burn v. Cole, Ambler 415 (1762). The notes taken by William Samuel Johnson, Connecticut agent and later a member of the Constitutional Convention, on the Rhode Island case of

Holmes v. Freebody (1770) are also in a form strongly suggesting this practice. Johnson's notes are indorsed on "The Case of Appellant" (CULL) and are printed in part in Goebel, *Cases and Materials on the Development of Legal Institutions*, 294-95. Some of the decisions noted by Robert Walpole, Clerk of the Council in Mansfield's time, are preserved in the Public Record Office and seem to us to be corroborative. *E.g.*, the Virginia appeal of Cleeve v. Mills (1764), WO 1/404/23; the Jamaica appeal of Beckford v. Jeake (1765), WO 1/404/56-57.

and even legislative regulations were issued in the same format; for it terminated a juristic controversy, and its execution depended upon further action by the colonial court where the original record of the cause lay. In this last particular it resembled a judgment of the House of Lords.

The Order itself was cast in a standard form—a recital of the petition, the averment that the Lords Committee had heard the parties and the tender of its advice. Then follows the Order by the King himself—an exertion of his ultimate prerogative in the dispensing of justice. In its prolixity the Order was more akin to a Chancery decree than the terse form of judgment in error.[152] It was this much better than a final judgment in the House of Lords, for it said more, the Lords having decided that it was a breach of privilege to publish anything of its conclusions. It was no worse than a colonial judgment which very rarely was remembranced by more than the traditional formula *ideo considera-tum est.*

Despite what the provincial bar may have thought of the short-comings of the form of final adjudication, there can be no doubt that in terms of imperial administration the Privy Council acting in its judicial capacity served an important and useful function. This is to be measured not in terms of the number of appeals from all the New World possessions, by no means inconsiderable, but by the adjudication of causes involving decisions as well on the constitutions of the provinces as on that of the empire itself, thus habituating the inhabitants to the maintenance of constitutional standards. Nevertheless, neither this nor the discharge of the historic role of doing justice *inter partes* has earned the Privy Council much attention from historians. In fact it has received but cavalier treatment at their hands. At the root of this may be the derogatory remarks of Thomas Pownall, onetime Massachusetts governor, in his work *The Administration of the Colonies* that ran through four editions between the years 1764 and 1768.[153] It was not only difficult to appeal, he wrote, but the redress was inefficient. The difficulties lay, however, not in bringing appeals but chiefly in the remoteness of this court of final resort, the protraction of proceedings and the lack of control over the sort of record to come up from below. That the redress was inefficient was untrue. This body, wrote Pownall, "scarce ever, in the temporary and occasional sittings, looks like such a court; but is rather accidentally or particularly, than officially attended." The point of irregularity of attendance was well taken, but the criticism that this seat of judgment scarce ever looks like a court was inane. Certainly to those who noted and so preserved the argu-

---

[152] Form of judgment in error, Blackstone, *Commentaries*, 1771 ed., III, App., xxvi.
[153] In the 1765 edition, at 83.

ments of counsel and the opinions of judges sitting, the Lords Committee sounded like a court. It could not have been otherwise during the faithful sitting of Hardwicke and, after 1760, of Mansfield and Wilmot before whom leaders of the bar argued in terms as learned as those heard in Westminster Hall.

From the standpoint of colonial justice, the chief drawback of the Privy Council as a Supreme Court of Appeal was not the appealable minimum, for this was correctible by use of the *doleance*, but rather the fact that it was not in any real sense an integral part of provincial judicial establishments. If something had been done to perfect a mandate as potent as the writ of error to get up the record, this situation might have been bettered. And yet, the manner in which appeals were managed via London agents or solicitors and eventually argued by luminaries of the English bar would in any event have preserved the aura of detachment. This does not mean, of course, that the judicial work of the Council was a matter of indifference on this side of the Atlantic. It was a factor that any individual involved in what he conceived to be important litigation had to take into account, and others with similar interests who might be affected on an ultimate appeal would have it no less in mind. A sovereign example is the celebrated Parsons' Cause in Virginia.[154] Nor was this jurisdiction solely of concern to the well-to-do. If popular excitement over the supposed attempt to review jury verdicts by the instruction of 1753 is not proof enough, one may throw into the scales the anxieties of the numberless freeholders whose titles were at stake in the settlement of boundaries by royal commission with appeal reserved.[155]

One achievement of the Privy Council as court that seems to us to have been of particular significance was the fact that it applied the living common law of England to causes arising in jurisdictions each of which had fabricated systems of law that were essentially adaptations but that, in many particulars, were vagarious. The Privy Council was able to do this because the colonies were dependent jurisdictions, and nothing illustrates better the Council's commitment to the authority of a supervening and supreme law than its requirement that plantation law be proved, much as the central courts in England required proof of deviations from common law. The Council might have succeeded better in developing a sense of the importance of its *modus operandi* among Americans had it developed a body of its own precedents. As it was,

---

[154] *Infra*, c. II, pp. 81 *et seq.*
[155] Discussed in Smith, *Appeals to the Privy Council from the American Plantations*, c. VII. The disputes taken up on appeal were the Massachusetts- New Hampshire and the Massachusetts-Rhode Island boundaries. The settlement of the Mohegan Indians-Connecticut controversy was similarly handled.

the import of the process of adjudication in terms of a general law was appreciated only when, after independence, the void left by the determination of the Privy Council's authority was experienced. The thirteen inferior jurisdictions had become independent polities each with its own fruit from the mother stem, and what had once been the supreme law of the land had become the law of a foreign power. This is why in default of a law of general application, recourse was had to the law of nations in interstate controversies immediately after the Revolution,[156] and why in the Constitutional Convention certain problems like the trial of civil actions in federal courts were left for future settlement.

Every discipline has a history proper to itself, and what has been sketched about the transplantation of English law and the proliferation of appellate devices has been largely so told. But in any society the law is inextricably part of life in its daily round and, indeed, of its larger movements. Something therefore remains to be said about this aspect of the remarkable development which we have been considering, particularly if we are to anchor our premise that the colonists' grasp of the law and its operations was broadly based. This is something that can be fully assessed only by a thorough canvass of the records of inferior courts, a task too remote from our main inquiry. But our sampling of such records for Massachusetts, Connecticut, New York, Pennsylvania and Virginia has been sufficiently extended to convince us of the broad base of participation. The availability of land, unlike England, a thing in commerce, and above all the general possibility of acquiring such in fee, produced a breed with a very different outlook from the tenants and copyholders of the old country. The independency thus promoted contributed to a litigious spirit and even more particularly to the reluctance to accept defeat. This state of mind, familiar to anyone who has been a litigator, was wonderfully served by the colonial "appeal" whether in its northern or southern form. No man need rest content with a judgment obtained in an inferior court, too often presided over by so many Justices Squeezum, Gobble or Shallow.[157] Nothing speaks more elo-

---

[156] William Samuel Johnson's argument in the Pennsylvania-Connecticut boundary trial, Ms. Joseph Reed Papers (NYHS); and Alexander Hamilton's ms. brief in the New York-Massachusetts case, printed in J. Goebel *et al.*, eds., *Law Practice of Alexander Hamilton: Documents and Commentary*, I, 611–31 (hereafter cited as *LPAH*).

[157] In a late edition of Matthew Bacon's *Abridgment, s.v.* Justices of the Peace F, it was stated: "A justice of the peace is strongly protected by the law, . . . He is not to be slandered or abused: . . ." Nevertheless, this gave him no immunity from the barbs of the satirists. Of all the literary caricatures, Shakespeare's Justice Shallow, who adorns two plays, is the most renowned. Henry Fielding, himself on the Middlesex Commission, was the creator of several objectionable magistrates of

quently of the pervasive passion for appealing than the statutes in divers jurisdictions that sought to stem it. Even in the jurisdictions that used the staider writ of error proceeding, such legislation was found necessary.[158]

Regarded in all of its ramification, the development of the law and its administration in the several American jurisdictions is an aspect of institutional history of the first magnitude that has deserved a great

---

which the lubricious Justice Squeezum in *The Coffee House Politician* is outstanding. Tobias Smollett fathered other worthies for the fictional bench. Justice Gobble, who fell afoul of Sir Launcelot Greaves, is remembranced above.

[158] This was handled in various ways. For example, the "action of review" in Massachusetts was subjected to a time limitation; there was to be no stay of execution. 1 *Acts and Resolves Prov. of Mass. Bay*, 466 (1701). In Virginia, also an appeal-ridden jurisdiction, it was provided as early as 1647 that appeals from county to General Court did not lie if the suit was for less than £10 or 1,600 lbs. of tobacco (a higher amount for the Eastern shore). 1 Hening, *Va. Stats.*, 345. In 1655 the amount was raised (*ibid.*, 398, and 477 [1658]). The jurisdictional amount was eliminated in 1660 (except as to the Eastern shore), but a new approach was tried—that of penalizing an appellant one half the amount of his "debt" and all costs should he be cast (*ibid.*, 541; and see 2 *ibid.*, 65 [1662]). From 1676 onward (*ibid.*, 362, 397) no limitation was set until 1748 when it was enacted that no appeals lay unless at least £10 or two thousand pounds of tobacco or title to lands were involved (5 *ibid.*, 467 at 482). This act was disallowed by the Crown. The provision was re-enacted in 1753 (6 *ibid.*, 325 at 340).

Maryland in 1713 limited appeals from county courts to the Provincial Court if the amount involved less than £6 sterling or 1,200 lbs. of tobacco, and from the Provincial Court to governor and council if the sum were less than £50 or ten thousand pounds of tobacco (Oct. Sess. 1713, c. 4,

§3, in T. Bacon, comp., *Laws of Maryland at Large* [1765]). In the small debts act of 1763 appeals would lie only if more than 33s. 4d. or four hundred pounds of tobacco were involved (*ibid.*, Oct. Sess. 1763, c. 21, §8). The same principle was operative in the small debts act of New Jersey of 1760 where at least 20s. must be claimed for appeals to lie. If there had been a jury verdict, no appeal would lie. 2 Nevill, *Acts of the General Assembly of the Province of New-Jersey, 1753–1761* (1761), 340.

In New York, when the jurisdiction of justices of the peace in small causes was increased to £10 (1769), the limitation was placed on serving writs of error or certiorari, requiring an affidavit in the Supreme Court of reasonable cause and a finding thereon. Failure so to do was penalized. 4 *Col. Laws N.Y.*, 1079 at 1086. The act was disallowed. Earlier, in 1765, similar restraints had been laid on "frivolous" use of certiorari or error in civil cases before justices (*ibid.*, 861). These provisions were carried into a 1772 act (5 *ibid.*, 304).

In Connecticut the appellate jurisdiction of the General Assembly was pruned in 1718 by an act limiting petitions to cases involving £15 or more. *Acts and Laws, of His Majesties Colony of Connecticut in New-England: passed by the General Assembly, May 1716 to May 1749* (Bates, facsimile, 1919), 234. Appeals from county courts to the Superior Court were foreclosed to defendant if the matter in issue involved only 10s.; plaintiff's right to appeal was barred if the original demand had not exceeded 20s. (Act of 1725, *ibid.*, 313). There was later restrictive legislation in 1736 (*ibid.*, 445).

deal more attention than it has received. The body of common law remedies and the rules which grew about these were weapons for the use of men prepared to assert or defend what they conceived to be their rights. For all that the courts regarded the law in terms of principle, wrestled with the problem of its inner logic and occasionally weighed the public interest, the Justinian *suum cuique* was always a dominant consideration. A phenomenon so highly individualistic is difficult to fit into the colonial story as it is usually told, whether in terms of the maturing of democratic ideals or of the class struggle. Furthermore, the place of the law in this story can only be fixed by reference to its muniments, which unhappily are of a nature that they yield grain only after tedious threshing through voluminous sheaves of formal documents. It is no wonder that colonial law has seemed to so many a matter of "technicalities" unrelated to life. Nevertheless, these materials and the degree of the inhabitants' familiarity with what they represented is as ponderable an element in the struggle over the ratification of the federal Constitution as the factors of economic or ideological involvement. There is otherwise no understanding of why the esoteric argument would have been advanced that federal courts would engross all litigation by employing fictions like the Bill of Middlesex unless the generality of voters would know enough to be frightened; or why, except for the variety of experience with the diversity of appellate procedures, the phrase "appellate jurisdiction in law and fact" should have engendered the emotion which it did; and of even more significance, why the willingness to entrust the safeguarding of the Constitution to the judicial. This we must next consider.

CHAPTER II

The Traditions of Judicial Control over Legislation

IF THE ENGLAND which the adventurous deserted for the New World was burdened with a superfluity of courts, it also abounded with law-making bodies. The emigrants were not less aware of the workings of these than of the judicial process. Both because their situation here demanded enactment, and because some of the groups which settled here had pronounced ideas about law reform, the legislative urge was to possess them betimes. This manifested itself not only in the fabrications of general law for province or colony, but also in the production of local enactments of varied provenance. To the array of indigenous creations there was to be added law-giving by proprietors, ordinances of royal governors, commands of the Crown and the Acts of Parliament, all of which, whether liveried as grants, or concessions or things done for the commonweal, were fiat law in the sense that those affected had no hand in the making.

In America as in England the motley of regulations posed problems of what may be called the order of laws, involving questions of relationship *inter se*, the degree of their imperative, but, above all, the control over areas of conflict. We shall examine in a moment how the English had earlier grappled with these problems, establishing in the process certain traditions that were vigorously alive when America was first peopled. They were traditions concerning both administrative and judicial control of enactments and had their roots in the early thirteenth century. Thereafter, although there were to be changes in the means of implementing the underlying notions, these concepts were so steadfastly sustained as to be of the very bone and marrow of the English constitution. This alone might have been enough to promote the influence of these traditions in America. Their translation by the Crown to the sphere of overseas government insured it. They thus became basic in the constitution of the empire—the first all-embracing constitution under which Americans lived—and, ineluctably, equally basic in American thinking.

The theories upon which this imperial constitution was founded, and which were to make relevant the old precedents in a new context, were themselves of ancient lineage. They were projections of postulates that, in England at least, had served to define the nature of the King's lordship in those lands without the realm that in the Middle Ages had acknowledged his suzerainty.[1] As already remarked, such lands were the King's demesnes, his possessions, where his prerogative was not subject to the restraints of English law. Only the merest remnants of the old empire survived when James I became king, but it is clear from the terms of the first Virginia charter (1606)[2] that old theories were still animate. They were to draw fresh life from a judgment in Exchequer Chamber (1608) when the Court restated the medieval rule that lands not acquired by descent the King had by conquest, and in such demesnes his prerogative over the laws was nearly absolute.[3]

This pronouncement by the English court to which the most difficult questions of law were referred and in which all the judges of the several benches and the Lord Chancellor participated was truly fateful. It imparted constitutional solidity to the doctrine of prerogative *extra regnum*, and there is no doubt but that it formed the legal basis of Crown policy thereafter. There was, of course, something anachronistic about it in the light of the progressive restraints under which the prerogative had been laid in England itself, and which were further to shackle it. There was, although at the time the judges may not have been aware of the fact, something absurd about projecting a theory, once applicable to Normans, Gascons and others who lived by their own law, to demesnes peopled by Englishmen.[4] At the moment when the old views were judicially refurbished and when the fate of the Virginia settlement still hung in the balance, there was momentarily the barest relations between legal doctrine and practical reality. The content of founding charters thereafter issued reflects the doctrine, but

---

[1] For details of the theory and practice, see Goebel, "Matrix of Empire," in J. H. Smith, *Appeals to the Privy Council from the American Plantations*, xiv *et seq.*

[2] Thorpe, *Constitutions and Charters*, VII, 3783–89.

[3] Calvin's Case, 7 Coke Rep. 1; 2 Howell, *State Trials*, 559. The distinction was drawn between lands conquered from a Christian kingdom—where the old laws remain until the King alters them—and a con-quest from infidels—where the laws are *ipso facto* abrogated. Until certain laws are established, the King himself, or judges delegated, judge causes according to natural equity. The conquest theory as applied to America rested upon the fiction of the state of perpetual hostility with infidels. This fiction was still applied as late as 1705 in Smith v. Brown, 2 Salkeld 666.

[4] Calvin's Case, 7 Coke Rep. 1 at 21b; Coke, *Fourth Institute*, 286.

not until Charles II's time were effective measures taken to exploit the implications.

The long interval during which the colonies, founded by instruments backed by a solid common law history, were more or less left to their own devices laid the basis for the adversarial situation that developed when, after the Restoration, agencies entirely associated with the prerogative were set over their affairs. For the authority exercised by these agencies there were parallels to be found both in administrative supervision of the "subalterne power" of legislation[5] within the realm, and in the doctrines applied to such by the courts. The agencies of imperial government performed more effectively than any of the administrative controls in use in England, but this together with the taint of their origin did not commend them to the inhabitants of America. Belligerently aware of the fact that they were Englishmen, they looked to doctrines prevailing in England to govern their relations to the Crown. There was in these but cold comfort.

ENGLISH CONTROLS ON LOCAL ENACTMENTS

EXCEPT FOR PLYMOUTH, and the pristine settlements in Rhode Island and Connecticut that later came into the fold, every mainland plantation owed its political origin to a grant from the King. Nothing was better settled in English law than that enactments by inferior jurisdictions thus created were subject to administrative or judicial review. The oldest and most relevant precedents related to the chartered boroughs, although the principles developed applied equally to individual grantees of franchises. The relevance of the borough charters consists in this, that like the colonial charters a complex of special privileges wholly in the gift of the King was conveyed, and among these privileges was the right to make enactments.[6] The control over unwarranted

---

[5] J. Wheeler, *A Treatise of Commerce* (1601), 25.

[6] The ordinance power derives from the grants confirming extant customs, or the "same liberties and customs" of other free boroughs, or grant of customs of some particular borough. As is elsewhere pointed out (J. Goebel, *Felony and Misdemeanor* [New York: Commonwealth Fund 1937], 226–33), the word "custom" on the Continent is applied indifferently to a usage, a due and an enactment, and there is evidence that the same ambiguous use of the word flourishes in England.

See T. Plucknett, *The Legislation of Edward I* (Oxford: Clarendon Press, 1949), 7. The existence and content of any "custom" was traditionally a matter of proof, and, as Maitland long ago pointed out, "the function of declaring customs could not always be marked off from that of imposing new rules." F. Pollock and F. W. Maitland, *History of English Law* (1903), I, 660. The charter formulas are in A. Ballard, *British Borough Charters, 1042–1216* (Cambridge: Cambridge University Press, 1913), 4–34; A. Ballard and J. Tait, *British*

exercise of any powers which only the King could grant had been first done through the General Eyres, those periodic local visitations by royal justices commissioned to discharge both administrative and judicial duties.[7] The justices were furnished with interrogatories to be put to jurors, the so-called articles of the eyre, that disclose the full scope of their investigative duties.[8] The content of the articles was relatively stable but from time to time additions were made. One such occurred twelve years after Magna Carta was signed, a direction that there be inquiry into "new customs raised."[9] The records establish that this wonderfully ambiguous term was understood to embrace both fiscal exactions and new enactments.

The justices pursued their inquisitorial task through the use of local presentment juries, and on the basis thereof might strike down the innovation, impose a penalty, or entertain, at the King's suit, a *quo warranto* proceeding. For nearly fifty years it was the novelty of an enactment that was under scrutiny. The dominating purpose was fiscal, but there emerged from the activity of the eyres the principle, thereafter embedded in the law, that a grantee of a franchise must observe the limitations set out in the grant. A change in the formula of instruction early in Edward I's reign was to establish a second principle.[10] Inquiry was to be made into misuse of liberties granted by the King as well as into liberties obstructive of "common justice" and subversive of royal power. The term "common justice" on its face comprehended violations of common law. At the great London Eyre of 1321, Justice Herle understood the article to mean against "comun dreit"[11] and it is

---

Borough Charters, 1216–1307 (Cambridge: Cambridge University Press, 1923), 7–29.

[7] On this generally, W. C. Bolland, *The General Eyre* (Cambridge: Cambridge University Press, 1922). The distinction of administrative and judicial duties is made advisedly, for the immixion of governmental functions was such at this period that such a differentiation would hardly then be made. Nevertheless, the ends for which the fact-finding was made by the presentment device were primarily informational, relating to a mass of non-judicial matters and concerning which other than judicial action might be taken.

[8] A critical discussion in H. Cam, *Studies in the Hundred Rolls, Oxford Studies in Social and Legal History* (Oxford: Clarendon Press, 1921), VI, 9–101, where the varia-

tions from eyre to eyre are indicated. A version of the so-called old articles is in 1 *Statutes of the Realm* 233; the "new" articles, at 235.

[9] In 1227 Cam, *Studies in the Hundred Rolls*, 21. But already at Worcester Eyre of 1221 inquest was made into "new customs." D. Stenton, *Rolls of the Justices in Eyre . . . for Lincolnshire 1218–9 and Worcestershire 1221*, Selden Society, vol. 53 (1934), 552.

[10] In connection with the great inquests of 1274–75. For the text, H. Cam, *Hundred and Hundred Rolls* (London: Methuen and Co., 1930), 248; and added to the articles of the eyre in 1280, see Cam, *Studies in the Hundred Rolls*, 96–97.

[11] Some of the proceedings of this eyre are in H. T. Riley, ed., *Munimenta Gildhallae Londoniensis*, pt. I, *Rolls Series* (1860), II, 285 *et seq.*;

clear from the proceedings there on the *modus operandi* of the London courts that the attack was conceived in terms of what was soon to be called a lack of due process of law.

That the exercise of any liberty, usurped or not, was put to the test of conformity with common law seems to us to have been of great constitutional significance. For a long time the courts had been applying this test to ancient community usages. Its application to the regulations of those enfranchised, or those, like many craft gilds, which were not, represents not only a magnification of the common law but of the judicial process as a means of control. Of further significance is the fact that at this time the courts coupled with the test of illegality the further criterion—did the ordinance run counter to public benefit? This was more than a policy consideration for it was contemporarily a necessary element in the dispensing of justice. The "Common profit" or commonweal of the people had already become a preambular piety in statutes and was to enjoy long lodgment in Acts of Parliament.[12]

The abandonment of the eyres in the mid-fourteenth century brought to a temporary halt efforts at systematic scrutiny of ordinance-making, not to be resumed until 1437. Meantime, the range of petty enactment had increased vastly with the chartering of gilds which were vested with extensive powers to manage and proctor their crafts in particular localities. On representations that these bodies under color of grants had made unlawful ordinances to the "common hurt of the people," it was enacted in Parliament that new ordinances must in the future be submitted to justices of the peace, or to the chief governors of cities, and made of record.[13] Ordinances in disherison or diminution of royal franchises or against the common profit of the people were forbidden, and the justices were empowered to revoke or repeal those found illegal or unreasonable. Penalties were imposed—loss of charters and a £10 fine for every ordinance made in violation of the statute.

---

the articles of the eyre, at 347. One Yearbook with some cases in R. V. Rogers, *Year Book, Eyre of London, 14 Edward II, Memoirs of the American Academy of Arts and Sciences* (Boston: The Academy, 1941), XIX. Another Yearbook version in M. Weinbaum, *London unter Eduard I und II, Beihefte zur Vierteljahrschrift fur Sozial- und Wirtschaftsgeschichte* (Stuttgart: Verlag von W. Kohlhammer, 1933) II, 113–27. On a plea of being quit of all pleas, "Herle: cest article de eire: franchises qe sount

contre comun dreit." Weinbaum, *London unter Eduard I und II*, 127.

[12] St. Westminster I, 3 Edw. I (1275); 7 Edw. I (1279); 21 Edw. I, St. 1 (1293). Some preambles are cast in terms of rectifying oppressions of the people. See further in relation to trade the comment in Cunningham, *The Growth of English Industry and Commerce*, I, 284, on Edward I's policies of substitution of general regulations for the realm in place of local regulations.

[13] 15 Hen. VI, c. 6; *Rotuli Parliamentorum* IV, 507.

II: *Traditions of Judicial Control*

There is reason to suspect that this statute was not effectively executed,[14] but it is in any event significant that the standards judicially established were put into statutory form. In 1504 Parliament, treating this act as expired, renewed the ban on ordinances by crafts, mysteries or gilds in diminution of royal prerogative or "of other" or the common profit of the people. To make such or to execute them was forbidden, and a penalty of £40 was provided. Examination and approval of ordinances was committed to the Chancellor, Treasurer, the Chief Justices of either Bench, or any three of them or before the Justices of Assize on circuit.[15]

As to the enforcement of this statute there is no question. This appears both from company records and from pleadings in litigation.[16] And there was every reason for compliance, for Parliament had a few years earlier declared void by statute a London ordinance,[17] and subsequently, by clapping a penalty on the execution of an ordinance of the Merchant Adventurers, had effected a nullification by implication.[18] Furthermore, the Privy Council in Star Chamber and out was in proc-

---

[14] B. H. Putnam, *Proceedings before the Justices of the Peace in the Fourteenth and Fifteenth Centuries, Edward III to Richard III* (1938), cx.

[15] 19 Hen. VII, c. 7. K. Pickthorn, *Early Tudor Government—Henry VII* (Cambridge: Cambridge University Press, 1934), 137, states the act originated in the policy of the King. However, a scribe of the Merchant Taylors' Company avers that the act was craftily procured by Sir Robert Sheffield, Recorder of London and Member of Parliament. C. M. Clode, *Memorials of the Guild of Merchant Taylors* (1875), 200.

[16] For the confirmation of the Merchant Taylors' Company ordinances (1502–08), C. M. Clode, *Early History of the Guild of Merchant Taylors* (1888) I, 36–39. See *Report and Appendix, City of London Livery Companies Commission* (1884) II, 6; Vintners' Company, Dec. 4, 1507, *ibid.*, 647; Salters' Company, 1507, *ibid.*, 524. Fishmongers' Company, Feb. 26, 1509, W. Herbert, *History of the Twelve Great Livery Companies of London* (1837), II, 32–33. Brewers' Company, July 15, 1508, *Report and Appendix, City of London Livery Companies Commission*

(1884), III, 123; Goldsmiths' Company, 1514, *ibid.*, II, 337. Companies newly chartered needed confirmation, *e.g.*, the Broderers' Company, 1562, *ibid.*, III, 201, or the Painters' Company, 1582, *ibid.*, 615. The confirmation of provincial gild ordinances is difficult to settle. The Hammermen's Company of Ludlow was confirmed Apr. 3, 1576, by justices of Assize, *Report of the Commission on Municipal Corporations, England and Wales* (1835), IV, 2802; that of the Gild Merchant of Kingston-upon-Thames in 1635, *ibid.*, 2898.

The process of confirmation under St. 19 Hen. VII, c. 7, continued well into the eighteenth century. See that for the Founders' Company, Feb. 3, 1783, *Report and Appendix, City of London Livery Companies Commission*, II, 404; and the Vintners' by-law confirmed, Nov. 3, 1829, *ibid.*, 661; Fishmongers, Dec. 14, 1843, and May 20, 1860, *ibid.*, 208.

For recitals in pleadings, Davenant v. Hurdis, Moore (K.B.) 576 (1599); Case of the Tailors of Ipswich, 11 Coke Rep. 53a (1615).

[17] 3 Hen. VII, c. 9 (1486).

[18] 12 Hen. VII, c. 6 (1496).

ess of becoming a forum where recourse against the extravagances of companies might be had, and where a police of their activities might be exercised.[19]

Contemporary with the enactment of 19 Henry VII, c. 7, the limitation to be standard in later American charters—that enactments be not contrary to the law of England—makes its appearance in letters patent. The earliest examples we have seen are in charters to two of the London livery companies, the Coopers Company (1501)[20] and the Merchant Tailors (1502).[21] There is desultory use of the formula thereafter in domestic charters, but in view of the settled rule of law respecting ordinances it is not clear why it should have been used at all. The companies or associations trading out of England were in a different case, for they were not within the statute. Furthermore, they were so particularly associated with the jealously guarded royal prerogative over foreign trade that one may properly doubt how far at this time they were deemed subject to the ordinary course of law. This peculiar status is reflected in the early forms of restraint embodied in the charters. The earliest of these which we have seen is the 1505 charter to the Merchant Adventurers which declared of no force and effect any act or statute "that shalbe or may be contrarious to us, our crowne, honnour, dignyte royall or prerogatif or to the dymynution of the common weale of our realme."[22] This formula safeguarding the public "welthe" or commonweal appears also in a charter of Henry VIII's reign,[23] and although a company was thus not subject to common law restraints, the limitations were severe enough for these were days when the prerogative was

---

[19] The earliest example found from the year 1477 in I. Leadam, *Select Cases before the King's Council in the Star Chamber*, Selden Society, vol. 16 (1903), I, 1; and see Leadam's introductory comments, *ibid.*, cli–cliii, and the case Butlond v. Austen, *ibid.*, 262 (1507), and contemporary proceedings against the Cowpers' Company, *ibid.*, 283, n. 3. See also the adjudication in 1504 of the jurisdictional dispute between the Merchant Adventurers and the Merchants of the Staple in C. Bayne and W. Dunham, *Select Cases in the Council of Henry VII*, Selden Society, vol. 75 (1958), 38, 149. For later controversy between these antagonists temp. Henry VIII, see the documents from the Star Chamber proceedings printed in G. Schanz, *Englische Handelspolitik gegen Ende des Mittelalters*, II, 556 *et seq.* References

to the later expanded jurisdiction of the Council in Holdsworth, *History of English Law* (1924), IV, 323.

[20] Apr. 29, 1501, in *Report and Appendix, City of London Livery Companies Commission* (1884), III, 273.

[21] Jan. 6, 1502/3, in W. Herbert, *History of the Twelve Great Livery Companies of London*, II, 520.

[22] Schanz, *Englische Handelspolitik gegen Ende des Mittelalters*, II, 549 at 552. A modernized version in G. Cawston and A. H. Keene, *The Early Chartered Companies* (1896), 249. In the more elaborate charter of Elizabeth (1564) "contrary to any of our Lawes and Statutes" is added, *ibid.*, 268.

[23] To the merchants trading to Spain. C. T. Carr, *Select Charters of Trading Companies*, Selden Society, vol. 28 (1913), 1 at 3.

in lush bloom and when the "common weal of the realm" was in process of being promoted as a para-constitutional principle for the enhancement of the prerogative.[24]

Beginning with the charter to the Russia Company (1555),[25] the prohibition on enactments contrary to the law of England is used with some consistency in the patents for such overseas adventures and was also written into patents granted to individual would-be colonizers.[26] The first Virginia charter (1606) was, however, an exception.[27] For in this charter, James I, who regarded himself as *jurisperitus clarus*, reserved the right of law-giving. In the second charter of 1609, when the Company was incorporated, the ordinance power was bestowed with words of limitation, that the statutes ordinances or proceedings "as near as conveniently may be, be agreeable to the Laws, Statutes, Government and Policy of this our Realm of England."[28] This formula was simplified in the 1612 charter,[29] the proviso being that which became almost standard in colonization charters, that the laws "be not contrary to the Laws and Statutes of this our Realm of England." But it was to be a long time before anything was done to implement the restraint. Nevertheless, the drastic remedies of *quo warranto* or *scire facias* to repeal a patent were there for the using, as the intractable men of Massachusetts Bay were to discover.

COMMON LAW REVIEW OF LEGISLATION

WHILE THE CHANGES in charter formula were in process of being tried and the new system of administrative supervision of gild ordinance was in operation, the common law courts were to revive their

---

[24] On this, Goebel, *Cases and Materials on the Development of Legal Institutions*, 188–90 and the statutes there cited.

[25] R. Hakluyt, *Principall Navigations, Voyages, and Discoveries of the English Nation . . .*, II, 304 at 311.

[26] See the charter to the Eastland Company (1579), in M. Sellers, *Acts and Ordinances of the Eastland Company*, Camden Society *Publications* (1906), 142 at 145; that to the Levant Company, Hakluyt, *Principall Navigations, Voyages, and Discoveries of the English Nation . . .*, V, 192 at 194; and to the Barbary Merchants, *ibid.*, VI, 419 at 421. Individual patents to Sir Humphrey Gilbert (1578), in C. Slafter, *Sir Humpfrey Gylberte*, Prince Society *Publications*

(1903), 95 at 100; and to Raleigh (1584), Hakluyt, *Principall Navigations, Voyages, and Discoveries of the English Nation . . .*, VIII, 289 at 294.

[27] Thorpe, *Constitutions and Charters*, VII, 3783. The reservation at 3785. Instructions later issued permitted limited legislative authority to be exercised consonant with the laws of England "or the equity thereof," subject to royal review and royal ordinance power. A. Brown, *Genesis of the United States* (Boston and New York: Houghton Mifflin Co., 1890), I, 73–74.

[28] Thorpe, *Constitutions and Charters*, VII, 3790 at 3801.

[29] *Ibid.*, 3802 at 3806.

own languishing traditions of controlling corporate enactments. One extremely important law-making group, the chartered boroughs, was neither covered by the Statute 19 Henry VII, c. 7, nor, except in a very few cases, did the charters require conformity with the common law. Individuals aggrieved by some ordinance had always been cast upon their common law remedies, but in the state of medieval law reporting it is impossible to say how often resort was had to them. Until the nineteenth century what appeared in law reports was wholly adventitious, and consequently one cannot assume from the sudden appearance toward the end of Elizabeth's reign of cases dealing with corporate by-laws that the common law courts were doing something novel. There was, thereafter, a steady succession of such cases reported but the foundations of "modern" doctrine were laid by those that appear in Sir Edward Coke's reports. The colonials held these books in almost biblical veneration, and consequently what Coke had to say about illegal ordinances has particular significance.

Coke's views were first set forth in the *Chamberlain of London's Case* (1590)[30] where he appeared as counsel for the city. An individual against whom debt had been brought for a penalty imposed for breach of an ordinance claimed that the city had no power to make an ordinance against the law and the freedom of the subject. Coke argued that the city had made ordinances time out of mind for the government of its citizens and consonant with law and reason—"and all such ordinances constitutions or by-laws are allowed by the law, which are made for the true and due execution of the laws or statutes of the realm, or for the well government and order of the body incorporate. And all others which are contrary or repugnant to the laws or statutes of the realm are void and of no effect." He added the further test that these ordinances should be for public good and not private benefit.

All of this was but a summation of the rules developed in medieval times, and although delivered *arguendo*, was to form a species of platform for cases to follow. Within a few years in *Clark's Case* (1596) a St. Albans ordinance providing imprisonment for any inhabitant refusing to pay an assessment was held to be a violation of Magna Carta, c. 29.[31] Although the ordinance was not explicitly declared void, the ruling that it could not be pleaded in justification amounted to an implicit avoidance.

At the end of the sixteenth century the first of the important gild cases was adjudicated. Here the Merchant Tailors Company of London, which had long before secured a clearance of ordinances in

---

[30] 5 Coke Rep. 62.   [31] *Ibid.*, 64.

Star Chamber, had concocted a monopolistic ordinance. This was adjudged to be against the common law because it was against the liberty of the subject, and, therefore, whether or not made by color of charter was void.[32] This particular by-law had been properly confirmed yet nothing was made of the point. The effect of such confirmation was, however, soon settled in the *Case of the Tailors of Ipswich* (1615),[33] more famous for the pronouncement on restraint of trade than the constitutional doctrine before us. Here the ordinance had been allowed by the Justices of Assize. Nevertheless, it was held by King's Bench that the statute of Henry VII did not "corroborate" any corporate ordinances allowed or approved as stipulated, "but leaves them to be affirmed as good, or disaffirmed as unlawful by the law." The sole benefit of allowance was to relieve from the £40 penalty for not complying with the statute. The ordinance here was adjudged to be against the common law and the commonweal.

These cases and others in other contemporary reports have usually been viewed by historians as but a phase of the aggressive reassertion of judicial authority by the common law courts in which Coke played so major a part. They are obviously something more. The Crown, secure in its ultimate weapon, the *quo warranto*, had done nothing better than to institute a system of administrative watch and ward over the enactments of inferior jurisdictions. The courts offered remedy for the protection of the common law rights of individuals, and in so doing reaffirmed the supremacy of this common law. The sovereign authority of this law was further emphasized by solemn judgment that not even a royal patent could validate a void ordinance, and further, that royal grants against common right were void.[34] To pronounce such judgments was no small thing at a time when these courts had dangerous competitors, and is properly to be accounted a bold vindication of a constitutional principle.

We have set forth the sum of English experience in dealing with the enactments of inferior jurisdictions because the handling of colonial problems was inevitably affected thereby. Much of this was living law when the Crown at long last undertook to deal with the plantations. In England the ordinances of companies were still being submitted, pur-

---

[32] Davenant v. Hurdis, Moore (K. B.) 576 (1599), where Coke was counsel for the plaintiff. The authorities were reviewed in the argument of the third point as to the legality of the ordinance. Coke refers to this case in The Case of Monopolies, 11 Coke Rep. 84b.

[33] 11 Coke Rep. 53a.

[34] The doctrine is laid down in Waltham v. Austin set out in The City of London's Case, 8 *ibid.*, 121 at 125 (1610), with the supporting "maxim" *potentior est vulgaris consuetudo quam regalis concessio*. Coke had already advanced the doctrine *arguendo* in Davenant v. Hurdis; it appears also in The Case of Monopolies (*supra*, n. 32). See also Norris v. Staps, Hobart 210.

suant to 19 Henry VII, c. 7, for allowance consistently by the Lord Chancellor who was of the Privy Council and the Chief Justices.[35] The courts were still holding void illegal enactments. And not far off was the concentrated attack on boroughs by *quo warranto*. The adaptation of any of these means of control to the plantations was a matter of practicality and convenience, and beyond this was the ultimate reality of royal pleasure as to what should be done. In the case of the corporate and proprietary colonies, there had been qualified yielding of prerogative, and the failure to make explicit provision for submission of laws was to produce controversy. Only in the royal provinces was the King, within limits of political prudence, free to exercise the prerogative *extra regnum* conceded by the judiciary. It was with respect to these provinces that future policy was set, a policy that was to establish a legal relationship between King and legislative unlike any hitherto known. The practices that fixed and defined the relationship became so stabilized that the policy as implemented hardened into a fundamental of the imperial constitution. The effect upon American political thinking was profound. Controls, administrative and judicial, were to be accepted, although sometimes with rancor, as a normal incident of dependent government. Indeed, after nearly a century of subjection to these controls, the Americans when they came to frame their own instruments of government were prepared to accept supervision of legislation as a constitutional principle and in some states to provide machinery to execute it.

ADMINISTRATIVE CONTROL OF COLONY LEGISLATION

THE SYSTEM which was so to mold the American opinion was in its fundamentals the work of a committee of the Privy Council to which plantation affairs were entrusted in February 1674/5—the Lords Committee of Trade and Plantations. This system was the fruit of the first thorough exploration of the nature and limits of the King's authority in the governments of his American possessions conducted in terms

---

[35] Needlemakers' Company, June 20, 1664, *Report and Appendix, City of London Livery Companies Commission* (1884), III, 602–03. Glass Sellers' Company, Nov. 28, 1664, *ibid.*, 483. Gunmakers' Company, July 13, 1670, *ibid.*, 505. Wheelwrights' Company, Oct. 12, 1670, *ibid.*, 858. Patternmakers' Company, June 20, 1674, *ibid.*, 641. Fishmongers' Company, Sept. 15, 1668, *ibid.*, II, 208. Haberdashers' Company, Dec. 23, 1675, *ibid.*, 478. Skinners' Company, Apr. 26, 1676, *ibid.*, 396. Salters' Company, 1676, *ibid.*, 524. Coach and Harness Makers' Company, July 17, 1677, *ibid.*, III, 249. Farriers' Company, Jan. 29, 1676, *ibid.*, 371. Masons' Company, 1678, *ibid.*, 575. Girdlers' Company, May 30, 1682, *ibid.*, 452.

both theoretical and practical. The anxiety to achieve a constitutional settlement based in law is evident from the consultations of the Committee with distinguished legal talent—William Jones and Creswell Levinz, Attorneys General, Francis North, Chief Justice of Common Bench, Heneage Finch, Lord Chancellor, and probably other judges. So important was the effect of these proceedings on the future constitutional control of legislation that they deserve close examination.

The proceedings began when late in 1675 there arrived a book of Jamaica laws which were conceived to be prejudicial to the prerogative. The Lords Committee of Trade and Plantations at first itself undertook to amend these laws.[36] The conception of its function and that of the local legislative is disclosed by the first declaration of policy (June 1, 1676) "Their Ldshps. on this occasion of altering a law do conceive that when any alterations are made by His Majesty in the Lawes transmitted, they are to be approved by the Governor, Council and Assembly there, without reenacting them, and sending them back for His Majesty's approbation again."[37] The intimation that the King was believed to be an indispensable party in the legislative process itself, a part of the magic that converts a bill into law, was made explicit a week later: "Their Lds. observe that the words (Be it enacted etc.) are irregular and not agreeable to the Law of England, before His Majesty's Assent be already given in the making of laws."[38] Throughout subsequent discussions the Committee was exercised about the style of enactments obviously because this was deemed to have substantive implications.

Nine months passed while the Jamaica laws were prepared for royal action. Finally in April 1677 the attendance of the Lord Chancellor and the Lord Treasurer was requested for an opinion on laws, amendments and "defalcations." The opinion of the Attorney General was also solicited as to how far the laws were fit to be allowed, in particular an act extending the common law to Jamaica.[39] It was also requested that he prepare a "Bill like Poynings' Law in Ireland directing the manner of Enacting, Transmitting and Amending these laws by

---

[36] Beginning May 18, 1676, Ms. Journal of the Lords Committee of Trade and Plantations, I, 118 (C.O. 391/1, LC Trans.). The standard account, but not free of inaccuracies, is E. B. Russell, *The Review of American Colonial Legislation by the King in Council.*

[37] Ms. Journal of the Lords Committee of Trade and Plantations, I, 126.

[38] *Ibid.*, 134.

[39] Ms. Journal of the Lords Committee of Trade and Plantations

(rough minutes), II, 22–29 (LC Trans.). This volume, Phillips Ms. No. 8539, is described in G. G. Griffin, *A Guide to Manuscripts Relating to American History in British Depositories* (Washington, D.C.: Library of Congress, 1946), 43, as a contemporary copy. The format indicates clearly that it is a rough minute book from which the engrossed Journal was made. The order to the attorney general is in *CSP Col.* 1677–80, No. 200.

His Majesty here in England."[40] The legislative serfdom of the Irish was to be projected into the New World.

It was another nine months before the Attorney General reported.[41] Meanwhile some Virginia laws were submitted to him and on the heels of this action arrived a fresh clutch of Jamaica laws "prejudicial to His Majesty's Prerogative and authority."[42] Their Lordships at once decided to apply the principles of Poynings' Law. It was resolved that in the future no colonial assembly could be called without special order from the King. The governor was to consent to no laws until first approved by the King. Even in cases of emergency the Crown must be notified and the projected laws sent over for approval.[43] On September 20, 1677, it was further decided that the enacting style be "By the King's most Excellent Majestie by and with the consent of the General Assembly."[44]

After the Attorney General finally reported in January 1677/78,[45] a "body of laws" for Jamaica including a perpetual revenue act was submitted to the Privy Council which ordered that these pass under the Great Seal February 15, 1678.[46] Never were labors more arduously spent to prove more fruitless. The Jamaica assembly refused to pass the menu of bills submitted.[47] The Jamaica agent and certain merchants appeared before the Committee to urge that the case of the Island be distinguished from Ireland[48]—a position their Lordships thought frivolous, despite the arguments of a Jamaica address embodying practical and constitutional reasons why the methods favored at Whitehall were

---

[40] Poynings' Law is in 1 *Statutes at Large* (Ireland), 10 Hen. VII, c. 4; corrected text in D. B. Quinn, "Early Interpretations of Poynings' Law 1494–1534," *Irish Historical Studies*, 2:242. By the terms of the statute, royal administrators in Ireland prepared bills in advance of summoning the Irish Parliament. These bills were required to be submitted to the Crown; those approved together with a license to summon Parliament were returned under the Great Seal. The role of the Irish Parliament was to vote. In 1556 a clarifying statute (1 *Statutes at Large* [Ireland], 3 & 4 Ph. & M., c. 4) recognized a right of amendment both by the Crown and the Irish Parliament. See further on the operation of the statutes, R. D. Edwards and T. W. Moody, "The History of Poynings'

Law 1494–1615," *Irish Historical Studies*, 2:415.

The Poynings' Law precedent was fresh in the administrators' minds, Charles II's one Irish Parliament having been prorogued in 1666.

[41] Ms. Journal of the Lords Committee of Trade and Plantations (rough minutes), II, 145.

[42] *Ibid.*, 167.

[43] *Ibid.*, 168.

[44] *Ibid.*, 187.

[45] *Ibid.*, 312.

[46] 1 *APC Col.*, No. 1202.

[47] Ms. Journal of the Lords Committee of Trade and Plantations (LC Trans.), III, 73. See also "A Breviate of What Passed in Ye Assembly," British Museum, Egerton Ms. 2395, fol. 576 (LC Trans.).

[48] Ms. Journal of the Lords Committee of Trade and Plantations, III, 115 (Jan. 13, 1679/80).

unworkable.[49] The heart of the Jamaicans' brief was that no law had been transmitted to them "for ascertaining the laws of England." As to this their Lordships thought it reasonable that the King "retain within himself the power of appointing the Laws of England to bee in force in that Island as Hee shall find necessary"[50]—a confirmation of the continued vigor of the doctrine of *Calvin's Case* that indicated there was to be no utter yielding of royal authority.

Despite this stiff-necked attitude, the Committee submitted to the Attorney General whether or not the colonists "have right to the Laws of England as Englishmen or by virtue of the King's Proclamation or otherwise." He was also to inquire whether or not, embraced in the claim to be governed by the laws of England, the inhabitants were not bound as well by laws beneficial to the King by appointing taxes as by other laws beneficial to themselves.[51] The Attorney General, Sir Creswell Levinz, reported that the Jamaicans had no right to be governed by the laws of England but "by such laws as are made there and established by His Majesty's authority."[52]

Before the Committee had finished with the Jamaica lawbook it had taken up the Virginia laws enacted "contrary to the power residing in the government of Virginia"—a first suggestion that the constitution established for a province was a restraint.[53] It was decided to apply the Poynings' Law procedure here, and three necessary bills were drawn, sealed and despatched to Virginia by the new governor, Lord Culpeper.[54] The Virginians proved to be more ductile than the Jamaicans. Two bills were enacted, a third passed with provisos later amended by the Lords Committee.[55]

The Virginia bills had not yet left England when the Jamaica protest arrived and within a few weeks complaints about Barbados laws

---

[49] 1 *APC Col.*, No. 1274; *CSP Col. 1677–80*, No. 1009.

[50] Ms. Journal of the Lords Committee of Trade and Plantations, III, 153.

[51] *Ibid.*, 160 (Mar. 11, 1679/80).

[52] *Ibid.*, 167 (Apr. 27, 1680).

[53] The entries in Ms. Journal of the Lords Committee of Trade and Plantations (rough minutes), II, 145 (Aug. 2, 1677), 165 (Sept. 6, 1677), 288–89 (Dec. 11, 1677), where it was recommended that the laws be "disannulled and abrogated by His Majesty and others more agreeable to His Majesty's justice be sent to Virginia." The report to the Council,

Jan. 18, 1678, in 1 *APC Col.*, No. 1198.

[54] The attorney general ordered on Dec. 14, 1678, to draft laws, Ms. Journal of the Lords Committee of Trade and Plantations (rough minutes), II, 447. Six days later it was voted to recommend to the King the same establishment for Virginia as for Jamaica. The laws were approved Apr. 16, 1679, *ibid.*, 327.

[55] *CSP Col. 1677–80*, Nos. 558, 612. The vote of the Lords Committee on the approval in Ms. Journal of the Lords Committee of Trade and Plantations, III, 209–10 (Oct. 10, 1680). See also 2 *APC Col.*, No. 44.

represented to be unreasonable, against royal prerogative and violative of the frame of government.[56] There was some brief consideration of resort to the Poynings' Law nostrum, but while it was coping with the Jamaica issue the Lords Committee, experienced in the dilatory ways of contemporary lawyers, submitted the Barbados laws to outside counsel.[57] It was not to be disappointed, for Sergeant Baldwin took a year to answer. Consequently the Barbados matter was not resumed until June 1680.[58] The decision reached was to provide a solution to the Jamaica problem.

At this juncture there are signs of a changed approach to the problem of keeping in hand the doings of far-off legislative bodies. The pains that were devoted to a careful framing of the commission to Sir Richard Dutton, destined to be governor of Barbados, indicates a resolve to cast this instrument into a form so that it would veritably be what the chief law officer had earlier said it was—the constitution of the province.[59] Changed opinion is indicated further by the questions to which the Secretary of the Committee, William Blathwayt, was to secure an answer.[60] Could the laws of Barbados remain in force perpetually without royal confirmation; could governor, council and assembly without royal consent repeal a law once confirmed; could laws sent to England be amended or must they all be granted or rejected; could the King at any time signify dissent to laws not confirmed and would such become void immediately?[61]

The Committee Journal does not indicate if an answer was submitted. Nevertheless, it was decided in relation to Dutton's commission: "As for the power of Enacting Laws it is thought fit that the method of Biennial Laws be laid aside, and that they continue in force untill they be disallowed by his Majesty. . . ."[62] Furthermore, laws must be sent to England within three months of enactment.

These dispositions were to be applied to Jamaica, but not before the advice of the law officers and the judges was besought.[63] This had

---

[56] Ms. Journal of the Lords Committee of Trade and Plantations, III, 30–38 (June 26, 1679).

[57] After consultation with the Barbados merchants and agents, ibid., 46–50.

[58] After the report of Sir Samuel Baldwin, ibid., 173, 179.

[59] The discussions, ibid., 183–84, 203. The commission is in British Museum, Additional Mss. 15896, 28–35.

[60] Ms. Journal of the Lords Committee of Trade and Plantations, III,

179 (July 10, 1680).

[61] Ibid., 180.

[62] Ibid., 186–87.

[63] On June 23, 1680, an Order in Council issued directing that the Crown law officers confer with the judges on whether by letter, proclamation or commission the King had excluded himself from the power of establishing laws in Jamaica, it being a conquered country. CSP Col. 1677–80, No. 1405. On the same day Blathwayt passed on the query to the judges, ibid., No. 1406.

evidently not been forthcoming by the fall of 1680, for Sir Francis North was requested to report on whether the King by proclamation, letter, commission or instruction had divested himself of the power he formerly had to alter the forms of government in the Island.[64] The Chief Justice's reply was not fully responsive, for he reported only that by a proclamation of Lord Windsor's time (1661) the King had settled the property of the inhabitants, not the government.[65] But it was not on points of law but by negotiation with the Jamaica agent and the merchants in London that the problem was finally to be settled. North, deputed to handle these parleys, reported that the Jamaicans had agreed to a perpetual revenue act provided that the inhabitants be restored to their "ancient form of passing Laws," and be assured of such of the laws of England as concerned their liberty and property.[66]

Since agreement on the revenue act had been reached, the Lords Committee, relying chiefly on a recommendation from Blathwayt, decided to extend to Jamaica the methods of keeping a hand on legislation settled for Governor Dutton's commission, viz., that the King would be free at any time to disallow an act not confirmed by him.[67] The clinching argument against adhesion to the scheme of Poynings' Law was advanced by William Blathwayt: "by the Irish Modell His Majesty establishes perpetual laws to the people and puts it out of His Own Power to allow or disallow them as His service shall require."[68] Eight months later the surrender of the Lords Committee was made complete by a direction respecting Virginia laws, that the style, "Be it enacted by the King's Most Excellent Majesty by and with the consent of the General Assembly is not agreeable to the powers in the commission."[69]

Although the drawn-out proceedings over the manner of royal participation in plantation legislation may seem but another instance of administrative dithering, the ultimate decision was portentous. In arriving at it, the Lords Committee not only set the pattern for its own future handling of colony acts but established the *modus operandi* to be followed by the Board of Trade and Plantations after this body was established in 1696. The standard procedure was to be that laws must be submitted to the Crown within a reasonable or set time limit for approbation or disallowance. In the Penn charter (1681)[70] and that

---

[64] Ms. Journal of the Lords Committee of Trade and Plantations, III, 216.

[65] *Ibid.*, 219 (Oct. 21, 1680).

[66] *Ibid.*, 220–21 (Oct. 27, 1680).

[67] *Ibid.*, 222 (Oct. 28, 1680).

[68] "The State of Jamaica with a Proposal Concerning the Method of Making Laws," British Museum, Egerton Ms. 2395, fol. 603 (LC Trans.).

[69] Ms. Journal of the Lords Committee of Trade and Plantations, III, 269 (July 5, 1681).

[70] Thorpe, *Constitutions and Charters*, V, 3035 at 3039.

later issued to Massachusetts (1691),[71] laws not acted upon by the Crown within a specified term were to become effective *sub silentio*. In other royal provinces, as noticed, disallowance could be signified at any time. Furthermore, in the settlement of the Jamaica imbroglio a constitutional issue of great significance was settled. This concerned the style of enactment, superficially a mere matter of form, although the implications were gravely substantive. The Crown relinquished the claim to the formula "Be it enacted by the King's Most Excellent Majesty by and with the consent of the General Assembly"[72] and permitted the prevalent colonial "Be it enacted by the Governor, Council and assembly."[73] The plantation enactment thus was not to be the act of the King as was the English or Irish Act of Parliament, but in English eyes stood on no more stately footing than the act of any inferior jurisdiction in England. The total effect in the colonies was to encourage the belief that they were possessed of legislative power beyond that of a mere corporation.

As a matter of constitutional theory what the King was about when he accepted or rejected a colonial act was done in exercise of his prerogative in his demesnes. For such action precedent did not have to be found in the common law or even in usages connected with the administration of the realm, although such was available. For the courts, on the basis of practice relating to the King's medieval demesnes, had recognized the existence of a mandate power, even in form current within the realm, that would extend to any land in his ligeance.[74] The directions about the law in the first Virginia charter and the first instructions had been a practical extension of this authority.[75]

A problem of greater legal complexity than the authority by which the Crown acted was the nature of what was involved in accepting or rejecting of a colonial act. The signification of royal pleasure was no whimsical act. It was arrived at only after extensive deliberation. Following the establishment of the Board of Trade (1696) upon which rested the duty of advising the Crown, consideration of a colony act involved not only advice from the Board's counsel or from the law officers of

---

[71] *Ibid.*, III, 1870 at 1883.

[72] And actually ordered to be effective Sept. 20, 1677. Ms. Journal of the Lords Committee of Trade and Plantations (rough minutes), II, 187.

[73] As to Jamaica, it was decided in the agreement reported Oct. 27, 1680, that "they may be restored to their ancient form of passing laws." Ms. Journal of the Lords Committee of Trade and Plantations, III, 220–

21. In the case of Virginia, the form given in the text was settled upon, *ibid.*, 269 (July 5, 1681). In practice this formula had certain minor local variations.

[74] Calvin's Case, 7 Coke Rep. 1 at 20a; Vaughan, *Process into Wales* (1677), 401.

[75] Thorpe, *Constitutions and Charters*, VII, 3783. The instructions in Brown, *Genesis of the United States*, I, 65 *et seq.*

the Crown, but also hearings attended by colony agents or other interested parties. The Board would report to the Lords Committee of the Privy Council and only after a report from this group to the Council itself[76] and a vote there would the Order in Council issue. Despite constant dealing with the question "approve or disallow?" the administrators appear never to have formulated a theory as to the legal implications of royal action. As we shall see, it was only in litigation that this problem was to be considered.[77] Nevertheless, it is difficult not to believe that some principles were active.

In the first place, the decision reached on the style of laws in the Jamaica affair removed the King as an indispensable factor in the legislative process itself as he was in England. An Act of Parliament was *brutum fulmen* without subscription of "the King wills it." Obviously, what the King did with colony acts was something different. In some colonies, like Connecticut, where no provision had been made for submission of acts, these were effective without royal pleasure being signified. In Massachusetts and Pennsylvania, as noticed, a time limit within which the Crown must act was set by charter. If there was no action the colony enactment was to be effective. In the royal provinces where no such limitation existed, the Crown could at any time overturn an act not previously approved.

The terms chosen to characterize royal action and used consistently in the governors' commission were "approbation" and "disallowance." The choice appears to have been deliberate, for the forms of commissions were thoroughly canvassed at the time the matter of the Barbados, Jamaica and Virginia laws was before the Privy Council. From what vocabulary the terms were plucked we cannot say. *Allocatur* and *non allocatur* had been used by the courts when liberties were claimed, and were also part of Exchequer jargon. Coke had described action on by-laws submitted pursuant to 19 Henry VII, c. 7, as "allowed or disaffirmed." In Charles II's reign the Lord Chancellor and the two Chief Justices when acting under the Tudor statute used "approve" or "ratify confirm [or allow] and approve," a formula closely patterned on that used to confirm deeds.[78] We have seen no instances where the officials rejected by-laws.

---

[76] And even after the recommendation of the Board of Trade parties could be heard before the Lords Committee, *e.g.*, on the Virginia Two-penny Act. See Smith, *Appeals to the Privy Council from the American Plantations*, 612–14.

[77] *Infra*, p. 77.

[78] Needlemakers' Company, June 20, 1664, *Report and Appendix, City of London Livery Companies Commission*, III, 602–03 (ratify, allow and approve); Glass Cutters' Company, Nov. 28, 1664, *ibid.*, 479 (ratify, confirm and approve); Haberdashers' Company, Dec. 23, 1675, *ibid.*, II, 472 (approve). The formula for confirming deeds in Coke, *Littleton*, 295b.

Whatever the source for the terms, it is apparent that approbation was deemed at Whitehall to possess constitutive force since counsel for the Board of Trade speak of a colony act thereby "passing into law."[79] The formula for signifying approval "confirmed, finally enacted and ratified" bears out this view, although taken singly the legal intendment of each word in this curious conglomeration suggests a confusion of ideas. In any event, so many acts, even in royal provinces, were operative as law without the royal pleasure ever being signified that we must conclude that whatever the theory, the Crown was practically not an indispensable party. Some further light on the royal role, whether conceived as participation or control, is thrown by formulas describing the effect of disallowance. The provision in the governors' commission dealing with the continuing right of disallowance states that acts not confirmed shall upon disallowance "thenceforward cease determine and become utterly void." The act of assembly thus is viewed as voidable, a law *sub modo* under which rights could attach until the law is avoided.[80] No wonder that the Crown strove to require suspending clauses, as a means of forcing acknowledgement that to be law a colony enactment needed an expression of the sovereign will.

Modern writers have sometimes used the term veto as a synonym for disallowance, but this is technically meaningless since an act without a suspending clause became operative upon signing by the governor. The formula long employed in Orders in Council "is hereby Repealed, declared void and of none affect"[81] is obviously adapted from the usual English statutory clause "repealed and made void."[82] But in English legislative usage a repeal could only be effected by the power which brought the law into being. Since the Crown had no hand in the making

---

[79] Chalmers, *Opinions*, II, 47 (1723), 56 (1723), 89 (1724), 94 (1748).

[80] See the opinion of Attorney General Ryder and Solicitor General Murray in 1753, Chalmers, *Opinions*, I, 295. Later, in the Virginia appeal of Howlett v. Osburn (1765), Mansfield is reported as saying, "They all take force from passing there. The King's Disapprobation is only of force from the time it is signified in the Colony—it's a Law there 'till then." P.R.O. WO 1/404/58. See also the earlier (1718) opinion of Board of Trade counsel West in Chalmers, *Opinions*, I, 115.

[81] The Orders in Council using the phrase are scattered in various collections. For a sampling, see those in *Docs. Rel. Col. Hist. N.Y.*, V, 71 (1708/9), 529 (1719); *ibid.*, VI, 137 (1738). 3 *Acts and Resolves Prov. of Mass. Bay* 509 (1752); 4 *ibid.*, 93 (1759); 111 (1758), 563 (1763). 5 *Statutes at Large of Pennsylvania*, 477 (1750), 532 (1756), 576 (1758). *Colonial Records of North Carolina*, VI, 53 (1759), 707 (1762), 723 (1762); *State Records of North Carolina*, XI, 212 (1767).

[82] *E.g.*, 12 Car. II, c. 24, sec. 3 (1660); 13 Car. II, c. 2 (1661) "repealed, annulled and made void"; 25 Car. II, c. 4 (1672) "stand repealed and be utterly null and void"; 30 Car. II, c. 5 (1677) "stand void and be repealed"; 5 Wm. & M., c. 9 (1694) "repealed, null and void."

of a colonial act, the word repeal was presumably used in the non-technical sense of annul. Even so, the formula is on its face ambiguous since it could stand as well for a declaration of nullity. When the troubles began after the French and Indian War, there appears to have been some experiment with the formula.[83] Eventually "disallowed, declared void and of none effect" becomes usual.[84]

While the attention given the formulas of disallowance may savor of pettifoggery, it is only through these that one can come to some estimation of what, as a matter of law, the Board of Trade and the Privy Council supposed they were doing. Furthermore, it is important to establish the normal mode of rejecting a colony act, in order to comprehend the full impact of the instances where the Crown exercised the prerogative in its plenitude by declaring certain enactments void *ab initio*. This was done both in process of administrative review, and judicially, upon appeal, and there was probably nothing done in Council that left a more lasting impress. The occasions were not many for even where colony enactments were reported to be unreasonable, or contrary to the common law or even an invasion of the prerogative—all grounds on which a common law court would avoid a by-law—the Privy Council with prudence again and again did no more than disallow. Since rights vested under an act before disallowance were unaffected, this manner of controlling legislation although disliked was not intolerable. A declaration of nullity was something close to catastrophic, for everything that might have been done under it was rendered nugatory.

It should be observed that the disallowance had been given constitutional status by being embodied in a royal direction in instruments under the Great Seal—charter or commission. Whether or not a waiver of prerogative to make a declaration of nullity could be implied never appears to have been raised. Out of the complex body of law relating to grants by the Crown some authority to support an argument of such waiver might be squeezed, but in view of the few restraints upon the King's power in his demesnes we believe the law to have been the other way. There was no question of the authority of the King in Parliament to declare void the enactments of inferior jurisdictions. Some early examples have been noticed. It was done again during Charles II's reign.[85]

---

[83] See 4 *Acts and Resolves Prov. of Mass. Bay*, 926 (July 24, 1767) "disallowed and rejected"; *ibid.*, 944 (May 13, 1767) "disallowed and rejected"; *ibid.*, 1045 (July 31, 1771) "disallowed and rejected."

[84] 5 *ibid.*, 283 (Apr. 13, 1774). *Colonial Records of North Carolina*, IX, 284–85 (Apr. 22, 1772); *State Records of North Carolina*, XI, 236 (June 7, 1771). This formula was used for the Virginia acts involved in the Parsons' Cause (*infra*, p. 81); see Smith, *Appeals to the Privy Council from the American Plantations*, 616–17.

[85] 20 Car. II, c. 6.

In 1696, the same year which saw the establishment of the Board of Trade, Parliament in the Act for Preventing Frauds,[86] designed to strengthen the enforcement of acts of trade, laid down a policy with respect to nullification of colonial enactments, past or future, that were counter to the complex codex of trade acts. The relevant section provided:

> And it is further enacted and declared by the Authority aforesaid, That all Laws, By-laws, Usages or Customs, at this Time, or which hereafter shall be in Practice, or endeavoured or pretended to be in Force or Practice, in any of the said Plantations, which are in any wise repugnant to the before mentioned Laws, or any of them, so far as they do relate to the said Plantations, or any of them, or which are any ways repugnant to this present Act, or to any other Law hereafter to be made in this Kingdom, so far as such Law shall relate to and mention the said Plantations, are illegal, null and void, to all Intents and Purposes whatsoever.

Nothing was enacted to implement this section. Since the disallowance of legislation, and the hearing of appeals, was by this time settled practice, this statute must be taken as a direction to the agencies of administration. It was so understood, for special instructions enjoining obedience were forthwith despatched to the plantations[87]—even Connecticut and Rhode Island which normally were not reached by these royal mandates were this time included.[88]

The occasions on which colonial acts were declared null and void both on administrative and judicial review have been so exhaustively and expertly examined by Professor Joseph Henry Smith that we need here advert but briefly to the main precedents. There is only a handful of instances where on administrative review a declaration of nullity was issued. The first occurred in 1699 with reference to a Pennsylvania act regulating abuses of trade. On representations from the Commissioners of Customs that the act was contra to the Act for Preventing Frauds, and upon the recommendation of the Board of Trade that it be declared void *ab initio*, the Privy Council declared the act "to have been and to be null and void from the time of making of the said act." The Privy Council appears to have read the Act for Preventing Frauds to have set up a standard of repugnancy "to the known laws and statutes of the Kingdom" and not merely to acts of trade or English statutes extending to the plantations, for the Order in Council recites

---

[86] 7 & 8 Wm. III, c. 22, §9.
[87] Labaree, *Royal Instructions*, II, No. 1053.

[88] In 1699, 2 *APC Col.*, Nos. 732 and 733.

that this colony act or any other colony act contrary to the known laws and statutes should be deemed void *ab initio*.[89]

This gloss on the statute made it cut much deeper than the statutory language directed. Since the Penn charter had provided only for disallowance, the Order in Council was in effect an amendment by process of the Privy Seal of an instrument under the Great Seal. The dispositions made in the case seemed to promise aggressive action on obnoxious legislation, but except for a pair of Carolina acts submitted in 1706 and 1718,[90] while the province was still in the hands of proprietors, and where the formula used was highly ambiguous, there were no further such administrative declarations of nullity until a Jamaica act fell under the axe in 1762.[91] The Board of Trade repeatedly recommended declarations of nullity, but the Council steadfastly adhered to mere disallowance. This may have been due to the exertions of colony agents.

There were to be three further declarations of nullity—at least the formula used in disposing of the enactments differed so radically from the conventional one that no other conclusion seems tenable. All three were Pennsylvania acts, one a public act, the other two private acts. The first,[92] in 1770, involved a new procedure that was reported to imperil title holders, a matter on which the English were traditionally hypersensitive. The Board of Trade counselled that "it may be advisable for Your Majesty to adjudge and declare under your privy seal, the said act to be void."[93] The Order issued in these terms.

The two private acts, one a legislative divorce,[94] the other naturalizing an individual,[95] both raised constitutional questions. The Board of Trade had been troubled with a variety of legislative divorces and had vainly sought the opinion of the Crown law officers. The Board's own counsel had delivered a report that was a masterpiece of irresolution.[96] It consequently took the bull by the horns in 1773 and advised that colonial divorce acts "are either improper or unconstitutional"[97]

---

[89] Smith, *Appeals to the Privy Council from the American Plantations*, 531–32.

[90] *Ibid.*, 534–35.

[91] *Ibid.*, 592.

[92] An Act for the Sale of Goods Distrained for Rent, 7 *Statutes at Large of Pennsylvania*, 334 (1770).

[93] *Ibid.*, 662; 5 *APC Col.*, 301–02. The action seems drastic in the face of the recommendation of the Board of Trade's counsel that an instruction to amend would suffice. It is

possible that what moved the Lords Committee was the notification from the Board that despite an earlier direction to cease and desist, the assembly had incorporated in its style of enactment the improper claim of proprietorship over Delaware.

[94] 8 *Statutes at Large of Pennsylvania*, 243 (1772).

[95] *Ibid.*, 256 (1772).

[96] *Ibid.*, 597–98.

[97] *Ibid.*, 599.

and that action be taken to prevent the Pennsylvania action from becoming a precedent. The constitutional point was the lack of due process.[98] Accordingly the Crown "adjudged and declared void" the divorce act.[99] As for the naturalization act which purported to bestow the privileges of a natural-born subject of Great Britain, the Crown law officers reported that such privileges were "considerably more extensive than any provincial assembly hath authority to give." The King himself could not naturalize and the assembly's power was derived from the King's charter. A further objection was that the naturalization would confer liberty of trading contrary "to the Plantation Act."[100] Again the Order in Council took the form that the King did "adjudge and declare void all the said act, which act is declared void by these presents."[101]

With respect to the raising of constitutional points it may be remarked that such references to what was and what was not constitutional were not unusual on the eve of the Revolution.[102] The resort to a formula that purported to invest an administrative procedure with the quality of an adjudication is no less noteworthy. This it was not in any technical sense of the word. Professor Smith has pointed out the hardening of opinion in the Lords Committee that a judicial declaration of nullity was to be preferred over an administrative one.[103] This being the case, it is conceivable that the Board of Trade and the Council between them were attempting to cloak their action with the semblance of a judgment.

The bias in favor of judicial proceedings if a question of voiding an act *ab initio* was posed may be laid to the indurated common law tradition that issues of such moment should be settled in true adversarial proceedings. For in point of fact, the occasions were few when the issue of nullity came before the Council in its judicial capacity. They were nonetheless portentous and must be examined in some detail.

---

[98] In this, the lack of "a suit instituted in any ecclesiastical court, nor any verdict previously obtained in a court of common law" (*ibid.*). The reference is, of course, to the conditions precedent for a Parliamentary divorce, viz., a decree for divorce *mensa et thoro*; a successful action at common law for criminal conversation.

[99] *Ibid.*, 600, for the order.

[100] *Ibid.*, 601–02. The "Plantation Act" referred to is, presumably, the Act for Preventing Frauds.

[101] *Ibid.*, 603. See also on the proceedings 5 *APC Col.*, 365–68.

[102] See the report on a South Carolina act, 5 *APC Col.*, No. 86 (1769); on a practice of that province regarding payment of monies, *ibid.*, No. 140 (1770); on a New York omnibus act adopting English statutes, *ibid.*, No. 168 (1770); on a New Jersey inheritance law, *ibid.*, No. 203 (1771); on a North Carolina anti-riot act, *ibid.*, No. 222 (1772); on a Dominica act regarding tax bills, *ibid.*, No. 227 (1772).

[103] Smith, *Appeals to the Privy Council from the American Plantations*, 635.

JUDICIAL CONTROL OF COLONY LEGISLATION

THE LANDMARK CASE is *Winthrop v. Lechmere*,[104] a protracted litigation involving the validity of a Connecticut intestacy act of 1699.[105] This provided that the estate, both real and personal, of an intestate decedent be divided into equal shares among decedent's children or their representatives, but allowing a double portion to the eldest son or his representatives. The decedent here had died in 1717 seised of a personal estate and lands in New York, Connecticut and Massachusetts. Common law rules obtained in New York, but Massachusetts had furnished the statutory model for Connecticut. A son, John Winthrop, and a daughter, Anne, married to Thomas Lechmere of Boston, survived the decedent. The cause began mildly enough when the son was granted letters of administration by the New London Court of Probates and bond was given conditioned upon making a true inventory of decedent's personal estate. From the outset Winthrop assumed that as heir at law he was entitled to all realty. The inventory was never exhibited, but no objections to Winthrop's administration were made until 1723 when the first gambits in a lamentable family fight, so familiar a feature of settling estates, were made.

The ramifications of the ensuing forensic battles have been so capably and thoroughly explored that it is unnecessary to recount them here. Every resource available by way of original action, of appeal and otherwise, that even at this early date the litigious temper of the colonies had brought to flower, was sought out and used. The first stage of the contest in which Winthrop was seemingly the winner ended when, on defendant's representations, the General Assembly of Connecticut ordered proceedings *de novo*, the resolve indicating that Winthrop's claim to inherit according to common law rules of descent would have to yield to the statutory rules of the colony.[106]

In the subsequent proceedings Winthrop suffered a series of defeats, and was, as he later averred, denied an appeal to the Crown.

---

[104] By far the best and most exhaustive study of this cause is in Smith, *Appeals to the Privy Council from the American Plantations*, 537–60. It supersedes completely the account in G. Washburne, *Imperial Control of the Administration of Justice in the Thirteen American Colonies, 1684–1776* (New York: Columbia University Press, 1923), 184–85,

and that of M. C. Andrews, "Influence of Colonial Conditions as Illustrated in the Connecticut Intestacy Law," in *Select Essays in Anglo-American Legal History*, I: 431 at 445, 1907.

[105] *Acts and Laws of the Colony of Connecticut* (1702), 60.

[106] *Public Records of the Colony of Connecticut*, VII, 525.

New letters of administration were granted Lechmere, who eventually petitioned the assembly for leave to sell realty to meet the cost of administration and a balance of decedent's debts. Over Winthrop's protest and his demand for an appeal to King in Council, a bill was ordered to be brought in permitting the sale for which Lechmere petitioned.[107]

Winthrop protested to the Governor and Company, warning that they would answer to King in Council. This gained him nothing but a citation to appear before the assembly to answer for contempt. Upon his appearance he again declared his intention of laying all the proceedings before the King in Council. This was viewed as a contempt and Winthrop was committed to the custody of the sheriff. He was fined £20. The bill to permit sale of realty was enacted. Irrelevant as these episodes were to the merits of the case, we believe that the ultimate decision at Whitehall may have been influenced by them.[108]

On January 16, 1726/7, Winthrop submitted to the Privy Council a petition for leave to appeal from two Superior Court sentences in favor of Lechmere, praying that the act enabling Lechmere to dispose of the realty be repealed, and requesting stay of pending actions for accounting.[109] Some three weeks later appellant submitted a further petition consisting of twenty-nine articles of complaint against the Governor and Company of Connecticut, alleging a variety of irregularities, breaches of the charter and deviations from English law.[110] The prayer here was that the charter be recalled. The Lords Committee heard counsel for both sides on the petition for appeal and advised allowance thereof, February 18, 1726/7. On the same day it advised despatch of the Winthrop complaint to the colony officials, setting a terminal date for an answer.[111]

The appeal came on to be heard by the Lords Committee on December 16, 1727.[112] Attorney General Yorke and Solicitor General Talbot, two future Lords Chancellor, appeared for Winthrop. Respondent's counsel were Willes and Booth, the former presumably John Willes, later Chief Justice of Common Bench. The colony was not heard on the appeal. Appellant's "case," on its face unduly prolix for the seeming irrelevancies embodied, was sagely drawn to convey the

---

[107] *Ibid.*, 37.

[108] The tale of Winthrop's tribulations at the hands of "severall Joabs and Judases" is in a letter to Cotton Mather (1725/6?) as well as the "Brief in Appeal to the Privy Council," both in *Winthrop Papers*, VI, at 423 and 440, respectively (hereafter cited as *Winthrop Papers*).

[109] Smith, *Appeals to the Privy Council from the American Plantations*, 544–45. The first part of the so-called "Brief" (*supra*, n. 108) is the petition.

[110] Calendared, 6 *APC Col.*, No. 367.

[111] 3 *ibid.*, 139.

[112] On the pre-hearing gambits, Smith, *Appeals to the Privy Council from the American Plantations*, 545.

sense of persecution through resort to manifold irregularities. The gravamen of the complaint was that nothing that had ensued upon the assembly's first resolve was warranted by the colony charter.[113] This charter was peculiar in this, that the grant of law-making powers was made with specific reference to the "Course of other Corporations within this our Kingdom. . . ."[114] It seems to us very likely that in the argument of the case the rules respecting exercise of corporate ordinance powers were ventilated upon argument, particularly because in the meagre notes of respondent's counsel (our chief source of their argument) the point is made "Not like a corporač. here. Corporač. here bound by laws here."[115]

The printed case of respondent has never been brought to light. But it appears from the notes of argument just mentioned that counsel had done no close reading of the charter. It was conceived that the colony had been empowered "to make all laws whatsoever." According to Willes, the limitation of nonrepugnancy was related only to statutes wherein the plantations were mentioned, apparently a reference to the Act for Preventing Frauds. Booth also picked this up, arguing that the charter clause of limitation related only to "public matters, trade, etc."[116] He went so far as to claim that only by particular act could the law of England extend to the colony. If it was conquered land, the law of the conqueror did not extend—ignoring thus the crucial sequitur of this theory that the law would be what the King pleased.

The Lords Committee reported to the Privy Council on December 20 advising that the colony act be declared null and void as contrary to the laws of England in making lands of inheritance distributable as personal estate, and as not warranted by the charter.[117] The act empowering Lechmere to sell realty and the court order pursuant thereto were also to be declared void. All the proceedings subsequent to the assembly resolve were reversed or set aside. Appellant was to be permitted to exhibit an inventory of personalty only and the Probate Court directed not to reject it. Winthrop was also to be restored to possession of realty taken from him, respondent was to account for rents and

---

[113] For the four chief points, *Winthrop Papers*, VI, 476–78.

[114] Thorpe, *Constitutions and Charters*, I, 529 at 534. The phrase occurs in the interminable passage conveying governmental powers that covers a closely printed page before a period is encountered. The punctuation is such that it was arguable that the phrase quoted above refers only to "for the Imposition of Lawful Fines Mulcts, Imprisonment or other Punishment upon Offenders and Delinquents. . . ." But in England there was strong judicial opinion that a corporation could not imprison. Clark's Case, 5 Coke Rep. 64; Case of the City of London, 8 *ibid.*, 121b, 127b.

[115] From the notes of argument, *Winthrop Papers*, VI, 495.

[116] *Ibid.*, 496.

[117] *Ibid.*, 506.

profits and was to pay costs. The Council approved and the formal order issued February 15, 1727/8.[118]

Viewed in terms of the long and solid English tradition of judicial avoidance of corporate enactments, the determination in *Winthrop v. Lechmere* was no bold *coup de main*. Connecticut Colony, however, regarded it to be such and made great exertions to undo or repair the injury the Privy Council was conceived to have done.[119] There was a certain irony in the situation. Since the early days of New England's settlement the charters had been treated by the inhabitants in their relations with their own governments as a species of constitution, and now the supreme judicature was holding their own law-making authority to the letter of the instrument. Whether or not counsel for respondent had been officially instructed, it is apparent from their argument that they strove to escape being classified as inferior jurisdictions, which indeed they were. Never again was the Privy Council to avoid an act in its judicial capacity. But it had asserted the power, and this was thereafter to be a factor in litigation before it.

The opportunity for further extension of the notion that colony acts contrary to the common law were void was not long in presenting itself. This time the Massachusetts Act of 1692, which had served Connecticut as a model, came before the Privy Council.[120] *Philips v. Savage* involved an attack on a Probate Court order approving the appraisal and division of both realty and personalty among the five next of kin of an intestate decedent. Decedent's brother had appealed the allowance and approval of the order to the governor and council, on the ground that he was by English law the heir at law, that the act of 1692 was repugnant to English law and so void, and that the Probate Judge had no jurisdiction over realty and the course of descent. The governor and council affirmed the order of the Judge of Probates and refused an appeal to King in Council. The Crown granted a petition for leave to appeal and after some delay the case was heard in January 1737-38.

Appellant's argument was compact. The legislative power under the charter was confined to acts not repugnant or contrary to English law. The acts in question subverted the established common law of

---

[118] *Ibid.*, 507-08. In a letter to his wife of Mar. 25, 1728 (*ibid.*, 509-11) Winthrop describes the hearing at which he alleges those present with one voice cried out, "Shame on the New England Collony's!" He further alleges that "the Lords said, W^t a strange madd sort of people are these, that are endeavoring to hurt a family that founded them!"

[119] Smith, *Appeals to the Privy Council from the American Plantations*, 551-60.

[120] 1 *Acts and Resolves Prov. of Mass. Bay*, 43. Again the best account of the litigation is Smith, *Appeals to the Privy Council from the American Plantations*, 562-72.

descent and introduced a new jurisdiction over realty. *Winthrop v. Lechmere* was proffered as a binding precedent. Respondent, whose cause was aided by the intervention of the province, offered a rich treasury of argument. Counsel fastened on the obvious point, not raised in *Winthrop v. Lechmere*, that the law of England to which Massachusetts enactments must conform tolerated usages similar to the acts in question.[121] But the nub of the case was the effect of the royal confirmation of the original act and one of the explanatory acts. Three other explanatory or supplementary acts had become law when the Crown failed to act within the three years stipulated in the charter.[122] Respondent in the first stage of argument treated royal action or inaction as a conclusive ratification.[123] This did not dispose of appellant's claim that the legislation was void, for in his behalf the long-established doctrine that "a Confirmation doth not strengthen a void estate" was put forward.[124] Respondent countered with cases relating to royal grants tending to establish that if the Crown was mistaken in its own affirmation even in matter of law, such grants were good.[125] There were better precedents to be found than in the law of real property, viz., those affirming that the Crown could not make grants in defeasance of the common law, and even more persuasive that a thing void by law could not be granted by the King.[126] Strangely enough, these do not appear to have been advanced.

From notes kept by Chief Justice Lee it appears that counsel for respondent persisted in treating royal approbation as a grant, for the ingenious argument was advanced that an enlargement of legislative powers beyond the limits of the charter had been effected by the confirming Order in Council. The charter proviso that laws not disallowed within three years should be in force had the effect of qualifying the nonrepugnancy clause so that only the "judgment" of the King was

---

[121] The "Cases" of the parties are printed in *Proceedings*, Massachusetts Historical Society, 5:64–80. Counsel for appellant were Attorney General Dudley Ryder and John Brown; for the one respondent who was heard, John Strange (later Solicitor General) and Jonathan Belcher. The information about the oral arguments derives from notes kept by Sir William Lee, Lord Chief Justice. These are in the Osborn Collection, Yale University Library (hereafter cited as Lee Ms.).

[122] One act, c. 46 of the Laws of 1692–93 (1 *Acts and Resolves Prov. of Mass. Bay*, 101), had been con-

firmed at the same time as the basic act. The three acts which became law because of royal inaction are in the Laws of 1710–11 (1 *ibid.*, 652); of 1715–16 (2 *ibid.*, 31); and of 1719–20 (2 *ibid.*, 151).

[123] *Proc.* Mass Hist. Soc., 5:72.

[124] Citing Coke, *Littleton*, 295b, Lee Ms. The formula of royal allowance (*supra*, p. 67) was obviously taken to have sufficient identity with that used to confirm deeds—"ratified approved and confirmed"—to make relevant the real property precedents.

[125] See 11 Coke Rep. 86a.

[126] *Supra*, p. 59.

the critical factor.[127] If he did not object, any law might subsist. The role of the Crown in relation to the colonial legislative process was characterized as not one of participation but as an exercise of a power of judgment in which he was restrained by nothing but the laws of England. It cannot, however, be said that in this case any solid determination was made on the dimensions or nature of royal power.

Winthrop v. Lechmere was apparently distinguished to the point of not being treated as in any way controlling. Both sides agreed that there had been no confirmation of the Connecticut act and that there was no reservation of a power to confirm or reject. This last was a witless concession by appellant's counsel, particularly because earlier a Connecticut act against Quakers had in fact been disallowed (1705).[128] Lord Hardwicke was reported as saying that although he had been of counsel in the Connecticut case, he was not satisfied with the decision, a dictum that may have been enough to knock out the chief prop of appellant's case. [129] In any event, the Lords Committee advised affirmance and on February 15, 1737/8, the Order in Council issued.[130]

With this case the jousting over American profanation of common law rules of descent virtually came to an end. It is true that another litigation involving the Connecticut act, Clark v. Tousey, came up on appeal, but this was never heard on the merits. The procedural grounds on which the appeal was dismissed are indicated in the margin.[131] It has been supposed by some that the effect was to overrule Winthrop v. Lechmere, but there is nothing in the record to justify such a conclusion. The adjudication of Winthrop v. Lechmere sat undisturbed, to remain a factor of which the advisers of litigants must ever be aware. This determination was given currency beyond even the confines of the profession for it was noticed in a mid-eighteenth century American history book[132] and so acquired the quality of a notable event, which indeed it was.

---

[127] Lee Ms.

[128] 2 APC Col., 832. This had been upon representation of the Quakers; see CSP Col. 1704–5, Nos. 1060, 1100, 1153, 1356, 1362.

[129] Talcott Papers, II, 81.

[130] 3 APC Col., 436.

[131] In 1737 Clark took an appeal from the sentence of the Superior Court of Connecticut (Mar. 6, 1732/3) in a proceeding again involving the common law rights of an intestate's heir. The appeal was allowed some six months later, but no steps taken to prosecute it. Meantime a writ of review was unsuccessfully prosecuted

in the Superior Court. Petition for leave to appeal from this judgment (February 1740/1) was allowed in 1742 and ordered heard in February 1742/3. Clark was unable to produce the record. He then sought to proceed with his earlier appeal. Coming for hearing in July 1745, the petition for leave to appeal was dismissed, obviously for failure to prosecute within a year or a year and a day. On the case, Smith, Appeals to the Privy Council from the American Plantations, 572–76.

[132] W. Douglass, A Summary, Historical and Political, . . . of the British

II: *Traditions of Judicial Control*

Modern opinion of *Winthrop v. Lechmere* has ranged from denying it any influence upon later American constitutional thinking, indeed denying even that it was an adjudication,[133] to the claim that is "the one clear-cut precedent for the American doctrine of judicial review."[134] That the case was not judicially determined is an absurdity; that it stands in solitary grandeur is claiming too much for it. This claim, apparently assuming an actual declaration of nullity to be crucial, overlooks the long traditions of judicial action that underlay the Privy Council's determination and equally what this body was yet to do. It is hardly to be denied that any case where the validity of legislation is taken under advisement is a precedent of judicial review regardless of the decision. The essence of the process is the assumption and exercise of the power to weigh the validity of an enactment against a constitutional standard as something proper to the judiciary. For Americans, the significance of *Winthrop v. Lechmere* was that the Privy Council adopted and projected to their legislation the principles and practice of the common law courts in dealing with the enactments of inferior jurisdictions in England. This having once been done, there was no escaping the immanence of the power and the imminence of its possible exertion, whenever a colonial act was *sub judice*.

The constitutional standards applied in colony appeals embraced not alone those developed by the common law courts to determine the illegality of ordinances, but also those embodied in royal grants, as well as those derived from the principles, judicially approved, on which imperial administration rested. This is clear from the discussion in *Philips v. Savage* and later in *Camm v. Hansford*.[135] There were consequently manifestations of judicial control peculiar to colony cases, most importantly in respect to the extension of Acts of Parliament. The basic rule, and one of considerable antiquity, was to the effect that Acts of Parliament were applicable only if the dominions were named.[136] In the several colonies the opinion developed that they were privileged

---

Settlements in North-America (1760 ed.), II, 174.

[133] E. Corwin, "The Establishment of Judicial Review," *Mich. L. Rev.*, 9:102 at 103, 1910. Partially corrected in *The Doctrine of Judicial Review* (Princeton, N.J.: Princeton University Press, 1914), 74–75.

[134] C. Rossiter, *Seedtime of the Republic*, 460, n. 24.

[135] *Infra*, p. 81.

[136] On the establishment of the rule as to Ireland, R. Schuyler, *Parliament*

and the British Empire, cc. I and II. The colonists' immediate source of reference, Calvin's Case, 7 Coke Rep. 1 at 17b. As to other demesnes, Goebel, "Matrix of Empire," liii. The rule in Calvin's Case reiterated by Chief Justice (C.B.) Vaughan in 1670 in Craw v. Ramsey (Vaughan 274), and see also his notes on *Process out of the Courts at Westminster into Wales* published in 1677 (*ibid.*, 395); and see Privy Council "Memorandum," 2 Peere Williams 75.

79

to avail themselves of pre-settlement English statutes,[137] and on occasion this view was supported by royal administrators.[138] Inevitably also American legislatures and courts would trespass into the forbidden ground of novel Acts of Parliament which did not mention the plantations. The Privy Council maintained the old rule with notable consistency. It not only disallowed acts of assembly that attempted to introduce English statutes,[139] but sitting in its judicial capacity denied as to particular colonies the vigor of such statutes, as the Elizabethan Statute of Charitable Uses,[140] the Statute of Frauds[141] and the Bankruptcy Acts.[142] In terms of the force and effect of statutes, such judgments were the equivalent of a nullification *quoad hoc.*

To the constitutional standards—already mentioned—an attempt was to be made to add another—the royal instructions. Unlike charters or commission, the authentication of instructions was by signet and sign manual. The instructions were private communications, as we have seen,[143] resembling the letters close of medieval times. The legal distinctions between letters patent and instructions and the constitutional implications had been set out in the *Case of the Lords Presidents,*[144] available to anyone with a set of Coke's *Reports* at hand. Thomas Pownall in his well-circulated book on colonial administration averred that commission and instructions together formed the constitution of the royal colonies.[145] This was true only in the sense that the governor was bound by the instructions; the subjects clearly were not. On divers occasions efforts were made to give the instructions the force of law by Act of Parliament, but these attempts came to nothing.[146] In the Privy Council the standard procedure had been merely to disallow acts

---

[137] Partly because of a disposition to take English law where they found it; partly because of the confusion in infant communities of common law with statute, *e.g.*, the use of the riot act of Hen. IV (on which see the 1696 record quoted in Goebel and Naughton, *Law Enforcement in Colonial New York,* 122, n. 277) and the bastardy provision of 18 Eliz. I, c. 3 (*ibid.*, 101, n. 183).

[138] See the opinion of Richard West, counsel to the Board of Trade, in 1720 regarding statutes "in affirmance of the common law" (Chalmers, *Opinions,* I, 194–95). In 1724 the law officers of the Crown, Philip Yorke and Clement Wearg, conceived that "long usage and general acquiescence" sufficed to effect a reception of statutes (*ibid.*, 220); and see Yorke's opinion

(1729) that post-settlement statutes could be effective through usage (*ibid.*, 197).

[139] Russell, *The Review of American Colonial Legislation by the King in Council,* 139 *et seq.*

[140] In the Antigua appeal Dunbar v. Webb (1753); see Smith, *Appeals to the Privy Council from the American Plantations,* 487–89.

[141] In the Jamaica appeal Orby v. Long (1710), *ibid.*, 476–78.

[142] In the Virginia appeal Rickards v. Hudson (1762), *ibid.*, 490–92.

[143] *Supra,* c. I, p. 12.

[144] 12 Coke Rep. 50.

[145] T. Pownall, *Administration of the Colonies,* 54.

[146] On this see Smith, *Appeals to the Privy Council from the American Plantations,* 599–605.

violative of instructions even where the Board of Trade had intimated such ought to be avoided. The question was not really fought out until after Virginia undertook in 1755 to legislate a radical change in methods of discharging obligations, leaving it to the obligor whether payment be made in tobacco or in money at a fixed rate of commutation (twopence per pound), or in some counties only in money; four acts were involved.[147] All had the effect of repealing an earlier (1748) act which had been confirmed by the Crown.[148]

The act which precipitated the loudest outcry was that commuting into currency the statutory salary payments to the Church of England clergy. The gravamen of clerical complaint was that salaries were being paid at half rate in paper currency. Resolute efforts were made to enlist episcopal aid in moving the Board of Trade to recommend a declaration of nullity. The 1755 act was temporary but in September 1758 it was re-enacted to be in effect a year.[149] The royal instructions had been disregarded in two particulars for the governor had been directed to refuse assent to laws enacted for a lesser time than two years, or to laws repealing any law, whether confirmed or not, without a suspending clause. The Virginia clergy despatched the Reverend John Camm to manage their cause. Hearings were held before the Board of Trade, which only advised disallowance. Subsequently before the Committee of the Council eminent counsel appeared to urge nullification.[150] Nevertheless, the several laws suffered only disallowance.

The Virginia parsons, whose exegetical powers were better spent on more sacred texts, affected to view the order of disallowance as an act of nullity. A number of actions were brought to collect what was owed under the 1748 act. The most important was that instituted in the Virginia General Court by the Reverend Camm, manager of the clergy's case in England, against one Hansford and another, collectors of the parish levy.[151] The pleadings put in issue the status of royal instructions, for it was alleged that the 1758 act was void as contrary to these and had been so declared by the King in Council. On demurrer, judgment was given for defendants, the collectors of the parish levy.

Camm was allowed an appeal to the King in Council (1764) that he perfected, but the cause did not come on for hearing until November 1766. His claim was here put forward more subtly, for it was averred

---

[147] 6 Hening, *Va. Stats.*, 568 (1755); acts applying to certain counties, *ibid.*, 369, 372, 502.
[148] *Ibid.*, 88.
[149] *Ibid.*, 240.
[150] Smith, *Appeals to the Privy Council from the American Plantations*, 611-15. Smith has the most

complete and accurate account of the events and the ensuing appeal. A more recent study, B. Knollenberg, *Origin of the American Revolution, 1759–1766* (1960), c. III, adds nothing.
[151] Smith, *Appeals to the Privy Council from the American Plantations*, 618 *et seq.*

that the governor's instructions were incorporated by reference in his commission. If this were correct they would have possessed the legal quality of something of public benefit conveyed under the Great Seal. There was the added embellishment that the act was against reason and natural justice, and once more the Committee was reminded of *Winthrop v. Lechmere.* Respondent argued that the Virginia act had been merely disallowed, and the instructions were private directions to the governor liable to be dispensed with on occasion.[152]

The Committee advised affirmance of the General Court judgment and dismissal of the appeal. Charles Yorke who had appeared for respondent noted that the question whether the disallowance voided the act *ab initio* or whether it was void "as being against natural justice" was not determined.[153] But the Clerk of the Council, Robert Walpole, who fortunately noted numerous cases and made a fuller report, wrote that the objection that the act was void *ab initio* "was not allowed." He indicates further that it was determined that the instructions "are private directions from the King." The only sanction for disobedience was upon the governor.[154]

The "Parsons' Cause" settled the constitutional status of instructions. Although the Virginia clergy readied another case for appeal, it was not pressed because it was believed that the political climate in England was unfavorable to their aim.[155] For in 1767, after submission of all the precedents of nullification on both administrative and judicial review, two attempts had failed in the House of Lords to have declared null the pardon provision of the Massachusetts Act of Pardon and Indemnity, aftermath of the Stamp Act riots.[156] The issue had been decided not on the merits but on factional party lines, yet the parsons conceived that a policy decision had been made. In this they were grievously mistaken, for a year earlier a truculent Parliament had affirmed its authority to nullify in the Declaratory Act which declared void any resolutions, votes, etc., calling into question Parliament's authority to legislate for the plantations.[157] And at the same session at which the

---

[152] *Ibid.,* 621–23.

[153] *Ibid.,* 624.

[154] P.R.O. WO 1/404/66.

[155] See the letter, Horrocks to the Bishop of London, July 6, 1769, in W. Perry, ed., *Historical Collections Relating to the American Colonial Church, Virginia,* I, 530.

[156] A brief account, Hansard, *Parliamentary History of England* (1813), XVI, 359; H. Walpole, *Memoirs of the Reign of King George the Third,* Barker ed. (New York: G. P. Putnam's Sons, 1894), III, 34–36; letter, Thomas Whately to John Temple, May 2, 1767, in "Bowdoin-Temple Papers," 80–84. The precedents sent in are listed in 5 *APC Col.,* No. 30, where see also the action of the Privy Council on the Massachusetts act.

[157] 6 Geo. III, c. 12 (1766), An Act for the better securing of the Dependency of His Majesty's Dominions in America upon the Crown and Parliament of Great Britain. The name "Declaratory Act" apparently

attack on the Massachusetts Act of Pardon failed, the act suspending the New York legislature included a similar declaration of nullity of votes or resolves by the assembly until provision had been made for supplying the troops.[158]

CHANGING THEORIES OF THE EMPIRE AND JUDICIAL CONTROL

THESE WERE TIMES when notions about the avoidance of legislation were in circulation as never before. For while the royal agencies and Parliament were recommending or declaring or threatening nullification of colonial enactments, the Americans were boldly asserting the proposition that Acts of Parliament could be void for unconstitutionality. This was a fresh way of formulating an idea with which from time to time divers English judges had toyed. It reflected an aggressive estimation by the Americans of their political situation, part and parcel of changing opinion on both sides of the water about the relations of the home government with the components of the empire. The basic premises, laid down long before there was much of an empire to be concerned about, were now to be questioned as they had not been in any of the earlier recurrent controversies. It was the events of the French and Indian War and its aftermath that disturbed the precarious balance of opinion about imperial relations, and, as new points of controversy developed, precipitated fresh explorations of how these should be regulated. The colonists, perpetually on the defense, had always been more alert to constitutional issues than their masters. But it is apparent from our evidences of Privy Council proceedings that during and after the war this body had become much more alive to the constitutional implications of questions that came before it; so had the courts, so had Parliament.[159]

Underlying the exchanges between the British administration and colonies over particular issues, *e.g.*, the tenure of judges, the extension of the Mutiny Acts, the appeal of verdicts, were truly profound changes in outlook. In England the colonies were still viewed as so many corporations, but the sovereignty over them had been redefined

---

derives from the popular name for the earlier Act for the better securing the Dependency of the Kingdom of Ireland upon the Crown of Great Britain, 6 Geo. I, c. 5 (1719). C. McIlwain, *The American Revolution: A Constitutional Interpretation* (New York: Macmillan Co., 1923), 50, argues its identity "except for a few phrases." The Irish Act purported only to avoid the assumption of judicial power by the Irish House of Lords. The American Act was politically much more far-reaching.

[158] 7 Geo. III, c. 59 (1767).
[159] *Infra*, n. 187.

by Parliament to the end that the prerogative was made less and the legislative power of Parliament greater. The diminution of the prerogative was the result of the Revolution of 1688 at which time the constitutional principle that the overseas demesnes were in the nature of the King's private possessions was abandoned. These were proclaimed to be annexed to the Crown, and it was on these terms that William and Mary accepted the "Crown and Royal dignity of King and Queen of England, France, and Ireland and the Dominions thereunto belonging."[160] This formula recurs in the two great constitutional documents, the Bill of Rights (1689)[161] and the Act of Settlement (1701),[162] indicating the importance attached to the principle that it was in the sovereign's politic and not his personal capacity that the dominions were to be ruled.[163] The implications of this change were not immediately appreciated specifically as regards Parliament's legislative authority, for to all intents the empire continued to be administered on principles that had prevailed under the Stuarts. But the change in the constitutional status of the dominions had been coincident with the establishment of Parliament's supremacy and was among the first manifestations of this plenary power.

A general challenge of Parliament's authority over components of the empire came belatedly. This may be laid to the fact that, barring a few divagations, the supreme legislative had, so far as the colonies were concerned, moved within defined limits for so long that these limits appeared to have acquired the sanction of custom—always a sovereign ingredient in the amorphous British constitution. Furthermore, the fact that parliamentary action had been sporadic served to keep colonial relations with royal administrative agencies (with which dealings were constant) in the forefront of American thinking about constitutional questions. And assuredly it contributed to the colonial conviction that they were not to be classed with English domestic corporations.[164]

---

[160] 1 Wm. & M., sess. 1, c. 1.

[161] 1 Wm. & M., sess. 2, c. 2, sec. 2, 4.

[162] 12 & 13 Wm. III, c. 2; and see also 11 & 12 Wm. III, c. 2 (1699), an Act granting an aid to His Majesty by Sale of the Forfeited and other Estates in Ireland. . . .

[163] That the distinction as to the two capacities was not extinguished see Blackstone, *Commentaries*, I, 109, where it is emphasized that any "foreign dominions which may belong to the person of the King by hereditary descent, by purchase or other acquisition, as the territory of Hanover, and his Majesty's other property in Germany . . . these do not in any wise appertain to the crown of these kingdoms. . . ."

[164] As done in Pownall, *Administration of the Colonies*, 31, 33; Soame Jenyns, *Objections to the Taxation of Our American Colonies by the legislature of Great Britain, Briefly Considered*, 2d ed. (1765), 11; the opinion of Attorney General Yorke and the lawyers quoted *infra*, p. 88.

II: *Traditions of Judicial Control*

Each plantation had in fact achieved a new species of identity, exercising a degree of independent authority that would not have been its own had it been integrated into the English judicial system. No corporation court in England was so little subject to central control as the superior courts in the colonies. A great deal of colony legislation was never questioned, and as for the system of supervision, it did not become intolerable until pressure mounted, at the last, for suspending clauses. If one can speak of a colonial constitutional approach in the first half of the eighteenth century general to all colonies and divorced from the acerbities produced by single crises, it was the philosophy of the *modus vivendi*—nurtured by the long period of "salutary neglect" begun under Sir Robert Walpole.[165] This philosophy had been imperilled by measures taken during the French and Indian War. It was shattered after 1763 by changes in English fiscal policy, and the concurrent alteration of the methods of enforcing trade laws.

The initial gambit in the new English policy was a statute (1763)[166] seeking to tighten enforcement by extending to the plantations an earlier hovering act, and authorizing use of the royal navy to prevent smuggling, thus converting these ships, as a New York merchant complained, into "floating Custom Houses."[167] In the colonies, penalties and forfeitures were committed at the option of the informer to courts of admiralty or to courts of record; in the realm, to common law courts. This was the first of a series of statutes that was to raise the question of deprivation of jury. In the next year the Sugar Act,[168] which, in addition to raising duties, enwrapped seaborne commerce in coils of red tape, was to precipitate the two constitutional issues of jury trial and of taxation without representation. The preamble of this act stated the purpose to be the improvement of "the Revenue of this Kingdom," and its introduction had been accompanied by a promise of a stamp tax to come. The provisions for suits to recover penalties and forfeitures had given an informer the option of proceeding either in a court of record or admiralty court, or a vice-admiralty court for all America, to be established. This court was in fact established in 1764 at Halifax.[169] In

---

[165] Walpole, *Memoirs of the Reign of King George the Third*, II, 50, n. 1.

[166] 3 Geo. III, c. 22.

[167] Gerard G. Beekman to his brother William, July 3, 1764, in P. White, ed., *The Beekman Mercantile Papers, 1746–1799* (New York: New-York Historical Society, 1956), I, 469.

[168] 4 Geo. III, c. 15.

[169] On the establishment, C. Ubbelohde, *The Vice-Admiralty Courts and the American Revolution*, 46 *et seq.* This writer indicates that it was the principle of establishing the court in an outlying port and not the reality of what was done there which aroused the merchants. Absent a documented analysis of business done, no firm conclusions seem tenable.

the final paragraphs of the act, the British really showed their teeth for those concerned in making seizures were given particular protection, and the remedies of "claimers" made nearly frustrate.[170]

The Sugar Act was read in America as designed to channel cases into admiralty courts, and so to eliminate jury trial. The impediments placed upon "claimers" by cutting down common law rights of action and the fact that within the realm itself suits were to be brought in courts of record gave color to this view. Obviously no writ of prohibition would lie, and it was equally apparent that any seizure made on the high seas could be prosecuted in any plantation vice-admiralty court with attendant difficulties of conducting a defense. What was particularly susceptible of being made an issue of principle was the discrimination made between subjects in the provision limiting suits in England to common law courts. The Stamp Act continued the policy of the colonial informer's choice of forum, and further extended this to suits for violation of the provision of the act itself and of revenue acts in general.[171] It offered the boon of an appeal to admiralty courts established or to be established in America. This was not seen as a benefit, but as a clear enough indication that revenue cases were to be forcibly channeled into courts proceeding according to the civil law. These provisions were repealed with the rest of the Stamp Act. They were, however, revived by an act of 1768 for the more easy and effectual recovery of penalties and forfeitures inflicted by Parliament for breaches of acts relating to trade and revenue in the plantations. This statute benignly offered relief from resort to the Halifax vice-admiralty court, but this relief was only to be sought in vice-admiralty courts, established or to be established, with liberty of appeal to such courts. The intendment of this was settled by the Order in Council establishing four new vice-admiralty courts upon which appellate jurisdiction was conferred.[172]

The Americans could not but regard this act as an assault upon the right to jury trial. Their attachment to this form of trial was then

---

[170] Where informations were brought to trial in America and the verdict or sentence was for the "claimer," if the judge certified there was probable cause for the seizure, defendant should be entitled to no costs and no right of action would lie against the captor. Where actions were brought against persons involved in seizures, prior to commencement or trial of condemnation proceedings, and the verdict or sentence was against the defendant, if probable cause was certified, the plaintiff would be entitled to but twopence damages. If the plaintiff were cast in any action against persons proceeding under the act or any customs legislation, the defendant was to be entitled to treble costs.

[171] 5 Geo. III, c. 12 (1765).

[172] 8 Geo. III, c. 22. For the Order in Council, 5 APC Col., No. 74 (July 6, 1768). The permissive "may be prosecuted . . . in any court of vice-admiralty" of the statute, the Council treated permissive as respected the Crown.

neither irrational nor a species of romantic illusion. In the harsh criminal procedure of the day it was only the jury that could dispense the leaven of mercy, and in civil proceedings it functioned as an immediate corrective for the lack-learned or overbearing judge. Insofar as the colonists had in their several jurisdictions settled their own constitutional standards, jury trial and by men of the vicinage was high among these, a palladium against officialdom. To subtract this protection, to the end that collection would be assured of revenues imposed without consent, amounted in colonial eyes to the employment of an unconstitutional means to effect an unconstitutional end.

Colonial juries have been so often represented as accessories to evasions of revenue acts[173] that the constitutional issue has been slurred over as if it were a mere gambit in the contest with Parliament. There is no doubt but that the sure sympathies of jurors was a factor in the formulation of the issue. Nevertheless, the sincerity of American beliefs is attested to not only by what has already been related about the extension of the institution to appellate proceedings, but also by what was done when the colonists became their own masters. The issue was kept vital because Parliament was to demonstrate that its view of trial by jury did not consist with that held here. In December 1768 a joint address of Lords and Commons to the Crown proposed,[174] indeed beseeched, that the provisions of Henry VIII's Statute of Foreign Treasons be invoked against Massachusetts rioters, provisions that would have involved transportation and trial in England.[175] The same *modus operandi* was to be embodied in the Dock Act (1772),[176] and ultimately in the Administration of Justice Act (1774),[177] one of the quintuplets

---

[173] Any accurate statistics are wanting and could be supplied only by reference to prosecutions in common law courts. No inferences can be drawn from vice-admiralty records as, *e.g.*, does L. Gipson, *The Triumphant Empire*, 228, n. 12.

[174] Hansard, *Parliamentary History*, XVI, 479.

[175] 35 Hen. VIII, c. 2 (1543). The Virginia Resolutions on this in *Journals of the House of Burgesses 1766–69*, 212–18; the Resolve of the Massachusetts House of Representatives (June 29, 1769) in A. Bradford, ed., *Speeches of the Governors of Massachusetts, from 1765 to 1775: And the Answers of the House of Representatives to the Same: With Their Resolutions*, 176.

[176] 12 Geo. III, c. 24. Induced by the firing of naval installations at Portsmouth, England, this act was directed at destruction of any naval property anywhere. Trial of overseas offenders could be abroad or in any shire in England. Proceedings under the act were initiated after the burning of the *Gaspée* by the Rhode Islanders (see 5 *APC Col.*, 356–57).

[177] 14 Geo. III, c. 39. The act was designed to protect magistrates or other persons charged with murder or other capital crime, where, if information was lodged with the governor that the offense charged had been committed in the course of suppressing riots or in support of laws or revenue, the governor was given discretion to direct trial of the inquisition, indictment or appeal in another province or in Great Britain before King's Bench.

famous as the Intolerable Acts. In the American credo trial by men of the vicinage was of the essence.

Reduced to its simplest terms the constitutional crisis stirred up and sustained by successive Acts of Parliament resolved itself into the issue—could Parliament lawfully legislate for the colonies in the areas invaded? The ministries and the parliamentary majorities, secure in the theory and practice of Parliament's supremacy within the realm, assumed that no distinction could be made between realm and dominions. It was not even conceived that in legislating for the latter a change in the constitution might be involved. The case for parliamentary authority was never better stated than by Attorney General Yorke and the "Gentlemen of the Long Robe" in the debate on the Declaratory Act (February 1766). They are reported by Charles Garth, Member of Parliament and Agent for Maryland and South Carolina to have said:[178]

> That the establishment of the Colonies was originally by Licence from the Crown, who by Charters gave them the Jura Regalia & powers of Government as necessary for their protection, Defence & support of Civil Government among them, being to be so far distant from the great executive Power of the Realm, which Power of Government so given by the Crown were of a Nature to those granted to the East India Company and to great Cities & Corporations in England, each having a power of raising money for their support, but neither of which coud by any Grant the King could make, be exempted from the supreme authority of King, Lords & Commons, That the Crown was but a part of the superior Authority of the Realm, & therefore coud give no more, indeed in some instances seemed to have Granted all that he had to Grant, but by no Construction cou'd be deem'd to have Granted that which he had no power to Grant, that which belong'd to the Supreme Legislative Power, which in all Ages extended wheresoever the Sovereignty of the Crown did extend; That the Colonists carried with them all the Subjection and Allegiance, they owed when resident in Great Britain, that no time nor Distance coud Terminate that Subjection and Allegiance which by the Law of Land must descend to their own immediate Heirs, and to all their Posterity; whatever Compact was stipulated between the Crown and these his Subjects upon their Emigration no condition whatever was made or woud have been suffer'd between them, and the Supreme Sovereign Power.

This conception of the imperial constitution was obviously unacceptable to the colonial remonstrants. Ironically, they stood, for all their

---

[178] *South Carolina Historical and Genealogical Magazine*, 26:80, 1925. Garth, also agent for Maryland, submitted a similar report to his principals there, *Maryland Historical Magazine*, 6:286–305, 1911.

incessant quoting from Locke, patron saint of the Whigs, upon the ground earlier prospected by the Tory Bolingbroke with whose writings various outstanding American political leaders were conversant.[179] It was Bolingbroke's thesis that government must be conducted in conformity with the constitution which he defined as "that Assemblage of Laws, Institutions and Customs, derived from certain fix'd Principles of Reason, directed to certain fix'd Objects of publick Good, that compose the general System, according to which the Community hath agreed to be govern'd."[180] The conformity or repugnancy of things to the constitution must be the rule by which they were accepted as favorable, or rejected as dangerous to liberty. Bolingbroke took issue with the view that there was nothing which Parliament could not do— "A Parliament," he wrote, "cannot annul the Constitution."[181]

The colonials shared Bolingbroke's belief in the fixity of the constitution. Their experience with the testing of their laws against set standards by the Privy Council afforded practical grounds for this belief. It was this principle of action to which they had recourse when they challenged the constitutionality of taxation without representation and the impairment of the right to jury trial. They invoked the common law precedents, the ancient rule that this law was their birthright, the more recent doctrine that an Englishman carries this law with him, and the guarantees of the rights and liberties of Englishmen granted in the charters. As a species of collateral assurance these arguments were buttressed by liberal references to natural rights.

In the early stages of controversy the Americans had not yet come to a clear distinction between the English and the imperial constitution.[182] The gravamen of their pleading was that the objectionable legislation was repugnant to the fundamentals of the English constitution—a position untenable because as matters then stood it lay wholly in Parliament's power to alter the constitution if it would. After the

---

[179] John Adams was a fervent admirer and read largely in Bolingbroke. See the entries in his Diaries, *Adams Papers*, I, 11, 35, 38, 40, 176, 200, 210; and the comments in his autobiography, *ibid.*, III, 264. Thomas Jefferson was equally addicted; see M. Kimball, *Jefferson: The Road to Glory, 1743-1776*, 113-14. James Wilson in his *Legislative Authority of the British Parliament* (1774) (reprinted in J. Andrews, ed., *The Works of James Wilson*, II, 505) refers to the *Dissertation upon Parties* (at 509).
[180] Henry St. John Viscount Bol-

ingbroke, *A Dissertation upon Parties*, 3d ed. (1735), Letter X at 108; Letter XII at 138.
[181] *Ibid.*, Letter XVII at 210.
[182] This is most marked in the "Declarations" of the Stamp Act Congress, the petition to the King and the addresses to the Lords and the Commons where "British" constitution and "English" constitution are sometimes used interchangeably and nowhere clearly distinguished. The *Journal* of the Congress and these documents are printed in H. Niles, *Principles and Acts of the Revolution in America*, 155–68.

passage of the Declaratory Act the first gropings toward definition of an imperial constitution are perceptible.[183] In the course of a few years the theory was fully elaborated. After the Intolerable Acts it became the platform of the Revolutionary leaders. Whatever one may think of the ingredients of this theory it was a legal-historical *tour de force* and is worth examining because in particulars it advanced political thinking to the threshold of independence.[184]

---

[183] By Franklin and Richard Bland. Franklin outlined major points in marginal notes on a copy of the printed *Protests of Certain Members of the House of Lords against the Repeal of the Stamp Act* (1766). The notes are printed in J. Bigelow, ed., *The Works of Benjamin Franklin* (Federal ed., 1904), 248–52. And see V. Crane, "Benjamin Franklin and the Stamp Act," Colonial Soc. of Mass. *Pubs.*, 32:56 at 69, 1937. The development of Franklin's thinking is traced in Crane's *Benjamin Franklin, Englishman and American* (Providence, R. I.: Brown University, 1936), 72 *et seq.*

Bland published a pamphlet in 1766—*An Inquiry into the Rights of the British Colonies*—where the lines of argument are more consecutively pursued than in Franklin's notes, and a variety of precedents recited. A curious perversion of history is Bland's use, to establish the legislative independence of the assembly, of the recital in the Revenue Act despatched by the King to Virginia when the Poynings' Law scheme was tried (*supra*, pp. 62–63). The pamphlet was reprinted in 1922 (E. Swem, ed.).

[184] The evolution of the new theory owed as much to the opposition as it did to the writing of proponents. The technique of interpreting a colonial argument so that it was made to say something more extravagant than intended often had the result that the opposition's interpretation was used as a stepping-stone to advance thinking. This was the case in the evolution of the new theory. The pamphlet by William Knox, one of the Under-Secretaries—*The Controversy between Great Britain and Her Colonies Reviewed* (1769)—with passages from John Dickinson's *Letters from a*

Farmer in Pennsylvania (1767), R. Halsey, ed., (New York: The Outlook Co., 1903) Letter XII, 137–38, by compression and elision of sentences were made to read as if the colonies were a separate political body of which each colony was a member—intimating a conception of independence Dickinson was certainly not yet advocating. Again, expatiating on the "pretense" that the American lands appertained to the King only, an argument at which James Otis barely hinted (*Considerations on Behalf of the Colonists* [1765], p. 13), Knox in replication elevated this argument to a position it had not yet achieved.

What Knox's pamphlet accomplished was to elicit a reply from Massachusetts-born Edward Bancroft, a protégé of Franklin's. This pamphlet, *Remarks on the Review of the Controversy between Great Britain and Her Colonies*, was printed in London in 1769, and reprinted in New London in the same year. It is in terms of an affirmative defense, elaborating the points Knox had undertaken to traverse. Bancroft develops, with historical references, the thesis that it lay with the King alone to dispose of American lands (44, 46), that in the foundation of the colonies they were emancipated from Parliament's authority (47–51). The King had constituted the colonies distinct states (51, 79, 87).

J. Boyd, in "Silas Deane: Death by a Kindly Teacher of Treason?," *Wm. and Mary Quarterly*, 16:165 at 181, 3d ser., suggests Franklin may have been useful to Bancroft in preparing the pamphlet. Franklin's 1769 notes on Pownall, *State of the Constitution of the Colonies* (Franklin, *Works, ut supra*, V, 139), and on *An Inquiry*

II: *Traditions of Judicial Control*

Taken as a basic premise was the old rule that the plantations were the personal possessions of the King, a rule that had obtained at the time of settlement. By successive charters the frames of government of the several colonies and the rights of the colonists had been so established that the arrangements were fixed beyond defeasance or alteration by an authority which had not only not participated in the founding but could not now lawfully do so. Under the circumstances, the colonies could not be part of the realm. The tie that bound their interests with those of Britain was the personal one of ligeance to the King. By him they had been constituted distinct states. As a matter of logic no room was left for legislative intervention by Parliament, and, indeed, the more truculent resolve writers came to denounce all acts for the colonies as unconstitutional. More moderate heads were prepared to concede authority in the sphere of imperial trade. On the grounds of necessity the First Continental Congress declared that it would consent to such regulation.[185]

For purposes of persuasion the colonial theory of an imperial constitution in its ramifications was less likely to induce a change of heart in the opposition than the arguments that had preceded it, particularly as the proffer of a substitute for the much lauded English constitution amounted almost to an impiety. The wonder is that a Parliament secure in the legal theory of its omnipotence would listen at all to charges about the unconstitutionality of its enactments for the dominions. Yet it is clear that there existed a body of opinion in England that there were fundamentals beyond tampering by the supreme legislative, and its most eminent judicial prolocutor was no less a figure than Lord Camden.[186] The strength of this opinion is evident from the numerous occasions

---

in to the Nature and Causes of the Disputes . . . (*ibid.*, 149), and still more in his letter to Samuel Cooper, June 8, 1770 (*ibid.*, 187), indicate his agreement with some of Bancroft's main points. In particular to be noted is Franklin's categorical statement that the colonies were originally constituted "distinct states" (*ibid.*, 188). This description used by Bancroft and Franklin seems to be the genesis of the designation accepted by the colonies upon independence, a designation which Jefferson's *Summary View of the Rights of British America* (1774) helped circularize at a critical time.

The further development of the theory cannot here be pursued. It had its best and fullest statement, making many of the points raised by Bancroft, in the two replies to the governor by the Massachusetts House of Representatives of January 26, 1773, and March 2, 1773 (in Bradford, *Speeches of the Governors of Massachusetts from 1765 to 1775 . . .*, 351–64, 384–96). Also in H. Cushing, *Writings of Samuel Adams* (New York: G. P. Putnam's Sons, 1906), II, 401–26, 431–54.

[185] W. C. Ford *et al.*, eds., *Journals of the Continental Congress 1774–1789*, I, 68–69, Resolve 4 (hereafter cited as *JCC*).

[186] In the debates on repeal of the Stamp Act and the passage of the Declaratory Act, Hansard, *Parliamentary History*, XVI, 168, 178–81.

when on measures before Parliament unrelated to American affairs the question of constitutionality was raised.[187]

In relation to purely English issues talk in Parliament about unconstitutionality never was more than political rhetoric because nothing was advanced as to where the authority to make a final determination lay. The Americans, in mutiny against the theory of Parliament's omnipotence, made do for a time with Coke's report of *Dr. Bonham's Case*.[188] What this case had to offer was the celebrated statement: "And it appears in our books, that in many cases, the common law will controul Acts of Parliament, and sometimes adjudge them to be utterly void: for when an Act of Parliament is against common right and reason, or repugnant, or impossible to be performed, the common law will controul it and adjudge such Act to be void."[189]

Much of what has been written about this statement has been directed at its worth as a correct statement of law. It has been assailed as obiter, as without support in the cases cited and as an almost disreputable doctrine. There have been defenses, or at least explanations, in terms of its relation to antecedent and then-contemporary canons of statutory interpretation.[190] All of this seems irrelevant to the purposes to which the doctrine was applied by the colonists. All the history back of the case, and the scattering of later cases that appeared to follow it, were immaterial in the 1760s. For like the immigrants who came to these shores, *Bonham's Case* began a new life in America in the context of the constitutional principles that had here been in process of formulation. These constitutional principles had a pronounced early seventeenth century cast because at their heart was the belief and conviction that the common law guaranteed certain rights to the subject that were indefeasible. For some five hundred years English courts had so understood "common right," and had maintained it as a standard even

---

[187] For random examples see the debate on the "Bristol Night Watch Bill" (1755), *ibid.*, XV, 479–87; on the motion respecting informations *ex officio* (1765), *ibid.*, XVI, 43–44; on the "Bill for Indemnity for those concerned in the Embargo" (1766), *ibid.*, 248–49; the protest against the East India Dividends Bill (1768), *ibid.*, 403–05; debate on thanks to the Crown (1770), *ibid.*, 658; on the motion for an inquiry into administration of justice (1770), *ibid.*, 1214–15.

[188] 8 Coke Rep. 107 (1610).

[189] *Ibid.*, at 118a.

[190] See B. Coxe, *An Essay on Judicial Power and Unconstitutional Legislation*, 154–56, 173–78; L. Boudin, "Lord Coke and the American Doctrine of Judicial Power," *N.Y.U. L. Rev.*, 6: 223 at 236, 1928–29; T. Plucknett, "Bonham's Case and Judicial Review," *Harv. L. Rev.*, 40:30, 1926–27; E. Corwin, "The 'Higher Law' Background of American Constitutional Law," *ibid.*, 42:365, 1928–29; S. Thorne, "Dr. Bonham's Case," *L.Q. Rev.*, 54:543, 1938; S. Thorne, ed., *A Discourse upon the Exposicion and Understandinge of Statutes . . .* (San Marino: Huntington Library, 1942), 85–89.

against the King when the greatest threats to it had emanated from that quarter and not from the Parliament.

What, then, was the impact of *Bonham's Case* upon American thinking? We believe that no more can be claimed than that it was a single ingredient in the complex corpus of ideas and usages from which a distinctively native doctrine of control over legislation eventually emerged. The case seems to have enjoyed only a brief usefulness in pre-Revolutionary polemics. It had been a main precedent in James Otis' argument against the issuance of writs of assistance,[191] and it was one of several precedents invoked in his *Rights of the British Colonies Asserted and Proved*, a tract inspired by the Sugar Act.[192] We know from Chief Justice Hutchinson that during the Stamp Act crisis there was, in Massachusetts at least, reliance upon the case.[193] But circumstances destroyed its worth as a cutting weapon. From Coke's language it was clearly to be inferred that a judicial declaration of nullity was anticipated as proper. In America this could not be secured from a court of any stature, assuming even that judges commissioned "at pleasure" would be bold enough to act. Furthermore, during the Stamp Act crisis public anger had taken fire so promptly and violently that the stamps or stamped paper necessary for the discharge of judicial business had either been returned or impounded. The rioters had made it too perilous to use any which might be made available. In consequence, the superior courts in all the colonies, except Rhode Island, were open, if at all, only for the trifling business that could be despatched without stamps.[194]

It was not only the impossibility of translating the doctrine of

---

[191] Quincy Reports 471 at 474 (1761). It may be noticed that the learned note of Mr. Justice Horace Gray (*ibid.*, App. I) has supplied much of the raw material for later writing on Bonham's Case. The reprint of this note in J. B. Thayer, *Cases on Constitutional Law* (Cambridge: George H. Kent, 1895), I, 48, seems to have contributed to an opinion about the continuing importance of Bonham's Case as a cornerstone of the American doctrine of judicial review.

[192] At 71–73. The pamphlet, published 1764, is reprinted in a collection by C. Mullett, "Some Political Writings of James Otis." Otis also used the case in Jeffries v. Edward (1762); see *Adams Papers*, I, 230–31. In 1765, before Governor Bernard on the Memorial of Boston to governor and council, Otis and John Adams again

appear to have used Bonham's Case. On the proceedings, *ibid.*, 266–67. The memorandum of authorities was reprinted in C. F. Adams' edition of the *The Works of John Adams*, II, 159n. (hereafter cited as Adams, *Works*). In the account of the argument (Quincy Reports 200–09) Adams' speech seems to have been scantily noted, a bare two pages, for Otis stated that Adams had entered "largely" into the validity of the Stamp Act.

[193] Hutchinson's letter relating to taxation, Mass. Archives (Ms. Hutchinson Correspondence), XXV, 129–30; a letter written to an unknown, Mar. 8, 1766, but not sent, *ibid.*, XXVI, 201–202; "A Summary of the Disaster in Mass. Province," *ibid.*, XXVI, 183.

[194] E. S. Morgan, and H. M. Morgan, *The Stamp Act Crisis*, c. 10.

93

Bonham's Case into action that led to its abandonment as an argument *ad captandum*, but also the fact that its usefulness as a precedent was impaired following the publication of volume one of Blackstone's *Commentaries*, late in 1765. In his tenth rule[195] for the construction of statutes over which Jeremy Bentham made merry,[196] Blackstone states that Acts of Parliament impossible to be performed are of no validity; and if there should arise out of them collaterally any absurd consequence manifestly contrary to reason, they are as to such consequence void. He conceded that it was generally laid down that Acts of Parliament contrary to reason were void, but if Parliament "positively enact a thing to be done that is unreasonable I know of no power that can control it."[197] In his opinion none of the cases usually cited proved that where the main object of the statute was unreasonable the judges were at liberty to reject it, "for that were to set the judicial power above the Legislature which would be subversive of all government." The most Blackstone would concede was as to unreasonable collateral matter arising out of the main words of a statute. Here the judges "in decency" might conclude that Parliament had not foreseen the consequence and as to this disregard it.

Whether or not His Majesty's judges, who are supposed to have examined Blackstone's manuscript before publication, meddled with his text, the tenth rule reads as if they might have. It resembles nothing so much as a composite of discordant views emanating from opinionated members of a bench at war with itself. The damage the "rule" did to the credit of *Bonham's Case* as a support for judicial review must have been considerable, for in the continuing contest over colonial rights references cease to this important incident of Coke's statement. The substantive premise that acts of Parliament could be void was not abandoned, for the claim that such were unconstitutional continued, a monotonous threnody. And some collateral support for this could be found in the shifty passages of the tenth rule. Indeed, the conduct of the colonists during the Stamp Act crisis, as a saturnine observer might have described it, was designed to establish that here was an act "impossible of performance"—and so also the non-importation agreements after the passage of the Townshend Acts.

So far as a solution of imperial relations was concerned, the lawless actions and para-legal measures resorted to by the American re-

---

[195] Blackstone, *Commentaries*, I, 91.

[196] J. Bentham, *A Comment on the Commentaries*, Everett ed. (Oxford: Clarendon Press, 1928), 152.

[197] This is the form of the statement in the first edition. In the 1783 edition it was altered to read, "I know of no power in the ordinary forms of the constitution, that is vested with authority to control it." It is likely that this addition revived the authority of Bonham's Case in post-Revolutionary thinking.

sistance produced short-lived results. The disputation of constitutional issues directed toward a rational resolution of pending issues produced none. Had the colonial position been defended mainly with the insubstantial weapons of natural law, as is so often represented, this would be understandable. But for all the reference to philosophers, it was with solid shot from the magazine of common law precedent that the American cause was chiefly vindicated. Since this had been traditional in English political controversy, some effect might have been anticipated. But all this came to nothing because the forum of final decision was not one at which the Americans could be heard on equal terms with their opponents.

If the American agitators and their English sympathizers were addressing deaf ears in the homeland, the impact of all the argumentation on this side of the Atlantic was incalculable. The quest for an area of agreement on the terms of the constitution sufficiently fixed to be relied upon was to be carried forward into the time of revolution and thereafter. The principle that government must be conducted in conformity with the terms of the constitution became a fundamental political conviction. What was not fully established was where the ultimate decision on conformity or repugnancy was to be lodged. Everything in the experience of the American lawyers, intellectual and practical, had prepared the way for committing this power to the judicial. The time was not far off when this would be done.

CHAPTER III

The New States and the Principle of Constitutional Authority

T HE AMERICAN REBELS who set about the fabrication of new constitutions were seemingly bent upon doing all they could to make
a future such as they desired. Because they and their forebears had
lived for generations according to the terms of the written instruments
establishing or regulating the structure of their governments, the conviction had been bred that only through matter of record could the
metes and bounds of the fundamental law be secured. This was a conviction afforced by the controversies which had led to revolt. That a
constitution in the nature of things must embody matter basic to the
governing of a polity and that its prescriptions be enduring had become,
so to speak, articles of faith and, consequently, chief objectives in the
process of constitution-making. These objectives, if there was to be
new building, invited protracted deliberation, yet the circumstances of
armed conflict and civil commotion that prevailed when most of the
new instruments were framed left little time for dalliance. What was
regarded as of emergent necessity, the correction of the patterns of
government which had hitherto prevailed, was in general achieved; and
in some jurisdictions the "rights and liberties" of the people were secured
to the degree that they were explicitly affirmed. Nevertheless, accounting even for the fulfillment of long-standing aspirations and for the
infusion of ideas derived from the philosophers, the several frames of
government all disclose how much was owed to the institutional structure of colonial times.

Nowhere was the hand of the past more directing than in the
treatment of the judicial. This is evident from the fact that in none of
the new constitutions was it dealt with much more explicitly than had

been the case in the charters or royal commissions.[1] This would seem to betoken a general attitude of satisfaction with the *status quo ante*, an attitude unaccountable in states like New Jersey and New York where the judicial establishment rested upon ordinances of royal governors. We believe, however, that the affirmation of the *status quo* was a mere stop-gap to be subject to future correction not by constitutional amendment but by statute, and this because of a deep-rooted and pervasive belief that the ordering of the judicial system should be committed to the legislative branch. For nearly a century the veritable *cordon sanitaire* maintained by the Crown against legislative trifling with the judicial structure had prevented the translation of beliefs into action, but they remained animate because of an enduring sense of grievance. The rebels gave tongue to this in the charge in the Declaration of Independence that the King had "obstructed the Administration of Justice by refusing his Assent to Laws for establishing Judiciary Powers."[2] This was fair warning that an overhaul of the old structure impended and that such was properly a task for the legislative.

For all the anxieties to make explicit the fundamentals proper to a constitution, the judicial generally came off with little more than an honorable mention because these anxieties were everywhere spent upon making less of the executive and more of the legislative branch. The clearest indications of intentions respecting the courts is found in those constitutions where provision was made for substitutions for the former jurisdiction of King in Council,[3] governor and council,[4] admiralty[5] and

---

[1] For the terms of surviving charters conveying power to erect judicatories see Thorpe, *Constitutions and Charters*: Connecticut (1662), *ibid.*, I, 533; Maryland (1632), *ibid.*, III, 1680; Massachusetts (1691), *ibid.*, III, 1881; Pennsylvania (1681), *ibid.*, V, 3037–38; Rhode Island (1663), *ibid.*, VI, 3215. Connecticut and Rhode Island elected to continue to be governed by their charters. By statute Connecticut, after approving the Declaration of Independence, asserted its right to be a free and independent state and provided that for form of civil government the charter was to be followed so far as adherence to it was consistent with absolute independence (*Acts and Laws of Connecticut*, Oct. Sess. 1776 [Green ed., 1783]). For Rhode Island's action see *infra*, n. 147.

[2] Thorpe, *Constitutions and Charters*, I, 5.

[3] Explicitly only in Delaware (1776), art. 17, *ibid.*, I, 565. Conceivably the institution of the Court of Appeals in Virginia had the same purpose, *ibid.*, VII, 3817.

[4] The authority to hear appeals in probate causes was conveyed by the Massachusetts Constitution to governor and council, subject to legislative change (c. III, art. 5), *ibid.*, III, 1906. In New Hampshire the Superior Court was substituted—also subject to legislative change, *ibid.*, IV, 2467. In New York the Court for the Trial of Impeachments and Correction of Errors —an imitation of the House of Lords —was the substitute (art. 33), *ibid.*, V, 2635. New Jersey continued the jurisdiction in governor and council (art. 9), *ibid.*, V, 2596.

[5] By Acts of Conventions, *infra*, c. IV.

probate.[6] In every case legislative action was obviously a necessity to make operative these replacements. The bundle of bills introduced into the Virginia legislature in 1776 dealing explicitly even with ancient and well settled bodies like the General Court establishes the point.[7] Similarly in Maryland legislation was needed to provide for Orphans' Courts to replace the Commissary General; and so in New York, to activate the Court of Probates and the Court for the Trial of Impeachments and the Correction of Errors.[8]

In some states the independence of the judiciary was regarded to be a matter sufficiently fundamental to warrant incorporation of provisions to secure it. Such were the stipulations regarding tenure and salary;[9] and here again was reflected colonial experience, specifically the altercations with the Crown over commissioning judges during pleasure, and the uproar over Grenville's civil list scheme. Good the intentions of the constitution-makers may have been, but they did not sufficiently take into account the fact that in the new order which they were setting up the provisions for salary and tenure designed to assure the independence of the judges were insufficient safeguards for the independence of the judicial function itself. The magnification of the legislative was a standing temptation to trespass even in those states where the separation of powers was specifically proclaimed. Thus in Massachusetts interferences in litigation by legislative resolve were per-

---

[6] In Maryland it was considered that it was the intention of the constitution to abolish the Commissary General (*Laws of Maryland*, Feb. Sess. 1777, c. 8). In New Jersey, by art. 8, the power was committed to the governor as theretofore (Thorpe, *Constitutions and Charters*, V, 2596); in New York, art. 27, to a court of probates, *ibid.*, V, 2634; in South Carolina, art. 16, establishing an ordinary, *ibid.*, VI, 3246. For the appellate authority of the governor in matters probate, *supra*, n. 4.

[7] The bills, drafted by Jefferson, are set out in J. Boyd *et al.*, ed., *The Papers of Thomas Jefferson*, II, 605 (hereafter cited as *Papers of Jefferson*).

[8] On probate jurisdiction, *Laws of Maryland*, Feb. Sess. 1777, c. 8; *N.Y. Laws*, 1 Sess. 1778, c. 12. On the Court for the Trial of Impeachments and Correction of Errors, *N.Y. Laws*, 8 Sess. 1784, c. 11.

[9] Tenure by good behavior was established for superior court judges in Delaware (art. 12), Thorpe, *Constitutions and Charters*, I, 564; Maryland (art. 40), *ibid.*, III, 1697; Massachusetts (c. III, art. 1), *ibid.*, III, 1905; New Hampshire, *ibid.*, IV, 2466; New York (art. 24), until sixty years of age, *ibid.*, V, 2634; North Carolina (art. 13), *ibid.*, V, 2791; South Carolina in 1776 (art. 20), *ibid.*, VI, 3246, and in 1778 (art. 27), *ibid.*, VI, 3254; Virginia, *ibid.*, VII, 3817.

The salary provisions were various —"adequate, fixed, but moderate" (Delaware); "permanent and honorable" (Massachusetts and New Hampshire); "fixed" (Pennsylvania); "adequate" (North Carolina and South Carolina 1778); "fixed and adequate" (Virginia). Inflation, of course, wrecked the well-intentioned concept of fixity as a form of insurance, and adequacy became a matter of legislative caprice.

sistent,[10] as they were also in New Hampshire.[11] In North Carolina such interposition both by statute and by private act was occasional.[12] We have Jefferson's testimony that in Virginia the legislature had "in many instances, decided rights which should have been left to judiciary controversy"[13]—a form of intervention as subversive as interference with litigation. Where the principle of separation had not been explicitly adopted, as in Pennsylvania, but was fairly to be inferred, the supreme executive not only exercised powers traditionally used by courts alone, but besought advisory opinions from the Supreme Court and also actively obstructed the due course of law.[14]

These evidences of meddling tend to establish that despite explicit or *de facto* recognition of the doctrine of separation of powers, what

---

[10] *E.g., Mass. Acts and Resolves 1782–83* (reprint), May Sess. 1782, cc. 49, 92, 112; Sept. Sess. 1782, cc. 107, 122; Jan. Sess. 1783, cc. 44, 88, 89; May Sess. 1783, cc. 48, 88; Sept. Sess. 1783, cc. 26, 39, 56.

[11] *E.g., 5 Laws of New Hampshire 1784–1792*, Oct. Sess. 1784, c. 9; Oct. Sess. 1785, cc. 4, 5, 13, 15; Feb. Sess. 1786, cc. 6, 18, 21, 25.

[12] The three notable interferences by public act occurred in 1783. The first directed that in pending actions where damages were laid in paper currency, judgments should be specie and no writ of error should lie for variance. 1 *Public Acts of the General Assembly of North Carolina* (Martin ed., 1804), Apr. Sess. 1783, c. 4. The second, *ibid.*, c. 5, discharged and made void all actions, prosecutions, etc., and judgments against persons who had done a variety of acts in defense of the state during the war. The third, *ibid.*, c. 7, suspended executions.

For private acts, see *A Collection of the Private Acts of the General Assembly of North Carolina* (Martin ed., 1794), Oct. Sess. 1784, c. 46; Nov. Sess. 1785, c. 43; Nov. Sess. 1788, cc. 26, 41; Nov. Sess. 1789, c. 38.

[13] "Notes on the State of Virginia" (1782), in P. L. Ford, ed., *The Works of Thomas Jefferson* (Federal ed. 1904–1905), IV, 21 [hereafter cited as *Works of Jefferson* (Ford, Federal ed.)].

[14] *E.g.*, committing persons to jail for offenses or letting to bail, Minutes of the Supreme Executive Council of Pennsylvania, in *Colonial Records of Pennsylvania* (1852), XI, 201, 226, 236, 268. It interfered in civil disputes that were properly judicial, *ibid.*, XI, 668; *ibid.*, XII, 75; issued a writ of assistance, *ibid.*, XII, 105. Interference in habeas corpus proceedings (1777), *ibid.*, XI, 308; on which see R. L. Brunhouse, *The Counter-Revolution in Pennsylvania 1776–1790*, 43, and the later case of Joseph Griswold (1780), *ibid.*, 101. Examples of soliciting judicial opinions in *Col. Rec. of Pa.*, XI, 560, 744; *ibid.*, XII, 44, 103, 105.

The attitude of the Council toward the judiciary is indicated in a message to the General Assembly, December 11, 1780, regarding a pending act empowering the Council as well as the judiciary to apprehend suspected persons. "It has been the policy of all other States, and even of our enemy, at this juncture, to repose a confidence in the Executive powers to guard the publick safety by commitments not subject to the examination of any other, and much less an inferior authority, for such we deem the Justices of the Supreme Court on this occasion, and we cannot help thinking the superior confidence in the Justices of the Supreme Court implied by this bill, not only degrading to the Council, but inconsistent with the spirit of the Constitution." *Col. Rec. of Pa.*, XII, 564–65.

Madison called "parchment boundaries" proved unavailing. One might suppose that things would have been otherwise because of general disillusionment with the commingling of governmental powers under the old regime, from governor and council to the level of justice of the peace. But the legislatures had at last been put in the way of having their earlier pretensions to the powers of Parliament made a reality. The tenor of the petitions which poured in at the commencement of their sessions indicates a widespread belief in their omnipotence. Obviously the judicial, so indifferently secured in the several constitutions, could not anticipate immunity.

From what is of record during the first decade of independence it is impossible to determine whether or not the courts rendered themselves vulnerable to forays against the judicial process itself. They were called upon both during the war and after to dispense justice under enactments that in many instances offended traditional standards of due process. With the coming of peace the attendant economic distress gave the color of injustice to the normal discharge of their functions. A further and imponderable factor was the fact that an old and indurated body of law and procedure was being administered in a world that in other particulars was one greatly changed. As we shall see, the continuance of the law as practiced had been assured by constitution or statute in nearly all of the states, subject, to be sure, to future legislative change. In spite of the heavy flow of legislation in some states during the first decade of independence, the impress of current libertarianism upon the corpus of the common law and the manner of its practice was hardly perceptible. The effect of all this was to leave blemished the image of the judicial and to make difficult the full and free exercise of its traditional role of molding the law within the framework of issues raised in litigation. This was to become manifest on the first occasions when courts undertook to vindicate as against the legislatures the specific restraints of particular constitutions.

These restraints, either accessory to or embodied in the constitutions of all those states which had established such new instruments, had the purpose of safeguarding and keeping viable the provisions of the fundamental law. They testify emphatically to a general determination that the principle of the controlling effect of the constitution upon law-making should be put on as solid a footing as the frame of government itself. Resort was had to a variety of expedients—bills of rights, solemn declarations in the instruments of government, and that most ancient form of collateral insurance, the oath. This deliberate conversion of what had been a matter of political dialogue into the most solemn form of law is so important an aspect of American constitutional development that it must here be considered at large.

DECLARATIONS OF SUPREMACY IN THE FUNDAMENTAL LAW

IN THE STATES which adopted declarations or bills of rights, and there were seven which had done so by 1784,[15] these declarations were devised to mark boundaries beyond which government could not trespass. The terms of this *ne intromittat* were broadly conceived, for in addition to safeguards of individual rights all these instruments embodied certain general restraints upon the exercise of powers elsewhere bestowed. The precedent for combining basic political principles and the statement of individual rights was, of course, the English Bill of Rights, and we shall later observe how the notion that such an amalgam was proper to any bill of rights persisted through the struggle over ratification of the federal Constitution.

When the states ordained their declarations of rights the times were hardly propitious for the provisions to be put to impartial trial. It is too much to say that various wartime measures which the legislatures saw fit to enact fixed a pattern of power hard to break, but there is no doubt that in some states the legislatures remained recusant and there was no effective means of bringing them to repentance. Not one of the declarations contained a guarantee of due process of law. All of them had guaranteed that no man should be deprived of his liberty or his liberty and property except by the judgment of his peers or the law of the land—a guarantee written also into the New York constitution and into South Carolina's second constitution of 1778. This phrase, taken from Magna Carta, the constitution-makers may have believed to be synonymous with due process.[16] It has elsewhere been shown that it was not,[17] for due process had developed at the hands of the courts with particular reference to settled procedural expectations—standards set and protected by the judiciary. Where legislative authority was supreme or close to being such, law of the land and due process were not interchangeable terms.

---

[15] Delaware, Maryland, Massachusetts, New Hampshire, North Carolina, Pennsylvania and Virginia. Four states—Georgia, New Jersey, New York and South Carolina—which did not frame discrete bills of rights singled out specific items, *e.g.*, jury trial, traditionally esteemed to be basic "rights and liberties" for incorporation into their instruments of government.

[16] Chiefly, we believe, because the rather obscure text in Coke, *Second Institute*, 50–51, appeared to make the identification. On this, see the comment in Goebel, "Constitutional History and Constitutional Law," 563, n. 24.

[17] Basic documents in Goebel, *Cases and Materials on the Development of Legal Institutions*, 168–72.

The declarations of rights were a climactic point in the articulation of rights, the militant assertion of which had been going on for better than a decade. The constitution-makers, however, appear not to have learned as they should have from this experience the profound truth of the old maxim "no writ, no right"—that without implementation a right remains a mere abstraction. The lack of attention to this crucial detail is most arresting where the proposition that legislation must conform to the terms of the constitution was expressly stipulated in the body of the constitution itself. In Delaware,[18] Georgia,[19] Maryland,[20] Massachusetts,[21] New Hampshire[22] and Pennsylvania[23] it was laid down as an injunction upon the legislature that there should be no enactments in violation of or repugnant to the constitution. The manner of expressing this was various but the intention was clear. North Carolina saw fit only to immunize its declaration of rights from any violation "on any pretence whatsoever."[24] In none of these instruments was there any indication of how redress could be had betimes for acts passed in despite of the injunctions.

NON-JUDICIAL DEVICES TO CORRECT OR PREVENT INFRINGEMENTS

NEW HAMPSHIRE and Pennsylvania had procedures for belated correction. The provision in the New Hampshire constitution of 1784 was actually one for amendment at the expiration of seven years, but it was introduced by a recital to the effect that the purpose was to preserve "an effectual adherence to the principles of the constitution," to correct any violation and to make alterations that might from experience be expedient.[25] The scheme in Pennsylvania was more complex. In the first place, it was ordained that to assure mature consideration and

---

[18] Art. 30; see Thorpe, *Constitutions and Charters*, I, 568.

[19] Art. 7 (*ibid.*, II, 779). See also the curious provisions, arts. 42 and 43, regarding juries being sworn to bring in verdicts according to law and the opinion entertained of the evidence "provided it be not repugnant to the rules and regulations contained in this constitution" (*ibid.*, II, 783).

[20] Art. 42 of the Declaration of Rights (*ibid.*, III, 1690–91).

[21] Pt. II, c. I, sec. I, art. 4 (*ibid.*, III, 1894).

[22] Pt. 2 (*ibid.*, IV, 2458).

[23] Sec. 9 (*ibid.*, V, 3085).

[24] Art. 44 (*ibid.*, V, 2794). See,

however, the restraint on the executive, art. 19, and the sanction of impeachment for officers violating the constitution, art. 23 (*ibid.*, V, 2792). It may be noticed that the legislature on occasion adverted in statutes to legislation or practices as being "contrary to the spirit of the constitution," *e.g.*, the 1783 statute repealing assessments on conscientious objectors (1 *Public Acts of North Carolina* [Martin ed., 1804], 331) and the 1784 statute to prevent persons holding offices of profit having seats in the General Assembly (*ibid.*, 360).

[25] Thorpe, *Constitutions and Charters*, IV, 2470.

to prevent hasty determinations all public bills should be printed and circulated among the people and except in cases of emergency be laid over for the following session of the assembly. The matter of repugnancy of such bills to the constitution was not mentioned, but obviously this was a consideration not excluded. This preventive measure was supplemented by a remedial one. A Council of Censors was to be elected in 1783 and every seven years thereafter, to sit for a year.[26] This Council was among other things to inquire "whether the constitution has been preserved inviolate in every part," whether or not the legislative and executive branches had done their duty or assumed or exercised greater powers than they were entitled to by the constitution. To this end a subpoena power was conferred, and the Council might pass censures, order impeachment and recommend to the legislature repeal of such laws as "appear to them to have been enacted contrary to the principles of the constitution."

The basic defect of the Council as a regulatory device was the fact that no account had been taken of the degree to which private interests might be affected by unconstitutional legislation. A censure or a belated repeal was no balm to one whose rights might have been impaired. Moreover, the fact that the Council, an elected body, was also authorized to call a convention to amend the constitution predestined its failure. The state of politics in Pennsylvania was such that when the Council convened in 1783, the many flagrant breaches of the constitution uncovered by the minority[27] were disposed of by partisan vote, apparently to quiet demands for revision of the democratical constitution.[28]

The scheme devised by the New York constitution-makers to hold the legislature in check, and for which Robert R. Livingston was chiefly responsible,[29] was reminiscent of the colonial system, although it was designed as a restraint upon both the legislature and the executive. Reciting that laws "inconsistent with the spirit of this constitution or with the public good" might be hastily or inadvisably passed, Article III ordained that there be a Council of Revision composed of governor,

---

[26] Sec. 47 (*ibid.*, V, 3091). This provision was copied by the Vermont rebels in their constitution of 1777, art. 40 (*ibid.*, VI, 3761) and reiterated in the state constitution of 1793, sec. 43 (*ibid.*, 3771).

[27] The calendar of grievances appears at the end of the formal proceedings in *Journal of the Council of Censors Convened, at Philadelphia* (1783). These were disposed of in the

course of the second session, June 1784.

[28] Brunhouse, *The Counter-Revolution in Pennsylvania 1776–1790*, 156–63.

[29] *Journals of the Provincial Congress, Provincial Convention, Committee of Safety and Council of Safety of the State of New-York: 1775–1776–1777* (1842), I, 860 (hereafter cited as *Journals of Provincial Congress, New-York*).

chancellor and the judges of the Supreme Court of Judicature, or any two of them, to which all bills passed by senate and assembly be submitted before they became laws. If it should appear "improper" that any such bills become law, these were to be returned together with a statement of objections. Both houses were then to reconsider the bills, and if approved by two thirds of the members the bills should become law.

The records of the Council, especially in the early years of its existence, demonstrate that the membership conceived that it possessed a broad mandate.[30] Its opinions rejecting bills were grounded as well upon the letter as the spirit of the constitution. The law of nations, common law and equity were regarded as no less controlling. There is nothing to indicate that hearings were held, and certainly nothing in the nature of adversarial procedure. No inference can be drawn from the association of the judges with the executive that the Council was a substitute for judicial review in the course of litigation.[31] Its functions were entirely connected with the legislative process.

The name of the Council was misleading, for unless the legislature corrected defects in accordance with the opinion of the Council there was nothing truly revisory about its work. It was essentially advisory and only as to defects, for no statement was constitutionally required where a bill was approved. In this particular lay one essential difference between the manner in which New York used the informed opinion of chancellor and judges and the procedure written into the Massachusetts and, later, the New Hampshire constitution.

Chapter III, Article II, of the Massachusetts constitution authorized each branch of the legislature as well as the governor and council to require the opinions of the justices of the Supreme Judicial Court upon important questions of law and upon "solemn occasions." Shortly after the adoption of the constitution of 1780 an opinion was requested by the General Court on the respective powers under that instrument of House and Senate.[32] In the years following, both the executive[33] and the legislature[34] availed themselves of the constitutional privilege

---

[30] Council's reports assembled in A. Street, *The Council of Revision of the State of New York.*

[31] On this see the comments of Duane J. in Rutgers v. Waddington (1784), reprinted in *LPAH*, I, 416 et seq.

[32] *Supplement to Acts and Resolves of Massachusetts* (Bacon ed., 1896), 42–49.

[33] A message of the governor to the General Court, Jan. 23, 1784, trans-

mitted a request of the governor of South Carolina re detention of Negroes allegedly the property of South Carolina "subjects" and enclosed an opinion of the justices (*ibid.*, 212–13). The legislature resolved Mar. 23, 1784, that the opinion be despatched to South Carolina (*Mass. Acts and Resolves 1782–83*, 898).

[34] In the Ms. Cushing Papers (MHS) is a request, October 27, 1784, from Samuel Adams inquiring whether the

—the latter requiring opinions on both its constitutional rights and the constitutionality of pending legislation.

THE OATH AS SAFEGUARD

BOTH THE Massachusetts advisory opinion and the New York conciliar "revision" were notionally outgrowths of the system of imperial review and control of colonial legislation. As this system had been administered, it was directed at preventing infractions of standards set by the Crown and was not in the least concerned with remedy. This outlook was dominant in all the new constitutions where obedience to their provisions was expressly enjoined. This injunction was thus left primarily as a charge upon the conscience of law-makers. Substance was lent to this visionary expectation by the oaths stipulated either in the constitutions or in statutes—the oaths of fidelity and allegiance, usually of universal application, and the new oaths of office. In the text of these oaths is manifest the profound constitutional change in process of taking place. In the case of the oath of allegiance it was a vehicle by which change was forwarded. For the duration of the Revolution and even thereafter the relation of the individual to the body politic was founded thereon. The oaths of office were supplementary, phrased with reference to the new allegiance. The obligations this imported were of a different order than the oaths traditionally exacted of officers in the colonies.

In eighteenth-century colonial America it was only the officials in the royal provinces who had been required to take oaths of allegiance and abjuration. These were the test oaths appointed in the English Bill of Rights (1689)[35] and subsequently rephrased in various Acts of Parliament.[36] The ligeance of colonial inhabitants at large was not founded upon oath but, like ligeance of subjects within the realm, was a "natural" allegiance to the King. This consisted in what Coke called the "obligation of duty and obedience"[37] on the part of the subject and of protection on the part of the King. Ligeance was deemed to be a personal bond beyond the power of the subject to sever. There was ancient authority to the effect that the King's "natural" protection was equally indefeasible even where a man was out of the protection of the

---

two branches of the General Court had the constitutional right to fill vacancies in the Council. Cushing's opinion is torn and has no date. See Ms. Journal of the House of Representatives of the Commonwealth of Massachusetts (1785), VI, 196–200 (Mass. Archives); *ibid.*, VII, (1786),

255; and the opinion in Ms. Senate Files (1785), No. 284 (Mass. Archives).

[35] 1 Wm. & M., sess. 2, c. 2, sec. 3.
[36] Listed in Bacon, *Abridgment*, IV, *s.v.* Prerogative C 2.
[37] Calvin's Case, 7 Coke Rep. 1, 4b (1608); and see Coke, *Littleton*, 129a.

law itself—not even Parliament could sever the bond.[38] Nevertheless, as the Americans saw it, this is precisely what Parliament did when it enacted the so-called Prohibitory Act (December 22, 1775)[39] and put the rebellious colonials irrevocably out of the King's protection. There had been no express statutory declaration to this effect, but the inference seemed inescapable from the directive that ships and cargoes were to be treated "as if the same were the ships and effects of open enemies."

That the Prohibitory Act was regarded as a final breach is apparent from the fact that the King's exclusion of the inhabitants of the United Colonies from the protection of his crown was chosen as the operative fact in the preamble of the Continental Congress's resolve of May 15, 1776,[40] advising the colonies which had not set up governments sufficient to the exigencies of their affairs to do so. The preamble further recited that it was "irreconcileable to reason and good Conscience" to take oaths necessary for the support of any government under the British Crown, but no recommendation as to a substitute was offered.

The divisions among the Americans and the clear and present danger which those still abiding in their natural allegiance presented to the patriot cause shortly induced the formulation of new oaths of allegiance by the several states. The impetus appears to have been given by the report of a Committee of the Congress appointed June 5, 1776,[41] to consider what should be done with those giving intelligence to the enemy or supplying them with provisions. Five lawyers—John Adams, Robert R. Livingston, James Wilson, Thomas Jefferson and Edward Rutledge—served on this committee. Its report, adopted by Congress June 24 in the form of a recommendatory resolve, was significant because a new definition of allegiance was devised coupled with a redefinition of treason, historically the ultimate sanction for breach of ligeance.

"All persons," read the resolve, "abiding within any of the United Colonies, and deriving protection from the laws of the same owe allegiance to the said laws and are members of such colonies." All persons members of or owing allegiance to any colony "who shall levy war" against any colony or be adherent to the King or other enemies, or should give aid or comfort to them "are guilty of treason against such colony." It was recommended that laws be passed in the several colonies to implement the resolve.[42]

---

[38] Calvin's Case, *ut supra*, 13b–14a.
[39] 16 Geo. III, c. 5. Also referred to this side of the Atlantic as the Piracy Act because of the provision that sole property in all prizes taken should rest in the captors.
[40] *JCC*, IV, 357–58. The resolve proper of May 10, *ibid.*, 342.
[41] *JCC*, V, 417.
[42] *Ibid.*, V, 475–76 (June 24, 1776).

III: *The New States and Constitutional Authority*

The dehumanization of ligeance by substituting the laws instead of a living being as the object of duty and obligation was typical lawyers' handiwork. A great deal of old law was thereby made meaningless and, as the courts were to discover, the legal implications of the new concept remained to be explored, in particular the matter of indefeasibility of the new allegiance and the extension of the obligation to the nascent union itself. That the Congress's resolve served to establish uniformity of opinion is patent from the state constitutional provisions or the statutes enacted for oaths of allegiance or of fidelity[43] and from the treason statutes.[44]

---

[43] In the oaths of allegiance or fidelity—the latter term obviously used to distinguish the new duty from the old—the duty pledged is to the state. So in New Hampshire, Jan. 17, 1777, 4 *Laws of New Hampshire*, 71; Massachusetts, Feb. 3, 1778, 5 *Acts and Resolves Prov. of Mass. Bay*, 771; Rhode Island, Test Act, June Sess. 1776, *Rhode Island Acts and Resolves* (facsimile ed.), 109, and Oaths of the Justices, May Sess. 1776, *ibid.*, 24; Connecticut, October 1776, *Acts and Laws of Connecticut* (Green ed., 1783), 433. New York, on taking the oath, Mar. 26, 1777, *Journals of Provincial Congress, New-York*, I, 853; art. 8, constitution of 1777; the form, *N.Y. Laws*, 1 Sess. 1778, c. 7. New Jersey, Sept. 19, 1776, *Acts of the General Assembly . . . of New Jersey*, 1 Sess. 1776, c. 2, and c. 34 (June 5, 1777). Pennsylvania, Sept. 5, 1776, 9 *Pennsylvania Stats. at Large*, 111–12; and the form, sec. 40, constitution of Sept. 28, 1776. Maryland, *Laws of Maryland*, Feb. Sess. 1777, c. 20, sec. 13; Virginia, May 1777, 9 Hening, *Va. Stats.*, 281; North Carolina, Apr. Sess. 1777, *State Records of North Carolina*, XXIV, 11; South Carolina, Constitution of 1778, art. 36, for all officials, Thorpe, *Constitutions and Charters*, VI, 3255, The Georgia oath, required of all voters, is set out in art. 14 of the 1777 constitution, *ibid.*, 780; see also the statute of general oblivion, Aug. 20, 1781, *Colonial Records of the State of Georgia*, XIX, Pt. II, 142.

On the oath exacted of Continental officials see the report, *JCC*, X, 68–73.

The form voted Feb. 3, 1778, *ibid.*, 115. Note further New Jersey's objections that the Articles of Confederation imposed no "oath, test, or declaration" upon delegates to Congress. It was argued that the United States had interests distinct from the states and an oath not to assent to a vote or proceeding in violation of the Articles was essential. This was rejected by Congress. J. Elliot, ed., *The Debates in the Several State Conventions, on the Adoption of the Federal Constitution . . . together with the Journal of the Federal Convention*, I, 87 (hereafter cited as Elliot, *Debates*).

[44] In the treason statutes the coupling of duty and protection of the laws as reported in Congress and the limits thereof is usual. See 4 *Laws of New Hampshire*, 71; 5 *Acts and Resolves Prov. of Mass. Bay*, 615; *Rhode Island Acts and Resolves*, May Sess. 1777, 30; *Acts and Laws of Connecticut* (Green ed.), 432; *Journals of Provincial Congress, New-York*, I, 527, for the Resolve of July 16, 1776; *Acts of the General Assembly . . . of New Jersey*, 1 Sess. 1776, c. 5; 9 *Pennsylvania Stats. at Large*, 18; *Laws of Maryland*, Feb. Sess. 1777, c. 20; *State Records of North Carolina*, XXIV, 9, where the acts constituting treason are elaborated. Virginia omitted reference to protection of the laws as an operative fact, 9 Hening, *Va. Stats.*, 168. South Carolina anticipated treason legislation by a sedition act, Apr. 11, 1776, *Public Laws of South-Carolina* (Grimké, 1790), 283. A temporary act re treason was passed in February 1779 which did not fol-

We are concerned here with the oaths taken by official persons, for in the new order and the changed political climate these undertakings had, we believe, a direct bearing upon the controlling effect of the constitution upon legislative enactment and how such control could be maintained. Wherever the supremacy of the constitution was in one form or another laid down and a constitutional oath of office to observe the constitution provided therein, as in New Hampshire, Massachusetts and Pennsylvania, the responsibility of upholding the supremacy of the fundamental law lay with all officers of government. Where, however, there was no declaration of supremacy of the constitution or where this rested only upon inference and nothing more than an oath of allegiance or fidelity was exacted, the limits of duty were less obvious. In South Carolina the oath to maintain the constitution of 1776 was supplanted in 1778 by a mere oath of allegiance,[45] and although by statute governor and councillors were sworn to observe the constitution,[46] the only judicial officer for whom a special oath was devised was the chancellor who swore to dispense justice according to law.[47] This was also the pattern in Maryland where a similar distinction between executive and other civil officers was drawn by statute.[48] In Virginia an ordinance of the Convention[49] required governor and privy councillors to swear among other things to maintain the constitution. Assemblymen made no such pledge. In the bills brought in in 1776 judges were required only to take the oath of fidelity and by their oaths of office "to do the law,"[50] an engagement that remained in the laws as enacted.

The statutory rules laid down in New York also reflect the then-pervasive uneasiness over executive encroachments.[51] The constitutional article relating to the Council of Revision indicated the intention of maintaining the constitution's supremacy, yet the legislators were required only to take the oath of allegiance. The governor and lieutenant governor were, however, sworn to execute the laws in conformity with the powers bestowed by the constitution. The judges undertook to execute their offices according to the laws and constitution of the state "in defense of the freedom and independence thereof and for the main-

---

low the terms of the congressional resolve, 4 *South Carolina Stats. at Large* (Cooper ed.), 479.

In W. Hurst, "Treason in the United States, Pt. I," *Harv. L. Rev.*, 58:226–72, 1944, is compiled the full list of the state laws. He does not enter upon the implications of the change in the underlying concept of allegiance; neither does B. Chapin, *The American Law of Treason, Revolutionary and Early National Origins* (Seattle: Uni-

versity of Washington Press, 1964).
[45] Art. 36.
[46] *Public Laws of the State of South-Carolina*, (Grimké, 1790), 297 (Mar. 28, 1778).
[47] *Ibid.*, 337 (Mar. 21, 1784).
[48] *Laws of Maryland*, Feb. Sess. 1777, c. 5.
[49] 9 Hening, *Va. Stats.*, 119.
[50] *Papers of Jefferson*, I, 607, 610, 621, 645.
[51] *N.Y. Laws*, 1 Sess. 1778, c. 7.

tenance of liberty and the distribution of justice"—a formula that might well have given rise to doubts as to the circumstances under which it would be proper to prefer the constitution over enactments.

In the jurisdictions where there was no explicit monition against the enactment of legislation repugnant to the constitution, and the conscience of the judges was bound by no more than an oath of fidelity to the state, defense of the supremacy of the constitution was not an obvious incident of judicial duty. This may serve to explain why, as we shall presently observe, there was resort to the established canons of judicial interpretation of statutes to avoid the effects of legislation without venturing upon the politically hazardous course of seeming to raise the judicial above the legislative.

THE RECEPTION PROVISIONS AND CONSTITUTIONAL CONFORMITY—THE ROLE OF THE COURTS

ALTHOUGH NEITHER the state constitutions nor the oath statutes indicate that the safeguard of the fundamental law against legislative encroachment was conceived to be the particular charge of the courts, the case was otherwise with respect to the existing body of law. All of the states except Connecticut and Rhode Island, which had elected to live under their old charters, found it expedient either by constitution or statute to declare, among other things, what law was there to be in force. These mandates were at once directions to the judiciary and affirmations of legislative authority to make future changes. They bear so importantly upon the power of the judiciary to maintain the constitution that they must be examined.

These declarations were induced by a variety of considerations— to resolve doubts as to what law obtained once the ties with Britain were severed; to settle the long-disputed question over the force and effect of the English common law without the realm; and to expurgate certain Acts of Parliament and other unwanted incidents of the old systems of law. The ordinance promulgated in May 1776[52] by the same Virginia Convention which was to settle the state constitution a month later was the first of these measures, and in succession ten other states took similar action.

The texts of these declarations, and so their quality as reception provisions, varied. The majority of the states explicitly or by inference proclaimed their law to be the common law, either with no reservation, or as used in the colony, or as used in the colony prior to a certain date. English statutes again prior to a certain date or as used in the

---

[52] 9 Hening, *Va. Stats.*, 127.

colony were included.[53] Finally embraced were acts of assembly in force or as "practiced." The caveat, already noticed, that the *status quo* was subject to legislative change was in every case included. Common to all these declarations was the monition regarding the repugnancy of any law or statute as affirmed or theretofore used to the constitution or the declaration of rights where one existed.

In each of the several states this latter mandate was variously expressed. In some cases certain particulars, *e.g.*, anything relating to royal prerogative, were singled out and declared abrogated, and this was coupled with a declaration of nullity of matter inconsistent or repugnant. In other cases the rejection was less forcefully put, the direction being no more than "except as altered in the constitution." Only two states made reference to the activities of the Continental Congress. Delaware excluded its own acts of assembly if contrary to the resolutions of Congress.[54] Georgia put the regulations and resolves of Congress on the same footing as the constitution as a criterion of validity.[55]

Because these provisions on their face anticipated some affirma-

---

[53] Virginia was the only state to receive the common law as such and English statutes prior to 1607 of a general nature. Maryland, in the Declaration of Rights, sec. III, fixed upon the common law as of the time of emigration as well as the then applicable statutes and those subsequent used and practiced. New York, in art. 35 of the constitution of 1777, opted for those parts of the common law, English statutes and acts of assembly "as together did form the law of the said colony" on Apr. 19, 1775. Pennsylvania, by statute of Jan. 28, 1777, chose May 14, 1776 as a terminus for the common law and English statutes theretofore in force (9 *Statutes at Large of Pennsylvania*, 29). The New Jersey constitution, art. 22, accepted the common law and statutes theretofore practiced. The North Carolina Convention by ordinance of December 22, 1776, adopted the statutes and common law theretofore in use (*State Records of North Carolina*, XXIII, 992). This was substantially re-enacted by the assembly in 1778 (1 *Public Acts of North Carolina* [Martin ed., 1804], 252). Neither New Hampshire nor Massachusetts used the words "common law." New Hampshire by statute in 1777 proclaimed that all the laws in force should re-

main in effect (4 *Laws of New Hampshire*, 87). This was restated in the New Hampshire constitution of 1784 —"all the laws which have heretofore been adopted, used and approved . . . and usually practiced in the courts" (Thorpe, *Constitutions and Charters*, IV, 2469). This latter formula had already been adopted in the Massachusetts constitution of 1780, Pt. II, c. 6, sec. 6 (*ibid.*, III, 1910). Since the body of private law had been common law in both jurisdictions, these declarations must be held to have been an adoption of it. By the South Carolina constitution of 1776, art. 29, "all laws now in force here" were continued (*ibid.*, VI, 3247). In 1712 an act of assembly had explicitly adopted the common law (Public Law 99, in 1 J. Brevard, *Digest of the Public Laws of South Carolina* [1814], tit. 44). Georgia initially (June 7, 1777) affirmed the continuance of the statutes and common law used and adopted only as related to crimes except treason (*Colonial Records of Georgia*, XIX, Pt. II, 58). This was enlarged Nov. 15, 1778, to include all of the common law used and adopted (*ibid.*, 128).

[54] Constitution, art. 24.

[55] Act of June 7, 1777, *supra*, n. 53.

tive action in rooting out unconstitutional ingredients of the system of law, they testify more emphatically to a determination that the principle of constitutional supremacy be carried into effect than some of the merely hortatory phrases of the instruments of government. Apart from the purpose of putting the citizenry on notice regarding the status of the law, they were, as remarked, essentially directions to the judiciary, and so operated as a license to the courts to settle what parts of the law were preserved and operative and what parts were unconstitutional. This was an inescapable incident of litigation, and until the legislature exercised the right reserved to make alterations, there was no other competent authority that could act.

The committal of these powers to the courts was nothing more than the addition of a new and greater dimension to an authority that they had long been exercising in the several colonies. This had been, of course, the business of accepting or rejecting matter from the formidable hotchpot of the rules and practices of English courts to suit the conditions and convenience of the jurisdiction. There were incidents, as it had turned out on appeal to the Privy Council, that the colonies were at liberty neither to use nor to reject. Yet in general, both in relation to the trial of actions and, as we have seen, in connection with devices for review, the colonial courts were little restrained in settling the *cursus curiae* of a particular jurisdiction.

Insofar as this phase of colonial judicial activity had related to procedure and the manipulation of such devices it is impossible not to ascribe to it great constitutional import. This is most strikingly demonstrated by the accommodations that had been made in the colonies to supply the lack of a Chancery office. It is equally demonstrable by the accumulation of changes in process and practice. All of this related to the establishment of a distinctive due process of law in the pristine sense of the Statute 28 Edward III, c. 3, which in English law was the constitutional basis upon which the subjects' procedural expectations rested.

The effect of the declarations that nothing repugnant to the constitution in the law hitherto observed or the common law, as the case might be, was to require the courts to make what amounted to political decisions. In colonial times there had been occasions when the courts had done just this, notably with respect to using Acts of Parliament which under then-constitutional principles did not extend to the plantations.[56] Obviously the scrutiny for repugnancy of English statutes theretofore a part of the law and even of colonial acts was calculated to harden opinion regarding the propriety of judicial review. The rejection

---

[56] *Supra*, c. II, n. 136.

of common law rules once used could add little to such opinion, for this is what colonial courts had consistently been doing for reasons of practicality and convenience.

It is impossible to assess with accuracy the contribution of the courts in purging the old law of unconstitutional matter. Apart from the fact that action depended upon the accidents of litigation, the muniments of such for the period when the hue and cry after obnoxious features of regal government was at its height are of little help. What was reported of judicial opinion for these years is sparse. Little or nothing can be harvested from a common law record or collateral documents relating to judicial action. The issue of constitutionality would normally arise only on demurrer, motion in arrest, motion for a new trial or by one of the devices for review. Unhappily rulings on motions were not then part of the record, although they might be entered in judges' books or occasionally in court minutes. Certainly the traditional formula for judgment on demurrer or on points of law assigned in error which was of record tells nothing except the court's conclusion that one party or the other prevailed. We are consequently cast upon the earliest published reports which by no means supply a satisfactory conspectus of judicial business in any jurisdiction. Nevertheless, they reveal something about the basic problems confronting the new state courts, including the question of repugnancy, and how these were approached.

In the first place, it is apparent that the chief problem posed by the constitutional or statutory directions regarding the status of the law was the judicial articulation of what the law of a particular jurisdiction had in fact been. This was a task fraught with difficulties because of the peculiar methods of adjudication that had prevailed during the eighteenth century. The working precedents on points of substantive law had been consistently culled from English reports and what had been used, what modified and what rejected was rarely remembranced. This had the result that although provincial courts resorted to English cases more or less as did the courts at Westminster, unless a provincial application of an English rule had recurred sufficiently to have become a matter of common knowledge at the bar, or unless a single occurrence was within the memory of the court, a fresh determination with reference to English authority would have had to be made when, after a lapse of years, the identical issue was again presented. What there was of native jurisprudence, whether by naturalization or by invention, rested upon oral tradition—it was, in other words, a memory jurisprudence.[57] The comments of early reporters and the sprinkling of

---

[57] On this see the comments in the preface to volume I of Caines' New- *York Term Reports of Cases . . . in the Supreme Court of that State*

cases where judges, like their medieval predecessors, would in their opinions recall the determinations of a colonial court establish the point.[58] In respect to forms of process there were surer guides than judicial recollection, for this was matter preserved by clerks of court, and in some jurisdictions lawyers had compiled manuscript "precedent" books of provincial variants.[59] Nevertheless, post-Revolutionary courts were sometimes obliged to confirm a local course of practice no matter how ancient.[60]

(1804) on the absence of reports: "The determinations of the court have been with difficulty extended beyond the circle of those immediately concerned in the suits in which they were pronounced; points adjudged have been often forgotten, and instances might be adduced where those solemnly established, have, even by the bench, been treated as new. If this can happen to those before whom every subject of debate is necessarily agitated and determined, what must be the state of the lawyer, whose sole information arises from his own practice, or the hearsay of others."

Johnson in his preface to 1 *Reports*, iv, remarking upon the changed status of English reports and the inapplicability of decisions there to cases here, states, "We must look, therefore, to our own courts, for those precedents which have the binding force of authority and law. But how are these decisions to be known? Must they float in the memories of those by whom they are pronounced, and the law, instead of being a fixed and uniform rule of action, be thus subject to perpetual fluctuation and change?"

In the address to the reader, an apologia for undertaking their task, the Maryland reporters Harris and McHenry in the first volume of their *Reports*, iv, remark, "Courts when obliged to rely on tradition or the uncertainty of memory have been often embarrassed between the different assertions of counsel."

[58] *E.g.*, Burrows v. Heysham, 1 Dallas 133 (Phila. C.P. 1785); Baldwin v. O'Brian, Coxe (N.J.) 418 (1789), where counsel recalled a pre-Revolutionary adjudication; State v. Farlee, *ibid.*, 41–42 (1790); Stille v. Wood, *ibid.*, 162 (1793), where the

court recalls practice in New Jersey had consistently followed English statutes on error proceedings; Grymes v. Pendleton, 4 Call (Va.) 130 (1788), where counsel recalls pre-Revolutionary practice on joinder; Birch v. Alexander, 1 Wash. (Va.) 34 (1791), where counsel recalled a determination by the "old General Court," but Pendleton C.J. states that he was misinformed. See also Butler v. Parks, *ibid.*, 76 (1792), and Kennon v. McRoberts and wife, *ibid.*, 96, 108 (1792); White v. Jones, 4 Call (Va.) 253 (1792), where Pendleton refers to decisions in the old General Court and the Court of Appeals never published and so known to few in the profession, perhaps not at all to those practicing in the country. Brisbane v. Lestarjette, 1 Bay (S.C.) 113 (1790), and State v. Blyth, *ibid.*, 166 (1791), where counsel urged earlier unreported precedents; and Eden v. Legare, *ibid.*, 171 (1791), where Rutledge C.J. adverted to earlier holdings; State v. Holly, 2 Bay (S.C.) 262, 266 (1800); State v. Harding, *ibid.*, 267, 268 (1800). Madox v. Hoskins, 2 Haywood (N.C.) 4 (1791); Strudwick v. Shaw, *ibid.*, 5, 10 (1791); Bradford v. Hill, *ibid.*, 22, 23 (1793); Kenedy v. Alexander, *ibid.*, 25 (1794). Palmer v. Horton, 1 Johns. Cases (N.Y.) 27 (1799); LeRoy v. Veeder, *ibid.*, 417, 427 (1798). Avery v. Ray, 1 Mass. 12 (1804); Henshaw v. Blood, *ibid.*, 35, 40 (1804); Hamilton v. Boiden, *ibid.*, 50, 53 (1804); Bangs v. Snow, *ibid.*, 181, 188 (1804).

[59] *LPAH*, I, 43–44. Some of the manuscript precedent books cited in *ibid.*, 44, n. 23, contain forms for both New York and New Jersey.

[60] *E.g.*, Campbell v. Richardson, 1 Dallas 131 (Phila. C.P. 1785); Cecil's

The resources for determining what had here been received being what they were, the fact that the Revolution had converted English law into an alien jurisprudence was of less moment to the immediate future of state law than the intellectual necessity for consultation which habit had ingrained. Although the courts were rarely articulate on the presumptions by which they justified recourse to English case law, what appears in the early reports conveys the impression that the judiciary was embarked upon a course that may be described as a process of republican restatement or reaffirmation of practices and doctrines the vigor of which had derived from the fact of royal sovereignty. The use of English sources depended on the view taken of the reception provisions[61] and might now and again be justified by assertions that the

---

Lessee v. Lebenstone, 2 *ibid.*, 95 (Sup. Ct. 1786); Schooley v. Thorne, Coxe (N.J.) 71, 73 (1791); Dickerson v. Simms, *ibid.*, 199 (1793); Tabb v. Gregory, 4 Call (Va.) 225 (1792); Meredith v. Kent's Ex'r., 1 Martin (N.C.) 17 (1792); Borden v. Nash's Adm'r., *ibid.*, 34 (1796); Daniel v. Cobb's Ex'r., *ibid.*, 80 (1797).

[61] In Pennsylvania McKean C.J., who appears to have dominated his court, early took the view that the Pennsylvania Act of 1777 (*supra*, n. 53) was one for the revival of the laws in a state of suspense since May 14, 1776, and that the effect was simply to bring to an end any "virtue or validity" derived from enactment under the royal authority (Respublica v. Chapman, 1 Dallas 53, 58 [1781]). The assembly enjoined observance of common law theretofore in force, but McKean used English case law regardless of this qualification. In New York we have the testimony of James Kent, written in 1786 shortly after his admission to the bar, that the courts proceeded selectively under art. 35 of the state constitution (quoted in *LPAH*, I, 50, n. 50). In what is reported of Virginia cases the judicial attitude seems to have approximated that in New York. Pendleton, C.J. of the Court of Appeals, was not the liberal citer that McKean was although he could hold his own, as in Thornton v. Smith, 1 Wash. 81 (1792), where the words "not local" in the Ordinance of 1776 were interpreted to knock out a variety of

precedents proffered. His penchant for recalling earlier Virginia cases has been noticed. However, in Kennon v. McRoberts and wife, *ibid.*, 96, 108 (1792), English precedent was preferred over an earlier General Court determination. The elaborately reported Commonwealth v. Posey, 4 Call 109 (1787), indicates the disposition of all the judges of the Court of Appeals to cleave to English case law. The most ingenuous explanation is offered by Mercer J. (at 119), "our ancestors brought the doctrine in Powlters Case [11 Coke Rep. 29] with them into this country."

In North Carolina there is little reported prior to 1790, but thereafter it appears that the judicial attitude is similar to that in Virginia. Although, as noticed above, there was a disposition to follow such native precedent as could be recalled, the reliance on English case law is striking even when it was plausibly argued that a rule was inapplicable to the local situation; see Quinton v. Courtney, 2 Haywood 40 (1794); State v. Long, *ibid.*, 154 (1795), where the court was divided. In Clark v. Kenan and Hill, *ibid.*, 308 (1796), the court refused to follow a Mansfield precedent after showing of earlier rejections by North Carolina judges, although two years before it had in State v. Webb, *ibid.*, 103, preferred a common law rule over any inferences to be drawn from an old act of assembly.

In South Carolina the wholesale common law reception act of 1712

rule had been received or that the case had been brought hither "by our ancestors." Where constitution or statute adverted to the common law, the currency of the Mansfield-Blackstone theory[62] that the cases were evidence of what the common law was explains why in some jurisdictions it was thought proper even to cite post-Revolutionary English precedents.[63]

---

had founded a tradition of using English case law, and was presumably affirmed by art. 29 of the constitution of 1776 and art. 34 of the 1778 constitution except as altered by the resolves of the South Carolina "Congress." Bay J., in the preface to volume I of his *Reports* (1809), comments that many of his cases may be similar to those in English reports "(and which continue to be of authoritative influence in our courts,) yet they derive a confirmatory, and more indisputable weight, when they are known to have received the decided and concurrent sanction of our courts of judicature. . . ."

The adjudications in New Jersey disclose a reliance upon English precedents no less resolute than in South Carolina, although it should be noticed that the editor of Coxe, the first reporter, made a variety of anachronistic interpretations. Note, however, the remarks of Kinsey C.J., in Mason v. Evans, Coxe 182, 188 (1793): "I do not (as Wilmot says in the case before cited) stir a pebble of the common law, neither have I the slightest wish to do it, because I look on it as the best and surest foundation of our rights and property."

[62] Blackstone, *Commentaries*, I, 69; Mansfield in Jones v. Randall, 1 Cowp. 37 (1774). For some discussion of the application of this theory in Virginia, see Goebel, "The Common Law and the Constitution," in *Chief Justice John Marshall, a Reappraisal*, W. M. Jones, ed., 108–12.

[63] See, for example, Morris v. Tarin, 1 Dallas 147 (Phila. C.P. 1785), where it was argued that a post-Revolutionary English case was not law, but it was held otherwise. The citation by counsel of such cases in the Supreme Court of Pennsylvania was consistent, without being checked by

the bench, and the court itself on occasion referred to these. On one occasion, in Steinmetz v. Currie, *ibid.*, 270 (1788), McKean C.J. ruled that a case from 1 Term Reports was law here because it was upon general mercantile law. Earlier, on a question of new trial, this report was referred to without such explanation, Steinmetz v. Currie, *ibid.*, 234. The Supreme Court of New Jersey had no doubts about using post-Revolutionary cases; see Stille v. Wood, Coxe 162 (1793); Mason v. Evans, *ibid.*, 182 (1793); and Waldron v. Hopper, *ibid.*, 339 (1795), where a case (5 Term Rep. 648) is spoken of as conclusive.

In New York the posture of the courts was ambivalent; see Hamilton v. Holcomb, Coleman 61 (1799), where a late English case was held to be conclusive. In the same year Lansing C.J., in Johnson v. Bloodgood, 1 Johns. Cases 51, 62, raised the question of whether "on sound legal reasoning" the construction assumed by English courts against the common law principle be adopted. He took the test of "the whole course of English adjudications." The great amount of New York litigation over marine insurance post-1793 and the obvious utility of recent English case law did much to induce tolerance. Nevertheless, the propriety of referring to it was occasionally raised; see the opinion of Livingston J. in Bogert v. Hildreth, 1 Caines Rep. 1, 3 (1803), and in Hildreth v. Ellice, *ibid.*, 192, 196 (1803).

Neither in Virginia nor Maryland was there hesitation in relying upon post-Revolutionary cases. For the former, see Shelton *et al.* Ex'rs. v. Shelton, 1 Wash. 53 (1791); Thornton v. Smith, *ibid.*, 81 (1792); Kennon v. McRoberts and wife, *ibid.*, 96 (1792); Taylor's Admx. v. Peyton's Admx.,

The consistent use of English common law precedents by state courts by no means imported abandonment of the well-tried test of their applicability to American conditions. This was a criterion flexible enough to include the question of constitutional conformity, and it is not improbable that in some decisions the test of applicability may have masked a determination on constitutionality. If the early reporters had seen fit to deal adequately and consistently with arguments of counsel, one might arrive at some estimate of how frequently and in what guise the question of the constitutional repugnancy of a common law rule was brought to the attention of a court. The ferreting out of such issues lay with counsel, and upon them rested the burden of persuading courts normally content to follow what was embalmed in their books. Rules so consecrated were regarded, as a New York judge put it, as "so many landmarks from which it would be dangerous to depart, except we have other guides equally safe and obvious."[64] This is why when a court declined to follow an English common law rule—sometimes categorically and sometimes with the explanation that it was unsuited to American conditions—it is impossible, lacking indications of what was proffered, to settle if a constitutional point was at issue, however much one may suspect it. Scarce a handful of cases from the generation following independence has been found where the constitutionality of a common law rule is reported to have been raised;[65] in

---

ibid., 252 (1794). For Maryland, see Calvert's Lessee v. Eden, 2 Harris & McHenry 279 (1789); Webster v. Stevenson's Ex'rs., 3 *ibid.*, 131 (1793); Martindale's Lessee v. Troop, *ibid.*, 244 (1793). The most extensive arguments of the problem that we have found occurred in North Carolina; see Hamilton v. Dent, 2 Haywood 116 (1794); Den ex dem. Young v. Erwin, *ibid.*, 323 (1796).

[64] Per Radcliff J., in Johnson v. Hart, 3 Johns. Cases 322, 326 (Ct. of Errors 1803).

[65] In Lessee of Allston v. Saunders, 1 Bay 26 (1786), counsel argued that the *nullum tempus* "principle" was not part of the common law adopted by the constitution of South Carolina. The court declined giving an opinion on the point. In neighboring North Carolina in an undated case, Smith v. Smith's Ex'rs., 1 Martin 14, but which occurred before 1790 as Iredell was of counsel, on the question when a statute came into operation, the English common law rule was put forward

that Acts of Parliament took effect from the first day of the session. Opposing counsel "relied on the words and spirit of the Constitution" and claimed an act came into effect when signed by the Speaker of the Assembly. The court affirmed the common law rule. A question of constitutionality later arose in Dalgleish v. Grandy, Cameron & Norwood 22 (1800), on error from a county court to the Superior Court and reserved for the Court of Conference. The action had begun with a warrant of distress issued by a landlord against his tenant to satisfy arrears of rent. Goods had been distrained. Defendant pleaded *nil debit*, payment, set-off, tender, release on satisfaction. Plaintiff had a verdict. On motion in arrest it was claimed that the verdict was contrary to the state bill of rights, the constitution and the law of the land. Assignment of error was presumed to be identical. It was held that there was no usage amounting to an adoption of the laws of England, nor was there

one of the most noted, *People v. Croswell*, it was only because one of participating counsel published the arguments that the fact of challenge emerges, for the reporter of the case fails to mention it—no doubt

---

adoption of an English statute. If this mode of procedure was ever sanctioned by pre-Revolutionary usage, "it is utterly irreconcilable to the spirit of our free republican government" (at 24).

The Virginia reports of cases decided before the revision of the laws was complete have yielded one instance, Commonwealth v. Ronald, 4 Call 97 (1786), where, on a rule to show cause why an attachment for contempt should not issue because the Chief Justice of the General Court had been served with process from a county court, the attorney involved relied upon the Virginia bill of rights which provided that no person should be entitled to privileges but in consideration of services. The court, however, instead of interpreting the obscure passage or otherwise disposing of its relevance, held that the privilege was one at common law which Virginia had adopted.

The peculiar circumstances in State v. Farlee (1790), a habeas corpus proceeding to bring up the body of a negro, induced the Supreme Court of New Jersey to refuse to apply the constitutional provision which "confirmed" trial by jury. Counsel claimed a right of property was involved and that the constitution guaranteed jury trial in such cases. The court asserted that the cause was one of personal liberty. The writ was one of right designed to protect the individual from arbitrary or illegal detention—"we are to decide upon it in our constitutional capacity, sitting here to superintend the liberty of the citizen" (Coxe 41–42). There was no constitutional provision of such tenor.

Subsequently counsel obtained a rule to show cause why a writ of error presented should not be allowed or appeal granted to the governor and council. The basis of counsel's claim was that it was a matter of constitutional right that no party could be deprived of a revision of a judgment or proceeding which affected his property. There was, however, no provision of the constitution to this effect. Opposing counsel claimed error would not lie in the case as it was not matter of record. The court dodged the constitutional question, remarking that the court which issued the writ must judge of the competency of the writ.

The defects in the New Jersey constitution which counsel sought to supply by unsupported inference are further illustrated by Den ex dem. Chews v. Sparks, Coxe 56 (1791). Chew had conveyed all his estate to his children in July 1776 with intent to preserve it from forfeiture should British arms prevail. He was then attached to the rebel cause. Later he joined the enemy, was convicted of treason and his property confiscated. Defendant claimed as purchaser from the commissioners of forfeited estates. Chew's children brought ejectment, relying on the father's conveyance. The jury found for the latter. On motion for a new trial it was urged that this conveyance was fraudulent against the King had he succeeded and precedents were cited. The court, having no convenient constitutional provision upon which to rely, repelled the proposition as improper to be considered by a court which derived its authority and its existence from the "principles" of the Revolution.

Barring People v. Croswell (*infra*, n. 66), the one case which indicates a rejection of common law rule is Palmer v. Horton, 1 Johns. Cases 27 (1799), where the court asserted that it had frequently been decided in the New York Supreme Court that forfeiture under the Confiscation Act of 1779 (*N.Y. Laws*, 3 Sess. 1779, c. 25) did not forfeit a widow's dower. Unlike statutes of this order in some states, the New York act besides a mere legislative attainder of named persons set up a machinery for indictment in the Supreme Court, Courts of Oyer and Terminer and Courts of General Sessions, not restrained by

because the judges did not deal with the point.[66] Even had there then been a rubric "constitutional law" in the abridgments, none of these cases would have been there arrayed as advancing doctrine. Their significance is limited to the fact that the bar and the courts were prepared to subject the common law, hitherto the repository and index of constitutional right, to the test of a law more fundamental.

THE COURTS AND THE REPUGNANCY OF OLD STATUTES

THE PRE-REVOLUTIONARY English statutes adverted to in the several reception provisions posed problems of a different order from those relating to the common law. All of the colonies had been at liberty to rummage at will in the stores of the latter, but Acts of Parliament had been on a different footing. There had been English judicial precedent only on the point that acts not naming the plantations did not extend to them. However, unless the question of extension was in issue, provincial courts had not hesitated to have recourse to any acts if these were regarded to be salutary. Beyond this, a further criterion concerning which there developed a consensus on this side of the Atlantic, was the proposition that pre-settlement statutes where applicable were in force—a projection of Holt's dictum that an Englishman going to countries newly found out carries his law with him. This view had had the occasional support of royal administrators although on occasion the Privy Council sitting judicially rejected the view as to particular statutes.[67]

What the dimensions of statutory reception had been in any jurisdiction remains to this day a matter of conjecture. It was no less so after independence. One consideration that could not but have weighed with lawyers and courts was the fact that pre-Stuart statutes had become so inextricably entangled in the general body of the law that to have denied their relevance to American conditions would have excluded a respectable amount of judicial precedent. The state of mind respecting such enactments is exemplified in the dictum of Wilmot C.J.,

---

the locus of the crime of treason, notice by publication and judgment of treason upon non-appearance. The common law rule was that a wife forfeited dower upon husband's attainder for treason. Consequently it seems to us probable that the New York courts had found constitutional grounds, viz., statutory infraction of art. 41 re jury trial, to save dower.

[66] Discussed at large in *LPAH*, I,

775 *et seq.* The constitutional question was raised in pre-trial maneuvers, *ibid.*, 787, and again by Van Ness in the argument for a new trial, *ibid.*, 797–98. The opinions of the evenly divided court are in 3 Johns. Cases 342.

[67] Discussion in J. Smith, *Appeals to the Privy Council from the American Plantations*, 26.

often quoted, to the effect that the common law was nothing else but statutes worn out by time[68]—a saying that would make easy the stomaching of any ancient enactment. So many of such were swallowed either as possessed of statutory force[69] or as "precedents"[70] or as having become the common law of a jurisdiction[71] that one is justified in attributing to the courts the formulation of a presumption that these were in fact parcel of pre-Revolutionary law. It was rare that inquiry was made into the validity of this presumption,[72] although there were occasions when a court would declare *ex cathedra* that an act had never been in force in the jurisdiction[73]—a simpler way of disposal than struggling with an issue of constitutional repugnancy. In an era when the tablets of memory substituted for written muniments, dicta of this sort were hardly to be challenged.

LEGISLATIVE REVISIONS AND THE OLD STATUTES

ONE FURTHER point regarding English statutes deserves comment because in view of the passions aroused post-1763 over Parliament

---

[68] Collins v. Blantern, 2 Wils. K.B. 341, 348 (1767). The quotation appears in a note to Runnington's edition of Hale, *History of the Common Law* (1779), 67. Hale himself, p. 66, intimates the same idea.

[69] See Morris's Lessee v. Vanderen, 1 Dallas 64, 67 (1782), re St. 32 Hen. VIII, c. 2; State v. Higgins, 1 Martin (N.C.) 59 (1792), an indictment based on 21 Hen. VIII, c. 7; State v. Grove, *ibid.*, 36 (1794), where held that 2 & 3 Ph. & M., c. 10, was in force as not repealed; Moore's Lessee v. Pearce, 2 Harris & McHenry (Md.) 236, 241 (1788), re 7 Geo. II, c. 20.

[70] See the opinion of Henry J. in Commonwealth v. Posey, 4 Call (Va.) 109, 115 (1787); Den ex dem. Hinchman v. Clark and Zilcar, Coxe (N.J.) 340, 356 (1795).

[71] Which practice in colonial New York with respect particularly to riot and bastardy clearly indicates. Goebel and Naughton, *Law Enforcement in Colonial New York*, 14, 101, 122; see Commonwealth v. Leach, 1 Mass. 59 (1804) re St. 1 Edw. III, c. 16, and 34 Edw. III, c. 1, per Dana C.J.: "Generally when an *English statute* has been made in amendment of the common law of *England*, it is *here* to

be considered part of *our* common law. . . . Usage of the country establishes and makes the common law of the country."

[72] Respublica v. Mesca, 1 Dallas 73 (1783), where testimony was taken re actual use of St. 28 Edw. III, c. 13. Apparently in Calvert's Lessee v. Eden, 2 Harris & McHenry (Md.) 279 (1789) proofs were adduced regarding actual adjudications on extension of statutes, because such are included in the specific findings of the special verdict (pp. 284, 290). In State v. Mairs, Coxe (N.J.) 335 (1795), it was submitted that the extension of an English statute prior to the Revolution must be proved, but the court declined to give an opinion.

[73] *Supra*, n. 61. See also Jackson ex dem. Trowbridge v. Dunsbagh, 1 Johns. Cases (N.Y.) 91 (1799), and Weaver v. Lawrence, 1 Dallas 156 (Phila. C.P. 1785). In the former case the Statute of Enrolments was said not to extend because of reference to the courts at Westminster; in the latter the same conclusion was reached regarding replevins under the Statute of Marlborough because of institutional differences.

legislating for the colonies it seems to involve a more fundamental question than the possible repugnancy of a statute here once put to use. This concerns the propriety of suffering acts of an alien Parliament to serve as law in the new sovereignties. Allowing even for the prevailing consensus that in time of revolution it was desirable to maintain the private law in a state of stability, it is remarkable that this question does not appear to have been seriously debated either in the courts or by most of the legislatures. Even in Virginia where the revision of the law was undertaken by the General Assembly when the fires of revolution were bright, the constitutional problem was not in the fore but republican and democratic principles and eradication of the vicious parts of regal government.[74] The revision involved preparation of substitutes for English statutes and the final bill (No. 126) provided that all pre-settlement Acts of Parliament "except such as shall be by this General Assembly enacted in express words to be in force" were repealed and declared void and "never had any force."[75] Whether or not this doom was based on the "style" of the acts or on more fundamental grounds of constitutionality does not appear. This bill was never enacted. When a new committee was appointed in 1790, a compilation of desirable acts or portions of acts theretofore in force was made, and a final statute ending the force and effect of Acts of Parliament with certain savings was the capstone of the new structure of laws. This action was based not on constitutional grounds but on the fact that "the good people of this commonwealth may be ensnared by an ignorance of acts of parliament which have never been published in any collection of the laws."[76]

In Massachusetts a committee to revise the laws was commissioned shortly upon adoption of the constitution. It was directed among other things to make them consistent with the constitution and put them in form "intelligible to the common people."[77] The direction was broad enough to have included the rooting out of English statutes, but over the years that the commission was in existence there was no explicit repeal of such, although among the enactments of the Massachusetts General Court, as their legislature was styled, there are some statutes

---

[74] Jefferson's *Autobiography*, in *Works of Jefferson* (Ford, Federal ed.), I, 57, 65.

[75] *Papers of Jefferson*, II, 656.

[76] 1 *Collection of Acts of the General Assembly of Virginia* (1803), cxlvii, 291.

[77] *Mass. Acts and Resolves 1780–81* (reprint), Oct. Sess. 1780, c. 98,

dated Nov. 30, 1780. Appointed were James Bowdoin, William Cushing, Nathaniel P. Sergeant, David Sewall, Robert Treat Paine, James Sullivan and John Pickering. There were subsequent resolves: May Sess. 1781, c. 53, to consider specific laws; Jan. Sess. 1781, c. 338, providing quarters, and c. 516, on allowances.

during the period of the revision, like that on forcible entries, identifiable as re-enactments or simplifications of earlier English models. Massachusetts was presumably that "one of the Eastern States" where the revisal, as Jefferson wrote to Madison in April 1784, was mangled by the legislature so that consistency was lost and the project reportedly abandoned.[78] Actually, far from there having been mangling, there had been inaction by the legislature, as James Bowdoin reported on June 5, 1784.[79] It would appear that the committee's work ground to a stop. If there had been an intention to consign English statutes to oblivion, this did not happen, for when the printed reports begin, these are referred to as still possessing vigor.[80]

In New York where a revision was set afoot in 1786, this was confined by the legislature to those English statutes and colony acts which, as the constitution declared, were part of the law April 19, 1775. These, it was recited, were scattered in many volumes and were "conceived in a stile and language improper to appear in the statute books" of the state. Accordingly, Samuel Jones and Richard Varick were commissioned to collect and reduce into proper form these enactments and to submit bills to the legislature.[81] Once these had been enacted by the legislature, none of the statutes of England or Great Britain should operate or be considered laws of the state. Whether or not the commissioners considered the question of constitutionality of some of the pre-Revolutionary law is not known. In any event, a succession of bills was fed to the legislature over the succeeding two years, and a great many English statutes passed through the purification process of state re-enactment. In 1788 the legislature formally ended the dominion of Acts of Parliament.[82]

---

[78] *Papers of Jefferson*, VII, 118. New Hampshire did not appoint revisors until June 12, 1784 (5 *Laws of New Hampshire*, 16).

[79] Bowdoin's report in response to an order of the General Court is in Mass. Archives, Ms. Senate Files, No. 167. Bowdoin states that more than fifty bills consolidating three times that number had been laid before the legislature. A further number prepared by individual committeemen had not been considered by the committee itself. These by special order of the House had been delivered to a member of a house committee and been tabled. "The greatest number of the bills which have been laid before the General Court, have not (as the Com^tee are informed) been yet taken into consideration by that Court."

[80] *E.g.*, Commonwealth v. Leach, 1 Mass. 59 (1804); Pitts v. Hale, 3 Mass. 321, 322 (1807). Finding list of citations of English Statutes in the Massachusetts reports is in C. W. Harris, *Massachusetts Statutory Citations* (Boston: Little, Brown and Company, 1894).

[81] *N.Y. Laws*, 9 Sess. 1786, c. 35.

[82] *N.Y. Laws*, 11 Sess. 1788, c. 46. For New Jersey, which in 1792 took the New York action as a model, see E. G. Brown, *British Statutes in American Law 1776–1836* (Ann Arbor: University of Michigan Law School, 1964), 76–82.

The New York act for the revision of the laws was from its tenor designed to dispose of the constitutional incongruity that laws that had been made in the name of the King should be enforced in the name of the People of the state of New York. Since the commissioners' working papers cannot be found, it is impossible to settle whether or not any Acts of Parliament once used were rejected by them because of repugnancy to particular provisions in the constitution. In any event, once the Acts of Parliament were declared to be of no force and effect, the courts were thereafter relieved of the task of determining which of these had been in effect and if they had been abrogated by the constitution.

In the margin is indicated the later action of New Jersey, North Carolina, Pennsylvania and Maryland to clarify the status of Acts of Parliament. In all four states the motive appears to have been to settle what acts were theoretically applicable or had in fact been used.[83]

THE COURTS AND REPUGNANT COLONIAL ACTS

UNLIKE THE ACTS of Parliament, colonial acts of assembly did not embody in their style of enactment the monarchic and aristocratic taint, for, as noticed, the concurrence of the Crown was signified col-

---

[83] For North Carolina, see 1 F. X. Martin, *A Collection of the Statutes of the Parliament in England in force in the State of North Carolina* (1792). The resolve of the General Assembly had directed retention of statutes which might affect titles to realty.

In Pennsylvania the legislative resolve of 1807 referred the problem to the judges of the Supreme Court. The resolve and the report in 3 Binney 593 *et seq.* The judges made clear that they viewed their task as one of making specific what had been laid down in the reception act of 1777. Accordingly, they excluded from the appended list of statutes all Acts of Parliament related to the prerogative, for they conceived such to be repugnant irrespective of any question of *de facto* extension to the colony.

In Maryland an inquiry launched in 1794 came to nothing. Then, in 1810, the question of pre-Revolutionary statutes—those applicable and those which had been used—was referred to the Chancellor and judges of the Court of Appeals. Chancellor William Kilty appears to have done the work single-handed. His report, published in 1811, was based upon research of the records. He relied also upon an earlier listing of Justice Samuel Chase supplied to Judge Matthew Tilghman. The report was divided into those English statutes not applicable, those applicable "but not proper to be incorporated," and those applicable and proper to be incorporated. Nowhere does Kilty make plain the sense in which "proper" is used; apparently it did not embrace the matter of constitutionality. In the case of a very few statutes, he states that these are not necessary under the Maryland Constitution to be incorporated. W. Kilty, *Report of all such English statutes as existed at the time of first emigration of the people of Maryland . . .* (1811).

laterally.[84] One might suppose that the Revolution would have made royal action constitutionally irrelevant, yet as late as 1793 the Virginia Court of Appeals took the view that proof of royal confirmation was essential to the validity of a colonial act.[85] In New Jersey a statute reviving all private acts expressly excluded those disallowed by the Crown,[86] but in New York, possibly because information on a disallowance was unavailable, this was regarded as immaterial.[87] Where, as in Massachusetts Bay, the habit had prevailed of passing acts of short duration as a means of frustrating royal action, the state legislature by reviving or extending temporary colonial laws bypassed the question of royal action.[88] Relief from royal controls was further manifested by the enactment of recently disallowed acts—a course which itself indicates the intellectual difficulty of discarding former constitutional standards.

The work of eradicating colonial acts regarded as repugnant was shared by legislatures and the courts. The evidence of judicial action is meagre, and before reports in any number became available, revisions, either wholesale or piecemeal, in the jurisdictions covered had already wrought great changes in the statutory structure. It is further to be observed that in the reported cases where colonial acts of assembly were considered, these related usually to matters of procedure or substantive private law not of a sort to invite inquiry into constitutional repugnancy. Furthermore, because such acts were native handiwork the courts appear to have been predisposed to accord them greater respect than might otherwise have been their due. An extreme example of over-tenderness toward a colonial act may be found in the defense by the Pennsylvania Supreme Court of judicial attainder and order for execution provided by the outlawry procedure of a 1718 act. One Doan outlawed for robbery had been so attainted. The Executive Council, vested with power of pardon by the constitution, addressed a series of questions to the judges of the Supreme Court that raised among other things the issue whether or not dispensing with a jury trial was against the letter and spirit of the constitution.[89] The court in its defense of the statute failed to come to grips with the meaning of the guarantees both in the declaration of rights and the frame of government but elected

---

[84] *Supra*, c. II, p. 66.

[85] Daniel v. Robinson's Ex'r., 4 Call 570.

[86] *Acts of the General Assembly . . . of New Jersey*, 3d Sess., 1st sitting, c. 3 (Nov. 26, 1778).

[87] *LPAH*, I, 115, n. 128.

[88] 5 *Acts and Resolves Prov. of Mass. Bay*, May Sess. 1778, c. 17 (p. 903); Nov. Sess. 1779, c. 18 (p. 1120).

[89] Respublica v. Doan, 1 Dallas 86, 87 (1784). The inquiry was signed by the President, John Dickinson, himself a lawyer of parts.

to stand on the English precedents sustaining the barbaric incidents of the medieval outlawry.[90] Although the issue was *sub judice* only in a manner of speaking, the opinion became a precedent.[91]

In contrast to the Pennsylvania court's evasion of the constitutional question was the action of the Supreme Court in neighboring New Jersey only two years earlier. Here, too, the jury trial provision of the constitution was in issue, but the supervening authority of the fundamental law was sustained. Involved was a 1778 statute designed to control traffic in and out of enemy lines.[92] Among other things, it provided for seizure of persons and goods, vested powers of adjudication in justices of the peace and, with explicit reference to a colonial act of 1775, allowed a six-man jury on demand of either party, and cut off all right of appeal.[93] In 1779 a seizure made under the new act was brought before a Monmouth County justice for adjudication and tried with a six-man jury. While the suit was pending, defendants secured from the Supreme Court a writ of certiorari to remove the cause. Prior to removal a verdict was reached, so that the certiorari operated as a writ to review. The case was ordered argued at the November term 1779. The chief ground offered for reversal was that the jury consisted of six men when by the "Laws of the Land it should have consisted of twelve men." This was later sharpened to a claim that the six-man jury was "contrary to the constitution of New Jersey." The court held the cause under advisement until September 7, 1780, when the judgment below was reversed. No trace of the opinion remains, but from petitions to the Assembly and the proceedings upon a new trial of the cause it appears that the reversal was grounded upon the unconstitutionality of the six-man jury.[94]

It should be observed that the six-man jury in small causes was a New Jersey statutory institution of more than thirty years' standing. The New Jersey constitution had provided that all the laws of the province contained in Allinson's edition of the laws (1776) except such "as are incompatible with this charter" remain in effect until altered by the legislature.[95] As to the jury, the constitution said no more than that "the inestimable right of trial by jury shall remain confirmed as

---

[90] The proceedings of the Council, *ibid.*, 93, indicate that the procedure of the colonial act had not been observed.

[91] According to a note by the reporter Dallas, *ibid.*, 86.

[92] *Acts of the General Assembly . . . of New Jersey*, 2d Sess., 4th sitting, c. 45 (Oct. 8, 1778).

[93] Allinson, *Acts of the General Assembly . . . of New Jersey* (1776), 468.

[94] The details are set out with reference to the records in Austin Scott, "Holmes v. Walton: The New Jersey Precedent," 456–69.

[95] Art. 21; see Thorpe, *Constitutions and Charters*, V, 2598. On the six-man jury see *supra*, c. I, p. 34.

a part of the law of this Colony, without repeal, forever."[96] English text writers were dogmatic that a jury of twelve was *de rigueur*, and furthermore, there was some English case law to the effect that local customs to try causes by six men were void.[97] It is plausible that the court acted on the basis of these authorities.

If the New Jersey constitution gave warrant to the court to strike down a colonial act, this was not the case under the South Carolina constitution of 1790, for the vaguely worded provisions of the two earlier instruments regarding constitutional conformity were not carried forward into it. In 1792 when a title was set up under an act of 1712 which had transferred the freehold of a tract of land from the heir at law to another, the Court of Common Pleas held, as counsel had argued, that the act was against common right as well as against Magna Carta and therefore *ipso facto* void.[98] The court's approach to the issue was in the ancient tradition of employing basic tenets of the common law as a test of constitutionality, an approach confirmed by a later adjudication in another cause.[99] But for the failure to advert to authority, the decision might be regarded as an application of a passage in Blackstone[100] to the effect that a private act against reason was void—a dictum in *Lord Cromwell's Case* (1578)[101] misrepresented as a holding.

JUDICIAL REVIEW OF NEW LEGISLATION

WE COME AT length to the early examples of judicial review of state legislation that embrace all discoverable instances where the courts assumed and exercised authority to test the validity of such statutes against a constitutional standard or one believed to be equally compulsive. The expression "judicial review" cannot, of course, be confined to those cases where there was an actual declaration of nullity, for as will

---

[96] Art. 22; see Thorpe, *Constitutions and Charters*, V, 2598.

[97] Coke, *Littleton*, 155; Blackstone, *Commentaries*, III, 365; and more importantly, because it was the breviary of the bar, Bacon, *Abridgment*, III, *s.v.* Juries A, where the cases re six-man juries are assembled. Mr. Scott suggests that the provisions of the "West Jersey Concessions and Agreements" and the 1699 "Declaration of Rights and Privileges" regarding a twelve-man jury may have been invoked ("Holmes v. Walton: The New Jersey Precedent," 459). This seems unlikely in view of the more

recent and long-term legislative authorization of a six-man jury.

[98] Bowman v. Middleton, 1 Bay 252.

[99] Lindsay et al. v. Commissioners, 2 Bay 38, 57 (1796), where the approach was used to sustain a power of eminent domain.

[100] Blackstone, *Commentaries*, II, 346.

[101] 4 Coke Rep. 12. In Spotswood v. Pendleton, 4 Call (Va.) 514 (1801), counsel argued that a colony private act was contrary to the principles of justice and Magna Carta and so "void by English law." The court held otherwise.

shortly be noticed, the application of long-established common law rules of interpretation enabled the courts to defeat legislative purpose as effectively as a blunt holding that an act was unconstitutional. The effect upon uninformed opinion was the same. For the *de facto* primacy of of state legislatures was so far advanced that any judicial rebuff of their expressed will had the appearance of a challenge to the established political order. What is here of record is meagre, particularly for the period before 1788. This is a significant date because, as we shall later observe, debate over the propriety of judicial review became national in scope, and consequently to the degree that the legal profession was influenced by these discussions, the issue of constitutionality may have been more readily raised.

These early cases together with those where a common law rule or pre-Revolutionary enactments were rejected for constitutional repugnancy are interesting mainly as exemplifications of the manner in which the principle of constitutional supremacy, originally a mere matter of political theory in America, became a rule of judicial action. The effect upon the law at large of the adjudications on state statutes was not, however, as widespread as might be assumed from the attentions of modern scholars. For, despite the publicity given such cases in the newspapers, accounts of only two useful to the legal profession had been published prior to the final ratification of the United States Constitution. The significance of the early cases as precedents, we believe, was local and depended upon the degree that the bar in a particular jurisdiction was acquainted with the litigation and its issue and may thus have believed a principle of judicial action to have been settled. The prospective effect of a judicial determination of constitutionality where nothing was reported depended thus upon survival by word-of-mouth tradition whereby, as noticed, matter peculiar to a state's jurisprudence was kept animate.

A persuasive instance of this may be found in the aftereffects in Virginia of *Commonwealth v. Caton*, decided in 1782 but not reported until 1827 from surviving memoranda, which included the notes of Pendleton C.J., a source here followed.[102] The case concerned a pardon to certain convicted traitors granted by the House of Delegates alone, although the Treason Act of 1776[103] had provided for pardons by the

---

[102] 4 Call 5. In the "Reporter's Preface," dated May 1, 1827, Daniel Call states that the materials for the volume had been collected over a period of years and that the notes and memoranda of judges and lawyers as well as the records had been consulted. It is clear that he consulted the notes of Pendleton C.J. (Force Transcripts, 8695–8716 [LC]), but there are variants in the reported version. Call's account of the opinion of Wythe C. is obviously based on another and unknown source.

[103] 9 Hening, *Va. Stats.*, 168.

General Assembly. An ambiguously worded provision in the constitution[104] gave color to the action of the House of Delegates. The matter came before the General Court when upon motion of Attorney General Edmund Randolph that a rule be made for the prisoners' execution, the pardon was proffered. The General Court adjourned the matter for novelty and difficulty to the Court of Appeals.[105] The latter tribunal was composed of the judges of Admiralty, General Court and Chancery, many of whom were to serve for years to come. Besides the Attorney General and counsel for the plaintiffs, various members of the bar at the request of the court argued the issues: first, did the General Court have power to adjourn a capital case into the Court of Appeals for difficulty; second, could a court of law declare a law void for repugnancy to the "Act for the Constitution of government"; third, was the Treason Act contrary to the constitutional provision?[106] The majority of the court answered the first two questions affirmatively. The Treason Act the majority held to be constitutional.

The issue as to the power of the courts had been presented not in the general terms of power to determine the constitutionality of the statute, but on the narrower ground—could courts declare a statute void? This was by no means a distinction without a difference, because the belief had taken hold at the time of the Stamp Act that an unconstitutional act need not be executed. It would require no more than a judicial declaration of constitutional repugnancy to activate such an anarchic result. During the war this notion had received support in a pamphlet of Lord Abingdon, *Thoughts on the Letter of Edmund Burke to the Sheriffs of Bristol on Affairs in America* (1777), wherein among other things it was preached that when laws were subversive of the constitution "disobedience instead of obedience is due." This opus was so esteemed in America that it had been reprinted within a year of its appearance in England.

Six of the eight judges met the issue head on. Five decided explicitly or by inference that the Court of Appeals had the power to declare a law void for unconstitutionality. Lyons J. denied this to be the case;[107] Dandridge J. "declined the question."[108] John Blair, who was to become a Justice of the United States Supreme Court, "waved the question."[109] As reported by Call, the most positive, indeed eloquent, assertion of the power was made by Chancellor Wythe.[110] According to Pendleton, Wythe "offered reasons of the nature of those used by Lord

---

[104] Thorpe, *Constitutions and Charters*, VII, 3816–17.
[105] For a dramatic account of the proceedings, D. J. Mays, *Edmund Pendleton, 1721–1803, A Biography*, II, c. XI.

[106] Force Transcripts, 8696–97 (LC).
[107] *Ibid.*, 8714.
[108] *Ibid.*, 8715.
[109] *Ibid.*
[110] 4 Call 7–13.

Abington" to prove that an anti-constitutional act of the legislature would be void.[111] Chief Judge Pendleton said only that the question of avoiding a statute was deep, important and awful, from which "I will not shrink if ever it shall become my duty to decide it."[112] In the instant case there was no need.

In dealing with the obscure and ambiguous sentence structure of the pardon provision of the constitution, both Wythe and Pendleton found occasion to put to use the intimate knowledge of the proceedings of the Convention which six of the judges had attended.[113] But in the main, both judges in their exigeses sought to solve the matter of meaning by resort to grammar and to familiar rules of statutory interpretation. Pendleton denied that any help could be had from Britain, pointing out that Lord Coke had both asserted the omnipotence of Parliament and had exalted the judiciary "above them giving courts power of declaring Acts of Parliament void."[114] Nevertheless, Pendleton did have recourse to the old English canons of statutory construction, viz., construing one part of a statute by reference to another, putting a construction on a statute that would best answer the intention of the makers and observing the distinction between affirmative and negative statutes.

The resort to the accepted rules of statutory interpretation to settle the intent and meaning of constitutional provisions was, as we shall see, a method used by courts elsewhere in the Confederation. This must be accounted an important stage in the evolution of the technique of dealing with constitutional questions. It was undoubtedly an approach that commended itself to the Virginia court because this state, unlike some sister states, had no explicit safeguards against legislation repugnant to the constitution. There was, indeed, no exploration of theory even on the issue of the power to void a statute.[115]

Theory was, however, to be advanced some years later in a judicial uprising against a legislative attempt to reconstitute the system of courts. This occurred not as a result of a litigated issue, but on the motion of

---

[111] Force Transcripts, 8716 (LC).

[112] *Ibid.*

[113] 4 Call 10–11. Wythe had had a hand in settling impeachment procedure (*Papers of Jefferson*, I, 365 n. 5), and we believe his relation of the pardon provisions to this is reflected in the printed opinion. That Pendleton also was relying upon his acquaintance with the doings in convention is indicated by his reference to the rejection of Jefferson's pitiless proposal that there be no pardon of criminals (*ibid.*, 360 and 365, n. 4) and to the consensus of the convention regard-

ing what should be done in respect of restraining executive prerogative (Force Transcripts, 8709–11 [LC]).

[114] Force Transcripts, 8706 (LC).

[115] It would seem that sometime before 1788 the General Court held an act of 1778 to be unconstitutional. St. George Tucker in his edition of Blackstone's *Commentaries* (1803), vol. I, note C at 126, makes an obscurely worded statement to this effect. The act was repealed in January 1788 as contrary to the spirit of the constitution (12 Hening, *Va. Stats.*, 507).

the Court of Appeals itself.[116] The statute, enacted in January 1788, imposed common law duties on the bench of both Chancery and Admiralty and loaded new tasks upon the judges of the Court of Appeals without additional compensation. The Court of Appeals conceived this to be an assault upon the independence of the judiciary implicit in the constitutional provisions for separation of powers, of tenure and of salary. At the April (1788) meeting the court declined putting into execution a power of appointing clerks and prepared a *Remonstrance* which was read from the bench and later delivered to the Governor for submission to the legislature. The *Remonstrance* declared that "the constitution and act are in opposition and cannot exist together; and that the former must control the operation of the latter."[117] Forestalling any claim that in championing the independence of the judiciary the court was countenancing encroachments upon the legislative, it was emphasized that when the judges "decide between an act of the people, and an act of the legislature, they are within the line of their duty, declaring what the law is, and not making a new law."[118]

This candid justification of authority to put statutes to a constitutional test was an important accretion to the law of Virginia.[119] Because the *Remonstrance* was published on the eve of the convention convened to ratify the new federal Constitution, with a special session of the General Assembly called for July to deal with the *Remonstrance*, the provenance of the document was to lend it greater political immediacy than the discussions in press and pamphlet then circulating.[120]

It subtracts nothing from the significance of the *Remonstrance* to suggest that the manner in which the Court of Appeals justified its authority may have owed something to an incident which occurred in connection with a recent North Carolina litigation involving the constitutionality of a statute.[121] This act (1785),[122] a belated thrust at the loyalists, sought to protect purchasers from the commissioners of forfeited estates from liability to answer in any suits or actions by persons specified or described in the earlier confiscation acts or persons claiming under them. The courts were directed to dismiss such actions on motion of defendants.

---

[116] 4 Call 135.
[117] *Ibid.*, 142.
[118] *Ibid.*, 146.
[119] Kamper v. Hawkins, 1 Va. Cases 20 (1793).
[120] See the speech of Pendleton in Elliot, *Debates*, III, 299, and of Patrick Henry, *ibid.*, 324–25.
[121] Den ex dem. Bayard and wife v. Singleton, 1 Martin 42 (1787).
[122] *Public Acts of the General As-* *sembly of North Carolina* (Martin ed., 1804), I, 396. Although Martin stated in his preface that when any part of Iredell's revisal (1791), which he reprinted, "has appeared improper to be retained" its omission or legislative alteration would be noted, yet he does not indicate that the act had been declared unconstitutional—and this despite the fact that he had reported the case.

In 1786 an action of ejectment was brought by one Bayard and wife whose title derived from a British subject once domiciled in the state who had shipped for England in 1775. He had returned in 1777 to remove his family and had executed a deed to his daughter, one of the plaintiffs. As a confiscation bill was pending in the legislature, the deed was dated eight days before it was actually executed. Defendant Singleton claimed title under a deed from the Superintendent Commissioner of Confiscated Estates. Of counsel for plaintiffs was James Iredell, future Supreme Court Justice; for defendants, Alfred Moore, who was to succeed him.

At the May term 1786 of the Superior Court counsel for defendants moved for dismissal of the action pursuant to the provision of the 1785 act. This precipitated "long arguments from the counsel on each side on constitutional points." The court made some comments on the separation of powers and took time to advise. The motion was not resumed until May term 1787. In the interval there appeared on August 17, 1786, in a Newbern newspaper an address, prepared by Iredell and signed "An Elector," assailing the theory of legislative supremacy and asserting the subjection of the assembly to the constitution and the right of the judicial to interfere where acts repugnant thereto had been passed and to declare them void.[123] The terms in which judicial action is justified—"they being judges for the benefit of the whole people, not mere servants of the Assembly"—so closely parallels that used in the Virginia judges' *Remonstrance* as to suggest this piece may have been known to them.

There was further debate on the motion, and the court, failing to persuade the parties to stipulate for a jury trial, proceeded with explicit reference to the judicial oath to hold the act unconstitutional and dismissed the motion. The ground of the ruling was the fact that the disabilities of plaintiffs' grantor were personal and could not be transmitted, and that by the constitution every citizen was entitled to have property rights decided by a jury.[124]

Den ex dem. Bayard v. Singleton was not published until 1796. Nevertheless, its effects in North Carolina were not delayed by this. For, in 1788, the Superior Court refused to give effect to a statute which directed judgment without notice against delinquent receivers of public moneys, apparently because of unconstitutionality.[125] There was a flat

---

[123] G. McRee, *Life and Correspondence of James Iredell* (1857–58) II, 145, 148 (hereafter cited as McRee, *Iredell*).

[124] The case was then tried by jury which found for the defendant. The resolution of the court on the con-

stitutional point upset Richard Dobbs Spaight, then attending the Federal Convention. For the exchange of views with Iredell, see *ibid.*, 168–70, 172–76.

[125] Related by Attorney General Haywood in State v. ——, 2 Haywood 28, 36–37 (1794).

holding to this effect on a 1793 revision of the law[126] by Williams J. who had participated in the decision in *Bayard v. Singleton*. He grounded his opinion on the "law of the land" provision of the Declaration of Rights which he understood to require compliance with common law standards.[127] The Attorney General was permitted to renew his motion, and his argument is worth noticing because he developed the theme with reference to English precedents that the "law of the land" chapter of Magna Carta adopted by North Carolina meant no more than any law adopted by the legislature—an exemplification of what has here been pointed out, that law of the land and due process were not identical.[128] Williams J. remained unconvinced. Later at a court held by two other judges the motion was granted.

The courts of Virginia and North Carolina resolved at least for their own jurisdictions the uncertainties regarding the locus of authority to deal with legislative invasions of their constitutions. The immediate effects of this may not have extended much beyond the confines of the local bar, but during the early decades of the Republic the progress of the law can be charted only in terms of its progress in the several states. Although in neither jurisdiction was there an explicit pronouncement that a statute was void, this can take nothing away from the fact that the power of judicial review, and on the explicit grounds of constitutional conformity, was asserted. Other jurisdictions resorted to the time-honored artifices of statutory construction to arrive at the conclusion that the legislature could not have intended the result which the language of an act imported.[129] This method, too, was an exercise of judicial review, but it was an antiquated approach and added nothing to the distinctively American enlargement of the judicial function then emerging.

The most noted of the cases of this genre is the New York case,

---

[126] 2 *Public Acts of the General Assembly of North Carolina* (Martin ed., 1804), 39–41, sec. 10.

[127] State v. ——, 2 Haywood 28 (1794).

[128] *Ibid.*, 30–40. The argument shows no trace of the arguments advanced during the struggle over ratifying the federal Constitution.

[129] *E.g.*, Ham. v. M'Claws and wife, 1 Bay (S.C.) 93 (1789), where the court adopted the comment in Dr. Bonham's Case that statutes against common right and common reason were void, but it did not follow this through with a declaration of nullity. Instead, by resort to the passage in Blackstone's tenth rule of statutory interpretation, it declared that such a result could not have been intended by the legislature and so refused to give effect to the letter of the act. See also Howell v. Wolfert, 2 Dallas 75 (Phila. C.P. 1790); Den ex dem. Hinchman v. Clark and Zilcar, Coxe (N.J.) 340, 360 (1795). Turner v. Turner's Ex'r., 4 Call (Va.) 234 (1792), is a borderline example. The court stated, regarding a 1787 act to explain a colonial act of 1758, that the legislature having made the law "have no authority afterwards to explain its operation upon things already done under it," and proceeded to interpret the law to avoid violation of the constitution.

Rutgers v. Waddington.[130] It was noted in its day because the court's opinion, forthwith published, made considerable stir. It has remained a species of landmark because it is the earliest reported case where the restraints upon a state legislature implicit in the national constitution, such as it then was, were brought in issue.

This was a statutory action of trespass brought in the Mayor's Court of New York City by Mrs. Rutgers, patriot owner of property in that city, against a British merchant who had occupied and used the premises while the British army was in possession of Manhattan. The statute,[131] one of several measures directed at loyalists, was enacted just before news of the provisional articles of peace had arrived. The act had not been objected to by the Council of Revision. Designed for the relief of those patriots who had fled occupied territory, the trespass action was given against persons who had occupied, injured or destroyed the estates real or personal within the power of the enemy or who had purchased or received goods. The statutory actions were peculiar in that they were declared to be transitory, that if brought in inferior courts they should there be finally determined, and defendants were barred from pleading in justification any military order or from giving the same in evidence on the general issue.

The occupation of Mrs. Rutgers' premises had originally been authorized (1778) by the Commissary General, civilian employee of the British Treasury. In 1780 and for three years thereafter the occupation had been under license of the Commander-in-Chief and rent had been paid during the term. Under the letter of the statute these licenses were of no avail. Unaccountably the proviso respecting military orders was omitted from plaintiff's declaration.[132] This enabled the defense, which pleaded the general issue as to the force and injury, to confess occupation, but to justify this on two grounds.[133] For the period authorized by the Commissary General it was averred that the latter had authority from the Commander-in-Chief of the army according to the law of war. For the period where occupation was by direct license of the Commander-in-Chief the law of nations was again pleaded. A second ground

---

[130] An account of the case and the documents including pleadings, briefs and the opinion of Duane J. are set out in *LPAH*, I, 289–419. The identification and publication of the briefs make this now the most fully documented of the early cases involving constitutional issues.

[131] *N.Y. Laws*, 6 Sess. 1783, c. 31.

[132] Counsel for plaintiff were John Lawrence, late Judge Advocate General of the Continental Army, Egbert Benson, Attorney General of New York, Robert Troup and William Willcocks.

[133] The plea was prepared by Alexander Hamilton. Co-counsel were Brockholst Livingston, later Justice of the United States Supreme Court, and Morgan Lewis, later Chief Justice of the New York Supreme Court.

advanced was the treaty of peace which was alleged to have operated as a mutual release of injuries arising out of the conflict.

In replication plaintiff made good the earlier omission to plead the proviso against justification, for against defendant's plea of the law of nations the statutory proviso was pleaded. To the plea of the treaty of peace, plaintiff demurred. Defendant demurred to the replication. The issue of law was thus clearly defined: could the statutory proviso avail against the law of nations and against the treaty?

The course of pleading has been sketched because it is an early and revealing example of how a constitutional issue could be raised. This issue was not entirely manifest until the demurrers were argued. Certainly counsel for plaintiff did not immediately apprehend it, for it would appear that their challenge was initially to the relevance of the law of nations because its content was vague, because in any event it could apply only in the case of a formal war, which the Revolution was not, and never in the case of an unjust war, which the Revolution was. The incident in question did not relate to war—the only circumstance under which the law of nations could apply. It was denied that the law of nations was a part of the common law, and even if it were, it was no more binding upon the legislature than the common law itself. As for the treaty, neither it nor the resolve of Congress signifying its approval nor the resolve enjoining observance would be effective in New York. Congress had no power to interfere with the internal law of the state. Were such a power construed to have been granted by implication, such a delegation would have been unlawfully made by the legislature. The Articles of Confederation had received only legislative ratification and could therefore be amended or repealed as any other act of the legislature. In that body was seated the supreme law-making authority in the state, subject only to the people, and the courts as agents of the state owed a primary and single duty to the laws of the state.[134]

For defendant, Alexander Hamilton began with an extended analysis of the law of nations and, in particular, the laws of war to establish their relevance, which plaintiff had denied. The affirmative part of the case and one which concerns us was the construction of the constitutional obligation violated by the Trespass Act. The sovereignty of New York derived from a federal act, the Declaration of Independence, in which the United States asserted their power to levy war, conclude peace and contract alliances. This declaration was a fundamental constitution

---

[134] No original papers relating to arguments for plaintiff appear to have survived. They are deduced from statements in the court's opinion and from Hamilton's notes and briefs where specific points are traversed.

of every state and the union established by it was adopted as a fundamental law in the New York constitution. The constitutional powers were not controllable by any state. True, the Articles of Confederation were an abridgment of the original compact, but the full and exclusive powers of war, peace and treaty were left to Congress.

The New York constitution had adopted the common law and the law of nations was a part thereof. Insofar as the direction of foreign relations pertained to the United States, they had become parties to the law of nations and no state singly had either the right or power to violate this law. Since defendant occupied the premises under authority of the British army, he derived the right of the captors sanctioned by the laws of war. To subject him to liability would involve a violation of the law of nations. So far as the treaty was concerned, which did not contain an express amnesty, counsel argued with considerable ingenuity the rules of international law which supported an amnesty by implication. The Trespass Act he conceived to be a breach of the treaty and so a violation of Congress's constitutional authority and so a breach of the Confederation. While the Confederation existed, any law in derogation of its authority was no law. The New York legislature might not alter the law of nations—this would be unconstitutional, for Congress had exclusive direction of all matters relating thereto.

Plaintiff's point that the judges were bound by the law of the state was countered by the proposition that since the Confederation had no judicial authority except in prize causes, the judges of each state must of necessity be judges of the United States. They must take notice of the law of Congress as part of the law of the land. Although obliged by the law of the state as to its own citizens, they must judge foreigners according to the law which alone the constitution knew as regulating their concerns. The argument concluded with a marshalling of precedents on the interpretation of statutes, including *Lord Cromwell's Case* and *Dr. Bonham's Case*, with the intent that if the act was not held void, at least the section relating to justification could be held not to be within the intent of the legislature.[135]

The judgment in the cause preceded the opinion by ten days. It was held that as to the period of initial occupation of the premises, defendant's plea was insufficient. As to the second period (under license of the Commander-in-Chief), the plea was good and sufficient in law. The effect of this was, of course, to negative *pro tanto* the proviso of the

---

[135] This summary is taken from Hamilton's Brief No. 6. Some of the points were already hit upon in the earlier briefs drawn as preliminary outlines. The brief used at the trial was turned over to Mayor Duane. Brief No. 6 seems to have been prepared for error proceedings, but for reasons indicated in *LPAH*, I, 332–34, it would appear that No. 6 was essentially identical with that used at the trial.

This is what is called the right of
Eminent domain.

Elements of Jurisprudence
p 62
vol. B 3 /12 §76
Para: 3

In theory one nation has no right to alter the general
law of nations.

Rules of Construction of Statutes

Coke Rep. P. 13 a
dito Pay 118 a & b

A statute against law and reason especially if
a private statute is void.

10 Mod 245 Bacon
Title Statute 648

Statutes are to be construed by the rules of the common law

Comm. Title Maxims Letter
. Pa. 351 & 1
Rep. 71 .
Raymond 7 Coke Littleton 49
. X: 659 . . . .

And if against the general policy of the common law
are to be qualified ~~expect~~ and controled by it

Reports Lib 4 pa 71 a
Bacon Title Statutes pa 514
27. 30. 31
Idem 524   pa 1.9
Idem 527   pa 125
Idem 528   pa 154 &156
Powers 1 pa 455 -

Especially if the provisions are general in which case
construction may be made against the Letter of the
statute to render it agreeable to natural justice.

mod Vol 10.7 §2
4 Bs C 12 pa 61

Many things within the letter of a statute are not within
its equity and vice versa.

Laws giving remedy where there was none before are to
be construed strictly.

Bacon Title Statute
pa 653. N.º 92

No Statute shall be construed so as to be Inconvenient
or against reason

Alexander Hamilton's Brief No. 4, page 5, for *Rutgers v. Waddington*.
(*Hamilton Papers, Library of Congress*)

statute. The opinion,[136] rationalizing the judgment and delivered by Mayor Duane, leaned heavily at critical junctures upon traditional canons of interpretations. Commencing with the proposition that the Trespass Act was a remedial statute, the court summarized the rules of construction upon which each party relied and arrived at the conclusion that remedial laws were to be expounded to have their full force in advancement of the remedy, upon an equitable interpretation, according to the intention of the legislature, to be sought after by a sound legal discretion. So viewed, the statute *prima facie* applied to defendant. Certainly the license from the Commissary General was repugnant to orders from the Commander-in-Chief and could not avail defendant for it was a mere nullity. The license from the Commander-in-Chief, if it depended abstractly "on the voice of reason," had no relation to the war. There were, however, other considerations.

The court here entered into a lengthy discourse on the law of nations. This had been adopted by the New York constitution as law of the land for it was part of the common law. Applying the law of nations, the court, repudiating plaintiff's contentions, decided that the war was of such a nature and the capture of New York such a conquest as to transfer right to rents to the British Commander-in-Chief. The rights of the latter could only be communicated by his immediate authority. Defendant could not derive any rights from the Commissary General. Consequently, where the tenancy was authorized directly by the Commander-in-Chief, the injury related to the war and was defensible. As for the treaty, the court adopted defendant's view that no state could alter either the Confederation or the treaty; the latter, however, could give defendant no benefit additional to that which the law of nations gave him.

On the final and crucial point, whether or not the court was obligated to follow the statute where it clearly militated against the law of nations, it was stated that the supremacy of the legislature need not be called in question. Where it saw fit "*positively*" to enact a law, no power could control it. When the main objective was clearly expressed, the judges were not at liberty to reject it even if it appeared unreasonable. But when a law was expressed in general words and some collateral matter arising therefrom was unreasonable, the judges in decency should conclude that the consequences were unforeseen, and therefore would be at liberty to expound the statute by equity and only *quoad hoc* to disregard it—a paraphrase of a passage in Blackstone's tenth rule of statutory construction. This was the case with the Trespass Act, and the

---

[136] *Ibid.*, 393 *et seq.* The portion quoting the Trespass Act and describ- ing the pleadings is there omitted.

court detailed the reasons why repeal or interference with the law of nations could not have been in contemplation.

Although Duane had carefully denied an intention to control an act of the legislature, he had in effect held nugatory the most noxious provision of the statute. The state of feeling toward the loyalists was such that the opinion produced violent reaction. The New York Assembly passed an indignant resolve at its next sitting[137] and an unsuccessful attempt to remove Duane and Recorder Varick followed. Angry citizens, which included some plaintiffs in pending Trespass Act cases, published a lengthy diatribe in a city newspaper inveighing against the notion of judicial control of legislation.[138]

Legislative repercussion in New York was trifling compared to the Rhode Island Assembly's angry reaction to the judgment of the Superior Court in *Trevett v. Weeden*. This was the second case dealing with judicial review published during the period before the flood of discussion on the subject precipitated by the submission of the federal Constitution. The account of the case,[139] chiefly devoted to the argument of defendant's counsel, is the only exhibit emanating from the New England states, for the Massachusetts case about which John Brown Cutting wrote Jefferson[140] has not been certainly identified.[141]

The Rhode Island case arose under a statute of August 1786, designed to implement earlier legislation[142] which had given a radical twist to the paper money policy on which the state had embarked. The enforcing act[143] was aimed at persons who refused to accept bills tendered in payment for articles offered for sale. A drastic procedure by

---

[137] Set out in *ibid.*, 312. The decision was apparently viewed as an example "dispensing" with a statute, an adversion to a royal prerogative cut off by the English Bill of Rights, 1 Wm. & M. sess. 2, c. 2.

[138] *The New-York Packet. And the American Advertiser*, Nov. 4, 1784. It was said, *inter alia*, "That there should be a power vested in courts of judicature, whereby they might controul the supreme Legislative power we think is absurd in itself. Such power in courts would be destructive of liberty, and remove all security of property." One of the signers was Melancton Smith who was to be Hamilton's most articulate adversary at the Poughkeepsie convention in 1788. *Infra*, c. IX, p. 397.

[139] James M. Varnum, *The Case,*

Trevett against Weeden . . . Tried before the Honourable Superior Court in the County of Newport, September Term, 1786. Also The Case of the Judges of said Court . . . (hereafter cited as *The Case, Trevett v. Weeden*). On Varnum, *DAB*, sub nom.; W. Updike, *Memoirs of the Rhode-Island Bar*, 145.

[140] In connection with the *Remonstrance* of the Virginia Court of Appeals, July 11, 1788, see *Papers of Jefferson*, XIII, 337.

[141] A. Goodell, "An Early Constitutional Case in Massachusetts," *Harv. L. Rev.*, 7:415-24, 1894.

[142] *Rhode Island Acts and Resolves* (facsimile ed.), June Sess. 1786, 8.

[143] *The Case, Trevett v. Weeden*, 58. See also *Rhode Island Acts and Resolves*, Aug. Sess. 1786, 5.

information without jury and without appeal was instituted. Complaints were to be brought before any judge of the Superior Court or either of the judges of the Superior Courts of Common Pleas within the county where the offense was committed. The judges were directed to draw up the informations and to convene a special court for trial. Defendants faced heavy fines, immediate performance of judgment or jailing until paid. In the hard money centers there was immediate protest that the act was unconstitutional.[144] The test came in September 1786 when Trevett tendered bills to Weeden, a butcher, in payment of meat offered in open market. Weeden refused them. Trevett then made complaint to the Chief Justice of the Superior Court. The latter convened a special court but as the complaint was made in term time the information was referred to the term for consideration.

The defendant's "answer"[145] was one of those curious New England mutants, essentially a discursive plea to the jurisdiction. It alleged that the act had expired; that complaints under the act were cognizable by special courts, uncontrolled by the Superior Court; that the court was not authorized to empanel a jury and so the act "was unconstitutional and void." This plea is interesting for it was in the colonial tradition of raising constitutional questions by questioning jurisdiction. One of the judges later referred to the averment that the act was unconstitutional as mere surplusage, but James M. Varnum, who with Henry Marchant appeared for defendant, dwelt at length upon this point and neither the prosecution nor the court objected.

The account of this case, argued September 25, was prepared after the event by Varnum and may well embody some afterthoughts. Only the argument for defendant is given and only the judgment of the court. The Attorney General prosecuted, but beyond a newspaper account that he stated that Rhode Island had no bill of rights, nothing more is known of what he had to offer.[146] The plea, undoubtedly drafted by Varnum, appears to us to have set up two grounds of constitutional repugnancy, for the claim that the act created special courts uncontrollable by the Superior Court was argued as an infraction of what amounted to a constitutional establishment. The other ground, deprivation of jury trial, was explicitly treated as unconstitutional. In certain respects Varnum faced a problem similar to that which confronted Hamilton in *Rutgers v. Waddington*—to establish a fundamental law to which the act was repugnant. The colonial view was that in the jurisdictions possessed of

---

[144] William Ellery to the Commissioners of the Treasury, Aug. 29, 1786, Ms. Loan Office Letter Book and Customs House Letter Book (Newport Hist. Soc.).

[145] *The Case, Trevett v. Weeden,* 2–3.

[146] "A Newport Letter," Sept. 26, 1786, in *The Providence Gazette; and Country Journal,* Sept. 30, 1786.

a charter this served as a constitution setting the frame of government and embodying certain limitations. When Rhode Island had elected to continue under its charter from Charles II, doing no more than changing the "style" of its "government" from colony to state,[147] it might be supposed that these limitations had been accepted; yet the legislature had thereafter proceeded as if the instrument imposed no restraints upon it. As an essential preliminary to an appeal to the bench to exercise control over legislation, Varnum laid down the premise that in all free governments there were three distinct sources of power: the legislative, the judicial and the executive.[148] By "our original constitution," the charter, authority had been specifically granted to erect courts without particularizing what these should be. But Varnum claimed that an act of 1729, never altered and on which the judicial system rested, had become a matter of common right.[149] Since the Superior Court was vested with the powers of the three central courts of England and since it possessed the supervisory powers of King's Bench, the subtraction of appellate authority by the legislature deprived the people of their right of access to the locus of ultimate pronouncements on the law.[150] It may be remarked that Rhode Island's record with respect to keeping open avenues of appeal or review gave point to this claim.

The silence of the charter on jury trial Varnum repaired by reference to the charter clause confirming all the liberties of Englishmen and to the accepted view that the settlers had in any event carried these rights with them. Varnum conceived that jury trial was one of such rights, confirmed by Magna Carta. Deft were the references to the invocation of this constitutional right against British acts prior to the Revolution. All of this was preparation for the allocution regarding the judges' duty under the constitution that came toward the end of the argument. Here the bounds of legislative power were described and the proper function of the judicial in respect to enactments—"the Legislative have the incontroulable power of making laws not repugnant to the constitution: The Judiciary have the sole power of judging those laws, and are bound to execute them; but cannot admit any act of the Legislative as law, which is against the constitution."[151] The judges were bound to support "fundamental, constitutional laws" by their oath of office and the oath

---

[147] *Rhode Island Acts and Resolves*, July Sess. 1776, 127. The change was made July 18, 1776, by enactment after the Declaration of Independence was approved.

[148] The argument on the temporary nature of the act is here omitted.

[149] Varnum's claim that the establishment had never been varied was misleading. The original act had provided for two Superior Courts (*Acts and Laws of . . . Rhode Island* [1730], 191). By act of 1746 a single Superior Court was provided (*Acts and Laws* [1752], 27). Certain minor amendments were later made (*Acts and Laws* [1767], 49).

[150] *The Case, Trevett v. Weeden*, 9.

[151] *Ibid.*, 27.

of allegiance to the state.[152] With a certain lack of candor Varnum quoted Blackstone's tenth rule only as to what was said regarding collateral consequences arising out of Acts of Parliament contradictory to common reason that render such acts void *pro tanto*. Nothing was said about Blackstone's opinion that he knew of no power that could control an unreasonable act, and his comment that there could be no evasion of a statute where parliamentary intent was couched in evident and express words. Instead Varnum quoted from Bacon's *Abridgment* the words of Coke in *Dr. Bonham's Case* to clinch his argument. Henry Marchant did not argue because he thought Varnum's defense was complete.[153]

The record shows that it was adjudged "that the said Complaint does not come under the Cognizance of the Justices here present, and that the same be and it is hereby dismissed."[154] According to a newspaper account, the court then adjourned until the next morning when explanation of the judgment was made *ore tenus*.[155] Howell J. stated that he was independent as a judge, that the law was repugnant and unconstitutional and therefore the court could not take cognizance of the information. Devol J. concurred. Tillinghast J. took notice of the striking repugnancy of the expressions in the act, "without trial by jury, according to the laws of the land," and for this reason gave judgment. Hazard J. merely voted against taking cognizance, and Mumford C.J. announced the judgment without giving his opinion.

The legislature, which convened a few days later, was indignant. In the week succeeding the trial a summons issued from both houses requiring immediate attendance of the judges "to render their reasons for adjudging an act of the General Assembly unconstitutional, and so void."[156] Three judges attended; the two others were unwell and were excused but were directed to appear at the next October session. What the judges had to say is in certain particulars an amplification of what was reported in the press. Howell J. harangued the assembly for six hours. He opened by stating that the court as "legal counsellors of the State" was ready to assist in framing new or repealing old laws. "But that for the reasons of their judgment upon any question judicially before them, they were accountable only to God and their own consciences."[157] He pointed out the objectionable parts of the act, demon-

---

[152] *Ibid.*, 28.

[153] *The Providence Gazette; and Country Journal*, Oct. 7, 1786; see also Ellery to the Commissioners of the Treasury, Sept. 28, 1786, Ms. Loan Office Letter Book and Customs House Letter Book (Newport Hist. Soc.).

[154] Entered in the legislative proceedings, *Rhode Island Acts and Resolves*, Oct. 2d Sess. 1786, 5–6.

[155] *The Providence Gazette; and Country Journal*, Oct. 7, 1786.

[156] *The Case, Trevett v. Weeden*, 37 (the Case of the Judges).

[157] *Ibid.*, 38.

strating by argument and authority that it was unconstitutional. Varnum indicates that the judge followed mainly what had been argued in court. As to the legislative summons, Howell took the technical and proper position that although the plea had mentioned that the act of the assembly was unconstitutional and so void, the judgment had been only in terms denying that the court had jurisdiction. Whatever might have been the opinion of the judges, "they spoke by their records which admitted of no addition or diminution."[158]

Howell entered at large into the matter of judicial independence of the legislative and the importance of maintaining the integrity of the judicial function. Neither Tillinghast J. nor Hazard J. had anything substantial to add. The assembly voted that it was not satisfied with the reasons given. A motion was then made to dismiss the judges from office. Before a vote was taken, the judges presented a memorial requesting a hearing before some proper and legal tribunal and an opportunity of answering certain and specific charges.[159] Varnum appeared as counsel and directed his argument chiefly to the impropriety, indeed unlawfulness, of the legislature sitting as a court where no criminality was charged, or in the event of impeachment, of the assembly acting as a court. The Attorney General, called upon for an opinion, spoke strongly to the effect that "their determination was comformable to the principles of constitutional law." There was some further debate in the house and ultimately the judges were discharged from further attendance as they "are not charged with Criminality in rendering Judgment" on the information.[160] At the next election in May 1787 all the judges were turned out except Mumford C.J. who had maintained astute silence.

Considered in relation to the task which fell to the courts of settling what the law of a state had been and the range of discretion explicit or implicit in their warrants of authority, it seems nearly inevitable that the power to expound statutes would be manipulated to encompass constitutional repugnancy. The precedents for judicial interpretation of legislative intent were many of them old and well pedigreed and so much a part of the accepted common law technique of adjudication as to minimize political objection. This last was a consideration of such delicacy that courts were reluctant to come directly to grips with issues of constitutionality The one area where they seemed free to act boldly was the protection of the guarantee of jury trial. Here judicial distaste for invasions of common law due process could be indulged because of popular sensitivity regarding any tampering with the "inestimable" right of jury trial. Even so, there was no immunity from criticism and not all of it came from offended legislatures.

---

[158] *Ibid.*, 39.
[159] For the text, *ibid.*, 44–46.

[160] *Rhode Island Acts and Resolves,* Oct. 2d Sess. 1786, 6.

Resentment over the exercise of a power of judicial review was perhaps in some degree induced by the fact that courts were moving into ground as yet untrodden in America, but a deeper-lying cause was the fact that events, in particular the inexorable tide of democracy, had blunted the edges of certain pronouncements of principle in the constitutions, e.g., the separation of powers and the even more fundamental precept of the supremacy of the constitution. Such provisions had been embodied without foresight as to the effects of the inflation of legislative authority, although the object lesson of Parliament was fresh in everyone's mind. It very soon became evident that theoretical limitations had as a practical matter been displaced by the incompatible reality of legislative supremacy. As a result, legislatures assumed the prerogative of themselves judging whether or not they had strayed beyond the bounds fixed in the constitution, but the occasions of open admission that they had acted "contrary to the spirit of the constitution" were very rare indeed. In all the states the drift was toward subversion of the original design of limited constitutional government and its replacement by the unrestraint of English parliamentary hegemony. In the climate thus created, even the most candid and eloquent assertion of judicial duty was not effective to still charges of usurpation.

It cannot be claimed that the occasions where, either directly or by the artifices of common law methods of adjudications, the courts ventured to vindicate constitutional purpose had more than a remote effect upon the then-current trend. What was established, however, was that issues of constitutionality might be raised in litigation, and that courts in discharge of their duty to administer justice must take cognizance of such and adjudicate them. The discussions in the Federal Convention indicate something of the advance of these ideas. The polemics of the months succeeding submission of the Constitution were further to promote them.

CHAPTER IV

The Continental Congress and National Judicial Authority

THE FACT THAT each of the newly independent states assumed as its right the whole power of judicature, and exercised in its courts an authority more plenary than had been permitted it as a dependency, served to prolong the territorialism which had hitherto prevailed and the consequent insulation of remedial justice. With law administration thus partitioned and localized, the areas of conflict where the supervening authority of the Crown had been exercised were left, as it were, in a state of nature awaiting some form of compact. This was neither easily formulated nor brought to quick conclusion. For in every jurisdiction the long-standing sense of corporate identity and self-sufficiency was often enough to blunt dedication to the "common cause," and to affect profoundly the nature of what participants in the prosecution of the war were prepared to yield to a centralized management and eventually to the government of common concerns. The circumstances under which the colonies had been severally founded and the royal policy of treating each as a discrete jurisdictional entity were basic operative causes of separatism. This afflicted the relations of the colonies *inter se* —the contests over boundaries,[1] the circumscription of process that created difficulties with extradition,[2] confinement of the credit of judgments to the jurisdiction where rendered[3] and the restraints put upon

---

[1] For an account of these and the literature relating to them, J. Smith, *Appeals to the Privy Council from the American Plantations*, c. VII.

[2] Goebel and Naughton, *Law Enforcement in Colonial New York*, 287–98.

[3] The difficulties here derived from the lack of English precedent on the enforcement of foreign judgments, the

several provinces being as to each other foreign jurisdictions. The earliest available reference was Wier's Case (1607), H. Rolle, *Abridgment*, I, 530, pl. 12, where King's Bench on habeas corpus had held that by the law of nations the justice of one nation should be aiding to the justice of another. This was the position taken by that colonial favorite E. Vattel, *Droit*

use of colony armed forces.[4] These causes of friction were little affected by the spirit of brotherhood that fired the association of the revolting colonies in its first stages. As the war dragged on, new irritations developed. The boast in the *Declaration of the Causes and Necessity of*

---

des Gens (1758), Bk. 2, c. 7, secs. 84, 85. The enforcement of foreign judgments, however, presented certain practical difficulties. Not until 1771 did the House of Lords hold in Sinclair v. Fraser that the foreign judgment was to be received as prima facie evidence of the debt but that defendant could impeach the justice or irregularity of it. This case was cited in the Duchess of Kingston's Case, 20 Howell, *State Trials*, 355, 468 (1776), and in Walker v. Witter, 1 Doug. 1 (1778).

The earliest instance we have regarding the American problem is a ms. petition of Ezekiel Fogg to Governor Andros of New York, Nov. 7, 1676, regarding a judgment obtained in Boston (Huntington Library, H.M. 9736). In this jurisdiction, although debt would later lie in the Supreme Court on a judgment from an inferior court, we have seen no instance of debt on a foreign judgment. Merchant practice was to retain local counsel to bring original actions in the jurisdiction where defendant was domiciled; see the various entries in the Gerard G. Beekman Letter Book, P. White, ed., *Beekman Mercantile Papers* (New-York Hist. Soc., 1956), I. Beekman employed William Samuel Johnson in Connecticut (*ibid.*, 172, 208, 236, 239) and Richard Law (*ibid.*, 381). In one instance, having obtained a judgment in Rhode Island against a sea captain, copy of the execution was sent to a Philadelphia correspondent with orders to attach the debtor's vessel or to arrest him (*ibid.*, 233). It would seem from a later letter that an action *de novo* was necessary (*ibid.*, 238).

In this connection should be noticed the colonial legislation for the ease of local creditors without pursuing debtors in other jurisdictions—foreign attachment and procedures against property of absent debtors, *e.g.*, the South Carolina Act of 1691, 2 *South*

Carolina Stats. at Large, 61; the Pennsylvania Act of 1705, 2 *Pennsylvania Stats. at Large*, 231; the Virginia Act of 1744, 5 Hening, *Va. Stats.*, 220; the New York Act of 1751, 3 *Col. Laws N.Y.*, 835; the Massachusetts Act of 1758, 4 *Acts and Resolves Prov. of Mass. Bay*, 168. On royal policy see J. Smith, "Administrative Control of the Courts of the American Plantations," 1210, 1234.

[4] The difficulties were rooted in the royal charters in which provisions for the training and maintenance of military forces were cast in terms of defense of the particular colony. See Maryland (1632), Thorpe, *Constitutions and Charters*, III, 1682; Connecticut (1662), *ibid.*, I, 534; Rhode Island (1663), *ibid.*, VI, 3216; Carolina (1663), *ibid.*, V, 2751; Pennsylvania (1681), *ibid.*, V, 3042. The Massachusetts charter of 1691 (*ibid.*, III, 1884) had a peculiar provision that no person could be compelled to march out of the province without his consent or that of the General Court. On the invocation of charter powers by Rhode Island and Connecticut during King William's War see H. Osgood, *The American Colonies in the Eighteenth Century*, I, 100–05. The preamble to St. 13 Car. II, st. 1, c. 3, recognized a supervening power of the Crown in matters military. The law officers of the Crown conceded ordinary power over militia but insisted on the Crown's authority in time of war (*Docs. Rel. Col. Hist. N.Y.*, IV, 102–08). On the difficulties during Queen Anne's War, Osgood, *American Colonies in the Eighteenth Century*, I, 401–04, 412–13, 442–50. Two expedients were resorted to eventually to avoid the political hazards of embodying the militia—enlistment and impressment. Sample statutes: 3 *Acts and Resolves Prov. of Mass. Bay*, 144 (1744); *ibid.*, 417 (1748); 3 *Col. Laws N.Y.*, 574 (1746); 4 *ibid.*, 60 (1756); *ibid.*, 167 (1757); *ibid.*, 343

Taking up Arms that "our union is perfect" was, even when written, an extravagance; the difficulties of putting truth into it were formidable.[5]

The difficulties stemmed from the fact that although circumstances forced changes in the objectives of the colonies, responsive adjustments in the machinery of combination were impeded by the participants' attachment to their own local concerns. This had come about naturally enough because from the start opposition to British policy had centered in the several jurisdictions and the primary task of the apparatus of resistance had been to secure local political support to make effective the work of protest. The activities of the Committees of Correspondence had the result that far from diminishing the sense of corporate identity of any colony, this was kept very much alive. Consequently, as the colonies moved into a union of sorts, although not yet claiming sovereignty, they dealt with one another as if they were each sovereign. The manner in which the First Continental Congress (1774) was constituted tended to affirm this attitude.[6]

The Congress was an assemblage of delegates from each colony (except Georgia) named in a variety of ways: by local election, by assemblies or by extra-legal agencies. Each group of delegates acted under instructions from what were referred to as their "constituents," the general purpose being to concert a common course of action. What was agreed upon was submitted to the delegates' principals, although certain manifestos like the petition to the King, the letter to the people of Great Britain and that to the inhabitants of the colonies were emitted on the responsibility of Congress itself. The economic sanctions embodied in the Association, the one measure which required implementation, were left to local enforcement.[7]

When Congress reconvened in May 1775, there was no change in the manner of its constitution. Indeed, its character as an international conclave was even more pronounced than when it first met, for the agencies enforcing the Association had in the interim moved far in supplanting the regular colonial governments and so toward full territorial sovereignty.[8] Although hostilities had begun, the delegates' credentials were framed in terms of conciliation[9] and reveal no purpose of committing governmental powers to Congress. But rapid developments in

---

(1759); 5 *Pennsylvania Stats. at Large*, 197 (1755) where the preamble justifies resort to voluntary enlistment, but the Crown disallowed the act, *ibid.*, 201 (1756); 6 Hening, *Va. Stats.*, 544 (1755), *ibid.*, 461 (1755); 7 *ibid.*, 26 (1756). The controversies over lack of or reluctance in cooperation related in D. S. Freeman,

George Washington: A Biography, I and II *passim*.
[5] Text and critical notes, *Papers of Jefferson*, I, 213.
[6] Indicated in the credentials of members, *JCC*, I, 15–24, 30.
[7] Secs. 10, 11, 12 (*ibid.*, 78–79).
[8] E. C. Burnett, *The Continental Congress*, 61 *et seq.*
[9] *JCC*, II, 13–21.

the course of the war forced upon it tasks of management demanding legislative initiative in coping betimes with problems continental in scope. Some of the provincial Revolutionary bodies were still thinking in terms of uniform action while Congress under the stress of events was assuming the lead in formulating measures of united action. The steps taken in June 1775 to create a Continental military establishment[10] and the emission of bills to finance the defense of the colonies[11] were actions of far-reaching implications, possible only because of the general language of most of the delegations' instructions and the terrible urgency of the moment.

The instrumentality used by Congress to record its action was the "resolve," a medium of registering legislative will hitherto most freely employed in the New England colonies, and there, as to subject matter, as legally effective as an act of assembly.[12] This was a quality that owing to the political constitution of Congress could hardly be claimed for its resolves, which more often than not embodied recommendations. These were on no better footing than the precepts of the law of nations to which colonial leaders so often adverted; vigor, as law, depended upon compliance by the jurisdictions affected. So it was with the resolve dealing with captures at sea wherein Congress recommended establishment of provincial prize courts and reserved to itself appellate authority. This assumption of powers of adjudication by Congress and later committed to a quasi-autonomous tribunal was wholly connected with the war.[13] Inquiry into its functioning would be a mere antiquarian exercise but for the fact that the efforts to make the jurisdiction properly effective very shortly revealed the formidable difficulties of exercising judicial authority on the Continental level in an atmosphere of reluctance. In a left-handed sort of way this experience was to affect future dispositions with respect to federal jurisdiction, for a succession of political leaders, later to have a hand in promoting a more perfect union, were directly involved both in the discharge of judicial duties and in vain legislative attempts to strengthen the appellate process. They came thus

---

[10] Beginning June 14 (*JCC*, II, 89–90) through June 23, 1775 (*ibid.*, 104–05) and perpetuating the policy of enlistment noted *supra*, n. 4. Steps to put the militia in a proper state, June 24 (*ibid.*, 106).

[11] June 22, 1775 (*ibid.*, 103). See also E. C. Burnett, ed., *Letters of Members of the Continental Congress*, I, 140 (hereafter cited as *LMCC*).

[12] For an analysis see the preface of A. C. Goodell to 6 *Acts and Resolves Prov. of Mass. Bay*, vii–xi. The purpose of evading the necessity of submitting legislative action to the Crown discussed by Smith, *Appeals to the Privy Council from the American Plantations*, 644–45.

[13] Some account of the jurisdiction is given by J. F. Jameson in an essay misleadingly entitled "The Predecessor of the Supreme Court," in *Essays in the Constitutional History of the United States*, 1–45. J. C. Bancroft Davis with greater caution entitled his examination "Federal Courts Prior to the Adoption of the Constitution," 131 U.S. Rep., Appendix, xix.

to the problem of establishing a national judiciary with a practical understanding of the impediments, and for this reason the working of prize appeals deserves examination.

THE ESTABLISHMENT OF APPELLATE JURISDICTION

IT WAS NOT at the instance of any of the rebel colonies that Congress undertook this enlargement of function but as a result of representations by General Washington, then conducting the siege of Boston. Incidental to these operations the Commander-in-Chief had caused vessels to be equipped to prey on British shipping.[14] Early in October 1775 Washington had inquired of Congress what disposition should be made of prizes.[15] Congress already had before it a memorial from Rhode Island regarding public armed vessels.[16] This and Washington's letter set in train the determinations regarding outfitting a navy. On November 8 Washington again wrote to Congress regarding establishment of courts, and on November 11 he forwarded an act of the rebel legislature of Massachusetts providing for letters of marque and establishing courts for the trial of captures.[17] Although the language of the act does not bear out Washington's view of it, he conceived it to be inapplicable to prizes taken by vessels armed at Continental expense. It was consequently suggested that a court be established by Congress to take cognizance of prizes made by Continental vessels.

Washington's letter of the 8th was read in Congress, November 17, and referred to a committee[18] which reported six days later a resolve approved by Congress, November 25, 1775.[19] The resolve was a patent attempt to reconcile emerging national and colony interests, for although only those persons commissioned by the Continental Congress or its agents would be entitled to cruise for prizes, it was recommended to the colonies that they erect courts or confer jurisdiction upon existing tribunals for the determination of prize captures. It was further recommended that trial in such colony courts be by jury. To avoid conflicts over jurisdiction, "all prosecutions" were to be in the court of the colony where the capture was made. If this took place on the open seas, the court which a captor found most expedient should be the forum.

---

[14] J. C. Fitzpatrick, ed., *The Writings of George Washington*, IV, 6 (hereafter cited as *Washington Writings*).

[15] *Ibid.*, 9 at 11.

[16] *JCC*, III, 274.

[17] *Washington Writings*, IV, 81 (Nov. 11, 1775). The Massachusetts act is in 5 *Acts and Resolves Prov. of Mass. Bay*, 436.

[18] *JCC*, III, 357. The committee consisted of George Wythe, Edward Rutledge, John Adams, William Livingston, Benjamin Franklin, James Wilson and Thomas Johnson. The November 11 letter was read November 20 (*ibid.*, 360).

[19] *Ibid.*, 371–75.

Once brought into port, a capture could not be removed to another jurisdiction. To secure the "common" interest it was provided that in all cases "an appeal shall be allowed to the Congress, or such person or persons as they shall appoint for the trial of appeals." Demand must be made within five days after definitive sentence and such appeal must be lodged with the Secretary of Congress within forty days, the party appealing to give security to prosecute to effect.

Although the resolve established the division of the proceeds of captured property if condemned, nothing beyond the recommendation for jury trials was laid down regarding procedure, admiralty or other, in the colony courts, nor was anything stipulated by what law the prize forum should be governed. Congress was equally silent on the law and procedure to obtain in appeals to itself. There were lawyers in Congress like William Livingston and James Duane who had participated in prize litigation during the French and Indian War.[20] Others had had experience in admiralty procedure on the instance side, and, like John Adams, in trade acts litigation in vice-admiralty.[21] Consequently the failure to proffer detailed advice to the emerging states must be attributed to reluctance to interfere in matters of internal police rather than to lack of informed opinion in Congress. Awareness of English practice was manifested in the measures taken March–April 1776 to regulate privateering.[22] The provisions requiring a Continental commission and the exaction of a bond were patterned, we believe, on Statute 32 George II, c. 25, regulating privateers. The instructions to masters of privateers were similarly drafted with reference to those issued by the Crown.[23] The directions respecting interrogatories and deposit of all relevant ship's papers with the admiralty suggest that Congress anticipated that the old prize procedure would be followed. As for substantive law, no general recommendations were issued, although on December 8, 1775, it was resolved that prizes taken by armed vessels in the service of the colonies and carried into Massachusetts should be

---

[20] C. Hough, ed., *Reports of Cases in the Vice Admiralty of the Province of New York and in the Court of Admiralty of the State of New York, 1715–1788* (1925), 86, 88, 93, 95, 116, 125, 131, 142, 146, 149, 156, 159, 163, 167, 168, 186, 188, 189, 200, 203, 205, 207.

[21] See L. K. Wroth and H. B. Zobel, eds., *Legal Papers of John Adams* (Cambridge, Mass.: The Belknap Press, 1965), II, 68 *et seq.* In his autobiography Adams recounts the

offer of the office of Advocate General in 1768, it being judged that he was the person best qualified (*Adams Papers*, III, 287–88). On the state of knowledge re appeals see the diary entry for Feb. 10, 1772 (*ibid.*, II, 56).

[22] *JCC*, IV, 229 (Mar. 23, 1776), 251 (Apr. 3, 1776); the instructions, at 253.

[23] For text of those issued Nov. 30, 1739, J. F. Jameson, ed., *Privateering and Piracy in the Colonial Period: Illustrative Documents*, 347.

proceeded against by the rules of the law of nations[24]—in the then state of prize literature, a recipe difficult to follow.

If Congress had seen fit to incorporate in the resolve of November 25 some concrete propositions regarding appellate procedure, it is conceivable that some regard would have been paid them by the legislatures of colonies yet to settle where and how prizes were to be adjudicated. As it was, the defects of the November resolve were to haunt the Congress for many a year. Some of these shortcomings may be attributed to the need for a quick answer to an urgent question, some to misguided libertarian fervor and some to the fact that by assuming appellate jurisdiction Congress was aware that it was grasping at a very prickly fruit. It might well have confined its resolves to recommendations that appeals in colony courts be assured or to have claimed jurisdiction over conflicts between colony and Continental interest. What seems probable to us is that with projects for expanding American trade before it,[25] and with some anticipation of infringements of neutral rights such as had come before prize courts in the previous war, a "national" forum was necessary. During the Seven Years' War the Lords Commissioners for Prize Appeals had served as the locus for correcting the often predatory sentences of the colonial courts.[26] Circumstances had left this jurisdiction derelict and it is possible that Congress was intent upon providing a substitute.

In terms of institutional history, central appellate authority passed through three stages. From the time of the first appeal, certified July

---

[24] A letter from Washington of Dec. 4, 1775 (*Washington Writings*, IV, 141) regarding prizes taken raised a question whether a former resolve against confiscation had passed. It was agreed that cargoes should be forfeited, tried in an admiralty court "by the course of the Law of Nations not of the Municipal Law" (Diary, Richard Smith, *LMCC*, I, 275). The *Journals* show no agreement (*JCC*, III, 428). A further letter of December 11 (*Washington Writings*, IV, 156), debated December 19, Smith reported, led to defeat of a motion to seize all ships of Great Britain (*LMCC*, I, 280). But it was resolved that all ships carrying munitions, food, etc., to the British army or navy in the colonies be liable to seizure and the cargoes confiscated (*JCC*, III, 437). On the following day the resolve regarding proceedings by the law of

nations was passed (*ibid.*, 439).

[25] See here the debates as reported by John Adams, *Adams Papers*, II, 188 et seq. (Oct. 4 and 5, 1775); 204–17 (Oct. 12, 13, 20, 21); 219 (Oct. 27). Also printed in *JCC*, III, 476 et seq. Comments by Adams in his letters to Joseph Warren, *LMCC*, I, 218, 236, 239, 243.

[26] Pursuant to St. 29 Geo. II, c. 34. Included in the Commission were all members of the Privy Council, the Chief Baron of the Court of Exchequer, all the justices of King's Bench and Common Pleas, and the Barons of the Exchequer. Any three were to be competent to hear and determine appeals. 4 *APC Col.*, 501. Cases heard on appeal, W. Burrell, *Reports of Cases determined by the High Court of Admiralty and upon appeal therefrom, . . . 1758–1774*, R. Marsden, ed., (1885), 155 et seq.

16, 1776, and presented September 7, 1776,[27] until January 30, 1777, Congress employed the device of special committees to take cognizance of individual appeals.[28] These committees appear to have discharged their duties more or less as referees; that is to say, they conducted hearings and reported to Congress. The findings were there read and, depending upon the terms of the reference, the ultimate decision lay with Congress through its action upon the committee report.[29] Since no minutes or records of committee proceedings (if such were indeed kept) can be found, it is impossible even to conjecture how closely such proceedings approximated a judicial one.[30]

According to surviving case papers a total of eight special committees was named to hear prize appeals between September 9, 1776, and January 30, 1777, when, as a second stage in handling appeals, a Standing Committee was appointed.[31] This committee was discharged May 8, 1777, because it was too numerous, and a new Standing Committee of five, three of whom could act, was appointed.[32] The Standing Committee, the membership of which changed as delegates to Congress were replaced, was a congressional fixture until the establishment of the Court of Appeals in Cases of Capture (May 1780)[33] and so enjoyed the advantage of a certain continuity. The resolve instituting the Standing Committee provided that appeals lodged with the Secretary of Congress were to be delivered to it. Whether for this reason or another, the Committee acted more or less independently of Congress, reversing or affirming on its own authority rather than submitting reports to Congress for action. However, when appeals had been denied in state courts or had not been demanded or filed within the prescribed time limit, petitions for relief were addressed to Congress, from which authority

---

[27] *JCC*, V. 741. The first two applications to Congress (Jan. 31 and Feb. 27, 1776) prayed for an exercise of original jurisdiction. Petitioners were referred to colony courts (Davis, "Federal Courts Prior to the Adoption of the Constitution," xxii).

[28] The first special committee (*JCC*, V, 747) was composed of Robert Stockton, Samuel Huntington, Robert Treat Paine, James Wilson and Thomas Stone.

[29] For example, the *Journals* show no action was taken on the committee's reversal in the case of the *Thistle* (Sept. 16, 1776), but in the case of the *Elizabeth* (Oct. 14, 1776) Congress by resolve accepted the committee report (*JCC*, VI, 873), The committee for Barry v. the Sloop *Betsey* (Nov. 27, 1776) was given

power to determine and consequently Congress did not need to resolve.

[30] The case papers and certain fragments of proceedings were arranged and numbered by J. C. Bancroft Davis and listed in 131 U.S. Rep., Appendix, xxxv–xlix. They have been microfilmed and bear the National Archives title Revolutionary War Prize Cases: Records of the Court of Appeals in Cases of Capture, 1776–1787 (NA Record Group 267). These are hereafter cited as RWPC. No papers are on file for Cases 12, 17, 22, 26, 27, 101 and 2 Dallas 36. Court records are missing for Cases 39, 64, 109, 2 Dallas 1 and 2 Dallas 39.

[31] *JCC*, VII, 75.

[32] *Ibid.*, 337.

[33] *Infra*, p. 171.

was needed before the Committee could proceed with the case. The parallel with the *doleance* procedure of the Privy Council[34] is manifest.

Incongruous though it may seem, the resemblance between the earnest republicans who made up the Standing Committee and the grandees commissioned as Lords Commissioners of Appeal is very striking. Both bodies were similarly constituted; both performed similar tasks and faced similar difficulties. The likeness is one the Standing Committee seems to have recognized for it often used the style "Court of Commissioners of Appeals of the United States of America." In both cases the bodies were composed of lay and professional persons; both were presumably engaged in settling problems on the basis of the law of nations, although in England this was overlaid with Orders in Council and treaty provisions that possessed primacy because of royal prerogative in matters of war, peace and the conclusion of treaties.[35] Both bodies were dealing with systems of trial practice of most diverse complexion. The great difference lay in the fact that the Lords Commissioners, whether adjudicating appeals from the High Court of Admiralty or from the vice-admiralty courts of the plantations, had before them proceedings conducted in the name of a common sovereign; the Standing Committee was faced with the procedural vagaries of thirteen jurisdictions, each laying claim to sovereignty. The nature of the appellate process during the Revolution was greatly affected thereby, and as a result the problems of maintaining central judicial authority in a federal system became apparent long before there was serious thought of something more than a wartime measure.

The Congress itself was responsible for some of the difficulties which lay ahead because of the recommendation in 1775 that trials should be by jury in prize cases. Since in matters of prize the course of admiralty had been followed in England with the whole of the evidence reduced to writing,[36] Congress's recommendation was procedurally subversive, tending as it did to immunize from review the

---

[34] *Supra*, c. I, p. 43.

[35] See the discussion and citations Holdsworth, *History of English Law* (1922), I, 563–67.

[36] The comments of Lord Mansfield in Lindo v. Rodney (1782), 2 Douglas (3d ed. 1790) 613n., that "the whole system of litigation and jurisprudence in the Prize Court, is peculiar to itself: it is no more like the Court of Admiralty than it is to any court in Westminster-Hall" can mislead. The High Court of Admiralty exercised prize jurisdiction by virtue of a royal commission issued at the outbreak of war. (Specimen commission, in R. Marsden, *Law and Custom of the Sea* [Navy Records Soc., 1916], II, 297.) The colonial vice-admiralty courts were authorized by warrant from the Lord High Admiral or Commissioners if the office was in commission. (Specimen warrant, in A. Stokes, *A View of the Constitution of the British Colonies in North-America and the West Indies at the Time the Civil War Broke Out on the Continent of America*, 280.) As noticed *supra*, the jurisprudence was based upon the law of nations, provisions of

Lemuel Palmer Appellant &c.

rs

Reuben Hussey &c. Appellee
} Appeal from the Court of
Admiralty of the State of
North Carolina

We the Commissioners appointed by the honorable Congress to hear try and determine All Appeals from the Courts of Admiralty of the several American States to Congress having heard and fully considered as well all and singular the Matters and Things set forth and contained in the Record or Minutes of the Proceedings of the Court aforesaid in the above Cause as the Arguments of the Advocates of the respective parties in the above Appeal do thereupon adjudge and decree that the Appeal of the abovenamed Lemuel Palmer on behalf of himself and others in the said Appeal named be dismissed hence with Costs And We do assess the said Costs at ninety five Dollars &c &c and do order and decree that the Appellants pay to the Appellees abovenamed the said ninety five Dollars &c &c for the Costs and Charges by the said Appellees expended in supporting and sustaining the Decree of the Court of Admiralty aforesaid against the Appeal of the said Lemuel Palmer &c

May 22d: 1777

James Wilson

John Adams

Tho Burke

Decree of the Standing Committee on Appeals in *Palmer v. Hussey*, Case No. 17, Revolutionary War Prize Cases.
(*The National Archives*)

salient features of a prize cause by the protective cloak of the unassailable jury verdict.[37] The Congress's advice spoke to the prejudices that had been aroused by the criticism of provincial vice-admiralty courts as the locus for trial of trade and revenue cases, prejudices which extended to the admiralty jurisdiction at large. This last is reflected in some of the earliest measures taken locally to provide for prize courts, notably Massachusetts,[38] Rhode Island[39] and Pennsylvania,[40] where the enactments seem to us to indicate that common law procedures were anticipated. In jurisdictions such as these the revival of procedural traditions which had earlier prevailed in the vice-admiralty courts obviously would depend upon the exertions of the bar and of the judges.

Apart from what may have remained in vice-admiralty records from the last wars, the two statutes enacted during the War of the

---

treaties and Orders in Council. Comparison with the statement of the jurisdiction and law of the instance side of admiralty in A. Browne, *A Compendious View of the Civil Law and of the Law of the Admiralty*, 2d ed. (1802), II, cc. 4 and 5, written shortly after Mansfield's death, throws light on what the latter had in mind. It is clear from St. 29 Geo. II, c. 34, sec. 3, that in the main the procedure on the instance and prize side was substantially identical.

[37] The confinement of proofs to written evidence was, of course, an inheritance of the civil law, although this was rationalized in the proposition that the evidence to acquit or condemn must come in the first instance from the ship taken, viz., the papers on board and the examination on oath of the master and other principal officers. See the report of Sir George Lee, G. Paul, Sir Dudley Ryder and William Murray (1753), in H. Wheaton, *Digest of the Law of Maritime Captures and Prizes* (1815), 310 at 311. R. Pares, *Colonial Blockade and Neutral Rights, 1739–1763*, 111 *et seq.*, has assembled evidence indicating how departures had been made in the colonial vice-admiralty from the strict rules regarding examinations *in preparatorio* and ship's papers, with great improprieties in the admission of irrelevant testimony or testimony of interested parties. Lewis Morris, the New York judge, was a particular offender. Obviously departures of this

sort would be cured by a verdict.

[38] 5 *Acts and Resolves Prov. of Mass. Bay*, 436.

[39] *Rhode Island Acts and Resolves* (facsimile reprint), Mar. Sess. 1776, 312; amended May Sess. 1776, 41, with reference to Congress's resolve.

[40] Act of Assembly, Mar. 26, 1776, *Pennsylvania Archives*, 8th ser. (1935), VIII, 7457. Note, however, the Connecticut act (*Acts and Laws of Connecticut*, May Sess. 1776) empowered county courts to try by jury "or otherwise" all cases of captures. Rule for adjudication to be the civil law, the law of nations and resolutions of Congress. The Maryland Convention established an admiralty court May 25, 1776, and provided that process and form of proceeding "be as usual in courts of admiralty: but if either libellant or defendant, or [sic] any controverted material fact between them demand a trial" thereof by jury, such should be summoned. *Proceedings of the Conventions of the Province of Maryland . . . , 155*. The North Carolina Provincial Congress used special courts and on May 11, 1776, empowered the Council of Safety to establish courts of admiralty in four ports. This was done June 22, 1776. All proceedings, determinations and decrees were to be consonant and agreeable with the rules and regulations of Congress. Jurymen were to have allowances as per the last jury law. *Colonial Records of North Carolina*, X, 542, 549, 580, 634.

Austrian Succession (13 George II, c. 4, and 17 George II, c. 34) and that enacted at the inception of the Seven Years' War (29 George II, c. 34) specified the course of prize procedure. Of procedural literature, only Clerke's *Practice of the Court of Admiralty* was of practical use.[41] There were then no available admiralty reports, for the jurisprudence as practiced and applied in the High Court was a memory jurisprudence of the most arcane variety.[42] The lack of specialized literature had necessarily affected practice in the colonial vice-admiralty courts for it was handled by a bar trained in the common law and so, as Judge Hough has pointed out, was subject to a variety of digressions from the strict *ordo judiciarius* of the civil law.[43] Some of the vagaries which turn up in prize case papers during the Revolution may be attributed to continuing adherence to colonial usages, others were the result of colonial legislation and still others were probably due to lack-learnèd lawyers and judges.

Since we are here concerned with appellate jurisdiction on the national level and not with reconstructing prize jurisdiction at large, only what came before the appellate forum is relevant to our inquiry. It is patent that much has perished, for in some appeals no papers at all have survived; in others only libel and claim have been preserved. Nevertheless, the extant corpus of case papers furnishes, as it were, useful *documents pour servir*. Not only do they portray something of the procedure peculiar to each jurisdiction, but they also indicate clearly the difficulties confronting the appellate authority in dealing with records of great diversity. Some jurisdictions, among which were numbered Maryland,[44] North Carolina[45] and South Carolina,[46] employed a relatively formal

---

[41] First published as *Praxis Curiae Admiralitatis Angliae* in 1667 after F. Clerke's death. The English edition was published 1722. For appellate practice Clerke referred to his *Praxis in Foro Ecclesiastico* (1684). The latter superseded by T. Oughton, *Ordo Judiciorum* (1728). Note further the comment by Stokes, *A View of the Constitution of the British Colonies in North-America* . . . , 271, that Clerke "is the book used by the practitioners in the Colonies." At 281, he states that he had not met with any admiralty proceedings in prize causes in print. He adds ruefully, "I would gladly have got some forms from the practisers in Doctors Commons, and I accordingly used endeavours for that purpose; but I did not succeed."

[42] Holdsworth, *History of English*

Law (London: Methuen & Co., Ltd.), XII, 105.

[43] Hough, *Reports of Cases in the Vice Admiralty of the Province of New York* . . . , xii–xiii. On the Massachusetts vice-admiralty procedure, L. Wroth, "The Massachusetts Vice Admiralty Court and the Federal Admiralty Jurisdiction," *Am. Jour. Legal Hist.*, 6:250, 265–68, 1962.

[44] *E.g.*, RWPC, Case 15, The *Montgomery* v. the *Minerva* (1777); Case 48, Fossett v. the Sloop *Jane* (1780); Case 63, Courter v. the Brigantine *Pitt* (1780).

[45] *E.g.*, RWPC, Case 16, Coor *et al.* v. the *Hanover* (1777–78); Case 20, Fowkes v. the *Roseanna*, Hussey claimant (1777).

[46] *E.g.*, RWPC, Case 24, Weyman v. Arthur (1778); Case 25, Norris v. the Schooner *Polly and Nancy* (1778).

admiralty procedure, tainted, of course, with the anomaly of jury trial. In others common law procedure and writs were used as well as admiralty instruments to produce an odd potpourri. Very occasionally replications and rejoinders appear. In only one case was a demurrer interposed. In the margin are listed documents filed in a South Carolina[47] and in a Virginia case.[48]

While the states were each fabricating a *cursus curiae* in matters of prize, the Congress and its appeal committees took their own good time over settling an appellate procedure. There was only a modest amount of appeal business and this was completely overshadowed by the staggering number of more urgent problems connected with war. Furthermore, procedure in prize appeals happened to be an area where it is clear from John Adams' account of a frantic search for enlightenment in 1772 little information was available.[49] The prize statutes were

---

[47] RWPC, Case 25, Norris v. the Schooner *Polly and Nancy* (1778):
Petition for the filing of the libel
Preparatory examinations followed by introduction of the libel
Petition of claimant
Claim
Exhibit A (certificate of agreement for the sloop of war which captured the prize and also the ship's crew)
Proctor for the libellant moved that the warrant of appraisement might be prolonged until the next afternoon and also that the jury be drawn.
He then moved that the *venire facias* might issue returnable on Friday at eight in the morning
Replication
Rejoinder
Interrogatories and depositions of witnesses
Proctor for the libellant spoke in support of the libel and cited cases
Proctor for the claimant spoke on behalf of the claim and cited cases
Proctor for the libellant responded in support of the libel and cited cases
The judge than gave his charge to the jury [not set out]
Jury withdrew and then returned verdict

Decree
Petition for appeal
Exhibition of appeal
[48] RWPC, Case 5, Joyne v. the Sloop *Vulcan* (1776–77):
Libel
Proclamation made three times against the *Vulcan*, no one appearing
Jury impanelled, declared the vessel to be lawful prize
Decree
Sale made by marshal after notice at public auction
Later claim set up to *Vulcan*, claimant moving for new trial; granted, as he was unable to make an earlier appearance
Answer to libel admitted
Answer replied to generally
Jury impanelled
Witnesses sworn upon *voir dire*
Jury heard witnesses and arguments of counsel on both sides
Verdict returned
Appeal prayed to the Continental Congress; granted upon giving security in the sum of £200 for payment of costs and prosecution of appeal
Depositions of witnesses on both sides were later taken and reduced to writing
Appraisement and account of the sale put into the papers
[49] See *Adams Papers*, II, 56.

nearly silent, there were no printed collections of appellate forms and Clerke's little treatise dealt but casually with appeals, and this from the instance side of the court. For details, as already noted, Clerke refers to his work on ecclesiastical court practice—an opus unlikely to have been widely owned in America. In England appeals both from the ecclesiastical and admiralty courts were in the hands of the civilians and both had been heard by the High Court of Delegates for so many years[50] that the procedural molds were set when in the course of the seventeenth century prize appeals were singled out for adjudication by Lords Commissioners of Appeals. Muniments from the time of the eighteenth century Intercolonial Wars establish that such appeals followed the course described by Clerke for appeals from the instance side of the High Court of Admiralty.[51]

It will be enough to summarize the methods by which in England prize appeals had been pursued in the more recent wars to indicate how amorphous was the procedure of appeals to Congress and its agencies.[52] Traditionally an appeal lay only from a definitive sentence or an interlocutory decree having that effect. It had to be interposed within fourteen days and could be *viva voce* before the judge or before a notary *in scriptis*. After the demand, letters dismissory (apostles) would be requested, signed by the judge. These embodied a summary of the case, the sentence, and a statement that in lieu of further apostles, the proceedings would be transmitted. When an appeal was *in scriptis*, apostles were unnecessary because the instrument of appeal contained the whole matter of the complaint.

Inland appeals had to be prosecuted within three months, colony appeals within nine months by appellant praying that an inhibition issue from the Lords Commissioners to the judge *a quo*.[53] This mandate inhibited the latter from proceeding further and operated also as an ar-

---

[50] By statutes 25 Hen. VIII, c. 19, sec. 4, and 8 Eliz. I, c. 5. The jurisdiction of the Court of Delegates and the procedure are set forth in the well-documented study of G. I. O. Duncan, *The Court of Delegates*, unpublished thesis, St. John's College, Cambridge, England [n.d.], 124–43 and cc. VI–IX.

[51] See the particulars in the proctor's bill, Feb. 10, 1744, in the appeal of the case of the *Revenge*, in Jameson, *Privateering and Piracy in the Colonial Period: Illustrative Documents*, 453–56; the notice of appeal and prayer for apostles (1761), *ibid.*, 569; the forms of inhibition issued by the

Lords Commissioners, instructions for serving and affidavit of service (1763), in Stokes, *A View of the Constitution of the British Colonies in North America . . .* , 318–24.

[52] Details from Clerke, *Praxis Curiae Admiralitatis Angliae*, 75 *et seq.*; and see Oughton, *Ordo Judiciorum*, tit. 276 *et seq.* The stability of practice indicated by Browne, *A Compendious View of the Civil Law and of the Law of the Admiralty*, II, 435 *et seq.* (instance), 454 *et seq.* (prize).

[53] Browne, *A Compendious View of the Civil Law and of the Law of the Admiralty*, II, 454.

rest of the respondent or appellee (in the then-procedural jargon, "the party appellate").[54] Simultaneously a monition issued ordering transmission of all proceedings. At one time it would appear that execution of the sentence was suspended by force of the appeal, for by Statute 13 George II, c. 4 §8, it was provided that execution should not be suspended if respondent gave sufficient security to restore to appellant ship, goods or effects, or the full value in case of reversal.[55] This course of proceeding premised a reviewing authority with power to issue and to have the necessary mandates obeyed. To such power Congress could not lay claim when it assumed appellate jurisdiction, and we shall see what came of efforts to secure it.

No evidence has been found that either the Continental Congress or its appeal committees ever issued an inhibition or any mandate resembling it having the force of staying proceedings in the state prize courts. There is no mention of this warrant in the surviving case papers. And it is worthy of remark that when *Penhallow v. Doane's Administrators*, a cause which had occupied both the Standing Committee and the Court of Appeals, was adjudicated by the United States Supreme Court, the form of an inhibition which the court had before it was one issued in England, July 1794.[56] It would appear that although there was nothing in the original resolve of Congress speaking to the problem, the force of the appeal itself, if allowed, would suspend proceedings in the state court. The Congress, as noticed, set times within which appeal should be demanded and lodged with the Secretary of Congress, yet although it stipulated appellant give security to prosecute the appeal to effect, no time limit was set and the bonds we have seen normally did not have a terminal date.

The appeals to the Continental Congress from state courts appear to have been made both *viva voce*[57] before the judge, or *in scriptis*,[58]

---

[54] Clerke, *Praxis Curiae Admiralitatis Angliae*, 81.

[55] The earlier act, 6 Anne, c. 37, sec. 8, intimates the same but is too crudely drawn to support firm conclusions. The provision mentioned in the text was carried forward by 29 Geo. II, c. 34, sec. 9.

[56] Mentioned in the opinion of Cushing J., 3 Dallas 54, at 118 (1795).

[57] For a common form see RWPC, Case 33, Taylor v. the Sloop *Polly* (Pennsylvania 1778–79):

Be it remembered that on the tenth Day of September anno Domini 1778 Before the honorable George Ross Esquire Judge of the Court of Admiralty for the Port of Philadelphia in the state of Pennsylvania Cometh John Bunik the Claim^t in the above cause and appeals from the verdict and sentence and from all interlocutory Orders and Decrees found and passed in the same cause to the honorable the Continental Congress and offers himself ready to give sufficient security to prosecute the said appeal to effect at such Time and Place as the said Congress or such Court or Authority as may be authorised to hear and determine the same shall appoint.

[58] A petition sometimes was made to exhibit the appeal, *e.g.*, RWPC,

setting forth the cause of the appeal and exhibited to the judge. Neither Congress nor its committees, nor later, the Court of Appeals, used the monition to bring up the proceedings, consistently called "the record."[59] And unless the trial court denied an appeal, no difficulties over transmission seem to have arisen, for almost without exception the records still surviving were certified prior to the date when an appeal was lodged with the Secretary of Congress and later with the Register of the Court of Appeals. Some of the case papers contain entries which show that after the decree of the state prize court, appellant moved that a copy of the proceedings be made and transmitted to Congress.[60] If the motion was granted, it obviated the necessity of an order from the appellate forum. The actual transmission seems, however, to have been appellant's responsibility.[61] In a scattering of cases, where appeals had not been allowed because of some procedural defect or because a state statute did not permit appeals to Congress, appellants nevertheless encountered no trouble in securing copies of the proceedings, then taking them to Congress, which accepted any certified copy. The difficulties arose in securing attendance by respondent; Congress resorted to direct order to appear[62] or an order to show cause why the appeal should not

---

Case 25, Norris v. the Schooner *Polly and Nancy* (South Carolina 1778):

That your petitioner humbly apprehends he hath cause of appeal from the verdict of the jury sworn and impanelled in the same Cause and also from the definitive sentence pronounced by your Honor in behalf of the Owner, Officers and Mariners of the Private Sloop or vessel of War called the . . . on the twenty-eighth day of February last past, and means to exhibit such appeal before Your Honor, when your Honor shall think fit to receive the same.

May it therefore please Your Honor to hold a court at such time and place as to Your Honor shall be most convenient, in order to receive the said Appeal, which is made to the Honorable Continental Congress, or to such person or persons as they shall appoint for the Trial of Appeals

And as in duty Bound your petitioner will ever pray.

[59] In England during the eighteenth century neither the High Court of Admiralty nor the plantation vice-admiralty courts were courts of record, this status having been consistently denied them by the common law courts. See Blackstone, *Commentaries*, III, 69.

[60] *E.g.*, RWPC, Case 16, Coor *et al.* v. the *Hanover* (North Carolina 1777–78); Case 42, Gibbs v. the Sloop *Conquerant* (North Carolina 1779).

[61] In the colonies which used the "appeal" in common law cases (*supra*, c. I) the transmission of the record appears everywhere to have been appellant's responsibility. So, too, in vice-admiralty appeals; see Jameson, *Privateering and Piracy in the Colonial Period: Illustrative Documents*, 448. See further c. XIII, n. 210 *infra*.

[62] In RWPC, Case 20, Fowkes v. the *Roseanna*, Hussey claimant, a North Carolina appeal affirmed June 9, 1777, by the Standing Committee, claimant petitioned that the case be reopened. On the basis of a committee report Congress resolved that Fowkes appear within forty days (*JCC*, VIII, 486). There is no evidence that the order was obeyed. But sentence

be heard,[63] leaving it to petitioner appellant to serve. There is no evidence that Congress undertook in any appeal to enlist the marshals of state courts to execute its orders. As we shall see in a moment, this was an item and an important one in various proposals to refound appellate jurisdiction and it was consistently voted down. The lack of effective process did not, however, deter Congress from hearing appeals if the proceedings were before it, even if the appellee did not deign to appear or the appellant failed to prosecute to effect.

It is to be inferred from a certificate of John Potts, Register of the Court of Appeals in Cases of Capture,[64] that minutes were kept by the Standing Committee. Except for one fragment[65] these have disappeared, and consequently, except for the final decrees which sometimes mention hearing counsel, there can be no reconstruction of how their proceedings were conducted. No documents resembling an appellatory libel have been found, but it is conceivable that extant petitions and "reasons" of appeal may have served this purpose. These instruments resemble those long used in the states, viz., the bills in Chancery and the "reasons" used in colony appeal procedure earlier discussed. An isolated occasion was an early attempt (1777) to deal with an appeal as if it were a common law case—the Committee ordered a new trial, and directed that separate issues be made on each material fact alleged or pleaded, that evidence be admitted according to rules of common law and that evidence offered be reduced to writing before the jury retired.[66] This last direction makes manifest how disillusionment over the practicality of jury trial in prize cases had set in.

The effectiveness of appellate jurisdiction, to say nothing of the conduct of prize causes in accordance with the law of nations, made

---

was reversed Oct. 26, 1777. The same procedure was apparently used where appeal had been denied below.

[63] In RWPC, Case 21, White v. the Ship *Anna Maria*, Daniel Bucklin claimant, the privateer *Revenge* libelled the *Anna Maria* in the Court of Admiralty for the Middle District of Massachusetts. Bucklin, for the Ship *Montgomery*, put in a claim alleging collusion between the libellant and first claimant. Bucklin appealed to the Superior Court which affirmed the decree below. Under the then Massachusetts statute an appeal was denied. Bucklin's petition to Congress was referred to the Standing Committee June 24, 1777. On Aug. 4, 1777, Congress resolved that White appear to show

cause why the appeal should not be granted (*JCC*, VIII, 602–03; *ibid.*, XII, 1022). White does not seem to have appeared. Much later, Aug. 18, 1780, the decree was affirmed by the Court of Appeals in Cases of Capture.

[64] Ms. Papers of the Continental Congress, 44, fol. 229 (NA) (hereafter cited as PCC).

[65] This is a document identified in Microfilm 15 of the RWPC as "Causes Pending in the Committee on Appeals Feb–May 1778." The entries against case names identify it as rough minutes.

[66] RWPC, Case 5, Joyne v. the Sloop *Vulcan* (Virginia 1776–77), case papers.

mandatory inquiry into the facts. Where the state court, despite use of jury, attempted to follow the old vice-admiralty procedure, examinations *in preparatorio*, interrogatories and depositions would be included in the record. In other cases appellant would request the trial judge to have the testimony reduced to writing.[67] This would usually occur after trial and in the form of depositions.

The scope of the examination by the committees is by no means clear. In instances observed in the case papers where respondent failed to appear or appellant failed to prosecute, the Committee seems to have examined the record for errors that might appear on its face as if it had come up on writ of error.[68] However, in cases actually contested, if one may properly suppose that the later Court of Appeals in Cases of Capture proceeded along lines established by the Standing Committee, it is inferable that the Committee hearing *de novo* was conducted much in the manner of a Chancery appeal, viz., an examination both of facts and law with full argument by counsel.

THE CONFLICT OF STATE AND CONTINENTAL INTEREST

A TOTAL OF sixty-four cases was submitted to the Committees of Congress between September 1776 and May 1780. Some appeals were settled; in a few there remains no clue to Committee action; in most of the cases there was a final decree. If the volume of business seems inconsiderable in the light of what is claimed for the activities of American privateers, it is well to remember that allowance of the appeal lay with the state prize court, and although the way of petition to Congress was theoretically open to a litigant, some of the state legislatures had

---

[67] *E.g.*, RWPC, Case 5, Joyne v. the Sloop *Vulcan*; Case 42, Gibbs v. the Sloop *Conquerant*, Pillas claimant (North Carolina 1779).

[68] See the decree of Sept. 8, 1779, in RWPC, Case 32, Murphy v. the Sloop *Hawke* (Delaware 1778–79): "We the commissioners appointed by Congress to hear try and determine all appeals from the several courts of admiralty of the United States of America to Congress, having heard and fully considered as well all and singular matters and things set forth and contained in the records and minutes of the proceedings of the court of Admiralty of the Delaware state in the above cause as the argu-

ments of the advocates of the respective parties to the above appeal do thereupon adjudge and decree that the appeal of the abovenamed Daniel Murphy and others entered in this court be and it is hereby dismissed with costs and that the judgment or sentence of the said court of admiralty pronounced and published in the said cause be and it is hereby in all parts confirmed and established. And we further do adjudge and decree that the party appellant pay unto the party appellees in the above cause four hundred and thirty dollars for their costs and charges by them expended in defending the said appeal in this court."

sought to limit any general right of appeal to Congress. Massachusetts, which had amended its original prize statute to conform to the original resolve of November 25, 1775, providing for appeals to Congress,[69] nevertheless limited the right to cases of captures by vessels fitted out at the charge of the United States. Subsequently, in 1778 in a statute enlarging the powers of its maritime courts, provision was made for appeals to the Massachusetts Superior Court in terms so ambiguous as to suggest that an intermediate appellate stage may have been intended.[70] This was clarified by an act of June 1779[71] in which the right of appeal was conceded in all cases whether or not the vessel had been fitted out at national expense. However, litigants were given a choice between appealing to Congress or to the Superior Court, the implication apparently being that if the latter were chosen, further appeal would be foreclosed. Rhode Island, which had patterned its first prize act on that of Massachusetts, in 1780 gave would-be appellants a choice between the highest state court and Congress.[72]

New Hampshire, also influenced by her neighbor's legislation, had in 1776 limited appeals to Congress to cases where the capturing vessel was fitted out at the charge of the United Colonies.[73] All other appeals were to be taken to the next Superior Court of Judicature. In 1779 the right of appeal to Congress was extended to either party in cases where a claim was interposed by a subject of a foreign nation or state with which the United States was in amity.[74] The first statute, pursuant to which an appeal had been locally denied, gave rise to the protracted proceedings in Congress, later to be noticed, over the right to assume jurisdiction when memorialized by a would-be appellant.

The statutory restraints which Virginia placed upon appeals are of particular interest because of the personalities involved in the formulation of the legislation. In December 1775 the Provincial Convention in the first of the Commonwealth's measures aimed at the loyalists and to enforce the Continental Association had erected an admiralty court, appointing as judges John Blair, James Holt and Edmund Randolph to try and determine on all matters relating to vessels and cargoes.[75]

---

[69] 5 *Acts and Resolves Prov. of Mass. Bay*, 474, 477. See also a committee report, *JCC*, XII, 1022–23, noting the conflict between the Massachusetts laws and the Resolve of Nov. 25, 1775.

[70] 5 *Acts and Resolves Prov. of Mass. Bay*, 806 (Apr. 29, 1778), and see the editor's note on legislative history, *ibid.*, 871.

[71] *Ibid.*, 1077 (June 30, 1779).

[72] *Rhode Island Acts and Resolves* (facsimile reprint), July 1780, 2d Sess., 9. This act established an admiralty court to replace the Maritime Court created in March 1776.

[73] 4 *Laws of New Hampshire*, 25 (July 3, 1776).

[74] *Ibid.*, 238 (Nov. 18, 1779).

[75] 9 Hening, *Va. Stats.*, 101, entitled "An Ordinance for establishing a mode of punishment for the enemies to America in this colony."

Trial was to be by jury and an appeal lay to the Committee of Safety. Whether or not Congress's resolve of November 25 had yet reached Williamsburg is not known. A year later (1776) the state legislature enacted a bill, drafted by Thomas Jefferson, that placed the court of admiralty on a broader foundation, for the jurisdiction conveyed[76] embraced all causes theretofore "of admiralty jurisdiction in this country." This court was to be governed by the regulations of the Congress, the acts of the General Assembly, English statutes prior to 4 James I, the laws of Oleron, of Rhodes, and Imperial laws as observed in English admiralty courts. If in any case the regulations of Congress should differ from those established by acts of the General Assembly, the regulations of Congress would apply only in cases of captures from an enemy. "In all other cases the supremacy of the laws of this commonwealth . . . shall prevail." Appeals in cases of captures from an enemy were to be allowed as directed by Congress; in all other cases appeal or writ of error would lie to the Virginia Court of Appeals. This court was not established until two years later (1778). The founding statute conferred upon that court power to determine "all suits and controversies whatsoever" brought before it by petition or appeal from the High Court of Chancery and the Court of Admiralty, or by writ of error from the General Court.[77]

The language of the Virginia Court of Appeals act will bear a reading that appellate jurisdiction in admiralty cases was plenary and consequently that appeals to Congress were excluded. However, at the May 1779 legislative session the revisors submitted two bills, one dealing with the admiralty court, the other with the Court of Appeals. Both were originally drawn by George Wythe who in 1776 had sat on four special committees hearing appeals to Congress. The admiralty statute[78] provided that the court was to be governed by the regulations of Congress and acts of the General Assembly, the laws of Rhodes and of Oleron and the Imperial laws so far as theretofore observed in English Courts of Admiralty and by the laws of nature and nations. It was further laid down that where regulations of Congress conflicted with those of the General Assembly, the latter were to be supreme in cases where Virginia citizens only were litigants, the former in all other cases.

---

[76] *Ibid.*, 202; and see the notes *Papers of Jefferson*, I, 649.

[77] 9 Hening, *Va. Stats.*, 522.

[78] *Ibid.*, X, 98. Boyd, in *Papers of Jefferson*, II, 440, indicates in a note that the admiralty court act had only two readings and was reintroduced by Madison in 1785. But the statute was included in *A Collection of all such Public Acts of the Gen-* *eral Assembly . . . of Virginia passed since the year 1768 as are now in force* (1785), 104. The title page states that the volume was "published under inspection of the Judges of the High Court of Chancery" pursuant to a resolve of the House of Delegates of 1783. The Chancery judges, of whom Wythe was one, presumably assumed that the statute was in force.

IV: *National Judicial Authority, 1775–1787*

The right of appeal to Congress was recognized except in cases between citizens of the Commonwealth, in which event appeal lay to the Virginia Court of Appeals. The sweeping language of the earlier statute describing the jurisdiction of the latter was modified accordingly.[79]

The Virginia admiralty court act was enacted months after Congress had categorically reaffirmed its appellate authority. Consequently the repudiation of congressional regulations in any matter relating to the admiralty jurisdiction where the litigants were citizens of Virginia, and the removal of such cases from the congressional appellate jurisdiction, was nearly as extravagant an exhibition of state sovereignty as that staged by New Hampshire. There was, nevertheless, no overt collision over jurisdiction as there was to be in the case of New Hampshire.

A final example of state effort to inhibit the congressional appellate process was the Pennsylvania statute of 1778 which, in providing for jury trial, declared that the findings of the jury "shall establish the facts without re-examination or appeal."[80] As it turned out, this proved to be more challenging than any of the other state meddlings, for as we shall see, a variety of circumstances drove the Congress to a much more truculent defense of its authority than had yet been made. All of these assertions of state sovereignty fell just short of overt hostility to central management of common concerns. What lent these statutes a peculiarly aggressive quality was the fact that in the first draft of the Articles of Confederation (July 1776)[81] Congress had been given power to establish rules of prize as well as courts to receive and finally determine appeals in all cases of captures. These provisions remained in the final version of the Articles sent to the states in November 1777. Since no state which suggested alterations or amendments of the Articles prior to ratification objected to this jurisdiction,[82] the legislation directed against it was a species of apostasy that was manifested also by state votes in the halls of Congress when attempts were made to put into execution the powers granted by the Articles.

The Articles[83] on their face contemplated the exercise by Congress of an autonomous ordinance power as to specific items, stipulating as to some a majority vote, as to others the vote of nine states. Since the system of instruction of delegates was not abandoned, the actions of Congress, always deliberate, were still subject to remote control. Nevertheless, once the requisite vote was secured on a matter cognizable by Congress, the vigor of an ordinance as law no longer depended upon

---

[79] 10 Hening, *Va. Stats.*, 89.

[80] 9 *Pennsylvania Stats. at Large*, 277 (Sept. 9, 1778).

[81] M. Jensen, *The Articles of Confederation*, 258.

[82] The objections conveniently assembled in Elliot, *Debates*, I, 85–92.

[83] Thorpe, *Constitutions and Charters*, I, 9; Art. IX, at 12–15.

voluntary compliance. Such, however, was still the case when Congress through the medium of the resolve acted on matters not stipulated in the Articles.

The constitutional changes embodied in the Articles were for a long time in abeyance because ratification by all the states, stipulated as a condition precedent to their coming into effect, was unconscionably delayed. By May 5, 1779, twelve states had ratified; Maryland held out until March 1, 1781. There was in this interval no question of erecting any court of appeal except in exercise of war powers and by resolve—a way that presumably would require some form of confirmation by the states. This was the method chosen by Congress to terminate adjudication by the Standing Committee and to vest this power in a Court of Appeals in Cases of Capture. That this should have been done in advance of ratification requires some explanation.

Two major factors were involved—reaction to the corrosive effects of state legislation upon the right of appeal to Congress as of course, and concern over the impact upon foreign relations of sentences in state prize courts. The denial of appeals was correctible by petitions to Congress, of which there were many; so, too, in the case of foreign claimants depending upon an adequate record to refer to the Standing Committee. The matter of a dozen procedural systems, to say nothing of differences in substantive law, created diplomatic problems that could be effectively met only when the powers conveyed in Article IX could be exercised. The need of federal legislation, as there authorized, on what captures should be lawful had been brought home to Congress by accounts from the American Commissioners in Paris, both before and after the French alliance, regarding the indiscretions of privateers. The commissions of these rapacious patriots were issued by congressional authority.[84] The Commissioners in Paris duly sent out a warning circular[85] and on May 9, 1778, the Congress issued a proclamation admonishing against violations of neutral rights[86]—the most it could do with the ultimate status of the Articles still unsettled. Events were to show that this was insufficient.

---

[84] On the despatch of commissions, F. Wharton, *Revolutionary Diplomatic Correspondence of the United States* (1889), II, 231, 249, 314 (hereafter cited Wharton, *Rev. Dip. Corr.*).

[85] Nov. 21, 1777 (*ibid.*, II, 425).

[86] *JCC*, XI, 486. In *ibid.*, XII, 1285, are noted two separate printings of the proclamation. It had been preceded by a resolve of Feb. 26, 1778, regarding instructions to privateers not to violate the law of nations or laws

of neutrality (*ibid.*, X, 196). The Marine Committee was instructed March 5 to revise commissions and instructions (*ibid.*, 225). The arrival of the French treaties produced a resolve, May 6, 1778, that all personnel of public or private armed vessels conform to the terms of the treaties (*ibid.*, XI, 469). The commissions, bonds and instructions were changed May 2, 1780 (*ibid.*, XVI, 404–09).

Much as the transgressions of privateers may have weighed with Congress, it was actually an act of defiance by a Pennsylvania admiralty judge at the very doorstep of Congress that was the immediate provocation of a sweeping assertion of Congress's jurisdiction in matters of prize and specifically over appeals. This was a first and important stage in the establishment of the Court of Appeals. The *causa causans* was an appeal in the case of the sloop *Active* which had been condemned in the Court of Admiralty for Philadelphia.[87] The Standing Committee in the course of hearing the appeal had re-examined the facts in disregard of the Pennsylvania statute which had declared jury findings to be conclusive. The decree was reversed December 15, 1778, but the state judge refused to obey the mandate issued pursuant to the reversal and ordered his own decree to be executed.[88]

It is not essential to our purposes to enter into details of the ensuing uproar in which the Pennsylvania Assembly joined and which continued to vex Congress for months to come. The Standing Committee[89] submitted a report of the proceedings on January 19, 1779, and this was referred two days later to a committee of five "who shall examine into the principles of the powers of the said Committee on Appeals and the causes for the refusal . . . to execute their decree."[90] The report, notable for the bold and forceful exposition of the source and nature of Continental appellate authority, was submitted February 2 and was set for early consideration by the Committee of the Whole.[91] This seemingly did not occur until February 13, and the *Journals* note further debate on March 3.[92]

At intervals during the course of these proceedings Congress was put on notice from several sources of its international responsibilities in the war at sea. The first in point of time were letters and a memorial from the captain of a Portuguese snow, *Nostra Senhora de Carmo è Santo Antonio*.[93] This vessel had been taken by an American privateer and acquitted in Massachusetts, but in 1778 was ordered by Congress to be sold with cargo because the captain allegedly had taken ship for home.[94] As we shall see, a later investigation of the capture was to uncover embarrassing facts. Of more immediate effect in forwarding the final passage of as forceful a statement of the Continental position as

---

[87] RWPC, Case 39, Houston v. the Sloop *Active*.

[88] The relevant documents printed in *JCC*, XIII, 86–92.

[89] William H. Drayton (S.C.), John Henry (Md.), William Ellery (R.I.), Oliver Ellsworth (Conn.).

[90] *JCC*, XIII, 97. The committee— Thomas Burke (N.C.), William Paca (Md.), Jesse Root (Conn.), Eliphalet Dyer (Conn.), Meriwether Smith (Va.).

[91] *Ibid.*, 134–37.

[92] *Ibid.*, 183, 270.

[93] The documents are in PCC 44, ff. 63, 71; *ibid.*, 42, III, fol. 371. One letter read in Congress Jan. 19, 1779 (*JCC*, XIII, 78), the other, Jan. 26 (*ibid.*, 115).

[94] *JCC*, XI, 487 (May 11, 1778).

could be made with the Articles yet unratified was the receipt of two communications—one from the French Minister Plenipotentiary, Gérard; the other from the American Commissioners in Paris. On February 22, 1779, there was laid before Congress the regulations of the King of France regarding prizes brought by American ships into French ports and by French ships into American ports.[95] Sartine, Minister of Marine, had consulted with the American Commissioners in Paris and had made modifications in accordance with their suggestions.[96] The aim was at uniformity of procedure which, as one might expect, was posited upon standard civil law practice regarding written proofs and their handling. These regulations, ironically enough, imposed duties upon state admiralty judges beyond what lay in Congress's power to legislate, yet with possibly as many American prizes now being brought into French ports as into those of this country, the pressures for compliance were considerable. The necessity for centralized management in the United States of prize jurisdiction was manifest and made even more so by the communication from the American Commissioners read in Congress, February 24, dealing with the proper rule to govern recaptures by American privateers in European waters. The fact that there was diversity of legislation on this side of the Atlantic had led Sartine to suggest a uniform rule to apply in both countries.

On the effect of the communications upon the final form of Congress's declaration there is nothing of record. But it is our belief that the reformulation of assertions regarding the law of nations and Congress's ultimate authority to decide on questions touching it were induced by these advices. A resolve was voted March 6, 1779. Opening with a recital of the circumstances of the *Active* case, the relevant sections of the Pennsylvania statute and Congress's resolve of November 25, 1775, it was resolved:[97]

> That Congress, or such person or persons as they appoint to hear and determine appeals from the courts of admiralty, have necessarily the power to examine as well into decisions on facts as decisions on the law, and to decree finally thereon, and that no finding of a jury in any court of admiralty, or court for determining the legality of captures on the high seas can or ought to destroy the right of appeal and the re-examination of the facts reserved to Congress:
>
> That no act of any one State can or ought to destroy the right of appeals to Congress in the sense above declared:

---

[95] *JCC*, XIII, 219. The regulations are in PCC 59, IV, fol. 99. The negotiations, in Wharton, *Rev. Dip. Corr.*, II, 673, 682, 684–88.
[96] *JCC*, XIII, 245. The correspondence, in Wharton, *Rev. Dip. Corr.*, II, 708, 720, 730. The Commissioners' report to Congress, Nov. 7, 1778, *ibid.*, 830.
[97] *JCC*, XIII, 281–84.

That Congress is by these United States invested with the supreme sovereign power of war and peace:

That the power of executing the law of nations is essential to the sovereign supreme power of war and peace:

That the legality of all captures on the high seas must be determined by the law of nations:

That the authority ultimately and finally to decide on all matters and questions touching the law of nations, does reside and is vested in the sovereign supreme power of war and peace:

That a controul by appeal is necessary, in order to compel a just and uniform execution of the law of nations:

That the said controul must extend as well over the decisions of juries as judges in courts for determining the legality of captures on the sea; otherwise the juries would be possessed of the ultimate supreme power of executing the law of nations in all cases of captures, and might at any time exercise the same in such manner as to prevent a possibility of being controuled; a construction which involves many inconveniencies and absurdities, destroys an essential part of the power of war and peace entrusted to Congress and would disable the Congress of the United States from giving satisfaction to foreign nations complaining of a violation of neutralities, of treaties or other breaches of the law of nations, and would enable a jury in any one State to involve the United States in hostilities; a construction which for these and many reasons is inadmissible. . . .

The resolve concluded with a statement that control by appeal had been exercised by Congress through committee and that the committee which had determined the *Active* appeal was duly constituted and authorized to act. A second resolve that the committee had competent jurisdiction to make a final decree and that therefore its decree ought to be carried into execution was also carried.[98]

Within weeks after the passage of this resolve the Congress was again apprised of the embarrassments existing state legislation could create in its foreign relations. On April 24 Minister Gérard transmitted a complaint of the Spanish "observer" at Philadelphia regarding the seizure of Spanish ships with alleged Spanish cargoes and the proceedings against these in Massachusetts courts.[99] Since this occurred at a time when the United States was angling to draw Spain into the war, resolute action must have seemed appropriate. The matter was referred to the Standing Committee on Appeals which was instructed to prepare

---

[98] On the main resolve only Pennsylvania voted no. Witherspoon of New Jersey voted no, but under the rules where no more than one delegate represented a state, the vote did not count. On the second resolve Pennsylvania again voted no and Witherspoon voted aye.

[99] Wharton, *Rev. Dip. Corr.*, III, 134–36.

"a system of regulations for marine jurisdiction"[100]—something suggested two years earlier by James Wilson.[101]

The report of the Committee,[102] which is not precisely dated, was apparently prepared before May 20. The report is significant because it was the first concrete proposal that a Court of Appeals be established. It pointed out that in the state of the Massachusetts law the cases of the two Spanish ships could not be appealed to Congress and that Congress could not interfere. A uniform and equal administration of maritime law within the states was of the highest importance to the welfare and interest of the United States. Accordingly, a resolve was proposed which recited the resolve of March 6, and referred to the powers set out in the Articles of Confederation. Because only twelve states had ratified, the latter remained without effect, yet it was as necessary for the tranquillity of citizens "as for the satisfaction of Foreign Powers" that their provisions be put into effect. The resolve proper consisted of a recommendation to each of the states that a law be enacted vesting Congress with the powers specified in Article IX relating to prizes.

The *Journals* do not indicate that this proposal was discussed before there came before Congress a second memorial transmitted by Gérard relating that appeals had been denied in the earlier cases and telling of proceedings against a third Spanish ship.[103] Action was prompt. On May 22, 1779, Congress ordered immediate transmission of the resolves of March 6 to all the states with a request that they conform therewith.[104] Massachusetts in particular was requested to take effective measures to facilitate and expedite appeals in all cases of vessels and cargoes claimed as neutral property. It was also voted to write the French Minister explaining that Congress would "attend" to the cases of the Spanish ships and that it would cause the law of nations to be strictly observed. If there had been violations of the rights of war and neutrality and the owners had suffered a damage, it would cause reparation to be made for violations. It could not consistently with the powers entrusted it and the rights of the states interfere with the ordinary course of justice.[105]

The fact that the "ordinary course of justice" fell short of the authority claimed by Congress was to become further manifest during the summer of 1779 when new remedial measures in cases of wrongful seizures had to be taken. One case concerned the Portuguese snow

---

[100] *JCC*, XIV, 508.
[101] In a letter to Robert Morris, Jan. 14, 1777, *LMCC*, II, 215–17.
[102] *JCC*, XIV, 508–10.
[103] Wharton, *Rev. Dip. Corr.*, III,
170; submitted May 19, read May 20, 1779.
[104] *JCC*, XIV, 635–36. The action by Massachusetts, *supra*, n. 99.
[105] Text in Wharton, *Rev. Dip. Corr.*, III, 174.

mentioned above. It developed that the seizure of *Nostra Senhora de Carmo è Santo Antonio* had been made by a privateer in which both Robert Morris and Carter Braxton had shares. Braxton had instructed the Captain that if he heard that the Portuguese were actually taking American ships, he was to seize theirs. Because of the personages involved, the illegality of the orders bordered on the scandalous.[106] A great deal of time was spent on the case and Congress took what measures it could to quiet diplomatic waters.[107] The second case involved seizure of a French ship by a privateer. The owners had recovered a judgment, but the defendant, an American captain, had absconded. Congress ordered the vacating of his commission and ordered the bond posted to be put in suit.[108]

The accumulation of episodes domestic and international ultimately led to affirmative action on a Court of Appeals. It was successfully moved, August 26, 1779,[109] that a committee be named to report a plan for establishing "one or more supreme courts of appeal in all maritime causes" within the United States. The form of this reference extended, of course, well beyond what had been conceded in the Articles. Huntington, Paca and Dickinson were named; their report was submitted October 29.[110]

The plan provided that the United States be divided into four districts, and that a Court of Appeals be established in each district for the trial of all appeals from the state admiralty courts within such district. These courts were to have all the powers of courts of record to impose fines or imprison for contempts or disobedience. The judges and officers of the several state courts of admiralty were enjoined to obey the orders and decrees of the Courts of Appeals under pain of imprisonment for contempts. All captures were to be tried "according to the antient and common mode of proceeding and not by a Jury." Jurisdiction of the state courts of admiralty over captures on waters should be subject only to the control of the Courts of Appeals, except in such cases in which no appeal was given. The exception provided by the plan was that no appeal should be permitted when the party appealing was "a subject or inhabitant" of the state where the trial in the Court of Admiralty had been held, and was appealing in his own right and not on behalf of a foreigner or a subject of another state. This sweeping limitation of appeals was obviously designed as a *douceur* to

---

[106] Findings of the Committee in *JCC*, XIV, 838–42.

[107] *JCC*, XV, 1021.

[108] *JCC*, XIV, 951.

[109] *Ibid.*, 1002. Moved by McKean and seconded by John Dickinson.

[110] *JCC*, XV, 1220. The report, in the writing of William Paca, is set out *ibid.*, 1220–23. Paca was then a member of the Standing Committee on Appeals.

state sentiment and revealed a sound appreciation of political realities. All appeals were to be heard and determined according to the civil law, the law of nations and the usage and practice of courts of admiralty in Europe. There were other provisions regarding execution and security that need not detain us.

Congress ordered the report to be considered November 8, but this did not occur until a week later.[111] In what state the bill stood after discussion, on which some time was spent, is not known. It would appear from a draft in Secretary Charles Thomson's hand, dated December 5 (obviously a mistake as the matter was considered December 6), that there had been drastic amendments.[112] Entitled an "Ordinance for establishing a Court of Appeals for finally determining captures," the amended bill provided for a single Court of Appeals with three judges, two constituting a court. Sessions were to be held at Philadelphia, Williamsburg and Hartford, or not farther east or south as the court chose. The provisions regarding powers to fine and imprison as a court of record were kept. Courts of admiralty and all officers must pay obedience to decrees and orders of the Court of Appeals so far as necessary to carry these into execution. Threat of contempt was excised. Trials in state admiralty courts were to be according to the usage of nations and not by jury, and all exhibits, evidence and proceedings were to be in writing. Other provisions are indicated in the margin.[113] Debate was resumed December 7 and the matter referred to the Committee of the Whole.[114] Nothing was reported from the Committee during the rest of the month.

In some manner, not indicated by the *Journals*, the report again came before Congress January 4, 5, 7 and 8, 1780. The special interest of the states became manifest in the motions and votes to save the old jury trial endorsement, to limit appeals when the parties were citizens of the same state and to excise the ambulatory sessions of the court. The resolves agreed upon were put to a vote. When the ayes and nays were demanded, the vote stood at an even division.[115] A new

---

[111] *Ibid.*, 1223.

[112] *Ibid.*, 1349–50. The report was considered and then postponed (*ibid.*, 1356).

[113] The judges were authorized to appoint a Register and Marshal with power of removal at pleasure. Fines were to be paid into the Continental Treasury. No appeal was to be admitted unless demanded within five days of definitive sentence and lodged with the Register within forty days thereafter and unless the party appealing gave security to prosecute the appeal

to effect and be answerable for costs in case sentence was confirmed. The judges were to receive $30,000 per annum for services and expenses. *Ibid.*, 1350.

[114] *Ibid.*, 1360.

[115] *JCC*, XVI, 13–14, 17–19, 22–24, 29–30. On the abolition of jury trial New Hampshire, Massachusetts and South Carolina voted no. Connecticut and New Jersey were divided. Delaware and Georgia were not present. Six states voted aye.

committee was then appointed—Oliver Ellsworth, Thomas McKean, W. C. Houston and R. R. Livingston[116]—to prepare an alternative plan. A report was made January 14 and was taken up the next day.[117]

The new plan embodied only the bare bones of that just defeated. It established the court for the "trial" of appeals from courts of admiralty in cases of capture. This court was to be kept by three judges, any two of whom could hold court. Trial was to be according to the usage of nations and not by jury. The first session was to be held at Philadelphia; thereafter at such times and places as the judges should deem conducive to public benefit but no farther east than Hartford or further south than Williamsburg. Congress by resolve agreed to these items January 15, 1780, and this resolve became the foundation of the court.[118] It should be noticed that powers of contempt were eliminated; postponed were a resolve recommending that the states make laws to assure execution of decrees and orders of the Appeals Court, as well as a resolve recommending that the states authorize trial by civil law, the law of nations and the resolves of Congress. In the weeks following, Congress proceeded to the election and commissioning of judges[119] and by resolve settled certain procedural items.[120] On May 24, 1780, cases pending before the Standing Committee were transferred and the court was officially designated as "The Court of Appeals in Cases of Capture."[121]

---

[116] *Ibid.*, 32.

[117] *Ibid.*, 56.

[118] On the provision regarding trial by usage of nations and not by jury, New Hampshire and Massachusetts voted no. Georgia was not represented. The other states voted aye. *Ibid.*, 62. New Hampshire, Massachusetts and Maryland voted against the provision regarding the place of sessions. The other states voted aye. A provision that 1 percent of the value of prizes adjudicated be paid into the Continental Treasury to defray expenses and any overplus be applied for support of seamen disabled in the Continental service was attacked by Gerry and Holten of Massachusetts who made the humanitarian proposal that any overplus be paid the states. The overplus provision was struck and the whole paragraph postponed. *Ibid.*, 63–64.

[119] On Jan. 21, 1780, nominations were made for judges (*ibid.*, 77; and see Lovell to Samuel Adams, Jan. 21,

1780, *LMCC*, V, 12). On January 22 George Wythe, William Paca and Titus Hosmer were elected (*JCC*, XVI, 79). The form of commission, in McKean's handwriting, was voted February 2 (*ibid.*, 121). Wythe declined the appointment (*ibid.*, 254), and Cyrus Griffin was elected in his room (*ibid.*, 366). Paca accepted February 8 (*ibid.*, 143), Hosmer April 12 and Griffin May 4 (*ibid.*, 411).

[120] A Committee report of May 24, 1780, recommended that appeals be lodged with the Register of the court and that the directions of Nov. 25, 1775, be repealed. Congress accepted the report and by resolve made provision that appeals should be so lodged, provided they were demanded within five days and filed with the Register within forty days thereafter. Appellant was required to give security to prosecute the appeal to effect. *JCC*, XVII, 457–59.

[121] *Ibid.*, 458–59.

THE COURT OF APPEALS IN CASES OF CAPTURE

THE NEW COURT, having come into being by resolve, rested on no firmer constitutional foundations than did the Standing Committee, and like the latter was unpossessed of the ultimate essential of a judicial body—the power to enforce its determinations. Even if Congress had awaited the event of ratification of the Articles of Confederation to establish the Court of Appeals, it is improbable that a solution of the troublesome problem of the relations of state prize courts and federal appellate authority could have been found. Final ratification ushered in no real change in the domestic political climate, and the Articles themselves were silent on means of securing obedience to what Congress might ordain. All that was stipulated was the undertaking in Article XIII that the states would abide by the determinations of Congress. There was no word about means of holding them to this promise. This last became an order of business less than a week after Maryland had ratified. Duane, Varnum and Madison were appointed a committee to prepare a plan for carrying into execution in the several states all acts and resolutions passed pursuant to the Articles.[122]

The committee reported March 16 that an implied power to enforce inhered in Article XIII. To avoid the contingency that lack of explicit power might be used as a pretext to question the legality of Confederation measures, an amendment was proposed to authorize moving with armed forces against recalcitrants and to take economic sanctions as well.[123] This bellicose proposition was not to survive the gantlet of congressional and committee discussion, although it was to reappear in the so-called Virginia Plan submitted by Edmund Randolph to the Federal Convention.[124]

Meantime, on April 12, 1781, a motion relating to the Court of Appeals, apparently designed to fortify its authority, was offered by James Madison.[125] In particulars it revealed the same obtuseness regarding what would be tolerable to the states that characterized the pending proposed amendment of the Articles. The places for sessions of the court were multiplied. When an appeal was prayed and granted in any case, a state was to order its judges to send up full and fair

---

[122] JCC, XIX, 236.
[123] Ibid., 272; ibid., XX, 469. Text of the report with critical notes in W. Hutchinson and W. Rachal, eds., The Papers of James Madison, III, 17–20. For an account of the "progress" of the proposals, see Burnett, The Continental Congress, 504 et seq.

[124] M. Farrand, ed., The Records of the Federal Convention of 1787, I, 21, Resolution 6 (hereafter cited as Farrand, Records).
[125] JCC, XIX, 374–75. Text with explanatory notes in Papers of James Madison, III, 66–68.

copies of the record to the Court of Appeals.[126] Furthermore, the states should be called upon to order their marshals to carry into immediate execution "the decrees of Judgments of the said Court" under penalty of dismissal by the Court of Appeals and liability to a common law action of damages at the suit of the party injured. Also stipulated were matters relating to costs, salary and travelling expenses, housing and robes. It was further moved that the judges of the Court of Appeals be made judges for the trial of piracies committed upon the high seas; and again, the states were to be called upon to order sheriffs and gaolers to attend the court and to remove prisoners to the gaol most convenient for trial.

Why the provision regarding trial of pirates was offered is inexplicable.[127] The Articles had granted to Congress power to "appoint" courts for the trial of piracies and felonies on the high seas. A week before Madison offered his motion, Congress had passed an ordinance relegating this jurisdiction to courts to be erected by the states.[128] Whether or not the framers of the Articles by design drew a distinction between "establishing" courts of appeal in cases of captures and "appointing" courts for the trial of piracies and felonies on the high seas, there can be no doubt that Congress did. The ordinance with a subsequent amendment remained the basis for subsequent state legislation.[129]

---

[126] As noticed above, the state courts generally made no difficulties about transmitting records; refusals were not usual. The fact that the expedient of the motion was hit upon instead of vesting the Court of Appeals with power to issue monitions and inhibitions suggests to us that Madison knew nothing of prize procedure.

[127] The editors of the *Papers of James Madison* suggest (vol. III, at 67, n. 5) that the purpose was to supplement the ordinance already enacted or that the Court of Appeals "was to have original rather than appellate jurisdiction over cases involving felonies and piracies on the high seas." No appellate authority had been reserved in the piracy-felony ordinance. This would have been unthinkable inasmuch as error did not lie in such cases at common law. The writ was grantable only as a matter of royal grace, rarely bestowed.

[128] *JCC*, XIX, 354–56, (Apr. 5, 1781).

[129] *JCC*, XXIV, 164 (Mar. 4, 1783). According to Madison's notes the amending ordinance was occasioned by difficulties encountered by the Pennsylvania legislature in drafting a statute, owing to alleged ambiguities in the original ordinance.

In 1785 there was an abortive attempt to revise the earlier ordinances. On Sept. 6, 1785, Charles Pinckney (South Carolina) moved that a new ordinance be drawn because of the variety of dispositions made by the states (*JCC*, XXIX, 682). The drafting of such an ordinance was referred to the Secretary for Foreign Affairs (John Jay). The draft submitted October 3 was designed to establish a uniform system in all the states primarily through the form of a commission embodied in the proposed ordinance, said commission to be issued by the executive of the state to which accused might be brought. This draft also stipulated that prisoners should be brought or sent to jurisdictions where witnesses were available (*JCC*, XXIX, 797–805). The report was referred to two successive com-

It is unnecessary to trace the vicissitudes of what developed into an effort to put the Court of Appeals on more solid constitutional footing, for it came to nothing. The familiar round of reference to committee, reading, recommittal, new text debate, postponement, recommittal, new drafts and the like extended from April 12, 1781, until March 30, 1782, after which date the *Journals* are bare of references.[130] Although we have no clear indications of what the difficulties were, it seems to us probable that the attempt to meddle with the authority and procedure of state courts was an operative cause. In July 1781, when the ordinance was sent back to the committee, to which Edmund Randolph had been added, there was a further instruction to prepare an ordinance regulating proceedings in state admiralty courts and to revise and collect into one body the resolves of Congress and other convenient rules of decision.[131] Ordinances for the Appeals Court and to regulate proceedings in state courts were reported August 14, 1781, together with one for deciding, as the Articles provided, what captures

---

mittees, but no report was ever made. Charles Thomson to W. S. Johnson, May 16, 1789 (LC Ms. Misc. Continental Congress).

It is beyond our purpose to review the state legislation. It may be noticed, however, that South Carolina does not appear to have legislated until Feb. 27, 1788, when it was provided that piracies be "tried" by the grand and petit juries of the Charleston Sessions Court. The statute is utterly ambiguous as to the actual locus of trial. However, on June 10, 1788, trials for piracy and murder were held at an admiralty session. *State Gazette of South Carolina*, June 12, 1788; Ms. State of South Carolina Court of Admiralty Record Book 1785–89, 122.

Compare the Massachusetts statute, Feb. 25, 1783, to carry into execution the April 1781 ordinance (*Mass. Acts and Resolves*, Jan. Sess. 1783, c. 10). We have found one reference to a case in the "Court for the Trial of Piracies and Felonies done and committed on the High Seas"—a resolve to adjourn the court to Boston (Suffolk Files, No. 104147, Nov. 25, 1785 [Office of Clerk, Mass. Supreme Judicial Court, Boston]). No further record found.

[130] The motion was referred to a committee—Varnum (R.I.), Bee (S.C.),

and McKean (Del.) (*JCC*, XIX, 375). Apparently the notion of re-establishing the Court of Appeals by ordinance originated in this committee. The report was made May 10, 1781 (*JCC*, XX, 496). The second reading occurred May 11 and it was ordered read a third time on May 14 (*ibid.*, 497). However, the report was evidently recommitted, for on June 4 the same committee reported a new ordinance which was debated and a second reading set for the next day (*ibid.*, 599). This reading took place June 25 and the ordinance was debated by paragraphs. A provision that the judges' tenure be by good behavior was defeated (*ibid.*, 694–95). Further consideration was postponed. Congress resumed consideration July 18, 1781, on which date the text of the ordinance is inserted in the *Journals* (*ibid.*, 761). Certain new procedures were introduced. Most important was a provision which subjected all judges, registers, marshals and other officers of state admiralty courts to the rules and decrees of the Court of Appeals. The report was recommitted and Randolph added to the committee (*ibid.*, 761–64).

The ordinance is in PCC 29, fol. 394. Some sections are marked "passed."

[131] *JCC*, XX, 764.

should be legal.[132] Only the *Ordinance Ascertaining what Captures on Water shall be lawful* was actually enacted, December 4, 1781.[133] Its most notable feature was the paragraph which made the rules of decision in prize courts "the resolutions and ordinances of the United States in Congress assembled, public treaties when declared to be so by an act of Congress, and the law of nations, according to the general usages of Europe. Public treaties shall have the pre-eminence in all trials." This last provision, embodied as it was in an ordinance, was the first solemn attempt, albeit within a limited context, to establish treaties as the supreme law of the land.

Sometime between January 3 and March 30, 1782, a new committee (Thomas McKean, Elias Boudinot and Richard Law) was assigned the task of drafting a new ordinance for the Court of Appeals and for regulating state admiralty courts. Report was made on March 30, 1782, the final mention of either ordinance in the *Journals*.[134] Significantly, what was submitted regarding state admiralty courts was entitled "Form of a law to be recommended to the States for regulating the courts of admiralty," suggesting that any attempt to impose a "national" act had been abandoned in favor of a try at securing uniform state laws.

The collapse of plans to establish the Court of Appeals more securely than by resolve, and to integrate the appellate authority and the state courts through some form of procedural regulation, may be laid to the abatement of hostilities. In April 1781, when the first steps were taken, the war had been going badly in the south, and during the summer of that year the prospects of an early end were remote. The surrender of Cornwallis in October had, however, brought dramatic changes; and although military operations continued in South Carolina, Yorktown had produced a general conviction that the long struggle was nearly over.[135] Prizes were still being brought in and condemned and appeals taken, yet obviously the reasons for a reconstruction of the prize jurisdiction, a reconstruction which might diminish power hitherto wielded by the states, were in process of losing their virtue.

It was more or less inevitable with the means of compulsion withheld from it that the Court of Appeals should have proceeded in the

---

[132] *Ibid.*, XXI, 861. Since a new ordinance was reported, the status of what was marked "passed" in the preceding report remains doubtful. Because this latter report is included in the list of postponed reports (PCC 31, fol. 371), it is reasonable to suppose that the sections marked "passed" were not regarded as having been finally enacted.

[133] The ordinance as finally enacted, *JCC*, XXI, 1153–58.

[134] *Ibid.*, XXII, 153–54. April 2 was assigned for a second reading. This apparently took place, for David Howell wrote William Ellery Aug. 10, 1782, that the ordinance had not had a third reading (*LMCC*, VI, 439).

[135] Burnett, *The Continental Congress*, 524.

270

withdrawn from the original owner shall be divided as in the case of a Capture of an enemy's Vessel commissioned as a man of War, or privateer

On recapture by an Armed Vessel belonging to the United States of a Vessel under the protection of an hostile Vessel not commissioned as a man of War or privateer

And where the Vessel retaken is not equipped in a warlike manner the proportion to be withdrawn from the original Owner shall be divided as in the case of an hostile Vessel not commissioned as a man of War or privateer

The rules of decision in the several Courts shall be the Resolutions and Ordinances of the United States in Congress Assembled, public treaties, when declared to be so by an Act of Congress, and the law of Nations, according to the general usage of Europe. Public treaties shall have the pre-eminence in all trials This Ordinance shall commence in force on the first day of ~~November~~ february which will be in the year 1782 next

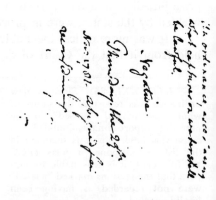

An Ordinance Ascertaining what Captures on Water shall be lawful (1781). Working draft. Papers of the Continental Congress No. 59, III fol. 270.
(*The National Archives*)

causes which came before it in much the same way as had the Standing Committee. The method of bringing up the record remained the same, viz., the appellant brought up the record himself. Reference has been found to one order to despatch certain papers not filed with the rest of the record,[136] but since there are no traces of either inhibition or monition, it must be assumed that neither mandate was used. Apparently state courts usually granted petitions for copies of their proceedings.[137] Again, except for a fragment,[138] there are no surviving minutes of the Court of Appeals and consequently it cannot be determined whether or not a stable *cursus curiae* developed. If the court promulgated any rules, these have not been found. The parties were usually represented by counsel and in two cases, prepared for appeal by James Iredell, a statement of the case and "reasons" that resembled the "Cases" submitted to the Privy Council are preserved.[139] The court occasionally made orders such as directions for testimony to be taken by commission, the execution of which seems to have depended upon counsel.[140] The depositions of witnesses heard below included in case papers indicate to us that the Court of Appeals re-examined facts after a jury verdict, a power claimed by Congress in the resolve of March 1779. There is no doubt that new testimony not presented in the state courts was received by the federal tribunal.[141] The final decrees are not en-

---

136 RWPC, Case 91, Jackson v. the Schooner *Dolphin*, Forman claimant: Admiralty

State of New Jersey, to wit:

In obedience to an order of the Honorable the Court of Appeals, of the sixth of the current month, I Joseph Bloomfield, register of the Court of Admiralty of said state—do transmit hereto annexed, fifteen letters, not included in the Record of the above cause, which (as is said) were found on board the said Sloop at the Time of her Capture and were filed in my office at the time of the trial of the above cause.

In testimony whereof I have hereunto set my Hand and affixed my Seal of Office at Burlington the twelfth day of May one thousand seven hundred and eighty three.

137 *E.g.*, Owners of the Sloop *Chester* v. Owners of the Brig *Experiment*, 2 Dallas 41; Case papers, RWPC Microfilm 15. That original documents might be taken to the Court

of Appeals is indicated by the agreement of captor and claimant in RWPC, Case 93, Manly v. the Ship *Bailey* and Russell, appellee (Mass. 1782–83).

138 For Sept. 10–11, 1783, found among the miscellaneous papers in RWPC Microfilm 15. The document labelled "Causes pending in the Court of Appeal," June 1780–March 1781, appears to be a docket.

139 McRee, *Iredell*, I, 476–79.

140 RWPC, Case 103, The Brigantine *Hope* (Conn.). The case papers contain a letter of Hamilton praying execution of the commission.

141 In some of the surviving case papers can be found depositions of witnesses taken in court. Whether this evidence was given orally in court and reduced to writing cannot be ascertained. There are also commissions to take testimony and the submission of such. The mass of new evidence presented in RWPC, Case 91, Jackson v. the *Dolphin*, Forman claimant (New Jersey 1783–84) is a classic example.

lightening and did not differ materially in form from those emanating from the Standing Committee.[142] Opinions survive in eight cases reported by Dallas; whether or not this was exceptional cannot be said.

It may be inferred from the report of a congressional committee, September 10, 1783, that the normal procedure for execution of a final decree of reversal by the Court of Appeals was the service by appellant of a certified copy of the decree upon the appellee.[143] Enforcement would depend upon state courts. That these were not invariably willing to cooperate is clear from the litigation in *Doane v. Tredwell and Penhallow*. It is known that the Court of Appeals did issue attachments but again, their effectiveness depended upon the willingness of the state to act.[144]

The Court of Appeals never enjoyed the status of a completely independent tribunal competent to implement the universal right of appeal that Congress had repeatedly affirmed. It was not only subject to a certain amount of direction by Congress, which, petitioned when appeals had not been perfected betimes or were otherwise defective,

---

In *Père Debade*, appellant v. the *San Antonio et al.*, libellants (RWPC, Case 95, Mass. 1783) one of the libellants petitioned Congress to reverse the Court of Appeals on the ground that it had allegedly exceeded its powers in receiving new evidence not presented in court. Francis Rendon writing to James Duane, Arthur Lee and Daniel Carroll, Sept. 11, 1783, about the case stated, "I should also add that I have been credibly informed that it has been the constant practice of that Court to take up new evidence on both sides in almost every cause that has been brought before them." Ms. James Duane Papers, Box 5 (NYHS).

[143] *JCC*, XXV, 546–48.

[144] The writ, dated July 24, 1783, is in PCC 78, XIX, fol. 451. A committee of Congress recommended that the executive of Massachusetts give assistance for the execution of the decree (*JCC*, XXV, 548).

We have one example of an individual petition to a state legislature for relief in enforcing appellate decrees; see *Acts and Resolves Prov. of Mass. Bay*, XXI, 604 (Sept. 18, 1780), summoning captors of the *Valenciana*, the *De La Merced* and the *Santander* to appear and show cause why the petitioner's prayer should not be granted.

[142] Typical is the decree in RWPC, Case 65, Bragg v. the Sloop *Dove*:

John Bragg Lib & Appee	
vs	In the Court of Appeals
The Sloop Dove & Her Cargo	in Cases of Capture
David Tatem claimt & appelt	

It is considered and finally decreed and adjudged that the judgment or sentence of the Court of Admiralty of the State of North Carolina pronounced and published in the above cause be and the same hereby is in all its parts revoked reversed and anulled.

And further that the Party Libellant do pay all and singular the costs and charges which have accrued on the prosecution of the appeal to this court.

Wm Paca
C. Griffin

would order such be admitted.[145] The court was also subjected to the importunities of the Secretary for Foreign Affairs.[146] There were numerous occasions when Congress was petitioned to authorize rehearings in particular cases, and in at least one of them did so,[147] until at last in June 1786, when the court was close to expiring, a resolve conferred upon it power to grant rehearings or new trials.[148]

The one serious attack upon the appellate jurisdiction of Congress and inferentially upon the constitutionality of the Court of Appeals came, as one might expect, long after the dangers of war were past. This arose as a result of the court's decree of reversal in the case of *Doane v. Tredwell and Penhallow and the Brig Lusanna.*[149] The Maritime Court of New Hampshire had condemned the ship as prize (December 14, 1777)[150] and had refused an appeal to Congress, for the capturing vessel had not, as the state law required, been fitted out at the charge of the United Colonies. An appeal was allowed to the New Hampshire Superior Court where a second jury found the ship lawful prize. Doane, tendering security, again demanded an appeal and was refused. A petition was directed to Congress (September 14, 1778)[151] which referred the case to the Committee on Appeals. The libellants were summoned to appear before the Standing Committee which on June 26, 1779, rendered an opinion that it had jurisdiction, but as the New Hampshire laws "militated" against Congress's resolve of March

---

[145] For example, the resolve Sept. 5, 1781 (*JCC*, XXI, 935–36) regarding reception of an appeal in Keane v. the Brig *Gloucester*, 2 Dallas 36; and Feb. 11, 1782 (*JCC*, XXII, 72) authorizing hearing of an appeal in RWPC, Case 101, McClure v. Sundry British Goods. In Spencer v. the Sloop *Sally*, Peters appellee (RWPC, Case 84) the Connecticut court denied an appeal; Congress granted leave May 10, 1783.

[146] See Secretary for Foreign Affairs Robert R. Livingston's account of his interventions in letters to Franklin, Mar. 26, 1783, and May 31, 1783 (Wharton, *Rev. Dip. Corr.*, VI, 343, 459, respectively); and Secretary Jay's letter to Congress Nov. 24, 1785, on the *Chester* appeal (Case papers, RWPC Microfilm 15).

[147] See *JCC*, XXVIII, 230. Rehearing authorized Apr. 7, 1785, in RWPC, Case 74, Ellis v. Sloop *Hannah,* and rejected by the Court

Nov. 14, 1785. Possibly Miller v. the Ship *Resolution*, 2 Dallas 1, 19, was reheard as a result of congressional intervention. The case papers are missing.

[148] *JCC*, XXX, 356 (June 27, 1786).

[149] RWPC, Case 30, Doane *et al.*, appellants, v. Tredwell and Penhallow, libellants, and the Brig *Lusanna.* There is confusion over the name of the brig, for in Penhallow *et al.* v. Doane's Administrators, 3 Dallas 54 (1795), it appears as Susanna. From the case papers it would seem the correct name is Lusanna.

[150] John Adams appeared for Doane; see *Adams Papers*, IV, 2–3. The history of this case is ably and exhaustively set forth in L. K. Wroth and H. B. Zobel, *Legal Papers of John Adams*, II, 352–95.

[151] Doane's petition is in PCC 44, fol. 187 (Claims for Captured Vessels).

6, 1779, despatched to all the states in May, the Committee would not proceed until advised of the result of the deliberations.[152]

The case was not adjudicated until after cases pending before the Standing Committee had been transferred to the Court of Appeals. In 1783 the court processed the appeal, notifying the libellants who sent a proctor to plead to the jurisdiction of the court and deny its authority. The plea was overruled and the sentences of the New Hampshire court reversed, September 17, 1783.[153] Penhallow and his associates memorialized Congress and the state of New Hampshire filed a remonstrance.[154] These were referred (January 2, 1784) to a committee— William Ellery (Rhode Island), Edward Hand (Pennsylvania), Richard D. Spaight (North Carolina), Thomas Jefferson (Virginia) and Arthur Lee (Virginia). General John Sullivan, who appeared as agent for petitioners,[155] attended the committee meetings and also wrote Jefferson, raising the questions whether or not the court was vested with power, and whether in any event this could be exercised "without any appeal had." He raised also the further question whether upon ratification the Articles of Confederation operated retrospectively to the time of their formation, whether each state was bound from the date of the signing by its own members or from the date of the first signature, viz., the first state's ratification.[156]

The committee's report, written by Jefferson, was made January 8, 1784. Although it recited the resolves and measures of Congress relating to appeals from 1775 to 1779, it made no assessment of their legal effect. It was otherwise with the establishment of the Court of Appeals for it was resolved "that the said capture having been made by citizens of N. Hampshire and carried in and submitted to the jurisdiction of that State before the completion of the Confederation, which appeals to Congress were absolutely refused by their legislature, neither Congress nor any person deriving authority from them had jurisdiction in the said case."[157]

Although the committee recited the several resolves of Congress upon which appellate jurisdiction in prize causes was grounded, it chose to ignore the matter of their justification, viz., that these were taken in exercise of the war power and in some degree based upon the authority over foreign affairs entrusted to the Continental agency. Jefferson himself was a delegate to the Congress which had voted the first resolve of November 25, 1775. Nevertheless, the "completion" of

---

[152] "Extract from the Proceedings of the Court of Appeals" (Committee on Appeals), *ibid.*, fol. 229.
[153] Case papers, *supra*, n. 149.
[154] PCC 44, fol. 203; the Penhallow *et al.* petition printed in *Papers of Jefferson*, VI, 448–52.
[155] PCC 44, fol. 207.
[156] *Papers of Jefferson*, VI, 447–48.
[157] *JCC*, XXVI, 17–20; printed with explanatory notes in *Papers of Jefferson*, VI, 452–55.

the Confederation (March 1781) was selected as the crucial operative fact upon which the lawfulness of the jurisdiction depended. Consequently, whether or not the committee was aware of the implications of its proposed resolve, adoption would have the effect of opening the door to successive impeachments of the dozens of decrees rendered by the Committees of Congress and, indeed, by the Court of Appeals as presently established.

The report was essentially a political document, expressing a view of jurisdiction embodied in the Virginia statutes, for the drafting of which Jefferson had some responsibility. It was a view not shared by a majority in Congress, for after some debates and postponements,[158] on March 30, it was moved by Jacob Read of South Carolina, seconded by Samuel Hardy of Virginia, to postpone consideration of the committee report to take into consideration a resolve that "it is improper for the United States in Congress assembled in any way to reverse or controul the decisions judgments or decrees of such court of appeals." The motion to postpone was lost.[159] A vote was then taken on the question to agree to the resolve reported by the committee. This was defeated.[160] The final answer to the committee's conclusions was to be formulated by the United States Supreme Court in *Penhallow et al. v. Doane's Administrators* where the jurisdiction was sustained by the four judges sitting.[161]

The Owners of the Sloop Chester v. the Owners of the Brig Experiment was the last case to be heard by the Court of Appeals and came before it after a long sojourn in the outer darkness of congressional committees. Owing chiefly to representations of the Netherland's Minister on behalf of Dutch claimants, Congress authorized the Court to take cognizance.[162] The decree dismissing the appeal was rendered

---

[158] *JCC*, XXVI, 39, 53. On March 19 a motion to submit the report to the judges of the Court of Appeals was defeated (*ibid.*, 151). Further postponement March 22 (*ibid.*, 156) and March 24 (*ibid.*, 163).

[159] *Ibid.*, 174–75. New Hampshire, Rhode Island, Connecticut, New Jersey, Pennsylvania and North Carolina voted no. New York and Massachusetts were divided; Maryland voted aye; South Carolina had only one delegate present and Delaware was not represented.

[160] *Ibid.*, 175. Six states (New Hampshire, Rhode Island, Connecticut, New Jersey, Pennsylvania and North Carolina) voted aye, but this, under the rules, was not enough to

carry it. Massachusetts and Maryland voted no. New York and Virginia were divided. South Carolina's vote did not count.

[161] 3 Dallas, 54, The last document in the case (PCC 44, fol. 233, *sub* May 6, 1784) is a petition of Shearjashub Bourne in behalf of Doane. He argued acutely that it did not lie with the judge *a quo* but with the judge *ad quem* to allow the appeal, for where such was *in scriptis* the matter did not have to be mentioned to the judge *a quo*.

[162] See *LPAH*, II, 892–903; 2 Dallas 41; Case papers, RWPC Microfilm 15. The appellants were Dutch merchants. The *Chester* had been libelled in the South Carolina

May 3, 1787, a few weeks before the Federal Convention assembled at Philadelphia.[163] During the term of the court's activities the records indicate that a total of fifty-six cases was disposed of; the actual number of appeals may have been greater for some of the cases were consolidations. There is little or nothing of contemporary opinion of the court to be found, and the attempts in Congress to have it held and kept by a single judge, and later, when business was sporadic, to determine the commissions, were due apparently to a desire to economize.

In surviving records the court was mentioned but once during the discussions at Philadelphia in the summer of 1787. This was a reference by James Wilson to the fact that the jurisdiction of the court had been construed to extend to facts as well as law and common as well as civil law.[164] Nevertheless, it is, indeed, difficult not to believe that the expansion of the limited national jurisdiction conferred by the Articles to embrace the whole of the admiralty jurisdiction was the result of rueful experience with a makeshift appellate jurisdiction which could never be converted into a more effective system because of the intransigeance of the states. It seems probable, also, that the decision that these inferior courts be established by Congress was influenced by the experiences with the prize jurisdiction. Dickinson, Madison and Wilson spoke out for this; only Sherman favored using state courts, but his objections were due to the probable expense of a federal establishment.

CONTROVERSIES BETWEEN STATES

A SUBJECT OF more vital concern to the new states than the review of the decrees of prize courts was the determination of disputes over territorial limits. This had been, as already remarked, a recurring source of friction between governments and of violence unrestrained when grantees of rival claimants resorted to self-help. The source of

---

Court of Admiralty and condemned July 14, 1777. No claim was interposed, but the owners, alleging illegal capture and condemnation of neutral property, directed a barrage of petitions for relief to Congress; see PCC 45, ff. 93–225. As early as Dec. 23, 1779, the Committee of Foreign Affairs laid papers before Congress; these were referred to the Committee on Appeals (*JCC*, XV, 1406). Later a letter of Nov. 23, 1783, from Van Berckel, Minister Plenipotentiary of the Netherlands, was submitted to Congress and referred to committee

(*ibid.*, XXV, 815). A report, June 2, 1784, advised application to the register of the state court for a copy of the proceedings. If there had been a breach of law, the bonds of the privateers were liable to suit (*ibid.*, XXVII, 509–10). Upon repeated representations, a report recommending that the Court of Appeals take cognizance was accepted July 24, 1786 (*ibid.*, XXX, 423–24). See *supra*, nn. 137, 146.

[163] 2 Dallas 41. See also *LPAH*, II, 896–97.

[164] Farrand, *Records*, II, 431.

these controversies was in the first instance the descriptions in the royal charters that were drawn in sublime ignorance of American geography, influenced sometimes by the royal pretensions vis-à-vis other nations, and not aided by the representations of suppliants for such charters. From the year 1664 onward,[165] numerous controversies were brought to at least tentative settlement by a variety of procedures—the exercise of original jurisdiction by the Privy Council as between feudatories, the negotiations of commissioners appointed by colonial governments involved, compacts between governors of contesting jurisdictions and commissions appointed by the Crown with appeal reserved.[166] Controversies outstanding when hostilities began in 1775 were those concerning the so-called New Hampshire grants (later Vermont), the survey of the eastern boundary between New York and Massachusetts, the dormant claim of the latter to New York western lands, the boundary between Pennsylvania and Virginia,[167] and finally Connecticut's claim to the Wyoming Valley lands in Pennsylvania.

The matter of establishing something resembling a neutral forum, as the Crown had been, was first bruited in 1775[168] when the Pennsylvania-Virginia and the Connecticut-Pennsylvania controversies were brought to the attention of Congress. The latter dispute was the most explosive, and although there were at the moment matters of more emergent concern than jurisdiction over a backwoods valley, the state of violence there prevailing and the tensions between the claimant

---

[165] The settlement of the Connecticut-New York line by the commission sent over in connection with the conquest of New York. D. Pratt, comp., *Report of the Regents of the University on the Boundaries of the State of New York*, I, 24–25. This had been preceded by an agreement in 1650 between the Governor of New Netherland and Commissioners of New England colonies. *Docs. Rel. Col. Hist. N.Y.*, I, 457, 541, 564, 610.

[166] The various devices considered in J. Smith, *Appeals to the Privy Council from the American Plantations*, 417 et seq.

[167] The Vermont problem was solved by political means; see A. Flick, ed., *History of the State of New York*, V, 3 et seq.; Burnett, *The Continental Congress*, 540–46. Documents in E. O'Callaghan, ed., *Documentary History of the State of New-York*, IV, 555 et seq. (hereafter cited as *Doc. Hist. N.Y.*). And see comment in H. Syrett, ed., *The Papers of Alexander*

Hamilton, III, 205, n. 2 (hereafter cited as *PAH*).

On the problems of surveying the Massachusetts-New York eastern boundary on which agreement had been reached in 1773, see *LPAH*, I, 545, n. 2. The Massachusetts-New York controversy over western New York lands is dealt with at large in *ibid.*, 553–656.

The Pennsylvania-Virginia boundary line was settled by commissioners appointed in 1779; documents in 10 Hening, *Va. Stats.*, 519–37. The basis of the settlement was an extension of the Mason-Dixon line. On the difficulties of running the line and for an account of the controversy, B. Crumrine, "The Boundary Controversy between Pennsylvania and Virginia, 1748–1785 . . . ," in *Annals of the Carnegie Museum*, I, 505–24; see also vols. II and III, *ibid.*

[168] See John Adams' "Notes of Debates" (Oct. 7, 1775), *JCC*, III, 487.

colonies made desirable some action to establish a truce. The situation was investigated by a committee[169] and eventually Congress voted an admonishing resolve that hostilities cease, property be returned, persons taken be released and peace be observed "until a legal decision" be had or Congress "take further orders thereon."[170]

What Congress meant by a "legal decision" is unfathomable. What is clear, however, is that this body at that date had no authority to issue any orders on a matter involving, as did this, the very constitution of a colony. For the basis of the Connecticut claim was its sea-to-sea charter, which antedated both the New York and Pennsylvania patents. Its bounds were so described that if projected to the South Sea as granted, the southern border overlapped the northern reaches of Pennsylvania and a belt along the south of New York Province.[171] The settlement of the Wyoming Valley, an enterprise of the Susquehannah Company organized in Connecticut, was undertaken under color of the royal grant.[172] Five other colonies—Massachusetts, Virginia, North Carolina, South Carolina and Georgia—were also the happy possessors of sea-to-sea charters, and very obviously the interests and claims of these colonies would be affected by any "order" of Congress regarding Connecticut.

In 1775 these interests were contingent, for the Crown had put a quietus upon them by forbidding settlement west of the so-called

---

[169] Petitions laid before Congress July 31, 1775 (JCC, II, 235); considered next day and put over (ibid., 238). A Pennsylvania Assembly resolve was submitted October 7 and referred to the delegates of that state and Connecticut (ibid., III, 283). The latter reported no agreement and, as the disputes "had proceeded to bloodshed," that a committee from other colonies be appointed (ibid., 295). On October 17 John Rutledge, Samuel Chase, Thomas Jefferson, James Kinsey and Stephen Hopkins were named (ibid., 297). Some notes on the issue made by Jefferson in Papers of Jefferson, I, 248. The report made November 4 resulted in a resolve that the assemblies of the two colonies take steps to prevent hostilities (JCC, III, 321). There was further discussion and on November 27 the committee was directed to hear evidence on possession and jurisdiction and to reduce to writing such parts as seemed proper and submit the same to Congress (ibid., 377). Sundry affidavits were submitted (ibid., 435), and on Dec. 20, 1775, Congress came to its resolve.

[170] Ibid., 439–40.

[171] The Connecticut charter discussed in LPAH, I, 547. The claim to New York lands—the so-called Connecticut Gore controversy—litigated in the United States Circuit Court for the District of Connecticut beginning in September 1796 was subsequently taken to the United States Supreme Court (ibid., 657 et seq.); cf. infra, c. XVII, p. 789.

[172] The chief source for the early years of the company are the four volumes of records, J. Boyd, ed., The Susquehannah Company Papers. For a résumé of the history of the company, see Boyd, "Connecticut's Experiment in Expansion: The Susquehannah Company, 1753–1803," in Journal of Economic and Business History, 4:38–69, 1931. An analysis of the business structure in S. Livermore, Early American Land Companies, 82–89.

Proclamation Line of 1763,[173] and Parliament by incorporating the trans-Allegheny lands north of the Ohio into the Province of Quebec had apparently put this region beyond exploitation by claimant colonies.[174] The final rupture with Britain rendered these measures meaningless and revived the expectations of the patentees and the entrepreneurs who now had only the woods and the Indians between them and the Mississippi.

How the pretensions to the western lands were to affect the framing and ultimate ratification of the Articles of Confederation is familiar history.[175] The rebel states had barely rid themselves of the incubus of imperial restrictions when on July 12, 1776, the so-called Dickinson draft of the Articles was submitted to Congress.[176] This conferred upon Congress broad powers over controversies between states concerning boundaries and jurisdiction, with authority to limit the bounds of colonies claiming to extend to the South Sea, to fix the boundaries of other colonies, to erect new colonies from land "separated," and theretofore obtained from the Crown or the Indians or thereafter purchased from the latter.[177] All such lands were to be disposed of for the benefit of the United Colonies. Since Dickinson proposed that future Indian purchases be placed wholly in the control of Congress,[178] the prospect of profitable exploitation of charter rights through this familiar expedient would be greatly impaired.

These proposals were to undergo drastic modification. The wardship of the Indians was ultimately reduced to authority to regulate trade,

---

[173] Text in *Annual Register* (1763), VI, 208–13. The primary purpose of the line was to reserve lands west of the Allegheny watershed to the use of the Indians. At the New York end, lands north and east of this ridge were reserved. There was a similar deviation in Georgia. See further C. Alvord, *The Mississippi Valley in British Politics*, I, 183–210; T. Abernethy, *Western Lands and the American Revolution*, 20 et seq. on the evasions, infractions and proposed changes.

[174] 14 Geo. III, c. 83.

[175] Jensen, *The Articles of Confederation*, cc. 6, 8, 10 and 11. Abernethy, *Western Lands and the American Revolution*, 170 et seq., 223 et seq., 242 et seq.

[176] A committee made up of representatives of each colony had been appointed June 12, 1776, to draft articles of confederation (*JCC*, V, 433). The direct evidence that Dickin-

son had drawn the original plan is in a letter of E. Rutledge to Jay, June 29, 1776, *LMCC*, I, 517–18. The extent of committee contributions is unknown. It should be noticed that on July 21, 1775, Franklin had submitted articles (*JCC*, II, 195), read in Congress but never subjected to discussion. The plan is printed in *ibid.*, 195–99. Burnett, *The Continental Congress*, 215–19, has demonstrated the degree to which Franklin's proposals were absorbed in the Dickinson draft. The text of this draft in Jensen, *The Articles of Confederation*, 254–62, and *JCC*, V, 546–54.

[177] In Art. xviii. The Franklin draft (Art. V) gave to Congress the power and duty of "Settling all Disputes and Differences between Colony and Colony about Limits or any other cause if such should arise; and the Planting of new Colonies when proper."

[178] Dickinson draft, art. xiv.

but otherwise the management of their affairs was subject to the legislative right of any state within its own limits.[179] As territorial claims stood when the Articles were completed, nothing barred the sea-to-sea patentees from Indian purchases, with a consequent reproduction of conflicts like that pending between Pennsylvania and Connecticut where claims overlapped and purchases had been made from the same chiefs. The further restraint which contemplated that all interstate controversies be subject to congressional action was expunged. In its stead was substituted what purported to be a power of adjudication, but it was nothing of the sort. It was provided that "The United States in Congress Assembled shall be the last resort on appeal in all disputes and differences now subsisting, or that may hereafter arise between two or more States concerning boundary, jurisdiction or any other cause whatever." The word "appeal," however, was a mere flower of rhetoric for no judicial authority was given Congress; indeed, it was assigned little more of a role in the settlement of disputes than that, in Bismarck's phrase, of "honest broker."[180] When a state engaged in a dispute with another state should petition Congress, setting out the controversy, notice should be given by Congress to the adversary state and a day assigned for appearance of the parties by their agents, who should then be directed to appoint, by joint consent, commissioners or judges to constitute a court for hearing and determining the controversy. In the event of a failure to agree, three persons from each of the states should be named by Congress. The parties were then alternately to strike names until the number was reduced to thirteen. From this number not less than seven nor more than nine names should be drawn by lot in the presence of Congress, any five to be commissioners.

Congress was also given power of nomination if a party failed to appear without giving reasons which Congress judged sufficient, or should refuse to strike. In either event the Secretary of Congress was to strike, and the determination of the court so chosen should be final; so, too, if a party refused to submit to the jurisdiction or to appear or defend. A similar procedure was provided for the settlement of controversies regarding "private rights of soil" claimed under different grants of two or more states. Nothing was stipulated regarding execution of decrees.[181]

---

[179] Articles of Confederation, Art. IX.

[180] Art. IX. Thomas Burke in his Notes on the Confederation (*LMCC*, II, 555) commented, "I have no Idea of an appeal or last resort unless there be some prior Jurisdiction and prior resort, and I know of no such thing between the States." His chief

criticisms related to the dangers of a partial tribunal where Congress did the appointing; this should be left to states not interested.

[181] The manner in which this part of Art. IX took form is obscure, and the few documents preserved in PCC 47 do not cast much light upon it chiefly because precise dating is im-

The institution of an *ad hoc* body of commissioners to settle inter-state disputes was obviously an adaptation of the commission procedure used in colonial times. Novel was the method of selection.[182] For the settlement of colonial boundaries the Board of Trade and Planta-

---

possible. The Library of Congress edition of the *Journals* has the first version of the revised procedure passed on Oct. 27, 1777 (*JCC*, IX, 841–43). This did not include the power of Congress to nominate where a party was absent without cause. However, on October 29, Samuel Adams wrote re settlement of boundary disputes that "The Representatives of Each State in Congress to be nominated, the contending States to strike off 13 each, and out of the remaining 13 not more than 9 nor less than 7 shall be drawn out by Lot . . . ," (*LMCC*, II, 536). There were two motions submitted by the New York delegates (undated, *JCC*, IX, 925–27) that proposed commissioners be balloted for by states not interested. The first motion imposed a similar restriction on the commissioners. The second motion would have limited commissioners to nine and allowed each of the parties peremptory challenge of two. The oath of the commissioners was Duane's suggestion (PCC 47, fol. 100). Connecticut moved for a court composed of a single judge from the Supreme Court of each state not interested chosen by ballot in Congress (*JCC*, IX, 927–28).

In the "second report" on the Articles (*ibid.*, 907) the interstate controversy provision is in Duane's hand. He also appears to have been responsible for the provision regarding adjudication of private rights to the soil (*ibid.*, 890).

[182] It is stated by Jameson, "The Predecessor of the Supreme Court," in *Essays in the Constitutional History of the United States*, 44, that "it seems obvious that we have here a reproduction of the machinery provided by Mr. Grenville's famous Act of 1770 for the trial of disputed elections in the House of Commons." To an attentive reader of 10 Geo. III, c. 6 (amended 11 Geo. III, c. 42, made perpetual 14 Geo. III, c. 15)

this conclusion is neither obvious nor probable. The English act made no provision for the contestants agreeing upon the Select Committee. The names of at least one hundred members were inscribed upon identical pieces of paper and placed in six glass boxes or bowls. From these the clerk would draw forty-nine names. The contestants were alternately to strike names to reduce the panel to thirteen. Each contestant could add a nominee of his own—a boon not conceded by the Articles. Grenville's Act made no provision for nomination by the Whole House as did the Articles. The function of the clerk was merely to draw the papers from the bowls. He was not authorized to strike for an absent party as in the Articles.

If the delegates in Congress were influenced by any model for a procedure when the contestants did not come to an agreement, it seems to us more likely that it was the procedure for selecting a panel when a struck jury was used. Upon return by the sheriff of a book of freeholders, the secondary in the presence of the judge would strike forty-eight names. From this list the parties would alternately strike twelve names each. In the event a party was absent, the clerk would strike in his behalf. See J. Lilly, *Register*, 155; Bacon, *Abridgment, s.v.* Jury D. Since there is some evidence of James Duane's interest in the procedure under Art. IX, it may be noticed that he had had immediate experience with the struck jury procedure (Goebel and Naughton, *Law Enforcement in Colonial New York*, 250).

With regard to the provision for the agreement of the parties upon commissioners, there was no exact precedent from inter-colony boundary disputes. However, a procedure similar to that established for the Confederation had been provided in 1769 by the New York Assembly to settle bound-

tions had named the commissioners and on occasion paid some regard to representations by colony agents. The normal practice had been to choose officials in other colonies. The Articles, it may be noticed, placed no such restriction on the formation of the court. Furthermore, they did not venture to provide a substitute for the most useful feature of the old system—the appeal to the sovereign. By the time the Articles were in the final stage of formulation it would have been idle even to have suggested that Congress should discharge such a function. The aftermath of one controversy, *Pennsylvania v. Connecticut*, adjudicated pursuant to the Articles suggests that even if Congress had reviewed the determination of the court, matters would not have been in any better case.

The genesis and progress of the bitter dispute over the Wyoming Valley lands has elsewhere been thoroughly explored.[183] The relation of the facts has been surcharged with anachronistic moral indignation because some of the principals in the controversy who were financially interested were also prominent in public service.[184] None of this has anything to do with the adjudication of the dispute, except as it may account for the fervor of some of the participants.

Proceedings under Article IX were initiated (November 3, 1781) by a Pennsylvania petition to Congress that commissioners be appointed pursuant to Article IX.[185] A form of notification to Connecticut was prepared by a committee and approved by Congress, November 14.[186] The first Monday of June 1782 was set for appearance of the two states

---

aries of the Kakiate and Cheesecocks patents (4 *Col. Laws N.Y.*, 1120). Committees of the respective patentees were authorized to appoint commissioners in writing under their hands and seals. The commissioners' determinations were to be conclusive, were to be acknowledged before the judges of the Supreme Court and lodged in the county records or the province secretary's office. The proceedings are in B V Orange County (NYHS) and are closer to a true judicial proceeding than that in Pennsylvania v. Connecticut. This procedure was later instituted with elaboration for settlement of the Waywayanda and Cheesecocks bounds (*N.Y. Laws*, 6 Sess. 1783, c. 29).

[183] *Supra*, n. 172. Dr. Boyd's editorial note, "The Connecticut-Pennsylvania Territorial Dispute," in *Papers of Jefferson*, VI, 474–87; G. Groce, *William Samuel Johnson*, 61–62, 87, 112–14. Documents also in *Pennsyl-*

vania Archives, 2d ser. (1890), XVIII. Whatever the merits of Connecticut's claim, some of the most distinguished counsel of England had thought it worth litigating if the colonists considered this prudent. The caveat was due to the danger of attack on the colony charter. See the report on the claim, *Public Records of the Colony of Connecticut*, XIV, 495–507; *Connecticut Courant*, Jan. 11, 1785. Counsel were Edward Thurlow, later Lord Chancellor; Alexander Wedderburn, later Chief Justice of Common Bench; John Dunning, recently Solicitor General; and Richard Jackson, Counsel of the Board of Trade.

[184] See Abernethy, *Western Lands and the American Revolution*, c. 26; M. Jensen, *The New Nation: A History of the United States, 1781–1789*, 330 *et seq.*; *Papers of Jefferson*, VI, 474 *et seq.*

[185] *JCC*, XXI, 1092.

[186] *Ibid.*, 1115–16.

by their agents. On June 24 Pennsylvania appeared by William Bradford, Joseph Reed, James Wilson and Jonathan Dickinson Sergeant, counsellors and agents, and Henry Osborne, solicitor.[187] Eliphalet Dyer laid before Congress powers of agency from Connecticut, naming himself, William Samuel Johnson and Jesse Root agents.[188] Only Dyer being present, a further day was requested. Two attempts initiated by Massachusetts to disqualify delegates in Congress of the differing states from sitting on the court failed.[189] On June 26 the Pennsylvania agents moved that the Connecticut agents having failed to appear pursuant to the resolve of November 14, Congress proceed to nominate three persons from each state. Dyer offered a counter-resolve that as Root was absent on congressional business, proceedings be postponed until a day in July.[190] No vote was taken on either resolve. On the following day the Connecticut delegates presented an instruction from the Assembly of their state that the agents move to postpone the appointment of commissioners until the termination of the war. The chief ground was that papers relating to the case were with counsel in England and could not be procured.[191] The resolve offered was postponed, and no vote appears ever to have been taken upon it.

Jesse Root returned to Congress July 15, and on the following day the Pennsylvania agents produced new powers.[192] The Connecticut agents objected to the powers and moved that it be shown that the Supreme Executive Council of Pennsylvania had a right to grant such powers. The question raised by Connecticut was not groundless, because in the Pennsylvania constitution of 1776 the power of making appointments had been partitioned between Council and Assembly. The Congress was thus faced with a decision upon the intendment of a state constitution. It was ordered that the agents withdraw and subsequently a motion to the effect that the powers were sufficient was lost. The agents were again called in and after a hearing Congress voted that the powers were sufficient.[193] The agents were then directed to proceed with naming the commissioners.

The procedure stipulated in the Articles invited further delay, but on August 12 the agents certified that they had with joint consent ap-

---

[187] *Ibid.*, XXII, 345–46; the powers dated June 19, 1782.

[188] *Ibid.*, 346–47; the powers dated Jan. 10, 1782.

[189] *Ibid.*, 348 (June 25, 1782); *ibid.*, 354 (June 27, 1782).

[190] *Ibid.*, 351–52. The Connecticut delegates reporting to Governor Trumbull (*LMCC*, VI, 376) commented that with Pennsylvania delegates striking on the one hand and "our Pennsylvania Secretary" (Charles Thomson) on the other, "what a set of judges we should be left with." Dyers' proffered resolve was hotly debated, for the discussions had taken up three or four days and on July 1 the matter was still being debated.

[191] *JCC*, XXII, 355.

[192] *Ibid.*, 389.

[193] *Ibid.*, 390–92.

pointed William Whipple of New Hampshire, General Nathaniel Greene of Rhode Island, David Brearley and William Church Houston of New Jersey, Cyrus Griffin and Joseph Jones of Virginia, and John Rutledge of South Carolina.[194] At the same time Congress was requested to settle on compensation for the commissioners, how and by whom they should be paid. The committee to which this query was referred could find no authorization in the Articles and tossed the matter back into the laps of the litigants.[195] It next developed that Rutledge declined serving and that there was no hope of securing General Greene's services. In their room were chosen Welcome Arnold of Rhode Island and Thomas Nelson of Virginia. Congress was so notified, August 23, 1782.[196] At the same time an agreement of the parties was submitted that Congress approve their choice, that the commissioners be commissioned by Congress, that each one be allowed $10 per day for services and expenses (this to be shared by the parties) and that the court meet at Trenton,[197] November 12, 1782. Congress directed the Secretary to prepare a commission.

If the Articles were silent on compensation, they were equally so on approval by Congress of the commissioners appointed by the litigant states. The Articles did authorize Congress to commission "all officers whatever in the service of the United States," but in light of the manner of appointment and Congress's disclaimer of any financial obligations, it is a strain on credulity to suppose that where the parties themselves named the commissioners, the commissioners were officers in the service of the United States. Nevertheless, the delegates in Congress, normally hypersensitive to any congressional excursions beyond the letter of the Articles, appear not to have demurred.[198]

As had been the case in colonial times, and was again to occur in

---

[194] JCC, XXIII, 461. The report is dated Aug. 8, 1782. See also the Connecticut delegates to Governor Trumbull, Aug. 10, 1782, LMCC, VI, 439.

[195] The Committee—John Morin Scott, James Madison and John Witherspoon—reported August 14 (JCC, XXIII, 466–68). The allowance to commissioners was viewed as costs of suit in private litigation, "yet the award of costs, as it implies not only a recompense for injury to the gaining party, but also a penalty on the losing party for litigiousness, would in the opinion of the Committee be inconsistent with the dignity of Sovereign and Independent States." But the commissioners "having been made by

voluntary act of the parties in the mode prescribed by the Articles of Confederation," might lawfully proceed at the expense of the parties. Before the Declaration of Independence the allowance to commissioners in similar cases had been a guinea a day and expenses. This had been equally borne by the parties.

[196] Ibid., 528.

[197] Ibid., 529. The commission, ibid., 533–36.

[198] The fact that the minutes of the commission recite that the court was held pursuant to the congressional commission (JCC, XXIV, 7) is the basis for the term "federal court" that came to be applied to this body.

the Massachusetts-New York controversy, the parties were not indifferent to supposed prejudices of those chosen to be commissioners.[199] The original and the substitute choices resulted in four citizens of so-called landless states and three from those with sea-to-sea charters. As finally constituted, only one judge from the latter sat, for neither Jones nor Nelson of Virginia chose to serve; Connecticut thus ended up with a very short straw. The selections can be explained only in political terms, for the issues of law were complex and only David Brearley, Chief Justice of New Jersey, was a judge of broad experience. Whipple had only recently been appointed to the New Hampshire Supreme Court. Houston had but shortly been admitted to the bar. Arnold was a merchant and Griffin's judicial career had been limited to a year and a half of service in the Court of Appeals in Cases of Capture.

The Court of Commissioners convened November 12, 1782, but a week passed before a full bench was present and proceedings could begin. The Connecticut agents, all of them experienced counsel, approached the controversy as if it were a common law action, resorting to what amounted to dilatory pleas, a practice that had been countenanced in colonial boundary litigations.[200] It is clear, however, from the meagre minutes of the court[201] that the Commissioners themselves were not prepared to conduct their proceedings according to familiar common law patterns. This appears from the short shrift given to Connecticut's more important motions. Then the initial motion for view of Pennsylvania's original petition to Congress, presumably to fix the grounds of claim, was denied. A second motion that citations for the appearance of grantees whose title might be affected was also denied on the ground that this could not be admitted according to the construction of the Ninth Article and the "tenor and design" of the court's commission.[202]

It was after this ruling that Pennsylvania's agents announced that they would tolerate no delays. Connecticut, however, professing willingness to proceed, made the caveat that a document deposited in England was not immediately available, and that should it develop such document was necessary, motion to postpone would be made. This was countered by a motion for the opinion of the court whether any motion to postpone would be proper after the case was opened and being heard on the merits. The court ordered these motions to be filed and later announced that it could not determine what motions would thereafter

---

[199] *Supra*, n. 190.

[200] Described by two historians as "delaying tactics" or "delaying game" (Boyd, in *Papers of Jefferson*, VI, 477–78; C. P. Smith, *James Wilson*,

173), as if there were an impropriety in a plea directed toward suspension of an action.

[201] *JCC*, XXIV, 6–32.

[202] *Ibid.*, 11.

be proper but "that they mean to govern themselves by the principles of law, so far as they ought to apply in the present case."[203] Unfortunately, the minutes do not reveal what law it was to which the court had reference.

When the parties on November 22 each submitted the "state" of its case,[204] it was clear that nothing resembling orderly pleading would be possible since both a variety of conflicting allegations of fact needed to be proved and inquiry made into the legal effect of certain acts of state. Connecticut asked at the outset for a ruling on the admissibility of depositions taken before justices of the peace regarding Indian purchases. This was resisted by Pennsylvania and the court determined that it could give no opinion upon admission of testimony until offered.[205] Pennsylvania then gave notice that it would oppose admission of *ex parte* depositions and that applications for commissions to take testimony would be opposed. It may be remarked that reposing among the few remaining papers of the proceedings is a commission to take testimony together with interrogatories and answers.[206] Some of the evidence was reduced to deposition form. Governor William Livingston's evidence was hearsay, but there is no indication that there were any difficulties over admission.

Twelve days were consumed in the taking of testimony and during argument some further witnesses were heard. Both sides submitted to the court memoranda of the "positions"[207] that it was proposed would be supported by "records and history." There have also been preserved exiguous and badly edited notes of all the speeches of counsel,[208] and an extensive set of notes made by Joseph Reed on the argument of

---

[203] *Ibid.*, 23.

[204] Pennsylvania, *ibid.*, 14–16; Connecticut, *ibid.*, 16–23.

[205] *Ibid.*, 24.

[206] PCC 77, ff. 57–70.

[207] Printed in *Papers of Jefferson*, VI, 488–97, where they are entitled "Arguments by James Wilson and William Samuel Johnson before the Court of Commissioners." These were published in somewhat abbreviated form in the *Connecticut Courant*, Jan. 25, 1785, where it is stated, "In order to bring the question to a point the agents on both sides then assumed certain positions, which they endeavored to support by records and history." It appears to us that these documents were more in the nature of "trial briefs" or memoranda for

argument. Only the last paragraphs of the Johnson document as printed by Dr. Boyd reads as if these were notes of the argument itself. These particular documents are in Cyrus Griffin's hand. Since the writer in the *Connecticut Courant* had access to "the positions," it seems probable that Griffin's version was a copy from originals submitted as an *aide mémoire* for the commissioners.

[208] *Pennsylvania Archives*, 2d ser. (1890), XVIII, 621–29. The nature of the editing is indicated by the manner in which citations of counsel are rendered, viz., T. Rutherforth, *Institutes of Natural Law*, obviously abbreviated "Inst. N. L.," is rendered "Ista. L. N."; 10 Coke Rep. appears as "10 Cohn."

William Samuel Johnson.[209] The arguments were obviously much more extended than any of these sources indicate; Wilson, for example, spoke for three and a half days, Johnson for three. The range of citation was considerable, encompassing leading treatises on the law of nations, the law of nature (upon which great reliance was placed) and English law. There was reference to some case law and to such works on geography and history as were available.

The Commissioners deliberated over a long weekend and on December 30 pronounced the following sentence or judgment: "We are unanimously of opinion that the State of Connecticut has no right to the lands in controversy. We are also unanimously of opinion, that the jurisdiction and preemption of all territory lying within the charter boundary of Pensylvania [*sic*], and now claimed by the State of Connecticut, do of right belong to the State of Pennsylvania."[210] Cyrus Griffin wrote to President Dickinson of Pennsylvania on January 1, 1783, that the Commissioners had agreed in advance that the reasons for the determination should never be given, and that the minority should concede the determination as the unanimous opinion of the court.[211]

The decree did nothing to ease the situation in the Wyoming Valley; indeed, conditions there remained as deplorable as they had ever been. The Connecticut settlers attempted to have their rights adjudicated by another commission pursuant to Article IX, but this came to nothing.[212] Despite protracted local acts of violence, years were to pass before the state of Pennsylvania finally took measures fairly to resolve the question of competitive individual claims.[213] This unhappy aftermath of the proceedings at Trenton did nothing to inspire confidence in the practicality of adjudication by commission. Apart from

---

[209] Ms. Joseph Reed Papers (NYHS), X, in Reed's hand and with some marginal comments. In W. Reed, *Life and Correspondence of Joseph Reed*, 388–92), are letters written to George Bryan describing his opinions as the case progressed.

[210] *JCC*, XXIV, 31. Jensen, *The New Nation: A History of the United States, 1781–1789*, 335, states that "a federal court decided that Pennsylvania had jurisdiction over Wyoming Valley, but declared that the Connecticut settlers in it should be confirmed in the possession of the lands on which they had settled." The court made no such declaration. The suggestion was in a letter the commis-

sioners wrote to President Dickinson, Dec. 31, 1782, as a representation of "private citizens." *Pennsylvania Archives*, 2d ser. (1890), XVIII, 629.

[211] Griffin to Dickinson, Jan. 1, 1783, *Pennsylvania Archives*, XVIII, 631–32.

[212] In an editorial note, *Papers of Jefferson*, VI, 480 *et seq.*, the stages of this attempt are related in some detail; R. Brunhouse, *The Counter-Revolution in Pennsylvania*, 175–76.

[213] Boyd, "Connecticut's Experiment in Expansion," 64–69. A colorful account of the disorders based chiefly on county histories, in J. B. McMaster, *A History of the People of the United States*, I, 212–16.

the fact that the absence of a *jugement raisonné* left prospective parties litigants in doubt as to whether or not the issues had been dealt with fairly and adequately, the lack of any constitutional power in a commission or in Congress to make the decree effective was itself a fatal flaw. It is true that both the controversy between Massachusetts and New York[214] and that between South Carolina and Georgia[215] proceeded through the stage of choosing commissioners, but in both cases the parties took the more prudent course of negotiation and compact.

Some modern writers have viewed the dispositions of the Articles for settling boundaries to have been wise and salutary—significant in that provision was made for the peaceful settlement of controversies between sovereign states, and consequently an important stage in constitutional development.[216] The design of the framers of the Articles was no doubt well intentioned, but the recent history of boundary troubles, a matter of general knowledge, should have served as a warning that the question of jurisdiction and the question of private rights to the soil were indisseverable if there was truly to be *pacem in terris*.

It is clear from the little we know about the framing of Article IX that the commissions to be set up in cases of interstate controversies were to function as bodies of arbitrators whose authority was to extend no further than the rendering of a decree. Anything more nearly resembling full-fashioned national judicial authority would have been "inconsistent" with the dignity of the sovereign states. This conception of the jurisdiction was the explicit ground upon which Congress based its refusal to permit costs to be awarded in the case of the Trenton commission. Congress's decision in this instance was entirely in accord with the "spirit" of the Confederation constitution which was not designed to accommodate a national judicial establishment; on the contrary, the constitutional structure was conducive to the growth of an antipathy to such. This was manifested most plainly in regard to the special and very limited jurisdiction bestowed over prize appeals, viz., the state legislation putting limits upon it, and Congress's own refusal

---

[214] On the Massachusetts-New York case see *LPAH*, I, 567–75.

[215] On the proceedings before Congress see *JCC*, XXVIII, 361, 365, 408; *ibid.*, XXXI, 622–29, 642, 650, 653, 654; *ibid.*, XXXII, 13. After matters had been initiated in Congress, the South Carolina legislature on Mar. 22, 1786, by statute indicated that a court should be sought only if negotiations by commissioners failed (*ibid.*, XXXI, 623–25). The final agreement is in *ibid.*, XXXIII, 467–74 (Aug. 9, 1787). Further data in *LMCC*, VIII, 83, 136, 468, 602.

[216] A. C. McLaughlin, *A Constitutional History of the United States*, 130, "one of the most important provisions in the Articles"; "This fortunate and wise provision." Boyd, in *Papers of Jefferson*, VI, 475, refers to Pennsylvania v. Connecticut as a landmark in our constitutional development.

to grant the Court of Appeals power to deal with contempts. Strength and durability were lent this bias by the conviction, already mentioned, that the whole power of judicature appertained to the states. This was not something easily to be disposed of, as the Framers of the Constitution were to learn. The full force of these beliefs, however, was to be experienced in the course of the struggle for ratification, and it was not until after the inauguration of the new government and the enactment of the Judiciary Act that they were brought in check.

CHAPTER V

The Constitutional Convention and the Judiciary

AT THE CLOSE of the conflict with Britain, the political temper of America still languished, as it had during the war, in that state of ambivalence which had afflicted the ancient Greeks—a "stubborn parochialism . . . and that essential unity, simultaneously felt, which made them aware that, despite local differences, they were bound together by a larger tie."[1]

The American states had advanced further toward unification than ever had the Greek city states, but the terms of confederation were such as to place parochial interests under slight restraint. What John Adams was to call "old Colony Habit" had been invigorated by the states' assumption of sovereignty, and we have observed how even the perils of war had little affected the tight-fisted yielding of authority during the formulation of the compact and in the implementation of what had been granted. The coming of peace brought no general change in attitude. Indeed, many states were not even willing to respect the acts performed pursuant to the powers already surrendered. Far from executing the terms of the Treaty of Paris, they resorted to contrivances to obstruct the collection of debts by British creditors, and by various means continued the harassment of loyalists. The requisitions for the support of the United States and the discharge of its debts were largely unpaid, and as a crowning sign of indifference to the Confederation there was pervasive neglect of representation in Congress. The attitude and behavior of the states makes patent that whatever may have been the legal nature of what had been compacted away, sovereignty in any real sense it was not. The locus of decision, even as to the matters yielded, remained dispersed in the contracting states.

---

[1] A. G. Woodhead, *The Study of Greek Inscriptions* (Cambridge: Cambridge University Press, 1959), 23.

V: *Constitutional Convention and the Judiciary*

The period of the Confederation has recently been depicted as a time of resurgence and vital growth[2]—a "springtime of all happiness," to borrow Sir Edward Coke's salute to the year of James I's accession.[3] If this was, indeed, ever the case, the vernal hopes were blighted as hard times overtook the nation. Money became increasingly tight; the pressure upon debtors mounted; the Confederation itself faced nearly insurmountable difficulties in meeting its obligations. And what was most parlous of all to the seaboard interests was the deterioration of our foreign relations. These last were matters that had been committed to the Congress. But the Articles of Confederation had made Congress a political gelding, and its resolves were puissant only as the states might make them so. Nothing reveals better the pathology of this government than the handling of the stern British protest against state infractions of the peace treaty.[4] This protest was laid before Congress in mid-October 1786. Five months elapsed before action.[5] Then Congress resolved that treaties were "part of the Law of the Land"; that states could in no way undertake to abridge these obligations; and, finally, that it be recommended to the states that they take steps to repeal the objectionable laws. Not until three weeks later were the states circularized.[6] Something better than a delayed pastoral admonition was needed here, but Congress was unused to energetic action, nor had it power of compulsion.

Apart from the fact that the implements of authority had been denied it, the constitution of Congress inhibited the growth of a corporate sense of a common mission. Perhaps the most that can be claimed is that this body served as a nursery for the propagation of what might be called a national conscience. Nowhere else was it possible to learn the dimensions of problems common to all the states and, at the same time, to experience immediately how defective was the machinery for coping with them. There were many who profited from this exposure, but there were also many who remained unaffected, and some of these men became resolute opponents of the Constitution. In that calamitous year of 1786 the weight of indifference was ponderable. In August a Grand Committee of Congress, on which each state was represented,

---

[2] M. Jensen, *The New Nation: A History of the United States, 1781–1789.*

[3] 4 Coke Rep., title.

[4] *JCC*, XXXI, 783. The Marquis of Carmarthen's note is dated Feb. 28, 1786. It was accompanied by a lengthy bill of particulars of grievances of merchants and other British subjects.

[5] *JCC*, XXXII, 124. The resolves were passed Mar. 21, 1787. Jensen's account of Congress's action (*The New Nation: A History of the United States 1781–1789*, at 280–81) is misleading because he sets this one year too early.

[6] *JCC*, XXXII, 177 (Apr. 13, 1787). In PRO: FO 4/5/266 *et seq.* are the communications in response and legislation passed in "compliance."

reported in seven amendments to the Articles designed to enlarge national powers.[7] But these were allowed to languish and expire. Members of Congress wrote about rumors of plans for the fragmentation of the nation into two or three separate confederacies—a by-blow of the passions aroused by the Mississippi negotiations with Spain.[8] They speculated about remedial measures. They did nothing. With such a political climate at the seat of government, it was inevitable that the drive for reform should elsewhere be activated.

THE CONVENTION—ITS WARRANTS OF AUTHORITY

MARYLAND AND VIRGINIA set afoot the conference on commerce at Annapolis that recommended appointment of commissioners by the states to meet at Philadelphia on the second Monday of May 1787 to consider the situation of the United States and devise such "further provisions" as might be deemed necessary to render "the constitution of the Federal Government adequate to the exigencies of the Union."[9] The Annapolis Report, prepared by Alexander Hamilton,[10] was addressed to the legislatures of Delaware, New Jersey, New York, Pennsylvania and Virginia, the only states actually represented, but was despatched to Congress and to the executives of other states. It anticipated no action by Congress, but, on the contrary, was an appeal by the delegates to their principals to take measures to secure the concurrence of other states in the appointment of commissioners.

It should be observed that although it had been provided by Article XIII of the Articles of Confederation that no alteration should be made in any of the Articles unless agreed to by Congress and afterwards confirmed by the legislatures of every state, the instrument was silent on how change could be initiated. Congress had, in the past,

---

[7] JCC, XXXI, 494–98. Three of the Committee members, William Samuel Johnson (Connecticut), Charles Pinckney (South Carolina) and William Houstoun (Georgia), were to be delegates to the Philadelphia Convention. Nathan Dane (Massachusetts) and Melancton Smith (New York) were to be important adversaries of the new Constitution.

[8] Theodore Sedgwick to Caleb Strong, Aug. 6, 1786, LMCC, VIII, 415; Monroe to Jefferson, Aug. 19, 1786, ibid., 443 at 445; Monroe to Madison, Sept. 3, 1786, ibid., 460.

[9] An account of the genesis in Madison's Introduction to his notes on debates in the Federal Convention of 1787 printed in Elliot, Debates, V, 109–22. This is reprinted in Farrand, Records, III, 539–51, but without the text of the resolutions adopted. The text of the Annapolis Report as submitted to Congress, JCC XXXI, 678–80. Some minutes of the proceedings in Ms. Emmet Coll., No. 9398 (NYPL). These are a fragment but fuller than the matter printed in Elliot, Debates, I, 116.

[10] So stated by Madison in his Introduction, Elliot, Debates, V, 115. A fanciful account of its genesis in I. Brant, James Madison, II, 386. On the authorship, PAH, III, 686, n. 1.

submitted proposals to the states, thus giving rise to the belief in some quarters that this was the only constitutional method of proceeding. Actually, however, Congress had assumed such power because it was a sort of *forum conveniens*, not because it was endowed with specific authority. Certainly there was respectable opinion that Congress was not the sole or even necessary medium by which change could be set in motion. As early as 1782 the New York legislature had resolved that a convention of states be called for this purpose.[11] A similar attempt had been made by Massachusetts.[12] Consequently the proposal of the Annapolis Report cannot be regarded as either novel or revolutionary.

The Virginia legislature took the initiative in carrying out the recommendation of the Annapolis Report. A bill passed the House of Delegates on November 8, 1786, and fifteen days later was agreed to by the Senate.[13] As enacted, the statute authorized the appointment of commissioners to meet with deputies of other states at Philadelphia "in devising and discussing all such Alterations and farther Provisions as may be necessary to render the Federal Constitution adequate to the Exigencies of the Union and in reporting such an Act for that purpose" to Congress. The confirmation procedure of the Articles was anticipated. The Governor was requested forthwith to transmit copies of the statute to Congress and to the executive of every state.[14]

New Jersey was almost as prompt. On November 24 the Assembly and the Legislative Council approved a resolution which followed

---

[11] In *PAH*, III, 110–13. The evidence of Hamilton's authorship, *ibid.*, 110, n. 1. A letter from Governor Clinton transmitting the resolves was laid before Congress August 15 and referred to a "Grand Committee," *JCC*, XXIII, 470, n. 2. On the subsequent adventures in Congress *PAH*, III, 113, n. 4.

[12] Recommended in Governor Bowdoin's speech, May 31, 1785, printed in "Supplement to the Resolves of the General Court of the Commonwealth of Massachusetts . . . 1785," in *Mass. Acts and Resolves 1784-1785* (reprint), 706 at 710. The resolves of the legislature, *ibid.*, 666 (May Sess. 1785, c. 76). The circular was addressed to executives of other states, *ibid.*, 667–68 (c. 78).

The Massachusetts delegation in Congress (Elbridge Gerry, Samuel Holten and Rufus King) conceived that there were reasons for suspending the presentation to Congress pending further instruction. See their letter of Aug. 18, 1785, to Governor Bowdoin, *LMCC*, VIII, 188, and the full argument in their letter of Sept. 3, 1785, *ibid.*, 206. Both letters also in C. R. King, ed., *The Life and Correspondence of Rufus King*, I, 59–66 (hereafter cited as *Life of King*). Until spring 1787, King was a convinced believer in the theory that the proper body to propose alterations was Congress; see his address before the Massachusetts House of Representatives, Oct. 11, 1786, *LMCC*, VIII, 478.

[13] *Journal of the House of Delegates of the Commonwealth of Virginia* (1786), 28; notification of Senate concurrence, *ibid.*, 55; House resolve that seven delegates be appointed, *ibid.*, 68; Senate agrees. *ibid.*, 70; delegates elected December 4, *ibid.*, 85–86.

[14] Text in 12 Hening, *Va. Stats.*, 256.

closely the language of the Annapolis Report.[15] Pennsylvania, referring to Virginia's action and defining its deputies' powers in nearly the same terms, enacted a statute on December 30.[16] A North Carolina statute was passed a week later.[17] New Hampshire acted on January 17, 1787,[18] Delaware on February 3[19] and Georgia on February 10.[20] Receipt of the North Carolina act set the wheels moving in South Carolina, and on February 26 a bill passed the House of Representatives.[21]

Meantime in Congress the Annapolis Report had reposed in the lap of a committee to which it had been referred on October 11, 1786.[22] Nothing appears to have been done. Indeed, between November 3 and January 17 it had not been possible for Congress to make a house. Not until February 12 was the committee reconstituted.[23] A week later a resolve was reported recommending that "the different legislatures" send delegates to the proposed convention.[24]

Congress took up the matter on February 21. After some political maneuvering,[25] agreement was finally reached on a resolution that was

---

[15] *Votes and Proceedings of the Eleventh General Assembly of the State of New Jersey* (1786), 73–74; *Journal of the Proceedings of the Legislative Council of the State of New Jersey* (1786), 30–31. The commission issued to David Brearley *et al.* is dated Nov. 23, 1786, as printed both in Elliot, *Debates*, I, 128, and Farrand, III, *Records*, 563.

[16] Farrand, *Records*, III, 565.

[17] Set out in the commission to William Blount, *ibid.*, 569.

[18] *Ibid.*, 571. A supplementary statute naming delegates was enacted June 27, 1787, *ibid.*, 572.

[19] *Ibid.*, 574.

[20] *Ibid.*, 576.

[21] Governor Moultrie's message of Jan. 25, 1787, urged participation in the Convention. Three days later the North Carolina act was transmitted. Discussion on this began February 8, and an act for South Carolina was advised. The bill passed February 26 and deputies were elected March 8. Obviously the resolve of Congress would not have reached Charleston when the bill was enacted. Ms. Journal of the House of Representatives of South Carolina (1787), at 18, 22–23, 92, 93, 181, 202, 211, 245.

[22] *JCC*, XXXI, 770 n. Edward Carrington of Virginia, who was on the committee, writing to Madison December 18, 1786 (*LMCC*, VIII, 523), lays the blame for Congress's inaction on the Annapolis Report upon the Massachusetts delegation. The reason given was that the mode of amendment was provided by the Articles, viz., that amendments must originate in Congress. This was nonsense, for the Articles said nothing on origination and it is clear from King's speech to the Massachusetts legislature (*supra*, n. 12) that the conclusion was reached by a tortuous process of reasoning. Nathan Dane, the Massachusetts delegate on the committee and who was to oppose the Constitution, in an address before the Massachusetts House of Representatives, Nov. 9, 1786 (*LMCC*, VIII, 500 at 504), refers to "the constitutional mode" pointed out in Art. XIII, implying necessity of amendments originating in Congress.

[23] From Jan. 18 to Feb. 2, 1787, no business was conducted because of insufficient representation. The committee appointed on the Annapolis Report is listed in *JCC*, XXXII, 42n.

[24] *Ibid*, 71–72.

[25] *Ibid.*, 71–72, and see the account in Madison's "Notes of Debates in the Continental Congress," *ibid.*, XXXIII, 723–24. Madison indicates

a masterpiece of ambiguity. The preamble, conceding that experience had revealed defects in the existing system, adverted to the fact that by instructions to their delegates some states had suggested a convention as a means to a remedy. It proceeded, "and such Convention appearing to be the most probable mean of establishing in these states a firm national government *Resolved* that in the opinion of Congress it is expedient that . . . a Convention of delegates who shall have been appointed by the several States be held . . . for the sole and express purpose of revising the Articles of Confederation" and reporting to Congress and the state legislatures "such alterations and provisions therein as shall when agreed to by Congress and confirmed by the states render the federal Constitution adequate to the exigencies of Government and the preservation of the Union."[26]

This resolution has been described as a "call for a convention."[27] This is supported neither by the language nor by events. If call there was, this had been voiced at Annapolis and all but five states had responded before the resolve of Congress was put in circulation. It was in the enabling legislation of the states that the source of the delegates' authority lay. The scope of this authority can be determined only by an analysis of the documents, something obviously slighted by those who have claimed that the delegates acted in disregard of them. A misunderstanding of the legal effects of Congress's resolution has undoubtedly contributed to this opinion.

When Congress had legislated on the few matters within its competence, it had enacted ordinances—*e.g.*, appointing courts for the trial of piracies[28] or the disposal of the western lands.[29] These alone could be said to have had the quality of statutes. Otherwise, when a matter depended upon state action, Congress used the resolve, usually in the idiom of recommendation. This was the case with the resolve of February 21, 1787. None of the five states which had not yet acted on a convention was likely to discover anything compulsive in the hortation "that it is expedient" that one be held. Rhode Island, indeed, decided otherwise. As for the restrictive words "for the sole and express purpose

---

that the peculiar language of the resolve was designed to sanction proceedings and appointments already made "as well as recommending farther appoint^ts from other States," but in such terms as not to point directly to the former appointments. The matter of separate confederations was raised. Madison states that this "had got into the Newspapers" for the first time—a fact that probably stimulated action.

[26] Text in *JCC*, XXXII, 73–74; Farrand, *Records*, III, 13–14.

[27] Jensen, *The New Nation: A History of the United States, 1781–1789*, at 421.

[28] 1 *Laws of the United States of America* (Bioren & Duane pubs., 1815), 670.

[29] *Ibid.*, 563.

of revising the Articles of Confederation," only three of the states yet to pass enabling legislation—Connecticut, Massachusetts and New York—made reference to the clause; Maryland ignored it.[30] Much was to be made of it in convention and out by opponents of change. In modern times it has been a foundation for imputations that the proceedings in Philadelphia were, at the least, *ultra vires*. But it should be patent from the pattern of state enactments and from their chronology that Congress was not delegating authority. It had in this particular none to delegate.

The scope of congressional authority was never allowed to come to an issue in convention. Indeed, it would have been as impolitic to have conceded the binding effect of the resolve as to have denied it. What was debated was the meaning of the resolve. As we shall see, the nationalists found the key to the meaning of the word "revising" in the words of the preamble, the "establishing in the States of a firm national government," and so denuded the "sole purpose" clause of all sense of limitation. This was in accord with a settled rule of statutory construction,[31] and every lawyer in the hall knew it, for all of them had been suckled on Coke's *Littleton*. The resolve was thus reduced to what it had been from the first, a blessing on the enterprise—but a benediction without force of law.

The state legislative instruments, whether resolves or statutes, from which the several delegations derived their authority had, with a single exception, one common characteristic—they were cast in general terms and did not impart specific instructions. Only Delaware qualified its warrant with a proviso that there should be no alteration of the unit voting rule of the Confederation.[32] There was no other intimation that the appointees were to be controlled representatives, as were the delegates to Congress. The unhappy precedent of direction by instruction set in the early days of the Second Continental Congress, and still persisted in, was thus ignored. The Philadelphia Convention was assured a greater freedom to act in the national interest than any assemblage yet convened.[33]

---

[30] Farrand, *Records*, III, 585 (Connecticut), 584 (Massachusetts), 579 (New York), 586 (Maryland).

[31] Coke, *Littleton*, 79a.

[32] Farrand, *Records*, III, 574.

[33] The list of delegates and the dates of their attendance set out in *ibid.*, 557–59, 587–90. Characterizations of individuals were composed by a delegate from Georgia, William Pierce (*ibid.*, 87 *et seq.*); and also in a report to the French Minister of Foreign Affairs (*ibid.*, 232–38). A good secondary account, C. Warren, *The Making of the Constitution*, pt. 1, c. 2.

The most exhaustive study of the background of the delegates, both to the Philadelphia and the state conventions, has been made by F. McDonald, *We The People: The Economic Origins of the Constitution*. This work is a traverse in detail of the thesis of Charles Beard, *An Eco-*

Although the delegates had the boon of being generally commissioned, divergencies in the operative words of the several resolves or enactments could not but raise some question as to whether or not all were equally empowered. The Convention abounded in lawyers used to treating questions of jurisdiction in advance of substance. Yet there was no preliminary exploration of powers.[34] Indeed, it was not until mid-June that the matter was debated, and then only because of the forcing tactics of the small states group.[35] There is in any event no substantial evidence of what the various delegations thought about the limits of their particular authority when they assembled at Philadelphia. One may infer, however, that the ideas of the Virginians, a closely knit group empowered under a broadly worded statute, had so far matured as to enable them to move with decision. They arrived in Philadelphia betimes and within less than a fortnight had agreed upon a plan.[36] This was presented by Governor Edmund Randolph on May 29.[37] On the same day Charles Pinckney of South Carolina submitted a plan of his own.[38] It was voted to refer both plans to the Committee of the Whole.[39]

---

nomic *Interpretation of the Constitution of the United States*. Beard's ideas became an article of belief among historians, working their way even into high school histories.

[34] On May 30, on a resolve offered by Madison that equality of suffrage established by the Articles ought not prevail in the national legislature, George Read of Delaware moved to postpone, reminding the delegates of the restraint in the Delaware commission. There were efforts by Gouverneur Morris and Madison to argue him out of his position. Finally it was agreed to postpone. This was the only early issue over powers. Farrand, *Records*, I, 36–37 (Madison).

[35] *Infra*, pp. 218–19.

[36] Madison, late in life, gave a sketch in his Introduction to his notes on the debates (Elliot, *Debates*, V, 121). Letters written to Jefferson and Randolph indicate the germination of his ideas (*ibid.*, 106–08). On the meeting of the Virginians see also Mason to George Mason, Jr., May 20, 1787, in K. Rowland, *Life and Correspondence of George Mason*, II, 100.

[37] Farrand, *Records*, I, 18 *et seq.* (Madison Notes). Madison took the

text from the *Journal*. J. F. Jameson, "Studies in the History of the Federal Convention of 1787," 89 at 103, analyzing the text of the Virginia Plan, casts doubts on whether or not Madison reproduced the *Urtext* of Randolph's presentation. The version preserved by John Lansing, Jr., of New York varies in some details from Madison; see J. R. Strayer, ed., *The Delegate from New York, or, Proceedings of the Federal Convention of 1787 from the Notes of John Lansing, Jr.*, (hereafter cited as *Lansing Notes*). Text also discussed in Farrand, *Records*, III, App. C.

[38] Partially reconstructed by Jameson, "Studies in the History of the Federal Convention of 1787," at 111–32; discussed in Farrand, *Records*, III, App. D, where the reconstructions are set out at large. *Lansing Notes* adds a few details but no full text. References here to Pinckney's plan are from Farrand, *Records*.

[39] Farrand, *Records*, I, 16 (*Journal*). The references in parenthesis to the Records are to identify the source—*Journal* or the note-taker, *e.g.*, (Madison), (King), (Yates).

THE VIRGINIA PLAN AND THE JUDICIAL

THE VIRGINIA PLAN was a succinct prospectus of a new organization that in its impact amounted to a total repudiation of the principles on which the existing frame of government rested. Consisting of fifteen resolutions, it struck at the very heart of the Confederation in two practical particulars. It created the nexus between the individual and the national government theretofore lacking. It amplified the governmental structure and so put an end to the concentration of functions in a single governing body. The plan was, in the language of the time, truly "national." In contrast, Pinckney's projected scheme was built upon the foundations of the existing order. It was, so to speak, a species of "halfway covenant." In this respect it resembled the plan later contrived by delegates of the so-called small states, in concert with two recalcitrants from New York, and submitted by William Paterson of New Jersey on June 15.[40] Items from both Pinckney's and Paterson's plans were eventually to be worked into the new Constitution, but the matrix was the Virginia Plan. For when the Convention first resolved itself into a Committee of the Whole on May 30, Randolph and his associates seized the initiative.

On one thing all the planners agreed—the separation of governmental powers. This was axiomatic in contemporary political thinking. If the philosophical fare of the Enlightenment on which the delegates had been nurtured did not make it so, colonial experience and that of certain state governments had provided disturbing examples of how objectionable the immixion of governmental functions could be. Immediate experience, too, had led to the conviction that implicit in the notion of separation was the principle of balance. Disbalance had always existed in the corporate colonies, Connecticut and Rhode Island, still living under their royal charters which had concentrated authority in the legislature. Elsewhere, as we have seen, in imitation of the English Parliament or in reaction to the disproportionate weight of authority wielded by royal governors in their triple role of executive, judge and legislator, the American rebels, when they revised their governments, had inflated the powers of their legislatures. To the predominance of these bodies many contemporary woes were attributed. This was a recurrent theme in private correspondence long before the Convention met—and wonderfully epitomized by William Blount: "Can any man be safe in his house while the legislature are sitting?"[41] At Philadelphia the delegates were similarly critical. Consequently, despite a

---

[40] *Infra*, p. 217.
[41] William Blount to Governor Cas-
well, Jan. 13, 1787, Blount Mss. (N.C. Hist. Comm., Raleigh, N.C.).

pervasive belief in the validity of the maxim of separation, the Convention was to temporize with a strict execution of the principle in its anxiety to guard against sacrifices of balance.

We shall here be concerned primarily with matters relating to the judiciary: how ideas developed with respect to its structure, its jurisdiction and the role of judicial power in the projected recommendations of the Convention. The ultimate determination on these matters was to be affected by the great and fundamental political question before the Convention—the role of the states in the projected government: whether it was to be a fat part or a lean one. The division of authority between states and nation was, again, a question of balance, but of a much different order than that involved in the partition of functions within the national government. Theoretically, it concerned the partibility of sovereignty. Practically, it concerned the feasibility of conceding just so much to the inflated claims of the states that they could, in their corporate capacity, participate in the projected system without perpetuating the disbalance of authority which had doomed the Confederation. State participation was an irrepressible issue, repeatedly raised in every imaginable connection—above all, in regard to the composition of the federal legislature. Both the state sovereignty men and their adversaries were embroiled in this, with the zeal of the former matched by the suspicious probings of the latter.

Unquestionably the vagarious procedure of the assemblage tended to keep matters animate that might otherwise have expired.[42] What was discussed in the Committee of the Whole for close on to three weeks was retravelled in Convention. When an impasse was reached on some particular, the question would be postponed, only to be later resumed and rehashed. Propositions once voted down were, like some favorite bone, dug up to be gnawed at to little or no purpose. When, finally, the report was made by a Committee of Detail (August 6) charged with fleshing out the resolutions thus far agreed upon, as many old arguments and doubts were revived as there were new ones provoked. It is no wonder that in mid-August Oliver Ellsworth exclaimed, in obvious despair, "We grow more & more skeptical as we proceed. If we do not decide soon, we shall be unable to come to any decision."[43]

The judiciary was subjected to much less critical working over than the other departments of government. Indeed, it is difficult to divest

---

[42] Facilitated by the rule adopted May 29: "That a motion to reconsider a matter, which had been determined by a majority, may be made, with leave unanimously given,—on—the same day in which the vote passed, but otherwise, not without one days previous notice; in which last case, if the House agree to the reconsideration some future day shall be assigned for that purpose." Farrand, *Records*, I, 16 (*Journal*).

[43] *Ibid.*, II, 301 (Madison).

oneself of the impression that, to some delegates, provision for a national judiciary was a matter of theoretical compulsion rather than of
practical necessity. In other words, it was received more in deference
to the maxim of separation than in response to clearly formulated ideas
about the role of a national judicial system and its indispensability.
Certainly, when specific provisions were under discussion there was
precious little divulged. The lawyers were undoubtedly aware of the
need for a national forum. Those who had represented British creditors
knew at first hand the defaults of justice in state courts; others were
aware of the difficulties of prosecuting successfully actions for out-of-
state citizens. But if there was debate in terms of need and utility, it
was not reported.

The two plans first laid before the Convention displayed a challenging divergence of outlook on what sort of judicial system was desirable. But their comparative merits were not canvassed once the Committee of the Whole launched upon an examination of the Virginia Plan.
That is not to say, however, that certain ideas and items in Pinckney's
project were not occasionally brought forward. In particular, his approach to a national judicial establishment suited those attached to the
status quo, and one feature was to be recurrently urged upon the Convention. For Pinckney sought to preserve, with certain elaborations, the
principles underlying the judicial arrangements of the Articles of Confederation. He made no provision for any proper tribunal the existence
of which would not be dependent on legislative creation. He left in his
bicameral Congress "appellate" authority over disputes between the
states.[44] This body was to be empowered to institute an admiralty court
in each state, and to institute a "federal judicial Court" vested with
power to try officers of the United States for all "Crimes &c. in their
Offices." To this court, too, appeals were to be allowed "from judicial
Courts of the States" in causes involving construction of treaties or the
laws of nations, regulations of the United States regarding revenue and
trade or "wherein the U.S. shall be a Party."[45]

Pinckney had been a member of the Grand Committee which in
August 1786 had recommended a judiciary amendment to the Articles.[46]
This amendment, except that it did not confer power to erect admiralty
courts, was identical with the Carolinian's instant proposal; but his plan
gained no added virtue from this history. In contrast, the Virginia Plan
projected an independent, self-contained system of tribunals of and for
the Union, and was patently influenced by certain provisions in the constitution of that state. As a matter of institutional structure, the plan
was premised on the long and indurated usage in the states of dividing

---

[44] As in Art. IX of the Articles of
Confederation.

[45] Farrand, *Records*, III, 608.
[46] *Supra*, pp. 197–98.

authority between inferior and superior courts with a power of superintendence via error or appeal vested in the latter. Randolph's ninth resolution, devoted to the judicial, was, alas, no model of draftsmanship, despite the fact that a future Supreme Court Justice (John Blair), the first Attorney General of the United States (Randolph) and a Chancellor of Virginia (George Wythe) presumably all sat in on the process of parturition. It provided:[47]

> Resd. that a National Judiciary be established to consist of one or more supreme tribunals, and of inferior tribunals to be chosen by the National Legislature, to hold their offices during good behaviour; and to receive punctually at stated times fixed compensation for their services, in which no increase or diminution shall be made so as to affect the persons actually in office at the time of such increase or diminution. that the jurisdiction of the inferior tribunals shall be to hear & determine in the first instance, and of the supreme tribunal to hear and determine in the dernier resort, all piracies & felonies on the high seas, captures from an enemy; cases in which foreigners or citizens of other States applying to such jurisdictions may be interested, or which respect the collection of the National revenue; impeachments of any National officers, and questions which may involve the national peace and harmony.[48]

In one way or another every delegate—whether man of affairs or lawyer—was familiar with the judicial structure of his own state and how it operated. Randolph's resolution consequently spoke to the practical understanding of the membership in a way that a scheme based on the principles of the Articles could not. It spoke even more trenchantly to the recollections of those delegates who had been involved in the difficulties encountered over review of the decrees of state prize courts. To be sure, the question of the exclusive use of state courts as

---

[47] The variant texts (Madison's and Yates') are conveniently published in sequence in C. C. Tansill, ed., *Documents Illustrative of the Formation of the Union of the American States*, House Document No. 398, 69th Cong., 1st Sess. (1927), 955 *et seq.* The version below is from this document. See also Farrand, *Records*, I, 21–22.

[48] Lansing's version, barring variants in spelling and punctuation, agrees with the above version with one important exception. In his specification of jurisdiction he omitted after "inferior Tribunals" the words "in the first instance, and of the superior tribunal to hear and determine,"

Lansing Notes, 116, n. 5. Lansing first attended June 2. He copied matter from Yates' notes for the early days of the Convention. The Virginia Plan was probably one item. This was missing from the Yates Ms. when it was published in 1821.

Jameson, "Studies in the History of the Federal Convention of 1787," at 105 *et seq.*, expressed doubts about the text of Resolution 9 in the Madison version. He believed that originally no provision was made for inferior courts. He found the clause "one or more supreme tribunals" to be "an improbable reading." Farrand, in *Records*, III, 594, disagrees with Jameson.

inferior tribunals in federal matters was to be raised repeatedly, and arduously contested. But this erupted not because anyone could know (or even believe) that such a plan was workable. It was promoted as a part of the resolute effort to preserve the underlying political principles of the Confederation. On the other hand, as we shall see, when Randolph's resolution was debated on the merits, the items which to all appearances engaged attention to a greater degree than even the heads of jurisdiction were the appointment of judges, tenure and salary. These were all matters that were variously handled in the states and to which first-hand knowledge could be applied: so, Nathaniel Gorham's championing of the Massachusetts method of appointment[49] and, we believe, Madison's attachment to the Virginia "fixed salary" provision.[50]

At no point did the local experience of certain delegates and their understanding of the role of the judicial in a government manifest itself more plainly than in the first great exploration of the general problem of how the "maxim" of the separation of powers was to be applied. This preceded immediately the initial consideration of Resolution 9 and consequently served as a sort of prologue, and a most revealing one, to the discussion of the judiciary resolution itself. The occasion was a consideration of the proposed arrangements for handling the veto of both state and national legislation.

The Virginians, anxious that the constitution be safeguarded against legislative invasion both by state and national legislatures, had proposed two different devices. Power to negative state laws contravening the Articles of Union was conferred upon the national legislature.[51] This was agreed to in Committee with the sole addition of acts contravening treaties.[52] This veto power was, however, to be subject to a further control. Resolution 8 provided for a Council of Revision composed of the executive and "a convenient number of the National Judiciary."[53] This Council was authorized to examine all acts of the national legislature before these became operative, as well as legislative vetos of state laws. Dissent of the Council would amount to rejection, unless the national law was again passed, or the state law again vetoed "by —— members of each branch." Both state and national legislation were thus to be subject to conciliar review.

This Council was obviously patterned on the one established by the New York constitution of 1777,[54] that, as already observed, owed something to the scheme of control exercised by the Crown over colonial

---

49 Infra, p. 224. Massachusetts constitution of 1780, pt. II, c. II, sec. 1, IX.

50 Infra, p. 225. The Virginia constitution of 1776 in Thorpe, Constitutions and Charters, VII, 3817.

51 Farrand, Records, I, 21 (Madison), Res. 6.

52 Ibid., 47 (Journal).

53 Ibid., 21 (Madison).

54 On this A. Street, The Council of Revision of the State of New York.

legislation. The proposal was rejected by the Committee of the Whole. In the course of debate something of current opinion respecting the judicial power and its role in the projected system was revealed.

Elbridge Gerry of Massachusetts did not like associating the judiciary with the executive. He believed that the judges had "a sufficient check agst. encroachments on their own department by their exposition of the laws which involved a power of deciding on their Constitutionality. In some States judges had actually set aside laws as being agst. the Constitution. This was done too with general approbation."[55] Gerry added that it was foreign to the nature of judicial office "to make them judges of the policy of public measures"—a revealing comment on the then limits of judicial action. His colleague, Rufus King, believed that judges should be able to expound the law free from the bias of having participated in its formation. They would no doubt stop the operation of such as might appear to be repugnant to the Constitution.[56] James Madison's defense of the provision failed to meet these objections. He believed that the judiciary should participate in order to protect itself. Similarly the negative of the executive was necessary for its own safety, and also for the safety of the minority which might be oppressed by an unjust majority. The executive would be a just judge because the eyes of the nation would be on him—"add the judiciary and you increase the respectability."[57]

It would appear that Madison conceived that the veto power should exist in the form proposed in order to safeguard the separation of powers or at least the balance between the departments. He was ready to yield strict separation to preserve the balance principle. John Dickinson of Delaware was quick to perceive this. He was willing to allow the executive a veto, for his office "is merely ministerial"; judges, however, interpret the law and should not be legislators; there was also precedent in English usage for executive veto.[58] It was probably this argument that led the majority to eliminate the judiciary from the resolution. A counter-proposal to vest a veto power in the executive subject to reversal by two thirds of each branch was voted 8–2.[59] On motion of James Wilson of Pennsylvania, seconded by Madison, it was agreed to reconsider.[60]

When the debate was resumed, on June 6, Madison undertook

---

[55] Farrand, *Records*, I, 97 (Madison).

[56] *Ibid.*, 98 (Madison), but more fully reported by Pierce, at 109.

[57] *Ibid.*, 108 (King). Madison's own report of his speech (at 99–100) is not enlightening. According to Pierce (at

110), it must have been a long oration.

[58] *Ibid.*, 108–109 (King). Madison does not mention Dickinson. Pierce (at 110) reports a truncated version.

[59] *Ibid.*, 94 (*Journal*).

[60] *Ibid.*, 95 (*Journal*), 104 (Madison).

to answer Dickinson. He thought that the logic which would exclude the judges from the revisionary power applied equally to the executive. Furthermore, even in England from which the maxim came, separation was not rigid—the executive had an absolute veto, and the supreme tribunal, the House of Lords, formed one of the branches of the legislature. In any event, only a small proportion of the laws coming in question before a judge would be those on which he would have been consulted previously, and of these but few would be so ambiguous as to leave room for his prepossessions.[61] Madison, who often spoke as a convinced believer in original sin, foresaw the executive as a figure envied and assailed by disappointed competitors, whose stake in the public interest was too transient to put him out of the reach of foreign corruption. He needed to be controlled as well as supported. This the judiciary could best do. Furthermore, "the Code of laws"[62] would be benefited by judicial perspicuity, conciseness and system. Gerry's comment on this watchdog theory was pungent—" it connects with the Executive numbers to divide the infamy of bad conduct."[63] Dickinson, too, believed that uniting judiciary and executive would destroy responsibility.[64] Since the Committee had thought it improper to have a plural executive, why should it be proper in this particular? The proposal was again voted down 8–3.[65]

THE FIRST DEBATE ON THE JUDICIAL

RANDOLPH'S NINTH resolution dealing with the judiciary was first debated in the Committee of the Whole on June 4 and 5, immediately after the initial discussion of the Council of Revision. At the day's end, June 4, it was voted unanimously "that a national judiciary be established."[66] The second clause of Resolution 9 was then moved in amended form: "to consist of One supreme tribunal, and of one or more inferior tribunals."[67] This was agreed to 8–2, but the next morning the words "one or more" were forthwith expunged.[68] At this juncture two issues developed, both of which were to impend for weeks to come. Who was to appoint the judges? Could the state courts serve as the inferior tribunals in the new scheme? On the first question three suggestions were made—appointment by the national legislature, by the upper house and by the executive with confirmation by the upper house.[69] No im-

[61] *Ibid.*, 138 (Madison); King (at 144) is much briefer.

[62] *Ibid.*, 139 (Madison).

[63] *Ibid.*, 144 (King).

[64] *Ibid.*

[65] *Ibid.*, 131 (*Journal*).

[66] *Ibid.*, 95 (*Journal*).

[67] *Ibid.*

[68] *Ibid.*, 116 (*Journal*). None of the note-takers explain why this was done.

[69] James Wilson wanted appointment by the executive, *ibid.*, 119

mediate decision was reached on this point. On the need for inferior national tribunals, it would appear that misgivings had germinated overnight. John Rutledge of South Carolina secured a rule for reconsideration of the clause establishing inferior national tribunals. He moved, June 5, seconded by Roger Sherman of Connecticut, that the clause be expunged. Both men believed that state courts were adequate to the purpose. Rutledge found in the right of appeal to a supreme court sufficient security for national interest and for "uniformity of Judgmts."[70] What was proposed involved an unnecessary encroachment on the rights of the states and would raise obstacles to the adoption of the new system. Frugal-minded Sherman dwelt on the expenses of a new set of courts.[71]

Ostensibly, the argument was in terms of expediency. Nevertheless, it must have been plain enough that concurrently with the drive to secure state participation in the legislative branch, a similar sharing in the judicial was being pushed. Rutledge's counter-proposal was in substance one to provide for partition of judicial authority between national and state tribunals linked by appeals. It resembled the dispositions made under the Articles where trials of captures were held in state courts and appeals lay to a Confederation court.[72] Institutionally the chief difference was that the appellate tribunal would be a constitutional and not a statutory court. Madison was alert to point out that without national inferior courts exercising final jurisdiction in many cases, there would be an oppressive multiplication of appeals. What was to be done, he asked, after improper verdicts in state courts, induced by biased directions or by the prejudices of undirected juries? It would be useless to remand for new trials, and trials at the supreme bar would oblige parties to transport their witnesses, though ever so far from the place of sitting.[73] James Wilson agreed, and added that the admiralty jurisdiction should be wholly committed to the national government. This related to cases not within the confines of the state and to a scene where controversies with foreigners were most likely.[74]

Rutledge's motion passed by a 5–4 vote, with two states divided.[75] Wilson and Madison then moved that "the national legislature be empowered to appoint inferior Tribunals."[76] They observed, so Madison

---

(Madison), 126 (Yates), 127 (King). James Madison suggested appointment by the upper house of the legislature, *ibid.*, 120. According to Pierce (at 128), Hamilton suggested appointment by the executive and confirmation or rejection by the Senate.

[70] *Ibid.*, 124 (Madison).
[71] *Ibid.*, 125 (Madison)
[72] *Supra*, c. IV.

[73] Farrand, *Records*, I, 124 (Madison).
[74] *Ibid.*
[75] *Ibid.*, 118 (*Journal*).
[76] *Ibid.* Madison's notes (*ibid.*, 125) use "to institute" in lieu of "to appoint." Yates' notes support the *Journal* version. The copy in *Lansing Notes* of the report of the Committee of the Whole also supports the *Jour-*

reports, that there was a difference between establishing such tribunals absolutely and giving the legislature discretion to establish them or not. Since Madison had just spoken warmly on the need for national inferior courts, this was hardly candid. Pierce Butler of South Carolina believed that the states would revolt against "such encroachments,"[77] but King, familiar with costly Massachusetts appellate proceedings, pointed out that the establishment of inferior tribunals would cost infinitely less than the appeals which they would prevent.[78] The motion passed 7–3, with one state divided.[79]

This was a swift change of mind, indeed. We believe that it may have been partly induced by the use of the ambiguous "appoint." For an understanding of this, the measures taken to put in effect the powers granted in the ninth of the Articles are relevant. This Article used both the words "appoint" and "establish." As we have seen, Congress had used its power of "appointing courts" for the trial of piracies and felonies on the high seas by designating state judges commissioned by the state. But the Court of Appeals in Cases of Capture was strictly federal, set up by Congress a year before the final ratification of the Articles had taken place.[80] In the bill introduced after ratification to regularize the constitutional status of the court, there was explicit reference to the power "to establish."[81] To delegates familiar with this history, the motion just adopted may have seemed to leave the door open to an "appointment" of state courts.

Although the provision in Randolph's Resolution 9 regarding tenure and fixed salary was this day voted, apparently without debate, the matter of jurisdiction was, inexplicably, postponed. This was typical of the capricious *modus operandi* of the Committee. The rising anxieties that encroachments upon the states were threatened might have been allayed if the proponents of a national system had entered fully into what federal courts were to do. As it was, the discussion on June 5

---

nal. H. Hart, and H. Wechsler, *The Federal Courts and the Federal System* (New York: Foundation Press, 1953), 17, have relied on Madison's language without explanation. In this they have followed Warren, *The Making of the Constitution*, 326, who also does not indicate why the *Journal* entry is rejected. The *Journal* has been subjected to much criticism for the slovenly way it was kept. Nevertheless, Madison used it frequently to pad out his notes. Where other independent sources support the *Journal* it has some claim to be treated as the

prime source. Under the rules established May 29, 1787 the *Journal* was open to inspection by members of the Convention.
[77] Farrand, *Records*, I, 125 (Madison).
[78] *Ibid.*
[79] See the *Journal, ibid.*, 118, and Yates, *ibid.*, 127.
[80] *Supra*, c. IV, p. 171.
[81] *JCC*, XX, 761 (July 18, 1781). The preamble was part of the ordinance passed before the whole was recommitted.

could only have intensified the uneasiness of the delegates from the small states that an engulfing national government was on the way. And before the definition of jurisdiction was reached a week later, things were to be said that were even more disquieting. On June 6 Pinckney moved to have the first branch of the national legislature elected by state legislatures, and there ensued blunt talk about the eventual fate of the state governments.[82] The motion was apparently an attempt to put before the house a feature of Pinckney's own plan, then languishing more or less in limbo. The effect of this motion was to raise obliquely the question whether or not the principle fundamental to the Confederation was to be jettisoned. Some of the delegates, looking beyond this, conceived that a government deriving from the people and not the states foreshadowed the destruction of the latter. On the heels of the vote to have the national legislature "appoint" inferior tribunals, the rejection of the motion was ominous.

At the end of the day's labors Pinckney gave notice of a motion for reconsideration of the clause providing for a negation of state laws.[83] The debate was set for June 8. If the delegates had expected that Pinckney would next attempt to have the Committee reverse its decision on this matter, they were to be surprised. Talented this young man was, but he was something of an intellectual *arriviste* and consistency was not in him. He now proposed that the national legislature be given a negative on all state laws "which to them shall appear improper."[84] He believed that the states should be kept in "due subordination" to the nation—something non-existent under the Confederation. The veto of the British Crown of colonial legislation, he claimed, had been beneficial and the states were now more one nation than they had been as colonies.[85]

Until the Convention finally adjourned, the British constitution was the subject of countless magnificats. None was more unaccountable than this homage to a feature of the imperial administration that, as colonials, Americans had hated. But the healing hand of time had worked its wonders not only on Pinckney, but on Madison who was also to use the same example. And there were others; for at that moment Congress, sitting in New York, had before it a proposed govern-

---

[82] Farrand, *Records*, I, 130 (*Journal*). Madison in his notes has a full account of the debate (*ibid.*, 132–38), and so has King (*ibid.*, 142–44). Yates' notes are relatively sparse (*ibid.*, 140–41); Lansing's even sparser.

[83] *Ibid.*, 131 (*Journal*).

[84] *Ibid.*, 162 (*Journal*); Madison seconded.

[85] *Ibid.*, 164 (Madison). *Lansing Notes*, 39, indicates Pinckney raised the question of ultimate control in the legislature which must act as arbiter.

213

ment for the Northwest that James Monroe described as a colonial government similar to that under which the states had earlier lived.[86] The plan, among other things, stipulated submission of territorial legislation to Congress.[87] This form of control was substantially what Pinckney was now arguing should be saddled on the states.

Madison, almost morbidly anxious to safeguard federal authority, spoke warmly in support. Others warned of enslaving the states,[88] of economic ruin for the small states[89] and of the cutting off of hope of equal justice to the distant states.[90] The amendment was defeated, indicating clearly that the delegates were not prepared to go further than the negative of unconstitutional state legislation, already voted on May 31.[91]

It is noteworthy that at no time during this discussion was it even hinted that, as an alternative, control over state legislation might be vested in the national judiciary. Within limits, this was implicit in the jurisdiction provisions of Resolution 9, not yet taken under discussion. And although those so warm for the use of state courts as inferior tribunals did not perceive it, the possibility of even broader control through appeals from these courts to the national Supreme Court was latent in this scheme. Madison, as reported by Robert Yates of New York, was the only member who even mentioned courts.[92] He warned that state courts must give effect to state laws, although these might abridge the rights of the nation. A general power of negativing such as Pinckney proposed was absolutely necessary—"this is the only attractive principle which will retain its centrifugal force, and without this the planets will fly from their orbits."[93]

Madison's figure of speech referred to a trope of Dickinson's of the previous day[94]—comparing the general government to the sun, the center, and the state governments to the other planets revolving around it. The version which Egbert Benson recalled being recounted to him by Rufus King elaborated: "Virginia was the earth and Kentucky her moon, Connecticut from her fondness for *Bundling* was Venus, and

---

[86] To Jefferson, May 11, 1786, *Papers of Jefferson*, IX, 510.

[87] The original report of the Committee, of which Pinckney had been a member, in *JCC*, XXXI, 669–73.

[88] Gerry; in Farrand, *Records*, I, 165 (Madison).

[89] Bedford of Delaware; *ibid.*, 167 (Madison), 170 (Yates).

[90] Pierce Butler of South Carolina; *ibid.*, 168 (Madison).

[91] *Ibid.*, 163 (*Journal*); lost 7–3, one state divided.

[92] *Ibid.*, 169; accord, *Lansing Notes*,

40.

[93] Farrand, *Records*, I, 169; and compare Madison's own account, *ibid.*, 165.

[94] In the course of the debate on Dickinson's motion that the second branch of the national legislature be chosen by the legislatures of the individual states, *ibid.*, 157 (Yates). Reported more briefly by *Lansing Notes*, 38. Lansing has Wilson answering "does not wish to extinguish State Governments—but believe they will neither warm or brighten the Sun."

thievish little Rhode Island was Mercury, etc."[95] Dickinson's image was the one flight of poetic fancy that seems to have captivated the Convention. For two days it invaded the speeches[96] and, we believe, served to obscure clear thinking about the state-national relationship.

The debates had resumed an utterly prosy tone by June 11, when Resolution 14 was reached. This contained the only explicit check on state courts in the Virginia Plan. It provided that the "Legislative, Executive and Judiciary powers within the several States ought to be bound by oath to support the articles of Union."[97] Randolph explained the oath was necessary to prevent competition between the constitution and laws of the nation and those of particular states. Since state officials were already under oath to the states, to preserve due impartiality they should be equally bound to the national government. He believed that despite the fact that the executive and judiciary were nominally independent of the states' legislatures, they were actually dependent; "unless they be brought under some tie to the Natl. system, they will always lean too much to the State systems, whenever a contest arises between the two."[98]

Williamson of North Carolina regarded the oath to be unnecessary "as the Union will become the law of the land."[99] This was a trustful comment. The Articles of Confederation were, indeed, the law of the land, and yet some state judges, sworn only to support their own constitutions, had acted as if this were not the case. The proposed oath, of course, would unseat the primary loyalties of judges to their states, and was opposed by Sherman as too greatly intruding into state jurisdiction.[100] Luther Martin, Attorney General of Maryland, newly arrived, alerted the scrupulous to the impropriety of requiring oaths conflicting with those already taken.[101] None of this availed and the provision was approved.

We cannot here chronicle all the skirmishes over the actual or threatened abridgments of state sovereignty that erupted during the first fortnight's consideration of the Virginia Plan. There was no lull in the hostilities when at long last (June 12) the examination of the judiciary resolution was resumed, for another effort was made to cut down the

---

[95] Egbert Benson to Rufus King, Feb. 18, 1799, 38 Ms. Rufus King Papers, no. 38 (NYHS).
[96] Not only used by Madison. *Lansing Notes*, 39, reports Pinckney using the figure in his opening on the veto of improper laws. Paterson referred to it in a speech, June 9, Farrand, *Records*, I, 179 (Madison); and see Paterson's Notes, *ibid.*, 187.
[97] *Ibid.*, 22.

[98] *Ibid.*, 203 (Madison). *Lansing Notes*, 47, reports Randolph: "There is no Constitution that does not contravene Confederation."
[99] Farrand, *Records*, I, 207 (Yates).
[100] *Ibid.*, 203 (Madison).
[101] *Ibid.* What has been recounted *supra*, c. III, regarding the weight attached to official oaths should indicate that Martin's point was not a captious one.

inferior national tribunals. Randolph's resolution, it will be recalled, had invested these with jurisdiction to hear and determine in the first instance, and the supreme tribunal to hear and determine in the dernier resort, all piracies and felonies on the high seas and captures from an enemy. It was moved to alter the resolution to read "that the jurisdiction of the supreme Tribunal shall be to hear and determine in the dernier resort all piracies, felonies &ca."[102] This was not put to a vote. Next it was moved and carried to strike out the clause conferring jurisdiction over piracies, felonies on the high seas and captures from an enemy.[103] The purpose of these moves was apparently to leave undisturbed the jurisdiction in the hands of state judges as it then stood. After a vote clarifying the proposed jurisdiction over causes between citizens of different states, the Committee adjourned.[104]

Although none of the note-keepers indicate detailed controversy, one may surmise that something sufficiently disturbing had occurred to induce Randolph, on the next day, to offer a substitute resolution which jettisoned all references to piracies, etc. (as earlier voted out), and the diversity jurisdiction. What he moved read: "the jurisdiction of the national Judiciary shall extend to cases which respect the collection of the national revenue, impeachments of any national officers, and questions which involve the national peace and harmony."[105] Randolph explained that there was difficulty "in establishing the powers of the judiciary." The present object was to establish this principle: "to wit the security of foreigners where treaties are in their favor, and to preserve the harmony of states and that of the citizens thereof."[106] Once the principle was established, a sub-committee would work out details. This resolution was unanimously agreed to. It was then voted that the legislature should appoint the judges to the supreme tribunal.[107] Later in the day the Committee of the Whole reported the resolutions to Convention.

The most remarkable thing about the vote on Randolph's substitute is that the formula "questions which involve the national peace and harmony" should at this juncture have been approved. It had, of course, stood in the original resolution but had never been discussed. Every source of conflict between nation and states and between the states themselves—the obligations of treaties, border disputes, land titles, the trespasses of state admiralty courts and the like—was obviously embraced. Furthermore, as the many lawyers present could hardly have failed to notice, the clause was an overt invitation to unrestrained ex-

---

102 Farrand, *Records*, I, 211 (*Journal*).
103 *Ibid.*
104 *Ibid.*, 211–13 (*Journal*).
105 *Ibid.*, 223–24 (*Journal*).
106 *Ibid.*, 238 (Yates).

107 *Ibid.*, 224 (*Journal*), 232–33 (Madison). There is confusion on the *Journal* entry. Madison and Yates (at 238) are correct. *Cf. ibid.*, 232, n. 12.

pansion of jurisdiction. In England the courts had been masters at this game, and some of the artifices they used had been copied by colonial courts. This formula, of course, was not to stand, but even with Randolph's soothing explanation, it sat in the record, a foreboding signpost of the nationalistic road its proponents were prepared to travel.

PATERSON'S PLAN AND THE GREAT COMPROMISE

THE WISDOM OF pursuing a nationalistic course was challenged by William Paterson of New Jersey, future Justice of the Supreme Court. On June 15 he laid before the Convention a plan, "purely federal," concerted by the delegates from the "small States"—Connecticut, Delaware, New Jersey and Maryland—and two from New York.[108] What Paterson and his associates proposed was to preserve the existing Congress, adding to its powers and superimposing a plural executive authority. They recommended a supreme judicial tribunal with original jurisdiction only over impeachments, and appellate jurisdiction in cases involving ambassadors, prizes, piracies and felonies on the high seas, those in which "foreigners may be interested, in the construction of any treaty or treaties, or which may arise on any of the Acts for regulation of trade, or the collection of the federal Revenue."[109]

The provision for inferior jurisdiction was embedded in a resolution dealing with additional power to Congress in the matter of revenue and the regulation of commerce, foreign and between the states. Cognizance of punishments, fines and forfeitures for breach of any such federal acts was conferred upon the "Common law Judiciaries of the State" where an offense might be committed, with liberty of commencing in the first instance all suits or prosecutions for that purpose in the superior common law judiciary of the state, subject to appeal to "the Judiciary of the U. States" for corrections of all errors "both in law & fact in rendering Judgment."[110] No explicit provision was made for original

---

[108] In *House Document* No. 398 (cited *supra*, n. 47), 967 *et seq.*, are given three variants of the text— one taken from G. Hunt, and J. B. Scott, *The Debates in the Federal Convention as Reported by James Madison*; one from *Documentary History of the Constitution of the United States* (1894), I (hereafter cited as *Doc. Hist. Const.*); one from *American Museum* (1788), III, 362–63. The references here are to the Madison version. Farrand, in *Records*, III, 615, states that Madison's copy of Paterson's plan (*ibid.*, I, 242–45) fairly reproduces the original. The text also examined by Jameson, "Studies in the History of the Federal Convention of 1787," at 133–43. Strangely enough, Lansing, who alone notes that Paterson moved his resolves and that he, Lansing, seconded, does not give a text. *Lansing Notes*, 52.

[109] *House Document* No. 398 (cited *supra*, n. 47), 968–69.

[110] *Ibid.*, 967.

jurisdiction over captures, piracies, felonies on the high seas or cases in which foreigners might be interested in the construction of treaties. Presumably this would remain in *statu quo*.

To give cohesion to his loosely jointed system Paterson offered a resolve (No. 6) that all acts of Congress made pursuant to his amended Articles of Confederation and all treaties "shall be the supreme law of the respective States, so far forth as those Acts or Treaties shall relate to the said States or their Citizens, and that the Judiciary of the several States shall be bound thereby in their decisions, any thing in the respective laws of the Individual States to the contrary notwithstanding."[111] The federal executive was authorized to call forth the power of the Confederation against states or bodies of men who might oppose the execution of any acts or treaties.

It was agreed in Convention to submit these proposals to the Committee of the Whole and to recommit what the Committee had already reported for the purpose of proper comparison. Debate was opened on June 16 by Lansing of New York.[112] He raised bluntly the question of the want of power in the Convention to discuss and propose the Virginia Plan. The "Act of Congress," as he called it, the tenor of the acts of the states, and the delegates' commissions restrained the Convention to amendments of a "federal nature—having for their basis the Confederacy in being."[113] Paterson, who on June 9 had already pointed to the restraints placed upon the Convention by the "Act" of Congress,[114] chimed in with Lansing, making a fervent plea for the maintenance of the sovereignty of the states. All of this was a sort of belated demurrer, and one on not too solid ground. The resolve of Congress had not the legal effect Lansing and Paterson attributed to it, and calling it an "act" could not infuse it with the normative quality it had never possessed. During the Revolution it had been customary to refer to resolves of the Continental Congress as "acts." This they were in a colloquial sense, but certainly not in the technical sense of an Act of Parliament or of a state legislature. In the rules of procedure adopted by Congress[115] after the Articles were ratified, the classification of ordinances, acts and resolves indicates an attempt to distinguish what Congress was authorized to do legislatively from its acts as executive and the amorphous area where its opinions were registered in resolves. Whether or not Paterson and Lansing were aware of this, there were plenty of delegates on the floor, past and present members of Congress, who were.

---

[111] *Ibid.*, 969.

[112] Farrand, *Records*, I, 249 (Madison).

[113] *Ibid.* Yates does not state the point clearly, and neither does Lansing in his brief account of his speech.

[114] *Ibid.*, 177 (Madison). Paterson had gone so far as to say that the Convention was formed pursuant to an Act of Congress.

[115] *JCC*, XX, 476–82 (May 4, 1781), Art. 8.

Nevertheless, issue was not joined on this important, if technical, point. The men who first answered Lansing disregarded Congress's resolve and faced up to the question of power by manifest reference to the legislation of their own states. Wilson boldly asserted that he conceived himself authorized to conclude nothing but to propose anything.[116] Pinckney thought the Convention authorized to go to any length in recommending cures for existing evils.[117] Randolph claimed that the resolves of his state had been adopted on the supposition that a "federal" government was impractical. When all was at stake he would consent to any mode to preserve the nation.[118]

It remained for Alexander Hamilton in his ardent speech of June 18 to come fairly to grips with the question of the resolve of Congress, on which New York's own resolve had been patterned.[119] Hamilton's analysis was as much in replication to Lansing, commissioned with him, as in explanation of his own view of their powers. The delegates, he said, had been appointed for the sole and express purpose of "revising the Confederation," and to alter and amend it so as to render it effectual for the purposes of good government. "Those who suppose it must be federal, lay great stress upon the terms *sole* and *express*, as if the words intended a confinement to a federal government; when the manifest import is no more than that the institution of a good government must be the *sole* and *express* object of your deliberations."[120] This was no fanciful characterization of the purview of the resolve or of the resolve of the state which had commissioned Hamilton. By recourse to a familiar prescript respecting the reading of enactments—the "Preamble of the Statute is a good Mean to find out the Meaning of the Statute, and as it were a Key to open the Understanding thereof"[121]—he linked up the "sole express purpose of revising" with Congress's avowed opinion in the preamble of its resolve that a Convention was the best means of establishing a "firm national government."

Hamilton then proceeded to explain what he believed the expectations of his own state to be. In the New York legislature of which he had been a member, he said, an attempt to restrain the delegates to prevent encroachment on the state constitution had not succeeded, because it was anticipated that such incursions might occur—possibly a new union would be formed. The delegates were free to propose and

---

[116] Farrand, *Records*, I, 253 (Madison).

[117] *Ibid.*, 255 (Madison).

[118] *Ibid.*, 262 (Yates); less pungently phrased by Madison, at 255.

[119] *Ibid.*, 282–93 (Madison), 294–301 (Yates).

[120] *PAH*, IV, 196 (Yates). This is the more detailed account of Hamilton's explanation and is to be preferred because penned by a member of the same delegation.

[121] Coke, *Littleton*, 79a.

recommend.[122] The power of ratifying or rejecting lay with the states. Hamilton then outlined his own plan—more boldly "national" even than the one the Virginians had contrived.[123]

Paterson's propositions were fated not to be considered as an integrated whole. The plan's proponents seemed unable to move beyond the narrow view that the country was committed to their own concept of federalism, and that it would be disastrous to abandon it. The nationalists, like a corps of knowledgeable physicians, expatiated on the ills of the body politic. In effect, they asked, which is more likely to cure, your nostrum or ours? Hamilton, of course, had his own physic, more drastic than any yet offered. Others, by comparing the probable effects of one remedy with the other and calling upon the resources of wide historical reading, concluded that only the Virginia Plan, as amended, would serve.[124] On June 19 it was voted again to report to the Convention the Committee resolves of June 13, viz., the revised Virginia Plan.[125]

This decision smothered the Paterson Plan, and did nothing to settle the uneasy stomachs of its proponents. It did nothing to resolve the conflict between opposing viewpoints that was to darken the ensuing weeks of debate. The discussions in Convention became less an examination into the abstract merits of particulars reported by the Committee than a continuation of the notable exchanges begun when Paterson reported his plan. It was in essence a controversy over what was conceived of as federalism versus consolidation. To the group which believed that it was neither prudent nor lawful to set the country adrift

---

[122] Farrand, *Records*, I, 295 (Yates); less clearly phrased by Madison, at 283.

[123] The text given at the end of Madison's Notes is in *ibid.*, 291–93. Text from the Hamilton Mss. in *PAH*, IV, 207–09. Various members took copies. Lansing's is in *Lansing Notes*, 119–22. Textual problems re Hamilton's plan discussed in Farrand, *Records*, III, App. F, and by Jameson, "Studies in the History of the Federal Convention of 1787," at 143–50. Variant readings in *PAH*, IV, 210–11.

The plan outlined on June 18 is not to be confused with that which Hamilton presented to Madison shortly before the Convention rose. Text of this in *PAH*, IV, 253–74.

Hamilton's plan of June 18 was never "before the Convention" in the technical and only meaningful sense of actual submission for discussion as

were the plans submitted by Randolph, Pinckney and Paterson. Consequently, we have not undertaken to use it in our discussion.

It should here be noticed that a document relating to the organization and jurisdiction of the judiciary found in the George Mason Papers has been accorded an attention which it does not deserve. It is reprinted in Farrand, *Records*, IV, 54–56. Charles Warren conjectured that it "probably" was in the handwriting of John Blair (*The Making of the Constitution*, at 538n.). Farrand states categorically that "there is no evidence that it was presented to the Convention."

[124] Interesting exhibits here are the notes on the two plans laid out in parallel columns by King (Farrand, *Records*, I, 263) and by Wilson (*ibid.*, 276).

[125] *Ibid.*, 312 (*Journal*).

from existing moorings, a federal union implied a compact by sovereign entities. In the nature of things, the contractants alone were competent to participate in the direction and exercise of powers yielded to the central organization. The direct operation of the latter upon individuals was inadmissible. No less admissible would be immediate representation of the people at large in the machinery of government, and so a responsibility of government to them. The intermediacy of the states was essential. The most extreme position in opposition was that already taken by Hamilton. A federal government he conceived to mean an association of independent communities into one: "two sovereignties cannot coexist within the same limits."[126]

In spite of their infatuation with historical example, the ardent nationalists were disinclined to face up to the fact that a long history supported the pretensions of the states to the lofty estate claimed by them. By way of special traverse, Wilson offered a reading of the Declaration of Independence to render irrelevant events antecedent to it. The Declaration, he claimed, had been an assertion of the political independence of the colonies as united and not of the colonies severally.[127] The answer to this was that upon separation from Britain the states had preferred establishing themselves as thirteen separate sovereignties instead of incorporating into one. The federal power had been formed for defense—against foreign nations and to protect the small states from the larger.[128] It was in the circumstances of confederation and the provision made to preserve the equality and independency of the states that the measure of their capacities and relations *inter se* were to be found. Inevitably, resort was had to the contract theory of government, then as much a matter of general conviction as was the "maxim" of the separation of powers. The application of this theory by the small states was countered by a variety of subtleties on the manifold types of contracts and the differences between them.

These forays into the realm of jurisprudence are interesting chiefly for what they reveal of opinion respecting the Articles and their political intent. They did not reach the true source of anxiety—that the plan voted in Committee would put the small states at the mercy of the large; that the very identity of the states would be snuffed out if they lost their role as intermediaries between the individual and the general government. There were dire predictions of failure if the Convention did not, as Ellsworth put it, "engraft" a general government on that of the individual states.[129]

---

[126] *Ibid.*, 287 (Madison), and at 294 (Yates), 301 (King).
[127] *Ibid.*, 324 (Madison); Hamilton agreed.

[128] *Ibid.*, 340–41 (Madison), speech of Luther Martin.
[129] *Ibid.*, 407 (Madison).

We cannot here enter into the ramifications of the debates which waxed in intensity and temper through the last days of June. The wrangle over the new way or the old way with the occasional taunts and incivilities reminds one irresistibly of the disputation between the Right Logic and the Wrong Logic in Aristophanes' *Clouds*. But it was no mere game of wits at Philadelphia, for the fate of the Convention was for days at stake.

The ground that was fought over was the constitution of the legislative—in particular the second branch. The most unbending nationalists were determined upon extirpating any features of the existing order that they believed to be its fatal flaws. They suffered a major setback when (June 25) the Convention affirmed the recommendation of the Committee of the Whole that the second branch of the national legislature be elected by the legislatures of the individual states.[130] The nationalists then took a new offensive. To kill the obnoxious rule of voting by states established by the Articles, these leaders sought to have proportional representation and proportional "right of suffrage" in both branches of the national legislature. The small state representatives, who believed that the extinction of their polities was threatened, consequently found themselves fighting, as it were, on two fronts. They strove to secure a larger voice in the first branch, but their major objective was to defeat proportional representation and voting in the second branch where they were resolved to stand on an equal footing with the large states. Controversy moved to a crisis between June 29,[131] when Ellsworth moved that each state should have an equal vote in the second branch of the legislature, and July 2 when a vote was taken.[132] The result was a tie, with Georgia divided. It was, thereupon, decided to refer this question and the matter of representation in the first branch to a committee composed of a representative of each state present. Three future appointees to the Supreme Court—Ellsworth, Paterson and Rutledge—were among those named.[133]

The committee's report, submitted on July 5, was utterly distasteful to the fervent advocates of a "national" government—Madison, Gouverneur Morris, Wilson. It provided, in brief, that in the first branch of the national legislature there should be one representative for each 40,000 inhabitants. This branch was to have the prerogative of initiating all money bills, not to be altered or amended by the second branch. In the second branch each state was to have an equal vote.[134] This last recommendation, the crux of the report, finally passed July 16 by a

---

130 *Ibid.*, 395 (*Journal*).
131 *Ibid.*, 474 (Yates); see also at 468 (Madison).
132 *Ibid.*, 509 (*Journal*).

133 *Ibid.*
134 *Ibid.*, 524 (*Journal*), 526 (Madison); *Lansing Notes*, 118–19.

vote of 5–4, Massachusetts being divided.[135] New York which had sided consistently with the small states, was not present—Hamilton was absent, to return late in August; Lansing and Yates had decamped forever on July 10. The New Hampshire delegates did not arrive until a week later.

The decision of July 16 settled the form of American federalism for decades to come.[136] If the states suffered a species of *capitis deminutio*, as a result of popular representation and election to the first branch of the legislature, they were, nevertheless, integrated into the new structure, in a way which seemed to assure opportunity of asserting their respective corporate wills. In the Convention the pattern of thinking underwent a perceptible change. The critical spirit of the assemblage lost some of its edge, although it was by no means entirely blunted. More importantly, mutual revisions of opinion induced by the settlement of principle brought to the fore the practical consideration of constructing a workable engine of government, and one that would be acceptable. This is apparent from the debate immediately following agreement on the compromise.

The debate concerned the resolve dealing with the powers of the legislative. But the judicial was collaterally involved. A general grant of legislative power in sweeping terms was voted. But when the clause giving the national legislature the negative on state laws contravening the Constitution and treaties was reached, this was rejected.[137] Gouverneur Morris was opposed because it was "likely to be terrible to the States." He believed that a law which ought to be negatived would be set aside by the judiciary department; if this failed, it might be repealed by national legislation.[138] Sherman thought that the courts of the states

---

[135] Farrand, *Records*, II, 13 (*Journal*). While the fight on the compromise was still raging, Edmund Randolph prepared a scheme for placating the small states. This provided among other things for a right in each state to appeal to the national judiciary against a negative of its laws—this power at the moment still being vested in the national legislature. This negative was to be void if it was adjudged contrary to the power granted by the Articles of the Union. Furthermore, every individual "conceiving himself injured or oppressed by the partiality or injustice of a law of any particular State may resort to the National Judiciary, who may adjudge such law to be void, if found contrary to the principles of equity and justice." This given to Madison on July 10 (Farrand, *Records*, III, 55–56; *Doc. Hist. Const.*, V, 437–38).

It should be observed that Randolph seems to have envisaged a declaration of nullity by an *ex parte* and certainly not an adversarial proceeding. The notion of a law being void for repugnancy to the principles of equity and justice suggests, of course, the doctrine of Dr. Bonham's Case, 8 Coke, Rep. 107a.

[136] What is here adverted to is the change brought about by the Civil War amendments to the Constitution, notably the Fourteenth Amendment.

[137] Farrand, *Records*, II, 21–22 (*Journal*).

[138] Two speeches, *ibid.*, 27, 28 (Madison).

would not consider valid any law contravening the authority of the Union.[139] Madison spoke earnestly in defense of the provision. He harped once more upon the propensity of the states to pursue their own interests, and upon the necessity of controls. Damage could be done by bad laws before they could be "repealed by the Genl Legislre. or be set aside by the National Tribunals."[140] He had, furthermore, no confidence in the state tribunals as protectors of the national interest. In all states, courts were in some degree under the thumb of the legislatures. He recurred to the beneficent effects of the supervisory control exercised by the British Crown over colonial legislation. The principle of this he approved, although he admitted it had sometimes been misapplied. The clause was rejected 7–3. Thereupon, Luther Martin moved:

> that the legislative Acts of the United States made by virtue and in pursuance of the articles of Union and all Treaties made and ratified under the authority of the United States shall be the supreme law of the respective States as far as those acts or Treaties shall relate to the said States, or their Citizens and Inhabitants—and that the Judiciaries of the several States shall be bound thereby in their decisions, any thing in the respective laws of the individual States to the contrary notwithstanding.[141]

This was almost verbatim the first portion of Paterson's sixth resolve, and was agreed to unanimously. The significance of this fresh approach was profound. The Virginia theory of controlling obstructive state enactments by legislative veto was supplanted by the concept of judicial control, for the resolve pointed irresistibly to this method.

THE SECOND DEBATE ON THE JUDICIAL

THE JUDICIARY resolves of the Committee of the Whole were reached on July 18. The Convention's attention was chiefly engaged by the power of judicial appointments and the freezing of judicial salaries. The Committee had lodged appointments in the second branch. But since this body had now been converted into a bastion of state interests, this disposition amounted to a sanction of state control of judicial patronage. Gorham of Massachusetts suggested and moved the system of his state—appointment by the executive with the advice and consent of the Senate.[142] One may infer that the state sovereignty men were aware of the virtues of the Committee's recommendation, for they sought to leave it undisturbed. The nationally minded were equally

---

[139] *Ibid.*, 27.
[140] *Ibid.*

[141] *Ibid.*, 22 (*Journal*).
[142] *Ibid.*, 41 (Madison).

resolute for the proposed change, alleging that the matter was one in which both the states and the people, through the executive, acting in their behalf, should have a say. The vote was evenly divided.[143] Madison then moved appointment by the executive with a right of dissent in the second branch.[144] This was held over to be debated on July 21, when it was rejected.[145] The discussions are interesting chiefly because the underlying divergence of viewpoint and purpose was masked by arguments of a "practical" nature. Legislatures were places of cabal and intrigue; the executive would toady to the large states—it would be easier for candidates to intrigue with him than with the Senate.[146] One wonders at the energies expended to perfect something for humans so unregenerate.

This misanthropic mood did not hinder a unanimous vote (July 18) that the tenure of judges should be during good behavior.[147] This, after all, was part of the American constitutional canon which obtained in most states, the result of a series of colonial struggles with the Crown over tenure at pleasure. But when a motion was made that judges' salaries be susceptible of increase, it was resisted by Madison, because he feared that the bench might be unduly complaisant toward the legislature should its members be interested in current litigation when salary increase was pending.[148] The "bad man" theory did not prevail, and a prohibition against increase failed.

When the clause empowering the national legislature to "appoint" inferior courts was reached, some delegates, obviously unwilling to trust the national legislature to interpret "appoint" as had the Confederation Congress, again sought to make the state courts participants in the national system. Conservation of state authority was involved. And, political considerations aside, there were, we believe, reasonable grounds

---

[143] *Ibid.*, 38 (*Journal*).

[144] *Ibid.*, 44 (Madison).

[145] *Ibid.*, 71–72 (*Journal*). Only Massachusetts, Pennsylvania and Virginia voted aye.

[146] *Ibid.*, 42–43 (Madison).

[147] *Ibid.*, 38 (*Journal*).

[148] *Ibid.*, 45 (Madison). Gouverneur Morris and Benjamin Franklin were advocates of permitting increase, on the ground that circumstances such as changes in the value of money or enlargement of judicial business must be taken into account. Madison believed that changes in the value of money could be guarded against by taking as a standard something of "permanent value" like wheat.

This idea cropped up again in Randolph's draft used by the Committee of Detail (*infra*, n. 180) in his provision for Senators' "wages." Every six years the supreme judiciary was to impanel a special jury of the most respectable merchants and farmers to declare what had been the "averaged value" of wheat during the last six years in the state where the legislature might be sitting. For the next six years the Senators were to receive the averaged value of —— bushels of wheat. This provision is struck out in the draft. The notion was typical of a *Naturalwirtschaft* like Virginia, and was unlikely to appeal to urban dwellers like Morris and Franklin, or Rutledge, who edited the above draft.

for anxiety. The new plan, as conceived and as it stood, conformed to the traditional American pattern of a hierarchical arrangement of courts with ultimate control at the apex, such as prevailed in all the states. Within each state, however, the writs of its courts did not run beyond its borders. Process in the proposed system of federal courts, however, would presumably be ubiquitous. This offered a tempting means of extending jurisdiction, and those who opposed a consolidated government might properly fear that courts might be agencies in bringing this about. The delegates were too familiar with the British constitution not to know that it was at the level of original jurisdiction that the three central courts at Westminster had each extended its authority.

In light of the fact that even a non-lawyer, Richard Henry Lee, was later to find warning in the English example, it is lamentable that the debate is so meagrely noted.[149] Luther Martin is reported merely as saying that federal courts would create jealousies and opposition in state courts and interfere with their operations—unbelievable brevity in one persistently wordy.[150] Nathaniel Gorham sought to allay his fears by pointing to the "federal" courts for the trial of piracies against which no complaint had been made by the states or by their courts.[151] These, of course, were but federal courts *sub modo*. Furthermore, they were subject to no appellate control, for error did not lie in such causes. Sherman, who had earlier argued for using state tribunals, was willing to give the power to the national legislature, but wished state tribunals might be made use of whenever this could be safely done. Both Randolph and Mason supported the power of the national legislature to "appoint" inferior courts. In the end this resolve was unanimously approved.[152]

Like the debate on using state courts as inferior tribunals, that which followed on the jurisdiction resolution was also inadequately noted. If Martin's later expanded report to the Maryland legislature is to be trusted, there was a fuller discussion than Madison indicates.[153] The latter had already exhibited an aversion to Martin's diffuse style and was possibly not prepared to report him at large. Madison notes the excision of jurisdiction over impeachment, and adds that "several criticisms" were directed at the definition of jurisdiction.[154] In place of the Committee resolution he offered a more sweeping substitute: "the jurisdiction [of the national judiciary] shall extend to all cases arising

---

[149] *Infra*, p. 290.
[150] Farrand, *Records*, II, 45–46 (Madison).
[151] *Ibid.*, 46.
[152] *Ibid.*, 39 (*Journal*).
[153] "His Genuine Information," on which see *infra*, c. VII, p. 301. Text in Farrand, *Records*, III, 172; the debate on inferior courts is recounted *ibid.*, 206; on jurisdiction, *ibid.*, 220–22.
[154] Farrand, *Records*, II, 46 (Madison).

SIR EDWARD COKE.
Propagator of Constitutional Doctrine.
(*Collections of the Library of Congress*)

JAMES MADISON.
Proponent of the Constitution. Portrait by Charles Wilson Peale.
(Courtesy of the Thomas Gilcrease Institute of American History and Art, Tulsa, Oklahoma)

ALEXANDER HAMILTON.
Proponent of the Constitution. Portrait by John Trumbull.
(Courtesy of the National Gallery of Art)

RUFUS KING.
Proponent of the Constitution. Portrait by Charles Wilson Peale.
(Courtesy of the Independence National Historical Park Collection, Philadelphia)

CALEB STRONG.
Proponent of the Constitution. Portrait by Gilbert Stuart.
(Courtesy of Frederick Strong Moseley, Jr., and the Frick Art Reference Library)

LUTHER MARTIN.
Opponent of the Constitution. Portrait by David Edwin.
*(Courtesy of the John Work Garrett Library at Evergreen House, The Johns Hopkins University,
Baltimore, Maryland)*

PATRICK HENRY.
Opponent of the Constitution. Engraving after the portrait by Thomas Sully.
(*Collections of the Library of Congress*)

RICHARD HENRY LEE.
Opponent of the Constitution. Portrait by Charles Wilson Peale.
(*Courtesy of the Independence National Historical Park Collection, Philadelphia*)

under the Natl. laws. And to such other questions as may involve the Natl. peace & harmony."[155] This was approved, but why the states' rights delegates agreed remains a mystery.

If the judiciary resolutions received short shrift in Madison's notes, he was lavish in his report of what ensued when Wilson (July 21) sought to resuscitate the scheme of associating the judiciary with the executive in the veto. Wilson believed that the judges should have the chance of remonstrating against projected encroachments on the people as well as themselves. There might be laws, unjust, unwise, dangerous or destructive, "yet not be so unconstitutional" as to justify the judges in refusing to give them effect.[156] Gerry, who denounced the mixing of departments as improper, exploded with the comment that this "was making Statesmen of the judges; and setting them up as the guardians of the Rights of the people."[157] This guardianship, he believed, was better entrusted to the people's representatives. He had, in short, no use for Madison's theory that the judiciary must be given a weapon for its own defense. But it was no easy matter to wean Madison from any idea which he had ever warmly embraced.[158] With considerable sophistical skill he explained that to each department must be added a defensive power in order to maintain in practice the principle of separation—an "auxiliary precaution in favor of the maxim."[159] As a political safeguard this was tantamount, as the old saying had it, to setting a fox to keep the geese. It was made plausible by reference to the British usage of the judges sitting both in Parliament and the Privy Council, a precedent which proved nothing. The English never had achieved a real separation of powers, although Montesquieu believed that they had.[160] The Convention was thus posed the problem whether a theory universally accepted as sound was to be applied with logical consistency, or whether it could safely rely upon British experience and make believable the pretext that it was in fact cleaving to principle.

---

155 *Ibid.*

156 Farrand, *Records*, II, 73 (Madison).

157 *Ibid.*, 75 (Madison).

158 Madison's tenacity is exemplified by remarks made September 12, five days before the signing. The question of permitting states limited power to lay export duties to defray inspection charges was before the house. Some members believed this threatened continuation of the existing oppression of states like New Jersey by the port states. Madison said that the Supreme Court would be the source of redress. In his opinion "A negative on the State laws alone could meet all the shapes which these could assume." *Ibid.*, 589 (Madison). The permission was granted (Constitution, Art. I, sec. 10), but state laws of this sort were made subject to revision or control by Congress.

See also Madison's complaints about failure to enshrine the negative of state laws in his letter to Jefferson, Oct. 24, 1787, *Papers of Jefferson*, XII, 280.

159 Farrand, *Records*, II, 77.

160 Montesquieu, *The Spirit of the Laws* (Dublin ed., 1751), I, 185–98, Bk. XI, c. 6.

But the motion before the house, whatever political-philosophical implications it bore for Madison and for other delegates, raised questions of a more practical nature. Would the hardly won struggles to establish and maintain the independency and integrity of the bench be imperilled? Was it compatible with these deep-seated traditions that a judge have anything to do with a statute except it be *sub judice*? Could a judge be party to the aborting of an enactment, or was he confined to what the lawbooks said he could do with a statute, or, as had been conceded generally in Convention, could he strike it down for repugnance to the Constitution?

The arguments of expediency in favor of Wilson's motion derived strength from the fact that at this time the judges were fettered in their handling of legislation by the canons of statutory construction inherited from England.[161] Under these rules, interpretation was less an art than an exercise in logic or grammar. If there had ever been much room for a court to indulge its own ideas of policy, it had shrunk to mere closet size once the hegemony of Parliament was settled. This was not without its effects in America, where legislatures were pretending to the same prerogative enjoyed by their prototype.

It is against this background of existing precedent concerning what judges could do with statutes that Wilson's comments must be viewed. Whether or not he expected that the exigent rules about statutory construction would be carried over to the exposition of the Constitution, it is manifest he anticipated no adventurous pronouncements on policy by the bench. This is inferable from his assertion that statutes might be infected with unconstitutionality and yet not to the degree that the judges could avoid them—a claim gainsaid by no one. Mason, indeed, agreed with Wilson; the purport of Gerry's remark about making statesmen of judges, as well as of Martin's speech in opposition, was to the same intent.

The motion to associate the judicial in the veto was defeated 4–3, two states being divided.[162] We cannot know what decided the issue— a rigorous view of separation, Ellsworth's intimation that the judges were free to employ standards other than the Constitution in the "revi-

---

[161] The standard books of reference at this time were, of course, Coke, *Littleton*, where various rules are scattered through Coke's own commentary, and Matthew Bacon's *Abridgment, s.v.* Statutes. Blackstone's rules of construction in *Commentaries*, Introduction, I, 85, were chiefly abstracted from Coke, *Littleton*, Coke's *Fourth Institute* and various cases in Coke's *Reports*. The continuing hegemony of Coke's precepts is obvious from J. Kent, *Commentaries on American Law* (1826), I, Lecture XX (hereafter cited as Kent, *Commentaries*). Examples of the rules of construction as applied by American courts, *supra*, c. III.

[162] Farrand, *Records*, II, 71 (*Journal*).

sionary" process[163] or the impact of Rutledge's final comment that judges ought never to give an opinion on a law until it was before them.[164] One thing remained: the judiciary was neither to meddle nor make with legislation except an issue of constitutionality should arise.

It is remarkable that neither in this discussion, nor at any time when any matter touching the judicial had been before the house, were there explicit statements concerning the basic jurisprudence that was to prevail in the new system. Madison's assumption, noticed above, that a "code of laws" would come into being[165] suggests that he anticipated a statutory solution. There was certainly no intimation that the common law would serve. It had, in America, undergone change from planting in new soil. It had, as we have observed, assumed as many variant forms as there were states. Unless the delegates were prepared to accept the parent English version, either as it presumably stood in 1787 or as of some other arbitrary date, they would be inviting bedlam. Madison was to make clear (August 17) that a "foreign law" was unacceptable and that there could be hope of "neither uniformity nor stability" by adverting to the laws of the states.[166]

There was a further and cogent reason why the common law was not to be embosomed in the new system. When, on July 23, the question of ratification by state conventions was before the Convention, Randolph asserted that particular states had set up the authority of the common law against that of the Confederation which had no higher sanction than legislative ratification.[167] The implications of this ran far beyond the matter then at issue in the Convention. Both in England and in the colonies the common law had served as a source of constitutional right.[168] In this country, in particular, the notion that the common law was the birthright of every man of which there could be no defeasance by legislative fiat had been a matter of conviction, a staple in the controversies on the eve of the Revolution. This was tolerable in a constitutional system as amorphous as was the British, where usage was so considerable an ingredient. It was a very different matter to welcome the common law into a constitution which was to define and make stable certain fundamentals. Some particulars of this body of law, involved in earlier constitutional controversies, were of

---

[163] *Ibid.*, 73–74 (Madison).
[164] *Ibid.*, 80 (Madison).
[165] *Supra*, p. 210.
[166] Farrand, *Records*, II, 316 (Madison). This was in the course of discussing the power of Congress "to declare the law and Punishment of Piracies and Felonies committed on

the high seas." Madison claimed that "felony at common law is vague. It it also defective." He argued for power "to define."
[167] *Ibid.*, 89 (Madison).
[168] Discussed in Goebel, "Constitutional History and Constitutional Law," 555 at 558 *et seq.*

incredible antiquity, but nonetheless viable. Others were utterly repugnant to republican principles. No one understood this better than the Virginians, fresh from the struggle over the revisal of their laws.[169] This had involved, among other things, the rooting out of anachronisms sanctioned by the ordinance of the Virginia Convention (1776) adopting the common law of England.[170] Reluctance to let the past take too great a command of the future may account in part for the Convention's judicious restraint in selecting only specific items from the vast storehouse of the mother law, e.g., habeas corpus, jury trial in causes criminal and, most importantly, the law-equity dichotomy. As things turned out, the Convention had not gone far enough to satisfy public opinion; the deficiencies were to be repaired by the first set of amendments.

THE PROBLEM OF RATIFICATION

RANDOLPH'S WARNING that the common law was viewed as a fundamental law superior to an instrument which purported to be such, but only had the sanction of legislative approbation, was evoked by an attempt of Ellsworth and Paterson to refer ratification to the state legislatures.[171] On its face this motion appeared to be an attempt to make the new Constitution depend on the procedures stipulated in the Articles of Confederation for their alteration. Inevitably it raised the problem from what source the Constitution would draw life and authority. Mason denied the powers of state legislatures to ratify, declaring that resort must be had to the people "with whom all power remains that has not been given up in the Constitutions derived from them." He declared bluntly that mere legislative ratification would leave the new Constitution "on the weak and tottering foundation of an Act of Assembly."[172] Taken together, the implications of Randolph's and Mason's remarks were inescapable—if the new instrument did not derive its vigor from a better source than did the Articles of Confederation or the constitutions of states like New York or Virginia, it would be no safeguard against the very evils it was designed to suppress or avert. Least of all could it be used effectively by the judiciary to strike down legislative excesses.

---

[169] Early stages discussed in M. Kimball, *Jefferson: The Road to Glory*, 209–28. The vicissitudes of the work of the first Committee of Revision are set out in the editorial note "The Revisal of the Laws 1776–1786" in *Papers of Jefferson*, II, 305–24; on the work of Madison at the 1785 and 1786 sessions of the legislature, *ibid.*, 321–22.

[170] 9 Hening, *Va. Stats.*, 127.

[171] Farrand, *Records*, II, 88 (Madison).

[172] *Ibid.*, 88–89 (Madison).

V: *Constitutional Convention and the Judiciary*

The nationally minded delegates knew well that only from the people themselves could come the Promethean fire to vitalize what might otherwise be as lifeless clay. They estimated that the fortunes of the Convention's work were better secured if the will of the people were expressed in conventions chosen for that purpose than if the decision be made by the keepers of state sovereignty—the legislatures. Adoption by the people was an unimpeachable postulate, for the one great principle established by the Revolution was that the people were the ultimate source of political authority. But it was a postulate the states' rights delegates were not prepared to accept; and it was repugnant to individuals like Gerry in whom a belated loyalty to the Articles of Confederation was beginning to stir.[173] The states' rights men took the ground that it was enough if legislatures, the people's representatives, speak for them.[174] As this was a principle underlying the Articles of Confederation, the argument assumed a certain constitutional plausibility. Gerry took the position that the Confederation was "paramount to any State Constitution."[175] Consequently he thought that Article XIII possessed this quality and implied that the Convention must conform to its terms.

The injection into the debate of the Articles of Confederation, and specifically Article XIII which required unanimous legislative confirmation of "alteration," not only threatened to revive the controversy over the authority of the Convention to do what it had been about for nearly two months, but also posed the prickly question whether it was in any event bound by Article XIII. Once more the contract theory was dusted off and urged in support of the need for securing action by sovereign states through their duly constituted organs.

In the end it was Rufus King who directed attention to the insurmountable obstacle to legislative ratification—the restraints of the state constitutions themselves.[176] This was elaborated by Madison. The changes which were being effected, he said, would make essential inroads on state constitutions. It would be a dangerous doctrine that a legislature could change the constitution upon which its existence depended. Some constitutions may have given the legislatures power to

---

[173] *Ibid.*, 89–90 (Madison).

[174] In the case of Ellsworth, he appears to have had a morbid distaste for conventions. This stemmed, of course, from the fact that the troubles in Massachusetts and on the borders of New Hampshire and Connecticut had been stirred up at local conventions and were regarded as defiant of the town meeting system. See *ibid.*, 91.

Gouverneur Morris in answer to Ellsworth claimed that legislative alterations not conformable to the Articles would clearly not be valid. "The Judges would consider them null and void." *Ibid.*, 92. This was good theory but, considering how the British treaty had been manhandled in the state courts, hardly realistic.

[175] *Ibid.*, 89 (Madison).

[176] *Ibid.*, 92 (Madison).

agree to changes in the federal compact; there were certainly some which did not. The difference between a system founded on legislatures only and one deriving from the people was the difference between a league or treaty and a constitution. In point of moral obligation both might be equally inviolable. In point of political operation there were two important distinctions. A law violating a treaty ratified by a pre-existing law might be respected by the judges as law, although unwise or pernicious. A law violative of a constitution ratified by the people would be considered by the judge to be null and void. The second difference was the doctrine of the law of nations in the case of treaties, that a breach of any article by any of the parties freed the other con-tractants from their engagements. In the case of a union of a people under one constitution, "the nature of the pact has always been under-stood to exclude such an interpretation."[177] And so it was determined that the instrument should be ratified by conventions.

THE COMMITTEE OF DETAIL

ON THE DAY following this determination (July 24) the Conven-tion balloted for a Committee of Detail to report a constitution con-formable to the resolutions passed by the Convention.[178] Chosen were Gorham, Ellsworth, Randolph, Rutledge and Wilson. It was also voted to refer Paterson's and Pinckney's plans to this Committee. The Con-vention continued to wrangle over the election of the executive until July 26 when it adjourned until August 6, on which day the Committee reported.[179]

The surviving papers of the Committee of Detail reveal virtually nothing as to how its perfected report was put together. A document in Randolph's hand with emendations by Rutledge is commonly regarded to have been the point of departure.[180] Something of the give and take of committee work may be inferred from the excisions and inserts.

Randolph's draft deals separately with legislature, executive and judiciary, but some matter touching the latter was placed in the legis-lative section, viz., authority "to provide tribunals and punishment for mere offenses against the law of nations" as well as to "appoint" tri-bunals inferior to the Supreme Court.[181] This last matter was repeated

---

[177] *Ibid.*, 92–93 (Madison).
[178] *Ibid.*, 97 (*Journal*).
[179] *Ibid.*, 176 (*Journal*).
[180] A facsimile of this document is published in W. M. Meigs, *The Growth of the Constitution in the Federal Convention of 1787*, following p. 316.

In a note Mr. Meigs not only identi-fied the handwritings but identified the document as relating to the delibera-tions of the Committee of Detail. The document is transcribed and printed in Farrand, *Records*, IV, 37–51.
[181] Farrand, *Records*, IV, 44.

in the judiciary section. There Rutledge substituted the word "establish."[182] Curiously enough, Randolph continued in the legislature the power to adjudicate disputes between states as then possessed by Congress. Rutledge amended to confine this to disputes over territory and jurisdiction.[183]

The section in this draft on the judiciary itself opened with the several provisions voted by the Convention on July 18, viz., that a national judiciary be established to consist of one supreme tribunal and of inferior tribunals which the national legislature was empowered to "appoint." The judges were to be appointed by the second branch of the national legislature, to hold office during good behavior and to receive a fixed compensation in which no diminution should be made during office.[184]

The draft next moves to the matter of jurisdiction. It opens: "The jurisdiction of the supreme tribunal shall extend 1. to all cases, arising under laws passed by the general; <Legislature:>"[185]—a particular agreed upon in Convention. The author then embroiders from a design of his own. He restored from the original Virginia Plan jurisdiction over impeachments and certain other matters upon which the delegates had earlier been unable to agree—apparently intending thereby to make precise the vague and slippery formula "national peace and harmony." Jurisdiction was to extend "to such other cases, as the national legislature may assign, as involving the national peace and harmony; in the collection of the revenue / disputes between citizens of different States / in disputes between different States; and in disputes, in which subjects or citizens of other countries are concerned."[186] Rutledge inserted: disputes between a state and a citizen or citizens of another state and "Cases of Admiralty Jurisdn."[187]

---

[182] *Ibid.*, 47.

[183] *Ibid.*

[184] Randolph inserted a direction that judges take an oath of fidelity to the Union. *Ibid.*, 49.

[185] *Ibid.*, 47–48. The word in the angle bracket was written over and obliterates a word in the original.

[186] *Ibid.*, 48.

[187] The Virginia Plan had contemplated establishment of diversity jurisdiction in language not too precise, but this had by amendment been combed out and was not embodied in the Resolves turned over to the Committee of Detail. There is nothing in the sources to indicate how it came to be resuscitated. H. J. Friendly, "The Historic Basis of Diversity Jurisdiction," *Harv. L. Rev.* 41:483–510, has adduced evidence from the meagre printed reports of the time that there was little cause to fear that state tribunals would be hostile to litigants from other states. It should be pointed out, however, that there were such variations in the judicial structure and the traditions of practice in the several states (here examined in cc. I and III) as to make it highly desirable that in the sort of union contemplated an out-of-state litigant have the option of pursuing a cause in a federal court. Obvious drawbacks in the existing scheme of things was the unavailability of equity remedies in their plenitude, in the New England states, Pennsylvania and Georgia, to say nothing of

The Randolph draft is here remarkable not because it embodied items rejected or disagreed to, but because it gave discretion to the national legislature to settle the circumstances under which the exercise of jurisdiction would be allowed. No such idea had hitherto been advanced. Far from stabilizing jurisdiction, it was left fluid. For weeks, legislatures had been so many whipping boys; now, amazingly enough, it was projected that the judiciary be prey to the caprices of the lawmakers. But this was not all. The draft had one further peculiarity. The Convention's resolve had conferred jurisdiction upon the "National Judiciary"; in Randolph's draft it was attributed to the supreme national tribunal. This "supreme jurisdiction" was to be appellate only, except as the national legislature might make it original. All or part of the jurisdiction might be assigned by the legislature to inferior tribunals to be exercised originally.

To the Convention's resolve on the supremacy of the national laws the Randolph draft originally appended: "All laws of a particular state, repugnant hereto, shall be void: and in the decision thereon, which shall be vested in the supreme judiciary, all incidents without which the general principles cannot be satisfied, shall be considered, as involved in the general principle."[188] This was possibly too cryptic for someone on the Committee, for it is struck out in the draft.

James Wilson, too, devised an amplification of the Convention's resolutions, but, as respects the judiciary, the remains of his plan are too fragmentary to support any conclusions.[189] He made extracts from Paterson's and Pinckney's plans, and the former, as will shortly be seen, influenced the statement of federal jurisdiction. There survives also of the Committee's work, and in Wilson's hand, what may be a next to last draft.[190] The provisions here for the judiciary are substantially identical with the final report.

By some stroke of draftsman's genius the judiciary article[191] as reported to the Convention on August 6 opened with the august words: "The Judicial Power of the United States. . . ." There followed the statement respecting the structure of the courts, and here the provision respecting inferior tribunals read: "such inferior Courts as shall when necessary, from time to time be constituted by the Legislature of the United States." The dispositions regarding tenure and compensation were specified as resolved. The definition of jurisdiction, as in Randolph's draft, was set out solely with reference to the Supreme Court.

the intricate system of appeals in Massachusetts, and the consistent recourse to legislatures to award new trials not only there, but in New Hampshire and Connecticut.

[188] Farrand, *Records*, IV, 45.

[189] One document, *ibid.*, II, 150–52; the second document, *ibid.*, 152–57, 159–63.

[190] *Ibid.*, 163–75.

[191] Art. XI, *ibid.*, 186–87 (Madison).

V: *Constitutional Convention and the Judiciary*

Everything that Randolph and Rutledge had stipulated respecting the heads of jurisdiction except collection of revenue was preserved; but the authority of the legislature to use the national peace and harmony as a criterion of their exercise was dropped. From Paterson's plan came jurisdiction in cases affecting ambassadors, expanded by including "other Public Ministers or Consuls." Presumably Paterson's grant of piracy and felonies on the high seas was intended to be subsumed under the Committee classification of "Admiralty and maritime jurisdiction."[192] The Supreme Court was to have original jurisdiction in cases of impeachments, ambassadors, etc., and those in which a state should be a party. Authority in the last instance was not plenary, for the states' pretensions to sovereignty were catered to by seating in the Senate the supervision of adjudications of interstate controversies over territory or jurisdiction as well as those arising from grants by different states. In the legislature was vested power to make regulations of and exceptions to the appellate jurisdiction.[193] Randolph's idea was also adopted of giving the legislature discretion to "assign" to inferior courts any part of the jurisdiction, except trial of the President; in other words, the stipulated original jurisdiction of the Supreme Court over cases affecting ambassadors and controversies between states was defeasible.

Into the judiciary article also went a provision respecting jury trial and venue of causes criminal that Rutledge had inserted in the Randolph document.[194] The provision respecting judgment in cases of impeachment, identical with the later Article I, section 3, was also embraced. The definition of treason and the dispositions respecting this crime, that with alteration were later to be tacked onto Article III of the Constitution, were in this report embodied in the article dealing with legislative powers. The appointment of judges of the Supreme Court remained with the second branch. This power was not finally transferred to the President by and with the consent of the Senate until September 7.

Two significant pieces of tinkering by the Committee of Detail with a Convention resolution concerned that declaring the supremacy of the acts of the national legislature. The *constitutions* of the states as well as their laws were made subordinate to the national laws.[195] And

---

[192] Paterson had invested the court with appellate jurisdiction in all cases of captures from an enemy and all cases of piracies and felonies on the high seas (*ibid.*, I, 244). Wilson copied this and added "or on the Law of Nations, or general commercial or marine Laws" (*ibid.*, II, 157). Pinckney, it will be recalled, authorized the legislature to institute in each state a court of admiralty for hearing and determining maritime causes (*supra*, p. 206). This was copied out by Wilson (*ibid.*, II, 159).

[193] Art. IX, secs. 2 and 3, *ibid.*, II, 183–85. In the Articles of Confederation this had been described as "the last resort of appeal" (Art. IX). This, as we have seen, it was not, for the power was merely supervisory.

[194] Farrand, *Records*, IV, 45.

[195] Art. VIII, *ibid.*, II, 183.

the latter were made binding upon the "judges in the several States" instead, as earlier resolved, upon "the Judiciaries of the several States." This had the effect of making personal the injunction, and laying it as well upon state as upon national judges functioning within any state.

The Committee did not explicitly grant jurisdiction to the Supreme Court to adjudicate matters arising under the Constitution itself. This, perhaps, may have been deemed to pass *sub silentio*. Nevertheless, to the literal minded it left without manifest implementation those provisions which the report lifted from the Articles of Confederation, viz., the clause which forbade the states to legislate on certain particulars,[196] and the clauses relating to full faith and credit,[197] privileges and immunities of citizens, and extradition.[198]

THE FINAL WEEKS

THE DEBATES IN the final weeks of the Convention had a somewhat different cast from those which preceded them. As the offering of the Committee of Detail was scrutinized and clause upon clause was rolled through the wringer of disputation, an increasing awareness of tough political reality pervaded the proceedings. Allusions to philosophers and to the past experience of mankind, that had lent the earlier discussions the quality of a search for enlightenment, were much less often made. Only the obsession with the British constitution continued, little abated. Most significantly, the mandate that something "adequate to the exigencies of the union" must be perfected was in the way of being eclipsed by the question latent from the very beginning—will this instrument be politically acceptable? Since there were thirteen respondents, each to answer, regional and particular state interests kept making themselves heard. The delegates were returning to their constituents and had to look to their reckonings. The spirit of accommodation for which much had been sacrificed in July was menaced by shortening tempers and by growing recusancy in a quarter not to be anticipated—Gerry, Mason and Randolph. All three had in varying degree been on the nationalist side.

The judiciary article suffered little if at all from these tensions. But before it was reached, late in August, there were motions which, if carried, would have been contaminating to the judicial function, and would have impaired the independency of this department. When the veto power was up for discussion, Madison and Wilson sought to confer upon the judges of the Supreme Court an independent and concurrent

---

[196] Articles of Confederation, Art. VI.

[197] *Ibid.*, Art. IV.
[198] Both in Art. IV.

power to veto legislative enactments.[199] The familiar arguments were repeated for and against, and once more the power of the court to pass upon the constitutionality of legislation was urged as the limit of judicial authority. The motion was beaten.[200] Three days later (August 18) Ellsworth suggested and Gouverneur Morris moved (August 20) the creation of a President's council.[201] On this the Chief Justice of the Supreme Court would have a seat, and he would preside in the absence of the President. The Chief Justice's duties were to include the recommendation of alterations and amendments to the "Laws of the United States as may in his opinion be necessary to the due administration of Justice, and such as may promote useful learning and inculcate sound morality throughout the Union."[202] This proposal to make the Chief Justice a sort of *custos morum*, with the rest of the elaborate resolution, was referred to the Committee of Detail. A greatly attenuated resolve was reported back.[203] This came to nothing after Mason's substitute of a council formed on a regional basis was rejected.[204]

If there had been some outward manifestation of preoccupation with "liberty," the Convention's uncompromising stand against extrajudicial employment of the bench might be attributed to respect for Montesquieu's warning that unless the power of judging was held separate from the executive and legislative "there can be then no

---

[199] Farrand, *Records*, II, 298 (Madison). Mercer of Maryland, who first attended the Convention August 6 and was not present after August 17, disapproved of the doctrine that judges as expositors of the Constitution should have authority to declare a law void. Mercer, of course, had no firsthand knowledge of the previous exploration of the question. During his fleeting visit at Philadelphia, he expressed opinions on a great variety of matter. Jefferson had a low opinion of Mercer's capacities; *cf.* his letter to Madison, Apr. 25, 1784, *Papers of Jefferson*, VII, 118.

[200] Farrand, *Records*, II, 295 (*Journal*). The vote was 8–3.

[201] *Ibid.*, 335–37 (*Journal*), 342–44 (Madison).

[202] *Ibid.*, 335 (*Journal*).

[203] On Aug. 22, *ibid.*, 367 (*Journal*). The Chief Justice was left on the Council, but the peculiar functions assigned him in the original resolution were eliminated. This Council was to advise the President in matters respecting the execution of his office that he might lay before them. He was not to be concluded by their advice.

[204] The report of the Committee of Detail was not acted upon. On August 31 all postponed matter was referred to a Committee of Eleven—one member from each state present. Technically the report on the Council was not "postponed" since no vote had been taken. On September 4 the Committee reported including a clause (eventually in Art. II, sec. 2) authorizing the President to require the opinion, in writing, of heads of executive departments. *Ibid.*, 473, 495 (*Journal*).

On September 7 the House had reached the section of the report dealing with the President. When the clause on requiring opinions from heads of departments was reached, Mason, seconded by Franklin, moved to postpone and asked an instruction for the Committee to prepare a clause establishing a Council based on regional representation. The motion to postpone was voted down. *Ibid.*, 541–42 (Madison).

liberty."[205] As it was, no word in the vocabulary of contemporary politics was used less often. Neither the task nor the idiom of discussion required it. "We are not working on the natural rights of men not yet gathered into society," wrote Randolph, "but upon those rights modified by society and interwoven with what we call the rights of states."[206] The "blessings of liberty" of the preamble, that last-minute inspiration of Gouverneur Morris, was not debated. In the state constitutions, drawn when liberty was on the lips of everyone but the Tories, the philosopher's dictum had in various cases been ignored. Even where the maxim of separation was enshrined in a constitution, as we have seen, violations were constant.[207] But there is nothing to show that the repulse of attempts to hybridize the judicial was in reaction to aberrations in the states. The discussions do reveal that some delegates cherished an austere conception of the judicial office as one the probity and detachment of which must be immunized from political taint.

The conviction that the power to pass upon the constitutionality of statutes lay with the courts involved no inconsistency of opinion, for, as already noticed, the consensus was that judgment on the policy of laws did not inhere in this power. This was precisely the point Wilson had made on July 21.[208] There existed, in any event, no body of judicial precedents upon which to found such criticism. Indeed, when John Dickinson, a lawyer of long experience, expressed misgivings about the power of judicial review on August 15, he could offer no better example by way of admonition than the justiciary of Aragon who "became by degrees the lawgiver."[209] But there prevailed far too much anxiety over legislative excesses for words of caution about judicial supremacy to be long pondered. If at any point there were more than a few delegates who doubted the prudence of committing the watch and ward over the Constitution to the courts, they could have gained but few recruits. For on August 23 the Convention unanimously approved Rutledge's motion to amend the article (VIII) declaring the supremacy of the laws, as follows:

> This Constitution and the Laws of the United States made in pursuance thereof, and all treaties made under the authority of the United-States shall be the supreme law of the several States, and of their Citizens and inhabitants; and the Judges in the several States shall be bound thereby in their decisions; any thing in the constitutions or laws of the several States to the contrary notwithstanding.[210]

---

[205] Montesquieu, *The Spirit of the Laws* (Dublin ed., 1751), at 185.

[206] In his discussion of what should go into a preamble in his draft for the Committee of Detail, Farrand, *Records*, IV, 38.

[207] *Supra*, c. III, pp. 98–100.

[208] *Supra*, p. 228.

[209] Farrand, *Records*, II, 299 (Madison).

[210] *Ibid.*, 381–82 (*Journal*), 389 (Madison). On the heels of this vote Pinckney sought to revive the negative of state laws by the national legisla-

V: *Constitutional Convention and the Judiciary*

The supremacy of the Constitution itself was thus at length expressly proclaimed, and the laws repugnant to it no less explicitly excluded from the imperative of obedience. The command of the article was directed equally at any law-making body and at all judges, the ultimate arbiters of enforcement and of enforceability. That this was to be the role of the bench is plain from all that had been said about the judicial function; and that is why the judiciary, alone of the departments of government, was singled out for mention.

The judiciary article at length came before the Convention on August 27. Again the notes on debates are so exiguous that it is not possible even to guess how extensively some of the most significant modifications by the Committee of Detail were scrutinized. First, as to what was moved and rejected. Madison, who might in an earlier age have borne on his shield the device *nil desperandum*, once again attempted to secure a prohibition on the increase of judicial salaries.[211] This was rejected. Dickinson came up with an amendment to qualify tenure by good behavior by a provision that the judges be removable by the executive on address of both houses of the legislature.[212] British precedent, to many always beguiling, was tendered in support. But the delegates would have none of this, either because, as argued, this example was not apposite, or because the proviso threatened the independence of the bench.[213]

No argument developed over the clause so freighted with contingent qualifications: "such inferior courts as shall, when necessary, from time to time be constituted by the legislature of the United States," despite the substitution of the verb "constitute" for the earlier "appoint." In terser form this had been unanimously approved on August 17, when the powers of the national legislature had been voted.[214] But when the Convention reached tentative settlement of the clause dealing with the original jurisdiction of the Supreme Court it was moved and seconded that "in all other cases before-mentioned original jurisdiction shall be in the Courts of the several States, but with appeal both as to law and fact to the courts of the United States with such exceptions and under such regulations, as the Legislatures shall make."[215] This motion was with-

---

ture if the general interest or harmony of the Union was involved. Madison and Wilson supported him. This recrudescence of the "peace and harmony" formula was savagely attacked by Rutledge: "If nothing else, this alone would damn and ought to damn the Constitution. Will any State ever agree to be bound hand & foot in this manner. It is worse than making mere corporations of them whose bye laws would not be subject to this shackle." *Ibid.*, 391 (Madison). A motion to commit was narrowly beaten 5–6.

[211] *Ibid.*, 429–30 (Madison).
[212] *Ibid.*, 428–29 (Madison).
[213] Beaten 1–7, three states absent.
[214] Farrand, *Records*, II, 315 (Madison). There is no vote recorded in the *Journal*.
[215] *Ibid.*, 424 (*Journal*). Madison does not mention this in his "Notes."

drawn. Hard upon this action followed an attempt to vest in the legislature discretion to determine whether or not jurisdiction should be original or appellate in cases where the United States should be a party. This was beaten 5–3.[216] Another proposal to permit the legislature to direct the manner in which jurisdiction (except that original with the Supreme Court) be exercised was also negatived.[217]

Finally the plan of the Committee of Detail to vest a large discretion in the legislature to assign jurisdiction was thrown out.[218] This was a most ambiguous proposal in that it made nonsense of the preceding assignments of appellate and original jurisdiction, for by its terms the original jurisdiction of the Supreme Court was made defeasible at the pleasure of the legislature. Taken from Randolph's draft, the clause had appeared in what we have called the next to the last draft of the Committee of Detail and was left in its final report. One can only conjecture that the purpose of including this curious provision was to gild the pill for those who hoped that the state courts might be used as inferior federal tribunals.

Journal entries are not the juiciest grapes from which to press wine. Nevertheless, some things of considerable import may be extracted from the successive repulse of propositions to increase the dependence of the judicial on the legislative. Clearly, it was the consensus of the Convention that there was to be no legislative meddling with the grant of jurisdiction. This, it would appear, was a necessary corollary to the earlier decision that the judges were not to participate in the process of enactment. The legislature was confined to the constituting of inferior tribunals if and when needed, and to the making of regulations and exceptions to the exercise of appellate jurisdiction. This latter provision was not debated, but it may be remarked that in contemporary state practice, regulation had been confined largely to such details as setting appealable minima or periods of limitation, and "exceptions" of certain proceedings where neither error nor certiorari had been traditionally available.

How earnestly the Convention this day (August 27) applied itself to create an effective judicial is borne out by what it added to the article before it—in every case notable. William Samuel Johnson's motion that the judicial power of the United States be "both in Law and Equity" was passed despite a pettifogging objection that these powers ought not be vested in a single court.[219] The specification of jurisdiction was fattened by the inclusion of controversies to which the United States might

---

[216] *Ibid.* Again, not mentioned by Madison.
[217] *Ibid.*, 425 (*Journal*), 431 (Madison).

[218] *Ibid.*, 425 (*Journal*), 431 (Madison).
[219] *Ibid.*, 428 (Madison). The objection was by Read of Delaware.

be a party,[220] and also of causes between citizens of the same state claiming lands under grants of different states.[221] In different form this last had been part of the supervisory powers of the Confederation Congress. The last vestige of the congressional powers which the Committee of Detail had retained—jurisdiction over disputes between states over territory or jurisdiction—had earlier been excised on the ground that this properly belonged to the judiciary.[222] The Convention on this day neglected to grant this explicitly. The oversight was later remedied by the Committee of Style.

The most significant alterations were those of general description, the import of which is revealed by their occurrence in point of time. The Committee of Detail had provided that "the jurisdiction of the Supreme Court shall extend to all cases arising under the laws passed by the legislature of the United States." Johnson moved the insertion of "this Constitution and the," so that the phrase read "the jurisdiction of the Supreme Court shall extend to all cases under this Constitution and the laws passed by the legislature. . . ."[223] The effect of this was to place beyond question the role of the Supreme Court as arbiter of the Constitution. Madison thought this authority should be confined to "cases of a Judiciary Nature."[224] His doubts were apparently allayed by assurances that the jurisdiction given was "constructively limited to cases of a Judiciary Nature." The vote on the motion was unanimous.

No less significant was the passage of Rutledge's motion to delete from the clause under discussion the words "passed by the legislature," already eliminated in the supreme law provision.[225] Even if the laymen present did not realize it, to a lawyer the words as they now read—"the laws of the United States"—opened the door to a substantial accretion of magisterial authority by the removal of the limitation to enactments. Almost as an afterthought, for it was to make the section further conform to the Committee's supremacy clause, cases arising under treaties were inserted.[226] Finally the two pugnacious nationalists, Madison and Morris, capped the repair of the section by moving the substitution of the words the "judicial power" in place of the words the "jurisdiction of the Supreme Court."[227] To speak of jurisdiction in terms of national power and not of a court was a noteworthy extension of the base of judicial authority. Considered in conjunction with the excision of the clauses that had sanctioned legislative direction, the purpose of the substitution seems plain—when the legislature came to constitute inferior

---

220 On motion of Madison and G. Morris, *ibid.*, 430 (Madison).
221 On motion of Sherman, *ibid.*, 431 (Madison).
222 August 24, *ibid.*, 401 (Madison).
223 *Ibid.*, 430 (Madison), 423

(*Journal*).
224 *Ibid.*, 430 (Madison).
225 *Ibid.*, 423–24 (*Journal*), 431 (Madison).
226 *Ibid.*
227 *Ibid.*

.... the United States of America, ... shall be removed from his
office on impeachment by the House of Representatives, and conviction in the
Supreme Court, of treason, bribery, or corruption. In case of his removal
as aforesaid, death, resignation, or disability to discharge the powers and duties of his office, the President of the Senate shall exercise those powers and
duties until another President of the United States be chosen, or until the
disability of the President be removed.

XI

Sect. 1. The Judicial Power of the United States shall be vested in one Supreme Court, and in such Inferior Courts as shall, when necessary, from time
to time, be constituted by the Legislature of the United States.

Sect. 2. The Judges of the Supreme Court, and of the Inferior courts, shall
hold their offices during good behaviour. They shall, at stated times, receive
for their services, a compensation, which shall not be diminished during their
continuance in office.

Sect. 3. The Jurisdiction of the Supreme Court shall extend to all cases ari-
ing under laws passed by the Legislature of the United States; to all cases affecting Ambassadors, other Public Ministers and Consuls; to the trial of
impeachments

[6]

peachments of Officers of the United States; to all cases of Admiralty and Maritime Jurisdiction; to Controversies between two or more States; between a State and citizens of
another State, between citizens of different States, and between a State or
the citizens thereof and foreign States, citizens or subjects. In cases of Impeachment, cases affecting Ambassadors, other Public Ministers and Consuls,
and those in which a State shall be party,
in all the other cases beforementioned with such excep-
tions and under such regulations as the Legislature shall make. The Legislature
may assign any part of the jurisdiction abovementioned (except the trial of the
President of the United States) in the manner and under the limitations which
it shall think proper, to such Inferior Courts as it shall constitute from time to
time.

Sect. 4. The trial of all criminal offences (except in cases of impeachments)
shall be in the State where they shall be committed;

Sect. 5. Judgment, in cases of Impeachment, shall not extend further than
to removal from office, and disqualification to hold and enjoy any office of
honour, trust or profit under the United States. But the party convicted shall
nevertheless be liable and subject to indictment, trial, judgment and punishment, according to law.

XII

No State shall coin money; nor grant letters of marque and reprisal; nor enter into any treaty, alliance, or confederation; nor grant any title
of nobility.

XIII

No State, without the consent of the Legislature of the United States, shall
lay imposts or duties on imports; nor keep troops or ships of war in time of
peace; nor enter into any agreement or compact with another State, or with
any foreign power; nor engage in any war, unless it shall be actually invaded

George Washington's annotated copy, Report of the Committee of Detail of
the Federal Convention, Article XI.
(Washington Papers, Library of Congress)

courts, any meddling with fundamentals was to be foreclosed. It should here be remarked that against what can be wrung from the muniments of the August 27 discussions nothing that was said or written during the ratification struggle by those privy to these proceedings can prudently be vouched. For, as we shall shortly see, this was to be a season of ardent advocacy—and not always advocacy without guile.[228]

By one addition, a well-intentioned clarification of the scope of appellate authority, the Convention unwittingly sowed seeds from which much trouble was soon to sprout. An inquiry by Gouverneur Morris whether or not appellate power extended to "matters of fact as well as law—and to cases of common law as well as civil law" was answered by Wilson that this was the Committee's understanding. The jurisdiction of the Confederation Court of Appeals had been so construed.[229] On motion of Dickinson the words "as to law and fact," suggested weeks earlier by Paterson, were added.[230] As we shall see, this was later to be attacked as an intended encroachment upon the finality of jury verdicts. The failure of the Convention to provide for jury trial in civil actions (for it made only one minor change respecting venue in the section dealing with trial of causes criminal) was to be advanced as proof of sinister intent.

---

[228] Hart and Wechsler, *The Federal Courts and the Federal System*, at 18, following Warren, *The Making of the Constitution*, take the position "it seems to be a necessary inference from the decision that the creation of inferior federal courts was to vest in the discretion of Congress that the scope of their jurisdiction, once created, was also to be discretionary." They find confirmation in a statement of Sherman's and in numerous indications that Congress would initially go no further than vest an admiralty jurisdiction in inferior federal courts. They express the belief that voting down the clause which gave the legislature power to assign jurisdiction "seems to have been part of a largely rhetorical change" induced by the substitution of the "judicial power" for the "jurisdiction of the Supreme Court."

We believe that this interpretation fails to take account of all the events of August 27: in particular, the withdrawal of the proposition that in certain cases original jurisdiction should be in the states; the rejection of power in Congress to direct whether jurisdic-

tion should be original or appellate in cases in which the United States was a party; and the repulse of the motion to add "In all the other cases before mentioned the judicial power shall be exercised in such manner as the Legislature shall direct." Farrand, *Records*, II, 424-25, 431. All these votes indicate that the majority wished to eliminate legislative direction and make the judicial a fully coordinate department. As we shall see (*infra*, pp. 246-47), a change by the Committee of Style robbed Congress of discretion whether or not to create inferior courts and left only discretion as to what courts were to be set up and to make changes.

Warren's statements about what the delegates believed are undocumented except for a quotation from a newspaper, the provenance of which is not indicated. It appears to be an account in *Massachusetts Gazette*, Feb. 22, 1788.

[229] Farrand, *Records*, II, 431 (Madison).

[230] *Ibid.*

With the discussion of August 27 the working over of the judicial in Convention was virtually finished. It had been made a fully coordinated department and was now armed with the potentials of power. The experience of most of the lawyers present was not such as to stir an awareness of the import of what had been done. Only William Samuel Johnson, who had attended upon the Privy Council for some years, had direct acquaintance with a court exercising appellate jurisdiction in causes often with political overtones.[231] His amendment giving the Supreme Court jurisdiction over cases arising under the Constitution may have been a reflection of this experience. Some opponents of ratification were to scent out political dangers in the language settled upon, but if on this day such criticisms were made we know nothing of them. Even Gerry, daily more waspish, was mute.

Since the judicial was to be taken under fire by Gerry and the two other delegates—Mason and Randolph—who refused to sign the Constitution, it is notable that not one of them appears to have availed himself of a nearly final opportunity to name chapter and verse. These men were already close to overt revolt. There is every reason to believe that Gerry and Mason were caucusing with other delegates at "private meetings."[232] Randolph, for better than two months an Achilles in battle, was to all appearances sulking, so infrequently and briefly is he mentioned in Madison's notes during the fortnight following August 13. The first threat of defection came on August 29, when a proposition was up requiring a two-thirds vote on navigation acts—a matter close to Mason's heart and one embodied but rejected in Randolph's draft constitution. Before the vote was taken, Randolph said bluntly that there were features so odious in the Constitution that he doubted whether he would be able to agree to it.[233] The threat was ignored and the proposal rejected.

The climate in the Convention had at no time been idyllic. Randolph's outburst gave hint of how supercharged with discontent the atmosphere had become. Two days after his initial warning, the storm broke over the assemblage. Before the house was a brace of articles deal-

---

[231] Johnson was present in London as Connecticut agent in the Mohegan Indian case. His interest in the functioning of the Privy Council is indicated by his collection of briefs on appeal and the ms. notes entered on them of various hearings. Volume labelled "Connecticut Cases" (CULL).

[232] Luther Martin's "Reply to Landholder, March 14, 1788," where he describes the August meetings initiated by Gerry. Martin claimed attendance

by Mason, the delegates from New Jersey and Connecticut, a part of the Delaware delegation, one member from South Carolina and one from Georgia. P. L. Ford, *Essays on the Constitution of the United States,* 353–59 (hereafter cited as Ford, *Essays*). Reprinted in Farrand, *Records,* III, 281–86.

[233] Farrand, *Records,* II, 452 (Madison).

ing with ratification.[234] One provided that ratification by ――――― states would suffice for "organizing this Constitution." The Convention settled on nine states. The second article concerned mechanics—submission of the plan to the Confederation Congress for its approbation, and an expression of the Convention's opinion that the plan be submitted for ratification to state conventions chosen under recommendation of the legislatures. It was moved and carried to strike out submission for Congress's approbation. Gerry, protesting the impropriety of destroying the Confederation without unanimous consent of the parties, sought postponement.[235] Mason, seconding, remarked that he would "sooner chop off his right hand than put it to the Constitution as it now stands."[236] He was reserving judgment, but if he was not satisfied with the decisions on various points, it would be his wish "to bring the whole subject before another general Convention." Randolph elaborated this by proposing that state conventions be at liberty to offer amendments to be submitted to another general convention.[237]

The rebellious suggestion that the summer's work would need doing over by another body and that such a conclave would have to wrestle with the whims of thirteen ratifying conventions could, at the very least, only have been dispiriting. To write such a provision into the Constitution would give it a hangdog look utterly destructive of its credit. A second convention was an idea that needed stifling at birth, but this did not happen. It flourished to do infinite mischief.

We do not know what private exertions were made to placate the fractious brethren. In Convention, decisions of the next ten days were to confirm them in recusancy. On September 10, on the eve of committing the determinations of the Convention to a Committee of Style and Arrangement, the matter of ratification was again raised by Gerry. He was supported by Hamilton, a strange bedfellow indeed.[238] After a series of sharp exchanges the Convention affirmed its previous stand—and this in the face of Randolph's ultimatum that he would dissent from the whole of the plan if the ratification dispositions were not changed.[239]

Near the end of this session Randolph set out the points in the plan with which he disagreed. Among them was the want of a more definite boundary "between the General and State Judiciaries," a charge which he never reduced to specific counts.[240] This came with ill grace, for no

---

[234] Report of the Committee, Arts. XXI and XXII; *ibid.*, 189 (Madison).

[235] *Ibid.*, 478–79 (Madison).

[236] *Ibid.*, 479 (Madison).

[237] *Ibid.*

[238] *Ibid.*, 559–60 (Madison). Hamilton wanted approbation by Congress, transmission to state legislatures and reference by them to conventions.

[239] *Ibid.*, 560 (Madison).

[240] *Ibid.*, 563–64 (Madison). He was still vague in his letter to the Virginia House of Delegates, Oct. 10, 1787 (Elliot, *Debates*, I, 482 at 491). Randolph came closest to being concrete in his answer to Grayson, June

one had had better opportunities than he, in Committee and on the floor, to have shown how this could be done. He moved a resolution for his second convention, but on Mason's urging this was tabled. Mason wished to see what the Committee of Style did with Randolph's objections. But this was not within its mandate. This Committee was only to revise the style and arrange the articles agreed upon by the house.

The Committee of Style, composed of Johnson, Hamilton, Gouverneur Morris, Madison and King, reported on September 12. Its solution of the ratification problem was ingenious. It left in the Constitution the article providing that ratification by conventions of nine states should be sufficient to establish the Constitution among them (Article VII). The hotly contested article regarding the mode of submission it converted into an appendant resolve that the "preceeding Constitution" be laid before Congress, and stated as the opinion of the Convention that it then be submitted to a convention chosen in each state, under recommendation of its legislature, for assent and ratification. The result was to be reported to Congress. A second resolve outlined the steps which, in the Convention's opinion, would follow after nine ratifications to put the new plan into effect.[241]

Convention determinations respecting the structure and jurisdiction of the judiciary suffered certain changes at the hands of the Committee, only two of which were important. The first was an alteration of language affecting the establishment of inferior courts. This was a change that gains in significance when considered in the light of the various mutations the phraseology had undergone. In the article specifying the powers of the legislature (renumbered Article I, section 8) the clause "to constitute tribunals inferior to the Supreme Court" was left untouched. But the specification in the judiciary article of the circumstances under which this power was to be exercised was recast and rewritten—and most significantly so. As submitted to the Committee, the article had read:[242]

> The Judicial Power of the United States both in law and equity shall be vested in one Supreme Court, and in such Inferior Courts as shall, when necessary, from time to time, be constituted by the Legislature of the United States.

The committee rewrote this provision to read:

> The judicial power of the United States, both in law and equity, shall be vested in one supreme court, and in such inferior courts as Congress may from time to time ordain and establish.[243]

21, 1788, at the Virginia ratifying convention (*ibid.*, III, 570–76).
[241] Farrand, *Records*, II, 603; for the resolve, 604 (*Journal*).
[242] *Ibid.*, 575.
[243] *Ibid.*, 600.

The effect of eliminating the words "as shall, when necessary" was to deprive Congress of power to decide upon the need for inferior courts and so to give full imperative effect to the declaration that "The judicial power . . . shall be vested in one supreme court, and in such inferior courts. . . ." That the Committee intended to convey the sense of an imperative is apparent from the choice of the most forceful words in the contemporary constitutional vocabulary—"ordain and establish"—to direct what Congress was to do. These were the words by which the state constitutions of the four stalwart nationalists on the Committee had called into being the new state governments.[244] These were the words of fiat used by the people of the United States in the preamble of the new Constitution. The selection of these words to replace the less affirmative "constitute" could only have been deliberate. We believe that their function was to assure that federal inferior courts must be created, and further that designation of state tribunals would not do.

The discretion left to Congress was the authority to settle the institutional pattern at the lower level of judicial administration and to arrange how the jurisdiction conferred by section 2 of Article III was there to be disposed. It is inferable that some appellate as well as original jurisdiction could be seated in these inferior courts since the power to regulate and make exceptions to the appellate jurisdiction of the Supreme Court was vested in Congress. The purport of the permissive phrase "may from time to time" was to secure the right of Congress to make such occasional rearrangements in the structure once set up as it might wish. In other words, the intendment of the new language was that considerations of public convenience, and not of necessity, were to govern Congress.

A second Committee change, and one that was not clearly embraced in its mandate, was the rectification of the Convention's oversight in failing explicitly to seat in Article III jurisdictional and territorial disputes between two states. In their task of arrangement, compression of articles and sectionalizing, the Committee found in Article III harborage for the treason section—the Convention's only striking adaptation of extant substantive law.

In one other particular that bore directly upon the effectiveness of the judicial, the second paragraph of Article VI, the Committee wrought a fine bit of rhetorical magic. This was the substitution of the terse "supreme law of the land" for the phrase "supreme law of the several

---

[244] Constitution of Massachusetts of 1780, Preamble, "agree upon, ordain and establish," Thorpe, *Constitutions and Charters*, III, 1889; of New York of 1777, "ordain, determine and de- clare," *ibid.*, V, 2628; of Pennsylvania of 1776, "ordain declare and establish," *ibid.*, 3082; of Virginia of 1776, "ordain and declare," *ibid.*, VII, 3815.

states and of their citizens and inhabitants." Thus, the essence of what had originally been conceived as a curb upon transgressions of the states was profoundly modified. What had read like a landowner's no-trespassing notice was transformed into a majestic expression of national authority.

After the Committee's report had been once read through, it was ordered to be printed.[245] A letter to Congress was next submitted and debated. The house then took under consideration the overriding of the executive's veto, substituting a two-thirds vote for the proposed three-fourths. At this juncture came a disturbing episode when Williamson of North Carolina observed that no provision had been made for jury trial of civil actions.[246] Gorham pointed to the difficulty of a rule applicable to both law and equity and claimed that the representatives of the people could be trusted to deal with the matter. This did not satisfy Gerry. Juries, he urged, were needed to guard against corrupt judges, and he proposed that the Committee of Style be directed to provide a clause securing the right. Mason, who professed to see the validity of Gorham's point, thought, nevertheless, that a general principle could be laid down. He wished that the plan had been prefaced with a bill of rights, and declared that he would second a motion for a committee to prepare such a bill. Gerry then so moved and Mason seconded.[247] With apparently little debate the motion was unanimously rejected.

In modern times the sentiments of the Framers on the bill of rights has been a matter so much stressed that it is desirable to indicate how little sensibility for federal protections of individual rights was exhibited at Philadelphia. Pinckney's plan, in which some bill of rights items were embodied, had been turned over to the Committee of Detail which had ignored these items. On August 20 Pinckney had submitted a variety of propositions among which were some of these guarantees. This list had also been referred to the Committee of Detail.[248] If the *Journal* is to be trusted, the "rights" were eliminated in this Committee's report on Pinckney's propositions.[249] Neither Mason nor anyone else is recorded as having made any inquiry as to the fate of these items. Pinckney did succeed on August 28 in salvaging a provision on the suspension of habeas corpus,[250] but no one that day undertook to use the occasion for opening up the question of other rights. This had also been the case, when the prohibition on bills of attainder and ex post facto laws had been proposed by Gerry (August 22).[251] The impres-

---

[245] Farrand, *Records*, II, 582 (*Journal*).

[246] *Ibid.*, 587 (Madison).

[247] *Ibid.*, 587–88 (Madison).

[248] *Ibid.*, 334–35 (*Journal*).

[249] *Ibid.*, 366–67 (*Journal*).

[250] *Ibid.*, 438 (Madison).

[251] *Ibid.*, 375–76 (Madison).

sion one has from the records is of a pervasive belief that provision for the security of the individual was a state matter, and that the delegates were wholly candid in their later representations that this had been the prevailing view at Philadelphia.

There can be no denying that everything that is of record testifies to the almost utter absorption of the delegates in the problem of the structure of government—no one more passionately so than Madison, who was to be the first mover in the new Congress of the amendments that became known as the Bill of Rights. One may, indeed, properly doubt whether these guarantees would so early have found lodging in the Constitution (1791) if, during the ratification struggles, opponents of the plan had not sounded the tocsin. As a result, political pressure had so built up that it was crucial to the success of the new government that a bill of rights be appended. Certainly on September 12, 1787, the mood of the Convention was frigid. It did not thaw in the remaining days of debate. For the body was seized by a sense of urgency and gave every sign of being intolerant of procrastination.

The main business of the discussions on September 13, 14 and 15 was the line by line scrutiny of the Committee's work. The Convention made but a single change in the judiciary article as reported by the Committee on Style. It excised from section 1 the modifying words "in law and equity" describing the judicial power of the United States, but retained them in section 2 as a description of the cases over which jurisdiction could be exercised. No one appears to have commented upon the substantial rewriting of section 1—not even Mason, who noted on his copy of the printed report a variety of suggested alterations.

The tedium of final furbishing was enlivened by a succession of almost feverish efforts by the dissatisfied and the perfectionists alike to secure additions or changes. A politically delicate situation was thus created, at least for those who hoped that the Convention would speak as a united body to the nation. Too many proposals advanced by the dissenters were voted down, however, to have made propitiation remotely possible. Among these proposals were final efforts to secure three of the standard bill of rights items—for a declaration against a peacetime standing army,[252] moved by Mason and Randolph; for a declaration that liberty of the press should be inviolably observed, moved by Pinckney and Gerry;[253] and, from the same pair, a proposal for guarantee of jury trial in civil actions.[254]

At the end of the final day of debate Gerry, Mason and Randolph announced that they would not sign.[255] Only Gerry referred to any of

---

[252] On September 14; *ibid.*, 616–17 (Madison).

[253] *Ibid.*, 617 (Madison).

[254] On September 15; *ibid.*, 628 (Madison).

[255] *Ibid.*, 631–33 (Madison).

the defeated bill of rights provisions. After listing a variety of particular objections, Gerry added that these he could have gotten over if the rights of the citizens had not been rendered insecure. This threat he found in Congress's powers under the necessary and proper clause, the power to raise money and armies without limit, and finally, the power "to establish a tribunal without juries which will be a Star-chamber as to civil cases."[256]

Constitutional protections of individual rights were so inconsequent in the objectors' schedules of faults unfolded on this lamentable occasion that one may fairly doubt the intensity of their immediate concern over the matter. As we have noticed, it is clear from the summer's record that a bill of rights, far from being something momentous in which there was general and sustained interest, was only fugitively an issue. Consequently, it is improbable that a yielding to belated scruples would have moved any of these three men to a change of heart. Their objections recited on September 15 were too many and too subversive of the new plan to have been so easily eradicated.

The Sunday which intervened between the announcements of final defection and Monday, September 17, when the engrossed Constitution was presented for signing did not bring grace to the schismatics. The ingenious formula to secure their signatures, devised by Gouverneur Morris and so persuasively supported by Benjamin Franklin, left them unmoved.[257] There were others who professed to be no less troubled over defects in their handiwork. Nevertheless, they set their hands to it.

---

[256] *Ibid.*, 632–33 (Madison).   [257] *Ibid.*, 641–43 (Madison).

CHAPTER VI

*The Appeal to the People and
the Molding of Opinion*

To OUR OWN generation, habituated by modern technology to view
the doings of men in terms of suspense and denouement, the afternoon of September 17, 1787, seems an occasion of high drama. The
months of secrecy were past. Rumor was to yield to fact. The people
of the United States were to know, as the news spread, whether or
not the signers had spoken for them rightly. Yet despite the "universal
anxiety" reported by Madison a few days earlier,[1] there is little to indicate that contemporaries were gripped by the theater of the moment.[2]
We hear of no post-riders impatiently waiting in State House Square
to speed the intelligence. The Pennsylvania Assembly, then in session,
was the first to be told of the signing. It apathetically suffered the letter
of notification to be subjected to a second reading and thereupon adjourned until the next morning.[3] There are, in short, small signs in
surviving documents to indicate instant appreciation of the drama of
the event, or indeed, excitement over it. Excitement there was to be,
but this lay ahead.

That there should be little immediate or widespread stir over the
completion of the Convention's task may be laid to the prevailing in-
sularity of outlook on public affairs. This was rooted in a primary and
traditional attachment to local community and state. It was sustained

---

[1] Madison to Jefferson, Sept. 6,
1787, *Papers of Jefferson*, XII, 102.
This and other letters addressed to
Jefferson as well as certain letters of
Washington are printed in *Doc. Hist.
Const.*, IV, *passim.*

[2] The *Pennsylvania Packet*, Sept. 18,
1787, printed on its third page a short
news statement about the signing, emphasizing the event only by leading

out the type. The "extra" was not unknown at this time, *vide* the *Supplement Extraordinary of the New-York
Independent Journal: or The Daily
Advertiser* when word arrived of ratification at Poughkeepsie—but this was
New York.

[3] The *Pennsylvania Packet*, Sept. 20,
1787.

by the political structure of the new nation and by deficiencies in means of communication. During the summer of 1787 there had been happenings in various parts of the land calculated to engage this parochial and fractionated public opinion more intensely than the deliberations in Philadelphia. In Massachusetts the citizenry had agonized for months over the pardon or execution of the convicted participants in Shays' Rebellion.[4] Virginia, in the grip of a searing drought, was alarmed over the burning of jails and courthouses by irate taxpayers.[5] The Kentucky district was being harassed by Indian raids.[6] North Carolina was girding for war with the Cherokees, and Georgia with the Creeks.[7] Against settings as immediately absorbing as these, the news that a Constitution had been completed may well have been something less than stirring.

To suggest that a public opinion on a national scale was virtually non-existent does not imply that something resembling this could not be brought into being. The very fact that there existed problems which touched all men, whether or not they were generally aware of these as national in scope, supplied a footing for reanimating in the Republic the sense of a common cause that had sadly abated since the war. Such a problem was the depression through which the country had been passing, and which had been a moving force behind the projected political change. The worst was past, although the public, lacking the hindsight of historians, was unaware of this. The bond of continuing adversity was yet sufficiently heavy upon men to dispose them even to risk in the application of remedy. Too many spoke in this tenor at the state conventions to doubt this. In any event, it was to be the hard times that everyone knew about that was to serve as a fundament for the *argumentum ad populum* of the proponents of the Constitution.

No one was then so naive as to suppose that improvement of what was still called a man's "estate" did not enter into individual calculations of what the promised future might hold. After all, the chief

---

[4] The tension is reflected in the summer issues of the *Worcester Magazine* beginning in vol. 3, at 117, with Cushing's sentencing of Shays, Wheeler, *et al.* Generally on the situation R. J. Taylor, *Western Massachusetts in the Revolution*, 164–66 and the matter cited in the notes thereto; A. E. Morse, *The Federalist Party in Massachusetts to the Year 1800*, App. D, "The Aftermath of Shays' Rebellion"; see also James Sullivan to Rufus King, June 14, 1787, *Life of King*, I, 222.

[5] Madison to Jefferson, Sept. 6, 1787, *supra*, n. 1. A piece from the *Virginia Independent Chronicle* printed in the *Pennsylvania Packet*, Nov. 28, 1787, mentions the jail burning.

[6] Harry Innes to John Brown, Dec. 7, 1787, Ms. Harry Innes Papers XXVIII, 113 (LC). He has estimates of losses since 1783. See also the report from Kentucky in the *Virginia Independent Chronicle*, Sept. 5, 1787.

[7] Wm. Blount to John Blount, July 19, 1787, in *LMCC*, VIII, 624; Sec'y of Congress to the Governors of North Carolina, South Carolina and Georgia, Oct. 27, 1787, *ibid.*, 667.

arguments for revision of the Confederation had been economic—the difficulties arising from state control of commerce and, notably, trade with foreign countries, the disorders of currency and the virtual bankruptcy of the central government. But so far as the proponents of the Constitution were concerned, their arguments were not to be cast in terms of individual economic benefaction,[8] for this would carry them no further than some of their adversaries who professed to believe that additions to the Articles giving Congress control over commerce and enlarged treaty-making powers would be equally efficacious.[9] Both sides were aware that the Constitution's answer to economic problems, as to others, was a political one, precipitating issues of state versus national sovereignty. Inevitably, therefore, the idiom of debate was to be political; more often than not economic considerations were to be raised or disposed of by inference.

THE ROLE OF THE PRESS

IF THE DELEGATES had ever supposed that the fate of their Constitution would not hang upon an intensive campaign of public education, the defection of Gerry, Mason and Randolph was warning enough. Weeks before this, the withdrawal of Lansing and Yates had been premonitory. All the delegates were familiar from pre-Revolutionary experience with the uses of propaganda; indeed, some of them had in those days been leading contributors. It was, of course, one thing to instruct a whole populace on the subject of invasions of their rights and move men to assert and defend these. A far different task was that of enlightening the voters on the probable workings of a complex instrument of government and of persuading to a surrender of powers. Then, as today, Americans were singularly susceptible to the beguilements of phrases. Five generations of them had been fired with a zeal for "rights and liberties." It was essential that the living generation should be made equally warm for "union." The opponents of the new plan had no such singleness of purpose, for some sought outright rejection; others, still intoxicated with the rhetoric of the Revolution, wished safeguards for "liberties"; and there were yet others who thought that features of

---

[8] See here the manner in which economic problems were handled by Hamilton in *Federalist* Nos. 6, 7, 11, 12, 13 and 15; by Madison in his famous No. 10 and No. 42; and by Jay in No. 4. There were, of course, others, notably "Landholder" I and II (Oliver Ellsworth), in Ford, *Essays*, 139–45; and a number of essays in the *Virginia Independent Chronicle*— "True Friend," Nov. 14, 1787; "Old State Soldier," Jan. 10, 1788, Apr. 2, 1788; "Old Planter," Feb. 20, 1788.

[9] See Madison to Randolph, Jan. 10, 1788, re antifederalist strategy in New York, *The Writings of James Madison*, V, 80–81; and the *Agrippa* letters in Ford, *Essays* 84, 98–99.

the old Confederation should be engrafted on the new system. Insofar as these men had a common interest it was in preserving the *status quo*, and they pled for it with all bethinkable cunning—prejudice, principle and prophecy were the chief lines their attack was to follow.

As a result of all the ardor spent upon the question of altering the national government, the people were the recipients of political instruction to a degree more intense than had hitherto been their fortune. Not the least significant aspect of this ten months of tutelage was the attention devoted to the judiciary.[10] This was something not usually a matter of lively public concern. It is true that in various colonies debates had recurred over the power to erect courts, over Chancery, the tenure of judges and the regulation of incidents of appellate jurisdiction. But, at bottom, these episodes had been mere gambits in the unending game of impugning royal or proprietorial authority. Despite the Americans' knowledgeability about the processes of the law, there had been no sober appraisal of how a judiciary ought to be organized, and what its role should be; such publicity as had attended earlier discussions had been largely local. In contrast, now not only was there a great deal written about the federal judiciary, much of it thoughtful and penetrating, but also a new awareness was stirred, for which the opposition was chiefly responsible, of how immediate a concern to the individual the courts and their functioning in fact were. The impact of these discussions and of the public's interest in them was not to be a fugitive one. It was to affect the form of the first Judiciary Act, the content of the first amendments, and ultimately, opinion of the actual operation of the new courts.

The apparatus of propaganda was not to be a replica of what it had been in pre-Revolutionary days. The Committees of Correspondence proved to be incapable of revival, as certain enemies of the Constitution were to discover. The pamphlet ceased to be a medium of first importance although some of the most significant tracts appeared in this form. Instead, the newspapers, of which many more were printed in many more different places than earlier, became the chief means of

---

[10] Except for the universal attention given to Hamilton's précis in *The Federalist*, writers have generally slighted the discussions of the judiciary that went on in the press. This may be laid to the fact that relatively more words were spilled on issues like taxation, representation, the powers of Congress and matter which more overtly threatened state sovereignty. The most recent study, J. T. Main, *The Antifederalists: Critics of the Constitution, 1781–1788* (1961), considers the discussion of the judiciary in a most fugitive way. Main concludes that "most Antifederalists were satisfied with all or with the greater part of the judiciary article; the need for a national court system was nowhere challenged and most of its powers were accepted without question." *Ibid.*, 158.

influencing opinion.[11] These journals had undergone the least of improvement since the war. They still printed a minimum of what a modern journalist would regard to be news, in particular of events occurring at the place of publication. Individually, their circulation was very limited.[12] If issues were despatched abroad at all, this had to be along some post route. There was no provision for their carriage as mail, and consequently it was the practice for a printer to have his papers conveyed by the carriers in exchange for some recompense, even if only a free copy of the sheet.[13] With such a system of distribution, it was too often a matter of chance if a newspaper reached its destination—assuming, of course, that there were out-of-town subscribers.

Miserable though these gazettes were as mirrors of current local events, they nevertheless possessed from the manner of their make-up certain potentialities for the cultivation of opinion. Relying as they did for filler upon clippings from whatever out-of-town newspapers that might come to hand, it was possible for a subscriber to a Boston or New York journal to learn belatedly of an event or opinion published weeks earlier in South Carolina or Virginia. Furthermore, in default of anything which even by the printers' standards might be deemed newsworthy, the proprietors were accustomed to open their columns to contributions from essayists, indignant readers or writers of verse. During the debates on ratification these potentialities of the press were fully exploited. Some writings which later appeared in pamphlet form made their debut in the journals.

The skirmishes in the press, sustained for so many months, should not be viewed as a species of decorative background for the several conventions. The writings were purposefully directed to sway the decision of legislatures on the calling of such conventions and thereafter

---

[11] A. M. Schlesinger, *Prelude to Independence* (New York: Alfred A. Knopf, Inc., 1958), advances the thesis that newspapers were then a more potent instrument of propaganda than has been hitherto thought to be the case. That these were in greater circulation than pamphlets and hence equally influential remains to be proven.

[12] The conclusions following are based on examination of leading newspapers of the Atlantic seaboard. See also J. B. McMaster, *A History of the People of the United States*, I, 35–38.

[13] The procedure is explained by the Postmaster General, Ebenezer Hazard, in a public statement reprinted in J. B. McMaster and F. D. Stone, eds., *Pennsylvania and the Federal Constitution, 1787–1788*, 530 (hereafter cited as McMaster and Stone, *Pennsylvania*). In a letter to Jeremy Belknap, May 17, 1788, Hazard explains that the contractors did send papers by stage. This was usually too expensive and the drivers careless, "Belknap Papers," II, 43–44. The best modern account is O. W. Holmes, "Shall Stage Coaches Carry the Mail?—A Debate of the Confederation Period," *Wm. and Mary Quarterly*, 20:555 at 570, 3d ser., 1963.

to influence the choice of delegates, and, indeed, to persuade the delegates themselves.[14] Above all, the basic design of molding and hardening opinion was so far successful that the printed word became common coin and was uttered by delegate after delegate in one assembly after another. Anyone familiar with the newspapers will be quick to recognize how much the speech-makers owed the scriveners. And, as we shall see, some delegates in different conventions had their fun with the matter.

There are characteristics of the pen-and-ink polemics over adoption that lead one to suppose that a great many more people of very different degrees of intelligence had to be enlightened or persuaded than the *communis opinio* of modern writers concedes. This opinion had its starting point in the dictum of a prominent historian that "the mass of men" was disfranchised.[15] As the "common man" more and more engaged the sympathies of publicists, this proposition assumed an apodictical quality although it originally rested upon inadequate studies of suffrage qualifications. It is a proposition deserving of not even a Scotch verdict, for more recent studies of the electorate in various states have demonstrated that earlier generalizations about defranchisement in those states are untrue.[16] And it may be observed that wherever, as was usual, a minimum valuation of property or income was made the criterion of qualification, there is at least a *prima facie* presumption that the body of voters had been swelled by monetary inflation. Whether or not persons thus qualified chose to exercise their franchise is quite another problem.

As a matter of sheer bulk, the intellectual fare proffered the public

---

[14] The most striking example of this is Hamilton's treatment of the judicial in *The Federalist* published on the eve of the New York Convention, long after the elections.

[15] C. Beard, *An Economic Interpretation of the Constitution of the United States* (1913 ed.), 24.

[16] These studies include P. A. Crowl, *Maryland during and after the Revolution*, 33 *et seq.*, and his "Antifederalism in Maryland," 446; J. A. Munroe, *Federalist Delaware, 1775–1815*; R. P. McCormick, *Experiment in Independence: New Jersey in the Critical Period, 1781–1789*; R. E. Brown, *Middle-Class Democracy and the Revolution in Massachusetts, 1691–1780*; R. E. Brown, and B. K. Brown, *Virginia, 1705–1786: Democracy or Aristocracy?*

The Beard thesis was challenged by R. E. Brown, *Charles Beard and the Constitution* (Princeton, N.J.: Princeton University Press, 1956); but, as already noted, substantial documentation was supplied by F. McDonald, *We the People: The Economic Origins of the Constitution*, where, in particular, an examination of the security holdings of the Framers and other participants in the ratification struggle (an essential for the support of Beard's thesis) disclosed a succession of errors by Beard. Main, *The Antifederalists: Critics of the Constitution, 1781–1788*, has at points not profited by McDonald's researches, for example, making out Edmund Randolph a rich man and Robert Yates as well off when the contrary was true.

from September 1787 to August 1788 is truly remarkable. This may be accounted for partly by the existence of a long-cultivated appetite for political homily, and partly to an even longer period of conditioning to diffuse harangue from rostrum or pulpit. Their political or spiritual salvation forming thus the burden of most of what Americans then heard or read about, they constituted an audience peculiarly susceptible to hearing out argument and pondering what was laid before them. Because, as already noticed, the journals borrowed lavishly from each other, not only were the compositions of some local sages served up to the reader, but also, as papers from elsewhere came to hand, the effusions of thinkers in far-off parts of the land. The enterprise of printers was responsible for much of this, but sometimes re-publication was engineered by earnest advocates. The federalists were at great pains to get their pieces reprinted,[17] and their opponents were no less zealous.[18] But whatever the initiative, the effect was the development of opinion on a national scale despite the fact that the issues themselves remained to be settled state by state. Not the least influential specimens put in circulation were the reproductions of newspaper reports of convention debates in Pennsylvania, Connecticut and Massachusetts. Ideas such as the power of the judicial to pass on the constitutionality of statutes, expressed by Wilson and then Ellsworth, thus gained a much greater currency than might otherwise have been the case. Of particular importance was the catalyzation of belief in respect to amendments. Here the program of the minority in Pennsylvania and Maryland, the recommendations of Massachusetts, and eventually of Virginia and New York, all played a part.

Since all this writing was published as much to persuade the voters

---

[17] Washington to Stuart, Nov. 30, 1787, re *Publius, Doc. Hist. Const.*, IV, 382; Tench Coxe to Madison, Dec. 28, 1787, re his pieces signed "An American," *ibid.*, 423. See also Hamilton to Madison, Apr. 3, 1788, *ibid.*, 545. The "American Citizen" pieces of Coxe were reprinted in the *Virginia Independent Chronicle*, Nov. 7 and 21, 1787. This paper ran the first three *Publius* letters Dec. 12, 19 and 26, 1787.

[18] The loss of the Mason–R. H. Lee correspondence for this period (*cf.* Rowland, *The Life and Correspondence of George Mason*, II, 184) and the destruction of George Clinton's papers in the Albany fire make difficult the documentation of these efforts. The activities of the Albany and New York Committees of the Federal Republicans are partially documented in the Ms. Lamb Papers, Box 15 (NYHS). The charges made regarding the cutting off of "southern" newspapers from Massachusetts during the convention there (*infra*, c. VIII, p. 352) lead one to infer that the despatch of inflammatory antifederalist matter had been deliberately undertaken and was likely deliberately frustrated. On Jan. 15, 1788, the *Pennsylvania Packet* ran a letter from Cambridge, Mass., reporting that A—— (Samuel Adams?) had encouraged publication of R. H. Lee's "hacknied trumpery" in a pamphlet circulated in Connecticut "lately brought here."

as to enlighten them, the diversity in the quality of the matter displayed itself suggests very strongly that it was not merely the now much suspected "upper classes" which were addressed. There were, indeed, pieces to appeal to any taste—from the polished periods of *Publius* to squibs of the sheerest vulgarity.[19] Much of what was written was pedestrian; much was repetitious to the point of intellectual benumbment. The same fashionable philosophers, notably Locke and Montesquieu, were vouched to warranty by both sides in the controversy. In tune with the contemporary bent for seeking security in historical example, the books were ransacked for precedents of leagues and confederations—*e.g.*, the Achaean, the Amphictyonic, the Helvetic. Over these auspices from the past, the Catos, the Caesars and other noble Romans of the journals spelled out auguries for the future. Protracted exposure to this literature tends to dull admiration for the skill with which the federal cause was often presented and to impair one's rueful appreciation of the prescience of some antifederalists. But one feels a warm kinship with the poetaster who sang:

---

[19] A few samples will suffice. *Marcus* in the New York *Daily Advertiser*, Oct. 15, 1787, commenting upon the lawyers' interest in the new judiciary: "It is *not* the Interest of Those who enjoy State consequences, which would be lost in the Assemblies of the States. These insects and worms are only seen on their own dunghill."

"A Man of no Party" commenting on pieces by Republican *Brutus*, etc.: "I wonder how the printer if he is delicately nosed could set his type so often to the obscene word S—t; which for that reason, I conceive to be no other S—t than his own." New York *Daily Advertiser*, Oct. 20, 1787. On a supposed federalist conversation in a beer house the following suggestions were offered for the treatment of antifederalists: "12. A Barber—I would *shave* the son of a ——"; "15. A Potter—And I would grind his dust afterward into a *chamber pot*." Philadelphia *Independent Gazetteer*, Sept. 20, 1787.

"A New Federal Song" which appeared in this same paper Apr. 24, 1788, describes how "a new federal sign" at a tavern was "All besmeared with the tagh of Jamie the Rover." The chorus of the song on the Poughkeepsie convention, printed in Greenleaf's *New-York Journal*, June 28, 1788:
"Federal, falderal, federal tit,
Beware of the dainty, the savory bit,
Keep fast all behind
  or you're surely b—t."

An example of vulgarity in respectable dress is supplied by "A Democratic Federalist" in the *Pennsylvania Packet*, Oct. 23, 1787. To drive home the enormities which people should be prepared to face at the hands of federal law enforcement officers, this writer dredged up an obscure English case more suited for telling in a pot-house than for public discussions—Ward's Case in Clayton, Reports and Pleas of Assises at Yorke, 44 (1651). The case concerned a constable who, searching for stolen goods, pulled the covers from a bed on which a woman was lying and pursued his inquiries beneath her smock. This case enjoyed a certain vogue in the journals. Samuel Chase cited it in his notes in opposition to the Constitution (*infra*, c. IX, pp. 368–69), and George Mason made oblique reference to it during the Virginia debates (*infra*, p. 388, n. 134).

Talk of *Holland* and *Greece* and of *purses* and *swords*,
Democratical mobs and congressional lords;
Tell what is surrendered and what is enjoy'd,
All things weigh alike, boys, we know, in a void.
Down, down, downderry down.[20]

THE SUBMISSION TO CONGRESS

ALTHOUGH THE anticipated changes in government had been the
subject of some preliminary sparring in the New York City newspapers
during the summer of 1787, it was the proceedings on the Constitution in the Congress immediately followed by the Donnybrook Fair in
the Pennsylvania Assembly that set the presses turning. On September
20 the Constitution, the recommendatory resolves of the Philadelphia
Convention and the letter of transmission were laid before Congress,
then sitting in New York.[21] This was a packet of surpassing political
potency, and in effect Congress was now to hear and determine the
matter of its own demise. As if the impact of the text of the Constitution itself were not sufficient, the resolves advising on ratification were
presented as an act of the states in Convention—almost as from one
equal to another. To cap it all, the new venture was winged on its way
by the wonderfully persuasive communication that carried the enormous
prestige of Washington's signature. Wednesday, September 26, was fixed
by Congress as the time for consideration. By this time ten members
who had participated in the Convention were on hand. It was well for
their plan that they were, for despite the brief time for study, the interval
had been long enough for major objections to have been formulated.
What is more, Madison had been advised on September 23 that his
fellow delegate to Congress, Richard Henry Lee, had set about "forming propositions for essential alterations in the Constitution" itself.[22]

This was something to have been anticipated in view of Lee's
previous disapproval of proposals for the expansion of federal power,[23]
and his close relations with George Mason. The gloss upon Article
XIII of the Confederation that had enjoyed currency, viz., that alterations of the Articles must be initiated by Congress,[24] gave some color
of constitutional right to what Lee was about, although the Articles

---

[20] New York *Daily Advertiser*, Nov.
23, 1787; reprinted *Worcester Magazine*, IV, 149; *American Museum*, II,
595 (Dec. 1787).
[21] Bingham to FitzSimons, Sept. 21,
1787, *LMCC*, VIII, 646.

[22] Ed. Carrington to Madison, Sept.
23, 1787, *ibid.*, 647.
[23] Lee to Samuel Adams, Mar. 14,
1785, *LMCC*, VIII, 66–67; Lee to
Madison, Aug. 11, 1785, *ibid.*, 180–
81.
[24] *Supra*, c. V, p. 200, n. 22.

actually said no more than that no alteration should be made in any of them "unless such alteration be agreed to in a Congress of the United States, and be afterward confirmed by the Legislatures of every State." The Convention, as we have seen, had twice voted down propositions to seek approval of Congress, and the resolution submitting the new instrument was coldly neutral. It was, however, too much to expect that those who did not like the new plan would not use Article XIII as a weapon of attack. The "Conventioners," as Lee called them,[25] having been haunted by this article at various junctures during their proceedings and having sought to exorcise it by Article VII of the new Constitution, were now to face it as a reality. Consequently, as delegates to Congress they were to seek the approval which as delegates to the Convention they had voted should not be sought.

There are no entries in the *Journal* of Congress for September 26, the day that discussion began. It would appear, however, from a report made by Madison to Washington that it was first urged that since the new plan was more than an alteration of the Articles and even subverted them, it would be a "constitutional impropriety" for Congress to take any positive agency in the work. This had been countered by reference to the preamble of Congress's resolve of February 21 with regard to the establishment of a "firm national government," and by reference to the fact that the powers of the Convention were defined in the Commissions in nearly the same terms as those given by the Articles to Congress. If the plan was within the powers of the Convention, it was within those of Congress, if beyond those powers, the same necessity which justified the Convention would justify Congress.[26] This was, of course, a reference to the *salus populi* argument which had been belabored in February to induce action by Congress, and it was to recur in the September discussions, although the skies were less dark than they had earlier been.

It cannot be certainly averred that at this stage a motion was before the house, but it seems probable from the tenor of Madison's report and from references in the *Minutes of Debates* kept by Melancton Smith of New York[27] that at some juncture on September 26 a motion had been offered by Nathan Dane.[28] These *Minutes*, recently come to light, cover some of the discussion of September 27 and open with a notation that a motion by Dane was under consideration. There is no record of this in the *Journals* for September 27, although other

---

[25] Lee to Samuel Adams, Oct. 27, 1787, *LMCC*, VIII, 669.

[26] Madison to Washington, Sept. 30, 1787, *ibid.*, 650–52.

[27] "Melancton Smith's Minutes of Debates on the New Constitution," *Colum. L. Rev.*, 64:26, 1964 (hereafter cited as "Smith's Minutes").

[28] Text taken from PCC in *JCC*, XXXIII, 543–44.

motions were entered. The resolve embodied in Dane's motion went no further than an agreement to transmit to the executives of the states the documents received from the Convention. But this was venomously fanged with a preamble which recited *inter alia* that the new Constitution appeared to be a new system in itself and "not as any part of, or alteration in" the Articles. By these, the powers of Congress were constitutionally confined to alteration. Congress could not with propriety proceed to examine or alter the proposed Constitution unless with a view so essentially to change the principles and forms as to make it an additional part of the Confederation. Thus the members of Congress did not feel themselves at liberty under the Articles to express an opinion on a form of government in no way connected with extant forms of government.

Apart from the procedural objection, it appears from a listing at the start of Smith's *Minutes* that certain major criticisms of the new plan had already been voiced, viz., that the consolidation was imperfect and would not work; if it did, it would not be on free principles, it must be supported by a standing army; it would oppress the industrious and advantage the few.[29] In the months to come these strictures were to become stock with the opposition.

The debate on the 27th took a new twist when Pierce Butler inquired what motive had produced Dane's motion because he thought that it was calculated to disapprove. Dane professed willingness to amend the motion to make it neutral, but he warned that if the Constitution was to be approved by Congress, it would be moved to take it up by paragraphs, with objections stated and amendments moved. Richard Henry Lee, however, insisted Congress had no right to recommend a plan subverting the government. What was proposed was a destruction of the Confederation of thirteen states and setting up one of nine states. Nevertheless, he thought it would be "indecent" not to send out the documents and consequently offered a substitute motion.

This motion, crossed out in the *Journal*, recited that Congress upon consideration of the constitution under which "it exists and acts" found that its power was limited by Article XIII to the amendment of the present Confederacy of thirteen states and did not extend to the creation of a new confederacy of nine states. Because the Convention had been constituted under authority of twelve states it was deemed "respectful" to submit the plan to the state executives to be laid before

---

[29] In "Smith's Minutes," at 34, Pierce Butler's query as to the motives which produced the resolve is followed by Dane's query as to what words were objectionable and then the listing of objections. This gives the appearance of these being voiced by Dane, but we believe the list to be a summary of what had generally been offered because later Butler states (*ibid.*, at 40), "Dane has leading objections but declines naming them."

On the constitution as reported.
by the Convention —
the motion of Mr Dane for sending
forward y.e Constil. with an opin —
renewed

Mr. Butler — wishes to know the motives y.t produced y.e motion. he
thinks it is calculated to disapprove —

Mr. Dane — Asks, to know what words are object —

1. the consolidate . imperfect & will not work —
2. If it does it will not work on free principles — it must
be supported by a standing army — it will oppress y.e honest
and industrious — will add. of a few — is not averse to an
is open to convict.n and if convinced will support — is willing
the pres.t motion should be amended so as to be neutral — If it
is to be approved it will be moved to take it up by paragraphs
— objections stated, amendments moved — Congress no concern be
to cons.d

Mr Lee — Every man to see with his own eyes — to judge for themselves
— Congress acting under y.e pres. constitution . defin.d limitting
y.e powers, have no right to recom.d a plan subverting y.e
Gov.t — this remark felt. as a Gent. yesterday justify. by y.e
necessity of the case — this dang.r because y.e prin.e has
been abus.d to bad footing. where it is used for good — the impor.t
Referred as an inst.e to justify — that within y.e powers. sent to
a.e y.e apph. of 13 S.s within y.e line — this by time — this plan
proposes destroy. y.e cons.f of 13 and a new one of 9 — yet it w.d be indisct.
not to send it to y.e S.s for 12 States sent del. as he und.d to amend y.e
pres. g.nt men of us Cho. have agreed upon y.t it sh.d before.d.

A Gen. yes.d said y.e Conf. says noth.g of Conven. — It is true it does n.t
point a cond. — but it does not prohib.d y.t to be prop.d by one, or any other
way. Conf. is only to agree — if this was not Restrict. but an amend.t
long might cons.r — proposes a Resolution, stating that as long.
have no right under y.e Conf. to alter sub.t alt. of y.e conf. unless agreed to
by 13 S. & y.e prop.r an am.t by 9

Mr King — Rec.d moderation. & is sorry m.r Dane is intemperate —

Mr Lee . approves y.e moti. of mr.l R.H. Lee; as being. y.e point. to view. whether y.e
shall be passed. with. incer. — a with.t thinks, mr.o has not app.d
int.

R.H. Lee . at a loss to under.d mr.k — feel his pulse & he will find no inten

the several legislatures.[30] This perversion of the intentions of the Convention was calculated to raise the hackles of the pro-Constitution men, and although Smith obviously did not note everything said, it is apparent that an angry exchange took place. Lee denied that he had any sinister intent but if he was called on to approve he would have to declare his sentiments. This he was shortly to do. Abraham Clark of New Jersey, who confessed he did not approve of the new instrument of government, could see no purpose in altering it and moved to postpone Lee's motion in favor of one "barely to forward" a copy to the states.[31] This was in accordance with what the Convention had wished, but as the debate in Congress had moved, the erstwhile delegates now were pressing for words of approval.

In the discussion of the merits of the two motions, the chief issue appears to have been whether or not the Convention had been bound as was the Congress. Madison insisted that the powers of both bodies were identical, and that if either motion were adopted, disapproval was implied. Lee, however, claimed that the Convention had not proceeded within the limits confining Congress, since nine states and not thirteen would be enough to make the Constitution the supreme law. Congress had never done anything "opposing the Confederacy." Madison's answer to this was that Congress itself had abandoned the federal idea and recommended a national government with the impost resolve of February 1781. Furthermore, the sale of the western lands and the Northwest Ordinance were instances of Congress exceeding its powers.[32] This was a telling thrust because Lee and Dane had been involved in securing passage of the Northwest Ordinance during the preceding summer. To this Lee made the woolly answer that the western lands had been Virginia's. She had given them to Congress which had a right to sell. The Western Government was temporary and not inconsistent. As for the new Constitution, there were so many bad things in it civil liberty would be in imminent danger and Congress, he believed, should have the liberty to amend.

The *Journal* shows that Lee called for the ayes and nays on the postponement of his motion, and it was voted to postpone, ten votes to one.[33] Whereupon Edward Carrington of Virginia moved to postpone Clark's motion to take into consideration a resolve to the effect that Congress agreed to the Constitution and recommended that the legislatures of the several states cause conventions to be called for the purpose of ratification.[34]

---

30 *JCC*, XXXIII, 540–41.
31 *Ibid.*, 541.
32 "Smith's Minutes," at 39.
33 *JCC*, XXXIII, 541–42. Only one Maryland delegate was present who voted aye, but under the rules his vote did not count.
34 *Ibid.*, 542.

This proposition did nothing to stem the pressure for amendments which Lee's remarks had made clear would be something in the nature of a bill of rights. The discussion at this juncture was befuddled by two suggestions. One had earlier been made by William Samuel Johnson that what was before the house was in the nature of a committee report which Congress must approve or disapprove.[35] Someone else had said that the Constitution was in the situation of a bill agreed to in one house.[36] This last, Madison said, would exclude amendments because the act if altered would not be the act of both. There was no probability of the members agreeing to alterations because of differences of opinion. A bill of rights was unnecessary because the powers were enumerated and only extended to certain cases. Lee, however, promised that a bill of rights would be brought forward. This had been unnecessary in the Confederation because only express powers could be exercised. To prevent exercise of constructive powers was the great use of the bill of rights.

Lee's announcement evoked the first lawyerlike denial of Congress's power. The house, said Rufus King, could not constitutionally make alteration. The idea of the Convention had originated in the states. Congress had been led to agree that the Convention should propose alterations which when agreed to in Congress and confirmed by the states would render the federal Constitution adequate. The resolve of February 21 consequently operated as an estoppel.[37] If the majority of the people manifested desire for a change, Congress might advise it but this was not obligatory. The house could agree or disagree, but if it disagreed, this would not prevent acceptance. Lee, adverting to Johnson's analogy of a report to Congress, found it a strange doctrine indeed that a report could not be altered. He was ready for the Constitution to go out as it stood but with amendments in a separate package. To send the instrument forth without amendments was like "presenting a hungry man 50 dishes and insisting he should eat all or none."[38]

Madison, treading the way taken by King, pointed out that one thing distinguished this report from any other: the Convention had not been appointed by Congress but by the people from whom Congress derived its power; Congress was only to concur. He admitted Congress might alter, but if it did, it would not be the act of the Convention but of Congress and so impose the trammels of Article XIII. Lee was not to be put off; he continued to worry the analogy of the report and finally put the question: "Is the Idea of Convention that not only Congress but the States must agree on the whole or else reject it?"[39]

---

[35] "Smith's Minutes," at 38–39.
[36] *Ibid.*, 40.

[37] *Ibid.*, 41.
[38] *Ibid.*, 41.   [39] *Ibid.*, 42.

This was to be a fundamental issue in the process of ratification. But Madison did not choose to meet the question head-on. The proper question, he asserted, was whether any amendments should be made and this the house should decide. If alterations were sent to the states, the Articles required the delegates to report to them. There would be two plans. Some would accept one, some another. This would create confusion. Lee retorted that some admitted the right but doubted the expediency. He then offered amendments—his so-called bill of rights.[40]

As we have elsewhere pointed out, the term "bill of rights" even at that time had political magic, and this description of the full content of what was offered can only be described as a crafty maneuver.[41] Lee's proposal opened with a statement that it had been found from universal experience that the most express declarations and reservations were necessary to protect the just rights and liberties of mankind from the silent, powerful and ever active conspiracy of those who govern. Consequently the new Constitution should be bottomed upon a declaration or bill of rights, clearly and precisely stating "the principles upon which this Social Compact is founded." The rights listed included those protections of the individual recited in the English Bill of Rights and already copied by various states. But whereas these, again imitating the English prototype, had embodied what were conceived to be basic political principles, Lee undertook to set out certain changes in the structure of the proposed government, *e.g.*, the creation of a Privy Council, abolition of the office of Vice President, abolition of diversity jurisdiction— items which, Madison wrote Washington, corresponded with the ideas of George Mason.[42]

Unfortunately, Smith's *Minutes* break off after four speeches— Dane announced that if amendments were precluded, he would vote no; Carrington thought that as amendments were offered, a member should have the right to support them; Clark stated that Lee's motion would do injury by being entered on the *Journal* and consequently the house upon cool reflection would do best to "agree to send it out without agreeing." Smith's notes end with inconsequential remarks by Grayson. It would appear, however, both from what Madison wrote Washington[43] and from a letter of R. H. Lee to Mason, that the debate had been furious. Melancton Smith supported Lee, and it may

---

[40] The text in *LMCC*, VIII, 648–49. As Mr. Burnett points out, there are some minor variations in the copy sent to Dr. William Shippen, printed in J. C. Ballagh, ed., *The Letters of Richard Henry Lee*, II, 442–44. Lee had other specific criticisms not added to what was presented to Congress.

Arthur Lee to Charles Cotesworth Pinckney, Oct. 29, 1787, Ms. Pinckney Papers, Box 2 (LC).
[41] "Smith's Minutes," at 33.
[42] *LMCC*, VIII, 650–52.
[43] Sept. 30, 1787, *LMCC*, VIII, 650–52. Until the Smith Minutes were published, this letter along with Lee's

be supposed from Dane's earlier comments that he did the same. What Madison called a "serious division" with popular alterations entered on the *Journals* with ayes and nays was avoided. The argument of expediency triumphed, for on September 28 Congress resolved unanimously to transmit the Constitution with the accompanying documents to the several state legislatures "in Order to be submitted to a convention of Delegates chosen in each state by the people thereof in conformity to the Resolves of the Convention." Eleven states and one delegate from Maryland were present at the vote.[44]

Richard Henry Lee reported to his friend Mason that the final resolve was a compromise—a statement of approbation of the Constitution having been abandoned.[45] Lee's own stand was a matter of great public significance, for he still bore the laurels of his service in promoting the Declaration of Independence. Washington expressed his displeasure over the course pursued by Lee—unusual candor in one who normally wrote with cold discretion.[46] It should be remembered, however, that the coolness between these men stemmed from Revolutionary days.[47] It was hardly to be expected that a plan of government approved and sponsored by Washington would engage Lee's sympathies. The General would have been even more disturbed had he known that Mason had been exhorted to organize opposition in Virginia as well as in Maryland and South Carolina.[48] To Washington, Lee wrote that his doubts over the Constitution were the result of long reflection upon the nature of man and government, and he assured him that his doubts of the new system were among the "first distresses" that had happened in his life.[49] Lee had already written his friend Shippen of his fears of the encroaching nature of power—"The malady of human nature in these States now, seems to be as it was in the years 1778 & 1779 with respect to the effect produced by a certain Combination."[50] Washington and Franklin were targets of the Lee faction at the time referred to; they had seemingly not yet moved out of range.

letters to Mason, Oct. 1, 1787 (*ibid.*, 652–53), and to Randolph, Oct. 16, 1787 (*ibid.*, 658), were the chief sources of what went on in Congress. See also Lee's bitter letter to Samuel Adams, Oct. 27, 1787 (*ibid.*, 669), regarding the "inconsistency" of members of the Convention passing on their handiwork in Congress. It was because of this dilemma, as Lee wrote John Adams on Sept. 5, 1787, that he had declined serving as delegate to the Convention (*ibid.*, 643). Note, however, that on Mar. 26, 1787, Lee writing to Governor Randolph had declined serving because of ill health (Ballagh, *The Letters of Richard Henry Lee*, II, at 415).

[44] *JCC*, XXXIII, 549. The letter of transmittal is in *Doc. Hist. Const.*, II, 23.

[45] *Supra*, n. 43.

[46] To Madison, Oct. 10, 1787, in *Washington Writings*, XXIX, 285.

[47] Wharton, *Rev. Dip. Corr.*, I, Introduction, sec. 11.

[48] Ballagh, *The Letters of Richard Henry Lee*, II, at 438–40.

[49] Oct. 11, 1787, *ibid.*, 448.

[50] Oct. 2, 1787, *ibid.*, 440 at 444.

COUP IN PENNSYLVANIA

IF THE DEBATE in Congress produced ingredients for the opposition's program, the events in the Pennsylvania Assembly, then meeting, provided an infusion of rancor which was to set public discussion over adoption off to an inflammatory start. The Pennsylvania Assembly had long been the situs of a guerilla war between the factions supporting the existing democratical constitution of the state and those working for revision. In 1787 the revisionists outnumbered the "Constitutionalists," and, as one might expect from adherents of a *status quo*, the latter opposed a change in the central government, the former favored it. In consequence, the fate of the federal Constitution was, as happened repeatedly, to hang upon the accidents of state politics.[51]

On the morning of the day Congress was to take its vote, it was moved in the Pennsylvania Assembly that a convention be called to meet in November to deliberate and determine on the new federal Constitution. This was vigorously opposed, chiefly on the ground that more time was needed by citizens to inform themselves and, further, that until Congress had acted, no state could do so. The resolution was fragmented into distinct propositions and the first of these—to call a convention in Philadelphia—was passed. The house then adjourned until four o'clock.[52]

At the appointed hour only forty-four members assembled. The opposition, well aware that forty-six were needed for a quorum, had remained away. The Sergeant at Arms, despatched to round up the truants, reported seventeen found who made clear their intention to remain absent. The house adjourned until the next morning. Fortunately, William Bingham, delegate to Congress, who had already undertaken to notify a member of the assembly of congressional action,[53] despatched a post-rider with the resolution of transmission. This was on hand when the faithful forty-four again assembled. Obviously this disposed of the only substantial objection of the minority. The Sergeant at Arms was again sent forth, armed with the resolution of Congress. He found various members to whom the document was exhibited but who were obdurate in their contumacy. But after he left the lodgings of two recalcitrants, a crowd broke in and hustled them to the State House. One of these unfortunates tendered his fine for breach of the rules and attempted to leave the chamber. Bystanders at the door prevented his exit. With a quorum thus present, the resolution fixing the date of the

---

[51] See Brunhouse, *Counter-Revolution in Pennsylvania*, c. VII.

[52] The assembly proceedings are reprinted in McMaster and Stone, *Pennsylvania*, 27–72.

[53] *LMCC*, VIII, 646.

state convention on November 28 and providing for details of representation and election was adopted.[54]

The dissident assemblymen lost no time in placing their grievances before the public in the form of an address to their constituents.[55] They were at pains to explain why they had withdrawn, detailed the performance which had produced a quorum and enlarged upon the insult to themselves and their constituents. The document then slides over into an attack upon the statutory authority of the Pennsylvania delegation to engage in forming a new constitution and sets out what the subscribers considered to be the major objections to the new instrument of government:

> You have a right, and we have no doubt you will consider whether or not you are in a situation to support the expense of such a government as is now offered you, as well as the expense of your state government? or whether a legislature consisting of three branches, neither of them chosen annually, and that the senate, the most powerful . . . are likely to lessen your burthens or increase your taxes? or whether in case your state government should be annihilated, which will probably be the case, or dwindle into a mere corporation, the continental government will be competent to attend to your local concerns?
>
> You can also best determine whether the power of levying and imposing internal taxes at pleasure, will be of real use to you or not? or whether a continental collector assisted by a few faithful soldiers will be more eligible than your present collectors of taxes?
>
> You will also in your deliberations on this important business judge, whether the liberty of the press may be considered as a blessing or a curse in a free government, and whether a declaration for the preservation of it is necessary? or whether in a plan of government any declaration of rights should be prefixed or inserted?
>
> You will be able, likewise, to determine whether in a free government there ought or ought not to be any provision against a standing army in time of peace? or whether the trial by jury in civil causes is becoming dangerous and ought to be abolished? and whether the judiciary of the United States is not so constructed as to absorb and destroy the judiciaries of the several States?
>
> You will also be able to judge whether such inconveniences have been experienced by the present mode of trial between citizen and citizen of different States as to render a continental court necessary for that purpose? or whether there can be any real use in the appellate jurisdiction with respect to fact as well as law?

---

[54] McMaster and Stone, *Pennsylvania*, 70–71.

[55] Reprinted in *ibid.*, 73–79.

The number of queries propounded that relate to the judicial process suggests that a lawyer or a judge had a large hand in drafting this document. Washington, whose plantation was a way-station for all manner of travellers and who thus was the recipient of much current gossip, wrote Madison that he had been informed that Richard Henry Lee had been at pains to disseminate his objections among the leaders of the Pennsylvania secessionists.[56] This may well have been the case. In any event, the "Address" is a cogent and adroit political tract, calculated to leave the impression that no knavery was beneath the pro-Constitution men. Even if a reader was not beguiled by the signers' protestations of high-minded purpose, he was nevertheless left with a store of solid objections for reflection.

The "Address," initially printed as a broadside,[57] appeared in the *Pennsylvania Packet* on October 4, 1787. A week later it was reprinted in Greenleaf's *New-York Journal* and presently made its way to other states. Swords were crossed at once in the Philadelphia papers, and the fray proceeded with liveliness and some bad temper. The matter of immediate grievance was quickly buried in discussion over the merits of the Constitution. These exchanges occurred with great intensity, for only a few short weeks ahead lay the election of delegates and the meeting of the state convention. Assuming the dissenting assemblymen were truly concerned that the people be afforded opportunity to inform themselves, the press of Pennsylvania met their wishes. Because these journals were widely copied, they informed—and misinformed—readers all over the Union.

THE APPEALS TO PREJUDICE

HAD THE CONTROVERSY over adoption of the new Constitution been conducted solely in the idiom of political philosophy, the debate would have been a very dull affair indeed. Fortunately, this was not the case. Since the object of the jousts in the journals preliminary to state conventions was as much to get votes as to instruct, great ingenuity was expended on emotional appeals. There was scarcely a prejudice susceptible of excitation that was not exploited by opposition writers. Some of this was of a low order and bore about the same relation to the sober

---

[56] Oct. 10, 1787, *Washington Writings*, XXIX, 285.

[57] According to a notation on the Library of Congress copy, the broadside appeared Oct. 2, 1787. A broadside version in German was also circulated (NYHS).

writing of *Cornelius* in Massachusetts,[58] *Fabius* in Delaware,[59] or *Aristides* in Maryland[60] as exists today between stump speeches for assemblymen and the sonorous periods of Presidential candidates. Even the most genteel figures, like the librarian of Harvard College,[61] the governor of New York,[62] and a future Chief Justice of the United States Supreme Court[63] deigned to the tactic of excitation. There were withal dozens of artful scriveners never to be identified whose compositions were of a sort to serve as the most effective vote swayers.

The appeals to prejudice were incessant, and in two particulars were related to the cries for a bill of rights. They tended to create an atmosphere of unreason, inimical to the exercise of sober judgment whether by the voter or by the delegate who represented him. Every argument for or against a provision in the Constitution, whatever its merits, was pondered, if at all, by men whose sensibilities—sectional, religious or social—had been played upon. So important was this phase of propaganda, so profoundly did it affect convention debates and press discussions on the merits of the Constitution, that some account must be given of it.

One of the most obvious bogeys was the military establishment.[64] Tensions between the colonists and the British regulars had reinforced a prejudice against a standing army that was a part of the English libertarian traditions of the seventeenth century imported by the settlers. The Americans developed an attachment to the ideal of the citizen soldier as exemplified in the militia, and the eventual defeat of the British became in popular imagination proof of the soundness of this belief. Certain events which occurred immediately after the war's end —the founding of the Society of the Cincinnati, and the bitter controversy over the pensioning of the veterans—had reanimated old fears about a military, and particularly an officer class. The reaction had been marked in New England. Consequently, when critics asserted that the intendment of a grant of Congress to raise and support armies was the establishment of an unnecessary standing army,[65] this was heard

---

[58] An unidentified writer of western Massachusetts. Reprinted in S. Harding, *The Contest over the Ratification of the Federal Constitution in the State of Massachusetts*, App. A.

[59] John Dickinson. His tract is in P. L. Ford, ed., *Pamphlets on the Constitution of the United States 1787–1788*, 163–216 (hereafter cited as Ford, *Pamphlets*).

[60] Presumed to be Alexander Contee Hanson. Tract in *ibid.*, 217–57.

[61] James Winthrop, who wrote in the *Massachusetts Gazette* as *Agrippa*.

Reprinted in Ford, *Essays*, 53–122.

[62] As *Cato*, George Clinton wrote in Greenleaf's *New-York Journal*. Reprinted in Ford, *Essays*, 247–78.

[63] Oliver Ellsworth writing as "Landholder"; *infra*, p. 229 *et seq.*, notes 1, 2, 3.

[64] The development of this is sketched in D. Goebel and J. Goebel, *Generals in the White House* (Garden City, N. Y.: Doubleday, 1945), c. I.

[65] The references to the creation of a standing army and the powers over militia were incessant. The fact that

by a large and receptive audience, nowhere greater than in the Eastern states. The provision respecting congressional control of the militia was represented as proof positive of the sinister intentions of the Framers. Because this injected a political element into the discussion, a great deal of states' rights feelings was aroused to compound the emotional reaction.

The appeal to religious sentiment[66] was of a different order because of the wonderful variety of sects and the multiformity of their beliefs. It was important to enlist the confessions with large membership or those which were well organized, and, above all, their pastors—what in Tudor times was known as "tuning the pulpits." The clergymen, of course, represented a vast pool of potential speakers whose admonitions their flocks were accustomed to follow. Objectors followed two lines of attack and they were diametrically opposed. On one hand was the clamor against the lack of any safeguard for liberty of conscience; on the other hand was the no less vociferous outcry against the failure to provide a religious test for office.

With what seems to us a lack of consistency these two lines of complaint were sometimes coupled. Typical was the backwoods publicist who scolded in the *Worcester Magazine* that with no religious test, Jews, Turks and heathen might hold the highest offices, "yet there is no liberty given the people to perform religious worship according to

---

three members of the Philadelphia Convention—Gerry (Ford, *Pamphlets*, 10), Mason (*ibid.*, 331) and Martin *The Genuine Information*, Farrand, *Records*, III, 207, 218; and letters, Ford, *Essays*, 342, 358)—had pieces in publications that had a good circulation gave impetus to the clamor. Others like R. H. Lee (Ford, *Pamphlets*, 304), Clinton (Ford, *Essays*, 258), *Agrippa* (*ibid.*, 68, 118), *Brutus I* (*New-York Journal*, Oct. 18, 1787), "Centinel," II (*infra*, p. 284) and Arthur Lee as *Cincinnatus* (*New-York Journal*, Nov. 15, 1787) raised the view halloo. A lot of smaller fry gave tongue. See "Officer in the late Continental Army," Philadelphia *Independent Gazetteer*, Nov. 6, 1787; *New-York Journal*, Nov. 19, 1787; *Worcester Magazine*, IV, 160 (December 1787); "Son of Liberty," *New-York Journal*, Nov. 8, 1787; an anonymous correspondent in the *Maryland Journal*, Oct. 16, 1787, who coined the expression "a Prussian militia." These pieces are much too numerous fully to list.

The pro-Constitution men took this seriously if for no other reason than that it related to the bill of rights clamor. *Publius* devoted Nos. 25 and 29 to the matter. Tench Coxe, answering *Brutus* (Ford, *Pamphlets*, 150), James Iredell, answering Mason(*ibid.*, 363), Alexander C. Hanson and others sought to quiet alarm. Numerous lesser known figures also contributed. An amusing comment combined gibes at two bogeys: "It [the Constitution] gives command of the whole militia to the President.—should he hereafter be a Jew, our dear posterity may be ordered to rebuild Jerusalem," New York *Daily Advertiser*, Jan. 18, 1788.

[66] Beginning with R. H. Lee's demand in Congress (September 27–28) for a guarantee of liberty of conscience this became a staple in antifederalist writing. It was reiterated in the first "Centinel" letter, by Lee in the "Federal Farmer" letters, *Brutus II*, and by a host of scriveners.

the dictates of their consciences."[67] This sort of addled thinking had good precedent, for constitution-makers in many states had done just what this Massachusetts critic believed should have been done in the federal Constitution. In one way or another, constitutional safeguards had been set up to protect freedom for worship, and simultaneously a declaration of belief was exacted for some or all public offices. These provisions fell far short of providing full freedom of conscience since a variety of believers were disbarred from places of trust.[68] What had been put into effect were variants of the English Toleration Act of 1688. In the case of Massachusetts the analogy is striking, for here, although peaceable Christians, good subjects of the Commonwealth, were assured equal protection under the law,[69] contribution to a Protestant faith was likewise enjoined.[70] Protestantism was thus constitutionally equated with Christianity.[71] This had a bearing upon the declaration required of the governor that he was of the Christian religion.

It seems probable that those who joined in the outcry for liberty of conscience wished something resembling the provisions of state constitutions. In any event, the response to this propaganda depended much upon the peculiar experience of a particular sect in a particular jurisdiction. This is illustrated by the case of the Baptists. Judging from a letter to Madison, February 1788,[72] the Virginia Baptists, who had waited ten years for the attenuated guarantee of the Declaration of Rights (1776) to be implemented and had only briefly enjoyed the fruits of

---

[67] "Watchman" in *Worcester Magazine*, IV, 242. The most distinguished representative of this school of thought was Luther Martin who, in *The Genuine Information* (Farrand, *Records*, III, 227), made himself out as a proponent of a religious test and later appeared as also a champion of a bill of rights with a guarantee of liberty of conscience (Ford, *Essays*, 365). Apparently a pamphlet in this tenor was circulating in North Carolina, for Iredell mentioned it in the debates there (Elliot, *Debates*, IV, 195).

It seems likely that the clergy was responsible for propagating much of this. The *Massachusetts Centinel* ran pieces to combat religious prejudice, *e.g.*, "Amen," Oct. 13, 1787, "Truth," Nov. 24, 1787: "Religion left to its guardian God—all tests, oaths, and hamperings of the conscience of our fellow men entirely done away."

[68] For example, by constitution in Delaware an office holder had to sign a declaration professing belief in the Trinity and the divine inspiration of both Testaments (Art. 22). North Carolina excluded from office persons who denied the being of God or the truth of the Protestant religion or the divine authority either of the Old or New Testaments (Art. 32). Pennsylvania set a form of declaration of belief in God and acknowledgment of the divine inspiration of both Testaments (sec. 10). New Jersey limited offices to those who professed a belief in any Protestant sect (Art. 19). In Maryland an office holder must subscribe a declaration of belief in the Christian religion (Art. 35).

[69] Constitution of 1780, Part the First, Art. II.

[70] *Ibid.*, Art. III.

[71] *Ibid.*, Part the Second, c. II, Art. II.

[72] *Doc. Hist. Const.*, IV, 525, enclosing objections of Rev. John Leland, a prominent Baptist. Earlier Madison's father had written him of Baptist opposition, *ibid.*, 462–63.

the Act for Religious Liberty, were deeply concerned over inclusion of a safeguard in the federal Constitution. On the other hand, in New York where toleration had long prevailed and where complete liberty of conscience was secured by the Constitution of 1777, the Baptist Association endorsed the federal Constitution as it stood.[73]

Whether or not the liberty of conscience issue was raised for mere partisan reasons, the extent of popular response is indicated by the anxieties expressed in the state conventions. More difficult to assess is the effect of appeals to bigotry and of the efforts to agitate sects which in the past had endured persecution. The Deists had long been bracketed with Belial in the clergy's index of evils, and consequently Luther Martin's innuendo that the Philadelphia Convention had been dominated by them[74] was bound to disturb some preachers of the Word and their congregations. In Pennsylvania and Virginia efforts were made to arouse the Quakers.[75] Piled on the embers of a recent conflagration over the consecration of American bishops in England was the charge that the adoption of the Constitution would be followed here by the establishment of the Anglican Church.[76] This last, of course, was designed to

---

[73] The circular is quoted in *New-York Journal*, Nov. 30, 1787. A "real Baptist" protested. See also *Pennsylvania Gazette*, Jan. 30, 1788.

[74] Martin, *The Genuine Information*, Farrand, *Records*, III, 227.

[75] Most important was the widely circulated "Centinel" who, in No. 3, Nov. 5, 1787, made direct appeal to them. Reprinted McMaster and Stone, *Pennsylvania*, 600. See also "Philadelphiensis," *Independent Gazetteer*, Nov. 28, 1787. See also rebuttals in *ibid.*, Jan. 15, 1788, and *Pennsylvania Gazette*, Jan. 30, 1788. Another Philadelphia piece with flicks at the Quakers reprinted in *New-York Journal*, Mar. 10, 1788.

The Pennsylvania Quakers were particularly vulnerable to the clamor for security of religious liberty. They had opposed the test laws of that state. In the summer of 1787 McKean C.J. had fined a Quaker for refusing the oath and so not qualifying for jury duty. Eleazar Oswald, who published the *Independent Gazetteer* and had earlier clashed with McKean, published a theatrical skit in which McKean appears as Lord Jeffreys—a skit reminiscent of the famous Penn case in Charles II's reign. McKean was

then an ardent federalist.

On the rousing of Virginia Quakers cf. *Virginia Independent Chronicle*, Feb. 13, 1788, and an answer by "One of the People," Mar. 12, 1788.

[76] "A Turk" in the *Independent Gazetteer*, Oct. 10, 1787, comparing the proposed government with that of the Ottoman Empire predicts Bishop Seabury "will be your Mufti." "A Baptist" in the Philadelphia *Freeman's Journal*, reprinted *New-York Journal*, Mar. 8, 1788, claims a deep-laid plot to establish the Episcopal Church. A "Real Baptist" apologizes to all Episcopalians, in *Pennsylvania Gazette*, Jan. 30, 1788, for the slur that an episcopacy would be established. In the *New-York Journal*, Dec. 28, 1787, *Democritus* claimed that "some priests" favored the Constitution and were going to excommunicate the Bible. It is not clear whether he referred to Roman Catholic or Anglican priests.

The political potency of attacks on the Anglicans was considerable as it was closely related in time to the imbroglio over the consecration of American bishops. The Tory Samuel Seabury had been the chief target. Unable to be consecrated in England owing to the necessity of taking an

have a double effect—to stir up the traditional dissenters and, because in many places Anglicans had been identified with Tories, to revive smouldering animosities.

Few of the defenders of the Constitution allowed themselves to be drawn into controversy over matters of religion. For the most part they contented themselves with attempting to meet the general bill of rights issue of which the liberty of conscience guarantee was a part.[77] Some of the wits, however, made merry over the matter. One of them in New York solemnly declared that the new Constitution admits to legislation, "1st Quakers, who will make the blacks saucy, and at the same time deprive us of means of defense—2ndly Mahometans who ridicule the doctrine of the trinity—3rdly Deists, abominable wretches—4thly Negroes, the seed of Cain—5thly Beggars, who when set on horseback will ride to the devil—6thly Jews &c. &c."[78] In far-off Pittsburgh another jeered, "The Rights of Conscience are swept away. The confessions of faith, the prayer-book, the manuel [sic] and Pilgrims Progress are to go. The songs of Watts, I am told, is the only thing of the kind that is to have any quarter at all."[79]

No less divisive than the incitement of sectarian feelings were the attempts to play upon sectional antagonism, often with particular reference to local economic interest. These were blows at a great underlying purpose of the new Constitution—the eradication, or at least abatement, of sectional differences. These pieces were the more serious for this reason. The South was the victim of unneighborly comment from Boston that it was common knowledge how the inhabitants of warmer climates were more dissolute and less industrious than those of colder regions, and so a code of laws for both Georgia and Massachusetts

---

oath of allegiance, he had resorted to the non-juring Scotch and there been consecrated. Because of his late Toryism and ritualistic leanings Seabury was faced with troubles in America. In 1787, thanks to a special Act of Parliament dispensing in certain cases with the oath of allegiance, Samuel Provoost of New York and William White of Pennsylvania were consecrated by the Archbishop of Canterbury. All this satisfied doctrinal scruples, but it fanned the anti-Episcopal prejudices of the myriad "dissenting" sects. The newspapers carried some very wounding propaganda in 1785–86. E. E. Beardsley, *Life and Correspondence of The Right Reverend Samuel Seabury, D.D.*, 3d ed.

(1882), 97–157, 292.

[77] Tench Coxe, as "An American Citizen," grappled with the issue (Ford, *Pamphlets*, 146) and these letters were widely printed. Ellsworth in *Landholder* (Ford, *Essays*, 168–69) entered into the matter more largely, apparently because this was being debated in Connecticut. No other widely distributed federalist writers seem to have entered this battle.

[78] *Curtiopolis* in the New York *Daily Advertiser*, Jan. 18, 1788, reprinted *Massachusetts Centinel*, Feb. 9, 1788.

[79] "Amos" in the *Pittsburgh Gazette*, reprinted in *Massachusetts Centinel*, Apr. 30, 1788 (*Extraordinary*).

was impossible.[80] It was averred by another writer that the rapid accumulation of wealth in the South had led to dissipation and a passion for aristocratic distinction.[81] These people could not know what it meant to acquire property by their own toil. It was questionable if they would be as tenacious of the liberties and interests of the Northern states as the legislatures of the latter. The principle upon which the representation of the South was fixed was also exploited to arouse misgivings of Northern freemen.

The "Federal Farmer," the Virginian Richard Henry Lee, was concerned about the Middle States and, anticipating that the seat of government would be settled there, predicted the rise of this group and the decline of the influence of both Northern and Southern states.[82] Pennsylvania was singled out by *Agrippa* of Massachusetts for the acid comment that it had expanded at the expense of religion and good morals.[83] The anonymous composer of a Boston broadside, however, pinpointed the true source of fear of the Quaker Eden by trumpeting "The *Trade* of *Boston* transferred to *Philadelphia*; and the Boston tradesmen *starving*."[84] George Mason was anxious about both the "northern and eastern" states because he thought the merchants there would ruin the South by exorbitant freights and by monopolizing the purchase of commodities at their own price.[85] These strictures, however, were solely for Southern consumption. They were eliminated from the version of his "Objections" published in Boston. As Mason's own constituents heard him, his regional dislikes were catholic. Hugh Williamson reported to his fellow North Carolinian, John Gray Blount, Mason's "beautiful Trope" in an election speech: "You may have been taught said he to respect Characters of the Members of the late Convention. You may have supposed that they were an assemblage of great men—There is nothing less true. From the Eastern States there were Knaves and Fools from the states southward of Virga: They were a parcel of Coxcombs and from the middle States Office Hunters not a few."[86] Mason believed in freedom of public expression and he practiced it.

---

[80] *Agrippa* in Ford, *Essays*, 64. Originally in the *Massachusetts Gazette*, he was partly reprinted *New-York Journal*, Dec. 5, 1787, Jan. 14, 1788.

[81] *Cato* in Ford, *Essays*, 258.

[82] Ford, *Pamphlets*, 290. Compare the South Carolinian Ramsay's assurance of Southern ascendancy, *ibid.*, 375. In the *Virginia Independent Chronicle*, Nov. 14, 1787, appeared a letter from New York to a friend in the House of Delegates prophesying ruin to the South at the hands of the carrying states. He claims a combination of "Eastern" delegates to Congress had rigged appointments in the Northwest territory to exclude Virginians.

[83] Ford, *Essays*, 79.

[84] Reprinted in the Boston *American Herald*, Nov. 19, 1787.

[85] Objections, Ford, *Pamphlets*, 331.

[86] June 3, 1788, *LMCC*, VIII, 747.

Of all the artifices used to sway men's passions there was none manipulated with greater constancy and with more lasting effect than the claim that the Constitution was an instrument designed to serve the interests of aristocracy, a claim which had definite economic implications.[87] The effects of this propaganda were lasting because the stigma was subsequently transferred to the Federalist Party which was unable to live it down. And in our own time historians with a predilection for the homespun have been so bewitched by what was palpably an appeal to the rough-and-ready voter that it has been treated as verity. An aristocracy, as it flourished and as the term was understood in the *grand monde* of Europe, did not exist in this country, and the English themselves would have been the first to deny that such had come into being in the colonies. Certainly the delegates to the Federal Convention did not conceive that an aristocracy existed here; indeed, they weighed various proposals in terms of a tendency to produce one, and with evident anxiety to forestall such a result.[88] That there were distinctions of wealth, education and ability there can be no question. But American society was too fluid to furnish that stability which is the *sine qua non* of an established aristocracy.[89]

It required perhaps a degree of intellectual sophistication, which a great many voters in 1787–88 were obviously not then thought to possess, properly to assess the issue over aristocracy. In any event, the issue was a weapon which circumstances had made ready for wielding. Since May 1787 there had been in circulation a book, more widely read than its literary merits deserved, expressing sentiments likely to

---

[87] The references to this are nearly endless. Virtually all of the leading antifederalist writers made some reference to the matter, and it was of course meat and drink for the minor scriveners. It was so much in issue that federalist writers could not avoid it, and even magisterial *Publius* was moved to special denials.

[88] The matter came up at various times, especially in the discussion of property qualifications, Aug. 7, 1787, and note in particular Gouverneur Morris's anxiety for safeguards against an aristocracy developing, Farrand, *Records*, II, 202 and 207; and Mason's comments, August 8, regarding the Senate's authority to initiate money bills, *ibid.*, 224; Williamson, September 5, on the appointing power, *ibid.*, 512; Wilson, September 6, *ibid.*, 522. When the question of making legislators ineligible for public office was

debated August 14, Mercer of Maryland, recently arrived, explained that the governments of America were already aristocracies, *ibid.*, 284. His acquaintance with governments like New Hampshire, New Jersey and Pennsylvania was obviously very limited.

[89] It should be noticed that both Madison and Hamilton analyzed the structure of society in terms of "interests," viz., the landed interest, the mercantile interest, etc. In other words, they classify in terms of the center of individuals' economic involvement. It is not a classification in terms of status, a concept into which entered such adventitious factors as birth, lineage, marriage and the like. The word "class" as used by them thus refers to their own grouping in terms of interest. See *Federalist* Nos. 10, 12, 60.

be obnoxious, or at least capable of seeming so. This was the first volume of John Adams' treatise *A Defence of the Constitutions of the United States against the attacks of M. Turgot.*[90] The bulk of this treatise was innocuous, being merely a tedious history of various polities, garnished by a chapter recounting the opinions of certain philosophers. In a preface and a conclusion Adams developed his own ideas about the three balancing powers necessary to good government.

Unfortunately, the disorderly character of Adams' text was a standing invitation to abstract quotable phrases. And so, despite the assertion that "there can be no free government without a democratical branch in the constitution,"[91] critics pounced on the passage, "The rich, the well-born and the able, acquire an influence among the people that will soon be too much for simple honesty and plain sense in a house of representatives. The most illustrious of them must, therefore be separated from the mass, and placed by themselves in a senate; this is, to all honest and useful intents, an ostracism."[92]

Adams might have escaped the indignity of being quoted out of context had he not, in his conclusion, counseled that the armed forces, offices of administration and justice, as well as those in foreign service, "must be gentlemen, that is to say, friends and connections of the rich, well-born and well-educated members of the house [of representatives]."[93] This sealed his reputation as a promoter of aristocracy. His openly expressed admiration of the British constitution was to some Americans a final damning self-incrimination.

Since the use to which Adams' words might be put could have escaped only the dullest of politicians, it was inevitable that he and his book should be forthwith injected into the fray. On October 5, 1787, there appeared in Philadelphia the first of the "Centinel" letters which bluntly raised the issue of an aristocratical plot.[94] The letters were said to have been composed by a "club" which included Judge George Bryan.[95] Bryan was the leader of the party to which belonged the recalcitrant Pennsylvania assemblymen. "Centinel" No. 1 had a great

---

[90] Reprinted in Adams, *Works*, IV, 271. The second and third volumes of the work appear in volumes 5 and 6 of this set. Adams' first volume was reprinted in Boston and Philadelphia. The book was soon read widely enough, or at least talked about, that during the summer of 1787 verses about it were printed in both Massachusetts and Virginia newspapers; see L. M. Miner, *Our Rude Forefathers: American Political Verse, 1783–1788*, 197–200, for sample stanzas.

[91] Adams, *Works*, IV, 289.
[92] *Ibid.,* 290.
[93] *Ibid.,* 583.
[94] Reprinted in McMaster and Stone, *Pennsylvania*, 565–76.
[95] So reported by Dr. William Shippen, Jr., in a letter to his son on a page dated Nov. 22, 1787, Shippen Mss. (LC). He also includes "Old Whig" as a club production. See, however, the statements in B. A. Konkle, *George Bryan and the Constitution of Pennsylvania* (Philadelphia: J. W. Campbell, 1922), 309.

circulation in many states and did a corresponding amount of damage to the federalist cause.

"Centinel" minced no words about "the wealthy and ambitious, who in every community think they have the right to lord it over their fellow creatures." He expressed his fears that "the principles of government inculcated in Mr. Adams' treatise . . . have misled some well designing members of the late Convention," and proceeded, after politely claiming that the balance which Adams preached was lacking, to charge that the Constitution "is a most daring attempt to establish a despotic aristocracy among freemen, that the world has ever witnessed." The Senate, he supposed, would be composed of the better sort, the well-born, etc. The President would become the head of "the aristocratic junto [of Congress] or its minion."[96]

With a speed that was dazzling for those slow-moving times, the charge of the aristocratic plot and the gibes at the "well-born" were spread before readers all over the country. The defenders of the Constitution did not at once perceive the mischievous potentialities of this propaganda, if we may take as typical James Wilson's casual dismissal of the matter at the start of the battle.[97] This obtuseness is the more inexplicable for, as noticed, there had been candid comment at the Convention on the peril of an aristocracy developing and conscious efforts at prevention. The pro-Constitution men were soon to discover that they had a bear by the tail. The measure of their enlightenment is established by the fact that *Publius* when he came to discuss the Congress did not hesitate to develop a careful refutation of the charges.[98] These traducements were in any event difficult to combat, and in retrospect it would appear that those who made fun of the whole thing were the most effective.

Adams, who was in London, might have given a helping hand had he known what was going on. He had earlier received a letter from Richard Henry Lee expressing the opinion that Adams' reflections in his book were "just."[99] Jefferson, too, had read the work and had written of his hope that its learning and good sense would "make it an institute for our politicians old as well as young."[100] This it had become, but not exactly as Jefferson intended. When Jefferson received the new Constitution he apparently did not see reflected in it a trend toward aristocracy. What engaged his fears, as he wrote Adams, was the Presidency.[101] This was not what worried Adams. He wrote in reply:

[96] McMaster and Stone, *Pennsylvania*, 567–68, 570, 574.
[97] Ford *Pamphlets*, 158.
[98] Madison in *The Federalist* No. 39, No. 52, No. 57, No. 63.

[99] Sept. 5, 1787, Ballagh, *The Letters of Richard Henry Lee*, II, 433.
[100] Jefferson to Adams, Feb. 23, 1787, *Papers of Jefferson*, XI, 176.
[101] Nov. 13, 1787, *ibid.*, XII, 349–51.

"You are afraid of the one—I, of the few . . . You are Apprehensive of Monarchy; I of aristocracy. I would therefore have given more Power to the President and less to the Senate."[102]

Unfortunately for his reputation, Adams did not make public either what his friends had written on his book or what his own reaction to the Constitution had been. All that the general body of men knew were the phrases wrested from the treatise, and they were constantly reminded of them by such *jeux d'esprits* as "John Adams' chickens (commonly called the Well-Born) are already in imagination, mounted upon the shoulders of the populace,"[103] or "Two classes of people—avoid as dangerous are lawyers and people of no property."[104] In newspapers, pamphlets, and even in convention, the opposition sought to inflame the voters with the red silk handkerchief of "the rich the well born and the able," resorting even to verse, as bad in its way as Mr. Adams' prose style:

> In evil hour his pen Squire Adams drew,
> Claiming dominion to his well born few.
> In the gay circles of St. James's plac'd,
> He wrote, and writing had his work disgrac'd.[105]

The intelligent and sober-minded voters may have been immune to such japes and may have made up their minds by reflecting upon the confutations in such sober and reasoned pieces as *Federalist* Nos. 57 and 63. Obviously, however, there was a segment of the enfranchised presumably susceptible to the versified sentiments, for "Squire Adams' Lament" was reprinted in various places. The proponents of the Constitution had poets no less fumbling on their side, yet no lyre was struck in behalf of Adams. Instead, the aristocracy issue was ridiculed in satirical prose—often the briefest squibs. For that part of the American public which thought the combinations of long words were comical, *Curtiopolis* jeered that the Constitution was "the most unheard of, unexampled, incomprehensible, motley, despotic, combination of biennial, quadrennial, and sextennial Aristocracies."[106] "Roderick Razor," who conceived that to some outlandish names were irresistible, assembled a cast, Squire Sour Crout, Squire Clip Purse Van Clink de Gelt and

---

[102] Dec. 6, 1787, *ibid.*, 396.
[103] Boston *American Herald*, Nov. 26, 1787, in a letter from New York.
[104] "Michaiah the Farmer" in *Norwich* [Conn.] *Packet*, Mar. 27, 1788.
[105] *New-York Journal and Weekly Register*, Feb. 14, 1788, allegedly from the *State Gazette of South Carolina*. It also appeared in the Philadelphia *Independent Gazetteer*, Mar. 10, 1788.
[106] New York *Daily Advertiser*, Jan. 18, 1788.

Domine Van Wrangletext, who used the password and countersign of "Stocracy" and "Montesque."[107] None of this availed—the "well-born" were to be belabored for years to come.

THE FIRST DEBATES ON THE JUDICIARY ARTICLE

THROUGHOUT THE months that the Constitution was under discussion the appeals to prejudice continued to sound a discord of rabid counterpoint to the sober development of the themes set in the several articles of the new Constitution by those who outwardly sought to deal dispassionately with them. We are here concerned with the disputations over the judiciary and matter relating to its functioning. The nature of these disputations was determined by the exiguous character of Article III, for it offered fewer handholds for the range of disagreement provoked by Article I. Nevertheless, it was thoroughly picked at, as much for what was actually set forth as for what had been left out. For some critics there had obviously been too little said about the structure of the projected judicial systems. It did not suit them at all that "the convention has only crayoned in the outlines. It is left to Congress to fill up and colour the canvas"—as one poetic Virginia defender wrote.[108] They believed that too much had been left to Congress, and so Article III was taken under collateral attack. And this was the case with those who joined the pack in the clamor over the absence of a bill of rights, specifically as respects jury trial and the safeguarding of individual rights.

Although these collateral attacks and the mere side thrust and parry were the most numerous, there were also direct assaults upon and defenses of Article III ranging from simple out-of-hand condemnation and denial to very elaborately reasoned arguments. Sometimes opponents elected to treat this article as no more than a piece of evidence in their case against the Constitution—an exhibit proffered among others to establish the malignant intent of the Framers or to support some forecast of disaster. An example of the first is the way the proposed judiciary was dragged in to buttress the claim that a vast consolidated government had been planned. Prophets, less interested in the conspiracy theory of the "dark conclave" and more concerned with maintaining the sovereignty of the states, were at pains to spell out predictions of doom for the state courts at the hands of the federal.

The generalized objections to the judiciary could be handled effec-

---

[107] *Ibid.*, Dec. 11, 1787. This amusing piece was obviously satirizing the Dutch of Clinton's party.

[108] *Civis Rusticus* in *Virginia Independent Chronicle*, Jan. 30, 1788.

tively only by a particularized affirmative answer; that is to say, by detailed explanations of the intendment of the several clauses with considerable emphasis upon limitations. This is how the ablest advocates of the new plan eventually proceeded. The prophecies were more difficult to counter. They were posited on the assumption that everything objectionable in the English legal system would be imitated, or that a wicked Congress would certainly set up an oppressive judicial establishment. Replication took the form of attacking the presumption of human iniquity, of pointing to the satisfactory record of state courts, or even of suggesting that these might bear some of the load of federal business.

The pro-Constitution men enjoyed one great advantage. No one seriously challenged the basic validity of the tripartite division of powers.[109] This had become a fundamental of the American political credo, thanks to the almost apocalyptic quality attributed to Montesquieu's *Esprit des Lois*. Consequently, even the most ardent advocates of the *status quo* conceded grudgingly or *sub silentio* the propriety of making better provision for the exercise of judicial power in matters of national concern than the very limited concessions in the Articles of Confederation. They advanced counter-proposals such as committing the power to state courts or restricting the new establishment to a supreme court. Of course, there was hot dispute over the limits of jurisdiction, and the supreme law of the land provision was assailed with particular vigor.

The attack on Article III did not develop in its full variety until the battle had for some time been under way. Nevertheless, within six weeks after the Congress had despatched the Constitution to the several states, the characteristics of opposition tactics just described were already manifest. This came about because of the intensity of the struggle in Pennsylvania where the election of delegates followed hard upon the fracas in the local assembly and the state convention itself was set to convene on November 28. To this sequence of deadlines local writers and press reacted with speed and volubility. The nation was thus afforded a preview of the course of future discussion. More than this, so much was turned out in such quick succession that journals everywhere had a seemingly inexhaustible source of filler. Adherents of both sides, of course, aided and abetted the out-of-state circulation of such materials. From Pennsylvania thus came early and important contributions to the molding of national opinion. Opposition writing was particularly effective, combining with ingenuity appeals to prejudice and seriously reasoned analysis of defects in the Constitution.

---

[109] What was challenged was the failure to observe the principle, *e.g.*, in the matter of impeachment.

Above all, it was aggressive. On the other side, federalist writing was largely a literature of rebuttal.[110] The Constitution itself stood as the affirmative statement of the proponents' case. Since the opposition by singling out particulars had elected to plead specially, as it were, the controversy was spun out in a succession of replications, rejoinders, rebutters, surrebutters and the like.

The anxiety of the pro-Constitution men over the "Address" of the dissident assemblymen is indicated by the fact that it was brought under prompt attack in a formal reply signed by some of the majority,[111] in a pamphlet of Pelatiah Webster's[112] and in the speech, already mentioned, made by James Wilson on October 6, four days after the broadside version appeared.[113] This speech, made at a meeting to fix on a ticket of delegates, was the most important of the three. Widely reprinted, it was much admired by some[114] but was given small quarter by those who did not agree with Wilson. It was at once a brief explanation of principle and a specific traverse of points raised by the assemblymen.

Wilson met the charge of an annihilation of states by indicating in particulars how dependent the new federal plan was upon the states. He did not deal with the judiciary as such, but he met directly two collateral issues related thereto—the lack of a bill of rights and the guarantee of jury trial. The first point he met by explaining the principles of extant American political organization. In the case of state governments the legislative was invested with every right and authority not in explicit terms reserved. In delegating federal authority everything not given was reserved. It would have been "superfluous and absurd, to have stipulated with a foederal body of our own creation, that we should enjoy those privileges, of which we are not divested either by the intention or the act that has brought that body [Congress] into existence." This argument was thereafter to be the standard explanation of why no bill of rights was needed.

What Wilson had to say about the absence of a provision for jury trial in civil cases was likewise to become a stand-by, useful and im-

---

[110] The defenders of the Constitution did not at the outset enter into any elaborate defense of the judicial. Tench Coxe (Ford, *Pamphlets*, 133) was casual, as was Noah Webster (*ibid.*, 25), and Pelatiah Webster's first pamphlet (McMaster and Stone, *Pennsylvania*, 90–106) and his answer to *Brutus* (Ford, *Pamphlets*, 117). In the latter he states that the supreme power will restrain the states from making angry and destructive laws, but does not explain how this would be accomplished.

[111] *Pennsylvania Packet*, Oct. 8, 1787.

[112] *Supra*, n. 110.

[113] Ford, *Pamphlets*, 155–61.

[114] Washington to Stuart, Oct. 17, 1787, and asking Stuart to try to secure re-publication, *Washington Writings*, XXIX, 290. The "Address" had already been reprinted in the *Virginia Independent Chronicle*, Oct. 24, 1787.

portant because it was a disclosure of why the Convention had failed to do what a great many people believed it should have done. Wilson explained that cases open to a jury differed in the several states; hence it was impractical to have made a general rule. It would have been idle to have made reference to the practice of the states; jury trial "as heretofore" would have been improper for there never existed a system of federal jurisprudence to which such a declaration could relate. He pointed out further that neither in admiralty nor in equity cases was jury trial required. The matter had therefore been abandoned—"in fullest confidence that no danger could possibly ensue, since the proceedings of the supreme court are to be regulated by the congress which is a faithful representation of the people."[115]

On its face, Wilson's address was aimed primarily at the "Address" of the assembly minority. A more formidable complaint, however, had appeared in the Philadelphia *Independent Gazetteer* the day before he spoke. This was the first of the "Centinel" letters, already mentioned.[116] Wilson would have done well to have directed his argument against this antagonist. The letter contained one of the first detailed attacks on the judicial power. It asserted that the objects of jurisdiction were so numerous and the "shades of distinction" between civil causes often so slight that the state judicatories would very probably be superseded, for the federal power as the more powerful was bound to prevail. Attention was drawn to England where, by "ingenious sophisms," the courts had extended their jurisdiction "out of the line of their institution, and contrary to their very nature." This manipulation of fictions was something familiar to every reader of Blackstone.[117] It was by no means an imagined danger, for at least one American jurisdiction[118] had made an adaptation of the King's Bench's Bill of Middlesex. Other pamphlets were also to resort to this argument.

"Centinel" further pointed to the supreme law of the land clause as one calculated to put beyond doubt the omnipotent power of Congress over state governments and judicatories. The argument moves to the familiar charge that the tendency will be to melt the United States into one empire, and the reader is cautioned that the opinion of the "greatest writers" is that a very extensive country cannot be governed on "democratical principles." No reflection of Montesquieu, bowdlerized as it was on this occasion, was of greater service to the opponents of the Constitution. Americans, accustomed to having biblical texts hurled

---

[115] Ford, *Pamphlets*, 157.
[116] McMaster and Stone, *Pennsylvania*, 565–76.
[117] *Commentaries*, III, 285–86.
[118] The so-called New York Bill. A form is in the Ms. William Living-

ston Precedent Book (NYSL Ms. No. 1329). A sample of the *latitat* in Dayton v. Parsons (1772), in Pl. K.18, N.Y.C. Hall of Records. On post-Revolutionary New York practice, see *LPAH*, I, 52, 55, 63–66.

at them as incontrovertible authority, were expected apparently to show the same deference to the philosophers.

"Centinel" made brief reference to the absence of a bill of rights and some comment upon the absence of a provision for civil juries. The "appellate jurisdiction in law and fact" clause was alleged to do away with such juries by implication. To this matter "Centinel" returned in his second letter (October 24) which was a reply to Wilson's speech.[119] He took issue with Wilson's statement that equity did not employ juries by adverting to the practice of sending issues to King's Bench for trial. What he did not disclose was that this concerned only the restricted common law jurisdiction of Chancery on the so-called Latin side, such as *scire facias* to repeal patents,[120] and had nothing whatever to do with equity. Similarly he traversed the statement regarding the admiralty jurisdiction by reference to the *qui tam* proceedings in Exchequer for violations of excise laws.[121] These, of course, were not a matter of cognizance in admiralty, but by tying this in with the power of the proposed federal government to lay imposts, the point had a certain popular appeal, reviving as it did memories of the long struggles against the trial of acts of trade violations in vice-admiralty courts, in particular the vice-admiralty court for all America at Halifax. "Centinel" offered a further reminder of old grievance in connection with his attack on appellate jurisdiction in law and fact by his reference to the angry controversy of 1764 over the power to review a jury verdict in the New York case of *Forsey v. Cunningham.*[122] This conflict, waged over an ambiguous use of the word "appeal" in a royal instruction, was well within the memory of mature men. Following "Centinel's" lead, a similar paper war was to be waged over the clause describing the Supreme Court's appellate jurisdiction.

The heads of federal jurisdiction were also taken under fire by "Centinel." The jurisdiction between citizens of different states implied a distrust of the impartiality of state tribunals; the jurisdiction between a state or citizens thereof and a foreign state, its citizens or subjects meant that a London merchant could come hither for a "supposed debt" and American citizens would be deprived of jury trial and subjected to an appeal (although matter of fact be in dispute) to a court five hundred or eleven hundred miles from home. This was ingenious special pleading, for even in Pennsylvania the collection of British pre-war

---

[119] McMaster and Stone, *Pennsylvania,* 576–91.

[120] Coke, *Fourth Institute,* 79.

[121] G. Beer, *British Colonial Policy 1754–1765* (New York: Macmillan, 1922), 289–91.

[122] Discussed in J. H. Smith, *Ap-* *peals to the Privy Council from the American Plantations,* 390–414. The case stirred interest beyond provincial borders because a pamphlet on the case (reprinted in a New York newspaper) was circulated.

debts, regulated by the Treaty of 1783, was a sore subject. Up to this time the creditors had been having a rough time indeed in state courts, and the creation of a more or less neutral forum was not a happy prospect for recalcitrant debtors.[123]

The establishment of inferior courts by Congress also worried "Centinel." There would have to be one or more such courts in each state, and laws and regulations provided to direct the judges. Contracts made under state laws would come before courts acting under new laws and new modes of proceedings not thought of at the time of contracting. A Pittsburgher, finding the goods of his Virginia debtor within reach of his attachment, would discover no writ to be had nearer than two hundred miles. By the time he secured his process the object would be eloigned. Furthermore, the expense of the new establishment would be enormous and be the source of needless interference with the judicial rights of the separate states. The writer had much to say about other provisions and, inevitably, made plea for a bill of rights.

"Centinel" was to produce twenty-four letters, the last of which was to appear on November 24, 1788.[124] Most of these pieces were written after Pennsylvania had ratified the Constitution. But the minority

---

[123] The matter of the pre-war debts became involved in antifederalist propaganda, but to a minor extent. The most blatant reference to this was in an alleged account from England when it was claimed that the merchants were "laughing in their sleeves" at the prospect of now having it in their power to collect with interest in new federal courts and being able to drag citizens from afar by appeal to the Supreme Court. Hitherto state juries had been favorable to their fellow citizens. Philadelphia *Independent Gazetteer*, Feb. 21, 1788; *New-York Journal*, Feb. 25, 1788.

The matter was obliquely involved both in the discussions over treaties as supreme law of the land and over the jurisdiction of the federal judiciary. In *Federalist* No. 22 (Dec. 14, 1787) Hamilton indicated the need of a supreme law and a tribunal with the ultimate word on matters in which our foreign relations were involved. Williamson in his Edenton, N.C., speech spelled out the matter in a more homely way (New York *Daily Advertiser*, Feb. 25, 1788; *Pennsylvania Packet*, Mar. 5, 1788).

The past attitudes of both state

courts and local juries had a bearing on the matter. In Maryland, where the alien creditors had had difficulties, *Civis* writing in the *Maryland Journal*, July 11, 1788, described the creed of the courts to be: "*let us procrastinate all decisions and thereby give ease to the people.*" Obviously federal jurisdiction was not to be preferred over this. Luther Martin had earlier (Mar. 19, 1788) explained that the supreme law of the land clause when introduced by him was not meant to imply superiority over the state constitution or bill of rights (Ford, *Essays*, 360–61). The dissenting minority in Pennsylvania (*infra*, pp. 336–37) actually demanded a similar limitation. This was among other things to assure juries of the vicinage, an institution the creditors had found to be hostile.

In Virginia a writer in the *Virginia Independent Chronicle*, Apr. 16, 1788, pinpoints opposition to the British debtors. On May 14 a local *Brutus* attacks the jurisdiction over controversies between foreigners and citizens.

[124] McMaster and Stone, *Pennsylvania*, 696–98.

in that state continued to fulminate, like retreating thunder, in hope of some way reversing the decision. Nothing significant regarding the judicial power was added by "Centinel," although it is interesting that in No. 8 he claimed that under the necessary and proper clause every possible law would be constitutional, for Congress would be the sole judges of the propriety of such laws.[125]

In spite of the air of reasonableness with which provisions of the Constitution were dissected, "Centinel" was not free of rabble-rousing matter. As we have seen, the first letter opened with long and acrid comments about the aristocratic plot, and John Adams came in for a share of abuse. A piece of bad political judgment was the denigration of Washington and Franklin. The former, it was hinted, was gullible, the latter senile. These innuendos did not sit well with many people. When the letters were translated into German, these aspersions were eliminated.[126] George Bryan had been the head of a Scotch-Irish-German coalition in Pennsylvania. But twelve German assemblymen had deserted the fold to vote for the state ratifying convention. So powerful was the German vote, no risks could be run. As time went on, "Centinel" tended to wax more abusive and, abandoning his earlier pose of dignity, sank to name calling: "James the Caledonian" for Wilson, "Gouvero the Cunning" for Gouverneur Morris, "Robert the Cofferer" for Robert Morris,[127] and "the Little Fiddler" for Francis Hopkinson.[128]

The early "Centinel" letters were first-rate propaganda, and they must be counted among the three or four most influential effusions of the opposition. They became a source book for the case against the Constitution at the Pennsylvania state convention, and they had an effect beyond the borders of that state for they were widely circulated. The first two letters were republished in pamphlet form. In the newspapers No. 1 appeared in Greenleaf's *New-York Journal* on October 18, 1787; No. 2 was published there November 1, 1787. *The Maryland Journal* ran No. 1 on October 30, and No. 2 on November 2. The Richmond *Virginia Independent Chronicle* ran No. 1 on November 7 and 14, and No. 2 on November 21 and 28. The Providence, Rhode Island, *United States Chronicle* republished No. 1 on December 6, and No. 2 on December 30. The Boston *American Herald* systematically

---

[125] Jan. 2, 1788, *ibid.*, 621–26 at 623.

[126] Brunhouse, *Counter-Revolution in Pennsylvania*, 291, n. 43. On Oct. 10 and 11, 1787, the Philadelphia *Independent Gazetteer* ran two communications denouncing the slurs on the two men.

[127] "Centinel" No. 10, Jan. 12, 1788, McMaster and Stone, *Pennsylvania*, 631.

[128] "Centinel" No. 17, Mar. 24, 1788, *ibid.*, 663.

reprinted the letters, and it should be noticed that with singular impartiality it also published an anti-"Centinel" letter from "A Citizen" (November 26) and reprinted from a Baltimore paper *Uncus*' replication to "Centinel." That the influence of these tracts disturbed the pro-Constitution men is indicated by the fact that after Pennsylvania had ratified, a spurious "Centinel" letter was confected, designed by its offensive tone to alienate the "Centinel" followers.[129] And, finally, some Connecticut "wit" inserted an "Advertisement" in the *New Haven Gazette* of December 13, 1787, to the effect that a large overgrown creature marked and branded "Centinel" had broken into Connecticut. The notice continues in a mocking, rustic vein.[130] It moved an indignant Pennsylvanian to answer, angrily predicting that "the time serving tools —the Phocions and Publiuses of our day—'will stink in the very nostrils of posterity.' "[131]

Shortly after "Centinel" No. 2 appeared in New York the printer Greenleaf offered for sale a pamphlet which to all appearances became the most widely read antifederalist tract.[132] This was the *Observations leading to a fair examination of the system of government, proposed by the late Convention*, better known as the *Letters of a Federal Farmer*, and was written by Richard Henry Lee.[133] His choice of a pseudonym was misleading and relates to the early days of discussion when the advocates of mere amendment to the Constitution were claiming that they were the true federalists. But things had moved rapidly, and by November the federalists had become the proponents of the Constitution. The opponents could do no better than assume the name of antifederalists, which seems more or less to have been thrust upon them.

Lee was himself active in securing circulation for his pamphlet. Samuel Powel, who had been mayor of Philadelphia before the Revolution, wrote Washington on November 13, 1787, that Lee had "escaped the Resentment of the People at Chester" where he had distributed printed papers against the Constitution.[134] He had harangued the populace of Wilmington and again "distributed many of his inflammatory

---

[129] *Pennsylvania Gazette*, Jan. 23, 1788; *Country Journal and Poughkeepsie Advertiser*, Feb. 19, 1788.
[130] Republished in the New York *Daily Advertiser*, Dec. 19, 1787.
[131] McMaster and Stone, *Pennsylvania*, 507.
[132] Nov. 15, 1787. The advertisement ran for weeks thereafter.
[133] Ford, *Pamphlets*, 277–325.
[134] *Doc. Hist. Const.*, IV, 378. The

New York *Daily Advertiser*, Nov. 24, 1787, ran a letter from Wilmington dated November 17 reporting that Lee had passed through the town "reading his Cincinnatuses," abusing Wilson and the new government, to a group of "school-boys and hostlers, who have since made themselves very merry at his expence." The writer attributes Lee's part to envy of Washington.

Papers." It is supposed that Governor Clinton and his committee attended to circulation of the *Letters* in western Massachusetts.[135] The *Letters* were advertised for sale in Boston just before the convention met there. Jeremiah Wadsworth informed Rufus King on December 16, 1787, that the *Letters* were already circulating in Connecticut and "calculated to do much harm."[136]

The objections expressed by Lee in Congress were considerably amplified in the *Letters,* and there was new matter added, particularly as respects the judiciary. He did not like the threat of a "consolidated" government, but apart from the familiar claim that a free government cannot be extended over a large territory, he adduced the novel argument that the diversity of laws and customs of the land would be unduly invaded by a uniform system of laws. This point he returned to by reference to the supreme law of the land clause, the effect of which he claimed would be to abolish ancient customs, rights, laws and institutions already established.[137] The specific complaints against the judiciary Lee conceived to be the improper blending of powers in the judges of the Supreme Court in whom was "lodged the law, the equity and the fact." Furthermore, "one judiciary" promised inconvenience. It would, even if moved once a year to the eastern and southern extremes of the union, involve a trip of 150 to 200 miles for the citizen.[138] Even if inferior courts were placed in counties or districts of the various states, the appellate jurisdiction would be intolerable and expensive.

The jurisdiction provided in Article III, section 2, did not suit the "Farmer" at all.[139] It was proper that the judiciary have powers coextensive with the federal legislature, but it was unnecessary that it have powers respecting questions arising upon the internal laws of the states. Except for suits by a state and citizens of another state, actions between citizens of different states or cases involving foreign states and their subjects were now brought in state courts. As matters stood, the state courts would have concurrent jurisdiction with inferior federal courts. In either case appeals would lie to the Supreme Court. In almost all cases either party might have a jury trial in the state courts; justice could be had on reasonable terms, and the state courts were obviously more competent to make proper decisions on the laws of their respec-

---

[135] Harding, *The Contest over the Ratification of the Federal Constitution in the State of Massachusetts,* 17, n. 3 but without citation. It is clear from a letter of Ledlie to Lamb, Jan. 15, 1788, that the New York people had sent "the books" to Connecticut. Ms. Lamb Papers, Box 5 (NYHS).

[136] *Life of King,* I, 264.
[137] Ford, *Pamphlets,* 288. *Cassius* addressed a severe letter to Lee in the *Virginia Independent Chronicle,* reprinted in New York *Daily Advertiser,* May 8, 1788.
[138] Ford, *Pamphlets,* 289–90, 298.
[139] *Ibid.,* 306.

tive states than federal courts could possibly be. Lee conceded that a prudent Congress might organize courts on "the common law principles of the country." But this was not secured by the Constitution, which provided jury trial only in criminal cases, yet no jury of the vicinage. He suspected that no jury at all was contemplated in the original jurisdiction of the Supreme Court.[140]

It is amusing that despite some slashes at his old friend John Adams, Lee did not disdain to refer to the British constitution as a *beau idéal*. Blending law and equity powers in federal courts involved abandonment of the safeguards which in Britain consisted in vesting law and equity in different hands. It was dangerous to abandon these, because a judge restrained by the law need "only to step into his shoes of equity" and give what judgment he pleased. "I confess in the constitution of this supreme court, as left by the constitution, I do not see a spark of freedom or a shadow of our own or the British common law."[141]

Lee had much to say about the necessity of jury trials in civil actions, and he reiterated his arguments for the incorporation of a bill of rights, in his version of which, laid before Congress, the jury trial amendment had been an important item.[142] With great artfulness the "Farmer" urged that common people should have a share in the judicial as well as in the legislative department. No purpose would be served to hold open to them such offices for which an expensive education was required. "The few, the well born, &c. as Mr. Adams calls them, in judicial decisions as well as in legislation, are generally disposed, and very naturally too, to favour those of their own description."[143] It was, of course, slightly absurd for Lee, who could be numbered among the Tidewater nabobs, to inveigh against the menace of aristocracy. His belief that this could be held in check by trial by jury because jurors were so situated as to acquire information and knowledge in the affairs and government of society was not the best argument that could have been advanced. It was, in any event, one which the Virginia planters with British creditors breathing down their necks were capable of appreciating.

At the time the *Letters of a Federal Farmer* was offered for sale Lee also addressed a letter to Governor Randolph, a précis of objections,[144] but in which ululations over lack of jury trial predominated.

---

[140] *Ibid.*, 307–08.
[141] *Ibid.*, 309.
[142] *Supra*, p. 265.
[143] Ford, *Pamphlets*, 316.
[144] Reprinted in Elliot, *Debates*, I, 503–05. It was printed in the *Virginia Gazette* and reprinted in Greenleaf's

New-York Journal, Dec. 22 and 24, 1787. The *Pennsylvania Packet*, Dec. 20, 1787, ran it under a Petersburg date. *Worcester Magazine*, IV, 181, reprinted the second week in January 1788; *The Providence* [R.I.] *Gazette and Country Journal*, Feb. 16, 1788.

This was reprinted and a plaintive letter from one of Madison's untutored friends indicates that plain people were affected by it.[145] Lee's letter was followed some months later by *An Additional Number of Letters from the Federal Farmer* in which some new ideas are developed.[146] By way of introducing a repetition of his attack on the judiciary, he comments that popular legislators have departed from the line of strict justice, while the law courts have shown a disposition to cleave to it. There was a tendency for the measures of popular legislatures to settle down and become mild and just, while the rigid systems of the courts became more severe. The "jurisdiction as to law and fact" in the Constitution establishes the essential principle of the civil law, and the "most noble and important principle of the common law [viz., the jury] [is] exploded."[147] He adds a new twist to the argument against a federal city by suggesting this will supply a footing for the increase of judicial power by means of fictions, as had happened in England.[148] He was equally concerned lest fictions on allegations of citizenship be used to give diversity jurisdiction. In this particular, events much later were to establish Lee's title as a prophet, for the corporate fiction was to serve as a device for just this purpose.

In the antifederalist writings just discussed most of the major objections to the judicial system are covered, and much of the literature which followed plodded over the same ground with an occasional minor gloss. Of course, the bulk of the criticism of the Constitution had to do with matters about which the average voter could be more deeply troubled than he could be about courts and litigation—representation, the powers of Congress over taxation, the militia, the necessary and proper clause, the executive. The basic source of anxiety was a concern over what a further surrender of powers to the Union would do to the states, or more exactly, the state where a reader or listener was denizened. The politicians, who had their own private forebodings over what might befall their own local factions, understood how indurated was the primary loyalty of the individual to his state and, as we have seen, did not hesitate to play upon it. There were others to whose

---

[145] From Benjamin Hawkins, Feb. 14, 1788, *Doc. Hist. Const.*, IV, 503. A wheelwright neighbor who had read Lee's letter posed some questions. Hawkins on a first reading saw Lee was "rong."

It drew comment from "An American" in the *Pennsylvania Gazette*, Jan. 16, 1788, in a piece obviously trying to eliminate sectionalism. On January

23 *Valerius* took Lee to task in the *Virginia Independent Chronicle*. On Mar. 19, 1788, *Senex* answered *Valerius* in the same journal.

[146] Published in New York; advertised for sale in *New-York Journal*, May 2, 1788.

[147] *An Additional Number of Letters*, 132–36.

[148] *Ibid.*, 176.

motives no suspicion can attach who were equally devoted to their states. In either case, many of the points made against the new plan were solidly based in reason, and it may be remarked that later events were sometimes to prove the objectors to have been right.

CHAPTER VII

The Framers as Propagandists

From the very onset of the discussions over ratification, the anti-federalist cause had been helped by the fact that several highly articulate members of the Convention had either withdrawn or had refused to sign. The chief irreconcilables were to publish justifications of their conduct, some of them, indeed, early in the campaign. This furnished the opposition with a sort of literary leg-up and added to the problems of the proponents of the new plan. The two earliest defectors, John Lansing and Robert Yates, held their fire for some time. Not until later, in December 1787, did they write Governor Clinton explaining their withdrawal from the Convention. This letter appeared in the press on January 15, 1788, probably for the purpose of influencing the action of the New York legislature then sitting.[1] Except as the letter may have reinforced belief in the accusation that the new national government would annihilate the states, it was not politically useful.[2] The writers had been too briefly present at the "dark conclave," and they impaired their assertion of principles by prefixing an exigent construction of their powers in a manner that only a small-town conveyancer was likely to relish.

---

[1] The letter is in Elliot, *Debates*, I, 480–82, where no date is given. As reproduced in the press it is dated Albany, Dec. 21, 1787. It appeared in the *New-York Packet*, January 15. On January 17 it was carried both in the *New-York Journal* and the *Pennsylvania Packet*. Reprinted upstate New York in *The Country Journal, and the* *Poughkeepsie Advertiser*, Jan. 22, 1788.

[2] It drew only two hostile comments worth noting: from "A Citizen" in the Lansingburg, N.Y. *Northern Centinel* reprinted in *Pennsylvania Packet*, Feb. 8, 1788; and by "Dutchess County Farmer" in *The Country Journal, and the Poughkeepsie Advertiser*, Feb. 26, 1788.

THE RECUSANTS

IF THE LANSING-YATES letter did little to arouse public interest, not so the contributions of the three who had refused to sign the Constitution and of Luther Martin who had slipped away before the moment of truth. Of these four men, all of whom were to write candidly of their objections, Governor Randolph alone was to produce a paper of highly ambiguous political utility. Randolph's letter to the Virginia legislature was dated October 10, 1787, but was not published until December.[3] He made clear his desire for amendments; indeed, he set out explicitly eight matters, including limitation and definition of the judicial power, that he believed should be repaired. He revealed that he had proposed at the Philadelphia Convention that state conventions be at liberty to proffer amendments which would then be considered at a second general convention. All this was, of course, welcome ammunition for those who were sincere in their profession that they would accept the Constitution provided it be amended. But Randolph had opened his report with a long and eloquent excoriation of the Confederation.[4] This made it a document almost too hot for advocates of the *status quo* to handle. Such were the New York antifederalists, and there little or nothing was made of the letter.[5] In Virginia, where there was a real division of purpose among the antifederalists, the Governor's lack of explicitness regarding his intentions, and the importance of his ultimate stand in the state convention, saved him from the rough treatment that befell others. He was wooed by leaders of both the federalists and their opponents, with a tenderness of approach as if he had been a timorous heiress.[6] Nevertheless, the Governor was not entirely spared.

---

[3] Reprinted in Elliot, *Debates*, I, 482–91; Ford, *Pamphlets*, 261–76. The correspondence on publication is in Carey's *American Museum*, 62 (January 1788), in *Virginia Gazette and Weekly Advertiser*, Jan. 3, 1788, and in *Virginia Independent Chronicle*, Jan. 2, 1788.

[4] Randolph's irresolution is revealed in a letter of St. George Tucker to his wife, Oct. 3, 1787. Reporting that he had dined with Randolph, Tucker wrote that his host wanted amendments but thought that the Constitution "is in its present state the less of two evils." Ms. Tucker-Coleman Collection, Earl Gregg Swem Library,

The College of William and Mary in Virginia.

[5] The letter was printed in the *Pennsylvania Packet*, Jan. 9, 1788, and in the *New-York Journal*, Jan. 11, 1788, and soberly discussed by the federalist *Americanus* in the New York *Daily Advertiser*, Jan. 12, 1788.

[6] Described in I. Brant, *James Madison*, III, 168, 191–92. See also R. H. Lee to Randolph, Oct. 16, 1787, Ballagh, *The Letters of Richard Henry Lee*, II, 450; K. Rowland, *Life and Correspondence of George Mason*, II, 210. This letter was run by the *State Gazette of South Carolina*, Jan. 14, 1788.

Two correspondents of the *Virginia Independent Chronicle*, irked by Randolph's efforts to carry water on both shoulders, had some sarcastic things to say. Particularly unkind was the comment of *A State Soldier* that the Governor had given out his objections to the Constitution and "then left them like a parcel of poor helpless orphans to be supported by a contribution of arguments from his friends."[7] *Philanthropos*, a Pennsylvania writer republished in this same paper, had dealt no less ironically and effectively with the Governor. He had taken the several published objections of the non-signers and demonstrated how little they agreed in disagreement. He concluded that there could obviously be no hope of securing a meeting of minds on any other plan at any second general convention.[8]

If Governor Randolph exhibited restraint over rushing into print, the same could not be said of George Mason. Early in October 1787 he published in broadside form his *Objections to the Proposed Federal Constitution*, a piece already adverted to—compact, hard-biting propaganda, written simply enough for common understanding.[9] It was soon disseminated the length of the seaboard, and was not without its effects. Not the least of these was the fact that national publicity made Mason into something of a celebrity. Like Governor Clinton of New York, his fame had been largely local. By mid-November Mason was sufficiently renowned to be made an ingredient in a Pennsylvania "Receipt for an Antifederal Essay," along with other staples, *e.g.*, the well-born, "liberty" of the press, aristocracy, jury trial and "great men."[10] The gibe at great men referred, of course, to antifederalist attempts to remove the glitter from that great federalist weapon—the prestige of Washing-

---

[7] "Plain Dealer" in the issue of Feb. 13, 1788; "A State Soldier" No. 3, on Mar. 12, 1788. The essays of this correspondent were all well done. The local writing carried in the *Chronicle* was of good literary quality and deserves rescue as much as some of the dull pieces reprinted by Ford.

[8] Originally in the *Pennsylvania Gazette*, Jan. 16, 1788; reprinted, *Virginia Independent Chronicle*, Feb. 6, 1788.

[9] Reprinted in Ford, *Pamphlets*, 327-32. Being in broadside form, it apparently circulated before the newspapers reprinted. The Boston *Massachusetts Centinel* ran it Nov. 21, 1787, the New York *Daily Advertiser*, November 30, the *Pennsylvania Gazette*, December 3, the Middletown, Conn. *Middlesex Gazette* the same day, the Newburyport *Essex Journal*,

December 12 and the *Maryland Journal, and Baltimore Advertiser*, December 21. The *Worcester Magazine*, which took its version from the *Virginia Gazette*, published the second week in December (IV, 130). The *American Museum* printed it in the December issue. Curiously enough the *Virginia Independent Chronicle* did not print Mason until Dec. 5, 1787. The *State Gazette of South Carolina* printed Jan. 7, 1788.

[10] *Pennsylvania Gazette*, Nov. 14, 1787. Another ingredient was "George Mason's right Hand in a Cutting-box, nineteen times." This was a reference, obviously, to Mason's speech in the Virginia House of Delegates reported four days earlier in the *Pennsylvania Packet*: "I would have lost this hand before it should have marked my name to the new government."

ton's and Franklin's support of the Constitution.[11] Then, as now, a body of ingenuous citizens existed, ready without more to follow the opinions of prominent personages. The comments of "Centinel," Gerry and others were intended to counteract this.[12] At the same time, undeterred by lack of consistency, the antifederalists promoted their own list of great names to which Mason was an important if controversial addition. A cynical Virginian, aware of the illogic of these tactics, produced at election time an essay "On the Influence of Great Names," devoted among other things to an examination of the antifederalist claims to eminence.[13] As we shall shortly see, there were other detractors among the federalists. And if the struggle did not gain thereby in distinction, it was lent a certain raffish liveliness.

It was meet and proper that the author of the Virginia Declaration of Rights should begin his *Objections* with the complaint that

---

[11] Both Washington and Franklin elected to remain aloof from the paper storm that broke out, and it does not appear that their influence in any way lessened because of this. It should be noticed that Washington was made an unwilling propagandist by the publication of a final paragraph in a letter written Dec. 14, 1787, to Charles Carter, *Washington Writings*, XXIX, 336, at 339. In his opinion, the choice was between the Constitution and anarchy. If one state or a minority believed that they could dictate a constitution, unless they had the power to administer the "Ultema ratio" they would find themselves deceived. The opposition arguments were more passion than reason. Another federal convention was likely to be less disposed to conciliation than the last. He could not prophesy what would be the consequence of a fruitless attempt to amend or delay. "I am not a blind admirer (for I saw the imperfections) of the Constitution to which I assisted to give birth, but I am fully persuaded it is the best that can be obtained at this day and that it or disunion is before us—"

Carter apparently had circulated copies of Washington's comments among friends and some zealot gave them to the press. Washington, who saw himself "running through all the newspapers" (to Carter, Jan. 12, 1788, *ibid.*, 380), chided his correspondent. His annoyance stemmed chiefly from

the fact that he had written in haste and he objected to an unpolished statement appearing in the press; *cf.* his letter to Madison, Feb. 5, 1788, *ibid.*, 402.

[12] *Supra*, p. 286 and *infra*, p. 298. See also "Officer of the Late Continental Army" in the Philadelphia *Independent Gazetteer*, Nov. 6, 1787, and the earlier innuendo of *Cato* in the *New-York Journal*, Sept. 27, 1787. The response to these statements was quick, *cf.* "Foederal Constitution" in *Pennsylvania Gazette*, Oct. 10, 1787, contrasting Washington with the dissenting assemblymen, and "One of the People" in *ibid.*, Oct. 17, 1787, reprinted as "Remarks on the late Insinuations against General Washington" in *American Museum* (Oct. 1787), II, 385. James Sullivan as *Cassius* (November 30, Ford, *Essays*, 22, 26) answered *Agrippa* who had cast doubts on the political sagacity of the Framers *ibid.*, 58 (November 27). Apparently the attack on federal great men was heavy in Connecticut. Roger Sherman, as "A Countryman" on November 22, cautioned against paying heed to this sort of talk, *ibid.*, 218.

[13] "A State Soldier" in *Virginia Independent Chronicle*, Mar. 12, 1788. Earlier, on February 13, this paper had carried an item with a Boston dateline stating that it was hinted that "R. M. Esq." and not "the great Fabius" was intended for President.

the Constitution provided no bill of rights, and that the paramountcy of federal law would make nugatory the state declarations of rights. "Nor are," wrote he, "the people secured even in the enjoyment of the benefit of the common law, which stands here upon no other foundation than its having been adopted by the several acts forming the constitutions of the several states." The judiciary, he believed, was "so constructed and extended, as to absorb and destroy the judiciaries of the several states." This would make the laws as "tedious, intricate, and expensive, and justice as unattainable" to most people as it was in England, and so enable the rich to oppress the poor.[14]

Mason's bill of particulars as respects the other defects of the Constitution was more detailed than Randolph's. Indeed, there were few vices to be laid bare in ensuing months which Mason did not here uncover. Mason, however, was almost alone in his concern that there be some declaration respecting the common law. Considering how emotions had been stirred over this very point some thirteen years earlier, it is strange that the antifederalists did not make more of it. So important had the matter seemed in 1774 that the Continental Congress had proclaimed in the Declaration of Rights that the respective colonies were entitled to the common law of England.[15] This they had secured, as Mason admitted. But what gave his point validity was the question it raised as to what the legal substratum of the new government was to be—a matter vital to the functioning of the federal judiciary.

James Madison with his accustomed acumen was apparently aware that Mason's complaint might reanimate an old shibboleth. He wrote at length to General Washington:[16]

> What could the Convention have done? If they had in general terms declared the Common law to be in force, they would have broken in upon the legal Code of every State in the most material points: they w^d have done more, they would have brought over from G.B. a thousand heterogeneous & antirepublican doctrines, and even the *ecclesiastical Hierarchy itself*, for that is a part of the Common law. If they had undertaken a discrimination, they must have formed a digest of laws, instead of a Constitution. This objection was surely not brought forward in the Convention, or it w^d have been placed in such a light that a repetition of it out of doors would scarcely have been hazarded. Were it allowed the weight which Col. M. may suppose it deserves, it would remain to be decided whether it be candid to arraign the Convention for omissions which were never suggested to them — or prudent to vindicate the dissent by reasons which either were not previously thought of, or must have been wilfully concealed. . . .

---

[14] Ford, *Pamphlets*, 329–30.
[15] *JCC*, I, 69.

[16] Oct. 18, 1787, *Doc. Hist. Const.*, IV, 334.

VII: *The Framers as Propagandists*

Madison was shortly to start upon his contributions to *The Federalist*. Although he might have slipped in some cautionary sentences in his first numbers, it was not until much later, when Hamilton took up the judiciary, that the federalist answer was given.[17]

Washington did not reply to Madison's inquiry about tactics.[18] But James Iredell, North Carolina lawyer and later Justice of the Supreme Court, took up the gage *sua sponte*.[19] So far as the people were now entitled to the common law, he wrote, they certainly would have the right to enjoy it under the Constitution until altered by Congress, "which even in this point has cardinal limits assigned to it."[20] Acts of assembly were nothing but deviations in degree from common law principles. Men were secured in their property by the prohibition on ex post facto laws. The principles of the common law, now applicable, must continue to apply except in those particulars in which express authority was given by the Constitution.

Iredell, it will be noticed, appears to assume that the common law would remain as a sort of "unwritten" substratum of the federal system. There is no question but that he acted upon this premise when he first became a Justice.

If the men of the South dealt gently with the two Virginia non-signers, the opposite was true of New England's reception of Elbridge Gerry's letter of explanation to the Massachusetts legislature.[21] Keying his composition to the need for securing the liberties of America, Gerry wrote briefly and circumstantially of the defects in the work he had refused to sign. In his opinion, the plan raised the question whether the "federal" government was to be dissolved, and whether the national Constitution now proposed should be substituted without amendment. He, too, raised the question of the sufficiency of the delegates' powers to do what they had done. The Convention had thought differently; nevertheless, he had acquiesced, because he thought an efficient govern-

---

[17] *Infra*, p. 312.

[18] Washington, from his reply of November 5, was apparently entirely engrossed in the Virginia situation, *Washington Writings*, XXIX, 303.

[19] "Answers to Mr. Mason's objections . . . ," Ford, *Pamphlets*, 333-70. McRee, in *Iredell*, II, 186, states that the pamphlet was dated Jan. 8, 1788, and that it was next reprinted in the *Newbern State Gazette*.

[20] Ford, *Pamphlets*, 336.

[21] Elliot, *Debates*, I, 492-94. A pamphlet entitled "Observations on the new Constitution" by a "Columbian Patriot" (Ford, *Pamphlets*, 2-

23), published in February 1788, was attributed by Rufus King to Gerry (King to Alsop, Mar. 2, 1788, *ibid.*, 1). Despite the stilted style and the display of pedantic learning, the New York antifederalists had the opus reprinted. It also ran in the *New-York Journal* beginning Apr. 2, 1788. If the re-publication was intended as an antidote to *Publius*, this was laughable misjudgment. Charles Warren, in Mass. Hist. Soc. *Proc.*, 64:143, 157, 1932, adduced evidence that the pamphlet was from the pen of the Bay State bluestocking, Mercy Warren.

ment essential to the preservation of the union. He admitted the Constitution in many respects had great merit and by proper amendment might be "adapted to the 'exigencies of government' and preservation of liberty." Should not such amendment, he asked, be better attained before ratification? Among existing defects were inadequate representation, ambiguous congressional powers, the status of the executive, the absence of a bill of rights, and his fear that "the judicial department will be oppressive."

All of this sounded very moderate. Gerry saw fit, however, to question whether it was proper to place implicit confidence in the Convention. "However respectable the members may be who signed the Constitution, it must be admitted, that a free people are the proper guardians of their rights and liberties." The greatest men might err and their errors were sometimes of the greatest magnitude. It was this particular paragraph, hardly essential to Gerry's justification of his course, that was to nettle some of his fellow delegates.

Gerry's letter was widely reprinted.[22] He was much more of a national figure than either Randolph or Mason, having signed the Declaration of Independence, and having labored long in the sterile vineyard of the Continental Congress. His actions were consequently eminently newsworthy. In Massachusetts the letter made trouble for the federalists,[23] and Madison thought it would "shake the confidence of some, and embolden the opposition of others."[24] It is not improbable that Gerry's comments led Madison in *Federalist* 37 to dwell on the Convention's objective of combining stability and energy in the government "with the inviolable attention due to liberty." A week later, in No. 40, he disposed of the charge that the Convention had not followed the mandate of the congressional resolution.

Gerry's letter began to circulate in the seaboard press early in November. "A.B." of Boston undertook to dispute his objections by suggesting, as respects the judiciary, that it was not in Mr. Gerry's power to show it was more probable that the federal judiciary would be oppressive than that of Massachusetts might so become.[25] It was possible that Congress might dispose of the courts so as to create public inconvenience and expense, but if a Constitution was to be rejected

---

[22] It was printed in the *Massachusetts Centinel* Nov. 3, 1787, in the *Boston Gazette* November 5, and a week later in *Worcester Magazine*, IV, 79. The New York *Daily Advertiser* carried it November 13, the *Pennsylvania Packet* on November 16,

the *Virginia Independent Chronicle* printed it Dec. 5, 1787.
[23] C. Gore to King, Dec. 30, 1787, *Life of King*, I, 266.
[24] To Washington, Nov. 18, 1787, *Doc. Hist. Const.*, IV, 380.
[25] *Massachusetts Centinel*, Nov. 14, 1787.

because it contained public inconvenience, it would be forever impossible to establish any government at all. Early in December, "A.B.'s" letter was reprinted in the *New-York Advertiser*,[26] which had run Gerry's objections three weeks earlier.

ELLSWORTH V. GERRY AND MARTIN

GERRY WAS DOOMED to fall afoul of a more formidable opponent than "A.B." Oliver Ellsworth, later Chief Justice of the Supreme Court, had been enlightening "The Holders and Tillers of Land" in a series of prosy articles signed "A Landholder" that ran in the *Connecticut Courant*.[27] Gerry's letter having come to his attention, Ellsworth, on November 26, published some "Remarks" on his late colleague's objections.[28] Except for an innuendo that Gerry might have "some state dignities or emoluments" which the new system endangered, this first letter was a reasonably temperate effort to traverse Gerry's allegations. In his second letter taking Gerry to task,[29] Ellsworth examined the future federal judiciary, and what he had to say about this in answer to Gerry's complaint is of particular interest because of his share in drafting the Judiciary Act of 1789. He commented that federal courts ought not to interfere with the internal affairs of a state, and the fear that they might do so was no ground for arguing against their existence when they were needed to execute national laws. State courts could not properly perform this task. Jealousies and friction would be inevitable, and there would never be achieved any uniformity in the application of national law. This was the intendment of the supreme law of the land clause. The Confederation had neither judiciary nor executive and consequently its resolves were not heeded.

A week later (December 10) Ellsworth pointed out the limitations on the judicial power.[30] There was no reason, he said, why the Supreme Court could not be held in different districts or in each of the states. All cases except those in which the Supreme Court had

---

[26] Dec. 4, 1787.

[27] The *Landholder* letters reprinted in Ford, *Essays*, 139–202. Ellsworth and Sherman had addressed a brief factual report on particular features of the Constitution dated September 26, Elliot, *Debates*, I, 491–92. Sherman later had five pieces in the *New Haven Gazette* in November and December signed "A Countryman," re-

printed in Ford, *Essays*, 215–28. They were moderate and mildly persuasive.

[28] Ford, *Essays*, 150.

[29] *Ibid.*, 155. In the "Landholder" sequence, No. 5.

[30] *Ibid.*, 161. Because of the attack on Mason, this letter was singled out for reprinting in the *Virginia Independent Chronicle*, Jan. 9, 1788.

original jurisdiction might be had in the first instance in state courts. The trials would be by jury as Congress should provide.

Ellsworth's ideas about how the judicial system might operate were quite overshadowed by his comments on Gerry and Mason. In his second letter "Landholder" had done no more than insinuate that Gerry suffered from defective understanding. The letter of December 10 was bellicose and scarcely polite. Coupling Gerry and Mason, he charged that their reasons for not signing were ex post facto. These reasons had been revised in New York by R. H. Lee and by him "brought into their present artful and insidious form."[31] He intimated that Mason's actions were motivated by sectional considerations. The reason Mason had not signed was the Convention's failure to require a two-thirds vote of both houses for any navigation act. The clause, said Ellsworth, was rejected as partial to the South. This objection of Mason's was undoubtedly in his *Objections* drawn for the South, but would not do for the Eastern states. This, of course, as we have noticed, was precisely the editing to which Mason's statement had been subjected when prepared for circulation in the North.

On December 24, 1787, "Landholder" addressed Gerry directly.[32] This savage letter, which opened with a lament over duplicity, advised Gerry that the New England version of Mason's *Objections* "would have come better from you," although in the New York coffee houses there was an excellent set of *Objections* which with some tailoring would have suited New England exactly. "Landholder" reminded Gerry that during the Convention no man had been more compliant than he until, at the close, he had made a motion that the old Continental money be placed upon a footing with other liquidated securities of the United States. Since Gerry was supposed to hold large quantities of this paper, his former plausibility and concession were accounted for, and the rejection of his proposal explained his present rage at the Constitution. Mockingly, "Landholder" outlined how Gerry should have conducted himself at the Convention, and suggested he should have consulted his New York friends in advance to know what objections he should have raised during the sittings.

Coming as this did on the eve of the Massachusetts Convention, Gerry was moved to a denial.[33] His proposal, wrote he, had been that the public debt be made "neither better or worse by the new system, but stand precisely on the same ground as it now does by the articles

---

[31] Ford, *Essays*, 161.
[32] *Ibid.*, 172.
[33] *Ibid.*, 127. This appeared in the *Massachusetts Centinel* on Jan. 5,

1788, four days before the state convention opened. Gerry had not been elected as a delegate.

of confederation." Neither then nor now did he own ten pounds of Continental money. He was not called on for his reasons for not signing but had stated them fully in the course of debate. This letter was dignified and temperate. But, as we shall see, it did not silence "Landholder."

It is difficult to estimate how much effect this exchange in fact had.[34] So far as popular appeal was concerned, an accusation twice made by Ellsworth was damaging. The Lee faction in Virginia, he wrote, was animated by hatred of Washington, as they had been during the war.[35] To this must be added "the madness of Mason." Had Washington neither attended the Convention nor disclosed his sentiments, the Lee party would have supported the Constitution, "and Col. Mason would have vented his rage to his own negroes and to the winds."[36] This was matter calculated to arouse the artless voter, and one the antifederalists were well advised to leave alone.

Meanwhile, a new combatant was to enter the lists. Luther Martin who had left the Convention on September 4, 1787, and so had not had occasion to refuse to sign, addressed the Maryland legislature on November 29, 1787.[37] A month later *The Genuine Information*, which purported to be his speech as delivered, began to appear in the *Maryland Gazette and Baltimore Advertiser*.[38] Martin undertook to explain the various articles of the Constitution, and at the same time to make clear his objections. Throughout he appears as a champion of the states. He comes first to his strictures on the judiciary in the course of a diatribe against the legislative powers of Congress. He pointed out that questions concerning the construction of tax laws and questions arising under them were taken away from state courts and confined to courts of the general government. He and others had thought the states better judges of the circumstances of their citizens.[39] He believed, in any event, that there was no need for inferior federal courts—the state tribunals were sufficient as courts of first instance and were now threatened with extinction. Like other antifederalists, he foresaw an army of federal officials at enormous expense.

The judicial power of the United States Martin envisaged as exclusive. With an abundance of italics he made clear that only judges who are *appointed* by Congress would have the power to decide whether

---

[34] In New England, the comment that Gerry had addressed himself to the feelings of the Shays faction was no doubt damaging. Ford, *Essays*, 176.

[35] *Ibid.*, 161.

[36] *Ibid.*, 177.

[37] Farrand, *Records*, III, 151–59. A speech by McHenry was made the same day, *ibid.*, 144–50.

[38] *Ibid.*, 172–232. Publication began in the newspaper Dec. 28, 1787, and continued until Feb. 8, 1788.

[39] Farrand, *Records*, 206

laws of Congress and acts of administrative officers "are *contrary to,* or not *warranted* by the Constitution."[40] The familiar arguments against the appellate jurisdiction were set out, with the usual argument that trial by jury was rendered worthless in criminal cases and was non-existent in civil cases. Martin charged that "they" did not trust *"State judges* so would they not confide in *State juries."*

As propaganda the Martin piece was potent, for he purported to portray the forces at work in the Convention, lay bare the designs of the larger states to aggrandize themselves at the expense of the smaller, and the wishes of the monarchy men to abolish state government. There were provisions the purpose of which he explained, in a manner not supported by other sources. But he pictured himself as a battler for the rights of small states and here Martin was substantially vera-cious. Because there existed a consuming curiosity over what had really happened in the course of the secret proceedings at Philadelphia, the disclosure of the alignment of states on various propositions had the effect of affording the public an intriguing keyhole view of something forbidden.

The Genuine Information was soon circulating in other states.[41] It engaged, of course, the attentive sympathy of "Centinel" in Pennsyl-vania, who proclaimed that the argument of unanimity of the Conven-tion and the sanction of great names could no longer be claimed. The Maryland attorney general had "opened such a scene of discord and accommodation of republicanism to depotism" as to arouse most serious apprehension. "Centinel" regarded Martin's production as furnishing proof positive of a conspiracy, and like a musician composing variations on a theme of another, developed with robust invective the villainies disclosed by Martin.[42]

For the federalists, of course, the ultimate villainy was Martin's breach of the secrecy agreement. The consensus was probably expressed by the rhymester, quoted by the New York *Daily Advertiser*[43] some months after *The Genuine Information* had appeared in the rival *Journal*:

---

[40] *Ibid.,* 220.

[41] The first installment appeared in the *Pennsylvania Packet* Jan. 5, 1788. On January 12, when another section was printed, the *Packet* also published an attack on Martin from a Maryland paper. The Philadelphia *Independent Gazetteer* also ran the piece. The *New-York Journal* regaled the readers with Martin off and on for two months be-ginning in the middle of January. The *State Gazette of South Carolina* began reprinting Apr. 10, 1788, and was still printing after the South Carolina Con-vention met.

[42] Nos. 11, 12, 14. McMaster and Stone, *Pennsylvania,* 633, 637, 646.

[43] New York *Daily Advertiser,* May 1, 1788, reprinted from the *Pennsyl-vania Mercury.* Miner, *Our Rude Forefathers,* 213–14, has some other verses on Martin's villainy.

> Did not the Devil appear to Martin
> Luther in Germany for certain?
> And can't the Devil, if he please,
> Come o'er to Maryland with ease?
> This being admitted, then 'tis certain
> He has got into L——r M——n.

The "Landholder," whose own breach of the pledge of secrecy was no less censurable, proceeded to beard the Marylander in his own lair. Martin had undertaken a defense of Gerry in the *Maryland Journal* in response to Ellsworth's accusations.[44] Six weeks later, and only a month before the Maryland elections, the same newspaper printed Ellsworth's rebuttal.[45] This was a personal attack in thoroughly bad taste, commenting upon the antagonism between Gerry and Martin during the Convention, and piling on a succession of rude remarks about Martin's garrulity, his contradictory positions, his vanity and his capacity for putting the delegates to sleep. Martin, he said, had originated the supreme law of the land clause, had voted for the appeal clause, and for the provision that agreement by nine states should put the government in motion.

Martin came to his own defense in three letters, and although he had explanations for the most telling points made by "Landholder," these were not entirely convincing.[46] But if anyone doubted what "Landholder" had written about Martin's prolixity, these letters settled the matter. In faraway Massachusetts Gerry, as if moved by a sense of *noblesse oblige*, wrote in aid of Martin—and also in his own behalf.[47] He, too, had a version of what had gone on in Philadelphia. It added nothing significant, and although reprinted in New York in May, it is doubtful if it affected opinion there.

In its outspokenness and detail Luther Martin's *Genuine Information* is a good example of one species of antifederalist technique. The principle on which these writers operated was basically to defend the *status quo* by emphasizing the perils to which the new Constitution would subject the nation, and in particular, the constituent sovereignties. In the maintenance of this position these antifederalists did not individually always act consistently. The concession made by certain leaders, notably R. H. Lee, that some things were wrong but that this Constitution was not the way to repair them, and the demand in almost the same breath for amendments, is an example. Such tergiversation, of course, weakened the position of the opposition *pro tanto*. The group, if such it may be called, lacked the cohesiveness of the federalists. The

---

[44] Ford, *Essays*, 341–43.
[45] *Ibid.*, 182–88.

[46] *Ibid.*, 344–71.
[47] *Ibid.*, 129–33.

latter were guided by men who for months had lived, wrangled and dined together. They had an affirmative program hammered out in concert. This the antifederalists did not have. The nearest approach to such was the demand for a bill of rights, although there was no agreement on what this should contain. The diehards, of course, did not conceive of the bill of rights issue as an affirmative program, for this would have been like attaching a tail to a kite they did not wish to fly. The issue was developed as a means to bring on defeat—circumstances were eventually to make it something else.

THE NEW YORK ROMANS

IT WAS THE peculiar political situation in the state of New York which precipitated the most notable piece of writing designed for the frustration of antifederalist tactics. George Clinton, Governor of New York since 1777, headed what today would be called a political machine that had little diminished in strength even after the southern counties were reunited with the rest of the state. Clinton's posture toward a change in the central government had been hostile, a fact which necessarily presaged political collision with Hamilton. Clinton's attack upon the Convention while it was yet sitting had precipitated a rebuke in the press from the hand of Hamilton in July 1787, the inevitable defense, and a sharp reply from Hamilton which appeared two days before the Constitution was signed.[48] This exchange was no more than a preliminary to the main bout yet to come. In Clinton's corner, to pursue our figure, were Lansing and Yates, and to this coterie also belonged John Lamb, Collector of the Port of New York, and the two Lees, Richard Henry and Arthur. Lamb, brevetted a general at the close of the Revolution, was to found the Federal Republican Committee to oppose the Constitution.[49] Arthur Lee was a commissioner on the Confederation Board of Treasury. He had been an intimate of John Wilkes, the English master of scurrility.[50] During the Revolution Lee had served abroad in various diplomatic capacities. The most notorious example of his prowess in this service had been the way in which he had discredited himself with the King of Prussia through the theft of his papers by British agents in Berlin.[51] His dislike of both Robert Morris and Benjamin Franklin was implacable.

---

[48] Hamilton's pieces are in *PAH*, IV, 229, and 248; the details of the counter-attacks are in the notes *ibid.*, 229, 249, 252. There is an account in B. Mitchell, *Alexander Hamilton*, I, 404-406.

[49] *Infra*, p. 295.
[50] Wharton, *Rev. Dip. Corr.*, I, Introduction, c. XII, §§138-40.
[51] Recounted in J. B. Moore, *The Principles of American Diplomacy*, 19 *et seq.*

VII: *The Framers as Propagandists*

A factor which worked to the advantage of Clinton and his friends was the fact that New York City was at this time the capital of the state and the seat of the Confederation government. The opportunity thus existed for spreading their views abroad. On September 27, 1787, there appeared the first of a series of articles signed *Cato*,[52] attributed to George Clinton, although without direct proof of identification. It appears, however, that New Yorkers of the time were guessing that it may have been their Governor. Innuendos were already circulating that antifederalist opposition there was inspired by fear of what the new system would do to entrenched state political interests. The scoffing comment of *Curtius* in the New York *Daily Advertiser* that the new federal establishment would leave *Cato* out in the cold scoffs at *Cato* in terms which leave no doubt that Clinton was meant.[53] Hamilton, in *Federalist* No. 67,[54] refers to *Cato*'s Letter No. 5 in terms indicating that he identified *Cato* with Clinton.

Cato began his writing with a pretense at non-partisanship. But he was immediately and intemperately attacked by *Caesar*, long supposed to have been Hamilton—an attribution that has been disproven.[55] *Cato* used *Caesar*'s attack as an excuse for dropping the guise of impartiality to appear as the people's advocate to help them in a cool and deliberate discussion of the subject. His object, he promised, was to take up the new plan, "compare it with the experience and opinions of the most sensible and approved political authors," and show that the principles of the Constitution and their exercise would be dangerous to liberty and happiness.[56] Five communications followed; the last appeared on January 3, 1788. They are undistinguished, and far from providing the promised intellectual feast, *Cato* seems to have had only three authors available for reference: Locke, Sidney and Montesquieu. This discrepancy between promise and performance was spotted by the nimble-witted "Examiner," who supplied a list of authorities not con-

---

[52] Reprinted in Ford, *Essays*, 247–78. The Boston *American Herald* ran *Cato I* on October 8, 1787.

[53] *Curtius* in the New York *Daily Advertiser*, Oct. 18, 1787: "See the Pennsylvania Farmer [Dickinson] has become a Duke. Phocion [Hamilton] is Prime Minister of State. The Pinckneys are Lords of the Queen's Wardrobe—a long train of nobility succeeds—and alas! the virtuous Cato is forgotten!"

[54] For the edition, *infra*, n. 64.

[55] The letters written in reply to *Cato* and signed *Caesar* (Ford, *Essays*, 283–91) were attributed by Ford to Alexander Hamilton (*ibid.*, 245, 281). The attribution was made on the basis of a letter the authenticity of which cannot be established. Professors Syrett and Cooke, editors of *The Papers of Alexander Hamilton*, have not included these letters in *PAH*, IV, 278, 284, because there is conclusive evidence that they were not written by Hamilton; see J. E. Cooke, "Alexander Hamilton's Authorship of the 'Caesar' Letters," *Wm. and Mary Quarterly*, 17:78–85, 3d ser., Jan. 1960.

[56] Ford, *Essays*, 254.

sulted.[57] He had the further impudence to doubt whether *Cato* ever saw or used more than scraps of Montesquieu.

Cato was aided by *Brutus*, who will later be considered, and *Cincinnatus*, a pseudonym allegedly assumed by Arthur Lee,[58] and, if so, injudiciously, since the Cincinnati members were commonly accused of being federalist plotters. *Cincinnatus* played freely upon current prejudice and was particularly abusive of James Wilson, whom he represented as using his craft as a lawyer to practice every fallacy to mislead the understanding and pervert judgment.[59]

It was in this milieu, where a rising clamor of local antifederalists was afforced by borrowings from the Pennsylvania newspapers, that two of the most original minds in America were moved to action. Some of the loudest and most articulate opponents of the Constitution happened to be congregated in New York for over a month following the signing of the Constitution, and it is clear from the pages of the leading city journals supporting the plan that no writer worth listening to was then speaking for it except the Pennsylvanians. James Madison, then attending Congress, had been serenely confident of public support. Not until October 18 did he mention the "vehement & virulent calumniations" in the newspapers.[60] Alexander Hamilton, whose profession took him about the state as he followed the Circuit, was in a better position to know the antifederalist sentiment of the back country. In any event, it was he who conceived the plan of doing precisely what Clinton had engaged to do, but for the exactly opposite purpose. To this end he enlisted Madison and John Jay.[61] Owing to illness, the latter was to

---

[57] *New-York Journal*, Dec. 14, 1787.

[58] The attribution was by Lee's brother-in-law, Dr. William Shippen, in a letter to his son, Nov. 22, 1787 (Shippen Mss., LC). The *Cincinnatus* pieces ran in the *New-York Journal* during the month of November.

[59] *New-York Journal*, Nov. 8, 1787.

[60] To Washington, Oct. 18, 1787, in *Doc. Hist. Const.*, IV, 334 at 336.

[61] Madison, writing to Jefferson, Aug. 10, 1788, stated that the proposal came from Hamilton and Jay (*Papers of Jefferson*, XIII, 497 at 498). In view of Hamilton's penchant for polemic writing, exhibited in his earlier *Publius* letters (1778), the letters of *Phocion* (1784) and later in the savage letters of "H.G." (1789), it seems highly probable that the initiative was his. Jay was a person of

great reserve. In November a canard was in circulation that Jay was opposed to the Constitution. This was published in the Philadelphia *Independent Gazetteer*, Nov. 24, 1787. Washington saw a reference to this in a Baltimore paper (*Washington Writings*, XXIX, 331, Dec. 7, 1787). Jay repelled the insinuation in typically modest fashion by writing a friend and giving him leave to publish the letter. New York *Independent Journal: or, The General Advertiser*, Dec. 15, 1787. See Madison to Washington, Dec. 20, 1787, *Doc. Hist. Const.*, IV, 416.

Jay was to publish "An Address to the People of the State of New York," a moderate and balanced tract, obviously timed to affect the elections, for it appeared around Apr. 15, 1788. Webb to Barrell, Apr. 27, 1788, W. C. Ford, ed., *Correspondence and*

produce only a few numbers. Madison, however, was to contribute many letters, some of remarkable acuteness, which regrettably cannot here be examined, for our inquiry limits us to the discussion of the judicial. On October 27, 1787, the first of the eighty-five *Publius* letters appeared.[62]

Judged in the light of contemporary politics, the merit of these letters, soon published collectively as *The Federalist*, was the fact that they were an exhaustive affirmative statement of the principles which underlay the succinct phrases of the Constitution itself. By way of example or contrast, historical precedents were used as support. Particularly effective were the references to the structure of state governments and of experience there. The use of political philosophers was relatively slight. Of necessity, the common criticism had to be met. This was done without falling into the prevailing mood of rebuttal that pervaded so much federalist writing. It is rare that a critique is quoted; even rarer is the identification of its source, although it is reasonably certain that at various junctures particulars of *Cato*'s complaints are being answered. The anonymity bestowed upon the traducers and the cold detachment with which their ideas are repelled inevitably remind the reader of Plato of the method of the *Dialogues*, except that here was no mere dialectical exercise.

The *Publius* letters were addressed to literate people, or at least those possessed of an active intelligence. To this extent their influence upon voters was restricted. Nevertheless, judging from various abusive comments in the press, their general effect must have been feared.[63] There is no doubt but that New York was literally saturated with copies of the earlier numbers, for three newspapers were printing them almost simultaneously: the *Independent Journal: or General Advertiser,* Child's *Daily Advertiser* and the *New-York Packet*, which carried little other propaganda. Essays 23 through 39 appeared in the antifederalist sheet, Greenleaf's *New-York Journal.*[64] One correspondent, indeed,

---

Journals of Samuel Blachley Webb, III, 98.

[62] In the New York *Independent Journal: or, The General Advertiser.*

[63] In the Philadelphia *Independent Gazetteer*, Dec. 27, 1787, as noted, it is predicted that "the time serving tools, the Phocions and Publiuses of our day,—'will stink in the very nostrils of posterity.'" "Centinel's" No. XI, which appeared Jan. 16, 1788, referred to the "deranged brain of Publius" and his torrent of misplaced words. In New York "Countryman" complained he could not find out what

Publius "would be at," *New-York Journal,* Jan. 10, 1788. In Boston "Bob Short" complained of the length of *Publius*' sermons as well as their insignificance: "His labor'd nothings, in so strange a stile/Amaze th' unlearn'd, and make the learned smile." Boston, *Massachusetts Centinel*, Dec. 29, 1787.

[64] On the publication history in the New York newspapers see the learned editorial note in *PAH*, IV, 288. Greenleaf, the antifederalist, ceased publication with No. 39, Jan. 30, 1788. In Jacob E. Cooke, ed., *The Federal-*

complained to the latter that his digestion was being ruined by all the *Publius* thrust at him in the several papers to which he subscribed. Because so many New York papers carried *The Federalist*, the chances of numbers reaching out-of-town papers and being there reproduced increased *pro tanto*. There is one important point to be noticed on its effectiveness as a campaign document. Appearing as it did in installments, the impression it could make upon the voters or the convention delegates in the several states was limited to the point to which analysis had been carried. The full impact of the complete work could have been felt only in Virginia, New York, and possibly New Hampshire, about which little is known.[65] Since the discussion of the judiciary was saved until the end of the enterprise, no other conventions had the benefit of *Publius'* reflections on this subject.

Although certain ideas which Hamilton was to develop in the *Publius* letters on the judiciary had been forecast in his briefs in *Rutgers v. Waddington*, his examination of Article III of the Constitution ranged over a greater variety of issues than had been raised in that celebrated litigation. We speak of issues, for these particular letters were not composed as a mere philosophical disquisition but as argument of a demurrer to the most searching piece of antifederalist pleading to appear during the ratification struggle—the letters of *Brutus*. The publication of these pieces in the months immediately preceding Hamilton's consideration of the judicial presented the species of challenge that invariably evoked his formidable powers of advocacy. And to one familiar with his manner of preparation for the argument of a cause, it should be apparent that it was this habit of painstaking analysis and composition which accounts for not only the delay in completing the last letters, but also the careful arrangement and articulation of the arguments.[66]

---

ist, the edition to which citations here are made, the newspapers' publishing dates are given for each essay so published.

[65] Tobias Lear had reported to Washington from Portsmouth, N.H., June 2, 1788, that "the valuable numbers of Publius are not known." *Fabius* [Dickinson], however, was in process of reprint. *Doc. Hist. Const.*, IV, 675.

On May 19, 1788, Hamilton informed Madison that the second volume of *The Federalist* would be ready for despatch to Virginia in a day or two, *ibid.*, 620. In a letter, which the editors of the *Papers of Alexander Hamilton* have dated June 8, 1788, he

claims these had been forwarded, *PAH*, V, 2–4.

[66] It should be noticed that nowhere does Hamilton advert to *Brutus* by name. Indeed, only twice is there explicit reference to any antifederalist writing in the letters on the judicial. To the sentence (*The Federalist*, 527) "Though I trust the friends of the proposed constitution will never concur with its enemies in questioning that fundamental principle of republican government, which admits the right of the people to alter or abolish the established constitution"— a note refers to the "Protest of the Minority of the convention of Pennsylvania, Martin's speech &c." *The*

VII: *The Framers as Propagandists*

Who was *Brutus*? He was identified by Paul Leicester Ford first as Thomas Tredwell of Suffolk County, and then as Robert Yates,[67] but no reasons for this final conclusion were advanced. The style of the first *Brutus* letters is substantially so different from the later ones on the judiciary as to indicate that the series was the work of a "club," such as we are told was the case with the "Centinel" letters, and as we know was the case with *The Federalist*. If we are to accept Yates as a participant in this enterprise, the contributions on the judiciary could only have been his, for he alone of the New York antifederalists was qualified by experience to have written knowledgeably on the subject. Tredwell has been described as a "distinguished Suffolk lawyer," but there is no evidence that he had been admitted to the bar.[68] From 1778 to 1787 he served as Judge of Probates, an office to which were committed the powers of the royal governor as Ordinary, and consequently one the duties of which were chiefly ministerial.[69] On the other hand, Robert Yates, who had been admitted to practice in 1760, had served for ten years as a puisne judge of the state Supreme Court of Judicature and was therefore intimately acquainted with the workings of both the trial and appellate jurisdiction of a tribunal exercising the powers of the three central courts in England.

Brutus first mentioned the judiciary in his opening essay, October 18, 1787.[70] What he had to say was mere repetition of arguments then making the rounds. But on the last day of January 1788 he launched into an attack, original and vigorous, which carried through until March 20.[71] Briefly stated, his argument was directed to establish that federal judicial supremacy was inevitable. He foresaw that this would come about in two ways: by the gradual dominance of the judicial arm over the legislative, and by the manipulation of jurisdiction to destroy the systems of the states.

Address and Reasons of Dissent of the Pennsylvania minority is expressly referred to in No. 83 (*The Federalist*, 567), viz., the recommendation "trial by jury shall be as heretofore."

[67] On the title page of Pelatiah Webster's tract, "The Weakness of Brutus exposed" (Ford, *Pamphlets*, 117), Ford fixed on Tredwell. However, in the bibliography appended at the end of this collection, on p. 424, Ford stated that the conjecture had been based on the fact that Tredwell had used the pseudonym in 1789, and he there stated that Robert Yates was Brutus but produced no proof. This conjecture was repeated four years later in *Essays*, 269n., 295, 417.

[68] The characterization from E. W. Spaulding, *New York in the Critical Period 1783–1789*, 240. Tredwell is not in the Ms. Roll of Attorneys for this period (McKesson Mss., NYHS).

[69] On the probate jurisdiction, *LPAH*, I, 24–25. Comments by Hamilton on both Tredwell and Yates in a letter to Robert Morris, Aug. 13, 1782, in *PAH*, III, 139–40.

[70] *New-York Journal*. The text of this was reprinted in *Debates and Proceedings in the Convention of the Commonwealth of Massachusetts* held in the Year 1788 (1856), 366–78.

[71] *New-York Journal*, Jan. 31, Feb. 7, 14, 21, 28, Mar. 6, 20, 1788.

The root of the future growth, in *Brutus'* opinion, was the grant of power over "all cases in law and equity, under this Constitution, the laws of the United States and treaties." Cases in law arising under the Constitution vested courts with power to apply as to words and context the usual rules of statutory construction. But the word "equity" empowered them "to explain the constitution according to the reasoning spirit of it."[72] Unhampered by rules, the "reason and spirit" of the Constitution would enable the federal courts to make of it what they wished. The opinions of the Supreme Court would have the force of law, for it would be the *dernier ressort* not subject to legislative control.

It was *Brutus'* opinion that the Supreme Court would "assume certain principles from which they will reason in forming their decisions." When fixed by a course of decisions, the Congress was bound to adopt such principles and thus form the rules by which their own powers were to be explained. If the legislature should "pass laws, which, in the judgment of the court, they are not authorized to do by the constitution, the court will not take notice of them . . . they cannot therefore execute a law, which, in their judgment, opposes the constitution."[73] The upshot of all this would mean that Congress would not pass anything which the courts would not execute and would not scruple to pass any law to which the courts would give effect. In short, the judgment of the judiciary would become the guide of the legislative arm.[74]

There were other particulars of Article III, section 2, which to *Brutus* were obnoxious. Treaties could be given whatever extension the courts wished by virtue of their equity powers.[75] Actions by citizens against states were humiliating and degrading.[76] The original jurisdiction of the Supreme Court in cases involving ambassadors embraced their meanest servants, and would force citizens who might seek to collect debts from them to go to the Supreme Court to do so.[77] *Brutus'* warning, if not inspired by a local *cause célèbre*, was at least underlined for New Yorkers by the event. In December 1787 a city constable, attempting to serve a civil process of arrest for debt on the coachman of the Netherlands Minister, had entered the legation and dragged out his victim. The ensuing uproar had not been quelled until a magistrate had intervened. Minister Van Berckel, properly indignant, did not confine his protest to Secretary Jay, but personally upbraided the alderman who had issued the warrant. Fuss at the top level was thus unhappily combined with fury at the municipal level. At the time *Brutus* wrote, the

---

[72] *Ibid.*, Jan. 31, 1788. This was, of course, what the New York Council of Revision was authorized to do under Art. III of the state constitution, and, in fact, did. As a Supreme Court judge, Yates sat on the Council.

For examples, *LPAH*, I, 286n.
[73] *New-York Journal*, Feb. 7, 1788.
[74] *Ibid.*, Feb. 14, 1788.
[75] *Ibid.*, Feb. 21, 1788.
[76] *Ibid.*
[77] *Ibid.*, Feb. 28, 1788.

hapless constable bound over to General Session, was awaiting action by the grand jury.[78]

Brutus was even more exercised over the Supreme Court's appellate jurisdiction. This, he claimed, obviously comprehended criminal as well as civil cases. This was a new and unusual thing and signified that even upon acquittal the government could appeal with all ruinous consequences to a defendant.[79] In civil cases the appellate power, since it extended over law and fact, was unknown to the common law. Habeas corpus, certiorari or writ of error were the only means of moving up a cause, and in no case were facts re-examined. If the intendment was to use a second jury, as was the Massachusetts practice on appeal, the verdict and judgment of the inferior court was made of no consequence. This had been, indeed, a chief cause of Shays' revolt.[80] Costs to the poor and middle classes would be endless, and moving the Supreme Court from place to place would do no more than make the oppression somewhat more bearable.

No court the world ever saw, wrote *Brutus*, had the immense powers of the Supreme Court. The determinations of English judges, whose tenure was during good behavior, were subject to correction by the House of Lords.[81] Their function was restricted to adjudication according to the laws of the land. Furthermore, these judges had never undertaken to control these laws by holding that they were inconsistent with the constitution, much less were they vested with power to give an equitable construction of their constitution. The tenure during good behavior established by the Framers was unobjectionable provided the judges were made responsible. This had not been done, for they had been made independent in the fullest sense, both of the legislature and of the people themselves. Men in such a situation generally feel themselves independent of Heaven itself. There would exist no power to correct their errors or to control their decisions. They could not be removed, nor their salaries reduced. The impeachment remedy was inadequate, restricted as it was to high crimes or misdemeanors. It could not be invoked for incompetence, saving proof of a wicked or corrupt motive.

---

[78] There were unfortunate delays in initiating proceedings, yet this could hardly excuse Van Berckel's conduct toward the alderman, a tailor. Having commanded the magistrate to attend him, the Minister not only made rude comments about his craft, but repeatedly threatened him with punishment. In May 1788 the grand jury indicted the constable. He finally confessed the indictment at the August Sessions and was sentenced to three months in jail. The papers relating to the case are in *The Diplomatic Correspondence of the United States of America, 1783-1789* (1833), VI, 497-512. The charge to the grand jury is in the New York *Daily Advertiser*, May 10, 1788.

[79] *New-York Journal*, Feb. 28, 1788.

[80] *Ibid.*, Mar. 6, 1788.

[81] *Ibid.*, Mar. 20, 1788.

With no less foreboding did *Brutus* view the impact of a federal judiciary upon the states. Using the preamble of the Constitution as the source from which the courts would find the premises of construction, it seemed to him that "to form a perfect union" (*sic*) logically would make necessary abolition of inferior governments; to "establish justice" would involve illimitable extensions of federal authority over controversies; to "insure domestic tranquillity" would involve jurisdiction over all private breaches of peace.[82] *Brutus* agreed with the "Federal Farmer" that by use of fictions, as in England, the apparent limitations on federal jurisdiction could be overcome.[83] Moreover, the federal courts would have authority to pass on the validity of state laws. Where federal jurisdiction was exclusive, they would adjudge all state laws in such cases void *ab initio*. Where there was concurrent jurisdiction, the law of the Union, being the supreme law of the land, would prevail and state law repealed, restricted or so construed as to give full effect to the former.[84]

In *Brutus'* opinion the state courts were wholly adequate for the administration of justice. Obstacles raised in the way of creditors was the fault of legislatures, not the judiciaries. These had sought by various means to restrict laws of this sort, and he cited the courts of wicked Rhode Island as an example—an obvious reference to the judgment in *Trevett v. Weeden*.[85] Claims under conflicting grants were sufficiently safeguarded in the state courts by allowing a writ of error to the Supreme Court; indeed, this was all that was needed as respects adjudications on laws of the Union. Thus would be preserved the "good old way of administering justice," and equally the inestimable right of trial by jury.[86]

Like many of his contemporaries, *Brutus* had a way of coming back to a point for further explanation, and like them he was repetitious. Nevertheless, as any pedagogue knows, the re-travelled road is a proven way to the enlightenment of the slow-witted. Even the dullest of such could be left in no doubt that *Brutus* had many reasons to believe that the projected judiciary was a very dangerous thing indeed. This was, then, the very point first taken up by Hamilton who, as remarked, was to write all of *Publius* on the judiciary.[87]

[82] *Ibid.*, Feb. 7, 1788.
[83] *Ibid.*, Feb. 14, 1788.
[84] *Ibid.*
[85] *Ibid.*, Mar. 6, 1788. On Trevett v. Weeden, *supra*, p. 138.
[86] *New-York Journal*, Mar. 6, 1788.
[87] Beginning with No. 78. The version here used is that of the most reliable critical edition of *The Federalist* (Cooke, 1961). The texts of numbers 78–85 published by Professor Cooke are taken from vol. II of the McLean edition. This volume appeared May 28, 1788. The Chancery Court and a Circuit Court were sitting in early April. Probably No. 78 was undertaken in that month, not long after the last *Brutus* piece. Newspaper publication began in the New York *Independent Journal: or, The*

The judiciary, in Hamilton's opinion, from the nature of its function would be the least dangerous to "the political rights of the constitution; because it will be least in a capacity to annoy or injure them."[88] With no influence over sword or purse, it might truly be said to have neither force nor will but merely judgment. Citing Montesquieu in support of the necessity of a complete separation of the judicial if liberty was to be secure, Hamilton asserted that the judiciary was in constant jeopardy of being overpowered, awed or influenced by its coordinate branches. Its independence was an essential ingredient in its constitution, and nothing could contribute to this more than permanency in office. This, it may be remarked, had been the view of New Yorkers in 1760, when a blistering quarrel had erupted over the Crown's refusal to commission the provincial Supreme Court judges by tenure of good behavior. This had terminated when the province was compelled to suffer the indignity of having a complaisant Massachusetts man imported to be Chief Justice.[89] Curiously enough, no one reminded the public of this episode.

Complete independence of the judiciary, continued Hamilton, was essential in a limited constitution, *i.e.*, one which had specific exceptions to legislative authority, such as no ex post facto laws. Such limitations could in practice be preserved in no other way than "through the medium of courts of justice; whose duty it must be to declare all acts contrary to the manifest tenor of the constitution void. Without this, all the reservation of particular rights or privileges would amount to nothing."[90]

Moving to a direct traverse of *Brutus'* theory that the exercise of such a power implied a superiority of the judiciary over the legislative power, Hamilton next set out his well-known defense of the doctrine of judicial control. There was no clearer principle than that every act of a delegated authority contrary to the tenor of the commission under which it is exercised is void. To deny this would be to assert that the deputy is greater than his principal; that the representatives of the people are superior to the people themselves; that men acting by virtue of powers may do not only what their powers do not authorize, but also what they forbid. The legislative body was not the constitutional judge of its own powers, nor could the construction it put upon them

---

General Advertiser, June 14. The numbers with which we are here concerned are also reprinted in *PAH*, IV, 655 *et seq.*

[88] *The Federalist* (No. 78), 522.

[89] The correspondence and the Royal Order in Council on the matter are in *Docs. Rel. Col. Hist. N.Y.*, VI,

792, 951; *ibid.*, VII, 466, 471, 479, 483, 489, 501, 503, 705. The appointee was Benjamin Pratt. The assembly refused to vote a salary and he was paid out of the provincial quitrents. He died in 1763.

[90] *The Federalist* (No. 78), 524.

conclude other departments. The contrary could not be presumed, for it was not inferable from particular provisions of the Constitution. This instrument could not be supposed to intend that the representatives of the people should be enabled to substitute their will for that of their constituents. It was more rational to suppose that the courts were to be the intermediate bodies between the people and the legislature to keep the latter within bounds. The interpretation of laws was the proper and peculiar province of courts. "A constitution is in fact, and must be, regarded by the judges as a fundamental law."[91] To the judges belonged the business of ascertaining its meaning as well as the meaning of any legislative act. Where there was irreconcilable conflict, the superior obligation of the Constitution must be preferred. This conclusion did not suppose a superiority of the judicial to the legislative power, but rather the superiority of the people to both.

The fact that the courts must be considered bulwarks of a limited Constitution against legislative encroachment was, in Hamilton's opinion, another argument for permanent tenure. It was equally requisite to guard the Constitution and the people from those "ill humours," designedly disseminated, that were likely to occasion dangerous innovations and oppressions of minority parties.[92] In the people was vested the right to change the Constitution by solemn act, but no presumption as to their sentiments warranted a departure from it prior to such an act. "But it is easy to see, that it would require an uncommon portion of fortitude in the judges to do their duty as faithful guardians of the constitution, where legislative invasions of it have been instigated by the major voice of the community."[93]

Independence of the judiciary was equally necessary to safeguard private rights of particular classes of citizens from injury by unjust or partial laws.[94] The firmness of the magistracy was important in mitigating mischief and also in checking the legislature. The benefits of moderation and integrity of the judiciary had already been felt in many states. This could not be expected of men holding temporary commis-

---

[91] *Ibid.*, 525.
[92] *Ibid.*, 527.
[93] *Ibid.*, 528.
[94] As to this passage, it would appear to be a reference to the measures taken against the former Tories, in particular the "Trespass Act," on which cf. *LPAH* I, 282–543, and the attempted "Exclusion Bill" which Hamilton and his friends had succeeded in beating in February 1787. This last related to a variety of disqualifications in the Bill for Regulating Elections, viz., (1) an oath of

abjuration in a form that would have excluded Roman Catholics; (2) persons receiving pensions from the United States or holding offices under the same to be barred from seats or votes as members of the assembly or senate; (3) officers or masters and owners of privateers who had cruised against the United States were to be disqualified from state offices of trust. Hamilton's speeches on these three issues in *PAH*, IV, 22–24, 25–29, 34–37.

sions who would be liable to an improper complaisance. Finally, Hamilton argued, the knowledge of the laws, as precedents cumulated, would demand long and laborious study. No one would quit a lucrative practice to accept a temporary post, and consequently the offices would fall to persons less able and less qualified.

In *Federalist* No. 79[95] Hamilton defended the salary provision for judges, a matter which had excited the rancor of *Brutus* and others, and also the exclusive sanction of impeachment as the only proper provision that could have been made consistent with judicial independence. The lack of any other scheme for removal he believed prudent. Removal for inability he regarded as subject to abuse at the hands of party politics.[96] The "mensuration of qualities of the mind" had no place in the catalogue of known arts. As for an age limit, as in New York where it was set at sixty, this was improper, for the deliberating and comparing faculties in men generally preserved their strength beyond that period.[97]

Publius' explanation and defense of the jurisdiction of federal courts in No. 80[98] followed in general the standard argument of pro-Constitution men, viz., application of the "just principle" that every government ought to possess means of executing its own provisions by its own authority. The extension of the judicial power over laws of the United States constitutionally enacted depended on the obvious consideration that a constitutional method was needed to give efficacy to constitutional provisions. Restrictions on state legislatures would be of no avail without a means of enforcing observance. The restrictions on the states could have been made effective only by a direct negative of their laws or an authority in the federal courts to overrule those in contravention of the articles of Union. This the Convention had chosen.[99] Because state tribunals could not be supposed to be impartial, controversies between different states and their citizens were properly left to federal courts. Hamilton was at pains to explain, but without reference to *Brutus'* ingenious interpretation, that the word "equity" was used in the Constitution to cover the ordinary heads of Chancery jurisdiction, such as relief in cases of fraud, accident, trust and the like.[100]

At no point in *The Federalist* is the influence of *Brutus* upon the

---

[95] *The Federalist* (No. 79), 531–32.

[96] This had been the subject of a considerable diatribe by *Brutus* in the *New-York Journal*, Mar. 20, 1788.

[97] *The Federalist* (No. 79), 533–34. The provision in the New York constitution had been motivated by the case of Daniel Horsmanden, first as a puisne judge of the Supreme Court (1737) and later as Chief Justice until his death in 1778 at eighty-five, long after he had been too feeble to function. See *Docs. Rel. Col. Hist. N.Y.*, VII, 528n.; *ibid.*, VIII, 685.

[98] *The Federalist* (No. 80), 534–41.

[99] *Ibid.*, 535.

[100] *Ibid.*, 539–40.

course of argument more patent than in the defense of the provision for the Supreme Court. The argument of No. 81[101] opens with a paraphrase, set out with quotation marks, of *Brutus'* objections published on March 20, 1788, where he reiterated the claim that the authority of the proposed Supreme Court would be superior to that of the legislature, and that it should be subjected to control, as in Great Britain by the House of Lords. This was a suggestion which New Yorkers might be deemed to favor since their own constitution had established in the Court for the Trial of Impeachments and the Correction of Errors an imitation of the House of Lords.[102] As we shall see, the creation of a supervisory power over the Supreme Court was to be urged in the New York Convention.[103] Nothing in the new Constitution, declared Hamilton, *directly* empowered the national courts to construe laws according to "the spirit of the constitution" or gave greater latitude in this particular than might be claimed by the courts of every state.[104] To insist that the ultimate resort be a branch of the legislature involved renouncing the doctrine of separation of powers. Furthermore, from a body which had even a partial agency in passing bad laws, a disposition to temper these could rarely be expected. Men who infringed the Constitution as legislators were unlikely as judges to repair the breach. The temporary tenure of legislators, their lack of professional knowledge and the dangers of party division together rendered the suggestion absurd. The courts had no force to support any such usurpations, and the sanction of impeachment was a sufficient means of punishing any judicial presumption.[105]

The notion that inferior federal courts were unnecessary and that the state courts were adequate to the purpose Hamilton rejected on the grounds that impartiality could not be found in the latter, and further that state judges commissioned at pleasure or from year to year would be too little independent to be relied on for an inflexible execution of national laws, even if there were reason for thus committing federal causes. This would give rise to a corresponding need for greatly extending appeals, a matter likely to cause public inconvenience. Hamilton suggested a division of the United States into four to six districts for federal courts where, together with state judges, the federal judges could hold circuits for trial of causes. Appeals could then be safely circumscribed.[106]

The original jurisdiction of the Supreme Court Hamilton believed to be unexceptional. As to the jurisdiction over the states, he digressed

---

[101] *Ibid.* (No. 81), 541–52.
[102] Art. 32 of the constitution of 1777, and *N.Y. Laws*, 8 Sess. 1784, c. 11. See also *LPAH*, I, 18.
[103] *Infra*, p. 400.
[104] *The Federalist* (No. 81), 543.
[105] *Ibid.*, 545–46.
[106] *Ibid.*, 546–48.

to answer a flight of fancy by *Brutus* to the effect that by assignment of public securities of one state to citizens of another, the federal courts under the diversity clause would become the agencies for ruining the states. Adoption of the new plan, said Hamilton, did not divest states of the privilege of paying their own debts in their own way. Such contracts were only binding on the conscience of the sovereign. Short of war, judgments or suits against states to recover debts could not be enforced.[107]

The Federalist's exegesis on the much disputed "appellate jurisdiction both as to law and fact" was the most logical and sensible handling of the question theretofore made.[108] The understanding of the word "appellate" varied according to the procedures in different states. It was improper, therefore, to fasten upon the expression anything derived from particular technical interpretations. In abstract, it meant no more than the power of one tribunal to review the proceedings of another either as to law or fact, or both. This depended on ancient custom, or, in the case of a new government, upon legislative provision. Hence if the re-examination of a fact once determined by a jury should in any case be admitted under the new Constitution, it might be so regulated as to be done by a second jury either by remand or by directing an issue immediately out of the Supreme Court. Did it not follow that a re-examination of a fact once found by a jury would be permitted in the Supreme Court itself? Could it not be properly said, asked Hamilton, that on writ of error to a superior court, as in New York practice, the latter had jurisdiction of the fact as well as the law? The superior court could not institute a new inquiry concerning the fact, but "it takes cognizance of it as it appears upon the record and pronounces the law arising upon it. This is jurisdiction of both fact and law, nor is it even possible to separate them."[109]

It must be confessed that Hamilton's explanation, while comprehensible to the intelligent layman, particularly if he had been involved in appellate litigation, and certainly to a lawyer, was probably not sufficient to assuage the popular unease that extinction of trial by jury was threatened. In New York the citizenry had cause for worry from long experience with summary proceedings before justices of the peace who, in their control of both law and fact, were the common and familiar example of such consolidated authority.[110] It may be observed,

---

[107] *Ibid.*, 548–49.

[108] *Ibid.*, 550–52.

[109] *Ibid.*, 551.

[110] This practice brought from England was given considerable extension by statute. A whole range of misdemeanors were handled summarily by single justices or two or three out of sessions. *Cf.* Goebel and Naughton, *Law Enforcement in Colonial New York*, 110–37. The continued vigor of the colonial legislation on summary jurisdiction had been assured by Art. 35 of the constitution and the further

however, that although all freemen over twenty-one had been qualified to vote for delegates to the New York Convention, the last of the *Publius* letters appeared long after the elections in New York, and for that matter, in Virginia. The matter of persuading a citizenry of limited experience was consequently no longer a problem.

Hamilton went on to distinguish the common law from the civil law—viz., equity and admiralty, where necessarily a jurisdiction over facts should extend in the broadest sense. No exception could be written into the Constitution respecting jury trial cases because in some states all cases were tried by jury. Obviously, future regulation of appeals by Act of Congress was the best answer to the problem in the service of public justice.[111]

There was one other matter relating to the judicial process discussed by Hamilton—the relation of the state and federal courts. Without referring to the Cassandras who prophesied the doom of the state tribunals, the theory is developed that the state and national governments were kindred systems and parts of one whole. The inference is drawn that in all cases arising under the laws of the Union, the state courts would have concurrent jurisdiction except where it was expressly prohibited.[112] These courts were divested of no part of their "primitive jurisdiction" except as respects appeals. The evident aim of the Convention's plan was that all causes of the "specified" classes should receive their original *or* final determination in the courts of the Union. The grant of appellate jurisdiction to the Supreme Court could not be confined to inferior federal courts, but must extend to state courts; otherwise the intent of the clause would be subverted. Hamilton, indeed, believed that there was no impediment to permitting appeals from state courts to subordinate national tribunals.[113] This would diminish the motives for multiplying federal courts and permit measures to contract the appellate jurisdiction of the Supreme Court.[114]

Hamilton's arguments have been considered at length not only because, like those of others, they had a bearing upon the form which the later Judiciary Act was to take, but also because they are relevant to what went on at the New York Convention. It does not appear from the sketchy surviving minutes that any federalist spoke there in the discussion of Article III. *Publius'* letters was their case, a case in particulars designed for a New York audience. For those who disdained the printed volume, the city journals, which began to reprint these

---

conservative jury trial as "heretofore been used" (Árt. 41).

[111] *The Federalist* (No. 81), 551–52.

[112] *The Federalist* (No. 82), 554.

[113] *Ibid.*, 555.

[114] *Ibid.*, 557.

pieces on the very day the delegates assembled, made them generally available. It is improbable that antifederalist leaders were ignorant of their content. In any event, antifederalist comment at Poughkeepsie and, above all, some of their proffered amendments were as much in refutation of *Publius'* views as they were in affirmation of ideas propounded by *Brutus*.[115]

Brief mention must be made of two further papers by Hamilton —one on the jury[116] and one dealing with a bill of rights.[117] The former is based on the familiar traverse of the claim that the mention of a trial jury in criminal cases was an exclusion of the jury in civil cases. Hamilton sought to reduce emotional fervor over the issues by establishing that juries in civil actions had nothing to do with liberty, but were basically an insurance against judicial corruption. The impossibility of setting up a constitutional rule on the matter was buttressed by a lengthy description of the variations of practice in the several states. Finally, the point was argued that there were certain types of jurisdiction, *e.g.*, equity and admiralty, where it would be improper to use a jury[118]—a viewpoint hardly acceptable to convinced libertarians.

Hamilton's remarks on the bill of rights were written almost particularly for New Yorkers. Unlike some states, New York's constitution had no discrete bill of rights.[119] It had been sought to remedy this by spelling out in a statute certain safeguards for the individual.[120] This statute was not yet two years old. With a certain sardonic pleasure, Hamilton intimated the inconsistency of demanding something for a federal constitution which no one had troubled to secure in the fundamental law of the state. The antifederalists had claimed that there was a variety of matter scattered in the New York constitution which amounted to a bill of rights.[121] The proposed federal Constitution, wrote Hamilton, also had several matters of this sort in it. The establishment of habeas corpus and the prohibition of ex post facto laws and titles of nobility were "perhaps greater securities to liberty and republicanism" than anything in the New York instrument.[122] As for a second

---

[115] *Infra*, p. 398. This supposition is strengthened somewhat by the various complaints of antifederalist delegates that they were hearing *Publius* warmed over.

[116] *The Federalist* (No. 83), 558–74.

[117] *The Federalist* (No. 84), 575–87.

[118] *Ibid.* (No. 83), 568–70.

[119] *Ibid.* (No. 84), 575.

[120] *N.Y. Laws*, 10 Sess., c. 1 (Jan. 26, 1787).

[121] *E.g.*, Art. 13, protection against disfranchisement except by law; Art. 24, tenure by good behavior for Chancellor, Supreme Court judges and the first judge of the county court; Art. 34, right to counsel; Art. 38, complete religious freedom; Art. 41, jury trial.

[122] *The Federalist* (No. 84), 577.

charge that no provision was made adopting the common law, Hamilton replied[123] that the New York constitutional article on this had made the common law subject to legislative repeal. This article had been inserted merely to remove doubts regarding "the ancient law" that might have been occasioned by the Revolution. Consequently this could not be considered a part of a declaration of rights.

Apart from these strictures, Hamilton's posture toward the inclusion of a bill of rights was substantially identical with that of James Wilson. The Constitution was designed merely to regulate the political interests of the nation, and a minute detailing of particular rights was not applicable as it would be in a constitution which regulated every species of personal and private rights. Hamilton believed that a bill of rights, to the extent demanded, was not only unnecessary, but might even be dangerous. It was absurd to make provision against abuse of authority which was not given. To do so, further, would imply a power to make proper regulation of such things as the press. In other words, handles would be supplied for a doctrine of constructive powers by indulgence of an injudicious zeal for a bill of rights.[124]

It is impossible to convey by paraphrase and brief quotation the qualities which make *The Federalist* a great book, particularly since so small a segment has here been so cursorily surveyed. There are few writings in the political literature of modern centuries that approach it in the loftiness of its tone, few that equal it in literary distinction. One can to this day still feel how portentous, how immediate was the issue to which the letters were addressed, for there is an urgency in the writing which has survived the event. Locke or Montesquieu, the household gods of the time, may have left posterity more to ponder; neither left his own people a heritage of more enduring vitality than did *Publius*.

With the publication of *The Federalist* the great period of propaganda came to an end. Never before and never again was there such soul-searching over the judiciary and its role in the structure of government as occurred in this nine-month period in 1787–88. In this protracted and far-flung exchange of hostilities, those Framers who took up their pens in defense or in repudiation of their deeds, if they did not all contribute greatly to political philosophy, at least added to the emotional pressures. Two of them, Dickinson and Williamson, whose writings have not been discussed, had nothing significant to say about the judiciary. Dickinson, writing as *Fabius*,[125] produced a tract larded with learning, but the fire had gone out of the *Pennsylvania Farmer* of pre-Revolutionary days. The address of Hugh Williamson of North Carolina

---

[123] *Ibid.*, 578.
[124] *Ibid.*, 579–80.

[125] Ford, *Pamphlets*, 163–216.

was reprinted in New York, but it was run of the mill, not calculated to spark controversy.[126] One other publication, printed in October 1787 by Charles Pinckney, must be mentioned. It could in no way be described as a defense of the Constitution as perfected, for it was a recension of the speech prepared for the presentation of his plan to the Convention, but never delivered.[127] Indeed, by displaying to public view a scheme containing ingredients ignored or rejected at the Philadelphia Convention, Pinckney's *Observations* might have proven a real apple of discord. Fortunately this did not happen, although the pamphlet brought on brief comment in New York when it appeared.[128]

There remains to be noticed another indiscretion which probably must be laid to the charge of one of the Maryland recusants, for it first appeared in the *Maryland Journal*. This was the publication of matter from the printed report of the Committee on Detail submitted to the Convention on August 6.[129] This was the grossest breach of the secrecy pact yet made. It was put out as something agreed upon in the Convention until "within a few days of their rising."[130] This was an untruth, but the contributor, among other things, made much of final changes in the supreme law of the land clause and also of the addition of the provision "appellate Jurisdiction, both as to Law and Fact." Reprinted in New York on June 17,[131] this disclosure was too late to have affected anything there except the convention debates, where, however, it does not appear to have been noticed.

---

[126] Ford, *Essays*, 397–406. Remarks on the judiciary at 399–400, chiefly a defense of jurisdiction over actions between foreign subjects and American citizens.

[127] Farrand, *Records*, III, 106–27. It was entitled "Observations on the Plan of Government submitted to the Federal Convention, in Philadelphia, on the 28th of May 1787. By Mr. Charles Pinckney, Delegate from the State of South Carolina. Delivered at different Times in the course of their Discussions." Farrand conjectures it represents a speech prepared for delivery when Pinckney presented his plan, plus some later additions.

The pamphlet was offered for sale in New York on Oct. 18, 1787, in the New York *Daily Advertiser*. Madison, on October 14, sent Washington a copy saying that Pinckney professed the print was for the perusal of his friends (*Doc. Hist. Const.*, IV, 329). Washington replied that Pinckney was unwilling to lose any fame that could be acquired by the publication of his sentiments (Oct. 22, 1787, *Washington, Writings*, XXIX, 291). It may be noticed that the *State Gazette of South Carolina* began running the "Observations" Oct. 29, 1787.

[128] See New York *Daily Advertiser*, Nov. 7 (*supp.*), Nov. 17, 1788.

[129] Printed in Farrand, *Records*, II, 177.

[130] There had been earlier leakage regarding the change in this clause. It will be recalled that the language had been changed by the Committee of Style (*supra*, p. 247) and a specific vote on the change had not been taken. In the debate on the Constitution in Congress, Nathan Dane had raised the matter but apparently received no answer ("Smith's Minutes," 37).

[131] *New-York Journal*, June 17, 1788.

How far were the voters affected by the torrent of propaganda? This is difficult to assess. In places like New Hampshire and Massachusetts where delegates came instructed, it may be assumed that the impact was considerable. Obviously, writers believed that they were reaching people, for it is striking how in a place like New York the flow of essays very nearly dried up after the elections there were over. That the delegates to the several state conventions were in countless instances the beneficiaries of what had been laid before them by the press has already been noticed. And it may be remarked that no matter how whimsical were the grounds parroted by delegates from their reading, these were always propounded as the firm conclusions of reason. This, too, reflected the nature of the propaganda. For it was characteristic of the Age of Enlightenment that propagandists optimistically, in such numbers, made appeal to the reason of their readers. For political purposes, of course, the appeals to prejudice may be cynically viewed as no less an appeal to reason—but a reason somewhat askew. Attempts to stir the imagination of readers took the form of conjuring dreams of better times, or, on the other hand, of playing upon fear which is a notable stimulant of antic ideas. Some of these gambits, as we have seen, were fanciful to the point of being bizarre, and they were countered by ribaldries and grotesqueries on a premise resembling the homeopathic *similia similibus curantur*.

There was, however, one flight of fancy, Francis Hopkinson's *New Roof*, which was at once an appeal to reason and to the mother wit of any man who had ever wielded hammer or saw.[132] Hopkinson set out the merits of the Constitution in a parable about the old house that needed a new roof. He relates how James, the architect, surveyed the old place and set about making plans for a new roof because the old one was too bad to repair. A fractious old woman, who lived in the house and whose apartment was to be made smaller, angrily made trouble. With humor and dexterity, the objections of the antifederalists are set out in builder's terms—in particular, the fuss over lack of a bill

132 The "New Roof" was first printed in the *Pennsylvania Packet*, Dec. 29, 1787. Other Philadelphia papers copied it almost at once, and the antifederalist papers soon attacked Hopkinson violently. The text reprinted in McMaster and Stone, *Pennsylvania*, 510–16, accords with that in the *Packet*. James, the architect in the allegory, is, of course, Wilson; Margery is George Bryan; the William, Jack and Robert whom she enlists are, respectively, Findley, Smilie and Whitehill, who carried the burden for the antifederalists at the Pennsylvania Convention (*infra*, p. 327). The lunatic whose ranting ends the piece has been identified as James Workman, a tutor at the university who, as *Philadelphiensis*, had been grinding out extravagances against the Constitution.

The "New Roof" was the origin of the ornament used by journals, the structure supported by columns inscribed with the names of states which had already ratified.

of scantlings. It is testimony to the enchantment evoked by this amusing story that within a few weeks the idea was versified by Hopkinson into "The Raising: A new song for federal mechanics":[133]

> Come muster my lads, your mechanical tools
> Your saws and your axes, your hammers & rules,
> Bring your mallets and planes, your level and line
> And plenty of pins of American pine;
> > For our roof we will raise, and our song still shall be—
> > Our government firm, and our citizens free.

The ballad continues with the details of a raising, and then, in the fifth verse, judges are celebrated in song for probably the first time in American history:

> Our *King Posts* are judges—how upright they stand,
> Supporting the *Braces*, the Laws of the Land—
> The Laws of the Land, which divide right from wrong,
> And strengthen the weak, by weak'ning the strong.
> > Chorus.

---

[133] G. E. Hastings, *The Life and Works of Francis Hopkinson*, at 409, states that Hopkinson published the verse in the *American Museum* in July 1788. Actually it appeared in the *Pennsylvania Gazette*, Feb. 6, 1788. It was reprinted in the New York *Daily Advertiser*, Feb. 11, 1788; the *Massachusetts Gazette*, Feb. 29, 1788; *Massachusetts Centinel*, Mar. 1, 1788; Rhode Island *Newport Mercury*, Mar. 3, 1788; the *Norwich Packet*, Mar. 6, 1788; the *Virginia Independent Chronicle*, Feb. 20, 1788.

CHAPTER VIII

The Raising I:
The Judicial before the States

THE RATIFICATION of the Constitution by the several states was a long drawn out process, involving as it did deliberations first by the legislatures and next by the conventions, with the attendant opportunities for political plots and stratagems. Yet it was high summer before the opposition was to discover the profound truth of the political maxim that "You can't beat something with nothing." At the time the ninth state, New Hampshire, had voted favorably, on June 21, 1788, the conventions of New York and Virginia were in session. No one apparently expected that the new government would be put into operation unless at least one or the other state should join with those which had already acted. North Carolina was not to meet until mid-July 1788—then only to reject the plan. Of Rhode Island no one expected anything except the worst. The North Carolinians were to recant better than a year later, but the Rhode Islanders remained obdurate until May 29, 1790.

Considering how generally and intensely public interest had been swiftly aroused by the parade of opinions in the press, it is a matter of some wonder that the proceedings in the conventions were, with three exceptions, badly or very incompletely reported—in three instances not reported at all. It is not improbable that in some states the apparent indifference was a reflection of an insular attitude that the matter was state business of no concern to outsiders, and that the result of the vote alone was important. There was, too, some anxiety over how politic it would be to broadcast the views of the opposition. Certainly, in Pennsylvania, care was taken to have a thoroughly federalist report. One reporter who had promised the public a full account was apparently suborned by the federalists. Another, publishing in the *Pennsylvania*

Herald, ceased after November 30[1] and "Centinel" charged that means had been found to suppress the publication.[2] In Maryland, where only the antifederalists spoke at length, there appears to have been a conspiracy of silence.[3] In certain places, as for example, New Jersey and Georgia, the unavailability of a good shorthand writer was likely the reason nothing was reported.

In general the speeches at the several conventions did not equal and rarely surpassed the best of what had been written in tracts and newspapers. That so much of what was said seems lacking in quality is in part attributable to the defects in reporting. At the same time it should be observed that a great many *minuti homines* attended these conclaves. These men, unskilled in expressing themselves, sometimes ventured to speak, and when they did, betrayed their limitations. It was not too often that the reporters deigned to record such speeches. The publishers' concern, after all, was in marketing their product, and there was no more reason then to suppose the public interested in the unedifying comments of some plain fellow than is the case today.

In Massachusetts, where the antifederalist attack came from such persons, the printers faced the dilemma of recording the speeches or of abandoning the semblance of reporting a debate. They solved their problem by doctoring the speeches for publication.[4] Nothing of this

---

[1] Thomas Lloyd, a shorthand writer, applied for the place of assistant secretary, but the convention "postponed" the request. *Minutes of the Convention of the Commonwealth of Pennsylvania . . . for the Purpose of Taking into Consideration the Constitution framed by the late Federal Convention . . .* (1787), 5. He undertook to report and publish and so advertised. He is supposed to have been bought up. Alexander James Dallas was the writer in *The Pennsylvania Herald and General Advertiser*. No documented explanation of why he ceased reporting has been published. R. Walters, *Alexander James Dallas*, 19–20, lays it to federalist pressure and the cancelling of subscriptions by *Herald* readers. This book is undocumented.

[2] Published in the Philadelphia *Independent Gazetteer: or, the Chronicle of Freedom*, Jan. 23, 1788, reprinted in McMaster and Stone, *Pennsylvania*, 637.

[3] *Infra*, c. IX, n. 57.

[4] David Sewall to George Thatcher, Mar. 4, 1788, "Thatcher Papers" (in *Historical Magazine*, 6:257–71, 337–53, 2d ser., 1869), no. 41: "The Printers here have really mended the diction and some of the Sentiments of A. federal Speakers If I may Credit some members of the Convention as well as some of the Spectators General T—— you may suppose for one—The Speakers on that Side in General were really Contemptible in every Sence indeed some of them had Speaches made out of Doors which they read, but read & pronounced in an awkward manner—Who fabricated Mr. N. last Speech I am uncertain—one thing I am satisfied of, he never made it himself not that I conceive it an Elegant one."
"General T——" was Samuel Thompson, windy delegate from Topsham (Maine). "Mr. N." was undoubtedly Samuel Nasson from Sanford (Maine). There are letters to Thatcher in 1788 from Nasson (he signed himself Nayson) indicating he

genre was reported in New Hampshire, although we know from sardonic comments by General Sullivan and John Quincy Adams that here there was town meetings oratory aplenty.[5] In New York Francis Childs concentrated upon the stars at the convention, ignoring remarks by the minor characters.[6] One may suspect that the same thing happened in Virginia. There is often not enough recorded to account for a full day of oratory. But in North Carolina very little appears to have been suppressed. Here the antifederalists' fears, as extravagant as those of timid spinsters peering at nightfall into places of concealment, were dutifully set down.[7] James Iredell handled the publication of these debates.[8] Except that his own able speeches thereby took on an added glow, it is incomprehensible why he did not eliminate these Boeotian harangues.

Allowing even for all the deficiencies in reporting, there is no question but that the new Constitution was thoroughly scrutinized. In the process a whole generation of American political figures was immersed in discussions over the ends of government and over the best means of securing these to a degree never before or since then equalled. It is beyond our purpose to survey in detail more than the debates on the judiciary and matter relating thereto. These debates were significant not alone for what they revealed of contemporary belief and prejudice; they had, too, a prospective potency in that later legislation and even the exercise of the judicial power were to be affected by the public exchanges of opinion. Every member of the first Bench of the Supreme Court and some of their distinguished successors were delegates to their respective state conventions, and so were many future members of the first Congress which was to frame and enact the Judiciary and the Process

---

was not well lettered (*ibid.*, Nos. 18, 37, 49). The like was true of William Widgery (*cf. ibid.*, No. 29) who was described as waging war on the Constitution "the same as a *new light* fighting the *Devil*" (from Jeremiah Hill, Jan. 1, 1788, *ibid.*, No. 9).

The affecting speech of a Berkshire farmer, Jonathan Smith, was apparently not touched up, judging from the reaction of Jeremy Belknap; he lauded it as "true natural eloquence." Belknap to Ebenezer Hazard, Jan. 25, 1788, in "Belknap Papers," II, 9, 10. R. J. Taylor, *Western Massachusetts in the Revolution*, 206, n. 25, describes Smith as "using a studied farmerish style."

[5] *Infra*, nn. 162, 165.

[6] The notes kept by John McKesson, clerk of the convention (NYHS), by Melancton Smith

(NYSL), and, beginning July 14, also by Gilbert Livingston (NYPL), furnish a check on Childs's report, Elliot's source. For example, the McKesson Ms. Notes of Debates for June 25 indicate unreported speeches of Harison and Tredwell on June 23. Speeches of Duane and Jones on June 26 are eliminated by Childs, and of Williams and Jones on June 30. During the last days, not reported by Childs, the Livingston Ms. Notes show a more general participation than theretofore. On the sources for these debates *cf.* the learned Introductory Note in *PAH*, V, 11–13.

[7] *E.g.*, in Elliot, *Debates*, IV, 95, 99, 201–05, 215.

[8] Note by McRee, *Iredell*, II, 235. See also B. P. Robinson, *William R. Davie*, 208–10.

Acts. The lawyers at the conventions had the unusual experience of having to construct and articulate a philosophic appraisal of the judicial process, what its structure should be and how it should function. They had also to weigh time-honored institutions for their value, to consider the relation of the law to the individual and to think a little about its improvement. These were exercises to which men trained in the common law were not prone. There could be no easy recourse to the comfortable generalities of natural law. The problems confronting them were practical and so they were called upon to exert in this context their gifts of prophecy as they would for a client ready to go to law. The impact of this experience was not one quickly spent, particularly as this was a time when circumstance compelled lawyers to make of memory a trustworthy and useful instrument in the practice of their profession. In these debates, therefore, the paradigm of what the Supreme Court should be was established in the minds of the men who were to mold its early history, and thus some of its unique characteristics were predetermined before even the first case was there argued.

DELAWARE, PENNSYLVANIA, NEW JERSEY

THE FIRST STATE to convene was Pennsylvania. But while the debates were going on in Philadelphia the Delaware Convention met. After a four-day sitting, the Constitution was ratified on December 7. Diligent search recently made by an able scholar has failed to yield any trace of the debates in that state.[9] Delaware was strongly federalist in sympathy and there appears to have been no public figure of consequence who was opposed.

Meanwhile, the Pennsylvania contest had been moving slowly along a very stormy track. The elections for the convention, held on November 6, had resulted in what appeared to be a federalist majority. Both Philadelphia City and County had returned a solid ticket of advocates. From the former came James Wilson and Chief Justice Thomas McKean, who were to do the bulk of the arguing for their cause. From Westmoreland County came William Findley, from Cumberland Robert Whitehill and from Fayette John Smilie. These were to be standard-bearers for the antifederalists. Findley and Whitehill had been among those who had sought to prevent a quorum in the assembly when the act to call a convention was moved.[10] Both had signed the *Address* of the assembly minority.

The convention which assembled on November 21 has been described as "a body as characteristic of the State as has ever been

---

[9] J. A. Munroe, *Federalist Delaware, 1775–1815,* 108.

[10] *Supra,* pp. 267–68.

gathered."[11] Religious belief was represented in virtually all of its indigenous manifestations. Nearly all the delegates had been active in public service or in the Revolutionary cause. Present were men of English and Scotch descent as well as of Scotch-Irish and German. In the turbulent state of Pennsylvania politics there was no counting on the result being a foregone conclusion. There was always the chance that the shattered alliance which had sustained the democratical constitution of the state might be repaired by its antifederalist leaders.[12]

The convention was singularly dilatory in proceeding to its main business, particularly as certain delegates had exhibited every sign of spoiling for a fight. On the first day there was a preliminary broil over opening proceedings with prayer. The second day the delegates had the dispiriting experience of attending a college commencement. Not until late in the third day was the Constitution first read. The uproar began on November 24 when McKean moved the ratification of the Constitution.[13] He was followed by Wilson, who in a speech which the *Packet* claimed that "the celebrated Roman orator" would not have blushed to own,[14] undertook to explain the principles that had produced the Constitution. While in form a disclosure of the current of political thinking in the Federal Convention, Wilson's remarks bear on the face of them signs of being rationalizations after the fact. Stripped of the didactic comments on the nature of governments, and the inevitable allusions to history and divers writers, the pith of the speech was, first, that a federal Republic had been decided upon which secured all the internal advantages of a republic and the external dignity and force of a monarchy. In the second place, it had been settled that "whatever object was confined in its nature and operation to a particular State" was to be subject to state government. Matters that involved more than a single state ought to be included in the federal jurisdiction. The interests of the collective body had transcended all else, for no form of government could exist unless private individual rights were subservient to the public and general happiness of the nation.[15]

Wilson's speech was not answered. Instead, for days there was

---

[11] McMaster and Stone, *Pennsylvania*, 13. This work contains the fullest reconstruction of the debates from Lloyd's account and from the newspapers, and is more satisfactory than Elliot (*Debates*, II, 415 *et seq.*), where the Lloyd version alone is used. A recent addition is R. C. Pittman, "Jasper Yeates's Notes on the Pennsylvania Ratifying Convention, 1787," *Wm. and Mary Quarterly*, 22:301, 3d ser., 1965. These notes begin November 30 (hereafter cited as Yeates's Notes).

[12] Brunhouse, *The Counter-Revolution in Pennsylvania, 1776–1790*, 202 *et seq.*

[13] McMaster and Stone, *Pennsylvania*, 218.

[14] *Pennsylvania Packet*, Nov. 27, 1788.

[15] McMaster and Stone, *Pennsylvania*, 218–31.

wrangling over procedures—the desirability of debating the Constitution section by section, whether or not this discussion was to be done in convention or by the body resolving into a committee of the whole,[16] what was to appear in the *Journal*, and in particular the recording of reasons for any dissents. Finally, on Tuesday, November 27, discussion on the merits began.

Wilson opened the debate with an explanation of the preamble. What he may have intended as a mere oratorical flourish—a comparison of its language with the English Bill of Rights and the Magna Carta, to the disparagement of the latter—excited the opposition to a violent attack upon the Constitution for lacking a bill of rights. In the course of this assault miscellaneous grievances were tossed into the discussion—the insufficiency of the commissions to the Federal Convention for the confection of a new Constitution, the creation of a consolidated government, the lack of annual elections to Congress and a variety of other familiar objections. Despite the resolution to have a section by section discussion, Wilson was trapped into a defense of the whole plan.[17] McKean, who followed, noted the point of order, but proceeded in a similar vein. Discoursing on the legislative powers, he listed those which were not objected to, and answered the complaints about others. The supreme law of the land clause, he asserted, meant no more than that laws made in pursuance of the Constitution were binding on all states. Said he, "I earnestly hope, Sir, that the statutes of the federal government will last till they become the common law of the land, as excellent and as much valued as that which we have hitherto fondly denominated the birthright of an American."[18] It is interesting to note that a day earlier McKean, in a speech not reported, had stated that among other means, Congress would be restrained "By the Judges deciding agst. the Legislature in Favor of the Constu."[19]

When the convention resumed on November 30, having again spent a day indulging its esoteric appetite for academic exercises,[20] the antifederalists continued their blunderbuss attack. Anthony Wayne noted Wilson as saying that he intended to answer objections worthy of an answer, otherwise he would "not trouble the Convention with any further observations."[21] He was soon goaded into more speech-making.

---

[16] This was moved by Whitehill on the ground that it would give more time for members to make up their minds. The federalists opposed on the grounds that no minutes would be kept and people would be left in ignorance of what went on. The motion was defeated. *Ibid.*, 236–37.

[17] *Ibid.*, 263–71.

[18] *Ibid.*, 277.

[19] Wilson's Notes, *ibid.*, 766.

[20] "Exercises of the Young Gentlemen of the German Lutheran Academy," *ibid.*, 283.

[21] Ms. Minutes 2 and 3, Anthony Wayne Papers (William L. Clements Library, University of Michigan).

For in spite of an effort by Timothy Pickering, seconded by Stephen Chambers, delegates from Lancaster, to have the antifederalists present their objections in an orderly manner,[22] they remained intractable. When, among other matters, the judiciary was listed by Findley as tending to the destruction of state sovereignty because its power was coextensive with the legislative,[23] James Wilson undertook to reply. It was the ablest speech Wilson had yet made and is particularly interesting because this future justice of the Supreme Court sets out his understanding of the judicial power in the federal system.

For judicial power to be coextensive with the objects of the national government was agreeable to the idea of magistracy in every government. The judicial department was considered as a part of the executive authority of every government. It should not be so restrained as not to be able to perform its functions with full effect. The legislature ought not to make laws which could not be carried out. At the same time, it was essential for stability and security that it be restrained: "There should not only be what we call a *passive* but an *active* power over it."[24] He pointed with scorn to performances in Pennsylvania where laws made at one session were so often repealed in the next.

Under the new plan the restraints existed in the division of legislative power itself. They might likewise arise from the interference of officers in the executive and judicial departments, and finally, from the people themselves. The restraints emanating from the judicial department derived from that fact that the Constitution was paramount to the power of the legislature acting under it. "For it is possible that the legislature, when acting in that capacity, may transgress the bounds assigned to it, and an act may pass in the usual *mode* notwithstanding that transgression; but when it comes to be discussed before the judges, when they consider its principles, and find it to be incompatible with the superior powers of the constitution, it is their duty to pronounce it void; and judges independent, and not obliged to look to every session for a continuance of their salaries, will behave with intrepidity and refuse to the act the sanction of judicial authority."[25]

This speech of Wilson's was published in full by the reporter Lloyd, and although there is no evidence of how widely this pamphlet was read,[26] the Pennsylvanians had opportunity to learn that one

---

[22] Yeates's Notes, at 305; Wilson's Notes, in McMaster and Stone, *Pennsylvania*, 770.

[23] McMaster and Stone, *Pennsylvania*, 300; Wilson's Notes, *ibid.*, 770–71, indicate both Smilie and Whitehill spoke and that more was urged against the judiciary than appeared in the newspaper account of Findley's speech. Yeates's Notes here are sparse.

[24] Taken from Lloyd's account, in McMaster and Stone, *Pennsylvania*, 304; Elliot, *Debates*, II, 445.

[25] McMaster and Stone, *Pennsylvania*, 304–05.

[26] The publication date of Lloyd's

Framer, at least, believed that judicial control of legislation was implicit in the system. What is strange is that the antifederalists, who were quick to pounce on anything that could be converted into a reproach of the proposed system, should not immediately have joined issue. As it was, some days were to elapse before they came up with an answer.[27]

With the disappearance of antifederalist speeches from the newspapers, the substance of their day-by-day objections can be gathered only from terse statements in the press, from the answering arguments of the federalists, from the brief notes kept by Wilson for his own replies and by Jasper Yeates. Unfortunately, the manner in which Wilson scrambled an opponent's points, and those with which he intended to meet them, often raises insurmountable difficulties. Yeates is usually meagre. Nevertheless, it is apparent that the debate spread over a very wide range of matter, such as the infrequency of elections, the taxing power, and treaty-making, to which, the opposition objected among other things, because a ministerial act was elevated to the supreme law of the land.

In the debate on December 4 Smilie of the opposition had ready his riposte to Wilson's claim that the courts would hold void unconstitutional Acts of Congress. He did not challenge the propriety of the claim, but averred that the independence of the judges was not secured, for if they refused to execute any law passed contrary to the Constitution, they would be impeached by the House and it would then be the duty of the Senate to determine whether or not the law was unconstitutional and whether the judges were not bound by it.[28] Wilson's answer was to ask what House would dare to impeach or Senate commit for the performance of their duty.[29] Puzzled, the *Pennsylvania Packet* queried whether the doctrine of an unconstitutional law being void *ipso facto* had been held by the Supreme Court of Pennsylvania.[30]

---

volume was Feb. 4, 1788 (*cf. Pennsylvania Packet*, Feb. 9, 1788). The newspaper version was in earlier circulation.

[27] Greenleaf in his *New-York Journal* of Dec. 14, 1787, published what appears to be an editorial setting out Wilson's ideas. Two weeks later the *Worcester Magazine* (IV, 163) printed part of the speech.

[28] Wilson's Notes, in McMaster and Stone, *Pennsylvania*, 774; amplified in Wilson's speech, *ibid.*, 340. Yeates records Wilson as saying this day, "I wish to hear and sub[sequently] answer every Objection against the new Constitution." What was offered concerned primarily the objection to the want of a bill of rights; that the government would be a consolidated one and swallow up the state legislature; that the Senate had a dangerous power of corrupting "by their Offices, the Representatives of the People." There follow notes of Wilson's answers to these points, but nothing on the judicial. Yeates's Notes, at 306–08.

[29] McMaster and Stone, *Pennsylvania*, 340.

[30] *Pennsylvania Packet*, Dec. 10, 1787.

It was not until three days later that a general assault on the judiciary was made. Whitehill[31] claimed that the judicial department was blended with and would absorb the judicial powers of the states —there was nothing to stop this. There must be a great number of inferior courts in the several states. One could not be enough—there should be one for each county with the resultant multiplication of officials. Any sort of action "by Contrivance" could be brought in federal courts; there could be equity as well as law courts—a horror to citizens of Pennsylvania which had no Chancery Courts. The appeals to the Supreme Court would put it in the power of the rich to oppress the poor. The "general Courts" might alter the course of descent and establish primogeniture. There would be no civil jury. Treaties might be made to absorb liberty of conscience, trial by jury and all liberties.

Mr. Smilie had some terrors of his own to add—adverting to the case of the sloop *Active*, he insisted that facts found by a jury should never be re-examined; he suspected an intention to substitute civil for common law; and that a system of double courts would be an unbearable expense. Mr. Findley, too, believed some provision for jury trial must be added since judges were better "for the Guard of Juries." He suggested, further, that there should be a declaration establishing trial by jury in civil cases as hitherto in the several states or in the state where the case arose. He objected to the diversity jurisdiction, which he said might introduce doubts in the dealings between citizens of Pennsylvania and New Jersey.[32]

To all this Wilson delivered a long analysis of Article III.[33] Most of what he said was a repetition of the explanations already standard in the federalist camp. What he did with particular effect was to underline existing difficulties inherent in the policies of the several states as respects the harassment of creditors, the things done to British creditors in defiance of the peace treaty that had postponed the surrender of the western posts. He pointed out that whenever the general government was a party against a citizen the trial was guarded by the Constitution itself—as in treason. As for a jury trial safeguard in civil cases, he had no doubt the legislative department would make regulations "as agreeable to the habits and wishes of the particular States as possible." He repudiated the contention of Whitehill that the Congress might enact laws inconsistent with the Constitution, and that therefore the power of judges was dangerous. If, said Wilson, a law was made inconsistent

---

[31] Wilson's Notes, in McMaster and Stone, *Pennsylvania*, 779; Yeates's Notes, at 310.

[32] Wilson's Notes, in McMaster and Stone, *Pennsylvania*, 780–81; Yeates's Notes, at 311.

[33] McMaster and Stone, *Pennsylvania*, 351–59. Yeates (at 310–11) recorded only a few remarks by Wilson.

with the powers vested by "this instrument" in Congress, the judges in consequence of their independence and the definition of the particular powers of government would declare such law null and void. "For the power of the constitution predominates."[34]

The following day was devoted to a discussion of jury trial, and every possible animadversion, too tedious to list, was paraded by the opposition.[35] There was a ludicrous exchange between Findley and Wilson over the question of whether or not Sweden had trial by jury, and subsequently an altercation over alleged "indecent" remarks by Smilie concerning Chief Justice McKean.[36] According to Wilson's notes the antifederalists cited a substantial body of authority in connection with virtues of the jury. Besides the inevitable Blackstone, they had numerous references to English precedents and came up also with *Forsey v. Cunningham*, the New York colonial case which "Centinel" had cited on the appeal question.[37] The *Pennsylvania Packet* reported that in consequence of the repeated call from the opposition for an answer to their argument McKean arose. He remarked that he had heard and read the objections in "Centinel," *Brutus* and *Cincinnatus*.[38] To this satirical comment he added that all the objections to the Constitution could have been delivered in two hours, and that the excess of time had been consumed in trifling debate. Smilie then remarked that McKean had treated the opposition with contempt, and spoke of his "magisterial air." This, Stephen Chambers, a federalist, objected to as indecent language, since he took it to be an allusion to McKean as a judge. A protracted wrangle ended with cries to adjourn.[39]

When the convention resumed on Monday, December 10, three more days were spent in speech-making. Chief Justice McKean con-

---

[34] McMaster and Stone, *Pennsylvania*, 354.

[35] The most exhaustive list of objections was kept by Wilson in his Notes (McMaster and Stone, *Pennsylvania*, 781–82). The listing in Yeates's Notes (at 311–12) is much shorter.

[36] The account in McMaster and Stone, *Pennsylvania*, 360–61, taken from the *Pennsylvania Packet*. Dr. William Shippen wrote to his son on Dec. 8, 1787, giving an account that varies some from the one in the *Pennsylvania Packet*. Findley, he thought, had proven himself superior to Wilson and the whole convention—"he triumphed over McKean & Wilson to their infinite mortification." When Wilson called for authority on trial

by jury in Sweden, Findley produced the "Modern Un. History & 3 Blackstone & severely remarked that it might be excusable in the Chief Justice of Pennsylvania & Counsellor of the City to forget such a circumstance in a history but I will observe that had my son been at the study of the law 6 months & not known such a passage in Blackstone I would be justifiable in whipping him." A newspaper writer thought that sufficient ground for impeachment existed. Shippen Mss. (LC).

[37] *Supra*, c. VI, p. 284.

[38] Wilson's Notes, in McMaster and Stone, *Pennsylvania*, 782.

[39] McMaster and Stone, *Pennsylvania*, 361 *et seq.*

sumed most of the first day summarizing the arguments of the anti-federalists and offering his answers.[40] He was followed on Tuesday by Wilson, who appears to have spoken virtually without interruption both morning and afternoon.[41] He assembled and correlated the arguments of the antifederalists to the articles of the Constitution to which they pertained, thus giving the tenor of the whole debate a quality of orderliness it had hitherto not possessed. Much of what he said in reply retravelled familiar ground. But there were two points which deserve notice. Wilson denied flatly that there was a trace of compact in the new system, and expressed his disbelief that the members of the convention thought that they were making a contract. This was a government founded on the power of the people. He well knew the "commonplace rant of state sovereignties" and that government was founded in original compact. This did not "accede very well with the true principle of free government." It did not even accord with experience, nor could it be supported consistently with the best principles of government. To admit it was to exclude the idea of amendment. Nothing of this inhered in the new system. It was the ordinance and establishment of the people.[42]

The second point arose in connection with a complaint that the judges would not be independent because they might hold other offices that might depend on the legislature. Wilson claimed that no sinecure could be conferred upon them except by the concurrence of the President and both houses of the Congress. Wilson did not come to grips with the basic question of the propriety of multiple office-holding, or of the compatibility of even casual employment *extra officio* with the dignity of the judicial office. Pennsylvania had forbidden its judges to hold other offices. Wilson argued that it was not to be expected that

---

[40] *Ibid.*, 364–65, from the *Pennsylvania Packet*; *ibid.*, 365–79, from Lloyd's report. Yeates's Notes (at 313–15) have a detailed summary of the main points.

[41] Yeates (at 315) states that the Convention began at 10:22 A.M. and ended at 1 P.M. Wilson resumed at 4:10 P.M. and spoke again for two hours.

[42] McMaster and Stone, *Pennsylvania*, 383 *et seq.* The version in Yeates's Notes (at 315) reads:

That Government is founded on Contract does not appear to be founded on Experience or supported upon the Principles of Freedom and Reason.

The Doctrine is politically true in Gr[eat] Brit[ain] because it was recognized at the Revolution.

It destroys the Rights of Amendment—because the Contract if made ought to be persued and kept up.

In America the Supreme Power resides [in] the People who have it in their Power to ordain such Systems as may be most suitable to their Interests. In this Instance they differ from Gr[eat] Brit[ain].

Why then talk of a Violation of the Confederation? Cannot the People change their Constitution if they find thereby their common Safety endangered?

other states should be required to accommodate themselves to Pennsylvania.[43] He was outspokenly an advocate of the superficial "best man" theory, and his own later conduct of his personal affairs shows clearly enough that he did not cherish a sufficiently lofty conception of the judicial office.

As matters drew to a close, the nature of the final decision was apparent. The antifederalists had cajoled no waverer into their camp. There is never a hint that they had effected any conversions. Nevertheless, on the morning of December 12 and into the early afternoon they launched a final assault on the Constitution.[44] Once more those resurrected paladins, Locke and Montesquieu, were thrown into the fray. Once more were made the dire predictions of inevitable monarchy, the threat of inevitable civil war. This was a hopeless effort. The newspapers barely noticed it, although in a special New Year's poem of the *Packet* it was inelegantly, if unintentionally, memorialized in the line: "Some in despair belch'd out their doubts and fears."

At the end of these harangues the question was called for on the motion of ratification. Dr. Benjamin Rush, who appears to have been relatively silent during most of the proceedings, thereupon craved the patience of the convention and then entered into a "metaphysical argument." He discoursed on the decay of morals and, commenting on the origin of the proposed system, declaimed that he believed that the hand of God had been employed in this work.[45] Unheeding of the Doctor's "pathetic appeal to the opposition," Mr. Whitehill remarked that he regretted that so imperfect a work should have been ascribed to God.[46] He thereupon presented petitions from Cumberland County praying no adoption without amendments. McKean opposed the acceptance of the petitions. Mr. Whitehill thereupon read and offered as the ground for adjourning to some remote day a list of articles either to be taken collectively as a bill of rights or as amendments to the proposed form of government.[47]

As for the judiciary, the proposed Article 14 eliminated the clause of Article III, section 2: "all cases, in law and equity, arising under this Constitution, the laws of the United States, and treaties made, or which shall be made, under their authority." Federal jurisdiction in criminal cases was to be limited to matter expressly stated in the Constitution. Congress was to be forbidden to pass acts altering laws of descent and distribution, or the regulation of contracts in the individual states.[48]

In the uproar which followed the presentation of the articles to

---

[43] McMaster and Stone, *Pennsylvania*, 401 *et seq.*
[44] Wilson's Notes, *ibid.*, 784–85.
[45] McMaster and Stone, *Pennsyl-*
vania, 419–20.
[46] *Ibid.*, 420.
[47] *Ibid.*, 421 *et seq.*
[48] *Ibid.*, 423.

the chair, Wilson finally demanded a written motion. This was done. The purport was that there should be adjournment to enable the people to study the proposals, to have opportunity to learn what other states would offer as amendments, and that these propositions be offered to Congress to be considered by the United States before final ratification. An apparently bitter debate followed and eventually the motion was lost 46–23. Then the main question was put which passed by the same margin.[49] "The mob in the streets," wrote Dr. Shippen sourly, "are huzzaing triumphantly on the great event, perfectly ignorant whether it will make them free or slaves."[50]

The convention reassembled to wrangle over the insertion of Whitehill's "articles" in its journal, and to sign the formal instrument of ratification. The opposition refused to join in this, Mr. Smilie remarking that he would never allow his hand in so gross a manner to give the lie to his heart and tongue.[51]

Six days after the Pennsylvania ratification New Jersey followed suit, but by a unanimous vote.[52] Nothing is known of the course of the debate there—the only record is the *Journal* of the convention that reveals nothing of significance.[53] But if the Pennsylvania federalists could rejoice that three states had acted favorably, the day of the New Jersey ratification (December 18, 1787) brought solemn warning that their adversaries were by no means finished.[54] The warning was in the form of an "Address," signed by twenty-one of the Pennsylvania minority, giving the reasons of dissent. A bitter and partisan review of the events leading up to the Constitutional Convention at Philadelphia where "the gilded chains" were forged, was followed by an account of the imbroglio in the Pennsylvania Assembly, the charge that only 13,000 of the eligible 70,000 freemen had voted in the elections for the state convention. The minority charged further that they had been prevented from voting on particular sections or entering reasons of dissent. They

---

[49] *Minutes of the Convention of the Commonwealth of Pennsylvania . . . for the Purpose of Taking into Consideration the Constitution framed by the late Federal Convention . . .* (1787), 12–14.

[50] To Thomas Lee Shippen, Dec. 12, 1787, Shippen Mss. (LC).

[51] The formal ratification in *Doc. Hist. Const.*, II, 27–45. For Smilie's comment, McMaster and Stone, *Pennsylvania*, 428.

[52] *Doc. Hist. Const.*, II, 46–64.

[53] *The Minutes of the Convention of the State of New Jersey . . .* (1787)

reveal nothing of consequence. Mr. R. P. McCormick, whose study, *Experiment in Independence: New Jersey in the Critical Period, 1781–1789,* is a remarkably thorough study of contemporary materials, failed to exhume any material on the course of the debates at Trenton. According to an account in the *Pennsylvania Packet,* Jan. 1, 1788, there were objections, but Breareley "bore down all opposition."

[54] Material on subsequent moves in McMaster and Stone, *Pennsylvania,* c. VI.

set out at large the amendments they had proposed. They entered at length into all the objections raised in convention.[55]

The *Address and Reasons for Dissent* was printed in the *Pennsylvania Packet*[56] as well as in broadside form and it had wide circulation. It appeared in the *New-York Journal* in three successive numbers, December 27–31. A month later it was reprinted in the *Providence Gazette and Country Journal*[57] and in *The United States Chronicle*.[58] It was offered for sale by the Boston *American Herald* when the Massachusetts Convention assembled there. One who signed himself "America" berated the Pennsylvania minority in the New York *Daily Advertiser*[59] and accused them of consummate arrogance. Even Hamilton deigned to take notice of the defects of their jury trial proposal.[60] It is not to be supposed from the to-do caused by this document that it was a state paper of distinction. It was not well drawn, the proposed amendments in particular were clumsily drafted. Nevertheless, the *Address* was politically significant in that it set out in its articles of amendment subject matter about which there had been much windy argument. It provided a species of platform and suggested the tactic of conditional ratification that was to afflict conventions in other states.

GEORGIA, CONNECTICUT

THE STORM AND strife in Pennsylvania had not subsided when the Georgia Convention met and after a week's debate, not reported, ratified on January 2, 1788.[61] Two days later the Connecticut Convention opened its sessions at Hartford.[62] This state, which had been content to continue its corporate charter as its fundamental law, enjoyed by custom a remarkably stable governing body. It was almost as if those free of the corporation were indisposed to remove directors whose government of the company had proven satisfactory.[63] In any event, the same names appeared year after year as assistants, and while

---

[55] Printed, *ibid.*, 454–83. It was issued in broadside form (copy in NYHS), a fact which greatly facilitated circulation.

[56] Dec. 18, 1787.

[57] Jan. 26, 1788.

[58] Jan. 31, 1788.

[59] Dec. 31, 1787.

[60] *Supra*, pp. 318–19.

[61] The ratification is in *Doc. Hist. Const.*, II, 65. The *Journal* of the convention, which is not informative, is reprinted in *Georgia Historical Quarterly*, 10: 223–37, 1926.

[62] The convention was authorized at the October session of the legislature. *Public Records of the State of Connecticut*, VI, 355. All those qualified in town meetings were qualified to choose delegates. This was a broader franchise than if it had been confined to those free of the corporation.

[63] The best available discussion of Connecticut background is in O. Zeichner, *Connecticut's Years of Controversy, 1750–1776*; it is considered somewhat also in G. Groce, *William Samuel Johnson*. Neither of these

one may applaud devotion to public service, the system there produced something very close to a governing class. The public employments of Oliver Ellsworth, future Chief Justice of the United States Supreme Court, are an example.[64] This stability, indeed near-stagnation, is reflected in the statute book and accounts for the absence of truly venturesome legislation to solve some of the problems that beset the state, dependent like New Jersey on the ports of its neighbors. This dependency played a role in Connecticut's attitude toward the new government.

Only six of the speeches made—two by Ellsworth—have been published.[65] Ellsworth's opening speech was on the need of union, and the need of an energetic system. There was a fine parade of historical examples of confederacies and their weaknesses—a demagogic reference to Connecticut's grievances as tributary to New York and Massachusetts, and the dangers threatened when even the present shadow of a national government should be gone. On Congress's power to tax, Ellsworth delivered a well-reasoned defense, again with a direct appeal to Connecticut's self-interest. He handled deftly the antifederalist objection that the two legislative powers, state and federal, could not coexist. In this connection was made the only reference to judicial power, but it was a significant one. If the United States went beyond its powers, said he, "if they make a law which the constitution does not authorise it is void; and the judicial power, the national judges, who to secure their impartiality, are to be made independent, will declare it to be void." Similarly, if the states overstepped with a law that was a usurpation on the general government, the judges would mete out the same treatment.[66] Sixty years earlier the Connecticut men had indignantly recoiled from this doctrine when the Privy Council had declared void the colony intestacy law.[67] It was now preached to them apparently without protest.

---

writers has noticed the translation and persistence in Connecticut of English corporate traditions and practices as related either to borough or commercial company organization.

[64] See W. G. Brown, *The Life of Oliver Ellsworth*. Additional data in Ms. Connecticut Archives, 1st ser., Towns and Lands IX, 321b; X, 53cq, 62; Ecclesiastical XV, 138b; Crimes and Misdemeanors VI, 149a, 151–53, 166b, 275b, 409a; Finance and Currency V, 159b, 160d, 161ac, 221a; Revolutionary War, 1st–2d ser., XXVII, 98; XXVIII, 346; XXXII, 390; and 3d ser., I, 3a; VI, 113a, 123a (Conn. State Lib., Hartford).

[65] The best assemblage of material has been made by Professor L. W. Labaree in *Public Records of the State of Connecticut*, VI, 548, App. B. It is more complete than the matter in Elliot, *Debates*, II, 185 *et seq.* There is an account of the convention by B. C. Steiner in his "Connecticut's Ratification of the Federal Constitution," Am. Antiquarian Soc. *Proc.*, 25:70–127, n.s., 1915.

[66] *Public Records of the State of Connecticut*, VI, 563.

[67] J. H. Smith, *Appeals to the Privy Council from the American Plantations*, 551 et seq.

Places Where the Supreme Court Held Its Terms

THE NEW YORK MERCHANTS EXCHANGE.
Here the first terms of the Supreme Court of the United States were held, 1790.
Original Drawing, Emmet Collection, No. 1129.
(Courtesy of the Manuscript Division, New York Public Library, Astor, Lenox and Tilden Foundations)

OLD CITY HALL, PHILADELPHIA,
on the far left, site of the Mayor's Court Room where the Supreme Court of the United States met,
August term, 1791–February term, 1800. The building to the right is the County Court House (Congress
Hall) where the August term, 1800, was held.

The Munro Clock Room

What was published about this convention discloses nothing of the temper of their discussions. The President of Yale described the assemblage as the grandest "of sensible & worthy Characters that ever met together in this State."[68] The *Connecticut Courant* lauded the learning and eloquence of Johnson, the genuine good sense and discernment of Sherman and the "Demosthenan energy" of Ellsworth.[69] Hugh Ledlie, onetime Son of Liberty, had another story to tell.[70] Writing to John Lamb, he complained that the federalists had carried on with a high hand. There were insinuations, he wrote, that Connecticut paid annually £8,000 of the New York impost, and that the salaries of Lamb, Clinton and other antifederalists were in this way paid by Connecticut; that Lamb got £900 from this source to print and circulate the *Federal Farmer*. Ledlie declared that he did not like the "guilded pill" and was thankful some could "discern Arsanac & poison through the outside cover." The antifederalists, he continued, were the best orators but they were browbeaten "by many of those Ciceros as they think themselves, & others of superiour rank as they call themselves, as also by the unthinking deluded multitude who were previously convened, as it is thought by many for that purpose, which together with the Shuffling & stamping of feet, coughing, Halking, spitting & Whispering as well by some of the members as spectators with other interruptions etc. etc. too many to be innumerated."[71]

As Ledlie noticed, midwinter in New England is not the most clement or salubrious time for holding a meeting. But the proceedings continued for five days until the final vote was taken. One hundred and twenty-eight voted in favor of ratification;[72] there were forty "righteous men that did not bow the Knee to Baal."[73]

MASSACHUSETTS

EXCEPT FOR RHODE ISLAND which had become a pariah in the minds of sober and propertied persons, the events in no state had contributed more to make Americans receptive to the idea of a stronger national government than those in Massachusetts. These events had been the fruits of circumstance, induced, it is true, by bad political

---

[68] F. Dexter, ed., *Literary Diary of Ezra Stiles*, (New York: Charles Scribner's Sons, 1901), III, 298.

[69] Quoted in *Public Records of the State of Connecticut*, VI, 564.

[70] Ledlie to John Lamb, Jan. 15, 1788, Ms. Lamb Papers, Box 5 (NYHS).

[71] But Collier's (Litchfield) *Weekly Monitor* of January 14, in a glowing and fulsome account of the convention, reported: "A very numerous and respectable audience attended the debates, with great decency." Quoted in *Public Records of the State of Connecticut*, VI, 572.

[72] The vote, *ibid.*, 569-71.

[73] Ledlie to Lamb, *supra*, n. 70.

management, but never seriously anticipated. The goings on in the western counties of the state in 1786–87—the seditious meetings, the forcible closing of the courts, and finally, armed rebellion—had, as nothing else, thoroughly alarmed political leaders everywhere.[74] Jefferson was perhaps the only illustrious contemporary who discerned benefit in these happenings, not because of the rebels' grievances, which were substantial, but because of their actions. Both to Madison and to John Adams' son-in-law he waxed almost lyrical on the therapeutic qualities of "a little rebellion now and then."[75] But officials, lawyers and people who were old-fashioned enough to regard an attack on a government arsenal as a step toward anarchy were understandably apprehensive.[76] To be sure, there had been occasions years not long past when the fractious inhabitants of western Massachusetts had closed the courts or had made riotous attempts to prevent sittings.[77] The western border,

---

[74] The insurrection was so unusually newsworthy that items on particular events were reported in newspapers all along the Atlantic coast. For a sampling of the coverage see App. C in A. E. Morse, *The Federalist Party in Massachusetts to the Year 1800*. The reactions to these events are registered in the published correspondence of contemporaries. There is no valid reason to discount this body of opinion solely because it came from propertied persons.

[75] To Madison, Jan. 30, 1787, in *Papers of Jefferson*, XI, 92, 93; to Madison, Dec. 20, 1787, *ibid.*, XII, 438, 442; to W. S. Smith, Nov. 13, 1787, *ibid.*, 355.

[76] A modern study of the Confederation period, Jensen's *The New Nation*, virtually ignores the rebellion. The most extensive reference (p. 56) is in connection with a denigration of Benjamin Lincoln—"the only successful military exploit he ever engaged in was during Shays' Rebellion when he marched mercenary troops against his fellow citizens in western Massachusetts. His conquest of the disorganized farmers who lived there was an unquestioned victory." The "mercenary troops" referred to could be none other than the militia who were sent out to cope with the rebellion. The governor's messages and the acts and resolves of the General Court consistently refer to the militia. In Febru-

ary 1787 Governor James Bowdoin asked for authority to empower Lincoln to enlist men to serve beyond the limit for which the militia had been called. When affairs had become critical and because the treasury was without funds, certain private individuals loaned money which Minot (*infra*) states was used for supplies. The General Court authorized repayment and also payment for the troops. The legislative picture can be gathered from *Mass. Acts and Resolves 1786–87* (reprint 1893); see the Act of Feb. 6, 1787, at 165–66; Resolves, *ibid.*, at 426–28, 441–42, 443, 449, 458–59, 495–96, 498–99, 502–05; Governor's Messages, *ibid.*, at 959–67, 972–73.

Shays had organized his men into a semblance of military order. But they were not obedient, as the attack on the Springfield arsenal shows. On the whole affair see G. R. Minot, *The History of the Insurrections in Massachusetts, in the Year MDCCLXXXVI, and the Rebellion Consequent Thereon*. An account with sympathy for the rebels' troubles in B. Hammond, *Banks and Politics in America from the Revolution to the Civil War* (Princeton, N. J.: Princeton University Press, 1957), 96–97.

[77] In Berkshire County the courts, closed in 1774, had not reopened until 1780 (D. Field, ed., *A History of the County of Berkshire* [1829], 111, 125). In 1782 an attempt was made to break

indeed, had a history of sporadic riots and affrays for more than thirty years.[78] Nothing on the scale of Shays' Rebellion, however, where resort to ordinary measures of law enforcement were utterly vain, had yet happened. Only when the Commonwealth administered the same form of violent physic as that applied by the rebels was a cure of recurrent tumult effected.

The temper of the western Massachusetts towns being one of long-standing truculence, there was no reason to believe them utterly chastened by the measures taken against the uprising. The pro-Constitution men had consequently serious cause to worry. On October 18, 1787, Governor Hancock had transmitted the Constitution and accompanying documents to the General Court in a tepid and non-committal message. The next day a joint committee reported on this portion of the message.[79] The senate perfected a resolution recommending that the several towns and districts of the Commonwealth elect delegates not exceeding their representation in the lower house. The Secretary was to send printed copies of the papers received from Congress to the sheriffs with directions that these be delivered to the selectmen of each town and district.[80]

A newspaper report indicates that only in the house of representatives was there sharp debate, the opposition raising the question of the sufficiency of the Philadelphia delegates' commissions. In the end, however, the resolution was approved 129–32.[81] William Jackson reported

---

up court sessions in Northampton (J. G. Holland, *History of Western Massachusetts* [1855], I, 231; R. Moody, "Samuel Ely: Forerunner of Shays," *New England Quarterly*, 5:105, 1932). For a 1783 attack at Springfield, see A. M. Copeland, *Our Country and its people: A History of Hampden County, Massachusetts* (Boston: The Century Memorial Publishing Co., 1902), I, 87. See also the documents appended to S. T. Riley, "Dr. William Whiting and Shays' Rebellion," *Am. Antiquarian Soc. Proc.*, 66:119 *et seq. n.s.* 1956. A measured account of the western problem is given by R. J. Taylor, *Western Massachusetts in the Revolution*.

[78] Beginning in 1752 and for years thereafter the Hampshire (later Berkshire) County men had engaged in a succession of violent affrays with New Yorkers in connection with disputed boundary lands. See *Doc. Hist. N.Y.*, III, for documents. After demarcation was agreed upon in 1773 (*Docs. Rel.*

Col. Hist. N.Y., VIII, 371), the troubles continued. In April 1775 Colden of New York reported the incitations of riots in newly created Cumberland County by the Massachusetts bordermen and the carrying of prisoners into that state. *The Colden Letter Books*, II, 395–400.

[79] *Debates and Proceedings in the Convention of the Commonwealth of Massachusetts held in the Year 1788* (1856), 19 (hereafter cited as *Massachusetts Debates*). This edition contains the *Journal*, which Elliot does not; only the debates are in Elliot, *Debates*, II, 1–183. For some additional light see the notes of the debates kept by the Rev. Jeremy Belknap and printed in Mass. Hist. Soc. *Proc.* for 1855–1858 (1859), 296–304. Some notes kept by William Cushing are among the Ms. Cushing Papers (MHS).

[80] *Massachusetts Debates*, 19.

[81] *Ibid.*, 21.

341

to General Knox that the majority was made possible by an amendment that the state treasurer and not the towns pay the delegates.[82]

The decorous tone of the proceedings in the General Court commented upon by the press was characteristic also of much of the propaganda written by Massachusetts leaders. There were exceptions. One writing as *Cassius*, and said to be James Sullivan, did not disdain to stoop to occasional invective. His comment on the supreme law of the land clause will serve as an example. It was, he wrote, an article "Knaves and blockheads have so often dressed up in false colors."[83] This writer took the position that laws not authorized by the Constitution were a nullity; but he did not take the final step of asserting that ultimate decision would lie with the courts.[84] As we have seen, James Winthrop, librarian of Harvard College, although not to be classed as a leader, did not regard appeals to prejudice to be beneath him.[85] But the deviations from intellectual sobriety were unusual.[86] The local diet was enriched by publication of some out-of-state writing—"Old Whig," *Cato, Publius*, "Centinel" and *Brutus*[87]—and selections from some of the raffish Philadelphia and New York publications served to ginger up matters.[88]

It may be supposed that copies of the Constitution having been sent abroad to all the towns, there was a very ample local discussion of its provisions. The Massachusetts voters had had practice at this sort of thing on the two earlier occasions when they had been called upon to pass on proposed state constitutions.[89] The fact that the

---

[82] Oct. 27, 1787, Ms. Knox Papers, XXI, 23 (MHS).

[83] Ford, *Essays*, 45. T. Amory, *Life of James Sullivan* (1859), I, 227, is non-committal. Ford misstates his position.

[84] Ford, *Essays*, 46.

[85] *Supra*, p. 270, n. 61. Some of the Massachusetts writing is discussed in S. Harding, *The Contest over the Ratification of the Federal Constitution in the State of Massachusetts*, *passim*. This work is strongly infected with a "class war" outlook.

[86] Even the pieces which aimed at wit resembled the leaden-winged flights of the "Hartford Wits," as, for example, the "Political Dialogue of Mr. Grumble and Mr. Union," Boston *Massachusetts Centinel*, Oct. 24, 1787; and the "Dialogue of Mr. & and Mr. Z," *ibid.*, Oct. 31, Nov. 7, 1787.

[87] "Old Whig," *Massachusetts Centinel*, Oct. 27, 1787; *Cato*, Boston *American Herald*, Oct. 8 and 22, 1787; *Publius, ibid.*, Nov. 12, Dec. 3, 10, and 24, 1787, Jan. 7, 1788; "Centinel," *ibid.*, Nov. 19, 1787, Jan. 7, 1788; *Brutus, ibid.*, Dec. 31, 1787.

[88] For example, "True Whig," *Massachusetts Centinel*, Dec. 22, 1787; "The Couching Needle," *American Herald*, Oct. 29, 1787; the rough piece, "Examiner No. III," *ibid.*, Dec. 31, 1787; *Curtiopolis*, in *Massachusetts Centinel*, Feb. 9, 1788. There were numerous others.

[89] Generally, H. A. Cushing, *History of the Transition from Provincial to Commonwealth Government in Massachusetts*, 214 *et seq.*, 264 *et seq.* On the 1778 submission see T. Parsons, Jr., *Memoir of Theophilus Parsons*, 46, App. I; Charles Francis Adams' notes, in Adams' *Works*, IV, 213 *et seq.*; letter to Timothy Pickering from his brother, May 30, 1778, and N. P. Sergeant to Timothy

suffrage, as we now have every reason to believe, was broadly based[90] made the education of opinion extremely important in the counties where the rebellious spirit had so recently manifested itself. General Knox, who was kept *au courant* by Boston friends,[91] described the three "parties" in the state as consisting first of the commercial interest, to which were added the bar, the clergy, all the officers of the late army and the neighborhoods of the great towns. This group, probably three sevenths of the whole, was "for the most vigorous government." The second group, formerly the province of Maine, amounted to two sevenths, and was disposed toward the Constitution solely as it might affect the possibility of Maine becoming an independent state. The third party was the insurgents and their sympathizers, "the great majority of whom are for an annihilation of debt public & private." This group, about two sevenths, was against the Constitution.[92]

As important as the divisions depicted by Knox was the fact that certain political figures had a following whose votes were bound to be affected by the stands of its leaders. Ex-Governor James Bowdoin had already indicated his support of the Constitution; not so Nathan Dane who had supported Richard Henry Lee in his moves against the new plan when it was submitted to Congress.[93] John Hancock had been noncommittal and most important of all, the old lion, Samuel Adams, was reputedly opposed.[94] He was the president of the senate, and R. H. Lee, knowing Adams' influence, had worked to draw him into the antifederalist camp.[95]

The convention assembled on January 9, 1788, and some 364 dele-

---

Pickering, May 28, 1778, Ms. Pickering Papers (Essex Inst., Salem, Mass.). On the 1780 submission see O. Handlin and M. F. Handlin, *Commonwealth: A Study of the Role of Government in the American Economy: Massachusetts, 1774–1861*, 25.

[90] R. E. Brown, *Middle-Class Democracy and the Revolution in Massachusetts, 1691–1780*, 384 et seq.

[91] Some of these letters from Gorham and Henry Jackson are reprinted in E. F. Stone, "Parsons and the Constitutional Convention of 1788," Essex Inst. *Hist. Coll.* (1899), XXXV, 88 et seq. Others from the same correspondents as well as from Dane and King are in Ms. Knox Papers, XXI (MHS). Letters in December 1787 to King from Gore and Gorham are in *Life of King*, I, 262 et seq.

[92] Knox to Washington, Jan. 14,

1788, *Doc. Hist. Const.*, IV, 441; *Massachusetts Debates*, 399 (in part).

[93] *Supra*, c. VI, pp. 260 et seq.

[94] Gore to King, Dec. 30, 1787, *Life of King*, I, 266. In addition to the piece by *Helvidius Priscus* mentioned by Gore, Adams was also supposed to have been the author of pieces signed *Candidus* published in the Boston *Independent Chronicle and the Universal Advertiser*. Gorham wrote to Knox on Jan. 6, 1788, that at a dinner of the Boston delegates, Adams had declared his unequivocal opposition (Essex Inst. *Hist. Coll.* [1899], XXXV, 89). See also Gore to King, Jan. 6, 1788, *Life of King*, I, 311.

[95] Lee to Samuel Adams, Oct. 5 and Oct. 27, 1787, Ballagh, *The Letters of Richard Henry Lee*, II, 444, 456.

gates were present. The *Journal* shows that a number of towns and districts were not represented and it does not appear that there ever was a full quota of delegates.[96] Most of the leading figures of Massachusetts were among the group: Hancock, Samuel Adams, James Bowdoin, Christopher Gore, William Cushing, (later Justice of the Supreme Court), Theophilus Parsons, Judge Francis Dana, Fisher Ames (to become the most irreconcilable of Federalists), Theodore Sedgwick, the generals Lincoln, Heath and Brooks. Three of the delegates to the Philadelphia Convention were there—Nathaniel Gorham, Rufus King and Caleb Strong. Lincoln reported to Washington that there were many ex-insurgents in the convention, including some of Shay's officers—"A great proportion of those men are high in the opposition."[97] But the antifederalists were lacking in distinguished leadership. Gerry had been defeated in the election of delegates. Samuel Adams, however, moved that he be allowed a seat on the floor to answer any questions concerning the Constitution.[98] Since three other delegates to the Philadelphia Convention were present, the motion, which passed, seems to have been aimed at strengthening antifederalist leadership. If this was the case, the plan failed. Gerry was called on to answer in writing one question on the last requisition by Congress.[99] Subsequently, unbidden and with considerable stage play, he set about to correct a statement of Caleb Strong's concerning the genesis of the Senate. His actions precipitated a violent and angry debate.[100] He left the hall in a "dudgeon," reported General Lincoln.[101] He did not return.

---

[96] The federalists, worried by the count of strength, bestirred themselves to secure the presence of absent members. *Cf.* Gore to King, Dec. 30, 1787, and Jan. 6, 1788, *Life of King*, I, 267, 311; Parsons to Michael Hodge, Jan. 14, 1788, Essex Inst. *Hist. Coll.* (1899), XXXV, 92–93.

There are interesting and sometimes entertaining details on the elections in letters to George Thatcher, himself a federalist, who had recently departed Massachusetts to represent the state in Congress. *E.g.*, David Sewall wrote on Jan. 5, 1788, that although Sanford (Maine) had voted in town meeting not to send a delegate, "Mr. S. come down full charged with Gass and Stirred up a 2nd Meeting and procured himself Elected, and I presume will go up charged like a Baloon" ("Thatcher Papers," No. 10). Apparently "Mr. S." indicates Samuel Nasson who sat for Sanford. According to reports from Jeremiah Hill (January 1 and 9), a petitioned second meeting in Biddeford brought on a heated election, and votes for the antifederalist victor were won on "hearing that he would not go, if he was chosen" (*ibid.*, Nos. 9, 13). *Cf.* also *ibid.*, Nos. 6, 8, 14.

[97] Feb. 3, 1788, *Massachusetts Debates*, 405.

[98] *Cf.* the *Journal* entries, in *Massachusetts Debates*, 55–57.

[99] *Massachusetts Debates*, 143.

[100] *Ibid.*, 147. And see the *Journal* entries and the notes appended thereto, *ibid.*, 64–75; King to Madison, Jan. 20, 1788, *Life of King*, I, 314; Belknap's Notes, in Mass Hist. Soc. *Proc. for 1855–1858* (1859), 297.

[101] To Washington, Jan. 27, 1788, *Massachusetts Debates*, 403; *Doc. Hist. Const.*, IV, 460. For circumstantial accounts, *cf.* also Lincoln to Washington, Jan. 20, 1788, *Doc. Hist.*

VIII: *The Raising I*

Adams alone might have spearheaded the opposition on the floor of the convention, much as Patrick Henry later did in Virginia. But two days before the convention met, a caucus of the mechanics and tradesmen in Boston unanimously passed resolutions favoring the Constitution and appended the blunt statement that the Boston delegates had been elected to promote adoption. If any opposed it, he would be acting "contrary to the . . . wishes of the tradesmen of Boston."[102] These were Adams' people; they were his political strength. Overt recalcitrance could compromise his political career. He was nearly silent during the debates; he supported the federalists on two vital votes.[103] Whether or not he participated in the nocturnal speech-writing sessions which the "antifederal junto" was alleged to have held we do not know.[104] At the very end, as we shall see, he broke bounds and nearly upset everything. Except for this, the deadfall which federalist leaders had helped set held him fast.[105]

In other particulars federalist management was admirable. It was decided in advance to make Hancock president in order to conciliate him and his followers.[106] Hancock was incapacitated by the gout and attended only toward the end of the sessions. Judge William Cushing, named vice president, acted in his stead. Cushing had charged grand juries in favor of the Constitution;[107] there was no doubt of his stand. The motion to admit Gerry was wisely not opposed in order to avoid a premature trial of strength.[108] The federalists caucused frequently, and the way in which the hesitant were won over was political legerdemain of the first order.[109]

Not until January 14 did the convention get through preliminaries and settle down to its main business. On motion of Strong it was decided to "enter into a free conversation on the several parts thereof by

---

Const., IV, 460; Belknap to Hazard, Jan. 20, 1788, "Belknap Papers," II, at 7–8; "Belknap's Notes," in Mass. Hist. Soc. *Proc. for 1855–1858* (1859), 299.

[102] *Massachusetts Centinel*, Jan. 9, 1788, A gaudy version given by Daniel Webster in an 1833 speech is in *Works of Daniel Webster*, 4th ed. (1853), I, 302.

[103] First, on January 24 when a motion to consider the Constitution as a whole was beaten (Parsons' Minutes, in *Massachusetts Debates*, 314; Adams' speech, *ibid.*, 196). Second, in siding with Hancock (*infra*, p. 351).

[104] *Massachusetts Gazette*, Mar. 7, 1788.

[105] Federalist implication in arranging the tradesmen's meeting is clearly indicated in Gorham to Knox, Jan. 6, 1788, Essex Inst. *Hist Coll.* (1899), XXXV, 89; Gore to King, Jan. 6, 1788, *Life of King*, I, 311–12; Jackson to Knox, Jan. 20, 1788, Ms. Knox Papers, XXI, 113 (MHS).

[106] Gore to King, Jan. 6, 1788, *Life of King*, I, 312.

[107] King to Knox, Oct. 27, 1787, Ms. Knox Papers, XXI, 30 (MHS).

[108] King to Madison, Jan. 16, 1788, *Life of King*, I, 313.

[109] On the constant caucuses *cf.* Tristam Dalton to Michael Hodge, Jan. 30, 1788, Essex Inst. *Hist. Coll.* (1899), XXXV, 94.

paragraphs," after which the question of ratification of the whole should be taken up.[110] The following day it was agreed that when a member conceived the clause under consideration to be connected with some other clause or paragraph he would be at liberty to deal with such other matter. Typical of an assemblage adorned with so many of the clergy, the propriety of this *modus operandi* was admitted on the principle of "elucidating scripture by scripture."[111]

It should not be inferred from this pious allusion that the convention was infused with a spirit of Christian forbearance. There are indications in Theophilus Parsons' *Minutes* of the exchange of galling personal remarks. Even in the newspaper accounts of the debates, edited with over-discretion, there were occasional innuendos published concerning pressures and improper manipulations. Nevertheless, the impression remains that despite sporadic flare-ups the proceedings were not particularly enlivening. Jeremy Belknap, indeed, described the antifederalists as "petulant, tedious and provoking."[112] No provision was made to have shorthand reporters present. On the petition of local printers, permission was granted them for a place on the floor.[113] By their own confession they were "inexperienced in the business and had not a very eligible situation to hear."[114] Consequently there were admitted omissions and inaccuracies. The most lamentable of these is the omission of the debates on Article III, obviously considerable. Unfortunately, Parsons' *Minutes* break off before this article was reached.

The debates for all their faults, as reported, have a flavor of their own, reflective of the Bay State's individuality. They are peppered with scriptural allusions—the driving of Jehu, the meekness of Moses, the counsel of St. Peter; "never . . . a greater general than Washington, except, indeed, Joshua, who was inspired by the Lord of Hosts."[115] The immense concern with the fishing, shipping and commercial interests is constantly manifest. The anxieties respecting the foreign relations of the nation are more pronounced than in any other state convention and with this a sense of diminished prestige abroad. The mortifying comment made by Captain Snow early in the proceedings that "this country [is] held in the same light by foreign nations as a well-behaved negro in a gentleman's family"[116] could hardly have been more shocking.

The Massachusetts men were disposed constantly to use their own constitution as a test for the propriety and the wisdom of provisions in the new plan. They had a knowledge of the history of their own

---

[110] *Massachusetts Debates*, 100.
[111] *Ibid.*, 109.
[112] To Ebenezer Hazard, Jan. 20, 1788, "Belknap Papers," II, at 6.
[113] *Journal*, in *Massachusetts De-* bates, 56–57.
[114] See the note, *ibid.*, xi, taken from the first printed edition of the debates.
[115] *Massachusetts Debates*, 152.
[116] *Ibid.*, 132.

state and a belief in the relevance of these past events to the course they might take in the future. As was to be expected of a state with a long and admirable tradition of public education, the references to the experience of antiquity and of later European history were frequent. They were so frequent as to provoke Mr. Randall of Sharon to protest that "quoting of ancient history was no more to the purpose, than to tell how our fathers dug clams at Plymouth."[117]

All of the various appeals to prejudice that had infested the newspapers during the fall and early winter were given an airing during the debates. Massachusetts added one peculiar to itself—a baiting of the lawyers. Over some years the lawyers had been an object of hostility culminating in the troubles of the preceding year. They had been subjected to a variety of attacks in the newspapers that had continued even during the convention.[118] This open antipathy to the profession in combination with the animus over the judicial process in the Commonwealth did not presage well for the fate of the judiciary article. General Thompson from Topsham (Maine) made the first thrust at the lawyers.[119] He was followed some days later by Mr. Singletary (Worcester County) who believed that the lawyers expected to be managers of the Constitution, seize all the power and money and then "swallow up all us little folks, like the great leviathan . . . yes, just as the whale swallowed up Jonah."[120] This was a new version of the conspiracy theory and it is regrettable that the reporters did not report more samples for the chastening effect upon the profession.

Despite the limitations of the reporters' judgment as to what was worthy of their notice, there is no question but that the delegates' interest was focussed primarily on Congress and its powers. The debates on Article I lasted through January 26. Only three days were spent on Articles II and III. What engaged the most attention were the terms of Representatives and Senators, the sufficiency of representation, Congress's power as respects elections and the arrangements respecting the taxing power. A variety of matter not immediately relevant, *e.g.*, the danger of a consolidated government, the need for a bill of rights, the unconstitutional method of the proposed plan, was dragged into the debate. It is perhaps indicative of convention thinking that when the question of checks on Congress's power was discussed by Bowdoin, no

---

[117] *Ibid.*, 169.
[118] On the early manifestations, L. Newcomer, *The Embattled Farmers* (New York: King's Crown Press, 1953), 134–36; on the attacks of *Honestus*, T. Amory, *Life of James Sullivan* (1859), I, 188–89. A writer in *The Boston Gazette, and the Coun-*

try Journal, Nov. 26, 1787, urged keeping lawyers out of the Convention. Another in the Boston *American Herald*, Feb. 4, 1788, wanted an amendment to exclude them from Congress.
[119] *Massachusetts Debates*, 168.
[120] *Ibid.*, 203.

mention was made of the judiciary beyond a reference to the oath taken by all officers to support the Constitution.[121] Of the same tenor were the remarks of Parsons.[122]

When Articles II and III were reached, the reporters assured their readers that every section was objected to and the objections were "obviated" by the proponents of the Constitution. This was a very cavalier way of disposing of discussion over matters that had excited so much controversy in the pre-convention press. Indeed, at the very time the delegates were assembling in Boston the *American Herald*[123] had published a prophecy in the form of a satirical piece from *"The Dependent Chronicle"* of January 1, 1796. This mythical gazette reported mournfully that a state convention had just adjourned after surrendering all state sovereignty to the King of America. Chiefly responsible for the rise of tyranny was the judiciary. The machinations of lawyers, use of fictions and removal of citizens had enabled the federal courts to take over all judicial business. Citizens who rebelled were thrown into jail by state warrants. When juries had convicted officers, the President had pardoned them. Actions of trespass lay at the mercy of judges even as to matters of fact. Finally, the overloaded federal courts had found it inconvenient to go on circuit and had holed up in the federal city fully out of sight of those subject to their pleasure.

With matter like this in circulation, editorial instincts should have been quickened to a thorough job of reporting.[124] As it was, only one antifederalist speech was published that purported to embody the main objections to the judiciary. This was delivered by Abraham Holmes of Plymouth County.[125] Holmes was concerned over safeguards for the citizen. The Constitution did not provide for a jury of the vicinage—a touchy point in Massachusetts since the repressions of the Intolerable Acts. There was, furthermore, no guarantee of protection against proceedings by information where a person could be taken and confined until the next session of a court, concerning the frequency of whose sessions nothing was said. Congress was given the power to settle the "mode of criminal process." There was no indication how jurors were to be selected, from whence or what the length of service was to be.

---

[121] *Ibid.*, 186.

[122] *Ibid.*, 194.

[123] Jan. 7, 1788.

[124] R. J. Taylor, *Western Massachusetts in the Revolution*, 172, notes as curious that the "published record" contains no mention of Art. I, sec. 10, regarding the prohibition on states to issue bills of credit or make anything but silver or gold legal tender. He surmises neither side wished this discussed. It seems more likely the reporters simply slighted the January 26 debate to which less than two pages were devoted. We find it incredible that of the unpalatable list in sec. 10 only the suspension of habeas corpus should have been mentioned.

[125] *Massachusetts Debates*, 211 *et seq.*

There was no word as to right to counsel, of confrontation or cross-examination. There was nothing to prevent Congress from instituting courts like the Inquisition of Spain. An "additional glare of horror" was the lack of restraint upon Congress's fixing cruel and unheard-of punishments, or of compelling a man to incriminate himself or to cast upon him the burden of proving his innocence.

Christopher Gore undertook to meet these objections.[126] He denied that a jury of the vicinage was promotive of justice for the object must be to determine on the real merits of a case uninfluenced by personal considerations. It was better a jury be perfectly ignorant of a person on trial. Gore denied, further, that lack of provision for indictment by a grand jury had the effect of authorizing *ex officio* informations. He pointed to the silence of the Massachusetts constitution on indictments and the fact that no dangers had resulted therefrom.

Apparently there was also the usual charge made that civil juries were done away with. Mr. Gore had explained the difficulties of fixing by Constitution a rule that could have applied to all states.[127] Mr. Dawes did not see how Article III took away jury trial, for the word "court" did not either in popular or technical construction exclude a jury to try facts.[128] He ridiculed the comparison of this article with the power claimed by Britain to try Americans without a jury, for it was in criminal cases they had sought to do this. The only instance he could recall was a piracy trial which under the statutes was by civil law.[129] Dawes further pointed to the parallel existing between the Massachusetts and the federal constitutions. The former empowered the General Court to erect judicatories and left the nature, number and extent of these to the discretion of the legislature.

The debate by sections ended on January 31 and Parsons moved that the convention assent to and ratify the Constitution.[130] There was some desultory discussion of the slave trade and the absence of a religious test, following which General Heath delivered a homily on the importance of adoption. Then rose President Hancock to apologize for his absences due to indisposition, and to note that he had learned of differences of opinion, to remove which he would offer some propositions in the afternoon.[131] These were apparently not of his making. More than a week earlier Rufus King had written to Madison that "we are now thinking of amendments to be submitted not as a condition of our

---

126 *Ibid.*, 213.
127 *Ibid.*
128 *Ibid.*, 215.
129 Under the provincial government, regulated by St. 11 & 12 Wm. III, c. 7. The intricate statutory picture is discussed by Goebel, "Ex parte Clio," 450, 478 *et seq.*
130 *Massachusetts Debates*, 221.
131 *Ibid.*, 224. He had appeared first on January 30 (Gorham to Knox, Jan. 30, 1788, Essex Inst. *Hist. Coll.*, XXXV, 94).

349

assent & Ratification but as the opinion of the Convention, subjoined to their ratification."[132] King believed that the scheme would gain a few members but he still thought the final issue to be in doubt. The most important one to convert, of course, was the Governor. There seems little doubt that the *douceur* with which he was won over was some assurance of political support and there may even have been intimations of help in securing him the Presidency.[133] A copy of the amendments in Theophilus Parsons' handwriting was found in the Hancock papers,[134] and while this is slim evidence on which to pin his authorship, there is little question but that Parsons had a share in formulating the propositions and that Hancock did not.[135]

The propositions opened with a wordy preamble and recited that in the opinion of the convention certain amendments and alterations would remove fears and quiet apprehensions, and guard against an undue administration of the federal government. The convention therefore recommended that the alterations "be introduced into the said Constitution."[136] As submitted, the propositions were simpler than when edited by the committee to which they were eventually referred. There were three amendments relating to the judiciary. One made indictment mandatory for crimes punishable by death or by infamous punishment.

---

[132] Jan. 23, 1788, *Life of King*, I, 316.

[133] The chief exhibit is a letter of King to Knox, Feb. 1, 1788 (*ibid.*, 319), announcing that Hancock "has committed himself in our favor." King goes on to say, "You will be astonished, when you see the list of names, that such an union of men has taken place on this question. Hancock will hereafter receive the universal support of Bowdoin's friends; and *we told him, that, if Virginia does not unite, which is problematical, he is considered as the only fair candidate for President.*" A letter of Tristam Dalton of Feb. 3, 1788, to an unknown correspondent (Essex Inst. Hist. Coll. [1899], XXXV, 88), tells of Hancock's adherence and proceeds, "We must, whether successful or not, support his interest. Are you willing that we should pledge yours? Do not say 'I will be damned first. He shall never have my vote.' Will you not if the Judge, Parsons and myself pledge ourselves? You will." The Letter of Laco, No. 7, published in 1789, sets out the "bargain" in detail. This work

was written by Stephen Higginson, an enemy of Hancock. *Letters of Laco* (Boston, 1789), 45–46.

[134] T. Parsons, Jr., *Memoir of Theophilus Parsons*, 71.

[135] Parsons (*ibid.*, 73) thinks it probable that the propositions originated with the Essex County group. Knox wrote to Livingston, Feb. 10, 1788, "As the motions and recommendations were the mature production of the Federalists there cannot be a doubt of the committee reporting in favor of the ratification" (Ms. Knox Papers, XXI, 140 [MHS]). Belknap, in a letter to Hazard on Feb. 3, 1788, wrote, "Hancock is the ostensible puppet in proposing amendments; but they are the product of the Feds; but in concert, and it was thought that, coming from him, they would be better received than from any other person" ("Belknap Papers," II, at 15). Higginson, in his *Letters of Laco* (*supra*, n. 133, at 45), stated that Hancock used the original paper handed to him.

[136] *Massachusetts Debates*, 79–81.

Another limited the jurisdiction of the Supreme Court in causes between citizens of different states to controversies involving more than a certain sum. This the committee fixed at $3,000; it also added a provision restricting the federal judicial power in actions between citizens of different states to cases involving $1,500 or more. Finally, there was the stipulation that in civil actions between citizens of different states, issues of fact arising in common law actions should be tried by jury if either or both parties should request it.

Samuel Adams moved that the propositions be taken into consideration by the convention. He declared his support of the Constitution, but in the terms of the amendments being a condition of ratification.[137] He frankly anticipated securing support from states yet to ratify as an assurance of the actual incorporation of the propositions into the fundamental law. It was over the issue of condition or recommendation that the maneuvering was to take place.[138] Curiously enough, there was little said about proposed limits on the judiciary. On the contrary, there was one forecast of the powers of the courts made by Adams himself which was of significance and was apparently not challenged. Adams had declared that he regarded Hancock's first proposition that all powers not expressly delegated to Congress were reserved to the several states to be exercised by them to be a summary of a bill of rights. This, said he, "gives assurance that if any law made by the Federal government shall be extended beyond the power granted by the proposed Constitution, and inconsistent with the Constitution of this State, it will be an error, and adjudged by the courts of law to be void."[139]

On February 3 King reported happily[140] that Adams had sided publicly with Hancock for the first time. King was certain, at last, of a favorable result. There were means of conversion besides reasoned argument. On the day Hancock presented the propositions, General Jackson wrote Knox that some of the antifederalists, feeling the pinch of poverty, had been to the state Treasurer who informed them he had no money available nor could he borrow it. The federalists consequently did not scruple to circulate the assurance that if the Constitution was

---

[137] Bancroft claims in *History of the Formation of the Constitution of the United States of America*, 270, n. 1, that Adams was not supporting conditional ratification. This is a misreading of his speech. Adams' remarks about the improbability of securing amendments pursuant to Art. V were made in support of conditional ratification (*Massachusetts Debates*, 226–27). They were so understood by the next speaker, Dr. Taylor.

[138] King to George Thatcher, Jan. 30, 1788, in "Thatcher Papers," no. 23. Lincoln to Washington, Feb. 3, 1788, in *Doc. Hist. Const.*, IV, 472; *Massachusetts Debates*, 404. As reported, the emphasis in the debates was upon the propriety of formulating amendments at all.
[139] *Massachusetts Debates*, 233.
[140] King to Madison, Feb. 3, 1788, *Life of King*, I, 318.

adopted, there would be no difficulty about pay.[141] It is small wonder that a motion to adjourn made on February 5 was beaten 214–115.[142]

Meantime, on February 2, a committee consisting of two members from each county had been named to consider the amendments. It reported, February 4, that a few alterations had been made and of the twenty-four members, fifteen agreed, seven voted adversely, one was absent and one abstained.[143] Three leading clergymen, Thatcher, Jarvis and Backus, spoke warmly and eloquently for the Hancock plan. Of these, the influence of Backus, a Baptist, was politically of great importance, for in Massachusetts this sect had been unfavorably disposed.

As the discussions reached an inevitable climax, with the antifederalists pushing for a bill of rights, Samuel Adams, despite his earlier professions of faith in the safeguarding of rights by the amendments on reserved power, offered a further amendment to be added to those reported. This was a provision that the Constitution should never be construed to authorize Congress to infringe on the liberty of the press, rights of conscience, or right to bear arms, to raise a standing army except for defense, to the right of petition, and to subject people to unreasonable searches and seizures. These propositions, the newspapers reported, did not meet "the approbation of those gentlemen whose minds they were intended to ease, after they were debated." Consequently Adams withdrew them.[144] A member, however, wrote privately that Adams had attempted to make the withdrawal but in the end had been obliged to vote against his own proposal.[145]

This same day (February 6) the final vote on ratification was taken—187 yeas, 168 nays.[146] The margin was uncomfortably close, but considering the lively apprehensions of the federalists, it was a triumph. Some of the opposition announced with fortitude their determination to support the Constitution—warm though Massachusetts politics were, the heat did not rise to the boiling point as it had in Pennsylvania. Nevertheless, there were charges made in the newspapers that there had been in effect a plot to keep out of Boston the productions of various antifederalist luminaries published in other states.[147] Due to hinted malfeasance in the post office, out-of-state newspapers had been deliberately withheld. These complaints had begun in New York three weeks before the Massachusetts Convention met and continued into the

---

[141] Jackson to Knox, Feb. 3, 1788, Ms. Knox Papers, XXI, 131 (MHS).
[142] *Massachusetts Debates*, 266.
[143] *Ibid.*, 250.
[144] *Journal*, in *Massachusetts Debates*, 86. For the comment see *ibid.*, 266.
[145] Belknap to Hazard, Feb. 10,

1788, in "Belknap Papers," II, at 17. See also his notes of the debates, in Mass. Hist. Soc. *Proc.* for 1855–1858 (1859), 302.
[146] *Journal*, in *Massachusetts Debates*, 83–92.
[147] *Massachusetts Centinel*, Feb. 16, 1788.

spring.[148] The Postmaster General was moved to issue a flat denial of irregularities in his office. He explained that newspapers were not considered part of the mail. The arrangements were between riders and printers. To "promote general convenience" postmasters undertook (not officially) to distribute papers brought by riders in exchange for a newspaper from each printer.[149] After a month the clamor subsided.

A final word must be said about the amendments as finally voted, for they had a prospective effect far beyond anything anticipated when the bargain concerning them was struck—because they set a pattern that was to govern similar demands elsewhere. They deal very briefly with the safeguard of individual liberties—probably because the proposition reserving to the states all powers not expressly delegated was believed to be sufficient—proposing only the requirement of indictment in cases of capital crimes or those involving infamous punishments, and jury trial in common law actions, strangely enough, at the option of the party or parties. Certain changes in the structure of the Constitution were advanced; one relating to the regulation of representation,

---

[148] *New-York Journal*, Dec. 17, 1787, Jan. 23, 1788; Philadelphia *Independent Gazetteer: or, the Chronicle of Freedom*, Feb. 6 and 7, 1788; Philadelphia *Pennsylvania Gazette*, Mar. 5, 1788; *Freeman's Journal*, Mar. 26, 1788. *Cf.* Samuel A. Otis to George Thatcher, Apr. 13, 1788 (*LMCC*, VIII, 716): "I think Hazzard is in a bad box. The foederalists frown upon him for being anti. The opposers of foederalism charge him hard with stoping the papers, and 'muzzling the press' to facilitate the purposes of despotism."

Then and today, Postmaster General Hazard was blamed for a situation over which he obviously had no control. The Papers of Congress and the *Journals* have considerable material on earlier difficulties with the mails. The troubles were not merely with the proprietors of stagecoaches who contracted to carry the mails but with the drivers, post-riders, etc. The latter were so unreliable as respects the mail there is no reason to suppose that they would be solicitous about newspapers which they carried as an accommodation. See Hazard's complaint to Congress, Sept. 25, 1786 (*JCC*, XXXI, 690–92), relating two examples of "inattention." In one

case the Philadelphia mail had been thrown at night on the wharf with the passengers' baggage by a negro boy who had ferried the lot over the river. When told that the bag belonged to none of the passengers, he threw it back into the boat. It remained there until 2 A.M. when it was removed to a neighboring house. Not until the next morning was the load found to be the mail and delivered to the post office. Alexander Hamilton, who was consulted, advised that the contractors' bonds could not be put in suit, for damage could not be shown.

[149] Printed in McMaster and Stone, *Pennsylvania*, 530–31. Complaints about the mails were made in Congress. On Feb. 20, 1788, a committee was appointed following a motion on better regulation of the postal service (*JCC*, XXXIV, 52, n. 1). *Cf. ibid.*, 116 (committee renewed); 131, n. 1 (a complaint of a letter opened in the post office); 142 (report thereon by Hazard).

Hazard's letters to Belknap show strong federalist feeling; in several of his letters he explains and defends the Post Office. "Belknap Papers," II, at 23 (Mar. 5, 1788); 29 (Apr. 12, 1788); 35 (May 10, 1788).

another a prohibition on the erection of companies with exclusive advantages of commerce, a third the restraint upon Congress consenting to acceptance by persons holding public office of any title of nobility or title or office from foreign kings or states. There were finally proposals designed to curb federal powers to the advantage of the states. These included the limitations upon the jurisdiction of the Supreme Court, already noticed, the requirement of resort to requisitions before Congress to exercise the power of direct taxation, and finally, limiting the power of Congress to make regulations for federal elections under Article I, section 4. We shall later have occasion to notice what was to befall these propositions when the first amendments to the Constitution were drafted.

NEW HAMPSHIRE

IF THE NEW ENGLAND federalists hoped that New Hampshire, where the convention met five days after the Massachusetts ratification was declared, would be guided by this example, they were grievously mistaken. Antifederalist feeling ran strong in New Hampshire for much the same reasons that it flourished in western Massachusetts. Lawyers and courts were anathema on both sides of the border; the clamor for paper money was equally loud. During the year before the Federal Convention met, the old pre-Revolutionary tactic of local conventions of protest had been resorted to, and had so far alarmed constituted authority that on September 30, 1786, President John Sullivan issued a proclamation enjoining the inhabitants to desist and resort to town meetings with their grievances.[150] At this time the threat to the legislature by a mob in which militia officers were implicated was met by resolute action, and matters consequently never got out of hand as they did in Massachusetts.[151] When Shaysites crossed into New Hampshire in February 1787, Sullivan issued a Proclamation of Rebellion[152] calling on all to aid in arresting the rebels and offering rewards. The Governor acted with resolution, but sympathies being what they were, the situation was difficult to handle. Indeed, as late as June 1787 Governor Hancock of Massachusetts laid before his legislature a report that armed bands were making incursions into his state from New Hampshire.[153]

When the New Hampshire legislature convened in December 1787,

---

[150] O. G. Hammond, ed., *Letters and Papers of Major-General John Sullivan, Continental Army: 1771–1795*, III, 484 (hereafter cited as *Sullivan Papers*).
[151] J. Belknap, *The History of New-Hampshire*, J. Farmer, ed., 400–

03. See the general order for court-martial, *Sullivan Papers*, III, 483.
[152] *Sullivan Papers*, III, 509.
[153] Message of June 5, 1787, *Mass. Acts and Resolves 1786–87* (reprint 1893), 988.

VIII: *The Raising I*

President Sullivan transmitted the Constitution with a warning that it could be there considered only insofar as the decision to appoint delegates was involved.[154] He added a cautious indorsement of the new instrument. The legislature finally resolved on December 14 to hold a convention on February 13.[155] Delegates were to be elected by the towns. The date chosen had indirectly an effect upon the course of the New Hampshire Convention, for, as rumor trickled in of the Massachusetts proceedings, towns instructed their delegates[156] in response to what it was thought was happening across the border. John Langdon reported that just as the elections were taking place in a principal county, word was circulated that Massachusetts was going to reject, and that the people had been frightened "almost out of what *little* senses they had."[157] As a result, a substantial antifederalist bloc was present when the New Hampshire delegates convened at Exeter. Among them, wrote President Sullivan, were some good men but shortsighted, "some few who longed for the onions of Egypt, many were Distressed & in Debt; numbers who conceived that This System would compel men to be honest against both their Inclination & their Interest, some who were blinded through excess of Zeal for the Cause of Religion and others who by putting on the masque of sanctity thought to win proselites."[158]

The *Journal* of the convention shows that debate began on February 14 and was over on the 21st.[159] Everything published in Massachusetts against the Constitution was "handed out here by Rote."[160]

---

[154] *Sullivan Papers*, III, 556.

[155] 5 *Laws of New Hampshire*, 294–95.

[156] Examples in J. B. Walker, *History of the New Hampshire Convention . . .*, 27–28. Jeremy Belknap reported to Ebenezer Hazard on Feb. 17, 1788, that he had been told that forty towns had been given instructions to vote against the Constitution ("Belknap Papers," II, at 20). Local suspicion of undue influence by Massachusetts antifederalists is reflected in a piece with a Portsmouth, N.H., address printed in the *Pennsylvania Packet*, Mar. 27, 1788. Dr. Kilham of Newburyport, who had tried to stall the calling of the Massachusetts Convention, is charged with having made two trips to Exeter while the New Hampshire Convention was sitting. He is threatened with rotten apples and eggs if he makes a reappearance.

[157] John Langdon to Washington, Feb. 28, 1788, in *Doc. Hist. Const.*, IV, 523. According to a report in the *Massachusetts Centinel*, Feb. 27, 1788, most of the New Hampshire people received their information from "factious demagogues" who disseminated misleading information.

[158] Sullivan to Jeremy Belknap, Feb. 26, 1788, in *Sullivan Papers*, III, 566. Sullivan states the division was seventy antifederalists to thirty federalists.

[159] The *Journal* is printed in *Provincial and State Papers . . . Relating to New Hampshire*, N. Bouton, ed. (1877), X, 12–22.

[160] The account of the February 14 debate is in the *Massachusetts Gazette*, Feb. 22, 1788. But John Pickering claimed that new arguments were advanced. *Cf.* Jeremiah Libbey to Belknap, Feb. 22, 1788, in "Belknap Papers," III, 389–90.

A variety of amendments, embellishments and disfigurements "as Ingenuity folly obstinacy & false piety could Suggest" were offered.[161] In the face of all this, converts were made by the federalists. But some thirty delegates were bound by town instructions. In consequence it was moved to adjourn until June 18, 1788.

It is regrettable no full report of the proceedings exists. Sullivan has preserved for us two samples of "New Hampshire Ingenuity" in argument. One pious deacon was for the plan if it had in it a guarantee that "the holy Scriptures continued to us in our mother Tongue." Another wanted a religious test at least for the office of President lest a Turk, a Jew, a Roman Catholic "and what is worse than all a universalist" might hold the office.[162]

Sullivan was not writing out of mere chagrin. Oratory as then taught in New Hampshire was not of a high order if a college sample given by the historian Jeremy Belknap was representative.[163] Furthermore, young John Quincy Adams, who had journeyed to Exeter from Newburyport by sleigh, wrote in his diary, "the debates I really think were not worth the ride in a cold day."[164] John Pickering he had found to be dull. He noted some would-be profundities of Joshua Atherton, and some absurdities from a speech of Parson Thirston who "did not even attempt to support the plan upon the fair and honourable basis of rational argumentation."[165] A son of the Enlightenment, Adams had no naive faith in the intellectual prowess of the common man.

The newspapers show the proceedings in a slightly brighter light. There is comment on the repetition of arguments advanced in Massachusetts. They fortunately noticed, rather particularly, the debate on Article III. Joshua Atherton objected to expense, to litigants being dragged to "Head Quarters" and the suspected partiality of federal judges in revenue cases. Judge Samuel Livermore in explaining the intent of the article quoted John Langdon as saying that "it was the meaning of the Convention that causes in which citizens of different states were the parties &c. should be commenced and tried before the several state courts, and that only an appeal lay to the federal court." Livermore insisted there was no compulsion in the words of the Constitution that these cases must originate in federal courts. A Mr. Parker called upon Langdon to say what was intended by the inferior courts

---

[161] *Sullivan Papers*, III, 567. *Cf.* John Langdon to Rufus King, Feb. 23, 1788, in *Life of King*, I, 321.

[162] *Sullivan Papers*, III, 567–68.

[163] Belknap to Hazard, May 15, 1788, in "Belknap Papers," II, at 40–41. The sample is from a commencement address at what Belknap calls that "hot-bed of literature," Dr. Wheelock's "*sylvan* academy."

[164] "Diary of John Quincy Adams," in Mass. Hist. Soc. *Proc.*, 16:385, 2d ser., 1902.

[165] *Ibid.*, 386.

to be established. Langdon replied that "they were courts of admiralty, maritime courts &c."[166]

President Sullivan himself made an able speech in defense of the proposed judicial system. He spoke to the heart of New Hampshire, harassed throughout its existence with troubles over boundaries and conflicting grants, when he proclaimed that only the justice of a cause would be considered in federal courts and not whether a party belonged to Massachusetts or to New Hampshire. He made the only discovered reference to the colonial system of appeals to the Privy Council. Those complaining of the proposed system had "quietly suffered an appeal to Great Britain in all causes of consequence. They then boasted of their liberties, boasted of the liberty of appealing to judges ignorant of our situation and prejudiced against the name of an American." He asked, could they be content under their former bondage and reject a Constitution because an American court operating under regulations set by their representatives was to be their judge in certain causes?[167]

When the convention resumed on June 18, a day was spent on general debate of the Constitution.[168] A committee was appointed to report amendments to be recommended. The report made on the afternoon of June 20 was a list identical with the Massachusetts amendments, except as to the judiciary. New Hampshire asked only that all common law actions must be commenced in state courts, and that appeals to federal courts be limited to cases where the amount in controversy exceeded $3,000.[169] An attempt by Joshua Atherton to hold up operation of the Constitution without the amendments was sidetracked. An attempt to adjourn was beaten down. On June 21 ratification was voted 57–47.

RHODE ISLAND

JAMES MADISON, sending Washington news of the February adjournment of the New Hampshire Convention, found it a "disagreeable subject of communication."[170] Perennially optimistic, he was neverthe-

[166] *Massachusetts Gazette*, Feb. 29, 1788; Boston *American Herald*, Mar. 3, 1788.
[167] *Sullivan Papers*, III, 569, which gives a wrong date. Also reported in the Massachusetts papers cited *supra*, n. 166. None of this is reported in Elliot's *Debates*. The Richmond *Virginia Gazette and Weekly Advertiser*, Mar. 20, 1788, printed a letter to an Alexandria man from a Boston correspondent who commented that Sullivan spoke for three hours "like a Roman."
[168] *Journal*, in *Provincial and State Papers . . . Relating to New Hampshire*, X, 16–19.
[169] *Doc. Hist. Const.*, II, 141.
[170] *Doc. Hist. Const.*, IV, 531.

less aware of the pressure the event put upon the federalists, and he expressed his fears that "the mischief elsewhere will in the mean time be of a serious nature." This does not seem to have occurred, although it is barely possible that the course pursued by the Rhode Island legislature may have been affected by the New Hampshire result. In any event, the action to which the Rhode Islanders were moved was typical of their treasured independency, and in the light of their feckless attitude toward their neighbors, not unexpected.

The new Constitution had been received with less than rapture. William Ellery, reporting on the event to Ebenezer Hazard, wrote, "The majority in this state wear long faces. The prospect of an abridgment of their powers to do mischief is extremely painful to them."[171] It was his opinion that the state would hold out to the end. He proved to be a good prophet. Not only did the legislature vote down a motion to call a convention, in accordance with the procedure recommended by Congress, but on February 24, 1788, the General Assembly passed an act providing that the Constitution be submitted to the several towns to be voted upon by the freemen and freeholders.[172] This was justified on the ground that no innovations "could be made" in a Constitution already agreed upon and "the Compact settled between the Governors and Governed" without the consent of the freemen individually in town meeting assembled. This pious sentiment coming from a citizenry long berated as an aggregation of contract breachers was truly inspired.

Federalist strength in Rhode Island centered in the two mercantile centers, Providence and Newport. Federalist leadership, however, showed none of the acumen to be expected of men of affairs. Indeed, it was as wrong-headed in its way as it accused the opposition of being. Federalists so objected to the mode of proceeding chosen by the legislature that they would not participate.[173] What they hoped to gain by abstention is a puzzle. By their abandoning the field without even the pretense of a fight, the levelling spirit that pervaded Rhode Island

---

171 Oct. 16, 1787, Ms. Loan Office Letter Book and Custom House Letter Book (Newport Hist. Soc.).

172 In the *New-York Journal*, Mar. 29, 1788, is an account of the proceedings in the Rhode Island General Assembly on calling the convention. The Rhode Island act is in *Doc. Hist. Const.*, IV, 556.

173 The *Pennsylvania Packet* on Apr. 11 and 15, 1788, carried news items from Providence on the political situation. It would appear that the local federalists in that town and in Newport having decided not to

vote concentrated their efforts on petitions to the legislature to call a convention. Antifederalist sentiment was reflected in the Richmond *Virginia Gazette and Weekly Advertiser*, Mar. 20, 1788, where under a Baltimore dateline a letter from Providence was run stating that a petition "was signing" impeaching with treason the several states which had ratified. The Rhode Island situation is discussed by H. M. Bishop, "Why Rhode Island Opposed the Federal Constitution," *Rhode Island History*, 8:33, 85, 115, 1949.

politics was to suffer no open challenge. The thousand copies of the Constitution printed and distributed to the towns were thus incontinently left to the ruminations of the rustics under the guidance of implacable enemies of the new system.[174] The new plan was rejected 2,708–237,[175] a majority which might have recalled to obdurate federalists the scriptural apothegm that "if the blind lead the blind, both shall fall into the ditch."

Governor Collins, reporting Rhode Island's action to Congress, did not justify the result by Scripture but by "pure Republican Principles, founded upon that Basis of All Governments originally deriving from the body of the People at large."[176] Collins added that the people in general conceived that the Constitution "may contain some necessary articles which could well be added and adopted to the present Confederation." These overtures no delegate in Congress could take seriously. Apart from the fact that Rhode Island had not been represented there for a year, no one was likely to forget the state's intractable attitude on the impost. The *Journals* of Congress indicate that no attention was paid to Collins' suggestion.[177] If Rhode Island had been a wayward and unforgiven daughter, the correspondence of members could not have maintained a more obdurate silence about her doings.[178]

---

[174] Among them Jonathan Hazard, described by Jeremiah Olney in a letter to Hamilton, Nov. 3, 1788, as an "Implacable & Powerfull Enimy to the New Systim, and the Leading Character in all the Vile politicks Carrying on in this *Devoted* State" (*PAH*, V, 229). Hazard was a leader in Rhode Island's paper money adventure. On his role, *cf.* McDonald, *We the People*, 328 *et seq.*

[175] The results of the vote in *Doc. Hist. Const.*, IV, 559–60.

[176] *Ibid.*, 555.

[177] It was "read and referred" (*JCC*, XXXIV, 131, n. 1).

[178] On the subsequent efforts to secure a convention and the steps leading to final ratification May 27, 1790, *cf.* McDonald, *We the People*, 322–23. On the pressures exerted by the national government, *cf.* Freeman, *George Washington*, VI, 268, n. 92. An interesting exhibit on Rhode Island strategy is the letter of Nicholas Brown of Providence to Senator Richard Henry Lee of Virginia, May 1, 1789 (Ms. Lee Family Papers, Library, University of Virginia). Brown explained that Rhode Island with its fine harbors was in a position to impede the collection of federal revenues. The towns of Newport, Providence, Bristol, Warren and Greenwich were federalist; the rest, antifederalist. The towns named proposed that if the assembly did not call a convention as recommended by Congress in September 1787, they wished to petition Congress to take them under its protection and include them in the Union with such representation as might be thought just and equitable. Brown explained how much Virginia tobacco they would take. He wished to be assured that they would be received and protected. Some federalists were holding back for such assurances.

CHAPTER IX

The Raising II:
The Judicial before the States

ALTHOUGH GEORGIA had ratified at the very start of the new year, the other states south of Mason and Dixon's line proceeded with great deliberation. Action depended, of course, upon the several legislatures, and none of them appears to have been anxious for a quick decision. The Virginia legislature was the first to convene and the steps there taken may have set a leisurely pattern for other states. The House of Delegates resolved on October 25 to have elections held at the March court days, the convention to meet on the first Monday in June. The Senate agreed to this on October 31.[1] It was provided, *inter alia,* that copies of the resolve should be transmitted by the executive to Congress and to the "legislatures and executives of the respective states." In an account of the debate, published in the *Pennsylvania Packet,*[2] it does not appear what purpose was supposed to be served by thus circularizing the states. The notion that a point of etiquette in state relations was being served is hardly borne out by the fact that other acts passed at this same session affected national or state interests and no such directions were appended. True, the earlier statute providing for appointment of delegates to the Philadelphia Convention[3] had contained an order that copies be sent to Congress and the executives of the several states. But this had been for the practical purpose of hastening the calling of the Federal Convention. Nothing of the sort was here involved. There is, however, some reason to believe that the resolve and its transmission abroad was a tactical move by the antifederalists who enjoyed a majority in the House of Delegates.

The antifederalists believed that time was on their side; for this reason it was insisted that the Constitution must be long and well

---

[1] *Doc. Hist. Const.,* IV, 367.
[2] Nov. 10, 1787.

[3] 12 Hening, *Va. Stats.,* 256.

360

pondered before action was taken. The House resolve of October 25 was an effective enactment of this policy, and since Virginia pretended to a role of leadership, it seems probable that the circulation of this document may have been designed to influence other legislatures to identical action.

The maneuvering which went on in connection with this resolve, as well as with certain other measures, indicates something of the antifederalists' intentions. Here both George Mason and Patrick Henry were active. Henry, it will be recalled, had declined to serve as a delegate to the Philadelphia Convention. He was described by his son-in-law to have been "most awfully alarmed" over the prospect of adoption. Alive to the threat to the country's liberties, he was determined "to buckle on once more the armour which he had hung up in the temple of peace."[4] In the debate on the resolve, he attempted so to amend it that the coming convention would have explicit power to propose amendments.[5] In this he did not succeed, and the impact of the resolve in other states was consequently infinitely less than it would otherwise have been. Nevertheless, he subsequently returned to this plan on November 30. The occasion was the discussion on a bill to provide for expenses of attendance at the June convention. The resolution of the House of Delegates sitting as a Committee of the Whole provided for defraying expenses "in case the said Convention should judge it expedient to propose amendments to the said Federal Constitution. . . ."[6] Archibald Stuart reported to Madison that Henry and Mason had seconded the proposal, the contemplated expense being the sending of deputies to other states.[7] Mason had earlier opposed any reference to amendments as an improper disclosure of legislative sentiment "to a body paramt. to us."[8] The friends of the Constitution felt likewise but the antifederalists prevailed.

The Committee designated to draft the statute pursuant to the resolution was overweighted with antifederalists; yet as finally enacted on December 12, 1787, the statute said nothing about amendments. This was probably the result of the debate on the bill which occurred on December 7 and 8.[9] The "whereas" clause of the statute was a masterpiece of indirection, and was pregnant with possible mischief.[10]

---

[4] W. Wirt, *Sketches of the Life and Character of Patrick Henry*, 262.

[5] *Pennsylvania Packet*, Nov. 10, 1787 (a letter from Petersburg, Va.).

[6] *Journal of the House of Delegates, Virginia* (1787) (reprint 1828), 77.

[7] *Doc. Hist. Const.*, IV, 384.

[8] Washington to Madison, Dec. 7, 1787, *Washington Writings*, XXIX, 333–34.

[9] *Journal of the House of Delegates, Virginia* (1787), 86, 88. Amended in Committee of the Whole on December 7 and again on December 8.

[10] 12 Hening, *Va. Stats.*, 462. This was printed as a broadside in 1787 by John Dix of Richmond and was also set in circulation by newspaper

It recited unctuously that it was essential to the safety and happiness of the people of all the states that the most friendly mutual sentiments be cherished and that unanimity should prevail, particularly during deliberations on the proposed change of government. Should, therefore, the convention deem it necessary to hold communication with sister states, or their conventions, or should it incur expense in collecting the sentiments of the Union respecting the Constitution in such manner as to sustain the friendly intercourse and to preserve unanimity on the proposed great change that it was the duty of the legislature to promote, the funds appropriated were to cover such expenses.

On December 26 the House of Delegates resolved that the governor "be desired" to transmit the statute to the executives and legislatures of other states. The Senate concurred, December 27.[11] On this same day Governor Randolph despatched letters to the other states.[12] Some two weeks earlier he had permitted publication of his letter of October 10, 1787,[13] withheld, as he claimed, in the interests of harmony. Since he had written in favor of amending, the arrival of the new statute with a covering letter from Randolph had the aspect of an official invitation to a cooperative movement by the states that had not yet ratified. A spark was struck only in New York. But by some mischance Randolph's letter was not received by Governor Clinton until March 7, 1788. Clinton did not reply, however, until May 8, 1788.[14] He explained that he had laid the Virginia act before the New York legislature, but the resolution calling a convention had already been passed and no action had been taken. He applauded the idea of friendly intercourse and the preservation of unanimity and assured Randolph that the New York Convention would hold communication with any sister state. There appears to have been a delay in transmission of this document. In any event, Randolph had a change of heart. He laid Clinton's reply before the Executive Council, which he claimed was of the opinion that it was a public communication directed to him in his capacity as governor.[15] As a delegate he did not exhibit it to the convention, and the Virginia General Assembly was given the full text of Clinton's letter only when it actually went into session after the

---

publication; see Richmond *Virginia Independent Chronicle*, Jan. 9, 1788; Richmond *Virginia Gazette, and Weekly Advertiser*, Jan. 10, 1788.

[11] *Journal of the House of Delegates, Virginia* (1787), 119, 120.

[12] The letter to Governor Caswell of North Carolina, Dec. 27, 1787, is in *State Records of North Carolina*, XX, 786. The text of the original resolve was published in the *Virginia Independent Chronicle* of Jan. 9, 1788. It appeared in the Philadelphia *Pennsylvania Packet* on Jan. 12, and in the Annapolis *Maryland Gazette*, Jan. 31, 1788.

[13] *Supra*, c. V, n. 240.

[14] Text in M. Conway, *Omitted Chapters of History Disclosed in the Life and Papers of Edmund Randolph*, 110–11.

[15] *Ibid.*, 112.

state convention had risen. There was fury in the antifederalist ranks. George Mason drafted an angry resolution[16] which was apparently not acted upon, for the turmoil in Richmond came to nothing.

This episode in its last stages belongs to the story of Virginia's ratification. But as the strategy of the antifederalists unfolded, particularly as respects the Southern states, the relevance of the early moves to the course of events in the South becomes apparent. While the October 1787 session of the Virginia legislature was still going on, reports began to circulate that Patrick Henry was promoting the idea of a Southern confederacy.[17] This was grounded upon a supposed community of Southern interest, and upon the familiar axiom adapted from Montesquieu that the country was too extensive to be compacted into a single republic. As a positive program this proposal could hardly have appealed to federally-minded critics like Randolph who were interested only in perfecting the Constitution by amendments.[18] Yet the creation of a bargaining position was not without attraction as a means of securing concessions. Jefferson, indeed, expressed in letters to Madison and Alexander Donald[19] his hope that nine conventions would ratify and the four last reject and refuse to accede until a bill of rights was offered. The North Carolina Convention alone was infatuated to the point of attempting this, and failed.

Whether or not there was substance in the charge that Henry was actively promoting the idea of a Southern confederacy, his adversaries had reason to suspect it. He was warm for the confederation principle of the existing government. His efforts to place Virginia in a commanding position, particularly in relation to its neighbors, estimated in connection with the propaganda that the South was to be put at the mercy of the Eastern states, seemed to point to a single conclusion. Not unnaturally, his espousal of amendments appeared to be a mere

---

[16] Text in K. Rowland, *Life and Correspondence of George Mason*, II, 275.

[17] *Cf.* Washington to David Stuart, Nov. 30, 1787, *Washington Writings*, XXIX, 323; Stuart to Madison, Dec. 2, 1787, re Henry on the subject of the South being driven to despair, *Doc. Hist. Const.*, IV, 385; Madison to Jefferson, Dec. 9, 1787, to the effect that Henry's party adheres to the confederation principle or to a "partition of the Union into several Confederacies," *Papers of Jefferson*, XII, 410.

Since the possibility of the Confederation breaking up into regional confederacies had been under some

discussion before the Philadelphia Convention met, Henry's plan was not as revolutionary as it was made to seem. There was also some scolding in the press about nine states having the power to dissolve the Union, *e.g.*, "C.D." in the *Virginia Independent Chronicle*, Dec. 26, 1787. The Henry plan was taken under attack as leading to war (*ibid.*, Apr. 9, 1788).

[18] He had in fact repudiated the idea of "partial confederacies" in his letter of Oct. 10, 1787 (*supra*, c. V, n. 240).

[19] To Madison, Feb. 6, 1788, *Papers of Jefferson*, XII, 568; to Donald, Feb. 7, 1788, *ibid.*, 570.

cloak for a more sinister basic design. Madison had been prompting his friends in late October to ask what would become of the "tardy remainder" when nine states had ratified.[20] This was an invitation to search for answers not necessarily to the liking of federalists. The rumors about disunion had, indeed, so far spread that in January 1788 a poetaster apostrophized Virginia with pleas not to hurl the Union into ruin.[21]

MARYLAND

NORTH CAROLINA was the only Southern state to fix its convention at a later date than Virginia's. Maryland's legislature, due to convene a few days after the passage of Virginia's resolve of October 25, proved laggard, for the lower house did not assemble a quorum until November 14. On this very date the Virginia resolve was despatched to the Maryland House of Delegates, before which it was laid November 23.[22] The next day a resolution was presented calling for a convention. The date was left blank.[23] On November 26 it was voted to hold elections on the first Monday in April, and hold the convention on April 21. Oddly enough, it was only after this vote was taken that two of Maryland's delegates to the Philadelphia Convention reported personally to the House. The versions of these speeches that survived[24] indicate that James McHenry's was a straightforward, factual account, typically federal. Luther Martin spoke provocatively as if to a jury he wished to inflame—one can almost smell the brimstone of his wrath over the new plan.

The Senate, which had not made a quorum until November 22, prepared its own bill. This provided for a £500 property qualification of convention delegates, and set the elections for the third Wednesday in January, the convention to meet on the first Monday in March.[25] However, on December 1 the Senate agreed to the House bill, con-

---

[20] *Doc. Hist. Const.*, IV, 354.
[21] *American Museum*, III, 92, January 1788:

Shall not fed'ral conduct crown
All thy acts of old renown?
Union into ruin hurl'd,
Shall a *tyrant* grasp a world?
Or shall sep'rate *unions* grow,
Endless source of war and woe!
The quality of the poet is revealed by the lines:
Maddison, above the rest,
Pouring from this narrow chest,

More than *Greek* or *Roman* sense,
Boundless tides of eloquence:
. . . .

[22] *Journal of the General Assembly of the State of Maryland*, November Session 1787: *Votes and Proceedings of the House of Delegates*, 9.
[23] *Ibid.*, 11.
[24] Texts in Farrand, *Records*, III, 144–59.
[25] *Journal of the General Assembly of the State of Maryland*, November Session 1787: *Votes and Proceedings of the Senate*, 5.

ceiving it best not to "run the hazard of protracting the session, by engaging in a conference or a train of messaging with the other house on the subject."[26]

The struggle for ratification in Maryland stirred national attention chiefly because Luther Martin on the heels of his speech to the legislature, November 29, set in train disclosures about the proceedings at Philadelphia. Apart from the exchanges already noticed,[27] only one native pamphlet, by the federalist Alexander Contee Hanson, was of superior literary quality, although it merely marshalled familiar arguments.[28] If Hanson's pamphlet may be taken as the statement of the Maryland federalists' case, there is no doubt but that Martin's *Genuine Information* may be accounted a brief for the opposition. Wholly apart from the intimate revelations about the Federal Convention, it is apparent to anyone with the patience to wade through its turgidities that the document was aimed at a repudiation of the Constitution. Martin was a diehard antifederalist. At the outset he and his fellows worked for rejection of the Constitution because nothing less than this offered hope of extrication from their financial embarrassments.[29] These men had overextended themselves in the purchase of confiscated loyalists' estates. They had sought succor in enactment of a paper money measure recently defeated. This they still hoped to secure and so wished no surrender of powers that would render it impossible.[30] They belonged to the coterie which had controlled public affairs for over a decade, and having broken with their associates on the issue of ratification, the contest had all the aspects of an internecine struggle.

By a quirk of fate in the guise of economic circumstances, the leaders of the opposing sides chanced to be men who were to be future Justices of the Supreme Court. The federalist leader, a staunch friend of Washington, was Thomas Johnson, an affluent lawyer who had served three terms as governor.[31] The federalists, because they were

---

[26] *Ibid.*, 7.

[27] *Supra*, pp. 301 *et seq.*

[28] *Cf.* Ford, *Pamphlets*, 217. In the Annapolis *Maryland Gazette* appeared two native pieces by "Federalist" (Nov. 8, 1787) and "Annapolitan" (Jan. 31, 1788). The James Wilson State House speech was run in the same newspaper Oct. 25, 1787. In addition to the Martin-Ellsworth letters, the *Maryland Journal and Baltimore Advertiser* ran some of the Pennsylvania pieces, including "Centinel" (*cf.* Oct. 16, Oct. 30, Nov. 2, Nov. 6, 1787) and George Mason's "Objections" (Dec. 21, 1787).

[29] The story of the finances of the various Maryland antifederalists is well and carefully told in P. A. Crowl, *Maryland during and after the Revolution.* The facts as to Samuel Chase and his associates were known at the time of the Convention; *cf.* the Baltimore letter dated Apr. 21, 1788, in the *Pennsylvania Gazette* of Apr. 30, 1788.

[30] John Brown Cutting to Jefferson, July 11, 1788, *Papers of Jefferson*, XIII, 332–33.

[31] E. S. Delaplaine, *The Life of Thomas Johnson.*

not vociferous, seem shadowy. Not so their adversaries. Commanding the antifederalists was Samuel Chase, former attorney general of the state, ardent patriot of Revolutionary days and said to be in financial difficulties.[32] Vigorous among them was Luther Martin, who is aptly described in the argot of the times as Chase's bludgeon man. There was William Paca, thrice governor, Jeremiah T. Chase, the attorney general, and James F. Mercer, who like Martin had decamped from the Philadelphia Convention. Mercer was against the payment of British creditors and currently of his own creditor, General Washington.[33] Daniel Carroll has left us a lively account of the campaign in Anne Arundel County where the voters, by handbills and a variety of canards, were terrified into returning a full slate of antifederalists. Only two other counties did likewise.[34] When the convention met at Annapolis on April 21, the pro-Constitution men commanded a large majority.

Apart from the harassments of the election, the federalists had cause to worry about the possibility of an adjournment of their convention until Virginia should act. Early in February it was reported that this was planned by the Maryland antifederalists.[35] There is nothing to indicate that the Virginians were the originators of the tactic, but before long word was circulating that they were making efforts to get both Maryland and South Carolina to postpone final action.[36] News that New Hampshire had met in convention, and on February 22 had voted to reconvene in June, had encouraged the Virginia antifederalists in the wholly mistaken belief that this had been done to await the issue of events at Richmond.[37] Madison, thoroughly alarmed, wrote to correspondents in both South Carolina and Maryland, for he believed that postponement would give a fatal advantage to the Virginia opponents of the Constitution.[38] His fears were well-grounded.

---

[32] The best extant biography of Chase is that by E. S. Corwin in *Dictionary of American Biography*, IV, 34–37.

[33] See his tract, *An Introductory Discourse to an Argument in Support of the Payments made of British Debts into the Treasury of Maryland during the Late War* (1789). Washington's letters attempting to secure payment of amounts owing at this time are scattered through Vol. XXIX, *Washington Writings*.

[34] *Doc. Hist. Const.*, IV, 636. The handbill enclosed "Bill of Rights./ Liberty of Conscience./ Trial by Jury./ No Excise./ No Poll Tax./ No Standing Army in Peace,/ With-

out Limitation./ No Whipping Militia,/ No Marching them out of / the State, without Consent / of the General Assembly./ No Direct Taxation,/ Without Previous / Requisition./ J.T. Chase, J.F. Mercer."

[35] Daniel Carroll to Madison, Feb. 10, 1788, *Doc. Hist. Const.*, IV, 497.

[36] George Nicholas to Madison, Apr. 5, 1788, *ibid.*, 551.

[37] Washington to Knox, Mar. 30, 1788, *Washington Writings*, XXIX, 449. A correct account had appeared in the Annapolis *Maryland Gazette* on March 13.

[38] Madison to Washington, Apr. 10, 1788, *Doc. Hist. Const.*, IV, 574.

A week later Governor Randolph, for whose conversion he and Washington had been striving, wrote that his final determination would not be taken until he heard something "from Maryland at least."[39]

On the eve of the Maryland Convention James McHenry besought from Washington a letter expressing his opinion on the effect that an adjournment would have.[40] The opposition, he wrote, intended to push for this on the pretext of a conference with the Virginia Convention on amendments. We do not know whether or not the Virginia statute of December 12 was circulating. In any event, the resolution of November 30 pursuant to which the Virginia statute was drafted, but which alone spoke of seeking amendments, had been published in the *Maryland Gazette*.[41] This apparently suggested the tactics of delay and consultation. On the same day that McHenry wrote, Washington on his own motion despatched a letter to Thomas Johnson setting forth his views on the dangers of adjournment.[42] This letter Johnson exhibited at Annapolis.[43] It was well that he had this document as an antidote to a letter of Jefferson's which the antifederalists were showing about.[44] This appears to have been what Jefferson had copied from a letter to Madison and sent to Uriah Forrest, member of the Maryland House of Delegates, who was responsible for producing it.[45] Daniel Carroll was properly indignant, for besides Jefferson's *idées raisonées* on the Constitution, the excerpt included the flighty remarks about the beneficence of revolutions.

As things turned out, the federalists need not have worried. When the delegates assembled on Monday, April 21, and before the convention was organized, the federalists held what amounted to a caucus. They decided that everyone was sufficiently informed, and that even if there were discussion, the "main question" had been decided by the voters whose will they were under obligation to carry into effect.[46] They should accordingly act with all speed consistent with decorum. Aware of their strength, they raised no question about the credentials of Chase, Martin and other antifederalists who, in spite of the statute, had been returned from counties where they did not reside. For reasons never

---

[39] Printed in Conway, *Omitted Chapters of History Disclosed in the Life and Papers of Edmund Randolph*, at 102.

[40] Apr. 20, 1788, *Doc. Hist. Const.*, IV, 580.

[41] Annapolis *Maryland Gazette*, Jan. 31, 1788.

[42] Apr. 20, 1788, *Doc. Hist. Const.*, IV, 581; *Washington Writings*, XXIX, 462.

[43] Text in Delaplaine, *The Life of Thomas Johnson*, at 459.

[44] Daniel Carroll to Madison, May 28, 1788, *Doc. Hist. Const.*, IV, 639.

[45] To Forrest, Dec. 31, 1787, *Papers of Jefferson*, XII, 475.

[46] Alexander C. Hanson, "Address to the People of Maryland," enclosed in Hanson to Madison, June 2, 1788, *Doc. Hist. Const.*, IV, 645 at 650.

explained, Samuel Chase, his "sure coadjutor"[47] William Paca and Luther Martin did not put in an appearance until the fourth day of the convention. Meanwhile, on the morning of the third day, the Constitution had been read through a first time. It was resolved that there should be no resolution as to particulars, but that there should be a second reading "after which the Subject may be fully debated and considered." The president was then to put the question "that this Convention do assent to and ratify. . . ." The second reading occurred that afternoon.[48]

When Chase and Martin appeared on Thursday, a vote was in order on the main question. Chase proceeded to lay out his objections, finally subsiding on the ground that he was exhausted and would resume the next day. Delegate William Smith wrote General Otho Williams that Chase had spoken for about two and a half hours. A profound silence had ensued for some time. Thomas Johnson rose and moved that as "there was nothing before them," there be an adjournment for dinner. "Martin had a sore throat which disqualified him from holding forth, & saved a great deal of time and money to the State."[49]

No report was made of Chase's speech; in fact, no speeches at all were reported by Lloyd, who had been engaged as shorthand writer. The story was that, being a federalist, and the federalists remaining obdurately silent, Lloyd would not report the opposition.[50] But Chase preserved some notes of his own objections to the Constitution indicating the tenor of his arguments in the convention, even if they were not actually used there. It is apparent from occasional citations that Chase had studied both the Pennsylvania and Massachusetts debates. He had consulted *Brutus*, *Cato*, the "Federal Farmer," "Old Whig" and some fall issues of the Pennsylvania newspapers. Most of the familiar arguments were arrayed—the defect of the delegates' authority, the pernicious tendency toward a consolidated government, the dangerous powers of the President, the taxing powers of Congress. He favored a bill of rights and amendment in advance of ratification. Curiously enough, he had only generalized objections to the judiciary. He opposed the diversity jurisdiction as there was no guarantee of jury trial. He objected particularly to federal jurisdiction over causes between citizens and foreign subjects. He believed that excise men were given an unrestrained power

---

[47] So described by John Brown Cutting in a letter to Jefferson, July 11, 1788, *Papers of Jefferson*, XIII, 330, 332.

[48] "Proceedings of the Maryland Convention," in *Doc. Hist. Const.*, II, 102–03.

[49] Otho Williams Mss., IV, No. 376, Apr. 28, 1788 (Maryland Hist. Soc.).

[50] "Anecdote," Annapolis *Maryland Gazette*, May 22, 1788.

of search (citing "Clayton's Rep 44—woman's shift") and were exempted from suing in state courts with jury trial.[51]

Chase was a Confederation man because he was passionately devoted to his state. He thought that the difficulties of the Union, which he described as a league, could be resolved if the states did their duty. He did not explain how this could successfully be brought about, but he believed that powers could be given "without surrendering our liberties." There is no reason to doubt the sincerity of his convictions, for even after he became a vocal Federalist Party man, his opinions in *United States v. Worrall*[52] and *Calder v. Bull*[53] disclose his respect for the state establishments.

In the afternoon following Chase's speech, William Paca turned up. He stated that he had many objections and wished to propose several amendments to accompany ratification. He prayed leave to prepare and submit them the following morning. Thomas Johnson thought this to be a reasonable request and moved for adjournment.[54] There was no division on this motion.

On Friday morning before Paca had an opportunity to present his amendments, delegates from each of eleven counties and one from each city one by one declared that they "were under an obligation to vote for the government."[55] They had no authority to propose amendments, and their constituents had given no directions. When Paca arose on the subject of amendments he was ruled out of order, the main question being still before the house. We have no adequate description of the antifederalist attack, but judging from some casual words of Washington, it must have been conducted with great vehemence.[56] All the rest of the day and the next morning the antifederalists spoke; the federalists remained "inflexibly silent." The motion for ratification was put early Saturday afternoon, April 27, and carried 63–11.[57]

Paca, who had voted with the majority, arose once more and read his amendments. He declared that he had voted for the Constitution in expectation of their future adoption; without amendments no man in the country would be more firmly opposed to the Constitution than himself and his constituents.[58] After debate it was agreed to appoint

---

[51] These papers in Chase's often indecipherable handwriting were generously loaned the writer by one of Chase's descendants. The format suggests, as does the occurrence of several repetitions, that the notes may have been set down for more than a single speech.

[52] 2 Dallas 384 (1798).

[53] 3 Dallas 386 (1798).

[54] Hanson, "Address . . . ," in *Doc. Hist. Const.*, IV, 652.

[55] *Ibid.*

[56] Washington to Madison, May 2, 1788, *Washington Writings*, XXIX, 491.

[57] Paca, "A Fragment of Facts Disclosing the Conduct of the Maryland Convention," in Elliot, *Debates*, II, 547, 549.

[58] *Ibid.*, 549.

a committee to consider the amendments, and to report on Monday, April 29, a draft of such amendments thought necessary to be submitted to the people, "if approved of by this Convention."[59] The committee, overloaded with federalists, met for two days and after heated wrangling emerged with nothing to report. Both Johnson and Samuel Chase were members of this committee.

Paca's propositions, twenty-eight in number, were a curious mélange of specific constituents of a bill of rights and a variety of limitations upon or additions to the Constitution.[60] All of these had been aired in the months of open controversy except number 28, proclaiming the right to revolution, lifted from the Maryland bill of rights. The articles dealing with the judicial process furnish a clue as to what the antifederalists may have raised on the subject in their one-sided debate. In criminal cases jury trial must follow the course of proceedings in the state where the offense was committed. No appeal should lie from matter of fact. There should be no second trial after acquittal. In actions on debts, contracts and all other controversies respecting property where inferior federal courts had jurisdiction, there was to be jury trial at the option of either party. State courts should have concurrent jurisdiction with an appeal in either case only as to matters of law to the Supreme Court. There could be no appeal unless the amount in controversy exceeded a certain amount. The jurisdiction of inferior federal courts was to be similarly limited, and in revenue cases both law and fact could be appealed. Congress was to be empowered to give the state courts concurrent jurisdiction in such cases. In trespass actions the plaintiff was entitled to jury trial. State courts were to have concurrent jurisdiction. Appeals were to be limited to matters of law. Federal courts "shall not be entitled to jurisdiction by fictions or collusion." Federal judges might not hold any other office of profit or take the profits of any office created by Congress.

The committee had tentatively agreed to these amendments and to the bill of rights items. It was when the restrictions on the use of the militia and upon the powers of Congress were reached that the majority proved adamant.[61] Meantime, the convention had voted that it would consider no propositions for amendment except such as were submitted by the committee.[62] The minority of the committee, holding out particularly for a requisition before any direct taxes could become operative for limits on congressional interference with elections and

---

[59] *Ibid.*
[60] Set out *ibid.*, 550–53. The Baltimore *Maryland Journal*, Apr. 29, 1788, published the text of the amendments signed by the clerk of the convention.

[61] Paca, "Fragment of Facts . . . ," in Elliot, *Debates*, II, 550–53; see also Hanson, "Address . . . ," in *Doc. Hist. Const.*, IV, 657–63.
[62] See Paca, "Fragment of Facts . . . ," in *Elliot, Debates*, II, 554.

for state consent to despatch of militia out of its borders, irritated the majority into refusing to recommend anything. When the committee returned to the house, Paca, the chairman, reported on the proceedings, read off the amendments initially agreed to and the three that were rejected. An attempt to get the amendments before the house failed and the convention adjourned.

The antifederalist leaders at once published in broadside form an address to the people of Maryland. They set forth their version of the happenings, including also their proposed amendments.[63] The latter were tendered as a program for future action; yet, the immediate publication suggests a play at influencing the impending conventions elsewhere. Coming, however, as the valedictory of a defeated group, it is unlikely that the paper had much effect except as particulars may have coincided with items in other lists of amendments then circulating.

Like the "Address" of the Pennsylvania minority, the tone of this document is one of grievance. But the Maryland leaders were themselves to blame for their mortification. Had they been as prompt in their attendance at the convention as they were in publishing their story, they might have had less cause for complaint. As it was, by their dilly-dallying they arrived to face a parliamentary situation that could not be undone. Their only triumph, if such it can be called, was the Pyrrhic one that for decades to come theirs was the only version to remembrance the events at Annapolis.

SOUTH CAROLINA

IF THE SCHEME of a Southern confederation was ever more than a political stalking horse in the calculations of its progenitors, the Maryland ratification was indeed a setback. There was, however, no cause to despair of South Carolina. In January, after extensive debate, a resolution to hold a convention had passed the House of Representatives by but a single vote.[64] Unlike the strategy elsewhere pursued of not having the issues pre-judged in legislatures, full discussion had been decided upon. The French consul reported that this had been done to smoke out the opposition under "pretext of enlightening the people."[65] The opposition gained nothing from this opportunity of airing its views, for it could muster no better leadership than Rawlins Lowndes who had made

---

[63] Copy in the NYHS Collection of Broadsides. It was printed in the Annapolis *Maryland Gazette*, May 1, 1788.

[64] For the vote on the question, Elliot, *Debates*, IV, 316–17; for the

preceding debate, *ibid.*, 253–316.

[65] M. Petry to the Duc de Noailles, Jan. 12, 1788, Archives Nationales, Affaires Etrangères B¹ 372, Correspondance Consulaires, Charleston I, 1784–1792, 266 (LC Trans.).

his personal peace with the British when they overran the state. In contrast, the Pinckneys and John Rutledge demonstrated that the federalist cause could be handled with skill. Their speeches were polished and adorned with learning. The self-interest of Carolina was adroitly handled, and if Rutledge toward the end showed the sharp side of his tongue, this only added spice to the proceedings.

Opposition leadership did not improve during the four months that elapsed before the convention met. Nothing indicates better the hollowness of the Southern confederation scheme than the fact that Virginia gazettes printed but the slightest intelligence from south of Cape Henry. This is true also of New York and Philadelphia journals, despite the fact that shipping news shows a constant intercourse between these ports and Charleston. The intellectual traffic, if flow of propaganda may be so described, was one way. Matter from the two great centers of polemical writing, New York and Philadelphia, was reprinted for the delectation of the Carolinians, but reciprocal publication of their effusions amounts to almost nothing. We have it from two sources, Charles Cotesworth Pinckney[66] and the French consul,[67] that the Pennsylvania minority was flooding the state with pamphlets and other writings to build up opposition, particularly in the back country.

The antifederalists were manifestly seeking to capitalize upon political grievances of some years' standing. Under the constitution of 1778, the scheme of representation, contrived to center power in the low country, had allotted the back country a meagre representation, grossly disproportionate to the number of inhabitants.[68] At the moment economic distress common to planters of the east and farmers of the *haut pays* might have provided a link between them.[69] But the social cleavage, resembling the Boston-western counties division, was an older and perhaps more ponderable factor. Here was fertile soil for the seeds sown by the antifederalists, in particular the threats of aristocracy and irreligion. Presumably, too, a population that not long since had suffered the savage man hunts of Tarleton and his legion would lend ready ears to warnings about the Turkish janissaries of a standing army. But here the federalists were in luck. The Creeks were an impending menace against whom the Carolinians well knew they would need all the help they could get.

The convention, due to open May 12, got under way the following

---

[66] C. C. Pinckney to Rufus King, May 24, 1788, *Life of King*, I, 328.

[67] M. Petry to the Duc de Noailles, Jan. 12, 1788, *supra*, n. 65. J. T. Main, *The Antifederalists*, 217, states that "no publications circulated."

[68] There is some discussion on this in Main, *The Antifederalists*, 23 *et seq.*

[69] The economic background is considered in McDonald, *We The People*, 205 *et seq.*

day.[70] Governor Thomas Pinckney submitted a letter from Governor Hancock of Massachusetts enclosing a copy of the proceedings of the convention in his state, which was ordered to lie on the table for the information of the delegates.[71] What prompted Hancock's gesture we do not know, unless it was to bring light to the benighted, in particular concerning the amendments recommended. On this the Carolinians had some ideas of their own.

It was decided to take up the Constitution by paragraphs and, when done, to vote to accept or reject. There is precious little available on the debates themselves and nothing of consequence on the judiciary. The discussion began May 14, and the *Journal* indicates that very little time could have been spent on Article III; on Monday, May 19, the assemblage was still debating Article II and the next day was on Article VII. There is so little reported of the actual debates that no adequate idea of the ebb and flow of argument can be formed.[72] On May 21, after the reading of the resolve of the Philadelphia Convention, Washington's letter and the resolve of Congress, General Sumter moved that further consideration of the Constitution be adjourned until the following October 20. This was beaten 135–89.[73] Sumter reportedly sought adjournment to give more time for reflection,[74] but it seems to us more probable that he may have wished to wait out action by Virginia and North Carolina.

George Miller, the British consul, reported to his government that the debate by the opposition had been feeble.[75] His French colleague, with Gallic volubility, was more descriptive: "the opposition did not distinguish itself either by its talents of eloquence or by the justice of its principles, or by its knowledge of forming a government originally by the liberality of its sentiments."[76] Nevertheless, enough of a fight was put up that, as Edward Rutledge reported to Jay, there were "sacrifices to make."[77] The sacrifices were presumably a list of recommended amendments. Rutledge was on the committee appointed May 23 to draft these. The report, made the same day, was composed

---

[70] A. S. Salley, Jr., ed., *Journal of the Convention of South Carolina*, 3.

[71] *Ibid.*, 20.

[72] In Elliot, *Debates*, IV, 318–38, are reprinted a few speeches which add nothing to our knowledge of what may have been said about Art. III.

[73] *Journal of the Convention of South Carolina*, 13, 21–23.

[74] Charleston *State Gazette of South Carolina*, May 22, 1788.

[75] Miller to the Earl of Carmarthen, June 6, 1788, PRO FO 4/6.

[76] M. Petry to the Duc de Noailles, May 24, 1788, *supra*, n. 65, at 289.

[77] Edward Rutledge to John Jay, June 24, 1788, Ms. Jay Papers (CUL): "We had a tedious but trifling opposition to contend with. We had prejudices to contend with & sacrifices to make. Yet they were worth making for the good olde Cause."

of two declarations and three resolves.[78] The convention declared that the right of prescribing time, manner and plans of election to the federal legislature ought to remain "to all posterity a perpetual and fundamental right in the local, exclusive of the interference of the General Government except in cases where the Legislatures of the States, shall refuse or neglect to perform and fulfil the same." The second declaration was that no section or paragraph of the Constitution "warrants a Construction" that the states did not retain any power not expressly relinquished and vested in the general government. The first resolve was a monition that the general government should not impose direct taxes except the yield of imports, duties and excises were insufficient or until Congress first resorted to requisitions. This followed the tenor and at points the language of the fourth Massachusetts-proposed amendment. The second resolve, dealing with Article VI, proposed merely insertion of a word so that the phrase of the last sentence would read "no *other* religious test." What the intendment of this may have been is obscure, unless it was by indirection to assure that oaths or affirmations exacted in the article be posited upon belief in a divine being.[79] Finally, it was resolved that it should be a standing instruction to state representatives to secure amendments conformable to the resolution.

These propositions did not go far enough to suit the antifederalists. Aedanus Burke, whose pamphlet on the aristocratical designs of the Cincinnati had brought him fame, moved to add a resolve making the President ineligible to succeed himself.[80] Otherwise, Burke claimed, the Presidency was calculated to terminate in an hereditary monarchy. This was rejected 139–69. In succession, a motion the purport of which was to make absolute the prohibition on gifts from foreign potentates (Article I, section 9) and another to deny Congress control of militia and to limit marching them out of the state were beaten. After the committee report was agreed to, a motion was made and defeated for an appointment of a committee to draw up a bill of rights to be proposed in amendment of the Constitution.[81] Ratification was resolved May 23 by a vote of 149–73.[82]

A month later Aedanus Burke, his wounds still green, wrote

---

[78] Set out in the instrument of ratification, *Doc. Hist. Const.*, II, 139–40.

[79] By Art. XXXVIII of the South Carolina constitution of 1778, "the Christian Protestant religion" was declared to be the established religion of the state. Governor, lieutenant governor, privy councillors, Senators and delegates to the House of Representatives were required to be "of the Protestant religion." Acknowledgment of the being of a God and belief in a future state of rewards and punishments were listed among the qualifications of electors. Thorpe, *Constitutions and Charters*, VI, 3249, 3251, 3255.

[80] *Journal of the Convention of South Carolina*, 25.

[81] *Ibid.*, 38–39.

[82] *Ibid.*, 49.

in a rancorous vein to John Lamb of New York that four fifths of the people "from the soul" detested the Constitution.[83] In Charleston it had been favored by merchants, mechanics, the professions, ex-Tories, the British consul—all classes down to the British scavengers. The journeymen printers, mostly of British origin, had with "servile insolence" discouraged opposition but pushed the publication of pro-Constitution matter. Burke admitted that previous to the convention the opposition had spoken or written "hardly a word." This was a misrepresentation. The Charleston *State Gazette of South Carolina* had reprinted Martin's verbose *Genuine Information* which was still running when the convention met. Obviously this was no doing of a federalist.

In Burke's opinion the chief reason Carolina had ratified was because the convention was held in Charleston. "The merchants and leading men kept open houses for the back and low country Members during the whole time the Convention sat."[84] This was in sharp contrast with the Massachusetts technique of starving the countrymen into submission. The chief prop of the Carolina antifederalists had been Dr. Fayssoux; but when on the sixth day of sitting word arrived of Maryland's ratification, he gave notice of throwing in his hand.[85] One by one others defected.

After the triumphal procession in Charleston, word drifted in from the back country that the people in places had held a funeral procession with a black painted coffin and buried it "as an emblem of the dissolution and interment of publick liberty." Half-clothed and half-armed, these people had fought British regulars for liberty. They "will join heart and hand to bring Ruin on the new plan unless it be materially altered."[86]

VIRGINIA

To HISTORIANS the Virginia Convention has always seemed to be the most interesting of all, if for no other reason than that it was the most fully reported. There were, besides, more eminences, contemporary

---

[83] June 23, 1788, Ms. Lamb Papers, Box 5, No. 25 (NYHS).

[84] Charleston hospitality may have been not without its effects. On May 29, 1788, Nicholas Gilman, attending Congress, wrote J. Wadsworth a summary of news from an "authentic" letter from South Carolina that had been written apparently before the vote on adjournment was taken. Gilman reported that some of the back-country members fettered with instructions "repugnant to their present sentiments" would probably vote in favor of the new system if unable to effect adjournment. Ms. Emmet Collection, No. 9442 (NYPL).

[85] See his statement in Charleston *State Gazette of South Carolina*, May 28, 1788.

[86] Burke to Lamb, *supra*, n. 83.

and future, attending than in any of the other state conventions. Not unnaturally, biographers of many of these leaders have severally depicted their subjects as if each alone had been the proper hero of the occasion. As a result, to one who has conned this literature, the struggle at Richmond is apt to seem one of epic proportions. But the debates themselves, without these adventitious embroideries, are something less than that— some extraordinarily well-reasoned speeches, some "pathetic" addresses, as the phrase then was, some shrewd ripostes and some wonderful sound and fury. There was little advanced that a reader of contemporary newspapers and pamphlets and the proceedings of other conventions will not already have come upon—for by this time everything had been written or said that ingenuity could produce. What gave the performance an excitement at the time was the signal importance of Virginia's accession to the new plan, and the fact that by consensus the issue was highly in doubt.

In both camps there were men of great political experience; in both prevailed that fierce pride of state for which Virginia was already renowned. Inevitably the question, was the new plan best for Virginia, tended often to crowd out the broader question of the nation's good. For this the nativistic zeal of the antifederalists was particularly responsible; and, of course, the exigencies of local politics were here no less involved. In this the Virginians were no different from their neighbors. Just as the delegates were assembling at Richmond, a writer in the *Virginia Independent Chronicle* addressed them, urging upon them the great economic advantages of the new plan and the disadvantages of separate confederations.[87] It was an able piece, but more likely to have affected opinion in Boston, New York or Philadelphia, for it did not address itself to the economic matters about which Virginians were exercised and which, because of their political implications, were to boil up at the convention.

The antifederalist cause had protagonists of greater ability than had yet spoken for the opposition in any other state.[88] Chief among them was Patrick Henry, the peerless orator of his time. No less eminent as a Virginian was George Mason, the chief architect of the state con-

---

[87] Reprinted in *The Virginia Herald and Fredericksburg Advertiser*, June 5 and 12, 1788.

[88] The part of the antifederalist leaders is described in Rowland, *Life and Correspondence of George Mason*, II, 219–71; W. Wirt, *Sketches of the Life and Character of Patrick Henry*, 263–311; W. W. Henry, *Patrick Henry: Life, Correspondence and Speeches*, III, 438 *et seq.* On Gray-

son, see H. B. Grigsby, *History of the Virginia Federal Convention of 1788*, I, 195–206, and *passim.* Grigsby's history was composed *c.* 1856 and he consequently had access to materials some of which were destroyed in the course of the Civil War. He was addicted to a florid Victorian style which makes it difficult on occasions to unravel fancy from now undocumentable fact.

stitution. Equally able in debate was William Grayson, who had long represented Virginia in the Confederation Congress, and who had fought the transmission of the Constitution to the states. These three carried the brunt of the debate. Richard Henry Lee, however, was not present. He had not stood for the convention, apparently for reasons of health. Mason was greatly chagrined, for as Arthur Lee wrote, "there will be no one in whom he can confide." Lee's absence undoubtedly subtracted from the strength of antifederalist leadership. For it is clear that unlike the federalists, the three chiefs of the opposition never achieved a well-planned and coordinated strategy.[89]

The federalists had succeeded in electing men of great capacity, some of them, indeed, from counties supposedly opposed to ratification. The most venerable of them, Edmund Pendleton, was Presiding Judge of the Court of Appeals and in the evening of a remarkable career in public service.[90] James Madison was, of all, the astutest of politicians, and despite his physical shortcomings, a deadly man on the floor.[91] George Nicholas, brother-in-law of the governor, a leader of the bar, has been described as "the *Ulysses* as well as the *Ajax Telamon* of the hosts which upheld the Constitution."[92] John Marshall, youngest of the group, was to make his mark in the discussion of the judiciary article.[93] Neither side was certain where stood the governor, Edmund Randolph. On the third day of the convention he threw in his lot with the federalists.

As happened elsewhere, the federalists appear to have organized their strategy in advance. On the field, as it were, their tactics in the choice of speakers were unsurpassed. This is very evident in the way Randolph was handled once he had made clear his decision. And skill was needed, for although the dream of Virginia heading a Southern confederation had been shattered by Maryland's ratification, and the arrival of word on the second day of the convention that South Carolina had acceded,[94] there were three practical issues of state politics to be met. The first of these concerned the thorny problem of the British debts and their collection through a neutral national forum. The second concerned the supposed dangers to titles in the western lands. The third was the question of the free navigation of the Mississippi. The delegates

---

[89] Arthur Lee to R. H. Lee, Feb. 19, 1788, Ms. Lee Family Papers Library, University of Virginia. Arthur urged his brother to stand for Tangier.

[90] On Pendleton in the convention see D. J. Mays, *Edmund Pendleton, 1721–1803, A Biography*, II, 217–72.

[91] On Madison in the convention, see I. Brant, *James Madison*, III, 185–228.

[92] Grigsby, *History of the Virginia Federal Convention of 1788*, II, at 286. There is here a sketch of the man and his career.

[93] On Marshall, see A. J. Beveridge, *The Life of John Marshall*, I, 357–480.

[94] William Grayson to Nathan Dane, June 4, 1788, Ms. Dane Papers (LC).

from the Kentucky counties were vitally interested in these last two matters, and without some of these votes the federalists believed that they could not succeed.[95]

Edmund Pendleton was elected president of the convention, June 2, the day of the first meeting. On the second day it was moved by Mason that the Constitution should be debated clause by clause before any question upon it be propounded. This being agreed to on motion of John Tyler, another antifederalist, it was resolved that the convention sit as a Committee of the Whole.[96] Nothing could have been more to the federalists' purposes than to have the opposition take the lead in a particular so important.[97] Nothing illustrates better the lack of concert in antifederalist leadership than the way in which their speakers refused to be confined by their own motion. This had the result that salvos of heterogeneous objections continued for days. When debate finally settled into a more orderly routine, the force of their projectiles was spent. The later repetition of an objection at a relevant point, far from persuading, could only induce tedium.

During the first week, once the debate was under way, Patrick Henry had, almost single-handed, carried the attack for the antifederalists. He had opened (June 4) mildly enough, with a query as to *"We, the people"* and by what authority the Framers had spoken for the people. Why was it not *"We, the states"*?[98] If the states were not the agents of this compact, it must be one consolidated government. Henry was fol-

---

[95] Mays, in *Edmund Pendleton*, II, 250, states that the Kentuckians were so alarmed over loss of the Mississippi that a convention had been called at Danville to instruct their delegates. Grayson, writing to Dane on June 4 (*supra*, n. 94), claimed that the District of Kentucky "is with us if we can get over the four counties which lye on the Ohio between the Pennsylvania line and big Sandy Creek the day is ours."

Apart from the two issues mentioned in the text it appears from a letter of Harry Innes to John Brown, Feb. 20, 1788, that the proposed federal judiciary was not liked in Kentucky. Citizens of the eastern states would not sue in Kentucky. Citizens of the latter "will be drawn away," and nine out of ten times would be sacrificed. Ms. Harry Innes Papers, XXVIII, (LC). Innes was later District judge.

[96] Elliot, *Debates*, III, 4. *The Virginia Herald and Fredericksburg Advertiser*, June 12, 1788, printed a letter of June 5 from Richmond recounting an interchange over permitting shorthand notes by David Robertson. The claim was breach of privilege, frequently determined so by the House of Commons. Mason feared a fatal stab from a perversion of language. In a letter to his son he later referred to Robertson as a "federal partizan" and expressed his suspicion that the report would be garbled in the "partial manner" of Lloyd's report of the Pennsylvania debates. Rowland, *Life and Correspondence of George Mason*, II, 298.

[97] *Cf.* Washington to Jay, June 8, 1788, *Washington Writings*, XXIX, 512. The antifederalists thought "this is in our favor." Grayson to Dane, *supra*, n. 94.

[98] Elliot, *Debates*, III, 21.

lowed by Randolph who disclosed his change of heart.[99] He proceeded to depict the necessities of the country that had made essential a more rigorous system of government. Stealing some of Henry's usual ammunition, he answered that it was *"We the people"* because government was for the people, and by misfortune the people had no agency in the existing government. Mason, who spoke next, picked up the theme of the "consolidated government," and in the process of his assault upon the Constitution claimed that the judiciary provisions would convince all that the annihilation of state governments would ensue. He then proceeded to admit that if amendments were introduced that would exclude the danger to the preservation of freedom and secure the rights of the people, he would put his hand to it. Most needed was an amendment that Congress should not have a power of direct taxation until the states should refuse to comply with requisitions.

That night Madison wrote Washington that Henry and Mason "appeared to take different and awkward ground."[100] Whether or not the opposition were cognizant of this does not appear. Nevertheless, Mason did not speak again for another week. Thenceforward, it was Henry, and for days he spread before the assemblage his awesome bill of particulars against the iniquitous document before it. To the allegations that the prostration of national affairs and the deficiencies of state government, which ran even to the failure of ordinary justice, made a constitutional change imperative, his replication was a series of vivid vignettes of the Revolution, and the patriotism of the citizenry, the effectiveness of the state systems and, above all, the florescence of liberty. This it was which the absence of specific safeguards for trial by jury, rights of conscience and the like imperilled.

There was no expedient to which Henry did not resort—the parade of all the bogeys which for months had inhabited the newspapers, the intimations of secession of southern Virginia, the invidious personal thrust, the solemn invocation of the opinion of Jefferson that four states should reject in order to secure amendments.[101]

---

[99] For antifederalist reaction, *cf.* Monroe to Jefferson, July 12, 1788, *Papers of Jefferson*, XIII, 351; George Mason to John Mason, Dec. 18, 1788, Rowland, *Life and Correspondence of George Mason*, II, 302, 304, where he calls Randolph "young A[rno]ld."

[100] June 4, 1788, *Doc. Hist. Const.*, IV, 683.

[101] This was the same excerpt apparently as that used in the Maryland Convention (*cf.* text at n. 19,

supra). Jefferson was so informed by Madison (July 24, 1788, *Papers of Jefferson*, XIII, 412–13). Henry first mentioned it on June 9 (Elliot, *Debates*, III, 152), and returned to the subject three days later (*ibid.*, 314). Randolph attempted to temper the effect of this (*ibid.*, 199–200). On June 12 Madison attempted to set out what he believed to be Jefferson's more recent thoughts (*ibid.*, 329 *et seq.*)

The federalists made no immediate effort to chain Henry to the orderly discussion of the Constitution by paragraphs. Randolph, Nicholas, Francis Corbin and pre-eminently Madison parried the orator's thrusts, explained, defined, met history with history. It was almost as if they sought to wear out their adversary before getting down to the pedestrian task of ploughing through the document they had met to ratify or reject. They, too, were not averse to making personal reflections. The most wounding of these was a charge made by Randolph in connection with his claim that there had been persistent violations of the Virginia constitution since 1776.[102] He recalled the case of the attainder of Josiah Phillips by the Virginia legislature during the governorship of Henry. As this had been in defiance of Section 8 of the Virginia bill of rights, it was a telling impeachment of Henry's sincerity. Henry helped himself none with his defense that the fellow was no Socrates, but a murderer and outlaw who might be struck out of existence as soon as apprehended.[103]

During these days of almost aimless circumambulation, the federalists were in serious trouble when Henry began pressing the Mississippi question. It was his contention that when negotiations were under way with Spain, the states with no interest in the future of inland navigation, in particular the carrying states to the north, had been willing to sacrifice the South. This was at once demagogic arousing of sectional feeling and an appeal to the self-interest of the Kentucky delegates. What made Henry's charges colorable, indeed, devastating, was the fact that James Monroe, whose political ethics were not invariably above reproach, proceeded to lay bare details of the late negotiation with Spain—a violation of Congress's rule of secrecy in the negotiations.[104] Monroe's breach of the rule was compounded by Grayson, who had further embellishments to add.[105] The federalists did their best to counteract

---

[102] Elliot, *Debates*, III, 66 *et seq.*

[103] *Ibid.*, 140. Randolph's statements that there was no trial were erroneous; *cf.* the documents in App. C, Wirt, *Sketches of the Life and Character of Patrick Henry.* The bill of attainder is in 9 Hening, *Va. Stats.*, 463; Jefferson's draft of the bill is in *Papers of Jefferson*, II, 189. The editor's note to the latter has a long account of the episode. Due to Jefferson's involvement it is there argued that the Virginia Declaration of Rights contained no specific prohibition of bills of attainder. Nevertheless, it must be observed that sec. 8 sets out all the then known safeguards of "capital or criminal prosecutions" except

right to counsel. Obviously if a man "hath a right" to demand the cause of prosecution, to confrontation by accusers and witnesses, to call witnesses in defense, to speedy jury trial by the vicinage, to a unanimous verdict and not to be compelled to give evidence against himself, the bill of attainder was in subversion of this provision and Jefferson could hardly have been unaware of this.

[104] Elliot, *Debates*, III, 335 *et seq.*

[105] Grayson admitted the rule of secrecy and thought since the Committee desired to develop the subject, "I shall stand excused" (*ibid.*, 340–41).

the baleful effect of these disclosures upon the Kentuckians who had been regaled with the dangers they would face under the new system which did not offer the security of the nine-state vote provided in the Articles of Confederation for the ratification of treaties. Madison's defense was inept, for he was frankly not prepared to "sully the reputation of our public councils"[106] as had the others. The final vote of the Kentucky delegates is proof of how little effect federalist arguments had upon them, although David Stuart seems to have believed the contrary.[107]

Until Saturday, June 14, the debate, which had ranged over a truly remarkable assortment of collateral and irrelevant matter, had ostensibly been over the first and second sections of Article I. It was that day moved by Corbin that the convention proceed "regularly" clause by clause. If he had hoped to end the unhappy Mississippi discussion, his seconder, the antifederalist Alexander White, promised to return to it when the Senate's treaty-making powers were taken up. The third, fourth and fifth sections were then read, and debate proceeded in a more orderly manner. That is not to say that there was no poaching in sections not before the house. The discussion (June 16) of the necessary and proper clause was an example.

The fears expressed that this provision was a *carte blanche* for Congress to forage about and legislate upon any conceivable subject, including abolition of jury trial, was a signal for Henry to have read certain articles from the Virginia bill of rights.[108] Nicholas explained that the intendment of the clause was that it was not related to the whole legislative power, but solely to the particular power of laying taxes for the purpose of paying debts and providing for common defense. If the Congress should exceed its powers, "the judiciary will declare it void, or else the people will have a right to declare it void."[109] Mason declared that artful sophistry and evasions could not satisfy him. He still believed there should be a clause expressly declaring that rights not given were retained by the states. Why was there no bill of rights? Unless there was one, "implication might swallow up all our rights."[110]

This put Henry on his feet to speak warmly for the necessity of such an addition—to give up power without a bill of rights was an absurdity. In Virginia when the state government was organized, the

---

106 *Ibid.*, 344.

107 Stuart to Harry Innes, June 29, 1788, Ms. Harry Innes Papers, XX, Pt. 2 (LC). He relates that the opponents of the Constitution had played on Kentucky feelings with the Mississippi question but that the Kentucky leaders now understood it and all fears were removed. It was proved that the Constitution was the best way of securing navigation of the river.

108 Elliot, *Debates*, III, 442.

109 *Ibid.*, 443.

110 *Ibid.*, 445.

common law of England was declared to be in force. This had protected the people as it had their ancestors. In addition, a bill of rights was adopted. In the proposed Constitution some of the best barriers of human rights were thrown away. At common law, trial of all facts was by jury of impartial men from the immediate vicinage. "This paper speaks of different juries from the common law in criminal cases; and in civil controversies excludes trial by jury altogether." Launching into a prophecy of the horrors of criminal law administration under the new plan, he protested that Americans should not be satisfied with less than Britons had. "That paper ought to have declared the common law in force."[111]

The weakness of Henry's ground and of Grayson's, who chimed in, was that the Virginia bill of rights was not in their constitution. Nicholas, who answered them, suggested that to establish that a bill of rights belonged in the federal Constitution, they must prove that it belonged in the Virginia constitution. The Virginia bill had, in any event, been violated in many instances—it was but a paper check. "You," obviously to Henry, "have violated that maxim, 'that no man shall be condemned without a fair trial.' That man who was killed, not *secundum artem*, was deprived of his life without the benefit of law and in express violation of this declaration of rights, which they confide in so much."[112]

As for the common law, Nicholas asked what would have been the consequence of a declaration that it was in force. It would be immutable. But the legislature, as matters stood, could legislate for the community freely. The common law was not excluded, for there was nothing in the paper to warrant such an assertion. There could be legislation for a jury of the vicinage. Henry's notion that Congress could by the Constitution define crimes and prescribe punishments was wrong. Treason was defined in the Constitution. Congress had power to define and punish piracies, felonies on the high seas and offenses against the law of nations; "but they cannot define or prescribe the punishment of any crime whatever, without violating the Constitution."[113]

The next day Henry came back to his favorite theme when the ninth section of Article I was read. The specific interdiction of ex post facto laws and the limitations on suspension of habeas corpus he took to prove that everything not expressly reserved was given up. This together with other matter made urgent the need for his bill of rights.

Randolph, who replied, undertook to answer the latest objections as well as what Henry had said the previous day.[114] He spoke particularly about the misleading statements that jury trial in civil cases had been abolished, and gave the usual explanation of why a general rule ap-

---

[111] *Ibid.*, 446–47.   [112] *Ibid.*, 450.   [113] *Ibid.*, 451.   [114] *Ibid.*, 463.

plicable to conditions in all the states could not have been embodied in the Constitution. As for the common law, this ought not to be immutably fixed. In Virginia it was secured only by statute and the legislature was free to alter it. What would have been the dilemma if it had been established in the Constitution? The writ of burning heretics (*de comburendo haeretico*) could have been revived. It would tend to throw property into the hands of the few; it would destroy the principles of republican government. It could be adopted by the legislature, its defective parts altered and modifications could be made as the convenience of the public might require.

The exchanges over the absence of a provision adopting the common law was the only important excursus on matter relating to law administration until Article III was reached, June 19. The night before, Grayson wrote Nathan Dane confessing that "our affairs in this quarter are in a ticklish situation." Only ten of the thirteen Kentuckians had been landed, and his group was not sure that one of the four upper counties had been secured. As for the judiciary, "we shall exert our whole force," since he anticipated securing two votes if the debate was conducted in an able manner.[115]

Pendleton opened for the federalists.[116] He regarded a judiciary to be an essential part of government, not only to check the executive arm, but also to serve as a protection for individuals. The arrangements for inferior courts were properly left to Congress, in order that change of circumstance could be met by legislative alterations. The use of state courts, he thought, would be Congress's first experiment, chiefly in the interests of economy. But even this mode might need to be changed and the Congress should have the power to do so. As for the jurisdiction, this was in all particulars of general and not local concern. The original jurisdiction of the Supreme Court he conceived to be susceptible of attenuation by Congress but not of enlargement.

Pendleton defended the appellate jurisdiction as essential not only to correct erroneous decisions of inferior tribunals, but also to introduce uniformity. He deprecated the words "both as to law and fact," which he wished "had been buried in oblivion,"[117] but he believed that Congress's power to make exceptions and regulations removed doubts. Obviously for the benefit of lay delegates, Pendleton explained the course of review in equity, admiralty and common law causes. He met the argument of the ruinous cost of appeals by the suggestion that these might be limited to a certain sum.

---

[115] Grayson to Dane, June 18, 1788, Ms. Dane Papers (LC). The dating in Elliot, *Debates*, III, 517, is in obvious error. Grayson states the debate was to open the next day.

[116] Elliot, *Debates*, III, 517.

[117] *Ibid.*, 519.

Mason, who replied, admitted that the judiciary "lies out of my line,"[118] but managed to talk for a long time. He challenged the friends of the Constitution to show what was left to the state courts. The supremacy of the laws of the United States and the extension of judicial power to all cases in law and equity in combination excluded no objects of jurisdiction. The effect and operation of the federal courts would be to destroy the state governments. As he explored this theme he spoke carelessly of persons he knew who favored a consolidated government. Madison interrupted and demanded an unequivocal explanation, as "these insinuations" might create a belief that every member of the Federal Convention was of that opinion.[119] Mason exculpated Madison and the Virginia delegates of such beliefs, an explanation that was accepted.

Mason continued, running through all the conventional objections to the jurisdiction. He believed that jurisdiction over causes to which the United States should be a party might, without restraint, be dangerously and oppressively extended. Jurisdiction over disputes between a state and citizens of another state was improper; equally so was the diversity of citizenship jurisdiction. Finally, jurisdiction over disputes between a state and citizens thereof was still more improper. At this point Nicholas rose and told Mason his interpretation was not warranted by the words. To this Mason made the astonishing reply that if he recollected rightly, the propriety of the power as explained to him had been contended for, but his memory was not good, and he would not insist upon it.

After painting a deplorable picture of indulgent federal judges dealing with the excesses of federal officers guilty of the greatest oppressions or who might behave with the "most insolent and wanton brutality to a man's wife or daughter" and the unendurable hardship of an appeal to a distant tribunal with jurisdiction over law and fact, Mason proposed what in substance was the amendment fourteen later recommended by the convention.[120] He had at this juncture reached a good stopping point, but he continued to spin out fanciful details as to how the various heads of jurisdiction would beget inconvenience and oppression. This was a skillfully confected *argumentum ad hominem*, specifically any man of Virginia—the inconveniences of Marylanders suing on a Virginian's bond in a federal court; the shame of a state being arraigned at the bar of justice like a delinquent individual; the British debts owed by Virginians; the peril to the Northern Neck by a revival of quitrents; the resuscitation of claims by companies to

---

[118] *Ibid.*, 521.　　[119] *Ibid.*, 522.　　[120] *Ibid.*, 525.

lands between the Blue Ridge and the Alleghenies; the claims of the Indiana Company to Kentucky lands.

This net was cast to catch a great variety of fish. Madison, who replied,[121] made no effort to counter the appeals to local prejudice or self-interest. He set out coldly the argument that jurisdiction must embrace any case that could arise under the Constitution. It was necessary, he said, that the judicial power should correspond with the legislative. It was perhaps a misfortune that in organizing any government the explication of its authority should be left to any of its coordinate branches. "There is a new policy in submitting it to the judiciary of the United States."[122] The expounding of treaties, cases involving foreign ministers, admiralty and maritime cases all affected foreign relations and hence were properly in federal courts. So, too, controversies affecting interests of the United States could not be left to partial, local tribunals. Controversies between two states were already provided for in the Articles of Confederation. Controversies between a state and the citizen of another state Madison conceived to be limited to cases where a state was plaintiff or would consent to be sued—a view which the Supreme Court later repudiated.[123]

Madison expressed the belief that disputes between citizens of different states might be left to the states but he thought it salutary that a federal jurisdiction exist for situations where a strong prejudice existed. He slid adroitly past the jurisdiction of controversies between a citizen and a citizen or subject of a foreign state, and confined his justification to the jurisdiction over disputes between an American state and a foreign state, as consonant with the law of nations. In any event, consent of both parties would be necessary. The regulatory powers of Congress, he believed, would make the judicial organization safe and convenient for both states and their citizens. The Supreme Court, he thought, might be ambulatory, and he cited the fact that this had been done with the Confederation Court of Appeals. Referring to the action of the Confederation Congress in vesting "state courts of admiralty" with jurisdiction over piracies and felonies on the high seas, he hazarded that "if there will be as much sympathy between Congress and the people as

---

[121] He began on June 19 and continued the next day.

[122] Elliot, *Debates*, III, 532.

[123] *Ibid.*, 532–33. It may be noticed that a paper in the Ms. George Mason Papers (LC), not in Mason's hand but with emendations in his hand, deals with the judiciary. It is printed in Farrand, *Records*, IV, 54–55. Far-

rand states that there is no evidence it was presented at the convention. The document's text provides that jurisdiction shall extend to controversies "between *a State and the Citizens thereof* and foreign States, Citizens or Subjects." Mason did not attempt to excise or amend this.

now, we may fairly conclude that federal cognizance will be vested in the local tribunals."[124] This was not an accurate statement of the ordinance for the trials of piracy; and unless Madison had had a lapse of memory, the cajoling comment about the states' exercising federal jurisdiction misrepresented what the Framers had sought to accomplish.

Like some minor Jeremiah, Henry rose to lament—"the purse is gone; the sword is gone; and here is the only thing of any importance that is to remain with us."[125] But not quite. The suggestion of vesting state judges with federal powers was a threat to the best barrier against strides of power—the Virginia judiciary. Who would prevail in case of a "concurrent dispute" between a state and the federal government? The laws of Congress being paramount, the judges must decide in favor of them. This was the end of judicial independence. Harking back to the grant of appellate jurisdiction, Henry harped upon the destruction of trial by jury. He scoffed at the idea of congressional regulation. If Congress should prohibit appeals as to facts, the federal judges, "if they spoke the sentiments of independent men, would declare their prohibition nugatory and void."[126] as being against the Constitution. Brushing aside the argument that the use of a technical term implied a reception of all matter incidental thereto, Henry declaimed this meant nothing to poor men whose rights should be secured in language of which they knew the meaning. He would rather the provision had been omitted. There was no right of challenge. "There is no common law of America (as has been said) nor constitution, but that on your table. If there be neither common law nor constitution, there can be no right to challenge partial jurors."[127]

Henry's diatribe on diversity jurisdiction revealed his unfamiliarity with the rudiments of conflicts of law. It was to him unthinkable that judges could know the law of various states. Recourse to a federal tribunal would consequently lead to the growth of a law destructive of local law. The jurisdiction of controversies between citizens and foreign subjects he regarded as a retrospective law, the effect of which was to alter the conditions of the original contract. He derided the idea that a state could be sued only by consent, and then recurring to his favorite theme, regaled the delegates with a reading from Blackstone's encomium of the jury. Henry's peroration began with a warning not to trust the wisdom and virtue of "our rulers." Congress in "all the plenitude of their arrogance, magnificence, and power" could take the privilege of jury trial from the American people. What reason was there to relinquish what Britain herself had preserved even to the point of rebellion when her rights were infringed. "This gives me comfort—that as long as I have

---

[124] Elliot, *Debates*, III, 536.
[126] *Ibid.*, 541.

[125] *Ibid.*, 539.
[127] *Ibid.*, 542.

existence my neighbors will protect me. Old as I am, it is probable I may yet have the appellation of *rebel*."[128]

Pendleton was helped to his crutches to reply.[129] He reiterated what had already been said about jury trial not being excluded and the point that the use of a technical term carried with it all incidents. To allay suspicion of the diversity jurisdiction, he conjured up the spectre of an outland obligee suing in Rhode Island and recovering under their laws but a third or less of his debt. The assignment of a bond to a Marylander to create diversity he disposed of by pointing out that action must be brought in federal court in Virginia. There could be no dragging of the defendant to the Supreme Court. He spoke critically of Mason's amendment as not meeting current practice in equity and admiralty. Mason answered briefly and was followed by John Marshall.[130]

Marshall had earlier crossed swords with Henry on June 10 and his comments then could only have made the latter uncomfortable. He had applauded the idea of adhering to fundamental maxims, and mockingly spun out three ugly "maxims" from Phillips' attainder.[131] He had referred to Henry's eulogy of the British constitution and queried innocently whether it would be more agreeable if the Senators were for life, and whether they would be safer if there were a constitutional maxim that the President could do no wrong. In his speech on the judiciary[132] it was not Henry alone, but Mason and Grayson as well who were to be belabored with good-humored and merciless logic.

The skill of Marshall's speech consisted in this—that he had searched out the most vulnerable of the absurdities and dire prophecies and cast these in the form of questions, some of which answered themselves, others of which he answered with reasonableness and temperateness. The principle on which the objections to the federal jurisdiction were based rested on the belief that there would not be a fair trial in these courts. Was there any reason to conclude that judges wisely appointed and independent in their office would countenance any unfair trial? Mason had objected to Congress's power to "create" inferior federal courts. Marshall owned that he had "an apprehension" that the gentlemen who placed no confidence in Congress would object that

---

128 *Ibid.*, 546.
129 Mays, *Edmund Pendleton*, II, 261. He had injured his hip in a fall from a horse in 1777. He was allowed to sit when presiding, but stood when addressing the Committee (*ibid.*, 228). Cf. also Grigsby, *History of the Virginia Federal Convention of 1788*, I, at 66. For Pendleton's speech *cf.* Elliot, *Debates*, III, 546–50.
130 Elliot, *Debates*, III, 551 *et seq.*

131 *Ibid.*, 222–23. "Shall it be a maxim that a man shall be deprived of his life without benefit of law? Shall such a deprivation of life be justified by answering, that a man's life was not taken *secundum artem* because he was a bad man? Shall it be a maxim that government ought not to be empowered to protect virtue?"
132 *Ibid.*, 551 *et seq.*

there might be no inferior courts. He admitted that he had thought that they would think there would be no inferior courts, as this depended on the will of Congress, but that all would be dragged to the center of the Union. What he had not conceived was the objection to the power of increasing the number of courts, for this would remove the inconvenience of being dragged to the center of the United States.

So far as concerned the items of federal jurisdiction, there was the supreme law of the land clause which was envisaged as giving authority to legislate on every subject. Did the United States have such power? Did Mason understand it so? Could they make laws affecting modes of conveyance or contracts or claims between citizens of the same state? Could they go beyond delegated powers? "If they were to make a law not warranted by any of the powers enumerated, it would be considered by the judges as an infringement of the Constitution which they are to guard. They would not consider such a law as coming under their jurisdiction. They would declare it void."[133]

On two other occasions in the course of this speech, Marshall had occasion to refer to the status of unconstitutional legislation. He did so in scoffing at Mason's extravagant picture of federal officers abusing a man's womenfolk, by declaring that a law authorizing such conduct would be void.[134] Again, in pointing out Virginia's deviations from a rule of invariable jury trial in civil cases, he insisted that the state bill of rights was merely recommendatory; otherwise many laws that were expedient would be void.[135] Much has been made in various quarters of these early expressions of Marshall's ideas on this subject. But, as already noticed, the conception of judicial control was in general circulation to the point of being a commonplace. As we have earlier seen, the Virginians themselves were due to grapple with the doctrine in a practical way on June 23. The Court of Appeals had addressed to the legislature a *Remonstrance* against a new act establishing district courts, assailing it as violation of the 1776 constitution. The text of the *Remonstrance* appeared in a Richmond newspaper on May 22, 1788.[136] Governor Randolph issued a proclamation calling a special session of the legislature for June 23 to the end that the act be examined according to the standard of constitutional right.[137]

Marshall made a variety of other points, the most important of which was his assertion that the state courts would have concurrent

---

[133] *Ibid.*, 553.
[134] *Ibid.*, 554. This is a reference to the case in Clayton's Reports referred to in antifederalist literature, and cited by Samuel Chase in the notes for his speech in Maryland (*supra*, n. 51).

[135] Elliot, *Debates*, III, 561.
[136] *Virginia Gazette, and Weekly Advertiser*, May 22, 1788.
[137] The proclamation appeared in this journal in successive issues while the convention was in session.

jurisdiction with federal courts in cases where the latter had cognizance.[138] This was important because by not committing himself to the suggestion that the state courts should serve as inferior federal courts—an idea which had outraged antifederalists—he knocked a prop from under the consolidated government argument. This was, further, an interesting disclosure of Marshall's notions of federalism. He delivered a brief lecture to Henry on conflict of laws,[139] he derided the idea that the "sovereign power" could be dragged before a court and he made it very clear that jury trial was secured neither by Magna Carta nor by the English Bill of Rights but could be meddled with by Parliament.

On Saturday, June 21, Grayson undertook a replication. Obviously the remarks of Marshall had made little impression on him for he was dully repetitious. His new points were objections to equity power because some states did not have Chancery courts. And he complained that if thirteen states, all different, had to legislate for all, they could not suit the genius of the people, "there being no such thing as a spirit of laws, or a pervading principle, applying to every state individually."[140] Randolph, who followed him, spoke to explain his reservations concerning the judiciary mentioned in his letter of October 10, 1787, that, as we have seen, the federalists believed had done damage. The pith of his dilemma was the fact that although the subjects of jurisdiction were proper, the article was not free from fault. It was ambiguous in some parts and unnecessarily extensive in others. What did the jurisdiction over all cases in law and equity arising under the Constitution mean? He believed that it involved all rights from inchoate rights to complete rights. "Arising under the Constitution" was to him very ambiguous— the possible source of interpretation to extend the federal jurisdiction. He saw no absolute necessity for the diversity jurisdiction, but he believed that Congress could take measures to prevent men from being harassed. With Pendleton he bewailed the phrasing of the grant of appellate power, but he was satisfied that Congress could apply the cure.

Randolph, remarking that "in this whole business we have had *argumenta ad hominem* in abundance,"[141] met Henry's imaginings about the claims of the Indiana Company by asserting even if they had rights, the remedy was against Virginia and not the settlers. As for the quitrents of the Northern Neck, there had been a complete confiscation. "I ask the Convention of the free people of Virginia if there can be honesty in rejecting the government because justice is to be done by it. . . . Are we to say that we shall discard this government because it would make us all honest?"[142]

---

[138] Elliot, *Debates*, III, 554.
[139] *Ibid.*, 556.
[140] *Ibid.*, 565.

[141] *Ibid.*, 574.
[142] *Ibid.*, 575.

Randolph closed his remarks by suggesting that in the form of ratification be included words stating that all authority not given was retained by the people and might be resumed when perverted to their oppression; further, no right could be cancelled, abridged or restrained by Congress or any officer of the United States.[143]

When the convention resumed on Monday, June 23, the shorthand reporter was absent. Most of what was said was hardly worth committing to paper, so repetitious were the comments. There were, however, exchanges of rude remarks and innuendos—such as General Adam Stephen's sneer at the "bugbears of hobgoblins"[144] used by Henry to frighten the delegates and his advice that if Henry did not like the new government he should go live among the Indians. Nicholas made some comments about fortunes made out of land speculations which aroused Henry's ire, and which elicited a denial of personal affront that was couched in terms as contemptuous as the original remark was provoking.[145] The discussion of the Fourth Article was desultory and added nothing.

On June 24 George Wythe, who had presided while the convention sat in Committee, offered a motion for ratification built on a preamble that followed what Randolph had already suggested respecting the reservation of rights not granted. Wythe's resolution specifically enumerated liberty of conscience and freedom of the press. The resolution recommended that any amendments be recommended to the first Congress to assemble.[146] Immediately Henry was on his feet, and in an impassioned speech once again marshalled spectres of ruin and oppression which he had conjured out of the future. He offered a resolution to refer a declaration of rights and certain amendments to the other states for consideration before ratification, an obvious attempt to implement the Virginia Act of December 12, 1787.[147] In the course of his speech,

---

[143] David Stuart wrote Harry Innes on June 29, 1788 (supra, n. 107) reassuringly about the judiciary, "the other great cause of dislike to the government with your members." Pendleton and "other good judges of that particular subject" were of the opinion that from a fair construction of the clause Congress would be able to establish courts with such restrictions and exceptions as it should deem necessary. The evils all would suffer would be the best security of the interests of all being consulted— a pedestrian summary of a long and brilliant debate.

[144] Elliot, *Debates*, III, 580.

[145] *Ibid.*, 581.

[146] *Ibid.*, 587. Without proof Beveridge (*Life of John Marshall*, I, 468) states that on the night of June 23 the federalists decided to deliver a final assault. Wythe was chosen to offer the resolution. See also Grigsby, *History of the Virginia Federal Convention of 1788*, I, at 307. This is, no doubt, probable. Henry already had his declaration of rights, for a copy had been sent on to the New York antifederalists (*infra*, n. 169). It was obviously good political tactics to move first.

[147] Elliot, *Debates*, III, 593.

Henry let drop some incautious remark about the possibility of his own secession.[148]

Randolph picked up these words at once, and although Henry interrupted to deny that he was a secessionist, his remark that he would remain and vote and afterwards "have no business here" Randolph regarded as an affirmation of the original threat. He said bluntly that a refusal to submit to the decision of the majority was destructive of every republican principle. The matter in Henry's bill of rights, he averred, was either secured by the Constitution or could not be infringed because these items lay beyond the powers delegated. The other amendments were unnecessary, dangerous or improper. He asked, could any man believe that twelve or even nine states would subscribe to these proposals? To insist upon them would be a farewell to the Union. "The Confederation is gone; it has no authority. If, in this situation, we reject the Constitution, the Union will be dissolved, the dogs of war will break loose, and anarchy and discord will complete the ruin of this country."[149]

Mason, Dawson and Grayson followed Randolph. Mason undertook to correct a statement of the governor's that at the Philadelphia Convention the provision respecting commerce and navigation was a condition *sine qua non* of the Union. Dawson and Grayson harped upon the need of previous amendment to safeguard "that unfortunate traveller Liberty." Grayson, indeed, with a calculated appeal to local pride suggested that Virginia was important enough to the Union to exact a price for adherence. In sharp contrast to the emotional overtones of his opponents, Madison replied with restraint and reasoned eloquence. To Grayson's cynical counsel he posed the question whether nine states having agreed, could it be expected that upon the demand of a single state they would decide that they had acted wrongly. Virginia had always spoken the language of respect to other states and had always been heeded.[150] This was language neither of confidence nor respect. Patiently he exposed the folly of some of the antifederalists' amendments, and made a plea for union.

The last speech of this day was made by Henry. Once again he interposed to Madison's warnings his fears of implied powers, of misuses of power, of catastrophe if liberties were not secured in advance. A penultimate passage, florid, but nonetheless affecting, was delivered in the accompanying roar and tumult of a great storm—"which put the house in such disorder" that Henry was obliged to conclude.[151]

On the following day, June 25, the balloting took place. The Wythe

---

148 *Ibid.*, 592–96. Threat of his own withdrawal was followed by repeated warnings of disunion.

149 *Ibid.*, 603.
150 *Ibid.*, 617.
151 *Ibid.*, 622–25.

resolution was moved, and thereupon an amendment by way of substitution was offered, resolving that previous to ratification a declaration of rights together with amendments "to the most exceptionable parts of the said Constitution" be referred to the other states for consideration.[152] Debate flared up again with various persons participating who had previously said nothing or little. Henry spoke his final words, making it clear that he would abide by the result. The substitute motion lost 88–80. On the main question of ratification the vote was 89–79. A committee was then appointed to prepare and report on the amendments to be recommended.

The report followed closely the Henry proposals of June 24.[153] The declaration of rights was modelled on the Virginia bill of rights with certain additions such as a rewording of the celebrated c. 29 of Magna Carta, an assertion of a right to remedies for all injuries, the right to bear arms and a freedom of speech guarantee. The amendments, twenty in all, embodied most of the points in which the antifederalists believed the Constitution to be inadequate. The most objectionable of these, a modification of the power to levy direct taxes and excises, Madison tried in vain to have eliminated. Amendment 14[154] vested the judicial power of the United States in one Supreme Court and such courts of admiralty as Congress might establish in the states. The judicial power was restricted to cases in law and equity arising under treaties; to all cases affecting ambassadors, foreign ministers and consuls; to all cases of "admiralty and maritime jurisdiction"; to controversies where the United States might be a party, to controversies between two states, and between parties claiming under grants from different states. The original jurisdiction of the Supreme Court was to extend to cases involving ambassadors, etc., and suits between states. Otherwise its jurisdiction was to be appellate as to matters of law only except in equity, admiralty and maritime causes where it encompassed both law and fact subject to congressional legislation. Finally, with an eye to prewar debts and other objections, it was provided that the judicial power of the United States should extend to no case where the cause of action should have arisen before ratification except territorial disputes between states, those between persons claiming under grants of different states and suits for debts due the United States. The fifteenth amendment secured the right of challenging jurors in criminal cases.[155]

In the test of strength on the taxation amendment, Pendleton and nine others who had voted for ratification supported Henry. Why this change of attitude took place has been explained on the theory of placating the Virginia General Assembly whose help would be needed

---

[152] *Ibid.*, 653.   [153] *Ibid.*, 593.   [154] *Ibid.*, 660–61.   [155] *Ibid.*, 661.

to set up the new government.[156] There was, wrote Monroe to Jefferson, "no circumstance on the part of the victorious that mar[ked] exultation, nor of depression on the part of the unfortunate. There was no bonfire illumination &c."[157] But in New York City, where the news arrived at 2 A.M. on July 2, the bells of the city began ringing "at the dawning" and at sunrise ten twenty-four pounders saluted the event.[158] The City, warm for union, had had served up to it in the press tales of the great parades held in celebration of successive ratifications. The citizens set about to honor Virginia in the same style.[159] At the moment it looked as if their own convention, then sitting, might not give them occasion for another such festivity.

NEW YORK

THE NEW YORK elections had been held the day after Maryland's ratification was signed.[160] The resolution of the legislature had pro-

---

[156] Mays, *Edmund Pendleton*, II, 270. This is highly probable. The temper of the assembly was indicated soon enough in the fall when it sought to activate a second convention. *Cf.* Madison to Washington, Nov. 5, 1788, *Doc. Hist. Const.*, V, 108; Edward Carrington to Madison, November 9, *ibid.*, 110; Corbin to Madison, November 12, *ibid.*, 113; Edward Carrington to Madison, November 15, *ibid.*, 116, and again November 18, *ibid.*, 118. The resolution of Nov. 20, 1788, respecting the convention is in W. W. Henry, *Patrick Henry: Life, Correspondence and Speeches*, II, 423–25. It was printed as a broadside.

[157] Monroe to Jefferson, July 12, 1788, *Papers of Jefferson*, XIII, 352.

[158] Samuel B. Webb to Miss Hogeboom, July 2, 1788, W. C. Ford, ed., *Correspondence and Journals of Samuel Blachley Webb*, III, 110.

[159] They did not get around to the celebration until July 23, three days before New York finally ratified at Poughkeepsie. It was apparently an extravagant affair. *Cf.* John Randolph to St. George Tucker, July 30, 1788, Ms. Emmet Collection, No. 9582 (NYPL); New York *Daily Advertiser*, July 23, 1788; *The New-York Journal*, July 24, 1788. S. A. Otis wrote

to George Thatcher, July 17, 1788 (*LMCC*, VIII, 763), conjecturing an adjournment of the New York Convention. "The Yorkers are determined however to have their frolic, and I don't know but are in danger of running into excess in regard to processions." *Forma regiminis mutata, non mutantur mores.*

[160] The New York ratification has been discussed in C. E. Miner, *The Ratification of the Federal Constitution by the State of New York*, where the emphasis is on the preliminaries to the convention. E. W. Spaulding, *New York in the Critical Period*, 204 *et seq.*, is strongly pro-Clinton. His work, *His Excellency George Clinton* (New York: The Macmillan Co., 1938), c. 13, adds nothing. The most recent study (L. G. De Pauw, *The Eleventh Pillar* [Ithaca, N.Y.: Cornell University Press, 1966]) deals briefly with the convention and does not deal at large with the substance of the debates. The Ms. Melancton Smith Papers do not appear to have been used. R. Brooks, "Alexander Hamilton, Melancton Smith, and the Ratification of the Constitution in New York," *Wm. and Mary Quarterly*, 24:339–58, 3d ser., deals mainly with the last stages of the debates. By ignoring the impact of

vided for extension of the suffrage to all male citizens of the age of twenty-one and over,[161] but despite the expenditure of much energy by both sides, there was no great surge of new voters to the polls.[162] When the votes were counted it was clear that except for Kings, New York, Richmond and Westchester counties, there had been an antifederalist sweep. Clinton and his "band of mutes," as his henchmen had been derisively described, were going to be in control.[163]

The New York City federalists were greatly chagrined over the election results, and now had every reason for serious concern over what Governor Clinton really planned. He was reported to have declared his opinion of the inutility of union, an opinion shared by others of his party.[164] His city followers were supposed to be in favor of a long adjournment of the coming convention, proposing to see how the new government would work before coming to a decision.[165] Hamilton and his friends would have been even more anxious had they been aware of the machinations of the Federal-Republican Committee. About the

---

the Virginia ratification, he makes Melancton Smith the "hero" of the deliberations.

[161] The resolve is in *Doc. Hist. Const.*, IV, 466. Clinton's January message is in *Journal of the Assembly of the State of New York* (1788), 6–7. The assembly proceedings of January 31, *ibid.*, 47–49; the Senate proceedings, in *Journal of the Senate of the State of New York* (1788), 20–21.

[162] The Albany antifederalists and federalists communicated with committees in New York City. On the antifederalists' connection see Ms. Lamb Papers, Box 5 (NYHS), for a letter to Albany, Apr. 8, 1788, regarding distribution of the "Columbian Patriot" (*supra*, p. 297), and the reply, April 12, complaining of its unsuitability and stating copies had been sent to Montgomery and Washington Counties. The federalist liaison is indicated in a letter of Mar. 12, 1788, from the Albany committee to James Duane, Ms. Duane Papers, Box 7 (NYHS). On activities in the countryside see Robert Livingston to Duane, Apr. 30, 1788, *ibid.*, complaining about emissaries poisoning his tenants and explaining his countermeasures. The campaign in Dutchess County was enlivened by exchanges between local letter writers; see *The*

Country Journal and Poughkeepsie Advertiser, Mar. 4 and 18, Apr. 8, 22 and 29, 1788. There is sharp criticism of Clinton's alliance with ex-Tory Samuel Jones by *Fabius* in the issue of Feb. 19, 1788.

Some of the handbills used are interesting, especially the two issued by the Albany antifederalist committee in which Jeremiah Van Rensselaer was a moving spirit. Among other things it was urged that after nine ratifications New York sit matters out. See also the election broadside of Mar. 16, 1788, containing the federalist ticket addressed to the "Independent Voters of Albany," and of Apr. 2, 1788, "On a move for the Liberties," signed by Melancton Smith and other antifederalist worthies. All in the Broadside Collection, (NYHS).

[163] Curiously enough, Arthur Lee wrote Charles Lee on May 31, 1788, that the results were close, that it was impossible to determine how the convention would go. Lee-Ludwell Mss. (Va. Hist. Soc.).

[164] Hamilton to Madison, May 19, 1788, *Doc. Hist. Const.*, IV, 620; *PAH*, IV, 649; and to Gouverneur Morris on the same date, *PAH*, IV, 650.

[165] Hamilton to Madison, June 8, 1788, *PAH*, V, 2–4.

middle of May and before the election returns were all in, General Lamb wrote to opposition leaders in various states, attempting to lay the groundwork for concerted action.[166] Whether or not the move was inspired by the Virginia statute of December 12,[167] it was only with that state, with New Hampshire and with North Carolina that anything resembling effective cooperation to stay the organization of the new government could be expected.

To Virginia the New York committee despatched an emissary, Colonel Eleazar Oswald, whose newspaper, the Philadelphia *Independent Gazetteer*, had continued the antifederalist bombardment throughout the spring of 1788. Oswald arrived in Richmond with a packet of pamphlets a few days after the Virginia Convention had convened. There he consulted with the leaders. Lamb's letter was laid before the "Committee of Opposition."[168] George Mason agreed to act as chairman of a Virginia Republican Society. Oswald was given copies of the bill of rights and the amendments which it was proposed to offer.[169] Henry, Grayson and Mason all sent approving letters to Lamb. What else Oswald may have brought back in the way of information and advice we do not know. He appears to have been closeted with Mason on June 7, for the latter was absent from the convention that day. It is tempting to suppose that he learned about Richard Henry Lee's suggestion to Mason[170] that the form of ratification embody amendments which must be obtained within two years after the new Congress should meet, otherwise Virginia should be considered as disengaged from ratification. This suggestion was in fact advanced at the New York Convention.

Madison advised Hamilton on June 9 that Oswald had had "closet

---

[166] Letters went out to Joshua Atherton and Nathaniel Peabody of New Hampshire; Chase of Maryland; R. H. Lee, Henry, Mason and Grayson of Virginia; Wilie Jones, Thomas Persons and Timothy Bloodworth of North Carolina (*cf.* McRee, *Iredell*, II, 231); Rollins Lowndes and Aedanus Burke of South Carolina. Replies from Chase, Lee, Henry, Grayson, Lowndes and Atherton are printed in I. Leake, *Memoir of the Life and Times of General John Lamb*, 307-13. Replies from Bloodworth and Burke are in Ms. Lamb Papers, Box 5 (NYHS). Mason's answer is printed in Rowland, *Life and Correspondence of George Mason*, II, 234.

Lamb's letter to Lee is in the Lee-Ludwell Mss. (Va. Hist. Soc.); the letter to Peabody is printed in *Historical Magazine* 2:280-81, 3d ser., 1873. To Lee and Peabody Lamb proposed correspondence to have a united front among the states that had not yet ratified.

[167] *Supra*, n. 9.

[168] Grayson to Lamb, June 9, 1788, in *Leake, Memoir of the Life and Times of General John Lamb*, at 311.

[169] Mason to Lamb, June 9, 1788, in Rowland, *Life and Correspondence of George Mason*, II, 234. A copy of the bill of rights is among the Ms. Lamb Papers, Box 5 (NYHS).

[170] To Mason, May 7, 1788, in Ballagh, *Letters of Richard Henry Lee*, II, 466; and to Pendleton, May 22, 1788, *ibid.*, 469.

interviews with the leaders of the opposition."[171] A week later he wrote
that it was conjectured that a policy was afoot to spin out the Virginia
session in order to receive overtures from the New York body.[172] There
is no doubt but that this was the strategy of the New York antifederalists.
Governor Clinton wrote from Poughkeepsie, four days after the convention had assembled there and news from Virginia had arrived, that
"the republican members" of the convention had appointed a "special
Committee of Correspondence, with the neighboring Conventions, &c.
of which the Honorable Judge Yates, is Chairman."[173] A letter to Mason
was enclosed for despatch "by such safe and expeditious mode of conveyance" as General Lamb might think expedient. All this was to no
avail, for by the time the letter could have reached Richmond, the
Virginians had ratified. Had the Federal-Republican Committee not
been so tardy in launching its scheme, things might have come to a
different conclusion.

If in choosing Poughkeepsie as the place of convention the New
York legislature aimed at a milieu free of distractions, they could not
have done better. A bard in *The New-York Journal*[174] asked scornfully:

> What means their wisdoms roving to Poughkeepsie
> Their heads with politics are surely tipsey?
> Why to the Druids ancient hunts be trotting
> Where naught but acorns on the ground be rotting?

So long drawn out were the proceedings in the bucolic quiet of this
river town that the fate of the acorns threatened the delegates. The
antifederalists arrived with a two-thirds majority. When the convention
assembled, therefore, on June 17, the issue could have been settled
forthwith, but for the need of waiting out the results of the Federal-
Republican Committee's negotiations, and the threat that the southern
counties might secede in the event of rejection. John Jay had written
Washington on May 29 that this idea "has taken Air"[175] and some days
later Hamilton informed Madison that fear over this was entering into
the calculations of the opposition.[176] It is noteworthy that on the convention floor no such threats were made until near the end of the
session after it was known that ten states had ratified.

The debates of the convention were extensively reported until
July 4.[177] From then until July 26, the day of adjournment, we are

---

[171] *PAH*, V, 4; *Doc. Hist. Const.*,
IV, 695; *cf.* also to Washington, June
13, 1788, *ibid.*, 703.
[172] To Hamilton, June 16, 1788,
PAH, V, 9.
[173] To Lamb, June 21, 1788, in

Leake, *Memoir of the Life and Times
of General John Lamb*, at 315.
[174] June 28, 1788.
[175] *Doc. Hist. Const.*, IV, 643.
[176] June 8, 1788, *PAH*, V, 2–4.
[177] Elliot, *Debates*, II, 205 *et seq.*

cast upon the scanty notes of Richard Harison,[178] of the more ample ones of John McKesson, clerk of the convention, of Gilbert Livingston, and of Melancton Smith, Dutchess County antifederalist.[179] For the federalists the brunt of argument was borne by Hamilton and Chancellor Robert R. Livingston, with some help from John Jay, James Duane and Chief Justice Richard Morris. The prolocutor for the antifederalists during the early weeks of debate was Melancton Smith, a well-to-do merchant, literate and more able in debate than in literary composition, if his *Address to the People of the State of New York* is a fair sample.[180] Lansing and Yates, who had deserted the Philadelphia Convention, spoke occasionally in the debates on the merits; but when the final maneuvering began, the former suddenly moved into a position of prominence. Strangely enough, Governor Clinton, the acknowledged leader of the New York opposition, had relatively little to say. Samuel Jones, ex-Tory lawyer who had been associated with Hamilton in various litigations,[181] was the antifederalist leader in the discussion of the judiciary article. There were numerous bitter personal exchanges,[182] and Chancellor Livingston affronted many by his sarcasms. He had a flair for giving a ridiculous twist to the most earnest of his opponent's arguments.[183] The occasional extravagance of the figures of speech used by some antifederalists was a recurrent incitation to such tactics. The gem of the debate was Gilbert Livingston's picture of the federal city surrounded by a "wall of gold—of adamant which will flow in from all parts of the continent."[184] This was nearly surpassed by Mr. Tredwell's reference to the Constitution as "this Goliath, this uncircumcised Philistine," from which he expected deliverance by the Lord.[185]

Taken as a whole, the quality of the New York discussions does not measure up to that of the Virginia debates. Yet when Hamilton spoke, he was incomparable. The convention was only five days old

---

[178] Printed in *Doc. Hist. Const.*, IV, 718–43, 751–53, 754, 758–59. The editors of *The Papers of Alexander Hamilton* have identified these as notes kept by Harison.

[179] McKesson, Ms. Notes of Debates (NYHS); Melancton Smith, Ms. Notes of Debates (NYSL); Gilbert Livingston, Ms. Notes of Debates (NYPL). See *supra*, c. VIII, n. 6.

[180] Ford, *Pamphlets*, 87.

[181] The most recent professional association had been in preparing New York's case in the controversy with Massachusetts over the western lands. *LPAH*, I, 571–72.

[182] The most violent altercation, that between Lansing and Hamilton, took place on June 28 and 30. This was not reported in detail by reporter Childs (Elliot, *Debates*, II, 376). However, John McKesson, clerk of the convention, did set down details. Lansing charged that at Philadelphia Hamilton advocated reducing the states to mere corporations. Hamilton vehemently denied this. Yates came in with references to his notes. See McKesson's Ms. Notes of Debates (NYHS).

[183] Elliot, *Debates*, II, 383, 384, 391, 392.

[184] *Ibid.*, 287.

[185] *Ibid.*, 405.

when Clinton wrote sourly that what had thus far been said by the federalists was "a second edition of Publius well delivered."[186] So far as Hamilton's speeches are concerned, they were more than this, for they were touched with fire, kindled by the ardors of forensic combat.[187] He had a worthy if unequal adversary in Melancton Smith, who was hampered, however, by the lack of a program more positive than the succession of emasculating amendments proposed as debate proceeded.

For more than two weeks the First and Second Articles were ploughed and harrowed. Representation and taxation were the subjects of the most discursive comments, which led to a parenthetical consideration of various clauses out of the section by section order that had been decided upon as the proper procedure of deliberation. Nothing that had been elsewhere objected and answered was overlooked. In the welter of detailed observation, what emerges as most significant is a pattern of exploring what the fundamental relations of state and national government were to be.[188] This was a philosophical problem that appealed to the intellectual tastes of Smith. Whether or not Hamilton sensed this, for once in his life, with immense patience, he shaped his discourse to the qualities of his antagonist's mind. It is difficult not to believe that this respect for Smith's intelligence itself was a subtle form of persuasion. There are junctures in the debates on the merits where the antifederalist leader seems ready for some yielding, only to harden in reaction to some suspected misrepresentation or bit of ridicule from the tongue of Livingston.[189]

The strategy of the antifederalists was settled upon almost fortuitously. Robert Yates, who headed the committee to correspond with

---

[186] Clinton to Lamb, June 21, 1788, in Leake, *Memoir of the Life and Times of General John Lamb*, at 315. On the same day Charles Tillinghast wrote Lamb regarding a quip that Williams's speech had been compiled out of New York newspapers, that he was no worse than Hamilton "who has Publius for retailing in convention." Ms. Lamb Papers, Box 5 (NYHS). On June 28 Clinton wrote Lamb that he was stealing a moment to write while the "little great man is employed in repeating over parts of Publius to us." *Ibid.*

[187] In Farrand, *Records*, III, 352, is printed a letter from Lansing to Yates and Smith, Oct. 3, 1788, which raises some implications that Childs submitted his report of the debates for revision. The letter has reference

apparently to the altercation between Lansing and Hamilton of June 28 and June 30 (*supra*, n. 182).

[188] This emerges with particular clarity in McKesson's Ms. Notes of Debates, especially for June 27–30 (NYHS). McKesson noted much that Childs left out.

[189] Chancellor Livingston, who seems to have enjoyed baiting Smith, would have done his cause good by keeping silent. Whereas Hamilton on several occasions apologized spontaneously for his vehemence on the ground of his great interest in the Constitution, Livingston only once in a mocking way made an explanation for an alleged slighting reference (*cf.* Elliot, *Debates*, II, 394). Many more of the rough exchanges were noted by McKesson than by Childs.

the Virginians, wrote George Mason on June 20 that the federalists had proposed that the Constitution be discussed in the Committee of the Whole without a question being put as to any part of the instrument. This had been agreed to, provided that in the course of the discussion amendments or "explanations" could be suggested where deemed necessary to any "exceptionable points." The agreement had been made to prevent the federalists from charging that the opposition acted precipitately. Yates confessed that no committee to draft amendments had been constituted, but he nevertheless sent on a copy of amendments "many of us have agreed on." Mason was assured that the opposition would not agree to the Constitution without previous amendments.[190]

The reports of debates together with the amendments offered as the Committee inched through section after section suggests that what had been agreed upon was the production of a New York version of what a national Constitution should be. A prime feature was the salving of the confederation principle. This was to be accomplished by preserving certain particulars of the Articles, and by attempting otherwise to assure maximum participation of the states *qua* states in the proposed government. Such were the amendments to secure the right of the states to recall their Senators; to require annual submission to state governments of accounts of receipts and expenditures; to safeguard extra-state service of militia by making this contingent on state consent; to use state courts as inferior tribunals except in maritime causes and those concerning crimes on the high seas.

In connection with these discussions of federal taxing power, there was some reference to the probable role of the projected national judicial establishment. This came about because Melancton Smith[191] and John Williams,[192] a delegate from Washington County, both conceived that the supreme law of the land clause would operate to destroy state taxing power. It was their belief that both national and state governments would impose taxes upon the same objects and that because of the supreme law provision the jurisdictional disputes would be settled in federal courts to the detriment of the states. Hamilton's explanation, twice made,[193] that the provision meant no more than that the laws of the United States were supreme as to their proper constitutional objects, and the state laws in the same way, fell on deaf ears. Lansing[194] continued to harp upon the inevitability of the supreme law provision destroying the authority of the states.

---

[190] Ms. Emmet Collection, No. 9528 (NYPL).

[191] Elliot, *Debates*, II, 332–33, for Smith's comment; but more precise and extensive in his own notes for his speech, Melancton Smith, Ms. Notes of Debates (NYSL).

[192] Elliot, *Debates*, II, 339.

[193] *Ibid.*, 355–56; 361–62.

[194] *Ibid.*, 374.

These exchanges took place on June 27 and 28 and presaged trouble with the judiciary article of the Constitution. This was reached on July 5, and far from there being debate, nothing but the brutal major operation which the antifederalists proposed to perform was made of record.[195] No federalist spoke. The reason for this counsel of silence was related by delegate Abraham Bancker in a letter to Ernest Bancker written on July 5: "the Gentlemen on the federal side on receiving news of Virginia have changed their System of proceeding; whereby it appears manifest no Reply will be made to any of their propositions untill after the whole of their Objections shall be stated."[196] Bancker had been elected as a federalist and was presumably privy to the plans of his party.

Samuel Jones opened the antifederalist case against Article III on July 5. He thought that the cases to which the article applied were not sufficiently defined. He adverted to the danger and expense of instituting many new courts, which, on Coke's authority, he claimed would tend to oppression. Another matter of great importance was this: "The Gen'l Gov't & State Gov'ts make one compact Gov't. They should therefore be kept so as to harmonize and prevent clashing of Jurisdictions—Without restrictions there would be a Contest for Power—and the Great National Court must Swallow the others—Great National Matters may be determined before them—There will be no Controul—They will be even superior to the Legislature."[197] Apparently Jones believed that the judicial power could be vested in state courts, although he conceded that this would be inconvenient. His suspicion of the Supreme Court led him to compare it with Star Chamber. There should be, he said, intermediate appellate courts. Following the ideas of *Brutus*, Jones wanted a body to correct errors of the Supreme Court and proposed a Commission of Review. He did not think that the judges would be corrupt, but they might be weak or ignorant. The knowledge that such an *ad hoc* body would stand over the court would make the judges cautious.[198]

Jones had objections to jurisdiction between a state and the citizen of another state, for many criminals "are citizens of other States and if not they may so plead." He believed, further, that a state must have some portion of sovereignty and therefore should never be impleaded

---

[195] Some matter set out in Harison's Notes in *Doc. Hist. Const.*, IV, 735 *et seq.*, and in McKesson's Ms. Notes of Debates for July 5 and 6 (NYHS). Gilbert Livingston's Ms. Notes of Debates (NYPL) begin on July 14; those for earlier days were apparently lost. On the margin of Chancellor Livingston's printed copy of the Constitution are a few annotations of antifederalist objections, (W. L. Clements Library, University of Michigan).

[196] Ms. Bancker Papers, No. 201 (NYHS).

[197] McKesson, Ms. Notes of Debates, July 5, 1788 (NYHS).

[198] Harison, Notes, in *Doc. Hist. Const.*, IV, 736–37.

by a citizen. As for citizens of different states or foreigners "in any contract," he asked why should they be entitled to any measure of justice different from the citizens of the state where the contract was made?[199]

Melancton Smith raised other doubts. He could not see how questions of equity could arise under the Constitution. The Supreme Court would be biased in tax cases, and it alone would decide in diversity cases if concurrent jurisdiction existed. He could not understand why federal courts should have jurisdiction over causes between citizens and foreigners since there had hitherto been no objection to the due administration of justice. There was no express provision for jury trial, appeals would lie in criminal cases as to law and fact, there was no safeguard of trial by the vicinage or even of indictment. States could be sued as private individuals.[200]

In the course of the discussions, nine amendments, one in duplicate, were offered.[201] The first was designed to restrain Congress from establishing any inferior courts with other than appellate jurisdiction except those necessary for the trial of admiralty causes and felonies or piracies on the high seas. State courts were to exercise original jurisdiction in all cases except when the Supreme Court had such jurisdiction, with an appeal either to courts established for that purpose by Congress or to the Supreme Court. Two resolves restrained jurisdiction in controversies over lands to causes involving grants from different states. The fourth resolve expressly restrained suits against any state, and the fifth excluded criminal prosecutions from the jurisdiction over cases where the state should be a party. Judges of the Supreme Court were to be disqualified from holding any other federal or state office. The jurisdiction of the Supreme Court or other federal court "ought not" to be extended by "any fiction, collusion, or mere suggestion." Finally was the resolve providing that a seven-man Commission of Review of Supreme Court sentences, judgments or decrees be appointed by the President, by and with the advice and consent of the Senate, subject to regulations established by Congress. Harison's notes indicate that Jones offered another amendment providing that New York appeals in common law cases be by writ of error.[202]

The work of going through the Constitution in committee was completed on July 7, on which day Lansing offered a bill of rights. But

---

[199] McKesson, Ms. Notes of Debates, July 5, 1788 (NYHS).

[200] Harison, Notes, in *Doc. Hist. Const.*, IV, 736. McKesson adds nothing significant.

[201] Printed in Elliot, *Debates*, II, 408–09. The ms. texts of the various motions are in McKesson Papers (NYHS).

[202] *Doc. Hist. Const.*, IV, 736. Accord, Chancellor Livingston's marginal notes on his copy of the Constitution (W. L. Clements Library, University of Michigan).

nearly three weeks were to elapse before a final vote was taken. Two events had occurred which stayed the hands of the majority. On June 24 had come an express with word of New Hampshire's ratification—the ninth state.[203] The antifederalists appear to have taken this in stride, although the Chancellor warned them that the Confederation was now dissolved and he gibed at the dream of a union with Southern states.[204] If this, indeed, had been a hope, it was dashed when on July 2 came the shattering news of Virginia's action.[205] Up to this moment the opposition leaders had believed that they could hold off and strike a bargain with the new government. Now, so John Jay reported, the resolve of the "southern District and their apparent Determination to continue under the Wings of the union, operates powerfully on the Minds of the opposite Party."[206] The question no longer was one of possible rejection; it concerned ratification and amendment. It was partly a question of the form and content of the amendments, and still more a question whether these should be conditions precedent or conditions subsequent.

The first step in coming to an issue occurred on July 10 when Lansing submitted an arrangement of the numerous amendments already offered. These he classified as explanatory, conditional and recommendatory.[207] The implications of conditional amendments were obvious. The federalists countered with a resolve moved by Jay (July 11) to the effect that the Constitution ought to be ratified, that doubtful parts ought to be explained and that useful or expedient amendments should be recommended.[208] The tenor of the debates on this may be

---

[203] Langdon to Washington, June 21, 1788, *Doc. Hist. Const.*, IV, 744; Schuyler to Madison, June 24, 1788, *ibid.*, 753. The bill for the express went to Hamilton with a surcharge for the laming of a horse. Sullivan to Hamilton, July 10, 1788, *Sullivan Papers*, III, 591.

[204] Elliot, *Debates*, II, 322. Smith's answer, *ibid.*, 324. McKesson's version in his Notes is briefer. He has Smith saying: "I am sorry the Gent. mentioned change of circumstances—I do not think them changed."

[205] The news arrived in New York at 2 A.M., July 2. Samuel Webb wrote Joseph Barrell that the express should be in Poughkeepsie by two o'clock in the afternoon. *Correspondence and Journals of Samuel Blachley Webb*, III, 109. The express run is said to

have taken about ten hours. The Poughkeepsie printer, Parsons, apparently ran off his broadside the same day.

[206] To Washington, July 4, 1788, *Doc. Hist. Const.*, IV, 766. In a letter of July 13 to Miss Hogeboom, Samuel Webb wrote: "The Southern District are determined on a Separation to join the union, and I do not believe the life of the Governor & his party would be safe in this place." *Correspondence and Journals of Samuel Blachley Webb*, III, 111.

[207] McKesson, Ms. Notes of Debates, July 10; the text of the amendments, in Ms. McKesson Papers (NYHS).

[208] Printed in Elliot, *Debates*, II, 410.

inferred from the elliptical notes of McKesson and Gilbert Livingston. There appear to have been "propositions" advanced that were not noted in the *Journal* but which raised the question whether or not Congress had the power to accept a conditional ratification, particularly to suspend the operation of certain provisions of the Constitution pending amendment. A second matter urged by the federalists was the limitation of the convention's power only to accept or reject under the terms of the legislative resolve pursuant to which it was sitting.[209]

With ten ratifications in the till, the federalists abandoned political theory for the tougher idiom of practical politics. Jay referred bluntly to the efforts that would be made to move the seat of government. It had been worth £100,000 per annum to have Congress at New York. In fact, all the hard money that had come into the state was due to its being the seat of government.[210] Chancellor Livingston was no less forthright. He dreaded "to mention perhaps the southern part of the state may separate." What would then become of the northern part? Could they reduce the southern counties by arms; would Vermont be still, and Canada? Was Montgomery County ready to resist the power of the British or the slaughter of the savages?[211] These were not mere phantasms. The Indian raids were only five years over; within New York's boundaries the British still held the posts at Fort Erie, Niagara, Oswego, Oswegatchie, Pointe-au-Fer and Dutchmans Point; New York still had not settled its score with Vermont.

If the upstate antifederalists were immediately affected by these appeals to self-interest, it is not apparent from their response. Melancton Smith moved July 14 that Jay's amendment be postponed, and offered as a substitute that ratification be on condition that until a convention be called and convened for proposing amendments, certain specified powers conferred by the Constitution be not exercised or exercised under stipulated conditions. The most important of these was the undertaking that there must be resort to requisition before direct taxes could be levied.[212] Philip Schuyler reported from Poughkeepsie to Stephen Van Rensselaer that the complexion of affairs on the 14th was "very alarming indeed. The question on the conditional adoption was called for and pressed with warmth. After an Argument by Jay and Hamilton which could not and was not answered, but which notwithstanding a predetermination against conviction made deep im-

[209] See particularly Gilbert Livingston's Ms. Notes of Debates, 37 *et seq.* (NYPL).

[210] McKesson, Ms. Notes of Debates, July 12 (NYHS).

[211] *Ibid.*

[212] Ms. Journal of the Proceedings of the Convention of the State of New York, 30–31 (NYSL) (hereafter cited as Ms. Journal of the Convention). For the dating of the motion, *cf. PAH*, V, 165, n. 3.

pression on some of the opponents who joined in a motion for the usual adjournment that time might be given for reflection."[213]

On July 15 Smith shifted ground and offered his proposal as an amendment to Jay's resolution.[214] The pressure for a vote was deflected that day by a new proposition of Hamilton's including certain amendments that showed the first sign of concession by the federalists.[215] Hamilton's proposal was described by Schuyler as being "much in the spirit of that of Virginia, but with a declaration of rights extended to objects which had not been contemplated by the anties, and with a string of recommendatory amendments, some altogether new and others although they appeared similar to those proposed by his opponents were evidently so framed as to be more decidedly in favor of liberty." The antifederalists were, he claimed, so deranged and embarrassed by this measure that there was hope for a better issue than had seemed possible.[216]

On the following day (July 16), before the convention had resolved itself into committee, John Sloss Hobart, puisne judge of the Supreme Court of Judicature, offered a resolution to adjourn to a stated date, the preamble reason being that the changes of circumstance made it desirable to consult with constituents.[217] Apparently the federalists believed this was the only way of forestalling an adverse decision. The motion was defeated but produced the first break in their opponents' ranks, for three of these voted with the federalists, the most important defection being Samuel Jones.[218]

The next federalist move was Duane's offer (July 17) of a substitute for Smith's motion (not yet voted upon).[219] Duane's substitute was a complex instrument, for it opened with a declaration respecting the reservation in the people or the states of delegated rights not granted in the Constitution, and the right of resuming these rights if

---

[213] July 15, 1788, Misc. Mss. Personal (LC).

[214] Gilbert Livingston, Ms. Notes of Debates, 38c (NYPL).

[215] The editors of *The Papers of Alexander Hamilton* have conjectured that what Hamilton offered was identical with the complex motion made by Duane to ratify the Constitution (*infra*, n. 219). The Ms Journal of the Convention (NYSL) notes this motion made on July 17. The draft in the McKesson Papers (NYHS) is dated July 15 (*PAH*, V, 168, n. 2; the text of the amendments, *ibid.*, 167–70). We do not quarrel with the matter of identity, but are not satisfied with the effort to pre-date Duane's motion in spite of the Journal entry.

[216] Schuyler to Van Rensselaer, *supra*, n. 213.

[217] Ms. Journal of the Convention, 25–26. The original motion was handed in with illegible excisions.

[218] Ms. Journal of the Convention, 26–27. Jones had been ill on the 15th. Schuyler believed it was lack of courage which kept him from disclosing his true sentiments. Schuyler also reported that several "anties" had engaged not to vote for the conditional proposition. Cf. Schuyler to Madison, *supra*, n. 203.

[219] Ms. Journal of the Convention, 31–35.

judged "necessary to their happiness." No right of any kind could be cancelled, restrained, abridged or modified by Congress or by any authority of the United States unless in conformity with the powers given in the Constitution. Liberty of conscience and of press "cannot be cancelled or abridged by any authority of the United States." There followed some homiletic matter, an assertion of reliance upon the mode of amendment prescribed in the Constitution, and a declaration that "in full confidence" that the amendments proposed would receive consideration and those tending to the security and advantage of the people would be adopted, the Constitution be ratified.

Then came a long paragraph explaining what was the true intent and meaning of parts of the Constitution "concerning which doubt had been raised." These "explanations and constructions" the convention enjoined their future Senators and Representatives to secure by a Declaratory Act. Among the constructions was an assertion that the judicial power of the United States in cases where a state might be a party did not extend to criminal prosecutions or to actions by private persons against a state. In the exercise of appellate jurisdiction, the Supreme Court could not authorize a second trial in criminal cases, or a second trial of any fact "determinable in the course of the common Law by a Jury." Presentment and indictment by a grand jury "ought to be observed" in all prosecutions for any crime. "Attending the preceding" declaration were thirteen amendments—a watered-down version of the long list offered by the antifederalists. These amendments appear to have been drafted by Hamilton.[220] When the yeas and nays were taken on postponing Smith's resolution in favor of considering this complex proposition, it was beaten; but Jones was still voting with the federalists.[221]

Before debate on Smith's resolution could be resumed, Smith himself confessed that he no longer believed that Congress "would receive us on the adoption proposed." He found that he was mistaken in believing that Congress could call a convention. Consequently it would be wise to relinquish "our plan" and adopt one which he would propose.[222] "We wish," said he, "to be received into the union but to insure if possible a submission of the amendments proposed to the people of America."[223] His "proposition," which at this juncture does

---

[220] This appears from McKesson's draft for the Journal for July 17, in McKesson Papers (NYHS), which reads: "Here insert the Draft of Ratification in the Handwriting of Mr. Jay and the Amendments in the hand writing of Mr. Hamilton."

[221] Ms. Journal of the Convention, 35–36.

[222] Gilbert Livingston, Ms. Notes of Debates, 44b–c (NYPL); Smith's notes for his speech in his Ms. Notes of Debates (NYSL).

[223] Melancton Smith, Ms. Notes of Debates (NYSL).

not appear to have been cast in the form of a motion, set out seven main grounds why the Constitution could not be approved without amendment. However, the convention was confident the Constitution would be amended, and consequently it was agreed to ratify with the reservation of a right to recede in case opportunity to amend was not given within a certain time. It was recommended that Congress should not exercise the power to tax, to call out militia, "&c &c" except as indicated in the New York amendments, until the sense of the people of the United States be taken on amendment. The other states were to be circularized, inviting cooperation in securing another convention. Zephaniah Platt seconded.[224]

On the following day some of the antifederalists made it clear that they did not like the proposal. But Jay said he would prefer it as a basis for discussion. A vote to adjourn was taken at once.

When the delegates reassembled on Saturday, July 19, the parliamentary situation could hardly have been more murky. Lansing claimed that there were three propositions before the house and he asked leave to proceed with his own plan.[225] This was a more complex confection than any yet before the Committee.[226] It opened with a "declaration" embodying the favorite reservations of rights plus an explicit disclaimer of federal powers by implication.[227] It recited all the matter in Lansing's own bill of rights as well as a variety of items culled from resolves theretofore offered by the antifederalists, such as the limitations upon suits where the state was a party, the use of writ of error in common law causes and the prohibition of extension of jurisdiction by the use of fictions. The ratifying paragraph had two "express condition" clauses. One was the express condition that the "Constructions"—viz., the rights and provisos previously recited—were to remain inviolable and that the Constitution "shall" receive them. The confidence was expressed that these would be submitted to a federal convention. The ratification was then expressed "upon Condition nevertheless" that until a convention was called, certain powers of Congress could not be exercised, or exercised only under limitations. As in Duane's resolution, a long list of amendments was subjoined which the convention admonished its future representatives to secure in the manner prescribed in the Constitution. These included the earlier resolves restricting jurisdiction of the Supreme

---

224 Jay sent the text to Washington on July 17, *Doc. Hist. Const.*, IV, 796. As there printed, it conforms in all but a few minor particulars with the original in the Ms. McKesson Papers (NYHS). A draft in Smith's hand is in Melancton Smith's Ms. Notes (NYSL).

225 Gilbert Livingston, Ms. Notes of Debates, 44d (NYPL).

226 *Ibid.*, 45a.

227 Ms. Journal of the Convention, 36 *et seq.*

Court, and a great variety of other crippling provisions. The motion to consider this substitute received solid support from the antifederalists.[228] It supplied the framework for the final resolution of ratification.

The consideration of Lansing's proposal began with a protracted examination of the several amendments that occupied the whole of the next three days. The federalists in what appears to have been an unexpected show of cooperation agreed to many of these, and in some instances minor changes suggested by them were accepted.[229] It was even agreed to remove some conditional amendments to the category of recommendatory amendments. Whenever the federalists disagreed, they were consistently voted down. In only one significant particular did Hamilton succeed in imposing his views. This was in restricting the commission of review that Jones had wished to set over the Supreme Court to cases where the Supreme Court exercised original jurisdiction.[230]

None of this touched, of course, the basic question of the form of ratification, and one cannot avoid the impression that the stab and parry over the wording of amendments was no more than a time-consuming diversion while exploration for an acceptable formula was proceeding outside the purlieus of the Dutchess County courthouse. One of these formulas was Smith's proposed ratification reserving a right to recede in the event amendments were not secured within a given time. For on July 19, while Lansing's amendments were still being considered, Hamilton wrote to Madison, who had returned to New York, inquiring whether or not New York would be received into the Union on the terms suggested by Smith.[231] Madison replied forthwith that this could not be: "the Constitution requires adoption *in toto*, and for ever."[232]

On July 23 the convention arrived at the moment of crisis—the paragraph of ratification. Melancton Smith moved to expunge the first sentence and offered another in which the words "Under the Impression and in Confidence" in lieu of the words "on the express Condition." This

---

[228] *Ibid.*, 45.

[229] It was sought to delete a direction regarding venue from the article providing protection for defendants in criminal prosecutions on the ground that trial by a jury of the county where the crime was committed was not invariably good, but this was rejected. The provision for jury trial in civil actions was rewritten to meet the objection that juries were not used in admiralty or equity. An amendment that the judicial power of the United States as to controversies between citizens of different states was not to be construed to extend to any controversy relating to real estate not claimed under grants of different states was shifted to the list of recommended amendments. However, the amendment which would confine inferior tribunals to appellate jurisdiction except for admiralty and trials for crimes on the high seas was left standing despite Hamilton's objection that it would increase appeals and operate to the prejudice of the poor. See *PAH*, V, 178–92.

[230] Gilbert Livingston, Ms. Notes of Debates, 45a (NYPL).

[231] *PAH*, V, 177–78.

[232] July 20, 1788, *ibid.*, 184.

was passed 39–19.[233] Samuel Jones then moved that in the second sentence the words "Upon Condition nevertheless" be obliterated and that the words "In full Confidence" be substituted. The vote on this was 31–29.[234]

After Jones had made his motion, Melancton Smith said he would vote against a condition. He believed the Constitution to be radically defective. Amendments had been the object of his pursuit, and until Virginia ratified he had thought these could be obtained before the new government was launched. He was now satisfied they could not be. It was the dictate of duty and reason to quit his first ground "and advance so far, as that they might be received into the Union." From the reasoning of his opponents he was sure the first plan would not work. He depicted the divisions between northern and southern New York if they did not ratify. The strength of his own party, anxious to amend, would be dissipated. Gilbert Livingston and Zephaniah Platt declared they would follow him. Governor Clinton, good machine politician that he was, declared that he would follow the sense of Ulster County which had elected him.[235]

The vote was next taken upon the things which the new Congress was not to do pending the convening of another convention. On the use of a state militia the vote was divided but on the rest the vote was unanimous. On July 24 Lansing offered an amendment, which he identified as Smith's earlier proposal, reserving the right to recede unless the various amendments had been submitted to a convention within a blank number of years.[236] This was debated into the next day. Both Jay and Hamilton spoke in opposition.[237] Hamilton asserted a distrust of other states was implied. It would awaken their pride and other passions unfriendly to amendments. Then as a *coup de grace* he read the letter from Madison. Smith was silent, but on July 25 announced that he

---

[233] Ms. Journal of the Convention, 55–56.

[234] *Ibid.*, 56–57.

[235] A letter from Poughkeepsie dated July 26, in the New York *Independent Journal: or, the General Advertiser, supp. extraordinary*, Monday, July 28, 1788. Livingston's Notes of Debates, 49a, merely state, "Smith gave Reasons—why he will not vote for the amendment." Platt stated he "shall pursue what he thinks will ultimately tend to the happiness of the people." Livingston reported that Clinton "does not rise to give a sentiment on this quest^n because Gent. may connect his character as Govr & representative."

A letter in *The Country Journal and Poughkeepsie Advertiser*, Mar. 4, 1788, had attacked Smith's nomination by Dutchess County because he was a New York City man and because he was believed to be too soft on the Constitution. Events proved this antifederalist to have been right.

[236] Ms. Journal of the Convention, 58. The pinning of this on Smith, in Livingston, Ms. Notes of Debates, 49b (NYPL).

[237] Gilbert Livingston, Ms. Notes of Debates, 49b *et seq.* (NYPL). See also New York *Independent Journal, supp. extraordinary*, July 28, 1788.

would vote against Lansing's proposal. He had originally submitted the proposition "as a middle ground," hoping both sides would be pleased with it. Neither was. It would not answer the end sought.[238] By his fellow antifederalists anxious doubts were expressed as to how the rights claimed were now secured. Smith replied, "What security can anyone have respecting any right—but the confidence you put in the government which is to exercise them?"[239] This seems to have irritated Clinton for he asked if confidence in the government "was to be our only safety why have we sat here so long?"[240] To this there could be no answer. Lansing's proposal was rejected 31–28.[241] A further change in the ratification clause designed to strengthen the statement regarding the inviolability of the listed rights was agreed to and the Committee report was then approved 31–28.[242] The convention voted its agreement 31–25. On motion of Duane a committee was elected—Jay, Melancton Smith and Jones—to prepare a circular letter on the matter of a second convention. There was some further tinkering with the amendments and on July 26 the final ratification was voted 30–27.[243] The circular letter was unanimously approved.

In its final form the New York ratification[244] runs to twelve printed pages—only four less than the Constitution itself—provoking the reflection that it was fortunate that New York was so fugitively represented at Philadelphia. The opening mélange of fundamental rights and "Explanations" which the delegates, as they ratified, declared they were under the "impression" could not be abridged or violated occupy better than four pages; the amendments desired are all of seven pages in length. More modest was the list of things they expressed confidence Congress would not do until a new convention to consider amendments was convened. But the only operative words in the instrument were the words of ratification, and if any of the antifederalists thought otherwise, they were deluding themselves. For once the resolve was shorn of words of condition; the various declarations possessed no more binding power than the promises of a political platform. Coupled as it was with the circular letter, this is, indeed, into what it had degenerated.

As for the circular letter, it was a moderate document designed to warm opinion for a convention to be called pursuant to Article V of the Constitution.[245] It referred to the desire of other states for amendments,

---

[238] Gilbert Livingston, Ms. Notes of Debates, 51d (NYPL).

[239] *Ibid.*, 52a.

[240] *Ibid.*, 52b.

[241] Ms. Journal of the Convention, 59.

[242] *Ibid.*, 65.

[243] *Ibid.*, 73.

[244] *Doc. Hist. Const.*, II, 190–203.

[245] Printed in Elliot, *Debates*, II, 413–14. The draft in the Ms. McKesson Papers (NYHS) indicates that the paragraph beginning "Our amendments will manifest . . ." was an addition drawn up by Lansing.

and characterized what New York had agreed upon as matters of general and not local interest. The request was made of the several state legislatures to take the necessary steps to activate the calling of a convention by Congress. A proposal for such a circular had been embodied in Melancton Smith's proposition of July 17.[246] It is not improbable that the pourparlers with the Virginia opposition had inspired this tactic and had given the New Yorkers some hope of its success.

Madison was worried and indignant over the "pestilent tendency" of the circular for he feared that the new system would be mutilated before it was fairly in operation.[247] Washington agreed; the letter would be attended with "parnicious" consequences.[248] Both men concluded it was the result of a bargain. What particularly irritated Madison, who wanted the new capital on the Potomac,[249] was the belief that the federalists had sold out to have the government seated at New York.[250] It is clear from the debates, however, that it was the federalists who were casting this bait, and if there was any snapping at it, this was done by the antifederalists.

No one who has examined Gilbert Livingston's notes on the final discussions can doubt that the federalists were lucky to get as good a bargain as they did, for up to the last moment in the voting their minuscule majority was imperilled. They were in the situation where they had no choice but to follow the counsel of the old proverb: "If you buy the cow, take the tail into the bargain." Fortunately the appendage of the circular letter was only a temporary embarrassment, for the fine scheme of the antifederalists came to nothing.[251]

There is no doubt but that circumstance had much to do with the Poughkeepsie result. Hard on the heels of Virginia's ratification had come the news that a committee of Congress had been named to report an act for setting in motion the new government.[252] Its report, made on

---

[246] *Supra*, p. 406, n. 224.
[247] Madison to Washington, Aug. 11, 1788, *Doc. Hist. Const.*, V, 14; to Jefferson, Aug. 10, 1788, *Papers of Jefferson*, XIII, 497; and same to same, Aug. 23, 1788, *ibid.*, 539.
[248] Washington to Madison, Aug. 17, 1788, *Washington Writings*, XXX, 52. He wrote to Hamilton on Aug. 28, 1788, that he supposed the circular letter was "the equivalent by which you obtained an acquiescence in the proposed Constitution" (*ibid.*, 66).
[249] Madison to Washington, Aug. 24, 1788, *Doc. Hist. Const.*, V, 29, at 32.
[250] *Ibid.*

[251] On the response to this, *infra*, c. X, p. 416 *et seq.*
[252] *JCC*, XXXIV, 281 (July 2, 1788). A letter from Poughkeepsie printed in the New York *Independent Journal: or, The General Advertiser*, July 9, 1788, stated that the act to put the new government into effect was being impatiently awaited. "This . . . will change the nature of the ground, and will beget a new relative situation betwixt the representatives and their constituents, which was not in contemplation at the time elected." This newspaper has also an extract of the *Journals* of Congress regarding the committee. A notice of the committee's appointment is in *The Country Jour-*

July 8, was published immediately,[253] and to the delegates at Pough-keepsie the only encouraging thing about it was the fact that it left blank the location of the new seat of government. For while settlement of this question was to the Southerners a question of prestige, the New Yorkers typically viewed it in terms of economics. Even so, this was not sufficient of itself to tip the balance.[254] It needed the utmost talents of Jay and Hamilton, particularly of the latter, to lure to their side the handful of necessary votes. Childs, the reporter, printed nothing of these fateful interchanges—possibly because these were not "high-toned" enough, as the phrase then was. Nevertheless, as a display of artful maneuvering they are fascinating. Above everything was the skill with which Hamilton imparted to arguments of expediency the quality of lofty purpose.

It was this in the end which persuaded the key figure, Melancton Smith, for it was after Hamilton's two speeches on the motion to adjourn that Smith made the reluctant admission that his plan would not work. This by no means implied a conversion. It was merely a retraction from a position which events had made untenable, and this is what Hamilton had persuaded him was the case. Smith had apparently never been for rejection. On June 28 he had written his friend Nathan Dane setting out his stand on amendments:[255]

> . . . my great object is to procure such amendments in this govt, as to prevent its attaining the ends, For which it appears to me, and to you calculated—I am therefore very anxious to procure good amendments— I had rather recommend substantial amendments, than adopt it con- ditionally with unimportant ones, leaving our critical situation out of the question. . . . hither to the amendments proposed are substantial, they will continue so—but as no question is taken in [*sic*] any, it is questionable, whether the most important will not be yielded under the idea of making previous conditional amendments—when I am per- suaded, if we can agree, to make the condition a subsequent one, that is to take place in one to two years after adoption of the ratification to become void, we can accomodate with the advocates of the Constitu- tion For more substantial amendm^t—

nal and Poughkeepsie Advertiser, July 15, 1788.

[253] *JCC,* XXXIV, 303–04. Sixty copies were printed (*ibid.,* 633).

[254] On July 9 Congress apparently put over the report (*ibid.,* 315, n. 1). Printed in the New York *Daily Ad-vertiser,* July 14, 1788, was a Pough-keepsie letter dated July 11 which stated that word had come by express that Congress had postponed fixing the seat of the federal government in order to have an opportunity of establishing it at New York. "But it had rather a bad tendency, for they treated it as a feint. One of their shrewd ones ridiculed the idea, and asked, whether a spider did not al-ways put himself in the middle of his web."

[255] Ms. Nathan Dane Papers (Beverly Hist. Soc., Beverly, Mass.)

When Smith became convinced that the new Congress on its own motion could not call a convention, and that New York should not put itself in the posture of opposing the whole country, he yielded. Apart from such considerations of public prudence, Smith was too seasoned in matters political to be heedless of the fundamental maxim of the craft that to be outside looking in is of no profit. New York, therefore, narrowly avoided the egregious mistake which North Carolina was to make just one week later. Deaf to the urgings of the federalist leaders, James Iredell, William Davie and Governor Samuel Johnston, the opposition in that state remained intransigeant to the end.[256] By a majority of ninety-nine the ultimatum was voted to require a bill of rights and a formidable array of amendments as a condition precedent to ratification. The antifederalist delegates, in obeying the mandate of those who had elected them, effectively deprived the state of a voice in organizing the new government. Only in Rhode Island could there be rejoicing—she at last had a companion to share her burden of disesteem.[257]

---

[256] The debates are in Elliot, *Debates*, IV, 1–252. See further, L. Trenholme, *The Ratification of the Federal Constitution in North Carolina*. Nothing not already broached elsewhere on the judicial was raised at the convention. The proceedings were not finally printed until the summer of 1789.

[257] Williamson to Iredell, Aug. 23, 1788: ". . . it appears that North Carolina has at length thrown herself out of the Union, but she happily is not alone; the large, upright, and respectable State of Rhode Island is her associate." McRee, *Iredell*, II, 236.

CHAPTER X

Unfinished Business—
The Bill of Rights

ON SEPTEMBER 13, 1788, the Continental Congress adopted a resolve reciting that the Constitution had been ratified "in a manner therein declared to be sufficient for the establishment of the same" and consequently setting the first Wednesday in January for the appointing of electors and the first Wednesday in February for the vote to be taken for President. The first Wednesday in March was fixed for commencing proceedings under the Constitution.[1] It was left, of course, to the states to settle the time, place and manner of the election of Senators and Representatives.[2] Because there were questions about the Constitution commonly esteemed to be yet unsettled, the resolve confronted politicians in the several states which had come into the Union with practical problems that bore some resemblance to those of a year earlier. The chief difference was the fact that there had emerged, as a result of the extended discussion over ratification, an awareness of national interests distinct from those of the states. The latter were no longer as predominant as they had been, although the nature of senatorial representation was tonic and certain rural districts like the South Carolina back country and upstate New York clung to old loyalties.

Insofar as there existed divisions of opinion susceptible of precipitation into political issues in the first national elections, these derived from ideas about the organization of the new government developed when the new Constitution had been under minute scrutiny. The most resolute of the pro-Constitution men wished the new instrument to be tried as it stood, effectively implemented without reference to any of the substantive suggestions and demands advanced by critics.[3] This did not

---

[1] *JCC*, XXXIV, 522–23.
[2] By U.S. Constitution, Art. I, sec. 4.
[3] Except in the case of Madison who wrote to Richard Peters, Aug. 19,

1789, that in Virginia the Constitution would certainly have been rejected "had no assurances been given by its advocates that such provisions would

suit their adversaries who were more impressed with the Constitution's defects than its virtues. Five states—New Hampshire, Massachusetts, New York, Virginia and South Carolina—held, as it were, promissory notes that something would be done about their amendments. To this the federalists had agreed as the price for unconditional ratification.[4] In three states—Pennsylvania, Maryland and South Carolina—there were defeated minorities with what may be termed non-negotiable paper who might be counted upon to make common cause. As events unfolded after September 1788, it became, as we shall see, the counsel of prudence that the promises earlier made be honored after a fashion, not *pro salute animae* but to quiet what had been represented to be public anxieties.

These anxieties, except as they related to safeguards for individual liberties, we venture to submit were mainly entertained by state politicians whose handiwork is evident in the several state programs for revision of the Constitution. All of these programs were weighted with political demands, and the fact that such were sometimes described as "unalienable rights" could not obscure their purpose. Some of these demands were directed at changes in the structure of the Constitution itself, such as the regulation of representation in Congress and the addition of restraints on commercial monopolies. Others were aimed at curbing national power to the advantage of the states. The most reactionary of these last was the proposal that there be resort to requisition before Congress exercise its power of direct taxation. Destructive of the judicial power were the proposals to emasculate diversity jurisdiction and to confine inferior courts to admiralty and maritime causes.

From the aggregate of the proposals of this genus there were few innocuous enough to be pressed without damage to the new Constitution. There were, however, the propositions relating to individual rights that were clearly severable from the political demands. Their inclusion would meet public expectations and so serve national interests without imperilling the highly sensitive operation of organizing the new establishment. These were to be the core of the first constitutional revision, and because some of these items affected the judicial process it is essential that some account of this significant episode be given.[5]

---

be pursued. As an honest man *I feel myself bound by this consideration.*" Ms. Madison Papers, XII, 9 (LC).

[4] Some of these provisions have been discussed *supra* in cc. VIII and IX. Texts are in *Doc. Hist. Const.*, II, 94–96 (Mass.), 139–40 (S.C.), 141–44 (N.H.), 190–203 (N.Y.), 377–85 (Va.).

[5] The most recent studies dealing with the bill of rights movement are R. A. Rutland, *The Birth of the Bill of Rights, 1776–1791*, and E. Dumbauld, *The Bill of Rights and What It Means Today*. The latter has valuable tables, and reprints not only the various proposals of state conventions, but also the chief documents relating the amendments' passage through the Congress.

INITIATION OF AMENDMENTS— BY CONVENTION OR CONGRESS

THE STORY OF THIS first revision might have been a different one if the device by which all five of the amendment-minded state conventions sought to insure ultimate acceptance of their programs had worked. With specific reference to Article V of the new Constitution, all laid it as an injunction upon future representatives in Congress to use all influence and reasonable means to obtain ratification of their proposals. The intendment of this was that the first of the alternative methods of Article V—viz., initiation of amendments by Congress—be pursued. This direction made in the name of the people of the state was manifestly an adaptation of the practice of state instruction of delegates to the Continental Congress that had so bedevilled its operations. Instruction was an expedient based on a misconception of the nature of representation in the lower house provided in the new Constitution.[6] It appears to have been anticipated, however, that the states might thus control their Senators. As we shall see, an attempt at the first Congress to engraft a right of instruction on the Constitution was to fail. And it is apparent from the record of the first session that although injunctions of the state conventions were sometimes adverted to,[7] these rested so lightly upon the representatives that no concerted effort by a whole state delegation to push the amendment program as directed was ever made.

The designs of the several conventions were overset not only by the disregard of their instructions by Representatives in the lower house, but also by the eccentric action of the New York Convention. This body, too, had resorted to the formula of instruction but, leaving nothing to chance, had also, as noticed in our account of the convention, authorized the circular letter to the governors of other states seeking to set in motion procedure according to the second alternative of Article V—viz., a convention called by the states.[8] This letter, signed by Governor Clinton as president of the convention, did not advert to the fact that two days earlier the convention had voted to press for amendment by the first alternative, nor did it even suggest that such a course would allay what were depicted as "apprehensions and discontents." Only a second convention would do, and one promptly called.[9]

One may infer from the circular's reference to "articles so ex-

---

[6] *Cf.* here J. E. Cooke, ed., *The Federalist*, No. 39, 254–55; No. 62, *ibid.*, 416; both by Madison.

[7] *E.g.*, on June 8, 1789, Gerry (Mass.), Livermore (N.H.), *Annals of Congress*, I, 464. On July 21,

Gerry, *ibid.*, 688. On August 13, Gerry, *ibid.*, 733. On August 24, Partridge (Mass.), Sedgwick (Mass.), *ibid.*, 807.

[8] *Supra*, c. VIII, pp. 409–10.

[9] Text in Elliot, *Debates*, II, 413–14.

ceptionable" which needed revision by a general convention that this expedient was advanced not out of fear that Congress would not initiate amendments to guarantee individual rights (for these were not even mentioned), but out of anxiety over the reception there of the propositions designed to retrieve states' rights. These were sown like dragon's teeth in the proposals of both the New York and Virginia conventions, and the supposition appears to have been that the irreconcilables would make themselves heard at the legislatures which convened in the fall.

The first two legislatures to which Clinton's circular was referred by the executive, New Jersey and Pennsylvania, gave it short shrift. The New Jersey Assembly referred it to the Council and heard of it no more;[10] the Pennsylvania Assembly, controlled by federalists, merely directed that it be entered upon the minutes.[11] Five days earlier (September 3) a conclave held by the so-called dissenting minority at Harrisburg had responded handsomely, if meaninglessly, to Clinton's exhortation by calling for a second convention in a petition addressed to the assembly and subjoining a menu of amendments conceived to be "essentially necessary."[12] This document produced no results beyond stimulating some fresh discussions of the amendment question in the newspapers, but these were not conducted *con brio* as they had earlier been.[13]

[10] *Votes and Proceedings of the Twelfth General Assembly of the State of New Jersey*, 2d Sitting, at 7. The letter was submitted Aug. 29, 1788. There is no further record. The letter was not mentioned in the list of unfinished business at the commencement of the next session. *Votes and Proceedings of the Thirteenth General Assembly*, at 7–9 (October 30). *The Journal of the Proceedings of the Legislative Council of the State of New Jersey*, 12th Sess., 2d Sitting, at 4 (Aug. 30, 1788), shows only delivery of the paper to the Council.

[11] *Minutes of the Twelfth General Assembly of the Commonwealth of Pennsylvania in their Third Session*, 219–21 (Sept. 8, 1788).

On Oct. 4, 1788, a motion to have Clinton's circular specially recommended to the next session was beaten 38–24 (*ibid.*, 276).

[12] This is discussed in E. P. Smith, "The Movement Towards a Second Constitutional Convention in 1788," published in J. F. Jameson, ed., *Essays in the Constitutional History of the*

United States . . . , 46 at 98. The text of the "Proceedings" in Elliot, *Debates*, II, 542–46. There is a more complete documentation including Gallatin's draft resolves referring to Clinton's circular in McMaster and Stone, *Pennsylvania*, 552–64.

There was critical comment in the *Pennsylvania Gazette*, Sept. 10 and Sept. 17, 1788; New York *Daily Advertiser*, Sept. 6, 1788, where it is claimed the Pennsylvanians were threatening civil war.

Richard Peters, writing to Washington Sept. 17, 1788, was of the opinion that the Harrisburg manifesto was oriented toward coming elections. *Doc. Hist. Const.*, V, 65. Cf. the opinion of "A Freeman" in New York *Daily Advertiser*, Sept. 29, 1788.

[13] *Massachusetts Centinel*, Sept. 20 and Sept. 27, 1788; New York *Daily Advertiser*, Sept. 20 and Sept. 29, 1788; *New-York Journal, and Daily Patriotic Register*, Sept. 25, 1788; Philadelphia *Independent Gazetteer: or, The Chronicle of Freedom*, Sept. 24, 1788; *Federal Gazette, and Phila-*

The response in New England to Clinton's appeal was one of indifference. The circular was read to the Connecticut Assembly,[14] but, as Jonathan Trumbull reported to Washington, "no one had hardiness enough to call up the consideration of that Letter."[15] The document was seemingly not even presented to the special session of the New Hampshire legislature called to make provision for electors, Senators and the choice of Representatives.[16] Only in Massachusetts was there a more positive reaction, for the circular was referred to a committee of both houses—an effective method of insuring delay, for no report was made at that session.[17]

The convention method of amendment seemed on the way to oblivion when events in Virginia infused it with new life. In October, before the House of Delegates was to convene, there was published in Richmond a pamphlet setting forth all amendments offered by various states, an obvious convenience for interested parties.[18] The members of the House of Delegates could be accounted such, for in the elections of the preceding spring when antifederalist sentiments were running high a legislature of this complexion had been returned. This assembly, moreover, was completely dominated by Patrick Henry. He declared, October 29, that he would oppose every measure tending to the organization of the new government unless accompanied by measures for amendment.[19] To this end he offered to the house, sitting as a Committee of the Whole, a resolution[20] introduced by a preamble in the manifesto

---

delphia Evening Post, Oct. 3 and Oct. 22, 1788; *Maryland Journal*, Sept. 12, 1788.

[14] If the text of the governor's message published in the *Connecticut Courant*, Oct. 27, 1788, is complete, the circular was not mentioned. The proceedings of the assembly do not record a reading as Trumbull states. The proceedings in L. W. Labaree, ed., *Public Records of the State of Connecticut*, VI, 469 *et seq.* The *Connecticut Courant*, Aug. 18, 1788, had printed the text of the circular.

[15] Oct. 28, 1788, *Doc. Hist. Const.*, V, 100–01.

[16] At least there is no record in Senate or House journals. *State Papers of New Hampshire*, XXI, 335 *et seq.* (Senate), 347 *et seq.* (House).

[17] Ms. Journal of the House of Representatives of the Commonwealth of Massachusetts, Oct. 29–Nov. 24, 1788, at 155. On November 1 the Senate requested a joint committee; *cf.* Sedgwick to Hamilton,

Nov. 2, 1788, in *PAH*, V, 228. It would appear from an entry (Jan. 8, 1789) in the House *Journal* at the next session that the Clinton circular was still pending business. *Cf. infra*, p. 421.

[18] *The Ratifications of the New Foederal Constitution, together with the Amendments, Proposed by the Several States* (1788; copy in LC). It appeared before Oct. 17, 1788, because Madison sent a copy to Jefferson with a letter of that date. *Papers of Jefferson*, XIV, 16, and *cf.* editor's note, *ibid.*, 22.

[19] Charles Lee to Washington, *Doc. Hist. Const.*, V, 101–03.

[20] *Journal of the House of Delegates of the Commonwealth of Virginia* (1788), 12 (October 30) (hereafter cited as *Jour. House of Delegates Va.*). According to Charles Lee, it was introduced the previous day. C. Lee to Washington, Oct. 29, 1788, in *Doc. Hist. Const.*, V, 101.

style of pre-Revolutionary days.[21] The resolution proposed an application to Congress to call a second convention, an answer to Governor Clinton and a circularization of the states. Before this came to a vote there was a motion to amend—in effect a substitute motion—to address Congress, praying that that body itself take steps to initiate amendments pursuant to Article V.[22] On this the antifederalists fell as ravening wolves and voted it down 85–39. On Henry's resolves, then approved, no ayes and nays were taken.

A committee was appointed to report the instruments resolved upon. These were presented November 14.[23] Again a counter-proposal was made, on this occasion to address Congress, leaving it to that body to decide whether to initiate amendments or to issue a call to the states for a second convention.[24] This was voted down 72–50. The committee report was agreed to and sent to the Senate, which made some minor amendments in which the House of Delegates concurred November 20.[25]

The diffuse and orotund style of the application[26] betrays the hand of Patrick Henry who, with James Monroe, was on the committee which prepared it. According to Monroe, Theoderick Bland revised the draft and imparted to it "his usual fire and elegance"[27]—a literary judgment in which it is difficult to concur. The document opens with an assurance that the legislature had thought it proper to make the arrangements necessary to carry the Constitution into effect. But the sense of the people of Virginia would not be complied with if something further were not done. The voice of the convention had pointed "to objects no less interesting." Ratification of the Constitution had been agreed to out of affection toward sister states despite dread of its operation in its present form. Consolation came from full expectation that imperfections would be speedily amended. Details need not be given. These were founded not on speculative theory but on principles established by "the melancholy example of other nations in different ages." The sooner public

---

[21] The preamble describes the Virginia amendments as involving "all the great essential and unalienable rights, liberties, and privileges of free men." The motivation of the resolve was to secure the clearest rights and liberties and for "preventing those disorders, which must arise under a government not founded in the confidence of the people."

[22] *Jour. House of Delegates Va.*, 13. This motion was drawn by Francis Corbin; see his letter to Madison, Nov. 12, 1788, in *Doc. Hist. Const.*, V, 113.

[23] *Jour. House of Delegates Va.*, 31.

[24] *Ibid.*, 32. Corbin had the assist-

ance of John Page and Edward Carrington in drafting this; *cf. supra*, n. 22.

[25] The Senate Journal has not been found. A comparison of the original and the printed resolve shows only minor changes.

[26] The text is conveniently available in *Annals of Congress*, I, 258–60. This is dated Nov. 14, 1788. A reproduction of the document in broadside form in *Papers of Jefferson*, XIV, 329. It is dated Nov. 20, 1788.

[27] Monroe to Jefferson, Feb. 15, 1789, in *Papers of Jefferson*, XIV, 557.

apprehensions were quieted and the government possessed of the confidence of the people, the more salutary would be its operation.

To infuse the application with some spirit the old shibboleth of the Revolution was enlisted: "The cause of amendments we consider as a common cause"; and hope was expressed that there would be zeal to obtain those provisions which experience had taught were necessary "to secure from danger, the unalienable rights of Human Nature." There must be no delay. "The slow forms of Congressional discussion and recommendation, if indeed they should ever agree to any change, would we fear be less certain of success." Happily, the Constitution provided the alternative of a convention of the states. Consequently Virginia was applying to Congress to call such a convention immediately. The circular letter to the states was a terse summary of Virginia's purpose.

Whatever its merits as a political manifesto, the application to Congress was not a candid representation of what Henry was after, which was nothing less than reversing the federalist victory. For surely the list of alterations in the structure of the new government selected by the Virginia Convention to correct imperfections could hardly be esteemed "unalienable rights of Human Nature." The purpose of the Virginia antifederalists was later to be bared by a flood of motions at the first session of Congress. Henry's motives were revealed by his measures of reprisal on the federalists which were executed with the thoroughness of Pride's Purge. Bent upon effecting Madison's political downfall, Henry had already managed to procure his adversary's defeat for election to the United States Senate and the naming thereto of Richard Henry Lee and William Grayson, of whose views on amendment there could be no doubt.[28] The full measure of Henry's animus was, however, made evident in the manner in which it was sought to exclude Madison even from the House of Representatives. In districting the Commonwealth for seats in the House, Madison's county of residence was coupled with five other counties, all reputedly antifederalist.[29] This, as we shall see, was a maneuver destined to fail. Henry's final assault upon the new system was to secure passage of a statute disqualifying all those employed in the administration of the federal government from holding any office or place under the Virginia government.[30]

As it turned out, the Virginia application, assiduously circulated, was based upon a misapprehension of popular temper elsewhere. The terms in which the application disparaged initiation of the amending

---

[28] Carrington to Madison, Nov. 9, 1788, in *Doc. Hist. Const.*, V, 110.

[29] 12 Hening, *Va. Stats.*, 653. *Cf.* Carrington to Madison, Nov. 15, 1788, in *Doc. Hist. Const.*, V, 116. The federalists had earlier been trapped into agreeing that residence in a district should be a condition *sine qua non.*

[30] 12 Hening, *Va. Stats.*, 694 (Dec. 8, 1788).

419

power by Congress itself suggests to us that the design was as much to influence the composition of a Congress hostile to such a procedure as it was to stimulate other states to echo Virginia's call. But the resolution was too badly timed to produce much effect upon the election of Senators, for seven other states had named their Senators before the application appeared in the Northern newspapers.[31] It could at best only affect the choice of Representatives, but when the returns were in, the number of second-convention Representatives was insignificant.

If it had been conceived that Clinton's circular was already doing its work and that Virginia's voice would be heard as a powerful second, this was an illusion for, as already observed, the New York letter had proved to be anything but a clarion call. Virginia's solicitation was to be harkened to only in that state. Two of Virginia's near-neighbors, Maryland and South Carolina, earlier marked for inclusion in Henry's phantom Southern confederation, were cold. In Maryland the utmost attempted was a resolve offered December 19, 1788, to the effect that the first Congress should adopt such mode of procuring amendments as appeared necessary and consistent with the Constitution. This was beaten 28–23.[32] Nothing was done by South Carolina. On January 9, 1789, the governor submitted the Virginia documents to both houses of the legislature. On the following day the House voted to take these into consideration on the 22nd, but the *Journal* records no further action. A committee of the Senate to which the Virginia documents were referred reported a resolve on February 18, 1789, that it would be premature to have another convention of the people of the state until the new government was organized and time allowed to consider there the South Carolina proposals for amendment. The *Journal* does not show that this was ever debated.[33]

The Virginia proposal fared little better in New England. The *Journal* of the New Hampshire legislature does not record that it was ever submitted to either house at the January session.[34] There is likewise no indication of action by the Connecticut Assembly, which met January 1, 1789, in an adjourned session.[35] In Massachusetts Governor Han-

---

[31] *Pennsylvania Gazette*, Dec. 10, 1788; New York *Daily Advertiser*, Dec. 10, 1788. There had been earlier but not specific pieces in the press indicating the temper in Virginia. The states which had elected Senators prior to December 10 were New Hampshire, Massachusetts, Connecticut, New Jersey, Pennsylvania, Delaware and Maryland.

[32] *Votes and Proceedings of the House of Delegates, State of Mary-land*, November 1788, 1st Sess., 77.

[33] *Journal of the Senate of South Carolina 1789*, at 8, the governor's message, Jan. 12, transmitting the papers. The report (*ibid.*, 123) was made February 18. Set for consideration the next day.

[34] *State Papers of New Hampshire*, XXI, 366 *et seq.* (Senate), 417 *et seq.* (House).

[35] *Public Records of the State of Connecticut*, VI, 493 *et seq.*

cock in his message of January 8, 1789,[36] laid the application before both houses, warning that a second convention would be costly if not dangerous and that the instructions of the Massachusetts Convention were sufficient security. In the House of Representatives, on January 20, a motion was made to refer to a committee the matter of a convention to take up amendments, but this was negatived.[37] When the legislature got around to framing a reply to the governor's message, finally decided upon in February,[38] it signified its concurrence in the opinion that a second convention would be expensive if not dangerous. Taking notice of Clinton's circular as well as Virginia's resolve, it spoke censoriously of the animadversion on the initiation of amendments in Congress; it pointed to the injunction laid by their own convention upon their representatives and expressed full confidence that this would be performed.[39] On February 17 it was resolved that the governor's reply to New York and Virginia be according to the tenor of this reply.[40]

The New Jersey Assembly had no chance to pass on the Virginia papers, for it did not meet until after Congress had despatched the amendments. In Pennsylvania the Council had presented the Virginia letter on February 6 and it was read a second time the next day,[41] but a motion to refer it to a committee was roundly defeated.[42] Nevertheless, the document was read a third time on March 3.[43] George Clymer then moved a resolve that the governor of Virginia be advised that the assembly did not see the necessity of a second convention. The resolve then proceeded to take issue with the Virginia arguments: "That though it is possible this constitution may not be a system exempt, in all its parts, from error, yet the House do not perceive it wanting in any of those fundamental principles, which are calculated to insure the liberties of their country. As it is, they conceive the happiness of *America* and the harmony of the union to depend altogether on suffering it to proceed, undisturbed in its operations by premature alterations or amendments, which, however plausible they may be in theory, or necessary perhaps to the idea of a perfect form of government, experience, after all, can demonstrate whether they would be real improvements or not." It could not consistently with its duty toward its own people and its affection for the rest of the citizenry concur with the legislature of Virginia.

---

[36] *Mass. Acts and Resolves 1788–89* (reprint), 741.

[37] Ms. Journal of the House of Representatives, of the Commonwealth of Massachusetts, Dec. 31, 1788–Feb. 17, 1789, *sub* Jan. 20, 1789.

[38] *Cf.* the entries *ibid.*, Jan. 23 and Jan. 31, 1789.

[39] The answer is published in full, *Massachusetts Centinel*, Feb. 7, 1789.

[40] *Mass. Acts and Resolves 1788–89* (reprint), Resolves, Dec. Sess., c. 121.

[41] *Minutes of the Thirteenth General Assembly of the Commonwealth of Pennsylvania in their Second Session* (1789), 55, 58.

[42] *Ibid.*, 60.

[43] *Ibid.*, 112–13.

After this resolve had had a second reading, antifederalist James McLene moved to postpone to introduce a resolve concurring in Virginia's declaration and directing that a committee be named to prepare a request for a second convention. This was beaten 42–18.[44] Clymer's resolve was voted 41–20.[45] In due course President Mifflin notified the Virginia governor.[46]

New York, as might be anticipated, took a different and more friendly course. The legislature had been called to meet in special session December 8. Governor Clinton laid before this body the Poughkeepsie ratification and the New York circular letter.[47] The epistle from the Virginia apostles was not submitted until December 27.[48] The newspapers had carried the text December 10. In reply to Clinton's speech, the antifederalist assembly engaged to carry out the governor's request that Congress be petitioned to call a second convention.[49] Not so the senate, where the federalists had a majority of one.[50] The dissensions between the two houses had the unhappy consequence that they were deadlocked both on the method of choosing electors and on that of electing Senators, with the result that New York did not vote for a Presidential candidate nor was that state represented in the Senate when Congress convened.[51] So pronounced was the aversion of the Clintonians for the new system that there was alarm lest the spirit of faction would lead to no representation in the lower house. Hamilton besought the aid of Samuel Jones who had earlier crossed party lines in the ratification struggle.[52] Whatever were the details of the "conversations" between the two, a statute making provision for the election of Representatives was signed January 27, 1789,[53] and on February 7 the president of the senate signed the assembly resolve petitioning Congress for a second convention.[54]

The New York result saved the Virginia scheme from a lonely death, but the reception accorded it elsewhere left no doubt of its ultimate

---

[44] Ibid., 123–24.

[45] Ibid., 124–26.

[46] Pennsylvania Archives, XI, 557–58.

[47] Journal of the New York Assembly, 12th Sess., 4.

[48] Ibid., 24. Governor Beverly Randolph's letter of transmittal was dated Dec. 2, 1788.

[49] Ibid., 19.

[50] Hamilton to Madison, Nov. 23, 1788, in PAH, V, 235.

[51] The struggle over "An Act for directing the manner of appointing Electors etc." continued all through

February 3, and was resumed the next day (cf. the Journal entries for those days) despite the fact that the legislature was sitting at Albany and February 4 was the day fixed for the Presidential election.

[52] Hamilton to Jones, Jan. 21, 1789, in PAH, V, 244.

[53] N.Y. Laws, 12 Sess. 1789, c. 12.

[54] Journal of the New York Assembly, 12th Sess., 108. For the printed text cf. Journal of the House of Representatives of the United States . . . (reprint 1826), I, 29–30 (hereafter cited as Jour. H.R.).

doom. This appears to have been the consensus in late March when the members of the new Congress came drifting into New York City, for Senator Paine Wingate of New Hampshire wrote Timothy Pickering, "Nobody thinks that a general convention will be called, and possibly in a convenient time Congress may take up the consideration of amendments or alterations, and may recommend some that may quiet the fears and jealousies of the well-designing and not affect the essentials of the present system."[55]

The question remained whether or not Representatives of states like Massachusetts and South Carolina would press the local amendments as their conventions had instructed, and whether some from other states which had no such programs would come up with new offerings. That the matter of amendments had become something of a political issue in the elections for the new Congress is clear from newspaper accounts. Little of this propaganda was directed at the respective merits of the alternative procedures of Article V,[56] but rather at the questions of haste, delay or complete inaction.[57] This aspect of the amendment question antedated the actual elections and threatened divisions among the federalists that were not expunged even when Congress convened.

An early manifestation of this threat was evident in the Massachusetts legislature[58] before the dispositions had been made for the choice of electors and Senators, and while action was pending on Clinton's circular. Apprised of this by Theodore Sedgwick,[59] Hamilton warned against suffering divisions on collateral points. "I do not think," he wrote, "you should allow any line to be run between those who wish to trust alterations to future experience and those who are desirous of them at the present juncture. The rage for amendments is in my opinion rather to be parried by address than encountered with open force. And I should therefore be loth to learn that your parties have been arranged

---

[55] C. E. Wingate, *Life and Letters of Paine Wingate*, II, 289–91, Mar. 25, 1789.

[56] *Infra*, nn. 72, 74. *E.g.*, New York *Daily Advertiser*, Jan. 7, 1789; *New-York Packet*, Jan. 13, 1789; *Pennsylvania Gazette*, Dec. 10 and Dec. 31, 1788; *Federal Gazette and Philadelphia Evening Post*, Oct. 18, 1788; *Massachusetts Centinel*, Jan. 31, 1789; *Maryland Journal*, Aug. 19, 1788.

[57] New York *Daily Advertiser*, Sept. 20, 1788; *New-York Packet*, Mar. 20 and Mar. 24, 1789; *Federal Gazette and Philadelphia Evening Post*, Oct.

22, 1788; *Pennsylvania Gazette*, Dec. 3, 1788; *Pennsylvania Packet*, Jan. 1, 1789; *Maryland Gazette: or, The Baltimore Advertiser*, Mar. 10, 1789; *Massachusetts Centinel*, Dec. 3, 1788.

[58] According to A. E. Morse, *The Federalist Party in Massachusetts to the Year 1800*, 61, n. 36, the campaign opened in late July. See also Christopher Gore to Rufus King, Aug. 10 and Aug. 30, 1788, in *Life of King*, I, 341, 343.

[59] Sedgwick to Hamilton, Nov. 2, 1788, in *PAH*, V, 228.

professedly upon the distinction I have mentioned. The *mode* in which amendments may best be made and twenty other matters may serve as pretexts for avoiding the evil and securing the good."[60]

Whether Hamilton in this last cryptic remark had in mind a distinction between political amendments and safeguards for the individual, or was seeking to remove amendment as a campaign issue, cannot be said. If the latter, he was reaching for the unattainable, because amendment was to prove something of a catalyst in the process of converting schools of opinion into perceptible party divisions. There was no way of keeping the letter writers out of the press, or the reports of electioneering. This was the case in Massachusetts where the candidacy of Samuel Adams and Elbridge Gerry alone was enough to precipitate such discussion.[61] The so-called Radicals in Pennsylvania made amendment their cause,[62] and in Maryland Samuel Chase injected the issue into elections for state office.[63] The efforts of the self-styled Federal Republicans of New York, whose pre-convention activities have already been noticed, were effective in keeping the issue alive through the spring elections of 1789 for Representatives in the House.[64] It was in Virginia, however, where the most fateful struggle over the revision of the Constitution took place, and this in the district where Madison confronted Monroe. Here, Madison was fighting for political survival. Contrary to the expectations of his adversaries, the contest, by his own choice, was not over amendment or no amendment or even the proper method of amendment, but over what amendments it would be expedient to adopt.

---

[60] Hamilton to Sedgwick, Nov. 9, 1788, *ibid.*, 230–31.

[61] Samples of the propaganda in *Massachusetts Centinel*, Sept. 3, 20, 27, Oct. 22, Nov. 5, Dec. 3, 1788. Gerry's letter to the electors of Middlesex announcing his stand in favor of amendments was reprinted in the *New-York Daily Gazette*, Jan. 30, 1789, and the *Pennsylvania Packet*, Feb. 6, 1789.

[62] Hopefully by resurrecting "Centinel" (*supra*, c. VI); and *cf.* also Philadelphia *Independent Gazetteer; or, The Chronicle of Freedom*, Nov. 7, 8, 1788. Other propaganda in this paper Sept. 6, 24, 26, Nov. 18, 22, 1788. See also *Pennsylvania Gazette*, Nov. 19, Dec. 24, 1788, and *Pennsylvania Packet*, Nov. 14, 1788.

[63] *Maryland Journal*, Sept. 19, 23, 26, Oct. 3, 1788.

[64] I. Leake, *Memoir of the Life and Times of General John Lamb*, 320 *et seq.* This group reorganized Oct. 30, 1788, circularized the counties and eventually sought to promote Clinton for the Vice Presidency. How far it was responsible for the legislative debacle which prevented choice of electors and Senators is unknown. The discussions pro and con of amendment were considerable in the New York papers, which used matter from Boston and Philadelphia. See for example *New-York Journal, and Daily Patriotic Register*, Nov. 27, Dec. 4, 11, 1788, Feb. 13, Mar. 12, Apr. 2, 1789; New York *Daily Advertiser*, Dec. 10, 11, 23, 1788; *New-York Daily Gazette*, Feb. 27, Mar. 9, 19, 1789; *New-York Packet*, Jan. 2, May 12, 1789.

THE CONVERSION OF A LEADER

BECAUSE MADISON was to take the lead in offering amendments for congressional action and, by his perseverance, to pilot through the House of Representatives its version of what was to become the federal Bill of Rights, some account of how he came to grace must be given. In his penultimate speech at the Virginia Convention Madison is thus reported:[65] "As to a solemn declaration of our essential rights, he thought it unnecessary and dangerous—unnecessary, because it was evident that the general government had no power but what was given it, and that the delegation alone warranted the exercise of power; dangerous, because an enumeration which is not complete is not safe." He added what under the circumstances was a mere gesture—that he would admit amendments that seemed in his judgment not dangerous.[66] The reaction to Clinton's circular letter and the alarming possibility of a second convention does not appear to have moved Madison to an immediate espousal of amendments recommended by Congress as a countermeasure. For in a letter to Jefferson, August 23,[67] he went no further than to write that a year's trial of the Constitution would suggest better amendments than those presently circulating. Even after the Harrisburg resolves, Madison remained uncommitted.[68] But by mid-October he had come to the conclusion that a "constitutional declaration of the most essential rights" would probably be added.[69] Possibly nudged by a suggestive letter from Jefferson,[70] Madison replied that his own opinion "has always been in favor of a bill of rights; provided it be so framed as not to imply powers not meant to be included in the enumeration."[71]

---

[65] Elliot, *Debates*, III, 626.

[66] Before the convention was Wythe's resolution of ratification (*ibid.*, 653) in the preamble of which was the declaration that all powers not granted remained in the people and no right could be cancelled, abridged, restrained or modified by any agency of the government of the United States except as power was conferred by the Constitution, and among other essential rights, liberty of conscience and the press "cannot be cancelled, abridged, restrained, or modified, by any authority of the United States."

[67] Madison to Jefferson, Aug. 23, 1788, in *Papers of Jefferson*, XIII, 539.

[68] Madison to Jefferson, Sept. 21, 1788, *ibid.*, 624.

[69] Madison to Jefferson, Oct. 17, 1788, in *ibid.*, XIV, 17.

[70] Jefferson to Madison, July 31, 1788, in *ibid.*, XIII, 440. Jefferson, then in Paris, was of the opinion that "the general voice from North to South" called for a bill of rights. "It seems pretty generally understood that this should go to Juries, Habeas corpus, Standing armies, Printing, Religion and Monopolies."

[71] Madison to Jefferson, *ut supra*, n. 69. Madison explained that he favored a bill of rights if it would be so framed as not to imply powers not meant to be included in the enumeration. He never had thought the omis-

Madison's anxiety to be an active participant in the organization of the new government under the Constitution for which he had so zealously labored had moved him to become a candidate for the House of Representatives and so to campaign against an adversary handpicked by his opponents as likely to win in a district contrived to assure this result. The clamor for amendments raised by the Virginia antifederalists made imperative public announcement of Madison's change of view regarding amendments, already privately expressed. This was done in letters to friends published and widely circulated.[72]

What Madison committed himself to in these letters were amendments securing liberty of conscience and of the press, trial by jury and exemption from general warrants—what Pierce Butler scathingly called "*milk-and-water* amendments."[73] He also favored provision for increase in representation and restraints upon vexatious appeals to federal courts. He expressed his conviction that action by Congress was preferable to a second convention. Whether or not this was an attempt thus to confine the campaign issue cannot be said.[74] There were, however, all the other Virginia amendments to which he then did not advert. We believe that these may well have been put in issue during the election contest, in particular that darling of Patrick Henry's—requisition before Congress might exercise its powers to tax—for late in January a Madison letter excoriating this proposal was published.[75] In the elections held shortly thereafter Madison prevailed.

It is worth remarking that Madison had openly committed himself to restraints upon appeals and passed over other revisions and safeguards which critics of a federal judicial claimed to be essential and

---

sion a material defect, nor been anxious to supply it by subsequent amendment for any other reason than that it had been anxiously desired by others.

[72] The earliest such communication was to his friend George L. Turberville, Nov. 2, 1788—chiefly an argument against a second convention, but in which Madison stated, "There are amendments wch I wish it to have received before it issued from the place in which it was formed. These amendments I still think ought to be made according to the apparent sense of America. . . ." Nowhere in the letter is there a specific commitment to a bill of rights. In the Madison Papers this is noted as a copy in substance of a letter to G. L. Turberville Esq. The text is printed in *Doc. Hist. Const.*, V, 103–06.

The first letter in which Madison committed himself to guarantees of individual rights was to George Eve, Jan. 2, 1789 (Ms. Madison Papers, X, 79a [LC]). The original of the second letter, written to Thomas Mann Randolph, apparently does not exist. In *ibid.*, 82a, is only a clipping from the *Virginia Independent Chronicle*, Jan. 28, 1789. See also *New-York Daily Gazette*, Feb. 13, 1789; *Pennsylvania Packet*, Feb. 10, 1789; *Maryland Gazette: or, The Baltimore Advertiser*, Feb. 4, 20, 1789.

[73] Butler to Iredell, Aug. 11, 1789, in McRee, *Iredell*, II, 263–65.

[74] On the campaign, I. Brant, *James Madison*, III, 238–42.

[75] *Maryland Journal*, Mar. 31, 1789. The letter is dated "Orange, Jan. 29, [1789]."

which were included in the docket of amendments awaiting action. Some of these needed constitutional protection as much as religious liberty, viz., the right to counsel, indictment or presentment in capital cases, double jeopardy and due process. Others, such as a trial jury of the vicinage and the right of challenge, being essentially procedural, were susceptible of being dealt with in the statutes for organizing the judiciary. The situation was one that invited consultation on the possible allocation of particulars, but we have seen no evidence that anything of the sort took place. The dillydallying which marked the convening of the first Congress was a circumstance unfavorable to such a preliminary.

On March 4, 1789, the day fixed for the Congress to convene, neither house mustered more than a corporal's guard. Indeed, the House did not have a quorum until April 1; the Senate not until April 6. Madison took his seat on March 14; Theoderick Bland, torchbearer for the Virginia second-convention postulants, on March 30. The federalists had so commanding a majority in the House, and so many were satisfied with the Constitution as it stood, that they were no less a source of anxiety to Madison and others who wished Congress to initiate amendments than were the advocates of the convention procedure.[76]

In the House of Representatives the urgency of providing revenue for the new government gave precedence to tariff[77] and tonnage acts over all other legislation needed to implement the directions of the Constitution. The Senate set promptly to work on a judiciary bill,[78] but the amendments to the Constitution which might have to be taken into account were inevitably delayed, yet not forgotten.[79]

On April 12 Madison, then deeply involved in the tariff debate, wrote Edmund Randolph that on the subject of amendments nothing had been said publicly and little privately. He was certain that whatever the amendments might be, they would be initiated by the Congress.[80] He must by this time have had clear in his own mind what he proposed to offer.[81] If Fisher Ames is to be believed, Madison had

---

[76] Writing to Edmund Pendleton, Apr. 8, 1789, Madison commented that there would be great difficulty obtaining reasonable amendments. "It will depend however entirely on the temper of the federalists, who predominate as much in both branches, as could be wished." Ms. Madison Papers, XI, 35 (LC).

[77] Opened by Madison April 8 in the Committee of the Whole in the form of a resolve. *Annals of Congress*, I, 106–08.

[78] *Infra*, c. XI, p. 458.

[79] As *e.g.*, the Virginia Convention's

proposal regarding inferior courts raised June 22, *infra*, c. XI, p. 494.

[80] Ms. Madison Papers, XI, 40 (LC).

[81] By the middle of March 1789 Madison had under consideration the form of a "declaration" in favor of religious liberty. Tench Coxe to Madison, Mar. 18, 1789, *ibid.*, 20. He was also toying with the idea of "introducing the houses of the union to an interposition between the state legislatures & their respective constituents" (*ibid.*) that later took form in his proposition that "no state shall violate

"hunted up all the grievances and complaints of newspapers, all the articles of conventions, and the small talk of their debates."[82] This was the sort of preparation customary with Madison, and it was a task which a busy floor leader, such as he had become, could have performed only in advance.

On May 4, despite the press of revenue business, Madison gave notice that on the fourth Monday (May 25) he intended to bring on the subject of amendments.[83] It has been asserted that notice was thus served to "get ahead of" Theoderick Bland[84] who presented the petition of the Virginia General Assembly on the day following.[85] Madison may have been equally concerned over the New York petition. This was, in fact, to be presented on May 6 by Representative John Lawrence,[86] to whom the task could hardly have been congenial for he had voted against the petition in the New York Senate. Madison himself wrote Richard Peters on August 19 that "if amend[ts] had not been prepared from the federal side of the House, the proposition would have come *within three days* from the adverse side."[87] As it was, under the House rules his proposition had priority. Bland's attempt to have his document referred to the Committee of the Whole was not, however, resisted on this point, but on the ground that under Article V of the Constitution application by two thirds of the legislatures of the states was a condition precedent for congressional action, and in such event the Congress had no option but to call a convention. It could not deliberate the matter.[88] In the opinion of both Boudinot of New Jersey and Madison any action such as commitment to the Committee of the Whole was therefore out of order. The House agreed and the document was entered in the *Journals* and filed. The New York petition was ordered to be filed.[89]

Despite Madison's purpose to push ahead with the amendments it was not until June 8 that he moved that the House resolve itself into a Committee of the Whole in order that he might present amendments and have full discussion.[90] The motion was opposed by some as untimely because legislation essential to the organization of the govern-

---

the equal rights of conscience, or the freedom of the press, or the trial by jury in criminal cases" (*infra*, p. 429).

[82] Ames to Thos. Dwight, June 11, 1789, in S. Ames, ed., *Works of Fisher Ames*, I, 52–53.

[83] *Annals of Congress*, I, 257.

[84] Brant, *James Madison*, III, 264.

[85] *Annals of Congress*, I, 258–60.

[86] *Ibid.*, 282.

[87] Ms. Madison Papers, XII, 9 (LC).

[88] *Annals of Congress*, I, 260–61.

[89] *Ibid.*, 282.

[90] *Ibid.*, 440–41. The discussion Friday, June 5, on a resolve of Benson of New York that Congress recommend that Rhode Island hold a ratification convention and the news that such a convention impended in North Carolina may have affected the timing of Madison's offering. North Carolina, of course, had demanded amendments as a condition precedent of ratification.

ment should have priority. Others thought that amendments should await experience with the Constitution as it stood, and one member asked how they could expect to deal with amendments affecting the judiciary until advised of what regulations the Senate would propose in the bill pending in committee. In the end, it was the always trenchant argument that the constituencies expected action that prevailed.

Madison proceeded to lay before the House the amendments which had "occurred" to him with the design that these should be interlarded at relevant places in the Constitution itself. If he had been under some academic mandate to shun controversy, his choice could not have been more politically temperate. Indeed, he wrote to Jefferson that "every thing of a controvertible nature" that might imperil acceptance was "studiously avoided."[91] Perhaps as a species of pacifier for his Virginia compatriots he proposed to prefix to the Constitution a general declaration that all power "is vested in, and originally derived from, the people," that government is instituted to preserve their rights of life, liberty and property, that the people have "an indubitable, unalienable, and indefeasible right to reform or change their Government"—a free version of the opening section of the Virginia bill of rights.[92] Whether this was to be by way of baroque embellishment of the wonderful preamble settled upon at Philadelphia or in substitution was not made clear. The substantive matter offered was mainly designed to secure the liberties of the citizen, but certain propositions were presented that affected the structure of the government, viz., a provision regulating representation in the House, a restraint upon any Congress benefiting from its own vote varying compensation, and a declaration "that no state shall violate the equal rights of conscience, or the freedom of the press, or the trial by jury in criminal cases."[93] The citizen's liberties which he was prepared to enshrine in the Constitution and which did not trench upon the judicial function included no abridgment of civil rights on account of religious belief or worship, liberty of conscience and a ban on a national religion, liberty of speech and of the press, the right of peaceable assembly and the right of petition, the right to bear arms and security against the quartering of soldiers.

The propositions relating to the judicial that were designed to allay

---

[91] June 30, 1789, in *Papers of Jefferson*, XV, 224 at 229.

[92] *Annals of Congress*, I, 451.

[93] This was original with Madison and was, of course, not suggested by any state convention. It stemmed, we believe, from his poor opinion of the state bills of rights. As he wrote Jefferson, Oct. 17, 1788, "[E]xperience proves the inefficacy of a bill of rights on those occasions when its controul is most needed. Repeated violations of these parchment barriers have been committed by overbearing majorities in every State. In Virginia I have seen the bill of rights violated in every instance where it has been opposed to a popular current." *Papers of Jefferson*, XIV, 19.

popular fears of its operation must here be set forth as first formulated. These were to undergo progressive revision and rearrangement, and it is our purpose to trace this process of metamorphosis. For whatever lay opinion may have been of the form in which historic rights were to be safeguarded, the prospective effect of the phraseology settled upon could not but have been a prime concern of lawyers whose business was the uses of language. Inevitably, honing the phrases of the projected amendments was attended by the lurking omnipresence of the state proposals. These were none of them models of draftsmanship and in some particulars aped the spongy language of state bills of rights. Those were fine enough as declarations of the principles to which people in revolution were committed but, because many provisions lacked precision and imperative, had not been effective restraints upon government. It was precisely the latter that the antifederalists demanded and what the first Congress was called upon to contrive.[94]

THE FIRST PROPOSITIONS

BECAUSE MADISON'S propositions were offered as a revision of the instrument of government itself, he fragmented those relating to the administration of justice in order to fit them in at points which seemed to him appropriate. Thus in Article I, section 9, of the Constitution which placed restraints on the federal government it was proposed to insert certain items between the bill of attainder and the direct tax clauses, among them the following:[95]

> No person shall be subject, except in cases of impeachment, to more than one punishment or one trial for the same offence; nor shall be compelled to be a witness against himself, nor be deprived of life, liberty, or property, without due process of law; nor be obliged to relinquish his property, where it may be necessary for public use, without a just compensation.
>
> Excessive bail shall not be required, nor excessive fines imposed, nor cruel and unusual punishments inflicted.
>
> The rights of the people to be secured in their persons; their houses, their papers, and their other property, from all unreasonable searches and seizures, shall not be violated by warrants issued with-

[94] No one was more critical of this than Fisher Ames when in the course of debate he asked the reasons upon which the amendments were founded. "He hoped it was not purely to gratify an indigested opinion." He challenged Madison's view that attention must be paid to the amendments recom- mended by the states. "If this position is true, we have nothing more to do than read over their amendments, and propose them without exercising our judgment upon them." *Annals of Congress*, I, 751 (Aug. 14, 1789).

[95] *Annals of Congress*, I, 451–52.

out probable cause, supported by oath or affirmation, or not particularly describing the places to be searched, or the persons or things to be seized.

In all criminal prosecutions, the accused shall enjoy the right to a speedy and public trial, to be informed of the cause and nature of the accusation, to be confronted with his accusers, and the witnesses against him; to have a compulsory process for obtaining witnesses in his favor; and to have the assistance of counsel for his defence.

It was further proposed to alter the judiciary article in two important respects. First, at the end of Article III, section 2, second paragraph (viz., following Congress's power to regulate the appellate jurisdiction of the Supreme Court), there was to be annexed:[96]

But no appeal to such court shall be allowed where the value in controversy shall not amount to —— dollars: nor shall any fact triable by jury, according to the course of common law, be otherwise re-examinable than may consist with the principles of common law.

Secondly, it was proposed to strike the whole of the third paragraph of Article III (dealing with the trial of all crimes) and substitute:[97]

The trial of all crimes (except in cases of impeachments, and cases arising in the land or naval forces, or the militia when on actual service, in time of war or public danger) shall be by an impartial jury of freeholders of the vicinage, with the requisite of unanimity for conviction, of the right of challenge, and other accustomed requisites; and in all crimes punishable with loss of life or member, presentment or indictment by a grand jury shall be an essential preliminary, provided that in cases of crimes committed within any county which may be in possession of an enemy, or in which a general insurrection may prevail, the trial may by law be authorized in some other county of the same State, as near as may be to the seat of the offence.

In cases of crimes committed not within any county, the trial may by law be in such county as the laws shall have prescribed. In suits at common law, between man and man, the trial by jury, as one of the best securities to the rights of the people, ought to remain inviolate.

What Madison had to say in presenting his amendments was eloquently and candidly stated; there are passages in his speech which so closely parallel what he wrote Jefferson on October 17, 1788, that one may properly suppose he had a copy before him.[98] Madison's de-

---

[96] *Ibid.*, 452.
[97] *Ibid.*, 452–53.
[98] Passages in the address, *ibid.*, 454–55. The copy of the letter of October 17 in *Papers of Jefferson*, XIV, 16, comes from the Madison Papers.

fense of the timeliness of his action was based upon the ethical ground of fulfilling the promises which had in places induced ratification, the prudence of allaying anxieties earlier aroused, and, heedful of the opinions of the "old revolutionists,"[99] spoke words of reassurance about securing the liberties for which they had bled. Inevitably there was reference to the effect upon the situation of Rhode Island and North Carolina.[100] As for the propositions themselves, these were moderate because any revision of the Constitution must be done cautiously. He declared his unwillingness to have the door opened for a reconsideration of "the whole structure of the Government." He was ready to open it for the security of rights.

A warm debate erupted even before the amendments were read, and it became clear that Madison's plan of action was threatened from two sides—the "wait and see" Representatives and those who wanted all the state proposals to be considered. To forestall the former he then retracted his motion for consideration by the Committee of the Whole and moved for a select committee.[101] The response from neither group was favorable, different reasons being advanced in favor of delay. "Fearing again to be discomfited," Madison then moved the propositions by way of resolutions to be adopted by the House.[102] But in the end it was decided to consider in the Committee of the Whole. Concerning these exchanges Patrick Henry's liegeman William Grayson had some gossip to impart to his leader. "I understood," he wrote, "that the mover was so embarrassed in the course of the business that he was once or twice on the point of withdrawing the motion, and it was thought by some that the commitment was more owing to personal respect than a love of the subject introduced."[103] The Senator was to learn something of Madison's determination.

In view of the passions earlier aroused over the absence of a bill of rights in the Constitution, it seems extraordinary that only General Sumter, who had received his comeuppance at the South Carolina Convention, expressed any sense of urgency.[104] George Clymer, writing to Richard Peters just before Madison's presentation, expressed the hope that "we shall be strong enough to postpone." He did not know whether Madison meant merely "a tub to the whale," e.g., declarations about the

---

99 The expression was James Sullivan's; cf. his letter to R. H. Lee, Apr. 11, 1789, in R. H. Lee, Memoir of the Life of Richard Henry Lee, II, 152.
100 Annals of Congress, I, 449.
101 Opposed by Gerry because he believed it would be "disrespectful" to the states which had offered amendments. Annals of Congress, I, 463–64.

Livermore of New Hampshire wanted the concurrence of the Senate before the matter was entered into at all. Ibid., 465.
102 Ibid., 467.
103 Grayson to Patrick Henry, June 12, 1789, in L. G. Tyler, The Letters and Times of the Tylers, I, 165 at 167.
104 Annals of Congress, I, 466.

press, or would be so far frightened of the Virginia antifederalists as to lop off essentials. In a postscript added the afternoon of June 8, Clymer reported that "Madison's had proved a tub or a number of tubs" and that Gerry proposed to treat the House to all the amendments of all the antifederalists in America.[105]

It was not until July 21, after the House had despatched a respectable volume of bills, that Madison once again prayed further consideration of his amendments.[106] During this interval there had appeared in the *New-York Daily Gazette*, in fact, commencing June 3, articles on the proffered state amendments by one who signed himself "Foreign Spectator." These articles ran through July 7. This writer, who belonged to the "wait and see" school of thought, examined all the proposals, including North Carolina's and those of the minorities in Maryland and Pennsylvania, and dealt very roughly with some of these. It is impossible to settle how generally these articles were read; if they were, the merits of the alterations and, indeed, the question of alteration at all was kept before the public, and presumably the congressmen, while long-winded struggles over other issues proceeded.

The discussions which ensued upon Madison's second attempt to induce action occupied the House the whole of July 21. The debates were not on the merits but on procedure. Fisher Ames at once moved reference to a select committee as a means of making some progress without interrupting the "principal business" of the House.[107] Those who wished to postpone the whole matter were disposed to agree.[108] Others, like Gerry and Tucker of South Carolina, who wanted to have the outpourings of all the conventions come before the House made their ultimate intentions so clear[109] that a majority voted (34–15) to discharge the Committee of the Whole of its task and to refer to a committee of eleven, directed to take into consideration Madison's amendments as well as the proposals of the several states and report to the House.[110]

John Vining of Delaware was chairman of the committee, and five members—Madison, Baldwin of Georgia, Roger Sherman, Nicholas Gilman and George Clymer—had been delegates to the Philadelphia Convention. Aedanus Burke, the South Carolina antifederalist, Egbert Benson of New York, Benjamin Goodhue of Massachusetts, George

---

105 Clymer to Peters, June [8?, 1789], in Ms. Peters Papers, IX, 96 (HSP). "Tub to a whale" from whaling lore had the derived meaning of creating a diversion to avoid a real danger.

106 *Annals of Congress*, I, 685–86.

107 *Ibid.*, 686.

108 Sedgwick (Mass.), White (Va.), Sherman (Conn.), Jackson (Ga.).

109 Gerry included here a promise to carry out the instructions to present the Massachusetts amendment. *Annals of Congress*, I, 688. Tucker appears to have believed that a select committee would either smother proposals or fatally delay matters. *Ibid.*, 689–90.

110 *Ibid.*, 690.

Gale of Maryland and Elias Boudinot of New Jersey were the other members. Of the lawyers on the committee only Egbert Benson, attorney general of New York for over a decade, and Roger Sherman, who had served as judge of the Connecticut Superior Court, could claim considerable professional distinction. We know a little about the committee's work from admissions made in the course of the debate on the report. In the first place, it is clear from a statement by Benson[111] that the merits of a separate list of amendments or the dissemination and incorporation of the items into the body of the Constitution were discussed and the latter method was chosen. Sherman had opposed this[112] and he was to do so again. A draft of amendments made by him, and preserved in the Madison Papers, was apparently drawn up as a project for appended amendments.[113] Furthermore, when the revised amendment dealing with freedom of speech and of the press and the right of assembly came up for discussion in the Committee of the Whole, Sedgwick rebelliously suggested that it was derogatory to the House to descend to minutiae. Benson asserted that the committee had proceeded upon the principle that these rights belonged to the people; "they conceived them to be inherent; and all that they meant to provide against was their being infringed by the Government."[114] The disposition of the various state proposals, included in the select committee's task of examination, was revealed by Vining in response to one of Gerry's nagging declamations. These amendments had not been reported, for, said Vining, "the committee conceived some of them superfluous or dangerous, and found many of them so contradictory that it was impossible to make any thing of them."[115]

It should finally be observed regarding Vining's report as a representation of committee opinion that when it was debated, the members seem to have felt free to disagree with the inclusion of particular items or with the form and intendment of particular provisions—none more candidly than Sherman.

The report of the Vining committee was submitted July 28[116] and reveals further that the members addressed themselves primarily to the task of clarifying and compressing the terms of Madison's amendments.

---

[111] *Ibid.*, 740.

[112] *Ibid.*, 734, 742.

[113] Ms. Madison Papers, XI, 120 (LC). As "A Citizen of New Haven" Sherman had gone on record before Congress actually convened in a newspaper article opposing amendments. *New-York Packet*, Mar. 20, 1789; *Pennsylvania Packet*, Apr. 4, 1789.

[114] *Annals of Congress*, I, 759.

[115] *Ibid.*, 770.

[116] *Ibid.*, 699. The text, printed in *Doc. Hist. Const.*, V, 186–89. It was published in the *New-York Journal and Weekly Register*, July 30, 1789; *Massachusetts Centinel*, Aug. 8, 1789; *Boston Gazette, and The Country Journal*, Aug. 10, 1789; *Gazette of the United States*, Aug. 1, 1789.

For example, in place of the discursive declamatory statement which Madison proposed to prefix to the Constitution it was recommended that before the words "*We the people*" of the preamble there be added "Government being intended for the benefit of the people, and the rightful establishment thereof being derived from their authority alone."[117] The religious liberty clause was sharply cut, and from the freedom of speech and press amendment was excised what may be called the stump-speech phrase "great bulwarks of liberty." A similar fate befell the description of jury trial—"one of the best securities of the rights of the people." One deletion—the words "unreasonable searches and seizures" from what ultimately became the Fourth Amendment—is inexplicable. The sentences in some of the propositions were rearranged and the net result of these several exercises was improvement. Other changes will be noticed in connection with the House debates. The report was tabled on the day that it was presented, but on August 3 Madison moved that it should be considered on the 12th.[118] Actually, discussion began the day following.

On a motion by Richard Bland Lee of Virginia that the House resolve itself into a Committee of the Whole to consider the report, the disposition to postpone again was manifest, and several members evinced an unexpectedly pressing interest in the claims of the Senate's Judiciary Bill to priority.[119] It was, however, decided to go into committee and there ensued a protracted wrangle over the propriety of incorporating the amendments into the body of the Constitution. Sherman's motion, the effect of which was to present the amendments as a supplement, was beaten.[120]

The debate in committee on the merits of the report consumed with minor interruptions a total of four days. The provisions which excited the most prolonged discussion were those over the proportion of representation in the House and the limitation of membership, the varying of compensation to members of Congress and the proper phrasing of the religious liberty clause. There was an acrimonious clash over Tucker's proposal to add to the right of assembly and petition amendment a guarantee that the people could instruct their representa-

---

[117] *Doc. Hist. Const.*, V, 186.

[118] *Annals of Congress*, I, 700.

[119] The Judiciary Bill had been sent to the House July 20 and had two readings that day. Apparently Sedgwick on August 13 raised the question of its priority, for Madison replied sharply that if the bill was of such importance, it should not have been postponed for the minor matters taken up. *Ibid.*, 731. Smith of South Carolina, Hartly of Pennsylvania and Gerry all agreed with Sedgwick.

[120] *Ibid.*, 744. The discussion involved interesting questions of theory concerning alteration by Congress and state legislatures of an instrument purporting to be established by the people.

tives.[121] The practice of instruction, as we have noticed, had been a means by which the states had controlled action by the Continental Congress, sometimes with stultifying effect. The Representatives, like Gerry and Tucker, who had served in the old Congress were certainly aware of this, but their commitment to state interests seems on this occasion to have been too much for them. They were able to make colorable their stand because both the New York and Virginia conventions had proposed a right of instruction, and a major tactic of the group to which these states' rights advocates belonged was to harp upon the need for all state amendments to be taken into consideration. The final vote rejecting Tucker's proposal was 41–10.[122]

On August 17 there came before the Committee of the Whole the first of the proposals affecting the judicial process. This was the due process amendment which Madison appears to have confected by combining two of the propositions advanced by the New York Convention.[123] The new version provided:

> No person shall be subject, except in case of impeachment, to more than one trial or one punishment for the same offense, nor shall he be compelled to be a witness against himself, nor be deprived of life, liberty, or property without due process of law, nor shall private property be taken for public use without just compensation.

The two lawyers, Benson[124] and Sherman,[125] objected to the provision of "one trial" because it was an abridgment of established rights. Sherman claimed that as the clause stood, a person found guilty could not move in arrest of judgment and obtain a second trial in his favor. A motion to strike "one trial" failed. A limitation moved by Lawrence of New York, familiar with chancery discovery proceedings in New York, to confine the self-incrimination phrase to criminal cases was passed.[126]

The excessive bail amendment, which had not been changed, was accepted, but the amendment designed to protect against unreasonable searches and seizures had been reported without these words and

---

[121] The debates (ibid., 761–76), allowing even for some of the antifederalist eccentricities, constitute in our opinion the most interesting compendium of opinion on the nature of representation of the time.

[122] Ibid., 776.

[123] The table in Dumbauld, The Bill of Rights and What It Means Today, at 161, showing the provenance of specific rights, lists the Virginia bill of rights no. 8 and that of the Virginia Convention no. 9 as source. The "right" in both was the well known Magna Carta "law of the land" clause. As indicated supra, c. III at n. 17 this clause was not the equivalent of "due process."

[124] Annals of Congress, I, 781.

[125] Ibid., 782.

[126] Ibid.

amounted to no more than a protection against general warrants.[127] On motion of Gerry the missing words were restored—his one affirmative contribution.[128] Over Tucker's expostulation and with a rearrangement offered by Livermore, the limitation upon state infringement of rights of conscience, freedom of speech or press and jury trial in criminal cases was accepted.[129]

To the proposed limitation on appeals the Vining committee fixed the amount at $1,000, and changed the phrase "be otherwise re-examinable than may consist with the principles of common law" to "be otherwise examinable than according to the rules of the common law"— a mode of expression more comprehensible to the bar, but one which implicitly raised the question whether the array of English amending statutes was thereby to be received. This point was not broached, but Benson moved to strike the monetary limitation because a case might be important although a trifling amount might be at stake.[130] Madison, who thought that the admission of "an appeal" would be at the discretion of a court, probably because in Virginia a writ of error had to be allowed by the court,[131] claimed that there was little danger that an appeal would be admitted if less than $1,000 was involved. He argued that the amendment was necessary to quiet the fears that the rich would use the appellate jurisdiction oppressively.[132] Sedgwick wanted a limitation of $3,000, but the proposition was accepted in its original form.

The Vining committee made one important shift of Madison's "points." The article dealing with the rights to speedy trial, confrontation, etc., which had been offered as an amendment to Article I, section 9, was now treated as a proposal of amendment to Article III, section 2. The whole of the third paragraph of this section was to be struck and the following three paragraphs substituted:[133]

> In all criminal prosecutions the accused shall enjoy the right to a speedy and public trial, to be informed of the nature and cause of the accusation, to be confronted with the witnesses against him, to have compulsory process for obtaining witnesses in his favor and to have the assistance of counsel for his defense.

The trial of all crimes (except in cases of impeachment, and in

---

[127] As reported, the text approximated the provision (sec. 10) in the Virginia bill of rights regarding general warrants (Thorpe, *Constitutions and Charters*, VII, 3814) which, as we have seen, was all Madison had committed himself to in his campaign letters.

[128] *Annals of Congress*, I, 783. Benson sought to make the direction "by warrants issuing" more commanding by substituting "no warrant shall issue," but this was beaten.

[129] *Ibid.*, 783–84.

[130] *Ibid.*, 784.

[131] In the General Court Act (1777), 9 Hening, *Va. Stats.*, 401, sec. 47.

[132] *Annals of Congress*, I, 784.

[133] *Doc. Hist. Const.*, V, 188–89.

cases arising in the land or naval forces, or in the militia, when in actual service in time of war or public danger) shall be by an impartial jury of freeholders of the vicinage, with the requisite of unanimity for conviction, the right of challenge and other accustomed requisites; and no person shall be held to answer for a capital, or otherwise infamous crime, unless on a presentment or indictment by a grand jury; but if a crime be committed in a place in the possession of an enemy, or in which an insurrection may prevail, the indictment and trial may by law be authorized in some other place within the same state; and if it be committed in a place not within a State, the indictment and trial may be at such place or places as the law may have directed.

In suits at common law trial by jury shall be preserved.

It will be observed that the one important change made in Madison's speedy trial amendment was to drop out, in the first paragraph, confrontation by an accuser. This point was not raised in the Committee of the Whole. The most significant objection to the first paragraph came from Aedanus Burke of South Carolina who moved to bar explicitly criminal prosecutions by way of information, but this he was induced to withdraw.[134] However, on a motion of Livermore of New Hampshire, it was agreed to provide that trial be in the state where the crime was committed.[135]

On August 18, before the House resolved itself into committee and before the second paragraph of the new amendment to Article III came up for discussion, Gerry and Tucker moved to have all the proposed state amendments considered.[136] Madison made the weak concession that he was about to move to refer these. But Vining, a tough tactician, pointed out that under the subsisting and limited order of the House such reference was improper.[137] After a "desultory conversation" the ayes and nays were taken and the motion voted down, 34–16.

The Committee of the Whole then moved to the second paragraph of the new proposal to amend Article III. Vining's committee had left intact Madison's confinement of the trial jury to freeholders, a Virginia rule[138] and a requirement that did not consist with practice in some states.[139] At this juncture the propriety of this was not raised. But it will

---

[134] *Annals of Congress*, I, 785.

[135] Stone of Maryland pointed out that full provision was made in the following clause, nevertheless Livermore's motion was carried. *Ibid.*, 785.

[136] *Ibid.*, 786–88.

[137] *Ibid.*, 788.

[138] 9 Hening, *Va. Stats.*, 401, sec. 49 (1777); 12 *ibid.*, 340 (1786). The latter bill had been presented in 1785 by Madison.

[139] *E.g.*, in New Hampshire, a freehold or other estate worth £50 (5 *Laws of New Hampshire*, 67, c. 3 [1785]); the same in Massachusetts (*Mass. Acts and Resolves 1784–85*, 15, May Sess. 1784, c. 7). In New York, in the cities of New York, Albany and Hudson, a freehold worth £60 or a personal estate of like value; elsewhere, a freehold of £60 value or rents in fee or for life of

be noticed that the rambling manner in which the *sine qua non* of indictment or presentment had been phrased by Madison was given more imperative form by recourse to a mode of expression which had its ancestry in the two due process statutes of Edward III.[140] The directions about the locus of indictment and trial, originally most discursive, chiefly to meet criticisms voiced by antifederalists, had been considerably pruned. No objection was offered to this curtailment, but a question was raised, as it was to be again, regarding the word "vicinage" because it would be inapplicable in states where "district" or "county" was the rule.[141] Nevertheless, the paragraph was approved; so was the simplified version of the jury trial guarantee in common law actions.[142]

PROCEEDINGS IN THE HOUSE

AFTER APPROVING, over considerable protest, an amendment offered as a new Article VII to the Constitution that proclaimed the principle of separation of powers, and in a separate paragraph declared a reservation to the states of powers not delegated by the Constitution or prohibited therein to the states, to which at the last moment was added the reservation "or to the people,"[143] the Committee of the Whole rose and reported to the House. Tucker at once moved that an array of amendments be referred to the Committee of the Whole.[144] Those designed to confine federal jurisdiction were the substitution of "courts of admiralty" for "inferior courts," and one which aimed at disemboweling diversity jurisdiction by limiting this to suits "between a State and foreign States, and between citizens of the United States, claiming the same lands under grants of different States."[145] The House refused to refer.

To manage the passage of the amendments through the House presented certain hazards because of the constitutional requirement of approval by two thirds of the members. Little can be deduced regarding the balance of opinion from the proceedings in the Committee of the Whole, for on the first day of debate there (August 13) the chairman had ruled in response to an inquiry that a majority vote was sufficient

---

like value (*N.Y. Laws,* 9 Sess. 1786, c. 41). In Pennsylvania, the sober and well behaved were eligible (11 *Stats. at Large Pa.,* 486 [1785]).

[140] St. 28 Edw. III, c. 3; 42 Edw. III, c. 3.

[141] *Annals of Congress,* I, 789.

[142] *Ibid.*

[143] By Carroll of Maryland, *ibid.,* 790.

[144] *Jour. H.R.,* I, 82–83 (August 18).

[145] Amendments to Art. III, sec. 1, and to Art. III, sec. 2, "clause 1" (*Annals of Congress,* I, 790–92). These were fractioned out of the Amendment 14 offered at the Virginia Convention (Elliot, *Debates,* III, 660).

to form a report.[146] An appeal from this ruling was unsuccessful. Two days later Fisher Ames pointed out that decisions reached in committee by a simple majority might be overruled by the House, and he moved to discharge the Committee. He was induced to withdraw this and offered a motion that a two-thirds majority be required.[147] This was apparently never voted. Committee votes were, of course, not noted in the House *Journal*, and the reporter furnishes insufficient clues of the votes in committee on many affirmative propositions to permit an accurate count of the strength of the "amendmentites," as they were dubbed in the press. But it may be noticed that when the vote was taken on the amendment to the preamble to the Constitution recommended by the Vining committee, this was adopted by a vote of only 27–23.[148] Madison himself appears to have sensed a precarious balance, for he wrote Edmund Randolph on August 21, two days after the House took up the report of the Committee of the Whole, about the opposition and expressed the opinion that "two or three contentious additions would even now frustrate the whole project."[149]

The House debate on the report of the Committee of the Whole consumed with some interruptions most of four days. Unfortunately the discussions were reported in a slovenly fashion, for there were certain emendations of language effected which are nowhere mentioned.[150] An example of the reporter's enterprise is indicated by his handling of the debate on Sherman's motion made on the first day of proceedings in the House, viz., that the amendments be added to the Constitution by way of supplement. The reader is merely directed to the account of the debate in committee.[151] It seems to us probable that new arguments were advanced in the House, because Sherman's motion was there carried by a two-thirds vote although it had earlier been beaten in committee.[152]

---

[146] *Annals of Congress*, I, 744.

[147] *Ibid.*, 776, 778.

[148] *Ibid.*, 747.

[149] *Doc. Hist. Const.*, V, 191–92.

[150] On the reporting *cf.* M. Tinling, "Thomas Lloyd's Reports of the First Federal Congress," *Wm. & Mary Quarterly*, 18:519–45, 3d ser., 1961. The most aggravating habit of Lloyd was the entry "a desultory conversation ensued," indicating to us inattention or absence from the chamber.

[151] *Annals of Congress*, I, 795.

[152] There is no entry in *Jour. H.R.*, I, 83–84, regarding Sherman's motion. Because of the manner in which the *Journal* was kept it is an inadequate check on Lloyd's reporting. It is strik-

ingly meagre compared with the journals of the Massachusetts House of Representatives or the New York Assembly. John Beckley of Virginia was the first clerk of the House of Representatives. There is nothing in the House rules to indicate why motions on important matters were not entered. Beckley's inattention to his clerical duties was apparently inveterate. When he was clerk of the Virginia Court of Appeals, by rule of court in August 1780 "the consideration of a proper allowance" was suspended until he showed cause for non-attendance on the court and for failing to furnish a transcript of a record on appeal. The rule was discharged in March

X: *The Bill of Rights*

The decision to abandon a revision of the Constitution in favor of a program of amendments offered by way of supplement had the effect of more or less stranding the profanation of the preamble approved in committee. No debate on this is remembranced, but this amendment was rejected because two thirds of the members present did not support it.[153] Nothing is noticed respecting changes in amendments affecting the judiciary and its functioning except abscission of the direction regarding venue in criminal trials where a crime was committed in a place not within a state.[154] The *Annals of Congress* indicate that otherwise these particular amendments were voted as they had been reported. However, a comparison of the text of the amendments delivered to the Senate with the votes and proceedings in the Committee of the Whole reveals that some verbal changes were agreed to in the House.

The first of these changes was in the searches and seizures amendment. As passed in committee this amendment had limited the safeguard of the right to be secure against unreasonable searches and seizures "by warrants issuing without probable cause," etc. Benson's attempt to amend the warrant phrase to read "and no warrant shall issue," to broaden the protection had been defeated by a considerable majority.[155] Nevertheless, in the version voted by the House this emendation appears.[156] On the other hand, the accretion to the speedy trial amendment that trial be in the state where a crime was committed voted by the Committee was apparently eliminated by the House. More importantly, the limitation of the petit jury to freeholders, accepted in committee, was also struck, for it does not appear in the articles finally approved.[157] On August 21 sixteen of the articles were approved by the House, two thirds of the members present concurring. When the seventeenth article was brought up, providing that the powers not delegated by the Constitution nor prohibited to the states were reserved to the states respectively, the Committee's addition "or to the people" had vanished. After a motion by Gerry to insert the word "expressly"

1781. Commonwealth v. Beckley, 4 Call 4 (1780). Any possibility of going behind the printed version of the *Journal* was eliminated by Beckley himself who saw to the destruction of both the rough and smooth ms. copies after the volume was printed. B. Rowland, "Recordkeeping Practices of the House of Representatives," 1. A ms. copy was then made from the printed version. According to the testimony of a clerk who served under Beckley this was done because Beckley claimed that the printed version was that authorized by the House and a ms. version of it would outlast printed copies. *Ibid.*, 17. On Beckley's political activities, N. Cunningham, "John Beckley: An Early American Party Manager," in *Wm. & Mary Quarterly*, 13:40, 3d ser., 1956.

For a scholarly account of House printed documents, *cf.* J. B. Childs, "Disappeared in the Wings of Oblivion," 91.

[153] *Annals of Congress*, I, 795.
[154] *Ibid.*, 796–97.
[155] *Supra*, n. 128.
[156] *Jour. H.R.*, I, 85.
[157] *Ibid.*, 85–86.

before "delegated" was beaten, Sherman, according to the *Annals,* moved to add the words "or to the people" and this was adopted. The *Journal* does not record such a motion or such a vote, and the seventeenth article went to the Senate without this qualification.[158] It was to be added by that body.

There was a final effort by the antifederalists to secure admission of their perennial favorites including the substitution of "Courts of Admiralty" for "tribunals inferior to the supreme Court," but these proposals were all rejected.[159] An "introduction" and the task of the "proper arrangement" of the articles were referred to a committee of three—Benson, Sherman and Sedgwick.[160] It will be noticed that the committee's mandate did not extend to any change in language. The seventeen articles voted by the House on August 21 had followed the order of the recommendations of the Vining committee, an order dictated by how the several revisions were to be distributed in the Constitution itself. The new committee effected something of a more rational arrangement when it reported August 24. A resolving clause prefixed to the "articles of amendment" was that day approved and the engrossed copy of the whole ordered to be sent to the Senate.[161]

As a means of conveniently checking the action of the Senate on the Articles of Amendment, their text is set forth in the margin.[162] They

---

[158] *Annals of Congress,* I, 797; *Jour. H.R.,* I, 86. It should here be noticed that the disappearance of Carroll's earlier amendment may have been due to the rules governing amendments of bills or reports in the Committee of the Whole. The body of a bill or report was not to be defaced or interlined, but all amendments noting the page or line must be entered by the clerk on a separate paper as agreed to by the Committee and so reported to the House. The possibility of error or loss was thus imminent. In view of the clerk's penurious practice with regard to noting motions in the House, and the absence of any evidence that the House itself paid any attention to the form of the *Journal,* it is possible that the reporter Lloyd was not wrong on both occasions.

[159] *Jour. H.R.,* I, 87–88.

[160] *Ibid.,* 88.

[161] *Ibid.,* 89.

[162] From *Journal of the First Session of the Senate of the United States of America . . .* (N.Y., 1789),

104–06 (Aug. 25, 1789) (hereafter cited as *Senate Journal,* 1st Sess.):

"Art. I. After the first enumeration, required by the first Article of the Constitution, there shall be one Representative for ever[y] thirty thousand, until the number shall amount to one hundred, after which the proportion shall be so regulated by Congress, that there shall be not less than one hundred Representatives, nor less than one Representative for every forty thousand persons, until the number of Representatives shall amount to two hundred, after which the proportion shall be so regulated by Congress, that there shall not be less than two hundred Representatives, nor less than one Representative for every fifty thousand persons.

"Art. II. No law, varying the compensation to the Members of Congress, shall take effect, until an election of Representatives shall have intervened.

"Art. III. Congress shall make no law establishing Religion, or prohibiting the free exercise thereof, nor

are not without interest in themselves because they serve to fix the degree to which the original propositions advanced by Madison underwent modification, and considering the latter's stiff-necked attachment to his own handiwork, testify to the fact that others besides the original projector deserve credit for the result. Furthermore, so far as the Articles of Amendment articulated safeguards for the individual, they

---

shall the rights of conscience be infringed.

"Art. IV. The freedom of speech, and of the press, and the right of the people peaceably to assemble, and consult for their common good, and to apply to the Government for redress of grievances, shall not be infringed.

"Art. V. A well regulated militia, composed of the body of the people, being the best security of a free State, the right of the people to keep and bear arms, shall not be infringed, but no one religiously scrupulous of bearing arms, shall be compelled to render military service in person.

"Art. VI. No soldier shall, in time of peace, be quartered in any house without the consent of the owner, nor in time of war, but in a manner to be prescribed by law.

"Art. VII. The right of the people to be secure in their persons, houses, papers and effects, against unreasonable searches and seizures, shall not be violated, and no warrants shall issue, but upon probable cause, supported by oath or affirmation, and particularly describing the place to be searched, and the persons or things to be seized.

"Art. VIII. No person shall be subject, except in case of impeachment, to more than one trial, or one punishment for the same offence, nor shall be compelled in any criminal case, to be a witness against himself, nor be deprived of life, liberty or property, without due process of law; nor shall private property be taken for public use without just compensation.

"Art. IX. In all criminal prosecutions, the accused shall enjoy the right to a speedy and public trial, to be informed of the nature and cause of the accusation, to be confronted with the witnesses against him, to have

compulsory process for obtaining witnesses in his favor, and to have the assistance of counsel for his defence.

"Art. X. The trial of all crimes (except in cases of impeachment, and in cases arising in the land or naval forces, or in the militia when in actual service in time of war or public danger) shall be by an impartial Jury of the vicinage, with the requisite of unanimity for conviction, the right of challenge, and other accustomed requisites; and no person shall be held to answer for a capital, or otherways infamous crime, unless on a presentment or indictment by a Grand Jury; but if a crime be committed in a place in the possession of an enemy, or in which an insurrection may prevail, the indictment and trial may by law be authorised in some other place within the same State.

"Art. XI. No appeal to the Supreme Court of the United States, shall be allowed, where the value in controversy shall not amount to one thousand dollars, nor shall any fact, triable by a Jury according to the course of the common law, be otherwise reexaminable, than according to the rules of common law.

"Art. XII. In suits at common law, the right of trial by Jury shall be preserved.

"Art. XIII. Excessive bail shall not be required, nor excessive fines imposed, nor cruel and unusual punishments inflicted.

"Art. XIV. No State shall infringe the right of trial by Jury in criminal cases, nor the rights of conscience, nor the freedom of speech, or of the press.

"Art. XV. The enumeration in the Constitution of certain rights, shall not be construed to deny or disparage others retained by the people.

"Art. XVI. The powers delegated

added up to the full sum of what the two-thirds majority of the House conceived to be essential. The Senate, as we shall see, was not moved to add any further affirmative propositions; indeed, that body was to discard some of those submitted to it. The pressures put upon the Senate were chiefly for the addition of amendments affecting political structure; all of such were in due course repelled. To all appearances the upper house was to function more as a covey of rhetoricians putting into form the composition of the representatives of the people, as if they were *in statu pupillarii*.

THE SENATE'S AMENDING HAND

WE ARE BADLY informed about the Senate debates on the amendments. For despite the recent clamor over the "dark conclave" at Philadelphia, the upper chamber conducted its business behind closed doors.[163] The chief source of information, consequently, is the Senate *Journal*, publication of which was enjoined by the Constitution excepting such parts adjudged to require secrecy. This *Journal* is a particularly unyielding one, and, what is more, as we shall have occasion to observe, not always to be trusted. Early in the session Senator Maclay of Pennsylvania noted in his private journal that Samuel Alleyn Otis, Secretary of the Senate, had made "the grossest mistakes . . . on our minutes" and it had cost an hour or two of the Senate's time to rectify

---

by the Constitution to the Government of the United States, shall be exercised as therein appropriated, so that the Legislative shall never exercise the powers vested in the Executive or Judicial; nor the Executive the powers vested in the Legislative or Judicial; nor the Judicial the powers vested in the Legislative or Executive.

"Art. XVII. The powers not delegated by the Constitution, nor prohibited by it to the States, are reserved to the States respectively."

[163] This was a decision not embodied in the Senate rules. *Ibid.*, 14–15. This leads us to suppose that action was taken as a matter of privilege, in imitation of the English Parliament. There, according to Blackstone, privileges claimed were not set down and ascertained lest it be easy for the executive to devise "some new case, not within the line of privilege."

Commentaries, I, 164. The Continental Congress had adopted a rule of secrecy Sept. 6, 1774 (*JCC*, I, 26), and reaffirmed this May 18, 1775 (*ibid.*, II, 55), explicable because of the precarious nature of the enterprise. This was so far loosened by the Articles of Confederation, Art. IX, as to require monthly publication of the *Journal* with certain matters excepted. However the Senate "rule" may have been settled, it was not one of secrecy, as witness the solicitation of learned opinion on the Judiciary Bill, *infra*, p. 467. For a comment, *cf.* Paine Wingate to Pickering, Apr. 29, 1789, "I do not desire that the private conduct or public proceedings of this body should be exposed to the daily inspection of a populace." C. E. Wingate, *Life and Letters of Paine Wingate*, II, 302.

CONGRESS OF THE UNITED STATES.

In the House of Representatives,

Monday, 24th August, 1789,

RESOLVED, BY THE SENATE AND HOUSE OF REPRESENTA-
TIVES OF THE UNITED STATES OF AMERICA IN CONGRESS
ASSEMBLED, two thirds of both Houses deeming it necessary, ~concurring~ That
the following Articles be proposed to the Legislatures of the several
States, as Amendments to the Constitution of the United States, all
or any of which Articles, when ratified by three fourths of the said
Legislatures, to be valid to all intents and purposes as part of the
said Constitution—Viz.

ARTICLES in addition to, and amendment of, the Constitution of
the United States of America, proposed by Congress, and ratified
by the Legislatures of the several States, pursuant to the fifth Article of the original Constitution.

ARTICLE THE FIRST.

After the first enumeration, required by the first Article of the
Constitution, there shall be one Representative for every thirty thousand, until the number shall amount to one hundred, after which
the proportion shall be so regulated by Congress, that there shall
be not less than one hundred Representatives, nor less than one Representative for every forty thousand persons, until the number of
Representatives shall amount to two hundred, after which the proportion shall be so regulated by Congress, that there shall not be less
than two hundred Representatives, nor less than one Representative
for every fifty thousand persons.

amendment

ARTICLE THE SECOND.

No law varying the compensation to the members of Congress,
shall take effect, until an election of Representatives shall have intervened.

ARTICLE THE THIRD.

Congress shall make no law establishing religion or prohibiting
the free exercise thereof, nor shall the rights of Conscience be infringed.

ARTICLE THE FOURTH.

The Freedom of Speech and of the Press, and the right of the
People peaceably to assemble, and to apply to the Government for a redress of grievances, shall
not be infringed.

Senate print of the House's Articles of Amendment with manuscript emendations, page 1.

(The National Archives)

them.[164] The situation was not improved with time for Maclay pounced on two other errors just before the debates on the Articles of Amendment began.[165] The watchdog of the *Journal* unfortunately was ill while these debates were going on and consequently missed them. Otherwise, the discrepancies between amended articles as returned to the House and the *Journal* entries regarding the wording approved in the Senate might have been then laid bare.

Collateral personal comment by Senators on the amendments is meagre. Even the letters of Richard Henry Lee, progenitor of the Bill of Rights movement, contain little but generalizations. He had written Patrick Henry months earlier (May 28)[166] that the sole reason that had compelled his attendance was the design to secure civil liberty. He took a pessimistic view of what Madison might present, for he feared that the ideas of Madison and those of the Virginia Convention were not similar. When the plan should come before the Senate, "we shall prepare to abridge, or enlarge, so as to effect, if possible, the wishes of our legislature." The Senate *Journal* does not identify the originator of any motion relating to the amendments. But it is fair to infer from Lee's letter and from the lament eventually addressed by Lee and Grayson to the Virginia legislature[167] that the successive motions to attach to the Articles of Amendment miscellany from the proposals of the Virginia Convention emanated from Lee or Grayson. On the other side of the aisle, so to speak, Senator Robert Morris could not contain his irritation over the "Nonsense they call Amendments." Writing to Richard Peters the day the House voted the Articles, he confessed his vexation at the precious time lost on them. He admitted he had not considered any of the propositions but condemned them "by the Lump." Representatives Clymer and Fitzsimmons had advised him that the Senate should adopt the whole as containing neither good nor harm, being perfectly innocent. He himself expected the Articles to lie on the table for some time.[168]

---

[164] *The Journal of William Maclay,* Introduction by C. A. Beard, 2 *sub* Apr. 25, 1789 (hereafter cited as *Maclay Journal*). According to Hamilton's "Report on the Estimate of the Expenditure for the Civil List . . . , Sept. 19, 1789," Schedule I, Otis had one principal clerk and one engrossing clerk. *PAH*, V, 385. Otis was a family connection of John Adams. Pressure to secure Otis the office began early; *cf.* Gerry to R. H. Lee, Feb. 9, 1789, in Lee, *Memoir of the Life of Richard Henry Lee*, II, 144.

[165] *Maclay Journal*, 139–40 *sub*

Aug. 29 and 31, 1789. Maclay had on August 29 checked the ayes and nays on the question of senatorial compensation and found them correct. When the minutes were read August 31 the figure had been changed. When Otis was called upon to explain, "He hummed, hawed; said his memory was bad."

[166] Ballagh, II, *Letters of Richard Henry Lee*, 486.

[167] *Ibid.*, 507 (Sept, 28, 1789).

[168] Morris to Peters, Aug. 24, 1789, Ms. Peters Papers, IX, 99 (HSP). Morris opens his comment on the

The House resolution came before the Senate August 25. According to Maclay, Izard of South Carolina moved to postpone consideration until the next session, but this was unsuccessful.[169] August 31 was the day set for consideration.[170] Actually, discussion began September 2. Then, off and on for a week, the Senate labored over the Articles. Whoever may have been responsible, the redrafting of certain provisions resulted in crisper phraseology. The recasting and combination of certain House articles into single amendments, notably the structure of what became Article I of the Bill of Rights and the text of the wonderfully magisterial Article V, were the work of skilled and articulate legal stylists, although Richard Henry Lee, who seems to have preferred tumid libertarian rhetoric, complained: "The english language has been carefully culled to find words feeble in their nature or doubtful in their meaning."[171]

The Senate was strongly federalist, but the size of the federalist majority did not deter their adversaries from persevering in attempts to implant provisions already rejected by the House. Since the ayes and nays were taken only four times and only once were there as many as six Senators voting with Lee and Grayson, it is impossible to determine how often some federalists may have crossed the line.

The debates on the amendments occurred September 2–4 and again September 7–9. On these days there were present never more than eighteen Senators of the total membership of twenty-two. Insofar as a pattern can be perceived in the Senate proceedings, these can be divided into two phases concerning which our chief source is ambiguous. A Senate rule provided that all bills on a second reading should be considered by the Senate in the same manner as if the chamber were in a committee of the whole, before such be taken up and proceeded upon according to the standing rules.[172] Nothing was stipulated concerning resolves. It would appear, however, that although a second reading was not noted in the *Journal*, the Senate proceeded as if the House resolve were indeed a bill. The style of recordation followed by the clerk makes no distinction, as was the case in the House *Journal*, between the manner

---

amendments with the sardonic reflection that "poor Madison" had taken one wrong step in Virginia by publishing a letter regarding amendments, "and you who knows everything, must know what a Cursed thing it is to write a Book." The consequence had been that he had been compelled to bring on his propositions.

[169] *Maclay Journal*, 131. The amendments "were treated contemptuously by Izard [S.C.] Langdon [N.H.] and Mr. Morris [Pa.]." Langdon seconded Izard's motion. "Mr. Morris got up and spoke angrily but not well."

[170] *Senate Journal*, 1st Sess., 106.

[171] Lee to ——, Sept. 27, 1789, Ballagh, *Letters of Richard Henry Lee*, II, 504.

[172] *Senate Journal*, 1st Sess., 39 (May 21, 1789).

of conducting proceedings as if in committee or as Senate. During the first phase (committee or no) the discussions were confined to alterations of words and phrases and to outright rejection of two articles—that forbidding the states to infringe certain rights,[173] and the amendment proposed originally by the Virginia Convention proclaiming the separation of powers.[174] Since the Senators represented the states, the first rejection was foreseeable. The second rejection may be attributed to the fact that the Senators had the wit to perceive what havoc this clause could wreak with a Constitution the terms of which did not strictly comply with the principle of separation.

As if obedient to some antiquated stage direction, the second phase of debate was ushered in by a peal of ordnance—the bombardment of the chamber with a succession of amendments from the ammunition readied at the Virginia Convention. The discussion and rejection of these occupied the Senate most of September 8.[175] It then moved to the final stage which consisted in reviewing what it had done, of combining certain House articles and compressing them, and making last changes in wording.

Of the seventeen articles transmitted by the House, eight concerned some aspect of the judicial process. On the first inspection by the Senate the seventh article, dealing with searches and seizures, was passed as it stood.[176] But the eighth article, which opened "No person shall be subject, except in case of impeachment, to more than one trial, or one punishment for the same offence," suffered a revision. From this clumsy and, to lawyers, mischievous mode of expression were struck the words "except in case of impeachment, to more than one trial, or one punishment," and in their place was substituted "to be twice put in jeopardy of life or limb by any public prosecution."[177] This was a variant of what Coke had called a common law maxim.[178] The reference to public prosecution may be accounted for by the fact that, except where specifically abolished, the ancient common law remedy of appeal of felony at the suit of an injured party, wife or kinsman was theoretically still available.[179] The appeal of felony had been used in

---

[173] Ibid., 122 (Sept. 7, 1789).

[174] Ibid., 124 (Sept. 7, 1789).

[175] Ibid., 123–27, beginning with: "That there are certain natural rights, of which men, when they form a social compact, cannot deprive or divest their posterity, among which are the enjoyment of life and liberty, with the means of acquiring, possessing, and protecting property, and pursuing and obtaining happiness and safety."

[176] Ibid., 119 (Sept. 4, 1789).

[177] Ibid.

[178] Vaux's Case, 4 Coke Rep. 44 at 45a.

[179] And, depending upon opinion regarding the continued vigor of the pre-settlement English statutes, e.g., 3 Hen. VII, c. 1, saving an appellor's suit for a year and a day after acquittal on an indictment for murder. The Virginia Revisors were aware of the legislation. 3 Hen. VII, c. 1,

colonial Maryland,[180] and the remedy had been given statutory recognition in New York as recently as 1787.[181] There the rights of private appellors were explicitly saved. We shall notice shortly the ultimate disposition of the clause.

Article IX, dealing with the specific protections of defendants in criminal cases—speedy trial, etc.—was left intact,[182] but Article X, in which the House had combined in antic fashion security for trial by a jury of the vicinage, etc., and the requirement for presentment or indictment, was disemboweled. All that was approved on September 4 was the following: "No person shall be held to answer for a capital, or otherwise infamous crime, unless on a presentment or indictment by a Grand Jury."[183] The direction regarding trial by the vicinage was eliminated, we believe, because the Senate had earlier rejected a proposal to embody such a provision in the Judiciary Bill, although subsequently (September 19) as a result of House recalcitrance a direction was added to the Judiciary Act (section 29).[184]

Since the Senate, as we shall see in the next chapter, failed to place a monetary limit on all cases in error to the Supreme Court, it was inevitable that the limitation included in the House's Article XI should be excised. All that was left of this article was the revised direction: "No fact, triable by a Jury according to the course of common law, shall be otherwise re-examinable in any court of the United States, than according to the rules of common law."[185] Considering the great alterations to which review procedures had been subjected in the several colonies and in the states, it is noteworthy that none of the lawyers in the chamber raised any question as to what common law was meant. Certainly there were at the moment such noticeable differences between New York, Virginia and English error proceedings as to have induced some doubts as to the serviceability of the amendment beyond quieting popular fears over impeachment of verdicts by new and tyrannical measures.

---

was on Jefferson's list of laws to be taken up (*Papers of Jefferson*, II, 660); and the statute 21 Hen. VIII, c. 11, providing a substitute for appeals of robbery by giving restitution to the owner of stolen goods if a defendant was convicted on indictment or "otherwise attainted by reason of evidence given by the party so robbed" was re-enacted almost verbatim in Virginia (12 Hening, *Va. Stats.*, 170). "Otherwise attainted" is not explained.

[180] Soaper v. Tom, 1 Harris & McHenry 227 (1765).

[181] *N.Y. Laws*, 10 Sess. 1787, c. 30.
[182] *Senate Journal*, 1st Sess., 119.
[183] *Ibid.*
[184] *Infra*, c. XI, p. 506.
[185] *Senate Journal*, 1st Sess., 119. Before the alteration was voted, a substitute was offered denying to the "Supreme Judicial Federal Court" jurisdiction over causes between citizens of different states unless at least $3,000 was in dispute. Federal judicial power was not to extend in actions between citizens of different states unless at least $1,500 was involved.

If the Senate was insensible to the mutations in review procedures, it was, nevertheless, fully aware of the American statutory developments regarding the dispensability of jury trial in petty civil litigation.[186] The House's Article XII was amended to read: "In suits at common law, where the consideration exceeds twenty dollars, the right of trial by jury shall be preserved."[187] A series of proposals, some of which had been rejected by the House, were next offered, all voted down, and the excessive bail article then was approved (Article XV). With this, the first working over of the amendments affecting the judicial process was completed.[188] After amending the House's Article XVII to extend the reservation of powers not delegated to the United States by the Constitution "to the people" as well as to the states,[189] the Senate voted to prefix to the House's "preamble" a species of *pièce justicatif*[190] to explain the reasons for the proffered amendments—a soothing elixir of phrases to quiet the disaffected.

On September 9 the Senate proceeded as Senate with the final consideration of the Articles. First of all, it settled upon the phrasing of the religious liberty clause with which it had had nearly as much trouble as the House. To the religious liberty clause it added prohibitions upon legislation by Congress abridging freedom of speech, or of the press or of the right of assembly, and eliminated the House's Article IV where these rights had been given only the imprecise guarantee "shall not be infringed."[191] Article V, already trimmed by lopping off the description of the militia as "composed of the body of the citizens" as well as the sentence exempting the religiously scrupulous from compulsory military service,[192] was now further amended by substituting for the encomium of the militia—"being the best security of a free State"—the more reserved "necessary to the security of a free state."[193] Conceivably some Senators who recalled the frequent flights of militia during the Revolution were prepared to be realistic about the citizen soldier. The Senate refused to limit the right to bear arms by voting down the addition of the words "for the common defence."

---

[186] *Supra*, c. I, p. 34.

[187] *Senate Journal*, 1st Sess., 121.

[188] *Ibid.*, 122.

[189] *Ibid.*, 123.

[190] The word "preamble" was consistently used for what is now called the "resolving clause." The justification was offered and passed as an amendment to the "preamble." As ultimately promulgated, it preceded the resolving clause and read: "The Conventions of a number of the States, having, at the time of their adopting the Constitution, expressed a desire, in order to prevent misconstruction or abuse of its powers, that further declaratory and restrictive clauses should be added; and as extending the grounds of public confidence in the Government, will best insure the beneficent ends of its institution—" (*ibid.*). This appears to have been drafted by Ellsworth, *cf.* Sen. 1A–C2.

[191] *Ibid.*, 129.

[192] On September 4, *ibid.*, 119.

[193] *Ibid.*, 129.

United States of America

In the Senate

Wednesday 9th Sept. 1789

On the question to concur with the House of Representatives, on their resolution of the 24th of Aug. proposing amendments to the constitution of the United States, with the following amendments viz:

to insert before the word "resolved" in the first clause

the convention of a number of the States having at the time of their adopting the constitution expressed a desire, in order to prevent misconstruction or abuse of its powers, that further declaratory & restrictive clauses should be added: And as extending the ground of publick confidence in the government will best ensure the beneficent ends of its institution —

To erase from the same clause the words "deeming it necessary" & insert — _concurring._

To erase from the third first article all that follows the word "hundred" in the 3d line, & insert _to which number one Representative shall be added for every subsequent increase of forty thousand, until the Representatives shall amount to two hundred;_

6

Although the right to bear arms amendment is irrelevant to the points upon which our discussion is focussed, it is here mentioned because it offers disquieting documentary evidence of the untrustworthiness of the Senate *Journal*. In the full text of the article as renumbered and voted, the *Journal* omits the words "necessary to" so that it appears "A well regulated militia being the security of a free State."[194] This is not the form in which the amendment went to the House. A copy of the official printing of the Senate's revised version of the amendments is preserved in the Madison Papers at the Library of Congress.[195] The text was also published in Greenleaf's *New-York Journal, and Weekly Register* for September 17, two days before the House took the Senate amendments into consideration. Both in the official print and in the September 17 *New-York Journal* the words "necessary to" in the militia article appear. There is nothing in the Senate *Journal* to indicate that a further vote was taken on this amendment after September 9.

An even more egregious example of bungling is the text of what was to become the Fifth Amendment. Whatever was the actual form of what was drafted and whoever drafted it, the Senate's objective was obviously to combine with some alteration the House's versions of Articles VIII and X into one article, reversing the order voted by the House. It will be recalled that Article X had been pared down to read: "No person shall be held to answer for a capital, or otherwise infamous crime, unless on a presentment or indictment by a Grand Jury."[196] The new version restored the exception of cases arising in land or naval forces or in the militia in actual service in time of war or public danger. At this point was added a newly revised version of Article VIII. As reported in the Senate *Journal* it reads: "nor shall any person be subject to be put in jeopardy of life or limb, for the same offence, nor shall be compelled in any criminal case to be a witness against himself. . . ."[197] The elimination of the words "public prosecution," voted September 4, was surely the work of the draftsman of the revised article. However, the muddling of the word order of the jeopardy clause and the omission of the word "twice" in the Senate *Journal* entry must be laid to Secretary Otis. For here, again, the form of the amendment sent to the House was not the Senate *Journal* version but the form ultimately sent to the states that became the Fifth Amendment to the Constitution.[198] And here, again, there is no evidence in the Senate *Journal* that after approval of the amendment it was further considered by the Senate

---

[194] *Ibid.*
[195] Ms. Madison Papers, LXXVI, 35 (LC).
[196] *Supra*, p. 499.
[197] *Senate Journal*, 1st Sess., 130.

[198] Senate's "Revision of the Amendments," *cf. supra*, n. 195. *New-York Journal, and Weekly Register*, Sept. 17, 1789.

beyond that chamber's refusing to retract from the version sent to the House.

The final coupling of House articles was the union of the already amended eleventh and twelfth articles, again in reverse order, to read: "In suits at common law, where the value in controversy shall exceed twenty dollars, the right of trial by Jury shall be preserved, and no fact tried by a Jury, shall be otherwise re-examined in any Court of the United States, than according to the rules of the common law."[199] The change of the earlier voted phrase "where the consideration exceeds twenty dollars" to "where the value in controversy shall exceed twenty dollars" had the effect of enlarging the scope of the limitation, because of the technical implications of the word "consideration."[200]

The remainder of the revised articles were approved after an attempt to secure a reconsideration of the House's Article X, the obvious purpose of which was to effect a commitment on trial by a jury of the vicinage, unanimous verdict, right of challenge and "other accustomed requisites." The vote was evenly divided so the question was lost.[201] After further renumbering, the original seventeen articles were reduced to twelve. The House resolve as amended was then approved with two thirds of the Senators present concurring. It was ordered that the House be advised accordingly. The new package was ordered sent to the House September 10.[202]

Richard Henry Lee was unhappy over the result. He wrote Patrick Henry on September 14 that the Senate had further weakened the House amendments, which fell short of what the Virginia Convention desired. "You may be assured that nothing on my part was left undone to prevent this, and every possible effort was used to give success to all the amendments proposed by our country."[203] Lee's fellow countryman Madison was reportedly equally unhappy, for on September 17 Paine Wingate wrote his absent colleague, John Langdon, regarding the amendments, that "Madison says he had rather have none than those agreed to by the Senate."[204] Three days earlier Madison had expressed himself more circumspectly in a letter to Edmund Pendleton.[205] The alterations, in his opinion, struck at the most salutary articles. He mentioned specifically the Senate's dislike of the restraint of the vicinage for the selection

---

[199] *Senate Journal*, 1st Sess., 130.

[200] Viz., as confining the phrase to actions on contracts.

[201] *Senate Journal*, 1st Sess., 131.

[202] Childs, "Disappeared in the Wings of Oblivion," at 119, offers evidence to show that the House did not receive the document until September 14.

[203] Ballagh, *Letters of Richard Henry Lee*, II, 501.

[204] Wingate to Langdon, Sept. 17, 1789, in Wingate, *Life and Letters of Paine Wingate*, II, 334-35.

[205] Ms. Madison Papers, XII, 30 (LC); see also *Doc. Hist. Const.*, V, 205.

of jurors in criminal cases (attributable to the great variance in state practice), and its refusal to put "a constitutional bar to appeals below a certain value" because such a limitation would be inconvenient and unnecessary. "The difficulty," he wrote, "of meeting the minds of men accustomed to think and act differently can only be conceived by those who have witnessed it."

The House, embroiled in the more exciting problem of the future seat of government, did not take up the amendments until September 19, and the reporter unfortunately noted nothing of the discussions. There was further consideration on September 21, and because some revised articles were approved and many more disapproved, a committee of conference with the Senate was desired.[206] Madison, Sherman and Vining were named as managers for the House. The Senate was prepared to recede only from its alteration of the representation amendment.[207] Ellsworth, Carroll of Maryland and Paterson were named managers at the conference on the part of the Senate.[208]

On September 23 Madison reported to the House the results of the conference.[209] In a letter to Pendleton of the same date he lamented that "it will be impossible I find to prevail on the Senate to concur in the limitation on the *value* of appeals to the Supreme Court. . . . They are equally inflexible in opposing a definition of the *locality* of juries." The proposal to restore to this article—after the word "juries"—the phrase "with the accustomed requisites," leaving the construction to the judgment of professional men, could not be obtained. The Senate managers supposed that the vicinage provision (recently added to section 29 of the Judiciary Act) would be sufficient.[210]

As we already have had occasion to observe, Madison was prone to regard as infallible his opinions on government, and he was not easily brought around to a change of view. His retreat from his original stand on amendments had come about gradually, but once converted and having presented a plan of his own, he had consistently resisted its

---

[206] *Jour. H.R.*, I, 115–16. The House agreed to ten and disagreed to sixteen of the Senate's amendments. Lacking any copy of the Senate document with the numeration noted, it is impossible to determine the precise particulars.

[207] *Senate Journal*, 1st Sess., 142. This had provided: "After the first enumeration required by the first Article of the Constitution, there shall be one Representative for every thirty thousand, until the number shall amount to one hundred; to which

number one Representative shall be added for every subsequent increase of forty thousand, until the Representatives shall amount to two hundred, to which one Representative shall be added for every subsequent increase of sixty thousand persons." *Ibid.*, 115.

[208] *Ibid.*, 142.

[209] *Jour. H.R.*, I, 120. The report was tabled and taken up the day following.

[210] Ms. Madison Papers, XII, 34 (LC); *Doc. Hist. Const.*, V, 210.

diminution or accretion. Now, with the end of the session less than a week off, there was no time for protracted wrangling, particularly with a group headed by Ellsworth, described as hanging "like a bat" to every particle of his own handiwork.[211] The result of the conference was to all appearances a bargain: the House would waive its objections to various Senate amendments provided that two articles be recast and a verbal change made in the representation amendment. The recasting concerned a rephrasing of the religious liberty clause (a matter close to Madison's heart) into the form in which it finally appeared in what became the First Amendment,[212] and a rewriting of what became the Sixth Amendment.[213] The significant change there was the compromise on the venue of trial juries—a provision rejected by the Senate—and its restoration and relocation from the article dealing with indictment, where the House had originally placed it, to the article dealing with protections in criminal trials, where it now properly belonged. The compromise consisted in the Senate's yielding to a mention of venue, and the House to the description: "by an impartial Jury of the District wherein the Crime shall have been committed, as the District shall have been previously ascertained by Law." The House approved the compromise on September 24, and the strength of the federalist majority was revealed when the ayes and nays were taken on the Senate's eighth article with its much altered venue provision. This was carried 37–14.[214] The Senate concurred September 25, and on the following day concurred in a House resolution of September 24 requesting the President of the United States to transmit copies of the amendments to the states which had ratified the Constitution as well as to North Carolina and Rhode Island.[215]

The vicissitudes of the amendments in the several states do not concern us here. It may be noticed, however, that after all the sound and fury expended on the issue of providing safeguards for the individual, the states were laggard in accepting what had been proffered them.

---

[211] *Maclay Journal*, 357.

[212] *Jour. H.R.*, I, 121; *Senate Journal*, 1st Sess., 145. In the Senate's version the article read: "Congress shall make no Law establishing articles of faith, or a mode of worship or prohibiting the free exercise of religion, or abridging the freedom of Speech, or of the Press; or the right of the People peaceably to assemble and petition the government for a redress of Grievances." Senate's "Revision of the Amendments," *supra*, n. 195.

[213] *Jour. H.R.*, I, 121; *Senate Journal*, 1st Sess., 145. The Senate version: "In all criminal prosecutions, the accused shall enjoy the right to a speedy and public trial, to be informed of the nature and cause of the accusation, to be confronted by witnesses against him, to have compulsory process for obtaining witnesses in his favour, and to have the assistance of Counsel for his defence."

[214] *Jour. H.R.*, I, 121.

[215] *Senate Journal*, 1st Sess., 150–51.

Indeed, it was not until Virginia finally ratified, December 15, 1791, that the amendments came into effect.[216] But not all of them, for two states rejected the first proposed amendment regulating representation, and three states rejected the second proposal regulating compensation of Representatives and Senators. With these exceptions, the proposals that had been agreed upon by the Senate and the House became the Bill of Rights. Meanwhile, the new federal courts had been functioning for two years, unbound by the pending constitutional restrictions; contrary to the expectations of some, the skies did not fall.

---

[216] The Congress was notified of this by Washington on Dec. 30, 1791. J. D. Richardson, ed., *A Compilation of the Messages and Papers of the* *Presidents, 1789–1897* (1899), I, 114 (hereafter cited as Richardson, *Messages and Papers of the Presidents*).

CHAPTER XI

The Judiciary Act of 1789

THE JUDICIARY ACT OF 1789[1] was not destined to acquire the numinous aura of the Bill of Rights, although it supplemented the Constitution by infusing with life the inert clauses of Article III; and, by detailing many concrete ingredients of due process of law, was to give substance to that guarantee. The first session of the first Congress enacted, as an old phrase had it, "many useful and honorable laws"; none was of greater prospective force than this act; none more astutely contrived. The leading spirits on the Senate committee charged with drafting this measure were federally minded and so politically disposed to take a bold view of the legislative authority conveyed by Article III. They were, nevertheless, as events proved, wholly sensitive to the variety of criticisms that had been directed at the judicial, and, for the future success of their handiwork, were prepared to meet these. At the onset the pendency of those amendments by which certain state ratifying conventions had sought to predetermine and confine structure and jurisdiction of a federal judiciary may have helped to establish a mood of concession, but they were without compulsive effect upon the decisions taken.[2] This is not to say that heed was not paid to certain particulars, as it was to other less formalized propositions like those earlier advanced by committee member Richard Henry Lee in his *Letters of a Federal Farmer.*

---

[1] 1 *U.S. Stats.*, 73. The correct title of the statute is "An Act to establish the Judicial Courts of the United States."

[2] It may here be remarked that the course of events in the House of Representatives respecting amendments to the Constitution was without demonstrable effect upon the contents of the Judiciary Bill, for its main features had been settled a fortnight before Madison presented his choice of amendments and the committee reported four days after the event. The bill passed the Senate six days before the House appointed the Select Committee headed by Vining (*supra*, c. X, p. 433).

If, as will be demonstrated, the Judiciary Act must be viewed in a political context as an instrument of reconciliation deliberately framed to quiet still smoldering resentments, in a juristic context it is a document of less fugitive nature and one of great historical depth. For when the provenance of various sections, in particular those of technical import, is explored, the statute is revealed to be rooted in the law and custom of divers American jurisdictions. That the "practick part" of the new system was thus planted in the soil of American tradition established a subtle species of continuity, afforced by the directions in the Judiciary Act regarding state laws as rules of decision, and the validation of state forms of common law process in the first Process Act.

THE DRAFTSMEN AND THE BILL

IF THERE IS ANY evidence of why the Senate took the initiative in proceeding to organize the judiciary, we have not seen it. But on April 7, 1789, the day after a quorum was made, a committee to bring in a bill for organizing the judiciary was appointed.[3] Chosen were Ellsworth of Connecticut, Paterson of New Jersey, Maclay of Pennsylvania, Strong of Massachusetts, Richard Henry Lee of Virginia, Bassett of Delaware, Few of Georgia and Wingate of New Hampshire. When Izard of South Carolina and Carroll of Maryland arrived, April 13, they were added to the Committee for Organizing the Judiciary, the Senate *Journal* recording that this was to secure a representation from each state.[4] Since the perfecting of a federal judiciary establishment was not a mere venture in the science of government but in its ramifications a technical undertaking of considerable complexity, the professional qualifications of the Committee members were a matter of first importance.[5] Izard, R. H. Lee and Wingate were laymen. Carroll had been a student of the civil law both in France and in England. Maclay had been a Common Pleas judge in Pennsylvania, but it is doubtful if he had more than a hornbook acquaintance with the law. According to a fellow Georgian, William Pierce,[6] Few's professional attainments were meagre, but he had been admitted to the bar. Bassett had been in active practice in Delaware but we know little of his abilities.[7] On the other hand, of the professional

---

[3] *Senate Journal*, 1st Sess., 10.
[4] *Ibid.*, 11.
[5] Biographies of all the committeemen are to be found in *DAB sub nom.*
[6] Farrand, *Records*, III, 97.
[7] According to H. S. Conrad, *History of the State of Delaware* (Wilmington: 1908), III, 828, Bassett had studied under Judge Goldsborough of Maryland. A letter of May 16, 1782, in W. T. Read, *Life and Correspondence of George Read*, 364, indicates Bassett had a command of procedure.

experience of Ellsworth, Paterson and Strong there can be no question. Ellsworth brought to his task not only immediate service as judge of the Connecticut Superior Court, but a knowledge of the problems of federal appellate authority gained from his service on the Standing Committee of the Continental Congress for appeals in cases of prize. Paterson had served as New Jersey's attorney general during the Revolution and, as was then the custom, had practiced privately. Strong, admitted to the bar in 1772, had for many years been county attorney in Massachusetts, as well as engaged in private practice. Like Paterson, he had been a member of his state's constitutional convention.[8]

These three lawyers were mainly responsible for the form and content of the Judiciary Bill. Paterson came to his task with the most pronounced common law background and probably better acquainted with the details of chancery procedure than his colleagues because a Chancery Court had long been seated in New Jersey. This was not a tradition in which either Ellsworth or Strong had been raised. In Connecticut, where the assembly had wielded equity powers, there had nevertheless been an appropriation of such by the common law courts, as well as an adaptation of certain chancery procedures. Massachusetts, which during the charter period had developed some equity doctrines of its own, had not, however, later proceeded beyond a limited reception of some features of equity jurisprudence. The appellate procedures in all three states have already been noticed.[9] We shall examine in a moment the evidence of how the work on the bill was shared, but it may be here remarked that Ellsworth by the power of his personality became the dominant figure. He brought to his assignment the powers of advocacy earlier exhibited in the "Landholder" letters, moving Maclay to write, "This vile bill is a child of his, and he defends it with the care of a parent, even in wrath and anger."[10] One would not suspect

---

[8] C. Warren, "New Light on the History of the Federal Judiciary Act of 1789," (hereafter cited as Warren, "Judiciary Act"), at 57, states that of the committee "Ellsworth, Paterson, Strong, Few, and Wingate had served in the Federal Convention of 1787 and were familiar with its intent as to the Judiciary." Wingate never attended the Convention, but Bassett, whom Warren overlooks, did. Ellsworth, no doubt, was conversant with the discussions although he had been absent August 27 when the crucial debate on Art. III occurred. Paterson had left the Convention on or about July 23, but returned to sign. Strong left the Convention before August 27 and so was not present when Art. III was taken up, and did not return. For dates of attendance *cf.* Farrand, *Records*, III, 586–90.

[9] *Supra*, c. I.

[10] *Maclay Journal*, 89. As early as April 29 Paine Wingate wrote John Pickering that "Mr Ellsworth seems to be the leading projector, who is a very sensible man and will do very well if he is not too much attached to the forms of law he has long been in habit of." C. Wingate, *Life and Letters of Paine Wingate*, II, 303.

from Maclay's frequent splenetic outbursts that Ellsworth possessed a capacity for accommodation, but what survives of Senate proceedings demonstrates this to have been the case.

The Committee took its time over setting anything to paper, and it would appear that by the last day of April it had proceeded no further than to settle what the judicial structure would be and to accept certain fundamentals respecting jurisdiction, not the least important of which were the principle of monetary limitation and the exclusion of questions of fact from appellate review by the Supreme Court. These details were communicated April 30 by Ellsworth in a letter to Richard Law, then Chief Justice of the Connecticut Superior Court.[11] Law's thoughts on the plan were solicited.

Law's reply has not been found but the tenor of his reaction may be inferred from a later letter of Ellsworth[12] in reply to two communications, one of which was certainly written after receipt of a copy of the draft bill. Law was generally in favor of the plan but he raised the question of using the state courts as inferior federal courts, a suggestion which Ellsworth adroitly disposed of. When Ellsworth wrote, the Senate bill was reposing in the House awaiting action.

That Caleb Strong also sought the opinion of judges in his own state of Massachusetts appears from an exchange of letters in May 1789 with Robert Treat Paine, then attorney general and later a judge of the Massachusetts Supreme Judicial Court. Paine reported May 18[13] that he had seen "sundry letters" which Strong had sent Judge David Sewall regarding the federal judicial system. Inferences regarding propositions earlier before the Committee may be drawn from Paine's comments. He did not favor the notion that in diversity cases citizens or foreigners might sue in any state where the defendant did not live. To require a defendant to answer "at a distance" would be a greater oppression of the individual than any from which liberation had been expected by the Revolution. Paine thought that to suppose a prejudice in "common cases" in the state of a man's domicil was contrary to "our

---

[11] F. Wharton, *State Trials of the United States during the Administrations of Washington and Adams* (1849), 37 note (hereafter cited as Wharton, *State Trials*). Compare Wingate's opinion in the letter *supra*, n. 10, that only "some general principles have been agreed to."

[12] Of Aug. 4, 1789, Wharton, *State Trials*, 38 note.

[13] Paine to Strong, Ms. R. T. Paine Papers (MHS). This letter is a copy, one page of which was written on a cover of a communication to "John Tucker Esq Clerk to the Honble Supreme Judicial Court County of Suffolk," and endorsed "to Caleb Strong—respecting the federal judicial System." The date there—May 1788—is in another hand, and was manifestly taken from the head of the letter itself—Boston, May 18, 1788—an obvious mistake made by Paine in copying because the body of the communication clearly refers to matters before the Senate Committee.

continued observation" and supposed a corruption of morals which would render it unsafe to go anywhere for justice. Some special provision could be made for "important popular causes."

Apparently at this stage of the Judiciary Committee's deliberations it had not yet settled the question of personal jurisdiction on the basis of the maxim *actor sequit forum rei* that was eventually written into section 11 of the act. The difficulties already noticed over execution of Article IV of the Treaty of Paris and the unhappy experience of British creditors in the state courts were probably the reason why a neutral ground was under consideration.

As for inferior federal courts, Paine reported that many had difficulties with the idea of casting the Massachusetts Supreme Judicial Court in such a role, although it would save expenditure of time and money if the state supreme courts could perform this function. Yet if this could not be done, "distant" federal inferior courts would be necessary. The number of such should be held down. There must be a court to determine matters of revenue, seizures and admiralty. It would not be inconsistent to vest jurisdiction over these matters in a single court. Paine was apparently not clear whether there were to be both inferior and separate admiralty courts. The Supreme Court, he believed, should be so regulated as to reduce the burden and expense of "going from home for justice."

One further fact emerges from Paine's letter—that Strong had sent for a copy of the bill for the reorganization of the Massachusetts judicial system submitted by a special committee of which Paine had been a member, and which had been under discussion in the 1788–89 session of the General Court. This bill had failed to become law.[14] No copy remains in the papers of either house but its purport can be established from the published text of the Committee report. It cannot be affirmed that the dispositions made would have advanced the work of the Senate Committee.[15]

Strong replied to Paine on May 24, and it is obvious from the

---

[14] The report came before the fall 1788 session of the Massachusetts House of Representatives and on Nov. 21, 1788, was referred to the next General Court. Ms. Journal Mass. House of Reps., *sub* Nov. 21, 1788. It was taken up again Jan. 2, 1789 (*ibid.*, 1st Sess. 1789), and referred to a committee. This committee reported adversely January 6, and after some debate a new committee was named Jan. 10, 1789 (*ibid.*). The final notice of rejection signed by Oliver Wendell is in Report 2888,

Mass. Archives. No copy of the rejected bill has been found in this repository.

The report of the Committee for Revising the Laws, dated Oct. 30, 1788, and signed by William Cushing, was printed in the Boston *Independent Chronicle and the Universal Advertiser*, Dec. 4, 1788.

[15] *The Maryland Journal*, June 2, 1789, carried a Boston item dated May 16 to the effect that members of Congress had sent for the Massachusetts bill.

letter that great progress had been made.[16] On May 11, so Maclay reports, a sub-committee had been named to draft a bill,[17] a fact generally overlooked but which has some bearing on the process of parturition. Maclay does not mention the names of the members. The terms in which Strong describes the status of the undertaking indicate clearly enough that he was a member, and the manuscript working draft to which we shall come in a moment indicates that Paterson and Ellsworth were Strong's associates.[18] If any others were on this sub-committee their identity remains unknown.

Before Strong entered into the details of what was being done, he reassured Paine that actions by aliens in a state where a defendant was not domiciled would be "guarded against." He referred Paine to his earlier letter to Sewall for explanations why it would be inconvenient to confer federal jurisdiction upon state courts. An added reason which he had earlier forgotten to mention was the Virginia enactment sponsored by Patrick Henry, the effect of which was to disqualify the courts of that state from having jurisdiction of causes arising under the laws of the Union. Such laws, wrote Strong, would enable every state to defeat the exercise of the judiciary powers of the general government. Clearly the Virginians had been hoist by their own petard.

It would appear from Strong's account, which he admitted was abridged, that the content of the first five sections of the plan was settled. He did not mention the following sections relating to the adjournments, appointments and the regulation of oaths. He proceeded then to detail the jurisdiction of District and Circuit Courts. At this time the directions regarding removals from state courts appear to have been embodied in the section dealing with the original jurisdiction of the Circuit Courts. The remainder of Strong's account is set forth below.[19]

[16] Strong to Paine, Misc. Bound Mss. (MHS).

[17] Maclay Journal, 29.

[18] Fisher Ames wrote to his friend Minot on July 8, 1789, in terms indicating this trio was chiefly responsible. Ames, Works of Fisher Ames, I, 61 at 64.

[19] "The Sup. Court to have exclusive Jurisdiction of all Causes of a civil nature where any of the United States or a foreign State is a party except between a State and its Citizens and except also between a State and the Citizens of other States or Foreigners in which latter Case it shall have original but not exclusive Jurisdiction, and original but not exclusive Jurisdiction of all Suits for Trespasses by Ambassadours other publick Ministers or Consuls & their Domesticks—the Trial of Facts in the Supreme Court in all actions at Law against the Citizens of the U. S. to be by Jury—to have appellate Jurisdiction from the Circuit Courts where the Value is 2000 Doll^{rs} but no Revision of Facts

"The Sup. Court may grant Writs of prohibition to the District Courts in Admiralty proceedings & Writs of Mandamus to any Courts appointed or Persons holding offices under the Authority of the United States Writs of Error may be brought to reverse the Errors in the District at the Cir-

XI: *The Judiciary Act of 1789*

To be noticed particularly is the confusion respecting the monetary limit upon the appellate jurisdiction of the Supreme Court. Some other details may already have been settled but are not mentioned, for Strong was anxious that the judges of the Massachusetts Supreme Judicial Court be advised of the *status quo* and that any objections be despatched betimes.

Strong was of the opinion that the bill would be reported within a week, but it is not clear whether he meant by the sub-committee or by the full Committee. Allowing even for the fact that Strong's account was abridged, there were to be, as it turned out, provisions in the bill that invited protracted discussion, particularly in the full Committee where the adversarial interests abided. Strong's prediction further failed to take into account the effect upon Committee business of the debate on the impost bill which had been taken up in the Senate the day after he had written. From then into early June he as well as other Committee members were to be mired, so to speak, in the molasses question. The Judiciary Bill was not reported to the Senate until June 12, 1789.[20]

What did the Committee, in fact, report? The answer to this is of first importance for settling a crucial stage in the legislative history of the statute.

There reposes today in the National Archives a collection of papers entitled "A Bill to establish the Judicial Courts of the United States."[21] This is the collection discovered years ago in the attic of the United

---

cuit Courts, in Causes not criminal and between 50 & 300 Dol.[rs] Value but Exon not to be staid and double Costs if no Reversal

"Writs of Error from the Circuit to the Sup.[r] Court in all Causes not criminal of which the Circuit Court has original Cognizance and the matter in Dispute does not exceed 2000 Dol.[rs]

"If in a Cause in a State Court the Question is whether a Law of the State or of the United States is constitutional and the Judgment is in favour of the State Law or against the Law of the U. S. a Writ of Error will lie to have *that Question & that only* determined in the Supreme Court. *No other power in the federal Courts to revise Judgments in the State Courts*—

"That all the Courts have power in the Trial of Actions at Law on Motion and due Notice to require the Parties to produce Books & Papers and the Defendant to disclose on oath in Cases & under Circumstances where such power has been usually exercised in Chancery, and if the Pl.[tff] refuse to produce Books &c to render judgment as in Cases of Nonsuit and if Def.[t] refuse to produce Books &c or to answer on oath to render Judgment by Default.

"That a Marshall be appointed to each District with power to execute Writs issuing under the Authority of the U.S. to appoint Deputies who may be removed by the District or Circuit Court at Pleasure

"The Mode of appointing Jurors is not yet agreed"

[20] *Senate Journal*, 1st Sess., 50.
[21] Senate Files, Sen. 1A–B1 (Safe #2.B–2, NA). Filed with the bill are the propositions for changes or amendments written on slips of paper.

463

A Bill

Be it enacted by ... and Representatives of the United States of America in Congress assembled, That the Supreme Court of the United States shall consist of a Chief Justice and five associate Justices; any four of whom shall be a Quorum, and shall hold annually at the Seat of the federal Government two Sessions, the one commencing the first Monday of February, and the other the first Monday of August. That the associate Justices shall have Precedence according to the date of their Commissions, or where the Commissions of two or more of them bear date on the same Day, according to their ages.

2. And be it further enacted, by the authority aforesaid, That the United States shall be and they hereby are divided into eleven Districts to be ... and called as ... to wit,

Manuscript draft, Senate Judiciary Bill, page 1, in the handwriting of William Paterson.

(*The National Archives*)

States Senate by the late Charles Warren, and described by him as "the original draft of the Judiciary Act as it was introduced into the Senate."[22] The text of this draft of the act is in four hands—the first portion is the writing of Paterson; the second of Ellsworth; one section is in Strong's hand; and the remainder, some eight sections, was indited by a clerk. The portions written by Paterson, Ellsworth and Strong bear section numbers, but only in the case of Paterson's composition is it clear that these numbers are in the writer's own hand. The portion done by the clerk has no section numbers. The manuscript in its several sections abounds in interlineations, insertions of single words, matter struck out and marginal additions, some of which are cancelled yet miraculously appear in the statute.

The whole appearance of this manuscript is such as to arouse a sense of caution over accepting it as the bill reported to the Senate. There is, indeed, evidence, close to being conclusive, that a different and more finished version was presented. This is the document which Maclay states the Senate ordered be printed June 12.[23] The official printer, Thomas Greenleaf, struck off 250 copies[24] and we know from a letter of George Read[25] that the copies were available for distribution June 16.[26] Three known copies of this print exist.[27] Whether or not it has hitherto been used for historical purposes we do not know.

In the margin we have indicated substantive particulars of how the manuscript and printed bill diverge.[28] Superficially, the printed bill

---

[22] Warren, "Judiciary Act," 50.

[23] *Maclay Journal*, 72. There is no entry to this effect in the Senate *Journal*.

[24] The printer's bill, now in the National Archives, is published by J. B. Childs, "The Story of the United States Senate Documents, 1st Congress, 1st Session, New York, 1789," 175 at 181.

[25] Read to John Dickinson, June 16, 1789, in Read, *Life and Correspondence of George Read*, at 480–81.

[26] Maclay sent off copies June 17 (*Journal*, 76).

[27] *Cf.* Childs, "The Story of the United States Senate Documents, 1st Congress, 1st Session, New York, 1789, at 184–85. The copy here used is in the New York Public Library and was acquired in 1918. The accession number is 626234. It is entitled "A Bill to establish the Judicial Courts of the United States." At the foot of the last page (16) is printed

"[NEW-YORK, PRINTED BY THOMAS GREENLEAF]."

[28] In the first place, in the section defining the jurisdiction of the Circuit Courts that became sec. 11 of the statute, the text of the working draft following the direction that these courts have concurrent jurisdiction with District Courts of crimes and offenses cognizable therein is mangled and incomplete. The printed bill and the statute both command that "no person shall be arrested in one district for trial in another, in any civil action before a circuit or district court." The working draft (here in Ellsworth's hand) originally had an approximation of this, but the operative words "arrested for trial" are struck out and over them is written "brought to trial" and the rest of the sentence in part cancelled so as to leave the command meaningless. In the margin of the manuscript is written a version of the text as it appears in the printed bill but with

differs radically from the manuscript draft in capitalization, punctuation and even spelling. Since there is no reason to suppose that the correction of a text was within the discretion of the printer Greenleaf, whose own newspaper, *The New-York Journal,* was no model of consistency, one is led to conclude that his compositors had before them a manuscript copy of a bill of a later recension than the manuscript in the National Archives. The latter we believe to have been no more than a working draft of the Committee in a late stage of its deliberations.

Apart from what a comparison of working draft and printed bill reveals, it should be noticed that whenever the meagre entries in the Senate *Journal* are specific, the references can be traced to the printed bill alone. This is true also of the chits or slips of paper still preserved on which proffered amendments or alterations were written and "delivered in at the table" pursuant to Senate rule VII. Many of these chits refer to pages—invariably to be found in the printed bill. Since the latter ran to only fifteen and a half pages and the manuscript draft to thirty-seven, attempts to fix the place of what was offered by reference to the manuscript are meaningless.

For reasons unknown, Richard Henry Lee was chosen to report the bill; there was mordant humor in the fact that "Landholder,"

---

considerable variation of language. This is cancelled.

The cancelled marginal insertion embodied also a limitation upon instituting civil actions against a defendant except in the district where he was an inhabitant or was found. Nevertheless, this provision in slightly different language did appear in the printed bill. But what is an even more curious feature of this rejected insertion is the elimination at this point of a provision denying to inferior federal courts cognizance of any suit to recover the contents of any promissory note or chose in action in favor of an assignee, unless the suit might have been prosecuted in these courts if no assignment had been made. This was a significant provision because its purpose was to prevent the establishment of diversity jurisdiction by subterfuge, a hazard against which the antifederalists, R. H. Lee among them, had warned. In the portion of the working draft in the clerk's hand the provision appears in a separate section coupled with another provision indecipherable because of

water damage. All of this section was struck. The effect of the two cancellations was to eliminate the provision entirely from the working draft, yet it appears in the printed Committee bill precisely where Ellsworth had placed the cancelled insertion. The Senate was to amend the clause. If it had been the working draft that came before this body, there would have been nothing to amend.

Another and no less peculiar aberration concerns a marginal addition, again by Ellsworth, to the section which provided that suits in equity might not be sustained in any case where an adequate remedy could be had at law. The addition read: "and the mode of giving testimony in suits in equity & in causes of admiralty & maritime jurisdiction shall be the same as in trials at common law, or as hereinafter specially provided." The substance of this appears later in the part of the working draft indited by the clerk in the section dealing with the taking of depositions where it was also placed in the printed bill.

chiefly responsible for its begetting, should have been ready to foist on the "Federal Farmer" the sponsorship of offspring which the latter soon showed he was ready to disown. June 22 was set for a second reading. Significantly, as soon as printed copies of the bill were available, individual Senators proceeded to solicit the views of judges and leaders of the bar in their own states and elsewhere. This was carrying out on a broader scale what Ellsworth and Strong had done while Committee discussions were proceeding—action that came close to being an infringement of the closed-door policy pursued as to Senate discussion. What was done with the reported bill which was made available to the newspapers was obviously no transgression. The poll of the profession was in a sense an approximation of a hearing on a bill—something not yet imagined—limited by the fact that it was conducted by correspondence. Many letters went out[29] but few of the replies have been found. The comments, some of which will presently be noticed, were in general of little constructive value, except those of Samuel Chase which arrived too late to be of use. Perhaps the chief effect of the answers was to supply some ammunition for debate and to induce the reassurance—if illusory—expected from consulting expert opinion. They had this effect on Maclay.[30]

If the members of the Senate Committee could have proceeded as it were, *ab ovo*, they might well have presented a bill different from the one reported. But theirs was a business already half hatched, for

---

[29] Dalton apparently sent a copy to Theophilus Parsons (J. Q. Adams to J. Adams, June 28, 1789, in W. C. Ford, ed., *Writings of John Quincy Adams*, I, 43). And it may be suggested that Strong probably sent copies to his correspondents. Ellsworth, as indicated *supra*, n. 12, sent a copy to Law. He also sent a copy to Chancellor Livingston (Livingston to Ellsworth, June 26, 1789, Livingston Mss. [NYHS], and see also a letter to an unknown correspondent, June 24, 1789 [Huntington Library Ms. No. 22577]). The poll of Pennsylvania worthies and others was thorough. According to Maclay, William Lewis, Richard Peters, Myers Fisher, Francis Hopkinson, McKean C.J., Tench Coxe and Thomas Mifflin were sent copies (*Maclay Journal*, 76, 97). House Speaker Muhlenberg sent a copy to Richard Peters (*cf.* his letter, June 18, in Ms. Peters Papers, IX, 95 [HSP]). The Philadelphia lawyers

held a conference on the bill and Alexander Wilcocks reported their views to Robert Morris (Shippen to Morris, July 13, 1789, Ms. Misc. Coll. Shippen [HSP]). George Read sent a copy to Dickinson who was asked to show the bill to Gunning Bedford, Jr. (*supra*, n. 25). Senator Henry of Maryland probably sent Chase a copy (*cf.* Lee, *Memoir of the Life of Richard Henry Lee*, II, 183). How the various Virginians received copies is not clear. Pendleton wrote his criticisms to Madison July 3, but his letter is lost (*cf.* Ms. Madison Papers, XI, 107 [LC]). Madison despatched a copy to Edmund Randolph June 17 (*ibid.*, 84). R. H. Lee apparently sent copies to Mann Page (*cf.* his letter to Lee July 23, 1789, Ms. Lee Family Papers, Library, University of Virginia) and to Richard Parker (*cf.* his letter to Lee July 6, 1789, *ibid.*).

[30] *Maclay Journal*, 100.

whatever was done had to be accommodated to the fact that the ultimate resort, the Supreme Court, was ordained by the Constitution itself. Furthermore, the specifications regarding jurisdiction, original and appellate, subtracted from calculation statutory modification of fundamentals. What Congress was at liberty to do was, however, substantial enough and embraced presumably freedom to act without reference to any model, state or other.

It was, nevertheless, hardly anticipated that there would be any radical departure from tradition, and as respects judicial organization, no belief was more ingrained in this country than that courts were properly to be ordered in terms of inferior and superior jurisdiction. This principle, indeed, had received explicit recognition in the federal Constitution itself. A corollary was the rule of action, no less inveterate, that the hierarchical arrangement of courts could properly serve as a means of controlling the appellate process. These became premises of Committee action, and since they were of such universal application, as we have had occasion to notice, no preliminary canvas of state laws was needed to make them acceptable. Where examination of state jurisprudence did become necessary was in respect to incidents of procedure and practice that found their way into the bill. As indicated below,[31] some items reflect individual experience at the bar—the *lex non scripta* that lawyers then carried around in their heads. Other items were adaptations of familiar statutes. It was wholly adventitious that

---

[31] There are provisions in the Committee bill adopting state usage, such as the manner of setting up an adverse title in the removal section and the compulsion of testimony by defendants in the books and documents section where the draftsman relied upon knowledge of state practice. The provisions which are renditions of state statutes could, we believe, hardly have been drafted from memory alone. This raises the problem of the availability of the sources. There were some good private law libraries in New York, but with practice localized as it then was, it is doubtful whether or not the statutes of sister states were to be found in such collections. It is, however, certain that the new Congress itself had inherited a collection of such statutes. On July 27, 1785, the Continental Congress by resolve requested from the states despatch of thirteen copies of all laws enacted since 1774 (*JCC*, XXIX, 582). The purpose was to preserve a set for Congress and distribute the residue to the several states to promote good understanding. *Cf.* the Secretary's circular, July 28, 1785, in *LMCC*, VIII, 173. A fresh circular was sent August 29 to states which had not complied (*ibid.*, 204), and again October 7 (*ibid.*, 230) and November 9 (*ibid.*, 252). There appears to have been such compliance as was possible under circumstances of paper shortage, limited printings, etc. The residue and remainder of what was submitted is now in Ms. Papers of the Continental Congress, Vols. 74–76 incl. According to a communication of ex-Secretary Thomson to Washington, July 23, 1789 (*LMCC*, VIII, 837–38), the books, letters and papers were deposited "in rooms in the house where the Legislature of the United States now assemble." The statutes were presumably available for the use of the Senate Committee.

A B I L L

TO ESTABLISH THE

JUDICIAL COURTS of the UNITED STATES.

BE IT ENACTED by the fenate and reprefentatives of the United States of America in Congrefs affembled, That the fupreme court of the United ftates fhall confift of a chief juftice and five affociate juftices, any four of whom fhall be a quorum, and fhall hold annually at the feat of the federal government two feffions, the one commencing the firft Monday of February, and the other the firft Monday of Auguft. That the affociate juftices fhall have precedence according to the date of their commiffions, or when the commiffions of two or more of them bear date on the fame day, according to their refpective ages.

AND BE IT FURTHER ENACTED by the authority aforefaid, That the United States fhall be, and they hereby are divided into eleven diftricts to be limited and called as follows, to wit, one to confift of the ftate of New-Hampfhire, and that part of the ftate of Maffachufetts, which lies eafterly of the ftate of New-Hampfhire, and to be called New-Hampfhire diftrict; one to confift of the remaining part of the ftate of Maffachufetts, and to be called Maffachufetts diftrict; one to confift of the ftate of Connecticut, and to be called Connecticut diftrict; one to confift of the ftate of New-York, and to be called New-York diftrict; one to confift of the ftate of New-Jerfey, and to be called New-Jerfey diftrict; one to confift of the ftate of Pennfylvania, and to be called Pennfylvania diftrict; one to confift of the ftate of Delaware, and to be called Delaware diftrict; one to confift of the ftate of Maryland, and to be called Maryland diftrict; one to confift of the ftate of Virginia, and to be called Virginia diftrict; one to confift of the ftate of South-Carolina, and to be called South-Carolina diftrict; and one to confift of the ftate of Georgia, and to be called Georgia diftrict.

AND BE IT FURTHER ENACTED by the authority aforefaid, That there be a court called a diftrict court in each of the afore-mentioned diftricts to confift of one judge, who fhall refide in the diftrict for which he is appointed, and fhall be called a diftrict judge, and fhall hold annually four feffions, the firft of which to commence as follows, to wit, in the diftricts of New-York, and of New-Jerfey on the firft, in the diftrict of Pennfylvania on the fecond, in the diftrict of Connecticut on the third,

Printed Senate Bill—An Act to Establish the Judicial Courts of the United States, page 1.

(Courtesy, Rare Book Division, The New York Public Library, Astor, Lenox and Tilden Foundations)

the superior professional attainments of Committee men from the "eastern states" resulted in a generous borrowing from these jurisdictions.

In terms of its arrangement the Committee bill, and so the statute, was put together logically enough up to and including the section dealing with error to state courts. The bill opens with a direction that the Supreme Court should consist of a Chief Justice and five Associate Justices, any four of whom should be a quorum, fixes the terms for February and August and where these should be kept, and establishes the order of precedence. With all deference, this first section bears resemblance to a playbill, and, indeed, served something of that purpose, for the Justices were characters who were to appear in other sections, and the terms of court were to bear a relation to other parts they were to play. The bill proceeds to settle the districts and District Courts, the circuits and how these were to be kept, the places and times. Then follow provisions regarding adjournment, the appointment of clerks, the oaths; then it moves to jurisdiction and certain specific judicial powers. The last sections of the bill cover a variety of matter so arranged as to withstand attempts at orderly rearrangement. One is tempted to suppose that these sections represent the residue and remainder of a much greater variety of propositions considered by the Committee. Here the act will be considered without strict reference to the sequence of its sections, for we are concerned with its chief features and not with subordinate though necessary provisions such as the form of oaths, powers of adjournment and the like. It will be on the bill as reported that our attention will be focussed, because it seems to us desirable to establish what out of past American experience was written into the act, and such choice was that of the Committee. Not everything fastened upon survived intact the passage through the fiery furnace of congressional debate. But so stubbornly did the chief draftsmen defend their work that they might fairly claim the statute to be of their creation.

Perhaps the most important initial decision made by the full Committee before the sub-committee was charged with preparing a draft was to inter the antifederalist proposal that state courts should serve as federal inferior courts. Two committeemen, Lee of Virginia and Wingate of New Hampshire, came instructed by their respective state conventions to press for amendments which touched on this.[32] New Hampshire desired to confine diverse citizenship litigation to state courts; Virginia among other restraints had voted to limit inferior federal jurisdiction to admiralty and maritime causes. Wingate makes no

---

[32] On the instructions *cf. supra*, c. X, p. 415.

mention in his letters that he sought to execute the New Hampshire direction. But we believe that Lee put forward the Virginia proposition in Committee, for on the first day of debate in the Senate he offered this as an amendment to the bill.[33]

The Committee not only refused to use state courts in lieu of new creations, but heedful of the multiform apprehensions that federal courts would obliterate those of the states, the Union was divided into districts coterminus geographically with state boundaries, except in the case of Maine (then parcel of Massachusetts) that was attached to the New Hampshire District. For the purposes of judicial administration, therefore, a species of artificial federal entities was to come into existence.

The idea of dividing the country into a number of districts with a federal court in each one in lieu of a federal court in each state had been advanced by Hamilton in *Federalist* No. 81 (May 28, 1788).[34] Districting was not a novel thing in state legislation, for Virginia had resorted to it in the District Court Act of 1787[35] which the Court of Appeals had conceived to be unconstitutional for other reasons.[36] This feature was retained when the statute was revised in 1788.[37] The purpose of districting had been to decentralize and make more convenient the administration of justice by transferring to the District Courts powers of the old General Court. An opposite purpose animated the districting of Massachusetts in the bill reconstituting the Supreme Judicial Court that failed of passage, a copy of which had been sent to Caleb Strong.[38] Currently the court sat in each county, and by throwing counties into districts it was sought to make the circuit less arduous. We may suppose that these precedents were of some use in aiding acceptance of the new and artful designation.

In each federal district there was to be a District Court to be held by a judge resident of the district for which he might be appointed. There were to be four sessions annually at both times and places set forth in the bill—in some districts the terms were to be held alternately at different cities with the obvious purpose of making justice accessible, a matter about which Lee had earlier made great to-do. Provision was added for special sessions.

The truly ingenious invention of the Committee was the scheme

[33] *Maclay Journal*, 83.

[34] *The Federalist* (Cooke, ed., 1961), 547. The suggestion thrown out was that the country be divided into districts, and that the federal with state judges make the circuit within each with appeals going directly to the Supreme Court. The Committee, of course, established districts, but the difficulty stemming from the varieties of judicial tenure in the states, and also a supposed difficulty of a conflict in judicial oaths, made the use of state judges impractical.

[35] 12 Hening, *Va. Stats.*, 532.

[36] *Supra*, c. III, p. 129.

[37] 12 Hening, *Va. Stats.*, 730.

[38] See here the report of the revisors referred to *supra*, n. 14.

of Circuit Courts. The districts were grouped into three circuits: the eastern, the middle and the southern—a division of the country that had been used for military administration in the first year of the Revolution.[39] In each district there were to be held annually in the spring and fall two courts to "consist" of any two Justices of the Supreme Court and the District judge. Considered in a historical setting, what the Committee did was to act upon one of the fundamental postulates of English law enforcement and one of tried antiquity, viz., the employment of judicial personnel of the courts at Westminster to dispense justice in the country, sometimes but not invariably in association with local officials.[40] The principle, if such it may be called, was well understood in America, although clumsily executed in Massachusetts and Pennsylvania where the whole or the majority of the bench of the highest court was bundled from county to county. Elsewhere, as in Virginia, New Jersey and New York, it underlay the commissions of Oyer and Terminer, and, of course, in the two latter states the *nisi prius* sittings were a manifestation of the same idea.

The consociation of the District judge with the two Supreme Court Justices seems to us to have resulted from a decision, or perhaps no more than an assumption, that features of state practice in the conduct of litigation would be followed at circuit. It is clear from what was embodied in the bill that it was not conceived to be a proper vehicle for the formulation of rules of pleading and procedure in common law actions, for the Committee went no further than to incorporate some general directions as to process and practice, together with others relating to appellate procedure. There flourished, however, divergencies from

---

[39] *JCC*, IV, 174 (Feb. 27, 1776); *LMCC*, I, 366.

[40] The advantages of the circuit in England had been eloquently expressed by Sir Matthew Hale in his *History of the Common Law*, published posthumously early in the eighteenth century and in its fourth edition in 1779. Hale's comments were particularly relevant to the problems confronting the Committee. After describing the close intellectual and professional relations of the judges at Westminster Hall, he proceeds: "[B]y this means their judgments and their administration of common justice, carry a *consonancy, congruity* and *uniformity one to another*; whereby both the laws and the administrations thereof, are preserved from that confusion and disparity that

would unavoidably ensue, if the administration was by several *incommunicating* hands, or by *provincial* establishments" (4th ed., 289). Prior to the appearance of Blackstone's *Commentaries*, Hale's book was a basic text for those commencing the study of law. It was used by John Adams (*Adams Papers*, ser. 1, I, 169); it was included in the curriculum prepared for apprentices by William Smith, Jr., the New York lawyer (P. M. Hamlin, *Legal Education in Colonial New York* [New York: New York University Press, 1939], App. VIII), and appears to have been used by William Samuel Johnson of Connecticut to whom a copy of Smith's curriculum was sent (G. C. Groce, *William Samuel Johnson: A Maker of the Constitution*, 17–18.

English common law procedures and native inventions in every state peculiar to its jurisprudence. It could not be expected that Supreme Court Justices bred in the procedure of one jurisdiction would be privy to the procedure of other states. The District judge, consequently, would serve as the resident expert. The importance of this role was to be further underlined by the Senate's addition of section 34, which will later be considered.

If what may be described as the localization of the federal inferior courts revealed an intention to quiet the alarums raised regarding the threatened inconvenience of the federal system, the handling of questions of jurisdiction indicates a similar sensitivity to other criticisms. Except for the admiralty jurisdiction, to which we shall come in a moment, the District Court was conceived as a very inferior court indeed.[41] The criminal jurisdiction, "exclusively" of state courts, was confined to crimes cognizable under the authority and defined by the laws of the United States, where punishment was limited to thirty stripes, a maximum fine of $100 or a six-month term of imprisonment "except where the laws of the United States shall otherwise direct." This exception was probably written in to give future elasticity to the criminal jurisdiction, but it was thrown out by the House of Representatives. In criminal cases trial of facts was to be by jury.

The heads of civil jurisdiction concerned actions by foreigners for torts only in violation of the law of nations or a treaty of the United States, cognizance of which was to be concurrent with state or Circuit Courts, and similarly concurrent were suits at common law where the United States or a common informer[42] sued and the amount in dispute exclusive of costs did not exceed $100. In respect to both types of cause, trial was to be by jury.

Sandwiched between the specification regarding criminal causes

---

[41] Although the printed bill bore no section numbers, that dealing with the jurisdiction of the District Court was the tenth (in the Judiciary Act, sec. 9). Interposed between the section fixing the terms of the Circuit and sec. 10 were: sec. 6, dealing with the adjournment of the several courts; sec. 7, providing for the appointment of clerks by the Supreme Court and the District Court and the oath to be exacted; sec. 8, stipulating oaths for the Justices of the Supreme Court and the District judges; sec. 9, containing a proviso for affirmations by Quakers wherever an oath was required. Maclay (*Journal*, 86) relates how in the Senate the proviso was broadened by striking the word "Quakers." This section was incorporated into sec. 7 of the printed bill to make sec. 7 of the statute. The Senate added the direction regarding the bonding of clerks. Ms. Senate Engrossed Bill, Sen. Files, Book 1 (NA).

[42] The Senate struck the provision regarding suits by a common informer. Ms. Senate Engrossed Bill, Sen. Files, Book 1 (NA). Why the Senate relucted is not clear, for ten days after the Judiciary Bill was passed, the "Collection of Duties Act" was approved which contained in sec. 38 provision for an informer's share. 1 *U.S. Stats.*, 48.

and the civil pleas just mentioned was the real meat of the District Court's jurisdiction—the exclusive original cognizance of "all civil causes of admiralty and maritime jurisdiction"—something that antifederalists generally had conceded was properly federal. This jurisdiction was to comprehend all seizures under laws of impost, navigation or trade of the United States where the seizures were made within the district on waters navigable by sea by vessels of ten or more tons burden, as well as upon the high seas. Since jury trial was expressly stipulated as to the other heads of jurisdiction, it may be inferred that here this was not to be the case. This was later to be made explicit.

That violations of customs and acts of trade were to be prosecuted as admiralty causes has seemed surprising to one commentator[43] aware of the pre-Revolutionary rage against this aspect of royal vice-admiralty jurisdiction. But the states of Connecticut,[44] New York[45] and, where a non-citizen was a party, Virginia[46] had adopted juryless procedure for enforcement of their impost acts and we have seen no evidence of local dissatisfaction publicly expressed. The Committee bill, furthermore, saved to suitors in all cases a right to a common law remedy where the common law was competent to give it.

At what the saving clause was aimed is obscure. The Framers of the Constitution had established "cases of admiralty and maritime jurisdiction" as a category to which the judicial power extended on the basis of the report of the Committee of Detail, but there had been no discussion of the implications of this combination. "Maritime jurisdiction" had no fixed technical meaning in English law. The expression, however, had been in the way of acquiring such in American usage because of the tenor of state legislation enacted beginning in 1775 and already noticed in connection with the establishment of admiralty and prize courts. Thus, the Virginia statute (1779)[47] conferred on its admiralty court jurisdiction over "all maritime causes," and by directing that proceedings and decisions be, *inter alia*, according to the laws of Oleron and the

---

[43] Warren, "Judiciary Act," 74.

[44] "An Act for levying and collecting a Duty . . . ," *Acts and Laws*, May Sess. 1784, appended to *Acts and Laws of the State of Connecticut* (1784 revision), 271 at 274.

[45] *N.Y. Laws*, 8 Sess. 1784, c. 7. In 1787 the option of proceeding in the court of exchequer, mayor's court or common pleas courts was added, but the option lay only with the collector or the Attorney General (*ibid.*, 10 Sess. 1787, c. 81). Hough, *Reports of Cases in the Vice-Admiralty of the Province of New York and in the*

Court of Admiralty of the State of New York, 1715–1788, reports one revenue case in admiralty (at 252).

[46] By sec. 44 of "An act to amend the several acts . . . concerning naval officers and the collection of the Duties" (1787) actions for forfeitures were fixed in the admiralty court. 12 Hening, *Va. Stats.*, 438. According to the statute constituting the admiralty court, a jury trial was available only if the parties were both citizens of Virginia.

[47] 10 *ibid.*, 98.

Imperial laws (so far as observed by the English courts of admiralty) and the laws of nature and nations furnished a passport for great enlargement of traditional English admiralty jurisdiction. The reference in the Massachusetts statute establishing its Maritime Court was, it will be recalled, to procedure according to the civil law, a less ample direction.[48] But the Massachusetts act gave this court exclusive jurisdiction over seamen's wages, a matter over which common law courts had had concurrent jurisdiction, as well as "other maritime matters" about which there existed no specific direction in the laws of the state.[49] This was a grant broad enough to include marine insurance contracts, something a part of the *droit maritime* of continental countries where civil law prevailed.

Until more is known about the operation of these new state courts, the extent to which they had overrun traditional Anglo-American lines is uncertain. It was James Kent's opinion that the expression "maritime jurisdiction" in the Constitution had been added *ex industria*,[50] and if this was indeed the case, the deliberate purpose was to extend the federal judicial power to everything theretofore handled by state courts under this heading. The purpose of the saving clause in the Judiciary Bill may therefore well have been to restore the jurisdictional balance between admiralty and common law courts as it had existed in the colonies. The explicit authority given the Supreme Court in another section to issue writs of prohibition to District Courts when proceeding as courts of admiralty and maritime jurisdiction lends some support for this opinion.

If the District Courts were viewed primarily as courts of special jurisdiction, the Circuit Courts were erected as courts of general original jurisdiction, so far as such was envisaged by the Constitution. Certain appellate powers were added, but spelled out in a later section. The Committee seems to have paid due regard to antifederalist criticism of a federal system by fixing a minimum above $500 (exclusive of costs) for civil actions in law and equity; by forbidding arrests of defendants in one district for trial in another; and by limiting actions by original process against an inhabitant of the United States in any district other than where he might be an inhabitant or be found at the time of service. At the end of this section was appended one of the most important pacifiers in the bill: neither District nor Circuit Courts should have cognizance of any action to recover the "contents" of any promissory note or chose in

---

[48] In 1778 and 1779.

[49] 5 *Acts and Resolves Prov. of Mass. Bay*, 807. And compare *Acts and Laws of Connecticut*, May Sess. 1776, "Civil Law" and "Laws of Nations"; *Acts of the Council and General Assembly of the State of New Jersey 1776–83* (Wilson ed.), c. 290, "Maritime Law and the Law of Nations."

[50] Kent, *Commentaries*, I, 369.

action in favor of an assignee unless an action might have been prosecuted in these courts as if no assignment had been made. Lee had warned against the establishment of diversity by subterfuge in his second pamphlet,[51] and at the Virginia Convention it was the assignment of specialties which George Mason chose as an example of how improperly the diversity jurisdiction might operate.[52]

The original civil jurisdiction of the Circuit Courts lay where the United States was a plaintiff or petitioner or where a "foreigner" or citizen of a state other than one in which suit was brought was a party. This jurisdiction was to be exercised concurrently with state courts, or (and here the Committee failed to consult the Constitution) with the Supreme Court. Upon the Circuit was also bestowed cognizance of all crimes and offenses against the United States, cognizable under the laws of the United States and defined by the laws of the same except where otherwise provided in the act or where the laws should otherwise direct. Concurrent jurisdiction with the District Courts of offenses there cognizable was also provided.

In a succeeding section some of the significance of the grant of concurrent jurisdiction with state courts was subtracted by establishing a privilege of removing causes commenced in such courts against a "foreigner" or a citizen of another state to the next Circuit Court in the district. Motion for removal had to be made at the time when appearance was entered in the state court. Security for appearance and other details relating to the transfer amounting to a removal of copies of the record as far as it went were set out. The bill stated that it "shall then be the duty of the state court to accept the surety, and dismiss further proceedings." In the Circuit Court the cause was to proceed as if brought there by original process.[53]

The Committee elected to place in the removal section the only dispositions made regarding jurisdiction over cases between citizens of the same state claiming lands under grants of different states. This was not made a head of original jurisdiction because it is patent that as respects civil actions or suits the premise upon which the Committee acted was to limit such original jurisdiction to diversity cases except where the United States was plaintiff. Consequently, it was provided that where action was commenced in a state court where the title of land was concerned, the parties being citizens of the same state and the

---

[51] *An Additional Number of Letters from the Federal Farmer* (1788), 177.

[52] Elliot, *Debates*, III, 526.

[53] This section did not on its face contemplate removal of the record itself but only copies. A change made by the House that the application be by petition and not by motion presumably had the effect of amplifying what would be transferred. It was evidently conceived that no writ would be necessary to effect the transfer but that this would be the responsibility of the moving party.

matter in dispute exceeding $500, and the defendant pleaded in bar, and set up a grant from a state other than that where the suit was pending and moved that plaintiff set forth his title, the latter "shall set it forth in his replication." If this title was founded upon a grant from the state where action was pending, defendant might on motion have the cause removed to the Circuit Court. Defendant then would have to abide by his plea in bar. These directions, insofar as they prescribed the course of pleading in the state court, amounted to something of an invasion of state prerogative and could only have given pause to the advocates of using state courts as inferior federal courts under federal regulation. The Senate was to amend the details of the procedure but did not retreat from the position of prescribing how the state courts were to act.

The regulation of original jurisdiction was rounded out by a section dealing with the Supreme Court—a section which was also to be amended by the Senate. The Committee bill provided that the Supreme Court should have exclusive jurisdiction of all controversies of a "civil" nature where any of the United States or a foreign state was a party except between a state and its citizens.[54] It was to have original but not exclusive jurisdiction over civil controversies between a state and citizens of other states or foreigners. For reasons unknown, the Committee undertook to confect variations on the constitutional direction that the Supreme Court should have original jurisdiction in all cases affecting ambassadors, other public ministers and consuls. The bill fragmented this by stipulating such exclusive jurisdiction as a court of law could have or exercise consistently with the law of nations of suits or proceedings *against* ambassadors, public ministers or consuls, and added *ex abundanti* their domestics or domestic servants. It was to have original but not exclusive jurisdiction of all suits for trespass brought by the same. The trial of facts in all actions in the Supreme Court against citizens was to be by jury. Nothing was stated regarding the mode of trial in cases involving diplomatic personnel. In this section, too, was the direction that this court should have power to issue writs of prohibition, as already noticed, and writs of mandamus "in cases warranted by the principles and usages of law, to any courts appointed, or persons holding office under the authority of the United States."

In the section next following, all the courts of the United States were empowered to issue writs of *scire facias*, habeas corpus and all other writs not specially provided for by statute that might be necessary for their exercise of their jurisdictions "and agreeable to the principles

---

[54] Warren, "Judiciary Act," 93, asserts that the words "except between a State and its citizens" were inserted by the Senate. The words appear in the printed bill and for that matter in the ms. draft.

and usages of law." Habeas corpus could issue to inquire into the cause of commitment, with the proviso that it extended only to prisoners in jail under color of the authority of the United States, committed by a federal court for trial at such or were "necessary to be brought into court to testify." The Committee's working draft had added writs of subpoena and protections of witnesses, but this was struck before the bill reached final form.[55]

The regulation of appellate jurisdiction by the Committee reveals an intention of placing restraints upon the native zest for pressing a cause through all possible stages of review. Appeals from final decrees of a District Court in admiralty and maritime causes where the matter in controversy exceeded $300 exclusive of costs were to be allowed to the next Circuit Court in the district. Similarly final decrees or judgments in civil actions in a District Court if the matter in dispute exceeded $50 exclusive of costs might be re-examined and reversed or affirmed in the Circuit Court for the same district. Procedure was to be by "petition in error"—a method once used to secure review by the House of Lords in England,[56] and still the method of pursuing a supersedeas for review in Virginia.[57] The petition in error had to contain an authenticated transcript of the record, an assignment of errors and a prayer for reversal with a citation to the adverse party annexed and signed by the District judge or a Supreme Court judge.[58]

That the Committee intended to make the Circuit Court the final resort on review of District Court judgments or decrees, except for one category, is apparent from the stipulations regarding the review by the Supreme Court of judgments and decrees from the Circuit Courts. Here, too, the process was to be by petition in error. As already noticed, Caleb

---

[55] Warren, *ibid.*, 95, claims that the striking was done by the Senate, but the provision is not in the printed bill.

[56] Coke, *Fourth Institute*, 21.

[57] So in the "Act for Establishing the General Court" (1777), sec. 46 (9 Hening, *Va. Stats.*, 401), and continued in the District Court Act of 1787 (12 *ibid.*, 532, c. 91) and of 1788 (*ibid.*, 730, c. 88). For an example of the petition, Peachy and Ford v. Cryer, Aug. 18, 1787, in Ms. Tucker-Coleman Papers, box and folder "Virginia High Court of Chancery" (Earl Gregg Swem Library, College of William and Mary in Virginia).

In 1788 Massachusetts by statute instituted a practice of allowing petitions to the Supreme Judicial Court where writs of review were not obtainable as of course (1 *Laws of the Comm. of Mass. 1780–1800* [1801], 423). John Rutledge when attorney general of South Carolina had reported in 1765 that error proceedings there were to be initiated by petition in error (Ms. Journal of the South Carolina Council 1765–1766, XXXII, 503 *et seq.*).

[58] Transcript of the record and assignment of errors was standard procedure in state error proceedings and patterned on English usage, on which *cf.* G. Crompton, *Practice common-placed: or . . . Practice in the Courts of King's Bench and Common Pleas*, 2d ed., (1783), II, 370 *et seq.*

Strong had written Paine in May that the Supreme Court was to have appellate jurisdiction "where the value is 2000 dollars." The bill, however, provided nothing of the sort, for the power of review extended to "final judgments and decrees in civil actions and suits in equity in a circuit court brought there by original process or removed there from the courts of the several states, or if the matter in dispute exceeds the sum or value of (2000) dollars exclusive of costs, removed there by appeal from a district court." The effect of this was to confine the monetary limitation to the review of cases brought up to the Circuit on appeal from the District Courts.[59]

Two peculiarities relating to proceedings in error deserve to be noticed. The first is the absence of any mention of a bill of exceptions, an instrument essential to secure review of mistakes of law that in strict common law practice never appeared on a record.[60] The second concerns the use of error to review chancery decrees, a strange departure from classical chancery practice. For this, however, there is the ready explanation that by statute in Connecticut error was the mode of reviewing chancery decrees, and consequently a normal procedure to Ellsworth.[61]

A section dealing with the effect of a writ of error as a supersedeas to stay execution confirms the fact that the Committee had not made a

---

[59] Warren, "Judiciary Act," at 102, claims that the words "brought there by original process or removed there from Courts of the several states" were added by the Senate. This is incorrect; the words were in the printed Committee bill. Warren was misled by the fact that in the ms. draft which preceded the printed bill the words were written in the margin and marked for insertion in the main text.

It should further be noticed that in error to the Supreme Court the citation was to be signed by a judge of the Circuit or a Justice of the Supreme Court, and upon signing security had to be taken that the petitioners in error would prosecute to effect and answer all damages and costs "if he fail to make his plea good." Such petitions had to be brought within three years after "rendering or passing" of judgment. There was to be no reversal either in the Circuit or Supreme Court for error in ruling on a plea in abatement other than to the jurisdiction or such plea to a petition or bill in equity in the nature of a demurrer.

[60] The failure to authorize the bill

of exceptions may possibly be attributed to the then precarious status of the instrument in Connecticut. When Ellsworth was on the bench of the Superior Court this bill was still a newcomer. This emerges from a dissent of Roger Sherman J. in Huntington v. Champlin (Kirby 166 at 168 [1786]) where it is stated that there had been not more than two or three instances of error brought on such a bill. In this case the bill had been drawn by the party excepting and Sherman thought it a self-serving document. In 1787 the point was further argued in McDonald v. Fisher (*ibid.*, 339). Here, too, the bill had been drawn by one party and signed by the judge. No opinion of the court was reported, but it would appear from the brief judgment on the pleading that only an agreed statement of facts as in Fabrigas v. Mostyn (20 Howell, *State Trials*, 82) would suffice. This may serve to explain the language of Ellsworth's amendment which became sec. 19 of the Judiciary Act, *infra*.

[61] *Acts and Laws of the State of Connecticut* (1784), 51.

sum in controversy in excess of $2,000 a condition precedent for error to the Supreme Court. Its mention of a minimum related only to the automatic stay of execution. And the petition could only operate as a supersedeas if the matter in dispute, exclusive of costs, exceeded the sum of $300 in District Court, or if in a Circuit Court, $2,000. More-ever, the further condition was imposed that the petition be served on an adversary by lodgment in the clerk's office, where the record remained, within ten days after the judgment rendered or a decree passed. Where the amount in dispute did not exceed the sums mentioned and there was no reversal, petitioner in error was liable to double costs. In the event of an affirmance when execution had been stayed, the Supreme or Circuit Court "shall adjudge or decree . . . just damages" as well as costs.

As to the judgments or decrees on error to the Circuit Court, the latter was empowered to render such judgment or pass such decree as the District Court should have done. The Supreme Court was to do the same on reversals there, except that where the judgment should be in favor of the plaintiff or petitioner in the original suit, and the damages to be assessed or the matter decreed were uncertain, "they shall send the cause back for a final decision." The Supreme Court was not to issue execution but to send a special mandate to the Circuit to award the same.[62] This section, it may be remarked, was passed intact by the Senate. The purists in the House substituted the word "remand" for "send back."

The succeeding section in the bill, the principle of which had been settled by May 24, was perhaps the boldest, for it furnished implementa-tion of the supreme law of the land clause. Briefly, it provided for the re-examination, reversal or affirmance by the Supreme Court on petition in error of a final judgment or decree in the highest court of law or equity of a state where was drawn in question the validity of a treaty, statute or authority exercised under the United States, and the decision was against this validity; or where the validity of a statute of or au-thority exercised under any state was drawn in question on the ground of being repugnant to the treaties or laws of the United States and the decision was in favor of this validity; or where the construction of any clause of the Constitution, a treaty, a statute of or a commission held under the United States was drawn in question. The assignments of error were explicitly confined to the questions of validity set out in the

---

[62] E.g., provided in New York for the Court for the Trial of Impeach-ments and Correction of Errors (N.Y. Laws, 8 Sess. 1784, c. 11) and in Virginia "An act constituting the Court of Appeals" (1779) (10 Hen-ing, Va. Stats., 89). The English practice summarized in Crompton, Practice common-placed: or . . . Practice in the Courts of King's Bench and Common Pleas, II, at 382, 387, 393.

section. The citation was to be signed by the chief justice or chancellor rendering judgment or passing the decree complained of, or by a Justice of the Supreme Court of the United States in the same manner and subject to the same regulations, and the petitions should have the same effect as if the judgment or decree had been rendered in a Circuit Court. The proceedings on reversal should also be the same, except where a cause had "been once so sent back before" the Supreme Court was given discretion to proceed to a final decision and award execution. This was a signal break with tradition in cases of error.[63] It was apparently devised to meet the situation where a judgment or decree of the Supreme Court would not be executed by a state court and supplementary proceedings in error were brought. Ellsworth had had first-hand experience with this species of state recalcitrance when he was a member of the Standing Committee for hearing prize appeals both in the case of the sloop *Active* and in *Doane v. Tredwell and Penhallow*,[64] and we consequently believe that this provision was the result.

The incidents of judicial power relating to practice that the Committee fastened upon for statutory mention were on the face of things capricious and were scattered through the bill. In addition to the power to issue writs, already noticed, all courts of the United States were authorized to grant new trials, in cases where there had been a trial by jury, for reasons for which new trials have been granted in courts of law. No other retrospective motions were specified. The lack of precision in the direction regarding new trials was the result of considerable variation in state practice. In New Jersey, New York and Virginia, for example, common law had been followed. Massachusetts had its ancient review procedure recently given fresh statutory footing,[65] while Connecticut was in process of executing a new and imprecise statute.[66] In

---

[63] This was the long-established common law rule that execution could issue only from the court where the record remained, a proposition on which there was substantial authority. Only a transcript of the record would be before the Supreme Court.

[64] *Supra*, pp. 165–67, 179.

[65] 1 *Laws of the Commonwealth of Massachusetts 1780–1800* (1801), 369 (1787). Colonial practice discussed *supra*, c. I.

[66] Cf. *Acts and Laws of the State of Connecticut* (1784), 6. The Connecticut history of motions for new trial was described by counsel in *Dorr v. Chapman* (1787), Kirby 205. "Anciently" new trials had only been obtainable by petition to the legislature. By statute the Superior and county courts had been authorized to grant new trials for mispleading, discovery of new evidence or "other reasonable cause appearing, according to the usual rules and methods in such cases." Application by petition was eventually supplanted by motion. It would appear, however, from Sumner v. Lyman (1787), *ibid.*, 241, and Noyce v. Huntington, *ibid.*, 282, that petition was still the accepted procedure. On this cf. Z. Swift, *A System of the Laws of the State of Connecticut* (1796), II, 270. In England it was rare to grant new trials on the ground of new evidence.

England, and in America where the *nisi prius* system had been instituted, the motion for a new trial was made before the full bench of the court where the record originated, and this bench had before it a report of the judge before whom the issue had been tried. Two of the chief grounds upon which such motions were based were incorrect rulings on the admissibility of evidence and misdirections of the jury by the judge.[67] In the system projected by the Committee, it was expecting the unlikely, that a judge of a District Court would admit to either transgression, and it did not occur to the Senate to correct this. Curiously enough, the Committee made provision to meet such a dilemma in a separate section dealing with such motions in the three-judge Circuit Courts, probably because these were to be forums for important civil actions. Here,[68] after judgment entered upon a verdict in a civil action, it was open to either party, at the discretion of the court and under such conditions for the security of the adverse party as might be fixed, to move for a stay of execution for forty-two days from the time of entering judgment. This was to give time to file a motion for new trial and a certificate from "either" of the judges permitting filing of the motion. It would be in the judge's discretion to refuse the certificate. If granted, execution would be stayed until a new trial was had.

Because a motion for a new trial *after* judgment was a Connecticut aberration, the draftsmen were again having recourse to the law of that state. Nothing resembling the procedure can be found in the contemporary English practice books. The Committee was presumably attempting to create a substitute for the new trial mechanism of the *nisi prius* system that would make available to litigants all the accepted grounds for new trial motions. Where the ground of such a motion was a misdirection by a judge, it is obvious that movant could anticipate relief only if, at the session of the Circuit next following a motion granted, the bench was differently populated. The Committee, it may be further observed, indicated nothing regarding a hearing on the application for a certificate or a review of a ruling.

Appendant to the section conveying power to grant new trials was authorization to establish rules for the orderly conduct of business in the courts, as well as power to impose and administer oaths and to punish by fine and imprisonment at the discretion of the courts all contempts of authority "in any cause or hearing" before them. It should be noticed

---

[67] The common law practice discussed in J. Sheridan, *Present Practice of the Court of King's Bench* (1785), 294. For New York, *cf.* *LPAH*, II, c. I.

[68] This became sec. 18 of the statute. For reasons unknown, the House provided in lieu of a motion that a petition be filed.

The United States Supreme Court Bench during Its First Decade

JOHN JAY.
First Chief Justice of the United States Supreme Court, September 1789–
June 1795. Portrait by Gilbert Stuart.
(Courtesy of National Gallery of Art)

JOHN RUTLEDGE,
South Carolina. Associate Justice of the United States Supreme Court, September 1789; resigned March 1791. Appointed Chief Justice, July 1, 1795; sat August term, 1795; rejected, December 15, 1795. Portrait by John Trumbull.
(*Courtesy of Yale University Art Gallery*)

WILLIAM CUSHING,
Massachusetts. Associate Justice of the United States Supreme Court, December 1789–September 1810. Pastel attributed to James Sharples.
(Courtesy of the Independence National Historical Park Collection, Philadelphia)

JAMES WILSON,
Pennsylvania. Associate Justice of the United States Supreme Court, September 1789–August 1798. Water color on ivory, undetermined artist.
(*Courtesy of National Collection of Fine Arts, Smithsonian Institution*)

JOHN BLAIR,
Virginia. Associate Justice of the United States Supreme Court, September
1789–January 1796. Portrait by Charles Wilson Peale.
(Collections of the Library of Congress)

JAMES IREDELL,
North Carolina. Associate Justice of the United States Supreme Court, February 1790–October 1799. Engraving after portrait by C. B. J. F. Saint-Mémin.
(Collections of the Library of Congress)

THOMAS JOHNSON,
Maryland. Associate Justice of the United States Supreme Court, November
1791–March 1793. Copy by Charles Wilson Peale of head in family portrait
by C. W. Peale at the Maryland Historical Society. This copy is now in the
State House, Annapolis, Maryland.
(Courtesy of Maryland State House)

WILLIAM PATERSON,
New Jersey. Associate Justice of the United States Supreme Court, March
1793–September 1806. Portrait by James Sharples.
(Collections of the Library of Congress)

SAMUEL CHASE,
Maryland. Associate Justice of the United States Supreme Court, January
1796–June 1811. Portrait by John Wesley Jarvis.
(Courtesy of National Portrait Gallery, Smithsonian Institution)

OLIVER ELLSWORTH,
Connecticut. Chief Justice of the United States Supreme Court, March 1796–
September 1800. Portrait by James Sharples.
(*Courtesy of the Independence National Historical Park Collection, Philadelphia*)

BUSHROD WASHINGTON,
Virginia. Associate Justice of the United States Supreme Court, December
1798–November 1829. Portrait by James Sharples.
(*Courtesy of the Independence National Historical Park Collection, Philadelphia*)

ALFRED MOORE,
North Carolina. Associate Justice of the United States Supreme Court, December 1799–March 1804. Portrait, American School (Nineteenth Century).
(Courtesy of Mrs. Iredell W. Iglehart and the Frick Art Reference Library)

that the draftsmen, scrupulous to mention jury trial where it was intended this be had, did not see fit to do so in this particular.[69]

Although in a separate section[70] the prescript was laid down that suits in equity should not be sustained in either of the courts of the United States in any case where a remedy might be had at law, the Committee was not averse to making certain equity procedures handmaidens of common law actions. One of these was the specification of authority to require production of books and papers in such actions "in cases and under circumstances where they might be compelled to produce the same by the ordinary rules of proceeding in chancery."[71] More than this, if plaintiff upon motion and notice could show to the satisfaction of the court that he without fault of his had been deprived of evidence to support his cause, defendant could be required to disclose under oath his knowledge of the cause, as a respondent might be so required under chancery rules. This was implemented by the threat of non-suit if plaintiff refused to produce books, and judgment by default if defendant failed to comply with an order so to do or to make disclosure on oath. The chancery sanction of contempt was conspicuously absent.

What was set out in this section was substantially the discovery procedure as it had been and was being used in the Chancery Court of New York.[72] This was an aspect of the chancery jurisdiction as assistant to courts of law, for at this time the powers of the latter to order production of books and papers were restricted in scope,[73] and the general rule of the incompetency of parties in interest to testify, a rule not regarded by Courts of Chancery, led litigants to that court for succor. In the Committee bill, however, the procedure was not conceived as an ancillary one but as incidental to any civil action. This was how the matter stood in Connecticut practice, where there was no bill of discovery but where it had long been the rule that plaintiff could call upon defendant to disclose any particular facts. Such disclosure, however, was conclusive of facts disclosed. We think that the Connecticut practice, so familiar to Ellsworth, was the source of this section, but without the rule of conclusiveness of defendant's testimony.[74] As we shall shortly see, the section was to be disembowelled by the Senate.

---

[69] Reflecting in this particular what has been established to have been the usage in all of the colonies; cf. the elaborate historical documentation in Appendix to the brief of the United States, Harris v. U.S., 382 U.S. 162 (Brief No. 6, Oct. Term, 1965).

[70] Sec. 16 of the statute.

[71] Sec. 15 of the statute.

[72] *LPAH*, I, 170, 173 and notes.

[73] F. Buller, *Introduction to the Law relative to Trials at Nisi Prius* (1791), 245 et seq.

[74] Z. Swift, *A System of the Laws of the State of Connecticut*, II, 475; Z. Swift, *A Digest of the Law of Evidence* (1810), 117. This last is for our purposes a late source, but the practice is depicted by Swift as of long standing.

A second borrowing from equity, not, indeed, from English Chancery practice but from the New England version of equity, was the procedure where action was brought to recover the forfeiture annexed to any agreement, bond, specialty, etc., and where forfeiture, breach or non-performance was found by a jury, default or confession of a defendant, or on demurrer, the court should render judgment for the plaintiff to recover so much as might be due according to equity.[75] This procedure was, of course, the New England practice of "chancering" bonds, described in the Massachusetts code of 1648 as a "matter of equitie,"[76] used in New Hampshire[77] and also in Connecticut.[78] This section, which in the manuscript draft was written by Strong, was a rendition of the first paragraph of a Massachusetts statutory revision of 1785.[79]

There was to be some selective borrowing from English Chancery practice in the long section dealing with methods of proof which, ironically enough, opened with a repudiation of the traditional methods of handling testimony both in Chancery and in Admiralty.[80] It was laid down that in the trial of all causes in the courts of the United States as well in causes of equity and admiralty as in common law actions the mode of proof by oral testimony and the examination of witnesses be identical. This amounted to a reception of the chanceryless New England procedure. Virginia had authorized *viva voce* testimony and jury trial in the statute erecting a High Court of Chancery (1777)[81] but in 1783 had repealed this section of the law.[82]

The general proposition with which this section opened called for some qualification to cope with the problem of securing the testimony of persons living out of a district or remote from the place of trial, an inconvenience about which the antifederalists had raised great clamor. This problem had been met variously by acts of assembly in some colonies and subsequently in some of the new states by validating the

---

[75] Sec. 24 of the bill. As amended, sec. 26 of the statute.

[76] *Laws and Liberties of Massachusetts*, Introduction by M. Farrand (1929 ed.), 32; repeated in the Code of 1660, *Col. Laws Mass.*, 167; Act of 1698, in 1 *Acts and Laws Prov. of Mass. Bay*, 356.

[77] Act of 1699, *Acts and Laws of His Majesty's Province of New Hampshire in New England* (1771), 7. Exemplified in Dering v. Packer, a New Hampshire litigation which was initiated in 1757, taken on appeal to the Privy Council and decided in 1760.

An account of the proceedings there in 4 Dallas, App., xxiii. See also Smith, *Appeals to the Privy Council from the American Plantations*, 500–02.

[78] *Acts and Laws of the Colony of Connecticut* (1769), 5; in the 1784 revision, *Acts and Laws of the State of Connecticut*, 6.

[79] 1 *Laws of the Commonwealth of Massachusetts 1780–1800* (1801), 251.

[80] Sec. 27 of the bill; sec. 30 of the statute.

[81] 9 Hening, *Va. Stats.*, 389.

[82] 11 *ibid.*, 342.

use of affidavits or depositions.[83] The New York practice was the most advanced for no conditions were imposed; it did not even provide that testimony taken by commission be *de bene esse*—a chancery procedure which the common law courts had appropriated for depositions of persons going abroad.

---

[83] In Massachusetts Bay Colony the Code of 1660 had authorized that testimony be taken in writing, not to be used if the witness lived within ten miles of the court and was not ill or in prison. After Massachusetts became a royal province, an act substantially in the same terms as the provision in the federal Judiciary Act of 1789 was enacted in 1695. 1 *Acts and Resolves Prov. of Mass. Bay*, 225. This statute was presumably still in force under c. VI, Art. VI, of the Constitution of 1780. It was not revised until 1798. 2 *Laws of the Commonwealth of Mass. 1780–1800* (1801), 800. New Hampshire copied the Massachusetts law in 1701. This was disallowed by the Crown in 1706 (2 *APC Col.*, 847), but the compiler of *Acts and Laws Prov. of New Hampshire* (1771), 22–23, included the act, indicating that no attention had been paid to the disallowance.

The Connecticut statutes which omitted the depositions to perpetuate testimony also were in debt to Massachusetts Bay; *cf. Acts and Laws of Connecticut* (1702), 116, and the compilation of 1769, at 254. The revision of 1784 left the matter on substantially the same footing as it had been. *Acts and Laws of the State of Connecticut* (1784), 263.

In New York it was not until 1746 that commissions to take affidavits from witnesses in the counties for use in the Supreme Court were authorized. 3 *Col. Laws N.Y.*, 546. The substance of this was continued by *N.Y. Laws*, 11 Sess. 1788, c. 46. For examination of out-of-state witnesses, *N.Y. Laws*, 12 Sess. 1789, c. 28, sec. 4. No statutory authorization has been found for New Jersey or Maryland, but both of these states had Chancery courts from which aid might be sought. A Pennsylvania act of 1706 (2 *Stats. at Large Pa.*, 271) re depositions of persons ill or leaving the province was disallowed Jan. 8, 1707/8. E. B. Russell, *The Review of American Colonial Legislation . . . ,* 163n. It would appear from the arguments and decision in Mifflin v. Bingham, 1 Dallas 272, 275–76 (1788), the question was settled by rule of the Supreme Court. If a subpoena was taken out, a deposition might be read in evidence if a witness was about to leave the country. Curiously enough, the Court of Common Pleas of Philadelphia County found its authority in Sheridan, *Present Practice of King's Bench*; *cf.* Gilpin v. Semple, 1 Dallas 251 (1788).

Virginia made provision for depositions in 1753, but despite the vast reaches of settled country did not allow such on the ground of remoteness of a place of trial (6 Hening, *Va. Stats.*, 337). This was carried forward after statehood in the General Court Act of 1777 (9 *ibid.*, 401). Richard Henry Lee, in 1787, made great to-do about attending far-off federal courts. The most his own state had conceded was to permit in the District Court Act of 1788 depositions to be taken of persons going to Kentucky or residing there (12 *ibid.*, 747).

No statute has been found for South Carolina, although in the "Act for establishing County Courts," 1785, sec. 16 (7 *South Carolina Stats.* [1840], 219) the reference to refusal to give evidence before commissioners appointed to take depositions indicates an existing practice.

On the limits of English common law indulgence of depositions, Crompton, *Practice common-placed: or . . . Practice in the Courts of King's Bench and Common Pleas*, I, at 229.

The New York law was clearly not the source used by the Committee. The indications all point to reliance upon the New England practice. The circumstances under which depositions *de bene esse* were to be allowed in civil actions in all United States courts were where a person lived out of a district and at a greater distance than one hundred miles from the place of trial, or was bound on a sea voyage or was about to go out of the United States, or out of the district more than one hundred miles from the place of trial and at the time of trial. Such depositions might be taken by any federal judge or state judge—even those of inferior courts. The adverse party was to be notified in advance and he was given leave to put interrogatories to be served on his adversary or attorney. Witnesses might be compelled to appear and depose in the same manner as to appear and testify in courts.

This same section set out the circumstances under which such depositions might be used in admiralty and maritime causes, and appended was the astonishing provision that in the trial of such cause in a District Court, the decree in which might be appealed from, if either party satisfied the court that "probably it will not be in his power to produce the witnesses there testifying, before the circuit court should an appeal be had" and should move that this testimony be taken down in writing, this should be done by the clerk. Nevertheless, if an appeal was had, such testimony could be used only if the court was satisfied that the witnesses had departed the United States, or were out of the district "where the trial is, and to a greater distance than as aforesaid [100 miles] from the place where the court is sitting or that by reason of age, sickness, bodily infirmity or imprisonment they are unable to travel and appear at court."

Apart from the light which this provision throws upon the Committee's understanding of procedure in admiralty appeals, it is a notable exhibit on how little seems to have been learned from the experiences of both the Standing Committee of Congress and the Court of Appeals in Cases of Capture with the problem of securing something resembling a record from state prize courts. The appeal was apparently conceived as a trial *de novo* in the New England tradition and it is difficult to believe that Ellsworth, familiar with prize appeals, supported the provision in Committee, particularly as he subsequently took corrective action in the Senate.[84]

Almost as an afterthought this section concluded with the proviso that nothing set out should be construed to prevent a federal court from granting a *dedimus potestatum* to take depositions "according to common usage" when it might be necessary to prevent a failure of justice—a

---

[84] *Infra*, p. 498.

power explicitly conferred—or to extend to depositions taken in *perpetuam rei memoriam*. Such, if related to matter cognizable in any United States court, a Circuit Court, when applied to as a court of equity, might direct should be taken "according to the usages in chancery."[85]

Two sections of the bill, the one a compact amendment and jeofails provision, the other relating to non-abatement of actions in the case of the death of one party or his adversary provided a cause of action survived, appear to have been drafted with reference to English mother statutes. The jeofails section was aimed at securing decision of a cause on the merits and consequently forbade considerations of form to govern except in cases of demurrer and permitted the court to amend all imperfections. No distinctions were drawn as to the nature of the proceedings. This section is not a rendition of either the Massachusetts[86] or Connecticut jeofails acts[87] but approximates the language of Statute 4 Anne, c. 16 §1 recently re-enacted by the New York legislature.[88] New Jersey had no such statute,[89] and in Virginia the District Court Act of 1788 had merely directed that all statutes of jeofails prior to 1750 were in force.[90] The Senate was to liberalize this section by empowering the courts to permit either party at any time to amend any defect in process or pleadings upon such conditions as the courts "shall in their discretion, and by their rules prescribe."

The model for the section providing that actions should not abate

---

[85] This latter part of the section suggests recourse to Massachusetts or New Hampshire practice, for Connecticut did not have the provision for perpetuating testimony, although it may be that elsewhere practice rested on other than statutory grounds. Hamilton, in his "Practical Proceedings" (*LPAH*, I, 94–95), describes the New York usage which at the time (1782) seems to have been without statutory sanction. In Maryland "An Act establishing a mode to perpetuate testimony" set out elaborate provisions (July Sess. 1779, c. 8, in I W. Kilty, *Laws of Maryland*), but no mention was made of Chancery. The reference to Chancery in the Judiciary Bill that was to make trouble probably derives from some English text or abridgment.

[86] I *Laws of the Commonwealth of Massachusetts 1780–1800*, at 207 (act of 1784). The colony act, very limited in scope, in I *Acts and Resolves Prov. of Mass. Bay*, 464 (1701). In England St. 18 Eliz. I, c. 14, was then in effect.

[87] *Acts and Laws of the State of Connecticut* (1784 revision), 2. See also the colonial act, *Acts and Laws of the Colony of Connecticut* (1769), 2.

[88] *N.Y. Laws*, 11 Sess. 1788, c. 32. The redrafting had not improved the original which in 1773 the provincial assembly had enacted virtually verbatim (5 *Col. Laws N.Y.*, 537).

[89] This may possibly be attributed to a reception of the English statute *sub silentio*. According to the ms. law notes of Edward Burd, *sub* Aug. 28, 1768 (Shippen Mss., HSP), 4 Anne, c. 16, was considered to be in force in Pennsylvania. In South Carolina the jeofails statutes were presumably received pursuant to their omnibus reception act of 1712. Maryland's version was enacted at the October Session 1763, c. 23 (Bacon, *Laws of Maryland* [1765]).

[90] 12 Hening, *Va. Stats.*, 749.

because of the death of one party or the other and permitting executors or administrators to prosecute or defend suits if the cause of action survived was the Statute 8 and 9 William III, c. 11 §6, 7. Some of the states, when colonies, had passed acts that were virtual copies of this statute. Following statehood these had been revised and simplified.[91] None of these revisions are cast in the language of the Committee bill—not even the Connecticut statute familiar to Ellsworth—and it consequently seems that this version probably was taken from the original act.

The most prickly problems which the Committee had to solve were those relating to bail and its administration in cases criminal and the manner of selecting juries. The warnings about a horde of minions necessary to make the federal judiciary effective and the consequent invasion of liberties were involved in the solution of the first problem. The almost irrefragable belief in the sanctity of the vicinage principle accounted for the difficulties presented by the second problem. The Committee bill provided for but two categories of administrative officers—the clerks to be appointed by the Supreme Court and by the District Courts,[92] and the marshals to be appointed for a four-year term in each district, removable at pleasure.[93] The marshal's duties, besides attendance upon the courts, were limited to the execution of all precepts directed to him issued under the authority of the United States, and to have the custody of prisoners. It is clear that the office was not modeled on that of the sheriff, and consequently there was no question of exercising such powers of bailing as the textbooks attributed to that officer.[94]

As we have elsewhere pointed out, three major considerations governed bail in the eighteenth century—the jurisdiction and powers of the judicial officer before whom a case came, the nature and quality of the offense, and the reputation of the parties.[95] This law was more a

---

[91] In Massachusetts the colonial acts were a peculiar variant; cf. 2 Acts and Laws Prov. of Mass. Bay, 422 (1727), 465 (1727/28). The revision was made in 1784, 1 Laws of the Commonwealth of Massachusetts 1780–1800 (1801), 122. For Connecticut Colony, cf. the act of May Sess. 1753, in Acts and Laws of the Colony of Connecticut (1769), 271; the state statute, in Acts and Laws of the State of Connecticut (1784), 2–3. In New York the English act was taken over in 1772 as to courts of record (5 Col. Laws N.Y., 287) and the provision extended to suits in equity in 1774 (ibid., 644). The revisors incorporated the provisions in 1788 (N.Y. Laws, 11 Sess. 1788, c. 46). Virginia adopted the act in 1748 (5 Hening, Va. Stats., 510); South Carolina, in 1746 (7 South Carolina Stats. [1840], 193).

[92] Sec. 7 of both the bill and the statute.

[93] Sec. 25 of the bill; sec. 27 of the statute.

[94] Hawkins, Pleas of the Crown, 6th ed. (1777), II, 147 et seq.; Blackstone, Commentaries, IV, 297.

[95] Goebel and Naughton, Law Enforcement in Colonial New York, 497.

congeries of rulings and statutory provisions than a systematic whole. The colonies had made what they could of it, but even post-Revolutionary statutes had not brought much order to the subject. The Committee for establishing a judiciary, however, produced what seems to us a reasonable scheme and one calculated to appeal to the frugal tastes of those who resented the expense of a new official establishment.

Every Justice of the Supreme Court and every District judge was authorized either on his own knowledge or upon complaint to cause any person to be taken for any offense against the laws of the United States and brought before himself for examination, and was vested with discretion to bail, to commit or to send the offender by warrant to the district where the crime was committed. The bill further enlisted the law-enforcing machinery of the states by authorizing any justice of the peace or magistrate of any of the states to arrest, imprison or bail offenders against the laws of the United States, agreeably to the customary mode of process of the states, for trial in the federal court which might have cognizance of the offense. To the clerk of such federal court copies of the process should be returned as speedily as possible, together with the recognizances of witnesses for appearance to testify. The state magistrate might require such recognizances under pain of imprisonment. Provision was made for the removal of persons committed to the district where trial was to be had. Whether by design or not this section in effect established the fundamentals of a right to bail as respects federal offenses—a subject left untouched in the Bill of Rights.

The power of the various magistrates to commit was limited by the rules laid down in the final sentence of the section that bail was to be admitted upon all arrests in criminal cases except where the punishment was death. In the latter case, the decision rested with the Supreme Court or a Circuit Court, or two Justices of the Supreme Court, or a single Justice of the Supreme Court and a District Court judge, who were given discretion regarding the nature and circumstances of the offense, and the evidence and "the usages of law." This was a cryptic direction, but to all appearances the Committee seems to have had in mind the large discretion of King's Bench to let to bail.[96]

The publication of Madison's proposed amendments for the Constitution presented June 8 and his pinpointing the requisite of a trial by men of the vicinage in cases criminal had no visible effect upon the text of the jury section of the bill reported in the Senate four days later. The Committee decided upon a rule that jurors, grand and petit, be returned from such part of the district from time to time "as shall

---

[96] On which *cf.* M. Hale, *Pleas of the Crown* (1778), II, 129; Hawkins, *Pleas of the Crown*, II, 176n.

be most favorable to an impartial trial, and as the court shall direct, so as not to incur an unnecessary expense or unduly burthen the citizens of any part of the district with such services." Jurors were to have the same qualifications as those requisite for jurors by the laws of the state for service in the highest court of the state. Writs of *venire facias* directed by the federal court were to issue from the clerk's office and be served by the marshal or his deputy. The jury list was to be made up by the marshal. In the event that in either a criminal or civil cause the panel was exhausted as a result of challenges or otherwise, the marshal, his deputy or elisors were to return jurors "de talibus circumstantibus." Needless to say, these specifications fell short of libertarian demands and left open the possibility of manipulation by the marshal.

The final section of the Committee bill again reveals the current state of incertitude regarding the probability of constitutional amendment, for it undertook to establish a statutory right of parties in all federal courts to plead and manage their own causes personally or by the assistance of counsel or attorneys at law "as by the rules of the said courts respectively shall be permitted to manage and conduct causes therein." Each District Court was authorized to appoint a person learned in the law to act as Attorney for the United States to prosecute "delinquents" for crimes cognizable under the authority of the United States and all civil actions in which the United States might be concerned, except before the Supreme Court in the district where it might be held and kept. The District Attorney was to be compensated by fees taxed by the courts. The Supreme Court was to appoint an attorney general to prosecute and conduct in the Supreme Court all suits in which the United States might be concerned. He was also to give advice to the President when required, and, when requested, to the heads of departments as to matters concerning such. His compensation was to be established by law.

The surviving letters of comments from lawyers and judges to whom the bill was submitted are generally a disappointing lot. Theophilus Parsons of Massachusetts was reported by young John Quincy Adams as doubting whether six judges of the Supreme Court were enough and he did not like joining the District judge with two Supreme Court Justices in the Circuit for it would give him a casting vote. Chancellor Livingston of New York also questioned if there were enough judges both to ride the circuit and do the business of the Supreme Court. He queried whether more than one circuit annually would be necessary. "The principal and most unnecessary business" of the federal courts would be the diversity jurisdiction. This should be confined to cases of great moment. Consequently he wished to increase the monetary limitations. Two practical suggestions were offered: that the attorney general be appointed by the executive, and that in granting new trials the courts have the power to impose terms at their discretion. Judgment in the first trial should be voidable, not void.[97]

None of the answers from the personages in Philadelphia to whom, as Maclay reports, the bill was sent have been found.[98] In a belated letter from Edward Shippen an entirely new plan was advanced.[99] We know that there were individual replies and that the lawyers in Philadelphia held a conference on the bill. John Dickinson and Gunning Bedford, Jr., then attorney general of Delaware, made notes on a copy of the bill and presumably sent it to George Read. Dickinson wrote George Read that the bill appeared to him "the most difficult to be understood of any legislative bill I ever read." Bedford claimed the time was too short for him to make a just criticism, but it appeared to him a "noble work." He had, however, difficulties with the terms "common law" and "statute," and raised the question of the impropriety of a possible reference to the law of England.[100]

The Virginia comments agreed in one point—that it would have been better to have had a series of separate bills. This was the opinion of Richard Parker, Edmund Randolph and Edward Carrington, no doubt inspired by the fact that this was the way the Virginia Revisors had approached their task. The letter of the most experienced and learned of all the Virginians, Edmund Pendleton, appears to have been lost, but it may be inferred from a letter of Madison's that Pendleton regarded

---

[97] For the present location of these letters see *supra*, n. 29.

[98] The replies appear to have been sent to Robert Morris, but a search of his papers at the Library of Congress and the Huntington Library has yielded none. Maclay saw a letter from Myers Fisher, but he complained bitterly (*Journal*, 97) that Morris would not show him letters received. Morris seems to have relented, for Maclay notes (July 8) that McKean C.J., James Wilson, Richard Peters, Tench Coxe and others had approved the general outline of the bill (*ibid.*, 100).

[99] Shippen to Morris, July 13, 1789, *supra*, n. 29. Shippen, then president of the Court of Common Pleas of Philadelphia County, was apparently privy to what the Philadelphia lawyers had decided. He offered "new thoughts." He disliked the Circuit Courts because it would hardly be practicable for two judges to ride circuits twice a year, and they would be inconvenient to suitors. He suggested

consolidating the jurisdiction in District Courts of three resident judges sitting four times a year. Appeals would lie to the Supreme Court in equity and maritime causes; in common law causes, writs of error. The Supreme Court was to have power to order new trials if the District Courts refused, the presiding judge to report the case. It was also important that the judiciary law should establish expressly "by what law we are to be governed." He suggested that the United States adopt the common law—"it should not be left to the Judges to make the Law, but only to declare it." The matter of amendatory English statutes troubled him and here he was willing to give the judges leeway. He was opposed to juryless trials of revenue cases.

[100] John Dickinson to George Read, June 24, 1789, in Read, *Life and Correspondence of George Read*, at 481; Gunning Bedford, Jr., to George Read, June 24, 1789, *ibid.*, 482.

the bill to be defective in general structure and in many of its particular regulations.[101]

Edmund Randolph's remarks are particularly interesting because later he was to submit as Attorney General a long report on the judiciary. To Madison he wrote that the number of Supreme Court Justices was too small "to make head against eleven state judiciaries, always disposed to warfare"—a strange application of a military metaphor. Nine or eleven would answer better and give opportunity of gratifying each state by a Supreme as well as a District judge. There was nothing improper in an even number of judges (as the bill provided), but a case decided at Circuit by a bare majority one of which would be the District judge but affirmed in the Supreme Court merely because the court was evenly divided would excite murmurs.

"The jurisdiction," wrote Randolph, and here he seems to be referring to the Supreme Court, "is inartificially, untechnically and confusedly worded." It would have been better to have left the point to the Constitution itself, for he doubted if the court would be bound by any definition of authority which the Constitution did not warrant. In his opinion resort to a separate bill would have brought forth the equitable jurisdiction with more lustre than it did in the bill where it had crept in seemingly uninvited and half forgotten, crammed in a corner. Detail ought to be left to the judges; every attempt to cope with it must be imperfect and arouse ridicule among technical men.[102]

It will be recalled that Randolph in his letter of October 10, 1787, to the Virginia legislature had recommended that steps be taken to limit and define the judicial power. The Virginia Convention had attempted to do so in its program of amendments, yet this thrawn and irresolute man was now ready to abandon even legislative regulation and leave detail to the judges. Neither he nor any of the other commentators exhibited the least perception of the Committee's sensitivity to antifederalist criticisms of a federal judiciary and the skill with which it had undertaken to meet or parry these.

Samuel Chase's letter mentioned above was written to R. H. Lee on July 16, the day before the Judiciary Bill was voted upon in the Senate. The two chief objects of his concern were the jury provisions and the chancery jurisdiction. His approach was wholly professional, for, as is noted in the margin, he wished the law to be a vehicle for some reform

---

[101] Richard Parker to R. H. Lee, July 6, 1789, Ms. Lee Family Papers (Library, University of Virginia); Edmund Randolph to Madison, June 30, Ms. Madison Papers, XI, 100 (LC); Edward Carrington to Madison, August 3, *ibid.*, XII, 2; Madison to Pendleton, Sept. 14, 1789, *ibid.*, 30.

[102] Ms. Madison Papers, XI, 100 (LC).

of the traditional jury trial. He championed an enlargement of chancery jurisdiction, and offered some practical suggestions on how to correct those features of procedure borrowed from the English that had served as a handle for antifederalist attack upon the constitutional grant of jurisdiction in equity.[103]

Whether or not he was aware of the fact, Chase was grasping nettles. Any suggestion that the jury system as then entrenched might be amended in any detail was beyond tolerance. No less so was his advocacy of a strengthened chancery jurisdiction, for the very word "chancery" was identified with prerogative in the popular mind, and so unamendably un-American. Equity was a word Americans had learned to live with as an ingredient of justice, but in states where there were no distinct chancery courts this forbearance did not extend to more than a niggardly borrowing of the procedures by which equity jurisprudence had been administered in England. It was unfortunate that the latent distrust of these procedures should have been aroused to the

---

[103] Chase thought that trial by jury had not been properly secured in criminal cases because here the jury should come from the place "where the fact is committed," not because a jury should give a verdict from private knowledge, but because the character of the accused ought to weigh in the truth of the charge against him. He opposed "a locality of trial in civil cases because such was generally attended with local prejudice." The bill, he believed, sought to provide for defects in common law jurisdiction but had not remedied defects in the jury system. He proceeded to set out a variety of suggestions regarding impanelling of juries including a provision for a struck jury. He opposed a unanimous verdict in civil cases and he thought that the court should have the power both to direct a verdict and to direct that counsel prepare a case stated and grant a writ of error upon it as on a bill of exceptions.

Chase, like others, believed that federal Chancery and common law courts should be distinct tribunals. The procedures of the common law courts were not adapted to intricate subjects of litigation arising from the growth of commerce and other factors.

In his opinion, the chief objections to Chancery jurisdiction were the examination of witnesses in private without cross-examination and that the Chancellor decided the facts. The first could be eliminated by depositions being taken in the presence of the parties or their counsel who might question as they pleased. The second objection could be met by a provision that, if requested, the Chancellor direct an issue be tried summarily by a common law court. If Chancery jurisdiction were restrained as by the bill, infinite mischief would result. Chase to R. H. Lee, July 16, 1789, Ms. Lee Family Papers (Library, University of Virginia).

Chase had earlier written Lee on July 2 (Lee, *Memoir of the Life of Richard Henry Lee*, II, 183) stating that the bill was ably drawn but that there were defects. He wanted District Courts to have civil jurisdiction up to $800, the Circuit Courts, over that amount. He thought the limitations upon courts of equity potentially harmful. Chase added that he had drafted a clause for "Mr. Housy"— an obvious misreading of Chase's execrable handwriting for Henry, Senator from Maryland.

point of obscuring the value of a federal jurisdiction in equity, and that what had seemed a minor critique in 1787 was to become an emotionally charged issue in the Senate.

THE SENATE DEBATE

WHAT THE SENATE did to the Committee bill can be settled by a comparison of the printed version with the engrossed bill sent to the House. The Senate *Journal* for the days when the third reading was in train indicates some of the backing and filling of the membership. The chits already mentioned, where they bear dates, supplement this and they also help in settling some details when the bill was discussed during the second reading in Committee. For this stage of the proceedings Maclay's journal is a prime source but inadequate in this, that the Senator, understandably enough, was mainly concerned with magnifying his own little triumphs and ignoring particulars which did not interest him. Consequently one receives the impression that the bill was not gone through systematically but was subjected to a species of grasshopper visitation.

Pursuant to the Senate rule, Committee consideration began upon the second reading June 22. The first two sections were postponed to take up that dealing with the District Courts.[104] After it was voted that there should be such courts, Richard Henry Lee moved "that no subordinate federal jurisdiction be established in any State, other than the Admiralty or Maritime causes but that federal interference shall be limited to appeals only from the State Courts to the supreme federal Court of the U. States."[105] He was seconded by Grayson. The argument on this ran into the next day when the motion was defeated. The number of Supreme Court Justices was next taken up with the question raised whether the number six was sufficient if the Circuit Courts should be established.[106] Maclay does not indicate if a vote was taken; nor does he mention the important decision to erect Maine and Kentucky as separate districts.[107] Neither was included in the definition of the circuits, although in section 11 Maine was made part of the Massachusetts Circuit in matters relating to this jurisdiction. The Kentucky District Court, however, besides the jurisdiction proper to such courts was vested

---

[104] *Maclay Journal*, 83.
[105] The resolve is written on a chit stamped 28 and filed with the ms. "Bill to establish the Judicial Courts of the United States." Senate Files, Sen. 1A–B1 (NA). Lee and Grayson were both, of course, charged with

presenting the limit on inferior courts proposed at the Virginia Convention.
[106] *Maclay Journal*, 85.
[107] Sec. 2, Ms. Senate Engrossed Bill, Sen. Files, Book 1 (NA). This embodies the changes made by the Senate.

with the jurisdiction of the Circuit Courts except as to writ of error and appeals. Error thence lay directly to the Supreme Court.[108] For reasons unknown the Senate did not choose to confer equal stature on the Maine District Court. This was, as we shall see, effected by amendment in the House of Representatives.

Three changes were made in the section dealing with the jurisdiction of the District Courts. There was added after the clause saving a common law remedy, jurisdiction, exclusive of the courts of the states, of all seizures on land or other waters than those defined as within the admiralty jurisdiction and all suits for penalties and forfeitures incurred under the laws of the United States. The second change was to confer "jurisdiction, exclusively of the courts of the several states, of all suits against consuls or vice consuls except for offences above the discription aforesaid."[109] The third alteration was to put beyond doubt the ambiguity of the bill regarding the mode of trial in cases of admiralty and maritime jurisdiction by the stipulation at the end of the section (9) that the trial of all causes except civil causes of admiralty and maritime jurisdiction should be by jury.

According to Maclay the debate on the Circuit Courts began with a consideration whether or not there should be courts of *nisi prius*, a matter raised by Johnson of Connecticut.[110] Since sittings at *nisi prius* were no more than trials of causes brought to issue in a court possessed of original jurisdiction, it is difficult to understand what Johnson was at unless he conceived that litigants would plead to issue in the Circuit Courts and that the District Courts would function as sittings for the trial of issues of fact. The suggestion came to nothing. The Circuit section was modified by throwing out the provision sharing original cognizance with the Supreme Court. A second change was to localize diversity jurisdiction by limiting jurisdiction as far as citizens were concerned to civil suits "between a citizen of the State where the Suit is brought and a citizen of another State."[111] The provision regarding assignments of choses in action was loosened by writing in the exception of foreign bills of exchange.

The Senate eliminated from section 11 as it had from section 9, dealing with the District Court, in the clauses pertaining to crimes cognizable under the authority of the United States, the words "and defined by the laws of the same." This has been made the basis of a conjecture that it was "clearly intended" to extend federal jurisdiction

---

[108] Sec. 10, *ibid.*
[109] This amendment is a chit stamped 39, Sen. 1A–B1 (NA), and is in Ellsworth's hand.
[110] *Maclay Journal*, 86 (June 24).

[111] Sec. 11, Ms. Senate Engrossed Bill, Sen. Files, Book 1 (NA); amendment is a chit stamped 32, Sen. 1A–B1 (NA).

to crimes at common law and under the law of nations.[112] There is no evidence to support this. On the contrary, it seems to us that the words may either have been regarded as redundant and so eliminated pursuant to a vote July 10 to expunge redundant words,[113] or to have been struck out by the Committee when the bill was recommitted July 13 for minor amendments.[114] There was at the moment expectation that the Senate would have before it a bill defining crimes against the United States, for a committee to bring in such had been named May 13.[115] This committee reported July 28,[116] and the bill passed the Senate August 31.[117] Under the circumstances the intention ascribed to the Senate is open to doubt.

The Senate amended section 12 on removals to make clear that it applied to suits commenced in state courts against an alien or by a citizen of the state where a suit was brought against a citizen of another state, and to eliminate the peremptory tone of the directions to state tribunals. The latter must be satisfied that the matter in dispute exceeded $500. Furthermore, while the state court was required to accept the surety, the Senate amendment provided only that such court proceed no further in the cause, rather than, as the Committee had it, dismiss further proceedings in the cause. Any attachment of goods was to hold to "respond the final judgment" in the same manner as by the laws of such state they would have been held to respond final judgment had such been rendered in the state court[118]—clumsy phrasing rectified by the House. As is indicated in the margin, the procedure in cases of action involving title to lands by citizens of the same state claiming under grants of different states was so revised as to relegate the directions on the course of pleading and simplify the manner of asserting title.[119]

In recasting the section dealing with the jurisdiction of the Supreme Court, the Senate eliminated from the exclusive jurisdiction controversies where a foreign state was a party. Eliminated also in the provision regarding suits against ambassadors was the reference to consuls. The

---

[112] Warren, "Judiciary Act," 73.

[113] *Senate Journal*, 1st Sess., 61.

[114] Wingate to Pickering, July 11, 1789, in Wingate, *Life and Letters of Paine Wingate*, II, 317.

[115] *Senate Journal*, 1st Sess., 34.

[116] *Ibid.*, 77.

[117] *Ibid.*, 113.

[118] Sec. 12, Ms. Senate Engrossed Bill, Sen. Files, Book 1 (NA).

[119] Before trial either party should state to the court and make affidavit if so required that he claimed and relied upon a grant from a state other than that where suit was pending, produce the grant or an exemplification, unless unable due to loss of public records. He should then move that the adverse party inform the court whether he claimed a right or title from the state where suit was pending, or otherwise be not allowed to plead the grant or give it in evidence. If the court should be informed that claim was made under such grant, it was open to the party raising the question on motion to remove the cause. The original form of this amendment is in Ellsworth's hand; *cf.* the chit stamped 29 with Sen. 1A–B1 (NA).

limitation in the Committee bill of suits brought by such functionaries to trespasses was excised, and here consuls and vice consuls were included but not domestics.[120]

The changes made in respect to error jurisdiction and procedure were substantial in this, that the "petition in error" containing transcript of the record, assignment of error and prayer for reversal was dropped in favor of a *writ of error* with record, etc., annexed. At some juncture, evidently in response to the clamor over finality of jury verdicts, there was added a prohibition that there should be no reversal either in a Circuit or the Supreme Court "for any error in fact." The period within which error could be brought was extended to five years. No question appears to have been raised as to whether a writ of error was the proper device for review of equity causes and nothing was done to clarify the obscure passage which, as written, placed the monetary limit in excess of $2,000 only on causes on appeal from District Courts to the Circuit and taken on error to the Supreme Court. This passage, it may here be remarked, was not a Senate amendment, as has been supposed,[121] but was in the printed Committee bill. A further amendment of error proceedings was that added to section 25 confining assignments of error to such as appeared on the face of the record.

For reasons which Maclay fails to impart, although he argued for the excision, Richard Bassett and George Read of Delaware moved and succeeded in having struck the limitations upon a writ of error operating as a supersedeas.[122] These had been inserted by the Committee presumably as a means of discouraging too free a resort to the appellate process. This change was voted in the course of the third reading[123] and at this stage a new section was offered and voted which had perhaps as liberalizing an effect as making general a stay of execution.

The formulation of this new section appears to have been the result of an upsurge of prejudice regarding the use of depositions. It will be recalled that what became section 30 of the Judiciary Act, the chief purpose of which had been to still the criticisms over the inconvenience of attending far-off courts, opened with the statement that

---

[120] Chit stamped 46, Sen. 1A–B1 (NA), in Ellsworth's hand, has the text of the second sentence of sec. 13 beginning "And shall have" and ending "a consul or vice consul shall be a party." This is an interesting paper because at the top of the page are three lines, all cancelled, directing words to be struck and insertions. This suggests a piecemeal alteration by words was begun and then abandoned in favor of a complete re-writing. At the foot of the document in another hand are the words "amended in print." This, we believe, refers to a later printing of the bill with amendments, no copy of which has been found (*cf.* Childs, "The Story of the United States Senate Documents, 1st Congress, 1st Session New York 1789," at 184).

[121] *Supra*, n. 59.

[122] *Maclay Journal*, 104.

[123] *Senate Journal*, 1st Sess., 62.

the mode of proof by oral testimony and examination of witnesses in open court should be identical in the trial of equity and admiralty causes as in actions at common law. This was followed by the directions for taking depositions *de bene esse* under the circumstances related above. Although these provisions went no further than the practice long seated in many of the states, they had the smell of chancery procedure. Maclay relates that on July 9 an amendment had been accepted to the effect "that in the Circuit Courts, under the name of equity they should have all the depositions copied and sent up on an appeal to the Supreme Court."[124] The Senate *Journal* records no such amendment for that date. Maclay, however, delivered himself of an attack on the use of depositions charging that an attempt was being made to introduce the methods of the civil law.[125] All that the Senate *Journal* shows is that the passage in section 30 which allowed testimony to be committed to writing if the parties could satisfy the court that in an admiralty cause which might be appealed they could not produce the witnesses before the Circuit Court had at some juncture been extended to hearings in equity in the Circuit Court for appeal to the Supreme Court. This extension was reconsidered and struck July 10.[126] The provisions regarding depositions stood.

On July 11 a new section was offered. The paper is in Ellsworth's hand and states: "that it shall be the duty of Circuit Courts in causes in equity and of admiralty and maritime jurisdiction, to cause the facts on which they found their sentence or decree, fully to appear upon the record, either from the pleadings and decree itself, or a state of the case agreed by the parties, or their counsel; or, if they disagree, by a stating of the case by the court."[127] Paterson offered a substitute: "That it shall be the duty of Circuit Courts in the trial of causes in equity and of admiralty, where the facts are contested, to cause the evidence exhibited at the hearing to be reduced to writing, if either of the parties require it, or a state of the facts to be made if the parties agree thereto."[128]

A vote was first taken on Paterson's motion and it was rejected; Ellsworth's was accepted and became section 19 of the statute.[129] A page is missing from Maclay's journal and we are consequently ignorant of whether or not he realized that the gentlemen of the bar whom he was constantly berating had presented him with something more radical

---

[124] *Maclay Journal*, 101.
[125] *Ibid.*, 102–03. What Maclay was unaware of was that by rule of court in Pennsylvania depositions could be taken of persons about to leave the jurisdiction (*supra*, n. 83).
[126] *Senate Journal*, 1st Sess., 61.

[127] Chit stamped 22, Sen. 1A–B1 (NA), in Ellsworth's hand, with the direction "between 17 & 18ᵗ Sectⁿ."
[128] Chit stamped 21, *ibid.*; cf. *Senate Journal*, 1st Sess., 61–62.
[129] *Senate Journal*, 1st Sess., 62.

than the provision he had succeeded in having excised. Indeed, had he known the pedigree of the procedure he would have recoiled in horror. For, as we have elsewhere pointed out, the "case made" could be and was manipulated to evade the finality of a jury verdict.[130] This incident of common law practice was used in Maryland, New York and Virginia, and it was marvelous indeed to observe that it should be appropriated for equity and admiralty causes. The alternative offered of a record, confected from the facts in pleadings or decrees, held promise of an immoderate inflation of instruments already insufferably prolix.

The prejudices of those who, like Maclay, believed that "twelve honest jurors are good chancellors"[131] were to be aroused by three other sections. The first occasion had been on June 29, when the section dealing with the production of books and papers was under discussion. The objections were directed at the provision that the defendant would be required to disclose under oath knowledge of the cause.[132] Maclay here is full of his own contribution to the argument and fails to pay adequate regard to the arguments of others. Whether or not the prime objection was to the admissibility of testimony of an interested party or to the fact that this was indeed modelled on chancery discovery procedure—a blemish exposed by a public reading from Blackstone—is not apparent. Ellsworth sought to save the provision by requiring the plaintiff also to testify.[133] This was voted down as doubling the invitation to perjury. Maclay conceived the provision to be a species of torture and to violate the privilege against self-incrimination, although the sanction for failure to disclose was no more than a non-suit. In Maclay's own state, although he seems to have been unaware of the fact, a recent bankruptcy statute had required a defendant to disclose assets under oath with much severer penalties;[134] and this was a characteristic of the insolvency laws of other states.[135] The discovery procedure except as to books and papers was struck out.[136]

On the heels of this vote a long debate ensued over the seemingly innocuous section which embodied the maxim that suits in equity should not be sustained where a remedy at law was to be had. Johnson of Connecticut spoke against the clause and it would appear that more was

---

[130] *LPAH*, II, c. I.
[131] *Maclay Journal*, 93.
[132] *Ibid.*, 89.
[133] *Ibid.*, 91.
[134] 12 *Stats. at Large Pa.*, 70, c. 1183, sec. 8, sec. 11 (1785). The procedure had been in existence since the Pennsylvania insolvency law of 1729. This appears in *Acts of Assembly of the Province of Pennsylvania* (1775), 162, a work published

by order of the assembly.
[135] *Cf.* 1 *Laws of the Commonwealth of Massachusetts 1780–1800*, at 401 (1787); *Acts and Laws of the State of Connecticut*, 35 (1784); *N.Y. Laws*, 11 Sess. 1788, c. 92; 1 Kilty, *Laws of Maryland*, Act of March 1774, c. 28, which remained in effect until revised, 2 *ibid.*, April 1792, c. 8.
[136] *Maclay Journal*, 92.

said in favor of Chancery than against. Maclay again aired his sentiments and managed to anger Read. On this date (July 1) the section was approved, with the addition of the modifying "complete" to the noun "remedy."[137] Nevertheless, on July 11 Paterson moved to delete the whole section and it was expunged.[138] If Paterson's motive was to leave the development of equity jurisdiction fluid, the Senate two days later reversed itself, restored the section and tightened it by requiring a "plain adequate" as well as "complete" remedy at law.[139]

There seems to us to be no doubt but that the inveterate belief in the virtues of jury trial had much to do with the apparent disinclination to implement the jurisdiction in equity. This was markedly the case when section 26, vesting the court with discretion to chancer the amount due on forfeited bonds, was debated. Strong, who apparently was unaware of the genesis of the Bay Colony's venture in "equitie" was hard put to defend the practice.[140] Because in Pennsylvania, Maclay's state, questions of equity were decided by a jury, this Senator led the battle to leave the matter to be thus determined. In the bill as passed by the Senate the section was so rewritten that no provision was made for the forfeiture or breach being found by the jury. The court was left discretion where the forfeiture or breach was by default or confession of defendant, or upon demurrer, to render judgment for plaintiff to recover so much as might be due according to equity. If the sum for which judgment should be rendered was uncertain, this should be assessed by a jury if the parties should so request.[141]

Although, as remarked, there were features of the section on the selection of juries open to criticism, the Senate agreed to it in Committee. However, on July 9 it was moved to insert "that Grand Jurors in all cases whatever, and petit Jurors in all cases not punishable with death" should come from that part of the district most favorable to an impartial trial. This was negatived.[142] It was next moved to insert that "petit Jurors, in all cases punishable with death, shall be returned from the body of the county in which the offence was committed." This, too,

---

[137] This is an inference from the entry in *Senate Journal*, 1st Sess., 63, coupled with Maclay's account of the debate of July 1. Cf. *Maclay Journal*, 92–94.

[138] The motion is on the dorse of the chit stamped 36, Sen. 1A–B1 (NA); the vote, *Senate Journal*, 1st Sess., 62.

[139] *Senate Journal*, 1st Sess., 63.

[140] *Maclay Journal*, 95–96 (July 2).

[141] This last recalls Jefferson's remembrance of Pendleton's amendment of the first High Court of Chancery

Act of 1776. Jefferson had provided for jury trial. Pendleton inserted "if either party chuse." In his *Autobiography*, Jefferson wrote: "The consequence has been that as no suitor will say to his judge, 'Sir, I distrust you, give me a jury' juries are rarely, I might say perhaps never seen in that court." *Works of Jefferson* (Ford, Federal ed.), I, 60. Of course, the real reason for disappearance of the jury was the Act of 1783.

[142] *Senate Journal*, 1st Sess., 61.

was rejected.[143] Just before the bill was recommitted on July 13, Lee and Grayson moved to insert a proviso that in "criminal cases where the punishment is capital, the petit jury shall come from the body of the county where the fact was committed." This was also passed in the negative. Maclay, who was usually more than alert on any meddling with the traditional practices respecting juries, recorded nothing of this. Evidently the vicinage principle was not held as sacred in Pennsylvania as it was in Virginia.

Except for the disposition of the Senate majority to limit what federal judges might do as Chancellors, the sources reveal little inclination to place restraints upon the exercise of the judicial function. At the instance of Grayson, supported by Bassett, it was decided July 7 that no District judge should give a vote in any case of appeal or error from his own decision, but that he might assign the reason for his decision.[144] Maclay records that a similar disqualification of Supreme Court judges who had sat in the trial of a cause at Circuit from voting in the trial of such causes in error in the Supreme Court had also been decided.[145] The Senate *Journal* does not bear him out. Two attempts to amend in this sense were made July 11. Both were beaten down.[146] Nothing is known of the debates on these motions. The only other occasion when any comment appears to have been made about the powers of judges had been when the bail section was under consideration. The authority which the Committee proposed to confer on federal judges on their own knowledge or complaint of others to order apprehension, take examinations, bail or commit for crimes and offenses against the United States was excised chiefly because this was depicted as an authority which might be abused because of the danger that judges might act out of personal resentment, to the detriment of the security of the citizen.[147] This was Maclay's opinion and the majority obviously sided with him. A final trimming of powers which the Committee had assigned to the judges was the appointment of District Attorneys and an Attorney General. The Senate agreed such should be appointed but did not specifically designate by whom.[148]

---

[143] *Ibid.*

[144] *Maclay Journal*, 99.

[145] *Ibid.*

[146] *Senate Journal*, 1st Sess., 62. The chits stamped 23 and 25, Sen. 1A–B1 (NA), have the texts of the motions and are marked "negatived."

[147] The chits stamped 30, 40, 43 (dorse) and 44, Sen. 1A–B1 (NA), have the texts of diverse motions. Ellsworth was apparently seeking a formula to save the grant of power to the judges. This authority was

embedded in the English statutes relating to justices of the peace.

[148] The only reference to this section we have seen is in a letter of John Adams to Francis Dana (Ms. Adams Papers, Reel 115 [MHS]) tentatively dated as written between July 5 and 14. The fact that Adams reported that the District judges might be eliminated, the number of Supreme Court judges and the number of circuits doubled, points to early discussions in the Committee of the

Something remains to be said about section 34, which provided that "the laws of the several states, except where the constitution treaties or statutes of the United States shall otherwise require or provide, shall be regarded as rules of decision in trials at common law in the courts of the United States in cases where they apply." Nothing more is known of its genesis than that the text is written out on a chit in Ellsworth's hand and marked for page 15.[149] The original form of the introductory sentence read: "That the Statute law of the several States in force for the time being, and their unwritten or common law now in use, whether by adoption from the common law of England, the ancient statutes of the same. . . ." All of this was cancelled, whether before debate or after we do not know, but since these memoranda were normally handed to a clerk, it was probably before discussion. As a capsulated description of state law, the original version could not be bettered.

The addition of section 34 was induced, we believe, by the need for some positive direction regarding the basic law by which the new courts were to be governed. The bill was replete with borrowings from the corpus of common law institutions, but the draftsmen with almost studied care had used the term "common law" itself only descriptively or as a term of classification. The mere use of the expression had troubled Gunning Bedford, Jr., who had written George Read that it would be derogatory to adopt English common law and that the time for emancipation was ripe.[150] This was the opinion of Maclay[151] and it would appear that other Senators shared it.

The Committee's bill at various junctures reveals an anticipation that federal judges would exercise the familiar and traditional function of molding the law by judicial decision, notably in the direction that all writs, even those not provided by statute, be issued agreeably to the "principles and usages of law," and in the jeofails-amendment section by authorizing courts to render judgment "according as the right of the cause and matter of law appear to them." Certainly, to a layman unfamiliar with the current credo that the common law was a body of principles, such expressions needed elucidation. We do not know if the point was debated, but we believe that some of the lawyers whose comments were solicited may have raised the question.[152]

Whole. The one specific amendment voted which was mentioned by Adams was that the Attorney General should be appointed by the President with consent of the Senate. Under consideration was appointment of deputies by the Attorney General.

[149] Chit stamped 45, Sen 1A–B1

(NA). The credit for discovering and rescuing this document belongs to Charles Warren.

[150] Read, *Life and Correspondence of George Read,* at 483.

[151] *Maclay Journal,* 93.

[152] Shippen's letter (*supra,* n. 29), belated though it was, may have re-

The solution was brilliant in its conception of bonding federal jurisprudence to extant American law in all its diversity, a result which Madison clearly perceived when he pointed out in the debate on judicial salaries that the judges must make a "new acquisition of legal knowledge," among other things "a familiar acquaintance with the laws of every State."[153] The section fell short in this, that it left out of account both admiralty and chancery causes and that it was limited to the trial stage of juristic controversy. Presumably an appellate court reviewing "rules of decision" in common law trials would exercise its corrective authority by reference to local jurisprudence—until the appearance of state law reports, a task one might suppose would tax judicial ingenuity but for the continued American dependence upon English books. The Judiciary Act, abounding with English words of art, itself invited such recourse, for what the terms were designed to communicate could only be so settled.[154]

On July 13 the bill was recommitted for "little alterations and amendments."[155] What these were we do not know; neither do we know for certain when the Committee reported.[156] It was an engrossed bill which came before the Senate July 17. Final speeches of dissent were made by Butler, Grayson and Lee.[157] A motion was made by Butler that "on the final question upon a bill or resolve, any Member shall have a right to enter his PROTEST or dissent on the Journal, with reasons in support of such dissent" if offered within two days after a final vote. This was rejected.[158] One fifth of the Senators present requiring that the ayes and nays be taken, the vote was so put. The bill passed 14–6. The dissenters were Butler of South Carolina, Maclay of Pennsylvania, Langdon and Wingate of New Hampshire, Grayson and Lee of Virginia.

PROCEEDINGS IN THE HOUSE

THE SENATE BILL had a first reading in the House on July 20 and was ordered committed to the Committee of the Whole for consideration

---

flected the opinion of the local bar which had met on the act.

[153] *Annals of Congress*, I, 937.

[154] We have earlier considered the matter in "The Common Law and the Constitution," in W. M. Jones, ed., *Chief Justice John Marshall, a Reappraisal*, 101–23, and *LPAH*, I, 31–34.

[155] Wingate to Pickering, *supra*, n. 114; *Senate Journal*, 1st Sess., 63.

[156] Maclay (*Journal*, 114) states

that "We read and corrected the long judiciary"—evidently referring to a Committee session, for he adds that the Senate met at the usual time, and that the "same judiciary was taken up and went over." The corrections were probably missing words inserted in the surviving Engrossed Bill.

[157] *Ibid.*

[158] *Senate Journal*, 1st Sess., 64.

July 27.[159] But weeks were to pass before there was any further action. Meanwhile, as Robert Morris wrote, the House had "been amusing themselves with proposing Amendments to the Constitution."[160] These were despatched to the Senate August 24. On the same day the Judiciary Act was taken up by the House in Committee.[161] Debate was resumed August 29 and 31, and not again renewed until September 8; after four more days of intermittent debate the Committee reported on the 14th.[162]

Of the content of these debates little is remembranced besides what the reporter Lloyd saw fit to set down of the proceedings on August 24, 29 and 31. Opponents took the initiative, for discussions opened with a motion to reduce the number of Supreme Court Justices, an attempt to dispense with a Chief Justice and a motion to eliminate the districts.[163] It soon developed that the antifederalists wished to jettison the whole proposed establishment, deeming the state courts sufficient to the ends of federal justice. The exchanges were hardly of a sort to whet the appetite, consisting as they did on both sides chiefly of warmed-over arguments from the days of the ratification struggle. On this occasion, however, the federalists stood on the firm ground of the law of the land, inspiring Aedanus Burke to exclaim that whichever way he turned, the Constitution stared him in the face.[164] A crucial vote was taken, August 31, on a motion by Livermore of New Hampshire to strike the third section. The motion was beaten 31–11.[165]

The tone of the debates apparently did not improve when discussions were resumed on September 8, for on the 13th Robert Morris wrote Richard Peters, "The Judicial Bill is working its way slowly through the House of Representatives. They have a Number of Lawyers that Keep snarling at it, but I fancy they are too Lazy or too Weak to make a bold attack on it. They must propose a better or pass this previous to the adjournment which will take place on the 22d of this Month."[166] It was this pressure which had much to do with saving the Senate bill. At that, more than fifty-two amendments were voted.

It has been averred that the House amendments were "merely verbal in nature and made no essential alterations in the Bill."[167] The record does not bear this out, even if one is prepared to accept as merely verbal the recasting of whole sentences to achieve the precision essential to a statute. At least four novel alterations were made. Three

---

[159] *Jour. H.R.*, I, 63; *Annals of Congress*, I, 685.

[160] Morris to Peters, Aug. 24, 1789, in Ms. Peters Papers, IX, 99 (HSP).

[161] *Jour. H.R.*, I, 90; *Annals of Congress*, I, 812.

[162] *Jour. H.R.*, I, 110.

[163] *Annals of Congress*, I, 812–13.

[164] *Ibid.*, 844.

[165] *Ibid.*, 866.

[166] Ms. Peters Papers, IX, 102 (HSP).

[167] Warren, "Judiciary Act," 130, n. 178.

were accepted by the Senate as framed. A fourth was then recast and both houses agreed to it. The list of amendments sent to the Senate has not been found, but a comparison of the statute as finally passed with the text of the engrossed bill as it had passed the Senate, conveniently marked at points where the House amended, establishes the purport of House action.

The first House alteration, which in light of antecedent stirrings for independence in Maine was of some political significance,[168] was an addition to section 10 endowing the District Court of Maine with the same original jurisdiction as the Senate had conferred upon the Kentucky District Court. It was, however, provided that while writs of error and appeals from the Kentucky jurisdiction would lie to the Supreme Court, writs of error from the District Court of Maine would lie to the Circuit Court for the Massachusetts district. To this court also were to go appeals from the Maine District Court in cases of admiralty and maritime jurisdiction.[169]

A second and procedurally highly significant change was the limitation of the amendment and jeofails section (33) to civil actions. As noticed, the Committee had excluded no type of proceeding from the operation of this provision, and the Senate had enlarged its effect by conferring upon the courts a broad discretion to permit amendment of pleadings and process. Although it had long been settled law that the jeofails statutes did not extend to criminal proceedings,[170] we believe that the House out of consideration for the rights of defendants was led to make the exception explicit, for in the harsh English criminal law here received, technical error had served as a defendant's first line of defense, and in the debates on constitutional amendments the House had already manifested its solicitude that there should be no subtraction of defendants' protections in criminal proceedings.[171]

For the exercise of appellate jurisdiction, the amendment of section 22 was a House contribution of undeniable importance because the monetary minimum of plus $2,000 was made applicable to all judgments and decrees of the Circuit Courts for purposes of review by the

---

[168] An account of the early agitation which commenced in 1784 was presented by Daniel Davis in Mass. Hist. Soc. *Coll.*, 4:25, 1st ser., 1795. At a convention held in January 1786, one of the grievances was to the effect that the business of the Supreme Judicial Court "from the extent of territories" was so great as to render a proper arrangement in that department exceedingly difficult; "and to repair to their office at Boston is very

expensive" (*ibid.*, 36). A petition to the Massachusetts General Court presented in 1788 was tabled January 1789. See also Mass. Hist. Soc. *Proc.*, 1:131, 134–37, 3d ser., 1908.

[169] Sec. 21. The removal section was also altered for transfer of causes to the Maine District Court.

[170] Hawkins, *Pleas of the Crown* (1777 ed.), II, 336.

[171] *Supra*, c. X, *passim*.

Supreme Court. The Senate version, it will be recalled, had imposed this only upon causes removed to the Circuit Courts by appeal from the District Courts. The House action was in effect a salvage by statute of the proposed limitation by constitutional amendment which the Senate had rejected on September 4.[172]

The text of the House's amendment of section 29 dealing with juries has not been found. The Representatives knew by September 10, if not earlier, that the Senate had stripped their Articles of Amendment of all reference to a jury of the vicinage. Possibly in reaction to this, two amendments were offered on September 14 while the House was sitting as a Committee of the Whole on the Judiciary Bill. It was reported in Greenleaf's *New-York Journal*[173] that William Smith of South Carolina had moved "that all juries which shall be summoned to serve in the courts of the United States, shall be formed according to the laws of each state respectively." This was adopted. Aedanus Burke of the same state then offered a second amendment, that "In cases of felony and treason, the offender shall be indicted and tried in the county, town or district wherein the offense shall have been committed, as hath been usual in each state before this law was enacted." This, too, was carried. The Committee reported to the House that day.

The House *Journal*, which was more miserably kept than that of the Senate, notes only one insignificant motion made on September 15 when the bill was ordered to be engrossed for a third reading.[174] We do not know whether the South Carolina amendments were among those finally voted September 17 when the bill as amended passed 37–16.[175] It was sent to the Senate the same day and referred to Ellsworth, Paterson and Pierce Butler.[176] All but four amendments were agreed to. As for the amendment of section 29 dealing with juries, a counterproposal was voted September 19[177] and, being agreed to by the House, became the first sentence and the first clause of section 29 of the Judiciary Act.[178] The Senate was unwilling to settle for any words of art such as

---

[172] *Senate Journal*, 1st Sess., 119.

[173] Sept. 17, 1789, reporting proceedings of September 14.

[174] *Annals of Congress*, I, 927. The House *Journal* makes no mention of the order (*Jour. H.R.*, I, 110–11).

[175] *Jour. H.R.*, I, at 113, notes only the fact of the passage of the bill. The tally of ayes and nays is in Greenleaf's *New-York Journal*, Sept. 24, 1789.

[176] *Senate Journal*, 1st Sess., 138.

[177] *Ibid.*, 139. The notes consisting of two pages stamped 26 and 47 are with Sen. 1A–B1 (NA). The official

notification dated September 19 is attached to the Ms. Senate Engrossed Bill, Sen. Files, Book 1 (NA).

[178] "That in cases punishable with death, the trial shall be had in the county where the offence was committed, or where that cannot be done without great inconvenience, twelve petit jurors at least shall be summoned from thence. And jurors in all cases to serve in the courts of the United States shall be designated by lot or otherwise in each State respectively according to the mode of forming juries therein now practised, so far

vicinage, felony or treason. The county was the extent of its yielding to the vicinage principle, and for the impanelling of jurors this needed to be regarded only in cases punishable by death. The selection of jurors by lot or otherwise in each state "according to the mode of forming Juries therein, now practised, so far as the laws of the same shall render such designation practicable" was so far an improvement over Smith's amendment that the choice was rescued from the whims of future state legislation, and an improvement over the Senate's original plan by depriving the marshal of a power it was hardly proper for him to possess. The House receded September 21 from the amendments to which the Senate had disagreed and agreed to the Senate amendment.[179] On September 24 the bill was signed by the President.

There was some unhappiness in both houses over the new act. At various junctures in his journal Maclay set out some individual criticisms, but as he had early made up his mind that the bill was "vile," one may suppose he was alert to find company. The two Virginia Senators obviously could not approve a statute which contained so much that was contrary to their instructions from the Virginia Convention. Paine Wingate viewed the system as too elaborate and too costly, but this did not deter him from advising a kinsman to seek judicial office.[180]

In the House, just before the final vote was taken, Gerry stated his objections which went to the principles of the bill and its operation. It had been "precipitated through the house" and he wished a clause to limit its duration. Jackson of Georgia, Burke of South Carolina and Stone of Maryland also had objections for they found the bill oppressive in nature and promising a mischievous operation. Benson of New York and Madison spoke in defense. The purport of their remarks was that the bill might not exactly suit every member in all its parts, but it was as good as at present it could be made. It was absolutely essential that a judicial bill pass the present session. Experience would show its defects. There had been no precipitation, for the bill had been in existence many months; it had been printed and had been a long time in the members' hands. It had been long discussed and many amendments had been added.[181] Madison's private opinion had been confided to Edmund Pendleton three days earlier.[182] He expressed his agreement with Pendleton that the bill was "defective both in its general structure

---

as the laws of the same shall render such designation practicable by the courts or marshals of the United States."

[179] *Jour. H.R.*, I, 115. The official notification attested by Clerk John Beckley was penned at the foot of the Senate notice.

[180] Wingate to Pickering, July 11, 1789, Wingate, *Life and Letters of Paine Wingate*, II, 318.

[181] *New-York Journal*, Sept, 24, 1789.

[182] Madison to Pendleton, Sept. 14, 1789, Ms. Madison Papers, XII, 30 (LC).

and, many of its particular regulations." Any radical alteration was prevented by the defect of time, the difficulty of substituting another plan with the consent of those who agreed in disliking the bill and because of the attachment of "Eastern members" to the Senate's bill. Well the latter might be, for so much out of their own law had been appropriated. The most Madison hoped for was that "some offensive violations of Southern jurisprudence" might be corrected, and the bill be reconsidered under the auspices of the judges. Madison did not detail what were the "offensive violations," but surely one item was the treatment of the venue question. The hope that the judges would assume responsibility for revising the act proved to be vain for, as we shall have occasion to notice, it was only as to occasional particulars that any advice was to be offered.

CHAPTER XII

The Process Acts

T HE SAME SESSION of the Congress which begot the Judiciary Act of 1789 brought forth also the Act to Regulate Processes in the Courts of the United States,[1] a younger brother, so to speak, of the more famous statute, but doomed to be little regarded by historians, for the subject matter was hardly such to captivate those to whom the larger aspects of institutional development were to be more beguiling. Nevertheless, this statute, because it supplemented the Judiciary Act and, as we shall see, projected into another area the political principle of section 34, was to exercise a profound influence upon the early functioning of federal law administration. For this and other reasons the history of the genesis and progress of this legislation deserves examination.

THE SENATE BILL AND ITS ANCESTORS

THE SENATE PROCESS BILL was the work of the same committee which had drafted the Judiciary Act[2] and which had assumed that the traditional mandates which set in motion civil litigation and kept it in train were to be at the disposal of the federal courts. The authorization was conferred by section 14 but in terms that were curiously obscure, viz., that

> courts of the United States, shall have power to issue writs of *scire facias, habeas corpus,* and all other writs not specially provided for by statute, which may be necessary for the exercise of their respective jurisdictions, and agreeable to the principles and usages of law.[3]

---

[1] 1 *U.S. Stats.,* 93.
[2] *Supra,* c. XI, p. 458.
[3] There were, of course, references elsewhere to other forms of process named in this act, *e.g.,* writ of error (sec. 10), attachment of goods by original process (sec. 12), *venire facias juratorum* (sec. 29).

This section had been adopted exactly as it had been framed in the bill reported to the Senate June 12, 1789, by the Committee for Organizing the Judiciary,[4] but it is clear from a letter of Senator George Read of Delaware to John Dickinson, dated June 16,[5] that the Committee had no intention of leaving matters on such a vague footing. "The same committee," wrote Read, "who reported this bill are preparing another, for prescribing and regulating the process of those respective courts."

The period of gestation was overlong, for it was not until September 17 that Senator Richard Henry Lee of the Committee reported "An Act to regulate Processes in the Courts of the United States,"[6] designed to supply specific directions for the guidance of the judiciary. The surviving materials relating to the history of this act, the revision of 1792 and the supplementary statute of 1793, are not rich, consisting as they do of committee bills, journal entries and exiguous reports of debates, yet it is manifest from these sources that a struggle took place between the legislators who favored creation of a uniform procedure for the new federal courts and those who conceived that in each district state forms and modes of process should prevail.

Considered in its historical setting the controversy may be viewed as an aspect of the sustained offensive conducted by the antifederalists against a "consolidated government." Richard Henry Lee himself had been one of the first to make this an issue in the fight over ratification of the Constitution.[7] And in the Senate during the opening stages of debates on the Judiciary Act he had sought, as noticed, to confine the jurisdiction of inferior courts to admiralty and maritime causes and to limit the judicial power to appeals from state to federal courts.[8] The proposal regarding inferior courts he had renewed early in September 1789, when the House's Articles of Amendment of the Constitution were debated in the Senate, and he had also presented the Virginia Convention's rewritten version of Article III, section 2.[9] On both occasions his motions were defeated. The federalists were too firmly in control to tolerate any tampering with Article III of the Constitution and with what was conceived to be the intendment of its language. Furthermore, the conviction that Article III of the Constitution must be properly

---

[4] *Supra,* c. XI, p. 465.

[5] W. T. Read, *Life and Correspondence of George Read,* 480–81.

[6] *Senate Journal,* 1st Sess., 137.

[7] In his "Observations leading to a fair examination of the System of Government, proposed by the late Convention . . . In a number of Letters from the Federal Farmer to the Republican," in Ford, *Pamphlets,* 277. Lee came to the matter in his

first "letter," Oct. 8, 1787 (*ibid.,* 286), and pursued the theme in the remainder of his discourse.

[8] The text of the resolve is written on a chit (stamped 28) filed with the ms. Bill to Establish the Judicial Courts of the United States, Senate Files, Sen. 1A–B1 (NA).

[9] *Senate Journal,* 1st Sess., 124–25. The Virginia proposals in Elliot, *Debates,* III, 659–61.

implemented without delay was sufficiently general that agreement was reached on the institutional structure and many of the procedural details embodied in the Judiciary Act. A Process Act was, however, something more difficult to promote, partly because it was legislation which was arguably less urgent, and partly because most of its provisions were of a sort to arouse professional provincialism. This had already manifested itself in debates on the Judiciary Act, and had led to the alteration or elimination of practice provisions such as the introduction of a discovery procedure.[10]

There is no evidence of how opinion on the Process Bill of 1789 divided in the Senate because no ayes and nays were recorded on any vote. It seems likely, however, that the eventual radical changes in its contents and the rejection of uniform process in common law actions were brought about by the lawyers who had had no hand in its making, those whom Jefferson called "demi-lawyers"[11] and ductile laymen.[12] This Senate, it will be recalled, was a small body, for only eleven states were represented when the bill was reported, neither North Carolina nor Rhode Island having yet ratified the Constitution. Half of the membership had been admitted to practice, and if only a few of these suffered from the age-old professional malady of resisting procedural change, which the Process Bill threatened in the newly created districts, the task of marshalling votes against the bill was not a strenuous one.

That some of the provisions of the bill should have seemed strange to anyone not familiar with the procedural vagaries of the jurisdictions laid under contribution by the draftsmen may be ascribed to the diversities in the practice of the several states. The English form and practice books had been the sires and dams of all the American systems, but the indicia of origin were not everywhere manifest in equal degree because something of the history of each colony or province had bred characteristic changes into its law. Nowhere was the native element more pronounced than in New England; nowhere was common law tradition more faithfully observed than in New Jersey, New York and South Carolina. The New England states had been most tenacious of the dispositions made before the establishment of imperial controls. Their scheme of process as originally instituted was patterned on that prevailing in English inferior jurisdictions—summons, attachment of chattels and ultimately distress infinite. Even when the New Englanders got around to authorizing the ultimate coercion of bodily arrest, this was

---

[10] *Maclay Journal*, 95–96, 89–92.
[11] Jefferson, *Autobiography*, in *Works of Jefferson* (Ford, Federal ed.), I, 71.
[12] *Cf.* the comment of Senator William Grayson of Virginia, himself a lawyer, reported by Maclay (*Journal*, 95): "The people who were not lawyers, on a supposition that lawyers knew best, would follow the lawyers, and a party were determined to push it."

permitted only for want of attachable goods. The scheme of progressively more severe mandates to compel appearance was a relic of medieval usage that the courts at Westminster had already abandoned and supplanted as respects personal actions by a first process of bodily arrest. It was this contemporary practice in the King's Courts that was to serve as the common law upon which process in certain royal provinces like New Jersey and New York was to be modelled.

The coexistence of two dissimilar approaches to questions of process is directly relevant to the drafting of the Process Bill, for our examination of the sources will reveal that the practice of Connecticut, Massachusetts and New Jersey was determinative of most of the bill's ingredients, and supplies support for the conjecture that it was Ellsworth of Connecticut, Strong of Massachusetts and Paterson of New Jersey who assumed the responsibility for drafting this document as they had in the case of the Judiciary Bill.[13] The task was one beyond the capacities of the laymen on the Committee, and although both Richard Bassett of Delaware and William Few of Georgia, also members thereof, were lawyers, no evidence of their participation has been found.

The manuscript text of the bill as reported is in Ellsworth's hand,[14] a fact suggesting his leadership; but if this was indeed the case, he was more ready to adopt practices from Massachusetts and New Jersey than he had been when the Judiciary Act was drafted. Since there was little of new invention offered to the Senate, the inquiry into the immediate sources as well as procedural variants in some jurisdictions not canvassed by the draftsmen should throw some light upon how responsibility was shared and why the bill ran into difficulties.

It is not our purpose to pursue the procedural diversities in all the states—indeed, it has proven in some instances, notably Georgia, a task impossible to perform because of the destruction of records. Furthermore, in some jurisdictions the provincial courts, aware of the rule that an Act of Parliament not naming the plantations was considered inapplicable, nevertheless had put into effect some English statutory innovation. It is wholly a matter of chance when such a covert reception, well known to the practitioners of the time, can be documented. What is here set forth, although it would not appease an appetite for procedural minutiae as consuming as that displayed by Uriah Heep in his study of Tidd's *Practice of the Court of King's Bench*, should be sufficient to indicate why, political considerations apart, this first attempt at uniform federal rules of practice was a daring and, in a way, an imaginative

---

[13] *Supra,* c. XI, p. 459.

[14] Senate Files, Sen. 1A–B1, tray 1, folder 1, 17 (NA).

An Act to regulate Processes
in the Courts of the United States —

Be it enacted by the Senate &
~ves of the United States
~rica in congress assembled, That
all Writs & Processes issuing out of any
of the Courts of the United States, shall
be in the name of the President of the
United States of America. And if they
issue from the supreme or circuit court,
shall bear test of the chief Justice of the
supreme court, & if from a district court,
shall bear test of the Judge of such
court; & shall be under the seal of the
court from whence they issue, & signed by
the Clerk thereof. The Seals for the supreme
& circuit co~ ~ to be ~~~ded by the supreme court,
& for the district courts, by the respective
Judges of the same.

And be it further enacted, That
in civil actions the Process shall commence
by a Summons or a *capias ad respondendum.*
The

Manuscript draft of an act to regulate Processes in the Courts in the handwriting of Oliver Ellsworth.
(The National Archives)

venture. It is further to be observed that in light of the final form of the Process Act, our survey of procedural variants should point up some of the complexities of law administration on the civil side of circuit jurisdiction more trenchantly than from surviving scraps in case papers. Major responsibility to provide guidance in state practice rested upon the District judges who were presumably masters of local procedural niceties. A Supreme Court Justice assigned to a circuit had, however, often to assume out-of-term responsibilities relating to process, and these local diversities could well give him moments of uneasiness.

The Committee bill[15] consisted of twelve sections. As we shall have occasion to notice, while some of these dealt with process in the strict sense of contemporary English practice books, others sought to regulate incidents of practice. The definition of process as proceedings in actions from the beginning to the end derived from the much venerated Giles Jacob,[16] and there is no better exhibit on the currency of this view than the fact that in various circuits the term "modes of process" used in the statute as enacted was by rule of court rendered as the "practice" of the state where the court was kept.[17]

The first section of the Committee bill opened with the direction that "all writs and processes issuing out of any of the courts of the United States, shall be in the name of the President of the United States of America." It proceeded to lay down how such process should be tested in the case of each court, the sealing and signature by the clerk. It directed how the seals should be provided. The section was provocative in this—that earlier during the Senate debate on the President's removal power (July 14–18) when the implications of the Constitution's grant of executive power were explored, Ellsworth had argued that by the Constitution such power was completely vested. The United States, he said, would be parties to a thousand suits and he asked "shall Pro-

---

[15] The references here are to the printed copy in the Library of Congress: "An Act to regulate Processes in the Courts of the United States," 4. At the foot of p. 4 is printed "[NEW-YORK, PRINTED BY THOMAS GREENLEAF.]" The printing was done after the first reading, for following the last section is printed "In Senate of the United States, September 17, 1789./ Read the first time./ SAMUEL A. OTIS. SEC." A comparison of ms. and printed bill reveals some minor discrepancies such as "a" Supreme Court (sec. 1) in the printed version whereas the ms. text version is "the" Supreme Court. As will be shown below, the printed copies were used in debate and curiously enough the printer's error of "a" Supreme Court survived in the statute.

No section numbers were printed. However, in the Library of Congress document these were written in the margins beginning with sec. 3. Hereafter the print will be referred to as the Committee bill.

[16] Blackamore's Case, 8 Coke Rep. 156, 157. And so far as concerned the run-of-the-mill American attorney, G. Jacob, Law-Dictionary, 7th ed. (1756), s.v. Process.

[17] Cf. infra, c. XIII on the Virginia doctrine.

scess issue in their Name vs. or for themselves?"[18] The intimation was, of course, that process should run in the name of the President, such mandates being esteemed an exercise of executive authority. Ellsworth's query, which seems irrelevant to the immediate issue, may, however, reflect a decision already reached by the draftsmen of the Process Bill. In any event, there was angry reaction summed up in the charge that this was "bringing in monarchy by a sidewind,"[19] a not unreasonable accusation in light of the fact that in pre-Revolutionary days process had run in the name of the King. The states, regarding the style of writs to be a manifestation of sovereignty, had severally elected that process run in the name of the Commonwealth or the People. Ellsworth was clearly not moved by the debate, for his notion was embodied in the Process Bill.

Section 2 of the bill provided "that in civil actions the process shall commence by a summons or a *capias ad respondendum.*" This was a curious turn of phrase the import of which seems to have been to bar rummaging in the treasury of English original writs for the instruments to initiate actions since such had served as first process until the bill procedure of King's Bench and the *capias* procedure of Common Bench made them dispensable. If it was this at which the draftsmen aimed, the language must be taken as limiting the generous but ambiguous grant of section 14 of the Judiciary Act. The section continued by setting forth the forms:

The form of the Summons shall be as follows:—
    The President of the United States of America,
To the Marshall of the District of
GREETING:
WE command you, that you summon A.B. of   if
he may be found in your District, to appear before our
Court, to be holden at   within the District of   on
the   day of   then and there to answer to C.D. of
      in a plea of   to the damage of the said C.D.   as
he saith.   And have you there this writ.
      Witness, E.F. Esq. at   the   day of
            in the year of our Lord

                    G. H. Clerk.

---

[18] Since the Senate conducted its debates behind closed doors, the few fragmentary notes kept by John Adams are the only sources approximating a verbatim account of proceedings. The notes on the removal debate are in *Adams Papers,* III, 218–19.

[19] Made by Grayson of Virginia, who proceeded, "You make him Vindex Injuriarum. The People will not like The Jurors of our Lord the President—nor the Peace of our Lord the President, nor his Dignity." *Ibid.,* 218.

AN ACT to regulate PROCESSES in the COURTS of the UNITED STATES.

BE IT ENACTED BY THE SENATE AND HOUSE OF REPRESEN-TATIVES OF THE UNITED STATES OF AMERICA IN CONGRESS ASSEMBLED, That all writs and proceffes iffuing out of any of the courts of the United States, ~~fhall be~~ in the name of the Prefident of the United States ~~of America~~. ~~And if they iffue from a Supreme~~ ~~Court, and if from a Diftrict Court, fhall bear teft of the Judge of~~ fuch Court, and fhall be under the feal of the Court from whence they iffue, and figned by the Clerk thereof. The feals of the Supreme and Circuit Courts ~~to~~ be provided by the Supreme Court, and ~~for~~ the Diftrict Courts, by the refpective Judges of the fame.

AND BE IT FURTHER ENACTED, That in civil actions, the pro- *for Debt or Damages* cefs fhall commence by a fummons or a CAPIAS AD RESPONDEN-DUM.

The form of the Summons fhall be as follows :—

The Prefident of the United States of America,

To the Marfhall of the Diftrict of

GREETING :
WE command you, that you fummon A. B. of if he may be found in your Diftrict, to appear before our ~~Circuit, particularly known as~~ within the Diftrict of on the day of then and there to anfwer to C. D. of in a plea of ~~to the damage of the faid C. D.~~ as he faith. And have you there this writ.

Witnefs, E. F. Efq. at   the   day of in the year of our Lord

G. H. Clerk.

And the form of the CAPIAS fhall be as follows :—

The Prefident of the United States of America,

To the Marfhall of the Diftrict of

GREETING :
WE command you, that you take A. B. of if he may be found in your Diftrict, and him fafely keep, fo that you have his body before our   Court, to be holden at within the Diftrict of   on the   day of then and there to anfwer to C. D. of in a plea of ~~to the damage of the faid C. D.~~ as he faith. And have you there this writ.

Witnefs, E. F. Efq. at   the   day of in the year of our Lord

G. H. Clerk

Printed Senate Bill—An Act to regulate Processes in the Courts of the United States.

And the form of the CAPIAS shall be as follows:—

The President of the United States of America,

To the Marshall of the District of

GREETING:

WE command you, that you take A.B. of   if
he may be found in your District, and him safely keep, so
that you have his body before our   Court, to be holden
at   within the District of   on the   day
of   then and there to answer to C.D. of   in
a plea of   to the damage of the said C.D.   as
he saith. And have you there this writ.

Witness, E.F. Esq. at   the   day of
in the year of our Lord

The projected form of federal summons corresponded with the form provided in the Massachusetts process act set out below and in effect at the time when the federal bill was drafted;[20] but the *capias* was a stripped-down version of the English form. The Massachusetts *capias* or attachment was significantly different because it provided that de-

---

[20] I *Laws of the Commonwealth of Massachusetts 1780–1800* (1801), 199, enacted October Sess. 1784.

[Summons]
COMMONWEALTH OF
MASSACHUSETTS.

To the Sheriff of our county of
S_____, *or his Deputy.*

GREETING

WE command you, that you summon A.B. of C. (if he may be found in your precinct) to appear before our Justices of our Court of   to be holden at B. within and for our said county of S. on the   Tuesday of   then and there in our said Court to answer to D.E. of R. within our county of M. in a plea of   to the damage of the said D.E. (as he saith) the sum of   *Pounds,* which shall then and there be made to appear, with other due damages. And have you there this writ, with your doings therein. Witness E.H. Esq.; at B. the   day of   in the year of our LORD
A.D. Clerk.

[Capias, *or Attachment*]
COMMONWEALTH OF
MASSACHUSETTS.

To the Sheriff of our county of
S_____, *or his Deputy.*

GREETING

WE command you to attach the goods or estate of R.F. of B. within our county of S. to the value of   *Pounds,* and for want thereof to take the body of the said R.F. (if he may be found in your precinct) and him safely keep, so that you have him before our Justices of our   Court of   next to be holden at B. within and for our said county of S. on the   Tuesday of   then and there in our said Court, to answer unto D.S. of R. within our county of M. in a plea of   to the damage of the said D.S. (as he saith) the sum of   *Pounds,* which shall then and there be made to appear, with other due damages. And have you there this writ, with your doings therein. Witness E.H. Esq. at B.   the   day of   in the year of our LORD
A.D. Clerk.

517

fendant could be arrested on original civil process only if his attachable property was of value insufficient to cover the damages claimed.[21]

By "An Act prescribing forms of Writs, Processes, &c.," Connecticut prescribed the language of a summons to appear before a justice of the peace and its county courts[22] that, except for the style, was identical with the pre-Revolutionary form.[23] The arrest process in this state resembled that of Massachusetts in specifically providing that defendant's person could be seized only for want of personal goods of sufficient value.[24]

The New England scheme of process was, as noticed, the product of more antiquated precedents than those which had governed in New York. Here personal actions were begun by bill—a precept for arrest—issuing directly from the Supreme Court of Judicature or by *capias* if defendant lived in a county where the Supreme Court was not held and kept.[25] In colonial New Jersey an action could also have been initiated by bill,[26] but by statute in 1783 it was provided that all actions which might be brought in the Supreme Court or in any Court of Common Pleas should be commenced by summons or *capias*.[27] The effect of this appears to have been a supplanting of bill procedure by the *capias*, and, of course, the latter was always preferred over summons because of the advantage of civil bail. In Pennsylvania, in 1724/25, the assembly acting in the interest of the liberty of the subject, had exempted freemen from arrest,[28] and the rule was still in effect in 1788.[29] The alternative offered by the proposed process act consequently ran counter to the policy of that state.

The last paragraph of the Committee's section 2 provided for notice to the defendant of the nature of the cause of action against him:

---

[21] The Massachusetts forms were not new; except for the style, they were identical with those provided by a provincial act of 1701. 1 *Acts and Resolves Prov. of Mass. Bay*, 464. New Hampshire had patterned its process on these forms in 1718. *Acts and Laws of His Majesty's Province of New Hampshire in New England* (1771), c. 80.

[22] *Acts and Laws of the State of Connecticut* (1784), 84.

[23] *Acts and Laws of the Colony of Connecticut* (1769), 75.

[24] *Acts and Laws of the State of Connecticut* (1784), 84.

[25] "Practical Proceedings in the Supreme Court of the State of New York," in *LPAH*, I, 55. The bill, alternatively Bill of New York or Bill of Albany, was an adaptation of the King's Bench Bill of Middlesex; forms, *ibid.*, 136–37.

[26] *Cf.* the form (Griffith v. Ball, 1768) in Ms. William Livingston Precedent Book, 149–50 (NYSL).

[27] *New Jersey Laws*, 8th Assembly, 2d Sitting (1784), c. 32, sec. 1.

[28] 1 A. J. Dallas, ed., *Laws of the Commonwealth of Pennsylvania* (1797), 223.

[29] Penman v. Wayne, 1 Dallas 241 (Phila. C.P. 1788).

> And the declaration in the cause shall be annexed to every summons
> or CAPIAS, as aforesaid, at the time of service; or, if not then annexed,
> the defendant shall be served with a copy of the declaration within
> days afterwards, and without charge to him.

The draftsmen's intent here seems to have been to furnish defendant
with fuller notice of the cause for which he had been taken to answer
than conveyed by the writ alone. Notice was, of course, a traditional
ingredient of due process, but that given by the original writs, and indeed the Committee's proposed process, was only *pro forma*. Where
causes were begun by bill or *capias* and originals became superfluous,
not even this modicum of advance notice had for a long time been given,
until by statute in England something resembling *pro forma* notice was
restored.

There is no doubt but that New England practice here furnished
inspiration. It was the practice in Massachusetts to incorporate in or
annex the declaration to process,[30] and the Connecticut legislature had
written into the first sentence of its process act in effect in 1789,[31]

> That the ordinary Process in Civil Actions in this State, shall be a
> summons or an Attachment . . . therein also containing a Declaration
> of the Substance of the Action. . . .

Thus Connecticut gave plaintiff no option to delay his declaration. New
Jersey's statute, however, did not require that plaintiff present his declaration to defendant along with the summons or *capias*, but only that

> within thirty days after the Return of any Summons or Capias served
> as aforesaid, the Plaintiff shall file his Declaration in the Clerk's Office
> from whence the Process issued, particularly stating his Demand, and
> on what the same is founded . . . which Declaration being filed in the
> Clerk's office as aforesaid, a Copy thereof shall be delivered by the
> Clerk to the Defendant. . . .[32]

Defendant was allowed fifty days to plead, but this time ran from the
date of return of the summons or *capias*, so long as plaintiff's declaration
was filed within thirty days after the return.[33] Both of these statutes
departed from the practice of England, in that defendant was presented
with the declaration before appearance. The contemporary rule in

---

[30] *Cf. Legal Papers of John Adams*,
I, xlv, where it is indicated that the
usage of entering the declaration on
process made such a rule unnecessary.

[31] *Acts and Laws of the State of
Connecticut* (1784), 3.
[32] *New Jersey Laws*, 8th Assembly,
2d Sitting (1784), c. 32, sec. 4.
[33] *Ibid.*, sec. 5.

England was that the declaration could not be filed in chief before appearance, although the declaration might be filed *de bene esse*.[34] The Virginia General Court Act of 1777 followed the rule of filing after appearance.[35] The New Jersey provision resembled English and Virginia practice because the writ and the declaration issued separately, but since it did not require entry of defendant's appearance prior to the serving of the declaration, the statute had the same virtues which Zephaniah Swift praised in Connecticut's law:[36]

> The writ is accompanied with the declaration, containing the substance of the action, and the demand of the plaintiff. The defendant becomes acquainted with it, and can determine whether he will make defence. . . . If he has no defence, then he may save the expence and trouble of an appearance, and the court having before them, the declaration which contains the claim of the plaintiff, they have a sufficient foundation laid to authorise them to render judgment on the default of the defendant.

Section 3 provided for the manner and time of service. In cases where the state was defendant, the "chief Magistrate" was to be served _____ months in advance of the court's sitting. Where a corporation was defendant, its clerk or a "principal officer" would be served _____ days before the court's sitting. A "common person" was to be served by delivery of the summons and declaration to him or to his "usual place of abode," the time he was allowed depending upon whether the writ was returnable to a District, a Circuit or Supreme Court.

Mere mention of process where a state was impleaded might have aroused latent state susceptibilities but for the fact that during the short life of the Articles of Confederation states had invoked the authority conferred upon the Continental Congress for the settlement of disputes and differences between two or more states[37] and something resembling process had been used by Congress pursuant to its constitutional authority in various interstate boundary controversies. These instruments had been no more than notifications issued in response to a petition requesting appointment of commissioners to determine the cause. Although the specimens used in the Connecticut-Pennsylvania dispute[38] and that between Massachusetts and New York[39] were pleonastic compositions devoid of the element of command, the directions of the

---

[34] Crompton, *Practice common-placed: or, the Rules and Cases of Practice in the Courts of King's Bench and Common Pleas*, 2d ed. (1783), I, 91.

[35] 9 Hening, *Va. Stats.*, 401.

[36] Swift, *A System of the Laws of the State of Connecticut*, II, 194.

[37] Articles of Confederation, Art. IX, Thorpe, *Constitutions and Charters*, I, 12–13.

[38] *JCC*, XXI, 1115–16.

[39] *Ibid.*, XXVII, 547–50.

Articles regarding further steps in the event of "neglect" imparted a minatory effect to the notification. The Senate Committee was proceeding beyond a mere notification, but it chose the mildest form of judicial order, viz., the summons. This was the form of process used in England for securing appearance of the "noble person" of a peer;[40] so, too, in republican Virginia, for actions against the governor, members of the Privy Council and, of all things, a sheriff.[41] Since it was long settled that no *capias* could issue against a corporation, the summons was here also to be the first process.

The rule for service on those whom the Committee with democratic candor called "any common person" reflects what had, with variations, become a surprisingly widespread practice in the United States. Because the original of process had to be returned with an indorsement of the serving official, in this country, as in England, a copy of the process was used in the ritual of service. What was novel in many jurisdictions and a departure from contemporary English usage, which required personal service,[42] was the authorization to leave a copy of process at defendant's abode. We know from Alexander Hamilton's little treatise on Supreme Court practice that in New York where actions were begun by *capias* or bill, English usage was closely followed.[43] The procedure chosen by the Committee appears to have been first introduced in Massachusetts in 1644,[44] and it was confirmed by acts of assembly 1701/02[45] and 1736/37.[46] It was probably from this source that the alternative of serving a defendant personally or by deposit of process at his abode made its way into the colonial law of New Hampshire[47] and Connecticut.[48] This was still the rule in these states and, of course, familiar to Strong and Ellsworth. But it may be noticed that an identical practice existed in Pennsylvania in 1785,[49] in Maryland, where the practice was tolerated if persons had left the province,[50] and in South Carolina.[51] In the Committee bill the times of return were left open to be settled by the Senate, presumably because the fancied inaccessibility of the new fed-

---

[40] J. Impey, *The New Instructor Clericalis*, 2d ed. (1785), 349.

[41] 9 Hening, *Va. Stats.*, 403.

[42] By virtue of St. 12 Geo. I, c. 29.

[43] *LPAH*, I, 55–56.

[44] *Laws and Liberties of Massachusetts*, Introduction by M. Farrand (1929 ed.), 3, limited to attachments of chattels or lands and hereditaments.

[45] 1 *Acts and Resolves Prov. of Mass. Bay*, 462—summons and attachment.

[46] 2 *ibid.*, 831—extended to summons alone.

[47] *Acts and Laws . . . Province of New Hampshire* (1771), 144 (c. 92).

[48] *Acts and Laws of the State of Connecticut* (1784), 10; and see *Acts and Laws of the Colony of Connecticut* (1769), 3.

[49] Case v. Hufty, 1 Dallas 154 (Phila. C.P.).

[50] Act of 1715, c. 40, sec. 3 (1 Kilty, *Laws of Maryland*), as to attachments.

[51] County Courts Act, sec. 31, March Sess. 1785 (7 *Stats. at Large South Carolina*, 224).

eral courts had been an item in the early critique of a national judiciary that had later manifested itself in niggling over the location of District and Circuit Courts when the Judiciary Act was under discussion.

Section 4 provided that in all suits begun by original process in a Circuit Court defendant should, _____ days before the first day of the term to which process was returnable, file notice of what plea he intended to rely upon or whether he intended to demur or what matter, if any, he would plead in abatement. In default of so doing, he would not be allowed to plead or demur, but judgment might be entered as upon a *nihil dicit* unless he could assign satisfactory reasons for his neglect. Defendant was further required to stand by the terms of the notice except as the court might permit amendment or alteration of a plea given in court.

The source of the regulation of section 4 has not been identified but the proposal was in several particulars a departure from English common law practice then obtaining. In both King's Bench and Common Pleas rules of court determined when a defendant ought to plead. In the second place, upon delivery of the declaration, plaintiff served defendant with a notice to plead within a specified time to so do. If the defendant failed to plead pursuant to the notice, a rule to plead would issue. On default of defendant's pleading, plaintiff might sign judgment by *nil dicit*.[52] The practice in New York where a twenty-day rule to plead obtained was similar.[53] It is further to be observed that both in England and New York what defendant delivered was the plea itself and not a mere notice of plea. Although the basic policy of the English courts was to hold defendant to his plea, the exceptions noticed in the practice treatises indicate a much less rigid approach than the proposed federal rule.[54]

Some of the American jurisdictions had by statute authorized a default judgment where defendant failed to file a plea,[55] but only in New Jersey and Virginia was a statutory time limit set.[56] Elsewhere the matter appears to have rested upon rule of court.[57]

---

[52] The rules of both King's Bench and Common Pleas are set forth in Crompton, *Practice common-placed: or, the Rules and Cases of Practice in the Courts of King's Bench and Common Pleas*, I, at 143–44.

[53] *LPAH*, I, 58.

[54] E.g., Crompton, *Practice common-placed: or, the Rules and Cases of Practice in the Courts of King's Bench and Common Pleas*, I, at 168.

[55] Act of 1763, c. 23, sec. 4 (1 Kilty, *Laws of Maryland*).

[56] *New Jersey Laws*, 8th Assembly, 2d Sitting (1784), 2d Sess. 1783, c. 32, sec. 5; 12 Hening, *Va. Stats.*, 743, sec. 32 (1788).

[57] As it was in New York, and had been in New Jersey before the statute of 1783; cf. "Rules of the Supreme Court Province of New Jersey 1740," in Ms. William Livingston Precedent Book, 202 (NYSL). For South Carolina, cf. Read v. Kennedy, 1 Bay 226 (1791).

XII: *The Process Acts*

Introduction of the *capias* into federal procedure by section 2 required some regulation of bail which allegedly "had come in with the *capias*" and had become a hardy American transplant. Conceived as a boon for a defendant, special bail, viz., the undertaking of responsible sureties for his appearance upon release from custody, also served the interest of a plaintiff as security.[58] Section 5 sought to fix the conditions under which special or money bail could be exacted.

It was provided that no person be arrested on a *capias* unless (1) plaintiff filed an affidavit giving his cause of action, stating that the debt owed exceeded _____ dollars, or (2) plaintiff sued for mayhem, battery or "other tort." A *capias* would be issued, however, without the meeting of these conditions if the United States or a "Body Corporate" were plaintiff. The affidavits could be filed with a justice, judge or clerk of any United States court, and the sum specified therein (or in the case of mayhem, battery or "other tort," an amount the judge deemed reasonable) was to be indorsed on the back of the writ, and bail could be taken for this sum and no more. Thus, although the New England states were more lenient in their use of *capias* in that they allowed defendant's body to be seized only if the value of his attachable goods was insufficient to cover the amount of plaintiff's claimed damages, the proposed federal rule required that the action be of a certain nature or for a specified sum before the writ could be used at all.

This section was apparently drawn with reference to the practice of states which had adopted common law usage and was obviously to be applicable where a declaration was not served with a *capias*. In England, because the original writ as first process had through the indulgence of fictions been displaced by precept or process ordering arrest of defendant, Parliament, to check abuse, had in 1661 made the disclosure of the true cause of action a condition precedent for special bail of defendants arrested on precepts or process based on a fictitious trespass.[59] Subsequently in 1725 it was required that plaintiff make an affidavit that

---

[58] Special bail was security taken from responsible sureties when a defendant was taken into custody on process in personal actions, upon conditions fixed initially in England by practice of the court, ultimately governed by statute. For the situations where such bail could not be exacted, although precept or writ ordered arrest of defendant, so-called common bail was entered which was no more than the nominal sureties John Doe and Richard Roe.

Special bail served as collateral security for the satisfaction of a judg-

ment; it was open to plaintiff to except to the sufficiency of the appearance bail (bail below). The procedure *coram judice* was called "justifying" bail, at which time, if the court was satisfied, the appearance bail became bail to the action (bail above). The liability of such bail to satisfy judgment attached in the event defendant could not do so or he had not been surrendered betimes by the bondsmen, and if plaintiff resorted to a *capias ad satisfaciendum* as final process to enforce his judgment.

[59] 13 Car. II, St. 2, c. 2.

the cause of action involved £10 or more.[60] The sum was to be in-dorsed on the back of the process and no more than that amount could be taken as bail. Because damages were uncertain in trespass actions, bail was allowed only on motion and order.[61] The practice in New York was closely patterned on the English and without local statutory inter-vention.[62] In New Jersey, by rule of court, the directions of 13 Charles II Statute 2, c. 2, were followed.[63] Maryland introduced some early statutory variations still in effect in 1789.[64] An attachment could not issue until a writ had been twice returned *non est* and with the attach-ment would go a *capias*. A note of the declaration would also be des-patched. Special bail would be taken at plaintiff's request. The Virginia General Court Act of 1777[65] contained elaborate directions which fol-lowed in the main English usage as delineated in the practice books. In *qui tam* actions, slander, trespass, assault and battery, trover or other wrongs, plaintiff was directed to indorse on original writ or subsequent process the true "species of action" (on pain of having his cause dis-missed with costs) to advise the sheriff whether bail was to be demanded. It lay with the judge to determine in the tort action upon proper affidavit or affirmation whether or not appearance bail be taken. In the case of debt actions founded upon obligations, all actions of covenant or detinue where indorsement of the true species of action and the demand for special bail appeared, the sheriff was to return the name of the bail and the bond before the day of appearance. If defendant de-faulted, or should not give special bail as ruled by the court, the ap-pearance bail should be liable to the action. In contrast with these elaborate directions, the Massachusetts[66] and Connecticut practice, chiefly because the declaration accompanied process, was simple.

Bail legislation in England had been aimed at preventing vexa-tious arrests; whether in imitation or independently, the same motive

---

[60] 12 Geo. I, c. 29.

[61] Crompton, *Practice common-placed: or, the Rules and Cases of Practice in the Courts of King's Bench and Common Pleas*, I, at 33.

[62] Because 12 Geo. I, c. 29, was fol-lowed there although it did not in terms extend to the plantations. *Cf. LPAH*, I, 57.

[63] "Rules of Supreme Court Prov-ince of New Jersey 1740," in Ms. William Livingston Precedent Book, 202 (NYSL). Absent statutory change, it may properly be assumed that the early rules remained in effect. This was clearly the case in New York, as indicated by the citations in W.

Wyche, *Treatise on the Practice of the Supreme Court of Judicature of the State of New York*, 2d ed. (1794).

[64] Maryland Law 1715, c. 46, sec. 3 (in 1 Kilty, *Laws of Maryland*).

[65] 9 Hening, *Va. Stats.*, 401, secs. 12–14.

[66] In Massachusetts the "Act Regu-lating Bail in Civil Actions of 1784" (1 *Laws of the Commonwealth of Massachusetts 1780–1800* [1801], 195) contains nothing resembling statutory provisions of England, for it lays down only rules as to when bail would become liable, provisions for surrender, service of *scire facias* on bail.

appears to underlie dispositions in this country. The American jurisdictions had, however, resorted to further means to protect defendants and section 6 of the Process Bill was of a piece with such legislation. It provided that:

> All original writs issuing from any District or Circuit Court, shall, before they are served, be endorsed by an Attorney of such Court, with his name thereon, or by such other responsible inhabitant of the district as shall be approved by a Justice, Judge, or Clerk of the court in which the action is to be tried; which endorser, in case the plaintiff fails to support his action, and an execution against him be returned unsatisfied, shall be liable to pay to the defendant the costs for which judgment shall be rendered.

Although, as noticed, this section owed something to American tradition and, indeed, to the immediate professional experience of at least two of the Committee, its incorporation was further motivated by an anticipation of vexations incident to the directions of the Judiciary Act regarding the locus of civil actions. The provision[67] that no such action could be brought by original process against an inhabitant of the United States except in the district where he was an inhabitant or where he might be found had been directed at disarming the criticisms of those who claimed the new system would victimize defendants, and of those antifederalists who wished actions between citizens of different states to be centered in state courts. Section 6 was designed as a further safeguard for defendants against non-resident plaintiffs.

What the Committee proposed went far beyond common law usage. Anciently a plaintiff offered only those storied characters John Doe and Richard Roe as pledges for prosecution of his action, but by the middle of the eighteenth century even this formality had been treated as dispensable.[68] It was only under particular circumstances in ejectment and in *qui tam* actions that, upon motion of defendant, a court could require security for costs.[69] Since the courts with characteristic British acumen conceived that the interest of commerce might be affected, non-resident plaintiffs were normally exempt from giving security until King's Bench in 1786 ruled this must be proffered or the action stayed.[70]

American dissatisfaction with English practice seems to have first manifested itself in Massachusetts where in 1695[71] an act of assembly required security for costs from non-resident plaintiffs. This act was

---

[67] Sec. 11.
[68] Littlehales v. Bosanquett, Barnes 163 (1742).
[69] Vat v. Green, 1 Strange 697 (1726); Lamii v. Sewell, 1 Wilson

K.B. 266 (1750).
[70] Pray *et al.* v. Edie, 1 Term Rep. 267 (1786).
[71] 1 *Acts and Resolves Prov. of Mass. Bay,* 222.

disallowed by the Crown, and in 1708, under cover of preventing vexatious arrests, the posting of security by plaintiffs in general was provided by a new act,[72] made permanent in 1714. New Hampshire followed suit[73] and so did Connecticut.[74] The Massachusetts Act of 1708 was re-enacted in 1784.[75] The text is set forth in the margin, for it is this which we believe served as a model for the Committee.[76]

It should be noticed that the Massachusetts statute allowed plaintiff himself to indorse the writ if he was an inhabitant of the state, but required that a "responsible . . . inhabitant" of the state indorse the writ if plaintiff, his agent or attorney resided without Massachusetts. The state's provision that the "Court may . . . order that the plaintiff shall procure a new indorser" seems changed only in phraseology by the Committee in its stipulation that the indorser-inhabitant "shall be approved by a justice . . . of the court."

The New England legislation was not an aberration peculiar to those parts, for there are entries in the minutes of the New York Supreme Court of Judicature as early as the year 1702[77] evidencing the practice

---

[72] Ibid., 739.

[73] Acts and Laws . . . Province of New Hampshire (1771), c. 74 (1718).

[74] In Connecticut a bond was required if resort was had to an attachment. Acts and Laws of the State of Connecticut (1784), 84, for the form.

[75] "An Act prescribing Forms of Writs in Civil Causes, and directing the Mode of proceeding therein," in 1 Laws of the Commonwealth of Massachusetts 1780–1800 (1801), at 199, 206, sec. 11 (October 1784).

[76] "That all original writs issuing out of the Supreme Judicial Court, or Court of Common Pleas, shall, before they are served, be indorsed on the back thereof by the plaintiff or plaintiffs, or one of them, with his christian and surname, if he or they are inhabitants of this Commonwealth, or by his or their agent or attorney, being an inhabitant thereof, and where the plaintiff is not an inhabitant of this Commonwealth, then his writ shall be indorsed in manner aforesaid, by some responsible person who is an inhabitant of this Commonwealth, provided that the Court may, upon motion, in consideration that the agent or attorney who indorsed the writ is not of ability for the purposes hereafter mentioned, order that the plaintiff shall procure a new indorser,

and such new indorser shall be held in the same manner as if the indorsement had been made before the writ was served, and unless the plaintiff shall procure such new indorser when directed thereunto by the Court, he shall become nonsuit, but no costs shall be awarded against him. And the plaintiff's agent or attorney who shall so indorse his name upon an original writ, shall be liable, in case of the avoidance or inability of the plaintiff, to pay the defendant all such costs as he shall recover, and to pay all prison-charges that may happen, where the plaintiff shall not support his action. And all goods and estate attached upon mean process, for the security of the debt or damages sued for, shall be held for the space of thirty days after final judgment, to be taken in execution. And if the creditor shall not take them in execution within thirty days after judgment, the attachment shall be void."

[77] The minutes are now printed in P. Hamlin and C. Baker, The Supreme Court of Judicature of the Province of New York, 1691–1704 (New York: New-York Historical Society, 1952), II. See the entries at 113 (Apr. 7, 1702); 139, 143 (Apr. 10, 1703); 169 (Oct. 9, 1703).

and suggesting that a rule of court was in existence.[78] This was still the case in 1794.[79] In colonial New Jersey the matter had also been regulated by rule of court[80] and there is no reason to suppose that the practice had been abandoned. Both in Virginia and South Carolina statutes had been enacted after the Revolution that required non-residents to post security. The Virginia law was one of the Revisors' bills that was not passed by the legislature until 1786.[81] The South Carolina statute had been enacted a year earlier.[82] It seems to us probable that both of these enactments were related to other measures directed at British creditors.

Section 7, the only one in the bill which is close to an exact copy of a state (Massachusetts) original, provided as follows:

> where a defendant shall be duly served with a process, and return thereof shall be made into the court where the same is returnable, and he shall not appear by himself or his Attorney, his default shall be recorded, and the court shall thereupon give judgment for the plaintiff for such damages as they shall find he hath sustained, unless the plaintiff shall move to have a jury to enquire into the damages, or the defendant shall come into court and request, or the court shall think such enquiry to be necessary, in either of which cases judgment shall be rendered for such damages as the jury shall assess: But if the defendant shall come into court at any time during the term, and shall offer to pay to the adverse party the costs which shall then have arisen, or so much thereof as the court shall judge reasonable, the court may in their discretion, admit the defendant to have a day in court in the same manner as if his default had not been recorded. PROVIDED, That if in any case it be doubtful to the court whether the defendant hath had actual notice and seasonably for his appearance, they shall continue the cause one term without an appearance.

Although the English practice books most used by lawyers who trained on the eve of the Revolution discuss the judgment by default in terms of defendant's failure to enter a plea according to court rule, confessing the action or failing to defend, the Committee, it will be noticed, drew its provision in terms of non-appearance. This had been

---

[78] That the Supreme Court had made a formal rule seems credible in light of the fact that the Mayor's Court of the City of New York, an inferior court, had by Rule 19 of Apr. 8, 1701, required "Forraigners" to give security for costs. R. Morris, ed., *Select Cases in the Mayor's Court of New York City* (Washington, D.C.: American Historical Association, 1935), 76.

[79] Wyche, *Treatise on the Practice of the Supreme Court of Judicature of the State of New York*, at 38–39.

[80] "Rules of the Supreme Court Province of New Jersey," Ms. William Livingston Precedent Book, 204 (NYSL).

[81] 12 Hening, *Va. Stats.*, 355.

[82] County Courts Act, sec. 43, Mar. Sess. 1785 (7 *Stats. at Large South Carolina*, 232).

regulated in England by Statute 12 George I, c. 29 (1725), which had exempted defendant from arrest in causes involving less than £10. He would be served only with a copy of the process, and upon failure to appear, plaintiff was privileged, upon submitting an affidavit of service, to enter an appearance for defendant, or file common bail (viz., John Doe and Richard Roe) and proceed as if defendant had himself entered an appearance. This procedure was applicable also where plaintiff had failed to submit an affidavit of the amount in controversy. At least two American states, New York[83] and Pennsylvania,[84] had treated this statute as if applicable. In English procedure where there was default as by *nil dicit* or *non sum informatus*, plaintiff was permitted to sign judgment.[85] Where the action sounded in damages such judgment was interlocutory and damages were normally ascertained by writ of inquiry. In debt, judgment was commonly said to be final.

Considered in connection with the section on special bail, it would appear that section 7 was designed to cover the situation where a mere summons had issued or a non-bailable *capias* where plaintiff had not complied with the conditions of section 5. That something may conceivably have been owed to the English statute noticed above is possible; nevertheless, section 7 follows so closely the language of a Massachusetts act of 1784[86] as to put beyond doubt the immediate source to which the Committee turned. The text of this statute is set forth in the margin,[87] and it is clear that a defendant in default was indulged to a degree not known in England, where the utmost allowed him was to have the advantage of technical errors and to offer evidence in mitigation to the jury of inquiry.

---

[83] *LPAH*, I, 57, n. 8.

[84] Per Shippen P., in Taylor v. Knox, 1 Dallas 158 (Phila. C.P. 1785), who states that the statute had been treated as applying, but in light of the Pennsylvania reception statute he believed it to be no longer law.

[85] Crompton, *Practice commonplaced: or, the Rules and Cases of Practice in the Courts of King's Bench and Common Pleas*, I, at 285.

[86] 1 *Laws of the Commonwealth of Massachusetts 1780–1800* (1801), 205, sec. 7 (October 1784). This was a substantial re-enactment of a provincial law of 1702. 1 *Acts and Resolves Prov. of Mass. Bay*, 464.

[87] "That when any defendant shall be duly served with process, and return thereof shall be made into the Court where the same is returnable, and he shall not appear by himself, or his attorney, his default shall be recorded, and the charge in the declaration shall be taken and deemed to be true, and the Court shall thereupon give such damages as they shall find upon inquiry that the plaintiff shall have sustained, unless the plaintiff shall move to have a jury to inquire into the damages, in which case the Court shall enter up judgment for such damages as the jury shall assess. *Provided nevertheless*, That if the defendant shall come into Court at any time before the jury is dismissed, and shall pay down to the adverse party the costs he has been at thus far, or so much thereof as the Court shall judge reasonable, then the Court may admit the defendant to have the same day in Court as if his default had never been recorded."

XII: *The Process Acts*

Statutory provisions resembling section 7 existed in other states at the time of the drafting of the Process Bill. Virginia had provided that

All judgments by default for want of an appearance . . . and not set aside, on the third day of the next succeeding district court, shall be entered by the Clerk as of that day, which judgment shall be final in actions of debt founded on any specialty, bill, or note in writing, ascertain[ing] the demand, unless the plaintiff shall chuse in any such case to have a writ of enquiry of damages, and in all other cases the damages shall be ascertained by a jury, to be impanelled and sworn to enquire thereof. . . .[88]

As Massachusetts in all cases, Virginia permitted plaintiff to move for a jury to inquire into damages only in cases founded on debt instruments; if no such motion were made in these cases, judgment was entered automatically. In all other cases a jury of inquiry would be impanelled.

New Jersey also had a provision, enacted in 1784, similar to section 7, and amended in 1788 to resemble more closely the Virginia and Massachusetts (and the Committee) provisions. The statute before amendment appeared as follows:

and in case the Defendant shall neglect to put in a Plea within the Time directed for that Purpose as above-said, the Charge in the Declaration shall be taken as confessed, and the Damages shall thereupon be assessed by the Court at the next Term thereafter, and final Judgment be then entered accordingly; at which Assessment of Damages the Defendant may, if he desires it, attend and be heard respecting the same . . . (in which case he shall be charged) *Six Shillings* to the Court for assessing the Damages. . . .[89]

Thus New Jersey in 1784 required that court, not jury, assess the damages. Both New Jersey and Virginia leave unclear the matter of defendant's erasing the default judgment by appearance, but both nevertheless provided that judgment could not be entered against defendant before the next term of court.

In 1788 New Jersey amended its default judgment statute to read as follows:

[if] any Plaintiff or Plaintiffs in any Cause, having filed a Declaration agreeably to the fourth section of the aforesaid Act, and the Defendant or Defendants shall not put in a Plea whereby the Court is directed to assess the Damages, and give Judgment, it shall and may be lawful,

---

[88] 12 Hening, *Va. Stats.*, 746, sec. 42 (October 1788).

[89] *New Jersey Laws*, 8th Assembly, 2d Sitting (1784), c. 32, sec. 5.

upon the Defendant or Defendants appearing to make a Defense in Mitigation of Damages, for the Plaintiff or Plaintiffs to request a Jury to ascertain the said damages, in which case the Court shall direct a Venire Facias, returnable to the same or the succeeding Term, that a Jury may be impannnelled [*sic*] for that Purpose, and the Court shall, upon the Verdict of the said Jury, give Judgment and award Execution accordingly.[90]

Where defendant appeared to mitigate damages, plaintiff had the option to demand jury trial.

Section 7, we have seen, differed from the state provisions in two important respects: jury trial was made available to either party regardless of the nature of the action, and defendant was specifically given the opportunity to set aside the default judgment simply by an appearance within the instant term and payment of costs. The section was probably not so much the child of reformers of procedure as of those anxious to see a strong judiciary the procedures of which would not be criticized by its foes as permitting judgment and execution against persons to whom the courts were physically unavailable, and summary assessments of damages by a court sitting without a jury.

Section 8 of the bill provided:

That the Marshall, or other officer, who shall take bail for appearance, shall, at the request and cost of the plaintiff, in such suit, or his lawful attorney, assign to the plaintiff the bail bond, by endorsing the same, and attesting it under his hand and seal. And if the said bond be forfeit, and assigned as aforesaid, the plaintiff, in such action, may bring a suit upon it in his own name.

This provision was a truncated version of the English Statute 4 and 5 Anne, c. 16, §20, that had recently been copied by the New York legislature although, as with so many other English statutes which did not extend to the plantations, it had been earlier adopted by the provincial legislature.[91] A reception had also taken place in New Jersey. There by a provincial act of assembly (1741)[92] bail in civil actions was to be regulated by rule of court, and this in fact had been done.[93] It

---

[90] *New Jersey Laws*, 13th Assembly, 1st Sitting (1788), c. 245, sec. 1.

[91] *N.Y. Laws*, 11 Sess. 1788, c. 46, sec. 8. The provincial assembly in 1767 had included the English statute in an omnibus bill adopting various Acts of Parliament (4 *Col. Laws N.Y.*, 953). This had been disallowed by the Crown. In 1773 the statute of Anne was enacted *in toto* (5 *ibid.*, 537).

[92] Allinson, *Acts and Laws of the General Assembly of the Province of New Jersey* (1776), 120, sec. 2. This statute remained in force until 1794 (*Laws of the State of New Jersey* [Paterson, 1800], 124).

[93] "Rules of the Supreme Court Province of New Jersey," Ms. William Livingston Precedent Book, 212 (NYSL).

seems probable therefore that the suggestion for incorporating section 8 may well have emanated from William Paterson. None of the New England states had attempted to establish the practice by legislation, the theory there apparently being that when the recognizance was delivered by the sheriff it became a record of the court. Maryland had adopted the English act *sub silentio*.[94] The Virginia Revisors had incorporated such a provision in their draft of an Act Regulating Procedure at Common Law presented in 1785 but this had died in the House of Delegates.[95]

Recourse against the bail after judgment had been traditionally dependent upon failure to secure satisfaction from defendant against whom execution should be first served and upon the form of execution chosen. If plaintiff proceeded by *fieri facias*, or by *elegit*, neither writ served to "fix bail" as the phrase was. This could be accomplished by *capias ad satisfaciendum* against the body of defendants—in effect a demand that he surrender himself in satisfaction.[96] In the event the writ was returned "not found," or if the bail did not surrender defendant, it was presumed that bail was ready to assume the debt and damages recovered. The bail could be proceeded against either by action of debt or by *scire facias*. This alternative, which prevailed in England, was seated in New York[97] and probably in other jurisdictions which followed the common law.

In section 9, which established certain rules regarding proceeding against bail, the Committee made no mention of the action of debt, apparently anticipating that *scire facias* was to be the sole method of proceeding. It was directed:

> That no SCIRE FACIAS shall be served upon the bail, in any civil action, but within two years after final judgment is rendered against the principal. And if the bail shall render the principal at any time before judgment is given against them upon a SCIRE FACIAS, and pay the cost which may have arisen thereon, they shall be discharged.

This provision was derived from the Massachusetts Civil Bail Act of 1784.[98] The period of limitation upon *scire facias* proceedings was, however, doubled—an indulgence which may have been due to the smoldering popular reaction against swift and inexorable collection of

---

[94] *Cf.* the opinion of Chase C.J. in Osborne v. Jones, 4 Harris & McHenry 5 note (1792).

[95] *Papers of Jefferson*, II, 660.

[96] Crompton, *Practice commonplaced: or, the Rules and Cases of Practice in the Courts of King's Bench and Common Pleas*, II, at 76.

[97] Wyche, *Treatise on the Practice of the Supreme Court of Judicature of the State of New York*, at 216.

[98] 1 *Laws of the Commonwealth of Massachusetts 1780–1800* (1801), 195–96.

debts. The right to render the principal at any time before judgment on the *scire facias* both in the proposed federal statute and the Massachusetts act was a departure from English practice which at this time required bail to render the principal only four days after return of a second *scire facias*, the court sitting, or they would be too late.[99]

Section 10 provided that a party who obtained a judgment in any civil action in any United States court would be entitled to have execution on the judgment at any time within a year after the rendering of the judgment, or, where the execution was stayed by law for a time, within one year after the expiration of the stay. A party would not after this time be entitled to execution without a writ of *scire facias*. This was standard common law practice, and so far as can be ascertained prevailed in all the states.

The opening words of section 11 dealing with the form of common law execution suggest that at this juncture the Committee had arrived at an impasse, and so, except for the proviso in the second paragraph, abandoned formulation of a uniform federal process of execution. In the several states there existed variations not only in the forms themselves, but also in what may be called the succession of remedies. Massachusetts,[100] New Hampshire[101] and Connecticut[102] had confected a so-called writ of execution which authorized in the same instrument levy on chattels, then, at the option of the judgment creditor, levy on lands, and finally a taking of defendant's body. In addition a second type of execution in Massachusetts and New Hampshire[103] combined a *habere facias possessionem* and a *fieri facias*. Because of the peculiar Connecticut procedure for trying title no *habere facias* appears to have been there used.

In New York a choice lay between a *fieri facias* and *capias ad satisfaciendum*,[104] and because of direct English legislative intervention (Statute 5 George II, c. 7)[105] the *fieri facias* included seizure of land as well as chattels; *habere facias* was used for judgments in ejectment.[106] In New Jersey the successful plaintiff had a choice between *fieri facias* or

---

[99] Simmonds v. Middleton and Another, 1 Wilson K.B. 269 (1750).

[100] 1 *Laws of the Commonwealth of Massachusetts 1780–1800* (1801), 200; originally enacted in 1702, 1 *Acts and Resolves Prov. of Mass. Bay*, 460.

[101] *Acts and Laws . . . Province of New Hampshire* (1771), c. 80, enacted 1718.

[102] *Acts and Laws of the State of Connecticut* (1784), 84.

[103] Originally enacted in 1701, 1

Acts and Resolves Prov. of Mass. Bay, 461; re-enacted in 1784, 1 *Laws of the Commonwealth of Massachusetts 1780–1800* (1801), 201. *Acts and Laws . . . Province of New Hampshire* (1771), c. 80.

[104] *LPAH*, I, 97.

[105] "An Act for the more easy Recovery of Debts in his Majesty's Plantations and Colonies in *America*" (1731).

[106] *LPAH*, I, 133; the form, *ibid.*, 159.

capias ad satisfaciendum.[107] Here by act of assembly in 1743[108] the *fieri facias* encompassed realty as well as chattels. The Pennsylvania Assembly had much earlier made a similar authorization.[109]

Although Maryland had put 5 George II, c. 7, into effect,[110] there is no indication that Virginia had so done. The provincial statute of 1748[111] which set out forms of execution had provided standard common law forms of *fieri facias* and *capias ad satisfaciendum* as well as the writ of *elegit*; post-Revolutionary legislation indicates that this writ was no longer available. No form of *habere facias* was provided in Virginia, neither was it in the South Carolina Act of 1785[112] which dealt only with *fieri facias* and *capias ad satisfaciendum*. There remains, of course, the probability that in those states which had a strong common law tradition some writs were used without particular statutory benediction.[113]

In the face of these jurisdictional peculiarities, it was manifestly too difficult and delicate a task to settle upon forms likely to be acceptable to the representatives of eleven states, and the Committee, we believe, was consequently led to proffer the following:

> That until further provision shall be made, the form of executions, in actions at common law, in the Circuit and District Courts, and the manner of issuing and satisfying the same; and the rate of fees in all cases in said courts, shall be, except where by this act or other statutes of the United States is otherwise provided; the same, as near as may be, in the respective States, where the proceedings shall be had, as in similar or the most analogous cases, now is used or accustomed in the respective courts of such States.

The full effect of this open-handed nostrification of state forms was, however, diminished by the proviso:

> That on all judgments in the cases aforesaid, the plaintiff shall have his election to take out a CAPIAS AD SATISFACIENDUM in the first

---

[107] Hustick v. Allen, 1 Coxe (N.J.) 168 (1793).

[108] Allinson, *Acts and Laws of the General Assembly of the Province of New Jersey*, at 129.

[109] In 1705, 1 *Laws of the Commonwealth of Pennsylvania* (Dallas ed., 1797), 67.

[110] *Cf.* Davidson's Lessee v. Beatty, 3 Harris & McHenry 594 (1797).

[111] The basic act of 1748 was presumably still in force (5 Hening, *Va. Stats.*, 526). The supplementary act in 1782 (11 *ibid.*, 75) seems directed

at eliminating the writ of *elegit*, for an amending act of 1783 made lawful tender of lands to the creditor (*ibid.*, 176). See 12 *ibid.*, 457 (1787), and 776 (1788).

[112] County Courts Act, sec. 35, Mar. Sess. 1785 (7 *Stats. at Large South Carolina*, 226–28).

[113] This is indicated in the case of Maryland by the Act of 1715, c. 40, sec. 3, which provided *fieri facias* and *capias ad satisfaciendum* "or otherwise" (1 Kilty, *Laws of Maryland*).

instance; and shall not be prevented levying the same by any other tender than that of payment in gold or silver coin: And all goods and chattels taken in execution shall, unless redeemed, be sold at public auction, for money of the like kind, to satisfy the same: And all executions shall be returned to the respective courts from whence they issue, at their next term.

By giving the plaintiff the option of electing execution upon the body of the judgment debtor, a federal rule was to be established by implication, for it was a long-established common law rule that by making such an election process against property was excluded—defendant's body being deemed the highest execution a plaintiff might have. There may well have been another reason for proviso, viz., to implement the antecedent directions regarding special bail. As already remarked, it is clear from section 9 that no action of debt against bail was anticipated—solely a proceeding by *scire facias*. A condition precedent for such proceeding was the issuance of a *capias ad satisfaciendum* against defendant. The proviso of section 11 may consequently be regarded as a necessary supplement to section 9. The requirement that tender of the judgment debt or the proceeds of the sale of goods and chattels taken in execution be in gold or silver followed the policy already laid down by Congress with respect to collection of duties.[114]

The final section of the bill has all the indications of something done in haste for it enjoined that proceedings in equity and in causes of admiralty and maritime jurisdiction be according to the course of the civil law, except as statutes of the United States might otherwise provide.

The direction as to equity proceedings was the one item of fresh invention produced by the Committee, and it could hardly have been more ill advised. Not only did a vulgar prejudice against the civil law prevail because of the American jury trial syndrome, but in New York, New Jersey, Maryland, Virginia and South Carolina Courts of Chancery had been in existence for varying periods of time and their procedure had been modelled on that of the English High Court. It was idle to suppose that the judges or the practitioners in any of these states were likely to set afoot unfamiliar and untried procedures. The mention in section 15 of the Judiciary Act of "the ordinary rules of proceeding in chancery" was focused on too minor an incident of practice to have been read as licensing a general exemption from the "rules of civil law." The Committee had earlier experienced the explosions over adopting English chancery practice during the Judiciary Act debates (related with relish by Senator Maclay in his journal) and it may have been conceived that something less contentious was being tendered.

---

[114] I *U.S. Stats.*, 29, sec. 30.

As for admiralty causes, the adversion to the civil law was not without precedent, for during the Revolution both Massachusetts and Connecticut[115] had signalized their antipathy of English admiralty law by adopting the civil law as the jurisprudence of their maritime or prize courts. There had been something unrealistic about this, also, for although the best-trained lawyers in the provinces had some familiarity with basic civil law treatises, it is open to doubt whether they had command of procedures.[116]

PROCEEDINGS IN THE SENATE AND HOUSE

WHEN THE BILL to Regulate Processes was reported, only five days remained before the scheduled adjournment of Congress. A first and second reading took place the day of the report (September 17). According to the Senate rules, as we have seen, the time of second reading was a consideration as by a Committee of the Whole.[117] Along with other business the second reading continued September 18 and 19; on the 19th it was voted to dispense with the rules for a third reading and the bill was ordered engrossed.[118] Although it was on a third reading in the Senate that motions or votes were recorded, nothing of the proceedings is to be found in the Senate *Journal*. For the protagonists of the bill these proceedings were little short of disastrous.

It may be inferred from the appearance of the printed bill as reported, now preserved in the Library of Congress, that the text was discussed systematically through section 5. This document has some handwritten textual additions or alterations, some redundant matter struck out in the forms of writs (section 2)[119] and figures written in the blanks

---

[115] *Supra*, c. XI, p. 475.

[116] As will be noticed, the provision regarding the civil law was retained in the act as passed, and this might be accounted a victory for the projectors of a uniform federal procedure in the areas of equity and admiralty but for the fact that the weight of history made it a Pyrrhic one. Wherever there existed longseated tradition of chancery or admiralty practice, the legal profession clung to old ways of conducting litigation. Peter Du Ponceau, a leader of the Supreme Court bar, wrote in 1795 regarding the "course of the civil law" in the Process Act of 1789: ". . . this is well understood with us to be the course of the Courts

of *Equity* and *Admiralty* in England and the United States before the adoption of the federal Constitution unless where Congress have by law declared it otherwise." To J. Y. Noel, Aug. 1, 1795, Ms. Du Ponceau Letterbook B, 124 (HSP).

[117] *Senate Journal*, 1st Sess., 39, additional rule voted May 21, 1789.

[118] *Ibid.*, 138–39.

[119] For example, the separate sentence in sec. 1 dealing with seals was coupled with the preceding sentence by addition of "and," and the clause further altered by changing the direction "the seals of the Supreme and Circuit Courts to be provided by the Supreme court and for the district courts by . . ." to read "the seals of

preceding the number of days, *e.g.*, to serve a declaration on defendant. There can be no doubt that the Library of Congress document was used by a Senator present at the debate because the handwritten alterations are identical with those in the piece of the printed bill abscised from the remainder and serving as section 1 affixed to the manuscript of revised sections 2 and 3. This conglomerate of print and script is indorsed "passed," and was probably the text committed to the engrossing clerk.[120]

The bill ran into trouble at section 4, whether on a first perusal or later cannot be said. The Library of Congress document is marked with a long bracket and the words "Struck out" are written in the margin. To those whose only weapons were taken from Blackstone, this section was not strictly a regulation of process and may have been excised for this reason. The Senator who used the Library of Congress print made no further additions beyond writing in "100" in section 5 dealing with plaintiff's affidavit of value in debt actions. This figure obviously did not come close to the minimum amount in controversy established by the Judiciary Act, and so threatened to open the door to vexatious arrests.

Our meagre indications suggest that it was at this point that the real assault on the bill occurred. Despite the dust-up in July over writs running in the name of the United States, section 1 was voted as it stood with but insignificant changes in wording. The weight of the attack fell upon sections 2 through 10. The Senate might not have gone as far as it did in its work of destruction, for all these sections were eliminated, but for the fact that since August 24 the Judiciary Act had been subjected to sniper's fire in the House. In the opening debate (August 24) the antifederalists had taken the initiative and this portion of the discussions had been generously reported and published.[121] The Judiciary Act had also been belatedly belabored in the Senate on September 8 when the House's Articles of Amendment to the Constitution were before the upper chamber.[122] This had occurred when Lee had pressed for acceptance of the Virginia Convention's emasculating amendments of Article III.[123] On September 17, 1789, the very day the Process Bill was reported, *The New-York Journal* had published a version of the

---

the Supreme and Circuit Courts *shall* be provided . . . and *of* the district courts. . . ." In the first sentence of sec. 2, "That in civil actions the process . . ." was expanded by insertion of the words "for Debt or Damages" after "actions."

[120] Senate Files, Sen. 1A–D1, tray 4, folder 1 (NA).

[121] *Annals of Congress*, I, 812–13, 826–51 (August 29), 851–66 (August 31); and see *supra*, c. XI, p. 504.

[122] The debates were partially reported by William Paterson; *cf.* Ms. Bancroft Transcripts (NYPL), "Paterson's notes on debate in the Senate, Sept. 1789."

[123] *Senate Journal*, 1st Sess., 126–27.

final bitter remarks about the Judiciary Act made September 14 when the House took a vote. It is difficult to believe that the forecasts of oppression and mischief to be expected from the new system did not have some effect upon the fate of the Process Bill.

The protagonists of the bill were hampered by the absence of Caleb Strong who had left with permission on August 20,[124] and it is conceivable that the effectiveness of Ellsworth and Paterson was blunted by the fact that they were named September 17 to the committee to deal with the fifty-two-odd House amendments to the Judiciary Act, which surely had a priority over other business.[125] In any event, it is impossible to say what swung the vote against the bill as reported, whether the prevailing sentiment was that the problem was too ramified for hasty action or that uniform federal rules were undesirable. It is clear, however, that the Senate was not prepared to permit the regulation of process to be settled by the courts pursuant to the rule-making power conveyed by section 17 of the Judiciary Act. Section 11 of the Process Bill which, it will be recalled, directed that state forms of executions in common law actions should, for the time being, prevail provided the footing.

This section was expanded and combined with the directions respecting proceeding in cases of equity and admiralty to read as follows:[126]

And be it further enacted, That until further provision shall be made, & except where by this Act or other Statutes of the United States is otherwise provided, the Forms of Writs & Executions & modes of process & rates of fees in the Circuit & District Courts, in Suits at common law, shall be the same in each State respectively as are now used or allowed in the Supreme Courts of the same. And the proceedings in Causes of Equity & of Admiralty & Maritime jurisdiction shall be according to the course of the Civil Law.

The original proviso was cut down to read:

Provided that on Judgments in any of the cases aforesaid where different kinds of Executions are issuable in succession, a *capias ad Satisfaciendum* being one, the Plaintiff shall have his election to take out a Capias ad Satisfaciendum in the first instance; & be at liberty to pursue the same until a tender of the debt & Costs in Gold or Silver shall be made.

The final section provided:

And be it further enacted that this act shall continue in force until the end of the next Session of Congress & no longer.

---

124 *Ibid.*, 100.
125 *Ibid.*, 138.

126 Senate Files, Sen. 1A–D1, tray 4, folder 1 (NA).

The text of this revised matter as passed and before being turned over to be engrossed is in Ellsworth's hand. While it represents a defeat of the Committee's purpose, it is a testimony to Ellsworth's capacity for accommodation. A surrender, perhaps, of predilection, the new section 2 was not an abandonment of principle, for it had been Ellsworth who had penned section 34 of the Judiciary Act directing that in trials at common law the laws of the several states "shall be regarded as the rules of decision."[127]

This truncated Process Bill was passed by the Senate September 19[128] and that day was sent to the House with a travelling companion— notice of Senate action on the House amendments to the Judiciary Act that embraced a venue provision which fell short of House expectations. That day feelings toward the Senate could not have been warm for its revisions of the House's proposed amendments to the Constitution came up for consideration.[129] What had been discarded from these were, among other things, a monetary limitation upon the Supreme Court's appellate jurisdiction, the right of challenge and the requirement of a trial jury of the vicinage, all matters dear to the hearts of the Southern members, and to the Northern antifederalists.

The time for adjournment having been postponed, the Process Bill was taken up in the House Committee of the Whole, September 23 and 24.[130] There was not much left to pick on in the second section, so complete had been the yielding to state interest. Nevertheless, fees to judges were excepted from the direction regarding compliance with state rates in common law actions, but in equity and admiralty causes it was voted that the rates were to be identical with those "last allowed by the States, respectively in the court exercising supreme jurisdiction in such causes." A design to clarify the word "proceedings" according to the civil law is manifest by the addition of the modifying "forms and modes."[131]

The first section did not fare so well. The Committee voted to strike the words "the President" so that process would run in the name of the United States. Nothing is known of the debate. This amendment was reported to the House and was voted 25–18. It was a curious conglomerate which made up the majority, for seventeen of the Representatives hailed from states where executive authority had been constitutionally fettered and the remainder were convinced antifederalists. James Madison, despite his earlier defense of executive power during the removal debate, voted with the majority.

The Senate was notified on September 25 and voted the next day

---

[127] *Supra*, c. XI, p. 502.
[128] *Senate Journal*, 1st Sess., 139–40.
[129] *Annals of Congress*, I, 938.

[130] *Ibid.*, 947, 949; *Jour. H.R.*, I, 120, 122.
[131] *Jour. H.R.*, I, 122.

to concur in all the amendments except that to the first section.[132] The House took up the matter forthwith. The reporter, Thomas Lloyd, whose application to his task had been steadily waning, published a brief account of one speech, by Stone of Maryland:[133]

> substituting the name of the President, instead of the name of the United States, was a declaration that the sovereign authority was vested in the Executive. He did not believe this to be the case. The United States were sovereign; they acted by an agency, but could remove such agency without impairing their own capacity to act. He did not fear the loss of liberty by this single mark of power; but he apprehended that an aggregate, formed of one inconsiderable power, and another inconsiderable authority, might, in time, lay a foundation for pretensions it would be troublesome to dispute, and difficult to get rid of. A little prior caution was better than much future remedy.

A vote to adhere carried 28–22.[134] On the 26th the Senate requested a conference.[135] Three hostile Representatives were named as managers for the House: Alexander White of Virginia, Aedanus Burke of South Carolina and James Jackson of Georgia.[136] The Senate chose three of its most accomplished members: Ellsworth of Connecticut, Rufus King of New York and George Read of Delaware.[137] The last reported September 28 that the conference had reached no agreement. A compromise amendment was offered on the Senate floor, the effect of which was to eliminate from section 1 any prescription as to style, the first sentence thus reading "all writs and processes issuing from a supreme, or a circuit court shall bear test of the chief justice of the supreme court and if from a district court shall bear test of the judge of such court." After an initial rejection, this was reconsidered and approved.[138] A second amendment to section 2 excepted the style of writs from the direction regarding state forms of writs and executions; this was likewise approved. On the same day the House agreed to these amendments.[139] The act was signed September 29, 1789.

If there was truth in the antifederalists' charge that the most ardent federalists were aiming at a "consolidated" government, the Act for

---

[132] *Senate Journal*, 1st Sess., 150–51.

[133] *Annals of Congress*, I, 951.

[134] *Jour. H.R.*, I, 124.

[135] The message requesting a conference Sept. 26, 1789, and the House reply are attached to the Engrossed Senate Bill (Sen. Files, Book 1 [NA]).

[136] *Annals of Congress*, I, 952.

[137] *Maclay Journal*, 163–64 *sub* September 26, relates how he found

John Adams, Ellsworth and Fisher Ames "railing against" the House's vote of adherence to reject the style of writs running in the name of the President. Maclay comments sourly, "This is only a part of their old system of giving the President as far as possible every appendage of royalty."

[138] *Senate Journal*, 1st Sess., 156–57.

[139] *Jour. H.R.*, I, 127.

Regulating Processes in its final form was a defeat for such ambitions. It is necessary only to point to the effects of the measure taken by the Treasury to organize and manage the fiscal arm of the federal government to appreciate the centripetal force of uniformity of administration. The Senate Committee bill fell far short of being even an adequate scheme of procedural regulation on the common law side—but there was something almost anarchic about the statute. There can be no doubt, however, that the principle settled upon was a boon to the lawyers who were to practice before the Circuit and District Courts, and, above all, to the clerks of court who, privy to the practice of a particular state, carried a considerable burden of attending to the policing of process, bail, pleadings and the like.[140] As already remarked, those who were most incommoded were to be the Supreme Court Justices. Their first critical encounter with the Process Act was to occur not long after its passage and was to be over the style of writs.

There is little reason to doubt that the style of process had been viewed in the Congress as a question of constitutional import involving the nature and scope of executive authority. By eliminating any directions whatever, the legislators had arrived at the absurd result that a marshal would receive a command to perform some act, such as an arrest, from an innominate source. John Jay, newly appointed Chief Justice of the Supreme Court, apparently took the initiative to correct matters, for on November 18, 1789, William Cushing, Associate Justice, wrote Jay that he had been informed that it was the Chief Justice's opinion that process should run in the name of the President of the United States to which the District judges would have to conform "and which I think is right."[141] Jay replied December 7, 1789, expressing his gratification that Cushing agreed with him about the style of process and that this would be the style of writs from the Massachusetts District Court. Jay suggested that there should be early informal meetings of the Justices to consider and mature some indispensable matters—"among those will be the stile of writs."[142] At February term 1790, the Chief Justice and three Associate Justices attending, the following rule was announced: "That (unless, and until, it shall be otherwise provided by law) all process of this court shall be in the name of 'the President of the United States.' "[143] That the Court possessed the power under sections 14 and 17 to formulate a rule of this sort, there can be no question. Nevertheless, in so doing, it settled what many had conceived to be a constitutional issue before ever there was a case on its docket.

---

140 *Supra*, p. 514.
141 Photostat of an autograph letter in the collections of the Massachusetts Historical Society.

142 Ms. R. T. Paine Papers (MHS).
143 Feb. 5, 1790. Sitting were Jay C.J., Cushing, Wilson and Blair JJ. 2 Dallas 400.

THE LATER PROCESS ACTS

CONGRESS WAS AGAIN in session when the Supreme Court held its first term. More than two weeks before the rule as to style had been made, the Senate appointed a committee to bring in a new process act.[144] The membership was confined to members of the bar—Strong, King, Johnson, Ellsworth and Henry—but it was overloaded with lawyers from the "Eastern States," for although King was Senator from New York, he had been trained and had practiced in Massachusetts. Henry of Maryland came closest to representing "southern jurisprudence." In terms of the result, all this turned out to be irrelevant, for the committee did no more than submit a bill to continue the extant statute until the end of the next session of Congress.[145] This was duly enacted.[146]

The committee's failure to come to grips with this assignment was explained in a letter of Caleb Strong to Robert Treat Paine written the day before the committee reported (April 23, 1790).[147] It appears that the committee had requested the Justices of the Supreme Court "to furnish them with such Remarks as should occur to them in this Business." The committee had determined nothing, for it was hoped that the Justices "would prepare a Bill or afford them some aid in doing it, but as the Judges from the Southern States were not present, those who attended, not being acquainted with the Forms used at the Southward, were unwilling to propose such as would be used in all the States and thought it prudent not to do it at present."[148]

If the Justices of the Supreme Court were unhelpful, the Attorney General, Edmund Randolph, was equally so. On August 5, 1790,[149] he was required by a resolve of the House to report on the judiciary system. Randolph submitted an extensive "report" December 31, 1790,[150] which consisted of an armchair critique of the Act of 1789 and a lengthy exposition of his own ideas on how the judiciary should be organized. He was critical of the civil law as a basis for equity and admiralty proceedings, but as for the forms and modes of process in common law actions,

---

[144] Jan. 19, 1790. *Senate Journal*, 2d Sess., 1st Cong., 13; *Annals of Congress*, I, 974.

[145] *Senate Journal*, 2d Sess., 1st Cong., 61; Senate Files, Sen. 1A–B1, tray 3, folder 2 (NA).

[146] 1 *U.S. Stats.*, 123 (May 26, 1790).

[147] Ms. R. T. Paine Papers (MHS).

[148] It should be noticed that on Jan. 29, 1790, Smith of South Carolina introduced a resolution "to this pur-

port, that the Judges of the Supreme Court be directed to report to the House a plan for regulating the Processes in the Federal Courts, and the fees to the Clerks of the same." This was tabled. *Annals of Congress*, I, 1143.

[149] *Annals of Congress*, II, 1719.

[150] *American State Papers: Miscellaneous*, I, 21 *et seq.* (hereafter cited as *Am. St. Pap.: Misc.*, I).

he stood by section 2 of the Process Act. His one suggested amendment was that Circuit and District Courts be authorized to use all known forms of execution in personal actions. Randolph's ideal judiciary act was drawn in utter disregard of the criticisms levelled at a federal judicial system during the ratification struggle, a fact which may account for the cavalier manner in which the House merely referred the report to the Committee of the Whole, where it rested in peace. This session of Congress, indeed, was disposed to no affirmative action for it did nothing about President Washington's suggestion, December 8, 1790, that it consider whether "an uniform process of execution on sentences issuing from the Federal courts be not desirable through all the States."[151] Instead, a bill was reported to the House in early February 1791 to extend the life of the original Process Act to the end of the following session "and no longer." Within ten days it had passed both houses and was signed by the President.[152]

The successive extensions of the Process Act are indicative that what had in some quarters been viewed as a temporary expedient was in the way of becoming a fixture. A bill introduced into the Senate on January 26, 1792, again was so worded as to suggest a provisional settlement. This language was to be struck in the House and the act emerged as a definitive treatment of the problem.[153]

This bill had a strange history because the Senate committee (John Henry, Caleb Strong and James Monroe) was appointed to bring in a bill providing compensation for officers of federal courts, jurors and witnesses.[154] For reasons unknown the first two sections of the bill reported dealt with process.[155] We are here concerned primarily with these provisions. The first section of the committee bill was taken almost verbatim from the Process Act of 1789 excepting a direction that seals of the courts be provided at the expense of the United States. The second section likewise parrotted the same statute with only the excision of the direction regarding state rates of fees in District and Circuit Courts. Fees in federal courts and certain contingent expenses were dealt with in the sections next following. A final section repealed the Process Act of 1789 and the statutes of 1790 and 1791 which had extended its vigor. But as earlier remarked, the proposed act was itself offered as a provisional one.

---

[151] Richardson, *Messages and Papers of the Presidents* (1899 ed.), I, 83.

[152] 1 *U.S. Stats.*, 191 (Feb. 18, 1791); *cf. Jour. H.R.*, I, 373–75, 381–82; *Annals of Congress*, II, 1756–57, 1928, 1960–62.

[153] *Journal of the Senate of the*

United States of America, Being the First Session of the Second Congress (1791), 100 (hereafter cited as *Senate Journal*, 1st Sess., 2d Cong.).

[154] *Ibid.*, 22 (Nov. 1, 1791).

[155] The ms. copy of the bill is in Senate Files, Sen. 2A–B1, tray 1 (NA).

Virtually nothing is known of the Senate debate. This began January 30 and continued with interruptions until February 13, when it was voted that the bill pass.[156] The changes made in section 2 were negligible. In the first place, the direction that "the forms of writs and executions, except their style and the modes of Process in suits at common law," was inflated by the insertion of the words "and proceedings" after the word "Process,"[157] the purpose of which, evidently, was to make clear that state practice was to be followed, a conclusion already arrived at by rule of court in various districts. The Senate let stand the provision "as are now used or allowed in the highest common law courts" (of the state)—an ambiguous direction which could be taken to mean that the federal court must keep in step with changes in state law. Added during debate was a section regulating costs in cases of prosecutions for fines and forfeitures.

The Senate's most drastic amendment related to the forms and modes of proceeding in equity and in admiralty causes. The course of the civil law was rejected. Instead, there should be followed "the course which hath obtained in the States respectively in like causes or in States which have not courts of equity jurisdiction, or have not had courts of admiralty and maritime jurisdiction, according to the course of proceedings in such courts respectively in any adjoining or the nearest state in which they have been instituted; subject however, to such deviations in each State by rule of court, as a difference of circumstances may require, or as may be requisite to prevent unnecessary delay and expence."[158]

The proviso of the 1789 act regarding the plaintiff's right to elect a *capias ad satisfaciendum* was preserved. Tender of the debt in gold or silver had apparently been voted out when the Senate sat as a Committee of the Whole. This was restored by a 14–13 vote.[159] It was this tender clause which agitated the House sufficiently to induce some reporter to leave the only account of the discussions in that body. The House sitting as a Committee of the Whole had unanimously voted to eliminate the provision, but subsequently the House had disagreed. On April 27, in the course of the third reading, Mercer of Maryland moved and it was agreed that the bill be recommitted to restore the amend-

---

[156] *The Senate Journal*, 1st Sess., 2d Cong., 113, notes that during the second reading certain amendments were agreed upon. Further amendments agreed to during the third reading, *ibid.*, 118.

[157] For the text, *ibid.*, 119; also *Annals of Congress*, III, 85–86. The sentence in question read: "The forms of writs and executions, except their style, and the modes of process and proceedings in suits at common law, shall be the same in each state respectively as are now used or allowed in the highest common law courts having original jurisdiction of the same."

[158] *Senate Journal*, 1st Sess., 2d Cong., 119.

[159] *Ibid.*, 118.

ment.[160] The summary of the arguments on both sides printed in the *Annals* is set out in the margin.[161] The motion was one of particular

---

[160] *Annals of Congress*, III, 581, 583.

[161] *Ibid.*, 581–82. "This amendment was, to strike out the clause that authorizes the creditor to pursue his action till a tender of the debt and costs in gold or silver is made. This motion was founded on the particular circumstances of persons indebted to foreigners. It was said that the law, with this clause in it, would annihilate the power of the several States to pass insolvent laws; and, in consequence, those unfortunate debtors would be entirely in the power of a set of persons who retained the most rancorous enmity against the Revolution, and the persons most conspicuous in their exertions to bring about that event. It was further said, that it vests a power in a merciless creditor to immure an unfortunate debtor within the walls of a prison for life. It confounds the unfortunate with the vicious and abandoned, and extends a regulation designed originally merely to produce a full discovery and delivery of all the debtor's property, to a most unrighteous and unreasonable punishment, to the shortening of life, and to the injuring of society. It was further observed, that its operation would place the citizens of the United States upon a very different footing from English debtors who owe money to the citizens of the United States. The Treaty of Peace which had been mentioned, was concluded during the existence of those laws under which the British debtors enjoyed privileges which will by no means be reciprocal, should this clause be retained. It was also observed, that if this law was passed, it would not be in the power of the Legislature to provide a remedy, as it would be an *ex post facto* law; it would place the debtors in a much worse situation than they were in at the time the contracts were made—by giving these foreign creditors an advantage which they did not contemplate at the time when the credit was given.

"In opposition to the motion for recommitting the bill, it was contended that the creditors alluded to had not discovered that rancorous and cruel disposition, in at least some of the States, which had been complained of; but, on the contrary, had treated their debtors in the most humane and generous manner. The provision contemplated by the bill is precisely the same with that contained in a law which has twice received the sanction of Congress under the new Constitution, of which no complaint had ever been made; that to prescribe a different rule, would excite great alarms, and be attended with embarrassments, and perhaps with injury to the debtor as well as to the creditor. To leave it optional with the debtor to say in what manner he will pay his debts, or to subject the creditor to the caprice of the several State Governments whose laws may be founded on very opposite principles, will put it out of his power to get his debts paid agreeably to the Treaty of Peace, and therefore will be a virtual infraction of that treaty. The provision, it was said, is strictly conformable to the letter of the Constitution. Uniformity, in connexion with justice, was a principal object contemplated by the Constitution. This was considered as one of its chief excellencies; but, to say that foreign creditors shall be subjected to the Legislative provisions of the several States, which are known to clash, some of which have made paper a tender, others of which have depreciated paper in circulation, is, to defeat every just expectation founded on the Treaty of Peace and the Constitution. It was urged that this clause ought to be retained on every principle of uniformity as a general provision. Nor could it be considered as an *ex post facto* law, since every contract would remain as it was, and always be determined according to its own principles; except by mutual consent, this general provision should be resorted to."

appeal to the soft money faction and beyond all else to sectional interests. For no sooner had the new Circuit Courts begun to function than the spate of actions by British creditors commenced, particularly in the Southern states. In view of the shortage of specie in these states, the debtor was placed in a peculiarly difficult situation. From an entry in the Order Book of the Circuit Court for the Virginia District shortly after passage of the statute, it is apparent that there were enough prior judgments entered up unsatisfied that the court was by rule prepared to extend to these the benefit of satisfaction in current money.[162]

The other changes made by the House in the process sections of the Senate bill are set out in the bill as amended that was sent to the Senate May 1, 1792, and ordered to be printed. There were minor changes in section 1.[163] Section 2, however, was recast. Not only, as already noticed, did the House eliminate the words suggesting that the measures were temporary, but it also jettisoned the reference to state forms and modes of process in common law cases and instead provided that "the forms and modes of proceeding in suits, in those at common law, shall be the same as are now used in the said courts respectively" in pursuance of the statute of 1789.[164] In effect this froze the procedures as they stood in all their diversity. The House rejected the eccentric Senate provisions regarding equity and the admiralty and maritime jurisdiction. The modes and forms of equity proceedings were to be "according to the principles, rules and usages, which belong to a court of equity as contra-distinguished from a court of common law, except so far as may have been provided for" by the Judiciary Act. Admiralty proceedings were to be according to the course of the civil law subject; however, to such alterations and additions as the courts "shall in their discretion deem expedient" or to such regulations as the Supreme Court should think proper from time to time to prescribe to any Circuit or District Court.[165]

It is noteworthy that while the bill was in the hands of the House, this body sought to make something of the office of Attorney General by transferring to him a species of jurisdiction over the District Attorneys. For in the course of departmental empire building that had been going on, Secretary of State Jefferson had assumed supervision over them.[166] This amendment was to be watered down by the Senate to a

---

162 1 Ms. Order Book, *sub* May 24, 1792, Circuit Ct. Virginia Dist.

163 Viz., provision for Supreme Court or Circuit writs to be tested by the senior Associate Justice if the office of Chief Justice was vacant; by the District clerk if the District Court judgeship was vacant.

164 The text is taken from the printed House Amendments, filed Sen. 2A–D1, tray 2 (NA).

165 *Ibid.*

166 L. D. White, *The Federalists: A Study in Administrative History*, 133, 406. It is possible that the House's effort to place the United States At-

form unacceptable to the House. No more was heard of it. Action on a February 1792 letter of Mr. Justice Iredell[167] regarding the dolorous effects of a Supreme Court decision that writs of error had to issue from the clerk of that court[168] produced a House amendment, agreed to by the Senate, making it lawful for such writs to be issued by the clerks of the several circuits.[169] There was agreement also on a further addition enlarging the authority of the clerks to take recognizances of special bail and certain other functions.

The Senate referred the House amendments to a special committee (Ellsworth, Bradley of Vermont, Monroe, Burr and Henry)[170] which reported three days later.[171] The chief difficulty appears to have been the dispositions regarding equity and admiralty procedures. There is preserved a draft of an amendment relating to this in Ellsworth's hand that is marked postponed, and which may have been presented when the Senator from Connecticut reported for the committee.[172] The purport of this was that the course of proceedings should be as "heretofore accustomed in causes of similar jurisdiction in the respective courts of England, subject however to such deviations by rule of court, as a difference in circumstance may require, or as may tend to uniformity with the practice heretofore adopted in the States respectively in like causes."

Explicit reference to practice of English courts was, of course, politically inexpedient. An amendment which was approved, apparently offered by Read of Delaware,[173] provided that equity forms and proceedings "and in those of admiralty and maritime jurisdiction, [be] according to the principles, rules and usages which belong to courts of equity and to courts of admiralty respectively, as contra-distinguished from courts of common law; except so far as may have been provided for by the act to establish the judicial courts of the United States."[174] Accepted and repunctuated was the House proviso "subject however to such alterations and additions as the said courts respectively shall in

---

torneys in a relation with the Attorney General may have been due to Randolph's representations to the President on Dec. 26, 1791. *Am. St. Pap.: Misc.*, I, 46.

[167] The letter, dated Feb. 23, 1792, is published in *PAH*, XI, 46, n. 1. The President consulted both Hamiltion and Jefferson. Nothing has been found to show how the matter was brought to the attention of the House.

[168] West v. Barnes, 2 Dallas 401 (1791).

[169] The form was to be approved by two Justices of the Supreme Court.

The writ was to issue under seal of the Circuit Court.

[170] *Senate Journal*, 1st Sess., 2d Cong., 196 (Apr. 28, 1792).

[171] *Ibid.*, 197.

[172] Attached to the printed House Amendments, *supra*, n. 164.

[173] On the printed copy (*supra*, n. 164) are marginal notations handwritten apparently by a clerk. Against the text of sec. 2 as amended by the House is written "amended by Mr. Read."

[174] Text from *Senate Journal*, 1st Sess., 2d Cong., 199.

their discretion deem expedient, or to such regulations as the supreme court of the United States shall think proper from time to time by rule to prescribe to any circuit or district court concerning the same."[175]

The redrafting of this section was artfully contrived. If punctuation meant anything at all, the House proviso had confined alteration by rule to proceedings in causes of admiralty and maritime jurisdiction. The Senate had cast the whole section into a single sentence, so that as a matter of grammatical construction, the scope of judicial rule-making was extended to proceedings at common law and in equity as well. The House agreed to the Senate's amendment to section 2, but it stood by its guns on its amendment to eliminations of the tender in gold or silver with which the Senate had disagreed. A conference brought no agreement[176] but in the end the Senate yielded[177] and the bill was signed May 8, 1792.

There can be no question but that the Supreme Court understood the new statute to validate the exertion of its rule-making power as to both common law and equity proceedings, for at the August term following "The Chief Justice . . . stated that—This Court consider the practices of the Courts of Kings Bench and of Chancery in England, as affording outlines for the practice of this Court and that they will, from time to time, make such alterations therein, as circumstances may render necessary."[178]

At this same term the Justices set in train further legislative tinkering with the judicial system that was to embrace an enhancement of the federal court's control over process. Two years of peregrinations to keep the Circuit Courts had induced the Supreme Court Bench to address representations to Congress, praying relief from the rigors of holding the Circuit Courts as well as the two terms of the Supreme Court. The document was despatched to the President for transmission to Congress. This he did November 7, 1792.[179] On November 21 the

---

[175] *Ibid.*; text from 1 *U.S. Stats.*, 275. A motion by Read to insert after "courts" the words "of Common Law, of Equity, of admiralty and Maritime Jurisdiction" was postponed and not voted upon. The motion is on a chit filed with Sen. 2A–D1, tray 2 (NA).

[176] The Senate, having struck all the House amendments regarding the Attorney General and District Attorneys, offered a substitute: "That it shall be the duty of the attornies in the several districts to correspond with the Attorney General of the

United States, on any matter relative to judicial business which shall arise within their respective districts, and upon which he shall request information from them." This was apparently one of the amendments to which the House disagreed May 3, 1792. *Jour. H.R.*, I, 595–96.

[177] *Senate Journal*, 1st Sess., 2d Cong., 207–09.

[178] Ms. Mins. U.S. Sup. Ct. *sub* Aug. 8, 1792. 2 Dallas 414 has an edited version.

[179] *Infra*, c. XIII, p. 565.

Honble: {
William Cushing
James Wilson
John Blair
James Iredell
Thomas Johnson Esq⟩ʳˢ
} Associate Justices.

met at the City Hall.

Proclamation is made and the Court opened.

The Chief Justice in answer to the motion of the Attorney General, made yesterday, informs him and the Bar, that this Court consider the practices of the Courts of Kings Bench and of Chancery in England as affording outlines for the practice of this Court and that they will from time to time make such alterations therein as circumstances may render necessary.

Edward Telfair for the
State of Georgia ----
v.
Samuel Brailsford Voth? }

bill

Rule of the Supreme Court of the United States, August 8, 1792, regarding practice in that Court.

(*Manuscript Minutes, The National Archives*)

Senate appointed Ellsworth, Strong, Monroe, Johnston of North Carolina and King a committee to take the judicial system under consideration and report.[180]

Ellsworth submitted for the committee a bill presented as an "Act in addition to the act entitled 'An Act to establish Judicial Courts of the United States.' "[181] Besides what was tendered for the ease of the Supreme Court Justices, other matter was incorporated that has the appearance of having been suggested by the federal judges or the Attorney General. The tenor of the Justices' representations was that they should be wholly relieved of circuit duties. The bill did no more than dispense with the attendance of one Supreme Court Justice and vest discretion in the Supreme Court to assign two. It made certain other dispositions that do not here concern us.[182] The procedural matters covered related to bail in criminal cases and the officials who might take such. Section 5 empowered any judge of the Supreme Court to grant writs of *ne exeat* and of injunction and laid down the conditions under which such writs could be granted. Section 6 provided that subpoenas issuing in one district might run into any other district provided that out-of-district witnesses in civil causes did not live more than one hundred miles from the place where court was being held.

The Senate apparently did not dally over the bill. It was amended during the second reading and was passed January 8 and sent to the House.[183] There it was committed on the same day to the Committee of the Whole. Not long thereafter a special committee was named which reported amendments February 15, 1793.[184] Three days later the House sitting as a Committee of the Whole made further amendments, and the bill as amended was returned to the Senate.[185] Neither the House *Journal* nor the *Annals of Congress* reveal the details of the amending process.

A surviving remnant of the printed revision of what was sent to the Senate establishes that it was the House which rewrote the first section of the bill and in connection with the Supreme Court's discretion

---

[180] *Journal of the Senate of the United States of America, Being the Second Session of the Second Congress* (1793), 16 (hereafter cited *Senate Journal*, 2d Sess., 2d Cong.).

[181] *Ibid.*, 28. Filed Sen. 2A–B1, tray 1 (NA). The bill is in Ellsworth's hand.

[182] Viz.: (1) That in case of disagreement between Circuit and District judge, the cause should be continued to the succeeding court. If, with a different Supreme Court Justice sitting, a like division take place,

judgment should be in accordance with the opinion of the presiding judge. (2) Provision for special sessions of the Circuit for criminal trials.

[183] *Senate Journal*, 2d Sess., 2d Cong., 30.

[184] *Jour. H.R.*, I, 684, 704. The special committee was Benson of New York, Hillhouse of Connecticut, William Smith of South Carolina, White of Virginia and Kittera of Pennsylvania.

[185] *Ibid.*, 705, 709.

to assign two Justices to attend a Circuit added the browbeating phrase "and it shall be the duty of the justices, so assigned, to attend accordingly."[186] The other House amendments of the Senate's work need not detain us; the significant changes were the addition of three further sections, but the text of only two has survived.

One of these additions directed that it should be lawful for federal courts to use the services of state-appointed appraisers of goods taken in execution on a writ of *fieri facias*, and to authorize the United States marshal to sell such goods if the appraisers failed to attend when summoned.[187] Of much greater significance was a new section which in effect was a supplement to the Process Act of 1792 and a revision of section 17 of the Judiciary Act. It provided that it should be lawful for the Supreme Court "from time to time, as occasion may require to make general rules or orders for the Circuit and District Courts throughout the United States, or special rules or orders" for such courts in particular districts, "authorizing the returning of writs and processes, the filing of declarations and other pleadings, the taking of rules, the entering and making up of judgments by default, and other matters, in the vacation, and otherwise to regulate the practice of these courts, as shall be fit and necessary for the advancement of justice and especially to that end to prevent delays in proceedings."[188]

This new section portended an abrupt break both with the policy of the Judiciary Act, section 17, which conferred the rule-making power "for the orderly conducting business" upon all federal courts, and of the Process Act of 1792. Clearly the House meant that the regulation of practice was in the future to be committed to the Supreme Court alone and the language was sufficiently sweeping to encompass equity and admiralty proceedings. It is surprising that this change should have originated in the House where factional attacks upon the national policies of the Federalists had become notably rancorous. Whether or not the opposition realized it, the door to an eventual uniformity was set temptingly ajar.

The Senate was not prepared to embark on the drastic change in policy charted by the House. On the motion of Richard Potts, newly appointed Senator from Maryland, it was proposed to confer the power to make general rules and orders upon the Supreme, the Circuit and District Courts.[189] The Senate modified the language to "the several Courts of the United States," and dropped the word "general." Potts had substituted the word "regulating" the return of writs, etc., for the House's

---

[186] The fragment is filed Sen. 2A–B1, tray 1 (NA).
[187] *Ibid.*
[188] *Ibid.*

[189] Text filed Sen. 2A–B1, tray 1 (NA). It is indorsed "Amendments Proposed by Mr. Potts to the Bill Judiciary Feb 25th 1793."

"authorizing" and the Senate voted for "directing" the return, etc. The general power "to regulate the practice" of their respective courts Potts limited by the words "in such a manner not repugnant to the laws of the United States"—a formula accepted by the Senate.[190] The final homiletic phrase regarding the advancement of timely justice was preserved:

> . . . it shall be lawful for the several courts of the United States, from time to time, as occasion may require, to make rules and orders for their respective courts directing the returning of writs and processes, the filing of declarations and other pleadings, the taking of rules, the entering and making up judgments by default, and other matters in the vacation and otherwise in a manner not repugnant to the laws of the United States, to regulate the practice of the said courts respectively, as shall be fit and necessary for the advancement of justice, and especially to that end to prevent delays in proceedings.

The House concurred in the amendments.[191] The act became law March 2, 1793.[192]

The most that can be claimed for the new statute is that it represented some relaxation of legislative control over process and practice. It did not purpose to overset the confirmation of the *status quo* in common law causes effected by the Act of 1792. The federal judges seem to have so understood the 1793 statute. There was no rush to alter procedural incidents by rule of court in the several circuits—at least such is to be inferred from the absence of entries in the minute books of divers jurisdictions. As a practical matter, the Process Act of 1789, despite its repeal, had yet to be taken into account because of the legitimation in 1792 of its procedural progeny. It remains a sovereign example of a comment made in 1814 by Attorney General Richard Rush: "A law once in full force, is apt to draw after it a sort of perpetuity in its effects, not capable of being wholly expunged, even if desired or aimed at, by the formal repeal of its provisions."[193]

---

[190] The Senate changes are set out in a separate chit, headed "In place of 7th Section proposed by the House of R," and are repeated with slight changes in punctuation and capitalization in the document indorsed "Judiciary as it passed both houses & was enrolled." Filed Sen. 2A–B1, tray 1 (NA).

[191] *Jour. H.R.*, I, 720 (Feb. 27, 1793).

[192] 1 *U.S. Stats.*, 333.

[193] "Plan of a New Edition of the Laws of the United States: In a Letter from the Attorney General to the Secretary of State" (June 10, 1814), in 1 *Laws of the United States* (Bioren and Duane pubs., 1815), iii.

CHAPTER XIII

The Circuit Courts—Organization, Civil and Appellate Jurisdiction

THE PROFESSIONAL QUALIFICATIONS of the personages whom Washington on September 24, 1789, nominated for places on the Supreme Court were, in the eighteenth century phrase, eminently respectable. All but James Wilson[1] had had judicial experience, although in the case of John Jay[2] it had been trifling. The most solid credentials were those of William Cushing[3] who had been appointed to the Superior Court of the Province of Massachusetts Bay in 1772, had become Chief Justice in 1777 and had been duly translated to the same office after the Supreme Judicial Court was established by the constitution of 1780. John Blair[4] had been elected to the Virginia General Court in 1777, had been chosen Chief Justice in 1779, and in this capacity had become *ex officio* a member of the Court of Appeals. He had been elected one

---

[1] C. P. Smith, *James Wilson*, gives some details, by no means exhaustive, of Wilson the lawyer. See also *DAB sub nom.*

[2] Jay, who had had an active practice in the New York Supreme Court of Judicature, was appointed Chief Justice thereof in 1777. He presided at a session of this court held in Ulster County Sept. 9, 1777, pursuant to a resolution of the Committee of Safety, but the minutes do not show that he sat thereafter (Ms. Mins. N.Y. Sup. Ct. of Jud. 1775–81, N.Y.C. Hall of Records). He was named delegate to the Continental Congress Nov. 4, 1778, re-elected Feb. 9, 1779, and attended that body consistently until Sept. 28, 1779 (*cf. LMCC*, III, lvii; *ibid.*, IV, lviii). He was elected Minister to Spain Sept. 28, 1779. Jay

may have attended on one or more commissions of oyer and terminer for which special allowances were made by statute (*N.Y. Laws*, 1 Sess. 1778, c. 35). No record of such has been found. Generally on Jay, see F. Monaghan, *John Jay*.

[3] *DAB sub nom.* In the Ms. Cushing Papers at Massachusetts Historical Society are some documents, *e.g.*, a notebook relating to the trial Comm. v. Mansfield and Huggins (1783), an advisory opinion (1784) and notes on piracy (*c.* 1788).

[4] On Blair's services, see J. E. Drinard, "Sketch of John Blair Jr., 1732–1800," reprinted from *Annual Reports* of the Virginia Bar Association (1927), XXXIX. See also *DAB sub nom.*

552

of the Chancellors of the High Court of Chancery in 1780. Rutledge of South Carolina[5] had been named one of the judges of the South Carolina Chancery in 1784, and Robert Hanson Harrison[6] had served for eight years as Chief Judge of the Maryland General Court.

Other factors which obviously entered into the process of selection were a proper geographic distribution of the posts, experience in public affairs, whether state or national, and a record of attachment to the new federal Constitution.[7] Washington would have done well to have inquired into the health and vigor of each candidate, for the task which lay ahead was such that its discharge would require *mens sana in corpore sano*.[8] Disease was a near-neighbor in those times and the rigors of travelling the circuit were a provocation for it to move in. This was a consideration that does not appear to have occurred to the law-makers when the Judiciary Act was in process of enactment. It determined Harrison to decline the commission tendered, for he suffered from some malady which had plagued him during his long period of service as Washington's wartime aide and was to cause his early death in 1790. James Iredell of North Carolina was then appointed in his place.[9] The

---

[5] No satisfactory biography of Rutledge has come to our attention. On him, see *DAB sub nom.*

[6] For details, see G. T. Ness, "A Lost Man of Maryland," *Maryland Historical Magazine*, 35:315, 1940. The reports of cases for the period in 2 Harris & McHenry throw no light on Harrison's judicial capacity.

[7] This emerges from a letter Washington to McHenry, Nov. 30, 1789, expressing doubt with regard to Paca's appointment to the Maryland District Court: ". . . his sentiments have not been altogether in favor of the General Government, . . ." *Washington Writings*, XXX, 471.

[8] The medical histories of the Justices, normally a matter between them and their physicians, happen to be relevant to the discharge of their Circuit duties and to their efforts to be rid of them. Jay appears to have suffered from rheumatism (Jay to Hamilton, Sept. 28, 1792, *PAH*, XII, 497). Cushing developed a growth on his lip (Blair to Cushing, June 12, 1795, Ms. R. T. Paine Papers [MHS]); Blair himself became afflicted with "a rattling distracting noise in my head," evidently a malady of the inner ear that made him cut short his

Circuit and led him to resign (*ibid.*). Rutledge suffered from gout (*infra*, n. 19). Both Iredell and Paterson appear to have been much sounder physically, although the former missed the February term of 1794 of the Supreme Court because of illness and Paterson was so severely "indisposed" in the spring of 1794 while on the Vermont Circuit, he wrote, he "nearly went out of my head" (Paterson to Cushing, Aug. 9, 1794, Ms. R. T. Paine Papers [MHS]). Washington's last two appointees, Samuel Chase and Ellsworth, were afflicted with gout and were martyrs to renal stones (Chase to Washington, June 28, 1798, Mss. Huntington Library; Adams to Jay, Dec. 19, 1800, announcing Ellsworth's resignation, Adams, *Works*, IX, 91). The complete nervous and physical breakdown suffered by James Wilson in the spring of 1797 that lasted until his death in August 1798 was brought on by the collapse of his speculations and the consequent harassment by creditors. We have found nothing regarding Bushrod Washington and Alfred Moore, both Adams appointments.

[9] On Iredell, see McRee, *Iredell.*

Circuit duty was also to cause Thomas Johnson of Maryland to demur at accepting a seat on the Court in 1791 after Rutledge's resignation. He was to yield when Washington assured him that the judiciary law would be changed.[10] Although Johnson was given comfortable assignments, he was shortly to resign and William Paterson, a more robust man, was appointed his successor in 1793.[11]

Even if the new Justices had elected to live at the seat of government, a step which only James Iredell essayed, the statutory travel schedule was foreboding. It will be recalled that in addition to the two terms of the Supreme Court, the Judiciary Act provided for two annually in each district of the three circuits. After North Carolina and Rhode Island had ratified the Constitution and Vermont had been admitted into the Union, the Justices of the Supreme Court in their capacity as Circuit judges had among them to hold a total of twenty-seven courts per annum.[12] The spring and fall circuits followed shortly upon the February and August terms of the Supreme Court, respectively, and consequently a considerable shuttling back and forth was inevitable, for the northern terminus of their perambulations was fixed at Portsmouth, New Hampshire, the southern at Savannah, Georgia. The exertions involved transcended anything within the experience of those who as lawyers or judges had followed a circuit in a particular state. Inevitably tensions were to build up in the relations of the Justices. No less inevitable was to be the straining for statutory relief.

THE REVOLT AGAINST CIRCUIT RIDING

INITIALLY CHANGE did not seem unattainable because of the widely held opinion that the dispositions of the Judiciary Act were provisional. The opportunity of offering concrete proposals for amendment, before the inevitable process of institutional ossification set in, was there to be seized when Washington, on April 3, 1790, solicited from the Supreme Court Justices suggestions regarding the judicial system.[13] Jay prepared a draft reply which he sent to his brethren in mid-September, soliciting alterations.[14] He raised the question of the incom-

---

[10] The standard biography of Johnson—E. S. Delaplaine, *The Life of Thomas Johnson*—while interesting on his career, throws little or no light on his professional capacity. The arrangement regarding the assignment was agreed to by the Justices at a dinner given them by the President. Washington to Johnson, Aug. 7, 1791, *Washington Writings*, XXXI, 332.

[11] On Paterson, see *DAB sub nom.*
[12] From November 1796 onward, twenty-eight, for two sessions annually were appointed for Vermont (1 *U.S. Stats.*, 475) and Rutland became the northernmost terminus.
[13] *Washington Writings*, XXXI, 31.
[14] McRee, *Iredell*, II, 292; the text, 293-96. The version there printed concludes: "We have the Honor to be,

To the Chief Justice and Associate Judges of the Supreme Court of the United States.

New-York.

Gentlemen,

I have always been persuaded, that the stability and success of the national Government, and consequently the happiness of the People of the United States, would depend in a considerable degree on the Interpretation and Execution of its Laws. In my opinion, therefore, it is important that the Judiciary System should not only be independent in its operations, but as perfect as possible in its formation. —

As you are about to commence your first Circuit, and many things may occur in such an unexplored field, which it would be useful should be known; I think it proper to acquaint you, that it will be agreeable to me to receive such Information and Remarks on this Subject, as you shall from time to time judge expedient to communicate.

(signed) George Washington

United States
April 3d. 1790.

President George Washington's letter to the Chief Justice and Associate Justices of the Supreme Court, April 3, 1790, on the eve of the first Circuits.
(*Washington Papers, Library of Congress*)

patibility of combining the duties of Circuit judges and Supreme Court Justices. The Constitution was opposed to the appointment of the same men to both offices and there was also a legal incompatibility—a proposition supported by a lengthy citation from Bacon's *Abridgment*.[15] Furthermore, he conceived that the designation of the Justices to be Circuit judges by an act of the legislature was "a departure from the Constitution and an exercise of powers which constitutionally and exclusively belong to the President and the Senate." Jay concluded with the comment that there were defects in the act "relative to Expediency" which merited attention by Congress, but as these were doubtless among the objects of the reference by that body to the Attorney General, "we think it most proper to forbear making any remarks on the subject at present."[16]

There is no evidence that this reply was ever sent to the President.[17] It is worthy of remark, however, that the Chief Justice was prepared to challenge the constitutionality of section 5 of the Judiciary Act, but for reasons of political decorum evaded enumerating defects because he supposed such would be considered by an executive officer. No sovereign example of advocacy, the composition reflects rather Jay's overlong exposure to diplomatic protocol. If any of the Associate Justices made comments on the reply, as they were invited to do, such have not been found. In the years following they may well have echoed the poet's lament, "to have held the bird and let it fly."

Many months were to pass before the Justices were actually to take affirmative steps to be relieved of the task of holding Circuit Courts. This was the result of a series of events the first of which was the resolute action of one of their number, James Iredell, to compel an equitable scheme of rotating assignments. Iredell had moved his family to New York some months after his appointment in February 1790 to the seat declined by Harrison. He had been advised, March 18, 1790, by Senator Samuel Johnston of North Carolina of an assignment to the

---

most respectfully,/ Sir/ your most obedient, and most humble servants." In the ms. copy in the Cushing Papers (MHS) this valedictory is altered by twice striking the word "most," leaving the Justices mere obedient and humble servants—a conclusion considerably less servile than the original. There are no indications otherwise that Cushing was displeased with the text.

15 Bacon's examples of incompatibility of offices included: the forester with a patent for life made a Justice in Eyre for the same forest *hac vice*,

the patent becomes void; a mandamus to be restored to the office of town clerk by one who had been elected mayor, the court was of the opinion that the offices were incompatible because of subordination. Jay gave no citation but the examples are *sub* Offices and Officers K.

16 On which see *supra*, p. 541.

17 Warren, in *The Supreme Court in United States History*, I, 85, assumes that the letter was sent. Mr. Fitzpatrick, editing the *Writings of Washington* (1932), found no evidence of receipt; see Vol. 31, at 31–32, n. 58.

Southern Circuit with John Rutledge.[18] Johnston had added that "it is expected that the Judges would take it in rotation." The Judiciary Act had specified nothing regarding assignments to the Circuit Courts and it may be inferred from what happened in 1791 that the matter was settled by the Justices in conference. The first assignments were obviously fixed to suit the convenience of the individuals, Jay and Cushing taking the Eastern, Blair and Wilson the Middle, Rutledge the Southern Circuit.

At the February term 1791 of the Supreme Court, present Jay C.J., Cushing, Wilson, Blair and Iredell, it was determined that the Justices be paired and confined permanently to one circuit. Iredell by his own confession was struck speechless. Blair was under a misapprehension regarding the significance of the vote. Rutledge, confined by the gout, was not present to vote. He had not even been informed that a vote would be taken. Greatly indignant, Iredell promptly addressed a remonstrance to Jay, Cushing and Wilson.[19] The only serious inconvenience of rotation which occurred to him was that two judges might hear a case and take time to deliberate, and it would then cause inconvenience if the same judges did not return. He suggested how this could be met. Against this, however, were considerations of greater weight. "I will venture to say," he averred, "no Judge can conscientiously undertake to ride the Southern Circuit constantly, and perform the other parts of his duty." He himself had ridden 1,900 miles on the last circuit; in addition, the distance there and back was 1,800 miles. Iredell concluded with the warning that if the decision remained unaltered, he would seek other means of securing relief.[20]

Iredell's threat must have come as a shock, for the Court, whether from commitment to principle or from a sense of propriety, had thus far steered clear of anything resembling political self-help. As noticed, it had declined to aid in the drafting of a process act;[21] it had never sent to the President its views regarding the defects of the existing system. Iredell's professional experience in turbulent and war-torn North Carolina, twice as attorney general and briefly as a state Superior Court judge, had bred a tough and independent outlook.

Cushing's answer is the only reply to Iredell's remonstrance that we have found.[22] Cushing expressed his regret that the Southern Circuit

---

[18] McRee, *Iredell*, II, 285.

[19] *Ibid.*, 322–25 (Feb. 11, 1791).

[20] Iredell also listed a personal reason for not attending the next Southern Circuit for proceedings were pending on a writ of certiorari issued by the North Carolina Circuit on the direction of Blair, Wilson and Rutledge, to which the state court had refused obedience. The cause was one in which Iredell as executor was a defendant. See *infra*, p. 558.

[21] *Supra*, c. XII, p. 541.

[22] Cushing to Iredell, Feb. 13, 1791, Ms. R. T. Paine Papers (MHS). Jay's attitude may be inferred from his con-

appeared tedious. "The Northern is not without its troubles—its green woods, rocks & mountains." He expressed his willingness to do his duty whenever the majority should determine on a rotation. He distinguished the English system (where, he wrote, "questions arising on motions for new trials on issues of fact tried in the Country, as well as issues of law are decided by the same Judges at Westminster") from the discharge of such duties at circuit where a rotation would cause frequent delay of causes, notwithstanding short notes of cases taken in a hurry at the term to be delivered over to another Justice. He suggested that Blair might be disposed to make an exchange, and held out the cold comfort that "the System may ere long meet with a legislative remedy."[23]

Iredell appears to have brought his grievance to the attention of Senator Samuel Johnston, his preceptor in the law and kinsman by marriage. Shortly after the first session of the second Congress convened, the latter wrote Iredell that the "House" had not given up the idea of the reform of the judicial system and that he would do everything in his powers to keep it before them. The Southern members complained loudly of being "neglected by the Judges."[24] The circuit was not among the matters included in the miscellany reported in the bill which became the second Process Act, presented on January 26, 1792.[25] Meanwhile, Iredell had again written Jay on January 17, 1792, remonstrating against taking the Southern Circuit once more, and adverting to the litigation in which he was involved as defendant in the North Carolina District.[26] Jay could see no remedy but by Act of Congress. There is nothing to indicate that the problem came up for discussion when the Justices met at the February term that year.

Iredell rode the Southern Circuit alone, for Johnson, also assigned, was ill and could not attend. The Georgia grand jury did not take kindly to the solitary visitation, for as Iredell wrote his wife, it "presented the neglect of the other judges."[27] The "presentment" is informally expressed but there is no doubt that the jury felt aggrieved at the neglect.[28]

---

tinued resistance to rotation. His Ms. Diary as Circuit Judge, Apr. 16, 1790–June 1, 1792 (CU), is replete with entries regarding the state of the inns and food offered along various routes in New England—a primitive *Guide Michelin* of the region. The South offered little in the way of such accommodations; *cf.* the comments on North Carolina, Daniel Huger to Hamilton, June 22–25, 1792, *PAH*, XI, 541 at 543.

[23] Cushing apparently conceived

that all the same judges sat at trials at *nisi prius* as they did at Westminster. This was, of course, not the case. For a discussion of the motion for new trial, case stated, case reserved, *cf. LPAH*, II, c. I.

[24] McRee, *Iredell*, II, 335–36 (Nov. 13, 1791).
[25] *Supra*, c. XII, p. 542.
[26] McRee, *Iredell*, II, 337–38.
[27] *Ibid.*, 346 (Apr. 25, 1792).
[28] Text, *ibid.*, 355–56.

XIII: *Circuit Courts—Civil and Appellate Jurisdiction*

While the second Process Bill was still pending, Iredell, on March 15, 1792, wrote to Jay the suggestion that the several Justices of the Supreme Court should relinquish of their salaries $500 apiece. In view of the relatively modest judicial salaries (Chief Justice $4,000, Associate Justices $3,500 per annum), from which travelling expenses had to be subtracted, Iredell's proposal was not ungenerous. Whether it was advanced to induce appointment of Circuit judges or for a partial relief is not known, for the letter has not been found.[29] Jay replied somewhat frigidly that if "our Brethren should think it advisable to make the offer informally we would concur—that is, I will consent to that Deduction if we are relieved entirely from the Circuit." He believed that the sentiments of Congress should be "pretty well ascertained" before the proposal was made. If it were regarded as conveying "an implication not flattering to their Ideas of their own Dignity it would produce disagreable strictures."[30]

Before Iredell could have received Jay's letter, Senator Johnston, on March 20, presented a bill for altering the times of holding the Circuit Courts in certain districts of the United States. This was referred to a committee (Johnston, Strong and Sherman) with directions to bring in a clause to establish such rotation "as will best apportion the burden."

The bill[31] as finally enacted provided that at each session of the Supreme Court the Justices attending should, in a writing subscribed with their names and deposited with the clerk of the Supreme Court, assign to the Justices attendance at the ensuing Circuit Courts. This was to be done in such a manner that no Justice, except he consent, be assigned to a Circuit already attended until the same had been attended by every other of the Justices. If the public service or convenience of the Justices at any time in their opinion should require a different arrangement, this might take place with the consent of any four of the Justices. The act became law April 13, 1792.[32]

---

[29] The substance of Iredell's proposition is contained in Jay's reply of Mar. 19, 1792, a copy of which he sent to Cushing on the same date. Ms. R. T. Paine Papers (MHS). The $500 figure represents, we believe, the sum laid out in travelling expenses, which it would appear the Justices themselves bore. There were no appropriations made by Congress, and the "Report on the Receipts and Expenditures of Public Monies to the End of the Year 1791" (Nov. 10,

1792) contains no item beyond the salaries paid. *PAH*, XIII, 34 at 52. The compensation act, 1 *U.S. Stats.*, 72.

[30] *Supra*, n. 29.

[31] *Senate Journal*, 1st Sess., 2d Cong., 160. The bill passed the Senate Mar. 22, 1792 (*ibid.*, 167). The House made one amendment (*Jour. H.R.*, I, 570–71), agreed to by the Senate.

[32] 1 *U.S. Stats.*, 252–53.

This statute was not calculated to bring happiness to the Justices who had not yet faced the insalubrious climate and the travel discomforts to and about the Southern Circuit, and consequently may have operated to induce concerted and more vigorous affirmative action for relief. To add to the existing burdens of constant perambulation, the Congress, only three weeks before its intervention in the rotation matter, had loaded upon the Circuit Courts unprecedented and tedious duties, and extended the time of sitting. This was the so-called Pension Act (March 23, 1792).[33] At the time of the February term of the Supreme Court, the House bill which had inflicted the duties on the District judges, was before the Senate.[34] It was the latter which had substituted the Circuit judges. Providentially, the Justices were to be furnished with something of substance on which to base their constitutional objections to Circuit duty.

The statute was drawn on the premise that officers who had not received commutation of half pay and all non-commissioned officers, soldiers or seamen disabled by wounds or otherwise in the actual service of the United States were entitled to be placed on the pension list for life or for the duration of the disability and should receive such compensation for arrears as the Circuit Court of the district might think just. The proofs which a claimant must present were specified, and the Circuit Court upon receipt thereof was directed forthwith "to examine into the nature of the wound" or the cause of disability. The court was to certify the degree of disability and its opinion, if the claim was allowed, to the Secretary of War together with "their opinion" of the proportion of monthly pay that would be equivalent to the degree of disability. The courts were to remain open five days at least from the time of the opening of the sessions. In the event the Secretary of War should suspect imposition or mistake, he was empowered to withhold applicant's name from the pension list and make report to the next session of Congress.

Remonstrances were despatched to the President from the Circuit judges in three districts in three circuits. The first, signed by Jay, Cushing and Duane, was an extract from the minutes of the Circuit Court for the New York District, April 10, 1792.[35] The second, signed by Wilson, Blair and Peters holding the Circuit for the Pennsylvania District, was dated April 18, 1792.[36] The third, dated June 8, 1792, was signed by Iredell and Sitgreaves holding the Circuit for the North Caro-

---

[33] *Ibid.*, 243.
[34] The text of the relevant sections of the House bill are set forth in

Senate Journal, 1st Sess., 2d Cong., 102 (Jan. 26, 1792).
[35] *Am. St. Pap.: Misc.*, I, 49–50.
[36] *Ibid.*, 51.

lina District.[37] Washington laid the first communication before Congress April 16, the second April 21, the third on November 7, 1792.[38]

The remonstrances of the several Circuit Courts, although variously phrased, were agreed in this, that the judicial power was constitutionally committed to a separate department, that the duties imposed by the Pension Act were not judicial, that subjecting the court's opinions to revision or control by an officer of the executive and the legislature was not authorized by the Constitution. The judges sitting at New York and North Carolina indicated their willingness to sit as commissioners; those at Philadelphia did not.[39] The judges could have made their point more bluntly, viz., that Congress could not by trick of language require performance of a duty not authorized by the Constitution, but for all that, their meaning was clear enough.

The House of Representatives had had notice of the action of the Circuit judges for the Pennsylvania District before Washington's letter of transmittal was sent, for on April 13, 1792, William Hayburn, of whose application the court had refused to take cognizance, petitioned Congress for relief.[40] Elias Boudinot of New Jersey informed the House that the judges "looked on the law which imposed that duty as an unconstitutional one" and explained the specific grounds for this opinion. It was also mentioned that in New York the judges had refused to act. A committee was appointed to inquire into the facts. A report made five days later (April 18) was tabled.[41]

Surprisingly enough there was nothing resembling debate reported, although then, as thereafter, the invalid veteran was an object of public sympathy, and the newspapers, according to their politics, were making a to-do over the Circuit judges' letters. The antifederalist faction, ap-

---

[37] *Ibid.*, 52–53. Veterans' petitions were presented at the October term of the Circuit for the South Carolina District, Thomas Johnson and Bee sitting. "But it appearing to the Justices now here that this court cannot constitutionally take Cognizance of and determine on the said Petitions and papers, they were ordered to be entered and filed with the Records of this court and no further proceedings be had thereon." Ms. Mins. Circuit Ct. South Carolina Dist. 1790–1800, *sub* Oct. 26, 1792.

[38] Richardson, *Messages and Papers of the Presidents*, I, 123, 133.

[39] The amount of extra labor is indicated in the tables appended to the letter of Knox to the House of Representatives, Dec. 14, 1792 (*American State Papers: Claims*, 56–67 [hereafter cited as *Am. St. Pap.: Claims*]), and his second report to the House, Apr. 25, 1794 (*ibid.*, 107–22), that included cases disposed of by Circuit judges. Iredell, on circuit with Wilson who refused to act as commissioner, wrote his wife from New Haven, Oct. 4, 1792: "The Invalid-business has scarcely allowed me a moment's time, and now I am engaged in it by candle-light, though to go at three in the morning." McRee, *Iredell*, II, 362.

[40] *Annals of Congress*, III, 555.

[41] *Ibid.*, 559.

parently blind to the implications of the judges' actions, assumed that a retreat by the federal judiciary was involved that would strengthen the state courts. This is reflected also in federalist Fisher Ames' sorrowful comment that the "decision of our Judges . . . is generally censured as indiscreet and erroneous. At best, our business is uphill, and with the aid of our law courts the authority of Congress is barely adequate to keep the machinery moving; but when they condemn the law as invalid, they embolden the States and their courts to make many claims of power, which otherwise they would not have thought of."[42]

Madison, obviously not looking beyond partisan advantage, was pleased that close upon the President's veto of the apportionment bill on the grounds of unconstitutionality a fresh check had been placed upon what he called the "unconstitutional career of Congress." Writing Henry Lee, governor of Virginia, on April 15, 1792, he commented further: "The Judges have also called the attention of the Public to Legislative fallibility by pronouncing a law providing for Invalid Pensioners unconstitutional and void—perhaps they may be wrong in the execution of their power—but such an evidence of its existence gives inquietude to those who do not wish Congress to be controllable or doubted whilst proceedings correspond with their views."[43]

If, as Ames indicated, the federalists needed the help of existing federal courts, and, as Madison suggested, the party then in process of emerging needed them as a makeweight against the dominant majority, the prospect of altering the circuit system was not favorable. We have not found that during the interval between the February and the August terms (1792) of the Supreme Court the Justices themselves were concerting anything for their relief, although in the case of those who were hearing claims as commissioners the burdens had increased. But at the August term there occurred proceedings which supplied a trenchant illustration of the incompatibility argument.

According to the minutes of the Supreme Court, on August 6, Attorney General Randolph gave notice of a motion for a mandamus to be directed to the Circuit Court for the Pennsylvania District commanding that court to proceed on Hayburn's petition.[44] On August 8 Randolph proceeded to show cause. The Court doubted the Attorney General's authority to make the motion *ex officio*.[45] He was heard August 10 on this point. Randolph described his actions in less technical language in a letter to Madison.[46] "I pressed an examination of the conduct of the

---

[42] Ames to Dwight, Apr. 25, 1792, *Works of Fisher Ames*, I, 117.

[43] Ms. Madison Papers, XV, 35 (LC).

[44] Ms. Mins. U.S. Sup. Ct. 1790–1805, *sub* Aug. 6, 1792.

[45] *Ibid.*, *sub* Aug. 8, 1792.

[46] Aug. 12, 1792, Ms. Madison Papers, XV, 75 (LC).

New York and Penn circuit courts on the pension law." His "exordium," he reported, was "strong and pointed."

According to a newspaper account,[47] Randolph relied upon the analogy of the Attorney General's office here and in England as well as the wording of the Judiciary Act. This bestowed upon him authority "to prosecute and conduct all suits in the Supreme Court in which the United States shall be concerned." Randolph is reported to have claimed that "this gave him a superintendance over the Courts of the United States"—a pretension no more likely to appeal to some of the Justices than the reference to the authority of the English Attorney General, because this depended upon a fundamental premise of the royal prerogative, viz., the King's ubiquity in every court and the Attorney General's being party in every cause for the King.[48]

The language of section 35 of the Judiciary Act could not bear the stress to which Randolph subjected it, for it confined the duties of the Attorney General to the prosecution or conduct of all suits in the Supreme Court in which the United States might be concerned, and said nothing about any of the other courts. It is further to be observed that the Congress had very recently backed away from any enlargement of the Attorney General's authority.[49] For a House amendment to the Senate bill that became the second Process Act, providing "that it shall be lawful for the Attorney-General, in any suit in which the United States shall be a party, and in any court whatsoever, to advocate the United States although such suit may not have been instituted by him or under his direction,"[50] had been rejected by the Senate and the House had concurred.[51]

Since this had occurred only a few months before the proceedings in the Supreme Court, Randolph could hardly have forgotten the legislative repudiation of his pretensions. But Randolph's concept of the office derived from his own experience as attorney general of Virginia, where the office seems to have been patterned on the English model. At least,

---

[47] *Gazette of the United States,* Aug. 18, 25, 1792.

[48] Coke, *Littleton,* 139b; Blackstone, *Commentaries,* I, 270.

[49] Randolph had initiated the attempt to enlarge his authority. *Cf.* his letter to the President, Dec. 26, 1791, *Am. St. Pap.: Misc.,* I, 46. The latter had transmitted this communication to Congress December 28 (*ibid.,* 45). The House had referred the matter to a committee and on Jan. 18, 1792, John Lawrence of New York had reported favorably (*ibid.,* 46). The House accepted the report by resolve in the same terms (*Jour. H.R.,* I, 495), and the text of this resolve was the basis of the amendment tacked to the Senate's Process Bill.

[50] Printed bill, Senate Files, Sen. 2A–D1, tray 2 (NA). The House amendment followed in general the text of the resolve of Jan. 23, 1792 (*Jour. H.R.,* I, 495). Other features of the resolve and the amendment were the transfer of supervision of District Attorneys to the Attorney General and the provision for a clerk.

[51] *Supra,* c. XII, pp. 545–46.

in 1779 when he was both state attorney general and delegate to the Continental Congress, he had resigned as delegate because "the interest of the Commonwealth makes an advocate necessary in the courts of appeals, Chancery and the general court."[52] That the Virginia theory went the full way of the English was evidenced a few years later by an indorsement of District Attorney Alexander Campbell on Daniel L. Hylton's petition in error, waiving citation: "The United States being always present in their courts"[53]—a notion without constitutional or statutory foundation.

It seems to us most unlikely that the Justices were unaware of the debacle that had befallen the House's attempt to make the Attorney General the law officer of the United States; yet the Court divided on Randolph's motion, made *ex officio*. Jay, Cushing and Wilson were against it, Blair, Iredell and Johnson in favor.[54] The Court then proceeded to hear the Attorney General, as counsel for Hayburn, on a motion for a mandamus to the Circuit Court for the Pennsylvania District. "The sum of my argument," wrote Randolph to Madison, "was an admission of the power to refuse to execute, but the unfitness of the occasion."[55] This was in substance Madison's own view of the Circuit Court's action. The Court put off final determination until the next term. This is the last entry in the minutes, and it may be supposed that the Justices conceived that the question was about to be moot because a bill relieving the Circuit judges and altering the procedure of the Pension Act reached the penultimate stage of a Senate-House conference during the February term 1793.[56]

Nothing was settled at the August term 1792 regarding the judges acting as commissioners, for awards were made at divers fall circuits.[57]

---

[52] Randolph to the Speaker of the House of Delegates, Oct. 15, 1779, *LMCC*, IV, 470.

[53] Ms. Case Papers U.S. Sup. Ct., Hylton v. United States, Case No. 13.

[54] Blair, of course, was familiar with the Virginia practice, and it appears that a similar usage prevailed in North Carolina. McRee, *Iredell*, I, 434–36. We have found nothing on the Maryland usage. Jay's stand can be explained by the long tradition of hostility toward the New York provincial attorney general, much of which was due to the prosecution of informations *ex officio. Cf.* Goebel and Naughton, *Law Enforcement in Colonial New York*, 370–79, 733–48. A study of the office in the several colonies still awaits doing.

[55] *Supra*, n. 46.

[56] The conference committee did not report until Feb. 19, 1793. *Annals of Congress*, III, 883.

[57] *Cf.* the lists appended to Knox's reports, *supra*, n. 39. The revision of the Invalid Pension Act enacted Feb. 28, 1793 (1 *U.S. Stats.*, 324), made it the duty of the Secretary of War, in conjunction with the Attorney General, to take necessary measures to obtain an adjudication of the Supreme Court on the validity of any such rights claimed under the original act, by the determination of "certain persons styling themselves commissioners." Attorney General Randolph accordingly arranged with Secretary Knox to move August term 1793 for a mandamus directed to the latter to

But the tempest over the pension law, for all the division and procrastination displayed by the Supreme Bench, produced one immediate practical result. This was the unanimous resolve to despatch representations to Congress, via the President, regarding the circuit duty and praying for relief. The letter to the President was dated August 9, 1792, the day after Randolph showed cause for his motion to move *ex officio*.[58] The representations struck an apologetic note in the comment "that as it would not become them" to suggest what alterations or system in their opinion ought to be adopted, necessity moved them to represent the rigors of holding twenty-seven courts per annum, in the most severe seasons of the year, the time spent on the road, the dangers to health and the improbability of enduring such severe duties for any length of time. The plaint then arrived at the solid policy argument, theretofore not submitted to Congress and one given point by the mandamus proceedings. "That the distinction made between the Supreme Court and its judges, and appointing the same men finally to correct in one capacity the errors which they themselves may have committed in another, is a distinction unfriendly to impartial justice, and to that confidence in the Supreme Court which it is so essential to the public interest should be reposed in it."[59] With the recollection of the dilemma in which the Supreme Court had been placed by Randolph's motions not yet faded, and the matter of Hayburn still *sub judice*, the argument of incompatibility possessed a certain immediacy.

President Washington, in his annual message of November 6, 1792,[60] again drew Congress's attention to a revision of the judiciary

---

put on the pension list a person approved by the Judges acting as commissioners. Two Justices expressed a disinclination to hear a motion in behalf of one who had not employed movant and Randolph let the matter drop. *Am. St. Pap.: Misc.*, I, 78. However, at the February term 1794, a motion by counsel for a mandamus, on behalf of one Chandler his client, was also denied. At this same term Attorney General Bradford brought an action of assumpsit against one Yale Todd to recover moneys received under an award by Jay, Cushing and Law sitting as commissioners. It was stipulated by Bradford and counsel for Todd that if the judges sitting as commissioners and not as a Circuit Court had authority and power to make the award, judgment should be for the defendant, otherwise for the United States. The court

gave judgment for the United States. Bradford reported to Secretary Knox that the court determined "that such adjudications are not valid." Case papers and minute entries, in W. J. Ritz, "United States v. Yale Todd," *Wash. & Lee L. Rev.*, 15:220, 1958. Mr. Ritz is disposed to believe that the case involved a declaration that an Act of Congress was unconstitutional. The statute, however, said nothing about the judges acting as commissioners and consequently the awards could be adjudged void on the theory that the acts were *coram non judice*. There was no constitutional warrant for assumption of original jurisdiction in this case.

[58] *Am. St. Pap.: Misc.*, I, 51.
[59] *Ibid.*, 52.
[60] Richardson, *Messages and Papers of the Presidents*, I, 125.

system, adverted to the Justices' letter, and on the following day transmitted this document together with Iredell and Sitgreaves' representations against the procedure of the Invalid Pensions Act.[61] As was noticed in the preceding chapter, the Senate took the initiative by appointing a committee to take the judiciary system under consideration. On January 3, 1793, Ellsworth brought in the bill[62] which among other matters gave the Supreme Court Justices some relief by dispensing with the attendance of more than one at each Circuit Court and by vesting the Supreme Court with discretion to assign two members when circumstances required the attendance of two Justices.[63]

After the President's message to Congress had been despatched, but before the bill had yet been brought in, the Chief Justice, who had hitherto been indisposed to energetic action, seems to have sought help from Alexander Hamilton. The latter informed him that Senator Rufus King would advise him of "the state of the business," and expressed his own opinion that the representation would probably produce some effect, although "not as great as ought to be expected."[64] If King indeed communicated with Jay, the news was not encouraging. The latter had been ill and was still feeling the effects when on January 9, 1793, he wrote Cushing, who had arrived in Philadelphia, that he had heard that "some Members of Congress doubt the Expediency of adopting our Plan—You will have many opportunities of conversing with them on the subject and I flatter myself it will be in your power to remove their objections—I wish to see the Business fully discussed—hitherto but little attention appears to have been paid to it."[65]

The prospects for fruitful conversations were not bright, for the bill had passed the Senate the day before Jay's letter was written, and what the Justices were after would have required a new approach to the Circuit and so a new bill. Cushing does not appear to have replied to Jay, or if he did, he offered little solace. For when Jay again wrote his colleague on January 27 announcing his expectation that if well enough he would attend the coming term of the Supreme Court, he merely expressed the hope that "the Benevolence of Congress would induce them

---

[61] Ibid., 133.
[62] Supra, c. XII, p. 549.
[63] Sec. 2 of the statute (1 U.S. Stats., 333 at 334) provided that if at any time only one Justice of the Supreme Court should sit with a District judge at a Circuit Court and if at the final hearing of a cause or on a plea to the jurisdiction they should be divided in opinion, it should be continued to the

succeeding court; and if upon the second hearing, a different Supreme Court Justice being present, a like division should take place, judgment should be rendered in conformity with the opinion of the presiding judge.

[64] The Jay letters have not been found. Hamilton's answer of Dec. 18, 1792, in PAH, XIII, 337–38.
[65] Ms. R. T. Paine Papers (MHS).

to fix the Terms at more convenient seasons—especially as the public good does not require that we should be subjected to the cold of Feby or the heat of August."[66]

As noticed, the postulants received from Congress but a half loaf and a meagre one at that. Jay, however, was to resume his exertions in December 1793 by attempting to interest Senator Rufus King shortly after Congress convened. A new and not too persuasive argument was advanced for confining the Justices to Supreme Court duties—viz., that in the same Circuit Court one set of judges would decide a matter in the affirmative and another set would decide a similar issue in the negative. Because writs of error did not reach every case "the evil has no remedy." He suggested a reduction of salaries and declared his willingness to consent to a sum equal to the expenses of attending the Circuits.[67] A few days later he advanced the astonishing opinion that "the important Questions expected to arise in the Circuit courts have now been decided in them." He could conceive of no reason for continuing to send the Supreme Court Justices to preside in them of "equal weight with the objections which oppose that measure."[68]

The Chief Justice's opinion of the dispensability of the Circuit Courts was apparently not shared by his colleagues. For when on February 18, 1794, the Justices belatedly thanked Congress for the relief granted by the Act of 1793,[69] only two minor affirmative suggestions were offered for legislative action. These were the solution, first, of the difficulty when a single judge by accident or illness was prevented from attending the court assigned to him, and second, of the dilemma of conflicting rulings in similar cases by different judges in the same court, already raised by Jay in his letter to King. The Justices concluded with the statement that it did not become them to take a minute view of the whole system, and to suggest alterations which appeared requisite to them. This hesitation was "increased by the reflection that some of those alterations would from the nature of them be capable of being ascribed to personal considerations."

The sole response of Congress to this letter was to empower the District judge, or in his absence the marshal, to adjourn the Circuit Court in any district to the next stated term if a Supreme Court Justice did not attend within four days after the time appointed by law for the opening of the session.[70]

---

[66] *Ibid.*

[67] *Life of King*, I, 469–70 (Dec. 19, 1793).

[68] *Ibid.*, 509 (Dec. 22, 1793).

[69] *Am. St. Pap.: Misc.*, I, 77–78.

The representations were transmitted by the President to Congress on Feb. 19, 1794. The signatories were Jay, Cushing, Wilson, Blair and Paterson.

[70] 1 *U.S. Stats.*, 369.

That Congress should have yielded little to ease the lot of the Justices may be attributed in part to the persistence of the belief that compared to state judges the federal Bench was well paid,[71] in part to the fact that the Supreme Court itself was not overburdened in these early years, and finally to the almost diffident tones of the Justices' representations. This last was deliberate on their part, in keeping with the resolve early settled upon to refrain from immixion either in legislative[72] or in executive business.[73] In this the Justices as a collegium viewed the doctrine of separation of powers more strictly even than had the Framers, and they held steadfastly to this position. Jay was at first ready to extend the Court's view even to personal approaches to individual law-makers, but later, as noticed, he overcame his scruples—or his timidity—and even tried his own hand at the game.

There was little to be hoped for from such tactics for they could not be consistently pursued. Except for the few days of the February term when the Congress would be in session[74] and conversations could be held, the Justices were on the road. Furthermore, the fact that they did not as a body elect to reside at the seat of government[75] was a factor which militated against the establishment of an institutional image, as much as did the lack of reports of decisions. It was, under the circumstances, remarkable that something of an *esprit de corps* did develop, evidenced by the assumption of unassigned Circuit duties when one or another brother was ill.[76]

---

[71] See the debate on judges' salaries in 1789 (*Annals of Congress*, I, 933–38); the comments during debate on reducing salaries, January 1795 (*ibid.*, IV, 1136–46); and the remarks during the discussion in January 1801 of the Judiciary Act of 1801 (*ibid.*, X, 900–05).

[72] *Supra*, c. XII, p. 541.

[73] *Infra*, c. XIV, p. 626.

[74] After the Supreme Court was first convened, only the second session of the first Congress sat during the August term of the Court.

[75] As noticed above, Iredell moved his family to New York. He removed to Philadelphia, but as a result of the yellow fever epidemic of 1792, he and his family resumed residence in North Carolina. McRee, *Iredell*, II, 399.

[76] See Cushing to Paterson, July 20, 1794, asking the latter to take New York on September 5. Paterson to Cushing, Aug. 9, 1794, signifying his agreement. Blair to Cushing, June 12,

1795, acknowledging receipt of $100 for expenses on account of his taking the Southern Circuit. Chase to Cushing, Mar. 10, 1796, asking him to take the April term at New York so that he could arrange some private business unfinished because of the short notice of his appointment and service at the Supreme Court. Ellsworth to Cushing, Apr. 15, 1798, advising him that Paterson had taken on New York and Connecticut. He would take New Hampshire and Vermont, but requested Cushing to take Boston and Newport. (All in Ms. R. T. Paine Papers [MHS]). Chase had been very ill in the winter months early in 1799 and asked Paterson to take New York; he thought that he could take New Haven and finish other parts of the circuit (Chase to Iredell, Mar. 17, 1799, McRee, *Iredell*, II, 548). The courts in Connecticut and Vermont fell through, however; and as they were in danger of again falling through owing to

No firm evidence of further attempts by the Justices to induce a fresh look at the judicial system has been found, although the question of some amendment was intermittently before the Congress from early in 1798 until the revision finally pushed through in February 1801. It is unnecessary to explore these various legislative maneuvers further than to notice that the first prospect of relief was offered by a March 1798 Senate bill which proposed that all the District judges of each circuit be associated to hold the Circuit Courts—a scheme which, if enacted, would perhaps have survived Republican attack.[77] As it was, the Judiciary Act of February 13, 1801, established a new and distinct category of Circuit judges. Six circuits were erected[78] and the offices filled with the party faithful. For one brief year the Justices were spared the dangers and miseries of overturned vehicles, runaway horses, rivers in full flood or icebound and scruffy taverns.[79] Unhappily, in March 1802 the act creating the new systems was repealed by the triumphant Republicans.[80]

ORIGINAL CIVIL JURISDICTION

THE COMPLAINTS about circuit riding were none of them directed at what is today repellently described as the "case load." This was, however, brought in issue when the victorious Jeffersonian Republicans prepared to assault the Judiciary Act of 1801 by establishing *inter alia* the dispensability of the new Circuit Courts. In his first annual message

---

Cushing's illness, Ellsworth was keeping the Connecticut court and purposed to go to Vermont (Ellsworth to John Adams, Sept. 18, 1799, Adams, *Works*, IX, 31). Ellsworth notified Cephas Smith, the Vermont District Clerk, on Sept. 22, 1799 (Mss. Boston Public Library). He was spared the journey because Cushing recovered (Ellsworth to Wolcott, Oct. 1, 1799, G. Gibbs, *Memoirs of the Administrations of Washington and Adams*, II, 266–67).

[77] Ellsworth to Cushing, Apr. 15, 1798, Ms. Cushing Papers (MHS).

[78] 2 *U.S. Stats.*, 89.

[79] For example, on overturned coaches, Cushing to his brother, Feb. 10, 1790, Ms. Cushing Papers (MHS). On a runaway horse and vehicle crash, Iredell to his wife, Apr. 26, 1792, McRee, *Iredell*, II, 346–47. The Philadelphia *Aurora*, Feb. 5, 1800, reported Chase taken almost lifeless from the Susquehanna while crossing it. An English traveller, Isaac Weld, Jr., describes the state of taverns in the mid-1790's, *Travels through the States of North America*, I, 27–29. He has a vivid description (*ibid.*, 99–103) of a crossing of the frozen Susquehanna and a stay at a tavern in January 1796. Among the company were "some eminent lawyers from Virginia and the southward, together with a judge of the supreme court, who were going to Philadelphia against the approaching sessions." The judge was probably Chase or Iredell, the Virginia lawyers, Marshall, Campbell and possibly Attorney General Lee, for both Hylton v. United States, and Ware v. Hylton were argued in February term 1796. Two lawyers from the "southward," Jacob Read and John Julius Pringle, also were present at this term.

[80] 2 *U.S. Stats.*, 132.

(December 8, 1801) President Jefferson laid before Congress what he described as "an exact statement of all the causes decided since the first establishment of the courts, and of those which were depending when additional courts and judges were brought in to their aid." The purpose was to enable Congress "to judge of the proportion which the institution bears to the business it has to perform."[81] The utility of the establishment was thus apparently to depend upon a quantitative analysis on the basis of statements of the clerks of the Circuit Courts and those of the Districts of Maine, Kentucky and Tennessee. The test chosen by the President might have been meaningful if applied to the business of quarter sessions or other inferior courts; it was delusive in the case of courts dealing with litigation frequently of great intricacy and often protracted.[82]

On February 26, 1802, Jefferson transmitted to Congress a letter from Secretary of State Madison submitting some further data as well as corrections and additions to the original lists. The President explained that the errors were partly due to inexactitude in some of the returns, "and partly in analyzing, adding and transcribing them." We consequently have to do with figures not as submitted by the clerks of courts whom Madison blamed for mistakes, but with returns subjected to some editorial work in the office of the Secretary of State.[83] Unfortunately the so-called Domestic Letters of the Department of State for the period in question, where directions to District Attorneys were normally recorded, were lost during the War of 1812, and it is consequently impossible to establish how the official tables were, in fact, put together.[84]

The form in which the statistics were presented to Congress was of the roughest and was evidently hit upon by one not conversant with the course of litigation. Against the several terms of courts, the terminal dates of which varied, were entered in columns: (1) Suits at common law; (2) Suits in Chancery; (3) Criminal prosecutions; (4) Admiralty causes; (5) Aggregate; (6) A total of "Decided, discontinued, dis-

---

[81] Richardson, *Messages and Papers of the Presidents*, I, 326 at 331. The accompanying document, in *Am. St. Pap.: Misc.*, I, 320 *et seq.*

[82] *Cf.* here the comment of Representative John Stanley of North Carolina, Feb. 18, 1802: ". . . I cannot but express my admiration of the novelty, if not the solidity of the argument, founded on this document, that courts are necessary and useful, in proportion to the quantity of business before them." *Annals of Con-*

gress, XI, 571–72.

[83] *Am. St. Pap.: Misc.*, I, 319.

[84] If the new administration followed established procedure, the orders were transmitted via the District Attorneys. Madison's letter settles the question as to who prepared the tables. The fact that the District clerks had their hands full dealing with the business of both Circuit and District Courts has some bearing on the thoroughness with which the data were processed.

missed and not prosecuted"; (7) A total of "Depending." The last two classifications were, of course, neither of them enlightening, for the data on which they were based were not revealed. One is, for example, at once moved to ask whether "not prosecuted" was limited to causes criminal, and if so, did it refer only to indictments non prossed or to bills returned *ignoramus*? Similarly, did the mere taking out of process, as occurred in some jurisdictions, make an action depending or did there have to be a return?

At this late date, what with the loss of minutes, praecipe, docket, judgment books and the like, it is impossible to put the figures reported to any trustworthy test for accuracy even if we had clues as to how the clerks made their compilations. Nevertheless, random samplings of minute books—not the most comprehensive guides to judicial business, in relation to items most easily traced—induces mistrust of the government's exhibits.

The return for South Carolina lists no criminal causes whatever. From the minute book, however, it appears that five indictments for piracy were returned, two for murder, two for obstruction of process and one for entering French service.[85] In 1797 fifteen indictments for piracy and two for trespass were presented to the grand jury but were returned *ignoramus*.[86] No less inexplicable is the return of admiralty causes. A total of fifty-six such was reported—the minute book has entries for only twenty-nine cases.[87] The Georgia return is no less difficult to reconcile with the minute book entries. These show a total of twelve identifiable indictments ranging from murder and piracy to "misdemeanor."[88] In the government's 1802 returns only one prosecution is entered. Only one admiralty cause is there listed. The minute book shows ten cases.[89]

---

[85] Ms. Mins. Circuit Ct. South Carolina Dist. 1790–1800, *sub* Nov. 3, 4, 1794, piracy, five cases; murder; Nov. 4, 1794, and May 13, 1795, obstruction of process, two cases; May, 1795, entering service of the French; May 9–11, 1797, murder.

[86] *Ibid.*, *sub* May 9, 1797.

[87] The figure of fifty-six may be based on entries of writs of error in the nature of appeals that were not prosecuted. We are led to this conjecture by the categorical statement of Senator Chipman, Jan. 19, 1802, that of the 423 suits brought in South Carolina in 1799, the greater part were filed by Miller and Co. for patent infringement (*Annals of Congress*, XI, 135). Since nothing of this appears in the minute book it is obvious some source like a docket or praecipe book had been used.

[88] Ms. Mins. Circuit Ct. Georgia Dist. 1790–1793, *sub* Nov. 10, 1792, piracy and felony, two cases; Ms. Mins. 1793–1798, *sub* Nov. 12, 1793, misdemeanor; Apr. 28, 1795, perjury; Nov. 10, 1797, forgery; Ms. Mins. 1798–1806, *sub* Apr. 22, 1800, and Nov. 11, 1800, murder; Apr. 22, 24, 1800, rescue and obstruction of process; Apr. 23, 1800, misdemeanor; Apr. 24, 1800, extortion. Two further indictments were found, but the offense is not indicated.

[89] *Ibid.*, Ormond v. Brig *Somerset* (May 1795); Penman v. Brig *Judith* (May 1795); Ross v. Ship *Elizabeth*

Minute books are of small help in any effort to test out the reported number of "suits at common law," although it may be remarked that in the case of New Jersey, where the minute book doubled as a praecipe book, the clerk seems to have included entries therefrom.[90] No case papers appear to have survived for this jurisdiction. Such do, however, exist in the case of Pennsylvania, although there are only fragments of minutes prior to 1792. The total of suits at common law was given as 722 in the 1802 report. The minutes reveal there were about 240 such actions. This figure is supplemented by some 158 actions for which case papers were found but no minute entries.[91] It seems to us probable that the returns of the Pennsylvania court were made up by an ill-informed deputy.[92]

There is no profit in adducing further evidence that the figures

---

(May 1795); Trabaduc v. Ship *Manamarana* (May 1795); Wallace v. Brig *Caesar* (May 1795); Wallace v. Brig *Everton* (May 1795); Horie v. Sloop *Peggy* (May 1796); Wallace v. *Granada* Packet (May 1796); Wallace v. Sloop *Casaldea* (May 1796). One appeal, U.S. v. Seven Pipes and Two Butts London Market Wine (April 1793), was probably a forfeiture case.

[90] Ms. Mins. Circuit Ct. New Jersey Dist. 1790–1806. After 1796 the entry of writs issued and returns falls off, indicating another book was in use by that time for praecipes.

[91] The count of the cases in the minutes is approximate because of occasional ambiguities in the entries, viz., the same case appearing under a different caption or the names of the parties being variously spelled.

[92] One theory to account for the total of 722 cases given in the 1802 report is that the clerk used the docket book and counted each entry. The docket entries in the famous case of Vanhorne's Lessee v. Dorrance suggest how this could happen. The first entry in October term 1791 is captioned "Richard Fenno Lessee of Cornelius Vanhorne vs. John Denn— John Dorance [*sic*] Tenants Ejectment." October 12, Rawle appeared for tenant in possession, entered common rule, pleaded not guilty. "It is agreed that a new Decl^n be filed agt. the sd. John Dorance as Dft." On

December 6 declaration was filed. In 1792, on August 4, "for Trial—"; October 5, "to be struck off trial list and continued." In 1793, "For trial by Special Jury." The entries are in Ms. Docket Books 1 and 2, Circuit Ct. Eastern Dist. of Pennsylvania, p. 63. On this page the names of counsel are written in the margin. However, on p. 68 where the entries are resumed, the caption appears "Sergeant —Richard Fenno Lessee of Cornelius Vanhorne vs. Rawle—John Denne— John Dorance Tenant." In 1793, on March 15, jury list was struck and sixteen *venires* issued; March 21 and 29, and April 11, blank subpoenas were issued. At April session, rules entered regarding taking depositions and issuance of commission; December 19, rule for trial by special jury. In 1794, on March 31, *venire* issued; April session, *venire* returned executed. In 1795, on March 12, rule for trial by special jury continued; March 24, jury list struck, *venire* issued; April 18, deposition of Jos. Shippen filed. On April 21, it is noted that the jury appeared, the names and the swearing or affirming of the jurors.

On p. 70 the cause reappears under the caption "Sergeant—The L^ee of C. Van Horne vs. Rawle—John Dorance." There are five April entries recording exceptions to testimony. On May 12, 1795, the charge of the court was excepted to; the verdict is entered and the judgment for plaintiff noted.

submitted in 1802 are not an exact representation of the volume of Circuit Court business. The "corrected" totals of "suits instituted" was given as 8,276; of "suits depending" as 1,539. How nearly these approximated the truth, no one at the time could have told, and because it was a political purpose these were to serve, truth was hardly in issue, although the federalists in Congress tried to make it so. What was more to the point, since one aim of the Act of 1801 was to relieve not only the Supreme Court Justices but also the District judges upon whom many and various labors had been loaded, was the fact that the tabulation in no way reflected the nature and extent of judicial burdens. In the case of the Circuit Courts, some of these are occasionally noted in court minutes, such as proceedings on recognizances, applications for habeas corpus, the drafting of decrees, the preparation of cases stated in equity and admiralty causes pursuant to section 19 of the Judiciary Act, and the formulation of rules.

There were other duties the scope of which the minute books do not illuminate: the preparation of general charges to grand juries, the formulation of instructions to petit juries, and finally the exacting task of the Justice familiarizing himself with the details of a protracted litigation, proceedings on which at earlier terms other Justices had presided, the writing of opinions and a certain amount of business done out of term.

There were still other and professionally no less formidable problems with which Supreme Court Justices in their capacity as Circuit judges had to wrestle, not susceptible of statistical analysis—certainly not by the formulas used in 1801. These were the result of the fact that on the common law side federal practice was conducted in conformity with the practice of the state where the Circuit Court was held, and the visiting Justices had to acquire some command of state procedural variants. Some of these diversities have already been noticed in connection with the Senate Committee's Process Bill of 1789,[93] and there were countless others rooted in statutes or in local usage. The accommodation of practice to that of each state resulted from the interpretation put upon the words "modes of process" in the first Process Act, taken as a direction to follow the procedure of the highest state court. We do not know whether or not this was agreed upon by the Justices at the first term held in February 1790. However, rules to this effect have been found for the Circuit Court for the Virginia District, May term 1790,[94]

---

[93] *Supra*, c. XII.
[94] 1 Ms. Order Book, Circuit Ct. Virginia Dist., *sub* May 22, 1790. In all civil cases where by laws and usages of the state bail was requirable, such could be demanded at Circuit and the recognizance entered into before such persons and in the form agreeable to present practice in the state District Court. The same rules which prevailed in causes depending before state District Courts on their rule dockets to be observed in the Circuit Court.

the South Carolina District, May term 1790,[95] the Georgia District, May term 1790,[96] the New Jersey District, October term 1790,[97] and the Maryland District, May term 1790.[98] Although no rules have been found for other districts, the case papers indicate that initially there was substantial conformity with state practice.

As already remarked, the language of the second Process Act indicates a legislative intention to leave the "modes of proceeding" at common law in the state in which these stood as of the effective date of the statute (May 8, 1792). Presumably this relieved the federal courts from accommodating themselves to every puff of the winds of change that might blow up in state legislatures, although whenever a drastic alteration was made in a form of action, as happened with ejectment in Vermont,[99] such alterations could not be ignored.

The second Process Act, it will be recalled, also enlarged the rule-making power of the federal courts, which would enable them to make adjustments of current procedures, but to all appearances no startling innovations were made by rule in most of the jurisdictions examined. Indeed, in New York the District Court in 1800 ordered that in all cases not specially provided for in its own rules, those rules established for regulating the practice of the New York State Supreme Court, so far as applicable, should be the rules regulating practice in the District

---

[95] Ms. Mins. Circuit Ct. South Carolina Dist. 1790–1800, *sub* May 13, 1790. This minute book appears to be an engrossed copy. In transcribing the rule the copyist did not complete the sentence. It reads: "The mode of proceeding in Causes at Common Law be conformable to the practice." Evidently the words "of the Supreme Court of this state" or "of the common law courts of this state" were skipped. The next rule directs that "proceedings in Causes of Equity be conformable to the practice of the Court of Chancery of this State."

[96] Ms. Mins. Circuit Ct. Georgia Dist. 1790–1793, 3 *sub* May 28, 1790. The order throws some light on the state of practice in that state. "That the mode of proceeding in this Court in Cases at Common *Law* shall be by Petition and Process as practiced in the Superior Courts on the twenty-ninth day of September last, which Petition shall contain the substance of the declaration, or state the complaint Allegation or demand of the plaintiff." Forms of proceeding in equity

"shall be conformable to the practice used in the Court of Equity which was established in the Province, now State of Georgia" so far as consistent with the Constitution and laws of the United States.

[97] Ms. Mins. Circuit Ct. New Jersey Dist. 1790–1806, *sub* Oct. 2, 1790: "Ordered that the general course of practice in the Supreme Court of New Jersey shall in all cases, to which that course is applicable, be the rule of practice in this court."

[98] Ms. Mins. Circuit Ct. Maryland Dist. 1790–1812, *sub* May 8, 1790. The same rule as to bail was laid down as in Virginia, the paradigm being the General Court of Maryland. "That the law proceedings of this court be conducted according to the usage & practice of the General Court of this state."

[99] *Vermont Laws* 1797; c. 3, sec. 88, whereby the "circuitous mode of prosecuting for the recovery of landed property," viz., the action of ejectment, was altered.

Court.[100] At the succeeding term of the Circuit Court the rules laid down by the District Court for regulating its own practice were adopted.[101] The New York Supreme Court in the preceding year had overhauled and enlarged its own rules,[102] and it may be supposed that the federal courts acted for the accommodation of the practicing profession. We have no such explanation for a rule similar to that of New York District Court, laid down April term at the Circuit for Pennsylvania District.[103]

One important exception has been found to the economical use of the rule-making power. This was the elaborate set of forty-one rules "for the orderly conducting business in the Circuit Court of Georgia in Cases at Common Law" ordered by Samuel Chase and Joseph Clay, Jr., the District judge, April term 1797. A set of twenty-one rules in Cases of Equity was also promulgated; but of course under the Process Act of 1792 this practice stood on a different footing.[104] Together these rules strike one as the boldest attempt made by any court during this early period to supplement the generalities of the statutes, and to settle details that we suspect were still at large. Diligent search has failed to exhume any trace of Georgia state rules for this period, and we do not know how competent Joseph Clay, Jr., may have been to have enlightened a visiting Justice on the nuances of local patterns of practice. From the first, such advice had been conceived to be the peculiar province of the District judge, but clearly at a time when practice depended upon usage and when there was no more trustworthy source than memory, the local oracle might not always have a correct answer.[105]

---

[100] Ms. Mins. District Ct. New York Dist. 1798–1800, *sub* Feb. 4, 1800.

[101] Ms. Mins. Circuit Ct. New York Dist. 1790–1808, *sub* Apr. 8, 1800.

[102] *Rules of the Supreme Court of the State of New York*, 3d ed. (1812), 25.

[103] Ms. Mins. Circuit Ct. Pennsylvania Dist. Apr. 1798–Apr. 1799, *sub* Apr. 20, 1799: "It is ordered by the Court that in the conduct and Management of suits depending on the common law side of this Court, the same Practice shall be observed as is at present observed in the Supreme Court of the State of Pennsylvania, so far as the same is not inconsistent with any former order of the Court, and subject to such Alterations and Additions as this Court shall deem expedient or to such Regulations as the Supreme Court of the United States shall think proper from time to time to prescribe to the Circuit Courts."

[104] These two sets of rules were recorded in Ms. Mins. Circuit Ct. Georgia Dist. 1793–1798, 297–313.

[105] *Cf.*, for example, the comments of Peters J. in Carson v. Jennings to the effect that the distinction between instance and prize sides of admiralty was unknown in this country (4 Cranch 6n.). Peters had been Register of the provincial vice-admiralty court of Pennsylvania and should have known better. Judge Cyrus Griffin was consulted by Chase on a ruling excluding certain testimony in U.S. v. Callender (*infra*, c. XIV). This ruling was made Art. III of the Articles of Impeachment; *cf.* C. Evans, *Report of the Trial of the Hon. Samuel Chase* . . . (1805), 66, testimony of William Marshall; *ibid.*, Exhibits, 4, for the article.

April Term 1794.

For the orderly conducting business in the Circuit Court of Georgia, in cases at Common Law It is ordered, by the said Court that the following rules be observed —

1st The defendant shall plead within sixty days after the expiration of the Term in which he appears —

2d The defendant with leave of the Court, may plead as many several pleas as may be necessary in his defence. Pleas to the merits only will be approved of by the Court: All sham pleadings will be discountenanced and attorneys guilty of such conduct will be censured or fined —

3d The Defendant shall not plead specially without the consent of the Plaintiff if by the rules of Evidence the special matter can be given in Evidence, on the general issue.

4th If the Defendant neglects to plead within the time limited, he may plead the general issue, on or before the first day of the next term:

5th If the Defendant neglects to plead within the time limited, he shall not plead the Act of Limitations, unless the plaintiff amends his declaration —

6th If the defendant neglects to plead the General issue within the time limited

Rules for the orderly conducting business in the Circuit Court of Georgia in Cases at Common Law, ordered by Samuel Chase and Joseph Clay, Jr., Circuit Judges.

(*Manuscript Minutes, Circuit Court for the Georgia District 1793–1798, page 297. Federal Records Center, East Point, Georgia*)

XIII: *Circuit Courts—Civil and Appellate Jurisdiction*

The itinerary, so to speak, of any action at common law, whether initiated by praecipe or otherwise, cannot in any jurisdiction be traced by reference to the formal record or even the court minutes. What may be described as necessary documentation varied from state to state, and from the residue and remainder of federal records it appears that the record-keeping practices of the Circuit Courts were patterned upon those of the particular states. The details are cheerless, but they establish the mechanics of administering justice and beyond all else demonstrate an aspect of judicial labors overlooked by the would-be saboteurs of the federal judiciary in Congress and out.

Prior to a cause coming to issue, these labors related both to process and pleading. As to the first, the most time consuming was the matter of bail, particularly in Pennsylvania where, as noticed, a freeman, as defined, was entitled to be summoned, and only in case of non-appearance could be taken on a *capias*. Since in the latter case the amount of bail lay in the discretion of the court, the hearings could be protracted.[106] A great deal of this type of business in jurisdictions like New York was despatched by the clerk of the court.[107] Nevertheless, wherever judicial intervention was necessary this could, in vacation, be handled in chambers.[108] The Process Act of 1792 apparently sought to relieve the judges by authorizing the clerk to take recognizances *de bene esse*, but gave no authority on propriety of bail or disputes over the amount.[109] Such issues were usually settled by the District judge, the workhorse of the federal system, but a Supreme Court Justice, if available, was no less qualified in his capacity as Circuit judge. However, James Wilson, not one to assume extra duties, refused in 1795 to hear a bail question at his residence on the ground that Justice Paterson had been designated for the next Circuit.[110]

---

[106] This was due in Pennsylvania to two factors: the law which required only one real person as surety for bail to the action, and the fact that out-of-state plaintiffs wished such person to be substantial. Plaintiff was allowed to refuse bail and notify defendant to justify. This was usually left to plaintiff's attorney. *Cf.* Lee v. Anderson, Ms. Case Papers 1793, Circuit Ct. Pennsylvania Dist. If the parties could not agree, defendant could move before the District judge that bail be reduced or he be admitted to common bail. *Cf.* Parasset v. Gautier fils, Ms. Case Papers 1795, *ibid.* An appeal would lie to the Circuit Court from such rulings.

[107] Which accounts for the numerous rules on the matter in individual cases entered in the minutes.

[108] Or the Supreme Court Justice might be consulted at long distance. *Cf.* the letter of Iredell to Peters from Edenton, N.C., June 16, 1797, Ms. Peters Papers, X, 49 (HSP), on proceedings to discharge on common bail, probably relating to Smyth v. Banks, Ms. Mins. Circuit Ct. Pennsylvania Dist. Apr. 1797–Apr. 1798, *sub* Apr. 27, 1797.

[109] 1 *U.S. Stats.*, 278 (sec. 10).

[110] Peter Du Ponceau to J. Y. Noel (Savannah, Ga.), Aug. 1, 1795, Ms. Du Ponceau Letterbook B. 108–10 (HSP).

As respects the course of pleading, the criteria for judicial ruling as against an entry of course by the clerk of the court—*e.g.*, a rule to plead—depended upon the usage in the state superior or supreme court of the district. Such usage was either a matter of professional tradition, as it seems to have been in Massachusetts,[111] or is attributable to rule of court, as in New York where the Supreme Court of Judicature distinguished between common and special rules (the latter requiring action by the court),[112] or derived from a statute, as in Virginia where was held a monthly meeting called the "Rules" based upon a direction in the state District Court Act of 1788.[113] Wherever docket books were kept and have survived, as in Pennsylvania, Maryland and North Carolina,[114] the progression of the pleading process, whether by interposition of motions or not, can be traced, often, however, only by reference also to the minute books or to case papers.

As for the pleadings themselves and indeed the various incidents of civil procedure in the several American jurisdictions, we have already remarked upon their common law ancestry. But this was a comment on pedigree, for insofar as Circuit Court case papers reflect state practice in some jurisdictions, the breeding out of the ancestral strain was well advanced.[115] This had been due in New England and Pennsylvania to

---

[111] This rests on inference from the fact that the "Rules of the Supreme Judicial Court 1779–1796" (in *American Precedents of Declarations* [1802], Appendix) do not deal with the matter.

[112] Hamilton, "Practical Proceedings," in *LPAH*, I, 58, 130–31. The Supreme Court revised and clarified its rules in April term 1796. *Rules of the Supreme Court of the State of New York*, 3d ed. (1812), 9 *et seq.*

[113] 12 Hening, *Va. Stats.*, 730. The Circuit Court "Rules" came to be scheduled once a month. *Cf.* Gist v. Mayo's Exrs., 7 Ms. Record Book, 193, Circuit Ct. Virginia Dist.: "1796 July Declaration and common order against the defendants. August common order confirmed and writ of Inquiry"; Murdock & Co. v. R. Anderson, *ibid.*, 208: "1797 June Continued for Decl. July Decl. & Common Order. August Common order confirmed." In the federal practice, default judgments had to be confirmed by the court during term.

[114] In Pennsylvania, Ms. Docket Books 1 and 2. Seven dockets were kept and have survived for Maryland:

(1) Original docket; (2) Imparlance and Continuance docket; (3) Judicials; (4) Reference docket; (5) Attachment docket (only for May term 1800); (6) Criminal docket; (7) Appeals and Errors docket (only entries for 1793). For North Carolina there are preserved a trial docket, an appearance docket, an equity docket and an execution docket.

[115] The editors of *The Legal Papers of John Adams*, Vol. I, have indicated how little recondite by English standards the Massachusetts pleading was in Adams' time. The usage of setting out the declaration at the foot of process persisted and is reflected in federal records. *E.g.*, O'Connor v. Gardner, on which see document dated Apr. 20, 1791, in Ms. Case Papers, and see also Ms. Final Record Book Circuit Ct. Massachusetts Dist. 1790–1799, *sub* November term 1791; Duncan v. Winship, document dated Sept. 4, 1794, in Ms. Case Papers, and Ms. Final Record Book 1790–1799, *sub* June term 1795; Bolton v. Browne, document dated Jan. 19, 1796, in Ms. Case Papers, and Ms. Final Record Book 1790–1799,

the persistence of usages established before the advent of men of professional training, and in North Carolina and Georgia to what may be called the countrifying of practice during and after the Revolution.[116] In four former royal and one proprietarial province—New Jersey, New York, South Carolina, Virginia and Maryland—there was the least deviation from the common law canon. These were what might be called the "high church" jurisdictions in contrast to the others which, to pursue our ecclesiastical figure, were in varying degrees "low church." Pennsylvania, although to be arrayed with the latter,[117] nevertheless was not uninfluenced by changes in English practice[118] and had, indeed, contrived some novelties of its own.[119]

It is perhaps not imagining too much to suggest that the Supreme Court Justices trained in conservative tradition (and most of them had been) when confronted with the instruments in one of the more aberrant jurisdictions may well have doubted that such exemplified what Hobart C.J. once called the "beauty and grace of pleading."[120] There is, indeed, a striking difference between the combination process and declaration and the short entries of pleadings in New England, or the verbose, repetitious instrumentalities of North Carolina, and the techni-

---

sub June term 1796. As might be anticipated from the fact noticed in the preceding chapter, the forms of pleading in Connecticut and New Hampshire were similar to those in Massachusetts. In Vermont, probably because it was settled mainly by Connecticut and New Hampshire emigrants, the pleadings there were cast in like form, viz., the declaration set forth on the process, and the pleadings usually entered short on the dorse.

[116] The pleadings in both jurisdictions, especially in the early years of the Circuit, were prolix and unartfully drawn. Prior to the Revolution professional expertise was centered in seaboard towns. Iredell resigned as Superior Court judge in 1778 because of the state of the court and practice there, a step that has led us to infer that practice had fallen into the hands of demi-lawyers (*cf.* McRee, *Iredell*, I, 395). John Williams, who succeeded Iredell, had been "raised to the trade of a house carpenter" (*ibid.*, 397).

[117] As late as 1823 Bushrod Washington commented, "The pleadings, . . . except the declaration are according to the loose practice in this state, entered short; neither the plea nor the replication being put in form." Bobyshall v. Oppenheimer, 4 Wash. C.C. 338. As in New England, the plea would be entered short on the dorse of the narrative. We think the simplified system in this state arose and persisted because the Common Pleas courts were vested with extensive jurisdiction and the bench in the country was not professionally served.

[118] *E.g.*, the case made or case stated, on which see *LPAH*, II, c. I. For examples at Circuit, see Duncan v. Koch, narrative in case, plea non-assumpsit, in Ms. Case Papers, also in Ms. Mins. Circuit Ct. Pennsylvania Dist. Oct. 1799–Apr. 1800, *sub* Apr. 18, May 2, 1800, and Ms. Mins. Oct. 1800–Feb. 1802, *sub* May 16, 20, 1801; Cowan v. Magauran, Ms. Mins. *sub* May 13, 1801; Thurston v. Koch, 4 Dallas 348 (1800).

[119] In particular the great variety of agreements, viz., to proceed with an amicable action without writ, to circumvent rules regarding joinder of actions or parties, and the not unusual agreements to refer.

[120] Slade v. Drake, Hobart 295 (1618).

cally expert pleadings used in New York. In most of the states the courts had long been vested with large powers of amendment[121] and of course the federal courts were similarly empowered. Unfortunately, in our period there was little remembranced of exchanges between court and counsel on points of procedure and practice so characteristic of English cases of this genus. We know little also of the individual convictions of the Justices, although it can be documented that Paterson did not regard himself as utterly bound by state practice,[122] and Chase consistently opted for the common law—state or English.[123] What is impossible to document is the extent to which Circuit practice was affected by the Supreme Court rule of August 1792, that it considered the practices of the King's Bench and the English Chancery as affording outlines for practice before it.

The probabilities that the rule respecting chancery procedure had direct effect upon the handling of equity suits at Circuit rest upon the fact that separate Chancery Courts had been maintained in only five states, and that federal legislation needed supplementation. It has already been noticed that equity procedure had at first been placed on the vague footing of "civil law" and in 1792 the second Process Act directed that it be according to the "principles rules and usage which belong to courts of equity."[124] Because the legal profession was hardly prepared to go to school to execute literally the injunction of the first Process Act, existing chancery practice was bound to be treated as substantial compliance. A rule making state practice obligatory has been found only for the Circuit Court for the South Carolina District. At May term 1790, Rutledge and Iredell sitting, it was ordered "That the proceedings in Causes of Equity be conformable to the practice of the

---

[121] Some of which are noticed in c. XI, *supra*. One example of the benefits was the mollification of the rule against duplicity—the privilege to "plead double" as it was called in New England. This is attributed to the effects of 4 & 5 Anne, c. 16 (Dane, *Abridgment*, VI, c. 180, art. 3), but in Massachusetts probably goes back to an act of 1702 (1 *Acts and Resolves Prov. of Mass. Bay*, 464). This was allowed at Circuit; see Douglass Ex'r. v. Rogers, *sub* June term 1797, Ms. Final Record Book Circuit Ct. Massachusetts Dist. 1790–1799. The Ms. Case Papers for New Hampshire reveal numerous instances where defendant was directed to plead double. In this District one

case was found (Rayson v. Jewett, Ms. Docket No. 6, May term 1795) where a faulty declaration was amended by attaching another paper containing the missing alteration.

[122] *Cf.* Brown v. Van Braam, 3 Dallas 344, 346 n. (Sup. Ct. 1797).

[123] *Ibid.* See also his comment in U.S. v. Parker, 2 Dallas 373, 380 n. (Circ. Ct. Pa. Dist., April term 1798), applying strict common law rules to the pleadings, and his remarks on the record in Wilson v. Daniel, 3 Dallas 401, 407 (Sup. Ct. 1798), that "every part of the pleadings, verdict and judgment, that is not conformable to the common law, I reject. . . ."

[124] *Supra*, c. XII, p. 546.

Court of Chancery of this State."[125] No such rule was laid down in Maryland, New York or Virginia. In New Jersey, in the first equity suit brought there in 1795, it was ordered April term 1797 that the cause be heard on plea or answer or such other pleadings as the parties might file "according to the practice of the Court."[126] Since no other causes had been entered prior to that term, one is at a loss to know what the court might have had in mind.

The Supreme Court rule of 1792 had, of course, the effect of validating the adoption of state practice in those districts where state Chancery Courts existed. It had the further effect of settling as to its appellate jurisdiction the meaning of "principles, rules and usages of courts of equity" by equating the phrase with the practice of the English Court of Chancery. Since this rule was subject to the restraints of section 30 of the Judiciary Act respecting oral testimony and examination of witnesses in open court, it could not be read to authorize the methods that prevailed in England of taking testimony by examiners, and keeping it secret until publication had passed.

The impact of the Supreme Court rule was probably greater in the chanceryless states than elsewhere, for assuredly no lawyer could be impervious to the shape of a record in case of appellate review. As for continuing reference to local procedure where Chancery Courts were functioning, it may be observed that neither in New Jersey, New York nor South Carolina was there significant legislative meddling with chancery procedure as established during colonial times after English models. The legislature in Maryland had introduced certain modifications, but as no equity suits were brought in the Circuit Courts held for this district, the changes are here of no concern. In Virginia, however, in 1792 there was a consolidation effected of existing legislation, and specific statutory rules of procedure were laid down.[127] A second act dealing with absent or absconding debtors contained provisions for procedure in chancery for dealing with such situations.[128]

---

[125] Ms. Mins., Circuit Ct. South Carolina Dist. 1790–1800. See also the entry in Bewly v. Hatter, *ibid.*, *sub* November term 1793, where in a suit brought by residuary legatees to establish their interest in an estate the clerk of the court was directed to settle the accounts of the said estate in the hands of the executrix "agreeable to the Mode Established before the Master in the State Court of Equity." For the rule in Georgia referring to provincial practice, *supra*, n. 96.

[126] Miers Fisher and Sam'l Fisher v. Walter Rutherford *et al.*, Ms. Mins. Circuit Ct. New Jersey Dist. 1790–1806, *sub* Apr. 4, 1797. The Ms. Case Papers U.S. Sup. Ct. (No. 77) on this case are the only evidence of practice found, the New Jersey case papers apparently having disappeared.

[127] *Collection of . . . Acts of the General Assembly of Virginia . . . now in force* (1794), 69 *et seq.*

[128] *Ibid.*, 122 (sec. 5).

The equity suits at Circuit in Virginia were with a single exception entered after the acts of 1792 and 1793. The suits, however, do not indicate complete conformity with the local statutory rules, or for that matter with English practice, and it may be conjectured that usages stemming from the first establishment of the state Chancery Court persisted. This is indicated by the use at circuit of an alias attachment after a failure to serve an attachment—a procedure not provided for in the Virginia acts.[129] In England the third process was attachment and proclamation of rebellion.[130] A further local peculiarity adverted to by Attorney General Charles Lee, an experienced Virginia practitioner, was the fact that attachment lay against the chattels as well as the person of the defendant.[131] The state of the case papers in this jurisdiction makes it impossible at this time to settle whether the Circuit Court adopted this practice.

In New York the tremendous body of records relating to the state Court of Chancery furnish firm ground for judging how faithfully Circuit Court practice followed state usage.[132] The Circuit minutes and case papers, so far as the latter have survived, testify to the fact that within the limits of the Judiciary Act and the nature of the suits filed there was no attempt to innovate. However, the present state of case papers and the fact that numerous important suits such as those involving the Yazoo lands[133] and the Holland land purchase[134] have vanished from the minutes render impossible reconstruction of a satisfactory picture of the equity side out of the Circuit papers.[135] It should further

---

[129] Bivin's Exr. v. Wayles Exr., 2 Ms. Record Book, 491 (1793), Circuit Ct. Virginia Dist.

[130] J. Wyatt, *Practical Register in Chancery* (1714), 22.

[131] Charles Lee to Oliver Wolcott, Jr. (copy), Dec. 12, 1797, Ms. Harison Papers (NYHS).

[132] Comment on chancery practice in New York and some sample documents, in *LPAH*, I, 167–96.

[133] Wilcox v. Phelps, Ms. Mins. Circuit Ct. New York Dist. 1790–1808, *sub* Apr. 3, 4, 1798. The bill, in the Ms. Case Papers, N.Y. Circ. Equity File, raised *inter alia* the question of the constitutionality of the Georgia Act of 1796. The Georgia lands discussed in *LPAH*, III (in preparation).

[134] Willinck, van Staphoorst *et al.* v. Robert Morris *et al.* Ms. Case Papers, N.Y. Circ. Equity File. The only minute book entry of April term 1800 relates to the issuance of sub-

poenas (Ms. Mins., *supra*, n. 133). The issues discussed in *LPAH*, III (in preparation).

[135] In a few cases there survive enough case papers which together with the meagre minute book entries permit a fair reconstruction of procedure. *E.g.*, Cavalier Jouet v. T. Jones, John Livingston and Brockholst Livingston, begun in 1796 and dismissed Apr. 9, 1800 (Ms. Case Papers, N.Y. Circ. Equity File). Rotch *et al.* v. Franklin *et al.*, bill filed Apr. 8, 1794, decree affirming clerk's report Apr. 7, 1797 (*ibid.*); six Supreme Court Justices and three District judges sat in this case at different times. Blair v. Bache, bill filed December 1794, dismissed finally Apr. 5, 1800, error to Supreme Court, decree affirmed there Mar. 5, 1806 (Ms. Case Papers U.S. Sup. Ct., Nos. 223, 259).

be noticed that as no provision had been made for masters in Chancery, the services performed by these functionaries were off-loaded on the clerk of the district. In addition, by the rule of the Circuit Court for this district, April term 1797, it was ordered that in the prosecution of suits on the equity side the clerk "may as a matter of course in the Vacation or in term time give rules for answering, replying, rejoining and producing Witnesses and may issue the usual process of Contempt for not appearing or answering or for the disobedience or non performance of any order or decree of this Court in the same manner as is practised by the Clerks of the Chancery of the state of New York."[136] No rule book for orders of this sort has been found.

Execution of the directions in the two Process Acts in the states which had never allowed themselves the indulgence of a separate chancery establishment presented problems of a different order from those in the states just discussed. Except for Connecticut, the New England states had but gingerly tested with their toes the waters of equity practice. But there had been considerable dabbling in them by Connecticut,[137] even if an English solicitor might not have admitted this to be the case. Pennsylvania, to use Justice Paterson's expression, had done something to "equitize" its law,[138] and in North Carolina the Superior Courts exercised both equity and common law jurisdiction as two distinct forms of proceeding.[139] About Georgia we have found nothing substantial.

Of the twelve men who served on the Supreme Bench during the period under consideration, seven had firsthand experience as lawyers and judges with classical chancery practice, five had not been so initiated, although the extent of individual involvement varied in terms of the degree to which incidents of such practice had been adopted. Iredell and later Moore were, we believe, better equipped than Cushing and Wilson. The professional background of the Justices was immediately relevant to the conduct of an equity suit in the situations where, for example, Paterson of New Jersey had to deal with Massachusetts counsel,

---

[136] Ms. Mins., Circuit Ct. New York Dist. 1790–1808, *sub* Apr. 8, 1797. *Cf.* Ms. Mins. Circuit Ct. South Carolina Dist., *sub* May 14, 1792: "Ordered that during the Vacation the Clerk of the Court be authorised to hear Motions, Issue Commissions and make necessary Interlocutory Orders in all Cases in Equity depending in this Court in the manner usually practised by the Master in the State Court of Equity in this State."

[137] Modest statutory acceptance of equity in *Acts and Laws of . . . Con-* necticut (1786), 29, 30, 48, 282. The account of equity jurisdiction in Swift, *System of the Laws of the State of Connecticut*, II, 419 *et seq.*, cites a few Connecticut cases but relies mainly on English authority.

[138] Hollingsworth v. Fry, 4 Dallas 345, 348 (1800).

[139] *Cf. Laws of the State of North Carolina* (Iredell, 1791), 432, Act of 1782, wherein are set forth some procedural details. *Ibid.*, 622, Act of 1787, introducing changes in process.

or Cushing of Massachusetts faced the highly experienced New York practitioners.

The role played by the bar in equity litigation can nowhere be adequately documented because of the difficulty of settling whether or not all procedural steps were made of record. In Massachusetts only a handful of equity suits were brought and in only one did the pleadings advance as far as a replication.[140] In New Hampshire the score was even less and but one cause proceeded to a decree.[141] As might be expected, a number of suits were filed in Connecticut and many were dismissed for one reason or another.[142] On two early cases, both prayers for injunction of a judgment at law, the clerk made notes of the proceedings and it appears that failure to make the proper allegations regarding the common law proceedings caused dismissal.[143]

Because the records of equity proceedings in Pennsylvania are more informative than those in New England, they furnish a better picture of the planting of chancery procedure in demi-virgin soil. The process is in particulars reminiscent of early common law reception in certain colonial jurisdictions with counsel sometimes floundering with book law and the judges evincing some discomfort with no tradition to fall back upon. The case of *Schermerhorn v. L'Espinasse* is an exhibit on this.[144] Complainant alleged that defendants, all residents of Amsterdam, had given him a power of attorney to receive interest on 6 percent United States certificates, but nevertheless had received the interest themselves

---

[140] Cook v. Soderstrom. In the Ms. Case Papers are the bill (1793), subpoena, answer, replication and prayer for a *dedimus* with interrogatories. The commission was granted upon complainant's stipulating costs. Because he failed to give bond the cause was dismissed. Ms. Final Record Book, Circuit Ct. Massachusetts Dist. 1790–1799, *sub* June term 1794.

[141] Bean v. Brooks, November term 1791, Ms. Case Papers, Circuit Ct. New Hampshire Dist. In Morton v. Langdon, November term 1790, *ibid.*, there was a demurrer to the bill—it had failed to recite that there was no adequate remedy at law. Ms. Records in Equity and Admiralty 1790–1795, Circuit Ct. New Hampshire Dist., 1–9 (Morton v. Langdon); *ibid.*, 10–19 (Bean v. Brooks).

[142] *E.g.*, Apthorp v. Bronson, April term 1790, dismissed by consent; Imlay v. Williams, April term 1791, same; Livingston v. Seymour, October

term 1791, dismissed, neither party appeared. The indorsement of non-appearance in numerous other cases indicates that the suit was probably dismissed. Ms. Case Papers, Circuit Ct. Connecticut Dist. Among the rare notes on judicial business entered in his Ms. Circuit Court Diary (*supra*, n. 22) Jay, *sub* April 22, 1790, indicates his puzzlement over Connecticut equity procedure. The next day he ordered that English equity practice obtain subject to the court's accommodating this to local and other circumstances.

[143] Burrell v. Hazzard, April term 1792, Circuit Ct. Minute Book 1791–1792, Ms. Simeon Baldwin Papers (YUL); Ms. Case Papers, Circuit Ct. Connecticut Dist. Thomas v. Pitts, *ibid.*

[144] 2 Dallas 360 (1796). The bill is in Ms. Du Ponceau Form Book, 423–27, n.d. (HSP).

and refunded the amount in 3 percent United States certificates. The bill asked for general relief, an injunction against the defendants and one directed to certain Treasury officials. The injunction issued probably sometime in early 1795.[145] On a motion to dissolve the injunction October 1796, the chief procedural question was compliance with the standard rule that an affidavit should have been filed respecting the truth of the allegations. The argument as reported is one of the few evidences we have of the books then being used, such as Mitford, Hinde, Harrison and English Chancery reports. Wilson and Peters, both Pennsylvania-trained, decided that the power of attorney was stronger evidence than an affidavit[146]—a contravention of traditional practice.

The action of the court in *Schermerhorn* seems to have been characteristic of how little the niceties of chancery practice might be regarded when the Supreme Court Justice at Circuit was uninitiated into its mysteries. If such a Justice was followed at the next term by one from a chancery state, the pace of an equity suit was leisurely enough for corrective measures to be taken. In *Boudinot v. Symmes,* petitioner, who had been one of the silent partners of John Cleve Symmes, brought suit against him for a specific performance of various land contracts relating to the notorious Miami purchase.[147] Defendant had been served with a subpoena in 1796 and at that time had entered an appearance by attorney. He put in no answer, so complainant took out an attachment and was proceeding to resort to "other process used at Westminster," viz., an attachment with proclamations, commission of rebellion and sequestration. At April term Iredell and Peters, sitting, were of the opinion that it was not necessary or practicable to pursue English practice. The bill might be taken *pro confesso* after failure to serve the first attachment. The cause next came before Chase and Peters. Chase came from a chancery state. Exercising his statutory prerogative as senior judge, the decree *pro confesso* was set aside because the "mode of proceeding was inadmissible" and the process as in England was then ordered.[148]

In one important phase chancery procedure originally regulated by sections 15 and 30 of the Judiciary Act was obviously loosened by

---

[145] Du Ponceau to James Beekman, May 27, 1795, Ms. Du Ponceau Letterbook B, 95–97 (HSP).

[146] 2 Dallas 364.

[147] *Cf.* S. Livermore, *Early American Land Companies,* 197, n. 115. Some of the facts in Wallace (3d Cir.), 139. The first minute entry is in Ms. Mins. Circuit Ct. Pennsylvania Dist. Apr. 1798–Apr. 1799, *sub* Apr. 14, 1798. Normally the first entries in chancery cases were made only when attachment was threatened.

[148] Wallace (3d Cir.), 139. See also Ms. Mins. Circuit Ct. Pennsylvania Dist. Apr. 1798–Apr. 1799, *sub* Apr. 12 and May 18, 1799; Ms. Mins. Oct. 1799–Apr. 1800, *sub* Apr. 14, 1800; Ms. Mins. Oct. 1800–Feb. 1802, *sub* Oct. 15, 1800, and May 25, 26, Oct. 14, 1801.

the directions of the second Process Act, for it gave meaning to the term "common usage" that governed the taking of depositions pursuant to a *dedimus*. There was free resort to such on interrogatories by rule or by agreement of the parties, sometimes with express stipulation that the evidence was to have the same effect as if the parties had personally testified. Ironically enough, considering the impassioned declamations of Senator Maclay against the chancery discovery procedure, the papers for the Pennsylvania Circuit disclose resort to it, and in one case a defendant defeated alleged diversity jurisdiction in law after it was revealed from plaintiff's answer to a bill for discovery that there had been a collusive conveyance to the lessor of the plaintiff in ejectment.[149]

One aspect of procedure not yet touched upon relates to the regulations set out in the Judiciary Act. That of most frequent occurrence was the matter of proper allegations respecting diversity. As we shall later have occasion to observe, it was not until 1798 in *Bingham v. Cabot II*[150] that the Supreme Court held that it was necessary to set forth the citizenship or alienage of the parties to bring a case within the jurisdiction of the Circuit Court. Initially the practice appears to have been very sloppy, and because Supreme Court decisions were long unavailable, it continued to be so. It was the responsibility of counsel to set out jurisdictional facts or to challenge such, and it was not the business of a court on its own motion to amend the mistakes of the pleaders. Both Wilson[151] and Iredell[152] advanced the proposition that a court was bound to take notice of a question of jurisdiction, or, more broadly, that it was the proper guardian of its jurisdiction, but this was each time in a different context, and we have found no evidence that at any Circuit the court ever raised the question of lack of diversity *sua sponte*. As for the bar, some of the difficulties with section 11 of the Judiciary Act stemmed from uncertainty over the intendment of the words "citizen of a state."

The difficulties were of two sorts. In common law jurisdictions it was unusual that plaintiffs identify themselves in pleadings by more than name, although as a result of the ancient Statute of Additions[153] the identification of defendants by the addition of places by towns, counties

---

[149] Maxwell's Lessee v. Levy, 2 Dallas 381 (1797).

[150] 3 *ibid.*, 382. The addition of "II" is to distinguish this removal from the earlier case of the same name.

[151] Ketland q.t. v. The *Cassius*, 2 *ibid.*, 365 (1796).

[152] Maxfield's [*sic*] Lessee v. Levy, 4 *ibid.*, 330, 337 (1797). This is the same case as that cited in n. 149, *supra*. Whether Iredell or Dallas is responsible for the change of name is unanswerable.

[153] St. 1 Hen. V, c. 5; and see the commentary in Coke, *Second Institute*, 665.

and the like "of which they were" had become settled. As noticed, it was the practice in New England to identify in the writs both parties litigant by name and place of habitation and this was carried on in the pleadings. A second difficulty arose, we believe, over the matter of state citizenship. The measures taken by the states during the Revolution to fix as a matter of law the citizenship of those within their territorial confines have already been related.[154] What their continued impact may have been prior to 1789, except as to state naturalization laws, is difficult to estimate, for other considerations, such as domicil, were of manifestly greater import in legislation, such as the election laws. The Constitution itself spoke both of citizens of the United States and of citizens of the states, but as to the latter, only in terms of privileges and immunities.

Some light was cast upon the question in *Collet v. Collet*,[155] at the Circuit for the Pennsylvania April term 1792. Here in an equity suit complainant alleged he was a British subject; and respondent excepting to the jurisdiction averred that complainant had taken an oath of allegiance to Pennsylvania pursuant to a state statute of 1789. The court sustained respondent's plea to the jurisdiction, holding that the states individually still enjoyed a concurrent right of naturalization, a fact recognized by the federal Act of March 26, 1790. This decision indicated that state citizenship was still a viable juristic concept. It did nothing to settle for purposes of diversity litigation what constituted such citizenship and how it was properly alleged. Uncertainty is reflected in declarations where nothing more than a city or state of residence or a place of business was named.

Lack of diversity was challenged by a variety of devices. In Massachusetts two instances have been found where the question was raised by plea in abatement.[156] In one plaintiff filed a replication on which issue was joined and submitted to the jury.[157] A similar plea in abatement was entered by Editor William Duane of the *Aurora*, defendant in a civil libel action in Pennsylvania,[158] the plea being in the form of a note sent by him to District Judge Peters advising him of the reasons why he considered himself to be an American citizen[159]—a fine example of the "loose practice" in that state. The question was here also submitted to a jury which found in favor of the court's jurisdiction.[160] In New York the lack of diversity was raised by demurrer to a replica-

---

154 *Supra*, c. III.

155 2 Dallas 294 (1792).

156 Duffield v. Greenleaf, Ms. Final Record Book Circuit Ct. Massachusetts Dist. 1790–1799, *sub* October term 1797; Pringle v. Russell *et al.*, *ibid.*, *sub* October term 1798.

157 Duffield v. Greenleaf, *supra*, n. 156.

158 Wallace (3d Cir.), 51.

159 Jan. 11, 1800, Ms. Peters Papers, X, 63 (HSP).

160 Wallace (3d Cir.), 57.

tion.[161] After issue joined, the court ordered plaintiff to withdraw his demurrer and exercising its power to direct amendment permitted a rejoinder to the effect that plaintiff was a citizen of Connecticut. One case has been found in Virginia where defendant raised the question on motion in arrest of judgment and the case was dismissed.[162]

There are a scattering of cases dealing with jurisdictional minimum[163] and attempts to establish jurisdiction by subterfuge,[164] but they are insufficient to establish any consistent body of practice in any jurisdiction. Some other questions of federal practice that were settled at the trial stage have also been noticed, as for example: refusal to assume jurisdiction over forfeitures committed by section 9 of the Judiciary Act to the District Courts;[165] the refusal to sign a citation in error when proceedings in the court's review were not final;[166] and the consistent resort to state statutes pursuant to section 34 of the Judiciary Act in trials at common law.[167] It is rare that truly informative entries appear

---

[161] Holmes v. Hayes. The narrative was filed in 1791 and the cause was decided April term 1797. Facts taken from Ms. Case Papers, Circuit Ct. New York Dist.

[162] Jas. Robb and Co. v. Hunter's Adm'r., 3 Ms. Record Book, Circuit Ct. Virginia Dist., 164 (1794).

[163] E.g., Douglass v. Enos, Ms. Final Record Book, Circuit Ct. Massachusetts Dist. 1790–1799, sub October term 1792—damages $312.50, costs $35.70; Neilson v. Cobb, ibid., sub October term 1793—damages $124.62, no costs, the court exercising discretion given by sec. 20 of the Judiciary Act. Newman v. Ward, Ms. Mins. Circuit Ct. New York Dist. 1790–1808, sub September term 1794 —damages $207.17, costs 6 cents. Martish v. Joranceau, Ms. Mins. Circuit Ct. North Carolina Dist. 1791–1806, sub November 1793—damages $206.34, no costs; Myers v. Brodie, ibid., sub November term 1796— damages $419.53 plus costs on motion of defendant.

[164] See text accompanying n. 149, supra. In Campbell v. Cogswell, May term 1799 (Ms. Docket No. 15, Circuit Ct. Vermont Dist.), the writ was abated on defendant's motion because it was not alleged that the assignor of the assigned note on which action was brought could also have brought action. On the same ground a de-

murrer was sustained in Grinage v. Hamilton, November term 1800 (Ms. Case Papers, Circuit Ct. Georgia Dist.)

In an 1800 action by an alleged New Jersey citizen against Robert Morris and John Nicholson, both in the Philadelphia debtors prison, on two notes, defendants elected to handle their own cause. No satisfactory answer having been elicited from plaintiff's counsel, they petitioned the court to grant oyer of the notes to determine whether the requirement of the Judiciary Act had been met. Spencer v. Morris and Spencer v. Nicholson, Ms. Mins. Circuit Ct. Pennsylvania Dist. Oct. 1800–Feb. 1802, sub Oct. 16, 1800. The petition is in the Ms. Case Papers.

[165] Ketland q.t. v. The Cassius, 2 Dallas 365 (1796). The discussions of questions of strategy in this case are in Ms. Du Ponceau Letterbook B, 127, 132 (HSP); Ms. Rawle Papers, III, 64–65 (HSP).

[166] Greenwood v. Higginson, Ms. Mins. Circuit Ct. South Carolina Dist. 1790–1800, sub Oct. 26, 1792.

[167] This is most consistently evident where statutes of limitation were pleaded. No conclusions can be made regarding reference to state decisions because the entries found are too ambiguously phrased to settle whether or not a rule is of statutory origin.

in minute books or that case papers yield such, and because of the substantial body of litigation in the Circuit Courts, it is difficult to believe that questions of federal procedure did not arise more frequently than our sources indicate. An overwhelming majority of the cases terminated at the trial stage, and consequently it was at this level that the *principia* of this practice were established. This was true not only of narrow issues of jurisdiction and cognizance, but also of the larger question of judicial review.

JUDICIAL REVIEW

IN HIS ACCOUNT of the argument of the carriage tax case (*Hylton v. United States*) at Circuit, John Wickham, counsel of the United States, explained why he had not raised the question of the court's power to pass on the constitutionality of the Act of Congress. He had been informed by the bench that although the Supreme Court had never decided this issue, it had come before each of the judges in his circuit and each of the judges had upheld the court's power.[168] Whether Justice Wilson, then presiding, was referring to the several determinations on the Invalid Pensions Act cannot be said. So far as we are aware, in only three cases prior to May 27, 1795, had the question of judicial review arisen in the Circuit Courts, and all concerned the constitutionality of state statutes.

The earliest of these cases, *Champion & Dickison v. Carey et al.* was heard at the Circuit Court for the Rhode Island District, June term 1792, before John Jay and Henry Marchant, District judge. Plaintiff, a British subject, brought an action for money had and received. Defendants pleaded in abatement a resolve of the Rhode Island State Assembly granting a stay of three years to get their affairs in order and to exempt them from all arrests and attachments. To this, plaintiff demurred and the demurrer was sustained.[169] Neither minutes nor case papers disclose the ground of the ruling, but from a newspaper account[170] it appears that the court conceived that the resolve was a law impairing the obligation of contracts, which the federal Constitution prohibited, and consequently could not operate to bar the action.

The second case, *Skinner v. May*,[171] came up on writ of error to

---

[168] J. Wickham, *The Substance of an Argument in the Case of the Carriage Duties* (July 1795), 15.
[169] Ms. Mins., Circuit Ct. Rhode Island Dist. 1790–1807, *sub* June 7, 1792. The Ms. Case Papers include

the *capias*, the narrative, the plea, the demurrer and the bill of costs.
[170] *The United States Chronicle*, June 14, 1792.
[171] Ms. Case Papers, Circuit Ct. Massachusetts Dist. The action was begun in 1791.

the Circuit Court for the Massachusetts District from the Maine District Court. This was a *qui tam* action of debt removed to the latter from a state court. The informer sued for a penalty imposed for violation of a Massachusetts Act of 1788 to restrain slave trade. In the Maine District Court plaintiff had had verdict and judgment, December 1792. In the special assignments of error, one relating to procedure was patently misconceived.[172] The substantive errors alleged were: first, that the Act of 1788 had been "repealed by the Constitution of the United States," in particular by Article I, section 8; second, that the Massachusetts legislature had no right or authority to make penal laws to regulate the conduct of citizens or aliens abroad. The cause came to be heard June term 1794, Cushing and Lowell sitting. The court ordered that the proceedings be revoked and annulled and that plaintiff in error be restored any losses suffered. A writ of restoration was awarded. The form of the judgment indicates that it was based upon the constitutional ground advanced.[173]

The third case, *Vanhorne's Lessee v. Dorrance*, which had been adjudged ten days before the trial of *Hylton* at Richmond, was an ejectment action tried at the Circuit for the Pennsylvania District, April term 1795, Paterson and Peters sitting.[174] Involved was the Pennsylvania confirming act, a statute relating to the conflicting titles in the Wyoming Valley lands—a controversy discussed in an earlier chapter.[175] As is well known, Paterson's views on the unconstitutionality of the state law were developed both as respects the state and the federal Constitution in the course of a lengthy charge to the jury.[176] His remarks justifying review and the power of the court to hold null a statute oppugning the Constitution, while not novel, acquired dramatic force from the fact that the charge was delivered at the same term where the western Pennsylvania rebels were tried. It was shortly published in pamphlet form.[177]

At this time, there appears to have been no questioning of the propriety of judicial review; indeed, at the argument of *Hylton*, the great states' rights advocate John Taylor, who appeared for defendant, emphasized its necessity.[178] The next instance where an issue of constitutionality was raised occurred in 1797 at the Circuit for Pennsylvania

---

[172] The procedural point, which was without merit, was to the effect that defendants should have severally impleaded.

[173] Ms. Final Record Book, Circuit Ct. Massachusetts Dist. 1790–1799, *sub* June term 1794.

[174] *Cf.* n. 92, *supra,* for a breviate of the docket entries.

[175] *Supra,* c. IV, pp. 188 *et seq.*

[176] 2 Dallas 304.

[177] The pamphlet, a copy of which is in the Wolcott Collection (LC), was printed in 1796, two years before publication of the charge in 2 Dallas.

[178] *An Argument Respecting the Constitutionality of the Carriage Tax* . . . (July 1795).

District in *United States v. Vilato*.[179] This was a habeas corpus proceeding, the defendant having been bound over out of term on charge of treason. By birth a Spaniard, he had in 1793 taken the oath prescribed by the Pennsylvania Naturalization Act of 1789. He had enlisted on a French privateer and had participated in capturing an American ship. On the return of the writ, April term 1797, the argument turned on the question whether or not the prisoner had become a citizen of the United States in consequence of the oath. The court held that the law of 1789 was inconsistent with the provisions of the new state constitution of 1790 and had ceased to exist; consequently that the declarations made pursuant to the act were void. The prisoner was released.

The early cases where the Circuit Courts exercised the power to pass on the constitutionality of state statutes appear to have excited no serious traverse of the propriety of judicial action. However, as we shall see in the next chapter, it was shortly to be contended, and for political reasons, that the function of deciding upon an issue of constitutionality was one to be exercised by a trial jury. The resulting agitation was to produce unfriendly comment about Justice Paterson's second excursion into the question of constitutionality.

In divers land grants made by the colonial governor of New Hampshire there had been reserved acreage for the Society for the Propagation of the Gospel, and glebe lands for the support of the Church of England to be established. The state of Vermont, by an Act of 1794, expropriated the Society's lands and also empowered the selectmen of the towns to take possession of glebe lands, lease them for a term of years and use the income for the support of teachers.[180] In April 1795 one *Pettibone (ex dem the Selectmen of Manchester)* brought an action of ejectment in the Bennington County Court against the tenant in possession of the glebe in that town, the Reverend Barber.[181] The case was continued until June 1796, when defendant, alleging that the lands exceeded $510 in value and that he claimed title under a grant from the state of New Hampshire and not of Vermont, petitioned for removal of the cause to the Circuit Court for the Vermont District.[182] The cause was entered on the docket of the Circuit Court, November term 1796, and continued until October term 1798, when it came to trial.

Except that issue was joined on defendant's plea of not guilty and

---

[179] Wharton, *State Trials*, 185. In the Ms. Minutes the defendant's name is rendered "Billato."

[180] The statute is set out in *Documentary History of the Protestant Episcopal Church in the Diocese of Vermont* (1870), 52.

[181] Summons and declaration, May 13, 1795, *cf.* Ms. Docket No. 2, November term 1796, Circuit Ct. Vermont Dist.

[182] Petition to Burlington County Court, June 1796, *ibid.*

that he had verdict and judgment,[183] neither docket nor case papers show anything. A historian of the Episcopal Church in Vermont states that it was argued for plaintiff that the grantees "were not in existence" to receive the grant. This was met by the argument that at the time of the grant the Church of England had a corporate existence.[184] We are on equally soft ground with respect to Paterson's charge to the jury, for the press said no more than that he "adjudged" the statute to be unconstitutional.[185] Some fifty years later a writer in the *Church Review* noted that a distinguished jurist had reported Paterson to have said "that Legislatures are not omnipotent. They cannot take this man's property and give it to that man."[186]

It is regrettable that no better account of Paterson's charge has been found. But at this same term of the Court for the Vermont District, Congressman Matthew Lyon was tried and convicted of violating the Sedition Act—a case that captured the interest of both press and public. As we shall see in the next chapter, in Lyon's case Paterson would not permit defendant to put the question of the constitutionality of the Sedition Act to the jury. From that moment and in the immediate future, the doctrine of judicial review was put to its defense.

REMOVAL

THERE HAD BEEN considerations of political expediency that led the first Congress to confer upon state courts concurrent jurisdiction in the limited class of civil causes over which the Circuit Court was to have original cognizance. Recourse to federal justice was manifestly viewed as a right of the qualified individual, for by section 12 of the Judiciary Act the procedure was established for the removal of a cause from a state to a federal court where an alien was impleaded or a citizen of a state other than that of the forum. As we shall notice in a moment,

---

[183] Entry for Oct. 5, 1798, *ibid.* Costs to defendant $42.15.

[184] *Church Review and Ecclesiastical Register* (1852), IV, 586–87.

[185] *Farmer's Museum, or Lay Preacher's Gazette* (Walpole, N.H.), Apr. 29, 1799.

[186] *Church Review*, IV, 587. The Philadelphia *Aurora* (Nov. 9, 1798) claimed that Paterson had told the jury that if legislatures assumed to themselves the power to enact unconstitutional laws, they ought not to be binding upon juries. It was further claimed that Paterson had said that courts and juries were the proper bodies to decide on the constitutionality of the laws. It seems to us improbable that Paterson, having asserted the authority of the judiciary in Vanhorne, would have made such a concession. Three days later at the same term in United States v. Lyon, Paterson would not permit defendant to address the jury on the question of constitutionality (*infra*, c. XIV, p. 646). This drew a charge of inconsistency from the *Aurora*.

the right was limited by the statutory procedure, and it is further to be observed that during the period here surveyed the statute was not understood to require that diversity exist as to all parties defendant,[187] although it was later to be held otherwise.[188]

In removal cases the state court was by the terms of section 12 only to be satisfied regarding the amount in controversy, yet the fact that a defendant proceeded by petition may have operated as an invitation to such court to exercise a fuller discretion. At least, in the period here under consideration, the Supreme Court of Pennsylvania so approached the statute, for it undertook to exercise an independent judgment on a petition for removal in three decisions, all involving William Cobbett who, as Peter Porcupine, was a particular scourge of the Republicans.[189] In 1798 Cobbett petitioned for removal of a libel action on the ground that the matter in dispute exclusive of costs exceeded $500 and that he was an alien, a British subject. The court denied the petition, stating that it could not determine damages in a summary way; furthermore, it was not the intention of Congress to provide removals in torts and vindictive actions. Its object was confined to property where the value of the thing in controversy could be satisfactorily ascertained.[190] In a second libel action at the same term, defendant's counsel, after hearing the determination in the first case, declined to argue the point, but moved that the court seal a bill of exceptions.[191] This the court refused to do, thus preventing a review of its action. A further gloss on the statute was written by McKean C.J. himself in refusing to grant a petition for removal of an action of debt on a recognizance in the amount of $2,000 for Cobbett's good behavior, brought on the supposition that the condition had been breached. It was asserted that section 12 did not contemplate removal where a state was a party, and in addition in an action criminal in its nature.[192]

Nothing resembling the Cobbett cases has been found elsewhere,

---

[187] Skinner v. May, the *qui tam* action for penalties imposed by a Massachusetts act of 1788 to prevent the slave trade, noted above, was begun in the Common Pleas Court of Cumberland County in 1791. One of the defendants was an alien, the others, citizens of Massachusetts. Ms. Case Papers, Circuit Ct. Massachusetts Dist.

[188] Strawbridge *et al.* v. Curtiss *et al.*, 3 Cranch 267 (1806).

[189] Wharton, *State Trials*, 24–25n., sets out some choice morsels of Cobbett's invective.

[190] Rush v. Cobbett, 2 Yeates 275 (Pa. S. Ct. 1798).

[191] Carey v. Cobbett, *ibid.*, 277.

[192] Respublica v. Cobbett, *ibid.*, at 352, 3 Dallas 467 (1798). McKean's judgment may have been clouded by the fact that his son-in-law to-be, the Spanish Minister Yrujo, claiming to have been libelled by Cobbett, elected to have proceedings brought against the latter in a Pennsylvania state court. Despite a spirited charge by McKean, the grand jury returned the indictment *ignoramus*.

the removals occurring without resistance, the form of record by which this was effected being substantially identical whether in Vermont,[193] Maine,[194] New York,[195] Pennsylvania[196] or Georgia.[197] How frequently resort was had to section 12 cannot even be conjectured, for it is usually in case papers that information is available; these have suffered such decimation that for statistical purposes they are not reliable. For example, only a handful of cases has been found for Pennsylvania, yet in 1799 Peter Du Ponceau, writing to a New Jersey attorney, remarked that "such removals are pretty frequent, when the Defendant conceives that he will have a better chance with the federal Judiciary."[198] A total of eleven cases has been found in the New York records, but there is reason to believe from Richard Harison's papers that there were others.[199] In Massachusetts indications in the minutes of six removals were found, but so many cases were discontinued or dismissed for non-appearance that these figures remain tentative.[200] It was, of course, entirely optional with defendant whether or not he would elect to remove, depending upon such factors as a quicker disposition wherever the state court maintained the classic four terms, or an advantage of delay or the anticipation of an atmosphere of greater neutrality in a federal tribunal.

During the first years of the Circuits' functioning two attempts were made at the instance of plaintiffs to effect a removal by certiorari, presumably in reliance on the all writs section (section 14). In England the certiorari was a prerogative writ by means of which the Crown exercised superintendence over the administration of justice, and lay

---

[193] Pettibone *ex dem* Selectmen of Manchester v. Barber, see n. 181 *supra*.

[194] Skinner v. May, n. 187, *supra*.

[195] Culbertson v. Godet, Ms. Mins. Circuit Ct. New York Dist. 1790–1808, *sub* April term 1795; Ms. Case Papers. Petitioner here was a Swedish ship captain against whom suit had been brought in a New York state court for failure to comply with a state statute requiring registration of aliens at the New York Customs House. A jury *de medietate linguæ* was summoned, but the case was dismissed because of plaintiff's failure to produce further evidence.

[196] Weber v. Moller (1792), removed but nonprossed by consent, Ms. Case Papers, Circuit Ct. Pennsylvania Dist.; Hodgson v. Ormond (1800), disposition post-1801, *ibid*. Here the whole "record" on removal is preserved.

[197] Grinage v. Hamilton (1799–1800), Ms. Case Papers, Circuit Ct. Georgia Dist.

[198] Ms. Du Ponceau Letterbook B, 102–03 (HSP).

[199] Opinions to James Thompson, Dec. 5, 1792, and to John Rutledge, n.d., in Ms. Harison Papers (NYHS). The cases were evidently of sufficient frequency for the Circuit Court to make a rule regarding the entry of special bail in such cases. Ms. Mins. Circuit Ct. New York Dist. 1790–1808, *sub* Sept. 2, 1800.

[200] In one of the cases, Villeneve v. Barrion, the removal was made to enable defendant to plead the improvident Consular Convention with France (1788) conveying to French consuls the right to try actions between French subjects. Ms. Final Record Book Circuit Ct. Massachusetts Dist. 1790–1799, *sub* May term 1792.

as well for causes criminal as for the transfer or review of administrative acts. It issued from King's Bench to inferior courts of record. Because of the fact that in some provincial American jurisdictions a petty civil jurisdiction was added to that traditionally exercised in causes criminal, the writ of certiorari had come to be used to transfer civil actions upon petition and showing of reasonable cause. This was the limit of American precedent, and failing any trace of how the applications to the Circuit Courts for certiorari were justified, it may be supposed that vis-à-vis the federal tribunal some rash litigants conceived the state courts to be inferior.

The first resort to certiorari occurred in November 1790 and is badly documented. It appears that Robert Morris and others had pending in the Superior Court of North Carolina a bill in equity to enjoin a local judgment against them. There were numerous respondents, one of whom was James Iredell.[201] The certiorari issued from the Circuit Court for the North Carolina District by the direction of Blair, Rutledge and Wilson JJ, and commanded the transfer of the pending case.[202] The Superior Court judges refused to comply. Their reasons, published in a newspaper,[203] were: First, as a court of "original, general supreme and unlimited jurisdiction," they were not amenable to any other judicatory, nor were proceedings depending before them subject to be taken from them by any mandatory writ of any court, least of all by a court of limited and inferior jurisdiction. Second, as judges of the "several Superior Courts of Law and Courts of Equity" they were not subject to the mandate calling for records or proceedings pending, or transcripts thereof by virtue of the federal Constitution or any "article of congress or, any law of the land." Third, the suit was not in a stage so as to be removable even by petition to themselves pursuant an Act of Congress, it not being in the first stage, but had been depending before the existence of any court established under the authority of the United States. Furthermore, the removal was not at "the instance of defendants, privileged to be sued in a federal court" but of complainants who had chosen the forum.

---

[201] Our information derives from a letter of Fisher Ames, Jan. 6, 1791 (*Works of Fisher Ames*, I, 91), and letters of James Iredell to John Jay, Feb. 11, 1791, and Jan. 17, 1792 (McRee, *Iredell*, II, 322 at 324, 337). Iredell was made a party to the action in his capacity as executor.

[202] The Judiciary Act was not extended to North Carolina until June 4, 1790 (1 *U.S. Stats.*, 126). The term for this June was not kept. The writ was therefore probably issued by Wilson and Blair who were holding court May term 1790 at Charlottesville, Virginia, and, because Rutledge at that time was assigned the Southern Circuit to which the North Carolina District was attached, the writ was also tested by him.

[203] *Virginia Gazette and General Advertiser*, June 1, 1791, taken from the *North Carolina Gazette*, May 14, 1791.

The action of the state judges was applauded by the North Carolina Assembly. The Supreme Court Justices seem to have come to no conclusion on how this flouting of federal authority was to be handled. Robert Morris eventually advised his counsel that since he was a member of the national legislature, "from motives of delicacy" he would rather the cause be proceeded on in the state courts.[204]

It was at the May term 1791 of the Circuit for the Virginia District that an attempt was again made by plaintiffs to secure a removal from a state court by certiorari. A firm of British merchants had had pending an action in the Virginia courts for some twenty years but had not succeeded in bringing it to trial. The petition was based on the claim that the Judiciary Act gave the Circuit Court jurisdiction in all cases where an alien was a party if the amount in controversy exceeded $500, ignoring the language that only alien defendants might remove. The court—Wilson, Iredell and Griffin—took time to advise and denied the petition. No reason was given, but apparently the court was not prepared to go out of the statute.[205]

APPELLATE JURISDICTION:
ADMIRALTY AND MARITIME CAUSES

DURING THE PERIOD here considered, it is only that parcel of the appellate jurisdiction relating to admiralty and maritime causes assigned to the Circuit Courts that demands some extended comment. This assumed dimensions and, concurrently, a significance wholly unanticipated as a result of the turn of international events and the measures here taken by the United States in reaction thereto. The involvement of the admiralty jurisdiction was precipitated by the extravagances of Citizen Genêt under color of the Franco-American Treaty of 1778, French pretensions under the Convention of 1788, the enforcement of the Neutrality Proclamation and the subsequent Act of Congress.[206] Later, new problems obtruded as a result of legislation induced by the so-called undeclared war with France.

All these events, which were to swell the dockets of District and Circuit Courts and were to bring in their train a build-up of an emotionally charged public opinion, rapidly turned to factional advantage. For the development of federal jurisprudence, it was the impetus given to the evolution of an appeal procedure at the hands of both District and Cir-

---

[204] Judge Sitgreaves to Iredell, Aug. 2, 1791, in McRee, *Iredell*, II, 333–34. Nothing has been found in the minute book, the first term there recorded being November 1791.

[205] Jones v. Syme, 1 Ms. Order Book, Circuit Ct. Virginia Dist., *sub* May 23, 1791. See also Waterman v. Syme, *ibid.*

[206] *Infra*, c. XIV.

cuit Courts that must be accounted of particular significance. The framers of the Judiciary Act had not seen fit to allow an appeal as this was understood in admiralty practice to be pursued beyond a Circuit Court, for, as noticed, further review by the Supreme Court could only be by writ of error. When at length Congress substituted review by appeal[207] for writ of error, the practices earlier settled at the Circuit level inevitably affected the later *cursus curiae* of the Supreme Court.

We have already had occasion to comment upon the difficulties experienced during the Revolution with the settlement of a workable appellate procedure in cases of captures at sea, and how the resolution of these difficulties was achieved without exact reference to English tradition.[208] Except for those who had participated in this venture as lawyers or in a judicial capacity, knowledge about the practice was never widely diffused, and it may be remarked that until the very close of the century[209] there had been no additions to the literature of English admiralty law beyond what had been available in 1776. Significantly, when Chief Justice Jay was in London negotiating his treaty, he solicited and obtained from Sir William Scott and Sir John Nicoll (retained in behalf of the United States as advocates) a statement concerning prize procedure including appeals.[210]

Sources of information regarding procedure relating to the incidents of instance jurisdiction remained equally meagre, although on some heads, *e.g.*, bottomry and seamen's wages, points of substance were sometimes to be found in common law cases. On the matter of appellate procedure, the literature of English ecclesiastical law was relevant, but it is open to some doubt how generally such books were here available. As a result of the curtain of secrecy with which the practitioners at Doctor's Commons had managed to envelop their doings,[211] adjective admiralty law on this side of the water had suffered a sea change. There had occurred an infiltration of common law terminology and modes of practice, and although some basic forms and their designations were

---

[207] Initially by sec. 33 of the ill-fated Judiciary Act of 1801 (2 *U.S. Stats.*, 89 at 98), later reinstated by the act of Mar. 3, 1803 (*ibid.*, 244).

[208] *Supra*, c. IV.

[209] When the second edition of Arthur Browne's *A Compendious View of the Civil Law and of the Law of the Admiralty* appeared (1802) and the first volume of Christopher Robinson's reports (1798).

[210] J. B. Moore, ed., *International Adjudications*, IV, 43–48. Text also in H. Wheaton, *Digest of the Law of Maritime Captures and Prizes* (1815),

310–17. Part of what was given Jay was subtracted from the famous report of Ryder, Lee, Paul and Murray of 1753. This had been published by authority in 1753; *cf.* E. Satow, *The Silesian Loan and Frederick the Great* (Oxford, Clarendon Press, 1915), 100. It seems to have been first cited here in the argument of the *Chester* appeal in 1787; *cf. LPAH*, II, 896, n. 21.

[211] Minister Rufus King in 1799 vainly sought light on the practice; *cf.* his letter to Robert Troup, Mar. 16, 1799, *Life of King*, II, 571.

retained, such as libel, citation, monition and inhibition, a great deal of the jargon peculiar to proceedings in the High Court of Admiralty had been jettisoned.[212]

The nexus between colonial vice-admiralty and state admiralty practice remains to be established—a matter beyond our mandate—but the probabilities favor the hypothesis that traditions were maintained. With little else but Clerke's brief treatise on admiralty practice at hand,[213] the profession's predilection for tried forms would work compulsively upon lawyers to seek out and use what remained of record from the provincial courts. If this was the case, it serves to explain why during the Revolution there were noticeable procedural variants in the several state records in prize appeals, and why diversities should have persisted in the several federal districts. Most of the jurisdictional variants were immaterial; indeed, their interest lies chiefly in their probative effect in establishing deviation from English practice and the longevity of provincial-state usage.[214]

The appellate procedure which obtained in admiralty causes required, as we have noticed, certain preliminaries before the trial, *e.g.*, the entry of the appeal *viva voce* before the judge when the definitive sentence was delivered or *in scriptis*.[215] The demand for apostles followed. In the district records examined, the appeals were consistently interposed *viva voce* and New York appears to have been the one jurisdiction where it was usual for apostles to be prayed, although this was done in the single appeal recorded in Connecticut.[216] However, "record and proceedings" became the standard term for the documents which went up on appeal and it may be conjectured that this was due chiefly to the wording in the Act of Congress (1793) regulating fees in admiralty.[217] The inhibition to stay proceedings on a sentence is a rarity and eventually disappears. It may be noticed, however, that in *Glass v. the Sloop Betsey*[218] where the District Court decreed it had no jurisdiction, and there was a sentence of condemnation by the French consul outstanding, libellant secured an inhibition from Paterson J., and again, when the District Court's decree was affirmed by the Circuit Court, ob-

---

[212] *Supra*, c. IV.

[213] Clerke, *Praxis Curiae Admiralitatis Angliae* (1722 ed.). Its continuing usefulness is attested by the fact that J. E. Hall made a translation which appeared in his treatise *Law and Practice of the Admiralty*, published in Baltimore in 1809.

[214] Indicated by Hall's choice of forms from various jurisdictions in his work cited above. The persistence is further exemplified by the com-

ments on district differences in S. F. Dunlap, *Treatise on the Practice of Courts of Admiralty . . .* , 2d ed. (1850), 189–91.

[215] *Supra*, c. IV.

[216] U.S. v. Schooner *Peggy* (June 1800), record and proceedings, in Ms. Case Papers, Circuit Ct. Connecticut Dist.

[217] 1 *U.S. Stats.*, 332.

[218] 3 Dallas 6 (1794).

tained a second inhibition tested by Chief Justice Jay and allowed by Iredell J. This second inhibition was necessary because libellant's proctor had undertaken to proceed by appeal to the Supreme Court instead of by writ of error.[219]

What came up on appeal was determined by the course of proceedings at the trial stage, and because at the outset the jurisdiction was professionally localized beyond even the mandate of the Judiciary Act, conditions favored the perpetuating of existing usages. The statute had required only that a District judge be resident in the district, but the initial appointments were made with regard to the individual's familiarity with the law and practice of the state where the district was situate. We do not know how far experience in admiralty practice weighed in the selections, but in this particular, Law of Connecticut, Duane of New York, Hopkinson of Pennsylvania and later Peters of the same state were eminently qualified. Whether or not Paca of Maryland, Lowell of Massachusetts, Marchant of Rhode Island and Griffin of Virginia were equally conversant with the traditions of their own states, except as such may have been reflected in records which came before the Standing Committee of the Continental Congress or the Court of Appeals, on one or the other of which these men had served, we do not know. As we have seen, the problem of these agencies had been to elicit from state courts a record adequate for appellate purposes. They had tolerated diversities; they were not concerned with uniformity.

The hand of the past was to retain its grasp upon many of the incidents of admiralty practice because of the eccentric way in which Congress had seen fit to regulate it. The Judiciary Act, it will be recalled, had said nothing of process and pleading. It had undertaken to deal only with methods of proof.[220] Later, in the hurry of readying a process act, the forms and modes of proceeding were ordained to be according to the civil law. Except as the fiction may have been indulged that the old way of handling admiralty causes was substantial compliance, we cannot find in the earliest District Court records examined (Maryland, New York and South Carolina) signs of bending to congressional command. For such sins of omission the second Process Act provided absolution, for thereafter the forms of writs, process and modes of proceeding were to be according to the principles, rules and usages which "belong" to courts of admiralty[221]—"except so far as may have been provided for" by the Judiciary Act, subject, however, to such alteration and additions as the courts might deem expedient. Whether

---

[219] For the inhibitions from Paterson (Aug. 20, 1793) and Iredell (Nov. 19, 1793), *cf.* Ms. Case Papers, Circuit Ct. Maryland Dist. For the text of the appeal, *cf.* Ms. Case Papers, U.S. Sup. Ct., Case No. 3.
[220] *Supra,* c. XI.
[221] *Supra,* c. XII.

or not this was designed to convey discretion regarding the execution of section 30 of the Judiciary Act respecting proofs cannot be said. We do not even know whether the courts conceived this to be the case. What is obvious from the muniments of litigation is that practice did not exactly conform to the mandates of this section. The record here is one of remarkable professional independence, successful because it seems to have been due to the cooperation of the bar and the judges.

Section 30, it will be recalled, extended to equity and admiralty trials the general rule that the mode of proof be by oral testimony and in open court. On its face the purpose of this direction was to secure a uniform method of proof, but it was evidently understood as a mandatory change in traditional modes. Depositions *de bene esse* in "any civil cause" were permitted only if witnesses lived more than a hundred miles from the place of trial, were bound on a sea voyage or about to go out of the United States or of the district more than one hundred miles, or were aged or infirm. For admiralty causes where a libel was filed in which an adverse party was not named, particular directions were made for taking depositions of persons situated as above set forth, but this had to be done before a claim was put in. The design thus far revealed indicates that it was only exceptionally (and in cases where the ecclesiastical law resorted to commission)[222] that written testimony was to be tolerated.

Identical limitations were placed upon appeals in a further provision which reveals a most curious concept of how such were to be conducted. In cases where an appeal might be had from the District Court, it was open to either party to suggest and satisfy the court that it would not be in his power to produce the trial witnesses before the Circuit Court. Upon motion that this testimony be committed to writing, this should be done by the clerk. However, should an appeal be had, the use of such written testimony depended upon satisfying the Circuit Court "which shall try the appeal" that the witnesses were dead, had left the United States or removed more than one hundred miles from where the court was sitting, or were unable to travel because of age, sickness, bodily infirmity or imprisonment, "but not otherwise."

It is obvious that the Judiciary Act instituted a method of taking proof at trial radically different from that which obtained in the English High Court of Admiralty[223] and, except for the occasional indulgence

---

[222] H. Conset, *The Practice of the Spiritual or Ecclesiastical Courts* (1685), 120.

[223] Clerke, *Praxis Curiae Admiralitatis Angliae*, at #19 (p. 27), states that the methods of proof were identical with those used in the ec-

clesiastical courts and refers to his volume on the subject. See also Conset, *The Practice of the Spiritual or Ecclesiastical Courts*, pt. III, c. 4. The resemblance with chancery practice derived from the same source is striking.

of *viva voce* testimony in provincial vice-admiralty courts,[224] from early American usage. As already remarked, Congress had not profited from the experience of some members with prize appeals during the Revolution. Furthermore, without regard to convenience or cost, Congress was envisaging an appellate procedure that was a complete retrial of the cause. To all appearances this was modelled on the New England appeal in common law actions[225]—a probability suggested when the appeal at Circuit was mentioned by the words "on the trial of the same." It is further to be observed that the statute was silent on the reception of new evidence upon appeal, and so said nothing regarding the taking of depositions. This was to cause difficulties where a Circuit Court following the usage in English admiralty appeals admitted new testimony, and except where it made reference to such testimony in its decree or a case was made pursuant to section 19, the effect of such testimony could not be brought to the notice of the Supreme Court on error. As we shall see, this is what happened in *Hills et al. v. Ross.*[226]

The fact that the final review by the Supreme Court of an admiralty cause was had by writ of error, an instrumentality designed and perfected for utterly dissimilar procedure, had, we believe, something to do with the complexion of the papers that went to a Circuit Court on appeal and ultimately to the Supreme Court on error. For in the period under consideration, the mandate of section 19—that it was the duty of the Circuit to have the facts on which a sentence of decree was founded "appear fully on the record either from the pleadings and decree itself" or from a case made—was loosely construed. Indeed, even where a case

---

[224] *E.g.*, Hough, *Reports of Cases . . . of Admiralty . . . New York, 1715–1788*, 24.

[225] *Supra*, c. I, pp. 26 *et seq.*

[226] Ross v. Ship *Elizabeth* and Cargo, Ms. Mins. Circuit Ct. Georgia Dist. 1793–1798, *sub* May 1, 2, 4 and 5, 1795. Decree of District Court affirmed. The error proceedings, Hills *et al.* v. Ross, in 3 Dallas 184; see also *infra*, c. XV. It was argued by Coxe and Du Ponceau for plaintiffs in error: "The judiciary act of the *United States* has greatly innovated upon the old system of Admiralty and Chancery proceedings, the forms and principles of the common law were interwoven with, and in many cases, entirely substituted to those of the *Roman* Jurisprudence. The 30th section of that act required, that the testimony of witnesses should be taken *viva voce*, instead of written depositions both in the District and Circuit Court. In the former of these tribunals, indeed, when either of the parties expressed an intention of appealing to the other, the depositions of the witnesses were to be committed to writing, but this was an exception to the general rule. In the Circuit Court, where new evidence was admitted, no provision had been made for committing the testimony to writing, except in the case of absent, aged, infirm or departing witnesses, whose evidence might be taken *de bene esse*, precisely as at common law." 3 Dallas 185. This last was obviously something counsel read into the statute, which was silent on the point.

was stated by the court, the evidence, whether offered at District or Circuit Court, reduced to writing, travelled with it.

The sampling of appeal papers we are about to examine tells a strange story, revealing unmistakable signs that an accommodation was effected between the traditional provincial-state admiralty practice and what had presumably been made mandatory by section 30. No doubt the second Process Act furnished some justification for this. Equally, however, it was in the interest of the bar that old ways should not be overturned, and of the Circuit judges, irked by the weight of their duties, that the appellate proceedings should not be a retrial, as it were, *ab origine*. Where, for example, as in the *Pintado* and *La Vengeance* cases,[227] the District Court had spent eleven days hearing testimony, it was unreasonable to expect that this routine should be repeated at Circuit, the schedule of the Supreme Court Justices often being a very tight one.

Each District Court had its characteristic method of remembrancing proceedings for the purpose of appeal. What was assembled does not always speak unambiguously on the practice with respect to the taking of testimony. An early example of an ambiguous record is that in a Massachusetts case, *Reynolds v. the Schooner Success, Debec claimant.*[228] Reynolds, a Briton resident in Boston, filed a libel September 5, 1794, on behalf of himself and others concerned. The *Success* was a British schooner, taken in Massachusetts Bay, September 1, 1794, by an armed boat, commanded by Debec, sent out from the French frigate *Concorde*, then lying in Boston harbor. The captors had allegedly looted the *Success* and had taken a large sum of money belonging to Reynolds, a passenger. An order issued to the marshal for the arrest of the schooner and the posting of a notification. At the same time the captain of the schooner was notified that depositions would be taken. One such is dated the day of notice, others the day that claim and answer were filed, and thereafter. The statements are all in simple narrative form signed and marked "sworn to." As to some witnesses, questions and answers regarding the American pilot of the French boat were appended —probably to form the basis of a later indictment.[229] Some of these statements were taken from residents of Boston. There is only one

---

[227] *Infra*, pp. 604–605.

[228] The record and proceedings including the testimony are recorded in the Ms. Case Papers. The appeal is entered as Citizen Debec, claimant v. Schooner *Success*, Ms. Final Record Book Circuit Ct. Massachusetts Dist. 1790–1799, *sub* October term 1794. The decree of affirmance dated Oct.

13, 1794, is filed with the case papers. Debec was a lieutenant in the French navy.

[229] Samuel Rogers was indicted, tried and convicted at the same term for violation of sec. 2 of the new Neutrality Act; see Ms. Final Record Book, *supra*, n. 228.

document which clearly establishes that witness testified in open court. There appears to have been no cross-examination by claimant's counsel— merely a notation on some "depositions" that he objected to them. There was a total of twenty-two "schedules" but these have not been found. The District Court in a long and reasoned decree ordered that the vessel and the property on board be restored. Debec, claimant, appealed and the proceedings described came before the Circuit Court; Cushing J. affirmed.[230] There is nothing to indicate that the witnesses testified orally once more.

The record and proceedings in *Talbot v. Jansen*,[231] which came to trial in the same year in the South Carolina District Court, are considerably more ample than in the case just discussed. It appears from the decree that in this court a term probatory was assigned, witnesses sworn and examined, interrogatories filed and depositions taken. If the probatory term was modelled on English usage, the testimony was taken down in writing before examiners, this procedure being deemed in England to be in the presence of the court.[232] The format of the writings resembles that in Massachusetts. Cross-examinations were separately recorded. In accordance with a practice peculiar to South Carolina, the District appeal proceedings were taken to the Circuit Court by writ of error with an assignment of errors, but the scope of review appears to have been the same as on an appeal.

The decree of the Circuit Court recites the examination of the record and proceedings below, the deposition, exhibits, etc., and in accordance with admiralty usage, the examination of new witnesses. The latter were examined in open court, but their testimony was nevertheless made of record. The minutes of the Circuit are explicit that at the outset of the hearing, Jacob Read, proctor for appellee, "proceeded to read over the papers and examinations of witnesses" below.[233] There was no indication that the testimony of the witnesses in the District Court was repeated orally at Circuit.

That the South Carolina District Court was cognizant of the restrictions imposed by section 30 is indicated by an entry in *Moodie v.*

---

[230] Ms. Final Record Book, *supra*, n. 228. The affirmance—a sentence on a scrap of paper—is among the Ms. Case Papers.

[231] The record and proceedings in Ms. Case Papers U.S. Sup. Ct., Case No. 9. The Circuit proceedings are also briefly noted in Ms. Mins. Circuit Ct. South Carolina Dist. 1790–1800, *sub* Oct. 28, 29, 30, Nov. 3, 1794. The Supreme Court report is in 3 Dallas 133 (1795).

[232] Browne, *A Compendious View of the Civil Law and of the Law of the Admiralty*, II, at 422.

[233] Ms. Mins., *supra*, n. 231, *sub* Oct. 28, 1794. The currency of this is attested by the entries in *ibid.* in Cook v. Kelly, *sub* Nov. 1, 1794; Delcol *et al.* v. Arnold, *sub* Oct. 3, 1794; Moodie v. Ship *Mermaid*, *sub* Oct. 30, 1795; Fisher v. Snow *Rebecca*, *sub* May 7, 1800.

Ship Betty Cathcart and Cargo and John Vidal et al. (1795), a suit brought by the British vice-consul to recover a ship taken by the *Citizens of Marseilles*.[234] Here there is a notation regarding interrogatories administered to certain named persons "who are transient persons and shortly to leave the United States." There is nothing to indicate that this was done on motion. However, in another case, *Moodie v. the Ship Britannia* (1795), it appears that testimony and cross-examination in writing were had by consent of the parties and order of the court.[235]

Concerning the practice in Georgia, the deficiencies of the records bar any firm conclusions, although it is worth noticing that a deposition taken by Joseph Clay, Jr., then a judge of an inferior state court (later, United States District judge), refers to the Judiciary Act and states that the witness represented that he was bound to "parts beyond the sea."[236] That it was not invariable there to remembrance testimony in writing emerges from a notation by the clerk that the testimony of witnesses sworn and entered on the minutes must have been taken *viva voce* in open court as no examination of the said witnesses appears in writing filed in the clerk's office.[237]

The procedure in the New York District is most precisely laid out in the case papers of two libels of information against the schooner *La Vengeance* and in *Pintado v. the Ship San Joseph*, the latter a prize of the *Vengeance*.[238] Instead of an account in the form of a common law memorandum entry, the core of the record and proceedings in the District Court consists of a transcript of the minutes there. The causes were carried to the Supreme Court, and the Circuit Court proceedings were in similar format. The District Court minutes record in the *Pintado* case that on July 10, 1795, "It is ordered by the Court that the testimony of all the witnesses which may be examined on either side of this cause be taken down in writing by the Clerk and preserved to the end that the same testimony may be used upon an appeal if any appeal should be had from the decree of this court in this cause." A similar order was made in the case of *La Vengeance*. An entry to this effect was made in the minutes as to each witness. This testimony, a massive amount, was not signed nor marked as "sworn to."

The examination of witnesses seems to have taken place at what amounted to a probatory term, for on November 11 the minutes recited in both cases that after reading the testimony together with the exhibits,

---

[234] Ms. Case Papers, U.S. Sup. Ct., Case No. 16.
[235] *Ibid.*, Case No. 23.
[236] Hills *et al.* v. Ross, *ibid.*, Case No. 12.

[237] Wallace v. Brig *Everton*, Cotton claimant, *ibid.*, Case No. 10 (Cotton v. Wallace).
[238] *Ibid.*, Case Nos. 32, 34.

"the cause" came on to be heard, and the same having been debated, the hearing was postponed. The arguments were resumed and on December 10, 1795, Pintado's libel was dismissed. The information against the *Vengeance* for illegally outfitting in the United States was dismissed, but the vessel was condemned in the prosecution for illegally exporting arms. An appeal was taken by Pintado, and by the French claimant, of the decree condemning the *Vengeance*.

In the appellate proceedings at Circuit, the apostles were read and filed on the day both the *Pintado* and *Vengeance* cases were called. Counsel had agreed in the course of the trials that the testimony taken in the causes should be consolidated and read upon the argument of the causes in the District Court and also at the hearings on appeal. The reading of testimony in the *Vengeance* appeal took place after new witnesses were heard. It was unnecessary to repeat the ritual in the *Pintado* case, although here, too, new witnesses were examined. The Circuit Court affirmed the decree in *Pintado* and reversed that in the *Vengeance*. Both cases went to the Supreme Court on writ of error, in each case with a section 19 statement signed by Justice Chase in which he referred to the "schedule annexed," a deliberate and artful designation of the avalanche of testimony that was part of the record and proceedings.[239]

Both in Connecticut and Pennsylvania the memorandum form of setting out proceedings was used. *The United States v. the Schooner Peggy* was the one case which went on appeal to the Circuit Court for the Connecticut District.[240] The schooner was taken prize by the U.S.S. *Trumbull* off the coast of St. Domingue in April 1800, during the hostilities with France. It carried a cargo and six guns. Buisson, claimant, alleged he was carrying despatches to France from Toussaint L'Ouverture, but was otherwise on a trading voyage. The record shows that the traditional rules of prize were followed, the only proofs considered being the papers on board the *Peggy*, and the "Declaration" of the officers of the *Trumbull* and the Captain's commission. Claimant offered other papers allegedly on board. Law, District judge, dismissed the libel. He

---

[239] Cf. *LPAH*, II, 788, 792–808. The form of the record and proceedings in two later New York cases, Talbot v. Ship *Amelia*, Seeman claimant (4 Dallas 34 [1801]; Ms. Case Papers, U.S. Sup. Ct., Case No. 89), and Topham v. Brigantine *Harriott* (unreported, 1800; *ibid.*, Case No. 75, docketed as U.S. v. Brigantine *Harriott*), exhibit some differences from the cases discussed in the text. In the former case the testimony is in each instance indorsed "sworn to" or "sworn" in open court, signed by the witness and the clerk. In the Topham case the record recites that testimony was taken down by the clerk and also that it was read at the trial.

[240] Ms. Case Papers, Circuit Ct. Connecticut Dist. The Circuit Court was reversed December 1801 (1 Cranch 103).

was reversed at Circuit by Cushing J. The Pennsylvania case, *Bas v. Tingey*,[241] was a libel for salvage of an American ship recaptured by the public ship *Ganges* from the French. The record and proceedings disclose that the testimony was taken on interrogatories but not whether these were taken in advance of trial. In some cases, *e.g.*, *Glass v. the Sloop Betsey*, the Circuit Court appears to have had before it only a deposition of Glass, sworn to in open court,[242] and an admission by proctors for appellant that certain operative facts on which the plea to the jurisdiction hinged be admitted as evidence. However, the practice in the Maryland District Court is indicated clearly enough by the few surviving papers, when this tribunal in March 1794 proceeded to try the cause by order of the Supreme Court "according to right and law." Here the witnesses were examined and the testimony recorded in the form of depositions.[243] This appears to have been the rule in the Maryland state Court of Admiralty,[244] and the survival of the practice is attested by divers bills of costs in District Court cases.

In relation to the matter of costs, what may be described as a left-handed congressional blessing on current practice is to be found in the admiralty fee statute of 1793.[245] Here, among the fees to which the clerk of the District might lay claim is the item: "Examining each witness and drawing his deposition, for each sheet of ninety words, ten cents." Whether or not this may be taken as reflecting current usage, the statutory establishment of any fee had a potential regulatory effect upon practice. The service involved was included in a draft fee bill prepared by Attorney General William Bradford in 1795.[246] By avoiding the equivocal term "deposition," the language used more correctly represents what the records show was going on: "For reducing the testimony of any witness to writing and engrossing a fair copy of same per sheet . . . 20."

There remains to be considered the purpose served by the re-membrancing of Circuit proceedings in the format of those in the District Court, their conflation and their despatch when a writ of error to the Supreme Court was pursued. This was, we believe, the result of a

[241] Ms. Case Papers, U.S. Sup. Ct., Case No. 87; 4 Dallas 37 (1800), where the name of the navy hero was spelled "Tingy."

[242] Deposition "sworn to in open court" Aug. 6, 1793. The admission was signed but the signature not acknowledged, filed Nov. 17, 1793. Ms. Case Papers, Glass *et al.* v. Sloop *Betsey* and Capt. Johannene, Circuit Ct. Maryland Dist.

[243] Testimony of Glass respecting ownership of cargo, filed Mar. 27, 1794, and of Lucas Gibbs, filed Mar. 20, 1794. The bill of costs for this proceeding has entries for "Exam'ing writ and Drawing Depose .42 Do. Do. .45"; "Copy Depositions 95, Copy Depositions 30." The total costs were $15.88. Ms. Case Papers, *ibid*.

[244] 1 Kilty, *Laws of Maryland*, Nov. Sess. 1779, c. 25, sec. 5, *sub* fees "To the Register of the Admiralty Court."

[245] 1 *U.S. Stats.*, 332.

[246] *Am. St. Pap.: Misc.*, I, 117–22.

superabundance of caution regarding compliance with section 19 of the Judiciary Act. So far as equity and admiralty causes were concerned, this had amounted to the introduction of a new definition of "record and process" which the writ of error commanded be transmitted. The purpose of section 19 was manifestly to spare the Supreme Court the task of wrestling with the prolixity of the mass of matter recorded on appeal below, and possibly to safeguard the prohibition of section 22 that there be no reversal for any error of fact. The alternatives offered—that the facts appear from the pleadings and decree itself, or in a case agreed on by counsel or stated by the court—would not necessarily offer a sufficient basis for the Supreme Court to settle whether or not correct inferences of law had been arrived at below. It is consequently arguable that the record of testimony, whether masquerading as "schedule" or not, was appended for the enlightenment of the Supreme Court. That it was so used is apparent from Paterson's opinion in *Talbot v. Jansen.*[247] As we shall observe, even after the Supreme Court decided that statements of the case by the parties or court were conclusive as to the facts set out in them, it, nevertheless, did not undertake to halt the transmission of evidence.[248]

---

[247] 3 Dallas at 152 (1795).

[248] Wiscart v. Dauchy, *ibid.*, 321 (1796), on which *cf.* c. XV, *infra.*

CHAPTER XIV

The Circuit Courts— Criminal Jurisdiction

W HAT CAESAR A. RODNEY called the "weeping voice of history"[1] has long deplored the administration of criminal justice by federal courts during the years 1790–1800. These jeremiads seem to us to have proceeded upon the assumption that the things laid to the charge of the Federalist administration by its opponents should be taken as incontrovertible. It is, of course, not possible to write of the courts in this period without referring to the political antagonisms of the time; nevertheless, tendentious sources, no matter how exalted, should be recognized for what they were. Surely, too, the judicial muniments deserve a professional scrutiny. This last demands some command of the conditions precedent of law and custom on which the functioning of the federal judiciary was based, and in terms of which it deserves to be judged.

All of those who were to be engaged as prosecutors or judges in the District or Circuit Courts, if they had dealt at all with causes criminal, had been blooded in provincial or state courts where the imprint of Crown law was still conspicuous. This was a factor imponderable but nonetheless real. For although the new courts were statutory courts and so first reference had to be made to Acts of Congress, yet what was presumed in these or left undefined could only be supplied by usages of

---

[1] 2 *Trial of Samuel Chase . . .* (S. H. Smith and T. Lloyd, reporters, 1805), 368. This does not appear in *Report of the Trial of the Hon. Samuel Chase . . .* (C. Evans, reporter, 1805). It should be noticed that at points there are substantial differences in the two accounts. The publishers of the Evans report state that the arguments and opinions of counsel were examined and corrected by the latter. The arguments of the managers were printed "literally" from Evans' notes. The publishers of the Smith and Lloyd version claim that the managers had revised their speeches. We here have used both versions.

the state where the federal court sat, if indeed, it conceived that these applied,[2] or by reference to the judges' own experience or reading in this grisly jurisprudence. In the new Republic recourse to extant literature was not without its snares, for these books dealt with pleas of the Crown and the rationale of many rules was the guarding of the king's interest.[3] During the period of colonial dependence, overt challenge of reasons for particular rules had been impractical, not to say impolitic. This was no longer the case, but such was the ascendancy of published authority that the disposition prevailed to accept a rule without reference to how it had been justified in the treatises.

The discretion left to the federal courts as respects procedure was considerable. For the organization and operation of federal law enforcement, this was of first importance and it is therefore worth noticing how casually the legislative branch dealt with it. Whether or not it was in anticipation that the Senate committee appointed May 13, 1789, to bring in a bill defining crimes against the United States would also deal with criminal procedure, the Judiciary Bill, and eventually the Act itself, contained only some general directions, already noticed, such as trial by jury, oral testimony in open court and the writ-issuing power.[4] It was, however, specific as to state forms of process for arrest, bail, venue in the case of capital crimes and directions for the selection of jurors. In the course of the squabble between House and Senate over the Senate bill, explicit reference to the grand jury and the authority of magistrates to take examinations disappeared.

Surprisingly enough, when the second session of the first Congress got around to the enactment clumsily entitled "An Act for the Punishment of certain Crimes against the United States" (April 1790),[5] there were only a few directions relating to procedure. That the statute was drawn on the assumption that common law methods of trial would be followed is evident from the random references to presentment and indictment. As the new amendments to the Constitution had not yet been ratified, something more precise would have been in order. Some of the items awaiting ratification were covered, viz., affirmation of the right to counsel, but to this there was a novel addition—the judges were required to assign such.[6] Defendant's right to a copy of the indictment and list of witnesses and compulsory process for his own witnesses were stipulated, as well as the number of peremptory challenges in indictments for treason and other capital offenses. The courts were authorized

---

[2] Pursuant to sec. 34 of the Judiciary Act.

[3] Goebel and Naughton, *Law Enforcement in Colonial New York*, 555.

[4] *Supra*, c. XI, p. 496.

[5] 1 *U.S. Stats.*, 112.

[6] *Ibid.*, sec. 29.

to proceed as if a defendant had pleaded not guilty when he stood mute, refused to plead or had not challenged peremptorily above twenty prospective jurors.[7]

No significant statutory directions relating to criminal procedure were added during the period here under consideration, except for the enlargement in 1798 of the jury's competence in trials for seditious libel and the alteration of the common law rule respecting defense in such prosecutions that will later be examined.[8] Because of legislative inaction or indifference a most important preserve of the law was thus left to be settled by the District and Circuit Courts. The dispositions which these courts might see fit to make were under no effective restraint by way of review for the reason that no statute authorized resort to writ of error in criminal cases. The matter does not seem to have been explored by Congress, either because the book learning about common law limitations upon the availability of the writ in criminal cases was generally accepted doctrine,[9] or because of the sentiment against enhancement of the scope of the Supreme Court's appellate jurisdiction.

Whether or not it was conceived that despite the silence of the Judiciary Act on error in causes criminal the writ could issue by virtue of section 14 is doubtful. Chase J. seems to have believed that he might allow such a writ, for in *United States v. Callender* (1800) he informed counsel for the defense that if the latter made his objection a matter of record, he would so do.[10] In Virginia, where the trial took place, error then lay in misdemeanor cases.[11] Because it had already been held (1795) in this Circuit by Iredell J. in *United States v. Mundell* that section 34 applied to criminal trials,[12] it was at least arguable that

---

[7] *Ibid.*, sec. 30. To be noticed also is sec. 24, extending to the crimes previously listed the constitutional prohibition (Art. III, sec. 3) regarding corruption of the blood or forfeiture; sec. 31, abolishing benefit of clergy in capital cases; sec. 32, limitations on time of prosecution.

[8] 1 *U.S. Stats.*, 596. "An Act in addition to the Act for the Punishment of certain Crimes against the United States" (Sedition Act).

[9] The source of first reference, at least for legislators, where are set out the limitations on use of the writ was Blackstone, *Commentaries*, IV, 391–92. The learning on the question was summarized in Rex v. Wilkes, 4 Burr. 2527, 2551–52, where it is indicated that the discretion over probable cause lay with the court.

[10] Wharton, *State Trials*, 707. Chase

indicates that he believed a bill of exceptions could be sealed, for he told counsel that if they would put their objections to his ruling on a question of evidence "on the record," he would allow the writ.

[11] Newall v. Comm., 2 Washington (Va.) 88 (1795); Jones v. Comm., 1 Call 555 (1799).

[12] 3 Ms. Record Book, Circuit Ct. Virginia Dist., 414 (1795). Defendant was indicted for "breaking away from the Marshall on a capias," an obstruction of process. The question before the court was whether a requisition of bail was correct. It was not required in state courts in such cases. Iredell held: ". . . I have no doubt that under the express reference by the act of congress to the laws of the several states as rules for our decision, . . . the law of Virginia . . .

exceptions might be taken at trial and so the question of the availability of error and bill of exceptions might have been adjudicated in the Supreme Court. Counsel, however, did not accept the invitation.

The only corrective procedure explicitly recognized in the Judiciary Act was the motion for a new trial, the power to grant which was conferred upon all courts. So far as such motions might be based upon matters such as misdirection of the jury, the law-makers had provided something which did not approach in fairness the practice of those jurisdictions where, after trial at sittings, new trial motions were argued at bar before the full bench with a report of the trial judge before it. This procedure was a reasonable approximation of an appellate review on points of law and it so operated in contemporary New York.[13] As the federal judiciary was organized, a motion for new trial at Circuit was heard by the trial judges. It is further to be observed that there appears to have been doubts whether or not such a motion could be entertained in criminal cases. The matter was argued at length at the Circuit Court for the Pennsylvania District in 1799 after verdict in the first Fries treason trial and settled in the affirmative.[14] The scantiness of available English precedent is evident from counsels' citations, but it is significant that in the face of English reluctance to apply precedents from civil litigation to Crown prosecutions, Iredell J. saw no reason here to distinguish civil from criminal practice.

PROSECUTION AND PRELIMINARIES TO TRIAL

THE CONGRESS having thus left the judiciary to its own devices, except as to the incidents already noticed, it came about that the procedure in causes criminal anterior to trial in many particulars duplicated the Americanized common law practice in each district. The initiation of prosecutions in federal courts, however, was *sui generis*, for although the Judiciary Act had directed that it should be the duty of each United States Attorney to prosecute in his district all delinquents for crimes and offenses cognizable under the authority of the United States, these officials became subject to a certain amount of executive control, once the first Secretary of State had made directive authority over them the business of his department. Orders from the Attorney General were rare, for in spite of some efforts by the first incumbent, Edmund Randolph, to promote his office into a department, he had been unsuccessful—

---

is that by which we are bound to decide on the present occasion." The quotation is from a ms. report of Call cited by Botts in United States v. Burr. 2 *Reports of the Trials of*

Colonel Aaron Burr, . . . 1807 (D. Robertson, reporter, (1808), 460.
[13] *LPAH*, II, c. I.
[14] United States v. Fries, Wharton, *State Trials*, 598–609.

indeed, he was not even allowed a clerk. As a result, when he was consulted, his advice was usually passed on to the local prosecutors by the Secretary of State.

The statute, on its face, left the District Attorneys with a large discretion over the initiation of prosecutions, a fact which critics of early federal law enforcement have not fully taken into account. These officers, however, appear in general to have acted circumspectly. Although one of the most important of federal law-enforcing officers, the District Attorney was ill provided for by Congress, and as his emoluments came from fees, what was allowed him was certainly no inducement to over-activity.[15] Since the pre-Revolution tradition that the law

---

[15] The Judiciary Act allowed him such fees as shall be taxed for his services in the courts. According to a letter from New York District Attorney Harison to Hamilton, Nov. 9, 1791 (*PAH*, IX, 483), since there was in New York no table of fees in the state courts for criminal cases because the Attorney General there was salaried, "it was thought most proper" to adopt the same allowance in the state Supreme Court for equal service in civil cases. These were inadequate because it was usual for counsel to receive additional compensation from the client. Harison had presented his bill earlier (*ibid.*, VIII, 511), and it had contained items of services for the Treasury which Hamilton told him would have to await congressional action. The bill was finally paid June 1792 for the 1791 services ($33 travel and $116.93 fees); see "Account of the Receipts and Expenditures of the United States, for the Year 1792" in *ibid.*, XV, 475 at 501.

In 1791 an allowance of 10 cents per mile travelling expenses was allowed (1 *U.S. Stats.*, 216 at 217), and by the second Process Act (*ibid.*, 275 at 277) practice respecting fees was confirmed by statute—"such fees in each state respectively as are allowed in the supreme courts of the same," plus the 10-cent-per-mile travelling allowance. Things remained on this footing until 1799 when the District Attorney was given in addition to the fees and mileage allowed by the 1792 act $5 per day when he "necessarily" attended District or Circuit Courts on

government business. In all districts *except* Massachusetts, New York, Pennsylvania and South Carolina, District Attorneys were allowed $200. Certain special fees were fixed for admiralty causes in the District Courts, and $6 for every other cause (*ibid.*, 624).

Pennsylvania District Attorney Rawle, writing the Secretary of the Treasury in 1794, commented upon his services performed in 1792 and suggested that although those relating to criminal business were "perhaps" compensated by fee schedules, others were not, and that it might be more satisfactory to wait for a "legislative sanction" to take place. RG 217, Miscellaneous Treasury Accounts 1790–1894, No. 6388 (NA). There was no legislation, but Rawle was paid $8 for services in April 1792, and $408 for services in August and September.

At the order of the Secretary of State, the Virginia District Attorney proceeded in 1794 to Norfolk to inquire into the capture of a vessel and to take depositions. He charged $8 per day for travel, subsistence and services. He wrote that he felt "considerable embarrassment from the novelty of the charges" and the lack of any standard by which to regulate them. *Ibid.*, No. 5747. For eight days' service he received $64.

Rawle wrote Comptroller Steele on May 8, 1800, to the effect that under the existing regulations the District Attorney received only attorney's and not counsel's fees, and for such he should be compensated as was any

officer of the province was free to conduct private practice was carried over into the new federal administration, it was here, and not in government work, that the District Attorneys earned their bread and butter. We have no doubt that the prestige of the office brought retainers their way. It is also clear that the office involved considerable counselling of local officials such as collectors. This last was something not embraced in any schedule of fees and consequently these tasks were undertaken with no more than a hope that the Treasury would eventually allow some compensation. We have not found in the surviving papers of early appointees to the District Attorney's office, all of whom were persons of solid and in some cases outstanding professional qualifications, anything substantial to indicate that the District judges normally were active in instigating prosecution by the local District Attorney.

While it lay with the District Attorney to set in motion the prosecution of delinquents whether at the instance of the Secretary of State, a collector, an informer or otherwise, the important preliminaries of issuing process to take offenders, the examinations and the recognizances for appearance were committed by section 33 of the Judiciary Act to any justice or judge of the United States or any state magistrate. Since the Supreme Court Justice officiated usually only at trial, although once assigned to a district he might be consulted,[16] these labors fell chiefly upon the District judge. The most dramatic illustration of this occurred during the so-called Whiskey Rebellion when District Judge Peters and United States Attorney William Rawle accompanied the armed forces to the western counties and shortly undertook the preliminary examinations of prisoners and witnesses.[17]

---

other gentleman of the bar. A lot of business was done, particularly in relation to the collection of the revenue, that he thought could not be compensated because these officials thought that they were entitled to call on him. *Ibid.*, No 11,484. It appears that jobs done for the Treasury itself were paid for; *cf.*, *e.g.*, *ibid.*, No. 9172 (deeds for Montauk Lighthouse).

[16] See, for example, the correspondence between Gunning Bedford, Jr., Delaware District judge, Justice Samuel Chase, and Maryland District Judge Winchester regarding the rendition of one Sanders, a postmaster at Georgetown, Maryland, who allegedly embezzled notes of the United States Bank which were uttered at Philadelphia. Sanders was captured in Delaware. The question was how he should be removed to Maryland, the locus of the crime. Ms. Case Papers, Circuit Ct. Maryland Dist. Sanders was tried and convicted, May term 1800.

[17] On Oct. 2, 1794, after the militia were on the march, United States Attorney Rawle requested of Secretary of State Randolph that he send an Associate Justice of the Supreme Court or the District judge "to issue process for & to administer oaths to witnesses, to issue process against the parties accused, to examine them, to judge from that examination whether a Committment or a bare recognizance will be expedient" (Ms. Peters Papers, X, 26 [HSP]). Randolph chose Peters J. who told the former he depended on military help to execute process if necessary (Oct. 7, 1794, *ibid.*, 27). Peters spent about two weeks with Rawle and others making

On these preliminaries depended a variety of questions such as the sufficiency of the evidence to proceed with a prosecution, the testimony to be submitted to a grand jury and the need of binding over witnesses to appear at trial. It will be convenient here to consider some of the problems which confronted the courts, the prosecution and the defense before trial. To some problems, such as the use at trial of examinations as a check on oral testimony of witnesses, no answer can be given.[18] On others, such as the examinations or confessions of witnesses, the evidence is meagre. The preliminary examination of defendants, a practice usual in some states, Iredell J. claimed was required by law, an inference from the wording of section 33 of the Judiciary Act.[19] Such examinations had traditionally been admissible as confessions.[20] The only discussion of the matter we have found appears to have been in the first trial of John Fries for treason. His confession was admitted without objection, but in charging the jury Iredell J. cautioned that no man could be convicted of treason except on the testimony of two witnesses or upon confession in open court.

In this case Peters J. had taken the confession during the preliminary round-up. Iredell charged the jury that the instrument could be taken as confirmation of what had been sworn to by the witnesses.[21] That confessions had to be signed to be admissible appears from a ruling in a North Carolina prosecution for piracy.[22] A document in the nature of a confession, but evidently written down and sworn to before defendant's attorney, seems to have been offered at the trial of Isaac Williams, indicted for accepting a commission on a French armed vessel and serving on the same against Great Britain in violation of Article 21 of the Jay Treaty.[23] The substance consisted in certain allega-

---

investigation. See also Hamilton to General Lee, Oct. 20, 1794, in H. C. Lodge, ed., *The Works of Alexander Hamilton*, VI, 445.

[18] See the justification for their use in M. Hale, *Pleas of the Crown* (1778 ed.), II, 285, and G. Gilbert's argument *contra* in his *Law of Evidence* (1769 ed.), 141.

[19] Wharton, *State Trials*, 535. The Committee bill had directly authorized that persons apprehended be brought before a federal judge for examination. A distinctive federal process was contemplated. In its final form the statute (sec. 33) provided for state process, excised the direct authorization to take examinations, but it retained a sentence authorizing magistrates to take recognizances of wit-

nesses, "which recognizances the magistrate before whom the examination shall be, may require on pain of imprisonment."

[20] Hawkins, *Pleas of the Crown* (1777 ed.), II, c. 46, sec. 29 *et seq.*

[21] Wharton, *State Trials*, 594.

[22] United States v. Maunier *et al.* The defendants were indicted in June term 1793. Ms. Mins. Circuit Ct. North Carolina Dist. 1791–1806, *sub* June 4, 1793; *cf.* 2 Martin (N.C.) 79. The Ms. Case Papers include a letter of June 22, 1792, from Blount to Sitgreaves J., the motion in arrest and the bill of costs.

[23] United States v. Isaac Williams (1799). The statement and the indictment in Ms. Case Papers, Circuit Ct. Connecticut Dist. The case was

tions regarding the acquisition of French citizenship and defendant's subsequent employment by that Republic. This document was apparently offered at the trial at Connecticut Circuit in 1799. The United States Attorney objected to its admissibility as the evidence was insufficient in law to justify the offense charged. Ellsworth C.J. ruled, however, that although the evidence was irrelevant, by the constitution of the court it should go to the jury.

During the whole of the period here under review the Circuit Courts were from time to time faced with the difficulty of securing the testimony of witnesses out of reach of their process, as in the case of mariners at sea or people living at great distances without the district. The Act of 1793 had provided that subpoenas "may run from one district to another," but in civil cases only, to a distance of one hundred miles from the place of trial.[24] There were no directions regarding attachment of a witness who, though served in a neighbor district, did not appear. The attendance of witnesses plagued both prosecution and defense at the trials of the Whiskey rebels; it was a hardship on defendants in custody to furnish bail and on witnesses who, similarly situated, had to wait out the chase for recalcitrants.

To all appearances the Circuit Courts were hesitant to extend to criminal proceedings the liberty conveyed by section 30 of the Judiciary Act to grant a *dedimus* to take depositions "according to common usage" in order to prevent a failure or delay of justice. If by common usage was meant the English practice, the weight of authority (except for a case recalled by Mansfield in *Mostyn v. Fabrigas*)[25] was against such an indulgence, and so far as state practice was concerned, it seems that only New York by statute tolerated the use of depositions in criminal cases.[26] But even if the state courts indulged the use of depositions more generally than we believe was usual, the federal courts were surely limited so far as the prosecution was concerned by the safeguards embodied in the Sixth Amendment. This was not deemed to apply to informations *qui tam*, for during the course of proceedings against some of the excise tax dodgers in western Pennsylvania, United States Attorney Rawle at the persuasion of A. J. Dallas, counsel for some defendants against whom informations had been filed for failure to register their

---

reported in the *Connecticut Courant*, Apr. 30, 1799, and thereafter copied by numerous newspapers. Wharton, *State Trials*, 652 *et seq.*, uses this account.

24 1 *U.S. Stats.*, 335.

25 The precedents are assembled in the margin of Hawkins, *Pleas of the Crown* (1777 ed.), II, c. 46, that breviary of early American criminal

practice. In Mostyn v. Fabrigas, Cowper 161 (1774), in the case referred to above, the court had threatened to hold up the trial forever if counsel would not agree to have the deposition made available.

26 *N.Y. Laws*, 11 Sess. 1787, c. 46; and *cf.* the use of a deposition in a criminal case by consent, *LPAH*, I, 764.

stills, agreed that depositions might be taken and used for trials at Philadelphia, where by statute the Circuit was held—a three-hundred-mile trip. The consent of the prosecutor was evidently deemed a waiver of the best-evidence rule.[27]

Beyond what has already been indicated it may be observed that Congress did not for a long time come to grips with the practical problem of adequate compensation and mileage for witnesses. The Process Act of 1792 had required that witnesses be compensated at the same rate as witnesses called in the Supreme Court of the state.[28] This ran as low as 25 cents a day in New Hampshire to $1.33 in Maryland. In 1796 Congress provided that an additional 50 cents per day be added to the state fees.[29] Not until 1799 was there legislation specifically authorizing compensation for travel—10 cents per mile.[30] At the same time, the compensation was fixed at $1.25 per diem. It is little wonder that witnesses who lived beyond the reach of a District or Circuit Court's process were reluctant to appear.[31]

As a practical matter all the advantages in securing testimony lay with prosecution, which had at its disposal the extant law-enforcing machinery of the government, in particular the collectors, the marshals and their deputies. Defendant, despite the guarantee of compulsory process, was disadvantaged to the extent that until he had view of the indictment and the list of witnesses against him, he could not settle on his own witnesses. By the Act for the Punishment of certain Crimes, three days before trial in treason cases, two in other capital cases, were allotted for this task.[32] It consequently became an item of defense tactics

---

[27] *Cf.* Rawle's report to the Secretary of State, July 30, 1794, Ms. Rawle Papers, I, 92; Dallas to Rawle, Jan. 18, 1794, *ibid.*, 13 (HSP).

[28] 1 *U.S. Stats.*, 275.

[29] *Ibid.*, 492 (June 1, 1796).

[30] *Ibid.*, 624 (Feb. 28, 1799).

[31] The reluctance would be increased by the element of chance in how costs might be awarded, as well as other incalculable factors. In United States v. Bank of United States (1800), Rawle, prosecuting some forgeries at the Circuit for the Pennsylvania District, had directed a witness from Virginia to attend. He claimed that he would have taken a deposition but for the fact that defendant would have objected under the best-evidence rule. Objection was, however, made to the live testimony, and it was stricken. Although costs were awarded against defendant, he did not have to pay the witness because the testimony was not used. Rawle intervened with the Comptroller to secure compensation. RG 217, Miscellaneous Treasury Accounts 1790–1894, No. 11,793 (NA).

Some further light on witness troubles is cast by an earlier application (1797) of Rawle for expenses owing to reluctance to testify. It had been necessary to employ several constables to bring forward witnesses who had absconded. To keep the witnesses taken on hand for the trials Rawle turned them over to the "Keeper of the Debtors' Apartment of the City and County of Philadelphia" with orders to supply the witnesses with rations and with wood for their warmth. One witness was confined for 127 days. *Ibid.*, No. 9224.

[32] Sec. 29, 1 *U.S. Stats.*, 118.

to move for postponement to secure witnesses. The matter was raised at the trials of the Whiskey rebels[33] and was probably more often raised than court minutes indicate. The English authorities were clear that such motions must be supported by affidavit showing that a witness was material and that without him defendant could not safely proceed to trial. If there was any cause for suspicion then, the court must be satisfied that the witness was material, that applicant had not been negligent and that there was reasonable expectation of securing attendance.[34] The rules in civil and criminal cases were identical.[35]

In some of the prosecutions under the Sedition Act defendants submitted affidavits which under the existing scale of compensation and travel expense were bound to excite some suspicion. Thus in the Circuit Court for the Vermont District (1800) the printer Haswell named a Virginia resident and Secretary of War McHenry.[36] At the trial of William Duane of the *Aurora* at the Circuit for the Pennsylvania District in October 1799 it was reported that Dallas moved for a postponement to secure as witnesses James Monroe of Virginia, General Clarke of Georgia and Timothy Pickering, archenemy of Republican printers.[37] The motion was here granted. In the *Callender* case, the defense listed witnesses as remote from Richmond (where the trial was held) as New Hampshire to the north and South Carolina to the south.[38] Callender also claimed that Adams' tract of 1765, *A Dissertation on the Feudal and Canon Law*, was material to his defense and that he would need weeks, even months, to procure it. Two Virginia witnesses, William B. Giles and Stephen T. Mason, were also on his list. The court then offered to put off trial for six weeks until after the Delaware Circuit. No reply was made. The defense was given five days for service upon the Virginia witnesses. Since William Giles, though served, did not appear, the defense moved to postpone until the next term. This was denied.

The only attempt by a defendant in a criminal cause to secure testimony by commission that has been found was engineered by counsel for William Duane, editor of the *Aurora*, indicted at the October term 1800 of the Circuit for Pennsylvania District for a libel on the United

---

[33] Wharton, *State Trials*, 172.
[34] Impey, *The New Instructor Clericalis*, 2d ed. (1785), 224–25; Tidd, *Practice of the Court of King's Bench*, 3d ed. (1803), II, 708–09.
[35] Rex v. D'Eon, 1 W. Blackstone 510, 514 (1766).
[36] United States v. Haswell, in Wharton, *State Trials*, 685.
[37] *Connecticut Courant*, Oct. 28, 1799. The prosecution was later dropped.
[38] According to the testimony of William Marshall, clerk of the court, two affidavits were filed—a general one and, at the discretion of the court, a special one. *Report of the Trial of the Hon. Samuel Chase . . .* (Evans, 1805), 64; text of the second affidavit, *ibid.*, Exhibits, 53; also Wharton, *State Trials*, 690.

States Senate. Duane named ten Senators as material witnesses. Congress was not then in session and had adjourned to meet at Washington, November 17, 1800.[39] Application had been made to United States Attorney Jared Ingersoll, who had succeeded William Rawle, to consent to a commission to take depositions of his witnesses. This was at once agreed to but defendant did not take out a commission until February 1801. The United States Attorney declined filing interrogatories for prosecution. Only three of the commissioners named accepted and a preliminary meeting was held. The commissioners for the adjourned meeting did not attend and the testimony was never taken.[40] At May session 1801 Duane asked for and obtained a postponement.[41] It should here be noticed that the short-lived Judiciary Act of 1801 considerably enlarged the powers of the new Circuit Courts, specifically granting authority to issue commissions to take testimony and to take depositions *de bene esse* with only the limitations "allowed by law."[42] The provisions of the Judiciary Act of 1789 were restored by the repealer of March 8, 1802.

Except for occasional reference to state statutes, and even rarer inquiries into what state practice might be, procedural questions were argued and settled at Circuit on the basis of English common law precedents.[43] The fact that the Supreme Court had by rule declared that the practice of the King's Bench afforded the outlines for its practice seems to have influenced the opinion of the judges at Circuit, for Paterson J. laid it down in the course of preliminary objections at the trial of the

---

[39] For the background, J. M. Smith, *Freedom's Fetters*, 288 *et seq.*

[40] United States v. Duane, Wallace (3d Cir.), 5. The interrogatories and stipulation are in Ms. Case Papers, Circuit Ct. Pennsylvania Dist., No. 106. Smith, *Freedom's Fetters*, 302, states that Ingersoll agreed to allow a "mixed commission" (*sic*) to go to the new capital to "interview" Senators whose testimony the defense deemed material.

[41] The indictment (Ms. Case Papers, *supra*, n. 40) is indorsed as nonprossed in July 1801.

[42] 2 *U.S. Stats.*, 89, 94 (sec. 15).

[43] Sec. 33 of the Judiciary Act of 1789, of course, directed that arrest for crimes against the United States be according to the usual mode of process in the state—the alleged failure to observe which was laid to Chase's charge. It should be noticed, however, that nothing was said in the act about

state practice regarding the closely related question of bail. In United States v. Mundell (*supra*, n. 12), except for an ambiguous reference to "Act of Congress," this matter was argued entirely on the basis of English authorities. See the two-page Memoranda in the Ms. Case Papers, United States v. Mundell, Ended Cases 1795, Circuit Ct. Virginia Dist. (Va. State Library).

In the case of the Western Insurgents, the defense claimed that an utter compliance with the Pennsylvania jury law was required by sec. 29 of the Judiciary Act. Apparently it was argued that this was afforced by sec. 34, for Peters J. held it was inapplicable. Neither he nor Paterson J. regarded the Pennsylvania law as governing beyond the mode of designating the jury and the qualifications of jurors. 2 Dallas 335 at 341–42 (1795).

Whiskey rebels (1795) that the Circuit Court was a court of original and permanent jurisdiction: "The proceedings in the King's Bench can alone be applicable."[44] The practical effect of such a doctrine would be to make citable any relevant precedents relating to pleas of the Crown insofar as such did not run counter to constitutional guarantees.

THE PATTERN OF COURT-KEEPING

LEST IT BE supposed that in making their accommodations in terms of common law practice the Circuit Courts were intruding on ground where, as an old statute has it, entry was not given by law, it should be recalled that not only did the Judiciary Act impart a certain license, but it was the assumption of the Bill of Rights that the procedures of the common law relating to crimes would be in effect. There was every reason for such an assumption, for a certain sameness in the routine of administering criminal jurisdiction had prevailed in the superior courts of the several provinces due to the sovereign influence of treatises like those of Coke, Hale and Hawkins, to say nothing of practice books like the *Office of the Clerk of Assize*, the *Crown Circuit Companion* and the like. There could be no expectation that the federal courts would depart from the general pattern, and as it turned out, the Circuit judges, all conditioned to it, proceeded to hold and keep their courts in accustomed ways.

The introduction of this routine at the first term of the several Circuit Courts appears to have occasioned no public surprise over the fact that the new courts should be conducted no differently than those of the states. The opening formalities, the calling over and swearing of the grand jury and the delivery of a general charge, seemingly an innocuous ceremony, excited no remark except as to the literary quality of the justices' compositions.[45] With the passage of time this attitude of amicable acceptance was to become one of angry criticism, because the judges' charges came to reflect an increasing sense of apostolic mission. The matter became one greatly, if temporarily, affecting the esteem in which federal justice was held in certain quarters and must consequently be examined in some detail.

---

44 *Ibid.*, 340 n.

45 The District Courts actually anticipated the Circuit Courts in establishing the routine. See, for example, the charge of Hopkinson J. in the Pennsylvania District Court, *New-York Daily Gazette*, Nov. 21, 27, 1789; Duane J.'s charge in the New York District Court, *Gazette of the* *United States*, Feb. 6, 1790. For typical Circuit Court minute entries, Ms. Mins. Circuit Ct. New Jersey Dist. 1790–1806, *sub* Apr. 2, 1790; Ms. Mins. Circuit Ct. New York Dist. 1790–1808, *sub* Apr. 12, 1790; 1 Ms. Order Book, Circuit Ct. Virginia Dist., *sub* May 22, 1790.

The function of the general charge was one of instructing the grand jury of its duty—in its barest form, a recitation of the offenses into which this body must make inquiry and presentment. No formal restraints upon any embellishments had ever been imposed. Such in England, at their most unexceptionable, were made by Assize judges, "more to inform the whole Country, and to shew their own Learning, and the Law therein, than that the Grand Jury should take them into Consideration, or make it the Duty of their Inquiry."[46] At their worst the general charges by English judges were to be found in the *State Trials* and so were well known to American lawyers. The political general charge was not unknown in pre-Revolutionary America, for John Adams had complained about Hutchinson's charges[47] and Cadwalader Colden of Chief Justice Horsmanden.[48] Drayton, South Carolina Chief Justice, had delivered a politically inflammatory charge in 1776,[49] and so had Iredell J. in 1778.[50]

Although it was general knowledge that An Act for the Punishment of certain Crimes against the United States was pending in Congress when the first term of the Eastern Circuit, and, indeed, the earliest in the Middle Circuit, were held, the only offenses then on the books and so to be brought to the grand jury's notice were certain ones under the Collection and Registration Acts. This may account for the fact that early charges were showpieces, or rather, lectures on the advantages of the federal system. Customarily a Supreme Court Justice during the period when he visited all districts within his circuit would use an identical charge. Samuel Chase, appointed after the system of rotation was introduced, kept a charge book[51] and seems on occasion to have thrown together items from divers charges. In some instances the place and term when the charge was delivered are noted. Frequently general charges received added circulation because admiring grand juries would call for publication.

Apart from homilies regarding good morals, a staple in many of the general charges we have seen, the presiding judge not only assumed the burden of explaining the elements of certain crimes, but also performed the useful function of propagating information about the federal penal law, and so of setting the bounds of permissible inquest. There had been no statutory clarification of a federal grand jury's powers

---

[46] J. Astry, *A General Charge to all Grand Juries* (1703), 2.
[47] *Adams Papers*, I, 281.
[48] *Colden Letter Books* (New-York Hist. Soc. *Coll.* [1878]), II, 171–72.
[49] W. H. Drayton, *A Charge, on the rise of the American Empire, delivered by the hon. William-Henry*

Drayton, esq; chief-justice of South-Carolina: to the grand jury for the district of Charlestown (1776).
[50] McRee, *Iredell*, II, 382–89.
[51] Ms. Chase Papers (Md. Hist. Soc.), entitled "Instructions to Grand Jury," n.d.

of independent inquest and presentment. This had been a function of grand juries in the colonies and was consequently still usual in various states. Conceiving themselves to serve as the voice of the county, these bodies were accustomed to present all manner of "grievances"[52] that ranged from matter such as the state of the jail or the dilapidation of buildings, to expressions of opinion on matters of public concern. In point of form such presentments differ markedly from those where a crime is presented on the jury's own knowledge. There is evidence that in some jurisdictions federal grand juries assumed they could speak for whole districts on broader matters of public concern. In the Georgia District the grand juries were evidently a very touchy lot for they seem to have found more crying evils to present than was the case in other districts. Their initial fusillade at October term 1791 consisted of eight separate grievances, and at April term 1793 they had collected six additional complaints. A few items, such as lack of a seaman's hospital and the pay of Georgia jurors, were purely local matters; most of the particulars related to national questions such as the cost of the judiciary, the iniquities of assumption and the Bank of the United States. One may suspect that elsewhere such presentments were more usual than court minutes indicate, for it lay in the discretion of the clerk what should be recorded.[53]

---

[52] This had been an incident of considerable importance in England. *Cf.* S. Webb and B. Webb, *English Local Government . . . The Parish and the County*, 452–56. Colonial records indicate that it was transplanted here with the institution itself.

[53] See Ms. Mins. Circuit Ct. Georgia Dist. 1790–1793, 26–27 *sub* Oct. 18, 1791; the presentment of the excise laws as oppressive and recommending repeal, *ibid.*, 45 *sub* Apr. 27, 1792; and the *omnium gatherum* presented April term 1793, Ms. Mins. Circuit Ct. Georgia Dist. 1793–1798, at 16–22. In 1798 the grand jury for the Maryland Circuit assured the President of support in the event of a war with France (*Gazette of the United States*, May 9, 1798). After the failure in Congress of the Non-intercourse Bill in 1794, the grand jury of the Circuit Court for the Virginia District at the May term 1794, "conceiving it our essential duty" to take notice of impediments to the happiness, etc., of the people of the United States, observing with concern the non-performance by Britain of the 1783 treaty, the violation of neutral rights, the injury to citizens by the recovery of pre-war debts, presented as "a national Greivance" the recovery of such debts by British subjects until the British had complied with the treaty and made reparation for spoliations (1 Ms. Order Book, 358 Circuit Ct. Virginia Dist.).

A presentment of truly explosive political effect was made at the May term 1797 (2 Ms. Order Book, 196, Circuit Ct. Virginia Dist.). On this occasion the grand jury presented as "a real evil" the circular letters of several members of Congress and "particularly Letters with the Signature of Samuel J. Cabell." These were conceived to endeavor at a time of real public danger to disseminate unfounded calumnies against the United States government, and to increase or produce a foreign influence ruinous to the peace, happiness and independence of the United States. See further, McRee, *Iredell*, II, 510.

It was this presentment which

It was obviously desirable to hold the federal grand juries to the limits of what was cognizable by the Circuit Court; but it is no less obvious that where a general charge incorporated comments on national policy or on current events, such could be taken to be invitations for the grand jury to present a version of district opinion. Even in the well-meant dissertations on the common law there might inhere some inducement for presentment of non-statutory offenses. And although it was within the power of the United States Attorney not to put such in form, we believe that in the early years of federal justice considerable uncertainty prevailed whether or not crimes at common law were cognizable in federal courts. Some of the judges themselves do not seem at first to have made up their minds on the point.

This was a question that arose at the first Circuit Court held in New York in April 1790, Jay, Cushing and Duane sitting. Two men were at this time under arrest on suspicion of piracy. The Act for the Punishment of certain Crimes against the United States was then (April 5) still before Congress, but the Chief Justice was not deterred thereby, for in his general charge he more or less nudged the grand jury into finding an indictment.[54] Early in his address Jay explained the obligations of the United States under the law of nations as a preliminary to a discourse on the rationale of the federal judicial system. When he moved to the enumeration of the grand jury's duties he declared that "the objects of your inquiry are all the offences against the United States in this district." He reminded the panel that "laws of nations make part of the laws of this and every other civilized nation." Unfortunately Jay did not enter into any specific argument why acts in violation of international law were subject to prosecution in federal courts. He did not even advert to the doctrine that the law of nations was part of the common law.

---

moved Jefferson, who twenty years earlier had been slaying the archaic dragons in the English statute books, then part of Virginia's laws, to suggest to Monroe a revival of a praemunire statute against all citizens who would take their causes to other than state courts (Sept. 10, 1797, *Works of Jefferson* [Ford, Federal ed.], VIII, 339–41). The first praemunire statute was 27 Edw. III, c. 1. *Cf.* Coke, *Third Institute*, 119 *et seq.*, for the uses to which it was put. As early as 1792 Jefferson had come to the view of the Congress as a "foreign legislature"; *cf.* his letter to Madison, Oct. 1, 1792, in *PAH*, XII, 85, n. 3.

Some historians have read the pre-sentment not as a presentment of the circular letters, but of Cabell personally, for they state that the latter was never brought to trial. *Cf.* A. Koch and H. Ammon, "The Virginia and Kentucky Resolutions: An Episode in Jefferson's and Madison's Defense of Civil Liberties," 152–53; J. M. Smith, *Freedom's Fetters*, 95. L. W. Levy, ed., *Freedom of the Press from Zenger to Jefferson*, 342–43, describes this as "an unprecedented case of seditious libel against the United States; it was wholly founded on the common law. . . ."

[54] H. P. Johnston, ed., *The Correspondence and Public Papers of John Jay, 1763–1826*, III, 387 *et seq.*

The prisoners were indicted for conspiring and confederating on the high seas to destroy the brig *Morningstar*, to murder the captain and passengers and to make a revolt on board. They were convicted and sentenced to stand in the pillory for an hour, to serve six months' imprisonment and on the last day to receive thirty-nine stripes each.[55] A pirate being *hostis humani generis*, the assumption of jurisdiction here aroused no outcry. But the time was to come when federal judges were to use their general charges as media for advancing particular opinions, not the least bold of which was the intimation that presentments at common law were proper. This last became a political issue of the first order, and the grand jury charges together with certain prosecutions which were popularly conceived to be at common law lent color to the view that the Circuit judges were in process of an unconstitutional magnification of the federal criminal law.

THE PROBLEM OF NON-STATUTORY CRIMES

IF A STARTING point for criticism of the judges need be pinpointed, this may be said to have followed upon the Neutrality Proclamation of April 22, 1793,[56] by the terms of which violators were threatened with prosecution. This was an item obviously not to be omitted from a general charge, and here the pattern was set by Chief Justice Jay, who at New York had already indicated his belief that the law of nations was part of the law of the United States. At the May term of the Circuit Court for the Virginia District in his general charge to the grand jury Jay was at pains to quote the President's proclamation, to advert to subsisting treaties and to expatiate on the duties of neutrality imposed by the law of nations. He admonished the grand jurymen that because the United States were in a state of neutrality as to all powers at war, those who committed, aided or abetted hostilities against these powers, or any one of them, offended against the laws of the United States. It was the grand jury's duty to inquire into and present such offenses.[57]

It cannot be inferred from this charge that presentments for violation of the proclamation were asked—there was an old and respected precedent against such action.[58] What may be inferred is that Jay con-

---

[55] United States v. Hopkins and Brown, Ms. Mins. Circuit Ct. New York Dist. 1790–1808, *sub* Apr. 13 and 14, 1790.

[56] Text in Richardson, *Messages and Papers of the Presidents*, I, 156–57.

[57] Wharton, *State Trials*, 49–59. The text of the charge printed in *Cor-*

respondence and Public Papers of John Jay, III, 478, as having been delivered at this time varies greatly from that used by Wharton, which we believe to have been the one actually delivered.

[58] Case of Proclamations, 12 Coke Rep. 74.

ceived that the law of nations was a part of the law of the United States and that prosecutions for violations were maintainable whether or not Congress had exercised its powers to provide for their punishment.

Jay's approach to the constitutional question was more that of a foreign affairs officer than of a judge. But there is reason to believe that the content of the charge had been the result of some conferring with members of the executive department, for on April 8, 1793, Jefferson had written Attorney General Randolph suggesting the utility of using the charge to the grand jury to deal with infractions of neutrality:[59]

> The Judges having notice of the proclamation, will perceive that the occurrence of a foreign war has brought into activity the laws of neutrality, as a part of the law of the land. This new branch of the law they will know needs explanation to the grand juries more than any other. They will study & define the subjects to them and the public. . . . It will be easy to suggest this matter to the attention of the judges, & that alone puts the whole machine into motion.

If there had been any hope that the judicial approach would exercise a calming effect upon the violently divided public opinion induced by the French Revolution, this proved to be vain. There was angry questioning of the President's authority to issue the proclamation and make punishable breaches of neutral duty, and no less passionate defending of the behavior of the French Minister, Genêt, who under color of subsisting treaties promoted the outfitting of privateers, enlistment or commissioning of American nationals and the holding of courts on American soil for adjudication of prizes by French consuls. The necessity of a test case was obvious. The opportunity presented itself early in May 1793 when the British ship *William*, prize of the French privateer *Citoyen Genêt*, was brought into Philadelphia port, Gideon Henfield, prize master. The latter, a citizen of the United States, had enlisted on the *Citoyen Genêt*, outfitted at Charleston. United States Attorney Rawle was directed by the Secretary of State to initiate proceedings against any citizens involved.[60]

Henfield and another were arrested. A special session of the Circuit Court for the district was appointed and convened July 22, 1793, Wilson, Iredell and Peters sitting. Justice Wilson's charge to the grand jury[61] was in part a discourse on the history and spirit of the common law and praise of its adaptability, one feature of which was its adoption of the law of nations, which in his view was the law of nature applied to states. He did not go the length of claiming that the common law was

---

[59] *Works of Jefferson* (Ford, Federal ed.), VII, 315, 318.

[60] Wharton, *State Trials*, 51n.
[61] *Ibid.*, 59–66.

a part of federal law. The obligation of a state was not to injure another state or suffer its citizens to do so. A citizen who in a state of neutrality might take a hostile part with any belligerent violated his duty and the laws of his country. Whether or not France was privileged by Article 22 of the Treaty of Amity of 1778 to outfit privateers in American ports, Wilson described as an "option" which the United States was free to exercise. It did not lie in the power of an individual citizen to "assist in a business of this sort." If he did, he was amenable to the justice of his nation.

The indictment in this case was drafted by Attorney General Randolph and District Attorney William Rawle.[62] Randolph had already rendered an opinion to Jefferson that because treaties were the supreme law of the land, Henfield was punishable for breach of treaties with nations with which the United States was at peace, and secondly, he was indictable at common law because his conduct came within the description of disturbing the peace of the United States.[63] This last was a tempting and dangerous suggestion, for to have used it might have opened the way to a reception of the English doctrines of acts done *contra pacem* and so a general common law jurisdiction. This idea was not pursued, although the phrase "against the peace and dignity of the United States" came to be used at the conclusion of the federal indictments as its equivalent was in the states. This was due to English book learning that indictments must so conclude, but its presence in a federal indictment to all intents and purposes came to be mere surplusage. Ultimately in the Henfield case the theory of the draftsmen consisted in this, that the United States had treaties with divers nations declaring a firm state of peace; the Constitution declared treaties to be the supreme law of the land; the acts of war in which defendant had engaged were violations of the treaties and so of the law of the land. This was the substance of the charge in each of the twelve counts of the indictment; in six counts violation of the law of nations was also charged.

Rawle, in his argument, touched briefly on the doctrine that the law of nations was part of the law of the land (citing Blackstone) but the defense did not meet this head on, claiming merely that no offense at common law was charged. Wilson J. did not advert to this in his instructions to the jury. These were not fully reported, for no more is noticed than that he made explanatory observations on the legal principles agitated in the case. He was explicit on the point that the United States being in a state of neutrality, Henfield's acts were an offense against its laws. By the law of nations he was bound to keep the

---

[62] *Ibid.*, 77n.
[63] *American State Papers: Foreign Relations*, I, 152 (May 30, 1793)

(hereafter cited as *Am. St. Pap.: For. Rel.*, I).

peace as to all nations with which the United States were at peace. The positive laws infringed were the treaties which by the Constitution were the supreme law of the land. Defendant was acquitted.

The efforts to bring to book the citizens who had enlisted in French service did not cease with the *Henfield* case. For at October term at the Circuit for the Massachusetts District, a true bill was found against one Batterman who had enlisted on the privateer *Roland*.[64] This indictment again relied upon the theory of breach of the treaties, but it was not as artfully drawn as the Pennsylvania instrument. At this term, too, a true bill was found against John Juteau, chancellor of the French consulate at Boston, for outfitting the *Roland* and making war upon the nations with which the United States were at peace. The defendants were not brought to trial, for on May 21, 1794, the indictments were ordered by the President to be non-prossed.[65]

How far the composition of general charges by the Justices of the Supreme Court at this time may have been affected by perusal of the well-known questions on neutrality and the treaties, submitted to them by the executive, is a matter of conjecture. Answers had been solicited July 18, 1793,[66] but with both Blair and Cushing absent, Jay put off a reply until all could participate.[67] This was only a few days before Wilson's general charge in the *Henfield* case (July 22, 1793). On August 8 a letter declining the President's request on constitutional grounds was despatched.[68] We find it difficult to believe that Wilson's charge was not a partial reply to some of the queries. Iredell's general charge of June 2, 1794, was even more responsive.[69]

In spite of the ingenuity displayed in formulating the charge of treaty violation, the *Henfield* case has been represented to be an example of a prosecution at common law.[70] Neither the indictment itself nor

---

[64] Ms. Final Record Book Circuit Ct. Massachusetts Dist. 1790–1799, *sub* June term 1794. George Batterman, with three other mariners, was indicted at October term 1793. The indictment, badly frayed, and related documents are in Ms. Case Papers, Circuit Ct. Massachusetts Dist.

[65] The indictment against Juteau is in Ms. Case Papers, *supra*, n. 64. The order signed by Secretary of State Randolph is likewise there filed.

[66] The questions are published in C. M. Thomas, *American Neutrality in 1793*, App. I; see also the draft version and notes in *PAH*, XV, 110–16.

[67] Ms. Misc. Letters of Dept. of State, 1790–1799 (RG 59, NA). In town were Jay, Wilson, Iredell and Paterson.

[68] *Ibid.* The objection was grounded on the separation of powers and on the impropriety of extrajudicial decision of the questions proffered.

[69] McRee, *Iredell*, II, 410. This charge was delivered in North Carolina three days before the Neutrality Act was signed.

[70] L. W. Levy, *Jefferson and Civil Liberties* (1963), 201, n. 72. Warren, in *The Supreme Court in United States History*, I, 115n., states: "In spite of the result in the Henfield Case, the Federal Courts continued to indict persons for violations of neutrality, the indictments being

Wilson's instructions to the petit jury made reference thereto; the most that the latter claimed was a violation of the law of nations which, as noticed, he conceived to be a universal obligation on all men. Fortunately for the United States District Attorneys, the burden of artful drafting which was cast upon them by the expediency of refraining from mention of the President's proclamation and the common law came to an end June 5, 1794. The enactment then of the so-called neutrality law making punishable certain unneutral acts supplied the necessary statutory footing for future prosecutions.[71]

At the same special Circuit Court at which Henfield was tried, the grand jury returned a true bill against Joseph Ravara, consul of Genoa, for a misdemeanor in sending an anonymous letter to the British Minister threatening violence to his person for the purpose of extorting money in violation of the law of nations and against the laws of the United States. Counsel for defense moved to quash the indictment, claiming that the Supreme Court had exclusive original jurisdiction.[72] The motion was denied on the ground that the offense was within the express delegation of jurisdiction to the Circuit Court.[73] The cause was postponed to the next Circuit, but owing to the yellow fever epidemic this term was cut short and defendant was not tried until April term 1794.

United States v. Ravara is badly reported.[74] The defense is represented to have taken the ground that the acts charged were not crimes by the common law or by any positive law of the United States. This was, of course, nonsense because by section 27 of the Act for the Punishment of certain Crimes, offering personal violence to a public minister was made punishable. It was also argued by defense that a criminal proceeding ought not to be sustained against an individual of defendant's official character. The court instructed the jury that the offense was indictable and that defendant was not privileged by virtue of his consular appointment. Ravara was convicted.[75]

---

based on common law and the law of nations." A. Beveridge, in *The Life of John Marshall*, III, 26, states: "Justice Wilson instructed the grand jury that Henfield could, and should, be indicted and punished under British precedents. When the case was heard the charge of the court to the trial jury was to the same effect."

[71] 1 *U.S. Stats.*, 381. This was an amendment to the "Act for the Punishment of certain Crimes." Being temporary, it was extended in 1797 and made permanent in 1800.

[72] He was indicted July 23, 1793, the day before a true bill was found in the Henfield case. Ms. Mins. Circuit Ct. Pennsylvania Dist. 1792–1795. The indictment, "plea" and demurrer to the plea are in Ms. Case Papers, Circuit Ct. Pennsylvania Dist., No. 17 (1793). The minutes and the papers are not in accord.

[73] Ms. Mins. Circuit Ct. Pennsylvania Dist. 1792–1795, *sub* July 24, 1793, for the motion.

[74] 2 Dallas 297.

[75] Ms. Mins. Circuit Ct. Pennsylvania Dist. 1792–1795, *sub* Apr. 14 and 15, 1794.

At a special Circuit Court of the
United States for the middle Circuits
and Pennsylvania Districts holden
at the City of Philadelphia in the
Districts aforesaid on the twenty
second day of July in the year
of our Lord one thousand seven hundred
and ninety three.

The Grand Inquest for the United States in the middle
Circuit of the said United States and in the Dis=
trict of Pennsylvania upon their respective
Oaths and affirmations do Present That Joseph
Ravara late of the district aforesaid Esquire on
the twelfth day of May in the year of our Lord
one thousand seven hundred and ninety three
in the district aforesaid and Circuit aforesaid he
the said Joseph Ravara then and there and yet
being Consul from the Doge and Governors of the
Republic of Genoa to the said United States at
the City of Philadelphia and being an evil
disposed person and seeking wicked gain and
practising contriving and intending to terrify
George Hammond Esquire Minister Plenepoten.
tiary to the said United States from the King
of Great Britain by threats of personal violence
and other Injuries and thereby wickedly and

Grand jury presentment, *United States v. Joseph Ravara*, July 22, 1793, at
a special Circuit Court for the Pennsylvania District, page 1.
(The National Archives)

Not long after the Ravara trial a second case involving the British Minister Hammond again presented the issue of action under Article III, section 2. In September 1794 Hammond complained about a defamatory article in Greenleaf's *New-York Journal.* Secretary of State Randolph submitted the piece to Attorney General Bradford who advised that it was *prima facie* libellous and might be made the subject of a criminal prosecution. The law of libel which protected the citizen was in the case of a diplomatic person "strengthened by the law of nations which secures the minister a peculiar protection not only from violence but also from injury."[76]

The generalities of the Attorney General's opinion offered a prosecutor no real handhold for framing an indictment. Bradford may have conceived that the language of the Constitution declaring the judicial power "shall extend . . . to all cases affecting ambassadors, other public ministers and consuls" was sufficient to confer jurisdiction *ratione personae.* He failed, however, to deal with the second problem, whether a federal court could ask cognizance of a non-statutory crime. This does not seem to have troubled Randolph who forwarded the letter to United States Attorney Harison of New York, directing him "to proceed upon it as the law directs."[77] At April term 1795 of the Circuit Court, the grand jury of the New York District found a true bill charging Greenleaf with criminal libel.[78] The defendant was bound over to appear at the next Circuit. There was apparently some settlement for no further record appears. However, in April 1797 Greenleaf was again arrested and indicted, this time for libelling Sir John Temple, British Consul General.[79] He was tried and convicted at the same term. This court was kept by Chief Justice Ellsworth and Robert Troup, District judge.

Ellsworth moved on to Boston to hold the June term for the Mas-

---

[76] 1 *Official Opinions of the Attorneys General of the United States* (1852), 52.

[77] Ms. Domestic Letters of Dept. of State, VII, 271 (Sept. 18, 1794) (NA).

[78] Ms. Mins. Circuit Ct. New York Dist. 1790–1808, *sub* Apr. 7, 1795.

[79] *Ibid., sub* Apr. 5, 6 and 7, 1797. The District Attorneys were already under general orders to take measures to prevent or to punish breaches of the peace or good behavior toward consuls. In a circular instruction to the District Attorneys of Massachusetts, New York, Pennsylvania, Baltimore and Charleston, dated Nov. 29, 1793, Secretary of State Jefferson had passed on complaints of Genêt that French consuls were exposed to insults and personal danger at the hands of French refugees from the West Indies. Consuls were entitled to protection as were other strangers but to a "more attentive enforcement" because of their commissions. Jefferson asked that the local consul be advised that the federal government would put into effect all the means of protection which the state laws provided. The laws to which Jefferson adverted were those punishing breaches of the peace and binding to good behavior or the peace. C. F. Jenkins, ed., *Jefferson's Germantown Letters,* 126. Not until 1798 were federal judges empowered to take security for good behavior and the peace. 1 *U.S. Stats.,* 596.

sachusetts District in this same year. Four indictments were prosecuted at this term for counterfeiting or passing counterfeit bills of the Bank of the United States, not then a statutory offense.[80] The Act for the Punishment of certain Crimes had made provision only for the forging, counterfeiting or uttering of securities of the United States,[81] and such the bills of the bank were not. In one of the cases, *United States v. Pardon Smith*, counsel for defendant made a motion in arrest of judgment on the ground that there was no federal statute on the subject and consequently that it was only an offense at common law exclusively within the jurisdiction of the state courts. In denying the motion, the court is reported to have held that the act incorporating the bank was a constitutional act and that by the Constitution the federal courts had jurisdiction over all causes or cases in law or equity arising under the Constitution and laws of the United States. This case was one arising under those laws, for the bills were made "in virtue" thereof; although there was no statute punishing counterfeiting, it was a misdemeanor against the United States, and punishable by them as such.[82]

The logical hocus-pocus employed by the court to avoid an outright admission that a prosecution at common law was maintainable in a federal court bears additional witness to the judicial policy manifested in other cases to find some constitutional or statutory foundation on which to base jurisdiction where no explicit warrant was authorized by Act of Congress. This was a position Ellsworth was to abandon within two years.

At the May 1799 term of the Circuit Court for the South Carolina District, he charged the grand jury that conduct clearly destructive of a government or its powers ordained to exist by the people must be criminal. It was not necessary to particularize facts because these were readily perceptible and were ascertained by known and established rules: "I mean the maxims and principles of the common law of our land." This law the ancestors had brought here and, with occasional "accomodating exceptions" in the nature of local custom, was the law in every part of the Union at the time of the national compact, "and did of course attach upon or apply to it for the purpose of the exposition and enforcement." Ellsworth conceived that the parties to the compact, acting in their sovereign capacity, might have discontinued the law with

---

[80] United States v. Naire Smith; United States v. Pardon Smith (two indictments); United States v. Samuel Spring and Richard Graham. Ms. Final Record Book Circuit Ct. Massachusetts Dist. 1790–1799, *sub* June term 1797. The indictments are among the Ms. Case Papers *sub nom.*

[81] Sec. 14.

[82] The report is from 6 Dane, *Abridgment* (1824), 718–19. The date there given, June 1792, is incorrect.

respect to their new relation but this was not to be presumed, "and it is a supposition irreconcilable with those frequent references in the constitution to the common law as a living code."[83]

Three months later Ellsworth was further to commit himself at the trial of Isaac Williams at the September term of the Circuit Court for the Connecticut District.[84] Defendant, as we have seen, offered a sworn statement the purport of which was to the effect that after entering French service in 1792 he had sailed to France and had there been naturalized and had become domiciled in Guadaloupe. In charging the trial jury, Ellsworth told them they were not to regard the offer of proof, for "The common law of this country remains the same as it was before the Revolution." The force and effect of this was that the common law rule of indelible allegiance was treated as remaining in effect. Ellsworth justified this not on the classical ground of the bond of ligeance between subject and king, but on the ground that all members of civil community were bound to each other by compact and that one of the parties to the compact could not dissolve it by his own act.

Ellsworth was well berated by the anti-Federalist press for this charge because, as will shortly be noticed, the question of the federal common law had become a matter of violent party controversy. It had also become a subject of differing opinions among the Justices of the Supreme Court, for in his instruction Ellsworth's views were in flat contradiction to those set out the year before by his colleague Samuel Chase in the famous case of *United States v. Worrall*.

At the Circuit for the Pennsylvania District, April term 1798, the grand jury had found an indictment against one Worrall for attempting to bribe Tench Coxe, Commissioner of Revenue, "in contempt of the laws and constitution of the said United States . . . and against the peace and dignity of the United States."[85] Defendant was found guilty April 26 and it was moved in arrest and argued that the common law was not the law of the United States and that the crime charged was "not recognized by the Federal Code, constitutional or legislative." United States Attorney Rawle retorted with a policy argument that the jurisdiction was essential to good government, and unless the offense was punishable in the federal courts, it was certainly not cognizable in state courts.

Chase J., who was sitting with Peters J., would have none of this.

---

[83] Text in *Farmer's Museum, or Lay Preacher's Gazette*, June 17, 1799. Ellsworth's change of heart is graphically illustrated by contrasting this charge with the pallid charge at Savannah, Apr. 25, 1796, reprinted in

H. Flanders, *Lives and Times of the Chief Justices of the Supreme Court* . . . , II, 189–91.
[84] *Supra*, p. 614, n. 23.
[85] The case is reported in 2 Dallas 384, and in Wharton, *State Trials*, 189.

In his opinion the United States as a federal government had no common law and consequently no indictment could be maintained in federal courts for offenses merely at common law. So far as the states were concerned, the settlers had brought with them as a birthright so much of the common law as was applicable to their circumstances. Each state judged for itself what this was. The result was that the whole of the common law had nowhere been introduced and the greatest diversity had resulted from this process of selection. The United States had not brought the common law from England, the Constitution did not create it and no Act of Congress had assumed it. Peters J. disagreed. He thought the power to punish misdemeanors to be one of which the United States was constitutionally possessed and that the indictment was within the jurisdiction of the court by virtue of section 11 of the Judiciary Act. The judges and the United States Attorney wished to put the case in such form that it would be taken to the Supreme Court, but counsel for the defendant declined, with the result that Worrall was fined and imprisoned.

The Chase opinion was cited almost immediately as a precedent by counsel in the proceedings initiated June 26, 1798, against Benjamin Franklin Bache, editor of the *Aurora*. He was taken on a warrant and charged with libelling the President and the executive government. Brought before Peters J., Dallas and Levy, counsel for defendant, on the strength of Chase's opinion, denied that the court could take cognizance of a libel at common law. They spoke to deaf ears, because Peters had disagreed with Chase, so Bache was bound over for trial.[86] At this juncture the Senate bill to "Define more Particularly the Crime of Treason and Punish the Crime of Sedition" had its first reading.[87] Whether in anticipation of passage or not, Secretary of State Pickering sent out instructions to the New York District Attorney regarding initiating proceedings for libel, obviously at common law, against one Burke, editor of the *Time Piece*, and one Durrell, an upstate printer.[88] Such

---

[86] Reliance on this defense noted by Bache in reporting his arrest (*Aurora*, June 27, 1798). The proceedings before Peters, *ibid.*, June 30, 1798. D. Malone, *Jefferson and the Ordeal of Liberty*, 384n., states that Bache was "brought into federal court," and his text indicates that the editor was indicted. This is, of course, not so as the Circuit Court was not in session and the next term was in the fall, by which time Bache was dead.

[87] *Annals of Congress*, VII, 589–90. The text of the bill "to define more particularly the crime of Treason, and

to define and punish the crime of Sedition" is in the *Aurora*, June 27, 1798.

[88] Pickering to Harison, July 7, 1798, Ms. Pickering Papers, XXXVII, 315 (MHS); same to same, June 20, 1798, *ibid.*, VIII, 604. In his letter of July 7 about Burke, Pickering expected Harison to function as an investigator of Burke's alienage. At this time all the alien statutes had been enacted. These acts are not being here discussed as there were no prosecutions.

were the bitter fruits of the successful coup of making the District Attorneys quasi-dependents of the Department of State.[89]

We do not know how competent a lawyer Pickering may have been or how conversant he was with the sometimes delicate questions of federal jurisdiction. The *Worrall* case could hardly have escaped his attention, for he was something of a newspaper reader, as events were to prove. It was consequently an incautious exercise of his supervisory authority to direct a local prosecutor to proceed as at common law. The Sedition Act was to afford the Executive through the Secretary of State the opportunity of ordering prosecutions *ad libitum*, and as to such, signs were to develop, disquieting to Republicans, of increased centralization of authority. This statute and its enforcement must be considered in some detail, not only because in the controversies over it the question of federal common law was raised, but also because of novel procedural problems. Liberty has probably not shed her last tear over its iniquities, but the questions that concern us here are best viewed with dry eyes.

THE SEDITION ACT—PROSECUTIONS AND THE PROBLEMS OF LAW

LONG BEFORE THE passage of the Sedition Act, the Federalists fancied they heard the deathwatch beetles at work on the beams of the New Roof. As criticism mounted, fomented by their adversaries, the Federalists developed a sensitivity to it unparalleled in our history, a sensitivity that even the prospect of a French war does not fully explain. But the pride of power was theirs, and so unregarding the old saw that "there is no fence against tyranny," they sought the illusory protection of an oppressive statute. Even if there had been agreement that under the Constitution prosecutions for seditious libel, as well as for unlawful

---

[89] J. M. Smith, in *Freedom's Fetters*, 182–83, casts Pickering in the role of a witch hunter. He omits to explain that directions to District Attorneys to prosecute for crimes had been settled in the Department of State. There is no doubt that Pickering activated both investigations and prosecutions under the Sedition Act. Cf. his letters to Rawle, July 5, 1799, regarding a German paper at Reading, Pennsylvania (Ms. Pickering Papers, XI, 390 [MHS]), and of July 24, 1799, regarding the *Aurora* (*ibid.*, 486); to Hollingsworth of Maryland, Aug. 12, 1799, regarding the *Balti-* *more American* (*ibid.*, 603); to Nelson of Virginia, Aug. 14, 1799, regarding the *Richmond Examiner* (*ibid.*, 611). But there were other directions about other law enforcement problems; cf. the circular to the District Attorneys of Georgia, South Carolina, North Carolina and Tennessee, Aug. 3, 1797, regarding a scheme of settling Indian lands (*ibid.*, VII, 16); and the circular to the District Attorneys of Massachusetts, New York and South Carolina, May 6, 1799, regarding a ring of counterfeiters (*ibid.*, XI, 40).

combinations to oppose government measures, would lie at common law, this would not have satisfied the Federalist legislators. It was their design to protect the "government," both houses of Congress and the President from public reproach in the form of "false scandalous and malicious" writings, and to make punishable combinations or conspiracies to oppose any measures of the government and the procurement or attempts to procure insurrections, riots and unlawful assemblies. As noticed, the bill had originated in the Senate but it underwent considerable modification in the House. The arguments there advanced by the promoters of the bill were not remarkable for consistency, for while Chase's opinion in *United States v. Worrall* was tendered as a reason why statutory regulation was necessary,[90] it was also argued that the common law had been adopted by the Constitution, and that this justified the enactment of the statute with its alteration and mitigation of the common law doctrine of sedition. The position of the Jeffersonian Republicans, founded on their doctrine of strict construction, was that full common law jurisdiction was not conferred by the Constitution, nor did this instrument give power to pass a law for the punishment of libels.[91]

Of no less import was the debate on the question of the conflict of the proposed law with the guarantees of the First Amendment, discussed at length, chiefly in the context of a free press. If there was any inquiry into trespass upon the safeguards of freedom of assembly and of petition, which were no less involved in the section dealing with seditious practices and conspiracies, this was not reported. Perhaps the evidence of Senator Blount's conspiracy[92] was too fresh in Congress's mind for this portion of the bill to have been given the flaying which the rest of it suffered. The act, to remain in force until March 3, 1801, was approved July 14, 1798.

The House debates had promised that in some way or manner the issue of constitutionality would be precipitated in prosecutions for violations of the act. This was a matter of moment, for the prosecutions were to be the first to raise the question of how the safeguards of the Bill of Rights could be practically asserted. This, as we shall shortly see, was a problem that confronted defense counsel from the very

---

[90] *Annals of Congress*, VIII, 2113.

[91] The debates in the House began July 5, 1798, and continued with interruptions into July 10 (*ibid.*, 2094–2171).

[92] Papers relating to this had been submitted by the President on July 3, 1797. The Senate had expelled Blount July 8, 1797. On this day the House appointed a committee to prepare articles of impeachment. Report was made Nov. 30, 1797; all the documents were appended. The two houses were occupied with procedural detail until Apr. 16, 1798. *Cf.* Wharton, *State Trials*, 200–321; see also *Annals of Congress*, VIII, 2319–2415. The impeachment proceedings were at the next session.

commencement of the enforcement of the new law. There were other problems novel to the judges bred to the common law that called for solution, because the legislators did not choose to adopt the practice standard in England until 1792, viz., that the jury was confined to finding the fact of publication and the truth of the innuendos, but that it remained with the court on the basis of such a verdict to determine whether there had been a libel as a matter of law.[93] Fox's Libel Act of 1792, which purported to be declaratory of the common law, had provided that on the trial of an indictment or information for libel the jury might give a general verdict upon the whole matter at issue and should not be directed by the judge to find the defendant guilty merely on proof of publication of the papers charged and of the sense thereof ascribed in the indictment.[94] It was further provided that the judge on a trial for libel should, "according to his discretion," give his opinion and direction to the jury on the matters in issue in the same way as in other criminal cases.

The effect of Fox's Libel Act upon the new Act of Congress[95] is apparent in the direction of its third section that "the jury which shall try the cases shall have a right to determine the law and the fact under the direction of the judge." The Congress, however, went further than Parliament for it provided that "it shall be lawful for the defendant upon the trial of the cause to give evidence of the truth of the matter contained in the publication charged as a libel."

The changes introduced by the Sedition Act posed some questions for the solution of which the available precedents of English trial of informations or indictments for libel were of little assistance. The most complete accounts of such trials were available in *State Trials*, but in the state of the common law prior to 1792 the rulings on questions of evidence were of no help in dealing with the Sedition Act. This was true also of instructions to the jury because questions of law had been withheld from it. Nevertheless, on the matter of intent the eighteenth century judges, and Mansfield among them, did not forbear in their charges from comment on this and from expatiating on the wicked character and tendency of the writing.[96] Such charges were not the best models for federally-minded judges.

---

[93] The classical statement of the old law was made by Mansfield in 1784 in Rex v. Shipley (known familiarly as the Case of the Dean of St. Asaph), published as a note to Rex v. Withers, 3 Term Rep. 428 (1789). The full proceedings including Erskine's speeches, in 21 Howell, *State Trials* (1814), 847 *et seq.* Erskine and Welch published their arguments and those of Judges Mansfield, Willes and Ashurst in 1785.

[94] 32 Geo. III, c. 60.

[95] 1 *U.S. Stats.*, 596.

[96] *Cf.* Erskine's speech in 21 Howell, *State Trials*, at 1011–12 (Rex v. Shipley). Mansfield's riposte, *ibid.*, 1035–36.

The most difficult questions that both counsel and courts had to face up to in the trial of indictments under the Sedition Act related to the limits of the burden on defendant when he sought to establish the truth of the alleged libellous matter. The statute did not authorize a special plea and consequently the matter in justification had to be offered under the general issue. The common law precedents were explicit that this could not be done. It had been attempted, but in the *Case of the Dean of St. Asaph* Mansfield had explained why it was not proper to leave evidence of lawful excuse to the jury. In his view this involved two questions: one of fact for the jury—whether the facts alleged existed; and one of law—whether the facts amounted to an excuse or justification in law—which was for the court. The effect of this under the then extant exclusion of the jury's right to consider matters of law in prosecutions for libel was to make irrelevant proof of justification except in mitigation of the sentence.[97]

English Crown law precedents were completely disestablished by the Sedition Act and so, too, the little fragments of law in the treatises on evidence. What remained to help the judges found their rulings were the precedents relating to civil actions for libel that were more liberally conceived than those relating to criminal prosecutions. Here the federal judges were prepared to show no more respect for the artificial distinctions observed in England between civil and criminal precedents than they had in the case of motions for new trial.[98]

The English courts had consistently been more stiff-necked about permitting justification in the case of written than of spoken defamatory words, the notion being that a libel was a durable scandal and one susceptible of broad circulation. Consequently it had been only in slander actions that justification was first tolerated, but this had been something narrowly conceived and confined to such defenses as that the words were spoken innocently or on an occasion that warranted publication, and initially this could only be done if defendant pleaded specially.[99] There was reluctance to permit evidence of the truth of the words, and the limit of tolerance appears to have been to allow such evidence to be offered in mitigation of damages.[100] However, in 1744 it was determined by a majority of the judges at a meeting that evidence of truth could not be offered under the general issue but must be pleaded so that the

---

[97] *Supra,* n. 93.
[98] *Supra,* p. 611.
[99] Lord Cromwell's Case, 4 Coke Rep. 12 (1578–81). This case has been taken to support the proposition that truth was always a defense, but the language does not bear out this contention. The special plea had to traverse and answer the whole of the declaration; it was defective if only a part was justified (Johns v. Gittings, Cro. Eliz. 239 [1590]).
[100] Per Holt, Smithies v. Harrison, 1 Ld. Raymond 727 (Summer Assizes, 3 Wm. III).

plaintiff might be prepared to defend himself as well as to prove the speaking of the words.[101]

Because the courts regarded libel as a distinct tort, the rules evolved respecting slander were not extended out of hand. Lord Hardwicke declared in 1735 that he had never heard justification being even hinted at; the most permitted had been to give evidence of the truth in mitigation of damage.[102] This was the doctrine propagated in the 1768 edition of Bacon's *Abridgment*,[103] the golden book of post-Revolutionary American practitioners. There is, however, some reason to believe that within less than a decade special pleas in justification in actions for libel were admitted.[104] Such, of course, would determine the scope of the evidence. This question came up for decision in King's Bench in 1787. Here the writing consisted of a statement charging plaintiff with being a common swindler, member of a gang of swindlers, sharing their spoil and diverse other inflammatory descriptive terms. Defendant's plea was no more than a repetition of the charge in terse form, "wherefor he printed and published etc." The plea was sustained in Common Pleas on special demurrer but on error to King's Bench the judgment was reversed. The plea was bad because of its generality. When defendant took it upon himself to justify generally the swindling charge, he must be prepared with the facts which constitute the charge. If defendant could support the charge that plaintiff had defrauded divers persons, it must be known to him who had been defrauded and they must be called to prove the particular acts of fraud. Defendant could not prove the justification as pleaded by "general evidence"; he had no justification unless he could prove the special instances.[105]

Although the decision here was in the context of a defective plea in bar, the statement regarding proof in justification was broad enough to be applied where evidence was offered under the general issue. Because the *Term Report* where the case reported can be proved to have been used here in the early 1790's,[106] it seems to us probable that it was to this source that the judges turned in settling upon what defendant's burden of producing evidence amounted to.

The five cases about which we possess information regarding the defense represent about one third of the total number of indictments for

---

[101] Underwood v. Parks, 2 Strange 1200.

[102] King v. Roberts, a ms. case cited in F. L. Holt, *Law of Libel* (1st Am. ed. 1818), 281.

[103] Bacon, *Abridgment*, III, 495.

[104] Newman v. Bailey (1776), a ms. case cited by counsel in J'Anson v. Stuart, 1 Term Rep. 748, 750 (1787).

[105] J'Anson v. Stuart, 1 Term Rep.

748 (1787), per Ashurst and Buller.

[106] *E.g.*, Webster v. Stevenson's Ex'r., Md. Gen'l Ct. 1793, 3 Harris & McHenry 131, 135; Hecking v. Howard, *ibid.*, 203 (1794); Marshall v. Montgomery, Pa. Sup. Ct. 1792, 2 Dallas 170; Haldane v. Duche's Ex'r., *ibid.*, 176 (1792); Cochran v. Street, Va. Ct. of Appeals, 1 Washington 80, 81 (1792).

violation of the second section of the Sedition Act that came to trial.[107] Our information is not the most trustworthy, for with the exception of *United States v. Callender* where a portion of the case was taken in shorthand by a practicing lawyer, details come from newspapers or other partisan accounts.

At the first trial under the act, *United States v. Matthew Lyon*, Paterson J. presiding, the indictment charged the truculent congressman with the writing, printing and publication of a libel which, among other things, had commented that on the part of the Executive he (Lyon) had seen that considerations of public welfare had been swallowed up in a continuous grasp for power, in an unbounded thirst for ridiculous pomp, foolish adulation and selfish avarice. A second count charged the publication of a letter from Joel Barlow, then in France, which referred to a "bullying" speech of Adams, a "stupid" answer by the Senate and a suggestion that the Congress had better have sent an order committing Adams to the madhouse. It does not appear from the notes of testimony kept by Paterson that Lyon made any effort to establish the truth of his publication. But according to the press, Lyon,[108] who was conducting his own defense, made an impertinent attempt to do so when he asked the judge whether he had not frequently dined with the President and observed his ridiculous pomp and parade. This was, to say the least, irregular, but Paterson replied that he had dined rarely with the President and had never seen pomp or parade but rather much plainness and simplicity. Paterson did not deign to reply to a question whether there was not more pomp and servants there than at the Rutland tavern. Paterson did not comment upon this phase of Lyon's defense. He did direct that in order to find a verdict of guilty the jury must be satisfied beyond all reasonable substantial doubt that "the hypothesis of innocence is unsustainable."[109] Lyon was convicted.

Paterson again presided more than a year and a half later at the Circuit Court for the Vermont District at the trial of Anthony Haswell.[110] The first count of the indictment charged publication in Haswell's news-

---

[107] Smith, *Freedom's Fetters*, 185, states that fourteen verifiable indictments under the Sedition Act were found. To his list may be added United States v. Shaw, in Ms. Docket No. 26, October term 1799, Circuit Ct. Vermont Dist. Smith's count obviously does not include some of the indictments under sec. 1 that were returned against some participants in the Fries rebellion. A number of the indictments under sec. 2 never reached the trial stage because defendants changed their pleas.

[108] The indictment is in Ms. Docket No. 24, October term 1799, Circuit Ct. Vermont Dist. There is an account of the trial in Wharton, *State Trials*, 333–44. The notes of the trial kept by Paterson are in the Bancroft Transcripts (NYPL).

Lyon was a Representative for Vermont in Congress from which he had narrowly missed expulsion for a violent fracas with Griswold of Connecticut.

[109] Wharton, *State Trials*, 336.
[110] *Ibid.*, 684–87.

paper of an advertisement inserted by a group of Lyon's friends to promote a lottery to raise money for payment of Lyon's fine but it embodied comment on the cruel treatment of Lyon by the marshal during the former's confinement. This count was inartfully drawn in that the prosecutor seems to have been under the misapprehension that all federal officers were covered by the Sedition Act. The second count charged publication in the *Vermont Gazette* of some remarks about Adams' appointment of Tories to office, "men who had fought against our independence who had shared in the desecration of our homes and the abuse of our wives, sisters and daughters."[111] To justify the statement regarding the marshal's harsh treatment, defendant produced witnesses to testify to this. Paterson charged the jury that unless the justification "came up to the charge" it was no defense.[112] It was for the jury to determine whether the violent language applied to the marshal had been sustained by the evidence. No attempt had been made to justify the remarks about the administration's employment of Tories "who shared in the desolation of our homes." If the jury believed beyond a reasonable doubt that the intent was defamatory and that the publication was made, they must convict. This they did.

Paterson's charge as published is not without its ambiguities, but it can be read as directing that what was offered by way of excuse or justification must traverse the alleged libellous publication in its entirety. Chase J., instructing the jury in *United States v. Cooper* (April 1800), described the burden upon the defendant clearly and pithily: "the traverser in his defense must prove every charge he had made to be true; he must prove it to the marrow."[113] The defendant, Thomas Cooper,[114] an English radical who had immigrated to the United States, had composed and printed as a handbill an attack on the President. He had invited arrest and prosecution by handing his composition to a justice of the peace, as if, in Chase's words, he "was going to part with an estate." Like Congressman Lyon, Cooper conducted his own defense. He had had some experience as a barrister, but the defects in his training are evident from his plea. It stated, "The above named defendant (protesting against The Insinuations and constructions in the said Indictment alledged against him) pleads not guilty of this he puts himself on his Country and will give the following facts in evidence on the

---

[111] The indictment is in Ms. Docket No. 24, October term 1799, Circuit Ct. Vermont Dist. The text in Wharton is not an exact copy.

[112] Wharton, *State Trials*, 686.

[113] *Ibid.*, 659 at 676. The minute entries, Ms. Mins. Circuit Ct. Pennsylvania Dist., Oct. 1799–Apr. 1800,

sub Apr. 14, 19 and 24, 1800. Among the Ms. Case Papers are the handbill containing the libellous matter charged and Cooper's plea.

[114] On his career, D. Malone, *The Public Life of Thomas Cooper 1783–1839.*

Trial in justification of the supposed Libel stated in the aforesaid Indictment." There followed twelve propositions, the text of which is set forth below.[115]

Cooper was given great latitude in what he was permitted to offer in his defense; indeed, he was given better than a week to collect his evidence. Chase J. had refused to subpoena the President. When, however, defendant requested invitations to testify be issued to members of Congress,[116] Chase ordered subpoenas, commenting that the Constitution gave the right of compulsory process and he knew of no privilege to exempt members of Congress. There was some delay in the arrival of the congressmen at court, but although they were in attendance for most of the trial, defendant called upon none of them to testify.[117] Cooper was found guilty and with commendable perversity refused Adams' pardon.

Chase was to make a further amplification of what he conceived to be the proofs that a defendant must offer in establishing the truth of the matter alleged to be libellous. This occurred in *United States v. Callender* at the May term (1800) of the Circuit Court for the Virginia

---

[115] Plea, United States v. Cooper, Ms. Case Papers, Circuit Ct. Pennsylvania Dist.:

I That Mr Adams either by himself or by the Officers of State acting under his authority has given the Public to understand that he w^d bestow no Office but on persons who conformed to his political Opinions.

II Mr Adams has declared that a Republican Governm^t may mean anything.

III Mr Adams did sanction the Alien Law, and thereby the abolition of the Trial by Jury in the Cases that fall under that Law.

IV Mr Adams did sanction the Sedition Law & thereby entrenched his public character behind the legal provisions of that Law.

V Under the auspices of Mr Adams the expence of a permanent Navy is saddled on the People.

VI Under the auspices of Mr Adams we are threatened with the existence of a Standing Army.

VII The Government of the United States has borrowed Money at 8 per Cent in time of Peace.

VIII The unnecessary Violence of official Expressions used by Mr Adams, and those in authority under him, & his adherents, might justly have provoked a War.

IX Political Acrimony has been fostered by those who call themselves his friends and adherents.

X Mr Humphries after being convicted of an assault and Battery on Benjamin Franklin Bache the printer of the Aurora merely from political motives, was before his Sentence was expired, promoted by Mr Adams to a public Office viz to carry dispatches to France.

XI Mr Adams did project and put in execution embassies to Prussia Russia and the Sublime Porte.

XII Mr Adams in the case of Jonathan Robbins alias Nash did interfere to influence the decision of a Court of Justice.

[116] 4 Dallas 341.

[117] A fact which was to cause some sardonic comment in Congress. *Annals of Congress*, X, 930, 934–37 (Jan. 21, 1801).

District.[118] The defendant, one of the reptilian adornments of contemporary journalism, had published a political tract, *The Prospect Before Us*, a rambling vituperative arraignment of Federalist administration past and present. The very diffuseness and variety of the book's calumnies made difficult the proofs in justification.

The indictment[119] consisted of two counts; in each count twenty different sets of words from *The Prospect Before Us* were set out and charged as libellous. Each set of words was taken, in the terminology of the times, to be a separate charge. When the prosecution had finished presenting the case for the United States and had summed up,[120] defendant's counsel made no opening statement but offered John Taylor of Caroline as a witness.[121] At the moment that he was sworn, Chase inquired of counsel what they intended to prove by the witness. Counsel answered that they intended to examine Taylor to prove that Adams had avowed principles in his presence that justified Callender in saying that the President was an aristocrat; that he had voted against the sequestration law, and against the resolutions concerning the suspension of commercial intercourse with Britain by which he had defeated every effort of those who were in favor of those beneficial measures that were calculated to promote the happiness of this country.

Counsel were evidently planning to begin *in medias res*, as it were, for the witness was to justify the twelfth charge. "He (meaning the said President of the United States) was a professed aristocrat; he (meaning the said President of the United States) had proved faithful to the British interest (innuendo against the interest and welfare of the United States.)"

Chase demanded that the questions to the witness be reduced to writing. Counsel objected that this had not been required of the pros-

---

[118] Wharton, *State Trials*, 688–721.

[119] The full text of the indictment is printed in *Report of the Trial of the Hon. Samuel Chase . . .* (Evans) Exhibits, 48 *et seq.* The grand jury presentment on which the indictment was founded is in Ms. Case Papers, Ended Cases 1800 (Va. State Library): "We the grand jury present James Thomson Callendar, whom we find to have been the publisher of a book with this title 'The Prospect before Us,' which contains several passages tending to defame the Government, the President and the Congress of the United States, and to bring them into contempt, and disrepute, contrary to an Act of Congress. . . ."

District Attorney Nelson did not include the title in the bill of indictment. When the prosecution offered the book in evidence defense counsel George Hay, who had already admitted that "he was but little acquainted with the doctrine of libels," objected because the title was not mentioned in the indictment. Chase's position was that the prosecutor must prove publication of a false, scandalous and malicious writing with intent to defame the President. This could be done without reciting the title.

[120] The complete summation in *Report of the Trial of the Hon. Samuel Chase . . .* (Evans) 82–88.

[121] Wharton, *State Trials*, 706.

We the grand jury present James Thomson
Callender, whom we find to have been the
publisher of a book, which contains several passages tending
to defame the Government, the President,
and the Congress, of the United States, and to
bring them into contempt, and disrepute,
contrary to an act of Congress, entitled "An Act
in addition to the act of Congress, entitled an
act for the punishment of certain crimes
against the United States.

James M. Glass foreman

ecution when he introduced his witnesses and that it was "not according to the practice of the State courts."[122] He did not know what the witness would exactly prove but he wanted the latter to state all that he knew which applied to the defense. Chase explained his reason: "Juries are only to hear legal evidence, and the court are the only judges of what is or is not legal evidence to support the issue joined between the parties." Illegal evidence once heard would make a wrong impression and therefore should not be heard by a jury at all. The prosecutor in opening his cause had stated the purpose for which he introduced the witnesses.

Counsel was claiming too much when they alluded to the practice of state courts. They were wrong as to neighboring Maryland, for at the Chase impeachment trial only five years later, Luther Martin, a Maryland practitioner of long experience and counsel for Chase, testified that it was the regular practice in that state for questions to be committed to writing either at the request of counsel or at the direction of the court.[123] They were wrong even as to Virginia, for Chief Justice Marshall, a reluctant witness at Chase's impeachment trial, testified that it was not unusual to require counsel to reduce questions to writing, and listed situations where this might be done. In response to a question whether this was done after the court had heard the questions and not before they were propounded, Marshall admitted of his own practice in Virginia he never knew it to be done in the first instance.[124]

As a result of Chase's ruling, Callender's attorneys wrote out the first questions it was proposed to put to Taylor: "1. Did you ever hear Mr. Adams express any opinion favorable to monarchy and aristocracy and what were they? 2. Did you ever hear Mr. Adams whilst Vice President express his disapprobation of the funding system? 3. Do you know whether Mr. Adams did not in the year 1794, vote against the sequestration law, and the bill for suspending commercial intercourse with Great Britain?"[125]

---

[122] *Ibid.* The objection here was made by defense counsel Philip N. Nicholas, attorney general of Virginia. There are ambiguities in the report, for the reference to the practice of the state courts may relate to the submission of questions in writing or to the rule that counsel should not call witnesses without opening to court the nature of the evidence it was intended to examine to. On this rule, King v. Rookwood, 4 F. Hargrave, *State Trials* (4th ed. 1777), 661 (1696); 1 L. MacNally, *Rules of Evidence on Pleas of the Crown* (Am. ed. 1804), 14.

[123] *Report of the Trial of the Hon. Samuel Chase . . .* (Evans), 209–10. Philip B. Key had already drawn attention to the Maryland practice (*ibid.*, 157).

[124] 1 *Trial of Samuel Chase* (Smith and Lloyd), 257. The version of Marshall's answer in the Evans edition of the trial (*supra*, n. 123) at 70 is different and more positive as to the court's power: "If doubts are suggested as to the propriety of the question, the judges will do right to have it reduced to writing."

[125] Wharton, *State Trials*, 706–07n.

Chase declared that the evidence was inadmissible. No evidence was admissible which did not prove the whole charge. There were two points embraced in the particular charge. Both had to be proved or nothing was proved. If counsel did not prove the whole of a particular charge but only a part of it, the evidence could not be received. This was the law in both civil and criminal cases; "he who justifies, must justify an entire charge or else his defense does not amount to a justification in law."[126]

Chase made it clear that he feared an argumentative justification of a trivial, unimportant part of a charge might be urged before a jury as a substantial vindication of the whole and would be misleading. Counsel suggested that it might be proper to prove one part of a charge by one witness and another part by another witness, but Chase would not have this—it would be irregular and subversive of every principle of law to admit an argumentative establishment of a minute part of a charge by one witness and another part by another.[127] With this District Judge Cyrus Griffin agreed.

Counsel for Callender then remarked that he supposed that the evidence would support the whole charge, which he wished to do, but did not know if it was in the power of the defense. He suggested that he could prove the statement that Adams was a professed aristocrat by reference to the President's opus *In Defence of the American Constitutions*, and the later part by establishing what had happened in the Senate on the two measures defeated by Adams' casting votes. Both these last occurrences had taken place when Taylor was Senator. The United States Attorney Nelson objected to the admission of irregular testimony, and claimed that under "universal principle of law" the *Journals* of the Senate were the best evidence of the votes there. Chase suggested to him that he permit the written questions be put, irregular though these were, but the District Attorney refused to consent. No further effort by defense to introduce testimony was made. Some of Chase's rulings and

---

[126] *Ibid.*, 707.

[127] Robertson, who took down part of the Callender trial in shorthand, when he later testified at the Chase trial read from the printed copy of his account which he had compared with his shorthand notes (*Report of the Trial of the Hon. Samuel Chase* . . . [Evans], 73 *et seq.*) At various junctures he explicitly recorded only the substance of argument or testimony, a fact not noted by Wharton. Unfortunately for the purposes of our inquiry, viz., the basis for the ruling on admissibility, Robertson's report of Chase's answer to counsel's suggestion is incomplete. He states: "Judge Chase, in answer, repeated some of his former arguments . . ." (*ibid.*, 90). William Marshall, Clerk of the Court, testified in 1805 that the judge had said: "Suppose a man should say that I was a scoundrel, a rogue, and an ugly fellow; he is indicted for it, and pleads not guilty. On the trial he proves I am a very ugly fellow, will any man say that this will justify him for saying that I was a scoundrel and a rogue?" (*ibid.*, 67).

his manner of expressing his conclusions reveal his familiarity with the relation of pleading and evidence in both slander and libel actions, and with the more recently established English rules respecting evidence in justification, viz., that where the necessity of pleading was waived and justification allowed to be given in evidence, this must go to the whole charge in each case.[128]

None of this weighed with contemporary and later critics of the federal judges' handling of the statutory defense of truth in justification, for these critics were either unaware of or ignored the fact that testimony in judicial proceedings was a matter regulated by rules of law, many of long standing. Defense counsel, where they possessed any competence, were under no illusions about the applicability of such rules. It is significant that no effort was made by them in any of the cases where truth was offered to move for a new trial, a course which offered little probability of success because no well-founded rules of evidence could have been advanced to counter those applied by the trial courts.

We come at length to the crucial gambit of the defense in the *Callender* case—the attack on the constitutionality of the Sedition Act and the bold but fruitless attempt to have this issue treated as one for the jury alone to determine. This was not an ingenious concoction of counsel. It had, so to speak, a pre-history which should be looked into before relating the climactic moments at Richmond. From the first the Jeffersonian Republicans had claimed that the statute was unconstitutional, a contention based upon their doctrine of strict construction of the Constitution. Collateral was the proposition that the issue of constitutionality was a matter for the jury. The attempt to throw into the hands of the jury a function which the Circuit judges had already been exercising was a direct challenge to the long-seated assumption that this was an incident of judicial power. It may properly be taken as a preliminary to the assault on the judiciary that was to follow. The state of our sources is such that we cannot be certain how often the issue of the jury competence was raised and pressed at trial, nor are the later mar-

---

[128] This is borne out by the later explanation in Chase's answer to the third article of impeachment: "Admitting, therefore, these two phrases [charge 12 of the indictment] to constitute one distinct charge, and one entire offence, this respondent considers and states it to be law, that no justification which went to part only of the offence, could be received. The plea of justification must always answer the whole charge, or it is bad on the demurrer; for this plain rea-son, that the object of the plea is to shew the party's innocence; and he cannot be innocent, if the accusation against him be supported in part. Where the matter of defence may be given in evidence, without being formally pleaded, the same rules prevail. The defence must be of the same nature, and equally complete, in one case as in the other." *Report of the Trial of the Hon. Samuel Chase . . .* (Evans), Exhibits, 22–23.

tyrologies of the prosecuted of much help. The matter was raised in the *Lyon* case, the first and widely publicized prosecution under the statute, and was definitively disposed of at the *Callender* trial less than two years later.

Ironically enough, it was not from the Republican but the Federalist side that warnings of a possible enlargement of the jury's function had first emanated. James A. Bayard, speaking in the House in opposition to a proposed amendment to the Sedition Bill that "the jury who shall try the cause shall be judges of the law as well as the fact," observed that "the effect of this amendment would be to put it into the power of a jury to declare that this is an unconstitutional law, instead of leaving this to be determined where it ought to be determined, by the Judiciary."[129] Congressman Matthew Lyon of Vermont was present and voting that day (July 9, 1798).[130]

It was three months later that Lyon was indicted for the publication of allegedly libellous statements in violation of the new statute. In addressing the jury in his own defense Lyon claimed among other things that the statute was unconstitutional, and it may be inferred from a newspaper account that he sought to have the jury so find.[131] Paterson J. opened his charge to the jury: "You have nothing to do with the constitutionality or unconstitutionality of the sedition law. Congress has said that the author and publisher of seditious libels is to be punished; and until the law is declared null and void by a tribunal competent for the purpose, its validity cannot be disputed."[132]

The publicity which the *Lyon* case received invited some consideration of judicial policy respecting the manner in which grand juries should be charged but concerning this there was no consensus. The Sedition Act being "An Act in addition to the Act, entitled An Act for the Punishment of certain Crimes against the United States," reference to its terms was properly included in a general charge. Comment on its constitutionality was a matter of judicial perspicacity. Ellsworth's charge to the grand jury for the South Carolina District in June 1799[133] represents

---

[129] *Annals of Congress*, VIII, 2136.

[130] Listed among those voted when the ayes and nays were recorded on the amendment. *Ibid.*, 2137–38.

[131] *Connecticut Courant*, Oct. 29, 1798. Paterson's notes of the trial indicate that the question of constitutionality was one of the heads of Lyon's defense. He does not elaborate. Bancroft Transcripts (NYPL).

[132] Wharton, *State Trials*, 336.

[133] *Supra*, n. 83. It should be noticed that some months earlier Ellsworth had expressed himself forthrightly in

a letter to Pickering, Dec. 12, 1798. Thanking Pickering for a charge of Addison of Pennsylvania, he commented that Addison was "doubtless" right in supposing that the Sedition Act did not create an offense, but by permitting truth to be offered in justification, had effected a diminution of punishable offenses. It had also cut down the rigor of previous penalties. As for the constitutional question, he asked who could say that negating the right to publish slander and sedition was "abridging the freedom of

the extreme of reticence. Iredell's charge at the April 1799[134] term of the Circuit for the Pennsylvania District incorporated a bold repudiation of the Jeffersonian doctrine and a defense of the Federalist view. Chase alone appears to have concerned himself with the question of where the power to determine the constitutionality of a statute was. He entered in his *Charge Book* a statement that:

> If the *Federal* Legislature should, at any time, pass a Law *contrary to the Constitution of the United States, such law* would be *void*; because the Constitution is the *fundamental Law* of the United States, and *paramount* to any Act of the Federal Legislature, whose authority is derived from, and delegated by that Constitution; and which imposes *certain restrictions* on the Legislative Authority that can only be preserved through the medium of the Courts of Justice. The *Judicial* power of the United States is *coexistent, co-extensive,* and *coordinated* with, and altogether independent of the *Legislature* & the *Executive*; and the Judges of the Supreme and District Courts are bound by the oath of office to regulate their decisions *agreeably to the Constitution*. The Judicial powers, therefore, are the only proper and competent authority to decide whether any Law made by Congress, or any of the State Legislatures is contrary to or in violation of the *federal* Constitution.

This charge appears to have been composed in the spring of 1799,[135] and from what we know of Chase's use of his *Charge Book* was probably repeated on a variety of occasions.[136] At this late day the passage quoted does not appear to be as politically abrasive as Iredell's comments on strict construction, but in the light of the doctrines ad-

---

speech & of the press" of a right which ever belonged to it.

Ellsworth reveals his belief in a federal common law when he suggests that if the act should be repealed, the preamble should run "Whereas the increasing danger and depravity of the present time require that the law against seditious practices should be *restored to its former rigor* therefore etc." Ms. Pickering Papers, XXIII, 362 (MHS).

[134] McRee, *Iredell*, II, 551 *et seq.*

[135] This inference is drawn from the changes made in the Ms. Chase Charge Book, 15 (Md. Hist. Soc.), where the original text read: "I have made these observations Gentlemen, in consequence of the former and present insurrections in the Common-

wealth of Pennsylvania." The word "present" is struck out and the word "later" inserted in Chase's hand; "the" before "Commonwealth" is struck and "this" substituted. The Northampton County insurrection occurred in March 1799. Chase was recovering from a long illness in early March and had asked Paterson to hold court for him in New York (Chase to Iredell, Mar. 17, 1799, McRee, *Iredell*, II, 548).

[136] *Cf.* here the testimony of District Judge Winchester describing Chase's use of his book, in I *Trial of Samuel Chase* (Smith and Lloyd), 296. The report of this testimony is less full in Evans' *Report of the Trial of the Hon. Samuel Chase . . . ,* [105*].

647

vanced in the Virginia and Kentucky Resolutions it had at the time definite political overtones.

The impact of these state pronunciamentos is manifest in the argument advanced by the defense in *United States v. Holt* at the Circuit Court for the Connecticut District, April 1800. Justice Bushrod Washington, like Paterson J. at the *Lyon* trial, made no effort to cut off counsel. According to a newspaper account,[137] defense counsel asserted that the powers of the general government, being carved out of the powers of the states, were not to be extended by construction; those powers not delegated to the United States remained with the states. The necessary and proper clause of the Constitution could not extend "to the case in question" and it would be dangerous to extend it by construction. Unfortunately no text of Washington's instructions to the jury has been found.[138] The account just referred to commingles the prosecutor's arguments with what the court said; although the familiar Federalist doctrine of broad construction was laid out, there is no indication that the jury was told that it had nothing to do with determining the constitutionality of the statute. Within a few weeks this was to emerge as the prime issue at the trial of Callender.

That the *Callender* case was planned as a major assault on the constitutionality of the sedition law was revealed a few years after the event. George Hay, who managed Callender's defense, testified at Chase's impeachment trial that he had appeared to defend the cause and not the man, the cause being the Constitution.[139] But whoever the mastermind behind the selection of counsel, it is clear that they were chosen more for their ardor than their professional experience.[140] The initial

---

[137] The New York *Spectator*, Apr. 26, 1800. The account in the *New York Commercial Advertiser*, Apr. 23, 1800, is substantially identical. The rough draft of the indictment is among the Ms. Case Papers 1800, Circuit Ct. Connecticut Dist.

[138] The *Connecticut Gazette*, Apr. 30, 1800, reported only, "Judge Washington in his charge (which was given in an unrivalled manner) established the act to be constitutional, by a train of reasoning too powerful to be resisted. He also proved the publication to be libelous beyond even the possibility of a doubt. . . ."

[139] *Report of the Trial of the Hon. Samuel Chase* . . . (Evans), 37–38.

[140] Wharton (*State Trials*, 718n.) commented that Chase had hardly entered the courthouse "when he saw that the most distinguished lawyers

even in that most distinguished body had been pitched upon to conduct the defence." The correctness of this judgment is open to doubt. George Hay admitted at the trial that he was "but little acquainted with the doctrine of libels" (*ibid.*, 692). At the Chase trial he admitted that the criminal law was "a branch of jurisprudence, with which I am but little acquainted," and in the face of reported cases denied that he had ever heard of a bill of exceptions being taken in a criminal case (*Report of the Trial of the Hon. Samuel Chase* . . . [Evans], 37, 110*).

Philip Norborne Nicholas was about twenty-five years of age at the time of the Callender trial (*DAB sub nom.*). He had been named attorney general of Virginia by Governor Monroe in March 1800 (S.

exertions of counsel had been to secure postponement of the trial. There was a conflict between bench and counsel over the form of challenge and a subsequent and belated objection to the form of the indictment and the admission of the book from which the passages recited in the indictment had been extracted. The propositions of law advanced by the defense were continually questioned by Chase who was at his most imperious and sardonic. The controversy over Taylor's evidence has been earlier related. It was at the conclusion of Chase's ruling on admissibility, when he offered to let counsel enter their objections on the record and indicated his willingness to grant a writ of error (an offer Callender's counsel did not accept), that there was some reason to suspect that Callender was not, as Jefferson had wished, being "substantially defended."[141]

The defense's intention became clear when William Wirt, associate counsel, proceeded to address the jury. He was later to make a name for himself for a florid style of oratory, but Chase at this trial gave him no opportunity. Wirt informed the jury that by the common law, which was part of the law of Virginia, the jury had a right to consider the law as well as the facts, and that their right to consider the law embraced the Constitution. If the law under which defendant was prosecuted was an infraction of the Constitution, it was without legal vigor, and if defendant was guilty under such an act, the jurymen would be violating their oaths.[142]

At this juncture Chase told counsel please to take his seat. The argument being advanced to the petit jury, he said, was irregular and inadmissible: "it is not competent to the jury to decide on this point."[143] If counsel would address themselves to the court, the reasons offered in support of the jury's right would be heard with pleasure. When he had come into Virginia he had heard that the question would be urged. He had deliberately considered the subject and he was ready to explain his reasons for concluding that the petit jury had no right to decide questions of constitutionality. Chase then proceeded to read an opinion (to which we shall later advert) at the conclusion of which he told counsel that he would be glad to hear arguments to show that he was mistaken.

M. Hamilton, ed., *The Writings of James Monroe*, III, 170), and consequently his experience as a prosecutor was hardly one aged in the wood. He admitted at the Chase trial that he had just begun to practice in the federal courts (*Report of the Trial of the Hon. Samuel Chase . . .* [Evans], 42). William Wirt was twenty-eight years of age. He had been a country lawyer practicing at

Culpeper until he came to Richmond in 1799 to be clerk of the House of Delegates (*DAB sub nom.*). Such eminence as these men achieved lay in the future.

[141] Jefferson to Monroe, May 26, 1800, *Works of Jefferson* (Ford, Federal ed.), IX, 135.

[142] Wharton, *State Trials*, 709.

[143] *Ibid.*

What counsel offered to convince Chase that he was mistaken was not impressive. Wirt proceeded with a loose analysis of the jury's right to consider the law and then came forward with what came to be known derisively as the Richmond Syllogism: "Since, then, the jury have a right to consider the law, and since the constitution is law, the conclusion is certainly syllogistic, that the jury have a right to consider the Constitution." "A *non sequitur*, Sir," and Chase, and Wirt sat down.[144] The remainder of the argument for the defense by Nicholas and then Hay, when it did not return to the original proposition, revolved about the question of the court's control of the jury and the right of the latter to determine every question before sentence could be pronounced on the defendant. There was no libel, Hay asserted, "because there is no law in force, under the government of the United States, which defines what a libel is, or prescribes its punishment. It is a universal principle of law," he continued, "that questions of law belong to the court and that the decision of facts belongs to the jury; but a jury have a right to determine both law and facts in all cases."[145] Piqued by a question from the bench on the correctness of this statement of the law, counsel refused further to proceed.

In Chase's charge to the jury he repeated the opinion already read to counsel respecting the role of the jury;[146] he explained the issue and what had to have been proved. The opinion is a document well argued and boldly expressed that at once demolished the claim regarding the jury's competence and laid out the reasons why under the Constitution the power to determine the constitutional validity of statutes resided with the judge. The wrath and anger it provoked in the homeland of the Virginia Resolutions is understandable. That it anticipated the justification of judicial review in *Marbury v. Madison* has earned a footnote.[147] It deserves perhaps more, for John Marshall was present at Callender's

---

[144] *Ibid.*, 710.

[145] *Ibid.*, 711–12.

[146] Text in *Report of the Trial of the Hon. Samuel Chase* . . . (Evans), Exhibits, 65. This is entitled: "A correct copy of the opinion of judge Chase in the case of Callender, as delivered, and refered to in Mr. Robertson's testimony." Wharton did not reproduce this at the point in his account where Chase addressed counsel, but prints it as the full charge to the jury (*State Trials*, 712 *et seq.*). At the Chase trial Robertson, using his notes, testified that the judge read his opinion to the jury, then explained the issue to them, and continued: "He

said that the fact of publication must be proved, and it must appear to be false, scandalous and malicious. He then stated the length of time Mr. Adams had been in the service of his country, and the eminent services that he had rendered it, and added that he was extremely happy that Callender was not a native American" (*Report of the Trial of the Hon. Samuel Chase* . . . [Evans], 94). This conclusion was not printed by Wharton.

[147] Beveridge, *Life of John Marshall*, III, 40, n. 1: "Chase advanced most of the arguments used by Marshall in *Marbury vs. Madison*."

trial when the opinion was delivered;[148] Chase attended the term of the Supreme Court when *Marbury* was decided.

Obedient to Chase's instructions regarding the limits of its competence, the jury returned a verdict of guilty, and thus was brought to a close the last important Sedition Act trial. The violence of the repercussions in the Republican press and the abuse heaped upon Chase served to efface in contemporary discussions consideration of all issues except those of the liberty of the press and the standards of judicial civility. The trial, however, had in two ways contributed to political issues still aflame. In the first place, Chase's pronouncement that the judicial power of the United States was the only proper and competent authority to decide whether any statute made by Congress (or any of the state legislatures) was contrary to, or in violation of, the federal Constitution was a direct challenge and contradiction of the doctrine which had been set out in the Virginia Resolutions in 1798[149]—that "it was competent to the states" to make such determination. In the second place, the Circuit Court had not fallen in with the theories of the defense that at every stage, from process to the role of the jury in formulating its verdict, the law of the state (in this case Virginia) should govern.[150] This theory had involved putting a tension on section 34 of the Judiciary Act which the language could hardly bear, but it was advanced to deny the governance of common law doctrine save only as it had been adopted by act of legislature of the state, was in consequence a part of state law, but in no wise a part of the law of the United States.

THE ATTACKS ON THE JUDICIAL

THE EXERTIONS OF defense counsel to draw the utmost advantage from what may be called the states' rights sections of the Judiciary Act (29 and 34) reflect the current views of Virginia Republicans on the limits of federal judicial authority. These views were, of course, shared

---

[148] See his testimony regarding the trial in *Report of the Trial of the Hon. Samuel Chase . . .* (Evans), 69–71; somewhat fuller in the Smith and Lloyd version, Vol. I, 254–61.

[149] Text in Elliot, *Debates*, IV, 528–32; G. Hunt, ed., *The Writings of James Madison*, VI, 326–31. The more radical Kentucky Resolutions, passed six weeks earlier, are in Elliot, *Debates*, IV, 540–44. Vice President Jefferson's drafts of the latter are in *Works of Jefferson* (Ford, Federal ed.), VIII, 458 *et seq.*

[150] The effort to secure a postponement of the cause on the ground that in Virginia misdemeanors were not triable at the same term at which an indictment was found is an example (Wharton, *State Trials*, 692). It does not appear that counsel referred to sec. 34, but this portion of Wharton's account comes from a newspaper. However, at Chase's impeachment, Art. VI charged his ruling against counsel to be a violation of sec. 34.

by party members elsewhere, but Virginia was the breeding place. Ironically enough, it had been from the Commonwealth that loudest complaint had earlier been raised that the Constitution had not adopted the common law.[151] It was from here that in 1798 the view halloo was raised to chivy unauthorized resort to it. The effects upon federal jurisprudence were to be long-lasting.

The Virginia Resolutions of 1798, a statement of a political philosophy, had made no specific repudiation of a federal common law, but the address to the people which accompanied the document (January 23, 1799)[152] had raised the issue. It was asserted that the argument that one accused under the Sedition Act was allowed to "prove the truth of the charge" did not for a moment disguise the unconstitutionality of the act. Where, it was queried, did the Constitution allow Congress to create crimes and inflict punishments, provided the accused was allowed to exhibit evidence in his defense? Such a doctrine, it was predicated, combined with the assertion that sedition was a common law offense and therefore within the power of Congress, opened at once "the hideous volumes of penal law" and the concomitant evils. Within weeks (February 25, 1799) a committee of the lower house of Congress, reporting in favor of retention of the Sedition Act as a war measure, reiterated the claim that the statute was in affirmance of the common law.[153] Issue may thus be said to have been joined.

It was James Madison who at the end of the year 1799 was to amplify and give specific content to the generalities of the Virginia Resolutions in his report on them—an apology in the classical sense of the word.[154] The purpose of this report was to establish that because the federal jurisdiction was limited to what had been explicitly granted in the Constitution, the Alien and Sedition Acts were unconstitutional. He set out at large the reasons why he believed that the common law had not been established by the Constitution. In this otherwise tedious composition, Madison made the arresting statement that the phrase "cases in law and equity" of Article III "is manifestly confined to cases of a civil nature, and would exclude cases of criminal jurisdiction."[155]

---

[151] *Supra*, c. VII, p. 296.

[152] Text in *Writings of James Madison*, VI, 332–40.

[153] *Annals of Congress*, IX, 2985 at 2989.

[154] *Writings of James Madison*, VI, 341–406; also in Elliot, *Debates*, IV, 546–80.

[155] *Writings of James Madison*, VI, 377. As a clinching argument Madison offered the text of the Eleventh Amendment: "The judicial power of the United States shall not be construed to extend to any suit in *law* or *equity* commenced or prosecuted against one of the United States by citizens of another State or by citizens of any foreign power." Madison stated: "As it will not be pretended that any criminal proceeding could take place against a State, the terms *law* or *equity* must be understood as

The Virginia General Assembly responded handsomely by voting an instruction to the state's Senators and Representatives to oppose passage of any law founded on the principle that the common law of England was in force "under the government of the United States," with exceptions noticed in the margin.[156]

Within less than a fortnight the scene of action moved once more to Congress where Representative Nathaniel Macon of North Carolina submitted a resolution to the effect that the second section of the Sedition Act ought to be repealed "and the offenses therein specified shall remain punishable as at common law" provided that a defendant might give in evidence the truth of the matter charged.[157] Macon's motive is unclear. He thought that the act was unconstitutional, but he failed to explain why a declaration that the offenses remain punishable as at common law was within Congress's powers. An amendment moved by Bayard that the offenses "remain punishable at common law"[158] precipitated a new debate on the subject of the federal common law, for his obvious premise was that the common law was to be regarded as part of the law of the land within the meaning of the Constitution.

Ground already well tilled was harrowed again, but it is worth remarking that except for comments by Robert Goodloe Harper there was no exploration of practical matters.[159] The common law was plainly a contrived issue, for the conflict was essentially one over opposing political philosophies. If there was harbored any notion of influencing the judiciary through the airing of legislative opinion, something better could have been furnished the judge on which to ruminate than the Federalist justification of *salus rei publicae* and the Jeffersonian Republican prediction of two Constitutions, the instrument itself and a rival one built

---

appropriate to *civil* in exclusion of *criminal* cases." Casuistry of this sort needs no comment.

[156] Excepting "such particular parts of the common law, as may have a sanction from the constitution, so far as they are necessarily comprehended in the technical phrases which express the powers delegated to the government; . . . and excepting, also, such other parts thereof as may be adopted by congress as necessary and proper for carrying into execution the powers expressly delegated." Text in St. George Tucker's *Notes on Blackstone's Commentaries* (1803), I, Appendix, 438-39.

[157] *Annals of Congress*, X, 404 (Jan. 23, 1800).

[158] *Ibid.*, 410. The text as given in *Annals* is obviously garbled. This is clearly enough indicated by Gallatin's speech immediately following the motion, and by the text as voted, *ibid.*, 423, upon which we rely. The House *Journal* is of no help—it was, as usual, carelessly kept.

[159] *Ibid.*, 422-23. In reply to those who claimed that there was no common law of the United States yet, "to clear themselves of what they could not get out of otherwise, they called it all a mere matter of form," Harper asked whether the rules of evidence were mere matter of form; where did one go to get a definition of murder except to Hawkins' *Pleas of the Crown*, etc.

by the judges out of the "dark and barbarous pages of the common law."[160]

Although there were lawyers of repute who defended one side or the other in the recurring congressional debates, there was nothing resembling a searching inquiry on a professional level into what was the constitutional warrant for judicial dependence upon the common law. Federalist Harrison Gray Otis in July 1798 had suggested a general reception because of the use of some technical terms from English law.[161] But this advanced the analysis of the problem no further than did Republican Gallatin's concession that only the "principles" of the common law were granted.[162] The problem was never adequately considered on the level it deserved to be because with one exception the chief Republican prolocutors were not professionally equipped so to deal with it. The naiveté displayed regarding rules of evidence when the question of continuing the Sedition Act was discussed in January 1801 attests to this.[163]

The Federalists seem to have been content that the Alien and Sedition Acts should remain the focus of the disputations over the federal common law, for, apart from any other considerations, these statutes could be and were vindicated as parcel of the legislation enacted for national defense, There were other statutes enacted by earlier Congresses, notably the Judiciary Act (for which even Madison had voted) and the Act for the Punishment of certain Crimes (which he does not seem to have opposed), that could have been pressed as *pièces justicatifs*. Demonstrably sections of these were either direct borrowings from the common law or were premised upon a belief that recourse to the common law was warranted by the Constitution. But such was the animus of the Jeffersonian Republicans toward the federal judicial, and in some localities so strong the delusion of the sufficiency of state courts, that except for one incautious reference to the Judiciary Act in July 1798[164] the Federalists seem studiously to have avoided adverting to any acts that dealt with the judiciary. This was a time of short political memories and of kaleidoscopic change in party affiliations, and in politics the doctrine of estoppel has never taken root.

It is apparent from legislative discussions of a federal common law,

---

[160] This prediction was Gallatin's. *Ibid.*, 421. The quotation is from Dallas' speech for the defense at the Blount impeachment trial. *Ibid.*, VIII, 2264 (Jan. 4, 1799).

[161] *Ibid.*, 2145 *et seq.*

[162] To the extent that the courts had jurisdiction. Gallatin, *ibid.*, 2157.

[163] Gallatin: "The gentleman from South Carolina [Harper] had said, that in a certain trial the judge had permitted a book or newspaper to be read, although it was not legal evidence. This shows that the accused was at the mercy of the judge, since he could not claim it as a right." *Ibid.*, X, 951 (Jan. 22, 1801).

[164] *Ibid.*, VIII, 2147.

1798–1801, that when the term "common law" was not qualified by the word "English," the speakers harbored a variety of opinions. Much favored was the view that the common law was a body of principles, a view that left the problem on as imprecise a footing as the law of nature. But there were some who used the term in the sense of legal institutions common to all states, and others who spoke of it in the sense of a law reduced to possession and altered by the several states. The lack of consensus on the meaning of what had become fighting words seems to have blocked consideration of the extent to which the Constitution as amended was an instrument of reception. With the exception of the general direction regarding the Supreme Court's original jurisdiction— and this last is surely a term of art—the explicit references by any definition were all to institutions and procedures of the common law. Neither jointly nor severally could the references support a claim that a general reception was intended. To be sure, the safeguards of the Fifth, Sixth and Seventh Amendments were premised upon the expectation that federal courts would have recourse to the rules and practices of the common law. The articles could hardly be read to authorize the exercise of substantive jurisdiction beyond what was prescribed by statute.

In the course of the disputations over a federal common law, the Republicans did not dissipate their efforts by questioning the application of common law rules in civil actions, although there is no question but that the Circuit judges made free resort thereto. The scope and conduct of commercial transactions had changed so materially since 1787 that state law was as yet unsettled or not to be found—thus precluding resort to the direction of section 34 of the Judiciary Act.[165] It is further to be observed that while the term "common law" was used in this act descriptively or as a word of classification,[166] the statute was so replete with words of art that could have come from no other body of jurisprudence as to amount to an invitation if not a warrant from Congress for the judges to treat the common law and its literature as a source of reference.

The Act for the Punishment of certain Crimes was another pair of shoes, for it ventured into substantive law, specifying certain crimes such as murder, manslaughter, felony on the high seas and perjury in federal courts, without further definition of these terms, and so driving the courts to the books. In other respects the statute held out temptation to the judicial to do things which strict constructionists believed it ought not to do because the statute contained grudging limitations on certain malefactions such as embezzlement, which was limited to military equip-

---

[165] On this *cf. LPAH*, II, cc. III and IV.   [166] *Supra*, c. XI, p. 502.

ment, bribery, which was confined to the judicial officers, and a narrowly conceived obstruction of process section. What had proved to be most immediately embarrassing was the failure to provide adequately for a jurisdiction over offenses against the law of nations.[167] Some of the deficiencies in the specification of acts punishable were to be repaired,[168] but there remained room for unsanctioned enlargement by the courts of this jurisdiction.

The encroachments of the federal judges seem on the whole hardly sufficient to have earned them the reproaches laid to their charge by what Fisher Ames in another connection called "hypochondriac imagination." Their control over the initiation of prosecutions was minimal, as Chase found out at Newcastle in June 1800,[169] and because the defendants were usually indifferently represented, it was rare that the courts were called upon to rule on questions of jurisdiction.

In two particulars, however, the control exercised by the bench over the admissibility of testimony, and the instructions to the petit jury, the judges were at liberty freely to appropriate from the common law. There was nowhere else to turn. The reception of English rules of evidence was arguably within the intendment of the due process of law clause which, although conceived as a safeguard for the citizen, implicitly required of the court the observance of long-established procedures. The instruction insofar as it was a matter of communicating the judge's understanding of the law was not so restrained, and offered

---

[167] The protection of diplomatic personnel and their domestics was the limit of congressional interest. By sec. 25 of the act (1 *U.S. Stats.*, 112) process of arrest, or of distraint or attachment of their chattels was declared to be void. By sec. 26 persons suing out or prosecuting such process and all attorneys or solicitors as well as officers executing such process were, upon conviction, to be deemed violators of the law of nations "and disturbers of the public repose," imprisoned for three years and fined at the discretion of the court. However, no citizen who had contracted debts prior to entering the service of a foreign minister and had not paid such could take any benefit from the provision. No persons proceeding against a domestic servant could be liable under the statute unless the domestic's name was registered. Sec. 28 punished violations of any safe conduct or passport issued under the

authority of the United States, and assaults or imprisonments of ambassadors or other public ministers, or offering violence to them.

[168] *E.g.*, Collection of Duties Act (Aug. 4, 1790), 1 *U.S. Stats.*, 145, sec. 66, giving or receiving bribes to or by customs officers. Excise Act (Mar. 3, 1791), 1 *U.S. Stats.*, 199, sec. 39, extortion by collectors; sec. 47, giving or offering bribes to revenue officers; sec. 48, obstruction of revenue officers. "Act establishing a Mint" (Apr. 2, 1792), 1 *U.S. Stats.*, 246, sec. 19, debasing coin. "Act to establish the Post Office" (May 8, 1794), 1 *U.S. Stats.*, 354, sec. 16, embezzling or destroying letters, etc., containing banknotes, securities, etc.; sec. 17, robbing the mail.

[169] *Cf.* the testimony of District Judge Gunning Bedford, Jr., *Report of the Trial of the Hon. Samuel Chase* . . . (Evans), 96 *et seq.*

Dorse of the indictment, *United States v. John Fries*, April term 1800 of the Circuit Court for the Pennsylvania District.

(*The National Archives*)

opportunity for the expansion of jurisdiction by what Peters J. called "supplementary interpretation,"[170] as Ellsworth did in the bank note case mentioned above. Equally, such interpretation could serve to direct the law into narrower channels than those marked in English books, as was the case with the law of treason growing out of the two Pennsylvania insurrections.[171]

In the course of all the fuss and fury over a federal common law little or nothing was made of accretions through interpretation such as those just mentioned, as well as resort to the common law to supply deficiencies in the statute regarding the impanelling of jurors,[172] and similarly to spell out the manner of challenging.[173] Even the most politically active Republican lawyers appear to have avoided making an issue of such use of the common law; they would otherwise have been taking the bread out of their own mouths. Their practice, after all, depended upon their burrowing in English case law no less diligently than did the judges.[174] Nevertheless, this was a vulnerable point, and we believe that it might have been taken under attack if the exchanges over a federal common law had been something more than political skirmishing.

There remains to be considered one further phase of the bush-

---

[170] United States v. Fries, Wharton, *State Trials*, 586.

[171] Chase had attempted at the second Fries trial for treason to exclude from argument allusion to English cases which the constitutional definition of treason had made obsolete and improper. Such had been referred to by counsel in the first trial. Chase prepared a paper setting out his view of the law, copies of which were proffered to Lewis and Dallas, counsel for Fries, before the trial began. Counsel spurned the papers. They claimed that the trial was being prejudged and that the bar had been affronted. They withdrew from the case, the honor of the bar evidently weighing more with them than their duty to their client. Fries refused other counsel and Chase, following common law tradition, undertook his defense. This episode formed the basis of Art. I of the Articles of Impeachment of Chase. He was acquitted 18–16. The most circumstantial account of the affair is to be found in Judge Peters's letter to Senator Pickering, Jan. 24, 1804, Ms. Peters Papers, X,

91 (HSP). Wharton's account of the episode in *State Trials*, 610–48, is biased; corrective are the comments in Horace Binney, *Leaders of the Old Bar of Philadelphia* (1859), 32–36. Binney was present at the trial; Wharton was not. A masterly summary of the law by Marshall C.J. in United States v. Burr, 4 Cranch 481 (1807).

[172] United States v. The Insurgents, 2 Dallas 335, 341 (1795).

[173] United States v. Callender, Wharton, *State Trials*, 695–96.

[174] See, for example, the arguments of A. J. Dallas and W. S. Lewis in United States v. Fries, *ibid.*, 537–48, 565–77. About these, Peters wrote to Timothy Pickering, Jan. 24, 1804: "All the abominable & reprobated Cases of constructive Treason in England, were suffered to be read such as the Innkeeper at the Sign of the *Crown*, who was condemned for Treason in saying his Son was Heir to it; & that of the unfortunate Wight who wished the Stagg's Horns in the King's Belly &c &c." Ms. Peters Papers, X, 91 (HSP).

fighting over federal justice that erupted shortly after the first Sedition Act trial. This concerns the attempts to change the method of impanelling juries, a cause which Jefferson and his close associates made their own.[175] This posed some delicate problems to the hard-shell states' rights faction because the Judiciary Act had knit such essentials as the designation and qualifications of jurors to state law, and this accommodation would be expunged by the enactment of a uniform federal procedure. It will be recalled that by section 29 of the Judiciary Act the designation of jurors was to be by lot or otherwise "according to the mode of forming juries now practised" in the several states—so far as the state laws rendered this practicable; the qualifications were to be the same as those requisite by the laws of the state for service in the highest law court thereof. The statute contemplated a divided responsibility. The designation of jurors was to be by court and marshal. The court was given discretion to settle the locality within a district from which jurors were to be returned. The *venire* was to be issued by the clerk and served by the marshal. As a practical matter, except as the District judge might become involved, the execution of the statute rested with the clerk and the marshal.

We are illy informed as to the mechanics of administration, but party tensions produced criticism that none but Federalists were included in panels, or that juries were packed with persons politically hostile to defendants. A two-pronged attack and reform of the system was planned by Jefferson: a modification of the Virginia law to the effect that jurors were to be elected and designated, and because he conceived that the words "now practised" in section 29 of the Judiciary Act froze the practice as of 1789, a change in the federal law to conform to the projected Virginia change.

The plan to alter the law of Virginia came to nothing,[176] but a resolute effort was made to change the Judiciary Act. On January 31, 1800, Senator Charles Pinckney of South Carolina offered a bill[177] to establish a uniform mode of drawing jurors by lot in all the courts of the United States. Pinckney was full of praise for the lot method of designating jurors[178] in South Carolina and the "Eastern States," and

---

[175] Jefferson's ideas were set forth in a draft petition to the Virginia General Assembly, *Works of Jefferson* (Ford, Federal ed.), VIII, 451–55; and in letters to Madison, Oct. 26, 1798, *ibid.*, 456, and to John Taylor of Caroline, Nov. 26, 1798, *ibid.*, 479.

[176] According to 2 Shepherd, *Stats. at Large Virginia*, nothing was enacted at the sessions of 1799, 1800 or 1801.

[177] *Annals of Congress*, X, 35–41, where his speech is set forth.

[178] The promotion of the selection of jurors by lot was wholly doctrinaire and launched without considering the practical difficulties the marshals were encountering where this existed. On this *cf.* a 1797 letter from the Connecticut District Clerk to the Comptroller of the Treasury, RG 217, Miscellaneous Treasury Accounts

expressed his revulsion at the state of the law in New York, Pennsylvania, Maryland, Virginia and New Jersey. He indicated the dangers faced by persons charged with libelling the President with the marshal free to pick a jury. It is unnecessary to trace the fortune of Pinckney's bill, for on March 11 it was postponed until the next session.[179] On the following day the Senate named a committee to inquire into necessary amendments to the Judiciary Act including methods of selecting a jury.[180] A new bill was presented April 8. This provided:

> that jurors to serve ordinarily in the courts of the U.S. shall be drawn by lot in each state respectively according to the mode practiced and from the selection made for jurors to serve in the highest courts of law therein—Provided, such selection shall be sufficient, and the laws of the State do or shall permit the same to the courts or Marshals of the United States.[181]

As might be surmised from the proviso, the majority of the committee were Republicans. The bill and an amendment were referred to a new committee composed of two Federalists and one Republican. A modification was reported April 28 that became the statute finally enacted, viz., "that jurors to serve in the Courts of the United States, shall be designated by lot or otherwise in each State or District respectively according to the mode of forming Juries to serve in the highest Courts of Law therein, now practised; so far as the same shall render such designation practicable by the Courts and Marshals of the United States."[182]

1790–1894, No. 9264 (NA): "By the laws of this State, one set of Jurors are summoned to attend the court as jurors for the trial of all issues, without reference to any particular case, and to prevent the necessity of talesmen from bystanders, it is a standing order of the Circuit Court to summon 18 instead of 12 Jurors, these according to the law of this State are to be drawn by lot from the Jury Boxes of those Towns named in the Venire. These towns are taken from different counties by direction of the court in rotation. As the laws of the United States require this service be made by the Marshal or his Deputy, he must necessarily travel many times several miles to the Jury Box of the Town to draw the names and then to the respective dwellings of the Jurors so drawn and so from

Town to Town till he obtains a Jury according to his warrant, the Towns being designated in his warrant. . . . Under these circumstances it is obvious that those dollars will be no compensation to the Marshal for executing a venire according to this practice when he may be obliged by the directions of the warrant to travel 150 miles to execute it."

For a lament from a South Carolina marshal in 1800 after having his account reduced, *ibid.*, No. 11,639.

[179] *Senate Journal*, 1st Sess., 6th Cong. (1821 reprint) 46.

[180] *Ibid.*, 47.

[181] Senate Files, Sen. 6A–B1, tray 1 (NA).

[182] *Senate Journal*, 1st Sess., 6th Cong., 81; Senate Files, Sen. 6A–D1, tray 2 (NA).

The committee also reported a new section to the effect that where it should not be practicable to form juries as provided in the preceding section, the jurors should be designated and returned "pursuant to the rules and practices of the Common Law as nearly as the Constitution of the sd. Courts will permit it." No debates on this were noted, but it was obviously voted down for the bill went through the House without this change.[183]

The new statute amounted to no more than a clarification of one sentence of section 29 of the Judiciary Act,[184] and since it did not purport to repeal the portions of that section left untouched, it may be supposed that such remained in effect. So far as federal legislation was concerned, the great objective of cutting down the marshal's powers about which Jefferson had fumed and Pinckney had fulminated in the Senate was brought to naught.[185] Anxiety over the marshal's powers ceased with the change of administration in 1801. He was, after all, appointed and removable by the President at pleasure, and could be expected to conduct himself more circumspectly in the new and salubrious political climate. There was now bigger game to be hunted, as events were to prove.

---

[183] *Jour. H.R.*, III, 689, 714, 717. It may be noticed that on the day the bill passed the Senate, Apr. 30, 1800, Jefferson wrote to Edward Livingston, "Our Jury bill in Senate will pass so as merely to accomodate N.York & Vermont." *Works of Jefferson* (Ford, Federal ed.), IX, 131–32.

[184] The one significant change was the elimination of reference to the "laws of the states" and some re-punctuation which seems to have vested courts and marshals with discretion to determine if the mode used in the state courts was practicable.

[185] The change of heart about the marshal is evident from sec. 30 of the Judiciary Act of 1802 (2 *U.S. Stats.*, 156) which took from the clerks of court the power of returning special juries and confided this to the marshals. The clerks, of course, were appointed by the District judges, most of whom were Federalists.

CHAPTER XV

The Supreme Court—
Appellate Practice

T HE DECADE FOLLOWING the inauguration of the new federal government was a time of mounting political excitement in which, however, the Supreme Court was but occasionally involved. As a result, its role during these dramatic years of national development has been treated by historians as an almost faceless one.[1] We shall later have occasion to examine the cases of pronounced political complexion docketed or adjudicated during this period. These represent but one tenth of the total business of the Court, even if to appellate cases are added those where its original jurisdiction was invoked, manifestly too slight a tally to invite extended inquiry, although all of these decisions possessed both instant and prospective force. More comprehensible has been the silence with which historians have passed over the no less significant area where the pre-Marshall Court made great contributions— the regulation of appellate practice—for this area has seemed peculiarly a bailiwick of the bar. For our purpose this does not make the subject less eligible for inquiry. Many ground rules, so to speak, were settled in those years and consequently this aspect of the Court's work must be examined at large.

A first and emergent task confronting the Supreme Court was to settle certain details more often than not of a formalistic nature. The

---

[1] For example, S. E. Morison, and H. Commager, *Growth of the American Republic* (New York: Oxford University Press, 1937), I, 216: "Under Chief Justice Jay the federal judiciary assumed its place as the keystone to the federal arch." N. Schachner, *The Founding Fathers*, 129, mentions only the decision in Chisholm v. Georgia; he summarizes: "the work of the Court was scanty, its judgments few." J. C. Miller, *The Federalist Era, 1789–1801*, 136, refers to Glass v. the *Sloop Betsey*, Chisholm and Calder v. Bull (*ibid.*, 180), Hylton v. United States (*ibid.*, 181–82). He states (p. 179) that there were "no epoch-making decisions handed down from that tribunal."

directions of the Judiciary Act were of the most general, and obviously judicial amplifications were anticipated. The use of common law terminology suggested recourse to the body of learning concerning error, although it is unlikely that any legislator supposed that there would be heavy borrowings from the bountiful harvest of case law assembled under this rubric in the popular abridgments. Furthermore, no one had the prescience to foresee that the dispositions of the Process Act would be read to mean that in each district state practice in common law actions was to be followed and thus would generate problems respecting the review of judgments, as, for example, the variety of usages respecting record, or what was properly included in any assignment of errors.

The Court early evinced its predisposition to settle procedural details in the context of litigation, although once the second Process Act had enlarged its rule-making power, some issues might have been disposed of by rule.[2] As it was, the rule of August term 1792, to the effect that the Court considered the practices of the English Courts of King's Bench and of Chancery as affording outlines for its practice subject to future modifications, seems to have been no more than a notice that English practice books would be a source of first reference. It is difficult to imagine how the rule could have meant more. The draftsmen of the Judiciary Act, relying largely upon native traditional usage, had made of the federal writ of error notionally a very different instrument than was the English, and the Congress had concurred. The constitutional limits upon jurisdiction being what they were—and this included the Seventh Amendment—the Court was constrained to produce its own glosses, its own commentary.

The tempo of eighteenth century litigation at common law, everywhere leisurely, was particularly so in the federal system because the Circuit Courts were confined to two terms annually. This is reflected in the Supreme Court docket book, for it was not until 1796 that a substantial amount of appellate business was ready for disposition. The statutory minimum had something to do with the quantum of business, but it may be remarked that Circuit minutes or dockets disclose the entry of numerous judgments sufficient to qualify that yet were not carried further. Allowing even for the dilatory pace of pursuing civil actions and the restraints built into the Judiciary Act, there was, nevertheless, a sufficient volume of appellate business during the decade here studied for general lines of approach to be established, for matter that needed amendment to be uncovered and for certain incidents of practice to be settled.

So far as we are aware, no satisfactory body of statistics on appellate causes in the Supreme Court has yet been compiled although it

---

[2] *Supra*, c. XII.

_? At the Supreme Judicial Court of the United States, begun and held at New York (being the Seat of the National Government) on the first Monday of February, and on the first day of said month Anno Domini 1790.

Present.

The Honble John Jay Esquire Chief Justice
The Honble { William Cushing, and
            James Wilson, Esq rs } Associate Justices.

This being the day assigned by Law, for commencing the first Sessions of the Supreme Court of the United States, and a sufficient number of the Justices not being convened, the Court is adjourned by the Justices now present, untill to morrow, at one of the Clock in the afternoone.

Tuesday, February 2nd 1790.

Present

The Honble John Jay Esqr Chief Justice
                William Cushing
The Honble { James Wilson, and } Associate Justices
            John Blair, Esq rs }

Proclamation

has long been known that what was reported by Alexander J. Dallas is by no means an accurate representation of the actual number of cases brought up for review and disposed of by the Court. The most reliable source still extant is the Court's smooth docket book (the rough book having disappeared),[3] and this has been made the basis for the tabulations set forth in the Appendix.[4] Prior to 1801 a total of eighty-nine cases was entered in the docket book as appellate, a figure to be corrected to eighty-seven because of duplication.[5] Two cases reported by Dallas, *West v. Barnes* et al. (1791)[6] and *Blair v. Miller* (1800),[7] were not entered on the docket. Another case, *Dewhurst v. Coulthard*,[8] was an attempt to secure via a case stated an advisory opinion and so is not properly to be characterized as appellate. Two other cases erroneously reported to have been decided in 1800 have also been omitted. The Supreme Court disposed of a total of seventy-nine appellate cases prior to 1801.

Although less than half of the dispositions by the Supreme Court were professionally reported, so far as the bar at large was concerned these reports came to be prime sources of information regarding the Court's jurisprudence. This was to be a belated enlightenment, for Dallas' second volume reporting the earliest term did not appear until 1798, his third in 1799 and his fourth not until 1807. Since, in general, newspaper accounts of decisions were of small use in disseminating information on points of practice,[9] counsel in most districts were at a considerable disadvantage in perfecting appellate cases, and they could only inform themselves by inquiries at the seat of government whether or not the Supreme Court had adjudicated certain issues.[10]

---

[3] On this see J. R. Browning and B. Glenn, "The Supreme Court Collection at the National Archives," 4 *Am. Jour. Leg. Hist.*, 4:241, 249, 1960. The original smooth docket book now has a stamped number by each appellate case, keyed to an index of cases by title prepared in the Library of the Supreme Court. See comment by Dr. Joseph P. Blickensderfer, *Law Library Journal*, 52:342, 1959. The number of docket entries does not reflect accurately the actual number of appellate causes because of instances where a writ was quashed for a defect of form and the same case brought up by new writ.

[4] *Infra*, p. 667.

[5] Where the writ was quashed or defective and a new entry made for resumption of the cause by a new writ.

[6] 2 Dallas 401 (1791). A full report of arguments and opinions is in *Gazette of the United States,* August 13 and 17, 1791.

[7] 4 Dallas 21 (1800). Both this case and West v. Barnes concerned the question of the process by which they had been removed to the Supreme Court.

[8] 3 *ibid.*, 409 (1799). The cause was presented by petition. There is nothing in the minutes or case papers of the Circuit Court for the New York District to indicate any action in that court after removal from the New York Supreme Court of Judicature.

[9] The report of West v. Barnes, *supra*, n. 6, is a notable exception.

[10] Alexander Hamilton to an unknown correspondent (undated), raising the question concerning Supreme Court adjudications on an appeal from a state Chancery Court and sug-

It came about during the decade with which we are concerned that practice in the Supreme Court was in the hands of a small group made up chiefly of Philadelphia lawyers—A. J. Dallas, Peter Du Ponceau, Jared Ingersoll, William Lewis, William Rawle and the two Tilghmans, Edward and William—although from time to time counsel from elsewhere appeared. It was upon this bar that the profession generally was dependent for information and ultimately for the management of a cause in the Supreme Court. The molding of appellate procedure consequently appears to have been accomplished in a manner approximating the club-like mode that prevailed contemporaneously in the English High Court of Admiralty.

THE APPELLATE PROCESS

THE REGULATIONS OF THE Judiciary Act have already been examined in detail.[11] But by way of refreshment, if such it may be called, it will be convenient here to take a brief view of the salient provisions. The Congress provided for an appeal in causes of admiralty and maritime jurisdiction from District to Circuit Courts; otherwise civil causes were reviewable only by writ of error. The jurisdiction and process were regulated by section 22, whether from District to Circuit Courts or from the latter to the Supreme Court. Final judgments and decrees in civil actions and equity suits brought in the Circuit Court by original process, or removed thereto from state courts or by appeal from a District Court where the amount in dispute exceeded $2,000 exclusive of costs, might upon writ of error be "reexamined and reversed or affirmed" by the Supreme Court. It was directed that to the writ there be annexed and returned at the day and place mentioned therein an authenticated transcript of the record, an assignment of errors and a prayer for relief together with a citation signed by a judge of the Circuit Court or Justice of the Supreme Court; the adverse party was to have at least thirty days' notice; the Justice or judge signing the citation was to take sufficient security that plaintiff in error prosecute his writ to effect and answer all damages and costs if he should fail to make good his plea. There was to be no reversal for error in ruling on a plea in abatement other than to the jurisdiction, or a plea in the nature of a demurrer to a bill in equity, or for any error in fact.

For review of final judgments or decrees of the highest state courts, section 25 authorized removal by writ of error in specified cases under

---

gesting inquiry be made at Philadelphia and Washington. In the margin are the names of Lewis, Tilghman,

Ingersoll and Rawle. Misc. Docs., Ms. Hamilton Papers (LC).

[11] *Supra*, c. XI.

regulations provided in section 22, but with the significant limitation that the error assigned or advanced as a ground of reversal be confined to such as appeared on the face of the record and immediately involved the validity or construction of the Constitution, treaties, statutes, commissions or authorities (mentioned in the section) in dispute. The citation could be signed by the judge of the state court passing judgment or decree, or by a Supreme Court Justice. There was no monetary limitation.

It should finally be noticed because of possible bearing upon appellate authority that section 13 conveyed authority to issue mandamus, and by section 14 the Supreme Court shared the authority of all federal courts to issue habeas corpus. There was respectable authority to the effect that this writ could serve as one of error.[12] This was, however, not to be put to the test during the terms of the Court examined here.

The Process Act furnished one procedural addition—the requirement that all writs issued from the Supreme or a Circuit Court should bear the test of the Chief Justice, be under the seal of the court from which they issued and be signed by the respective clerks.

Nothing has been found to establish how the form of the writ of error was settled. Samples were available in English form or practice books and those used in various states more or less conformed to these models. There is some reason to suppose that Chief Justice Jay assumed responsibility for deciding the form. In the first place, he tested a writ purporting to be a writ of error issued by the clerk of the Circuit Court for the Rhode Island District and directed to that same court, returnable to the Supreme Court. This was the instrument presented August term 1791 to the Supreme Court in *West v. Barnes* et al. and it was moved that defendants rejoin to the errors assigned. It was objected by defendants that the cause was not properly before the Court because the writ issued from the wrong court. Bradford, for plaintiff in error, argued that only a matter of form was involved and that a stay of execution was impossible if litigants were compelled to secure their writs at the seat of government. The Justices who delivered their opinions seriatim sustained defendants' objection. They were agreed that the fact that the writ was a mandate was determinative. It was an absurdity that a court should order itself to do something. The inconvenience that execution could not be stayed was for the legislative to repair. Writs of error could only issue from the office of the clerk of the Supreme Court.[13] Following

---

[12] Hale, *Pleas of the Crown* (1778 ed.), I, 584; Bacon, *Abridgment* (1768 ed.), *s.v.* Habeas Corpus A.

[13] See n. 6, *supra*. The account in the *Gazette of the United States* (Aug. 13, 1791) states that the substance of the opinions was printed. In the Supreme Court Iredell, Blair, Wilson and Cushing set out their objections at large. Jay merely commented that

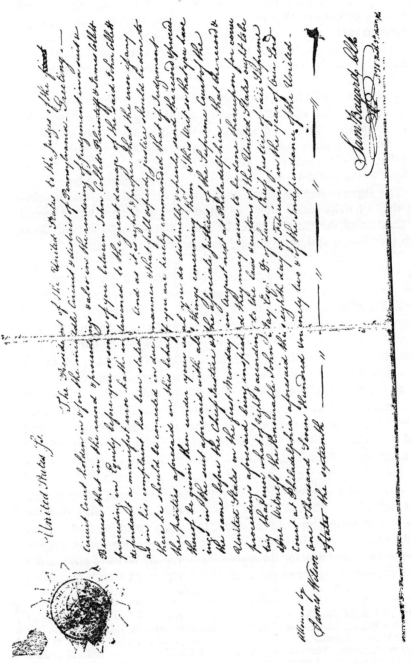

Writ of error, *Collet v. Collet*, February 8, 1792.
(The National Archives)

this decision, on February 8, 1792, there issued the writ of error used in *Collet v. Collet* (the first appellate case docketed), the text of which is set forth in the margin.[14] Again one is led to suspect that the Chief Justice may have had a hand in drafting it because of the addition of the honorific title of Doctor of Laws newly bestowed upon him.[15]

As we have seen, the decision in *West v. Barnes* et al. was not without result, for Justice Iredell, holding the Southern Circuit, drew the President's attention to the fact that under the existing statutory rule (section 23) which required service of the writ of error within ten days to operate as a supersedeas, no stay of execution was possible in a district as remote as Georgia.[16] This difficulty, he wrote, had been considered by the Supreme Court but it had taken the position that the solution was a matter of legislative and not judicial action. Iredell seems to have been the one Justice resolute enough to initiate remedial action. The second Process Act, as noticed, authorized the clerk of the Supreme Court to transmit the form of the writ of error, approved by two

---

the reasons assigned were explanatory of his own opinion, and he "suggested" his concurrence. The question remains why he tested the writ in the first place.

[14] Ms. Case Papers U.S. Sup. Ct., Case No. 1:

United States ss.

The President of the United States to the Judges of the Circuit Court holden in & for the middle Circuit and district of Pennsylvania—Greeting—

Because that in the record & proceedings & also in the rendering of Judgement in a suit & proceeding in Equity before you or some of you between John Collett Plaintiff & James Collett defendant a manifest error hath intervened to the great damage of the said John Collett as in his complaint has been stated. And as it is right & proper that the error if any there be should be corrected in due manner & that full & speedy justice should be done to the parties aforesaid in this behalf you are hereby commanded that if Judgement thereof be given then under your seal you do distinctly & openly send the record & proceedings in the suit aforesaid with all things con-

cerning them & this Writ so that you have the same before the Chief Justice & the associate Justices of the Supreme Court of the United States on the first Monday in August next at Philadelphia—that the record & proceedings aforesaid being inspected they may cause to be done thereupon for correcting that error what of right & according to the laws & customs of the United States ought to be done Witness the Honourable John Jay Esq.ᵣ D.ᵣ of Laws Chief Justice of said Supreme Court at Philadelphia aforesaid this eighth day of February in the year of Our Lord One Thousand Seven Hundred & ninety two & of the Independence of the United States the sixteenth—

Allowed by
James Wilson
Sam¹ Bayard Clk
N° 58. North 3.ʳᵈ Street. Phil.ª

The writ correctly indorsed, Collet v. Collet.

[15] Jay had been awarded the LL.D. degree by Harvard in 1790. *Harvard University Quinquennial Catalogue of the Officers and Graduates: 1636–1930* (1930), 1151.

[16] *Supra*, c. XII, p. 546.

Justices, to the clerks of the Circuit Courts, who were empowered to issue the writ returnable to the Supreme Court.[17]

There were no specific statutory directions regarding removals from state courts pursuant to section 25. The touchiness of certain states suggests that the situation was one for application of the procedure by petition that had originally been proposed in the Judiciary Bill. Early Supreme Court minutes indicate that writs of error to state courts did not issue immediately as of right. In February 1793 one James Martin offered papers to the Court which were suggested as the foundation for a writ of error to the Supreme Judicial Court of Massachusetts. At the succeeding term he applied for allowance of a writ which the Chief Justice had erroneously refused. The Supreme Court held that under the circumstances of the case the writ could not be allowed.[18] The first docketed state case, *Olney v. Arnold* (1796), had annexed an assignment of error cast in the form of a petition reciting the foundation of the Court's jurisdiction under section 25.[19] It is doubtful, however, that

---

[17] *Ibid.*

[18] Ms. Mins. U.S. Sup. Ct. 1790–1805, *sub* Feb. 4, 14, and Aug. 6, 1793. Martin had applied in the Supreme Court on February 4 to be sworn to the truth of a deposition, an application refused until expressions imputing corrupt motives to the judges of the Supreme Judicial Court were expunged. On February 14 Martin was sworn. The nature of the case is not known.

In another case, Pagan v. Hooper, the minutes indicate that on Feb. 16, 1793, the Court heard a copy of the record and decided that the writ applied for should not issue.

[19] 3 Dallas 308. The assignment, in Ms. Case Papers U.S. Sup. Ct., Case No. 7:

To the Honorable the Supreme Court of the United States holden at Philadelphia on the first Monday of February AD 1795.— Humbly shews Jeremiah Olney of Providence in the District of Rhode Island Esquire Collector of the District of Providence—That in the proceedings and rendition of Judgment at the Superior Court of Judicature, Court of Assize and general Jail delivery holden at Providence within and for the County of Providence, in the State of Rhode Island and Providence Plantations, on the third Monday of September in the Year of our Lord Seventeen Hundred & Ninety four in a certain action of Trespass on the Case, between Welcome Arnold Pltf: and the said Jeremiah Defendant, there is manifest Error in this, to Wit. That in the same Cause, the said Jeremiah by his Plea therein Stated, justified his refusal, as Collector as aforesaid, to grant a Permit to unlade the Cargo of the Brig therein mentioned untill the Duties on the same Cargo were paid, or the Bond of the said Welcome, for duties then due, and unsatisfied, should be paid and discharged, and claimed a right so to do under the Law of the United States set forth in the said Plea. And the said Superior Court decided in the same cause against the right claimed by the said Jeremiah in manner and by Virtue of the Law aforesaid: As by the Records of the said case fully appears. Wherefore the said Jeremiah prays that the same

much weight can be attached to this form, for counsel in seeking review of Circuit Court judgments sometimes used the form of petition, and since there are no minute book entries after 1793 to show that the Court considered applications for writ of error, it may be assumed that the writ came to be issued as of right.

Because the Judiciary Act provided that a writ of error with the record annexed was to be returned at the "day and place therein mentioned" counsel were bound to fall upon discrepancies. The first occasion was in *Hamilton v. Moore* (1797)[20] where the writ, returnable February term, was sued out January 2, 1797, and served on defendant twelve days later, but was not returned until August term. The Court held that it could not be amended pursuant to section 32 of the Judiciary Act, as there was nothing to amend, evidently refusing to treat the matter as a defect of form. Subsequently, process was quashed in the unreported case of *Ross v. Maul* (1800)[21] and in the non-docketed case of *Blair v. Miller* (1800),[22] in both of which the writ was returned a term later than the return date. In the latter case the Court explained that the writ was a nullity and could not be a legal instrument to bring the record before it for revision.[23]

An irregularity of even greater import was presented by the record in *Wilson v. Daniel* in February 1797.[24] Here only a copy of the writ of error was transmitted, signed by William Marshall, the clerk of the Circuit Court for the Virginia District, with his marginal notation that the writ had been allowed by Cyrus Griffin. Only a copy of the citation accompanied the record with an affidavit of service. There was no certificate that the record was returned in obedience to the writ. Although counsel for defendant in error, objecting to the return, raised the question of the sufficiency of a mere copy of the writ, the Court is not reported to have ruled specifically on this point. It did hold that the verification of the record was defective and that it could not under the statute dispense with the return of the original citation. Pursuant to an agreement of counsel the cause was continued, diminution of the record alleged and certiorari issued. There is reason to suppose that much more ground was covered in the argument over the state of the record in *Wilson v. Daniel* than was reported by Dallas, for on February 13, 1797,

---

Judgment may be reversed and he be restored to all that he has lost thereby.

           Jereᵇ Olney Collᵣ
     Wᵐ Bradford
[20] 3 Dallas 371.
[21] Ms. Docket Book U.S. Sup. Ct., p. 94, is not clear on the point in the

text.
[22] 4 Dallas 21.
[23] In Mossman v. Higginson, *ibid.*, 12 (1800), a writ which was blank for the return was held amendable by leave of court under the Judiciary Act, sec. 32.
[24] 3 Dallas 401.

the Court by general rule had ordered that the clerk of the court to which any writ of error was directed "may make a return of the same, by transmitting a true copy of the Record, and the Proceedings in the Cause, under his hand, and the Seal of the Court."[25]

A second point, which surely invited argument but about which nothing was reported, was the allowance of a writ of certiorari where diminution of the record was alleged. This was a long-settled incident of English error practice,[26] and consequently we have here the adoption of common law usage evidently in reliance upon the "all writs" section of the Judiciary Act.[27]

THE IMPACT OF STATE PRACTICE

IN TWO PARTICULARS, the assignment of error and the bill of exceptions—both being the responsibility of counsel—the diversity of state usage, if, indeed, this had stabilized in any jurisdiction, was to have the effect of keeping Supreme Court procedure respecting these incidents more or less at large. As to the assignments of errors, there is no evidence that either by general rule or in the context of litigation the Court did establish any precise rules. As noticed, the Judiciary Act directed that the assignment of errors, together with a prayer for reversal, be attached to the record on return; but, as we shall see in a moment, the bar dealt very inattentively with this provision. In contemporary English common law practice, and as the logical consequence of the rule that the writ of error was an original writ,[28] the assignment of error was conceived to be in the nature of a declaration,[29] and lay for either error in law or fact. This last was, however, limited to such facts as that a defendant had died before verdict or interlocutory judgment, or that a feme plaintiff or defendant was under coverture when the action was begun, neither of which would appear on the face of the record, but if true, proved the judgment erroneous.[30] Here, however closely state usage may have followed the common law, section 22 of the Judiciary Act introduced an alteration by forbidding reversal of any error in fact, and, indeed, carried matters further by limiting reversals for error in a ruling on a plea in abatement, a standard means of attacking capacity to sue.

By the direction that the assignment of errors be attached to the

---

[25] *Ibid.*, 356 (Feb. 13, 1797).
[26] Tidd, *Practice of the Court of King's Bench*, 3d ed. (1803), II, 1103 *et seq.*
[27] The only discussion of this use of certiorari occurred August term 1797 in Fennimore v. United States,

3 Dallas 357 at 360, but solely in the context of the rule of Feb. 13, 1797.
[28] *Supra*, c. I, n. 19.
[29] This doctrine was based upon a reading of Y.B. 9 Edw. IV, Mich. 32 pl. 5.
[30] Tidd, *Practice of the Court of King's Bench*, II, at 1107.

record, the statute presumably contemplated that such be made in the Circuit or state court. This appears from case papers to have been the usual but by no means invariable practice. One of the difficulties in the way of framing a categorical description of practice is that when assignments were in the form of a declaration, they were not always dated and, consequently, there is no telling when the document was filed or with what court. That the lack of an assignment probably would not defeat jurisdiction may be inferred from the fact that none of the rules obtained by counsel for defendants were framed in such terms.[31] This is not to say that this was not seen as a danger, for in *Pintado v. the Ship San Joseph, Berard claimant*, and *United States v. La Vengeance*, by agreement of counsel it was stipulated that the assignment of errors was to be annexed to the return of the writ (then in the office of the clerk of the Supreme Court) and considered as taken as part of the return and to have the same effect as if originally annexed.[32]

In the great majority of cases general error was assigned either by asserting that the declaration or libel was insufficient in law to maintain the action, or that judgment was given for defendant in error when by the law of the land (or a similar phrase) judgment should have been given for plaintiff in error.[33] Assignment of special error was made in a relatively large number of cases and with very few exceptions general error was assigned as well.[34] Occasionally, when general error was

---

[31] For example, in Dorrance v. Vanhorne's Lessee (1799, unreported) a rule was obtained Feb. 14, 1799, to assign error in two days or the writ non-prossed, a rule made absolute February 18. The case was originally docketed August term 1796. Ms. Docket Book U.S. Sup. Ct., p. 28.

[32] Pintado v. the *Ship San Joseph*, Berard claimant (Ms. Case Papers U.S. Sup. Ct., Case No. 32), decided in 1796, is unreported. United States v. *La Vengeance* (Case No. 34) is reported 3 Dallas 297 (1796). The agreement in the Pintado case made by Hamilton and Du Ponceau is printed in *LPAH*, II, 804. The agreement in the *Vengeance* case was between United States Attorney Harison and Du Ponceau.

[33] The following is a partial list of cases where only a general assignment was made: Cases No. 16, Moodie v. *Ship Betty Cathcart*; No. 18, Moodie v. *Brig Eliza*; No. 17, Moodie v. *Ship Mermaid*; No. 15, Geyer v. *Ship Den*

Onzekeren; No. 21, Moodie v. *Ship Alfred*; No. 19, Moodie v. *Ship Phyn*; No. 20, Moodie v. *Brig Tivoly*; No. 24, Moodie v. *Snow Potowmack*; No. 23, Moodie v. *Ship Britannia*; No. 22, Moodie v. *Brig Favorite*; No. 26, Moodie v. *Ship Phoebe Anne*; No. 9, Talbot v. Jansen; No. 35, Fennimore v. United States; No. 36, Emory v. Greenough; No. 39, Wilson v. Daniel; No. 29, Hunter v. Goodtitle ex dem Fairfax; No. 28, MacDonough v. *Ship Mary Ford*; No. 43, Court v. Van Bibber; No. 14, Delcol v. Arnold; No. 87, Baas v. Tingey; No. 79, Paine and Bridgman v. United States. In addition there are several cases for which the case papers contain indications that no assignment was made but where general error may have been assigned at some time in the proceedings.

[34] An example of an elaborate special assignment is that in Penhallow *et al.* v. Doane's Administrator, 3 Dallas 54 at 64-66 (1795). That filed in Brown v. Barry *ibid.*, 365

assigned below, specifications of error were later filed in the Supreme Court. The review of causes from state courts under section 25 of the Judiciary Act had, of course, been confined to the special errors set out in the statute. In the first two such cases adjudicated, *Olney v. Arnold* and *Olney v. Dexter*,[35] and following these *Calder v. Bull*,[36] the statutory prescriptions were observed. However, in four cases from the Maryland High Court of Appeals, general error was averred.[37]

Despite its putative quality as a declaration, the assignments of errors in this period were frequently cast in the form of petition. The case records indicate they were also made *viva voce* before the Circuit Court judges and noted on the record. Sometimes the assignment was made *in scriptis* merely by stating that general error was assigned. There

---

(1797), is taken from the Ms. Case Papers U.S. Sup. Ct., Case No. 48:

To the Honorable Oliver Ellsworth chief Justice and the associate Judges of the supreme court of the .United States.—

The Petition of James Brown a citizen of, and resident in, the State of Virginia

Humbly Sheweth Unto Your Honors, that hereunto is annexed an authenticated copy of the record and proceedings in an action of debt lately depending in the honorable the circuit court for the district of Virginia, in which James Barry of the State of Maryland was plaintiff and the said James Brown was defendant. And your Petitioner is advised, and humbly suggests, that in the said record and proceedings there are various and manifest errors, and amongst others the following, to wit, first, that parol evidence was admitted to vary a written contract upon which the plaintiff's action was founded; secondly, that the said plaintiff's declaration and the matters contained therein, are not sufficient in law to maintain the said action of the said James Barry against the said James Brown; thirdly, that the reasons offered in arrest of judgment on the verdict rendered in the said action were all of them over-ruled, when they

or some of them ought to have been sustained; and finally, that judgment in the said action was given for the said James Barry against the said James Brown, where by the law of the land the said judgment ought to have been given for the said James Brown against the said James Barry.

Whereupon for these and other errors apparent in the said record and proceedings, the said James Brown prays that the judgment aforesaid may be reversed, annulled and entirely set aside, and that he may be restored to all that he hath lost by occasion of the said judgment &ca.

James Brown

To the Clk of the Court
U.S.V.D.

Let a Writ of Error & Supersedeas
issue in the suit above mentioned.

Cyrus Griffin Judge

[35] Ms. Case Papers U.S. Sup. Ct., Cases No. 7 and No. 8. Olney v. Arnold is reported in 3 Dallas 308 (1796); Olney v. Dexter (1796) is unreported but involved the same issues.

[36] 3 Dallas 386 (1798).

[37] Clerke v. Harwood, *ibid.*, 342 (1797); Court v. Van Bibber, Court v. Wells and Court v. Robinson, all of 1797, were none of them reported.

Leaders of the United States Supreme Court Bar during Its First Decade

EDMUND RANDOLPH,
Attorney General of Virginia, 1776–1786, first Attorney General of the
United States, 1789–1794. Copy of lost portrait by F. J. Fisher.
(Courtesy of Virginia State Library, Richmond)

WILLIAM BRADFORD,
Attorney General of Pennsylvania, 1780–1791, Justice of the Supreme Court
of Pennsylvania, 1791–1794, second Attorney General of the United States,
1794–1795. Portrait by C. B. J. F. Saint-Mémin.
(Courtesy of the Independence National Historical Park Collection, Philadelphia)

WILLIAM TILGHMAN
of Pennsylvania. Portrait by Rembrandt Peale.
(*Courtesy of American Philosophical Society, Philadelphia*)

ALEXANDER J. DALLAS
of Pennsylvania. Portrait by Gilbert Stuart.
(*Courtesy of the Pennsylvania Academy of the Fine Arts, Philadelphia*)

JARED INGERSOLL,
Attorney General of Pennsylvania, 1790–1799, United States Attorney,
Pennsylvania District, 1800–1801. Portrait by Charles Wilson Peale.
(Collection of Miss Anna Warren Ingersoll, reproduced through the courtesy of Miss Ingersoll and the Frick Art Reference Library)

WILLIAM RAWLE,
United States Attorney, Pennsylvania District, 1791–1800. Portrait by T. S. Duché.
(*Courtesy of the Historical Society of Pennsylvania, Philadelphia*)

WILLIAM LEWIS,
United States Attorney, Pennsylvania District, 1789–1791, United States
District Judge, Pennsylvania District, 1791–1792. Engraving from an original
portrait by Gilbert Stuart.
(*Courtesy of the Historical Society of Pennsylvania, Philadelphia*)

CHARLES LEE
of Virginia, third Attorney General of the United States, 1795–1801. Portrait
by Cephas Thompson.
(Courtesy of National Portrait Gallery, Smithsonian Institution)

EDWARD TILGHMAN
of Pennsylvania. Portrait by Rembrandt Peale.
(Courtesy of the Law Association of Philadelphia)

Peter S. Du Ponceau
of Pennsylvania. Portrait by Thomas Sully.
(*Courtesy of American Philosophical Society*)

SAMUEL DEXTER,
member of the United States House of Representatives from Massachusetts,
1792–1795, United States Senator from Massachusetts, 1799–1800. Portrait
by John Johnston.
(Courtesy of American Antiquarian Society, Worcester, Massachusetts)

JACOB READ,
United States Senator from South Carolina, 1795–1801. Portrait by John
Trumbull.
(Courtesy of Yale University Art Gallery)

were no statutory directions with respect to the response to the assignment. Consequently, here again, common law usage, at least as understood in particular jurisdictions, manifestly influenced the development of Supreme Court practice. In England a defendant could either demur or plead.[38] The plea was either special or common (joinder)—*in nullo est erratum*—the usual plea in Supreme Court cases. If then made, and if recorded at all, joinder usually appears in the docket book. Such pleas were also made in the Circuit Court, particularly if general error had been there assigned, either *viva voce* or *in scriptis* by a short notation often written on the assignment itself. Only one case has been found where plaintiff in error obtained a rule from the Court for defendant to appear and plead by a certain date.[39]

The effect of the long-seated rule that error might be assigned in every part of the record, when applied to the "record and proceedings" in admiralty causes, so fundamentally unlike a common law record, was to give some such assignments the appearance, in particulars, of bills of exceptions, a device unknown to admiralty procedure. The basic difference between the assignment and the bill of exceptions was that the former was a complaint drawn after verdict and judgment—a confection of the party aggrieved; the bill, on the other hand, the genesis of which has already been noticed, was a record of party remonstrances in the course of the trial on points of law, tendered to the judge presiding to affix his seal. The bill of exceptions was available only in the context of appellate review by writ of error.

No federal statutes made specific reference to the bill of exceptions during the period here studied, and the question whether the bill was included by implication in the directions respecting writs of error in the Judiciary Act or by the language of the first Process Act was apparently not explored by the Court. The only indication that the question may have been judicially considered has been found in the minutes for the April term 1793 of the Circuit Court for the Pennsylvania District in the case of *Livingston v. Swanwick*,[40] Iredell sitting with District Judge Peters. The defendant had taken a number of exceptions at the trial and when it was over had tendered a bill of exceptions to be sealed. The somewhat ambiguous minute entry indicates that it was left with the judges if the bill was legal, a mode of expression which suggests that it

---

[38] Tidd, *Practice of the Court of King's Bench*, II, at 1116. There is ambiguity in Tidd's account, for in almost the same breath he states that *in nullo est erratum* "is in the nature of a demurrer, and at once refers the matter of law arising thereon, to the

judgment of the court."

[39] Mossman v. Higginson, 4 Dallas 12 at 13 (1800), and see the entry Ms. Docket Book U.S. Sup. Ct., p. 65.

[40] Ms. Mins. Circuit Ct. Pennsylvania Dist. 1792–1795, *sub* Apr. 27, 1793.

was not the particulars of the bill that were taken under advisement, but rather the reception in federal practice of this incident. The bill was allowed and a writ of error obtained, but this was never pursued.[41]

In the course of the years 1790–1800 three cases came up to the Supreme Court with bills of exceptions but only two of them were adjudicated and in neither of these was anything substantial said about form or content. The first case, *Bingham v. Cabot* (1795),[42] was an action of assumpsit, the subject matter of which was the proceeds from the sale of a cargo of a ship unlawfully taken as prize in 1777. The bill was in the form of a petition.[43] The exceptions related to the exclusion

---

[41] 2 Dallas 300 at 302 n.

[42] 3 *ibid.*, 19. During the Revolutionary War William Bingham had been the agent for the Continental Congress in Martinique. In 1778 the Danish vessel *Hope* was taken as prize by the American privateer *Pilgrim* and was brought into St. Pierre in 1779. After the ship's papers had been delivered to Bingham he had laid them before the admiralty court in Martinique; the judge held that the capture was illegal because of the evidence indicating the neutral ownership of the *Hope*. Bingham had disposed of the cargo in Martinique because of its perishable nature and deposited the proceeds to the credit of the Commercial Committee of the Continental Congress. The owners of the *Pilgrim* subsequently sued Bingham in trover in the Court of Common Pleas in 1779 in Massachusetts. Judgment on demurrer was given for Bingham in that court, and on appeal there was a verdict for Bingham in the Supreme Judicial Court in 1784. In June of 1794 the owners of the *Pilgrim* instituted the present action against Bingham in the Massachusetts Circuit Court on a declaration in assumpsit.

[43] John Cabot *et al.* Pltfs v. William Bingham (bill of exceptions, in Ms. Case Papers U.S. Sup. Ct., Case No. 57):

And the said William Bingham now here in Court by James Sullivan and Christopher Gore Esqʳˢ his Attornies, the issue is joined in the same case, and a jury in the same is duly and legally impanelled, prays leave to file a bill of exceptions to the determination of the said Court here had on the evidence, which by the said Bingham is offered in this case, and by which determination the said evidence is excluded, and the said Bingham is denied the advantage of giving the same to the Jury in the same case, *viz!* The several copies attested by Thomas Jefferson, and which are hereunto annexed, and numbered from one to eighteen inclusively; and also three other papers numbered 23, 24 & 25; all which papers had a tendency to prove that no interest ought to be allowed by the Jury on the sum, for which the Pltfs declare, in their third count, or damages for the detention of the money therein mentioned, and declared on, and by the exclusion whereof the said Bingham does sustain manifest injury and wrongs as he conceives.—And the said Bingham further files his exception to the determination of the same Court, by which the papers numbered from 27 to 36 inclusively were excluded—and which papers contain a complete record of the Supreme Judicial Court of the Commonwealth of Massachusetts, wherein William Carlton, who had been, as the said Bingham avers, and as appears by the evidence in the case, in possession of the same flour, declared on in the said third count in the Pltfs declaration, had sued in an action of trover for the same, and by which rec-of certain papers tending to prove that no interest should have been allowed by the Circuit jury on the third count claiming damages (money received to the use) and the exclusion of other papers relating to a Massachusetts action of trover for the same cause in which Bingham had had judgment. A third exception related to the refusal of the Circuit judge to permit the reading of certain resolves of the Continental Congress relating to the matter in controversy. The assignment of error included general error, lack of jurisdiction in the Circuit Court (raised for the first time) and the refusal to admit the evidence stated in the bill of exceptions. Plaintiff in error also prayed a writ directed to Justice Cushing, the trial judge, to confess or deny his seal—establishing that the procedure of Statute Westminster II (1285) was deemed operative.

The argument of this cause was beclouded in the first place by the misapprehension of counsel for defendant in error that the bill of exceptions should have included the evidence of the plaintiff below, a claim which may have been inspired by a form in Buller's *Nisi Prius*.[44] The Court did not enter into any explanation of the nature of the bill or what it should or should not contain. It merely stated that it was conclusive upon the Court, which would not presume that any part of the evidence was omitted. A second element of confusion emerged in

ord it appears, that such proceedings were had in the same Court as would fully shew, as the said Bingham conceives, that the Pltfs had no legal right to change the same action, after the Judgment in the same record specified, into an action of assumpsit, or as principals to implead the said Bingham again, after the cause of action had been tried adjudged and determined, in an action of Trover, wherein the special bailiffs of the Pltfs as the said Bingham avers, in this suit had so impleaded the said Bingham to verdict and Judgment in the same cause, and for the same cause of action. And that the determination to reject the same papers is wrong—because that if the same papers are admitted to be given to the Jury, the evidence therein contained will have a legal tendency to lessen the damages if not wholly to defeat the action of the Pltfs—

And the said Bingham further files in this his bill of exceptions,

that the Court did reject and refuse to have read to the Jury in the trial as evidence, a resolution of the Congress of the United States of America, of the thirtieth of November 1779—also another resolution of the same Congress of the twentieth of June 1780—both which were concerning the subject matter of the suit.

Wherefore, that Justice by due process of Law, may be done in this case the said Bingham by the undersigned his Council prays the Court here that this his bill of exceptions may be filed and certified as the Law directs.

Ja Sullivan

C. Gore

June 16 1794—allowed to be filed, per

Wm Cushing   Judge of said Circuit Court

District of Massachusetts

Circuit Court

filed June Term A.D. 1794

Att: N. Goodale Clerk

[44] At 317.

the course of a colloquy over what constituted the record,[45] for Cushing asserted that in Massachusetts the declaration and pleadings were entered in a book and this alone was deemed the record; the papers and depositions were referred to only to ascertain what writ issued and what depositions were taken. Dallas' report does not indicate that any clear decision was reached on the point whether common law or Massachusetts practice was to be adopted for the purpose of determining what constituted the record. However, Cushing eventually agreed that the papers and depositions transmitted were to be regarded as part of the record. Paterson, Iredell and Wilson concurred. The judgment below was reversed, but because the Court was divided on the question of jurisdiction, it did not order a *venire facias de novo*.

There was some further consideration of the effect of the bill of exceptions in *Clarke v. Russell* (1799).[46] This was an action of assumpsit stemming from Russell's indorsement of several bills of exchange which had not been paid. They had been protested for non-payment. Russell, a citizen of South Carolina, had originally brought action in the Circuit Court for the Rhode Island District against Clarke and one Nightingale. There the defendants had demurred to the evidence; plaintiff's objection to joinder was overruled but judgment was given for him. The cause was taken on error to the Supreme Court where, in 1798, judgment was reversed, whether on the merits or because of Nightingale's death cannot be ascertained.[47] A second action was brought in the same Circuit against Clarke, surviving partner. In this action the disputed evidence was submitted to the jury. This consisted, among other items, of letters from Clarke and Nightingale to Russell that the latter in his declaration represented as an undertaking to see him secured, and a deposition taken under a commission, the tenor of which was to confirm the interpretation of the letters. Defendant had sought to put off the cause and filed an affidavit in which it was claimed that his absent witness could testify traversing the facts averred in the deposition. Cushing, who tried the cause alone, stated that the trial would be put off unless plaintiff agreed that the facts alleged in defendant's affidavit be considered at the trial as proven. Plaintiff had a verdict and judgment on one count of his declaration.

The cause was heard by the Supreme Court, February term 1799. The bill of exceptions was attached to the record, averring *inter alia* that the bills of exchange had been submitted in evidence without pro-

---

[45] 3 Dallas 19 at 27n.
[46] *Ibid.*, 415; the bill is printed at 416.
[47] Ms. Case Papers U.S. Sup. Ct., Case No. 55. The Ms. Mins. U.S. Sup.

Ct., *sub* Feb. 8, 1798, read: "Ordered that the Judgment of the Circuit Court . . . be reversed, and A Venire facias de novo is awarded. The Death of Joseph Nightingale is suggested."

tests for non-acceptance, that certain letters written by defendants[48] did not import a promise that Murray and Company of New York (on whose application the bills had been indorsed) would comply with any contract made with Russell, and that parol evidence had been admitted wrongfully to explain the promises in the letter. Objection had not been made when the evidence was introduced; this was done in relation to Cushing's charge to the jury.

At the beginning of the argument Ellsworth, presumably for the Court, held that acknowledgment of the seal of the Justice was unnecessary when the bill was attached to the record. On the authority of *Brown v. Barry*, which the Court had decided in 1797,[49] it was held that a protest for non-payment was sufficient. As for the admission of parol testimony, the Court split 3–2 on the point whether the deposition taken under commission could be regarded. Washington J. thought that since it accompanied the record, it might be considered as part of the record, but since it was not referred to in the bill of exceptions, the Court could not presume that it was the evidence objected to and so must be excluded. Ellsworth and Iredell agreed with this conclusion but denied that it was part of the record. Paterson and Cushing considered the reference to be sufficient. That part of the charge to the jury which asserted that the letters of the defendant partners could be explained by parol evidence was incorrect. Judgment was reversed and a *venire de novo* awarded.

A final example of a bill of exceptions appears in the record of the unreported case of *Ross v. Maul* (error from Virginia, 1800).[50] Here defendant had moved for leave to file a bill of exceptions before the jury retired. This was sealed. The writ of error was, however, quashed, probably because it was returned to the wrong term.

APPELLATE RECORDS AND THE REQUIREMENTS OF JURISDICTIONAL FACTS

SOME OF THE jurisdictional requirements written into the Judiciary Act, such as the amount in controversy and the finality of the judgment, were not novelties to American lawyers conversant with statutes, domestic and English, as well as the lore of practice books. They seem, how-

---

[48] Evidently those printed in Dallas' report. There were others in the record.

[49] 3 Dallas 365. In the record of Clarke v. Russell was included a statute of South Carolina (Act of Mar. 22, 1786) which gave a right of action for either non-payment or non-acceptance. This suggests a possible reference to sec. 34 of the Judiciary Act, but nothing of the sort was reported by Dallas.

[50] Ms. Case Papers U.S. Sup. Ct., Case No. 82.

ever, to have been slow to appreciate the tactical advantages which a non-conforming appellate record offered. It lay, of course, with counsel to alert the Bench to defects in a record. Neither as a matter of tradition nor of statutory direction was the Supreme Court Justice obliged to assume the burdens of those practicing before the Court. This is clearly exemplified by what went on in *Hylton v. United States*,[51] decided in February term 1796. Here the record had offered an opportunity for inquiring into the amount in controversy. An action of debt had been brought for the sum of $1,000, the taxes due on 125 coaches, and a like amount in penalties. Defendant had pleaded *nil debet* and further averred that the statute was unconstitutional. Issue had been joined but jury trial was waived. The parties, however, had submitted a case agreed upon by their counsel to serve in lieu of a special verdict. This included an agreement[52] that if it was adjudged that defendant was liable for fees and penalty, judgment was to be entered for the United States in the sum of $2,000, to be discharged by defendant by payment of $16—the tax and penalty on one chariot. Curiously enough, the flat sum of $2,000 had been suggested by Alexander Hamilton,[53] apparently under the misapprehension that this would suffice to satisfy the jurisdictional requirement. No attention was drawn to the defect in the Supreme Court and the Bench paid none. Counsel were present to argue the constitutionality of the carriage tax. This is what they did and the Court confined itself to this issue.[54]

It was one year later that the question of the amount in controversy came squarely before the Court in *Wilson v. Daniel*.[55] The action was one of debt on bond for the penal sum of £60,000. Judgment below was for the face value of the bond, but incorporated the finding of the jury, impanelled pursuant to section 26 of the Judiciary Act, that the debt be discharged by payment of $1,800. The judgment was operative only as to this amount.

The cause was twice argued, at February term 1797 and August term 1798. On the first argument Chase, Cushing and Paterson concurred in considering the judgment to be as one at common law for the penalty of the bond. Wilson noted a dissent; Iredell took no part. On

---

[51] Hylton v. United States, 3 Dallas 171 (1796).

[52] The agreement in Ms. Case Papers U.S. Sup. Ct., Case No. 13, Hylton v. United States.

[53] The correspondence relating to the case will appear in *LPAH*, III (in preparation).

[54] It may be remarked that little would have been gained except delay if the Court had declined to take cognizance of the cause. Since the allegations were fictitious, a new action adding tax on another coach and penalty would have taken care of the earlier oversight.

[55] 3 Dallas 401 (1798). Dallas states incorrectly that judgment was affirmed. Actually it was reversed. Ms. Case Papers U.S. Sup. Ct., Case No. 39.

reargument Ellsworth was of the opinion that the thing demanded, and not that found, constituted the matter in dispute in cases where the law gave no rule. And where the nature of the action governed, this was decisive—in this case debt for the full amount of the bond. Chase was much of the same opinion. In actions of tort or trespass he conceived that the damages laid in the declaration furnished the only practicable test. The instant action he considered to be an action at common law, and judgment to be for the full amount. The stipulation for discharge Chase treated as surplusage. Iredell dissented. He viewed the writ of error as in the nature of a new suit, and evidently thought that in this situation the chancering of the bond by the jury furnished the basis of the amount in controversy. The judgment of the Circuit Court was reversed.

Within two years after the opinions in *Wilson v. Daniel* the Court, in *Williamson v. Kincaid*,[56] settled a further detail of practice respecting the amount in controversy. In a common law action for dower plaintiff below had judgment on demurrer to a replication. A preliminary objection was made by counsel in the Supreme Court that the value of the matter in dispute did not appear upon the record. Since there was no Act of Congress or rule of Court prescribing a mode of ascertaining value in cases of this sort, it was proposed to continue the cause to afford opportunity to satisfy the Court by affidavits of the actual value of the property. This the Court accepted with the stipulation that the writ of error was not to be a supersedeas.[57] At the same term a similar rule was made in the preliminary proceedings in *Course* et al. *v. Stead* et ux. et al.[58]

Only twice in the period here considered did the Court have occasion to rule on the finality of the judgment or decree before it. In *Wilson v. Daniel* there had been no joinder of issue on one plea, and the judgment at Circuit had been only on a second plea. It was claimed that the judgment was so defective that error would not lie upon it. The Court, however, decided that the judgment was not interlocutory but final and went to the merits. Ellsworth took as his test the fact that an

---

[56] 4 Dallas 20 (1800).

[57] The declaration in dower demanded of defendant one-third part of 300 acres of woodland, 300 acres of pine land and 218 acres of rice land in Chatham County, Georgia. Ms. Case Papers U.S. Sup. Ct., Case No. 73. Dallas erroneously reports judgment reversed for lack of sufficient allegation of diverse citizenship. The records show the cause continued until Feb. 14, 1803, when the writ of error was non-prossed.

[58] 4 Dallas 22 (1800). In this period the only writ of error which we are reasonably certain was quashed by the Court because of insufficient jurisdictional amount was the unreported case of Paine and Bridgman v. United States (1800). The face value of the bond sued on was $1,441.90, damages alleged $100. Verdict was returned for the United States, damages 1 cent. Ms. Case Papers U.S. Sup. Ct., Case No. 79; Ms. Docket Book U.S. Sup Ct., p. 86.

execution could issue upon it. In a second case in 1800, *Rutherfurd v. Fisher and Fisher*, an equity suit involving a great tract of land in New Jersey, the Court held the obvious, that error would not lie on an interlocutory decree below which overruled pleas to several statutes of limitation and ordered defendants to plead over.[59]

The most aberrant form of "final judgment"—that in *Hylton v. United States*—the Court did not undertake to examine. The Circuit Court for the Virginia District was divided on the issue of the constitutionality of the carriage tax, a situation for which the Act of March 2, 1793,[60] had provided by directing that the case be continued to the succeeding court, and if, with a different Supreme Court Justice attending, the bench was again divided, judgment was to be rendered in conformity with the opinion of the presiding judge. However, by agreement,[61] Hylton confessed judgment with the stipulation that this would not preclude his suing out a writ of error and assigning error in the Supreme Court. In England the ancient rule that error lay in certain cases where judgment had been confessed[62] had undergone some enlargement,[63] and it may be inferred from a statute of Anne[64] directing that there should be no reversals of judgments entered upon confession for defects curable by statutes of jeofails, that the courts had tolerated much broader departures from the old rules than case law indicates. The reservation in Hylton's confession of judgment indicates that the pristine common law rule may have been esteemed to be in effect.

From what we know about the circumstances of this case, both the government and the Virginia politicians who resented the carriage tax were anxious for a speedy determination. The bar already had become alert to take advantage of the words of the writ "if judgment thereof be given" or its equivalent to expedite matters by procuring the issuance of the writ in advance of judgment being entered. Thus in *Collet v. Collet* the writ was tested as of February 8, 1792,[65] but judgment was not entered until April 21; and so in *Delcol v. Arnold* the writ was tested as of October 25, 1794, and judgment entered a month later.[66] Agreements approximating that in *Hylton* are those in *Jennings v. Read*

---

[59] 4 Dallas 22 (1800). Defendants had pleaded in bar provisions of 32 Hen. 8, c. 2, and 21 Jac. 1, c. 16, claimed to have been practiced in New Jersey, as well as New Jersey Acts of 1729, 1787 and 1799, all limiting the time within which land title and mortgage actions might be brought. The decree overruled the plea and ordered defendants to answer. Ms. Case Papers U.S. Sup. Ct., Case No. 77.

[60] 1 *U.S. Stats.*, 333.

[61] Ms. Case Papers U.S. Sup. Ct., Case No. 13.

[62] Fitzherbert, *Natura Brevium* (1794 ed.), 21 K; and see Beecher's Case, 8 Coke Rep. 58a at 62a.

[63] Viner, *Abridgment* (1792 ed.), *s.v.* Error.

[64] 4 Anne, c. 16, sec. 2.

[65] Ms. Case Papers U.S. Sup. Ct., Case No. 1.

[66] *Ibid.*, Case No. 14. See also Moodie v. *Ship Betty Cathcart* (unreported; *ibid.*, Case No. 16), the writ

(1799)[67] where it was agreed that the decree of the District Court be affirmed by consent as of a certain date in order that a writ of error be sued out from the Supreme Court, the affirmance to be as of April term 1798; in *United States v. Brig^t Harriott and George Topham* (1800)[68] the case papers and docket book reveal that the writ of error was issued by consent more than a month before judgment and returnable as of February 1800 term of the Supreme Court.

It was not until the 1798 decision in *Bingham v. Cabot II*[69] that the Supreme Court belatedly took corrective action to put an end to the lackadaisical practice regarding the showing of diversity enjoined by the Judiciary Act in implementing the constitutional provision. As noticed, case papers from various circuits indicate that local attorneys were not always attentive to allegations of citizenship,[70] and since the responsibility for having the record in error perfected rested upon counsel or attorney for plaintiff in error, aberrations from statutory requirements in such records must be attributed to professional negligence. The actual preparation of the records appears to have been done by the District clerk or his deputies. Counsel for plaintiff in error in *Brown v. Van Braam Houchgueest* (1797) had commented sarcastically about "the errors of clerks, and the blunders of yearlings (to whom often the business of keeping and making up a record is confided)."[71] Whether or not this was said by Samuel Dexter of Massachusetts, one of three counsel in this cause, it was he who represented defendant in error a year later in *Bingham v. Cabot II.*

The assignment of error in this case averred that there was not a sufficient allegation of the citizenship of the parties to sustain the jurisdiction of the court below. Attorney General Charles Lee for plaintiff in error argued in the Court that citizenship was not co-extensive with residence and further that there was no entirety of parties. The dec-

---

was tested Aug. 3, 1795, judgment entered October 26; Moodie v. *Brig Eliza* (unreported; *ibid.*, Case No. 18), the writ was tested Aug. 3, 1795, judgment entered Sept. 5, 1795.

[67] Unreported; *ibid.*, Case No. 6. This was a writ of error to the Circuit Court for the Pennsylvania District, where a decree of the District Court dismissing a libel brought to enforce the decree of the Court of Appeals in Cases of Capture had been affirmed. The Supreme Court reversed and remanded to the District Court with instructions. The merits later decided in Jennings v. Carson, 2 Cranch 2 (1807). The agreement signed by Edward Tilghman and Jared Ingersoll on July 10, 1798, reads: "The Decree of the District Court is to be affirmed by consent in order that a Writ of Error be sued out from the Supreme Court of the United States— the affirmance to be as of April Term 1798." Ms. Case Papers Circuit Ct. Pennsylvania Dist.

[68] Unreported; Ms. Case Papers U.S. Sup. Ct., Case No. 75.

[69] 3 Dallas 382. This second action was also framed in assumpsit; most of the disputed evidence had been admitted (*supra*, p. 676), and again plaintiff had a verdict.

[70] *Supra*, c. XIII, p. 586.

[71] 3 Dallas 344 at 350.

laration filed in the Circuit Court had merely described several of the plaintiffs as "of Boston" or "of the same place" with the citizenship of one of the plaintiffs, Cabot, depicted as "of Boston aforesaid, now resident at Philadelphia aforesaid, merchant."[72] Counsel for the defendant in error argued in opposition that citizenship could be changed without going through the forms required of an alien and that a citizen of the United States was to be considered as one of the state in which he was domiciled. The Court held that to bring the case within the jurisdiction of the Circuit Court it was necessary to set forth the citizenship or alienage of the parties. Judgment below was accordingly reversed.[73] The Court did not rule on the question of the entirety of parties.

The effect of this holding, if earlier arrived at, would have been to throw out a majority of the cases in which jurisdiction was based on diversity which theretofore had come to the Court. In some records there is no description either of the citizenship or the residence of domicil of any of the parties. The immediate effect of the decision was to present a new and lethal weapon to counsel for appellants seeking reversal in the Supreme Court. On the same day that the *Bingham* decision was handed down, the Court also held that the process must aver the diverse citizenship of the parties.[74]

After *Bingham II* lack of description became a common assignment of error.[75] The decision was logically extended to an alienage case

---

[72] See the declaration, filed June 1, 1797, Ms. Case Papers U.S. Sup. Ct., Case No. 5. The case papers in the two Bingham cases have been intermingled.

[73] Dallas erroneously states (at 384) that the case "and many others" were accordingly stricken from the docket. Actually, judgment was reversed. Lack of jurisdiction in the court below would not defeat the Supreme Court's jurisdiction on writ of error to correct the assumption of jurisdiction. As to the "many others" Dallas speaks of, only one other case was decided the same day.

[74] Emory v. Greenough, 3 Dallas 369; Ms. Case Papers U.S. Sup Ct., Case No. 36. Dallas reports the case under the 1797 term of the Court. Argument had begun in that year but the decision was given in 1798. *Cf.* Ms. Docket Book U.S. Sup. Ct., p. 30. The declaration did aver the plaintiff's Massachusetts residence and the Pennsylvania residence of the defendant. Although it is not clear from the

report (and not included in the record) if that were a sufficient description, the process omitted the requirement. This is another interesting conflicts case. The action in assumpsit was based on a loan of public securities and loan office certificates. Pleaded in bar was a discharge in bankruptcy under Pennsylvania proceedings. The plaintiff's reply was his Massachusetts citizenship and domicil, the execution and suit in Massachusetts, and what amounts, stripped of the verbiage, to a claim of lack of *in personam* jurisdiction in the Pennsylvania proceedings. The Circuit Court ruled the plea insufficient, and a verdict and judgment was subsequently given for the plaintiff.

[75] Of the twelve cases adjudicated by the Court in 1799 and 1800, four were reversed on this formal jurisdictional basis. Assignments of error on that basis were made in a number of others which did not reach an adjudication.

in 1799, *Turner v. Enrille*, where the plaintiff's residence had been left blank in the declaration and the defendants described as "merchants and partners at Newbern."[76] In 1800 two additional cases were reversed on the same basis, *Jones* et al. *v. Pearce* (unreported)[77] and *Mossman v. Higginson*.[78]

The *Bingham* rationale was further extended in *Turner v. The Bank of North America*[79] by requiring not only that there be an adequate description of the parties, but also that where the suit was upon a promissory note prosecuted by an assignee, the citizenship of the original promissee had to be set forth by the record.

---

[76] 4 Dallas 7 (1799); and see Ms. Case Papers U.S. Sup. Ct., Case No. 64. Counsel for the defendant in error, A. J. Dallas, "lamented the obvious irregularities on the face of the record." Dallas attempted to distinguish the case from *Bingham II* on rather tenuous grounds, alleging that in the instant case the plaintiff was described specifically as of "an island" and only generally of Massachusetts in *Bingham*, and that the defendants were described as merchants at Newbern whereas in *Bingham* their residence had not been stated at all.

[77] Error from Delaware (1800, unreported); Ms Case Papers U.S. Sup. Ct., Case No. 83. The declaration averred the plaintiff's Maryland citizenship but only the Philadelphia residence of three of the defendants and no description of two others. No assignment of errors is among the case papers. The writ of error reveals that reversal was being claimed on the basis that one of the defendants had died before final judgment in the Circuit Court. (Sec. 31 of the Judiciary Act provided for non-abatement of the action if the cause survived to the surviving plaintiff or the surviving defendant, directing the action to proceed after the suggestion of death is noted on the record. The death of the deceased defendant was not so noted.) The circumstances of the inadequate description favor the view that the judgment below was reversed on that basis.

[78] 4 Dallas 12 (1800); Ms. Case Papers U.S. Sup. Ct., Cases No. 62

and No. 71. The declaration averred the alienage (English) of the orator in equity but gave no description of the defendants. The suit was a bill in equity to foreclose the equity of redemption on a mortgage. Counsel for the defendant in error (Tilghman and Read) contended that the prayer of process against one defendant, who had never held the land, was irregular and mere surplusage (Mossman, however, answered the bill), and that as to the other defendant (Mein), the Court should take judicial notice of the law of Georgia under which no alien could hold real estate. They also argued that it was sufficient under the Constitution and sec. 11 of the Judiciary Act that an alien was a party to the suit, effectively here a proceeding *in rem* and not a personal recovery, and that in any event the Court would permit the defect to be amended. The Supreme Court held that sec. 11 of the Judiciary Act could and must receive a construction consistent with the Constitution and that while sec. 11 was framed generally (cognizance of suits "where an alien is a party") the legislative power conferring jurisdiction in this respect was confined to suits between citizens and foreigners. The Court rejected the *in rem* proposition on the basis that both the Constitution and the Judiciary Act contemplated the parties and not the subject of the suit. A description of the parties was indispensable to the exercise of jurisdiction. The writ was quashed.

[79] 4 Dallas 8 (1799).

THE SCOPE OF REVIEW

OTHER THAN ITS few ventures into the thickets of constitutional law and those undertaking to define the jurisdictional boundaries of the federal courts in admiralty,[80] the decisions delimiting the Supreme Court's scope of review present the single most important group of decisions handed down prior to 1801. Certainly no other issue involved a comparable volume of litigation in the Court, marked, it would seem, by an unexcelled intensity and displaying some of the best examples of the skill and analytical resourcefulness of the early Supreme Court bar. This should occasion no surprise for the monetary stakes in many of this group of cases involved contemporarily remarkably large sums,[81] a factor always affecting viability in the pursuit of appellate review. As a group these decisions, because they included the equity and admiralty causes brought up on error, were to suffer decimation as precedents after the 1803 amendment to the Judiciary Act which authorized removal by appeal proper and allowed new evidence to be introduced on appeal in admiralty cases.[82] The short-lived Act of 1801[83] that had so enraged the Republicans had provided the pattern for change, and we believe that the experience of the Supreme Court in wrestling with the adjustments necessary to fit the appeal below into the corselet of writ of error proceedings before itself may have led to this first alteration. Why, after the repeal of the 1801 act, the Congress, nevertheless, had a change of heart respecting appeals to the Supreme Court we do not know.

The majority of the cases examined here are admiralty suits. There were proportionately a greater number of these; and because of

---

[80] Discussed *infra*, c. XVII.

[81] For example, in Talbot v. Jansen (3 Dallas 133, 170 [1795]; Ms. Case Papers U.S. Sup. Ct., Case No. 9), the final recovery of the libellant-defendant in error, including costs, demurrage and interest plus recovery of the proceeds of the ship and cargo, amounted to over $60,000. In Hills *et al.* v. Ross (*ibid.*, 331, 332 [1796]; Case No. 12), the final recovery was nearly $38,000. In Delcol v. Arnold (*ibid.*, 333, 334 [1796]; Case No. 14), final recovery amounted to over $33,000. In some suits the owners of condemned ships stood to lose from the value of the cargo alone over $50,000 (Talbot v. Jansen). These judgments were the "big" suits which came to the Court in this period, excepting some suits involving the

title to great tracts of land. Of the latter see, *e.g.*, Hunter v. Goodtitle *ex dem.* Fairfax, writ non-prossed (1797, unreported; Case No. 29), where the ejectment itself was for only 788 acres; however, the principle established would have affected the title of over a quarter of a million acres in the Northern Neck of Virginia. Also compare Rutherfurd *et al.* v. Fisher and Fisher (4 Dallas 22 [1800]; Case No. 77), *supra*, p. 581.

[82] 2 *U.S. Stats.*, 244.

[83] *Ibid.*, 89. This act expressly barred reception of new evidence. It also stipulated that appeals should be subject to the same rules, regulations and restrictions "as are prescribed by law in case of writs of error," a provision also written into the 1803 act.

the nature of the appellate records in admiralty causes that came up from the Circuit Courts, the ingredients of which have already been examined, it is not improper to claim that here the scope of review, even though the instrument of removal had been writ of error, was broader than it was in actions at law. In the latter the common law record and the whole body of practice respecting review on writ of error and the inherent limitations were both familiar and accepted. Furthermore, review of fact in common law cases in which there had been a jury trial was restricted not only by the force of section 22, but after 1791 by the Seventh Amendment as well. But in admiralty suits it was basically review of fact which was crucial; review of law was available irrespective of the removal process, whether by writ of error or by appeal.

It is unnecessary to recapitulate the details of the Senate discussions over the review provisions of the Judiciary Bill further than to recall the upsurge of prejudice against the methods of the civil law, and the expedient devised by Ellsworth to make workable error proceedings in admiralty and equity causes.[84] The agreement to incorporate what became section 19 into the act had the effect of creating a new species of record that, like some fabled beast of classical mythology, was left to be bridled by the traditional process of writ of error.[85] Although it may have occurred to some that section 19 by committing to the control of the Circuit judges the exemplification of operative facts might have the effect of undercutting the prohibition of section 22—that there should be no reversal in the Supreme Court for any error in fact—this point was not mooted at the time.

Before proceeding to the dissection of the more difficult and subtle questions involved in the scope of review, it should be emphasized that the Court paid careful, indeed, almost fastidious, attention to the regulations under which a case was brought before it. This is not to claim that there were no irregularities perceptible in the history of the appellate process during this period. *Glass v. the Sloop Betsey* is an obvious example, the jurisdiction here being obtained by an appeal *in scriptis* before a notary,[86] an established incident of English practice, rather

---

[84] *Supra*, c. XI, p. 500 *et seq.*

[85] It has already been suggested that the procedure of case reserved or case stated where a point of law was to be settled *en banc* may have furnished inspiration for the agreement of counsel or under the pre-Mansfield procedure for the statement by the Court. There was, of course, the further usage of counsel agreeing upon the form and content of special verdicts.

[86] 3 Dallas 6 (1794). The appeal,

in Ms. Case Papers U.S. Sup. Ct., Case No. 3:

Alexander S. Glass [et al.]
vs.
The Sloop Betsy and Cargo and Capt Pierre Arcade Johannene

Circuit Court for the District of Maryland

A Plea to the Jurisdiction in this cause having been pleaded by the Defendant in the District

than by writ of error. Exceptions to the process were, however, waived by counsel, and waiver was one device, and probably the only one, by which irregular process could be converted into efficacious process. The Court did not usually object on its own motion to the propriety of process; the division in *Hayburn's Case* (which Attorney General Randolph seems to have conceived as in nature appellate) occurred because of doubts of his authority to act *ex officio*.[87]

How far the doctrine of waiver could be extended is not known, but it obviously was deemed to have limits. In *Dewhurst v. Coulthard* (1799) counsel for both parties, resorting to a perversion of the New York case-reserved procedure, joined in a request to the Court to assume jurisdiction to settle the point of law at issue. This was presented by way of petition.[88] The Court, however, remained firm in its stand that it could not take cognizance of any case not brought before it but by the "regular process" of law.[89]

Court for the District of Maryland and the said Plea having been allowed by the Judge of the said District of Maryland, and a Decree made for the restoration of the said Sloop Betsy and her Cargo to the said Defendant, the Libellants prayed an Appeal from the said Decree to the next Circuit Court of the District of Maryland to be held at Easton on the seventh day of November 1793 which said Appeal was then and there heard before the Judges of the said Circuit Court, when by the said Court it was adjudged and Decreed that the said Appeal should be dismissed with Costs and that the Decree of the said District Court should be affirmed from which said Opinion and Decree of the said Circuit Court the said Libellants and Appellants have this day at Baltimore Town before me George P. Keeports Notary Public by lawful Authority Commissioned and sworn dwelling in Baltimore Town in the presence of John Hollins and Daniel O'Sullivan Witnesses prayed an Appeal to the Supreme Court of the United States to be held at the City of Philadelphia on the fourteenth day of Feb-

ruary next—

In testimony whereof I, the said Notary in the presence of the said Witnesses have hereunto set my Hand and affixed my Seal Notarial the eighteenth day of November in the Year of Our Lord one Thousand seven Hundred and ninety three—

Witnesses

John Hollins
Daniel O'Sullivan

George P. Keeports
Notary Public of
Balt County

Whether this appeal was actually ever filed with the Circuit Court is not known. It probably was filed with the Supreme Court directly with a transcript of the record when the writ of inhibition was sued out.

Dallas (at 7n.) states that the Court would not allow "any judicial countenance" to be given to the proceeding before the notary. The Ms. Docket Book U.S. Sup. Ct., p. 6, notes the proctors' agreement was filed February 8. Note further that the record name of the sloop is spelled *Betsy*. In other cases Dallas has his own version of party names.

[87] *Supra*, c. XIII, p. 562.
[88] 3 Dallas 409 (1799).
[89] See Wilson v. Daniel, *ibid.*, 401.

Although it was not until *Bingham v. Cabot I*[90] that the Court made plain some of the considerations that would determine its scope of review, a year earlier attention had already been directed to an important one—the state of the record. This had occurred in *Glass v. the Sloop Betsey*.[91] Here, by consent, argument was restricted to errors appearing on the face of the record. This was particularly attenuated, consisting of the libel, the plea to the jurisdiction (sustained below), the decree of the French consul acting as a prize court, the proceedings in the District Court on staying execution, writs of inhibition and the appeal proceedings at Circuit. As will later be noticed, the argument had revolved about the nature of the District Court's jurisdiction under the Constitution and laws of the United States. After keeping the case under advisement for several days, the Court informed counsel that another question arose upon the record: whether any foreign nation had a right without express treaty provision to establish in this country an admiralty jurisdiction for taking cognizance of prizes. The Court meant to decide it and hear it discussed. Peter Du Ponceau, retained by the French Minister, "observed that the parties to the appeal did not conceive themselves interested in the point and the Minister had given no instructions for arguing it." The Court proceeded to answer its own question in the negative.[92]

The decision in *Bingham v. Cabot I*, on the exceptions to the jurisdiction of the Circuit Court, was to clarify what seems to have come as a surprise to counsel in *Glass*, viz., the sovereign role of the record. For in *Bingham* the four Justices who heard the case (Cushing, Iredell, Paterson, and Wilson) eventually agreed that all the papers transmitted upon the return of the writ of error were considered as forming part of the record.[93] In this case the significant effect was that the Court was at liberty to examine the depositions and other evidence excluded at trial for the purpose of determining the Circuit Court's competence. Here, as remarked, the evidence had been specifically referred to in the bill of exceptions which the court regarded as conclusive upon it. Subsequently,

---

[90] *Ibid.*, 19 (1795).

[91] *Ibid.*, 6 (1794).

[92] What is published by Dallas as the "unanimous opinion" of the Court is in fact a truncated version of the final decree in this case. See the decree which accompanied the mandate to the District Court, in Ms. Case Papers, Circuit Ct. Maryland Dist. This document was set out in John Trumbull's opinion on the case of the *Elizabeth* before the Mixed Commission under Art. VII of Jay's Treaty (J. B. Moore, ed., *International Adjudications*, IV, 545–46).

[93] In this connection note the colloquy reported by Dallas (vol. 3, at 27n.) over the preliminary question whether the "peculiar" practice of Massachusetts or the general common law practice as to what constituted the record was to be followed. Cushing made a somewhat defensive speech on the Massachusetts record. *Cf. supra*, p. 678.

in *Clarke v. Russell*,[94] Iredell and Ellsworth rejected the proposition that papers ambiguously referred to in a bill formed part of the record.

One further dimension was added in *Bingham* to the Court's conception of the scope of review, viz., that jurisdiction over subject matter could be challenged in the appellate court even though it had not been raised below.[95] Counsel for defendant in error claimed that the objection came too late, thereby advancing a claim of waiver.[96] The Court did not speak explicitly to this point, but it is apparent from a remark of Paterson's[97] and from the tenor of the opinion that it was conceived that a question of jurisdiction could never be waived. This holding was subsequently enforced in the second *Bingham* case and its successors with respect to the requisite statement of citizenship or alienage necessary to give a Circuit Court jurisdiction over a cause. The question of waiver was not even ventilated by counsel for the obvious reason, one may suppose, of the limitations written into Article III of the Constitution.

In 1796, the Supreme Court's first year of abundance, a substantial number of suits involving questions of the scope of review were litigated with consequent significant accretions to the law, nowhere more evident than in respect to review of equity and admiralty causes.[98] Basically the issues fought over concerned three interrelated problems: the jurisdictional need for a statement as provided by section 19 of the Judiciary Act and the effect thereof; the reception of new evidence in the Supreme Court; and the effect of the evidence transmitted on the return of the writ of error. The nature of the record and proceedings that went up on appeal from the District to the Circuit Court has already been examined, as has also the conflation of this by addition of the proceedings at Circuit.[99] Section 19 contemplated only a showing of facts from pleadings and decree as an alternative to a judicial statement or one by the parties or their counsel. It seems probable that the occasional monstrous documentation of which the record on error consisted was due to the desire to have review of the sufficiency of the evidence and the facts found from it.[100] This conjecture gains in plausibility from evidence of attempts to proceed by appeal instead of error.

---

94 3 Dallas 415 at 422–23n. (1799).

95 Plaintiff in error contended that the subject matter of the action was prize and therefore exclusively of the admiralty jurisdiction. The Court divided on the question.

96 3 Dallas 28.

97 *Ibid.*, 32n.

98 The admiralty suits mostly involved infractions of the Neutrality Act, and claimants generally set up in bar the seventeenth article of the Treaty of Amity and Commerce of Feb. 6, 1778, granting to the privateers of the contracting parties free entry and immunity from arrest in the ports of either country. This was usually coupled with or preceded by a plea to the jurisdiction.

99 *Supra*, c. XIII, p. 602 *et seq.*

100 See here Peter Du Ponceau in an opinion given to Capt. Martin Jorris in 1795 relative to an appeal from the District to the Circuit Court suggesting that it was material that the evidence should be made part of the

Two of the problems mentioned above had presented themselves in 1795 when *Talbot v. Jansen*[101] came before the Court. Before argument on the principal questions, counsel for defendant in error offered to introduce a certificate not produced below. But without resolving the question whether or not new evidence could be presented on appeal, the Court held that under rules of evidence the document was inadmissible. The lack of a section 19 statement had been assigned as error, but the Court had no occasion to pass on this, for the objection was waived because the parties desired a decision on the merits.[102]

At February term 1796, in *Hills* et al. *v. Ross*, another admiralty case, the alleged error—lack of a section 19 statement—was again assigned, but on this occasion was argued. A short discussion of the record of the *Hills*[103] case is relevant here to comprehend the proceed-

record (it had been omitted in the District Court and the judge's impression of the evidence substituted) in case the cause be subsequently appealed to the Supreme Court for the purpose of controverting the findings below. Ms. Du Ponceau Letterbook B, 58, to Captain Martin Jorris, Apr. 8, 1795 (HSP).

[101] 3 Dallas 133 (1795). The action began in the South Carolina District Court with a libel in admiralty against the Dutch vessel *De Vrouw Christina Magdalena* prosecuted by the owners of the ship and cargo. The *Magdalena* had been captured by a French vessel commanded by one Ballard and later taken into Charleston by another French vessel, *L'Ami de la Point a Petre*, commanded by William Talbot. Discussed *infra*, c. XVII.

Specifications of error filed on August 5 included (1) the possession of the prize by Ballard could not impair the rights of Talbot acquired by his capture and possession, (2) the facts were contrary to the finding that *L'Ami de la Point a Petre* was illegally armed in the United States and owned by American citizens and (3) the facts and law proved Talbot a French citizen. Ms. Case Papers U.S. Sup. Ct., Case No. 9.

[102] 3 Dallas 137–38n.

[103] *Ship Elizabeth* and Cargo and Hills, May and Woodbridge, Plaintiffs in Error v. Walter Ross (error from Georgia), 3 Dallas 184 (1796). The

facts of the suit, not delineated by Dallas, are interesting and necessary to the damages problem discussed *infra*. A libel was filed in the Georgia District Court by Ross, a British subject, for the owners of the ship and cargo alleging that the *Elizabeth* had been captured illegally by two French ships commanded by Talbot and Ballard (the same privateers involved in Talbot v. Jansen, *supra*) in 1794 near the Bahamas and that these ships had been built originally in the United States, were owned by American citizens, and that one of them was largely manned by Americans. The libel also averred that Hills, May and Woodbridge of Savannah as agents for Talbot and Ballard had taken the *Elizabeth* under a fictitious sale, the vessel subsequently coming into the hands of Joseph Miller. Neither Talbot nor Ballard appeared. Answers were interposed by Hills *et al.*, claiming ownership of one third of the ship and all the cargo for their own account and the reception of the residue for Talbot on agency by virtue of a sale from the French consul, and averring that the cargo had been disposed of prior to the filing of the libel. Miller also answered, claiming a *bona fide* purchase without notice. The District Court ordered the ship and cargo restored to the libellant, Hills *et al.*, however, only being held liable for the residue of the cargo in their hands.

On appeal to the Circuit Court the

ings and argument in the Supreme Court, for these were somewhat garbled by Dallas in his report of the case.

After the original decree in the Georgia District Court, an appeal was prosecuted to the Circuit Court, with the hearings held in May of 1795. A fragment of the minutes included in the record disclose that a number of witnesses were examined *viva voce* in the Circuit but that this testimony had not been committed to writing. Consequently the record included solely the testimony and evidence which had been taken in the District Court.[104] There was no elaboration of the decree in the Circuit Court or a statement of the case which might have satisfied section 19; the decree merely ordered the affirmance of the decree below as to the ship and otherwise substituted a new one. There is some reason to doubt how carefully the Court considered the appeal. District Judge Pendleton, who had heard the case below, withdrew, and it was at this term that Justice Blair was so distracted by colic and a rattling noise in his head that he felt himself unfit to do business, but was persuaded to do so.[105] The possibility of an attack on the record as an imperfect one appears to have made an impression on counsel for the defendant in error at some point after the Circuit Court decree—evidently between May and December of 1795. In August Peter Du Ponceau cautioned Noel, the attorney for the Hills' interests in the District, against agreeing with opposing counsel to remedy the defect in the record arising from the want of facts, even though it might be productive of delay to their clients.[106] In the same letter Du Ponceau elaborately outlined the attack which was to be made on a possible attempt to remedy the lack of a section 19 statement of facts through the use of Justice Blair's notes, and the argument to be advanced for reversal, if error was confined to the record in its extant state. This was to be directed chiefly to the failure to fulfill the section 19 requirement.[107]

---

decree below was affirmed as to the ship, and Hills *et al.* were ordered to pay the full value of the cargo. There was no specific reversal of the District Court's order making Hills *et al.* liable only for the small amount of cargo subsisting in their hands (a couple of hogsheads of rum and one of sugar). The omission was later argued as a basis for reversal in the Supreme Court by the plaintiffs in error. However, this evidently was not given much play, if seriously pressed at all. Du Ponceau, writing to attorney J. Y. Noel who had handled the litigation in the District Court and delineating the tactics to be used on argument, conceded he was not in-

clined to rely on the omission as it was so trifling that it probably would be considered as an error of the clerk in drawing up the decree. Ms. Du Ponceau Letterbook B, 108 at 121, Aug. I, 1795 (HSP).

[104] Ms. Case Papers U.S. Sup. Ct., Case No. 12.

[105] *Supra*, c. XIII, n. 8.

[106] Ms. Du Ponceau Letterbook B, 108 at 109, to J. Y. Noel, Aug. 1, 1795 (HSP).

[107] *Ibid.*, 121. Du Ponceau contemplated the insistence of the Court on a statement of the case by the parties or perhaps by Justice Blair, who had been the Circuit Court judge; he noted, however, that both possibilities would

Either previous or subsequent to this letter counsel for the defendant in error (Ross) had served notice on plaintiffs that an examination of four witnesses would be taken and transmitted to the Supreme Court. The proctor for the plaintiffs in error attended and objected to the examination on the ground that section 30 of the Judiciary Act defined the cases in which testimony *de bene esse* might be taken and confined them to cases in which they might be used on trial in the District or Circuit Court. Also argued in objection was that section 30 contained no provision for taking testimony where there might be an appeal to the Supreme Court but restricted it to the cases where there might be an appeal from District Court to Circuit Court, and that otherwise the method prescribed by the Judiciary Act for the recital of facts on error taken from the Circuit Court was a section 19 statement.[108] There is no indication that these depositions were taken at this time. The motion to take the depositions of the witnesses examined in the Circuit Court was later renewed in the Supreme Court after the decision on the preliminary question involving section 19.[109]

---

be opposed. If a statement were to be made through the use of Blair's notes, Du Ponceau intended to object on the basis that: (1) Blair was no longer a judge of the Circuit Court of Georgia —this was supported with the notation that Wilson had refused to hear questions of bail during vacation time because Paterson was the judge appointed for the next circuit; (2) if Blair were still judge, his statement ought to have been made and annexed to the record while the case was before him as was the rule with respect to special verdicts, bills of exceptions, etc.; (3) the certificate of a judge where required, as in actions of trespass, probable cause and so forth, could not be made out of court; (4) the power given by the Judiciary Act to a Circuit judge to find facts in causes by his own special verdict is erroneous and before unheard of in this country and ought not to be extended beyond the strictest rules; and (5) the report of a *nisi prius* judge on motions *en banc* for a new trial (the most analogous case he could find) was not conclusive as to the statement of the evidence laid before the jury below but might be corrected by the notes of counsel, but that here when Judge Blair's certificate was committed to writing and became part

of the record no recollection, even his own, could help it. With the help of these and other arguments Du Ponceau hoped "to prevent being saddled with an inaccurate statement of the case, which might be productive of the greatest mischief."

[108] Ms. Case Papers U.S. Sup. Ct., Case No. 12. One of the papers in the record relates these proceedings, but it gives no firm date or place where held. The notice was signed by District Judge Pendleton. The arguments here used were basically the same as those later advanced in the Supreme Court.

[109] The application was made either in February or March. Counsel for the plaintiffs in error had previously argued in the Supreme Court and conceded that the record was imperfect and that it would be impossible to obtain a fair view of the proceedings as they then stood; consequently counsel did not object but insisted on the rule being made generally to examine all and any new witnesses. Ms. Du Ponceau Letterbook B, 143–45, to Messrs. Hills, May and Woodbridge, Philadelphia, Mar. 3, 1796 (HSP). The objection to the insufficiency of the facts was, of course, made to obtain a reversal in the Court.

On argument of the case in the Supreme Court at the February term 1796,[110] it was conceded by both sides that it was impossible to obtain a fair view of the proceedings because of the failure of the record to contain the evidence produced below in the Circuit Court. However, Du Ponceau and John B. Coxe contended that the decree below must be reversed because of the lack of the section 19 statement. Counsel for the defendant in error opposed this on the ground that the decree ought to be affirmed unless shown to be erroneous, that the omission could not be assigned as error and did not vitiate the proceedings, and that it was the result of the neglect of plaintiffs in error who ought to have applied to opposing counsel in the Circuit Court to agree to a statement of the case, and, if they refused, then to the Circuit itself.[111]

In developing their theory for reversal, the plaintiffs in error insisted that section 30 required that testimony of witnesses should be taken *viva voce* rather than by deposition, both in the Circuit and District Courts, with an exception noted in the District Court where there might be an appeal to the Circuit Court; that in the Circuit Court where new evidence was submitted, no provision was made for committing the testimony to writing except for evidence taken *de bene esse*. Consequently, the whole testimony could not come before the Supreme Court in case new witnesses were heard, or the same witnesses examined in the District Court were produced *de novo* in the Circuit, without the consent of the parties.[112]

It was claimed, therefore, that by these provisions it was the intention of Congress to vest the power of trying facts in the District and Circuit Courts exclusively and that the decision of the Circuit Court was final, section 22 disabling the Supreme Court from reversing errors in fact.[113] Consequently, an appeal did not lie to the Supreme Court, but only a writ of error. However, because the admiralty and equity forms of proceedings were still retained, crowding the record with a variety of facts, section 19 made it the duty of the Circuit Court to cause the facts on which it founded its decree to appear on the record. As the omission was the fault of the court below, it could be assigned as error.

The Supreme Court was unanimously of the opinion that the error assigned was not a sufficient ground for reversing the decree and recommended that the parties come to an agreement which might bring the

---

110 The argument occupied only part of one day. Ms. Mins. U.S. Sup. Ct. 1790–1805, *sub* Feb. 26, 1796.

111 3 Dallas 184–85.

112 If this argument is correctly reported it involved a misinterpretation of sec. 30, because testimony could not be taken by deposition generally if there was to be an appeal, but only if it would not be within the party's power to produce the witnesses at the trial in the Circuit Court.

113 3 Dallas 185–86.

controversy fairly before them.[114] This was accomplished by stipulating that new evidence could be taken on both sides and that the whole matter of fact and law be brought before the Court "as upon an appeal."[115]

The day before the consent agreement in the *Hills* case was arrived at, the Supreme Court had affirmed the decree in *Cotton v. Wallace*, another case from the Circuit Court for the Georgia District involving another prize taken by Talbot who commanded the French privateer *Egalité*, formerly the *L'Ami de la Point a Petre*, concerning which it had twice been decreed that she had been armed and equipped in the United States.[116] The Georgia District Court decree that the ship be restored to the libellants was affirmed generally by the Circuit Court. The lack of a section 19 statement was among the assignments of error. It may be noticed, however, that the facts were fully stated in the District Court's decree. Dallas reported only the question of damages which was argued at the succeeding term (August 1796).[117] There is no entry in the docket to suggest that an agreement similar to that in *Hills* was ordered. As events were to prove, it is significant that Chief Justice Ellsworth, father of section 19, did not attend the Court for these arguments.

---

[114] Unfortunately we have only a paraphrase by Dallas of the opinion of the Court. Apparently no opinions were delivered nor was there any specific discussion of the question. The defendants in error probably wanted to confine the agreement to a stipulation for the taking of the testimony of the witnesses examined *de novo* in the Circuit Court and not committed to writing, to which Du Ponceau objected and insisted the rule be made general.

[115] 3 Dallas 187–88; Ms. Docket Book U.S. Sup. Ct., p. 18 (original entry in August term 1795). The agreement also provided that if the defendant in error should not be able to obtain the deposition of Gideon Davis Pendleton, his deposition taken on June 23, 1795, before Judge Nathaniel Pendleton could be given in evidence if otherwise competent (Ms. Docket Book, *sub* Mar. 3, 1796). Evidently this deposition was taken in the proceedings discussed *supra*. There were two basic reasons apparently why Du Ponceau wanted the order to take new evidence made general. The first was the deficiency of proof re-

garding the payment of money by Hills *et al.* to Talbot's order (evidently for the proceeds of the ship), for the payment of a balance only had been provided in the lower courts. This had not been contested below, but Du Ponceau thought that it probably would be in the Supreme Court (Ms. Du Ponceau Letterbook B, 143–45, to Messrs. Hills, May and Woodbridge, Mar. 3, 1796 [HSP]). The second point on which Du Ponceau wanted to produce additional evidence was the testimony of Gideon Pendleton, a notary public. This involved the sufficiency of the notice given to Hills *et al.* that the prize, the ship *Elizabeth* and her cargo, was claimed by the owners. By this he hoped "to discredit the testimony of one Gideon Pendleton (on whom they directly rely) by proving him to be a man of bad character, and also by proving that he gave a different Testimony at the District & at the Circuit Court" (*ibid.*).

[116] Ms. Case Papers U.S. Sup. Ct., Case No. 10.

[117] 3 Dallas 302 (1796), and see *infra*, p. 697.

We have no more litigation on the scope of review in the February 1796 term regarding the inquiry of the Court into facts. One record does indicate another consent order to attach additional exhibits to the record.[118] This, however, was not uncommon and may have been merely the result of clerical omissions below. The February term also saw the affirmance of a substantial number of unreported prize cases,[119] but little can be gleaned from the records as to any procedural errors argued and litigated, for general error was assigned in the majority of the cases, and the important substantive issues concerned the legality of augmentation of arms by French privateers in American ports.[120]

In the August term of the Court three important cases were argued and decided—*Pintado v. the Ship San Joseph, Berard claimant,*[121] *United States v. La Vengeance*[122] and *Wiscart v. Dauchy,*[123] the first a suit for restoration of a prize, the second a libel of information for forfeiture for illegal exportation of arms and the third an equity suit. The cases are of prime importance for their bearing upon the Court's

---

[118] Delcol v. Arnold, Ms. Case Papers U.S. Sup. Ct., Case No. 14; 3 Dallas 333 (1796). The evidence made part of the record was the minutes of the District Court indicating the order selling the ship *Friendship* and paying the proceeds to a Charleston bank subject to the order of the court, and the stipulations for security for prosecuting the writ of error to effect and for damages in case of reversal. The District Court opinion is reported at Bee 5, Arnold v. Delcol (1794). For the facts of the suit, *infra*, p. 713 *et seq.*

[119] Wallace v. *Brig Caesar* (unreported); Geyer v. Michel and *Ship Den Onzekeren*, 3 Dallas 285 (1796); Moodie v. *Ship Betty Cathcart* (unreported); Moodie v. *Ship Mermaid* (unreported); Moodie v. *Brig Eliza* (unreported); Moodie v. *Ship Phyn* (unreported); Moodie v. *Brig Favorite* (unreported); MacDonough v. Dannery and *Ship Mary Ford*, 3 Dallas 188 (1796).

[120] On this see Geyer v. Michel and *Ship Den Onzekeren*, 3 Dallas 285 (1796).

[121] Don Diego Pintado v. *Ship San Joseph* and Jean Antoine Berard, claimant (unreported, 1796). Dallas was absent from the Court the day the case was argued and the opinion handed down. The action began in

the New York District Court with the filing of a libel by Pintado, a Spanish merchant, against the *San Joseph* captured by the French privateer *La Vengeance*, alleged to have been fitted out and armed in the United States. On appeal in the Circuit Court the decree dismissing the libel was affirmed, Justice Chase holding that the *La Vengeance* had been armed in St. Domingo rather than the United States. Ms. Case Papers U.S. Sup. Ct., Case No. 32.

[122] 3 Dallas 297 (1796). This was a companion case to that of *Pintado*, the proceedings below discussed in c. XIII, p. 604. It was argued in the Supreme Court that the cause was a criminal one and should not have been removed to the Circuit Court, and that even if civil, it was not one of admiralty and maritime jurisdiction and so should have been remanded by the Circuit Court for a jury trial. The Supreme Court affirmed on the basis that it was a case of admiralty and maritime jurisdiction, that it was a civil suit and, process being in the nature of a libel *in rem*, did not touch the person; the appeal therefore was regular.

[123] *Ibid.*, 321 (1796), instituted as a suit in chancery to set aside allegedly fraudulent conveyances.

construction of section 19. They are not without interest on a second point—whether an appeal rather than a writ of error was not a more appropriate method of removing a case for review by the Supreme Court. Curiously enough, before any of these cases came up for consideration, Justice Paterson, on August 2, in the course of the argument on damages in *Cotton v. Wallace,* a question held over from the previous term, remarked that he always had and still entertained great doubts whether a writ of error was the proper remedy to remove an admiralty cause. Counsel—Read, Lewis, E. Tilghman, Ingersoll and Du Ponceau—then left the question of damages with the Court and entered into a discussion of the "regularity of process."[124] One week later *Pintado v. the Ship San Joseph, Berard claimant* was argued. The case was not reported, but the fact that Du Ponceau appeared for defendant in error and was party to an agreement the intendment of which was to raise the question of appeal or error suggests that this question was indeed argued. The circumstances in *Pintado* were these: The ship was a prize of *La Vengeance.* After the libel had been dismissed by the District Court, an appeal was prosecuted to the Circuit Court where the dismissal was affirmed by Justice Chase. A writ of error was next produced to the court by counsel for Pintado, to remove the case into the Supreme Court under date of April 20, 1796. The indications that the plaintiffs in error considered prosecuting an appeal to the Supreme Court are contained in two agreements found in the case papers. On June 28, 1796, in *Pintado,* an agreement between Edward Livingston and Alexander Hamilton, counsel for the defendant in error and plaintiff in error, respectively, was filed stipulating that the annexing of the testimony to the writ of error should not prejudice the right of counsel for Berard to insist in the Supreme Court that the facts found by the Circuit Court were conclusive upon the parties and the Supreme Court, and could not be examined on writ of error.[125] By agreement between Richard Harison and Edward Livingston this was extended to the *United States v. La Vengeance.*[126]

Precisely at what point the record was returned is not known. However, no assignment of error had been made for the Supreme Court previous to the return. On July 8 Hamilton and Du Ponceau, who acted for the French Republic, agreed that the assignment of error and the citation were to be annexed to the return and taken as part of the

---

[124] *Ibid.,* 302 at 304n.
[125] The document is printed in *LPAH,* II, 803–04.
[126] *Ibid.,* 804. The Supreme Court case papers for Pintado v. the *San Joseph,* Case No. 32, and for United States v. *La Vengeance,* Case No. 34,

are now commingled and all are filed under Case No. 32. The minute book, *sub* Aug. 9, 10, 11, 1796, indicates, however, that they were not joined for argument. See also the Ms. Docket Book, pp. 28, 29.

return and have the same effect as if originally annexed. This, however, was conditioned on the proviso that counsel for the plaintiff in error was not admitting that section 22 of the Judiciary Act applied to this case.[127] This stipulation was also extended to the *La Vengeance* by an agreement between Du Ponceau and Richard Harison.[128] It is probable that it was Hamilton who intended to insist in the Supreme Court that an appeal was the correct process by which to bring an admiralty case before the Supreme Court and that section 22 applied only to civil causes, which admiralty suits were not. No evidence has been found that Hamilton in fact argued the case in the Supreme Court for Pintado. However, in the assignment of error made for the Supreme Court (signed by Hamilton) the caption reads: "Upon appeal from the decree of the Circuit Court of the United States. . . ." The error assigned was that the evidence did not warrant the statement of facts made by the Circuit Court and general error.[129] Why, with victories in both cases in the Circuit, Du Ponceau acquiesced in the agreements, other than perhaps to prevent delay, is not known. *Hills* et al. *v. Ross*, of course, had not settled the point that a section 19 statement was conclusive upon the Supreme Court; there had been no such statement in that case. If the Court were to hold that the statement was not conclusive and that section 22 did not apply to the case, the annexing of the testimony would obviously save a considerable amount of time and not involve the taking of numerous depositions as was done in *Hills* et al. *v. Ross*.[130]

The statement of the case in *Pintado* made by Justice Chase in the Circuit Court consisted of a recitation of the claims of the libel and answer, the decree of the District Court and the notation of appeal to the Circuit Court, ending with the following:

The facts upon which the decree of the said Circuit Court was founded are as follows that is to say—

---

[127] This document is printed in *LPAH*, II, 804–05.

[128] *Ibid.*, 805.

[129] *Ibid.*, 802–03 for text of the assignment.

[130] Du Ponceau exercised every care that all the evidence be included and annexed to the record. On July 11 he had written Troup, clerk of the New York District and associated with Hamilton, that the agreements were satisfactory to him but noted that some of the evidence was missing, ending with the *caveat*, "Permit me to observe to you that if the whole of the Evidence is not annexed to the record it will be a strong argument with us for admitting the Judge's statement of facts as Conclusive, for reasons which must be very obvious to you." Ms. Du Ponceau Letterbook B, 164–66 (HSP). This evidence was later stipulated in an agreement signed by Du Ponceau, Hamilton and Richard Harison, filed July 22, 1796, with the Court. Ms. Case Papers U.S. Sup. Ct., Case No. 32; printed *LPAH*, II, 805–08.

1 That the said armed Schooner was not furnished, fitted out and armed within the United States

[2 That the said armed schooner was furnished, fitted out and]*
armed at the Island of St. Domingo in the Territories of the
republic of France and at no other place

All of which will more particularly appear from the Schedule hereunto annexed

Samuel Chase[131]

As noted previously, there is no report of *Pintado*; that of *United States v. La Vengeance* is confined to the discussion of whether a libel in admiralty on an information was a criminal case, and, even if civil, whether it was one of admiralty and maritime jurisdiction, the Court answering the first proposition in the negative and the second in the affirmative. However, it is known that both cases were affirmed on the basis that the statement of facts made by the Circuit Court was conclusive upon the Supreme Court, for on August 17, 1796, Du Ponceau wrote to Robert Troup that "I forgot to tell you that the Supreme Court affirmed both decrees on the ground that the statement of facts by the Circuit Court was conclusive."[132] There is regrettably nothing to show whether or not the Court considered the attempt at an appeal. This question was not settled until February term 1800, when in *Blane v. the Ship Charles Carter* it was held that removal of suits from the Circuit Court must be by writ of error in every case, whatever the original nature of the suit.[133]

The problem relating to section 19 raised in *Pintado* and then in *La Vengeance* was explored further on August 10 in the argument of *Wiscart v. Dauchy*, an equity suit removed on writ of error from the Circuit Court for Virginia.[134] No express statement of the facts similar to Chase's statement in *Pintado* appeared in the record of *Wiscart*. The decree of the Circuit Court as set forth in the record[135] opened with the recital of the substance of bill and answer plus a reference to a return by commissioners of accounts—a standard formula made widely current by its inclusion in Jacob's *Law Dictionary*[136]—then proceeded, that

---

*Struck out.

[131] Ms. Case Papers U.S. Sup. Ct., Case No. 32; printed *LPAH*, II, 800–02.

[132] Ms. Du Ponceau Letterbook B, 180–81 (HSP).

[133] Reported in 4 Dallas 22 as Blaine v. *Ship Charles Carter et al.* Libellant's correct name was Thomas

Blane. Ms. Case Papers U.S. Sup. Ct., Case No. 76.

[134] 3 Dallas 321 (1796).

[135] Ms. Case Papers U.S. Sup. Ct., Case No. 33.

[136] G. Jacob, *Law-Dictionary*, 7th ed. (1756), *s.v.* Decree. See also G. Jacob, *Compleat Chancery-Practiser* (1730), II, 603 *et seq.*

in consideration of the matter, the Court (Iredell and Griffin) was of opinion that certain deeds conveying chattels and slaves were fraudulent and intended to prevent the satisfaction of an earlier decree in equity made by the Circuit Court. The decretal portion followed. Despite the fact that Iredell, as Dallas reports, stated that the court below did not intend the decree to have the force of a statement of facts but transmitted the record in its present form "in compliance with precedents established in other circuits,"[137] the force and effect of the recital became focal. Two questions were initially argued—whether the statement of facts was conclusive and whether the decree in the present case was such a statement as the law contemplated. The record of *Wiscart* contained all the depositions and exhibits which had been produced below.

Ellsworth, for the Court, noted that the question of how far the statement was conclusive, having already been decided in a previous case (obviously referring to *Pintado*), submitted two rules:

1. If causes of equity or admiralty jurisdiction are removed hither, accompanied with a statement of facts, but without the evidence, it is well; and the statement is conclusive as to all the facts which it contains. This is unanimously the opinion of the court.
2. If such causes are removed, with a statement of the facts, and also with the evidence—still, the statement is conclusive, as to all the facts contained in it. This is the opinion of the Court; but not unanimously.[138]

The Court was split 4–2 on the second proposition,[139] Justice Wilson articulating for the occasion one of the most vigorous dissents recorded in Dallas' *Reports*.[140] Wilson stated that notwithstanding the provisions of the Judiciary Act, an appeal was the natural and proper mode of removing an admiralty cause, and that such an appeal was expressly sanctioned by the Constitution. As there were no words in the Judiciary Act restricting the power of proceeding by appeal, it was to be regarded as still permitted and approved. If there were a restriction on appeal, Wilson thought that it would be superseded by the superior authority of the constitutional provision. His interpretation of section

---

137 3 Dallas 322n.

138 For the arguments of counsel, *ibid.*, 322–24. Dallas has the arguments for the parties reversed. Furthermore, he has Du Ponceau appear for plaintiff in error whereas it is clear from a letter of Du Ponceau to John Chevalier of Richmond, Aug. 15, 1796, that he was retained by Dauchy and was to receive $200. Ms. Du Ponceau Letterbook B, 176 (HSP).

139 3 Dallas 324. In both *Wiscart*

and *Pintado* the evidence produced below was included in the record.

140 While only the opinions of Wilson and Ellsworth are recorded in Dallas, Paterson stated in Jennings *et al.* v. *Brig Perseverance, ibid.*, 336 (1797), that the Court was divided 4–2 in *Wiscart* and that he had concurred with Wilson there. Thus the majority must have consisted of Ellsworth, Cushing, Iredell and Chase.

22 proceeded on this basis: Section 21 authorized removal to the Circuit Court by appeal from the District Court of final decrees in admiralty, and the first part of section 22 authorized removal to the Circuit Court on writ of error of final decrees and judgments in civil actions in a District Court, deducing therefrom that while "civil" was often used in contradistinction to criminal cases, it was used here in contradistinction to admiralty and maritime suits. Consequently, to preserve consistency in section 22, admiralty actions could not be comprehended within the term "civil" used later in section 22 authorizing removal to the Supreme Court on writ of error.[141] Thus, as the Judiciary Act made no provision for admiralty suits to be removed to the Supreme Court, jurisdiction over them on appeal flowed as a consequence from Article III.

In rebuttal, Ellsworth vigorously rejected Wilson's concept of residual non-statutory jurisdiction, asserting that the appellate jurisdiction of the Court was dependent upon the exceptions and regulations provision of Article III, articulating one of the indestructible maxims of constitutional law which survives one hundred and seventy-three years later as the basis of that jurisdiction:

> Here, then, is the ground, and the only ground, on which we can sustain an appeal. If congress had provided no rule to regulate our proceedings, we cannot exercise an appellate jurisdiction; and if the rule is provided, we cannot depart from it. The question, therefore, on the constitutional point of an appellate jurisdiction, is simply, whether congress has established any rule for regulating its exercise?[142]

Ellsworth's reply to Wilson on the interpretation of section 22 was that the Judiciary Act preserved the technical distinction between a writ of error and an appeal, that "civil" in that section was used in contradistinction to criminal cases and that admiralty cases were comprehended within the term "civil" because admiralty cases are the only ones which could be removed from the District Court by appeal and that "decree" referred to admiralty suits, since there could not be a decree in the District Court in any suit except one of admiralty or maritime jurisdiction.

---

[141] The flaw in this theory, as Ellsworth succinctly pointed out in his opinion, was that sec. 22 in authorizing removal to the Supreme Court extended it to civil actions begun in the Circuit Court or brought there by appeal from the District Court, and that the only actions which could be brought to the Circuit Court by appeal were admiralty and maritime actions under sec. 21.

[142] 3 Dallas 327. The most famous of the cases is probably *Ex Parte McCardle*, 7 Wall. 506 (1869), involving the repeal of the appellate jurisdiction of the Court under the Habeas Corpus Act of 1867, and in which Chief Justice Salmon P. Chase cited *Wiscart*. On this point generally, see Hart and Wechsler, *Federal Courts and the Federal System*, 288–322.

Since Congress had only prescribed removal by writ of error, the Court was bound to adopt that process. In speaking to the conclusiveness of the section 19 statement, Ellsworth held that it could not be deemed a denial of justice if a man was not permitted "to try his cause two or three times over." If he had one opportunity to have all parts of his case tried, justice was satisfied. The imputation of denial could not be made because in appeal the law directed that the facts be tried below, the law by the Supreme Court. Addressing himself to the section 19 problem, Ellsworth commented that there was nothing in the nature of fact which rendered it impracticable or improper to be ascertained by a judge. If the Justices were competent to ascertain facts in the Supreme Court, they were equally so sitting in the Circuit Court.

Two days after the original argument in *Wiscart*, Ellsworth, for the Court, held that the decree of the Circuit Court satisfied the requirements of section 19 and therefore the facts found were conclusive.[143] The opinion noted that if the decree had stopped with the statement that the conveyances were fraudulent, some "doubt might reasonably be entertained, whether it was not more properly an inference, than the statement of a fact." However, by describing the fraud ("the conveyances were intended to defraud the complainant, and to prevent his obtaining satisfaction for a just demand"), a statement of the fact was effected and the facts therefore appeared from the pleadings and decree according to section 19.

It should be observed that Ellsworth appears to have ignored the first alternative of section 19, viz., the coupling of pleadings and decree as the source of the facts on which the latter was founded. This had been raised by counsel but the point was not met. The consistent emphasis upon a "statement" of facts—the second and third alternatives—suggests that the Chief Justice had come to entertain second thoughts about the section which he had fathered. This, of course, had been contrived in the heat of debate on the Senate floor.[144] Later reflection upon the inadequacies of pleadings as disclosures of fact, particularly as this had been earlier urged by counsel in *Hills* et al. *v. Ross*,[145] may well have moved Ellsworth the judge to revise Ellsworth the legislator.

The inquiry as to the scope of section 19 and its interpretation under the two rules established in *Wiscart* was carried forward February 1797 in *Jennings and Venner v. Arcambal and the Brig Perseverance and Cargo*.[146] This cause had had a peculiar history. The brig had been taken by two French privateers. On complaint of the British vice-consul prompted by Jennings and Venner, residents of New Brunswick, the governor of Rhode Island, acting under color of general instructions

---

[143] 3 Dallas 329.
[144] *Supra*, c. XI, pp. 498–99.

[145] 3 Dallas 186.
[146] *Ibid.*, 336.

from Secretary of War Knox, convened a council of inquiry August 25, 1794.[147] Here it was decided that one privateer had been outfitted in Hispaniola and that the proofs did not support the allegation that the other had been equipped at Charleston. The prize was turned over to the prize master Barnard and sold and the proceeds deposited with the marshal of the District.

Jennings and Venner then filed a libel against the brig in the District Court, September 20, 1794, but because they failed to offer proofs, the libel was dismissed for failure to prosecute.[148] An appeal was taken to the Circuit Court where the French vice-consul was admitted to file a claim against appellants and certain evidence was submitted by agreement. On June 25, 1796, the Circuit Court affirmed the decree of dismissal and formulated a new decree regarding proceeds, damages and costs. After the decree, Henry Marchant, the District judge had died and Justice Chase had left the district.

The record removed to the Supreme Court contained all the evidence heard in the Circuit Court but did not contain a statement of the facts. Counsel for defendants in error insisted that plaintiff could not go into a consideration of errors of fact because the rules established in *Wiscart, Pintado* and *La Vengeance* were conclusive. E. Tilghman, for the plaintiff in error, asserted that although the case of a record transmitted with the evidence but without a section 19 statement had never been expressly decided, it appeared to be embraced by Ellsworth's reasoning in support of the second rule in *Wiscart v. Dauchy*. If the Court were also of this opinion, he would not trouble with further argument.[149]

Justice Paterson made this the occasion to explain that he had agreed with Wilson in *Wiscart*, for he thought that excluding consideration of the evidence (which he conceived amounted virtually to a statement of fact) "was shutting the door against light and truth," and left property too much at the discretion of a single judge.[150] On the point before the Court, "it was the subject of discussion among the

---

[147] The letters from Henry Knox accompanied the record. These related to policy initiated by the Executive in the summer of 1793 and continuing after passage of the Neutrality Act of 1794 of enlisting the aid of the state governors to enforce the Neutrality Proclamation and subsequently the statute. On the decisions of the Cabinet see *PAH*, XV, 168 *et seq.*, 181 *et seq.* See also *infra*, c. XVII.

[148] The cause had been continued to permit procurement of evidence,

but in August 1796 the Court refused further continuance—possibly the ground why libellants refused to offer proofs.

[149] 3 Dallas 337.

[150] Paterson's view was of long standing, for it will be recalled that when Ellsworth offered sec. 19 to the Senate Paterson moved a substitute that did not mention a judicial statement and proposed that the evidence be reduced to writing or a statement of the facts be made if the parties agreed (*supra*, c XI at n. 128).

Judges at their chamber." An opinion was formed but not delivered by the same majority that established the second rule in *Wiscart*. The reasoning of the Chief Justice in the support of that rule went clearly to "this case." He felt bound by decisions where there was no statement of facts there could be no error.[151]

After *Jennings v. the Brig Perseverance* there was no further litigation dealing with section 19. That the decision in *Wiscart* had the effect of alerting the Justices to their responsibilities as Circuit judges is evidenced by the fact that in the following November at the Circuit Court for the Georgia District in the appeal of *Wallace v. the Grenada, Hills, May and Woodbridge and Capt. Talbot claimants*, Paterson prepared an appropriate statement although at the time no writ of error appears to have been sought.[152] Ellsworth himself, in *Franklin* et al. *v. Rotch* at April term of the Circuit Court for the New York District, 1797, prepared with Troup J. an elaborate statement of the facts on which the decree in this equity suit was based.[153] The bar, at least in New York and Pennsylvania, became aware of the advantage of counsel formulating the statement. In the former jurisdiction such were prepared in *United States v. the Brig^t Harriott and George Topham* (1800),[154] and in *Talbot v. the Ship Amelia* (1801);[155] in Pennsylvania, in *Priestman v. the United States*[156] and in *Baas v. Tingey* (1800).[157]

One further incident relating to the scope of review deserves to be mentioned. This relates to the two cases where the review of state enactments was considered. The most significant comment here is recorded in an opinion of Samuel Chase in *Calder v. Bull* (1798)[158] discussing the awarding of a new trial by the Connecticut legislature to probate a will attacked as an ex post facto law and otherwise rendered without legislative competence. In reply to the argument by counsel that the legislature of Connecticut had no constitutional power to make the resolution in question, Chase said:[159]

> Without giving an opinion, at this time, whether this Court has jurisdiction to decide that any law made by Congress contrary to the Con-

---

151 What this case did to Hills v. Ross is conjectural. Presumably the latter was no longer precedent for remedying lack of a sec. 19 statement by agreement of the parties in the Supreme Court.

152 Ms. Mins. Circuit Ct. Georgia Dist. 1793–1798, 239–42, *sub* Nov. 16, 1796. A writ of error was undoubtedly anticipated here for the total award against one group of claimants ran to $89,386.37. Of this Hills, May and Woodbridge were to pay $27,873.79 less $300 allowed them for wharfage and storage.

153 Ms. Case Papers U.S. Sup. Ct., Case No. 54 (unreported).

154 *Ibid.*, Case No. 75 (unreported); see *LPAH*, II, 858–60.

155 Ms. Case Papers U.S. Sup. Ct., Case No. 89; 4 Dallas 34; see *LPAH*, II, 914–18.

156 4 Dallas 28.

157 *Ibid.*, 37.

158 3 Dallas 386.

159 *Ibid.*, 392–93.

stitution of the United States, is void; I am fully satisfied that this court has no jurisdiction to determine that any law of any state Legislature, contrary to the Constitution of such State, is void. Further, if this court had such jurisdiction, yet it does not appear to me, that the resolution (or law) in question, is contrary to the charter of Connecticut, or its constitution, which is said by counsel to be composed of its acts of assembly, and usages and customs. I should think, that the courts of Connecticut are the proper tribunals to decide, whether laws contrary to the constitution thereof, are void. In the present case, they have, both in the inferior and superior courts, determined that the Resolution (or law) in question was not contrary to either their state, or the federal, constitution.

None of the other Justices who delivered opinions in *Calder* met the issue raised by counsel, most of the discussion being confined to a discussion of ex post facto laws and whether the power exercised by the legislature was judicial or legislative, indicating if the former, it was not touched by the prohibition of the Constitution in any event.[160] Chase made no express reference to section 25 in promulgating his views on the jurisdiction of the Court to void statutes alleged to be in violation of the state constitution. By its terms, however, that section recognized no such jurisdiction, for the state statute or authority exercised must be assailed on the basis of repugnancy against the "constitution, treaties, or laws, of the United States."

That Chase's comment was confined to cases in error under section 25 is evidenced by a later decision of the Court in 1800, *Cooper v. Telfair*.[161] This was an action of debt on a bond, instituted in the Circuit Court for the Georgia District, and involved the validity of an act of the Georgia legislature passed in 1782 attainting by name the plaintiff, then a Georgia citizen, and subsequent enactments in 1786 and 1787 liquidating claims relative to confiscated estates. These statutes were pleaded in bar to recovery. The replication pleaded that the statutes passed were in violation of the Georgia constitution (1777) at the time they were passed.[162] The Circuit Court held that the plea in

---

[160] See *infra*, c. XVII.

[161] 4 Dallas 14 (1800). Dallas' spelling of plaintiff's name has been retained although it is rendered as Cowper in the minutes of the Circuit Court for the Georgia District and in various papers in the Supreme Court case papers.

[162] Ms. Case Papers U.S. Sup. Ct., Case No. 72. The plaintiff claimed that he had never been tried, convicted or attainted for the treason alleged in

the plea; he claimed that the Georgia constitution provided that the legislative, executive and judicial departments were to be separate and distinct and that neither was to exercise the power of the other (Art. 1), that the assembly could not pass any law repugnant to the true meaning of the constitution (Art. 7) and that all matters of treason against the state were to be tried in the county where the crime

bar was sufficient and gave judgment on demurrer for defendant.[163] The errors assigned for the Supreme Court stripped of verbiage amounted to an averment of legislative incompetence under the Georgia constitution.[164] The Supreme Court unanimously affirmed. Dallas sets out four opinions but unfortunately it is only their "substance" which he reports. Nevertheless, despite shortcomings, these are interesting in the light they shed on this problem.

Justice Washington rested his conclusion on the observation that the Georgia constitution did not expressly interdict a legislative bill of attainder and confiscation. It made no provision for a trial where the offense was not committed within some county in the state. If the plaintiff in error had shown that the offense with which he was charged had been committed within any Georgia county, he might have raised the question of conflict between the constitution and the legislative enactment. This factor did not appear and consequently there was no ground on which he was prepared to say that the law was void. Chase was in basic agreement, noting that there was a material difference between laws passed during the Revolution and those passed subsequent to the organization of the federal government. However, he declined giving an opinion on whether the power of declaring an act of the legislature unconstitutional could be exercised in cases where the state law had been enacted prior to the present constitution. Paterson thought that it must be a clear and unequivocal breach of the constitution to authorize the Court to pronounce any law void, and that this had not been demonstrated in the present case. Cushing remarked that while the Supreme Court had the same power that a state court in Georgia would possess to declare a law void, the occasion did not warrant an exercise of the power, as the right to confiscate and banish must belong to every government, and not being within the judicial power, it must belong to the legislature.

---

was committed (Art. 39). Also pleaded were the state constitutional provisions for habeas corpus (Art. 60) and the guarantee of trial by jury (Art. 61).

[163] Ibid. By leave of court, payment was also pleaded in addition to the demurrer.

[164] Ibid. Assigned as errors were: (1) general error; (2) the court's ruling on the plea; (3) that the defendant had not specially pleaded that the legislature was constitutionally empowered to deprive Cooper of his rights as a Georgia citizen and to pass on their own authority a sentence of confiscation and banishment; (4) that

the judgment of the Circuit Court decided that the legislature could take cognizance of treasons alleged against Cooper and try, convict and banish him whereas upon constitutional principles the legislature had no such power; (5) that by the judgment individuals might be stripped of their lives and property without trial by jury or inquest of office by legislative acts alone whereas the decision was in contravention of the Georgia constitution; and (6) that the judgment gave efficacy to an act of the legislature which was an usurpation of the judicial and legislative powers.

It may be remarked that *Cooper* was a section 22 case. Cushing alone seems to have been convinced that the Supreme Court possessed the same power to declare a law void as would the Georgia court. The others were more wary. Chase did not apparently abandon the position he took in *Calder v. Bull*, a section 25 case. He regarded the question where the power to declare acts of the legislature void resided to be an open one, and evidently thought that a declaration by the Supreme Court of its power to void an Act of Congress to be a condition precedent. What is most interesting in the development of his ideas is that it was at February term 1800 that he asked his question regarding lodgment of the power to pass on the constitutionality of statutes. It was in June of the same year that he delivered his magisterial answer at the Circuit for the Virginia District.[165]

COSTS

BUT FOR THE diatribes of 1788 about the expense of the projected federal judiciary, the matter of costs in the Supreme Court during the 1790's would be hardly worth noticing. The records show no litigation there over the amount of costs, and from what such papers yield in the way of figures, the charges were trifling. How the particulars such as the charge for a writ of error were arrived at is not known. The Judiciary Act laid down no more than the direction in section 22 that security must be taken of a plaintiff in error that he prosecute his writ to effect and answer all damages and costs if he fail to make good his plea,[166] and the provision in section 23 that upon an affirmance the Supreme Court would have discretion to adjudge damages for delay and single or double costs. The first Process Act did, of course, refer to state schedules of fees for the computation of costs, but the tenor of the statute is such as to put in doubt whether it was supposed to extend to the Supreme Court. It is not until the second Process Act (May 8, 1792) that the clerk of the Supreme Court was authorized to charge double the fees of the clerk of the supreme court of the state where the United States Supreme Court was held.

The bill for August 8, 1792, in *Hayburn's Case*,[167] is the first one we have found after the passage of the second Process Act. For reading

---

[165] *Supra*, c. XIV, p. 650.

[166] It should be noticed that the amendment to sec. 22 of Dec. 12, 1794, enacted to remove doubt as to the amount of security, provided that where the writ of error was not a supersedeas to stay execution, the amount was limited to a sum suf-

ficient to answer all costs upon affirmance as might be decreed or adjudged to the respondent in error. The act said nothing of damages. I *U.S. Stats.*, 404.

[167] RG 217, Miscellaneous Treasury Accounts 1790–1894, No. 6494 (NA).

and filing Randolph's motion *ex officio* $1.31 was charged: "—Opinion of the court—taxing bill etc. 2.57—cryer .40." This bill the United States Treasury paid.[168] Similarly, small charges were made in *United States v. John Hopkins* (1793) and *United States v. Yale Todd*. The fee for a writ of error was $3.60 and appears to have remained constant, plus $2.00 for seal and certificate.[169] In *Hylton v. United States* (1796)[170] the Attorney General was furnished with two copies of the record which, plus seals and certifications, came to $16. He had also undertaken that the United States would pay the bills for clerk's fees. This totalled $9.72. Bills of costs that occasionally appear in the case papers are similarly modest. What appears to be a deviant, the case of *Talbot v. Jansen* where the judgment awarded costs of $91.93 (not, however, identified as those incurred in the Supreme Court),[171] may be explained as including travel charges for co-counsel Jacob Read of South Carolina, an item authorized by the Act of 1793, already noticed in connection with Circuit Court operations.

DAMAGES AND COUNSEL FEES

THE AUTHORITY OF THE Supreme Court to award damages was founded on the same sections (22 and 23) of the Judiciary Act that dealt with costs. But unlike practice with respect to the latter, there was a substantial amount of controversy over questions of damages.

The first of these cases was *Penhallow v. Doane's Administrators*. The libel in admiralty, originally filed in the New Hampshire District Court and subsequently transferred to the Circuit Court,[172] was brought to enforce a decree of the long-defunct Confederation Court of Appeals in Cases of Capture rendered in 1783.[173] The libel did not request damages occasioned by the non-compliance of the respondents with the decree of the Court of Appeals, but did request damages for the

---

[168] *Ibid.*
[169] Earliest reference found is in *ibid.*, No. 5898, an account of the Pennsylvania Marshal to Bayard, Clerk of the Supreme Court, for fifteen writs of error totalling $54. See also the entry on the margin of Ms. Docket Book U.S. Sup. Ct., p. 11 (Bingham v. Cabot).
[170] RG 217, Miscellaneous Treasury Accounts 1790–1894, No. 8000 (NA).
[171] Ms. Docket Book U.S. Sup. Ct., p. 15.
[172] 3 Dallas 54 (1795). Although neither the record nor the opinion of

the Court makes it clear, the case was presumably transferred to the Circuit Court under sec. 11 of the Process Act of 1792 (1 *U.S. Stats.*, 278–79) authorizing removal where the judge had been in interest or of counsel for either party. John Sullivan, the New Hampshire District judge, had been counsel for the Penhallow interests and represented them in the proceedings before the Court of Appeals in Cases of Capture.
[173] On the early proceedings see *supra*, c. IV, p. 179.

illegal capture and for general relief.[174] The decree of the Circuit Court, however, provided that the respondents there (plaintiffs in error above) should pay the libellants such damages and costs as were the result of non-compliance with the earlier decree.[175] On the prosecution of the writ of error to the Supreme Court this allowance of damages (among numerous other items) was assigned and pressed in argument as error.[176] The response of defendants in error to this was that damages was the substance of the whole proceeding and thus lawfully allowed, and that in any event the damages could be awarded because of the sufficiency of the prayer for general relief.[177] Justices Paterson, Iredell and Cushing all considered that the prayer for general relief was a sufficient answer to the objections raised.[178] Blair's opinion is not as explicit, but he appears to have concurred in this holding. Damages were, however, reduced in the Supreme Court because of an error made by the Circuit Court with respect to the date from which interest was to be calculated. This disposition followed a challenge whether the Supreme Court had power to rectify the decree of the Circuit Court which had run against the respondents there jointly for a sum in excess of $38,000. In the assignment of errors to the Supreme Court it was claimed that the moneys arising from the sale of the prize in question had been paid to Joshua and George Wentworth as agents to be distributed according to law (one half to the captors and the other half to the owners of the privateer) and that the decree was erroneous, running against all the parties jointly. In the argument of the case this was pressed by the plaintiffs in error as a basis for reversal,[179] the defendants in error countering that, even if erroneous, the Supreme Court could correct it and give such judgment as the Circuit Court ought to have done.[180] The Supreme Court agreed that the interests were several, but that as the facts were spread on the record, it was within the power of the Court to sever the damages and to apportion them to "effectuate substantial justice."[181]

---

[174] See the libel in Ms. Case Papers U.S. Sup. Ct., Case No. 6.

[175] Decree, *ibid.*

[176] See the assignment of errors, 3 Dallas 64–68.

[177] *Ibid.*, 78.

[178] Iredell J. (*ibid.*, 103): "It is alledged, damages were not prayed for by the libel. It is a sufficient answer, that there is a prayer for general relief. And so little do I think of this objection, and so much of the duty of a court, unaided by formal applications, where there is a substantial one, that I am strongly induced to think, if a case proper for a specific relief was laid before a civil law court, and the direct contrary to the proper relief was prayed for, yet the court, even in this case, would be justified in granting the relief that might be properly afforded, if the party who had committed the mistake consented to it: without that, indeed, it might be improper, for no court ought to force a benefit on a party unwilling to receive it."

[179] *Ibid.*, 73.

[180] *Ibid.*, 79.

[181] *Per* Paterson J., *ibid.*, 88.

In arriving at this conclusion there was virtually no reliance upon English common law precedent relating to judgments in error either by counsel or the Court. The difficulty of applying such to the review of an admiralty cause is reflected by a passage in Iredell's opinion:[182]

The 4th question is—

whether this court can now rectify the decree in respect to the parts of it considered to be erroneous or must affirm or reverse in the whole.

The latter is certainly the general method, at common law, and it has been contended, that as this proceeding is on a writ of error, it must have all the incidents of a writ of error at common law. The argument would be conclusive, if this was a common-law proceeding, but as it is not, I do not conceive, that it necessarily applies. An incident to one subject cannot be presumed, by the very name of such an incident, to be intended to apply to a subject totally different. I presume, the term, "writ of error," was made use of, because we are prohibited from reviewing facts, and therefore, must be confined to the errors on the record. But as this is a civil law proceeding, I conceive the word "error" must be applied to such errors as are deemed such by the principles of the civil law, and that in rectifying the error, we must proceed according to those principles. In a civil law court, I believe, it is the constant practice, to modify a decree, upon an appeal, as the justice of the case requires; and in this instance, it appears to me, under the 24th section of the judicial act, we are to render such a decree as, in our opinion, the district court ought to have rendered. If this was a case, wherein damages were uncertain, and wherein, for that reason, the cause should be remanded for a final decision (which it does not appear to be, because the libellants in the original suit had a decree in their favor, which is now to be affirmed in part), yet the damages here are not uncertain, because we all agree, that interest ought to be allowed from the date of the decree, in September 1783, upon the value of the property, as specified in the report, against those who are to be adjudged to pay the principal.

At the succeeding term of the Court the question arose of what damages and the amount thereof that could be additionally assessed upon the affirmance of the decree in *Talbot v. Jansen.*[183] After the libel had been filed in the District Court the cargo of the captured vessel *Magdalena* had been sold. The decree of that court awarded restitution of the ship and cargo to the libellant owners; on appeal to the Circuit Court the decree was affirmed on November 5, 1794.[184] In addition the ap-

---

[182] *Ibid.,* 107–08.
[183] *Ibid.,* 133 (1795).

[184] Ms. Case Papers U.S. Sup. Ct., Case No. 9.

pellant was ordered to pay to Jansen two guineas *per diem* as damages and demurrage from August 6 (the date of the District Court decree) until November 5, plus 7 percent interest on the proceeds from the sale of the cargo.[185] Subsequently, in the Supreme Court and before the cause was heard, a consent order was entered authorizing the sale of the *Magdalena* with the proceeds to be deposited in the Bank of Carolina subject to the definitive sentence of the appellate court.[186]

After affirmance of the decree, counsel for defendants in error moved the Court to assess additional damages, opposed by Dallas for the plaintiff in error.[187] There is no report of the reason for the Court's action on the motion. However, the decree of the Court indicates that additional damages for demurrage and detention of the vessel from the date of the Circuit Court decree to the date of actual sale of the ship (June 6, 1795) was assessed at the rate of $9.33 *per diem* plus interest at 7 percent on the proceeds of the cargo from the date of the District Court decree, and also interest at the same rate on the proceeds from June 6 to the date of the Supreme Court decree (August 22, 1795).[188]

Two other cases involving activities of French privateers that presented questions of damages came before the Court in February 1796 term—*Cotton v. Wallace*[189] and *Delcol v. Arnold.*[190] In *Cotton v. Wallace* the District Court had ordered restitution of the ship *Everton* and cargo to the libellant, the British vice-consul. The ship had been taken by the French privateer *L'Ami de la Point a Petre*, commanded by William Talbot.[191] This privateer and Talbot had both been involved previously in the *Talbot v. Jansen* litigation, and the Georgia District Court decree noted that it had been twice decreed that the *Point a Petre* had been armed and equipped in the United States contrary to law. At this juncture *Talbot v. Jansen* had already been affirmed on appeal in the Circuit Court for the South Carolina District. In *Cotton*, on appeal to the Circuit Court for the District of Georgia, the decree below

---

185 *Ibid.*

186 Ms. Docket Book U.S. Sup. Ct., p. 15, entry under February term 1795. The date of the order is Mar. 3, 1795.

187 3 Dallas 169.

188 Ms. Docket Book U.S. Sup. Ct., p. 15. The award of interest on affirmation of judgment on error in King's Bench was regarded as damages for delay, and was computed as such but added to the costs taxed for plaintiff in the original action. Tidd, *Practice of the Court of King's Bench*, 3d ed. (1803), II, 1132–33.

In two cases also from the South

Carolina District—Geyer v. Michel and *Ship Den Onzekeren* (3 Dallas 285 [1796]) and Moodie v. *Ship Betty Cathcart* (unreported, 1796; Ms. Case Papers U.S. Sup. Ct., Case No. 16)—the Ms. Docket Book U.S. Sup. Ct., p. 22, discloses that the judgments in both cases were affirmed with costs but without damages, which evidently had been requested.

189 3 Dallas 302.

190 *Ibid.*, 333.

191 Ms. Case Papers U.S. Sup. Ct., Case No. 10, for decree of District Court.

awarding restitution was affirmed generally.[192] On March 2, 1796, this Circuit decree was affirmed in the Supreme Court with costs and the question "whether any and what damages shall be recovered to lie over until the next Term."[193] Ingersoll, E. Tilghman, William Lewis and Jacob Read, who had all served previously as counsel in *Talbot v. Jansen*, were engaged in the present case, and thus were aware of the significance of damages which might be awarded in the Supreme Court. According to the report in Dallas, when the decree was affirmed at the February term, counsel for defendant in error (erroneously given in the report as the plaintiff) suggested that he was entitled to damages and urged the Court to sanction some procedure to assess them.[194] This was evidently rejected although the question of damages was held over. The defendant in error subsequently applied to the Circuit Court where the presiding judge was in favor of appointing auditors, the District judge dissenting.[195] On notice to the opposite party, Wallace had the damages certified "by respectable citizens" and the resulting certificate was offered in the Supreme Court at the hearing in August. Read, counsel for Wallace, argued that if the proceedings were "irregular," "further time might be allowed, to ascertain the proper remedy for an evident right."[196]

In opposition to the introduction of the certificate, Du Ponceau urged that as the damages were requested by the libel, the decree of the District Court amounted to a negation of the claim. He further urged that the cause had come up on an assignment of error, that no restitution ought to have been awarded, and that on a plea of *in nullo est erratum* on which issue was joined, there had then been a general affirmance of the decree below. The proceedings were consequently complete and the jurisdiction of the Court expended as to everything brought into controversy upon the record.[197] He argued further that the damages mentioned in sections 23 and 24[198] of the Judiciary Act applied only to damages for delay from the date on which the writ of error was brought. It neither authorized an assessment of general

---

[192] *Ibid.*, for decree of Circuit Court.

[193] Ms. Docket Book U.S. Sup. Ct., p. 16.

[194] 3 Dallas 302. Defendant in error was the British vice-consul. Du Ponceau consistently represented the French.

[195] *Ibid.*

[196] *Ibid.*

[197] *Ibid.*, 303.

[198] 1 *U.S. Stats.*, 85. "That when a judgment or decree shall be reversed in a circuit court, such court shall proceed to render such judgment or pass such decree as the district court should have rendered or passed; and the Supreme Court shall do the same on reversals therein, except where the reversal is in favour of the plaintiff, or petitioner in the original suit, and the damages to be assessed, or matter to be decreed, are uncertain, in which case they shall remand the cause for a final decision. And the Supreme Court shall not issue execution in causes that are removed before them by writs of error, but shall send a special mandate to the circuit court to award execution thereupon."

damages nor did it embrace a proceeding *in rem* except in cases where a liquidated sum was awarded by an inferior court. Moreover, since the decree in the District Court was in the favor of the defendant in error, he could either have claimed damages or applied for immediate restitution on giving security. He also urged that even if the Circuit Court had awarded damages without assessing them, the Supreme Court would have to remand if there were a reversal, according to section 24, the case being even weaker here because the defendant in error prayed only an affirmance.

The questions elicited from the Bench on argument are particularly interesting on this question. Paterson had originally questioned Read whether he meant to go outside the record to prove the damages or whether the estimate was founded upon the record itself. Read admitted the record did not show the extent of the damages, although the decree entitled the defendant to recover the full amount and the defendant wished therefore to ascertain that amount "by matter *dehors* the record."[199] Paterson later noted that in every case in which there had been allowed an increase or decrease in damages the facts regulating the decision appeared on the record, though he questioned whether a writ of error was the correct process to remove an admiralty case.[200] Iredell thought the present case was distinguishable from *Penhallow* because the damages were decreased there to the benefit of the plaintiff in error, but that *Talbot* had apparently increased the damages allowed the defendant.[201] Chase queried whether the increase in *Talbot* went back beyond the decree of the Circuit Court to increase damages or whether the increase allowed was merely for the delay in executing that decree.[202]

Ellsworth, for the Court, held that where the judgment or decree was affirmed on a writ of error there could be no allowance of damages except for the delay. Interest at 8 percent from the date of the decree of the Circuit Court on the proceeds of the sale of the *Everton* and her cargo was consequently assessed as damages.[203]

In *Delcol v. Arnold* a part of the argument was held during February term 1796; the question relating to damages was argued and

---

[199] 3 Dallas 302n.
[200] See *supra*, pp. 703–04.
[201] 3 Dallas 304 n.
[202] *Ibid*. In fact the decree in *Talbot* did not go beyond the decree of the Circuit Court. Interest on the proceeds of the cargo at 7 percent was given in the Supreme Court from the date of the District Court decree. The same rate of interest on those proceeds had been awarded by the Circuit Court from the date of the District

Court decree to that of its own decree. Whether the awarding of demurrage damages from the date of the Circuit Court decree until the date of the sale of the vessel under order of the Supreme Court can be viewed as damages beyond an allowance merely for delay in executing the decree is not known.
[203] *Ibid*., 304; Ms. Docket Book U.S. Sup. Ct., p. 16, Aug. 9, 1796 (case entered in February term 1796).

decided by the Court on August 11 of the same year.[204] This did not involve the measure or propriety of the assessment of additional damages in the Supreme Court, but the damages awarded in the District Court and the legal responsibility therefore of the owners of a privateer. This litigation was unusual in that it began with a libel by Arnold, owner of the vessel *Grand Sachem* and her cargo, against Delcol and others, owners of the privateer *La Montagne* and of the ship *Friendship* (alias *The Industry*) and cargo, the latter a prize of the *La Montagne* moored in Charleston, South Carolina, harbor. The *La Montagne* had taken the *Grand Sachem* in August 1794 and she had subsequently been run ashore and scuttled outside of the Charleston harbor when *La Montagne* was chased and captured by the British ship *Terpsichore*.[205]

When the marshal of the District attempted to serve process on the *Grand Sachem*, then in the joint possession of the prize crew and customs officers, the prize crew prevented execution of the process.[206] Consequently, the *Friendship* was attached by libellants; later she was sold by the consent of the parties, the proceeds to abide the decree of the District Court. In November of 1794 the District Court ordered the claimants to pay $33,329.87 plus interest at 10 percent from the date of the capture, the proceeds of the *Friendship* being subjected to satisfaction of the decree with a stipulation not here relevant. On appeal the lower court decree was affirmed by the Circuit Court and costs adjudged against the appellant.[207] The libel in the District Court had averred that the *Grand Sachem* was an American ship and that the cargo was also owned by Americans, the vessel engaging in the coastal trade between Philadelphia and New Orleans.[208] The claim alleged, on the contrary, that an examination of the ship's papers showed that she was actually owned by two New Orleans residents and naturalized Spanish citizens, carried a set of Spanish documents and colors, and that the neutral ownership of the cargo was irrelevant because by the Treaty of Amity and Commerce the cargo found on board enemy ships was constituted prize.[209]

In the Supreme Court four questions were argued:[210] (1) whether there was sufficient probable cause for seizing the *Grand Sachem* and

---

[204] 3 Dallas 333; Ms. Docket Book U.S. Sup. Ct., p. 21, Aug. 11, 1796 (case entered in February term 1796).

[205] Ms. Case Papers U.S. Sup. Ct., Case No. 14, for libel and claim.

[206] 3 Dallas 333. The bit about execution is not in the record, but comes from Dallas. The claim merely denied that the crew of the *Grand Sachem* had been put out of possession by American revenue officers and

that the damages to the ship had been occasioned by their neglect.

[207] Ms. Case Papers U.S. Sup. Ct., Case No. 14, for decree of Circuit Court.

[208] *Ibid.*, libel.

[209] *Ibid.*, claim. The French and Spanish were then at war.

[210] 3 Dallas 334. There had been a general assignment of error.

bringing her into port for further examination; (2) whether if there was sufficient cause, the captors could be made liable for the consequent injury and loss; (3) whether if the immediate captors who ran the vessel into shoal waters and scuttled her were responsible, that responsibility could be attributed to the owners of the privateer; and (4) whether the *Friendship* prior to condemnation could be attached and subjected to the satisfaction of the decree. The first two questions were argued in February of 1796, the Court holding that while there was probable cause for the seizure, this did not excuse any spoliation and the captors proceeded at their peril and were liable for all consequent loss.[211]

In August the Court decided as to the third question, that the owners were responsible for the conduct of their agents and crew and that the measure of damages was the full value of the property injured or destroyed; and on the fourth question, that any objection to the attachment of the *Friendship* had been waived on the consent to sale made in the District Court.[212] The other interesting aspect of the case is the tainted and tendentious report of the evidence given by Dallas, counsel for the plaintiff in error.[213]

On the day following the decree in *Delcol* the Supreme Court in

---

[211] *Ibid.*

[212] *Ibid.*, 335.

[213] Dallas reports that on the evidence it appeared that the *Grand Sachem* had been engaged in a smuggling trade at New Orleans and the Spanish Main, for that purpose had procured a register in the name of Spanish subjects, sailed under Spanish colors and had carried on board a number of Spanish documents that had been collusively delivered to the owner, defendant in error Arnold, by one of the sailors. *Ibid.*, 333–34. Nothing is said of the other contradictory evidence in the record. Dallas' rendition of the case directly contradicts the findings of Judge Thomas Bee. Bee sat on the appeal from his own decree and assigned the grounds of his opinion reported in Arnold v. Delcol, Bee 5 (1794). Bee found that that *Grand Sachem* had a regular register to show she was an American vessel, that Arnold's property (as an American citizen) was fully proved, that by art. 25 of the French treaty the production of sea letters was sufficient to prevent any detention of the vessel, that the witnesses who maintained that trade to New Orleans could be carried on only by Spanish ships (averred in the claim) referred to a period prior to that when Arnold's ship had been there, that the requisite of obtaining Spanish colors to proceed up the Mississippi River to New Orleans did not divest the *Sachem* of her American character, that the allegation of doubtful papers and fraud was not supported by the proof, and that the paper found on board showing the cargo as belonging to Cox and Clark of New Orleans had been signed by the *Grand Sachem*'s captain who was ignorant of Spanish. Bee's opinion, of course, did not come up with the record and it is questionable whether Dallas had access to it. However, this does not exculpate that reporter from slanting the statement of the case entirely in favor of the parties whose interest he was serving. This is the most egregious example found in the reports, but it raises some question as to the other reports, particularly those involving the French Republic, which often paid Dallas for arguing its cases.

Hills et al. *v. Ross*, which again came before it, also decided another question relative to damages assessed in the lower courts. In the Circuit Court Hills *et al.*, agents for a French privateer, had been ordered to pay to the owners the full value of the cargo of the captured ship ($75,000) with costs. The Court held that the plaintiffs in error (Hills *et al.*) were not trespassers *ab initio* and that as agents they were responsible only for the cargo which came into their hands, modifying the decree from the annexed sales accounts and decreeing interest from June 6, 1794 (the date of the District Court decree), to August 12, 1796, making a total of $37,695.70.[214]

On the same day that *Hills* et al. *v. Ross* was decided (August 12, 1796), there was submitted to the Court the question whether or not counsel fees could be reckoned as an element of damages. This occurred in *Arcambal v. Wiseman.*[215] Here two cases were actually involved as the result of cross appeals from the decree of the Rhode Island District Court later to the Circuit Court. In the District Court the suit was instituted by the Spanish vice-consul for Rhode Island, Joseph Wiseman, as agent for the owners of the *Nuestra Senora del Carmen*, a prize of the French ship *Brutus*, allegedly armed unlawfully in the United States, and commanded by J. A. Gariscan. Two claims were interposed to the *Carmen*: the first was by Louis Arcambal, vice-consul of the French Republic, averring that the *Brutus* was owned by the French government; the second was made by John Jutau as agent for Gariscan.[216] In March of 1796 Wiseman and Arcambal, by written motion to the Court, stated that the ministers plenipotentiary of France and Spain had decided that the legality of the capture was in doubt for it was not clear at what point hostilities had ceased between the two countries, and requested that the proceeds from the sale of the *Carmen* and her cargo be deposited in the French consulate until the two governments decided the question of legality.[217]

Jutau objected to the request, urging that the disposition of the property was improper unless all the parties to the suit concurred, that the motion was collusive with intent to defeat the interests of the party he represented (Gariscan) and that the ship should be restored to him if the allegations of the libel were unfounded. In May of 1796 the objection was sustained. Subsequently, the District Court dismissed the libel and ordered that the moneys be paid to the claimants jointly, to be withdrawn only by mutual consent.[218] Wiseman was ordered to pay the claimants damages occasioned by the detention ($8,000) plus costs.

---

[214] 3 Dallas 332.
[215] *Ibid.*, 306 (1796).
[216] Ms. Case Papers U.S. Sup. Ct., Cases No. 37 and No. 38.

[217] Ms. Case Papers U.S. Sup. Ct., Case No. 37.
[218] *Ibid.*, decree of District Court.

From the decree separate cross appeals were taken, one by the libellant, Wiseman, and the other by Arcambal.[219] On June 20, 1796, the Circuit Court (Justice Chase) affirmed the dismissal of the libel and reversed the rest of the decree, ordering that the net proceeds from the sale of the ship and cargo be paid to Gariscan for the use of the owners and crew of the *Brutus*, the libellant to pay the claimant for the detention of the ship damages of $9,328.82 plus costs of both courts.[220] From this decree both Wiseman and Arcambal sued out writs of error to remove to the Supreme Court—Wiseman's entered on the docket as case 37, *Wiseman v. the Ship Nuestra Senora del Carmen and Jutau, agent of Gariscan, and Louis Arcambal*, and that of Arcambal as case 38, *Ship Nuestra Senora del Carmen* et al. *v. Wiseman*,[221] where Wiseman was only the formal party defendant, the bone to be picked involving only Jutau as agent for Gariscan.

In the Supreme Court both decrees were affirmed on the principal question which had been decided only a few days earlier in another case involving the *Brutus*.[222] The argument then turned to the question of damages computed below, which in the record, under the heading of "Estimate of Damages," included a charge of $1,600 for counsel fees— $400 apiece for two counsel in the District Court and a similar item for services in the Circuit Court.[223] Ingersoll contended that this item "might be fairly included under the idea of damages." The Court held that the charge could not be allowed, the general practice in the United States being the contrary, and that this practice was entitled to respect until changed or modified by statute.[224] If correctly reported, the Court made no allusion to the Act of March 1, 1793, for ascertaining fees in admiralty proceedings in District Courts[225] by the terms of which a counsellor or attorney could claim at most $3.00 for drawing and exhibiting libel, claim or answer, $3.00 "for drawing interrogatories,"

---

[219] It is interesting to note the differences in the appeals used by the two parties, indicating the practice in that Circuit. One appeal was apparently made *viva voce* before the District judge, Henry Marchant. The other was made *in scriptis* and filed in the office of the clerk of the Circuit Court.

[220] *Ibid.*, decree of Circuit Court.

[221] Ms. Docket Book U.S. Sup. Ct., pp. 30–31.

[222] See Moodie v. *Ship Alfred*, 3 Dallas 307. The *Brutus* had been involved in a substantial number of prize suits in the South Carolina District. The ship had originally been built in New York for use as a privateer in case the controversy between Britain and the United States terminated in war; later sent to Charleston, she was sold to Gariscan and one Morel and was equipped in French territory. The Court held, without discussion in Moodie v. *Ship Alfred*, for Gariscan over Read's contention that this amounted to an original construction for war.

[223] Ms. Case Papers U.S. Sup. Ct., Case No. 37.

[224] 3 Dallas 306. The Court recommended that the easiest way to correct the error was for counsel to enter a *remittitur* for the amount.

[225] 1 *U.S. Stats.*, 332.

and for all other services $3.00. By section 4 of the same act such fees in the Circuit Court were determined by the schedule of the state supreme or superior court. Since the total damages awarded for detention came to $9,328.82 plus Circuit costs of $6.14 in addition to District Court costs of $22.75, it is clear that counsel had not regarded themselves restrained by the statute.

The purpose of the schedules of fees was to fix the items and charges taxable as costs in the bills of costs to be submitted to a court for allowance. As we have elsewhere pointed out,[226] practitioner's records, where available, indicate a great variety of charges to clients, e.g., retainers, consultations and the like which were not taxable costs, but which, as between attorney and client, were remuneration for services rendered not traditionally embraced in official tariffs. Considered in relation to the items in the admiralty fee statute, the amount of the charges in *Arcambal* suggests a subterfuge—to secure judicial blessing on non-taxable charges.

At the next term of the Court (February 1797), in *Jennings v. the Brig Perseverance*, after the Court had affirmed the decree below, Edward Tilghman for the plaintiff in error asserted that damages were very high and that an allowance for counsel fees was included in the damages assessed below.[227] Chase answered that it was a sufficient answer to that objection that the allowance did not appear on the record, an opinion in which the Court concurred.[228] Du Ponceau for the defendant in error then attempted to obtain an increase in damages for the delay occasioned through suing out the writ of error on the ground that by section 23 of the Judiciary Act, damages for delay were peremptorily prescribed and that the discretion of the Court went only to single or double costs.[229]

The opinion of the Court, as reported by Dallas, is no model of clarity, but the holding seems to have been that as the defendant in error (the French vice-consul) was a party to an agreement for the voluntary sale of the vessel, the decree should be affirmed without an increase in damages, the interest to run on the debt only and not on the damages assessed in the Circuit Court, calculated from the date of the

---

[226] *LPAH*, II, c. I.

[227] 3 Dallas 337.

[228] And compare here Cotton v. Wallace, *supra*, p. 713, where the Court had refused to venture outside the record.

[229] ". . . and whereupon such writ of error the Supreme or a circuit court shall affirm a judgment or decree, they shall adjudge or decree to the respondent in error just damages for his delay, and single or double costs at their discretion." Cotton v. Wallace had not settled the issue here because the Court had held only that where judgment was affirmed on writ of error there could be no allowance for damages but for the delay. No opinion was given on whether such damages must be given in the Supreme Court.

decree of the Circuit Court to February 13, 1797. Du Ponceau suffered one further setback—the Court refused his prayer for an allowance of $12.50 for a printed state of the case because no rule authorized such a charge.[230]

The last case involving problems of damage assessment on which there is a report is *Brown v. Van Braam Houchgueest*,[231] decided in the February 1797 term of the Court. The importance of this case as an exposition of section 34 of the Judiciary Act of 1789 appears to have been overlooked. The action was prosecuted in the Circuit Court for the District of Rhode Island, with jurisdiction there obtained through alienage.[232] The suit was brought on several sets of bills of exchange drawn by the defendants and indorsed to the plaintiffs and not paid, the bills before suit having been protested both for non-payment and non-acceptance.[233] After a plea of the general issue was entered, the plaintiff prayed judgment, which was given to him on the defendant's default. The judgment rendered was for over $30,000 damages plus costs, a note to that decree indicating that the damages included the principal and interest on the bills from January 15, 1795, to November 19, 1796, plus 10 percent damages and $29.22 charges of protest.[234] In the Supreme Court two principal errors were argued[235] (other than a procedural point not here relevant)[236]—that the 10 percent damages and 6 percent interest were included in the judgment whereas no damages ought to have been given, and that the Court assessed the damages when a jury should have done this.[237] For present purposes, the arguments of counsel, reported very extensively by Dallas, involved basically the construction of the laws of Rhode Island, the inquiry proceeding under both the Process Act and section 34 of the Judiciary Act. The defendants in error insisted that the practice of Rhode Island and its construction by the courts of that state must dictate the grounds of decision. Counsel entered at large into the form of the record usual in Rhode Island upon the controverted points and adduced some English authority in support of local practice. At the suggestion of the Court, counsel's statement of

---

[230] 3 Dallas 338.

[231] *Ibid.*, 344 (given as Brown v. Van Braam).

[232] Ms. Case Papers U.S. Sup. Ct., Case No. 41. The plaintiff was a resident of Canton, China. The defendants were Rhode Island residents. The pleading of the jurisdictional fact of citizenship and alienage would not have withstood attack under Bingham v. Cabot II, discussed above.

[233] The declaration was in special assumpsit on the separate bills and general assumpsit on the whole amount.

[234] Ms. Case Papers U.S. Sup. Ct., Case No. 41, for Circuit Court judgment.

[235] General error was assigned in the Circuit Court. The specifications were evidently subsequently assigned.

[236] Viz., whether after the plea of the general issue there was a discontinuance of the case and that therefore no judgment could be rendered. 3 Dallas 345.

[237] *Ibid.*

Rhode Island practice was reduced to the form of a certificate. Unfortunately the reported decision is painfully cryptic, Justice Wilson holding for the Court that "under the laws and practical construction of the courts of Rhode Island, the judgment of the circuit court ought to be affirmed."[238] Interest on the principal and interest adjudged below were ordered to run to the date of the Supreme Court judgment.[239]

Something remains to be said concerning the manner in which cases in error were presented to the Court and the reliance upon authority by both counsel and the Court. These are matters on which the case papers help not at all and one is cast upon Dallas' reports for such inferences as they may yield. Unlike some of his contemporaries, this reporter made no explicit statement about his *modus operandi* but we know that he solicited copies of opinions from Cushing and probably from other Justices.[240] The very circumstantial accounts of the arguments of counsel, in particular where these were adorned with clumps of citations not susceptible of speedy reproduction in shorthand, lead one to suppose that Dallas often had access to briefs of counsel. On one occasion he acknowledged the help of William Tilghman.[241] No rule of the Supreme Court required that briefs be filed. The Court did, however, on February 4, 1795, give "notice to the Gentlemen of the Bar, that, hereafter, they will expect to be furnished with a statement of the material points of the Case, from the Counsel on each side of a cause."[242]

Only one manuscript "points of the case" has been found, a clerk's incomplete copy of one presumably used by Hamilton in *Hylton v.*

---

[238] *Ibid.*, 356. A note to the report states that Justice Chase concurred in the Court's affirmance but "that it was on common law principles, and not in compliance with the laws and practice of the state."

[239] *Ibid.*, 356; Ms. Docket Book U.S. Sup. Ct., p. 34 (entry under February term 1797). The Docket Book records the interest as "by way of damages." This obviously was for the delay occasioned by the prosecution of the writ of error. On this see Cotton v. Wallace, *supra*, p. 713.

[240] See Dallas to Cushing, Oct. 1, 1796, Ms. Cushing Papers (MHS); copy of the reply (n.d.) to Dallas, written on the cover of Dallas' letter to him, acknowledging receipt. Cushing explains that what minutes he might have of an opinion in any of the cases he supposed were in Phil-

adelphia, particularly Talbot v. Jansen and Ware v. Hylton. His opinion in McDonough v. *Ship Mary Ford* was stated in his decree. A copy of the case was with the clerk, who would lend it. He had given no opinion in the carriage tax case, being indisposed, and he had no recollection of an opinion in writing in Bingham v. Cabot. Ms. Cushing Papers (MHS).

[241] 3 Dallas 207n. (Ware v. Hylton, 1796). Dallas states that he had not been present during the argument and had hoped to obtain the briefs of counsel. He had been disappointed but had been helped by the notes of William Tilghman to whom he was indebted for similar communications in compiling his reports.

[242] Ms. Mins. U.S. Sup. Ct. 1790–1805, *sub* Feb. 4, 1795.

United States.[243] In the reports some cases, *e.g., United States v. La Vengeance, Olney v. Arnold, Wiscart v. Dauchy, Delcol v. Arnold* et al., the substance of such appear in the summation of arguments. Only one brief has been found—a draft by Hamilton of that used in *Hylton v. United States.*[244] The printed case submitted by Du Ponceau in *Jennings v. the Brig Perseverance* was not a brief, but a résumé of the record with the "points" set out at the end.[245] We do not know whether or not it was common practice to submit such printed statements, for no others have been found.

The reports of cases where procedural questions were settled have one feature which to the modern eye is arresting. This is the degree to which judicial opinions are innocent of citations. Of course, in numerous instances nothing more than a memorandum opinion is set out, which leads to some wonder whether or not the reporter was present to hear the decision delivered, particularly in those causes where arguments of counsel were reproduced at large.[246] Many of these arguments are gravid with citations to treatises and English case law, yet even in the reports of some causes where it is obvious that the Justice was not speaking from notes but was delivering a prepared written opinion, there are enough examples to suggest that the Justice felt under no compulsion to rest conclusions upon a meticulous examination of the precedents proffered.

---

[243] Ms. Hamilton Papers, Nos. 2636–38 (LC).

[244] *Ibid.*, Nos. 93871–82.

[245] 3 Dallas 338–42n.

[246] *E.g.*, Olney v. Arnold, Brown v. Van Braam Houchgueest, Clarke v. Russell.

CHAPTER XVI

The Supreme Court—
Political and Constitutional Issues I

Those MAJOR and indeed minor antifederalist prophets who claimed that the Supreme Court was a political instrument endowed with a potential to obliterate state authority were not to see their direst forebodings come true. Soon enough, however, there were to be portents that the gift of second sight might be theirs, notably with regard to an emergent cause of contemporary anxiety. This concerned the pursuit in federal courts of remedies for the liquidation of certain obligations[1] which had remained undischarged or uncollectible because of state impeditive legislation or the shortcomings of extant judicial machinery. So acute was the fear that state jurisdiction would be deterred that, as noticed, some of the ratifying conventions had proffered amendments to Article III—barring causes of action arising before ratification,[2] prohibiting suits against states,[3] and finally, vesting inferior jurisdiction in state courts subject only to superintendence by appellate process.[4]

The valiant though abortive efforts to make something of these proposals when the Judiciary Bill and the Bill of Rights were under discussion have already been related. Thereafter the proposed amendments no longer amounted to a program; but the underlying complex

---

[1] These embraced, of course, the category of private debts unimpeded discharge of which had been mutually agreed upon in art. IV of the Treaty of Paris (1783).

[2] Virginia, June 1788 (Elliot, *Debates*, III, 660–61); North Carolina, Aug. 1788 (*ibid.*, IV, 246).

[3] Virginia and North Carolina by confining the judicial power to suits between states (*ibid.*, III, 661, and *ibid.*, IV, 246, respectively). New York, July 1788, included among its "unabridgable" rights a denial that the judicial power extended to suits by any person against a state (*ibid.*, I, 329).

[4] Virginia (*ibid.*, III, 660); New Hampshire, June 1788, as to all common law diversity actions (*ibid.*, I, 326); the North Carolina restriction was copied from Virginia's (*ibid.*, IV, 246); New York (*ibid.*, I, 331).

of pretensions and political ideas regarding the sovereignty of the states suffered no abatement. This the Justices of the Supreme Court were to discover when some of the first cases docketed came to be heard. Indeed, as to these and to causes later to surface, state sovereignty was an immanent presence—a sort of *inimicus curiae.*

State sovereignty, as the new Court had to deal with it, was a term of historical rather than of philosophical signification. This was because of the nature of the issues that arose and because transactions were involved that stemmed from the moment when the relations of the states *inter se* had not advanced beyond the stage of joint venture for limited ends. Then, and for a considerable time to come, not only did the states exercise what Leibniz had called the *ius superioritatis,* but the *ius suprematus*[5] as well; to the latter they did not utterly resign their pretensions even after ratification of the Articles of Confederation.[6] With this the tacit or admitted reliance by each state upon the common law which embraced the body of doctrine relating to the prerogatives of the Crown had much to do. Insofar as incidents of supreme power appertaining to the king-sovereign were compatible with republican forms of government, they were susceptible of appropriation by each state as sovereign, or, indeed, of being treated as devolving by way of succession. The several legislatures manifestly acted upon such assumptions as respects escheats, forfeitures and other fiscal prerogatives; some particulars susceptible of being uncrowned, such as the immunity of the sovereign from suit, were left for judicial determination.

STATE SOVEREIGNTY AND ORIGINAL JURISDICTION

TWO INNOCENT-APPEARING cases, the first to be entered on the Court's docket, were the harbingers of a political outburst over state sovereignty, although at the moment there was no reason to suspect this.

---

[5] *Tractatus de jure suprematus* (1677), written under the pseudonym Caesarinus Furstenerius, in O. Klopp, ed., *Die Werke von Leibniz,* (1869), IV, 20 *et seq. Cf.* Goebel, *The Equality of States* (New York: Columbia University, 1923), 87.

[6] Of course, two sovereign powers were not relinquished by the Articles, viz., over commerce and taxation. Upon occasion laws were passed in contravention of the treaties, notably those impeding collection of pre-war debts. Even after Congress's admonition in April 1787 regarding the force of the treaty as supreme law of the land (*supra,* c. V), Virginia suspended the operation of its repeal until the western posts were surrendered (12 Hening, *Va. Stats.,* 528). In 1784 Massachusetts prohibited export of all goods in British bottoms and levied a tonnage duty of 5s. per ton on all foreign ships (*Mass. Acts and Resolves 1784–1785* [reprint], 439–43). This was imitated by New Hampshire in June 1785 (5 *Laws of New Hampshire,* 78). The French government protested the breach of the treaty (*JCC,* XXIX, 817–20).

In both cases the Court's original jurisdiction was invoked. The first was an action of assumpsit by the Amsterdam bankers Nicholas and Jacob Van Staphorst against the state of Maryland, February term 1791;[7] the second, an action by the antifederalist editor Eleazer Oswald, a resident of Pennsylvania, surviving administrator of the printer John Holt, against the state of New York, was begun the same term.[8] No case papers remain in the Maryland case although a declaration, plea and replication were filed. We know also that a summons was returned and that Luther Martin appeared for the state. At the next term the Court, apparently relying upon section 30 of the Judiciary Act, and on motion, ordered a commission to take testimony issue.[9] The cause was continued until August 6, 1792, when it was ordered that the action be discontinued, the matter having been compromised.[10]

Oswald's action against New York was based upon a 1777 agreement between the state and Holt by the terms of which Holt had undertaken to print laws and resolutions of the legislature and such other public papers as should be required. For this he was to be paid £200 per annum. The services were to be performed from February 1777 onward, as long as the printer gave satisfaction. In March 1781 a payment was authorized by the legislature for moneys owing up to February 17, 1781. The action in the Supreme Court was for services performed from that date until 1784 when Holt died. The sum of $3,558.35 was alleged to be owing the estate and $20,000 damages were claimed. At August term 1791[11] the writ was returned served on Governor Clinton and Attorney General Burr. The state failed to appear at February term 1792, and Oswald's counsel moved for a *distringas* to compel appearance.[12] This was taken under advisement. Three days later plaintiff was given leave to withdraw his motion and discon-

---

[7] Ms. Docket Book U.S. Sup. Ct., p. 1.

[8] *Ibid.* The docket entry is ambiguous, but the summons bears the date Feb. 8, 1791. Ms. Original Case Papers U.S. Sup. Ct., Oswald v. State of New York.

[9] The Ms. Mins. U.S. Sup. Ct. 1790–1805, *sub* Feb. 8, 1791, note return of the summons. In 2 Dallas 429 it is reported that Martin "voluntarily appeared." The motion for commissions to issue was made Aug. 1, 1791, and it was so ordered August 3 (Ms. Mins., *supra*).

[10] The discontinuance is entered Ms. Docket Book U.S. Sup. Ct., p. 1; and see Ms. Mins. U.S. Sup. Ct. 1790–

1805, *sub* Aug. 6, 1792. In 2 Dallas 429 it is stated that the case was compromised.

[11] The facts are reconstructed from the Ms. Original Case Papers U.S. Sup. Ct., Oswald v. State of New York. These include a copy of the New York Convention's resolve of Jan. 31, 1777; copy of a certification by James Duane, Apr. 1, 1786; depositions by John Lamb, Jan. 22, 1795, and by Governor Clinton, Jan. 17, 1795; copy of Account, Estate of John Holt (undated). Elizabeth Holt's efforts to secure full payment from New York produced only £200.

[12] Ms. Mins. U.S. Sup. Ct. 1790–1805, *sub* Feb. 11, 1792.

tinue.[13] New process issued at once and for the next two years the energies of counsel were spent upon securing an appearance by the state.

It is proper to remark here that process against a state was a troublesome question, for manifestly the Process Act was inapplicable. Recourse to the all-writs section of the Judiciary Act was the sole statutory warrant, but there was every reason for hesitating, as the Court seems to have done in *Oswald*, to introduce the sequence of progressively more exacting process of the common law. As we shall have occasion to notice, the dignity if not the temper of some states was such as to find even the mere notification by summons intolerable.

This was markedly the case in two causes initiated in 1792 while Oswald's action was still pending—*Grayson* et al. *v. Virginia* (later retitled *Levi Hollingsworth* et al.) and *Alexander Chisholm exr. of Farquhar v. the State of Georgia.* The first mentioned was a suit in equity brought on behalf of the shareholders of the Indiana Company for damages and losses suffered in consequence of Virginia's nullification of the Company's title to an extensive tract of land which the state maintained was located within Virginia's western boundary.[14] A subpoena issued August term 1792, ordering Governor Henry Lee and Attorney General Harry Innes to appear before the Supreme Court on February 4 next, under penalty of $400.[15] They did not obey.

The Court was evidently following the old rule that a subpoena might issue before filing of a bill, for the docket established that the filing was not done until December 4, 1792.[16] This bill does not appear to have been preserved. It had evident flaws for William Grayson had died in 1790 and had been a citizen of Virginia. At some juncture expert counsel, William Lewis and William Rawle, were retained who moved successfully February term 1793 for leave to amend the bill. This was drawn with careful attention to allegations of citizenship.[17] A new subpoena issued February 11, 1793, in the name of Levi Hollingsworth and others.[18] The Virginia officials remained contumacious and the case was continued from term to term, until in March 1796, as will be later noticed, counsel moved for a *distringas* to compel appearance.[19]

---

[13] *Ibid., sub* Feb. 14, 1792. The docket book dates the discontinuance July 17, 1792. This was evidently a mere discontinuance of process, possibly because of doubts about a *distringas.*

[14] See Note A at the end of this chapter for a summary of the Company's claim.

[15] Copy of Subpoena, Aug. 11, 1792, Ms. Original Case Papers U.S. Sup. Ct.

[16] Ms. Docket Book U.S. Sup. Ct., p. 4.

[17] Ms. Mins. U.S. Sup. Ct. 1790–1805, *sub* Feb. 20, 1793.

[18] Subpoena, Feb. 11, 1793, Ms. Original Case Papers U.S. Sup. Ct., Hollingsworth v. Virginia. The amended bill is printed and is signed by Lewis and Rawle.

[19] Ms. Docket Book U.S. Sup. Ct., p. 4.

It was the second cause in which process had issued in 1792 that was to precipitate the constitutional issues latent in the other original actions. That this case should have been pressed with vigor may be attributed to the fact that Chisholm had retained as counsel Attorney General Randolph whose official emoluments were so meagre that his living depended upon the effectiveness with which he represented private clients.

Chisholm's action was based upon a claim for the delivery of goods by decedent to the state of Georgia in 1777 and for which no payment had been received. Both Chisholm and Farquhar were citizens of South Carolina. There is reason to believe that Chisholm first pursued an action in the Circuit Court for the Georgia District because the minutes of that court for October term 1791 note a cause—*Exr. of Farquhar v. the State of Georgia*—where the court granted a motion to amend process so as to describe plaintiff as a citizen of South Carolina. The next entry notes a plea to the jurisdiction, demurrer, joinder and the fact that the demurrer was overruled and the writ quashed.[20] Thereafter, Chisholm brought an action of assumpsit in the Supreme Court. The summons was served on the governor and attorney general of Georgia and the return filed July 11, 1792.[21] When the state failed to enter an appearance, Randolph moved August 11, 1793, that unless the state after reasonable notice of the motion cause an appearance to be made by the fourth day of the next term or show cause to the contrary, judgment be entered and a "writ of damages" be awarded.[22] The Court postponed action until February term 1793.[23] There appears to have been some discussion when Randolph's motion was made, for Iredell left him with the question whether or not assumpsit would lie against the state.[24]

When the Court reconvened, Ingersoll and Dallas presented a written remonstrance from the state of Georgia protesting against the exercise of jurisdiction, but because of positive instructions, both declined to participate in the argument.[25] Randolph proceeded solo. Regrettably he explicitly forebore to enter into "a wide history" of the

[20] Ms. Mins. Circuit Ct. Georgia Dist. 1790–1793, *sub* Oct. 21, 1791. The decedent Farquhar was also a citizen of South Carolina.

[21] The summons dated Feb. 8, 1792, in Ms. Original Case Papers U.S. Sup. Ct., Chisholm, Ex'r. of Robert Farquhar dec. v. the State of Georgia, is partly obliterated, as is the marshal's return on the dorse. The action named is case—still the common usage to designate assumpsit. The declaration filed Mar. 1, 1793 (*ibid.*) gives the details. The value of the goods sold and delivered was alleged to be $169,613.33. Damages of $500,000 were claimed.

[22] Ms. Mins. U.S. Sup. Ct. 1790–1805, *sub* Aug. 11, 1792.

[23] Ms. Docket Book U.S. Sup. Ct., p. 3.

[24] 2 Dallas 419 at 430.

[25] *Ibid.*, 419.

August Term 1792

Hallowell. Attr⟩ Alexander Chisholm
Randolph. Counsel⟩ Exor of Robert Farquhar dec⟩ ⟩ Summons in Case

The State of Georgia

1792.
August 11   On motion of Plaintiffs Counsel ordered that the rule now moved for
to compel the appearance of the State of Georgia be postponed for
Consideration until the next term.

1793
February 5   The Court heard the Attorney General in support of his motion in this
"   Cause.

19   Ordered on argument that Judgment by default be entered against the
State of Georgia in this suit unless she appear or shew cause to the
Contrary by the first day of next term.

August 6   Continued by consent of plaintiffs Counsel.

1794 February 13   On motion of the Attorney General of the United States the Court
direct that Judgment be entered for the Plaintiff and award
a Writ of Enquiry of damages.

1794 August 5   On motion of the Attorney General of Counsel for the plaintiff the Court do
award that the General Jury to be summoned at the next Court do enquire
upon their Oaths & Affirmations what damages the plaintiff has sustained by
reason of the promises and the Nonperformance of the promises and assumption,
in the declaration of the Plaintiff contained and that three months notice of
the holding such Enquiry be given to the Governor and Attorney General of the State
of Georgia.

1795 February 2   Continued.
"   August   Continued
1796 March 14   Continued
   Augt   continued.
1797 Feb.y ——   contd
1797 Augt   cont?

Costs paid

Docket entries, Chisholm, Exr. of *Farquhar v. the State of Georgia*.
(*Manuscript Docket Book, Supreme Court of the United States, The National Archives*)

Constitution as too dangerous, and applied himself to its language and spirit. He was at pains to establish that jurisdiction over controversies between a state and citizens of another state was not confined to causes where a state was plaintiff, a view earlier and artfully advanced by federalists during the ratification debates. To give substance to his claim that the Constitution contemplated that a state might also be impleaded as defendant, Randolph pointed to possible breaches of the restraints of Article I, section 10, such as a law impairing the obligation of contracts. Not denying sovereignty to the states, he asserted, nevertheless, that the Constitution derived its origin from the people, that the states were in fact assemblages of individuals amenable to process. The limitations which the federal government admittedly imposed upon state powers were at least equal to making them defendants.

Randolph rounded out his discourse with the policy argument that adjustment by a judicial forum was preferable to the danger of warring sovereignties,[26] and some of the well-fingered chestnuts of the pamphleteers—the confederacies of antiquity and of modern times—were once more dispensed. The point earlier made by Alexander Hamilton, that an action against a state was impractical because of the impossibility of execution,[27] Randolph sought to meet by referring to the all-writs section of the Judiciary Act, and he suggested that the choice lay in the bosom of the Court. The question raised by Iredell, whether or not assumpsit would lie against a state, was lightly dismissed.

According to a newspaper account,[28] when Randolph had concluded, the Court "expressed a wish to hear any gentlemen of the bar, who might be disposed to take up the gauntlet in opposition to the attorney general." None was so disposed. The Court had the matter under advisement until February 18, on which day the Justices delivered their opinions seriatim. There are hints in two of these that there may have been no conference and that each Justice arrived at his conclusion independently without knowing what each of his brethren had decided. The opinions in *Chisholm* deserve to be considered more or less at large, for not only was this the first great case to be decided by the Court, but also the opinions were delivered at a moment when factional divisions over the limits of national authority lent explosive force to the issue *sub judice*.[29]

---

[26] The "harmony between the states" argument had already been advanced by Randolph at the Virginia ratifying convention. Elliot, *Debates*, III, 570–71.

[27] *The Federalist*, No. 81 (Cooke ed., 1961), 549.

[28] *Dunlap's American Daily Advertiser*, Feb. 21, 1793, p. 3.

[29] The divisions had their immediate origin in differences over the fiscal policies of the national government. Hamilton's account of the growing opposition as of late May 1792 is in his well-known letter to Edward Carrington, May 26, 1792, *PAH*, XI, 426 *et seq.* Opposition peaked in the so-called Giles Resolutions, Jan. 23,

The first opinion was Iredell's. The particular issue before the Court, abstracted, as he said, from the general question—could a state be sued—was whether or not assumpsit would lie against a state. If so, it must be by virtue of the Constitution and of some Act of Congress conformable thereto. The Constitution, Article III, section 2, and section 13 of the Judiciary Act, which he described as "conveying the authority of the Supreme Court under the Constitution," Iredell conceived must be taken together. The terms of each he set out in his opinion, but clearly he regarded the provision of section 13 that the Supreme Court should have original but not exclusive jurisdiction over civil controversies between a state and citizens of another state to be governing. He did not explore the implications of the second paragraph of Article III, section 2, that in cases "in which a state shall be a party the Supreme Court shall have original jurisdiction"—viz., the intendment that the jurisdiction might be considered exclusive, and thus the dispositions of section 13 a mere legislative embellishment. He was, however, quick enough to notice that the phrase of the Judiciary Act, section 13, "controversies of a civil nature," was a legislative gloss, but, he claimed, one a reasonable man would think well warranted.

The importance attached to the Judiciary Act became obvious when Iredell expressed his disagreement with Randolph's theory that once the Supreme Court was formed, it was to exercise by its own authority all the judicial power vested in it by the Constitution. In his opinion all the courts of the United States must receive not only their organization, but also all their manner of proceeding from the legislature. Congress's authority was to be found in the necessary and proper clause. This authority was subject only to the limitation that acts must not be inconsistent with the Constitution, in which event such acts would be void.

In the all-writs section of the Judiciary Act, in particular the modifying phrase "agreeable to the principles and usages of law," Iredell found the directions for the Court's manner of proceeding. The only principles, he concluded, that could be regarded were those common to all states. Of such there were none but those derived from the common law. No other part of the common law could be applicable here except that respecting remedies against the Crown. This was an explicit rec-

---

1793, challenging the regularity of Secretary Hamilton's administration. The exchanges over these resolutions were proceeding while *Chisholm* was before the Court. There is an excellent note on the Giles-Hamilton clash in *PAH*, XIII, 532 *et seq.* The state sovereignty aspect of the controversy appears in a memorandum of Jefferson's (*Works of Jefferson* [Ford, Federal ed.], VII, 223–24) that opens "Divide the Treasury Department/ Abolish the bank/ Repeal the Excise law & let states raise the money/ Lower impost. . . ." Ford places this sometime in February 1793.

ognition of the transfer of royal prerogatives to the states, which he said were completely sovereign except as to powers surrendered to the United States. Amenability to federal judicial authority could depend only upon pre-existent laws or those passed under and conformable to the Constitution. Because the Judiciary Act failed to confer upon Circuit Courts jurisdiction to entertain suits against states, this authority, in Iredell's opinion, could be exercised concurrently only with the states. Consequently, applying the test of pre-existent laws—in this case the hypothesis of the reception of prerogative—the exercise of federal jurisdiction was made contingent upon whether an action against the state would lie in a state court.

There followed a thorough examination of book learning on the amenability of the Crown to actions at law. Iredell concluded that only the way of petition lay open—assumpsit would not lie. A deceptive analogy suggested by Randolph of the amenability of corporations was summarily reasoned out of the picture. Consistent with his view of the case that the question at issue was whether assumpsit would lie, Iredell was not prepared to enter upon a construction of the Constitution, although he thought it not improper to intimate that his present opinion was strongly against any construction that would admit under any circumstances a compulsive suit against a state for the recovery of money.

Justice Blair confined his argument to an analysis of constitutional language, suggesting that the words "between a State and a citizen of another State" could not support the inference that the jurisdiction was limited to where a state was plaintiff because it was probable that the state was first named "in respect to the dignity of a State." Elsewhere in the same article it was patent that maintaining a jurisdiction against a state was contemplated in the category of controversies between two or more states. As for controversies between a state and a foreign state, the inference that a state could only be plaintiff was to lose sight of the policy underlying the provision, viz., that no state by withholding justice should have the power to embroil the whole Confederacy.

The direction of Article III that the Supreme Court possessed original jurisdiction where a state is a party, passed over by Iredell, Blair contended could not be renounced, for refusal to take cognizance of the pending cause would amount to a refusal by the Court to do part of its duty. As for the question of execution, Blair believed that the exercise of jurisdiction was not conditioned by any such consideration, for the means had been furnished by the Judiciary Act, section 14. The Court should go as far as it could, and if insurmountable difficulties should arise, the matter should be left to the departments of the government with higher powers. He would have nothing of proceeding by petition, for "we are not now in a state Court" where the sovereign might claim exemption. But when a state by adopting the Constitution agreed to be amenable to the judicial power of the United States, she had in this particular given up her right of sovereignty.

Wilson's opinion was an example of his judicial style at its fussiest.[30] Here, as in his general charges at Circuit, the learned Justice was a compulsive lecturer, disposed to decorate his text with all the furbelows of learning, a great deal of which was dispensable. He proposed to examine the question whether a state was amenable to the jurisdiction of the Supreme Court first by the principles of general jurisprudence, second by the law and practice of particular states and kingdoms and finally by the Constitution of the United States. Neither of the first two heads of Wilson's argument, whatever their merits as an essay in political science, need detain us. He found neither supported Georgia's claim.

Although the literary ornamentation of Wilson's discussion of the Constitution itself is a constant distraction, his analysis, nevertheless, was not wholly unprofessional. A major premise was to establish the role of the people, for "in almost every nation which has been denominated *free* the state has assumed a supercilious preeminence above the people who have formed it: Hence the haughty notions of state independence, state sovereignty and state supremacy." The support for this observation was taken from French and English writers only; yet it was a comment calculated to stir the bile of state legislatures.

Wilson proceeded to elaborate his premise that all political power in America derived from the people, who upon the failure of the Confederation had ordained and established the Constitution. If the people could alter their former work, there could be no doubt but that they could bind the states to the terms of the Constitution. That this was the intention emerged from the words of the preamble. Here Wilson had resort to the ancient rule of interpretation used so effectively by Hamilton at the Constitutional Convention, viz., that a preamble was a key to the understanding of a statute. To "establish justice" pointed to the judicial authority; to "ensure domestic tranquility" could be achieved only by the exercise of a superintending judicial authority. The language of Article III made inescapable the conclusion that the action would lie.

The opinion of Cushing was a journeyman's job. The question before the Court did not turn on the law and practice of England or upon the law of any country, but upon the Constitution. The prime objection extracted from Article III, section 2, that to subject a state to be a defendant would affect the sovereignty of the state, he thought was

---

[30] William Davie, writing to Iredell, among other sharp comments remarked on the opinion that "perhaps, notwithstanding the tawdry ornament and poetical imagery with which it is loaded and bedizened, it may still be very 'profound.'" McRee, *Iredell,* II, 382.

answered by the preceding clause "between two or more states" where a state must of necessity be a defendant. If any exception was intended, he asked, why was one not made? That the clause "controversies between a state or the citizens thereof and foreign states or citizens" contemplated that one of the United States stand to right as a defendant he related to the provisions of the Constitution conferring the control of defense and foreign affairs on the federal government. Incident to these powers and to prevent controversies with foreign powers or citizens from rising to extremities a national tribunal was necessary. Similarly, it was to avert civil commotion that jurisdiction over controversies between states and between states and citizens of other states had been granted. In other particulars state prerogatives had been curtailed. He had no doubt that if a state was capable of contracting, assumpsit would lie.

According to the *American Daily Advertiser*,[31] Chief Justice Jay delivered "one of the most clear, profound and elegant arguments perhaps ever given in a court of judicature." It was considerably less than this but must be considered at large because it is the chief exhibit on Jay's judicial prowess. Jay prefaced his discussion with a bit of hand-tailored history. The lamentable standards of American judicial historiography may thus be said to be of his founding. The Chief Justice asserted that "from the crown of *Great Britain*, the sovereignty of their country passed to the people of it," and that it was not an uncommon opinion that the unappropriated lands of the Crown passed not to the colony or state where these were situate, but to the whole people. Jay's views are hardly borne out by contemporary records; but these views were necessary to the further comments that thirteen sovereignties had emerged, but the people, nevertheless, continued to consider themselves "in a national point of view as one people." They made a confederation of states, and when disappointed by it, the people in their collective and national capacity established the new Constitution. The opening words of the preamble established that the people were acting as sovereign, and in the language of sovereignty established a Constitution by which it was their will that the state governments be bound and state constitutions be made to conform to it.

Following a diversion comparing the differences of the feudal governments of Europe with governments by compact, or those of the states and the Union, Jay arrived at the question whether suability was compatible with state sovereignty. His argument here took a fanciful form. One citizen could sue any number on whom process could be served. In certain causes a citizen might sue forty thousand, for where a corporation was sued, all members were actually sued though not

---

[31] *Dunlap's American Daily Advertiser*, Feb. 21, 1793.

personally served. The city of Philadelphia had forty thousand free citizens who might be collectively sued by one citizen. In the state of Delaware there were fifty thousand freemen. Was there any reason why a free citizen with demands against them could not prosecute such? Was it not as easy to serve a summons on the governor and attorney general of Delaware as on the mayor and officials of the corporation of Philadelphia? Did Delaware citizens, being associated under a state government, stand in a rank so superior to those of the corporation of Philadelphia that it would not comport with the dignity of the state to meet an individual on equal footing in a court of justice?

It was clear, said Jay, that suability was not incompatible with state sovereignty. One state might sue another state in the Supreme Court, so it was not thought to be a degradation to make an appearance there. He could not perceive that it was more incompatible to appear at the suit of one citizen than of 100,000. At the moment there was pending an action by Georgia against two citizens of South Carolina, a circumstance which took away half the force of the argument of incompatibility.[32]

A review of the situation prior to the Philadelphia Convention brought Jay at length to the Constitution itself. Here he entered into consideration of the relation of the preamble to the contents of Article III, section 2, more at large than had Cushing. The extension of the judicial power to controversies between a state and citizens of another state was remedial and should therefore be construed liberally. If, as had been contended, the language extended only to controversies where a state might be a plaintiff, there would at least have been some intimation. When power was extended to a controversy, it extended necessarily as to all judicial purposes to those between whom the dispute subsisted.

The Chief Justice made an unnecessary digression into the suability of the United States, and concluded his discussion of the main issue with the policy argument that the extension of the judicial power to the controversy before the Court was wise because it was honest, and because it was useful. It was wise because it provided for doing justice without respect of persons; useful because not even the most obscure citizen was without means of obtaining justice from a neighboring state. There was a lot more of this. Jay concluded by again affirming the amenability of the state to suits by citizens of other states, warning, however, that this might not extend to all demands and to every sort of action.

On February 19 the Court ordered that plaintiff file his declaration

---

[32] This was State of Georgia v. Brailsford, 2 Dallas 415, on which see *infra*, p. 743.

on or before March 1, 1793; certified copies were to be served on the governor and attorney general on or before June 1. It was further ordered that unless the state show cause by the first day of August term, judgment by default be entered.[33] The marshal of the Georgia District duly served the papers and when the August term opened, Dallas and Ingersoll appeared to show cause. Dallas moved to postpone argument until the next term. By consent the cause was continued.[34] On February 13, 1794, Randolph moved that judgment be entered for plaintiff.[35] After argument the Court unanimously agreed that judgment be directed for Chisholm and awarded a writ of inquiry to ascertain damages.[36] The subsequent fate of the cause is indicated in the margin.[37]

The furor aroused by *Chisholm* among militant believers in the sovereignty of states was widespread, not only because the suability of states had earlier been hotly contested by antifederalists, but also because at February term 1793 process had been returned in *Oswald v. New York* and an order issued that unless the state appear at the following term and show cause, judgment would be entered against her.[38] On the same day (February 20, 1793) a second subpoena was awarded in the case of *Grayson* et al. *v. Virginia.*[39] Massachusetts was drawn into rebel ranks when, in June 1793, process issued against the state at the instance of William Vassal, a loyalist whose property had been confiscated in 1779.[40] The prospect of being called to account for the liquidation of claims, just or not, was a powerful stimulant to political theory.

The reaction of the Georgia legislature was the most intemperate, reflecting not only wounded pride but also the hot-headedness that was later to mark its proceedings in the Yazoo land business. On December 14, 1792, while the show cause motion had yet to be argued, a resolve was offered in the state house of representatives declaring that the state would not be bound by an unfavorable decision and would regard it as unconstitutional.[41] After the default was entered in the Supreme Court,

---

[33] Ms. Mins. U.S. Sup. Ct. 1790–1805, *sub* Feb. 19, 1793. The declaration, partially destroyed, is in Ms. Original Case Papers U.S. Sup. Ct., Chisholm v. Georgia.

[34] Ms. Mins. U.S. Sup. Ct. 1790–1805, *sub* Aug. 5 and 6, 1793.

[35] *Ibid.*, *sub* Feb. 13, 1794.

[36] *Ibid.*, *sub* Feb. 14, 1794.

[37] At August term 1794 Randolph moved that a general jury be summoned to inquire at the next sitting into the damages (*ibid.*, *sub* Aug. 5, 1794). It is stated, 2 Dallas 479n., that the writ was not sued out. In the

Ms. Original Case Papers is an undated List of Jurors but no indication if summoned. The Ms. Docket Book, p. 3, indicates continuance to August term 1797. The effect of the decision in February 1798 (*infra*, p. 741) was to discontinue the cause.

[38] Ms. Docket Book U.S. Sup. Ct., p. 5 (Feb. 4 and 20, 1793).

[39] *Ibid.*, p. 4 (Feb. 20, 1793).

[40] *Ibid.*, p. 5 (June 4, 1793).

[41] H. V. Ames, ed., *State Documents on Federal Relations*, 7–8; U. Phillips, *Georgia and State Rights*, 26.

the grand jury of the Circuit for the Georgia District, perennially querulous, at April term presented as a grievance the action of the Supreme Court.[42] Seven months later Governor Telfair, on November 4, 1793, delivered a defiant message that was followed fifteen days later by "An act declaratory of certain parts of the retained sovereignty of the State of Georgia."[43]

There was no less anger in Massachusetts but response was more sedate. The lower house, on March 18, appointed a committee to look into the Supreme Court's decision and make a report on the circumstances relating to the case.[44] After process had been served in *Vassal v. Massachusetts,* Governor Hancock addressed both houses, September 18, 1793, directing attention to the dangers to the sovereignty of the states.[45] Nine days later both houses concurred in a resolution to the effect that the doctrine laid down by the Court was unnecessary and inexpedient, dangerous to the peace, safety and independence of the states, and repugnant to the first principles of a federal government. It was further resolved that the Senators be instructed and the congressmen requested to adopt speedy measures to secure such amendments to the Constitution to remove any clause or article that could be construed to justify a decision that a state was compellable to answer any suit by an individual in a federal court.[46]

In November 1793 the Virginia General Assembly, addicted to the tactic of defiant resolutions, voted one similar to that of Massachusetts, assailing the decision as "incompatible with, and dangerous to the sovereignty and independence of the individual states, as the same tends to a general consolidation of these confederated republics."[47]

The Massachusetts and Virginia resolves were laid before the

---

[42] "We present as a grievance the decision of the Supreme Court, in a question relative to the liability of the State of Georgia to answer an Action commenced against her by one individual of another State, exclusive of the incompatibility of Sovereignty and liability to be sued. We observe that circumstances may and situations will alter cases, and actions against the States of New Hampshire or Georgia may be finally concluded by the Verdict of a Jury formed at the seat of Government wherever it may be, influenced *perhaps* by a State prejudice, for such may exist, uninformed of the real merits as it may be too distant amidst the hurry of State business to be attended to, and totally repugnant to the Idea of tryal by vicinage, unless the State concerned

as a party, should possess within its borders the seat of Federal Government." Ms. Mins. Circuit Ct. Georgia Dist. 1793–1798, 20–21 *sub* Apr. 29, 1793.

[43] Phillips, *Georgia and State Rights,* at 27.

[44] Ms. Journal of the House of Representatives of Massachusetts, May 30, 1792 to Mar. 28, 1793. The report of the committee is in the *Salem Gazette,* July 2, 1793.

[45] *Mass. Acts and Resolves 1792–93* (reprint 1895), 699–702.

[46] *Ibid.,* 590–91.

[47] *Journal of the House of Delegates of the Commonwealth of Virginia,* 1793, at 99 (Nov. 28, 1793). The concurrence of the Senate is noted *ibid.,* 110.

New York legislature by Governor Clinton on January 8, 1794.[48] Under his intractable antifederalist leadership, New York no less than Virginia was dedicated to preserving its sovereignty inviolate. There was, however, considerable disagreement as to how this could best be effected. The *Oswald* action posed the practical question of whether a defense should be interposed, and if so, whether this should be confined to a denial of the jurisdiction. The sense of both houses was that the attorney general should appear for the state.[49] Resolutions of protest were offered but not voted, for on March 27 the Eleventh Amendment to the Constitution was laid before the legislature and was ratified the same day.[50]

Despite the presence of state rights' standard-bearers in Congress, action there had been deliberate. On the day after the Court's order in *Chisholm* there was introduced in the Senate a resolution for a constitutional amendment to render the states immune to suits, but this never came to a vote, for on February 25 it was postponed to the next session.[51] Finally on January 2, 1794, the text of what became the Eleventh Amendment was presented in the Senate as a joint resolution.[52] Attempts to amend this failed and the original text passed in the affirmative on January 14.[53] In the House an attempt to amend also failed, and on March 4 the resolution passed[54] and was enrolled March 10.[55]

Oswald's action was to fare better than Chisholm's. Because of his antifederalist activities in 1788, Oswald himself was something of a minor hero in New York and Clinton was under political obligation to him. As noticed above, a show cause order threatening judgment by default had issued February 20, 1793.[56] Both the governor and attorney general were served, and at August term Ingersoll showed cause why New York should be exempt from appearing because it was a "free, sovereign and independent state," and that it refused so to do.[57] On motion of plaintiff's counsel the cause was continued.[58] Docket entries

---

[48] *Journal of the Assembly of the State of New York*, 1794, at 7–8.

[49] House vote, *ibid.*, 17 (Jan. 15, 1794); Senate substitute, *ibid.*, 20 (January 16); rejected by the House, *ibid.*, 21 (January 18). The difference was mainly over a general duty to defend the state *ex officio* or a specific direction as to Oswald's action.

[50] *Ibid.*, 180.

[51] *Annals of Congress*, III, 651 (Feb. 20, 1793); *ibid.*, 656 (Feb. 25, 1793).

[52] *Ibid.*, IV, 25.

[53] *Ibid.*, 29–31.

[54] *Ibid.*, 476–78; *Jour. H.R.* II, 78–80.

[55] *Jour. H.R.*, II, 87. The text, 1 *U.S. Stats.*, 22: "The judicial power of the United States shall not be construed to extend to any suit in law or equity commenced or prosecuted against one of the United States by citizens of another State, or by citizens or subjects of any foreign State."

[56] *Supra*, n. 38.

[57] Show cause paper, Aug. 5, 1793, Ms. Original Case Papers U.S. Sup. Ct., Oswald v. New York.

[58] Ms. Mins. U.S. Sup. Ct. 1790–1805, *sub* Aug. 6, 1793.

to this effect appear for both of the 1794 terms, although on August 5, 1794, a *venire* issued to the marshal of the Pennsylvania District to cause forty-eight to sixty men to appear to serve as petit jurors.[59] In October the New York attorney general consented that divers depositions *de bene esse* be taken pursuant to section 30 of the Judiciary Act, notwithstanding that witnesses might not live precisely one hundred miles from the place of trial, and agreed that these be read at trial.[60]

The depositions were returned and ordered filed February 2, 1795; trial was set for February 5. On that day a plea of non-assumpsit and payment was entered by the state.[61] The docket entry indicates that issue was joined.[62] There is no entry in the minutes to indicate that the jury was charged. A verdict was returned for plaintiff in the amount of $5,315 damages and 6 cents costs. Judgment *nisi* was entered.[63] Grudgingly the New York legislature voted in April 1795 that Oswald be paid the sum of £2,144.13.11 provided that he execute a release and discharge in full from a certain judgment, and from any execution thereon and for all costs and charges accrued, including expenses and disbursements by the New York attorney general in defending the action.[64]

Despite the uproar precipitated by the *Chisholm* decision, it was close to four years before a sufficient number of states had ratified to put the Eleventh Amendment into effect. In the meantime *Vassal v. Massachusetts* slumbered on the docket, kept animate by a succession of continuances; but the suit in equity by Hollingsworth and others against Virginia exhibited signs of activity. Two new original actions were also initiated in 1795, one by John Brown Cutting, citizen of Pennsylvania, against the state of South Carolina to recover a debt owing the estate of the Prince of Luxembourg,[65] a second by Alexander Moultrie and others, citizens of South Carolina, against Georgia for specific performance of a contract for the sale of lands to the so-called South Carolina Yazoo Company.[66]

---

[59] Ms. Docket Book U.S. Sup. Ct., p. 5. The *venire* and a panel of forty-eight jurors are in Ms. Original Case Papers U.S. Sup. Ct., Oswald v. New York.

[60] Consent executed Oct. 4, 1794, filed Jan. 30, 1795, Ms. Original Case Papers U.S. Sup. Ct., Oswald v. New York.

[61] Ms. Mins. U.S. Sup. Ct. 1790–1805, *sub* Feb. 2, 1795. The depositions included those of Clinton, John Lamb, Robert Harpur, John Broome, Richard Bogardus, John Jay and James Duane.

[62] Ms. Docket Book U.S. Sup. Ct., p. 5. The plea is in Ms. Original Case

Papers U.S. Sup. Ct., Oswald v. New York.

[63] Ms. Mins. U.S. Sup. Ct. 1790–1805, *sub* Feb. 5 and 6, 1795.

[64] *N.Y. Laws*, 18 Sess. 1795, c. 76.

[65] Summons, Aug. 6, 1795, Ms. Original Case Papers U.S. Sup. Ct., Cutting adm'r. v. State of South Carolina.

[66] Apr. 13, 1795. The original bill is lost; the date is taken from the supplemental bill of complaint, Ms. Original Case Papers U.S. Sup. Ct., Moultrie *et al.* v. Georgia. For an account of the cause see Note B at the conclusion of this chapter.

That the Court, having decided upon the construction of Article III, section 2, considered itself bound by precedent is evident from the proceedings in *Hollingsworth, Cutting* and *Moultrie.* In the first of these cases, counsel on March 12, 1796, moved for a *distringas* to compel the appearance of Virginia.[67] This was held over until the next term when the Court established two rules.[68] The first ordered that when process at common law or in equity issued against a state, the same should be served on the governor or chief magistrate and the attorney general of the state. The second rule ordered that process of subpoena issuing out of the Court in an equity suit should be served on defendant sixty days before the return date. If defendant did not then appear, complainant should be at liberty to proceed *ex parte.* The motion for a *distringas* in *Hollingsworth* was withdrawn and an alias subpoena issued that was duly served.[69] At February term 1797 a commission issued to take testimony. At this term a similar commission issued in *Moultrie v. Georgia,* plaintiff having leave to proceed *ex parte,* for the state had failed to appear after service of process.[70]

At this term, also, Cutting's action progressed further than the other original actions then pending. A breviate of the genesis of the claim is set out in the margin.[71] It is to be noticed that the jurisdiction of the

---

[67] Ms. Docket Book U.S. Sup. Ct., p. 4.

[68] Ms. Mins. U.S. Sup. Ct. 1790–1805, *sub* Aug. 12, 1796; 3 Dallas 320–21.

[69] *Ibid.* The subpoena is in Ms. Original Case Papers U.S. Sup. Ct., Hollingsworth *et al.* v. State of Virginia.

[70] Ms. Docket Book U.S. Sup. Ct., p. 32. This is noted in 3 Dallas 339 *sub nom.* Huger *et al.* v. South Carolina. There was no such case of this title. Huger was one of the plaintiff members of the South Carolina Company.

[71] This is presumably the case referred to by Warren in *Supreme Court in United States History,* I, 104, n. 2, as Catlin v. South Carolina, apparently relying upon H. L. Carson, *The History of the Supreme Court of the United States,* I, 169, n. 1. No case of that name appears on the docket. *Cutting* arose out of a contract (1780) between an agent for South Carolina and the Prince of Luxembourg for a three-year charter of the frigate *L'Indien,* renamed the

South Carolina. The frigate was the property of the French King, who had granted the Prince the use of her for three years. The Prince received a down-payment of 100,000 livres and was to receive a share of prize money and other benefits and 300,000 livres if the ship was lost or captured. The *South Carolina* had been in the service of the state for over two years when she was captured. The attempts to settle the Luxembourg claims in South Carolina are detailed in D. E. Huger Smith, "The Luxembourg Claims," 92. These included an award by arbitrators authorized by the legislature (1784), resolves of the legislature liquidating the amounts due (1786), and an agreement to fund the debt. The Prince having died in exile, Cutting, who had been handling the claims, commenced proceedings as principal creditor in the Court of the Ordinary (1794). The French vice-consul claimed jurisdiction by virtue of the Consular Convention of 1788 and further that the Republic had succeeded to the claims of the French King. The vice-consul's claim of

Supreme Court was invoked only after the South Carolina Court of the Ordinary had concluded in 1794 that it could not dispose of the claim interposed by the French Republic as a principal creditor of the late Prince's estate. The state had not denied that the moneys were due the estate; it admittedly stood in the position of a stakeholder. Consequently, as between it and Cutting the cause was not adversarial in the sense that other original actions brought by individuals were. Nevertheless, South Carolina made no appearance February term 1796. An alias summons issued March 6.[72] This was returned at August term when plaintiff was ordered to file his declaration within a month, the same to be served on the governor and attorney general; unless the state appeared or showed cause to the contrary by the first day of the following term, judgment by default would be entered.[73]

The declaration and the copy of the Court's order were served betimes, but again the state failed to enter an appearance. A judgment by default was consequently entered February 8, 1797.[74] Two days later a writ of inquiry of damages was awarded.[75] The immense patience of the Court is evident from the order that three months' notice to the governor and attorney general be given.

The recalcitrance of the South Carolina executive is the more remarkable because the legislature by joint resolution on December 19, 1796,[76] acknowledged the debt, professed its lack of capacity to settle the litigation and recommended that the attorney general be directed to file a bill of interpleader in the United States Supreme Court to make all parties interested in the claim come before the Court. The attorney general was further to be directed when the interpleader was filed to attach a "Declaration against the Exercise of any Jurisdiction by the Supreme Court of the United States coercive on the State. And a protest against this Example being drawn into precedent."

News of this action had reached Philadelphia, for in March 1797 A. J. Dallas, counsel for the plaintiff, in despatching to the South Carolina governor the rule for judgment and the rules for the jury of inquiry, advised him that the proceedings had been "conducted with utmost delicacy and deference towards the State." As counsel for plaintiff he agreed that on executing the writ of inquiry the state and all other claimants would be heard as if an issue had been directed and joined

---

jurisdiction was rejected, but the Ordinary held that the Republic's claim was a question for a federal court.

[72] Summons, Mar. 6, 1796, Ms. Original Case Papers U.S. Sup. Ct., Cutting v. South Carolina.

[73] Ms. Docket Book U.S. Sup. Ct., p. 21 (Aug. 11, 1796).

[74] *Ibid.*

[75] *Ibid.*

[76] Exhibit "C," in Ms. Original Case Papers U.S. Sup. Ct., Cutting v. South Carolina.

agreeable to the prayer of a bill of interpleader.[77] The rules and letter were served before May 10, 1797,[78] but apparently the state did not appear until after the jury, on August 8, found damages, $55,002.84.[79] A bill for an injunction was filed August 9, by Jacob Read for the South Carolina attorney general,[80] but a rule for final judgment in Cutting's action was entered August 11.[81]

The tactics of South Carolina seem to have been directed beyond all else at avoiding the role of defendant and appearing as complainant. The state was so far successful that its suit was docketed as a new cause.[82] On August 15 the Court ordered that an injunction issue staying all proceedings on the judgment until January 1, 1798. It was further ordered that an injunction also be awarded to stay all further proceedings on condition that the state on or before that date bring into Court £10,855.8.5 sterling money of South Carolina equal to $46,523.25 plus interest at 7 percent since March 13, 1789, to the time of payment into Court deducting from the amount of interest £1,000 already paid Cutting, subject to the Court's further order and decree. At the same time the state was to pay costs in the suit.[83] This cause was continued February term 1798 by consent[84] and thereafter no further proceedings took place. Nothing has been found to indicate that the money was ever brought into Court; indeed, the subsequent protracted proceedings in South Carolina tend to establish that it was not.[85]

The February term 1798 marked the demise of the jurisdiction of the Supreme Court over actions brought by individuals against states. Despite the turmoil precipitated by the decision in *Chisholm* (February 1793) there had been no frantic rush to ratify the Eleventh Amendment, for it was not until January 8, 1798, that President Adams notified Congress that three fourths of the states had ratified and that the amendment "may now be declared" to be part of the Constitution.[86] On February 10, 1798, Attorney General Lee submitted to the Court the question whether the amendment did or did not supersede all suits depending as well as prevent the institution of new suits against a state

---

[77] Dallas to the governor of South Carolina, in Ms. Original Case Papers U.S. Sup. Ct., Cutting v. South Carolina. The exact date is obliterated.

[78] Marshal's return, *ibid.*

[79] Ms. Docket Book U.S. Sup. Ct., p. 21.

[80] Bill in Equity, Ms. Original Case Papers U.S. Sup. Ct., State of South Carolina v. John B. Cutting adm'r. for the Prince of Luxembourg, the French Republic and the Duke of Luxembourg.

[81] Ms. Docket Book U.S. Sup. Ct., p. 21.

[82] *Ibid.*, 49.

[83] *Ibid.*

[84] Ms. Mins. U.S. Sup. Ct. 1790–1805, *sub* Feb. 14, 1798.

[85] Smith, "The Luxembourg Claims," at 101 *et seq.*

[86] Richardson, *Messages and Papers of the Presidents*, I, 260.

by citizens of another state.[87] William Tilghman and William Rawle argued that the amendment must be considered as introductory of a new system. They advanced the odd theory that the amendment was void because it had not been proposed in the form prescribed by the Constitution, for they conceived that the concurrence of the President was necessary. The words "commenced and prosecuted" looked to the future suits, for the Constitution was opposed to everything in the nature of ex post facto or retrospective regulation. Support was sought in certain rules of statutory interpretation, none of which had been developed in a political context.

Attorney General Lee replied that the amendment was merely explanatory. From the moment those who gave the power to sue a state annulled it, this power ceased to be a part of the Constitution, and if it did not exist there, it could not be exercised. The policy and rules regarding ex post facto laws did not apply to the formation or amendment of a constitution. The question whether the proper forms had been observed in proposing the amendment Chase answered from the Bench to the effect that the President had nothing to do with the amending process. Lee proceeded to repudiate the theory that rules for applying statutes were relevant: the people had chosen to cut off a branch of judicial power supposed to authorize a particular jurisdiction—"the words being so extended as to support that policy will equally apply to the past and to the future." On February 14 the Court decided unanimously that the amendment being constitutionally adopted, no jurisdiction in any case past or future could be exercised in any case in which a state was sued by citizens of another state or by citizens and subjects of any foreign state.

PRE-WAR DEBTS

THE ELEVENTH AMENDMENT relieved the anxieties of the states, excited by the *Chisholm* decision, that they might be subject to a deluge of actions in the Supreme Court by refugee loyalists if for nothing else than for debts forfeited by acts of attainder and similarly directed

---

[87] 3 Dallas 378, *sub nom.* Hollingsworth v. Virginia. The minutes of the Court indicate that on Feb. 10, 1798, the argument was heard without reference to any pending cause. The entries for Feb. 14, 1798, start with Hollingsworth, followed by Moultrie, Brailsford v. Georgia, and Cutting, which alone was continued. Brailsford v. Georgia was an action for assumpsit. The declaration, noted in the Court minutes as filed Feb. 7, 1798, alleged a loan to the state of $10,000, never repaid. The pleading is so badly stained that the date of the loan is indecipherable. Ms. Original Case Papers U.S. Sup. Ct., Brailsford v. Georgia.

legislation. These apprehensions were by no means baseless, for by the fifth article of the treaty of peace (1783) it had been agreed that all persons who had any interest in confiscated lands, either by debts, marriage settlements or otherwise, should meet with no lawful impediment in the prosecution of their just rights.[88] There was, furthermore, in relation to the collection of private debts owed British subjects some question of liability for sums paid into state treasuries wherever by statute a debtor was privileged thus to liquidate his obligation in current money.

Article IV of the treaty stipulated that creditors on either side should meet with no lawful impediment to the recovery of the full value in sterling money of all bona fide debts theretofore contracted. The removal of impeditive legislation had been the subject of negotiations with Britain during the Confederation. The action of the Congress in 1787 to press the states into honoring a national undertaking has already been noticed.[89] The difficulties of securing more than *pro forma* compliance were very great, not only because hard money was in critically short supply, but also because of the pervasive conviction that the British by not surrendering the northern and western posts had not carried out their part of the bargain. In the Southern states, where the pre-war debt burden was the greatest, the fact that the British had carried off the slaves in the hands of the evacuating armies despite the terms of the treaty[90] was regarded as an outright breach thereof.

The currency of such opinions inevitably militated against the effective pursuit of remedies by creditors in state courts even after the federal judiciary was established, as respects demands below the jurisdictional limit. For creditors with substantial claims the new Circuit Courts offered hope, although it may here be remarked that owing to the ingenuity of counsel this often was to be hope deferred before judgment was finally entered.

The first debt case to reach the Supreme Court was peculiar in this, that it was as a result of Georgia's invocation of the Court's original jurisdiction because of a procedural dilemma that arose in the course of some actions for recovery of debts at the Circuit Court for the Georgia District.[91] The earliest mention of the problem is contained in a letter of Iredell J. to President Washington, February 23,

---

[88] This was the concluding sentence of the undertaking by Congress "earnestly" to recommend legislation by the states for restitution of confiscated properties. For the treaty, see W. M. Malloy, *Treaties, Conventions, . . . between the United States of America and other Powers,* *1776–1909,* I, 586 (hereafter cited as Malloy, *Treaties, Conventions . . .*).

[89] *Supra,* c. V, p. 197.

[90] Art. VII.

[91] Among which was Brailsford *et al.* v. Spalding, Ms. Mins. Circuit Ct. Georgia Dist. 1790–1793, 19, *sub* Oct. 17, 1791.

1792.[92] Plea had been put in by the defendants, not denying the existence of the debt but showing a right in the state of Georgia to recover under certain acts passed prior to the treaty of peace. The law officers of the state were directed to interfere in the defense, but counsel for the defendants refused to permit this. Application was then made to the Court for leave to interplead. Iredell could find no precedent where an interpleader in an action at law had been directed except on application of a defendant much less against his consent, and consequently rejected the motion. It was also deemed questionable whether, if the state thus became a party, the cause would not have to be tried in the Supreme Court. A bill of interpleader in equity might have been appropriate but no such bill had been brought. Even then there was a question whether the Circuit Court was a proper forum. The problem was submitted to the President because it might be resolved in the projected revision of the judicial system.

There is no reason to doubt that one of the cases Iredell adverted to was the action by Samuel Brailsford, Robert Powell and John Hopton against James Spalding, surviving partner of Kelsall and Spalding, merchants of Georgia, who, in 1774, had executed a bond for the sum of £7,058.9.5 to plaintiffs that remained unpaid.[93] At the time action was brought (1791) Brailsford was a British subject; the other two plaintiffs were citizens of South Carolina. Defendant pleaded in bar the Georgia confiscation act of 1782; plaintiffs demurred and defendant joined issue. The Georgia statute had provided *inter alia* that "all debts, dues, or demands, due or owing to merchants or others residing in Great-Britain, be, and they are hereby sequestered."[94] Commissioners were to be appointed to recover and deposit these in the state treasury. The statute also subjected to confiscation estates within Georgia together with debts owing, belonging to persons convicted of offenses leading to the confiscation of their property in states whereof such persons were citizens.

The application of the Georgia attorney general to be made a party having been denied, plaintiffs' demurrer was sustained. The substance of the opinion was that Brailsford's debts were only sequestered by Georgia law, upon which no proceedings had taken place, the treaty of peace

---

operating as a repeal of that part of the act which barred recovery. Hopton's and Powell's debts had not been confiscated by South Carolina[95] and therefore could not be confiscated by Georgia.

The action in the Circuit Court was decided April term 1792. To prevent execution a bill in equity was brought in the Supreme Court, August term 1792, by the governor of Georgia in behalf of the state. The bill recited the Georgia statute and charged a "confederacy" between the parties to the Circuit Court action to defraud the state. An injunction was prayed to stay in the hands of the marshal all moneys raised or to be raised upon execution, and that he be directed to pay over such funds to the state. On August 8 Dallas moved that the injunction issue. After argument, the Court granted the motion and ordered that the moneys be stayed in the hands of the marshal until further order.[96] The decision was 4–2. Iredell repeated much of what he had already written to the President and emphasized that justice and honor required that the claim of Georgia should not be defeated by a judgment upon a trial at which she had not been heard. Blair agreed substantially with this, considering the injunction necessary while the Court inquired into the merits of the claim. Wilson and Jay concurred because of the peculiar circumstances. Cushing and Johnson dissented because they believed that Georgia had an adequate remedy at law.[97]

Subpoenas were ordered to be served on Brailsford, Hopton and Powell for appearance February 4, 1793.[98] They filed a demurrer on that day alleging that there was an adequate remedy at law and that section 16 of the Judiciary Act did not apply.[99] According to Dallas' report, Randolph moved to dissolve the injunction and dismiss the bill on two grounds—that Georgia had no remedy at law, and that even if it had, no equitable right existed to justify the present form of proceeding.

The minutes show that argument was had February 6, 7, 8 and 9. The cause was at this stage when on February 18, 1793, the opinions in *Chisholm* were pronounced. The *Brailsford* case was adverted to only in the wry comment by Jay that a rule was a bad one which did not work both ways, viz., that the citizens of Georgia were content with a right to sue citizens of other states, but were not content that the latter should have the right to sue them.[100] Two days after the *Chisholm* opinions, the Court decided, again 4–2, that if Georgia had a right, it must be pursued at common law. The injunction would be continued until the

---

[95] "An Act for disposing of certain Estates" (Feb. 25, 1782), 4 *South Carolina Stats. at Large*, 516.

[96] Ms. Mins. U.S. Sup. Ct. 1790–1805, *sub* Aug. 8, 9, and 11, 1792.

[97] 2 Dallas 404–09.

[98] Subpoenas, tickets, affidavits and affirmations in Ms. Original Case Papers U.S. Sup. Ct., Georgia v. Brailsford.

[99] *Ibid.*, for the text of the demurrer.

[100] 2 Dallas at 473.

next term when, if no action had been instituted, it would be dissolved.[101]

To prevent dissolution, the parties agreed that an action be docketed with the Supreme Court and that a plea of non-assumpsit be entered. This was filed June 3, 1793.[102] The cause was continued August term when the Court sat but two days. On February 4, 1794, the pleadings—declaration, plea and replication—were "filed and issue." The indebtedness alleged was $80,000. At some juncture a *venire* had issued for a special jury which was struck by the parties prior to the 4th. The Court heard arguments February 4–7.[103] Ingersoll and Dallas appeared for the state, William Bradford, United States Attorney General, E. Tilghman and William Lewis for defendants.

The argument for the state needs to be noticed because counsel deliberately injected into the controversy the rights of a sovereign state and the question of the applicability of Article IV of the treaty of peace regarding pre-war debts. The sovereign state, it was claimed, had the right to transfer the debt in question by her confiscation law without any of the traditional common law formalities.[104] Among a variety of authorities, two recent English cases were cited—one in which Lord Loughborough had characterized the New York confiscation law of 1779 as the law of an independent country.[105] The other, even more to their client's heart, was Chancellor Thurlow's opinion to the same effect in a cause relating to the confiscation of the property of former Georgia governor Sir James Wright pursuant to the 1782 act.[106] The laws of confiscation and sequestration, it was claimed, were not touched by the treaty for they were not the object of the fourth article. The situation was unaffected by the federal Constitution. The exception of debts in the South Carolina law on which Hopton and Powell relied was of no avail as that law was referred to only "for the manner and form and not for the subject of confiscation."

To all this, defendants answered that as Hopton's and Powell's debts had not been confiscated by South Carolina, they could not be by words of reference in the Georgia law. That state had no right to confiscate the property of citizens of other states. Brailsford's debt had only been sequestered, and this had not been enforced by any inquest of office,

---

101 Ms. Mins. U.S. Sup. Ct. 1790–1805, *sub* Feb. 20, 1793; 2 Dallas 415–17.

102 Ms. Docket Book U.S. Sup. Ct., p. 6. The agreement is in Ms. Original Case Papers U.S. Sup. Ct., *sub nom.*

103 The pleadings are in Ms. Original Case Papers U.S. Sup. Ct., Georgia v. Brailsford; see also Ms. Docket Book U.S. Sup. Ct., p. 6.

104 3 Dallas 1–3.

105 Folliott v. Ogden, 1 H. Blackstone (C.P.) 123 (1789). On error to King's Bench, Lord Kenyon expressed a contrary view although the judgment itself was affirmed (3 Term Rep. 726).

106 Wright v. Nutt, 1 H. Blackstone 136 (1788).

seizure or other act tantamount thereto. The peace alone, without compact, had restored Brailsford's right of action; the treaty expressly revived it and by the Constitution the treaty was the supreme law of the land.

A four-day argument seems more appropriate in the context of a demurrer than of a request for instructions to a jury. It invited certainly a more extended comment from the Bench on the treaty provision respecting debts and the effect of the supremacy clause of the Constitution than it was to receive. This reticence may be accounted for by the fact, as the Chief Justice, who delivered the charge, stated, that it represented the unanimous opinion of the Court.[107] He and Iredell had differed sharply on the debt question at the Circuit proceedings in *Ware v. Hylton* in June 1793 (a case to which we shall come in a moment), and it is conceivable that to secure unanimity exploration of the issue of the treaty provision raised by counsel was avoided. It was unnecessary, said Jay, to follow the investigation into the extensive field to which it had been carried. The instructions were limited to a brief statement of the effects of the statutes. The debts due Hopton and Powell were not confiscated by South Carolina because they were expressly excepted; the Georgia statute had enacted the like degree and extent of forfeiture and confiscation with respect to these. The debts due Brailsford were subjected by the Georgia act not to confiscation but to sequestration. His right to recovery revived at the peace both by the law of nations and the treaty of peace.[108]

The jury retired and later returned to ask whether the Georgia act at the time of passage completely vested the debts due defendants in the state. If so, did the treaty or any other matter revive the rights of defendants? Jay replied that the act did not vest the debts in the

---

[107] 3 Dallas 1 at 3–5.

[108] Although not material to the main issue, Jay's instruction on the respective roles of court and jury deserves remark. He refers to "the good old rule, that on questions of fact it is the province of the jury, on questions of law it is the province of the court to decide. But," he continued, "it must be observed that by the same law, which recognizes this reasonable distribution of jurisdiction, you have nevertheless a right to take upon yourselves to judge of both and to determine both the law and the fact in controversy. . . . We have no doubt you will pay that respect which is due to the opinion of the court—But still both objects are lawfully within your power of decision." James Bradley Thayer (*Preliminary Treatise on the Law of Evidence at the Common Law* [Boston: Little, Brown, 1898], 254) surmises that this "extraordinary doctrine" is partly explicable by the "lack of learning on the bench." If he means by this that neither bar nor judges were aware of Hargraves's careful analysis of the "maxim" *ad quaestionim facti*, etc., in his note on Coke, *Littleton*, 155b, which was already in circulation, his explanation is acceptable. Certainly the federal bench was far from being lack-learnèd. Because of Jay's office his statement was to have more influence than it deserved.

state; no sequestration divests the property in the thing sequestered. Brailsford had remained the real owner; Georgia had interposed her authority to prevent recovery. The right of action was revived by the peace and by the treaty. Never in law or in fact had the property been taken from defendants. If it were otherwise, the sequestration would remain a lawful impediment to recovery in opposition to the fourth article of the treaty. A verdict was returned for defendants and judgment was entered for them.[109]

The February term 1794 marked Jay's last appearance on the Bench, for in April of that year he accepted an appointment as envoy to Great Britain to negotiate a settlement of outstanding differences. He did not resign his judicial office until June 29, 1795, after his return to the United States.[110] The Jay appointment was roundly denounced as a violation of the principle of separation of powers.[111] Because the Court was already strongly committed to this doctrine, this charge was difficult to counter. At the bottom of the opposition, however, was a strong current of anti-British sentiment inflamed by the seizures of American ships and cargoes, and the suppuration of old sores such as the continued occupation of the northwest posts, the debts and the abducted negroes. Emotional tensity over the debt question reached, indeed, such a point that sentiments of disunity manifested themselves.[112] In the Congress a bill suspending commercial intercourse with Britain had failed of passage by Adams' casting vote in the Senate;[113] bills to sequestrate the pre-war debts had been introduced into both House and Senate but had failed of adoption.[114]

---

[109] Ms. Docket Book U.S. Sup. Ct., p. 6.

[110] Jay to Washington, H. P. Johnston, ed., *The Correspondence and Public Papers of John Jay*, IV, 177. According to RG 217 Miscellaneous Treasury Accounts 1790–1894, No. 6951, Jay was paid his salary as Chief Justice Apr. 1–June 30, 1795. This was a final payment.

[111] Bache's *General Advertiser*, Apr. 19, 28, 29, and May 2, 1794; *Dunlap's American Daily Advertiser*, May 12, 1794.

[112] Ellsworth wrote Oliver Wolcott, Sr., Apr. 5, 1794, that "the debts of the South, which were doubtless among the causes of the late revolution, have ever since operated to obstruct its benefits, by opposing compulsive energy of government, generating mist and irritation between this country and Great Britain,

and, of course, giving a baleful ascendancy to French influence." G. Gibbs, *Memoirs of the Administrations of Washington and Adams* (1846), 134. According to a memorandum Senator John Taylor of Virginia sent to Madison, May 11, 1794, Ellsworth and Rufus King had broached the question of a peaceful separation of North and South. The debt issue was among the reasons advanced. Facsimile in G. Hunt, ed., *Disunion Sentiment in Congress in 1794*.

[113] The House voted 58–34, Apr. 25, 1794 (*Annals of Congress*, IV, 605–06). The Senate voted April 28 (*ibid.*, 90).

[114] The House resolve of Mar. 27, 1794 (*ibid.*, 535); an attempt to vote it beaten on May 23 (*ibid.*, 715–16). The move in the Senate on May 6 was for leave to bring a bill suspending

The settlement of the pre-war debt problem was among the items in Jay's instructions.[115] No major federal case raising the chief issues involved in Article IV of the treaty of peace had yet advanced to judgment even in the Circuit Courts. But while Jay was en route to England, final judgment had been entered in the case of *Ware admr. of Jones v. Hylton*, an action brought by bill in November 1790 by a British creditor against a Virginia debtor in the Circuit Court for the Virginia District. A writ of error dated June 6, 1794, tested by Jay, was served returnable to the Supreme Court August term of that year. This was the cause in which Jay had ruled on a certain demurrer in favor of the plaintiff creditor, June 1793, but had been outvoted by Iredell and Griffin. The case had lain over for the trial of an issue of fact, an event which did not occur until a year later.[116] For reasons unknown the cause had been continued on the Supreme Court docket until February 1796.

By the time *Ware v. Hylton* came to be argued in the Supreme Court ratifications of the treaty concluded by Jay had been exchanged. The wrathful indignation that publication of the treaty's terms excited no similar event in our history can equal.[117] Not only those who suffered from what Senator Uriah Tracy called *Gallicus Morbus*,[118] but also some normally level-headed persons were carried away. One otherwise sensible statesman who succumbed to the hysteria was John Rutledge whom Washington had appointed to succeed Jay. An intemperate speech delivered in Charleston denouncing the treaty[119] cost him Federalist support in the Senate, which refused to confirm the appointment.[120]

---

art. IV of the treaty (*ibid.*, 94). Only the two Virginia Senators voted affirmatively.

[115] *Am. St. Pap.: For. Rel.*, I, 472–74.

[116] Ware *admr.* v. Hylton, Ms. Case Papers U.S. Sup. Ct., Case No. 4. This case is a prime exhibit on the delays and frustrations of plaintiffs, for the action was begun Nov. 27, 1790. A default judgment was recorded in the clerk's office. Upon motion to set aside, the cause was sent back to the rules docket (1 Ms. Order Book Circ. Ct. Va. Dist., 7), and in November 1791 a change of plea was granted (*ibid.*, 65). The trial itself did not take place until June 1793.

[117] The liveliest account is in J. B. McMaster, *A History of the People of the United States*, II, 213 *et seq.*

Details also in D. S. Freeman, *George Washington*, VII, cc. IX and X.

[118] Tracy to Wolcott, Sr., May 27, 1797, Gibbs, *Memoirs of the Administrations of Washington and Adams*, I, 537.

[119] For the text of the speech, *Connecticut Courant*, Aug. 10, 1795.

[120] There were rumors afloat to the effect that Rutledge was "sottish, deranged and had conducted himself improperly in financial transactions." These charges were brought to Hamilton's attention by Rufus King. King's letter has not been found, but the substance is deducible from Hamilton to King, Dec. 14, 1795 (H. C. Lodge, ed., *Works of Alexander Hamilton*, X, 135–36). Hamilton was noncommittal. Jefferson attributed the rejection to Rutledge's stand on the treaty (*Works of Jefferson* [Ford,

Jay's treaty embodied an article (VI) dealing with pre-war debts. On the basis of allegations by British creditors that, by operation of various legal impediments since the peace, full recovery of the debts had been delayed, their value and security impaired so that by the ordinary course of judicial proceedings the creditors "cannot now obtain" full and adequate compensation, it was agreed that in cases where in the ordinary course of justice full compensation could not be obtained, the United States would make compensation.[121] Jay had been instructed that the debt question should be treated as a judicial question; what was settled on was the appointment of a mixed commission to examine the claims and make awards which the United States agreed to pay in specie. This article had, of course, a direct bearing upon continuing litigation by British creditors in American courts, for despite some ambiguities, an exhaustion of ordinary legal remedies was contemplated. Whatever might be decided in *Ware v. Hylton* had an obvious bearing upon this.

When the February term 1796 opened, the Supreme Court was without a Chief Justice. After the Senate had refused to confirm Rutledge, William Cushing had been nominated and confirmed but he declined the post because of age and infirmity.[122] Not until March 4 was Oliver Ellsworth commissioned in his room, but he did not take his seat until March 8.[123] He attended only one other day of the term. The seat left vacant by the resignation of John Blair was filled by the appointment of Samuel Chase. If the states' rights faction, remembering Chase's antifederalist activities, hoped that by this addition the federalist complexion of the Bench would be a little bleached, Chase's inaugural opinion disabused them.

As already remarked, *Ware v. Hylton* had had a long pre-history in the Circuit Court for the Virginia District. It was distinguished by massive defensive pleading for which there is some reason to suppose that John Marshall may have been responsible. The pleadings,[124] of course, are directly relevant to the ultimate decision and must be briefly stated. The action was brought on a bond dated July 7, 1774, for the

---

Federal ed.], VIII, 204). The Senate rejected Rutledge on Dec. 15, 1795. In RG 217, Miscellaneous Treasury Accounts 1790–1894, No. 7905 (NA) is a letter of George W. Craik (May 10, 1796), who had been acting as Washington's amanuensis, stating that he had found a letter from Rutledge dated Charleston, Dec. 28, 1795, containing his resignation and enclosing his commission. This raises the nice question whether or not the resignation anticipated notice of the rejection.

[121] Malloy, *Treaties, Conventions . . .*, 590.

[122] *Washington Writings*, XXXIV, 424n. The reasons he declined recounted by Iredell in a letter to his wife, Feb. 20, 1796 (McRee, *Iredell*, II, 460).

[123] Ms. Mins. U.S. Sup. Ct. 1790–1805, *sub* Mar. 8 and Mar. 14, 1796.

[124] 3 Dallas 199–207.

penal sum of £2,976.11.6 sterling. Pleaded in bar were: (1) payment; (2) that under the Virginia sequestration act of 1777 defendants in 1780 paid £933.14 into the state loan office and received a certificate to the effect that the sum paid be applied to the credit of their accounts with plaintiff creditors, thus discharging a part of the debt; (3) that a Virginia Act of 1779 declared that all property real and personal within the commonwealth belonging to British subjects be deemed to vest in the commonwealth; further, by an Act of 1782 it was declared that no demand originally due a British subject should be recoverable in any of the state courts although transferred to a citizen unless the assignment was made in good faith for a valuable consideration before May 1, 1777; that the debt was personal property within the Act of May 3, 1779, and never transferred under the 1782 act; (4) that the British had breached the agreement in the treaty to withdraw forces without carrying away negroes or other American property, and further by failing to give up the western posts, and by inciting the Indians; (5) that the effect of the Declaration of Independence and the dissolution of the then-government had been to annul the debt.

To these pleas, plaintiff replied to the first, non-payment, and on this issue was joined. To the second plea he made replication, especially setting up the fourth article of the treaty of peace and the supreme law of the land clause of the Constitution. Defendants rejoined, averring breach of the treaty by Britain and reiterating that the debt was not bona fide. Plaintiffs demurred to the rejoinder. To the third, fourth and fifth pleas plaintiff also demurred and issue was joined. The Circuit Court found for plaintiff on pleas 3, 4 and 5. On the demurrer to the rejoinder to the replication (plea 2), Iredell and Griffin found for defendants, Jay contra. When the issue on plea 1 was finally tried, the jury found a verdict for only $596 plus 5 percent interest from July 2, 1752, and costs.

On the return of the record to the Supreme Court the error assigned was that judgment had been given for defendants instead of plaintiff upon the demurrer to the rejoinder to the replication to the second plea. Defendants were represented by John Marshall and Alexander Campbell of Virginia, plaintiff by E. Tilghman, William Lewis and Alexander Wilcocks of Philadelphia.

The arguments which occupied five days are not well reported, for as noticed in the preceding chapter, what Dallas published was abstracted from notes of William Tilghman taken presumably for his own convenience and not for publication.[125] Consequently these arguments will be considered only as they were touched on by the Court.

---

[125] *Supra*, c. XV, p. 720.

The fundamental position of defendants in error was that the Virginia act was a bar to recovery independent of the treaty and that the treaty did not remove the bar. The Justices delivered their opinions seriatim, and although the Court had sometime earlier settled upon the practice that a Justice who had sat below would forbear to give an opinion, Iredell felt so strongly that he read his Circuit Court opinion.

Chase delivered the first opinion,[126] his maiden effort in the Court, and it was something of a *tour de force*—a close and exhaustive analysis and a trenchant presentation of the issues. His composition was structurally dramatic for he devoted a good third of his argument to the establishment of elements of defendants' claim before proceeding to demonstrate that all this availed them nothing. The arguments of plaintiff's counsel were first considered, viz., that Virginia had no right to confiscate British property because the debt was contracted when both parties were British subjects, and consequently the law of nations between independent nations did not apply; that Congress alone had the power to confiscate; and, in any case, that the modern law of nations exempted debts from confiscation. To this Chase answered that the exclusive power of confiscating all and every species of property within Virginia's limits resided in her legislature. From the moment the people of Virginia abolished the old government and set up the new, the supreme power was vested in the legislature with the sole exception that laws enacted should not be repugnant to the constitution. There was no question but that the Act of 1777 was within the authority granted the legislature with the necessary result that it was obligatory on the courts of Virginia and, in Chase's opinion, on the courts of the United States. He went on to say that in June 1776 the Virginia Convention had declared the state to be a free, sovereign and independent state. On July 4, 1776, the United States declared the United Colonies free and independent states. This he considered as a declaration not that the United Colonies jointly in a collective capacity were independent states, but each of them was a sovereign independent state in the sense that each had a right to govern itself by its own authority.

It was immaterial that creditor and debtor were members of the same empire when the debt was contracted. The British creditor by the conduct of his sovereign became an enemy of Virginia and his debt subject to forfeiture as compensation for an unjust war. The authorities supporting the right of confiscation were set out by Chase. As for Vattel's reference to the modern law of nations exempting debts by general custom, this was not binding on Virginia for custom was a matter of tacit consent which Virginia had not given. Since the British adhered

---

[126] 3 Dallas 220–45. The opinions were delivered Mar. 7, 1796, more than three weeks after conclusion of the argument on February 12.

with all rigor to the old law, even Vattel admitted an adversary could do the like.

Up to this point Chase's opinion could hardly have been more gratifying to the defense. The Justice was not, however, prepared to accept John Marshall's argument that the effect of the 1777 law was to discharge the debtor, the foundation for the further argument that the treaty did not apply since there was in this case no debtor. Resorting to the pleadings, it appeared to Chase that defendants' plea of the statute and payment agreeably to its provisions was a bar "for so much of his debt" as he had paid into the Virginia loan office unless the plea was avoided or destroyed by plaintiff's replication setting up the fourth article to the treaty of peace. Marshall had doubted that Congress had the power to make a treaty nullifying any state act; Campbell had denied "with great zeal" that Congress possessed such a power. The inadmissibility of this objection to Congress's power, said Chase, was evident from the fact that all state legislatures had taken property for public use, uniformly compensating owners; that the state legislatures had often divested vested rights, impaired and almost annihilated the obligations of contracts as by the tender laws. If Virginia could by law annul a former law, the effect would destroy all rights acquired under the law so nullified. Finally, if Virginia could not do such things by an ordinary act of legislation, she could in the exercise of supreme sovereign power have done this by treaty if she had not parted with the treaty-making power. This power had been delegated to Congress by Article IX of the Articles of Confederation.

The treaties made by Congress, during the period of Confederation, pursuant to Article IX, the Congress itself on April 13, 1787, had declared to be the supreme law of the land. Any doubts were removed by the second paragraph of Article VI of the new Constitution declaring all treaties made or to be made under the authority of the United States to be the supreme law of the land. This provision was retrospective; the constitutions or laws contrary to the treaty of 1783 were prostrated by it; the treaty had superior power to the legislatures of the states; it was the declared duty of any state judge to declare any state constitution or law contrary to the treaty to be null and void; federal judges were bound by duty and oath to the same conduct.

Chase next launched into an examination of the treaty, the objects and the considerations underlying its provisions. There was a meticulous analysis of the language of Article IV evidently designed to counter some of the silly things that had been said about its meaning. When he was done, even the dullest pettifogger could have retained few doubts. In answer to the question, did Article IV intend to annul a law of the states and destroy rights acquired under it, Chase replied that it intended to destroy all lawful impediments, and such was the law of Virginia. It was not a mere repeal, as defendants' counsel claimed, for this would not have destroyed acts done. It was a total annihilation. To the argument that there was no creditor at the time of the treaty if a debtor had been legally discharged, Chase pointed out that it was not creditors generally described in the treaty, but only those with whom debts had been contracted before the treaty; this was a description of persons and not of their rights. Adhering to the letter destroyed the plain meaning, for if the treaty did not extend to debts paid into loan offices, it had done nothing.

Chase concluded that he was satisfied that the words of the treaty in their natural import and common use gave a recovery to the British creditor from his original debtor of the debt contracted before the treaty notwithstanding payment into a state loan office or treasury under any state law. The judgment of the Circuit Court should be reversed and judgment given on the demurrer for plaintiff in error.

For what the Justices (Paterson, Wilson and Cushing) who concurred in Chase's conclusion had to offer, they might as well have let his opinion stand as that of the Court. Paterson and Cushing agreed that the Act of 1777 did not confiscate the debts, the preamble expressing intent not to do so unless the British Crown should, an event which did not happen. Both Paterson and Cushing inclined to the belief that the "modern" law of nations which regarded confiscation of debts as disreputable should apply. Paterson did not explore the right of Virginia to confiscate; Wilson, however, thought that all powers of war and peace belonged to Congress. Paterson's view of the treaty differed from Chase's in that he believed that it repealed the act of Virginia, but as to the creditor, annulled everything done under it. Cushing thought that there had been nullification *ab initio* of all laws in the nature of impediments.

Iredell's dissent, which, as noticed, was the opinion delivered at Circuit in June 1793, has none of the cogency of the opinion delivered a few months earlier in *Chisholm*. This is to be explained by the pressures of the brief Circuit term. His continuing interest in maintaining watch and ward over the rights of states is manifest. Iredell believed that no absolute confiscation had occurred in this case, and so he would give no conclusive opinion on the right to do so. Nevertheless, the legislature in fact had confiscated. This action would be obligatory within the limits of the state.

If the state *de jure*, according to the law of nations, as Iredell was disposed to think, had a right to confiscate the whole of the debt, it had a right to proceed a partial way toward this by receiving the money and discharging the debtor. Even if only *de facto*, such action would be binding. By payment of money to the government, the debtor was wholly discharged. That payment was made in paper money was irrelevant, as

753

this was legal tender dictated by necessity. Plaintiff's action was barred unless the creditor's right was revived by something in the peace treaty.

Article IV Iredell regarded as a provision executory in nature. Under the Confederation it could not act as a repeal of impeditive laws; this could be done only by state laws and the Congress's letter of April 1787 served to establish this. After ratification of the Constitution, the supremacy clause so operated that every impediment was expressly repealed. However, everything done under the Act of 1777, while it was in existence, so far as private rights were concerned was unaffected by repeal. Under the circumstances, and referring to Marshall's idea that there could be no creditor without a debtor and a debt, Iredell concluded that if the debtor had been discharged, there was no one whom the creditor could sue.

Under ordinary conditions the judgment in *Ware v. Hylton* would have had much greater political repercussions than seems to have been the case.[127] At the moment it was still Jay's treaty with Britain with which political opinion was obsessed in places both high and low. On February 29, 1796, four days before the decision in *Ware* was announced, Washington had proclaimed the treaty to be in effect.[128] It was in the hands of the House March 1.[129] The following day Edward Livingston moved that copies of Jay's instructions and relevant documents be delivered. The ensuing debate which centered on the House's constitutional rights was concluded March 24 by an affirmative vote 62–37.[130] Washington, taking his time to consider, declined the request for copies of instructions and documents on March 30.[131]

The House discussions thereafter were concerned with the question whether or not the appropriations requisite for execution of the treaty should be voted. These discussions involved a protracted examination of the terms of the instrument, including the sixth article. This, as noticed, provided for a mixed commission to arbitrate the debts still due British merchants and other subjects in all cases where, by operation of lawful impediments, full recovery had been delayed, the value and security thereof also impaired and lessened so that by the ordinary course of judicial proceedings British creditors "cannot now" receive full compensation. The commission was authorized to take into consideration the question of interest. The United States undertook to pay the awards.

---

[127] It had an immediate impact upon pending debt litigation in Virginia where the Circuit records suggest from the innumerable earlier continuances that joinder of issue had been held up pending the Supreme Court decision. Thereafter there was a wholesale withdrawal of pleas.

[128] *Washington Writings*, XXXIV, 481n.

[129] Richardson, *Messages and Papers of the Presidents*, I, 192.

[130] *Annals of Congress*, V, 800–01.

[131] Richardson, *Messages and Papers of the Presidents*, I, 194.

One might suppose that the decision in *Ware v. Hylton* would have been brought into the debate at least for its prospective effect upon the "ordinary course of judicial proceedings," but the case was only fugitively mentioned.[132] It was surely relevant when talk erupted over the amount for which the United States would be liable. On this no firm figures were available although it was generally believed that the greatest share was owed by Virginia, for as William Giles of that state remarked, among the "fashionable calumnies of the day," Article VI had been a fertile source of misrepresentation against his state. He admitted that Virginia might be advantaged by assumption, but as the class of debtors was small, the burden of contributing to the amount settled upon would fall upon the bulk of the inhabitants.[133]

Giles had been actively involved professionally in debt litigation,[134] and since the judgment in *Ware* had been noticed in the *Aurora*,[135] the Republicans' favorite newspaper, he could hardly have been unaware of the fact that the way had been opened for the pursuit of reasonably complete remedy in federal courts. This was not mentioned.[136] What was emphasized by Giles and his fellow Representative John Nicholas[137] was the fact that the commission would not be confined to common law procedure.

One further episode in the subsequent history of *Ware v. Hylton* deserves to be noticed. After the mixed commission provided for by Jay's treaty was organized in 1798, it developed that Thomas McDonald, the bellwether of the British delegation, had never heard of the case.[138] Even after he had been set aright, he took the ignorant position that the reversed judgment of the Circuit Court of 1794 was controlling.[139] He and his colleague and the fifth member of the com-

---

[132] By Hillhouse of Connecticut, Mar. 21, 1796 (*Annals of Congress*, V, 665), and by Moore of Virginia, Apr. 21, 1796 (*ibid.*, 1123).

[133] *Ibid.*, 1030.

[134] Giles to Jefferson, May 6, 1792, *Am. St. Pap.: For. Rel.*, I, 234.

[135] *Aurora, General Advertiser*, Mar. 10, 1796.

[136] Giles to Jefferson, May 6, 1792, *supra*, n. 134. That Giles should ignore Ware v. Hylton may perhaps be attributed to the fact that the Virginians took the stand that no adjudications would be an effective defense because of their claim that the courts had uniformly denied interest. But see the judgment in Ware v. Hylton, Ms. Mins. U.S. Sup. Ct. 1790–1805, *sub* Mar. 7, 1796.

[137] *Annals of Congress*, V, 1008–09.

[138] J. B. Moore, ed., *International Adjudications*, III, 60. McDonald's "notes" were submitted July 25, 1798 (*ibid.*, 58).

[139] *Ibid.*, 227 (claim of Lidderdale); and see the letter of the American Commissioners to the British, Sept. 2, 1799, *ibid.*, 276 at 291–92. This was done in face of the fact that in February term 1797 *Ware* was treated as controlling in Clerke v. Harwood, a Maryland case (3 Dallas 342), and again in August term 1797 in Court v. Van Bibber, Court v. Wells, and Court v. Robinson, all involving the same Maryland act (all unreported; see Ms. Case Papers U.S. Sup. Ct., Cases No. 43, 44, 45).

mission, also a Briton, decided against requiring creditors to exhaust judicial remedies before claims could be considered by the board.[140] As is well known, the commission's proceedings were suspended in 1798. Thereafter a new treaty was concluded, in 1802,[141] by which the United States agreed to pay the sum of £600,000 in satisfaction of claims for pre-war debts. By the second article of this convention,[142] Article IV of the treaty of peace was confirmed as to its future operation—a belated recognition of the controlling effect of *Ware v. Hylton*.

The questions of state versus national authority involved in the cases thus far examined, and viewed politically, were a legacy of smoldering antifederalist opinion. To this, new heat had been imparted by factional alignments during Washington's administrations, compounding the difficulties of dealing with constitutional issues as questions of law. There was little to guide the Court in formulating its approach. English constitutional decisions would not serve as exemplars, for the British constitution was differently founded. Beyond some traditional rules of statutory interpretation, and the construction of writings that in the nature of things were of limited use, the Justices necessarily were put on their mettle to find a satisfactory technique for dealing with constitutional issues. Apart from recourse to learned discourses on the law of nations in the debt cases that the treaty of 1783 made relevant, what is particularly worth noticing is the resort to federalist constitutional theory advanced during the struggle over ratification of the Constitution and the inquiry into constitutional history since the outbreak of the Revolution. This approach was also used in one of the admiralty causes about to be examined.

NOTE A

The Indiana Company's claim to title arose prior to the Revolution. In the year 1763, the closing year of the French and Indian War, members of the Shawnee and other Indian tribes, tributaries of the Six Nations, seized goods and property belonging to certain traders to the value of £85,916.10.8 (New York currency). Through the agency of Sir William Johnson, Royal Superintendent of Indian Affairs, compensation for the "sufferers of 1763" was secured. At Fort Stanwix on Nov. 3, 1768, the chiefs of the Six Nations, for themselves and their tributary tribes, conveyed to the King of Great Britain for the express use of the injured traders a tract of 1,800,000 acres lying west of the Allegheny Mountains, in what is today the northern part of West Virginia and the southwestern section of Pennsylvania. Among the officials and representatives of various colonies who witnessed the transaction was a representative from Virginia who gave his "full assent and approba-

---

[140] Moore, *International Adjudications*, III, 225.

[141] Malloy, *Treaties, Conventions . . .* I, 610.

[142] *Ibid.*, 611.

tion." (Printed Bill in Equity, undated, Ms. Original Case Papers U.S. Sup. Ct., Hollingsworth v. Virginia; Copy of Conveyance, *ibid.*; Bill in Equity, and Exhibit "A," *ibid.* For a survey of the history of the Indiana Company see S. Livermore, *Early American Land Companies*, 113–19.)

The cession was divided into 85,916 shares, each trader receiving the number of shares proportionate to the value of his loss. (Bill in Equity, and Exhibit "B," Ms. Original Case Papers U.S. Sup. Ct.) Between 1768 and 1775 the proprietors tried but failed to secure royal confirmation of their title. Beginning in September 1775, by a series of meetings and agreements they organized as a practical corporate group. On Mar. 20, 1776, it was decided to open a land office through which persons already settled within the Company's bounds as well as future settlers could purchase land; this was advertised on Apr. 1, 1776. (Bill in Equity, and Exhibits "C" and "D," *ibid.*; Livermore, *Early American Land Companies*, 115–18. Livermore, at 116, incorrectly dates the first general meeting Sept. 21, 1776.)

The onrush of the American Revolution precipitated conflict between the Company and Virginia. Commencing with a resolution passed by the Virginia Convention June 24, 1776, by a series of measures the emergent state asserted its title to the western lands under its "sea to sea" charter of 1609. Despite memorials and representations by the Indiana Company, on June 9, 1779, the House of Delegates adopted resolutions (concurred in by the upper house on June 12) asserting Virginia's "exclusive right of pre-emption from the Indians of all lands within the limits of its own chartered territory" and declaring all purchases made by the Crown from any Indian nation within said limits and specifically the Fort Stanwix conveyance "utterly void and of no effect." On the 17th of the same month the General Assembly embodied the sense of these resolutions in a statute (10 Hening, *Va. Stats.*, 9). It was alleged that on the following day the legislature provided for the opening of a land office for the sale of all ungranted lands. (Bill in Equity, Ms. Original Case Papers U.S. Sup. Ct.; see also M. Jensen, *The Articles of Confederation*, 122–23, 206–08.) On the dating of the Land Office Act see Boyd's note, *Papers of Jefferson*, II, 133 *et seq.*

Subsequent attempts by the Company to obtain redress from the Continental Congress failed. In a final effort to obtain compensation from Virginia, the proprietors, through their agent George Morgan, petitioned the Virginia legislature on Nov. 23, 1790, and Oct. 17, 1791. As these petitions were disregarded, remedy was sought in the federal judiciary. (Bill in Equity, also Exhibits "E," "F," and "G," Ms. Original Case Papers U.S. Sup. Ct.; see also Jensen, *The Articles of Confederation*, 212–18, 232–33.)

NOTE B

This suit was brought in 1795 by Alexander Moultrie, Isaac Huger and William Clay Snipes on behalf of the South Carolina Yazoo Company for specific performance of a contract by the state of Georgia. This was one of three companies formed in the flush of land speculation of the 1780's for the sale of lands in the unsettled region of the southwestern United States. (C. H. Haskins, *The Yazoo Land Companies*, Amer. Hist. Assoc. *Papers*, 5:398–400, No. 4, 1891.) By an act of the Georgia legislature, Dec. 21, 1789, a tract of 10,000,000 acres, lying in the area of what is now southern Alabama and Mississippi, was reserved to the South Carolina Company as a preemption for two years. Confirmation of title was made contingent upon payment into the state treasury of $66,964 before the expiration of that period. (Copy of Georgia statute, Dec. 21, 1789, Ms. Original Case Papers U.S. Sup. Ct., Moultrie v. Georgia.)

Six months later (June 11, 1790) the Georgia legislature passed a resolution to the effect that no payment would be accepted in discharge of debts to the state except in "Gold or silver" or the paper money issued under a Georgia act of August 14, 1786, ". . . such paper medium to be received until the 14th day of August next and no longer." (Copy of Resolutions of House and Senate, *ibid.*) On Aug. 13, 1790, the Company paid into the treasury the sum of $4,846.92 in Georgia paper currency in part payment of the stipulated purchase price. (Certificate of Receipt, July 13, 1797, *ibid.*; Copy of Receipt Aug. 13, 1790, *ibid.*; this refers to $2,703.96 deposited by William Gibbons. Receipt of Secretary of Georgia, Sept. 11, 1790, *ibid.*; this refers to $2,142,96 deposited by William C. Snipes.)

The South Carolina Company failed to secure either settlers or confirmation of title to the grant. On Dec. 19, 1791, the deadline for payment in full, the Company tendered the remaining amount due in various kinds of paper money—South Carolina paper, Continental money of 1776 and Georgia certificates of various dates. This the Georgia Treasurer refused to accept on the ground that the act of 1789 contemplated payment in specie and that the resolution of June 19, 1790, governed. (Haskins, *The Yazoo Land Companies*, 407–08.) Some years later the Georgia legislature by the notorious "Yazoo land act" of Jan. 7, 1795, contracted to sell the tract which the South Carolina Company still claimed to two new companies—the Georgia and the Georgia Mississippi companies. (Act, in *Am. St. Pap.: Pub. Lands*, I, 152–55.)

The exact date of the inception of the South Carolina Company's suit in equity in the Supreme Court is not known, as the original bill of complaint is not among the case papers, but a supplemental bill of complaint was filed Apr. 13, 1795. (Supplemental Bill in Equity, Ms. Original Case Papers U.S. Sup. Ct., Moultrie v. Georgia.) In this, petitioners stated that they had previously filed a bill against the state of Georgia and against the original members of the Georgia and the Georgia Mississippi companies (including James Gunn, United States Senator) for specific performance of the contract set forth therein. Petitioners further alleged that at the time of the 1795 contract for sale of the tract, contained in the earlier South Carolina Company grant, the parties were apprised of the rights of the petitioners in this land. They requested that writs of subpoena issue and that members of the two new companies and their associates (including Justice James Wilson) be interrogated *inter alia* as to their particular interests in the parcels of land in question. (For the list of persons against whom suit was brought see Ms. Docket Book U.S. Sup. Ct., p. 32.)

Early in 1796, in response to popular outcry, a so-called Rescinding Act declared "null and void" the Jan. 7, 1795, Yazoo land act. (Act of Feb. 13, 1796, in *Am. St. Pap.: Pub. Lands*, I, 156–58.) In contrast to the fevered political temper in Georgia, the South Carolina Company's suit moved at a leisurely pace during the two years following. Process issued "in the summer of 1796" (Complainants' Brief, undated, *ibid.*, 167 *et seq.*), and the affidavit of service was read at February term 1797 (3 Dallas 339). At this term, as noted above, the Court granted rules for commissioners to examine witnesses upon certain interrogatories in South Carolina, Georgia and Pennsylvania.

XVI: *Political and Constitutional Issues I*

(Ms. Mins. U.S. Sup. Ct. 1790–1805, 82–82v *sub* Feb. 10, 1797.) The examination of witnesses and taking of depositions took months. (Commission with commissioners' and clerk's oaths attached, Feb. 13, 1797, Ms. Original Case Papers U.S. Sup. Ct., Moultrie v. Georgia; Interrogatories, *ibid.*; Statement of Commissioners Keppele and Reed, undated, *ibid.* Depositions were taken August 15, 16, 17, 23 and 25; for these, see *ibid.* See also *Am. St. Pap.: Pub. Lands*, I, 168–71, for a summary of the depositions.) At August term 1797 the Court ordered that the cause be continued. (Ms. Docket Book U.S. Sup. Ct., p. 32. For orders relating to the commissions see also Ms. Mins. U.S. Sup. Ct. 1790–1805, 87 *sub* Aug. 11, 88–89 *sub* Aug. 15, 1797. For a list of exhibits see *Am. St. Pap.: Pub. Lands*, I, 168.) But the merits of the case were never reached, for on Feb. 14, 1798, the Court gave its opinion that "on Consideration of the Amendment of the Constitution respecting Suits against States it has no Jurisdiction of this Cause" and dismissed the bill against Georgia. (Ms. Mins. U.S. Sup. Ct. 1790–1805, at 95.)

CHAPTER XVII

The Supreme Court—
Political and Constitutional Issues II

AT NO TIME in the history of the Supreme Court were questions relating to the enforcement and interpretation of treaties so persistently obtrusive as during the decade here studied. We have considered the chief cases in which the treaty of 1783 with Britain was involved. There remain to be examined the problems posed by the treaties with France. These were problems that blew in from the sea, so to speak, precipitated by war and by the prompt commitment of the United States to a policy of neutrality. Circumstances made it imperative that there should be early definition of the scope and meaning of the grant of "admiralty and maritime jurisdiction"—one of the most ill-documented phrases of the Constitution. And it may be remarked here that with the exception of one case, a relic of the Revolutionary War that presented an opportunity for definition unconnected with current events, the causes involving admiralty jurisdiction and the French treaties accounted for one quarter of the Court's appellate business.

The Neutrality Proclamation of April 22, 1793, already noticed in connection with enforcement problems,[1] had been decided upon and issued in advance of news about the activities of French Minister Genêt, who had started commissioning privateers shortly after his arrival at Charleston, April 8. Genêt believed that France had a treaty right to have any prizes brought into United States ports by ships commissioned by him, and as we shall see, claimed (and so acted) that consuls had been authorized to function as prize courts. Owners and captains sought relief in the District Courts, but the District judges entertained conflicting opinions of the limits of their jurisdiction; their dilemma was to be settled by the Supreme Court in *Glass* et al. *v. the Sloop Betsey.*[2]

---

[1] *Supra*, c. XIV.   [2] 3 Dallas 6 (1794).

THE ADMIRALTY JURISDICTION

SOME OF THE procedural gambits in *Glass* have already been noticed.[3] The *Betsey* was a Swedish-owned sloop taken by the *Citoyen Genêt*, a privateer outfitted at Charleston, and commissioned by the Citizen himself. Taken off Cape Henry, June 26,[4] the sloop had been brought into Baltimore where on July 9, 1793, she was condemned by the French consul as prize.[5] Glass, alleging that the sloop was neutral property and that two thirds of the cargo was his own property, filed his libel July 16, 1793. The master of the *Citoyen Genêt* pleaded to the jurisdiction and the plea was sustained by Paca, District judge, on August 16.[6]

Alexander Glass was one of those resolute litigators dear to lawyers' hearts. After Paca had refused to issue an injunction against the sale of the *Betsey*, Glass proceeded to Philadelphia and was apprised of the Executive's decision that all prizes taken by French privateers subsequent to June 5, 1793, should be restored, and that the governors had been ordered to expedite this. He notified Luther Martin and others[7] that the Secretary of State had recommended prompt application to the governor of Maryland.[8] At the same time he took the precaution of securing an inhibition under the seal of Justice William Paterson;[9] Glass was well advised to have taken this step for the Cabinet's decision contemplated restitution by Genêt and indemnification by the United States if the French Minister did not do so.[10] In any event, since the affair of the *Betsey* was still *sub judice*, it is open to doubt whether the governor could interfere. An appellatory libel was filed in the Circuit Court. Paterson, later at Circuit, affirmed the decree of the District Court, November 7, 1793.

---

[3] *Supra*, c. XV, pp. 687–88.

[4] The date is from the libel. It should be noticed that the Executive did not decide upon the extent of marginal seas until a Cabinet meeting Nov. 8, 1793 (*PAH*, XV, 381). The French Minister was notified the same day (*Am. St. Pap.: For. Rel.*, I, 183). See also Jefferson to the British Minister, Nov. 8, 1793, C. F. Jenkins, ed., *Jefferson's Germantown Letters*, 42.

[5] Text in Ms. Case Papers U.S. Sup. Ct., Case No. 3. This assumption of jurisdiction was allegedly profitable. John E. Howard wrote Hamilton Aug. 26, 1793, that it was said that out of two Dutch vessels condemned as prize, "the agents" would make £ 10,000 and the French consul was to have one fifth for his trouble (*PAH*, XV, 278–79).

[6] Ms. Case Papers U.S. Sup. Ct., Case No. 3.

[7] Glass to Luther Martin, Gustavus Scott and Robert Smith, Aug. 20, 1793, Ms. Corner Papers (Md. Hist. Soc.)

[8] The letter of Martin *et al.*, Aug. 22, 1793, to the governor of Maryland, *ibid.*

[9] Dated Aug. 20, 1793.

[10] See *PAH*, XV, 169–71.

The fact that Paterson within three months changed his mind invites some conjecture. The summer of 1793 had been agitated by the arrogant, not to say outrageous, conduct of the Minister of the French Republic, punctuated by recurrent breaches of neutrality. The tensions between the pro-French, pro-British and pro-neutrality groups had been kept at full stretch by publicists good and bad. The focus of much of this was the extent of American treaty obligations, and what this country's rights and duties were by the law of nations. These were likewise matters embraced in the questions submitted by the executive to the Supreme Court in July 1793, answers to which, as noticed, the Justices had declined for constitutional reasons.[11] Some of these questions, not the least important of which was the legality of consular prize courts, were involved in the *Glass* case. It is conceivable that Paterson affirmed to get the case before the Supreme Court.

The appeal in *Glass v. the Sloop Betsey*, for, indeed, this was the form of review, came before the Supreme Court February term 1794. Argument began February 8 and ended February 10. Edward Tilghman and William Lewis appeared for appellants, James Winchester, later a District judge, and Peter Du Ponceau for the appellee.[12] In the opening for appellants it was argued that if there was no jurisdiction in admiralty, there could be none in a common law court. There was no reason to distinguish ownership of ship and cargo, for friendly aliens were entitled equally with Americans to have their property protected by law. This was undoubtedly a civil cause of admiralty and maritime jurisdiction and so within the terms of the Judiciary Act. The point at issue was restitution or not; this involved a question of prize. Once the admiralty was possessed of a cause, it had a right to try every incidental question. A captor bringing a prize into an American port "has himself submitted to the American jurisdiction," to be exercised by the judicial not the executive department.

For the appellees it was argued that no act subsequent to capture would give jurisdiction if the seizure itself did not. Even if the present capture was unlawful, the District Court had no jurisdiction over prize by the Constitution and laws of the United States. Prize was not a "civil cause of admiralty" within the meaning of the Judiciary Act which did not vest the whole of admiralty causes provided for in the Constitution; furthermore, relying upon English authority, counsel insisted that prize was not a civil cause. No jurisdiction was conferred by the law of nations. If any injury had been done a subject of Sweden or an American citizen, it lay with Sweden to take cognizance and for the American to apply to his government, for the injury was of national not

---

[11] *Supra*, p. 689.   [12] 3 Dallas 6–16.

judicial inquiry. By the law of nations only the courts of the captor could determine the question of prize. Article XVII of the treaty of 1778 with France[13] barred American courts from taking cognizance. Dallas does not spell out the argument here, but it may fairly be supposed that Du Ponceau, attorney for the French, made something of the claim that had been advanced by Genêt in May 1793, and concerning which there had been newspaper controversy. This was to the effect that the provision of the treaty respecting prizes brought into United States ports— "nor shall the searchers or other officers of the places search the same or make examination concerning the lawfulness of the prizes"—conferred an immunity to come and go at will.[14]

The reply to all this by appellants was: (1) that Article XVII expressly extended only to "ships and goods taken by *France* from her *enemies*"; (2) that in section 9 of the Judiciary Act civil jurisdiction was used in contrast to criminal, for elsewhere in the statute (sections 12, 13, 19, 21) the word was dropped—indeed, in section 30 provision was made expressly for a case of capture; (3) that in the American system of government with its separation of legislative, judicial and executive powers, recourse to sovereign authority was a different thing than in Europe—the Constitution designated the portion of sovereignty to be exercised by the judicial, among other things "all cases of admiralty and maritime jurisdiction."

It has already been related that the Supreme Court took some time to advise and then informed counsel that there was another question on the record, viz., whether a foreign country had a right without positive stipulations of a treaty to establish a prize court in this country,

---

[13] "It shall be lawful for the ships of war of either party, and privateers, freely to carry whithersoever they please the ships and goods taken from their enemies, without being obliged to pay any duty to the officers of the admiralty or any other judges; nor shall such prizes be arrested or seized when they come to and enter the ports of either party; nor shall the searchers or other officers of those places search the same, or make examination concerning the lawfulness of such prizes, but they may hoist sail at any time, and depart and carry their prizes to the places expressed in their commissions, which the commanders of such ships of war shall be obliged to show; on the contrary, no shelter or refuge shall be given in their ports to such as shall have made prize of the subjects, people or property of either of the parties; but if such shall come in, being forced by stress of weather, or the danger of the sea, all proper means shall be vigorously used that they go out and retire from thence as soon as possible." Malloy, *Treaties, Conventions . . .* I, 474.

[14] Genêt to Jefferson, May 27, 1793, *Am. St. Pap.: For. Rel.*, I, 149. The newspaper controversy was in *Dunlap's American Daily Advertiser* between *A Jacobin* (July 13, 1793) and *No Jacobin*. The latter was Alexander Hamilton, who wrote a total of eight essays beginning July 31 through August 1793. *PAH*, XV, 145. *No Jacobin II* (*ibid.*, 184) deals with the clause in question.

and it meant to decide the question. Du Ponceau replied that "the parties to the appeal" were not interested in the point and he had no instructions from the French Minister.

In government circles the grounds on which consular jurisdiction was based were well known. There was in the first place the Consular Convention of 1788 negotiated by Jefferson,[15] ratification of which Jay had advised when Secretary for Foreign Affairs.[16] Article VIII provided that consular officers should exercise police over all the vessels of their respective nations and should have on board said vessels all power and jurisdiction in civil matters in all disputes which may arise. They were not permitted to interfere with the police of the ports. It was further claimed by Genêt that French consuls had been invested by the National Assembly with the powers of courts of admiralty.[17] On September 7, 1793, Jefferson circularized the French consuls at the direction of the President requiring them to cease exercising prize jurisdiction under pain of revocation of exequaturs.[18]

On February 18, 1794, the Supreme Court pronounced its decree in *Glass*.[19] This is referred to by Dallas (who excised the opening paragraphs) as the "opinion" of the Court, but there can be no doubt concerning its true character. It was decreed that the Court being decidedly of the opinion that every District Court of the United States possessed all the powers of a court of admiralty whether considered as an instance or prize court, the plea to the jurisdiction was insufficient and consequently overruled and dismissed. The decree of the Maryland District Court founded upon the plea was revoked, reversed and annulled. It was further decreed that the District Court of Maryland had "jurisdiction competent to enquire and decide, whether, in the present case restitution ought to be made to the claimants, or either of them in whole or in part (that is whether such restitution can be made consistently with

---

[15] Malloy, *Treaties, Conventions . . .*, I, 490.

[16] A consular convention earlier negotiated by Franklin had been opposed by Jay because of the excessive privileges and immunities bestowed on consuls. He did, however, somewhat grudgingly support the 1788 instrument. The best historical review of the matter is in the editorial introduction in *Papers of Jefferson*, XIV, 67–92.

[17] Jefferson to Gouverneur Morris, Aug. 16, 1793, *Am. St. Pap.: For. Rel.*, I, 167 at 169. See also the claim in the protest of Consul Hauterive, *ibid.*, 153 (June 21, 1793).

[18] Circular, Sept. 7, 1793, to the French consuls at Philadelphia, Maryland, Charleston and New York, *Am. St. Pap.: For. Rel.*, I, 175. This issued after the Cabinet meeting, Aug. 31, 1793, where the violent behavior of Duplaine, consul at Boston, was discussed, and his prosecution considered. *PAH*, XV, 314. Duplaine's exequatur was revoked Oct. 3, 1793. *Am. St. Pap.: For. Rel.*, I, 181–82. An account of Duplaine's conduct and his obstruction of process is in C. M. Thomas, *American Neutrality in 1793*, 211–19.

[19] Ms. Mins. U.S. Sup. Ct. 1790–1805, *sub* Feb. 18, 1794. Original text in Ms. Case Papers U.S. Sup. Ct., Case No. 3.

the law of nations and the treaties and laws of the United States)." The cause was remanded with directions to determine the libel agreeably to law and right.

As a sort of postscript the Court added that no foreign power could of right institute or erect any court of judicature of any kind in the United States except as warranted by treaty. It was therefore decreed and adjudged that the admiralty jurisdiction exercised by the French consul, not being warranted, was not of right.[20]

The Court, by electing to use the decretal form to register its unanimous opinion, evaded entering into the reasons for its conclusion respecting the powers of the District Court. Nevertheless, the passage giving directions to the Maryland District Court on how it should proceed on remand offers some basis for inferring on what grounds the Court itself arrived at its construction of the grant of jurisdiction. The formula chosen was substantially the same as that embodied in the Confederation Ordinance for Ascertaining what Captures on water shall be Lawful (1781), setting out the rules of decision. Recourse to the law of nations had been provided for in the prize legislation of various American state enactments post-1775; the Continental Congress in 1781 had been explicit that it must be the law of nations according to the general usages of Europe. It was this ordinance by which the Court of Appeals in Cases of Capture had been guided until it shut up shop in 1787. The Supreme Court, consequently, was not initiating a bold departure; it was giving fresh vigor to an established and independent American approach.

The Court went no further than was expedient in its decree. At the moment, when the whole neutrality policy of the United States rested upon executive orders or directions, albeit justified by the opinions of respected jurists like Bynkershoek and Vattel and not upon statute, it was no doubt prudent to resist the temptations held out in the arguments of counsel. With the passage of the so-called Neutrality Act, June 5, 1794,[21] the way was opened to a frank examination of the limits of treaty obligations vis-à-vis a statutory affirmation of what had hitherto been a matter of executive policy.

Before any causes arising after the Act of 1794 became law reached the Supreme Court, a somewhat unwelcome opportunity was

---

[20] In Georgia, at least, where France had a vice-consul the decree was no deterrent. When the *Elizabeth* (see Hills v. Ross, *supra*, c. XV) was brought into Savannah port May 27, 1794, the vice-consul condemned ship and cargo. This fact emerges from the claim preferred before the mixed commission arbitrating claims under art. VII of the Jay Treaty. Moore, *International Adjudications*, IV, 530, the Opinion of Mr. Trumbull.

[21] 1 *U.S. Stats.*, 381; properly "An Act in addition to the Act for the Punishment of certain crimes against the United States."

presented to deal finally with the barnacled litigation over the brigantine *Lusanna* that raised again questions of state sovereignty as well as of District Court jurisdiction. This was the case of *Penhallow* et al. *v. Doane's Administrators*[22] which came up on error from the Circuit Court for the New Hampshire District February term 1795, a year before the decision in *Ware v. Hylton*. We have already dealt with the first stages of *Penhallow*,[23] and it will be recalled that after the refusal of the Superior Court of New Hampshire to allow an appeal, Doane had petitioned Congress; the case was then turned over to the Standing Committee which ruled that it had jurisdiction. The cause was among those transferred to the Court of Appeals in Cases of Capture which in 1783 reversed the New Hampshire decree. The attempt in 1784 by New Hampshire to induce Congress to vacate the decree failed.

The Court of Appeals had, of course, no means of compelling execution of its decrees. Doane died in 1783 and his administrators sought unsuccessfully by actions first in Massachusetts and then in Pennsylvania to obtain redress.[24] A fresh opportunity was presented when the new federal courts were established. In March 1792 Doane's representative filed a libel in the New Hampshire District Court setting out the decree of the Court of Appeals and praying that it be carried into execution. Because John Sullivan, District judge, had represented the state in the 1784 proceedings, the cause was transferred to the Circuit Court pursuant to section 11 of the second Process Act, and came to be heard October 1793. The libellants had an interlocutory decree, the amount of damages to be fixed by commissioners. The definitive sentence passed October 1794.

The cause came before the Supreme Court on error February term 1795. No light is shed on the issues by the pleadings—indeed, in Justice Paterson's words, the cause "has been much obscured" by their irregularity, being "partly according to the common, and partly according to civil, law."[25] In the assignment of errors, summarized in the margin,[26] the principal points of attack were the lack of jurisdiction in

---

[22] 3 Dallas 54.

[23] *Supra*, c. IV.

[24] There is an account of these efforts in L. K. Wroth and H. B. Zobel, eds., *Legal Papers of John Adams*, II, 372–73. These editors give an exhaustive history of the case.

[25] 3 Dallas 54 at 79.

[26] *Ibid.*, 64–66:

(1) That the Court of Appeals had no jurisdiction in the original case.

(2) That if the Court of Appeals had jurisdiction, the decree was

erroneous and impossible to perform as Doane had died before the Court of Appeals reversed and that the decree had ordered restoration be made to Doane.

(3) That the case was not brought before Congress by way of appeal but by way of complaint in the nature of an appeal; and also that no appeal had been allowed by the New Hampshire courts or by Congress.

(4) That in the libel exhibited in the Circuit Court damages were not

the Court of Appeals, the irregularity of the procedure by which the cause had been brought before Congress, the failure of the copy of the record of the Court of Appeals used at Circuit to show how the case came before it and whether the court was validly constituted. The assignments regarding damages have been dealt with in an earlier chapter.

Counsel for plaintiffs in error, Attorney General Bradford and Jared Ingersoll, attacked every conceivable defect in the procedure of the appellate prize structure before and during the Confederation. They missed, however, the most vulnerable item bearing on the constitutional status of the Court of Appeals—the fact that it had been ordained before the Articles of Confederation had been finally ratified. Counsel's heaviest barrage, which might have been aimed from the banks of the Rivanna instead of the Schuylkill, was directed at the lack of jurisdiction in the Court of Appeals because of Congress's want of authority. This was predicated upon the retention of state sovereignty in all its plenitude, even as to waging war. Congress's power was one of recommendation only.

For defendants in error, Samuel Dexter, Tilghman and William Lewis disposed first of some procedural points not here relevant, and proceeded to develop a theory that Congress possessed the whole power of war—"the incidents as well as the full jurisdiction." A succession of measures including those relating to prize and jurisdiction, all tending to establish this proposition, was then recited. Particular emphasis was placed upon the resolution in the case of the sloop *Active*,[27] and the fact that New Hampshire had voted affirmatively for the same.

The Justices delivered their opinions seriatim, that of Justice Paterson being the most notable. He addressed himself to the basis of

---

asked for and should not have been given.

(5) That the decree of the Circuit Court was not made on the merits of the capture, but that the decree of the Court of Appeals had been received and admitted as the only evidence.

(6) That the money arising from the sale of the *Lusanna* was paid to Joshua and George Wentworth, as agents, to be distributed according to law, viz., one half to the owners of the privateer *McClary* and the other half to the crew, and that by the decree of the Circuit Court the plain-

tiffs in error and the Wentworths, as agents, were made liable for all the damages.

(7) That it did not appear from the filed copy of the record of the Court of Appeals how the case came before that court, the day of the decree, or whether that court was validly constituted.

(8) That the Circuit Court in its proceedings and in passing its final decree had acted as a court of admiralty, where by law that court had no jurisdiction.

[27] *Supra*, c. IV, p. 165.

jurisdiction of the three tribunals—the Standing Committee or Court of Commissioners, the Court of Appeals and the District Court. His argument reflects throughout the federalist constitutional theory born at the Convention of 1787. The powers of the Continental Congress, revolutionary in nature, arose from emergency and were coextensive with the objects to be attained. The specific powers in fact exercised he characterized as high acts of sovereignty "acquiesced in and approved of by the people of America." In Congress were vested the powers of peace and war because of this very approval. Paterson derided the notion that the states did or could with safety exercise such powers. It had been necessary for the people or colonies to coalesce and act in concert and they accordingly grew into union and formed one great political body of which Congress was "the directing principle and soul."

Paterson, who knew very well what the actual political conditions had been, was evidently transported by his own rhetoric. He was to toss in another observation, evidently to corroborate his conclusions. The states individually, he said, were not known or recognized by foreign nations as sovereigns, "nor are they now." The states collectively, under Congress as the connecting point, were acknowledged as sovereign— e.g., in rights of war, making treaties and exchanging ambassadors.[28] These reflections were unnecessary to his decision, but they are noticed here because almost a century and a half after they were voiced, they were made to buttress a historically indefensible judicial pronouncement on the control of foreign affairs.[29]

The concentration of war powers in the Continental Congress led to the conclusion that anyone who accepted a privateering commission from Congress was responsible to the latter for his conduct. If under color of such a commission the law of nations had been violated, Congress would have been called upon for redress. In the instant case, the captain of the privateer had his commission from Congress—for the legality of his capture he must be ultimately responsible to Congress. The authority to commission had been approved and ratified by the states because they received, filled up the commissions and bonds and returned them to Congress, New Hampshire with the rest.

To establish at once the authority of the Standing Committee on Appeals and New Hampshire's acquiescence, Paterson proceeded to review the steps taken by Congress in the case of the sloop *Active* (examined here in an earlier chapter), citing book and verse and retailing New Hampshire's affirmative votes in favor of the assertion of national jurisdiction. As for the Court of Appeals, Paterson found its authority in the Ninth Article of the Articles of Confederation. This court, he said,

---

[28] 3 Dallas at 81.
[29] United States v. Curtiss-Wright Export Corporation, 299 U.S. 304, 317 (1936).

had decided the point of jurisdiction in Doane's appeal. This was a decree of a court constitutionally established, of competent authority and of the highest authority, and was conclusive. It could not be opened or investigated. As for the jurisdiction of the District Court, there could be no question. The Court of Appeals and the New Hampshire admiralty court had expired with the old government. The decree in favor of defendants in error had not been satisfied; there was no remedy at common law or in equity; the only competent forum was the District Court because it had admiralty jurisdiction.

Iredell's view of the genesis of congressional powers was more nearly in accord with the facts than was Paterson's. The high powers of external sovereignty, which he conceived were exercised with the acquiescence of the states, did not imply that authority had actually been given. Every particle of authority which originally resided in Congress or in any branch of the states was derived from the people of each province originally and was conveyed by each body politic separately and not by all the people in the several provinces or states jointly. This view led him to the conclusion that while it was reasonable that Congress should exercise war powers, the authority was not possessed unless given by all the states. This view, of course, challenged the validity of the resolve of 1779 asserting the appellate authority in Congress induced by the *Active* case, for, as noticed, Pennsylvania voted against it. It could not be decided whether the Standing Committee was the superior court in respect to New Hampshire without deciding whether it was constitutionally so by virtue of power from all the states.

The Court of Appeals posed no problem because at the time Doane's appeal was decided it was the only court of final appellate jurisdiction in all cases of capture. At a suggestion of counsel that this court "could have no retrospect," Iredell commented that if Congress possessed the authority before, the Articles amounted to a solemn confirmation. Whether Article IX gave power to receive appeals circumstanced as was the *Doane* case was for the Court itself to decide. A case found depending before the Standing Committee was *sub judice* when taken over; no other court on earth could have decided it. As to the District Court, Iredell had no trouble. He had been ill February term 1794 when *Glass v. the Sloop Betsey* had been decided. He took this occasion to affirm his concurrence in the decision and rest his conclusion upon it.

It had been shown at the bar, said Iredell, that a court of admiralty of one country could carry out the determination of such a court of another country. Since a prize court was equally grounded on the law of nations as a court of admiralty and proceeded also on principles of the civil law, such a court must have the same authority. The District Court having "sole authority in cases of this kind, it must have equal power as to such subjects with the power possessed by this court in any case, where it has original jurisdiction."[30] The Court of Appeals having expired, there was as much reason for a court of similar jurisdiction to give effect to its decisions as a foreign court of admiralty. Curiously enough, nothing was made of the fact that the whole of the admiralty and maritime jurisdiction had been yielded by New Hampshire when it ratified the Constitution. Blair J., whose view of the Continental Congress's authority was close to Paterson's, did not enter into a justification of the powers of the District Court. Cushing, who dealt mostly with procedural points, commented, "the admiralty of England gives credence and force to the decisions of foreign courts of Admiralty; why not equal reason here?" As we have seen, the decree of the Circuit Court was affirmed, subject to a re-reckoning of how damages were to be apportioned.[31]

The New Hampshire legislature had been outraged by the decree of the Circuit Court, and despatched to the United States Senate a remonstrance against what was conceived to be a violation of sovereign rights. There was a sympathetic report on this by their Senator, Samuel Livermore, but nothing more appears to have been done.[32] There were worries enough about the rumors of war then circulating for the happenings of a war long past to exercise the Senate. A second remonstrance was sent to the House on January 14, 1795. On this, Madison reported frigidly, February 27, 1795, the matter had been settled by the Supreme Court's decision.[33]

At the August 1795 term of the Supreme Court, John Rutledge, newly appointed Chief Justice, was to preside. On the docket was the case of *Talbot v. Jansen*,[34] the first cause involving a breach of the Neutrality Act to come before the Supreme Court, and one destined to precipitate international controversy. As noticed in an earlier chapter, *Talbot* came up on error from the South Carolina District. Since the time of Genêt's landing at Charleston, this place had become a center of rabid pro-French sympathy, and so happy a place of refuge for French privateers that for a time it became the place of origin of much appellate litigation. The brigantine *Vrouw Christina Magdalena* and her cargo, both the property of citizens of the United Netherlands, were taken off the Cuban coast by an armed schooner, *L'Ami de la Liberté*, commanded by one Ballard. A prize master was put on the Dutch ship. A rendezvous was had with another French privateer, *L'Ami de la Point a Petre*, commanded by William Talbot, who took off the mate and

---

[30] 3 Dallas at 98.
[31] *Supra*, c. XV.
[32] *Am. St. Pap.: Misc.*, I, 79, for the remonstrance; *ibid.*, 81, for the report.

[33] *Ibid.*, 124, for the remonstrance; *ibid.*, 123, for Madison's report.
[34] 3 Dallas 133 (1795). The opinion of the District Court in Bee, **Reports**, 11 (1794).

four men from the *Magdalena* and ordered the ship sent to Charleston. The three ships arrived there May 25, 1794. The libel filed in the District Court by Jansen, master of the *Magdalena*, averred that Ballard was a United States citizen, and his schooner was owned by citizens of the United States, that Ballard had no valid commission and that the capture was a violation of the United States treaty with the United Netherlands.

Ballard defaulted, but Talbot filed a claim averring that he was a regularly admitted French citizen at Pointe-à-Pitre, December 28, 1793, and that he had a commission from the French Republic. His schooner was owned by Samuel Redick, a French citizen. Talbot claimed that the prize was his. Libellant's replication set forth that Talbot was an American citizen, an inhabitant of Virginia, that his schooner was American built, owned by American citizens, armed in the United States. In his rejoinder Talbot protested against the jurisdiction of the court. The evidence showed that Talbot was a native Virginian, until naturalized at Pointe-à-Pitre. His schooner was American built and owned until sailed to Guadeloupe where, with cannon and ammunition aboard, she was sold to Redick. Ballard, also a Virginian, had renounced his citizenship in April 1794 in a Virginia county court pursuant to a 1792 act of that state. At the time of the capture he had acquired no other nationality. His so-called commission was one issued to one Sinclair by a French admiral with the French fleet lying in Chesapeake Bay and assigned later to Ballard. The *L'Ami de la Liberté* had been supplied with arms by the *L'Ami de la Point a Petre* near Savannah.[35] The District Court ordered cargo and vessel to be restored to the owners. This decree was affirmed by the Circuit Court, November 5, 1794. A writ of error was issued the same day.

On August 5, 1795, assignments of error were filed in the Supreme Court alleging: (1) that possession of the prize by Ballard could not impair Talbot's rights acquired by capture and possession; (2) that the finding in the decree that the *L'Ami de la Point a Petre* had been illegally armed in the United States and was the property of American citizens

---

[35] Jansen's libel had been filed fifteen days after the Neutrality Act became law. Claimant's attack upon the jurisdiction of the District Court, it may be noticed, included not only a denial that the new statute extended to a capture made in May, but also an assertion that its sec. 6 ousted the District Courts of all jurisdiction except as therein stipulated. This section declared that "the district courts shall take cognizance of complaints by whomsoever instituted, in cases of captures made within the waters of the United States, or within a marine league of the coasts or shores thereof." Bee, District judge, held that the section extended the decision in *Glass* to cover restitution to a party belligerent should there be violation of American jurisdictional limits. Joost Jansen v. *The Brigantine Vrow Christina Magdalena*, and Edward Ballard, in Bee, Reports, 11, 20–21 (1794).

was contrary to fact; (3) that the facts and law proved Talbot was a French citizen; (4) that the Circuit Court had not caused the facts on which its decree was founded to appear on the record.[36]

The questions of law argued by Ingersoll, Dallas and Du Ponceau who appeared for plaintiff in error related chiefly to jurisdiction over the cause and the matter of citizenship and expatriation. It was asserted that capture of the *Magdalena* and carrying her in for adjudication were acts performed under the authority of the French Republic; the *Magdalena* did not fall within the rationale of *Glass*, for the Netherlands was an enemy of France. By Article XIII of the treaty of 1778, France had the right to bring into and carry from American ports all prizes taken from an enemy. The facts did not support the allegation that Talbot's ship was an American ship, illegally fitted out in the United States. The Act of June 5, 1794, punished illegally outfitted ships; there was no provision for restitution of their prizes. If a capture was made under a French commission, the nationality of the person commissioned was immaterial —had not America commissioned Lafayette and a train of French officers?

The argument on citizenship and expatriation was lengthy and reminiscent of the rhetoric of the Jacobin clubs that had sprouted along the seaboard. Expatriation was represented as a natural right; allegiance was a feudal concept, the "offspring of power and necessity." Citizenship was a political tie, the substitute for allegiance—"the charter of equality." "Citizenship is freedom, allegiance is servitude." The power of declaring whether a citizen was entitled to expatriate himself was not given to the Supreme Court. The conclusion of the argument for appellant was devoted to establishing that whatever the legal position of Ballard may have been, it could not affect the validity of Talbot's capture.

What E. Tilghman, William Lewis and Jacob Read (S.C.) offered for defendant in error was briefly reported. They asserted that the capturing vessels were American, and even if French, the agents used to effect capture were American. As both ships were of American outfit, the capture was unlawful. Ballard acquired no right by capture, and Talbot, "coming under him," could have no higher pretension. The whole association of the two was fraudulent. As respects expatriation, it was not enough to leave a country with the design to expatriate; a residence must be taken up in another country with an avowed declaration of intention.[37] The power over emigration was vested exclusively in

---

[36] Ms. Case Papers U.S. Sup. Ct., Case No. 9.

[37] Citing J. G. Heineccius, *A Methodical System of Universal Law* or the Laws of Nature and Nations . . . (1741), II, Bk. 2, c. 10, sec. 230, p. 220.

Congress. The Virginia act could have no effect upon the political rights of the Union. Talbot's pretended expatriation was itself an offense as he left the United States with intent to privateer against a nation with which the United States was at peace. The circumstances of the Ballard-Talbot adventure amounted to a fraudulent concert. The gist of the controversy before the courts of the United States was whether American citizens under color of a foreign commission should be permitted to make prize of the property of friends of America.

The Supreme Court's decision was rendered August 22, 1795. Again, the first opinion was delivered by Paterson J. To determine, he said, whether or not the decree of restitution was properly awarded it was necessary to consider the capture as made first by Ballard, second by Ballard and Talbot. Although justification of Ballard's act had been virtually abandoned in the argument, Paterson, nevertheless, proceeded to inquire into his national status and so to set out some conclusions about expatriation. It is apparent from his remarks that like counsel for appellees he linked emigration and expatriation. He arrived at the proposition that a mere renunciation of allegiance or declaration of expatriation, unless followed by removal and settlement in another country, was not sufficient to effect a change of national status. This Ballard had not done. Instead he had left this country *cum dolo et culpa* to cruise against friendly powers.

So far as the Virginia expatriation statute was concerned, it was inapplicable. If it affected Ballard's citizenship as respects the state, it nevertheless could not touch his citizenship as respects the United States. The sovereignties were different and so the allegiances and perhaps the rights. He indicated the need for a federal statute, particularly because in some states the common law of England had been expressly adopted. The reference here was, of course, to the doctrine of indefeasible allegiance.

On another ground, the seizure by Ballard was unjustifiable. The *L'Ami de la Liberté* was American built and owned and illegally outfitted in this country. It was idle to talk of Ballard's commission; if he had one, it was not to cruise as a privateer, and if so, it was of no validity because it was granted to an American citizen by a foreign officer within the jurisdiction of the United States—a flagrant violation of national sovereignty. The evidence that the ship was French property merited no attention. The capture by Ballard alone was illegal.

Paterson had no difficulty in supporting the decree of restitution even if the capture was due to joint exertions. The sum of the evidence of the association of Ballard and Talbot disclosed a succession of acts that were direct and daring violations of neutrality, and criminal by the law of nations. Talbot's commission afforded him no protection for it did not authorize abetment of a predatory scheme of an illegal cruiser

773

on the high seas. Talbot was an initial trespasser for he was concerned in the illegal outfit of Ballard's vessel. His possession of the *Magdalena* was gained by a fraudulent cooperation with Ballard, a United States citizen. He then brought the ship within the jurisdiction of the United States. It was the duty of competent authority to have her restored.

Iredell considered the points in the case under two heads: the jurisdiction *prima facie* of the District Court over the subject matter, and, if this was so, whether Talbot had supported a case to exempt him from such jurisdiction. Both by the law of nations and the French treaty, if a French privateer should bring in an enemy ship as prize taken on the high seas, the United States would have no right to detain her; but this exemption applied only to a privateer lawfully commissioned. If a vessel claimed such an exemption but did not appear to be entitled to it, it was the express duty of the court to make inquiry. If the vessel pretending to be a privateer used a colorable commission for purposes of plunder, such vessel must be considered for purposes of property transfer as having no commission at all. *Prima facie,* all piracies and trespasses committed against the law of nations were enquirable to be proceeded against where no special exemption by treaty or law of nations obtained.

So far as Talbot's claim was concerned, the first question was whether he was a French citizen. It was perhaps unnecessary to discuss the question of expatriation, said Iredell, but he would express his sentiments. He entered consequently into something of a philosophical discourse on the subject, indicating the limits of a "natural right" of emigration. From the record it was probable that Talbot was a citizen of Virginia. He must certainly be a citizen of the United States. The steps taken in Guadeloupe did not completely discharge the duty owed his own country. There was no satisfactory evidence that Talbot had ceased to be an American citizen. The same applied to Redick, the alleged owner of the *L'Ami de la Point a Petre.* The proof of the commission was sufficient, but its operation Iredell denied because the vessel was owned by Americans with an American captain on board. Finally, the fact that Talbot was a confederate of Ballard and the circumstance of capture destroyed any basis for claiming the property as prize. Cushing and Rutledge in brief opinions concurred in affirming the decree. On expatriation, both thought it unnecessary to give an opinion.

It should be noticed that although the neutrality law had put on statutory footing various executive measures such as the rules sent to Collectors of Customs on August 4, 1793,[38] and otherwise spelled out details of neutral policy, the sanctions of the new statute were penal and the federal courts were not in terms specifically authorized to decree

---

[38] *PAH*, XV, 178.

restitution. Nevertheless, it is not to be doubted that Congress recognized that the power to order restitution inhered in the courts exercising jurisdiction in admiralty and maritime causes, for by section 7 of the statute the President was authorized to use land or naval forces "to the restoring of such prize or prizes in the cases in which such restoration shall have been adjudged." In the instant case, no mention was made of this section. Both Paterson and Iredell regarded the decree of restitution as justified by the law of nations, although the latter remarked that "the new act had provided" a particular method of enforcing it. Cushing referred to every "principle of justice law and policy." *Talbot v. Jansen* may thus be taken as making explicit the grounds on which the Court had acted in *Glass*. This had also been the basis for the Cabinet's decision, approved by the President, to authorize the governors of the several states to secure prizes brought in after June 5, 1793,[39] and for the assurances to the British Minister to make compensation for prizes unlawfully taken.[40]

One other aspect of the opinions in *Talbot* that invites comment is the handling of the question of expatriation, because the discussion was not inhibited by mistaken commitment to English common law doctrine, in particular the doctrine that the sovereign's consent was essential to expatriation. The problems presented by the record were two: the effect upon national citizenship of a state statute of expatriation—solved by attributing only local effect to the latter; and the definition of expatriation, to which two Justices gave consent by requiring a bona fide removal, and two of them believed that there must be settlement in another country. This was enough to settle the status of the two knaves who had taken the *Magdalena* without venturing upon the dangerous waters into which Ellsworth later plunged at Circuit in *United States v. Williams*.[41]

After the decree of the District Court in *Jansen v. Talbot* and before the appeal was heard by the Circuit Court, the French Minister to the United States, Jean Fauchet, vigorously protested the exercise of jurisdiction in this as in other cases.[42] Fauchet, and his successor Pierre Adet, were both practicers of the ill-mannered style of diplomacy that revolutions seem to breed. Secretary of State Randolph's explanation[43] that the executive could not dictate to the judiciary was apparently be-

---

[39] *Supra*, p. 761 at n. 10.
[40] Jefferson to Hammond, Sept. 5, 1793, in *Works of Jefferson* (Ford, Federal ed.), VIII, 18.
[41] *Supra*, c. XIV, p. 631. Ellsworth's instruction is treated by Henry Adams, *History of the United States of America*, II, 338, as a Supreme Court decision. It may be noted that Thomas

Sergeant, *Constitutional Law* (1822), 304 *et seq.*, represents the remarks on expatriation in Talbot v. Jansen as a holding of the Court.
[42] Fauchet to Randolph, Sept. 13, 1794, *Am. St. Pap.: For. Rel.*, I, 590.
[43] Randolph to Fauchet, Oct. 28, 1794, *ibid.*, 593.

yond Fauchet's comprehension. He supplemented his earlier protestations with the charge that the American admiralty courts always "ceded" to the importunities of France's enemies to interfere with prizes.[44] In the seemingly interminable correspondence over the admiralty jurisdiction all the cases from *Glass* through *La Vengeance*[45] were put forward as grievances—the culminating conclusion of Minister Adet being his charge that the United States "by its chicaneries" had "abandoned French privateers to its courts of justice."[46]

That the judiciary should have been thus brought under attack was inevitable because of the sharp differences of opinion over the interpretation of the treaty of 1778. However, the record to any except the belligerents, none of which cared a fig for the rights of neutrals, was a fair one. This is borne out by the final disposition of what may be described as a fleet of admiralty causes that came up from the South Carolina District. In all of them the allegations of the libels were to the effect that some breach of the neutrality law had occurred, the most usual being an averment of illegal outfitting or augmentation of armament.[47] The standard defense was the French treaty of 1778, in particular Articles XVII and XVIII—the latter stipulating a right to repair ships in port. The questions presented in nearly all the augmentation cases were questions of fact, and no considerations of national policy beyond what was spelled out in the Act of 1794 were involved. Indeed, at August term 1796, when Jacob Read in *Moodie v. the Ship Phoebe Anne* drew attention to repairs in addition to the privateer's original outfit, and argued the "impolicy and inconveniency of suffering privateers to equip in our ports," Ellsworth C.J. remarked that "suggestions of

---

[44] Fauchet to Randolph, June 8, 1795, *ibid.*, 614.

[45] The documents relating to *La Vengeance, ibid.*, 621 *et seq.*

[46] Adet to Pickering, Nov. 15, 1796, *ibid.*, 579 at 583.

[47] Most of these are unreported. They are here noted by case number in the arrangement of the Ms. Case Papers U.S. Sup. Ct. and, where reported, by the citations to Dallas. Geyer *et al.* v. Michel and the *Ship Den Onzekeren* and Cargo (1796), No. 15 (3 Dallas 285); Moodie v. the *Ship Betty Cathcart* and Cargo and John Vidal *et al.* (1796), No. 16; Moodie v. the *Ship Mermaid* and Cargo and John Gaillard *et al.* (1796), No. 17; Moodie v. the *Brig Eliza* and Cargo and John Gaillard *et al.* (1796),

No. 18; Moodie v. the *Ship Phyn* and Cargo and John Gaillard *et al.* (1796), No. 19; Moodie v. the *Brig Tivoly* and Cargo and Abraham Sasportas *et al.* (1796), No. 20; Moodie v. the *Ship Alfred* and Cargo and John Gariscan *et al.* (1796), No. 21 (3 Dallas 307); Moodie v. the *Brig Favorite* and Cargo and Alexander Bolchos *et al.* (1796), No. 22; Moodie v. the *Ship Britannia* and Cargo and Jean B. Carvine *et al.* (1796), No. 23; Moodie v. the *Snow Potowmack* and Cargo and Jean B. Carvine *et al.* (1796), No. 24; Moodie v. the *Brig Eliza* and Cargo and Paul Beltrimeaux *et al.* (1796), No. 25; Moodie v. the *Ship Phoebe Anne* and Cargo and John Bouteille *et al.* (1796), No. 26 (3 Dallas 319).

policy and conveniency cannot be considered in judicial determination of a question of right."[48]

If Ellsworth's comment had been made in the course of deciding a case of greater public interest, it might have been remembered longer than it seems to have been. His position was not novel, for, as already remarked, it was not then conceived to be a part of a judge's function to indulge his ideas of policy.[49] It is evident from meagerly reported opinions of the Chief Justice that he consistently observed these limits. There is no indication that in the decision of *United States v. La Vengeance*, decided August term 1796,[50] there was a departure. The conclusion, that a libel of information for breach of a statute prohibiting exportation of arms[51] where the exportation was a water transaction was a civil cause in the nature of a libel *in rem* and that jury trial was unnecessary, had the effect of eliminating resort to the clause "saving the right to a common law remedy" in cases of seizures under impost, trade and navigation laws. James Kent was to disapprove of this decision because it represented a departure from English Exchequer practice where there was jury trial.[52] The practice in Ellsworth's own state had been otherwise. He and his brother Paterson had participated in the drafting of section 9 of the Judiciary Act. They could well have repeated the boast of Hengham C.J.: "Do not gloss the statute, we know it better than you for we made it."[53]

Until Ellsworth took his seat on the Bench such evidence as we have does not indicate that the place of Chief Justice had been one of leadership. This was a quality which Ellsworth possessed and which Cushing, who had declined the office, then did not. The volume of Supreme Court business from February 1796 onward was so far increasing as to induce some changes in the presentation of decisions, particularly because several days were often allowed counsel for argument. The way in which an American court tendered the rationale of its judgments was at the time of which we are writing, of course, much affected by the English precedent of the judges severally arguing their conclusions. Guidance, if not control, over any change in this tradition which had already gained a foothold in the Supreme Court would, one might suppose, rest with a Chief Justice. The manner in which Ellsworth piloted the Judiciary Bill through the Senate indicates his capacity to

---

[48] 3 Dallas 319 (1796).

[49] *Supra*, c. V, p. 209.

[50] 3 Dallas 297 (1796). Richard Harison, who had directed the prosecution below, stated in a draft opinion Apr. 6, 1802, that *La Vengeance* had been imperfectly reported. *LPAH*, II, 854 at 856.

[51] 1 *U.S. Stats.*, 369 (May 22, 1794).

[52] Kent, *Commentaries*, I, 376.

[53] Y.B. 33–35 Edw. I (*Rolls Series*), 83 (1305).

take charge. His tenure was, however, short of four years and out of these he missed almost all of his first term and other terms completely because of illness. Nevertheless, there are signs that his predilection for brief opinions was not without effect. In a number of cases no opinions at all were offered, but, as noticed, this may have been due to the reporter's lack of enterprise.[54] There is one indication of record that the Justices had arrived at a consensus that the Chief would speak for the Court. In 1800 while Ellsworth was abroad on a diplomatic mission to France, Paterson, having the oldest commission, presided.[55] In *Baas v. Tingey*, where the opinions were delivered seriatim, Chase remarked that as the Justices had agreed unanimously in their opinions, "I presumed that the sense of the Court would have been delivered by the president." He therefore had not prepared "a formal argument" but proceeded nevertheless to assign his reasons for agreement.[56]

THE CONSTITUTIONALITY OF LEGISLATION

ELLSWORTH DID NOT participate in the decision of *Ware adr. v. Hylton* or of *Hylton v. United States*, both of which were argued before he took his seat March 8, 1796. The latter case was one of no less political portent than the debt case for it involved the first clear-cut challenge of the constitutionality of an Act of Congress to come before the Court. This was the statute, ambiguously titled An Act laying Duties Upon Carriages for the Conveyance of Persons, that imposed "duties and rates" upon carriages kept by persons for their own use, or to be let out to hire or for the conveyance of passengers.[57] The rates were graduated, descending from $10 for every coach to $1.00 for a two-wheel carriage. This statute was enacted over vigorous opposition in the House of Representatives where among other objections the question of its constitutionality was raised—was it a direct tax within the meaning of Article I, section 2, which required apportionment of representation and direct taxes according to population, in reckoning which three fifths of the slaves were to be added to the whole number of free persons, including those bound to service for a term of years and excluding Indians not taxed? Relevant also was Article I, section 8, empowering Congress to lay and collect taxes, duties, imposts and excises, all of which "shall be uniform throughout the United States," and section 9 which provided that no capitation or other direct tax should be laid unless in proportion to the census or enumeration.[58]

---

[54] *Supra*, c. XV, n. 241.
[55] *Gazette of the United States*, Aug. 16, 1800.
[56] 4 Dallas 37 at 43 (1800).

[57] 1 *U.S. Stats.*, 373 (June 5, 1794).
[58] The background is discussed at large in *LPAH*, III (in preparation).

In September 1794, the month when liability for tax and the penalties for refusal became effective, Daniel Hylton of Richmond, Virginia, refused to pay, and a number of distinguished Virginia leaders did likewise.[59] The administration early came to a decision to test the constitutionality of the new law. We have elsewhere examined the evidence relating to questions of strategy; the details of the procedure by which the issue of constitutionality was presented for argument at the Circuit Court and the removal on error to the Supreme Court were examined in an earlier chapter.[60]

At the May 1795 Circuit ex-Senator John Taylor of Caroline, exponent of state sovereignty, had appeared for Hylton; for the United States, John Wickham, about whom Hamilton advised a client that he could not be in better hands.[61] Their arguments were both published within a few weeks after the term's end.[62] Wickham's argument was terse and to the point; Taylor's was so diffuse and so tangled that to get through it all is much like swimming through pickerel weed.[63] Attorney General Bradford played with the idea of submitting the cause to the Supreme Court "upon the two arguments." After his death in August 1795, it was decided that counsel should be retained at government expense to represent Hylton, for Taylor had refused to appear. Jared Ingersoll and Alexander Campbell, United States Attorney for Virginia District, were chosen. Alexander Hamilton was retained to appear with Attorney General Lee for the United States. The United States footed the bills.[64]

Dallas reported nothing of the arguments. What was offered by counsel for plaintiff in error can be deduced only from the Justices' opinions, from which it is evident that there had been some reliance on

---

[59] These included Chief Judge Pendleton, ex-Senator John Taylor, Spencer Roane and one of the Pages. St. George Tucker to James Monroe, Mar. 8, 1795, Ms. James Monroe Papers (Earl Gregg Swem Library, the College of William and Mary in Virginia).

[60] *Supra,* c. XV.

[61] Hamilton to Nathaniel Terry, Apr. 21, 1803, Ms. Hamilton Papers, Misc. Docs. (LC).

[62] J. Taylor, *An Argument Respecting the Constitutionality of the Carriage Tax . . . 1795;* J. Wickham, *The Substance of an Argument in the Case of the Carriage Duties . . . 1795.*

[63] See the comment of John Randolph of Roanoke concerning one of Taylor's pamphlets, quoted by E. T.

Mudge, *The Social Philosophy of John Taylor of Caroline,* 2: "for heaven's sake, get some worthy person to do the second edition into English."

[64] Hamilton received $500; Campbell and Ingersoll, $233.33 each. See RG 217, Miscellaneous Treasury Accounts 1790–1894, Nos. 7712, 7684, 7705, respectively (NA). Lee appeared *virtute officii.* Account No. 8000 includes: "Feb. Term 1796 To two copies of the Record Hylton v. U.S. furnished the Attorney General as counsel for the United States— 23½ pages @ 50¢ / 2 seals and certifications $—16. Same term, the bill of clerks fees in the same cause, which the Attorney General undertook that the United States should pay at all events $9.72."

Taylor's argument. There are still extant a brief of Hamilton and a partial copy of his heads of argument.[65] From these it is plain that Hamilton had analyzed Taylor's argument and purposed to traverse the tax doctrines of Sir John Steuart, the British economist, upon which Taylor relied. Affirmatively he advanced against these the views of Adam Smith and indicated that Smith's definition of direct tax was "probably contemplated in his sense by the Convention." He emphasized the utility of resort to the statutory language "of the Country from which our jurisprudence is derived"—a source of reference earlier derided by Taylor. The reliance upon the views of political economists is an arresting feature of this case, and to the Court if not a welcome, at least a refreshing, change of diet from the repeated servings of Vattel, Bynkershoek and Grotius.

The argument in *Hylton* continued from February 23 to February 25; judgment was rendered March 8. Cushing had been ill and had not heard the whole argument. Three opinions were delivered—by Chase, by Paterson and by Iredell. Wilson having participated below, and whose views were affirmed, did not submit an opinion. The decision was unanimous that the law was constitutional; the tax was not a direct tax requiring apportionment.

Chase's opinion is less impressive than the one delivered in *Ware*, upon which he seems to have spent himself.[66] After reciting the relevant sections of the Constitution, he asserted that the burden was on "Plaintiff's counsel in Error" to prove that the tax was direct; they had not satisfied him, but left doubts. He would accept the construction of Congress, which considered the tax to be a duty, if the case were doubtful. He was inclined to think that the tax on carriages was not a direct tax within the letter or meaning of the Constitution. The great object of this instrument was to give Congress power to lay taxes according to the exigencies of government. The general power to lay taxes was of every kind and nature without restraint save as to exports. Only two rules were prescribed—uniformity as to duties, imposts and excises; apportionment as to capitation or other direct taxes.

The Constitution, Chase thought, contemplated as direct taxes only such as Congress could lay in proportion to the census. The rule of apportionment could only be adopted where it could reasonably apply

---

[65] Ms. Hamilton Papers, Nos. 93871–82 (LC). These will be printed in *LPAH*, III (in preparation).

[66] The argument in Ware v. Hylton had concluded Feb. 12, 1796. The Court recessed for three days because of Cushing's and Paterson's indispositions. The judgment was pronounced March 7. Chase was laid up with gout March 2–6 (McRee, *Iredell*, II, 462). The indispositions of Cushing and Paterson were apparently due to influenza (*ibid.*, 460). The former had been absent from February 2 until he returned March 2. The report of the case, 3 Dallas 171.

"and the subject taxed must ever determine the application of the rule." To tax any specific article by the rule of apportionment would obviously create great inequality and injustice; and it was unreasonable to suppose the Constitution intended such a tax to be laid by that rule.

One antic notion derived from Taylor's argument was advanced by counsel for plaintiff in error. This was the proposition that the carriage tax was a direct tax, and that such could be apportioned by Congress fixing the gross sum to be raised and then apportioning it according to the census, placing it on carriages in one state, on horses in another and so forth. Chase found this liable to the same objection as the selection of one article in all the states. The tax on carriages was within the power to lay duties. He fell in with the view of Adam Smith, advanced by Hamilton, that a tax on expense was an indirect tax and the carriage tax was of that kind because a carriage was a consumable commodity and the annual tax on it was on the expense of the owner.

Paterson's opinion was considerably more persuasive than Chase's.[67] Like his brother Wilson, who did no more than affirm that the tax was constitutional, Paterson had been present at the Federal Convention when the rule of apportionment of taxes as well as representation was decided. He was thus qualified to speak with some assurance about the intentions of that body. After commenting that the arguments on both sides turned in circles, he laid it down that the Framers of the Constitution intended that Congress should have full power over every species of taxable property except exports. The only objects that these men contemplated to fall within the rule of apportionment were a capitation and a land tax. They had been moved to this to favor the Southern states which were so circumstanced that they would otherwise have been at the mercy of the other states. In such an event, Congress could tax slaves at discretion or arbitrarily, and land throughout the Union at the same rate without regard to density of population or productivity. Plaintiff in error contended that the rule of apportionment should be favored rather than the rule of uniformity. With this Paterson did not agree. The Constitution was a work of compromise and of this nature was the rule of apportionment; it was radically wrong, it was irrational. Why should slaves, he asked, be represented more than any other form of property? The rule should not be extended by construction.

The contention of counsel for plaintiff in error that the primary object of the Framers was an equal participation by the states in expense he found to be nothing more than the old system of requisition. He

---

[67] Chase concluded his opinion with the remark that it was unnecessary "at this time" to declare whether or not the Court had constitutionally the power to declare an Act of Congress void for unconstitutionality. If the Court had such power, he was free to declare that he would not exercise it except in a very clear case, 3 Dallas 175.

proceeded at some length to expose its defects, and to set out the difficulties and injustices of an apportioned land tax. He found the same objections to the scheme of assessment with choice of different articles in the several states from which the apportioned sum would be raised. None of these objections applied to the rule of uniformity. It operated directly upon individuals without intervention of assessments or any regard to the states. All taxes on expenses or consumption were indirect taxes and such was the carriage tax. He concluded his opinion with two quotations from Smith's *Wealth of Nations*—passages cited by counsel for the United States.

Most of Iredell's brief opinion was devoted to a calculation of how inequitably an apportionment of the carriage tax would operate, and to a dissection of the weaknesses of the Taylor notion of selecting different objects under a general assessment scheme. He accepted the principle contended for by defendant in error, and concluded that since the tax could not be apportioned, it must necessarily be uniform.

The affirmance of the judgment in *Hylton* was no doubt a blow to the Virginia politicians who had gone even to the length of securing and having published in a Philadelphia paper shortly after the term opened a letter from Chief Judge Edmund Pendleton assailing the constitutionality of the carriage tax.[68] The Republicans were to effect a repeal of the tax after they came to power; they could not destroy the great prospective effect of the decision.

Two years after *Hylton* the Supreme Court was again presented with a constitutional issue that had certain political overtones, for among other grounds an attack was made upon the indurated New England practice of legislative grants of new trials because of a lack of constitutional power. This was the case of *Calder v. Bull*,[69] argued February term 1798 and decided at August term.[70] What was brought under attack was the constitutionality of a resolve of the Connecticut state legislature setting aside a decree of a court of probate that refused to record a will, and granting a new trial with right of appeal in six months. At the second probate hearing the court approved the will; the appeal was taken to the Superior Court which affirmed, and this decree was in turn affirmed by the Court of Errors. It was the contention of the plaintiffs in error that the resolution or act of the state of Connecticut granting the new trial was an ex post facto law repugnant to the Constitution

---

[68] See Madison to Pendleton, Feb. 7, 1796, Ms. Madison Papers, XIX, 21 (LC). The letter appeared in Bache's *Aurora* (Feb. 11, 1796) thinly disguised as reflections of a "gentleman of the Judiciary Department of the State in which he resides"

and as "some remarks on the argument of Mr. Wickham."

[69] 3 Dallas 386.

[70] The cause was argued over two days. Ms. Mins. U.S. Sup. Ct. 1790–1805, *sub* Feb. 8 and 13, 1798. The opinions were delivered August 8.

of the United States and so void, and that the Supreme Court possessed the power to declare such a law void.

The four Justices who participated in the decision were unanimous that the resolve of the state legislature was not an ex post facto law. The longest opinion was delivered by Chase who, though troubled by the question whether or not the legislature was acting in a judicial capacity, restricted himself to an inquiry into the meaning of the term "ex post facto," relying upon definitions in various state constitutions and upon the explanation of Blackstone. He concluded that an ex post facto law was one confined to criminal proceedings. To the argument that the Connecticut legislature had no constitutional power to make the resolve in question, Chase answered that he was fully satisfied that the Supreme Court had no jurisdiction to determine that any law of any state legislature was contrary to the constitution of the state. This was a matter for state courts.

Paterson, relying upon the same data as Chase—an interesting exhibit on the degree of consultation among the Justices—came to the same conclusion. He had something to add about the understanding of the Framers who, he said, had used the words "ex post facto" in their known signification as referring to crimes and punishments. He confessed that he had an ardent desire to have extended the provisions in the Constitution to retrospective laws in general, for there was neither policy nor safety in such laws.[71] Paterson, who left the Convention in July 1787, is believed to have returned only in time to sign the Constitution, September 17. Since it was on September 14 that an attempt was made to reconsider the ex post facto clause, it is probable that this was the occasion referred to by Paterson.

Iredell, who usually had his own characteristic approach, conceived that Connecticut had at an early date empowered its legislature to superintend courts of justice, finding the sanction for this in the history of Parliaments. This power was judicial and when exercised as in the case before the Court was an exercise of judicial and not legislative authority. Iredell agreed that the term "ex post facto law" referred to such dealing with crimes and punishments. If the act of the legislature here was a judicial act, it was not within the words of the Constitution;

---

[71] These comments, we believe, throw some light on the badly documented events at the Convention on Sept. 14, 1787. Paterson had left the Convention in July, and Professor Farrand (*Records*, III, 589) conjectures that he returned in time to sign the Constitution, September 17. The only occasion Paterson would have had to seek an extension of language would have been on September 14 when the Convention was going over the report of the Committee of Style and the motion was made to reconsider the ex post facto clause. Madison does not note Paterson as speaking, but his jottings for this day were almost telegraphic (*ibid.*, II, 617). The motion was negatived.

even if it was a legislative act, it was not within the meaning of the Constitution. Cushing said nothing about the meaning of the phrase, for he remarked only that if the act was judicial, it was not touched by the Constitution; if legislative, it was justified by the ancient and uniform practice of Connecticut.

THE POWERS OF SUPERINTENDENCE

ONE FINAL QUESTION relating to the constitutional authority of the Court requires some comment. This is the delicate one of its powers of superintendence over the federal judicial system, a power exercised in England by King's Bench over courts of the realm and assumed by the superior or supreme judicatories of the states wherever by constitution or otherwise King's Bench had furnished the paradigm. The historical reasons why supremacy and supervision were thus associated were none of them relevant so far as the constitutional foundation of the Supreme Court of the United States was concerned. Indeed, except it might be supposed that the reference to inferior courts implied some supervisory power beyond what might be exercised as an incident of appellate jurisdiction, the supreme law offered no handhold.

In 1789 Coke's *Fourth Institute*[72] still remained the classical statement of the King's Bench's powers of superintendence and their rationale. Although it was about a court of plenary jurisdiction that Coke was writing, it is evident that the lawyers who put together the Judiciary Bill thought it appropriate that some implements of supervision be conveyed. These instrumentalities had traditionally been the so-called prerogative writs. Of these, as noticed,[73] the draftsmen designated in section 13 two by name—mandamus and prohibition—to be at the disposal of the Supreme Court. In the fourteenth section the Supreme Court, as well as the District and Circuit Courts, was empowered to issue *scire facias* (not a prerogative writ), habeas corpus[74] and all other writs which might be necessary to the exercise of their jurisdiction. This qualification left open the question under what circumstance *quo warranto* and certiorari might properly be added to the

---

[72] Coke, *Fourth Institute*, 71.
[73] *Supra*, c. XI.
[74] It is by no means clear whether or not the species of habeas corpus referred to in sec. 14 was the *habeas corpus ad subjiciendum*, because the language of the proviso at the conclusion of the section indicates that the *habeas corpus ad testificandum* was to be available. The various forms of the writ are discussed in Blackstone, *Commentaries*, III, 129 *et seq*. The *habeas corpus cum causa* was, of course, a familiar device for removal of causes that in England and in some states was an instrument of superintendence.

Supreme Court's armory of process. This section seems to us to be wholly ambiguous as a recognition of powers of superintendence.

The battery of prerogative writs in England had come into existence and, indeed, had been used primarily to exercise a sort of police over inferior courts and those of special jurisdiction, like the ecclesiastical and admiralty courts. In the federal system only the District Courts were properly inferior courts. The Circuit Courts, although brought into being pursuant to the constitutional license to constitute tribunals inferior to the Supreme Court, Congress had made into something more. This we believe contributed to what was the evident embarrassment of the Supreme Court in *Hayburn's Case*, the mandamus proceedings, already related,[75] that were to disappear from the docket. It was not until 1799 in *Turner adm. v. The Bank of North America*[76] that the Court held, per Ellsworth, that the Circuit Court, though an inferior court in the language of the Constitution, was not so in the language of the common law. It was, however, a court of limited jurisdiction with "cognizance, not of cases generally, but only of a few specially circumstanced." So it was a fair presumption that a cause was without its jurisdiction unless the contrary appeared. These remarks were made in the context of the necessity of setting forth on the record the facts or circumstances which gave jurisdiction. Nothing was said to indicate that the observance of limitations might be subject to control otherwise than by writ of error.

During the period here under consideration at least six mandamus applications came before the Court,[77] and so far as the meagre records show, the writ was refused in all of them. Nothing is reported regarding

---

[75] *Supra*, c. XIII.

[76] 4 Dallas 8 (1799).

[77] The count includes the two Hayburn proceedings. John Chandler v. Secretary of War, motion for mandamus to direct the Secretary to place Chandler on the pension list conformably to an order and adjudication of Iredell and Richard Law of the Circuit Court (Ms. Mins. U.S. Sup. Ct. 1790–1805, *sub* Feb. 5, 1794); mandamus refused (*ibid.*, *sub* Feb. 14, 1794). United States v. John Hopkins, rule to show cause why a mandamus should not issue to the Commissioner of Loans requiring him to admit one Smyth to subscribe to the loan proposed by an Act of Congress of May 8, 1792 (*ibid.*, *sub* Feb. 13, 1794). The Court held that the right was not sufficiently clear to authorize the Court to issue a mandamus (*ibid.*, *sub* Feb. 15, 1794). In an account submitted by the clerk of the Supreme Court, the Attorney General certified that the motion had been made pursuant to directions of the Secretary of the Treasury founded on an agreement between him and the executive of Virginia (RG 217, Misc. Treasury Accounts 1790–1894, No. 6494 [NA]). The fifth case is United States v. Lawrence, discussed below. The sixth is Fitzbourne and Allard v. Judge of the District Court of the District of New York, mandamus to compel the judge to proceed to judgment in what appears to have been a naturalization proceeding (Ms. Mins. U.S. Sup. Ct. 1790–1805, *sub* Aug. 12, 1800; no further entries).

the Court's view of its power to issue the writ although in *United States v. Judge Lawrence*, elaborately argued by counsel, there was opportunity to express it. This was a proceeding initiated by the Executive upon complaint of the French Minister, and the motion for issuance of a mandamus to the judge of the New York District Court was made by Attorney General Bradford.[78] One Captain Barré, a deserter from a French frigate, had become a New York resident. The French vice-consul had made a demand in writing that Judge Lawrence issue a warrant for Barré by virtue of Article IX of the Consular Convention between France and the United States. This article required that the ship's register or crew list be exhibited to establish that a deserter was in fact part of the crew of the ship from which desertion was alleged. Judge Lawrence, adhering to the letter of the Convention, declined to accept a copy of the *rôle d'équipage* certified by the French vice-consul at Boston and so refused to issue the warrant. The Supreme Court was unanimously of the opinion that a mandamus ought not to issue. The District judge was acting judicially when he determined that the evidence was insufficient. The Supreme Court had no power to compel a judge to decide according to the dictates of any judgment but his own.

What is remarkable about this case is the approach of counsel. Ingersoll and W. Tilghman, who opposed the motion, did not go beyond the words of the Judiciary Act that mandamus was issuable in cases warranted by the principles and usages of law, and proffered an assemblage of English precedents to establish that a default was necessary to found issuance of the writ. Attorney General Bradford evidently subscribed to the view that the Court possessed what he called "this controuling jurisdiction"[79] where no other specific remedy existed for the party, and this upon the principles of justice and good government. He, no more than his adversaries, examined the text of the Constitution, for he referred only to "the spirit of our Constitution" which made it essential that the judicial department decide the question on the ground that it was essential to the independence of that department that judicial mistakes be corrected by judicial authority.[80]

Questions regarding prohibition, the second prerogative writ mentioned in section 13 of the Judiciary Act, were raised for the first time at August term 1795.[81] One Yard was the owner of a schooner and her

---

[78] 3 Dallas 42. By agreement with Judge Lawrence the issue was argued on the motion before return of the writ. Bradford to the Secretary of State, Mar. 21, 1795, in 1 *Official Opinions of the Attorneys General of the United States* (1852), 55.

[79] 3 Dallas 53.

[80] The case was made the subject of complaint from the Minister of Foreign Affairs de la Croix to Monroe, Mar. 11, 1796, *Am. St. Pap.: For. Rel.*, I, 732.

[81] 3 Dallas 121. The facts are from the libel and the suggestion for a prohibition.

cargo, taken on the high seas by the *Cassius*, a public-armed vessel of the French Republic, and sent to Port de Paix for adjudication. When the *Cassius* arrived at Philadelphia she was libelled by Yard in the District Court in order, as libellant alleged, to be compensated for his loss. He further alleged that the *Cassius* was originally equipped and armed at Philadelphia. It lay in the cards that the French Minister would protest, and in this case it took the form of a demand for direct executive intervention.[82] From surviving correspondence there appears to have been considerable consultation on the proper course to pursue consistent with what Minister Adet conceived to be national honor. On August 19 Peter Du Ponceau reported to Adet that he, Ingersoll and Dallas were agreed that to proceed by way of prohibition in the Supreme Court "is in no way repugnant to the Constitution or laws of the United States."[83]

A suggestion for a prohibition was filed by the captain of the *Cassius*; in support of a motion grounded thereon, counsel, who had advised this procedure, appeared, although only Dallas' argument is reported. Lewis and Tilghman opposed. What Dallas had to offer on the constitutional question was ingenious. The three great objects of the judicial power, he said, were authority to administer justice, to compel the unwilling or neglectful magistrate to perform his duty and to restrain the ministers of justice within the boundaries of their respective jurisdiction. The judicial power was, therefore, "either abstract or relative; in the former character the court for itself declares the law and distributes justice; in the latter, it superintends and controuls the conduct of other tribunals, by a prohibitory or mandatory interposition. This superintending authority has been deposited in the Supreme Court by the Federal Constitution; and it becomes a duty to exercise it upon every proper occasion." Dallas failed to point out where in Article III this authority was bestowed, for he refers specifically only to section 13 of the Judiciary Act.

Dallas reported no more than his adversaries' heads of argument, viz.: (1) that the District Court had jurisdiction; (2) that even if this was doubtful, a prohibition ought not to issue until after sentence; (3) that on a plea to the jurisdiction the party injured by the sentence might have an adequate remedy by appeal. This third point has the appearance of a challenge of the exercise of original jurisdiction, and so a traverse of Dallas' theory of constitutional authority. A clear-cut ruling on this issue was not forthcoming, possibly because "French papers" had been received in the course of argument which indicated that a French

---

[82] See Adet to Randolph, Aug. 9, 1795 (*Am. St. Pap.: For. Rel.*, I, 629); the notes of Aug. 11, 1795 (*ibid.*, 630); and the peremptory demand of Aug. 18, 1795 (*ibid.*, 631).

[83] The correspondence is in Ms. Du Ponceau Letterbook B, 127, 129, 132 (HSP).

admiralty court had decided the case of the *Cassius'* prize. If the translation of the message proved this to be the case, counsel for Yard were prepared to withdraw the libel. Argument was resumed, but as the translations were not finished, and the Court was about to "break up *sine die*," counsel not yet having arrived at a compromise, Chief Justice Rutledge announced that although difference of sentiment existed, the majority was "clearly of the opinion" that the motion should be granted. The writ accordingly issued.[84] Whether or not this case was considered a precedent, the Court a year later granted a prohibition on a libel pending in the District of Virginia involving a mortgage on a ship, presumably grounded on the saving of a common law remedy of section 9 of the Judiciary Act.[85]

Only one attempt appears to have been made to move for a prohibition directed to a Circuit Court, obviously on the assumption that section 14 of the Judiciary Act conferred discretion upon the Supreme Court to issue such a writ under circumstances unrelated to the admiralty jurisdiction. This occurred in *United States v. Bache*, but owing to Bache's death, the proceedings abated.[86]

The occasions for the Court to consider its power to issue a writ of habeas corpus were confined to certain applications made during the February term 1795, and it is clear from the circumstances that *habeas corpus ad subjiciendum* was sought.[87] The motions were made on behalf

---

[84] The rule for a prohibition was granted Aug. 24, 1795 (Ms. Docket Book U.S. Sup. Ct., p. 17). A *qui tam* proceeding was immediately begun in the Circuit Court (see Ketland q.t. v. The *Cassius, supra*, c. XIII, n. 165). In breaking the news to Minister Adet on Aug. 25, 1795, Acting Secretary of State Pickering took pains to point out that the *Cassius* was in fact the same vessel which had left Philadelphia in December by the name of *Les Jumeaux* and which had openly resisted in arms the authority of the United States (*Am. St. Pap.: For. Rel.*, I, 631).

[85] United States v. The Judge of the District Court of the United States for the District of Virginia, Ms. Docket Book U.S. Sup. Ct., p. 27; Ms. Mins. U.S. Sup. Ct. 1790–1805, *sub* Mar. 1, 12, and 14, 1796. The ship was the *Charles Carter*. The conjecture that a question of common law remedy was involved is based upon an examination of the record in

Blane v. The *Ship Charles Carter* and Alexander McCauley *et al.*, Ms. Case Papers U.S. Sup. Ct., Case No. 80.

[86] Bache, it will be recalled, had been taken up on a warrant charged with libelling the executive and bound over in advance of the passage of the Sedition Act (*supra*, c. XIV, n. 86). The suggestion was filed the last day of the term, and the motion was for a prohibition to stay proceedings in the case and that the motion be continued until next term (Ms. Mins. U.S. Sup. Ct. 1790–1805, *sub* Aug. 8, 1798). The Court ordered the continuance (Ms. Docket Book U.S. Sup. Ct., p. 61).

[87] The business began with a motion on behalf of John Corbley and others to fix the time of trial (Ms. Mins. U.S. Sup. Ct. 1790–1805, *sub* Feb. 4, 1795); a similar motion was made in behalf of John Lockery (*ibid., sub* Feb. 6, 1795). The following day it was moved that a special Circuit be directed. On February 14, on motion

of individuals committed in the course of the round-up of suspects implicated in the Whiskey Rebellion. All were charged with treason. Motions were also made for the appointment of a special session of the Circuit Court. In only one case, *United States v. Hamilton*, did the Court admit one of two petitioners to bail. The question of the Supreme Court's powers of supervision was in issue because of petitioner's claim that he had not been heard, nor had he knowledge of who the witnesses were against him or of the scope of the depositions taken against him. District Attorney Rawle argued that section 33 of the Judiciary Act bestowed a discretion upon the District judge and that his decision could be revised by the Court, which had merely concurrent authority, only if new matter occurred or upon a charge of misconduct.[88]

The Court did not enter into an examination of the authority; the only report is of Wilson's comments on the appointing of a special Circuit Court that the petitioners sought and which he denied. In a second case involving two prisoners the writ was denied. Nothing more can be claimed for the 1795 cases than that the Supreme Court entertained motions for writs of habeas corpus and that in one case the writ issued and prisoner was let to bail.[89]

A final occasion on which the question of superintendence was presented arose in connection with litigation over the so-called Connecticut Gore. This was a strip of land, roughly eight miles wide running the length and north of the New York-Pennsylvania line, that Connecticut claimed by virtue of her sea-to-sea charter.[90] Certain entrepreneurs obtained a patent to the Gore from the state of Connecticut, and although some of the territory was already settled by New York patentees, sought to oust them. We have elsewhere dealt at length with this controversy, and consequently only the most relevant details need here be mentioned.[91] On the theory that the Gore was part of the District of Connecticut, actions of ejectment were brought in the Circuit Court for

---

of William Lewis, a habeas corpus was ordered to bring up John Hamilton and Thomas Sedgwick (*ibid., sub* Feb. 14, 16, 17, and 18, 1795). On February 20 Hamilton was discharged on bail; Sedgwick was returned by consent (Ms. Docket Book U.S. Sup. Ct., p. 13). The motion for habeas corpus as to Sedgwick and also John Corbley, mentioned *supra*, was made on February 26. The following day the Court declared that it was divided in opinion and refused the motion (Ms. Mins. U.S. Sup. Ct., *sub* Feb. 27, 1795; Ms. Docket Book U.S. Sup. Ct., p. 13).

[88] 3 Dallas 17.
[89] United States v. Hamilton was the authority for the decision in *Ex parte* Burford, 3 Cranch 448 (1806), although there had been no consideration of the question of the statutory limitation "necessary to the exercise of their respective jurisdictions." Marshall noted this in *Ex parte* Burford. His solution is set forth in *Ex parte* Bollman and *Ex parte* Swartwout, 4 Cranch 75 (1807).
[90] Fowler *et al.* v. Lindsley *et al.*; Fowler *et al.* v. Miller, 3 Dallas 411 (1799).
[91] *LPAH*, I, 657–84.

that district against divers New York grantees who were allegedly in unlawful possession. At September term 1797 defendants pleaded to the jurisdiction, averring that the lands lay in the District of New York. On this issue was joined and a jury summoned. There was a challenge to the array to which plaintiffs demurred, and defendants joined. The Court quashed the array on the ground that the deputy marshal was an interested party, being a shareholder of the Gore Company. The action was continued.

At April term 1798, a new panel having been returned, there was again a challenge to the array, demurrer and joinder. The gist of defendants' objection was that the jurors, as members of the Corporation (viz., Connecticut), were interested, and since there was a question of disputed sovereignty, the interest was direct. It was consequently advanced that the cause be removed by certiorari to the Supreme Court. Paterson indicated doubt that the interest of the states was direct. A second suggestion was made that a *venire* be directed by the Circuit Court to another district. This last, Paterson said, the Court had no power to do and the demurrer was sustained.[92]

The scene of action next shifted to the Supreme Court where on August 8 William Lewis moved, as to both the ejectment actions, for a rule to show cause why a *venire* should not be awarded to summon a jury from a district other than Connecticut or New York and the show cause order issued.[93] According to Dallas, this was changed by consent to a rule to show cause why a certiorari should not issue to remove the cause to the Supreme Court as exclusively belonging to that jurisdiction.[94]

The motion regarding the *venire* to a district other than New York or Connecticut was evidently based on the belief that the Supreme Court possessed powers to provide for a *casus omissus* in the statutory structure.[95] The motion that a certiorari issue rested upon a theory of superintendency, for this was the instrumentality *par excellence* by which the King's Bench supervised inferior courts of record.[96] Judging from the arguments at Circuit for the New York grantees, the ground underlying the motion was that the interest of the grantor states could be properly protected only by removal to the Supreme Court because

---

[92] See the extensive minutes taken by a private hand, *ibid.*, 678–84.

[93] Ms. Docket Book U.S. Sup. Ct., pp. 59, 60.

[94] 3 Dallas 411. The certiorari to remove had been a prerogative writ, and is to be distinguished from the use of certiorari where diminution of the record was alleged. This last was regarded as supplementing the command to transmit the record included in the writ of error. See Fennimore v. United States, 3 Dallas 357 (1797), and Wilson v. Daniel, *ibid.*, 401 (1798).

[95] This is the substance of Hamilton's final argument at Circuit (*LPAH*, I, 683).

[96] Fitzherbert, *Natura Brevium* (1794 ed.), 245.

the Circuit Court was without jurisdiction. A judgment at Circuit would be as to them *coram non judice*. All that the report in Dallas has to say about the argument in the Supreme Court is that it concerned the question whether or not the actions could be considered to be virtually between New York and Connecticut.

The question was decided by three Justices, two of whom, Cushing and Paterson, had sat at the Circuit proceedings. Ellsworth took no part because of the interest of Connecticut. Chase and Iredell were ill. The three Justices who wrote opinions agreed that the rule to show cause should be discharged. They were further agreed that for a state to invoke the jurisdiction of the Supreme Court because of an interest in the controversy the cause must be one in which a state was either nominally or substantially a party. This was not the case here. The controversy was one between individuals respecting title to a particular tract and could not be extended to third parties or states. All three thought that jurisdiction and right to the soil were matters independent of each other, a position challenged by grantees of New York.

Whether or not the conclusion of the Court was at all affected by the remedy prayed cannot be said. There is, however, no doubt that the Justices would have none of it. Washington J., in the face of some respectable precedent,[97] asked whether it had ever happened that a certiorari issued from a superior to an inferior court from a defect of jurisdiction.[98] Cushing said that the case must be decided by the Constitution and laws and not by "remote analogies drawn from English practice." Paterson with his accustomed acuity perceived that the certiorari was here a procedural device to effect a change of venue or to direct a jury from another district. For this sort of authority no power had been given by the Constitution or law. "The authority must be given—we cannot usurp or take it."

In this terse, almost epigrammatic sentence was summed up what had been a fundamental of the Supreme Court's approach to the discharge of its functions. From the beginning it had recognized how dependent its operation was upon enabling legislation, and where this was wanting, as in the matter of process in original actions, it was

---

[97] Tidd, *Practice of the Court of King's Bench*, 3d ed. (1803), I, 330, and the cases there cited.

[98] 3 Dallas 414. In the course of his opinion Washington suggested that New York bring a bill in equity against Connecticut, praying to be quieted of the boundaries of the disputed territory and that the Court "in order to effectuate justice, might appoint commissioners to ascertain and report those boundaries." This was in fact done (Ms. Docket Book U.S. Sup. Ct., p. 67), and an injunction prayed to stay the ejectment actions. Connecticut did not appear and the bill for discovery could not be determined. The injunction was denied on the ground that New York was not party to the suits below nor interested in them. 4 Dallas 1; *ibid.*, 3 (1799).

gravely embarrassed. Its posture toward Acts of Congress, except for a few instances of individual critique, was one of respect. There were, indeed, occasions, as in *United States v. Peters*, that invited inquiry into the constitutional basis for congressional action where less deference would have been appropriate. These opportunities were not seized, nor was there succumbing to the temptation to a loose construction of statutory language sometimes advanced by counsel in argument.

When the Court was constrained to explore the intendment of statutory language, it did so as a court of law in terms familiar to the profession and not by flights of fancy about the "spirit" of the Constitution. In the very first fully reported case, *West v. Barnes* (1791), the Justices then sitting made clear their conviction that, in Iredell's words, "It is of infinite moment that Courts of Justice should Keep within their proper bounds and construe, not amend acts of legislation."

This view of the limits to be observed in statutory construction was governing also in dealing with the text of the Constitution. This was manifest in the majority opinions in *Chisholm*, for these did not follow Iredell's use of the Judiciary Act to dispose of the critical clause of Article III but dealt with it immediately as if it meant what it said—an exhibition of candor that earlier none of the proponents of the Constitution had dared risk. Similarly, Ellsworth in *Wiscart v. Dauchy* (1796) was to recur to the explicit language of Article III to establish the dependence of appellate jurisdiction upon legislative regulation, a view reaffirmed by Chase in *Turner v. The Bank of North America*. This commitment to literal meaning did not make dispensable collateral inquiry, whether in the nature of historical investigation as in *Ware v. Hylton*, local and common law usage as in *Calder v. Bull*, or prevailing economic theory as in *Hylton v. United States*. These excursions were not, however, pursued as exercises in judicial power, but because of long-seated traditions in the technique of decision-making.

The Justices who had attended at Philadelphia in 1787, where the role of the judicial had been explored, had no reason to be emboldened to depart from familiar prescripts of interpretation. It had been only after repulsion of proposals to associate the Supreme Court Justices in the exercise of veto power that the judicial had emerged as a department of government fully coordinate with the legislative and executive, but privileged by the provision for tenure to assure its independence. This had been settled upon to prevent encroachments by other branches and not to license trespasses upon their demesnes. The Supreme Court during its first decade made clear its agreement, not only by refusal of its counsel to Congress on statutory revisions, but also to the executive on questions of neutrality. In other words, it left the formulation of policy to the branches of government where it conceived such belonged.

Within the confines of what the Court considered to be the bounds of its authority there was no lack of professional acumen or, indeed, of moral courage. Notable was the absorption of current jurisprudence, state or other, in settling of rules, substantive or procedural, essential to the adjudication of issues presented by the appellate records—a process so far advanced that when the ranting about a federal common law began, the Supreme Court was not singled out for attack. No less sagacious was the handling of the cases of admiralty and maritime jurisdiction—the resort to the same ordinance that had furnished the rules of decision for the Court of Appeals in Cases of Capture, the later reading of the Neutrality Act to fortify the rationale of the law of nations respecting restitution of ships unlawfully taken.

Of the moral courage of the Supreme Bench the leading admiralty cases that came before it are testimony enough. Not only did it proceed undeterred by the pressure of foreign powers, but also in disregard of factious American opinion. Similarly, it remained coldly unaffected by the political sentiment in the war debt cases. There were outcries against particular decisions; whether or not these were based upon an examination of sources better than newspaper accounts cannot be said. From our own reading of the Court's record it is clear that in this tribunal the Justices neither spoke nor comported themselves, in Myles' phrase, as "princes of the bench." Had it been otherwise, the storms ahead might not have been weathered.

APPENDIX*

The Business of the Supreme Court, 1789-1801[1]

APPELLATE JURISDICTION

INTRODUCTORY NOTE TO STATISTICAL TABLES

A S FAR AS CAN BE determined, no statistics have ever been compiled which accurately reflect the adjudication and disposition of appellate and original cases in the Supreme Court prior to 1801. It has been recognized for some time that the cases reported in Dallas' *Reports* are not indicative of the actual number of cases in error and disposed of by the Court.[2]

The tables incorporated in this section set out reasonably correct compilations,[3] assuming, of course, that an accurate docket book was kept by the Court and granting also the validity of the criteria here used to decide what constituted an appellate case.[4] A partial explanation of these criteria follows.

---

* Prepared by Mr. Donald J. McLachlan of the Illinois Bar.

[1] The tables in the following section do not include the extraordinary writ proceedings. No cases decided in 1801 have been used in the tables. Consequently two cases reported in 4 Dallas of the August 1800 term of the Court but actually decided in 1801 have been omitted: Course *et al.* v. Stead *et al.*, 4 Dallas 22 (1801), and Talbot v. the *Ship Amelia*, Seeman, Claimant, 4 Dallas 34 (1801), also reported in 1 Cranch, *sub nom.* Talbot v. Seeman, 1 Cranch 1 (1801), in somewhat more detail. The 1801 cutoff date has been used throughout unless otherwise indicated. The citations to Dallas' *Reports* normally follow the spelling used by that reporter.

[2] For example, see Warren, *The Supreme Court in United States History*, I, 158, n. 2.

[3] As to the total number of cases, the error should be no greater than 2 percent (one case), at least with the acceptance of the assumptions adumbrated on this and the following pages.

[4] Only the Court's smooth docket book is extant. Possibly other cases were entered on the rough docket book. However, the lack of extant papers relating to those cases militates against this assumption. Some writs of error were initially sued out of the Supreme Court to remove Circuit

For the purpose of the statistical tables, the entry of a case on the docket book was made a condition precedent to the characterization of a case as appellate.[5] Consequently, two cases reported by Dallas but not entered in the docket book are omitted: *West v. Barnes* et al., 2 Dallas 401 (1791), and *Blair v. Miller*, 4 *ibid.* 21 (1800).[6] Both of these decisions involved the validity of the process by which the cases had been removed to the Supreme Court.[7] Basically, however, they do not differ from other cases which were entered in the docket book on the return of a writ of error and subsequently dismissed by quashing the writ on the grounds that the removal was irregular.[8] A definitive assessment of the Court's disposition of cases probably should include these decisions so that the total business of the Court is fairly reflected.

One other case not entered on the docket but reported by Dallas is omitted, *Dewhurst v. Coulthard*, 3 Dallas 409 (1799), again involving a question of removal but differing substantially from the issues presented in *West v. Barnes* and *Blair v. Miller*.[9]

Court cases. However, as noticed in the text, with the enactment of the Process Act of 1792 writs of error issued from the clerk of the Circuit Court returnable to the Supreme Court to remove a case.

[5] The entry of a case on the docket probably indicates the initial acceptance of the writ of error and the attached record and papers. The absence of any papers relative to West v. Barnes and Blair v. Miller, *infra*, n. 6, is plausibly explained by the fact that in neither case was the writ initially accepted and thus no records would have been filed in the Supreme Court clerk's office.

[6] On West v. Barnes, see *supra*, c. XV, p. 667. Blair v. Miller, 4 Dallas 21 (1800), held that a writ of error which was not returned to the term of the Court stated on the writ was defective and would not remove a case, that deciding that the defect was not merely formal which could be amended pursuant to sec. 32 of the Judiciary Act (1 *U.S. Stats.*, 91) but jurisdictional. In this context also note that Hayburn's case, 2 Dallas 409 (1792), is not entered on the smooth docket of the Court.

[7] Problems relating to the removal process discussed *supra*, c. XV, p. 000.

[8] For example, Blane (correctly spelled Blaine) v. the *Ship Charles Carter*, 4 Dallas 22 (1800), holding that an appeal could not be sustained to remove a case and that all removals must be by writ of error. The reason that some of these cases are entered in the docket book and others are not is probably a question of timing of the objections made to the return. The clerk's doubts as to the regularity of the process may have played a role in this determination. No papers are available either for West v. Barnes or Blair v. Miller in the files of the Court. There are papers for Blane v. *Ship Charles Carter*, but probably only because the case was subsequently removed to the Court on a writ of error after the appeal process had been quashed. Probably the writ of error in case 82, Ross v. Maul (1800, unreported), was quashed for return to the wrong term of Court, though this is conjecture based upon the dates appearing on the docket book and the writ.

[9] In Dewhurst a case stated was presented to the Court relative to an action pending in the New York Circuit Court with a request for a decision by the Supreme Court. The Court held that it could not take cognizance of any suit not brought before it by regular process, *cf. supra*, c. XV, p. 665.

Appendix

Another facet of Supreme Court practice bearing on the statistical analysis is worth noting. In three cases the original writs of error were either quashed or amended but subsequently perfected through the amendment of the writ or by suing out a new writ to remove the case. As a result, two entries were made in the docket book for each case.[10] All of these have been treated as a single case (a total of three) with the consequence that the initial quashing of the writ of error is not considered as a disposition of the case.

Separate tables have been calculated to reflect: (1) the various[11] interests relevant to the cases removed to the Court on error, whether or not disposed of prior to 1801; (2) cases disposed of by the Court through an adjudication on the merits or jurisdictional bases,[12] the entry of a *non-prosequitur*, voluntary discontinuance or by quashing of the writ of error, and a third classification comprised of cases adjudicated, either on the merits or on jurisdictional grounds.

---

[10] Mossman v. Higginson, 4 Dallas 14 (1800), cases 62 and 71; Course v. Executors of Stead, 4 Dallas 22 (1800), cases 74 and 84; and Doe ex dem Lambert v. Payne, 3 Cranch 96 (1805), cases 81 and 92. Full entries were then kept for the duplicate entries, with the second entry either noting the rule for amendment or a continuance in the case.

[11] In other cases where the writ was quashed and it did not appear that the case had been reinstated on a new writ (though there is a remote possibility that it had been because sec. 22 allowed five years after judgment in the Circuit Court for a writ of error to be sued out, and the unreported appellate docket has not been completely checked through 1805), the quashing was considered as a disposition of the case. An example is Ross v. Maul, case 82 (1800, unreported). Cases 76 and 80, Blane v. the *Ship Charles Carter*, by this criterion could have been treated as a single case. *Blane* was originally brought up by appeal but the process was subsequently quashed as unauthorized by sec. 22 of the Judiciary Act, 4 Dallas 22 (1800). That decision has been treated as a disposition even though the case was again brought up to the Court on a writ of error and entered on the docket book

of case 80. See note 13, *infra*, for an explanation of the *Blane* case.

[12] Jurisdictional grounds refers only to questions relating to the jurisdiction (all those decided in this period pertain to questions of competence) of the lower federal courts and involved cases appealed in which the District or Circuit Court had held that it had no jurisdiction to entertain the suit (*e.g.,* Glass v. the *Sloop Betsey*, 3 Dallas 6 [1794], Jennings v. Read [1799, unreported]); and also cases in which the lower court had taken cognizance of the action but which were reversed in the Supreme Court for want of jurisdiction, frequently for failure of the record or process to aver the requisite diversity of citizenship (*e.g.,* Bingham v. Cabot, 3 Dallas 382 [1798]). A determination that the Supreme Court itself had no jurisdiction, even though there may have been valid jurisdiction in the lower court, either through lack of the requisite amount in controversy or because of the irregularity of the removal process had been characterized as a disposition of the case indicated by the quashing of a writ of error, but not an adjudication on the merits or jurisdictional grounds. The tables which appear subsequently give the precise breakdown between these various categories if one disagrees with our rules.

Prior to 1801 eighty-six or eighty-seven[13] cases were entered on the docket book of the Supreme Court as appellate either from the Circuit Courts or from the state courts pursuant to section 25 of the Judiciary Act of 1789.[14] Of these, seventy-nine had been disposed of by the Court at the end of August 1800 term, including one case which disappears from the docket book without a final entry and which it is assumed was either voluntarily discontinued or non-prossed.[15]

The three volumes of Dallas' *Reports* contain forty-six separate reports of appellate cases,[16] including *West v. Barnes, Blair v. Miller* and *Dewhurst v. Coulthard*. Omitting these cases, two cases actually decided in 1801,[17] and combining two reports dealing with different phases of the proceedings of a single case,[18] there are reports for forty cases and arguably for several more because of the identity of one or both of the parties and the similarity of the facts although on separate records and appeals.[19] However, note that some of the reports pertain

[13] This number does not include West v. Barnes, Blair v. Miller or Dewhurst v. Coulthard nor any proceedings for extraordinary writs considered as an exercise of appellate jurisdiction. The 87 number includes a double entry in effect for a single record, Blane v. the *Ship Charles Carter* (cases 76 and 80). This inclusion has been justified on the basis that the decision reported in 4 Dallas 22 (1800) was a final disposition with respect to the particular effort to remove the case by appeal, and that the subsequent removal by writ of error (entered on the docket as case 80) constituted an entirely different and separate proceeding. However, in the cases listed in n. 10, *supra*, for which there are also double entries in the docket book, the amendment or suing out of a new writ of error is characterized as a single proceeding. The total number of cases listed in the docket book is eighty, corrected to eighty-four for doubling (the second entry for case 81 was not made until 1801).

[14] 1 *U.S. Stats.*, 85–86. Seven cases were removed in error from the state courts: four from the High Court of Appeals of Maryland, one from the Supreme Court of Errors of Connecticut and two from the Superior Court of Judicature, Providence County, Rhode Island. All were decided on the merits prior to 1801, six reversed and the judgment of one lower state court affirmed, Calder v. Bull, 3 Dallas 386 (1789). One case was appealed from the Kentucky District Court which had Circuit Court jurisdiction under sec. 10 of the Judiciary Act except over appeals and writs of error. Case 30, Doe *ex dem*. Gist v. Robinette (no decision).

[15] Doe *ex dem*. Gist v. Robinette (error from the District Court for the District of Kentucky).

[16] This does not include any reported proceedings relative to extraordinary writs.

[17] Talbot v. *Ship Amelia*, Seeman, Claimant, 4 Dallas 34 (1801), also reported as Talbot v. Seeman, 1 Cranch 1 (1801); and Course v. Executors of Stead, 4 Dallas 22 (1801).

[18] Hills *et al.* v. Ross, 3 Dallas 184 (1796), 3 Dallas 331 (1796).

[19] The record set out in the report of Brown v. Barry, 3 Dallas 365 (1797) is that of case 48. However cases 47, 49, 50, 51 and 53 involved the same parties and identical issues. Separate actions were brought on a number of bills of exchange. Also the *et al.* of Hazelhurst *et al.* v. United States, 4 Dallas 6 (1799), probably

Appendix

only to the entry of a *non-prosequitur*[20] or a rule for continuance.[21] Consequently, somewhat less than half of the dispositions made by the Supreme Court in the first decade of its existence are reported.[22]

The tables immediately following contain the various statistical breakdowns by which the cases have been segregated. Explanations where necessary precede each table.

Of the total number of cases in error entered on the docket book of the Supreme Court, those pursuant to section 25 of the Judiciary Act accounted for about 8 percent, the rest coming from the Circuit Courts under section 22 with one exception.[23] South Carolina provided the largest volume of litigation (twenty-two), chiefly admiralty cases

refers to the plaintiffs in error of cases 66, 67, 68, 69 and 70. These were separate suits and removals with different plaintiffs in error but involved identical issues (arising out of suits on customs bonds) and identical assignments of error in the Supreme Court. There are a number of other examples. The Minute Book shows that a number of suits were consolidated for argument in the Supreme Court.

20 For example, Hazelhurst *et al.* v. United States, 4 Dallas 6 (1799).

21 For example, Hunter v. Fairfax's Devisee, 3 Dallas 305 (1796), writ of error non-prossed, 1797. The reporting of cases by Dallas is not at all consistent. Some of the cases are reported extensively—a complete statement of the facts if not a transcript of the record, a paraphrase of the arguments of counsel including citations and occasionally questions from the Court and responses made by counsel, and the opinions of the Supreme Court Justices if delivered seriatim or the opinion of the Court. Other reports are extremely terse even where it is known that opinions were delivered by the Court or the individual Justices. Also, there are inaccuracies in Dallas both as to the date of a particular decision (Emory v. Greenough, 3 Dallas 369 [1798, given as 1797]) and as to the judgment of the Court (Williamson v. Kincaid, 4 Dallas 200 [1800], reported as having been reversed but actually non-prossed in 1803).

22 The reports are more complete as to the cases adjudicated on the merits or jurisdictional grounds, with about 60 percent reported. Correcting this for nearly identical cases adjudicated at the same time, the percentage of reported decisions probably exceeds 70 percent. Some cases were apparently submitted without argument and affirmed or reversed on a precedent case, today what would be designated as a *per curiam* or memorandum decision. Also, most of the unreported cases adjudicated on the merits probably could have been or were in fact decided on an exposition of substantive or procedural law promulgated in a previous case which is reported. Admittedly there is a serious disadvantage in not having reports of cases in which the fact situations varied even though a reported proposition of law ostensibly applied. The cases which may have precipitated novel problems of constitutional law for the Court were either reversed on formal jurisdictional grounds or non-prossed, obviating a decision on the merits. An example of the latter is case 29, Hunter v. Goodtitle *ex dem.* Fairfax (non-prossed, 1797), involving title to land in the Northern Neck of Virginia.

23 One case was appealed from the Kentucky District Court which had Circuit Court jurisdiction except over writs of error and appeals under sec. 10 of the Judiciary Act of 1789. No direct appeal from District Courts was provided in the Judiciary Act.

involving prize captures, followed by Virginia (sixteen), with the bulk arising out of actions at law.[24]

Viewing the cases in the context of jurisdiction, slightly over 40 percent were the result of diversity actions with approximately the same figure based on federal question jurisdiction obtained through the admiralty clause, two thirds of which were prize cases. The United States as plaintiff (nine cases)[25] and error from state courts (seven cases) accounted for the remainder.

Viewing all appellate business in terms of the nature of the action brought, admiralty suits accounted for roughly 40 percent, actions at law just under 50 percent, equity bills 9 percent, and one probate case.[26] Thirty-three of the cases in error or appeal originated in the District Courts, forty-three in the Circuit Courts and eight in the state courts, one of which was removed to a Circuit Court pursuant to section 12 of the Judiciary Act of 1789.[27]

Of the cases actually adjudicated by the Supreme Court prior to 1801, South Carolina again provided the largest number (fourteen) followed by Virginia with ten; four states provided only one case each in the first decade—Delaware, Maryland, New Hampshire and New Jersey. On the jurisdictional plane, admiralty causes exceeded diversity by six cases,[28] and by the nature of the suit brought exceeded actions at law by two cases.[29]

With respect to dispositions made by the Court, fifty-three cases were adjudicated on the merits, eight on jurisdictional grounds, the writ of error non-prossed in nine cases, the writ or appeal quashed in five cases (either by virtue of a defect in the removal process, lack of finality in the judgment below or lack of the requisite amount in controversy to sustain the Court's jurisdiction), the writ discontinued in three cases and one case which disappears from the docket.[30]

With respect to the action taken by the Court, on jurisdictional cases six were reversed absolutely and two reversed and remanded. On the merits forty-one of fifty-three cases were affirmed and eleven reversed (of these a new trial awarded in two, the judgment of a lower court affirmed in six, new judgment in favor of the original plaintiff awarded in one, judgment entered for the original defendant in one, judgment reversed in one on an evidence question but no new trial

---

[24] See Table I, *infra*.
[25] Libels in admiralty by the United States for forfeitures or fines accruing by force of the navigation or customs statutes are included in the admiralty section.
[26] Calder v. Bull, 3 Dallas 386

(1798), a sec. 25 case from the Supreme Court of Errors of Connecticut.
[27] 1 *U.S. Stats.*, 79–80. Generally, see Table IV and notes following.
[28] Tables V and VI.
[29] Table VII.
[30] Table VIII.

awarded because of a split in the Court on jurisdiction below) and one case reversed in part and affirmed in part.[31]

Looking at the volume of business in the Court by years, 1796 was the great year of decision, the Court disposing of twenty-eight cases, adjudicating twenty-seven of these on the merits or jurisdictional grounds. Prior to 1796 there was virtually no business in the Court other than original cases. Seven appellate cases were disposed of in the six years between 1790 and 1796, four of these on the merits or jurisdictional grounds. After 1796 the dispositions fluctuated between seven in 1798 to thirteen in 1799.[32]

---

[31] Table IX.   [32] Table XI.

STATISTICAL TABLES
APPELLATE JURISDICTION 1789–1801

TABLE I
ORIGIN OF APPEALS AND CASES IN ERROR[1]

CIRCUIT COURT	CASES	
Pennsylvania	7	
New York	5	
Delaware	1	
Rhode Island	6	
South Carolina	22	
Virginia	16	
Georgia	9	
North Carolina[2]	2	
Kentucky (District Court)[3]	1	
Massachusetts	7	
Maryland	1	
New Hampshire	1	
New Jersey	2	
TOTAL CIRCUIT		80

STATE COURTS	CASES	
Rhode Island[4]	2	
Maryland[5]	4	
Connecticut[6]	1	
TOTAL STATE		7
TOTAL		87

[1] All cases entered on the docket regardless of the date of disposition.

[2] Jurisdiction established by Act of June 4, 1790, 1 *U.S. Stats.*, 126.

[3] Kentucky District Court exercised Circuit Court jurisdiction except over appeals and writs of error by sec. 10 of the Judiciary Act of 1789.

[4] Both cases from the Superior Court of Judicature, Providence County, Rhode Island.

[5] All four cases from the High Court of Appeals.

[6] From the Supreme Court of Errors.

Appendix

TABLE II
BASIS OF FEDERAL JURISDICTION[7]

JURISDICTION	CASES
Diversity:[8]	
a. State citizenship	23
b. Alienage	13
TOTAL DIVERSITY	36
Admiralty (including seizures under impost and navigation laws):	
a. Libel for restitution and/or damages for ship allegedly seized illegally as prize	23
b. Libel in admiralty to enforce judgment of Court of Appeals in Cases of Capture[9]	2
c. Libel in admiralty by U.S. for condemnation under impost or navigation laws[10]	4
d. Libel in admiralty on bottomry bond	2
e. Libel in admiralty for salvage for recapture on statute	2
f. Libel in admiralty for salvage[11]	1
g. Not known[12]	1
TOTAL ADMIRALTY	35
Civil Action, United States Plaintiff	9
TOTAL CIVIL ACTION	9
Section 25 Cases	7
TOTAL SECTION 25	7
TOTAL	87

[7] All cases entered on the docket regardless of date of disposition.

[8] Includes cases reversed in the Supreme Court for failure of the record to aver diversity.

[9] The Court of Appeals in Cases of Capture was erected by the Continental Congress prior to the establishment of the Constitution. See *supra,* p. 171.

[10] Includes cases prosecuted by the United States and by the Collector of Customs for the United States.

[11] District Court jurisdiction obtained by libel for salvage. Appeal by adverse claimants only claiming the proceeds of ship after salvage deductions. Mac-Donough v. Dannery and the *Ship Mary Ford*, 3 Dallas 188 (1796).

[12] Record not available. Probably a libel to compel the execution of the judgment of the Court of Appeals in Cases of Capture.

TABLE III
SIDE OF COURT AND ACTION[13]

COURT SIDE	ACTION	CASES
Admiralty:[14]		
a.	Libel for restitution and/or damages for ship allegedly seized illegally as prize	23
b.	Libel in admiralty to enforce judgment of Court of Appeals in Cases of Capture	2
c.	Libel in admiralty by U.S. for condemnation under impost and navigation laws	4
d.	Libel on bottomry bond	2
e.	Libel for salvage for recapture on statute	2
f.	Libel for salvage	1
g.	Not known	1
	TOTAL ADMIRALTY	35
Law:		
	Debt (including *scire facias* proceedings)[15]	24
	Covenant	1
	Ejectment	5
	Assumpsit	9
	Dower	1
	Case (malicious interference with property)	2
	TOTAL LAW	42
Equity:		
	Various (bills for accounts, specific performance, setting aside fraudulent conveyances, foreclosure, equity of redemption, etc.)	9
	TOTAL EQUITY	9
Probate:		
	Bill to affirm a will	1
	TOTAL PROBATE	1
	TOTAL	87

[13] All cases regardless of date of disposition.

[14] See the explanations covering admiralty jurisdiction in Table II, *supra.*

[15] Includes one case whose record was not available but which is thought on the basis of similar actions brought by the same plaintiff to have been in debt.

Appendix

TABLE IV
ORIGIN OF CASES[16]

ORIGINAL COURT	CASES
U.S. District Courts[17]	34
U.S. Circuit Courts[18]	43
State Courts[19]	8
TOTAL ACTIONS	85

[16] All cases regardless of date of disposition.

[17] Includes one case decided in the Kentucky District Court which had Circuit Court jurisdiction under sec. 10 of the Judiciary Act of 1789. The other thirty-three cases were sec. 9 admiralty jurisdiction cases (including seizures under the navigation and impost laws). However, two appeals were taken from a single District Court action, one by the original libellant and the other by an adverse claimant, cases 37 and 38. Also cases 76 and 80 represent a single District Court action from which two removals were made, one attempted by appeal proper (process quashed) and the other by writ of error. This accounts for the total being stated as eighty-five rather than eighty-seven removals. The number also includes one case started in the New Hampshire District Court and then removed to the Circuit Court pursuant to sec. 11 of the Process Act of 1792 (1 *U.S. Stats.*, 275, 278–279) which provided for removal in cases where the judge had been in interest or of counsel for either party. John Sullivan, the District judge, had been of counsel for the Penhallow (respondents in case 6) interests and represented them in proceedings before the Court of Appeals in Cases of Capture. *Supra*, c. XVII.

[18] Does not include any suits brought there by transfer legislation or sec. 12 removals.

[19] Includes one case removed under sec. 12 of the Judiciary Act of 1789. Possibly other Circuit Court cases were removed from state courts; however, it was not set out in the record. The other seven actions were removed to the Supreme Court under sec. 25 of the Judiciary Act of 1789.

TABLE V

ORIGIN OF APPELLATE RECORDS

DISPOSITIONS AND ADJUDICATIONS PRIOR TO 1801[20]

CIRCUIT COURT	DISPOSITIONS	ADJUDICATIONS
Pennsylvania	6	4
New York	4	3
Delaware	I	I
Rhode Island	6	6
South Carolina	22	14
Georgia	6	5
North Carolina	2	2
Virginia	13	10
Kentucky[21] (Dist. Ct.)	I	0
Massachusetts	7	6
Maryland	I	I
New Hampshire	I	I
New Jersey	2	I
TOTAL CIRCUIT	72	54

STATE	DISPOSITIONS	ADJUDICATIONS
Rhode Island	2	2
Maryland	4	4
Connecticut	I	I
TOTAL STATE	7	7
TOTAL DISPOSITIONS	79	
TOTAL ADJUDICATIONS		61

[20] Dispositions include withdrawal of the writ of error by consent of the parties. Adjudication refers either to a judgment on the merits or jurisdictional grounds. For a breakdown of the various dispositions see Tables VI–XVI, *infra*.

[21] Circuit Court jurisdiction except over writs of error and appeals, sec. 10, 1 *U.S. Stats.*, 77 (1789).

Appendix

TABLE VI

BASIS OF FEDERAL JURISDICTION

CASES DISPOSED AND ADJUDICATED PRIOR TO 1801

JURISDICTION	DISPOSED	ADJUDICATED
Diversity:		
a. State citizenship	22	16
b. Alienage	9	7
TOTAL DIVERSITY	31	23
U.S. Plaintiff, Civil Action, Circuit Court		
TOTAL	9	2
Section 25 State Removals	7	7
TOTAL	7	7
Admiralty (including seizures under impost and navigation laws):		
a. Libel for restitution of ship and/or damages, allegedly seized illegally as prize	23	22
b. Libel to enforce judgment of Court of Appeals in Cases of Capture	2	2
c. Libel in admiralty by U.S. for condemnation under impost or navigation laws	4	3
d. Libel on bottomry bond	1	0
e. Libel for salvage on statute for recapture	1	1
f. Libel for salvage[22]	1	1
TOTAL ADMIRALTY	32	29
TOTAL DISPOSITIONS	79	
TOTAL ADJUDICATIONS		61

[22] District Court jurisdiction obtained by libel in admiralty for salvage. Error to Supreme Court by adverse claimant only, claiming proceeds of ship after salvage deductions. MacDonough v. Dannery and the *Mary Ford*, 3 Dallas 188 (1796), United States citizens, libellants; claimants, British and French.

TABLE VII
ALIENAGE OF PLAINTIFF IN TABLE VI—DIVERSITY

PLAINTIFF[23]	DISPOSED	ADJUDICATED
Great Britain	6	4
France	2	2
China	I	I
TOTAL	9	7

[23] Nationality regardless of particular residency.

TABLE VIII
NATIONALITY OF LIBELLANT IN TABLE VI—ADMIRALITY (a)

NATIONALITY	CASES DISPOSED
British	15
Spanish	4
Dutch	2
U.S.[24]	2
TOTAL	23

[24] Includes one case prosecuted jointly for United States and Swedish citizens.

TABLE IX
CHARACTERIZATION OF ACTIONS UNDER TABLE VI—
U.S. PLAINTIFF, CIVIL ACTION, CIRCUIT COURT

ACTION AND INTEREST	CASES DISPOSED
Debt on customs bonds	7
Assumpsit for Continental Loan Certificates	I
Debt on statute[25]	I
TOTAL	9

[25] Case 13, Hylton v. United States, 3 Dallas 171 (1796), Carriage Tax statute, Act of June 5, 1794, 1 *U.S. Stats.*, 373.

Appendix

TABLE X

COURT SIDE	ACTION	DISPOSED	ADJUDICATED
Admiralty:			
a.	Libel for restitution of ship and/or damages, allegedly seized illegally as prize	23	22
b.	Suit to enforce decree of Court of Appeals in Cases of Capture	2	2
c.	Libel by U.S. for condemnation under navigation or impost laws	4	3
d.	Libel on bottomry bond	1	0
e.	Libel for salvage on statute for recapture	1	1
f.	Libel for salvage	1	1
	TOTAL ADMIRALTY	32	29
Law:[26]			
a.	Ejectment	4	1
b.	Assumpsit	9	9
c.	Covenant	1	1
d.	Debt	20	11

		Disposed	*Adjudicated*
	1. specialty	10	4
	2. statute	1	1
	3. record[27] (judgment)	1	
	4. simple contract	7	7
	(a) on promissory note	1	1
	(b) on bills of exchange	6	6
	5. not known[28]	1	

	ACTION	DISPOSED	ADJUDICATED
e.	*Scire facias* proceeding against terre tenants[29]	3	3
f.	Case (malicious interference with property)	2	2
	TOTAL LAW	39	27
Equity:			
	Various (bills for accounts, discovery, specific performance of covenants, foreclose equity of redemption, injunction against state court proceeding and against recovery of Circuit Court judgment, etc.)	7	4
	TOTAL EQUITY	7	4
Probate:			
	Libel to prove will	1	1
	TOTAL PROBATE	1	1
	TOTAL DISPOSITIONS	79 79	
	TOTAL ADJUDICATIONS		61 61

[26] Where several counts were made in the declaration the one recovered on was used for characterization purposes.
[27] Debt on *scire facias*, proceeding against special bail.
[28] Record not available, thought to be debt on conjecture from various proceedings by same plaintiff.
[29] Perhaps should be characterized as action in debt. Proceeding on record of judgment, recovered against terre tenants of land conveyed by original defendant judgment debtor.

TABLE XI

DISPOSITION OF CASES PRIOR TO 1801

ACTION TAKEN	CASES	
Adjudication:		
a. On the merits	53	
b. On jurisdictional grounds	8	
TOTAL		61
Writ of error non-prossed	9	
TOTAL		9
Removal Process Quashed:[30]		
1. Writ of error quashed		
a. writ returned to term of Court different from that stated on writ[31]	2	
b. appeal not taken from final judgment	1	
c. insufficient jurisdictional amount[32]	1	
2. Appeal dismissed as not sustainable as removal process under section 22[33]	1	
TOTAL		5
Writ of Error Discontinued:		
a. On motion of plaintiff in error	1	
b. By consent on specified conditions	2	
TOTAL		3
Not Known (Case disappears from docket—Probably either withdrawn or non-prossed)	1	
TOTAL		1
TOTAL DISPOSITIONS	79	79

[30] In addition to the cases entered on the docket, see comments on West v. Barnes and Blair v. Miller, *supra*, p. 796.
[31] One of these is based on conjecture, made by comparing the writ of error to the term of court when the record was returned.
[32] Based on conjecture, but the record indicates that the amount sued for in the Circuit Court was over $500 less than the jurisdictional amount to remove to the Supreme Court.
[33] Appeal as used here indicates the civil law proceeding. The Supreme Court held that all removals must be by writ of error, Blane v. *Ship Charles Carter*, 4 Dallas 22 (1800).

Appendix

TABLE XII

ADJUDICATIONS PRIOR TO 1801

BASIS	ACTION TAKEN	JURIS.	MERITS	TOTAL
Jurisdictional Grounds:[34]				
a.	Affirmances	0	0	
b.	Reversals:			
	1. absolute (failure of record or process requisite diversity to confer jurisdiction on lower court)	6		
	2. decision below holding District Court had no competence to entertain action reversed and ordered to take cognizance of libel	2		
	TOTAL JURISDICTIONAL ADJUDICATION			8
Merits				
a.	Affirmances (with or without costs and regardless of whether additional damages were assessed in Supreme Court)		41	
b.	Reversals:			
	1. (a) Judgment below reversed and *venire facias de novo* awarded		2	
	(b) Judgment below reversed and that of lower court affirmed		6	
	(c) Judgment below reversed and new judgment in favor of original plaintiff entered by Supreme Court		1	
	(d) Judgment reversed on merits (in favor of original defendant)		1	
	(e) Judgment reversed on merits but no *venire* awarded as Court divided on question of jurisdiction below		1	
	2. Reversed in part, otherwise affirmed		1	
	TOTAL ADJUDICATION MERITS			53
Affirmances, Jurisdiction		0		
Reversals, Jurisdiction		8		
Affirmances, Merits			41	
Reversals, Merits			12	
TOTAL ADJUDICATIONS				61

TOTAL REVERSALS: 20 (including one case affirmed in part)
TOTAL AFFIRMANCES: 41

[34] Does not include one case reversed on merits but on which Court was equally divided as to jurisdiction below. Does not include any cases where jurisdiction was attacked but upheld in Supreme Court and adjudication proceeded on the merits.

TABLE XIII
DISPOSITIONS AND ADJUDICATIONS BY YEAR[35]

YEAR	DISPOSED	ADJUDICATED
1790[36]	0	0
1791[37]	0	0
1792	1	0
1793	1	1
1794	1	1
1795	2	2
1796	28	27
1797	15	13
1798	7	6
1799	13	5
1800	10	6
Not known	1	0
TOTAL DISPOSITIONS	79	
TOTAL ADJUDICATIONS		61

[35] All cases disposed prior to 1801.

[36] No cases were entered on docket of Court prior to June 30, 1792, when the writ of error and record from case 1, Collet v. Collet (discontinued, 1792, no report), was returned.

[37] West v. Barnes, *supra*, was decided in 1791.

TABLE XIV
CASES DISPOSED PRIOR TO 1801, TREATY INVOLVED[38]

Treaty relied upon as defense either to merits or jurisdiction of Court	22
Treaty relied upon by plaintiff	9
TOTAL	31

[38] This only includes cases definitely known where it could be ascertained either from the pleadings or the report of the case that a treaty was involved. The treaties involved included the Treaty of Paris (1783), the French Treaty (1778), the Jay Treaty (1794) and the Dutch Treaty of Amity and Commerce (1782).

Appendix

TABLE XV
ECONOMIC BASES, REGARDLESS OF FORM OF ACTION[39]

ECONOMIC BASE

Maritime:
a.	Prize questions (ship and cargo)	29
b.	Fines and condemnations under impost and navigation laws (ship, cargo and imported articles)	4
c.	Maritime liens (bottomry bond)	I
d.	Salvage on statute for recapture	I

Non-Maritime (but including customs bonds and related questions):
a.	Credit (bills, promissory notes, bonds, etc.)	32
b.	Land title (public land grants)	4
c.	Contracts, sale of goods	2
d.	Partnership accounts	I
e.	Contracts relating to land (rents, mortgages, sales, etc.)	3
f.	Fines and penalties, civil, under statute	I
g.	Estate (underlying question regarding title to land)	I

TOTAL	79

[39] This table is subject to a considerable degree of error. *E.g.*, three *scire facias* proceedings involved the question of subjecting land to the satisfaction of a prior judgment obtained in an action of debt on a specialty (bond under seal). These have been incorporated in the credit section but they might arguably fall under questions relative to the title of land. Also, two tort actions involved the question of the right of the Collector of the Customs to refuse to execute customs bonds. These have also been put in the credit section.

TABLE XVI
CASES DISPOSED INVOLVING THE CONSTITUTION OR U.S. STATUTES[40]

Total dispositions	79
Cases involving federal statute or Constitution	53

[40] This includes resolutions of the Continental Congress. This table is subject to some error. It includes only those cases from which it could be definitely shown either from the pleadings or from the report that the Constitution or a federal statute was involved. It does not include cases involving the Judiciary Act as a basis for jurisdiction unless there was a controversy over the interpretation of a particular section of the Judiciary Act.

Manuscript Sources

ABBREVIATIONS OF LOCATIONS

Bev. Hist. Soc.	Beverly Historical Society, Beverly, Massachusetts
CUL	Columbia University Library, New York, New York
CULL	Columbia University Law Library, New York, New York
FRC	Federal Records Center
HSP	Historical Society of Pennsylvania, Philadelphia, Pennsylvania
LC	Library of Congress, Washington, D.C.
Mass. Archives	Massachusetts Archives, State House, Boston, Massachusetts
Md. Hist. Soc.	Maryland Historical Society, Baltimore, Maryland
MHS	Massachusetts Historical Society, Boston, Massachusetts
NA	National Archives, Washington, D.C.
Newport Hist. Soc.	Newport Historical Society, Newport, Rhode Island
NYHS	New-York Historical Society, New York, New York
NYPL	New York Public Library, New York, New York
NYSL	New York State Library, Albany, New York
PRO	Public Record Office, London, England
S. Car. Hist. Soc.	South Carolina Historical Society, Charleston, South Carolina
SCHC	South Carolina Historical Commission, Columbia, South Carolina
Va. Hist. Soc.	Virginia Historical Society, Richmond, Virginia
YUL	Yale University Library, New Haven Connecticut

814

Location of Manuscript

FEDERAL JUDICIAL RECORDS
CONSULTED

SUPREME COURT OF THE UNITED STATES

Minutes 1790–1805[1]	NA
Docket Book 1791–1809	Same
Case Papers (Appellate)[2]	Same
Original Case Papers	Same

CIRCUIT COURTS[3]

Connecticut District

Docket Book 1791–1799	FRC, Waltham, Massachusetts
Case Papers	Same

Georgia District

Minutes 1790–1793; 1793–1798; 1798–1806	FRC, East Point, Georgia
Case Papers	Same

Maryland District

Minutes 1790–1812	FRC, Suitland, Maryland
Docket Books (7)	Same
Case Papers	Same

Massachusetts District

Final Record Book 1790–1799	FRC, Waltham, Massachusetts
Case Papers	Same

---

[1] Transcriptions of the Minute Book 1790–1801 are published in *The American Journal of Legal History*, Vols. 5, 6, 7 and 8.

[2] The Appellate Case Papers are here referred to as Case Papers, followed by the number assigned in the Docket Book.

[3] For jurisdictions such as New Jersey and South Carolina where case papers appear to have been lost, the records which went to the Supreme Court on error throw light on the state of practice. The search of Circuit Court records began in 1957. Since then, great progress in classifying and reclassifying the case papers, transferred in some instances to District clerks in a state of nature, as it were, has greatly progressed. These muniments are here consistently referred to as Case Papers.

New Hampshire District
    Records in Equity and Admiralty   Same
       1790–1795; 1813–1818
    Dockets   Same
    Case Papers   Same

New Jersey District
    Minutes 1790–1806   FRC, Suitland, Maryland

New York District
    Minutes 1790–1808   Same
    Case Papers   Same

North Carolina District
    Minutes 1791–1806   Same
    Dockets (4)   FRC, East Point, Georgia
    Case Papers   Same

Pennsylvania District
    Minutes 1792–1795; 1796–1797;   FRC, Suitland, Maryland
       1797–1798; 1798–1799; 1799–
       1800; 1800–1802
    Docket Books (2)   Same
    Case Papers   Same

Rhode Island District
    Minutes 1790–1807   FRC, Waltham, Massachusetts
    Case Papers   Same

South Carolina District
    Minutes 1790–1800   FRC, East Point, Georgia

Vermont District
    Dockets   FRC, Waltham, Massachusetts
    Case Papers   Same

Virginia District
    Rule Book   Office of the United States District
                            Court, Richmond, Virginia
    Order Book   Same
    Record Books   Same
    Case Papers   Virginia State Library

DISTRICT COURTS

Maryland
    Case Papers   FRC, Suitland, Maryland

New York
    Minutes 1789–1796; 1796–1798;   Same
       1798–1800
    Case Papers   Same

South Carolina
    Minutes 1790–1795   FRC, East Point, Georgia

Manuscripts

OTHER THAN FEDERAL JUDICIAL
RECORDS

Adams Papers: MHS
Archives Nationales, Affaires Étrangères B¹, Correspondances Consulaires:
LC Trans.
Simeon Baldwin Papers: YUL
Bancker Papers: NYHS
John Gray Blount Papers: North Carolina Department of Archives and
History, Raleigh, North Carolina
British Museum, Additional Mss: LC Trans.
British Museum, Egerton Mss: LC Trans.
Calendar of Proceedings of the Court of Assizes, 1665–1672: NYPL
Samuel Chase, letters: The Huntington Library, San Marino, California;
University of Virginia Library, Charlottesville, Virginia
Samuel Chase, Notes for Debates on the Constitution: Privately owned
Samuel Chase Papers: Md. Hist. Soc.
Connecticut Archives: Connecticut State Library, Hartford Connecticut
Connecticut Cases: CULL
Corner Papers: Md. Hist. Soc.
William Cushing Papers: MHS
Nathan Dane Papers: Bev. Hist. Soc.
Nathan Dane Papers: LC
Domestic Letters of the Department of State: NA
James Duane Papers: NYHS
Peter Du Ponceau Form Book: HSP
Peter Du Ponceau Letterbook B: HSP
Oliver Ellsworth, letters: Boston Public Library, Boston, Massachusetts;
The Huntington Library, San Marino, California; In Pickering Papers,
MHS
Oliver Ellsworth, Public Services: Connecticut Archives, Connecticut
State Library, Hartford, Connecticut
Emmet Collection: NYPL
Force Transcripts: LC
Great Britain. Public Records: Colonial Office Papers. CO 391/1, Jour-

nal of the Lords Committee of Trade and Plantations, 1670–1686:   PRO.
LC Trans. Foreign Office Papers. FO 4/5, FO 4/6:   PRO. War Office
Papers. WO 1/404:   PRO
Alexander Hamilton Papers: LC
Richard Harison Papers: NYHS
Thomas Hutchinson Correspondence: Mass. Archives
Harry Innes Papers: LC
John Jay Papers: CUL
Thomas Jefferson, Fee Book: The Huntington Library, San Marino,
California
Thomas Jefferson, Register of Cases: The Huntington Library, San Marino,
California
Journal of the House of Representatives of the Commonwealth of Mas-
sachusetts: Mass. Archives
Journal of the House of Representatives of the State of South Carolina;
Journal of the Senate of the State of South Carolina: SCHC
Journal of the Proceedings of the Convention of the State of New York,
1788: NYSL
Rufus King Papers: NYHS
Henry Knox Papers: MHS
Lamb Papers: NYHS
Lee Family Papers: University of Virginia Library, Charlottesville,
Virginia
Lee-Ludwell Mss: Va. Hist. Soc.
Sir William Lee Papers, "Notes on Philips v. Savage":   Osborn Collection,
YUL
Livingston Mss: NYHS
Gilbert Livingston, Notes of debates on the Constitution: NYPL
Chancellor Robert R. Livingston, annotations on printed copy of the Con-
stitution: William L. Clements Library, University of Michigan
William Livingston Precedent Book: NYSL
Loan Office Letter Book and Custom House Letter Book: Newport Hist.
Soc.
James Madison Papers: LC
George Mason Papers: LC
Massachusetts Judicial, 1683–1724:   Mass. Archives
Massachusetts Senate Files: Mass. Archives
McKesson Papers: NYHS
Minutes of the Court of Common Pleas, Westchester County, 1723–1773:
Office of County Clerk, White Plains, New York
Minutes of the General Court of North Carolina, 1725–1751:   North
Carolina Department of Archives and History, Raleigh, North Carolina
Minutes of the New York Provincial Council: NYSL
Minutes of the Supreme Court of Judicature of the State of New York,
1775–1781:   Hall of Records, New York County, New York, New York
Miscellaneous Bound Mss: MHS
Miscellaneous Letters of the Department of State, 1790–1799:   NA
Miscellaneous Mss Continental Congress: LC

Manuscript Sources

Miscellaneous Mss Personal: LC

Miscellaneous Treasury Accounts, 1790–1894: NA

James Monroe Papers: Earl Gregg Swem Library, The College of William and Mary in Virginia, Williamsburg, Virginia

"Observations on the Present State of the Courts of Judicature in His Majesty's Province of South Carolina": LC

Robert T. Paine Papers: MHS

William Paterson, Notes on Debate in the Senate, September 1789: Bancroft Transcripts, NYPL

William Paterson, Notes on *United States v. Lyon*: Bancroft Transcripts, NYPL

PCC. Papers of the Continental Congress: NA

Edmund Pendleton, Notes on *Commonwealth of Virginia v. Caton*: Force Transcripts, LC

Richard Peters Papers: HSP

Pickering Papers: Essex Institute, Salem, Massachusetts

Pickering Papers: MHS

Pinckney Family Papers: LC

Pleadings, 1754–1837: Hall of Records, New York County, New York, New York

William Rawle Papers: HSP

Records of the Proceedings of the Court of the Ordinary, 1764–1771: S. Car. Hist. Soc.

Joseph Reed Papers: NYHS

RWPC. Revolutionary War Prize Cases, Records of the Court of Appeals in Cases of Capture, 1776–1787: NA

Shippen Mss: HSP

Shippen Mss: LC

Melancton Smith Papers: NYSL

South Carolina Council Journal, 1765–1766: SCHC

State of South Carolina Court of Admiralty Record Book, 1787–1789: FRC, East Point, Georgia

Suffolk County Court Files: Office of the Clerk, Supreme Judicial Court of Massachusetts, Boston, Massachusetts

Tucker-Coleman Collection: Earl Gregg Swem Library, The College of William and Mary in Virginia, Williamsburg, Virginia

United States Senate Files: NA

Anthony Wayne Papers: William L. Clements Library, University of Michigan

Otho Williams Mss: Md. Hist. Soc.

Contemporary Newspapers
and Periodicals Cited

CONNECTICUT

Hartford: *Connecticut Courant*
Middletown: *Middlesex Gazette*
Norwich: *Norwich Packet*

MARYLAND

Annapolis: *Maryland Gazette*
Baltimore: *Maryland Gazette, or the Baltimore Advertiser*
  Maryland Journal and the Baltimore Advertiser
    (short title: *Maryland Journal*)

MASSACHUSETTS

Boston: *American Herald*
  The Boston Gazette, and the Country Journal
  The Independent Chronicle. And the Universal Advertiser
  Massachusetts Centinel
  Massachusetts Gazette
Newburyport: *The Essex Journal & New-Hampshire Packet*
Salem: *The Salem Gazette*
Worcester: *The Worcester Magazine*

NEW HAMPSHIRE

Walpole: *Farmer's Museum, or Lay Preacher's Gazette*
    (short title: *Farmer's Museum*)

NEW YORK

New York City: *Daily Advertiser*
  The Independent Journal: or the General Advertiser
  New York Commercial Advertiser

820

Contemporary Newspapers and Periodicals Cited

New-York Daily Gazette

The New-York Journal and Weekly Register; variant titles: *The New-York Journal and Daily Patriotic Register, Greenleaf's New-York Journal*

    (short title: *New-York Journal*)

New York Packet; variant title: *New York Packet. And the American Advertiser*

Spectator

Poughkeepsie: *The Country Journal, and the Poughkeepsie Advertiser*

PENNSYLVANIA

Philadelphia: *American Museum* (Carey's)

Aurora. General Advertiser

Dunlap's American Daily Advertiser

The Freeman's Journal: or the North American Intelligencer

    (short title: *Freeman's Journal*)

Federal Gazette, and Philadelphia Evening Post

Gazette of the United States

General Advertiser (Bache's)

Independent Gazetteer: or the Chronicle of Freedom

Pennsylvania Gazette

The Pennsylvania Herald, and General Advertiser

Pennsylvania Packet

RHODE ISLAND

Newport: *The Newport Mercury*

Providence: *The Providence Gazette: and Country Journal*

United States Chronicle

SOUTH CAROLINA

Charleston: *State Gazette of South Carolina*

VIRGINIA

Fredericksburg: *The Virginia Herald, and Fredericksburg Advertiser*

Richmond: *Virginia Gazette and General Advertiser*

Virginia Gazette and Weekly Advertiser

Virginia Independent Chronicle

Short Titles and Abbreviations

LEGAL PUBLICATIONS MOST FREQUENTLY CITED IN THIS VOLUME

Bacon, *Abridgment*	Bacon, Matthew. *A New Abridgment of the Law.* 5 vols. 1736–66. 3d ed., corr. London: H.M. Law-Printers, for J. Worrall and Co., etc., 1768–70.
Blackstone, *Commentaries*	Blackstone, William. *Commentaries on the Laws of England.* 4 vols. 1765–69. Various editions are cited.
Charter and Laws Prov. of Pa.	*The Charter to William Penn, and Laws of the Province of Pennsylvania Passed Between the Years 1682 and 1700: Preceded by Duke of York's Laws in Force from the Year 1676 to the Year 1682.* Staughton George *et al.*, eds. Harrisburg: L. S. Hart, state printer, 1879.
Coke, *Littleton*	Coke, Edward. *The First Part of the Institutes of the Laws of England: Or, A Commentary upon Littleton.* 1628. 16th ed., rev. and corr. Francis Hargrave and Charles Butler, eds. London: L. Hansard, for E. Brooke, etc., 1809.
———, *Second Institute*	———. *The Second Part of the Institutes of the Laws of England: Containing the Exposition of Many Ancient and Other Statutes.* 1642. 2 vols. London: W. Clarke and Sons, 1809.
———, *Third Institute*	———. *The Third Part of the Institutes of the Laws of England: Concerning High Treason, and Other Pleas of the Crown, and Criminal Causes.* 1644. London: W. Clarke and Sons, 1809.
———, *Fourth Institute*	———. *The Fourth Part of the Institutes of the Laws of England: Concerning the Jurisdiction of Courts.* 1644. London: W. Clarke and Sons, 1809.

Short Titles and Abbreviations

Col. Laws Mass.	*The Colonial Laws of Massachusetts, Reprinted from the Edition of 1660, with the Supplements to 1672, Containing also the Body of Liberties of 1641.* William H. Whitmore, ed. Boston: City Council of Boston, 1889.
Col. Laws N.Y.	*The Colonial Laws of New York from the Year 1664 to the Revolution.* 5 vols. Albany: J. B. Lyon, state printer, 1894.
Colum. L. Rev.	*Columbia Law Review*
Harv. L. Rev.	*Harvard Law Review*
Hening, *Va. Stats.*	Hening, William W., ed. *The Statutes at Large: Being a Collection of All the Laws of Virginia, from the First Session of the Legislature in the Year 1619 [to 1792].* 13 vols. Richmond, 1809–23; Philadelphia and New York, 1823.
Kent, *Commentaries*	Kent, James. *Commentaries on American Law.* 4 vols. 1826–30. 12th ed., edited by Oliver Wendell Holmes, Jr. Boston: Little, Brown and Co., 1873.
L.Q. Rev.	*Law Quarterly Review*
N.Y. Laws	*Laws of the State of New York Passed at the Sessions of the Legislature Held in the Years 1777 [to 1801].* 5 vols. Reprint. Albany: Weed, Parsons, 1886–87.
N.Y.U.L. Rev.	*New York University Law Review*
U.S. Stats.	*United States Statutes at Large.* Vols. 1–5, titled *The Public Statutes at Large of the United States of America, from the Organization of the Government in 1789, to March 3, 1845.* Richard Peters, ed. Published by authority of Congress. Boston: Little and Brown, 1850.
Wash. & Lee L. Rev.	*Washington and Lee Law Review*
Wharton, *State Trials*	Wharton, Francis, ed. *State Trials of the United States during the Administrations of Washington and Adams.* Philadelphia: Carey and Hart, 1849.

For the older English legal publications full bibliographical details may be found in *A Bibliography of English Law to 1650*, Vol. 1, W. Harold Maxwell, comp., and *A Bibliography of English Law from 1651–1800*, Vol. 2, Leslie F. Maxwell, comp. (London: Sweet and Maxwell Ltd., 1925, 1931).

Abbreviations of law reports as well as standard legal terms and their abbreviations may be found in *Black's Law Dictionary*, 4th ed. (St. Paul, Minn.: West Publishing Co., 1951).

A Select Bibliography

AND SHORT TITLES OF WORKS OTHER
THAN LAW BOOKS CITED IN THIS VOLUME

Abernethy, Thomas Perkins. *Western Lands and the American Revolution.* New York: Appleton-Century Co., 1937.

Adams, Henry. *History of the United States of America* [1801–1817]. 9 vols. New York: Charles Scribner's Sons, 1889–91.

Adams, John. *The Diary and Autobiography of John Adams.* Lyman H. Butterfield *et al.*, eds. 4 vols. The Adams Papers, 1st ser. Cambridge, Mass.: Harvard University Press, Belknap Press, 1961. Short title: *Adams Papers.*

————. *The Works of John Adams.* Charles Francis Adams, ed. 10 vols. Boston: Little, Brown and Co., 1850–56. Short title: Adams, *Works.*

Adams, John Quincy. "Diary of John Quincy Adams." Massachusetts Historical Society *Proceedings* for 1902, 2d ser., 16: 291–464 (November 1902).

————. *Writings of John Quincy Adams.* Worthington C. Ford, ed. 7 vols. New York: The Macmillan Co., 1913–17.

Adams, Samuel. *The Writings of Samuel Adams.* Harry Alonzo Cushing, ed. 4 vols. New York: G. P. Putnam's Sons, 1904–08.

Alvord, Clarence Walworth. *The Mississippi Valley in British Politics: A Study of the Trade, Land Speculation, and Experiments in Imperialism Culminating in the American Revolution.* 2 vols. Cleveland: Arthur H. Clark Co., 1917.

Ames, Fisher. *Works of Fisher Ames.* Seth Ames, ed. 2 vols. Boston: Little, Brown and Co., 1854.

Ames, Herman Vandenburg, ed. *State Documents on Federal Relations: The States and the United States.* Philadelphia: Department of History of the University of Pennsylvania, 1906.

Bancroft, George. *History of the Formation of the Constitution of the United States of America.* 2 vols. 5th ed. New York: D. Appleton and Co., 1885.

Beard, Charles A. *An Economic Interpretation of the Constitution of the United States.* New York: The Macmillan Co., 1913.

A Select Bibliography

Belknap, Jeremy. "Belknap Papers." Pts. 1 and 2, "Correspondence between Jeremy Belknap and Ebenezer Hazard," Charles Deane, ed., in Massachusetts Historical Society *Collections*, 5th ser., Vols. 2 and 3 (1877). Pt. 3, "Miscellaneous Correspondence," Charles C. Smith, ed., in Massachusetts Historical Society *Collections*, 6th ser., Vol. 4 (1891).

———. *The History of New-Hampshire*. Vol. 1. John Farmer, ed. Copy of Dover ed., 1831. Dover, N.H.: G. Wadleigh, 1862.

———. "Notes of Debates in the Massachusetts Ratifying Convention, January, 1788." Massachusetts Historical Society *Proceedings* for 1855–58, 1st ser., 3: 296–304 (March 1858).

Beveridge, Albert J. *The Life of John Marshall*. 4 vols. Boston: Houghton Mifflin Co., 1916–19.

Bishop, Hillman Metcalf. "Why Rhode Island Opposed the Federal Constitution." *Rhode Island History*, 8: 1–10, 33–44, 85–95, 115–26 (1949).

Bolingbroke, Henry St. John, Viscount. *A Dissertation upon Parties*. 3d ed. London: Printed by H. Haines, 1735.

Bowdoin, James, and Temple, Sir John. "The Bowdoin and Temple Papers." Massachusetts Historical Society *Collections*, 6th ser., Vol. 9 (1897).

Boyd, Julian Parks. "Connecticut's Experiment in Expansion: The Susquehannah Company, 1753–1803." *Journal of Economic and Business History*, 4: 38–69 (1931–32).

———, ed. *The Susquehannah Company Papers, 1750–1772*. 4 vols. Wilkes-Barre, Pa.: Wyoming Historical and Geological Society, 1930–33.

Brant, Irving. *James Madison*. 6 vols. Indianapolis, Ind.: Bobbs-Merrill Co., 1941–61.

Brown, Robert Eldon. *Middle-Class Democracy and the Revolution in Massachusetts, 1691–1780*. Ithaca, N.Y.: For the American Historical Association, by Cornell University Press, 1955.

———, and Brown, B. Katherine. *Virginia, 1705–1786: Democracy or Aristocracy?* East Lansing, Mich.: Michigan State University Press, 1964.

Brown, William Garrott. *The Life of Oliver Ellsworth*. New York: The Macmillan Co., 1905.

Browning, James R., and Glenn, Bess. "The Supreme Court Collection at the National Archives." *American Journal of Legal History*, 4: 241–56 (1960).

Bruce, Philip Alexander. *Institutional History of Virginia in the Seventeenth Century: An Inquiry into the Religious, Moral, Educational, Legal, Military, and Political Condition of the People*. 2 vols. New York: G. P. Putnam's Sons, 1910.

Brunhouse, Robert L. *The Counter-Revolution in Pennsylvania, 1776–1790*. Philadelphia: Pennsylvania Historical Commission, 1942.

Burnett, Edmund Cody. *The Continental Congress*. New York: The Macmillan Co., 1941.

————, ed. *Letters of Members of the Continental Congress.* 8 vols. Washington, D.C.: Carnegie Institution, 1921–36. Short title: *LMCC.*

Carson, Hampton Lawrence. *The History of the Supreme Court of the United States: With Biographies of All the Chief and Associate Justices.* 2 vols. Philadelphia: P. W. Ziegler and Co., 1902.

"The Case of Phillips vs. Savage." Massachusetts Historical Society *Proceedings* for 1860–62, 1st ser., 5: 64–81 (October 1860); 5: 164–71 (March 1861).

Chalmers, George, comp. *Opinions of Eminent Lawyers on Various Points of English Jurisprudence, Chiefly Concerning the Colonies, Fisheries, and Commerce of Great Britain: Collected and Digested from the Originals in the Board of Trade and Other Depositories.* 2 vols. London: Reed and Hunter, 1814. Short title: Chalmers, *Opinions.*

Childs, James B. " 'Disappeared in the Wings of Oblivion': The Story of the United States House of Representatives Printed Documents at the First Session of the First Congress, New York, 1789." Bibliographical Society of America *Papers,* 58: 91–132 (1964).

————. "The Story of the United States Senate Documents, 1st Congress, 1st Session, New York, 1789." Bibliographical Society of America *Papers,* 56: 175–94 (1962).

"Church Lands in Vermont." *Church Review and Ecclesiastical Register,* 4: 580–90 (1851–52).

Colden, Cadwallader. "The Colden Letter Books, 1760–1775." 2 vols. New-York Historical Society *Collections,* Publication Fund ser., Vols. 9–10 (1876–77).

Connecticut. "Proceedings of the Constitutional Ratifying Convention, Hartford, January 3 to January 9, 1788." Leonard W. Labaree, ed. *Public Records of the State of Connecticut,* 6: 548–73, Appendix B (1945).

————. *The Public Records of the Colony of Connecticut.* James H. Trumbull and Charles J. Hoadly, eds. 15 vols. Hartford: State printer, 1850–90.

————. *The Public Records of the State of Connecticut.* Charles J. Hoadly et al., eds. 11 vols. to date. Hartford: State printer, 1894–   .

Conway, Moncure Daniel. *Omitted Chapters of History Disclosed in the Life and Papers of Edmund Randolph.* New York: G. P. Putnam's Sons, 1888.

Coxe, Brinton. *An Essay on Judicial Power and Unconstitutional Legislation, Being a Commentary on Parts of the Constitution of the United States.* Philadelphia: Kay and Brother, 1893.

Crowl, Philip A. "Anti-Federalism in Maryland, 1787–1788." *William and Mary Quarterly,* 3d ser., 4: 446–69 (1947).

————. *Maryland during and after the Revolution: A Political and Economic Study.* Baltimore: Johns Hopkins Press, 1943.

Crumrine, Boyd. "The Boundary Controversy between Pennsylvania and Virginia, 1748–1785: and Early Court Records of the Region around the Headwaters of the Ohio River." Carnegie Museum *Annals,* 1: 505–24 (1901–02).

A Select Bibliography

Cunningham, William. *The Growth of English Industry and Commerce.* 3 vols. 5th ed. Cambridge: At the University Press, 1910–12.

Cushing, Harry Alonzo. *History of the Transition from Provincial to Commonwealth Government in Massachusetts.* New York: Columbia University Press, 1896.

Davis, Daniel. "The Proceedings of Two Conventions, Held at Portland, to Consider the Expediency of a Separate Government in the District of Maine." Massachusetts Historical Society *Collections*, 1st ser., 4: 25–40 (1795).

Delaplaine, Edward Schley. *The Life of Thomas Johnson: Member of the Continental Congress, First Governor of the State of Maryland, and Associate Justice of the United States Supreme Court.* New York: F. H. Hitchcock, 1927.

Dickerson, Oliver Morton. *American Colonial Government, 1696–1765: A Study of the British Board of Trade in its Relation to the American Colonies: Political, Industrial, Administrative.* Cleveland: Arthur H. Clark Co., 1912.

Dickinson, John. *Letters from a Farmer in Pennsylvania, to the Inhabitants of the British Colonies.* First printed in Philadelphia, New York, Boston, London, 1768. Reprint, with Introduction by Richard T. H. Halsey. New York: Outlook Co., 1903.

Dictionary of American Biography. Allen Johnson *et al.*, eds. 22 vols. and Index vol. New York: For the American Council of Learned Societies, by Charles Scribner's Sons, 1928–58. Short title: *DAB.*

The Documentary History of the Protestant Episcopal Church in the Diocese of Vermont, Including the Journals of the Conventions, 1790–1832. Edited by an appointed committee for the Diocese of Vermont. New York and Claremont, N.H.: Church printers, 1870.

Drinard, J. Elliott. "John Blair, Jr., 1732–1800." Virginia State Bar Association *Annual Reports*, 39: 436–49 (1927).

Dumbauld, Edward. *The Bill of Rights and What It Means Today.* Norman: University of Oklahoma Press, 1957.

Elliot, Jonathan, ed. *The Debates in the Several State Conventions on the Adoption of the Federal Constitution, as Recommended by the General Convention at Philadelphia in 1787. Together with the Journal of the Federal Convention, Luther Martin's Letter, Yates's Minutes, Congressional Opinions, Virginia and Kentucky Resolutions of '98–'99, and Other Illustrations of the Constitution.* 5 vols. 2d ed. Philadelphia: J. B. Lippincott Co., 1881. Short title: Elliot, *Debates.*

Farrand, Max, ed. *The Records of the Federal Convention of 1787.* 4 vols. New Haven, Conn.: Yale University Press, 1911, rev. ed. 1937. Short title: Farrand, *Records.*

The Federalist. By Alexander Hamilton, James Madison and John Jay. Edited, with Introduction and Notes, by Jacob E. Cooke. Middletown, Conn.: Wesleyan University Press, 1961.

Flanders, Henry. *The Lives and Times of the Chief Justices of the Supreme*

Court of the United States. 2 vols. Philadelphia: J. B. Lippincott and Co., 1855–59.

Flick, Alexander C., ed. *History of the State of New York.* 10 vols. New York: Columbia University Press, 1933–37.

Ford, Paul Leicester, ed. *Essays on the Constitution of the United States, Published during Its Discussion by the People, 1787–1788.* Brooklyn, N.Y.: Historical Printing Club, 1892. Short title: Ford, *Essays.*

————. *Pamphlets on the Constitution of the United States, Published during Its Discussion by the People, 1787–1788.* Brooklyn, N.Y.: n.p., 1888. Short title: Ford, *Pamphlets.*

Franklin, Benjamin. *The Works of Benjamin Franklin.* John Bigelow, ed. 12 vols. Federal ed. New York and London: G. P. Putnam's Sons, 1904.

Freeman, Douglass Southall. *George Washington: A Biography.* 7 vols. Vol. 7 completed by John Alexander Carroll and Mary Wells Ashworth. New York: Charles Scribner's Sons, 1948–57.

Georgia. *Colonial Records of the State of Georgia.* Allen D. Candler, comp. 26 vols. Atlanta: State printer, 1904–16.

Gibbs, George. *Memoirs of the Administrations of Washington and John Adams, Edited from the Papers of Oliver Wolcott, Secretary of the Treasury.* 2 vols. New York: For the subscribers, W. Van Norden, printer, 1846.

Gipson, Lawrence Henry. *The British Empire before the American Revolution.* 14 vols. New York: Alfred A. Knopf, 1958–69. Vol. 10, *The Triumphant Empire: Thunder-clouds Gather in the West, 1763–1766,* 1961.

Goebel, Julius, Jr. *Cases and Materials on the Development of Legal Institutions.* 7th rev. ed. Brattleboro, Vt.: Vermont Printing Co., 1946.

————. "The Common Law and the Constitution." In *Chief Justice John Marshall, a Reappraisal,* William Melville Jones, ed. Ithaca, N.Y.: For the College of William and Mary, by Cornell University Press, 1956.

————. "Constitutional History and Constitutional Law." *Columbia Law Review,* 38: 555–77 (1938).

————. "*Ex Parte* Clio." *Columbia Law Review,* 54: 450–83 (1954).

————. "King's Law and Local Custom in Seventeenth Century New England." *Columbia Law Review,* 31: 416–48 (1931).

————, and Naughton, T. Raymond. *Law Enforcement in Colonial New York: A Study in Criminal Procedure (1664–1776).* New York: Commonwealth Fund, 1944.

————, et al., eds. *The Law Practice of Alexander Hamilton: Documents and Commentary.* 2 vols. to date. New York and London: Columbia University Press, 1964– . Short title: *LPAH.*

Great Britain. *Acts of the Privy Council of England, Colonial Series, 1613–1783.* William L. Grant and James Munro, eds. 6 vols. Hereford: Anthony Bros., for H. M. Stationery Office, 1908–12. Short title: *APC Col.*

828

A Select Bibliography

————. *Calendar of State Papers, Colonial Series, America and West Indies . . . [1574–1738], preserved in the Public Record Office.* William Nöel Sainsbury *et al.*, eds. 44 vols. to date. London: H. M. Stationery Office, 1860–   . Short title: *CSP Col.*

————. Historical Manuscripts Commission. "Manuscripts of the Most Honourable the Marquis of Landsdowne: Shelburne MSS, Colonial Affairs and Peace with America, 1766–1783." In *Fifth Report and Appendix* (*Reports*, Vol. 4), pp. 215–60. London: Eyre and Spottiswoode, for H. M. Stationery Office, 1876.

————. *Journal of the Commissioners for Trade and Plantations, from April 1704 to . . . [May 1782], preserved in the Public Record Office.* 14 vols. London: H. M. Stationery Office, 1920–38.

————. *The Parliamentary History of England from the Earliest Period to the Year 1803.* William Cobbett *et al.*, eds. 36 vols. London: Hansard, 1806–20.

————. *Parliamentary Papers.* Vols. 23–26 (1835) (*Reports from Commissioners*, Vols. 3–6). "First Report, and Appendices, of the Commissioners appointed to inquire into the Municipal Corporations in England and Wales," Report No. 116, in 4 vols.

————. *Parliamentary Papers.* Vol. 39 (1884) (*Reports from Commissioners*, Vol. 23). "Report and Appendix of the Commissioners appointed to inquire into the Livery Companies of the City of London," C. 4073, in 5 vols.

Grigsby, Hugh Blair. "The History of the Virginia Federal Convention of 1788: With Some Account of the Eminent Virginians of that Era who were Members of the Body." Robert A. Brock, ed. 2 vols. Virginia Historical Society *Collections*, n.s., Vols. 9–10 (1890–91).

Groce, George C., Jr. *William Samuel Johnson: A Maker of the Constitution.* New York: Columbia University Press, 1937.

Hakluyt, Richard. *The Principal Navigations, Voyages, Traffiques, and Discoveries of the English Nation. . . .* 12 vols. Glasgow: J. MacLehose and Sons, 1903–05.

Hamilton, Alexander. *The Papers of Alexander Hamilton.* Harold C. Syrett *et al.*, eds. 15 vols. to date. New York and London: Columbia University Press, 1961–   . Short title: *PAH.*

————. *The Works of Alexander Hamilton.* Henry Cabot Lodge, ed. 12 vols. Constitutional edition, 2d ed. New York: G. P. Putnam's Sons, 1904.

Handlin, Oscar, and Handlin, Mary F. *Commonwealth: A Study of the Role of Government in the American Economy. Massachusetts, 1774–1861.* New York: New York University Press, 1947.

Harding, Samuel Bannister. *The Contest over the Ratification of the Federal Constitution in the State of Massachusetts.* Harvard Historical Studies, Vol. 2. New York: Longmans, Green and Co., 1896.

Hastings, George Everett. *The Life and Works of Francis Hopkinson.* Chicago: University of Chicago Press, 1926.

Henry, William Wirt. *Patrick Henry: Life, Correspondence and Speeches.* 3 vols. New York: Charles Scribner's Sons, 1891.

Herbert, William. *The History of the Twelve Great Livery Companies of London, Principally Compiled from Their Grants and Records: With an Historical Essay, and Accounts of Each Company.* 2 vols. London: By the author, 1834–37.

Hunt, Gaillard, ed. *Disunion Sentiment in Congress in 1794: A Confidential Memorandum hitherto unpublished Written by John Taylor of Caroline, Senator from Virginia, for James Madison.* Washington: W. H. Lowdermilk and Co., 1905.

Hunt, Gaillard, and Scott, James Brown, eds. *The Debates in the Federal Convention of 1787, which Framed the Constitution of the United States of America: Reported by James Madison, a Delegate from the State of Virginia.* Publication of the Carnegie Endowment for International Peace. New York: Oxford University Press, 1920.

Jameson, John Franklin, ed. *Essays in the Constitutional History of the United States in the Formative Period, 1775–1789.* Boston: Houghton Mifflin Co., 1889.

——, ed. *Privateering and Piracy in the Colonial Period: Illustrative Documents.* New York: The Macmillan Co., 1923.

——. "Studies in the History of the Federal Convention of 1787." American Historical Association *Annual Report* for 1902, 1: 89–167 (1903).

Jay, John. *The Correspondence and Public Papers of John Jay, 1763–1826.* Henry P. Johnston, ed. 4 vols. New York: G. P. Putnam's Sons, 1890–93.

Jefferson, Thomas. *Jefferson's Germantown Letters: Together with Other Papers relating to his Stay in Germantown during the Month of November, 1793.* Charles Francis Jenkins, ed. Philadelphia: W. J. Campbell, 1906.

——. *The Papers of Thomas Jefferson.* Julian P. Boyd *et al.*, eds. 17 vols. to date. Princeton, N.J.: Princeton University Press, 1950– . Short title: *Papers of Jefferson.*

——. *Summary View of the Rights of British America.* Williamsburg, Va.: 1774.

——. *The Works of Thomas Jefferson.* Paul Leicester Ford, ed. 12 vols. Federal ed. New York: G. P. Putnam's Sons, 1904–05. Short title: *Works of Jefferson.*

Jensen, Merrill. *The Articles of Confederation: An Interpretation of the Social-Constitutional History of the American Revolution, 1774–1781.* Madison: University of Wisconsin Press, 1940.

——. *The New Nation: A History of the United States during the Confederation, 1781–1789.* New York: Alfred A. Knopf, 1950.

Kimball, Marie. *Jefferson: The Road to Glory, 1743–1776.* New York: Coward-McCann, 1943.

King, Charles R., ed. *The Life and Correspondence of Rufus King.* 6 vols. New York: G. P. Putnam's Sons, 1894–1900. Short title: *Life of King.*

A Select Bibliography

Koch, Adrienne, and Ammon, Harry. "The Virginia and Kentucky Resolutions: An Episode in Jefferson's and Madison's Defense of Civil Liberties." *William and Mary Quarterly*, 3d ser., 5: 145–76 (1948).

Labaree, Leonard Woods, ed. *Royal Instructions to British Colonial Governors, 1670–1776.* 2 vols. New York: For the American Historical Association, by D. Appleton-Century Co., 1935. Short title: Labaree, *Royal Instructions.*

Leake, Isaac Q. *Memoir of the Life and Times of General John Lamb.* Albany: Joel Munsell, 1850.

Lee, Richard Henry. *An Additional Number of Letters from the Federal Farmer to the Republican.* [n.p.], 1788.

———. *The Letters of Richard Henry Lee.* James Curtis Ballagh, ed. 2 vols. New York: The Macmillan Co., 1911–14.

Lee, Richard Henry. [Grandson] *Memoir of the Life of Richard Henry Lee.* 2 vols. Philadelphia: H. C. Carey and I. Lea, 1825.

Levy, Leonard W., ed. *Freedom of the Press from Zenger to Jefferson: Early American Libertarian Theories.* Indianapolis, Ind.: Bobbs-Merrill Co., 1966.

Livermore, Shaw. *Early American Land Companies: Their Influence on Corporate Development.* New York: Commonwealth Fund, 1939.

McCormick, Richard Patrick. *Experiment in Independence: New Jersey in the Critical Period, 1781–1789.* New Brunswick, N.J.: Rutgers University Press, 1950.

McDonald, Forrest. *We the People: The Economic Origins of the Constitution.* Chicago: University of Chicago Press, 1958.

McLaughlin, Andrew C. *A Constitutional History of the United States.* New York: D. Appleton-Century Co., 1935.

McMaster, John Bach. *A History of the People of the United States, from the Revolution to the Civil War.* 8 vols. New York: Appleton-Century, 1883–1913. Library edition; New York: D. Appleton and Co., 1914.

———, and Stone, Frederick D., eds. *Pennsylvania and the Federal Constitution, 1787–1788.* Philadelphia: Historical Society of Pennsylvania, 1888. Short title: McMaster and Stone, *Pennsylvania.*

McRee, Griffith John. *Life and Correspondence of James Iredell, One of the Associate Justices of the Supreme Court of the United States.* 2 vols. New York: D. Appleton and Co., 1857–58. Short title: McRee, *Iredell.*

Maclay, William. *The Journal of William Maclay, United States Senator from Pennsylvania, 1789–1791.* Edgar S. Maclay, ed. 1890. Reprint. With Introduction by Charles A. Beard. New York: A. and C. Boni, 1927. Short title: *Maclay Journal.*

Madison, James. *The Papers of James Madison.* William T. Hutchinson and William M. E. Rachal, eds. 6 vols. to date. Chicago: University of Chicago Press, 1962– .

———. *The Writings of James Madison.* Gaillard Hunt, ed., 9 vols. New York: G. P. Putnam's Sons, 1900–10.

Main, Jackson Turner. *The Antifederalists: Critics of the Constitution, 1781–1788.* Chapel Hill: University of North Carolina Press, 1961.

Malone, Dumas. *Jefferson and His Time.* 4 vols. to date. Boston: Little, Brown and Co., 1948– . Vol. 3, *Jefferson and the Ordeal of Liberty,* 1962.

———. *The Public Life of Thomas Cooper, 1783–1839.* New Haven: Yale University Press, 1926.

Maryland. *Archives of Maryland.* William Hand Browne *et al.,* eds. 70 vols. to date. Baltimore: Maryland Historical Society, 1883– .

———. *Proceedings of the Conventions of the Province of Maryland Held at the City of Annapolis, in 1774, 1775, & 1776.* Baltimore: Lucas and Deaver, 1836.

———. *Votes and Proceedings of the House of Delegates of the State of Maryland, November Session, 1787;* and *Votes and Proceedings of the House of Delegates . . . November Session, 1788.* Annapolis: Frederick Green, printer, 1788–89.

———. *Votes and Proceedings of the Senate of the State of Maryland, November Session 1787.* Annapolis: Frederick Green, printer, 1788.

Massachusetts. *Speeches of the Governors of Massachusetts, from 1765 to 1775: And the Answers of the House of Representatives to the Same: With Their Resolutions and Addresses for that Period.* Alden Bradford, ed. Boston: Russell and Gardner, 1818.

———. *Debates and Proceedings in the Convention of the Commonwealth of Massachusetts, Held in the Year 1788, and Which Finally Ratified the Constitution of the United States.* Bradford K. Peirce and Charles Hale, eds. Printed by authority of Resolves of the Legislature, 1856. Boston: W. White, 1856. Short title: *Massachusetts Debates.*

———. *Records of the Governor and Company of the Massachusetts Bay in New England, 1628–1686.* Nathaniel B. Shurtleff, ed. 5 vols. Boston: W. White, 1853–54.

Matthews, Albert, ed. "Massachusetts Royal Commissions, 1681–1774." Colonial Society of Massachusetts *Publications,* Vol. 2 (1913).

Mays, David John. *Edmund Pendleton, 1721–1803, A Biography.* 2 vols. Cambridge, Mass.: Harvard University Press, 1952.

Meigs, William Montgomery. *The Growth of the Constitution in the Federal Convention of 1787.* 2d ed. Philadelphia: J. B. Lippincott Co., 1900.

Miller, John Chester. *The Federalist Era, 1789–1801.* New York: Harper and Bros., 1960.

Miner, Clarence Eugene. *The Ratification of the Federal Constitution by the State of New York.* New York: Columbia University, 1921.

Miner, Louie May. *Our Rude Forefathers: American Political Verse, 1783–1788.* Cedar Rapids, Iowa: Torch Press, 1937.

Minot, George Richards. *The History of the Insurrections in Massachusetts in the Year MDCCLXXXVI, and the Rebellion Consequent Thereon.* Worcester, Mass.: Isaiah Thomas, printer, 1788.

Mitchell, Broadus. *Alexander Hamilton.* 2 vols. New York: The Macmillan Co., 1957–62.

832

A Select Bibliography

Monaghan, Frank. *John Jay.* New York and Indianapolis, Ind.: Bobbs-Merrill Co., 1935.

Monroe, James. *The Writings of James Monroe.* Stanislaus Murray Hamilton, ed. 7 vols. New York: G. P. Putnam's Sons, 1898–1903.

Montesquieu, Charles Louis de Secondat, Baron de. *The Spirit of the Laws.* Dublin: 1751.

Moore, John Bassett, ed. *International Adjudications, Ancient and Modern: History and Documents. Modern Series.* 6 vols. Publication of the Carnegie Endowment for International Peace. New York: Oxford University Press, 1929–33.

————. *The Principles of American Diplomacy.* New York: Harper and Bros., 1918.

Morgan, Edmund S., and Morgan, Helen M. *The Stamp Act Crisis: Prologue to Revolution.* Chapel Hill: University of North Carolina Press, 1953.

Morse, Anson Ely. *The Federalist Party in Massachusetts to the Year 1800.* Princeton, N.J.: The University Library, 1909.

Mudge, Eugene Tenbroeck. *The Social Philosophy of John Taylor of Caroline: A Study in Jeffersonian Democracy.* Columbia Studies in American Culture, No. 4. New York: Columbia University Press, 1939.

Munroe, John A. *Federalist Delaware, 1775–1815.* New Brunswick, N.J.: Rutgers University Press, 1954.

New Hampshire. "Journal of the Proceedings of the Convention of the State of New Hampshire, which Adopted the Federal Constitution, 1788." Nathaniel Bouton, ed. In *State Papers of New Hampshire,* 10: 1–22 (1877).

————. *Provincial Papers of New Hampshire,* or *State Papers of New Hampshire.* Nathaniel Bouton *et al.,* eds. State Papers Series, 40 vols. Concord: State printer, 1867–1943. Volumes in the series are titled to several sub-series: Provincial Papers, State Papers, Town Papers, Court Records, and other categories. Footnote citations are to the sub-series title and the main series volume number.

New Jersey. *Journal of the Proceedings of the Legislative-Council of the State of New-Jersey, First Sitting of the Eleventh Session [Oct. 24–Nov. 24, 1786];* and *Journal of the Proceedings of the Legislative-Council . . . Second Sitting of the Twelfth Session [Aug. 27–Sept. 9, 1788].* Trenton: Isaac Collins, printer, 1786–88.

————. *Minutes of the Convention of the State of New-Jersey, holden at Trenton the 11th day of December 1787.* 1788. Facsimile reprint. Trenton: Clayton L. Traver, 1888.

————. *Votes and Proceedings of the Eleventh General Assembly of the State of New-Jersey, First Sitting [Oct. 24–Nov. 24, 1786]; Votes and Proceedings of the Twelfth General Assembly, Second Sitting [Aug. 27–Sept. 9, 1788];* and *Votes and Proceedings of the Thirteenth General Assembly, First Sitting [Oct. 28–Dec. 1, 1788].* Trenton: Isaac Collins, printer, 1786–88.

New York. *Documentary History of the State of New-York*. Edmund B. O'Callaghan, ed. 4 vols. Albany: Weed, Parsons and Co., 1850–51. Short title: *Doc. Hist. N.Y.*

————. *Documents Relative to the Colonial History of the State of New-York*. Edmund B. O'Callaghan and Berthold Fernow, eds. 15 vols. Albany: Weed, Parsons and Co., 1853–87. Short title: *Docs. Rel. Col. Hist. N.Y.*

————. *Journal of the Assembly of the State of New-York, Eleventh Session* [*Jan. 9–Mar. 22, 1788*]; and *Journal of the Assembly . . . Twelfth Session* [*Dec. 11, 1788–Mar. 3, 1789*]. Poughkeepsie, Albany: Samuel and John Loudon, printers, 1788. *Journal of the Assembly . . . Seventeenth Session* [*Jan. 7–Mar. 27, 1794*]. Albany: Childs and Swaine, printers, 1794.

————. *Journal of the Senate of the State of New-York, Eleventh Session* [*Jan. 9–Mar. 22, 1788*]. Poughkeepsie: Samuel and John Loudon, printers, 1788.

————. *Journals of the Provincial Congress, Provincial Convention, Committee of Safety and Council of Safety of the State of New-York: 1775–1776–1777*. 2 vols. Albany: T. Weed, printer, 1842.

Niles, Hezekiah. *Principles and Acts of the Revolution in America*. 1822. Reprint. New York: A. S. Barnes and Co., 1876.

North Carolina. *Colonial Records of North Carolina*. William L. Saunders, ed. *State Records of North Carolina*. Walter Clark, ed. 26 vols. Goldsboro and Raleigh: State printer, 1886–1905.

Osgood, Herbert L. *The American Colonies in the Eighteenth Century*. 4 vols. New York: Columbia University Press, 1924–25.

————. *The American Colonies in the Seventeenth Century*. 3 vols. 1904–07. Reprint. New York: Columbia University Press, 1926–30.

Otis, James. *Some Political Writings of James Otis*. With Introduction by Charles F. Mullett. University of Missouri *Studies*, 4: 257–432 (1929).

Pares, Richard. *Colonial Blockade and Neutral Rights, 1739–1763*. Oxford: At the Clarendon Press, 1938.

Parsons, Theophilus. "Minutes Kept by Chief Justice Parsons of the Debates in Convention." Printed in *Debates and Proceedings in the Convention of the Commonwealth of Massachusetts, Held in the Year 1788, and Which Finally Ratified the Constitution of the United States*. Bradford K. Peirce and Charles Hale, eds. Pp. 285–320. Boston: W. White, 1856.

Parsons, Theophilus, Jr. *Memoir of Theophilus Parsons, Chief Justice of the Supreme Judicial Court of Massachusetts: With Notices of Some of His Contemporaries*. Boston: Ticknor and Fields, 1859.

Pennsylvania. *Colonial Records of Pennsylvania*. 16 vols. Philadelphia and Harrisburg: State printer, 1851–53.

————. *Journal of the Council of Censors, Convened, at Philadelphia, on Monday, the Tenth Day of November, One Thousand Seven Hundred and Eighty-Three*. Philadelphia: Hall and Sellers, printers, 1783.

A Select Bibliography

Continues to September 25, 1784, covering the first and second sessions.

——. *Minutes of the Convention of the Commonwealth of Pennsylvania, Which Commenced at Philadelphia, on Tuesday, the Twentieth Day of November, One Thousand Seven Hundred and Eighty-Seven, for the Purpose of Taking into Consideration the Constitution Framed by the Late Fœderal Convention for the United States of America.* Philadelphia: Hall and Sellers, printers, 1787.

——. *Minutes of the Third Session of the Twelfth General Assembly of the Commonwealth of Pennsylvania* [*Sept. 2–Oct. 4, 1788*]; and *Minutes of the Second Session of the Thirteenth General Assembly* . . . [*Feb. 3–Mar. 28, 1789*] Philadelphia: Hall and Sellers, printers, 1788–89.

——. *Pennsylvania Archives.* Samuel Hazard et al., eds. 138 vols. in 9 series. Philadelphia and Harrisburg: State printer, 1852–1935.

Perry, William Stevens, ed. *Historical Collections Relating to the American Colonial Church.* 4 vols. Hartford, Conn.: Church Press, 1870–78. Vol. 1, *Virginia,* 1870.

Peterson, Arthur Everett, and Edwards, George William. *New York as an Eighteenth Century Municipality.* New York: Longmans, Green and Co., 1917.

Phillips, Ulrich Bonnell. *Georgia and State Rights: A Study of the Political History of Georgia from the Revolution to the Civil War, with Particular Regard to Federal Relations.* Washington, D.C.: American Historical Association, 1902.

Pownall, Thomas. *The Administration of the Colonies.* 2d ed. rev. London: Printed for J. Dodsley, 1765.

Pratt, Daniel Johnson, comp. *Report of the Regents of the University on the Boundaries of the State of New York.* 2 vols. Albany: Argus Co., printers, 1874–84.

Read, William Thompson. *Life and Correspondence of George Read.* Philadelphia: J. B. Lippincott, 1870.

Reed, William Bradford. *Life and Correspondence of Joseph Reed.* 2 vols. Philadelphia: Lindsay and Blakiston, 1847.

Rhode Island. *Records of the Colony of Rhode Island and Providence Plantations, in New England.* John Russell Bartlett, ed. 10 vols. Providence: State printer, 1856–65.

Robinson, Blackwell P. *William R. Davie.* Chapel Hill: University of North Carolina Press, 1957.

Rossiter, Clinton L. *Seedtime of the Republic: The Origin of the American Tradition of Political Liberty.* New York: Harcourt, Brace and Co., 1953.

Rowland, Buford. "Recordkeeping Practices of the House of Representatives." National Archives *Accessions,* No. 53, pp. 1–19 (January 1957).

Rowland, Kate Mason. *The Life of George Mason, 1725–1792, Including His Speeches, Public Papers, and Correspondence.* 2 vols. New York: G. P. Putnam's Sons, 1892.

Russell, Elmer Beecher. *The Review of American Colonial Legislation by the King in Council*. New York: Columbia University Press, 1915.

Rutland, Robert Allen. *The Birth of the Bill of Rights, 1776–1791*. Chapel Hill: University of North Carolina Press, 1955.

Schachner, Nathan. *The Founding Fathers*. New York: G. P. Putnam's Sons, 1954.

Schanz, Georg von. *Englische Handelspolitik gegen Ende des Mittelalters*. 2 vols. Leipzig: Duncker and Humblot, 1881.

Schuyler, Robert Livingston. *Parliament and the British Empire: Some Constitutional Controversies Concerning Imperial Legislative Jurisdiction*. New York: Columbia University Press, 1929.

Scott, Austin. "Holmes vs. Walton: The New Jersey Precedent." *American Historical Review*, 4: 456–69 (1898–99).

Smith, Charles Page. *James Wilson, Founding Father, 1742–1798*. Chapel Hill: University of North Carolina Press, 1956.

Smith, D. E. Huger. "The Luxembourg Claims." *South Carolina Historical and Genealogical Magazine*, 10: 92–115 (1909).

Smith, James Morton. *Freedom's Fetters: The Alien and Sedition Laws and American Civil Liberties*. Ithaca, N.Y.: Cornell University Press, 1956.

Smith, Joseph Henry. "Administrative Control of the Courts of the American Plantations." *Columbia Law Review*, 61: 1210–53 (1961).

———. *Appeals to the Privy Council from the American Plantations*. New York: Columbia University Press, 1950.

Smith, Melancton. "Melancton Smith's Minutes of Debates on the New Constitution." Edited, with introduction and notes, by Julius Goebel Jr. *Columbia Law Review*, 64: 26–43 (1964). Short title: "Smith Minutes."

South Carolina. *Journal of the Convention of South Carolina which Ratified the Constitution of the United States, May 23, 1788*. Alexander S. Salley, Jr., ed. Atlanta: Historical Commission of South Carolina, 1928.

Spaulding, Ernest Wilder. *New York in the Critical Period, 1783–1789*. New York State Historical Association Series, Vol. 1. New York: Columbia University Press, 1932.

Stanwood, Edward. "The Separation of Maine from Massachusetts." Massachusetts Historical Society *Proceedings* for 1907–08, 3d ser., 1: 125–64 (June 1907).

Stokes, Anthony. *A View of the Constitution of the British Colonies in North-America and the West Indies at the Time the Civil War Broke Out on the Continent of America*. London: B. White, printer, 1783.

Stone, Eben F. "[Theophilus] Parsons and the Constitutional Convention of 1788." Essex Institute *Historical Collections*, 35: 81–102 (1899).

Strayer, Joseph Reese, ed. *The Delegate from New York, or, Proceedings of the Federal Convention of 1787 from the Notes of John Lansing, Jr.* Princeton, N.J.: Princeton University Press, 1939. Short title: *Lansing Notes*.

Street, Alfred Billings. *The Council of Revision of the State of New York: Its History, A History of the Courts with which Its Members were*

Connected, Biographical Sketches of Its Members, and Its Vetoes.
Albany: W. Gould, 1859.

Sullivan, John. "Letters and Papers of Major-General John Sullivan, Continental Army: 1771–1795." Otis G. Hammond, ed. 3 vols. New Hampshire Historical Society *Collections*, Vols. 13–15 (1930–39). Short title: *Sullivan Papers.*

Talcott, Joseph. "The Talcott Papers: Correspondence and Documents (chiefly official) during Joseph Talcott's Governorship of the Colony of Connecticut, 1724–41." Mary Kingsbury Talcott, ed. 2 vols. Connecticut Historical Society *Collections*, Vols. 4–5 (1892–96).

Taylor, John. *An Argument Respecting the Constitutionality of the Carriage Tax, which Subject was Discussed at Richmond, In Virginia, in May, 1795.* Richmond: 1795. [Wolcott Pamphlets, Library of Congress.]

Taylor, Robert Joseph. *Western Massachusetts in the Revolution.* Brown University Studies, Vol. 17. Providence, R.I.: Brown University Press, 1954.

Thatcher, George. "The Thatcher Papers." *Historical Magazine*, 2d ser., 6: 257–71, 337–53 (1869). The letters are numbered in sequence and are so identified in the footnote citations.

Thomas, Charles Marion. *American Neutrality in 1793: A Study in Cabinet Government.* New York: Columbia University Press, 1931.

Trenholme, Louise Irby. *The Ratification of the Federal Constitution in North Carolina.* New York: Columbia University Press, 1932.

Tyler, Lyon Gardiner. *The Letters and Times of the Tylers.* 3 vols. Richmond, Va.: Whittet and Shepperson, 1884–96.

Ubbelohde, Carl. *The Vice-Admiralty Courts and the American Revolution.* Chapel Hill: University of North Carolina Press, 1960.

United States. "An Act to Regulate Processes in the Courts of the United States." New York: Printed by Thomas Greenleaf, [1789]. [Library of Congress.]

——. *American State Papers: Documents, Legislative and Executive, of the Congress of the United States.* Walter Lowrie *et al.*, eds. 38 vols. in 10 classes. Washington, D.C.: Gales and Seaton, 1832–61. Short titles:
Am. St. Pap.: Claims.
Am. St. Pap.: For. Rel.
Am. St. Pap.: Misc.
Am. St. Pap.: Pub. Lands.

——. [*Annals of Congress.*] *The Debates and Proceedings in the Congress of the United States: With an Appendix, Containing Important State Papers and Public Documents, and All the Laws of a Public Nature: With a Copious Index.* 42 vols. Washington, D.C.: Gales and Seaton, 1834–56. Covers the first 17 Congresses and the first session of the 18th Congress (1789–1824). Short title: *Annals of Congress.*

——. "A Bill to establish the Judicial Courts of the United States." New York: Printed by Thomas Greenleaf, [1789]. [New York Public Library, accession 626234.]

——. Department of State. *The Diplomatic Correspondence of the United*

States of America, from the Signing of the Definitive Treaty of Peace 19th September, 1783, to the Adoption of the Constitution, March 4, 1789. 7 vols. Washington, D.C.: F. P. Blair, 1833–34.

————. Department of State, Bureau of Rolls and Library. *Documentary History of the Constitution of the United States of America, 1786–1870.* 5 vols. Washington, D.C.: Department of State, 1894–1905. Short title: *Doc. Hist. Const.*

————. *Journal of the House of Representatives of the United States . . . [from the First Session of the First Congress, through the Second Session of the Sixth Congress].* Reprint, by authority of the House of Representatives. Washington, D.C.: Gales and Seaton, 1826. Vols. 1–3, covering March 1789 to March 1801. Short title: *Jour. H. R.*

————. *Journal of the Senate of the United States of America . . . [from the First Session of the First Congress, through the Second Session of the Sixth Congress].* Annual vols. New York, Philadelphia, and Washington, D.C.: 1789–1801. Specific volumes are indicated at the place first cited. Short title: *Senate Journal.*

————. *Journals of the Continental Congress, 1774–1789.* Worthington C. Ford *et al.*, eds. 34 vols. Library of Congress edition. Washington, D.C.: Government Printing Office, 1904–37. Short title: *JCC.*

————. Malloy, William M., comp. *Treaties, Conventions, International Acts, Protocols, and Agreements between the United States of America and Other Powers, 1776–1909.* 2 vols. Washington, D.C.: Government Printing Office, 1910. Short title: Malloy, *Treaties, Conventions.*

————. *Official Opinions of the Attorneys General of the United States, Advising the President and Heads of Departments in Relation to Their Official Duties.* Benjamin Franklin Hall *et al.*, ed. 41 vols. to date. Washington, D.C.: Government Printing Office, 1852– . Vol. 1, covering 1791–1825.

————. Richardson, James Daniel, comp. *A Compilation of the Messages and Papers of the Presidents, 1789–1897.* 10 vols. Washington, D.C.: Government Printing Office, 1896–99. Short title: *Messages and Papers of the Presidents.*

————. Tansill, Charles C., ed. *Documents Illustrative of the Formation of the Union of the American States.* Library of Congress edition. Washington, D.C.: Government Printing Office, 1927.

————. Thorpe, Francis Newton, comp. *The Federal and State Constitutions, Colonial Charters, and Other Organic Laws of the States, Territories, and Colonies Now or Heretofore Forming the United States of America.* 7 vols. Washington, D.C.: Government Printing Office, 1909. Short title: Thorpe, *Constitutions and Charters.*

————. Wharton, Francis, ed. *The Revolutionary Diplomatic Correspondence of the United States.* 6 vols. Washington, D.C.: Government Printing Office, 1889. Short title: Wharton, *Rev. Dip. Corr.*

Updike, Wilkins. *Memoirs of the Rhode-Island Bar.* Boston: T. H. Webb and Co., 1842.

Varnum, James M. *The Case, Trevett against Weeden . . . Tried before the*

Honourable Superior Court in the County of Newport, September Term, 1786. Also the Case of the Judges of said Court. . . . Providence: 1787.

Virginia. *Journal of the House of Delegates of the Commonwealth of Virginia, 1786; Journal of the House of Delegates . . . , 1787;* and *Journal of the House of Delegates . . . , 1788.* 1786–88. Reprint. Richmond: Thomas W. White, printer, 1828. *Journal of the House of Delegates . . . , 1793.* Richmond: Augustine Davis, printer, 1793.

Walker, Joseph Burbeen. *Birth of the Federal Constitution: A History of the New Hampshire Convention for the Investigation, Discussion, and Decision of the Federal Constitution; And of the Old North Meeting-House of Concord in which It was Ratified by the Ninth State, and thus Rendered Operative . . . on . . . the 21st of June, 1788.* Boston: Cupples and Hurd, 1888.

Walters, Raymond, Jr. *Alexander James Dallas: Lawyer, Politician, Financier, 1759–1817.* Philadelphia: University of Pennsylvania Press, 1943.

Warren, Charles. *The Making of the Constitution.* Boston: Little, Brown and Co., 1928.

———. "New Light on the History of the Federal Judiciary Act of 1789." *Harvard Law Review,* 37: 49–132 (1923). Short title: Warren, "Judiciary Act."

———. *The Supreme Court in United States History.* 2 vols. Rev. ed. Boston: Little, Brown and Co., 1947.

Washington, George. *The Writings of George Washington.* John C. Fitzpatrick, ed. 39 vols. Bicentennial ed. Washington, D.C.: Government Printing Office, 1931–44. Short title: *Washington Writings.*

Webb, Samuel Blachley. *Correspondence and Journals of Samuel Blachley Webb.* Worthington C. Ford, ed. 3 vols. New York: Wickersham Press, Lancaster, Pa., 1893–94.

Webb, Sidney, and Webb, Beatrice. *English Local Government from the Revolution to the Municipal Corporations Act: The Parish and the County.* London: Longmans, Green and Co., 1924.

Weld, Isaac, Jr. *Travels through the States of North America, and the Provinces of Upper and Lower Canada, during the Years 1795, 1796, and 1797.* 2 vols. 2d ed. London: Printed for John Stockdale, Piccadilly, 1799.

White, Leonard Dupee. *The Federalists: A Study in Administrative History.* New York: The Macmillan Co., 1948.

Wickham, John. *The Substance of an Argument in the Case of the Carriage Duties, Delivered before the Circuit Court of the United States, in Virginia, May Term, 1795.* Richmond: 1795. [Wolcott Pamphlets, Library of Congress.]

Wilson, James. *The Works of James Wilson. James DeWitt Andrews,* ed. 2 vols. Chicago: Callaghan and Co., 1896.

Wingate, Charles E. L. *Life and Letters of Paine Wingate.* 2 vols. Winchester, Mass.: J. D. P. Wingate; Medford, Mass.: Mercury Printing Co., 1930.

Winthrop, John. "Correspondence of John Winthrop, F.R.S." In "Winthrop Papers: Pt. 6," Charles C. Smith *et al.*, eds. Massachusetts Historical Society *Collections*, 6th ser., 5: 371–511 (1892).

Wirt, William. *Sketches of the Life and Character of Patrick Henry*. 2d ed. Philadelphia: J. Webster, 1818.

Wroth, L. Kinvin, and Zobel, Hiller B., eds. *Legal Papers of John Adams*. 3 vols. The Adams Papers, 3d ser. Cambridge, Mass.: Harvard University Press, Belknap Press, 1965.

Yeates, Jasper. "Jasper Yeates's Notes on the Pennsylvania Ratifying Convention, 1787." R. Carter Pittman, ed. *William and Mary Quarterly*, 3d ser., 22: 301–18 (1965). Short title: *Yeates's Notes*.

Zeichner, Oscar. *Connecticut's Years of Controversy, 1750–1776*. Chapel Hill: University of North Carolina Press, 1949.

Index

Abingdon, Lord, *Thoughts on the Letter of Edmund Burke*, on disobeying laws subversive of the constitution, 127–28.

Act to establish Judicial Courts of the United States *see* Judiciary Act.

Act to Regulate Processes in the Courts of the United States *see* Process Acts.

Adams, John, on Massachusetts country court practice, 18; legal background, 148; *A Defence of the Constitutions of the United States*, used as evidence of aristocratic plot, 277–79, 644; prize appeals, 147.

Adams, Samuel, opposes ratification of Constitution at Mass. convention, 343, 345; supports ratification conditional upon Hancock propositions, 351; adds further amendment concerning rights, 352.

Administration of Justice Act of 1774, 87–88.

Admiralty Jurisdiction, 85–86, 147–82, 478–82, 596–607, 760–76.

Allyn v. Pratt, 28.

Ames, Fisher, federalist delegate to Mass. ratification convention, 344; on Hayburn's Case, 562.

Andros, Sir Edmund, Governor of New England, effects reorganization of courts, 13–14, 15.

Annapolis Report (1787), recommends appointment by the states of commissioners to a constitutional convention, 198–99.

Appeal, 24–35, 156–59, 166–67, 478, 486, 598, 666, 686–707. *See also* Admiralty Jurisdiction.

Ap-Richarde v. Jones, 22.

Apthorp v. Bronson, 584.

Arcambal v. Wiseman, 716–18.

Armstrong v. Reinolds, 28.

Arnold, Welcome, Rhode Island, commissioner in Wyoming Valley lands controversy, 190, 191.

Articles of Confederation, gave Congress power to establish rules of prize and appeals courts in all cases of capture, 163–64; powers conferred upon Congress over controversies between states concerning boundaries and jurisdictions, 185–88, 189–90, 194; difficulties arising from states' assumption of sovereignty under, 198–99; on alterations, 198–99; ordinance power, 201.

Debates in Constitutional Convention and in Congress on relation between Constitution and Articles, 230–32, 260–66.

Attorney General (U.S.), office established, 490, 501; failure to improve stature of, 545–46; represents private clients, 564, 726.

See also District Attorneys (U.S.).

Atherton, Joshua, delegate to New Hampshire ratification convention, objections to Article III, 356, 357.

Avery v. Ray, 113.

Bail, 488–89, 523–32.

Baldwin, Abraham, Representative from Georgia, serves on Vining Committee to consider proposed amendments to Constitution, 433.

Baldwin v. O'Brian, 113.

Bancroft, Edward, *Remarks on the Review of the Controversy between Great Britain and Her Colonies*, 90.

Bangs v. Snow, 113.

Barry v. the Sloop Betsey, 150.

Bassett, Richard, Senator from Delaware, serves on committee which drafts Judiciary Act of 1789, 458.

Den ex dem. Bayard and wife v. Singleton, 129–31.

Bean v. Brooks, 584.

Beckford v. Jeake, 44.

Bedford, Gunning, Jr., Attorney General of Delaware, writes letter of comment on the Judiciary bill, 491.

Beecher's Case, 682.

Bennett, J. J., "History of New England," on judicial administration in Bay Colony around 1740, 29.

Benson, Egbert, Representative from New York, serves on Vining committee to consider proposed amendments to Constitution, 433, 434.

Bewly v. Hatter, 581.

Bill of Rights: state declarations of rights, 101–102.

tempt by Henry to effect his political downfall, 419, 424.

On the dangers in a bill of rights, 425; comes to support amendments securing basic liberties, 426–27; presents amendments for Congressional consideration, 428–30; propositions affecting the judicial, 429–30. *See also* Bill of Rights.

On the Judiciary Act of 1789, 507–508; on the Justices' objection to the Pension Act, 562; defense of the Virginia Resolutions of 1798, 652.

Madox v. Hoskins, 113.

Mandamus, Writ of, 562–64, 667, 785–88.

Manly v. the Ship Bailey, 177.

Marbury v. Madison, 650–51.

Marchant, Henry, Rhode Island, counsel for defendant in *Trevett v. Weeden*, 138, 140.

District judge, Circuit Court, Rhode Island, 589, 599.

Marshall, John, federalist delegate to Virginia ratification convention, 377, 387; on jurisdiction of federal courts, 387–88; on the status of unconstitutional legislation, 388; on concurrent jurisdiction, 388–89; on conflict of laws, 389.

Counsel for defendant in *Ware v. Hylton*, 749, 750, 752.

Marshall v. Montgomery, 637.

Martin, Luther, Attorney General of Maryland, delegate to Constitutional Convention from Maryland, opposes oath to support articles of union from state officials, 215; offers resolve pointing to judicial review of state legislation, 224; on possible conflict between federal and state courts, 226.

The Genuine Information, purported text of address to Maryland legislature opposing ratification of the Constitution, 301–303, 365, 375; defense of Gerry in Gerry-Ellsworth exchange, 303.

Antifederalist delegate to ratification convention, 364, 365, 366, 367, 368.

Martin v. Joranceau, 588.

Martindale's Lessee v. Troop, 115.

Maryland—The Colony. Early development of the judicial, 7, 15, 16; probate jurisdiction, 8, equity courts, 8; role of the Crown, 10; use of the writ, 22; initiation of the appeal, 25–26, 31–32, 48; subject to Privy Council as ultimate appellate authority, 41; royal control over colonial legislation, 71.

Maryland—The State. Judicial independence and legislative interference, 98; constitution contains declaration of rights, 101, 102; lacks procedure for redress of legislative violation of constitution, 102; oath of allegiance required, 107, 108; declaration regarding the law that is to be in force, 109–10; revision of laws, 122; employs formal procedure in admiralty cases, 154.

Initiates with Virginia the Annapolis conference leading to the Constitutional Convention, 198.

Ratification convention, 364–71 (*see also* Constitution—The Ratification Conventions: Maryland); response to appeals for amendment by convention, 420.

State court procedure, 521, 524, 531, 533, 534.

Mason, George, delegate to Constitutional Convention from Virginia, supports power of national legislature to "appoint" inferior courts, 226, 228; supports the necessity of ratification by the people rather than the legislatures, 230; opposes provisions for the judiciary, 244–45; refuses to sign Constitution, 249–50.

Publishes *Objections to the Proposed Federal Constitution*, 294–97; attacked by Ellsworth, 300–301.

Actively opposes Virginia ratification of the Constitution, 361; delegate to ratification convention, 376–77, 378, 391; objects that judiciary provisions would annihilate state governments, 379, 380, 384; opposes Article III on relation of national and state courts, on jurisdiction, 384–85; communicates with New York antifederalists, 395.

Mason v. Evans, 114, 115.

Massachusetts—The Colony. Early development of the judicial, 7, 13–14, 15; probate jurisdiction, 8; equity courts, 8, 9; inferior courts, 17–18; initiation of the appeal, 25–29, 39, 48; royal administrative control over colony legislation, 66; judicial control, 76–78, 82–83.

Massachusetts—The State. Judicial independence and legislative interference, 98–99; constitution contains declaration of rights, 101; lacks procedure for redress of legislative violations of constitution, 102; oath of allegiance and treason statute, 107, 108; declaration regarding the law that is to be in force, 109–10; legislative revision of laws, 120–21, 123.

pate in Constitutional Convention, 199–200.

Ratification convention, 336; response to appeals for amendment by convention, 416, 421.

State court procedure, 511, 519, 522, 524, 527, 529–30, 530–31, 532–33, 534.

New York—The Colony. Early development of the judicial, 5, 7, 8, 13–14; Chancery court, 8; inferior courts, 17; initiation of the appeal, 26, 48.

Suspension of legislature by Parliament, 83.

New York—The State. Judicial independence and legislative interference, 98; constitution contains a limited declaration of rights, 101; provisions for check on possible legislative violations of constitution, 103–104, 108; oath of allegiance and treason statute, 107, 108; declaration regarding the law that is to be in force, 109–10; revision of laws, 121–22, 123; judicial review via statutory construction, in *Rutgers v. Waddington*, 131–37.

Border controversy with Massachusetts, 183, 191, 194, 520–21.

Ratification convention, 393–412 (*see also* Constitution—The Ratification Conventions: New York); response to Clinton's appeal and Virginia's application for amendment by convention, 422–23.

State court procedure, 511, 518, 522, 524, 526–27, 528, 532, 534, 578, 580, 582–83.

Newall v. Comm., 610.

Newman v. Baily, 637.

Newmann v. Ward, 588.

Nicholas, George, federalist delegate to Virginia ratification convention, 377, 380, 381, 382, 384, 390.

Norris v. the Schooner Polly and Nancy, 154, 155, 157.

Norse v. Endicott, 27.

North, Sir Francis, Chief Justice of Common Bench, consulted by Privy Council Lords Committee, 61, 65.

O'Connor v. Gardner, 578.

Olney v. Arnold, 670, 674, 721.

Olney v. Dexter, 674.

Ormond v. Brig Somerset, 571.

Osborne, Henry, solicitor for Pennsylvania in Wyoming Valley lands controversy, 189.

Oswald, Colonel Eleazar, emissary to Virginia from New York antifederalists, 395–96.

Oswald v. State of New York, 724–25, 734, 736–37.

Owner of the Sloop Chester v. Owners of the Brig Experiment, 177, 181–82.

Paca, William, delegate to Continental Congress from Maryland, serves on committee to establish Court of Appeals, 169.

Antifederalist delegate to Maryland ratification convention, 366, 368, 369–70, 371.

District Judge, Maryland, 761.

Pagan v. Hooper, 670.

Paine, Robert Treat, Attorney General of Mass., consulted by Senate committee preparing Judiciary Bill of 1789, 460–61.

Paine and Bridgman v. United States, 681.

Palmer v. Horton, 116.

Parker, Richard, Virginia, wrote letter of comment on the Judiciary Bill of 1789, 491.

Parsons, Theophilus, delegate to Mass. ratification convention, 344; moves adoption of Constitution, 349; participates in formulation of propositions to be subjoined to ratification as method of appeasing opponents, 350.

Parson's Cause, 46.

Paterson, William, delegate to Constitutional Convention, submits alternative to Virginia Plan, 203, 217 (*see also* Constitutional Convention: Paterson's Plan); supports ratification by state legislature, 230.

Senator from New Jersey, serves on committee which drafts Judiciary and Process Bills, 458, 459, 509, 512.

Justice of the Supreme Court: appointment, 554.

Service on the Circuit Courts: 580, 590, 592, 638–39; charge in *United States v. Lyon*, 646.

Service on the Supreme Court: 583, 598, 607, 678, 679, 680, 689, 697, 708, 718, 761–62, 766, 790, 791; opinion in *Wiscart v. Dauchy*, 703–704; opinion in *Cooper v. Telfair*, 706; opinion in *Penhallow v. Doane's Administrators*, 709, 767–69; opinion in *Ware v. Hylton*, 753; opinion in *Talbot v. Jansen*, 773–74; opinion in *Hylton v. United States*, 781–82; opinion in *Calder v. Bull*, 783.

Peachy and Ford v. Cryer, 31.

Pendleton, Edmund, Judge of Virginia Court of Appeals, federalist delegate to Virginia ratification convention,